COMPARATIVE CONSTITUTIONALISM
Cases and Materials

Norman Dorsen
Frederick I. and Grace A. Stokes Professor of Law
and Founding Director, Hauser Global Law School Program
New York University School of Law

Michel Rosenfeld
Justice Sidney L. Robins Professor of Human Rights,
Benjamin N. Cardozo School of Law, and President, International
Association of Constitutional Law

András Sajó
Professor of Law, Central European University,
Budapest, and Global Professor of Law,
New York University School of Law

Susanne Baer
Professor of Public Law and Gender Studies,
Faculty of Law
Humboldt University, Berlin

AMERICAN CASEBOOK SERIES®

Mat #16918849

American Casebook Series and West Group are trademarks registered in the U.S. Patent and Trademark Office.

COPYRIGHT © 2003 By WEST GROUP
                610 Opperman Drive
                P.O. Box 64526
                St. Paul, MN 55164–0526
                1–800–328–9352

All rights reserved
Printed in the United States of America

ISBN 0–314–24248–1

 *TEXT IS PRINTED ON 10% POST CONSUMER RECYCLED PAPER*

Preface

The accelerating trend toward globalization, combined with recent transitions from authoritarian regimes to constitutional rule, has dramatically increased the relevance of comparative constitutional analysis. The reason for this is that the world is becoming increasingly integrated as, in the words of a report of the Center on International Cooperation at New York University, "transnational flows of capital, goods, services, people, ideas, and information accelerate in velocity and swell in volume." Accordingly, just as the contemporary business lawyer must reach beyond the boundaries of domestic law to meet the needs of clients who are involved in the global economy, and just as lawmakers must be aware of the transnational constitutional standards that will be applied to their laws and regulations, so lawyers in all fields are increasingly handicapped if they are unaware of constitutional trends abroad, or if they lack the skills to assess foreign or transnational constitutional developments.

A strong impetus for scholarly examination of comparative constitutional systems and norms came with the collapse of communist and authoritarian regimes in the 1990s and the subsequent wave of constitution writing. A new generation examined the range of constitutional models to determine their limitations and advantages, their idiosyncrasies and transportability. Further, the tendency of vexed issues—from crime and terrorism, to human rights, to migration and environmental disputes—to spill across borders, coupled with the rising importance of international and regional adjudicatory bodies, means that no single system can exist in isolation or escape wide scrutiny. Of course, there have been earlier casebooks in this field, going back at least to 1968, when Thomas Franck's notable *Comparative Constitutional Process* appeared.

One sign of the cross-fertilization and dialogue in constitutional law is the increasing practice of supreme and constitutional courts to cite to international instruments and foreign decisions. Many newer courts, as in South Africa, and many courts interpreting relatively new constitutional instruments, as in Canada, routinely cite to other jurisdictions. Even some justices of the U.S. Supreme Court, older and more insular than its brethren, have cited foreign cases and foreign examples. For example, in his dissent in *Printz v. United States*, 521 U.S. 898 (1997), Justice Stephen Breyer referred to German federalism in discussing the constitutional limits of U.S. federal power. More recently, Justice John Paul Stevens's opinion for the Court in *Atkins v. Virginia* cited to a brief of the European Union as amicus curiae in a related case, pointing out that "within the world community, the imposition of the death penalty for crimes committed by mentally retarded offenders is overwhelmingly disapproved." 122 Sup. Ct. 2242, 2249 n.21 (2002).

This casebook does not merely parse constitutional developments and trends in other countries or survey constitutional doctrine across jurisdictions. The book also aims to show through varied examples that comparative constitutional law can deepen our understanding in three principal ways: (1) it pushes us to evaluate the foundations of individual legal systems: the assumptions, choices, trade-offs, and values that have formed them; (2) it gives us a better purchase on our own systems and legal cultures by revealing how other constitutional democracies address similar problems; and (3) it helps us to apprehend the nature and problems of regional and international institutions and adjudicatory bodies. We also recognize that there are democratic traditions beyond the Western democracies, and we signal the importance of countries in transition to democracy and in some cases away from it. We have included cases or other materials from more than 50 jurisdictions.

As far as possible, the casebook presents issues generically. In particular, we avoid characterizations and classifications that present the U.S. position as the norm and other positions as departures. For example, Chapter 4, Federalism and Vertical Separation of Powers, does not track the presentation of federalism found in most U.S. casebooks but rather sorts the material according to how decentralization works in different federal and unitary states. This arrangement exposes the similarities and differences among types of federalism and permits a more systematic evaluation of local autonomy and control in varied institutional settings—supranationalism, regionalism, and federalism—as well as in centralized or decentralized unitary states.

This methodology also allows for comparisons across customary subject boundaries. For example, *R.A.V. v. City of St. Paul*, 505 U.S. 377 (1992), a U.S. Supreme Court decision on the constitutionality of a state statute prohibiting burning a cross as an expression of racial hatred, is usually included in U.S. casebooks as a free speech ruling. While there is a free speech issue in the case, the Court's opinion cannot be adequately understood until one recognizes that it is also grounded in equality norms. Similarly, the casebook discusses abortion, euthanasia, and the death penalty within the context of privacy and dignity, a linkage meant to prompt readers to consider whether there are relevant ties among the legal issues surrounding life and death. The chapter on criminal justice, a subject now omitted from most U.S. constitutional law books, is included, both because it implicates several constitutional rights and because procedural rights in criminal cases are among the most important, and the most hotly contested, constitutional issues in many countries. On the other hand, we have reluctantly omitted certain subjects—for example, pornography in the context of free speech and sex equality—in order to permit deeper discussion of other issues. We have included cases decided by early 2002, as well as a few cases decided after that time.

The casebook is divided into three parts. Part One, Defining and Elaborating the Constitution, treats foundational subjects, such as the distinction between constitutions and constitutionalism, written and unwritten constitutions, the conditions necessary for constitution-making, different models of constitutional adjudication, and different approaches to constitutional interpretation.

Part Two, The Division of Governmental Powers, explores the ways in which limitations on government powers have been pursued in different constitutional systems. Particular attention is devoted to distinguishing among political and institutional settings—for example, presidential versus parliamentary democracy, and among various ways of apportioning power among local, regional, national, and supranational governments.

Part Three, Fundamental Rights, provides a comparative framework for discussion of free expression, privacy, dignity, autonomy, equality, and liberty. Of particular note is Chapter 10, the Constitutional Basis of the Economy, which brings together a cluster of related issues usually scattered under distinct rubrics and which highlights the striking contrast between the U.S. and other constitutional democracies. The chapter on equality includes racial and gender equality as well as group rights and linguistic rights, issues highly visible and contentious in most parts of the world but generally not emphasized in the U.S. The chapter on religion focuses on differences between countries with an official church and those where the state must remain neutral among religions, and it suggests how various religions tend toward different conceptions of religious freedom and of the proper relation between religion and the state. The final chapter, Constitutional Guarantees of Democracy, brings together topics such as elections, political parties, and campaign financing, the constitutional constraints on which vary widely in different systems. The chapter permits a broadened understanding of the roles of constitutions and citizens in preserving democratic systems.

We hope this casebook will facilitate the systematic and fruitful study of this rich and challenging field. While grounded in doctrine and in the structural, institutional, and cultural context in each country, comparative constitutional law requires an openness to outside ideas, a willingness to go beyond traditional conventions and assumptions, and an ability to see patterns and perspectives. Our experience in writing the book— authors of varied backgrounds, academic training, and ideas—convinced us that comparative constitutional law is a collaborative endeavor. It is best pursued jointly, with the opportunity to discuss and disentangle issues with colleagues from different countries and legal systems.

NORMAN DORSEN
MICHEL ROSENFELD
ANDRÁS SAJÓ
SUSANNE BAER

*

Acknowledgements

Our primary debt is to Karen Johnson, who served in effect as our managing editor, and whose background in law and Russian history, as well as her exceptional editorial skills and good sense, contributed significantly to the final product.

We are deeply grateful to Dwight Semler, whose incisive questioning and editing improved and facilitated completion of the book.

We also appreciate the contribution of Amanda Norejko, who assisted us greatly in reviewing and correcting a complex set of proofs.

Norman Dorsen thanks Karen Johnson, Maria McFarland, and Jeremy Zucker for their research assistance and Evelyn Palmquist for secretarial support.

Michel Rosenfeld thanks Matthew Hirsh, Claudia Hoefs, and Christina Ostergaard for research assistance and Stephen Kampmeier for translation assistance.

András Sajó thanks Dr. Renáta Uitz for substantive help and comment, Dr. Petra Bárd and Arun Thiruvengadam for research assistance, and Zsuzsa Kovács for secretarial support.

Susanne Baer thanks Olexandr Vodyannikov for translation and research assistance and Gisela Stuecken for secretarial support.

We also acknowledge the assistance of Priti Dave, Sandra Maja Fabula, David Koller, Jonathan Magidoff, Amanda Norejko, Andras Pap, Andrew Robertson, Naveen Thakur, and Mami Ushio for research, source-citing, and securing permissions to republish certain material.

Hungarian cases are unofficial translations by courtesy of the Secretary General of the Hungarian Constitutional Court. The translations from the Korean Constitutional Court, Japanese Supreme Court, Polish Constitutional Tribunal, Latvian Constitutional Court, and Estonian Supreme Court are from their official web sites.

Finally, we jointly acknowledge our gratitude to John Sexton, former dean of New York University School of Law and now president of the University, for his strong support of this project from the outset, and to NYU School of Law for important financial assistance.

*

Permissions

The authors gratefully acknowledge the right to reprint extracts from the following works:

Ackerman, Bruce A., *The New Separation of Powers*, 113 HARVARD LAW REVIEW 633 (2000). © 2000 by the Harvard Law Review Association.

_____, *The Rise of World Constitutionalism*, 83 VIRGINIA LAW REVIEW 771 (1997). Reprinted by permission of the Virginia Law Review.

Amar, Vikram David, and Alan Brownstein, *The Hybrid Nature of Political Rights,* 50 STANFORD LAW REVIEW 915 (1998). Reprinted by permission of the Stanford Law Review.

Amman, Diane Marie, *Harmonic Convergence? Constitutional Criminal Procedure in an International Context*, 75 INDIANA LAW JOURNAL 809 (2000). © 2000 by the Trustees of Indiana University. Reprinted with permission.

Arendt, Hannah, ON REVOLUTION (1965), © 1963 by Hannah Arendt. Used by permission of Viking Penguin, a division of Penguin Putnam Inc.

Baer, Susanne, *Constitutional Equality: The Jurisprudence of the German Constitutional Court*, 5 COLUMBIA JOURNAL OF EUROPEAN LAW 249 (1999). Reprinted by permission of the author.

Banks, William C., and Alejandro D. Carrió, *Presidential Systems in Stress: Emergency Powers in Argentina and the United States*, 15 MICHIGAN JOURNAL OF INTERNATIONAL LAW 1 (1993). Reprinted by permission of the Michigan Journal of International Law.

Barendt, Eric, AN INTRODUCTION TO CONSTITUTIONAL LAW (1998). © 1998 Oxford University Press. Reprinted by permission of Oxford University Press, Inc.

_____, FREEDOM OF SPEECH (Oxford University Press, 1987). © Eric Barendt 1985. Reprinted by permission of Oxford University Press, Inc.

Bartole, Sergio, *Regionalism and Federalism in the Italian Constitutional Experience*, in AUTONOMY: APPLICATIONS AND IMPLICATIONS (Markku Suksi ed., 1998). © Kluwer Law International.

Bassiouni, M. Cherif, *Human Rights in the Context of Criminal Justice: Identifying International Procedural Protections and Equivalent Protections in National Constitutions*, 3 DUKE JOURNAL OF COMPARATIVE & INTERNATIONAL LAW 235 (1993). Reprinted by permission of the Duke Journal of Comparative & International Law.

Beatty, David M., *The Forms and Limits of Constitutional Interpretation*, 49 AMERICAN JOURNAL OF COMPARATIVE LAW 79 (2001). Reprinted by permission of the University of Washington Press.

Beer, Lawrence W., and Hiroshi Itoh, THE CONSTITUTIONAL CASE LAW OF JAPAN, 1970 THROUGH 1990 (University of Washington Press, 1996). Reprinted by permission of the University of Washington Press.

Bell, John, *Devolution French Style*, 6 EUROPEAN PUBLIC LAW 139 (2000). © Kluwer Law International.

_____, FRENCH CONSTITUTIONAL LAW (Oxford University Press, 1992). © John S. Bell 1992. Reprinted by permission of Oxford University Press, Inc.

Bork, Robert H., THE TEMPTING OF AMERICA (Free Press/Simon & Schuster, 1990). Copyright 1990 by Robert M. Bark. Reprinted with the permission of the Free Press, a Division of Simon & Schuster Adult Publishing Group.

Butler, Judith, EXCITABLE SPEECH: A POLITICS OF THE PERFORMATIVE (1997). © 1997. Reproduced by permission of Routledge, Inc., part of The Taylor & Francis Group.

Capra, Daniel J., *Access to Exculpatory Evidence: Avoiding the Agurs Problems of Prosecutorial Discretion and Retrospective Review*, 53 FORDHAM LAW REVIEW 391 (1984). Reprinted by permission of the Fordham Law Review.

Cassels, Jamie, *Judicial Activism and Public Interest Litigation in India: Attempting the Impossible?*, 37 AMERICAN JOURNAL OF COMPARATIVE LAW 495 (1989). Reprinted by permission of the American Journal of Comparative Law.

Choper, Jesse H., *The Religion Clauses of the First Amendment: Reconciling the Conflict*, 41 UNIVERSITY OF PITTSBURGH LAW REVIEW 673 (1980). Reprinted by permission of the University of Pittsburgh Law Review.

Coomaraswamy, Radhika, *Uses and Usurpation of Constitutional Ideology*, in CONSTITUTIONALISM AND DEMOCRACY: TRANSITIONS IN THE CONTEMPORARY WORLD (Douglas Greenberg, Stanley N. Katz, Melanie Beth Oliviero, and Steven Wheatley eds., 1993). © 1993 by Oxford University Press, Inc. Reprinted by permission of Oxford University Press, Inc.

Cossman, Brenda, and Ratna Kapur, *Secularism's Last Sigh?: The Hindu Right, the Courts, and India's Struggle for Democracy*, 38 HARVARD INTERNATIONAL LAW JOURNAL 113 (1997). Reprinted with permission of the authors.

Dalton, Harlon Leigh, *Taking the Right to Appeal (More or Less) Seriously*, 95 YALE L.J. 62 (1985). Reprinted by permission of The Yale Law Journal Company and William S. Hein Company.

Daniel, Krystyna, and W. Cole Durham, Jr., *Religious Identity as a Component of National Identity: Implications for Emerging Church–State Relations in the Former Socialist Bloc*, in THE LAW OF RELIGIOUS IDENTITY: MODELS FOR POST-COMMUNISM (András Sajó and Shlomo Avineri eds., 1999). © Kluwer Law International.

Jackson, Vicki C., *Narratives of Federalism: Of Continuities and Comparative Constitutional Experience*, 51 DUKE LAW JOURNAL 223 (2001). Reprinted by permission of the Duke Law Journal.

Jörg, Nico, Stewart Field, and Chrisje Brants, *Are Inquisitorial and Adversarial Systems Converging?*, in CRIMINAL JUSTICE IN EUROPE (Christopher Harding, Phil Fennell, Nico Jörg, and Bert Stewart eds., Oxford/Clarendon, 1995). Reprinted by permission of Oxford University Press, Inc.

Karst, Kenneth L., *Paths to Belonging: The Constitution and Cultural Identity*, 64 NORTH CAROLINA LAW REVIEW 303 (1986). Reprinted by permission of the North Carolina Law Review.

Keir, D. L., and F. H. Lawson, CASES IN CONSTITUTIONAL LAW (5th ed., Oxford University Press, 1967). Reprinted by permission of Oxford University Press, Inc.

Kingsbury, Benedict, *Reconciling Five Competing Conceptual Structures of Indigenous People's Claims in International and Comparative Law*, 34 NEW YORK UNIVERSITY JOURNAL OF INTERNATIONAL LAW & POLITICS 189 (2001). © Benedict Kingsbury. Reprinted by permission of the author.

Kirby, Michael, *Law and Sexuality: The Contrasting Case of Australia*, 12 STANFORD LAW & POLICY REVIEW 103 (2001). This article originally appeared in Volume 12, Issue 1 of the Stanford Law & Policy Review. Reprinted by permission of the Stanford Law & Policy Review.

Kommers, Donald P., THE CONSTITUTIONAL JURISPRUDENCE OF THE FEDERAL REPUBLIC OF GERMANY (2d ed. 1997). © 1997 Duke University Press. All rights reserved. Used by permission of the publisher.

Kretzmer, David, *Freedom of Speech and Racism*, 8 CARDOZO LAW REVIEW 445 (1987). Reprinted by permission of the Cardozo Law Review.

Krug, Peter, *Civil Defamation Law and the Press in Russia: Private and Public Interests, the 1995 Civil Code, and the Constitution*, PART ONE, 13 CARDOZO ARTS & ENTERTAINMENT LAW JOURNAL 847 (1995); PART TWO, 14 CARDOZO ARTS & ENTERTAINMENT LAW JOURNAL 297 (1996). Used by permission of the Cardozo Arts & Entertainment Law Journal.

Kübler, Friedrich, *How Much Freedom for Racist Speech?: Transnational Aspects of a Conflict of Human Rights*, 27 HOFSTRA LAW REVIEW 335 (1998). Reprinted by permission of the Hofstra Law Review Association.

Kuo, Joyce, *Excluded, Segregated and Forgotten: A Historical View of the Discrimination of Chinese Americans in Public Schools,* 5 ASIAN L.J. 181 (1998). Reprinted by permission of the Asian Law Journal.

Kymlicka, Will, POLITICS IN THE VERNACULAR: MINORITY NATIONALISM AND MULTINATION FEDERALISM (Oxford University Press, 2001). © 2001 by Oxford University Press, Inc. Used by permission of Oxford University Press, Inc.

Lessig, Lawrence, and Cass R. Sunstein, *The President and the Administration*, 94 COLUMBIA LAW REVIEW 1 (1994). Reprinted by permission of the Columbia Law Review.

Lev, Daniel S., *Social Movements, Constitutionalism and Human Rights: Comments from the Malaysian and Indonesian Experiences*, in CONSTITUTIONALISM AND DEMOCRACY: TRANSITIONS IN THE CONTEMPORARY WORLD (Douglas Greenberg, Stanley N. Katz, Melanie Beth Oliviero, and Steven C. Wheatley eds., 1993). © 1993 by Oxford University Press, Inc. Used by permission of Oxford University Press, Inc.

Levinson, Sanford, Book Review, *Regulating Campaign Activity: The New Road to Contradiction,* 83 MICHIGAN LAW REVIEW 939 (1985). © Sanford Levinson. Reprinted with permission of Princeton University Press.

Ludwikowski, Rett R., CONSTITUTION-MAKING IN THE REGION OF FORMER SOVIET DOMINANCE (Duke University Press, 1996). Copyright, 1996, Duke University Press. All rights reserved. Used by permission of the publisher.

Lutz, Donald, *Towards a Theory of Constitutional Amendment*, in RESPONDING TO IMPERFECTION: THE THEORY AND PRACTICE OF CONSTITUTIONAL AMENDMENT (Sanford Levinson ed., Princeton University Press, 1995). © 1995 by Princeton University Press. Reprinted by permission of Princeton University Press.

MacKinnon, Catharine A., *Reflections On Sex Equality Under Law*, 100 YALE L.J. 1281 (1991). Reprinted by permission of The Yale Law Journal Company and William S. Hein Company.

Mahmud, Tayyab, *Freedom of Religion & Religious Minorities in Pakistan: A Study of Judicial Practice*, 19 FORDHAM INTERNATIONAL LAW JOURNAL 40 (1995). Reprinted by permission of the Fordham International Law Journal.

Matsuda, Mari J., *Public Response to Racist Speech: Considering the Victim's Story*, 87 MICHIGAN LAW REVIEW 2320 (1989). The article appeared in final form in WORDS THAT WOUND, eds. Matsuda, Lawrence, Delgado, and Crenshaw (Westview Press, 1993). Used by permission of the author.

Mayer, Ann Elizabeth, *Universal Versus Islamic Human Rights: A Clash of Cultures or a Clash with a Construct?*, 15 MICHIGAN JOURNAL OF INTERNATIONAL LAW 307 (1994). Used by permission of the Michigan Journal of International Law.

Morton, F. L., *Judicial Review in France: A Comparative Analysis,* 36 AMERICAN JOURNAL OF COMPARATIVE LAW 89 (1988). Reprinted by permission of the American Journal of Comparative Law.

Muni, S.D., *Ethnic Conflict, Federalism and Democracy in India*, in ETHNICITY AND POWER IN THE CONTEMPORARY WORLD (Kumar Rupesinghe and Valery A. Tishkov eds., United Nations University Press, 1996). Used by permission of the publisher.

Munro, Colin R., STUDIES IN CONSTITUTIONAL LAW (2d ed. 1999). Reproduced by permission of The Butterworth Division of Reed Elsevier (UK) Ltd.

Murphy, Walter F., *Merlin's Memory*: *The Past and Future Imperfect of the Once and Future Polity*, in RESPONDING TO IMPERFECTION: THE THEORY AND PRACTICE OF CONSTITUTIONAL AMENDMENT (Sanford Levinson ed., Princeton University Press, 1995). © 1995 by Princeton University Press. Reprinted by permission of Princeton University Press.

Nimmer, Melville B., *The Right to Speak from* Times *to* Time: *First Amendment Theory Applied to Libel and Misapplied to Privacy*, 56 CALIFORNIA LAW REVIEW 935 (1968). © 1968 by the California Law Review, Inc. Reprinted from California Law Review by permission of the Regents of the University of California.

Nino, Carlos, RADICAL EVIL ON TRIAL (Yale University Press, 1996). © 1996 by Yale University Press. Reprinted by the permission of the Journal of Law & Religion.

O'Connell, Rory, *Theories of Religious Education in Ireland* 14 JOURNAL OF LAW & RELIGION 433 (1999-2000). Reprinted by permission of the journal.

Olowofoyeku, Abimbola A., *Devolution: Conceptual and Implementational Problems*, 29 ANGLO-AMERICAN LAW REVIEW, 137 (2000). Reprinted with permission of Vathek Publishing.

Parikh, Sunita, and Barry R. Weingast, *A Comparative Theory of Federalism: India* 83 VIRGINIA LAW REVIEW 1593 (1994). Used by permission of the Virginia Law Review.

Preuss, Ulrich K., *Patterns of Constitutional Evolution and Change in Eastern Europe*, in CONSTITUTIONAL POLICY AND CHANGE IN EUROPE (Joachim J. Hesse and Nevil Johnson eds., Oxford University Press, 1995). © 1995. Reprinted by permission of Oxford University Press.

_____, *Constitutional Powermaking for the New Polity: Some Deliberations on the Relation Between Constituent Power and the Constitution*, in CONSTITUTIONALISM, IDENTITY, DIFFERENCE AND LEGITIMACY: THEORETICAL PERSPECTIVES (Michel Rosenfeld ed., Duke University Press, 1994). Copyright 1999, Duke University Press. All rights reserved. Used by the permission of the publisher.

Quint, Peter E., *Free Speech and Private Law in German Constitutional Theory*, 48 MARYLAND LAW REVIEW 247 (1989). © Peter E. Quint. Reprinted by permission of the author.

Rapaczynski, Andrzej, *Bibliographical Essay: The Influence of U.S. Constitutionalism Abroad*, in CONSTITUTIONALISM AND RIGHTS: THE INFLUENCE OF THE UNITED STATES CONSTITUTION ABROAD (Louis Henkin and Albert J. Rosenthal eds. © 1990, Columbia University Press). Reprinted with permission of the publisher.

Reich, Charles, *The New Property*, 73 YALE LAW JOURNAL 733 (1964). Reprinted by permission of The Yale Law Journal Company and William S. Hein Company.

ATIVE LAW REVIEW 617 (1999). © 1999 by University of California, Hastings College of Law. Reprinted by permission.

Sartori, Giovanni, *Constitutionalism: A Preliminary Discussion*, 56 AMERICAN POLITICAL SCIENCE REVIEW 853 (1962). Reprinted with permision of Cambridge University Press.

Savigear, Peter, *Autonomy and the Unitary State: The Case of Corsica*, in FEDERALISM AND NATIONALISM (Murray Forsyth ed., 1989). © Murray Forsyth. Reprinted with permission of Palgrave.

Schauer, Frederick, *Easy Cases*, 58 SOUTHERN CALIFORNIA LAW REVIEW 399 (1985). Reprinted by permission of the Southern California Law Review.

_____, FREE SPEECH: A PHILOSOPHICAL INQUIRY (Cambridge University Press, 1982). Reprinted with permission of Cambridge University Press.

Schuck, Peter H., *The Perceived Values of Diversity, Then and Now*, 22 CARDOZO LAW REVIEW 1915 (2001). Reprinted by permission of the Cardozo Law Review.

Schulhofer, Stephen J., Miranda*'s Practical Effect: Substantial Benefits and Vanishingly Small Social Costs*, 90 NORTHWESTERN UNIVERSITY LAW REVIEW 500 (1996). Reprinted by permission of Northwestern University Law Review.

Senelle, Robert, *The Reform of the Belgian State*, in FEDERALIZING EUROPE: THE COSTS, BENEFITS AND PRECONDITIONS OF FEDERAL POLITICAL SYSTEMS (Joachim Jens Hesse and Vincent Wright eds., Oxford University Press, 2001). Reprinted by permission of Oxford University Press.

Shiffrin, Steven H., *Defamatory Non-Media Speech and First Amendment Methodology*, 25 U.C.L.A. LAW REVIEW 915 (1978). Reprinted by permission of the author.

Silverstein, Steven, *Medical Confidentiality in Israeli Law*, 30 JOHN MARSHALL LAW REVIEW 747 (1997). Reprinted with permission from the John Marshall Law Review.

Singh, Mahendra P., *Securing the Independence of the Judiciary—The Indian Experience*, 10 INDIANA INTERNATIONAL & COMPARATIVE LAW REVIEW 245 (2000). Reprinted by permission of the Indiana International & Comparative Law Review.

Solozábal, Juan José, *Spain: A Federation in the Making?*, in FEDERALIZING EUROPE: THE COSTS, BENEFITS AND PRECONDITIONS OF FEDERAL POLITICAL SYSTEMS (Joachim Jens Hesse and Vincent Wright eds., Oxford University Press, 1996). Reprinted by permission of Oxford University Press, Inc.

Stein, Eric, *International Law in Internal Law: Toward Internationalization of Central-Eastern European Constitutions?*, 88 AMERICAN JOURNAL OF INTERNATIONAL LAW 427 (1994). Reproduced with permission. © The American Society of International Law.

Stepan, Alfred, and Cindy Skach, *Presidentialism and Parliamentarism in Comparative Perspective*, in THE FAILURE OF PRESIDENTIAL DEMOC-

RACY (Juan Linz and Arturo Valenzuela eds., Johns Hopkins University Press, 1994). © The Johns Hopkins University Press.

Stone, Adrienne, *The Limits of Constitutional Text and Structure: Standards of Review and the Freedom of Political Communication*, 23 MELBOURNE UNIVERSITY LAW REVIEW 668 (1999). Reprinted by permission of the Melbourne University Law Review.

Sunstein, Cass R., *On Property and Constitutionalism*, in CONSTITUTIONALISM, IDENTITY, DIFFERENCE AND LEGITIMACY: THEORETICAL PERSPECTIVES (Michel Rosenfeld ed., Duke University Press, 1994). Copyright, 1997, Duke University Press. All rights reserved. Used by permission of the publisher.

Sweet, Alec Stone, GOVERNING WITH JUDGES: CONSTITUTIONAL POLITICS IN EUROPE (Oxford University Press, 2000). Reprinted by permission of Oxford University Press, Inc.

_____, THE BIRTH OF JUDICIAL POLITICS IN FRANCE (1992). © 1992 by Oxford University Press, Inc. Reprinted by permission of Oxford University Press, Inc.

Taylor, Greg, *The Commerce Clause—Commonwealth Comparisons*, 24 Boston COLLEGE INTERNATIONAL & COMPARATIVE LAW REVIEW 235 (2001). Reprinted by permission of the Boston College International & Comparative Law Review.

Thio, Li-Ann, *The Secular Trumps the Sacred: Constitutional Issues Arising from* Colin Chan v. Public Prosecutor, 16 SINGAPORE LAW REVIEW 26 (1995). Used by permission of the author.

Traynor, Roger, *Quo Vadis, Prospective Overruling: A Question of Judicial Responsibility*, 28 HASTINGS L.J. 533 (1977). © 1977 by University of California, Hastings College of Law. Reprinted by permission of the Hastings Law Journal.

Tribe, Laurence H., AMERICAN CONSTITUTIONAL LAW (2d ed., Foundation Press, 1988). Reprinted by permission of Foundation Press.

Troper, Michel, *The Problem of the Islamic Veil and the Principle of School Neutrality in France*, in THE LAW OF RELIGIOUS IDENTITY: MODELS FOR POST-COMMUNISM (András Sajó and Shlomo Avineri eds., 1999). © Kluwer Law International.

Van Kessel, Gordon, *Adversary Excesses in the American Criminal Trial*, 67 NOTRE DAME LAW REVIEW 403 (1992). Reprinted with permission. © by Notre Dame Law Review, University of Notre Dame.

Van Kessel, Gordon, *European Perspectives on the Accused as a Source of Testimonial Evidence*, 100 WEST VIRGINIA LAW REVIEW 799 (1998). Reprinted with permission of the author.

Weiss, Jonathan, *Privilege, Posture and Protection—"Religion" in the Law*, 73 YALE L.J. 593 (1964). Reprinted by permission of The Yale Law Journal Company and William S. Hein Company.

Whitman, James Q., *Enforcing Civility and Respect: Three Societies*, 109 YALE L. J. 1279 (2000). Reprinted by permission of The Yale Law Journal Company and William S. Hein Company.

Witte, Jr., John, *A Dickensian Era of Religious Rights: An Update on Religious Human Rights in Global Perspective*, 42 WILLIAM & MARY LAW REVIEW 707 (2001). Copyright © 2000 by the William and Mary Law Review. Reprinted with permission.

Würtenberger, Thomas, *Equality*, in THE CONSTITUTION OF THE FEDERAL REPUBLIC OF GERMANY (Ulrich Karpen ed., Nomos, 1988). Reprinted by permission of the publisher.

Zupancic, Bostjan M., THE PRIVILEGE AGAINST SELF-INCRIMINATION AS A HUMAN RIGHT (unpublished manuscript) (1999). Reprinted by permission of the author.

*

Summary of Contents

*

Table of Contents

*

Table of Cases

The principal cases are in bold type. Cases cited or discussed in the text are roman type. References are to pages. Cases cited in principal cases and within other quoted materials are not included.

Table of Authorities

References are to Pages

A Note on Citations

This book cites to cases and secondary authorities from a large number of jurisdictions. Sometimes it is not clear what reporter or form of citation is appropriate, and although we have diligently tried to achieve accuracy there may be miscitations of one kind or another.

Where there is an official or preferred reporter, such as the U.S. Reports or the South Africa Law Reports (SALR), we have cited to it whenever possible.

When reproducing cases and other authorities, we have retained the American or British spellings of words and the form of citations as used by courts and authors.

Footnotes retained from excerpted material include their original numbering. Footnotes inserted by the editors are indicated by lower case letters. Omitted material from excerpted text or footnotes is indicated by asterisks, and material we have added is placed in brackets.

We have used the following acronyms:

BCCL, Bulletin on Constitutional Case-law

ECHR, European Court of Human Rights

ECJ, European Court of Justice

European HR Convention, European Convention for the Protection of Human Rights and Fundamental Freedoms

GFCC, German Federal Constitutional Court

HCC, Hungarian Constitutional Court

ICC, Italian Constitutional Court

ISC, Indian Supreme Court

RCC, Russian Constitutional Court

SACC, South African Constitutional Court

USSC, United States Supreme Court

*

COMPARATIVE CONSTITUTIONALISM
Cases and Materials

*

Chapter 1

WHAT IS A CONSTITUTION?

This chapter tackles the major, general subjects central to the issues and concerns surrounding comparative constitutional law. Section A., titled Why Comparative Constitutional Law?, explores the uses, benefits, rewards, drawbacks, and pitfalls of comparative analysis in constitutional law. Section B. analyzes the concept of "constitutionalism," which remains elusive and contested, and is distinguished from the concept of the "constitution." Section C. focuses on the relation among "constitutionalism," "justice," and "the rule of law." Section D. deals with constitutional models implemented throughout the world, including the contrast between written and unwritten constitutions; the major types of contemporary constitutional systems; and in light of the recent consolidation of supranational governing systems, such as the European Union, the prospects for cogent supranational constitutions. Finally, Section E. examines the issues surrounding the making and altering or revising of constitutions and focuses particularly on the relationship between constitution-making and constitutional amendment.

A. WHY COMPARATIVE CONSTITUTIONAL LAW?

Comparison is at the center of all serious inquiry and learning. Moreover, our natural curiosity prompts us to compare our experiences, beliefs, customs, traditions, and natural and institutional settings with those of others far and near. Consistent with this, the study of law, naturally, should be drawn to—and benefit from—comparative analysis in general and comparative constitutional analysis in particular. This has grown more common, as the world becomes increasingly interdependent, constitutional law expands beyond national boundaries, and national courts responsible for constitutional adjudication look more frequently to their counterparts in other countries for ideas and guidance.

Interest in comparative constitutional law has palpably increased in recent decades, due to, among other developments, (1) the proliferation of new constitutions and transitions to constitutional democracy in various parts of the world, such as Eastern Europe, sub-Saharan Africa, and Latin America, and (2) the growing trend toward internationalization of constitutional rights, begun after World War Two. Even before, by the end of World War One, a large number of national constitutions already gave clear recognition to the fundamental rights of the individual. In the aftermath of World War Two, upon the creation of the United Nations, in 1945, and its proclamation of the Universal Declaration of Human Rights, in 1948, the trend toward the internationalization of fundamental rights was decidedly on its way. Although the 1948 Declaration wielded no legally binding force, clearly it thrust the kinds of rights promoted by the French Declaration of the Rights of Man and of the Citizen of 1789 and the American Bill of Rights of 1791 to the forefront of the international arena. The 1948 Declaration was followed by the International Covenant on Civil and Political Rights (ICCPR) and the International Covenant on Economic, Social and Cultural Rights (ICESCR), which became binding after ratification by a sufficient number of states, in 1976, ten years after initial approval by the UN. Concurrent with the expansion of international human rights, several regional charters for the protection of human rights emerged, including the European Convention for the Protection of Human Rights and Fundamental Freedoms (hereafter, European HR Convention) and its African and American counterparts. Although both international and regional schemes for the protection of human rights emanate from international treaties rather than constitutions and often differ significantly in application and implementation from rights enshrined in domestic constitutions, transnational rights share much in terms of content and scope with many of their domestic counterparts. Moreover, in some cases, such as the rights protected by the European HR Convention, judicial enforcement is akin to what is generally available under many domestic constitutions. For instance, an aggrieved individual in a country party to the European HR Convention may pursue claims arising under the Convention before the European Court of Human Rights (ECHR), seated in Strasbourg, France. See, generally, Mark Janis, Richard Kay, and Anthony Bradley, *European Human Rights Law: Text and Materials* (2d ed. 2000).

In more recent times, contacts among judges from different countries have increased sharply, and foreign judicial decisions have become more readily available through the Internet.[a] Moreover, interest in, and opportunities for, exchanges among constitutional scholars from different parts of the world have risen in the past couple decades.[b] Notwithstanding these evolving trends, comparative legal studies in general and comparative constitutional law in particular are subject to special challenges and objections. Possible objections, concerning the feasibility, desirability, and utility of meaningful comparative analysis, concentrate around the danger of misinterpreting foreign legal and constitutional

a. See, e.g., Elizabeth Greathouse, *Justices See Joint Issues with the EU*, Wash. Post, July 9, 1998 (Justices O'Connor and Breyer commenting on a meeting between four U.S. Supreme Court justices and the judges of the court of the European Communities, in Luxembourg, and indicating that they might use, and refer to, European Union court decisions).

b. For example, the International Association of Constitutional Law regularly organizes meetings, bringing together constitutionalists from all parts of the world. In its 1999 World Congress, in Rotterdam, more than 400 scholars from 55 countries gathered to discuss various comparative constitutional law issues.

materials by taking them out of context. Legal norms and institutions are embedded in particular sociopolitical and cultural settings, and their meaning and import are linked, at least in part, to such settings. Accordingly, to the extent that the comparativist is unfamiliar with the context of foreign materials examined for purposes of comparison, he or she may misinterpret apparent similarities or misunderstand the import of apparent differences.

These difficulties seem more daunting in constitutional law than in private law. For example, to the extent that contract law is predominantly concerned with facilitating economic exchange and maximizing efficiency, political and cultural differences may play a rather minor role in meaningful comparison of various national contract law regimes. In contrast, constitutional frameworks and objectives may differ so markedly from one country to the next as to raise serious questions about the worth of comparative analysis. How can separation-of-powers problems or solutions in a presidential democracy, such as the U.S., be relevant for a parliamentary democracy, such as Germany or India? Or, how does the teaching of religion in public schools in a country where it is clearly constitutionally permissible, such as Germany, bear any useful relation to the same issue in countries with constitutions committed to the separation between religion and the state, such as France or the U.S.? Cf. Otto Kahn–Freund, *On the Uses and Misuses of Comparative Law,* 37 Mod. L. Rev. 1, 6, 7 (1974) (arguing that private law is much more amenable to transplant from one country to another than constitutional law).

Although these difficulties should not be overlooked, they can be adequately managed through proper consideration of significant contextual differences. Moreover, in the case of basic human rights, which are widely incorporated in national constitutions as well as in international and regional conventions, there are strong indications of widespread overlap—if not underlying universalism—at the core. For an enlightening and thorough discussion of the controversy over the "universalism" or "relativism" of human rights, see Yash Ghai, *Universalism and Relativism: Human Rights as Framework for Negotiating Interethnic Claims,* 21 Cardozo L. Rev. 1095 (2000). For a defense of a workable overlap in the context of cultural diversity, see Charles Taylor, *Conditions of an Unenforced Consensus on Human Rights,* in *The East Asian Challenge for Rights* 124–46 (Joanne R. Bauer and Daniel Bell eds., 1999); Abdullahi Ahmed An–Naim, *Towards an Islamic Reformation: Civil Liberties, Human Rights and International Law* (1990) (arguing for universal standards subject to culturally diverse interpretations); Michel Rosenfeld, *Can Human Rights Bridge the Gap Between Universalism and Cultural Pluralism? A Pluralist Critique Based on the Rights of Minorities,* 30 Colum. H.R.L. Rev. 249 (1999) (rejecting both universalism and relativism and arguing for a pluralistic approach resulting in widespread convergence amid certain inevitable divergences).

Another compelling reason for the pursuit of comparative constitutional analysis stems form the fact that constitutional norms elaborated in one country have often been adopted in others. Thus the Canadian Charter of Rights and Freedoms (Constitution Act of 1982, pt. I) has influenced the drafting of bills of rights in South Africa, New Zealand, and Hong Kong and the Basic Law in Israel. See Sujit Choudhry, *Globalization in Search of Justification: Towards a Theory of Comparative Constitutional Interpretation,* 74 Ind. L.J. 819, 821–22 (1999). Such borrowings, moreover, have occurred not only in the context of constitution-making but also in constitutional interpretation. See, e.g., Gary J. Jacobsohn, *Apple of Gold: Constitutionalism in Israel and the United States* ch VI (1993) (discussing the Israeli Supreme Court's adoption of American First Amendment free speech doctrine in the elaboration of its own free speech jurisprudence). See also the *Ahmadis* cases in Chapter 8.

The sharing of constitutional materials from one country to another has also led to rejection rather than adoption. In this case a country considers constitutional norms or doctrines prevalent in another country and deliberately decides to reject them in the course of instituting its own constitutional norms or doctrines. Typically such rejections follow from a conclusion that the norms originating abroad are either inefficient or contrary to the basic values, ideology, or constitutional objectives of the potentially borrowing country. Thus, after careful analysis of U.S. free speech jurisprudence in the context of a hate speech case, the Canadian Supreme Court rejected the American approach for reasons both of ideology and efficiency. See *R. v. Keegstra,* [1990] 3 S.C.R. 697. In short, as Jon Elster noted in examining constitutional elaboration in the course of transition to democracy in Eastern Europe, upon the collapse of the Soviet empire, "in constitutional debates, one invariably finds a large number of references to other constitutions," in some cases "as models to be imitated" but in others "as disasters to be avoided, or simply as evidence for certain views about human nature." Jon Elster, *Constitutionalism in Eastern Europe: An Introduction,* 58 U. Chi. L. Rev. 447, 476 (1991).

References to constitutions other than one's own are thus important not only in terms of searching for similarities but also in terms of looking for relevant or useful differences. This is true from the standpoint of constitution-makers or interpreters and from those engaged in comparative analysis. Moreover, both users and analysts of foreign constitutional materials confront the need to deal successfully with relevant context-dependent variables. Accordingly, the tasks performed by comparativists bear strong similarity to those confronting all legal practitioners and scholars. In both cases analogical reasoning—that is, drawing analogies and ferreting out disanalogies—is crucial. Cf. Cass R. Sunstein, *On Analogical Reasoning*, 106 Harv. L. Rev. 741 (1998) (stressing prominence and superiority of analogical reasoning in law). The key difference between those who use foreign constitutional materials and those who remain within their own national scene is that the former will typically confront greater difficulties than the latter concerning access and proper evaluation of the relevant contextual issues.

Because of the multiplicity and complexity of contextual variables, apparent similarities or differences stemming from diverse national constitutions may sometimes prove misleading. For example, a cursory review of various freedom of speech provisions drawn from numerous constitutions throughout the world, reveals a striking similarity in the formulation of that right. Examination of how freedom of speech is construed in various countries, however, reveals vast discrepancies, ranging from virtually unconstrained liberty to extensive speech regulation. See Frederick Schauer, *Free Speech and the Cultural Contingency of Constitutional Categories*, in *Constitutionalism, Identity, Difference and Legitimacy: Theoretical Perspectives* 353 (Michel Rosenfeld ed., 1994). What consequences should be drawn from Schauer's conclusions? That the constitutional text matters little? That not all cultural traditions share the same respect for fundamental constitutional rights? Or that different cultures genuinely disagree on the proper scope of freedom of expression? Or else, that they may not so much disagree as they confront, respectively, varying degrees of threats to political stability?

Conversely, what appears to be clearly different may turn out in the end to be quite similar. Compare, for example, the nearly contemporaneous abortion decisions issued by the U.S. Supreme Court (USSC) and the German Federal Constitutional Court (GFCC). In *Roe v. Wade*, 410 U.S. 113 (1973), (see Chapter 5, Subsection C.1.) the USSC recognized a constitutional right to abortion predicated on a woman's privacy and liberty rights. In contrast, the GFCC, in the *Abortion I Case*, 39 BVerfGE 1 (1975), (see Chapter 5, Subsection C.1.) stressed above all the paramountcy of the right to life, noting the German Constitution's great commitment to reversing the Nazi regime's wanton disregard for life evinced by its implementation of the extermination plan embodied in its "final-solution" policy. In spite of their markedly different approaches, however, both courts carved out abortion rights that seem nearly equivalent in terms of their practical scope. Are the differences between the two abortion jurisprudences or the similarities between the practical results worthy of greater emphasis? Are the differences merely a matter of rationalization in the context of different political cultures? Or do they carry important legal or constitutional implications? Noteworthy in this connection is that both Germany and the U.S. later narrowed the scope of constitutionally protected abortions. See Chapter 5, Subsection C.1., for the relevant cases.

There is one crucial difference between the use of foreign constitutional materials by constitution-makers or interpreters on the one hand and comparativists on the other. The former typically adopt a *participant* perspective, while the latter are properly confined to embracing an *observer* perspective. While a participant may approach foreign constitutional materials with due concern for relevant contextual nuances, he or she may also have recourse to such materials for *strategic* purposes. An interpreter in a recently established constitutional order, for instance, may borrow materials from an established constitutional order to imbue domestic constitutional interpretations with an aura of greater legitimacy. But in borrowing material from other constitutions a participant may have less concern with a true fit than with the appearance of a fit in order to achieve greater legitimacy. See, e.g., Jacobsohn, *op. cit.* at ch 6 (pointing out that although the Supreme Court of Israel has widely embraced American First Amendment doctrine in the context of its hate speech jurisprudence, it has nonetheless reached results that are diametrically opposed to those in American courts).

For reasons of principle and experience it seems quite natural that new constitutional democracies should borrow constitutional materials from older, more-established constitutional orders. A recent example is South Africa, which established a new constitutional order upon repudiation of its apartheid past. The South African Constitution specifically empowers courts to consider foreign law when interpreting the Bill of Rights. S.Afr. Const. § 39(1) (c.). Consistent with this mandate, the South African Constitutional Court (SACC) has relied heavily on foreign constitutional materials. See Margaret A. Burnham, *Cultivating a Seedling Charter: South Africa's Court Grows its Constitution,* 3 Mich. J. Race & L. 29, 44 (1997) (SACC's use of comparative jurisprudence as means for South Africa to claim "its place among the world's constitutional democracies"); *State v. Mhlugu,* 1995 (3) SALR 867, 917 (CC) (According to Justice Sachs, South Africa's constitutional jurisprudence must take its place "as part of a global development of constitutionalism and human rights.").

Conversely, one might expect that older, more-developed constitutional systems might be less prone to drawing materials form other constitutions. While this may have been true in the past, it is certainly less so now. There are several reasons for this shift, including the trend toward internationalization of constitutional norms and the increased availability of foreign materials for comparison, both mentioned above. Additionally, scientific advances and changing material conditions give rise to new constitutional issues that the older systems have not yet encountered and that on occasion may be adjudicated first within more recently established constitutional democracies. See, e.g., *Washington v. Glucksberg,* 521 U.S. 702 (1997) (in ruling on constitutionality of assisted suicide the USSC referred to earlier decisions on the subject by courts in Australia and Colombia).

Traditionally, the U.S., which boasts the world's oldest living constitution, has been particularly resistant to comparative approaches to constitutional law, but this is changing. Significantly, Professor Bruce Ackerman, a foremost constitutional theorist, appears to have altered his views on the uses of comparative law within less than a decade. In 1991, he wrote that "to discover the [American] Constitution we must approach it without the assistance of guides imported from another time and place. Americans * * * have * * * built a genuinely distinctive pattern of constitutional thought and practice." Bruce A. Ackerman, *We The People: Foundations* 3 (1991). By 1997, however, he was focusing on the rise of "world constitutionalism." See Bruce A. Ackerman, *The Rise of World Constitutionalism,* 83 Va. L. Rev. 771, 774–75 (1997), where he wrote:

> First and foremost, we must learn to think about the American experience in a different way. Until very recently, it was appropriate to give it a privileged position in comparative study. Other experiments with written constitutions and judicial review were simply too short to warrant confident predictions about which if any, would successfully shape long run political evolution. But as we move to the next century, such skepticism is no longer justified. Places like Germany or Italy or the European Union or India will be passing the fifty-year mark in their

experiments with written texts and constitutional courts; France and Spain will soon be experiencing the distinctive challenges of a second full generation of judicial review * * *. [A]ll these initiatives * * * add up to a formidable fund of experience for comparative investigation. Against this emerging background, we must learn to look upon the American experience as a special case, not as the paradigmatic case.

Given the increasing role of comparative constitutional law, what can be gained from the study of foreign constitutional materials and from acquiring the skills of comparative analysis? To the extent that one's own domestic courts use and refer to foreign constitutional materials, law students and legal practitioners need to become familiar with such materials and learn how to deal with them, much as they must with their equivalent domestic materials. Beyond that, there is no consensus on the potential of comparative work in constitutional law. This is due, in part, to the different uses that may be made of comparative materials. While a casebook may suggest the primacy of comparing cases in the context of judicial interpretation of constitutional norms, consideration of foreign materials can be useful for other purposes, such as making or amending a constitution. Thus in rejecting the relevance of foreign constitutional experience in the context of adjudicating a dispute concerning the limits of the national government's powers under American federalism, in *Printz v. United States,* 521 U.S. 898 (1997), (see Chapter 4) Justice Scalia emphasized that "comparative analysis [is] inappropriate to the task of interpreting a constitution though it [is,] of course, quite relevant to the task of writing one." *Id.* at 921 n.11. But see Justice Breyer's dissenting opinion in *Printz* (see Chapter 4). Moreover, assuming comparative analysis is appropriate both in constitutional interpretation and in constitution-making, its value may vary, depending on which of the two is at stake. Thus Justice Breyer argued for consideration of foreign experiences with federalism in *Printz* for the limited purposes of dealing with open questions and for these to be resolved pursuant to empirical evaluation. In contrast, in determining what kind of federalism to embrace in the making of a new constitution, a much broader use of foreign materials may be warranted.

The lack of consensus concerning the proper role of comparative analysis is also due to broader ideological disagreements about the nature and function of law. At one end of the spectrum are those who believe that the legal problems that confront all societies are essentially similar and that their solutions are fundamentally universal. See, e.g., Konrad Zweigert and Hein Kötz, *Introduction to Comparative Law* 36 (Tony Weir trans., 2d ed. 1987); David M. Beatty, *Constitutional Law in Theory and Practice* (1995) (arguing that basic principles of constitutional law are essentially the same throughout the world). At the other pole are those who maintain that all legal problems are so tied to a society's particular history and culture that what is relevant in one constitutional context cannot be relevant, or at least similarly relevant, in another. Compare Montesquieu's observation that "the political and civil laws of each nation * * * should be so appropriate to the people for whom they are made that it is very unlikely that the laws of one nation can suit another." Charles de Secondat, Baron de Montesquieu, *The Spirit of*

Laws 8 (Ann M. Cohler et al. eds. and trans., 1989). Between the two extremes are various other positions. Some believe that the problems confronted by different societies are essentially the same, see, e.g., Mary Ann Glendon, *Rights in Twentieth–Century Constitutions*, 59 U. Chi. L. Rev. 519, 535 (1992), but that the solutions are likely to be different, owing to varying circumstances that distinguish one society from the next. See Mary Ann Glendon, *Comparative Legal Traditions* 10 (2d ed. 1994). Consistent with this view, the principal benefit of comparative work stems from its ability to highlight the specific presuppositions, distinct conditions, and particular cultural and ideological commitments that circumscribe domestic constitutional norms and practices that tend to be taken for granted. In this view the most important function of comparative constitutional analysis is to enhance the knowledge and understanding of one's own system.

Without regard to whether problems and solutions are essentially similar across different constitutional systems, one can maintain that there is a significant degree of congruence between problems and their possible solutions across the spectrum of contemporary constitutional democracy. Accordingly, comparative analysis can be useful even if the specific constitutional norms or practices prevalent in one system are unlikely to have a direct impact on another constitutional system. For example, although systems of constitutional review vary greatly (see Chapter 2), their proliferation since the end of World War Two has yielded much information for fruitful comparative analysis.

Constitutional "transplants" and influences are proper subjects of comparative analysis, but their evaluation is bound to depend on the particular take one has on the dynamic between similarities and differences across separate constitutional orders. One important variable is how one construes the nexus between constitutional norms and national identity. If the nexus is weak, then transplants may be relatively unproblematic. Cf. Cass R. Sunstein, *On Property and Constitutionalism*, in *Constitutionalism, Identity, Difference and Legitimacy: Theoretical Perspectives* 383, 398 (Michel Rosenfeld ed., 1994) (arguing for implantation of Western-type private property rights and against constutionalization of social rights in new constitutions for formerly socialist Eastern European polities in transition to market economies). Professor Sunstein stated:

> It is often said that constitutions, as a form of higher law, must be compatible with the culture and mores of those whom they regulate. In one sense, however, the opposite is true. Constitutional provisions should be designed to work against precisely those aspects of a country's culture and tradition that are likely to produce harm through that country's ordinary political processes. There is a large difference between the risks of harm faced by a nation committed by culture and history to free markets, and the corresponding risks in a nation committed by culture and history to social security and general state protection.

Some have argued that the link between a country's constitution and its national identity may vary greatly. For example, Professor Tushnet has contrasted the Indian Constitution, which he characterizes as quite removed from the country's identity, to the American Constitution, which he claims expresses the national character. Mark V. Tushnet, *The Possibilities of Comparative Constitutional Law,* 108 Yale L.J. 1225, 1270–71 (1999). Does this mean that a country like the U.S. should be less susceptible to constitutional transplants than one like India? Or does it simply mean that countries are open to different kinds of transplants, depending on how closely their constitutions are linked to their national character?

Constitutional influence or transplants can be either positive or negative. See Andrzej Rapaczynski, *Bibliographical Essay: The Influence of U.S. Constitutionalism Abroad*, in *Constitutionalism and Rights: The Influence of the United States Constitution Abroad* 405, 407–08 (Louis Henkin and Albert J. Rosenthal eds., 1990):

> By "positive influence" I mean the adoption or transformation of a legal concept, doctrine, or institution modeled in whole or in part on an American original, where those responsible are aware of the American precedent and this awareness plays some part in their decision. An example is the adoption of the American type of federalism in Australia, or the influence of American First Amendment doctrines on the free speech jurisprudence of Israel. * * * By "negative influence," I mean a process in which an American model is known, considered, and rejected, or in which an American experience perceived as undesirable is used as an argument for not following the American example. Examples of this kind of influence are provided by the Indian decision not to include a due process clause in the Indian constitution, or the portrayal of judicial review as a reactionary American institution in preventing its establishment in France in the first half of the twentieth century * * *.

Whether positive or negative, influences and transplants are more likely to involve transformation rather than mere copy and are more prone to being dynamic rather than purely static. For example, the Indian rejection of a due process clause stemmed from a consideration of the American experience in enshrining substantive property norms in the early twentieth century. See, e.g., *Lochner v. New York*, 198 U.S. 45 (1905), in Chapter 10, Subsection B.1. (New York law limiting number of hours of work of bakery employees held to violate due process property rights of employers and employees). Although this interpretation of the Due Process Clause was repudiated by the USSC in the 1930s (see Chapter 10), the Indian framers, acting in the late 1940s, considered the American experience and specifically opted to exclude property due process rights form their new constitution to ensure against repeating the American *Lochner* experience. See Soli J. Sorabjee, *Equality in the United States and India*, in *Constitutionalism and Rights*, above, at 94, 96–97.

Perhaps the most daunting task confronting the comparativist is that of properly evaluating similarities and differences. Initial appearances may not prove accurate. See Michel Rosenfeld, *Justices at Work: An Introduction,* 18 Cardozo L. Rev. 1609, 1609–10 (1997). In part, however, as critical theorists have warned, comparativists may overestimate similarities for ideological reasons. See Günther Frankenberg, *Stranger than Paradise: Identity & Politics in Comparative Law,* 1997 Utah L. Rev. 259, 262–63 (criticizing mainstream comparativists as

"Anglo–Eurocentric" paternalists prone to imposing Western hegemonic approaches on the subject and characterizing comparative law as "a postmodern form of conquest executed through legal transplants and harmonization strategies"). Critical scholars have also contended that domestic law is ideological. See, e.g., Roberto Mangabeira Unger, *The Critical Legal Studies Movement,* 96 Harv. L. Rev. 561 (1983). Are ideological distortions likely to be more problematic in the context of comparative law than in domestic law? Or are differences in ideology or perceptions of such differences likely to play similar roles in both fields?

B. WHAT IS CONSTITUTIONALISM?

"Constitutionalism" cannot be equated with "constitution," though the two concepts are linked. At present, most countries—and numerous subnational political units, such as the states in the U.S., the *Länder* in Germany, and the cantons in Switzerland—have constitutions, but not all such constitutions satisfy the requirements of constitutionalism. Whether a country has a constitution is a question of fact, easily answered in most cases and particularly in those where an institutionalized, written constitution is involved. In contrast, whether a constitution conforms to the dictates of constitutionalism cannot be determined without some kind of *normative* evaluation. Constitutionalism is an ideal that may be more or less approximated by different types of constitutions and that is built on certain *prescriptions* and certain *proscriptions*. Determining whether a particular constitution approximates the ideal of constitutionalism, and to what extent, depends on an evaluation of how the institutions and norms promoted by the constitution in question fare in terms of the constitutionalist ideal.

What does the ideal of constitutionalism require? No consensus exists in answering this question. Consider, however, the following.

Louis Henkin, A NEW BIRTH OF CONSTITUTIONALISM: GENETIC INFLUENCES AND GENETIC DEFECTS, in CONSTITUTIONALISM, IDENTITY, DIFFERENCE AND LEGITIMACY: THEORETICAL PERSPECTIVES

39, 40–42 (Michel Rosenfeld ed., 1994).

Sources of political ideas and models for institutions or instruments are rarely single or simple, and they are notoriously difficult to identify. The ideas that fed the spread of constitutionalism, and the earlier expressions of constitutionalism that shaped recent constitutions, cannot be determined with confidence. Locke, Montesquieu, Kant, Rousseau, and their successors (Bentham, Mill, the socialists) have fed the stream of relevant ideas, but contemporary framers of constitutions rarely go back to original sources for guidance. There can be little doubt, however, of the immediate influence of two prominent instruments of constitutional character: the United States Constitution and its Bill of Rights, now 200 years old, and the International Bill of Rights—the common designation for the Universal Declaration of Human Rights and the two principal international covenants on human rights[1] born in our times and still maturing.[2]

* * *

Constitutionalism is nowhere defined. We speak of it as if its meaning is self-evident, or that we know it when we see it. Constitutionalism is commonly identified with a written constitution, yet not all constitutional texts are committed to the principles and serve the ends of constitutionalism. A constitution generally provides a blueprint for governance and government, but the system that is blueprinted may not satisfy the demands of constitutionalism. Some constitutions merely describe the existing system of government, proclaim societal goals, promise programs and policies, or serve other purposes that may not be intimately related to the concerns of constitutionalism.

The following sets out, in summary form, my understanding of the principal demands of constitutionalism.

1. Contemporary constitutionalism is based on popular sovereignty. "The people" is the locus of "sovereignty"; the will of the people is the source of authority and the basis of legitimate government. The people alone can ordain and establish the constitution and the system of government. The people remain responsible for the system which they establish.

2. A constitutionalistic constitution is prescriptive; it is law; it is supreme law. Government must conform to the constitutional blueprint and to any limitations the constitution imposes. There can be no legitimate government other than as constitutionally ordained.

3. With popular sovereignty have come related ideas, namely, government ruled by law and governed by democratic principles. Constitutionalism therefore requires commitment to political democracy and to representative government. Even in times of national emergency, the people remain sovereign. Constitutionalism excludes government by decree, except as authorized by the constitution and subject to control by democratic political institutions.

4. Out of popular sovereignty and democratic government come dependent commitments to the following: limited government; separation of powers or other checks and balances; civilian control of the military;

1. Universal Declaration of Human Rights, G.A. Res. 217A (III). U.N. Doc A/810, at 71, (1948); International Covenant on Civil and Political Rights, Dec 16, 1966, 999 U.N.T.S. 171; International Covenant on Economic, Social and Cultural Rights, Dec. 16, 1966, 993 U.N.T.S. 3.

2. No doubt other influences should be credited. England contributed to the idea of limited government, beginning with the Magna Carta, and to the idea of parliamentary government, through the Glorious Revolution and the Bill of Rights (1688). The French Declaration of the Rights of Man and of the Citizen helped spread the idea of inherent rights around the world. The French Declaration itself borrowed from American instruments. * * *

In a number of respects, notably the movement to a Constitutional Court (as distinguished from constitutional review by the ordinary national judiciary as in the United States) the Basic Law of the Federal Republic of Germany has served as a model, and various other European constitutions have doubtless been studied by constitution makers in Eastern and Central Europe and elsewhere. Many of those instruments also derived ideas and followed examples from the United States and from the international human rights movement.

police governed by law and judicial control; and an independent judiciary.

5. Constitutionalism requires that government respect and ensure individual rights, which generally are those same rights recognized by the Universal Declaration of Human Rights. Rights may be subject to some limitations in the public interest, but such limitations themselves have limits. Some rights may be suspended in times of national emergency, but the derogation from rights in an emergency must be determined by constitutional bodies and subject to democratic review and scrutiny, must be strictly necessary, and must be temporary.

6. Constitutional governance includes institutions to monitor and assure respect for the constitutional blueprint, for limitations on government, and for individual rights.

7. Today, constitutionalism may also imply respect for "self-determination"—the right of "peoples" to choose, change, or terminate their political affiliation.

Daniel S. Lev, SOCIAL MOVEMENTS, CONSTITUTIONALISM AND HUMAN RIGHTS: COMMENTS FROM THE MALAYSIAN AND INDONESIAN EXPERIENCES, in CONSTITUTIONALISM AND DEMOCRACY: TRANSITIONS IN THE CONTEMPORARY WORLD

139–141 (Douglas Greenberg, Stanley N. Katz, Melanie
Beth Oliviero, and Steven C. Wheatley eds., 1993).

Constitutionalism

Like other complex ideologies, constitutionalism is often obscured by a haze of mythology that makes it difficult to deal with realistically. Believers cannot help but see in it an end to a thousand vices and the source of as many virtues. But uncritical enthusiasm, without pause to examine assumptions, complicates any effort to understand clearly what is at issue. * * *

What exactly do we mean by constitutionalism? Rather than take for granted that we share an understanding of it and risking the intellectual abuse that accompanies such terms as "development" or "modernity" or those grand obscurantisms "East" and "West," I want to sketch the meanings that inform this discussion. As I use the term here, "constitutionalism" implies that political process, with or without a written constitution, is more or less oriented to public rules and institutions intended to define and contain the exercise of political authority. At the core of constitutionalism is legal process. The point should not be exaggerated beyond the capacity of any state to represent the genre. For the centrality of law and legal process does not mean that nothing else counts. The influence of economic interests, elite leverage, and popular values all matter in every society, contrary governing principles notwithstanding. But constitutional regimes necessarily foster a common appreciation of, or orientation to, legal rules and the general principles that underlay them. This orientation depends not only on appropriate institutions and roles, but on the widely accepted myth that legal process is efficacious and that its principles are eternally valid.

By contrast, religious, aristocratic, military, or charismatic regimes, whatever their constitutional or other overlay, imply quite different orientations with other institutional arrangements and legitimating ideologies. If the going myth is that law counts, people will use law to the limits of its assumed capacity to get things done. But if a god or gods alone provide, then priests will exercise authority. If the understanding of politics suggests that powerful men get things done, then patron-client relations are likely to prevail. The analytical problem is to ascertain in any society what exactly are the most sensible means, or mix of sensible means, of reaching objectives. Within society most people understand this implicitly, and those who object to the prevailing means, for whatever reasons, may try to change them if they can.

Historically, the rise of constitutional regimes has had to do with hemming in the state and confining its managers. Constitutionalism, a slightly higher abstraction than the rule of law or *rechtsstaat,* hence means little more (nor less) than the limited state, one in which official political power is surrounded by knowable laws whose acceptance transforms power into *legally* specified legitimate authority. In Weberian terms, constitutionalism grows out of the rational-legal form of domination, and is no less a means of political domination than any other. It may be a peculiarity of constitutionalism, however, that it presupposes at least a distinction, perhaps an antithesis, between state and society, without which there is little reason to make rules of the state.

Understood in this way, constitutionalism, like any other structure of state/society relations, is a matter of the distribution of power and authority. All organizations, including the state, are fundamentally coercive, their responsibilities ranging from subtle pressure and approving acquiescence to frank brutality and reluctant surrender. Political orders may be distinguished by how they apportion coercive power and legitimate authority, and what instrumentalities are differentially available to state institutions and social organizations to enforce their wills or to defend themselves from one another. The more power available in society, the more likely something like a "constitutional" order may exist. The more power available to the state, the more likely it is that a constitution, if it exists will be beside the point. Constitutionalism is meaningless without resources of power, in some form, both to achieve it and sustain it.

There is, however, nothing particularly compelling or inevitable about the constitutional republic. The view that constitutionalism represents the natural course of history, morally superior at that, is an ideological conceit that should have dissipated long ago but like other such myths, has infinite staying power. Far from inevitable, the demand for constitutional definitions of state authority grows from identifiable changes in economic and social structures that are likely to extrude new conceptions of group interest and political value. Without such transformations, it is hard to conceive the source of serious pressures for change at all. The most fundamental of changes is that in class structure, for the emergence or expansion of a social class causes tension as those who belong to it seek security and advantage by redefining political, social, and economic rules to accommodate themselves. Historically, constitutionalism has been the peculiar ideological haven of the middle class that could not claim an inherently legitimate right to govern but were dissatisfied with their lack of regular access to and influence over those who did govern. Persuasive evidence from around the world now suggests that this pattern remains fairly constant.

The social movements I have in mind are largely the product of new or growing middle classes, whether the groups they encompass are or are not self-consciously "middle class," bent on reordering state and society to their own purposes. The nature of middle-class ideologies in search of serviceable change is that their appeal cannot be restricted to middle-class interests alone. Although royalty and aristocracy naturally claim restrictive rights, justified by birth, and religious hierarchies are blessed by heaven, middle-class groups, lacking innate legitimacy, have no choice but to generalize the appeals to all who own property or to all citizens or even to all humanity. It is in this connection, in part, that human rights have become so prominent in the repertory of reform ideology now. I do not mean to imply that human rights appeals are no more than politically instrumental, but they do have to be understood in terms more complicated than those of the Universal Declaration. In some ways, human rights today serve precisely the same ideological purpose as natural rights did in Europe a few centuries ago, which may help to explain (only partially) why the political "rights" of the Universal Declaration remain generally more prominent than the social and economic "rights."

Because the political contentions that bracket constitutionalist demands are local matters, fed by local issues, interests, values, and historical circumstances, the outcomes (constitutionalist or not in whatever measure) are comprehensible essentially only in local terms. Neither constitutions nor constitutionalism can be transferred. The point should be obvious, but is often obscured by proprietary claims to the correct model. The dimensions of French constitutionalism are not altogether clear to Americans or to Japanese, the Indian or Norwegian cases seem odd anywhere else, and so on because the political compromises worked out historically, the tacit social and economic agreements made along the way, the play of local habit and values and cultural assumptions, the ways in which change proceeds, are all taken for granted at home but are unfathomable away. Without an understanding of the conflicts that go on in state and society, and between the two, of the ways in which power is generated and authority actually exercised, of the values and ideologies that inform political structure and behavior, we cannot comprehend constitutionalist (or any other) movements as they have evolved. We are left puzzled, for example, by the apparently cavalier attitudes of the constitutionalist French toward constitutions, or the strong patrimonial edge to Japanese practice, or the reverence in which Americans hold their constitution without bothering much to read it, or by any of the institutional outcomes along the routes of change anywhere. Finally, it should go without saying but usually does not,

constitutionalism is not the obvious solution to many of the most
serious, compelling problems that humanity has to deal with. It does not
eliminate economic poverty, or social discrimination, or political abuse,
or the incompetence, greed, or stupidity of political leadership. For all
these miseries the only sensible solutions remain relevant knowledge,
clearly articulated ideology, and effectively organized power in whatever
kind of political structure exists.

Notes and Questions: Constitutionalism as Ideal or Ideology?

1. A comparison of the excerpts from Professors Henkin and Lev raises
the question of whether constitutionalism is a universal ideal or an ideology
linked to class and culture. Moreover, when Lev contrasts French to American constitutionalism, or when he asserts that French constitutionalists have
a cavalier attitude toward constitutions, how does he portray the relationship between constitution and constitutionalism? Are French and American
constitutionalism two different ideals? If they are, how are the actual
constitutions of these two countries related to their respective ideals? In
thinking about these questions, consider that France has known more than a
dozen constitutions since its 1789 Revolution—the most recent one being
that of 1958—while the U.S. has had but one since 1787. Notwithstanding
this disparity, France's various constitutions bear certain definite resemblances and share certain norms in common, while the American Constitution endured major changes, leading to the adoption of amendments prohibiting slavery, instituting equality, and guaranteeing the vote to African-
Americans at the end of the Civil War, in the 1860s. See David A.J. Richards,
Revolution and Constitutionalism in America, in *Constitutionalism, Identity,
Difference and Legitimacy: Theoretical Perspectives* 85 (Michel Rosenfeld ed.,
1994); George Fletcher, *Our Secret Constitution: How Lincoln Redefined
American Democracy* (2001).

2. Is constitutionalism a purely Western ideal? Professor H.W.O. Okoth–Ogendo argues that there has been a movement in postcolonial Africa to
adopt constitutions as a means to attain political legitimacy, but, paradoxically, this movement has pitted constitutions against constitutionalism.
While constitutions have furnished an aura of legitimacy on postcolonial
leaders, they have not served to limit government powers. Leaders have
either abused their constitutions' emergency provisions or simply ignored
their constitutions altogether. Furthermore, the social, political, and economic conditions prevalent in postcolonial Africa account for this paradox of
constitutions against constitutionalism. See H.W.O. Okoth–Ogendo, *Constitutions without Constitutionalism: Reflections on an African Political Paradox*, in *Constitutionalism and Democracy: Transitions in the Contemporary
World* 65 (Douglas Greenberg, Stanley N. Katz, Melanie Beth Oliviero, and
Steven Wheatley eds., 1993). See also Radhika Coomaraswamy, *Uses and
Usurpation of Constitutional Ideology*, in *id.* at 159 (arguing that nationalism and cultural and religious traditions in South Asia have stood against
Western-type constitutionalism and democracy).

Professor Coomaraswamy concludes with the following:

> To survive and grow as an important aspect of political life, constitution-
> alism must develop internal processes relevant to the actual struggles

taking place in South Asian societies. The involvement of constitutional processes in elite concerns and in elite rights, such as property, lessens their legitimacy in the society at large. If, in the coming years, the processes of constitutionalism were to be attached to issues of poverty, political repression, social justice, regional backwardness, etc. it would be more likely that constitutionalism would enhance and enrich the democratic process in South Asian societies * * *. The use of constitutionalism in the future cannot be restricted to that of a watchdog or an errant executive. Its uses must be extended to become active and dynamic, to protect values by the use of language, discourse, and doctrine that have some resonance in South Asian reality.

Id. at 170.

C. CONSTITUTIONALISM AND THE RULE OF LAW

Michel Rosenfeld, THE RULE OF LAW AND THE LEGITIMACY OF CONSTITUTIONAL DEMOCRACY

74 S. Cal. L. Rev. 1307, 1308–1309, 1313–1314, 1318–1320, 1326, 1328–1330, 1333–1336, 1339–1340, 1345, 1349 (2001).

Although it is widely believed the rule of law and constitutional democracy go hand-in-hand, closer scrutiny reveals that constitutionalism and democracy might not always be in harmony, resulting in a clash between the rule of law and democracy. Additionally, the proper role and scope of the rule of law within constitutionalism is itself ambiguous inasmuch as the rule of law may spill over to the other two essential features of constitutionalism, rather than figuring exclusively as one of the three [the other two being limitations on the powers of government and protection of fundamental rights]. Indeed, a written constitution may have the force of law, and thus its provisions limiting the powers of government and those devoted to the protection of fundamental rights may become part and parcel of the rule of law regime instituted by the relevant constitutional regime. Moreover, the rule of law may encompass the entire field coming within the sweep of constitutionalism or it may only play a limited role in the maintenance of a prescribed constitutional order.

Compounding the above difficulties is the fact that there is no consensus on what "the rule of law" stands for, even if it is fairly clear what it stands against. An important part of the problem stems from the fact that "the rule of law" is an "essentially contestable concept", with both descriptive and prescriptive content over which there is a lack of widespread agreement * * *. Consistent with this, the rule of law has come to mean different things to various legal traditions, as evinced by the contrasts between Anglo–American "rule of law", German *Rechtsstaat* and French *État de droit*. Even within a single tradition, it is not clear whether the rule of law ought to be largely, if not exclusively, procedural or substantive or whether it should be primarily concerned with predictability or fairness. Finally, at least in the context of constitutional democracy, the rule of law appears to rest on a paradox. In terms of the institutional framework necessary for constitutional democracy, and of implementation of the will of the majority through law, the rule of law seems definitely on the side of the state, and often against the citizen. In contrast, in connection with protection of fundamental constitutional rights, the rule of law seems to be on the side of the citizen, at least to the extent that constitutional law can be invoked by citizens against laws and policies of the state.

* * *

The "rule of law" is often contrasted to the "rule of men"[25] * * * (or, as we might say today, "the rule of individual persons") [which] generally connotes unrestrained and potentially arbitrary personal rule by an unconstrained and perhaps unpredictable ruler * * *. At a minimum, therefore, the rule of law requires fairly generalized rule through law; a substantial amount of legal predictability (through generally applicable, published and largely prospective laws); a significant separation between the legislative and the adjudicative function; and, widespread adherence to the principle that no one is above the law. Consistent with this, any legal regime which meets these minimal requirements will be considered to satisfy the prescriptions of the "rule of law in the narrow sense".

* * * For the rule of law to measure up to the requirements of a legitimate constitutional democracy, it must be more than the rule of law in the narrow sense.

To become legitimate, the rule of law would seem to need democratic accountability, procedural fairness, and even perhaps substantive grounding. However, satisfying these requirements may be necessary without being sufficient to produce legitimacy. Democratic laws may be oppressive to minorities, procedural fairness may be consistent with a significant measure of substantive inequity, and the substantive values vindicated by any particular instantiation of the rule of law may be rejected by a sizeable portion of the polity, particularly in pluralist settings marked by clashing conceptions of the good.

* * *

Any attempt to put more flesh and bones on the concept of the rule of law should be mindful that diverse conceptions of the rule of law have taken root in different traditions. * * *

The *Rechtsstaat* is often treated as the German equivalent to the concept of the rule of law in the Anglo–American tradition. Both concepts share some important elements in common. Chief among these is the relationship between the state and the institutionalization of a legal regime or, in other words, the state's duty to wield its power through laws in accordance with fundamental principles of legality—including consistent implementation of publicly disseminated, generally applicable rules giving citizens notice regarding what conduct is subject to legal

---

25. *See* Marbury v. Madison, 5 U.S. 137, 163 (1803) (contrasting a "government of laws" to a "government of men").

sanctions, coupled with fair procedural safeguards. Beyond that, however, the two concepts differ significantly, particularly in terms of their understanding of the relationship between the state and the law * * *. [The] German * * * [*Rechtsstaat*] is squarely predicated on a veritable symbiosis between the law and the state. In the broadest terms, in the *Rechtsstaat,* law becomes inextricably tied to the state as the only legitimate channel through which the state can wield its power. Accordingly, "state rule through law" would be a much better approximation in English for *"Rechtsstaat"* than "rule of law" * * *.

As it evolved from its Kantian roots toward more positivistic configurations in Bismarck's late nineteenth century Germany, the *Rechtsstaat* became increasingly tied to issues of form rather than substance. What binds together both the Kantian and the positivistic conceptions of the *Rechtsstaat,* however, is the rejection of older notions that anchored the state's legitimacy in the pursuit and implementation of transcendental religious or ethical values. Accordingly, the *Rechtsstaat* opened the door to a state rule-through law that could function properly without having to rely on a value system derived from any particular religion or transcendental conception of ethics. In other words, the *Rechtsstaat* made possible the systematic deployment of a legal regime poised to accommodate a plurality of conceptions of the good.

* * *

* * * [T]he positivistic *Rechtsstaat* affords protections through the institutional framework of state rule through law and through imposition of the requirement that the state act through promulgation and implementation of laws, rather than through mere deployment of the will of the monarch.

* * *

Set against the horrors of the Nazi era, the contemporary German *Rechtsstaat,* shaped by its new constitution, the 1949 Basic Law, subordinates positive legality to entrenched substantive principles and values. Chief among the latter is human dignity which is enshrined as an unamendable constitutional value in Article I of the Basic Law, and which has been interpreted as the paramount value in the German constitutional order in numerous decisions of the German Constitutional Court. More generally, today's *Rechtsstaat* has become inextricably tied to constitutional democracy framed by fundamental substantive values, and its legality has become subjected to a set of substantive norms embodied in constitutional justice. * * *

[T]oday's *Rechtsstaat* * * * tends to constitutionalize all politics and to convert the *Rechtsstaat into a Verfassungsstaat* (i.e. a state rule through the constitution) as some German scholars have argued. Finally, even beyond constitutionalization as such, today's *Rechtsstaat* judicializes realms, such as the promotion of welfare, which were clearly relegated to politics in both of its nineteenth century predecessors. Thus, the Basic Law commands the German states—the *Länder*—to promote the *sozialer Rechtsstaat* or *Sozialstaat* (i.e. the social welfare state through law) as well as democracy and republicanism.[83]

* * *

The French *État de droit* is much more recent than the German *Rechtsstaat* and was originally derived from the latter. However, even though the French term *"État de droit"* is a literal translation of the German *"Rechtsstaat"*, the French adapted and transformed the concept * * *. *"État de droit"* does not mean "state rule through law", but rather "constitutional state as legal guarantor of fundamental rights" (against infringements stemming from law made by parliament).

The French *État de droit* has come to supplement and, in an important sense, limit the *"État Légal"*, which may be roughly translated as "democratic state rule through law." The *État Légal* is what comes closest in France to the positivistic *Rechtsstaat*, with the key difference that the French concept is inextricably linked to parliamentary sovereignty and parliamentary democracy. Accordingly, whereas the positivistic *Rechtsstaat's* primary function is to set institutional limitations on the uses of governmental powers by the monarch against the people, the *État de droit* embodies the democratic will of the French nation as transformed into law by the parliament.

* * * [There was a conviction during] the French Revolution * * * that the democratic fate of the nation would be best served by a single nationwide legislature entrusted with the transformation of the will of the people into law. This was set against an *Ancient Régime* marked by absolute rule in favor of those privileged within the prevailing feudal hierarchy. In contrast, the representatives of the people as a whole acting after the repeal of feudal privileges could easily be expected to legislate in the common interests of all, particularly to the extent that bourgeois interests were projected as being universal. Consistent with this, all laws of Parliament, regardless of their outcome, were perceived as expressions of the general will. Today, however, there seems to be no inherent reason for believing that parliamentary democracy will necessarily give voice to the common good—hence the need to balance the *État légal* with the protections afforded by the *État de droit*.

* * * [T]he Anglo–American tradition, relying on the common law, has developed a strong sense of the rule of law * * * [that] is not exclusively dependent on the state as such, but rather functions as a buffer between the interests of the state and those of its citizens.

In its American version, the rule of law is grounded on a written constitution designed a to provide legal expression to preexisting, inalienable fundamental rights. These rights are deeply steeped in a Lockean vision of natural rights as belonging to the individual and as preexisting and transcending both the social contract and civil society * * *.

In the context of an idealized minimal state almost exclusively concerned with better securing preexisting natural rights, the rule of law would by and large consist of the deployment and enforcement of

---

83. *See* GERMAN BASIC LAW, Art. 28, para. 1.

procedural safeguards. This presupposes that the legitimacy of natural rights would remain beyond dispute and that effective protection of such rights would guarantee the welfare of society either because it would allow citizens to be self-sufficient or because it would enable them to remedy any lack of self-sufficiency through private contracts * * *. Accordingly, the rule of law would boil down to the deployment and maintenance of procedural safeguards, which mediate between right holders, the state, and potential or actual rights infringers * * *.

It becomes clear from this rough outline how the rule of law can be invoked against the state * * *. [T]he common law * * * itself gives rise to * * * serious paradoxes that pose * * * great threats within the Anglo–American tradition. Two of these paradoxes raise serious questions about the existence and viability of the rule of law: first the one produced by the tension between the need for legal certainty and predictability and the common law's experimental and incremental approach; and second, that generated as a consequence of the clash between the need for binding and transparent criteria of judicial application of relevant legal norms and the great latitude enjoyed by common law judges prone to blurring the distinction between law making and judicial interpretation.

* * *

Many key constitutional provisions, such as the "due process" and the "equal protection" guarantees contained in the American Constitution are stated very generally and at a high level of abstraction. This allows for a wide range of plausible interpretations, and common law trained judges who have dealt with such constitutional provisions, have widely differed in their interpretations, making these provisions nearly as unpredictable as constantly evolving common law standards.

* * *

The rule of law in the narrow sense is firmly established in the United States and can be traced back to the Supreme Court's landmark decision in *Marbury v. Madison*. Thus, even if one considers common law trained judges unpredictable or at times arbitrary, the rule of law in the narrow sense does ensure some checks on the exercise of the power of the state in the name of the law. Furthermore, to the extent that judicial decisions must be made public and the reasons for such decisions revealed in published opinions, the likelihood of blatant judicial abuses seems rather remote. In short, the rule of law in the narrow sense appears to ensure a significant amount of legality and [favors] the promotion of legal norms that do not stray too far from the well of commonly accepted values.

* * *

[T]he common law proceeds in a way that is in some sense diametrically opposed to the way civil law is supposed to be implemented in the context of the *Rechtsstaat* or the *État légal*. In the civil law setting, the judge is supposed to apply a previously enacted law to a set of facts in a deductive process modeled on the syllogism. The legal rule figures as the major premise; the facts of the case, as the minor premise; and the syllogistically derived judicial decision as the conclusion. In contrast, the common law not only involves an inductive process * * * but also a future-oriented act of law making grounded in the very process of adjudicating a present dispute concerning past acts. * * * [N]o rule appraising the parties involved of likely legal consequences existed at the time of the act giving rise to litigation—the rule (although still incomplete) being announced only at the moment of adjudication. On the other hand, the very act of adjudication constitutes an announcement * * * of how similar cases will be adjudicated in the future. Consistent with this, moreover, the conscientious common law judge should be at least equally concerned, if not more so, with the future effect of his or her ruling than with achieving backward looking justice in the dispute at hand. To the extent that this is so, the common law, in contrast to the civil law, involves both an act of (judicial) legislation and an act of adjudication which is not sufficiently constrained by any pre-existing rule * * *.

* * *

At least under certain propitious circumstances * * * the rule of law can promote both predictability and fairness; this seems equally possible in an Anglo–American common law setting as in a continental civil law system. Beyond that, however, it is not clear whether the link between the rule of law and predictability and fairness is an intrinsic or an extrinsic one. In other words, does the rule of law [itself or] certain [external] circumstances make for predictability and fairness? * * *

C.1. THE RULE OF LAW: PREDICTABILITY VS. FAIRNESS AND JUSTICE

PRINCESS SORAYA CASE

Federal Constitutional Court (Germany).
34 BVerfGE 269 (1973)[c].

[This dispute arose out of a civil damage suit for defamation brought by the ex-wife of the Shah of Iran against *Die Welt* and a freelance journalist. The defendants published a fictitious interview with Princess Soraya, revealing intimate details of her private life. The German Civil Code precludes awarding civil damages for an invasion of privacy. Such an invasion constitutes a criminal offense in German law. Tort recovery for such injuries is possible only "in cases provided by [written] law." No law allows recovery for the injury sustained by the plaintiff. But the Federal High Court of Justice authorized such recovery, in the light of changing social conditions and the fundamental values of the Basic Law—one value being the right to protect one's personality. The affirmation of a monetary damage award in the present case was contested, in part, on the ground that the courts had exceeded their proper authority under the Basic Law.]

Judgment of the Second Senate: * * *

c. Reproduced from Donald P. Kommers, *The Constitutional Jurisprudence of* *the Federal Republic of Germany* 124–28 (2d ed. 1997).

C. IV. I. The judge is traditionally bound by the law. This is an inherent element of the principle of separation of powers, and thus of the rule of law. Article 20 of our Constitution, however, has somewhat changed the traditional formulation by providing that the judge is bound by "law and justice." The generally prevailing view implies the rejection of a narrow reliance upon [formally] enacted laws. The formulation chosen in Article 20 keeps us aware of the fact that although "law and justice" are generally coextensive, they may, not always be so. Justice is not identical with the aggregate of the written laws. Under certain circumstances law can exist beyond the positive norms which the state enacts—law which has its source in the constitutional legal order as a meaningful, all-embracing system, and which functions as a corrective of the written norms. The courts have the task of finding this law and making it a reality in binding cases. The Constitution does not restrict the judge to applying the language of legislative mandates to the particular case before him. This concept [of the judicial function] presupposes that no gaps in the written legal order exist—a condition which may be desirable in the interest of legal certainty but which in practice is unattainable. The judge's task is not confined to ascertaining and implementing legislative decisions. He may have to make a value judgment (an act which necessarily has volitional elements); that is, bring to light and implement in his decisions those value concepts which are inherent in the constitutional legal order, but which are not, or not adequately, expressed in the language of the written laws. In performing this task, the judge must guard against arbitrariness; his decision must be based upon rational arguments. He must make it clear that the written law fails to perform its function of providing a just solution for the legal problem at hand. Where th[e written law fails], the judge's decision fills the existing gap by using common sense and "general concepts of justice established by the community."

The only remaining question is what limits to impose upon such creative [judicial] decision making. We must keep in mind that the judge is bound by written law, a principle which [we] cannot abandon if the rule of law is to be maintained. We cannot reduce these limits to a formula equally applicable to all areas of the law and to all legal relationships.

2. For purposes of the present decision, [we] confine the formulation of the issue to the area of private law. In this area, the judge is confronted with a great codification, the Civil Code, which has been in force for over seventy years. This [fact] has dual significance: first, the judge's freedom to creatively develop the law necessarily grows with the "aging of codifications" with the increased distance in time between the enactment of the legislative mandate and the judge's decision in an individual case. The interpretation of a written norm cannot always or for an unlimited period remain tied to the meaning the norm had at the time of its enactment. One must explore what reasonable function the [norm] initially served. The norm always remains in the context of the social conditions and sociopolitical views it affects. As these conditions and views change, the thrust of the norm can, and under certain circumstances must, be adjusted to such change. This is especially true

when, between the time of enacting and implementing a law conditions of life and popular views on legal matters have changes as radically as they have in the present century. The judge cannot, by simply pointing to the unchanged language of the written law, avoid the conflict that has arisen between the norm [as written] and a changed society's substantive notions of justice. If he is not to be derelict in his duty to pronounce "justice," he must implement legal norms more freely. Second, as experience dictates, legislative reforms encounter particularly great difficulties and obstacles when they are intended to revise great bodies of legislation which shape the system and character of the entire legal order as does the codification of private law contained in the Civil Code.

3. The decisions presently being challenged concern an issue [i.e., the question of recoverability of money damages for injury, to an intangible interest] which was already controversial when the preparatory work on the draft of the Civil Code was in progress. Criticism of the solution chosen by the legislature was immediate and has never ceased, although it did not at that time involve constitutional arguments. Critics referred to legal development in other countries of the Western world which have taken a more liberal approach toward the possibility of recovering money damages for injuries to intangible interests. [The Court, here, cited several comparative studies.] Consequently, [critics] could point out that nowhere in the West did an unlawful act so frequently remain without civil sanctions as in Germany and for the sole reason that the act had "only" caused nonphysical damages.

The courts faced the question of whether to close this gap by the methods at their disposal or wait for legislative intervention. When the courts chose the first alternative, they found support from the writings of influential legal authors who had advocated the former course. For this reason, legal scholars widely approved the relevant decisions of the Federal High Court of Justice and of other courts from the very beginning. This [fact] illustrates that these decisions were consistent with generally recognized concepts of justice and were not regarded as intolerable restrictions upon freedom of opinion of the press. * * *

The other alternative, to wait for legislative regulation, cannot be regarded as constitutionally mandated under the circumstances. It is true that the federal government has tried twice to bring about a legislative solution to the problem or protecting an individual's personality right in the area of private law. But the bills drafted in 1959 and 1967 died early in the legislative process, even though there was no indication of any legislative intention to perpetuate the status quo. One cannot blame the judge if, compelled to decide every case submitted to him and convinced that he cannot rely upon the uncertain future intervention of the legislature, he does not adhere to the literal meaning of the existing written law in a case where adherence would largely sacrifice justice in a particular case.

The method by which the Federal High Court of Justice reached the decisions in question is constitutionally unobjectionable for a further reason: This method deviated from written law only to the extent absolutely necessary to resolve the legal problem presented by the instant case. The court has * * * merely added one situation to the legislature's own enumeration of situations in which money damages can recovered injury to intangible interests. The Federal High Court of Justice found this addition to be compellingly justified by the evolution of social conditions as well as by a new law of higher rank; to wit, Articles 1 and 2 of the Constitution. Thus, the Federal High Court of Justice and other courts following its holdings have neither abandoned the system of the legal order nor have they exhibited an intention to go their own way in making policy. They have merely taken a further step in developing and concretizing basic ideas inherent in the legal order molded by the Constitution, and they have done so by means which remain within this system. Therefore, the legal rule found [by creative judicial decision] is a legitimate part of the legal order, constituting a limitation upon the freedom of the press as a "general statute" within the meaning of Article 5 of the Constitution. The rule's purpose is to guarantee effective protection of the individual's personality, and dignity—i.e., of interests at the center of the constitutional ordering of values—and thus, within a particular area of the law, to strengthen the effect of constitutionally protected fundamental rights. For these reasons, complainants' constitutional arguments must fail.

RETROACTIVE CRIMINAL LEGISLATION CASE

Constitutional Court (Hungary).
Decision 11/1992 (III.10.) AB hat.

[The issue arose, in Hungary, in the context of demands for justice for acts of murder and torture in the aftermath of Hungary's failed 1956 uprising against Soviet rule. The murders and torture that occurred were generally illegal under the then-prevailing law but were not prosecuted for political reasons. By 1990, when victims and relatives of those killed demanded that the new democratic government bring the perpetrators to justice, the relevant statutes of limitation for the crimes involved had expired. The Hungarian law, struck down by the Constitutional Court, would have removed the statute-of-limitations impediment and allowed for the prosecution of the perpetrators.]

The President of the Republic having declined to promulgate Act IV/1991 on the Prosecution of Serious Criminal Offences not previously prosecuted for Political Reasons, petitioned for a preliminary review of its constitutionality.

He sought to know whether s. I of the Act violated the principle of the rule of law under the Constitution. Art. 2 (1) and, further, Art. 57 (4). In particular, he petitioned, inter alia, as to whether (a) the recommencement of the statute of limitations conflicted with the principle of the rule of law, an essential component of which was legal certainty; (b) s. I of the Act amounted to an unconstitutional retroactive criminal law which violated the doctrine of *nullum crimen sine lege,* especially since the statute of limitations relating to acts criminalized by the section might have already expired according to the Criminal Code in force at the time the acts were committed; (c) the recommencement of the statute of limitations, which had already expired, violated the rule of law. especially legal certainty; (d) overly general provisions and vague concepts violated the principle of legal certainty, e.g., "the State's failure to prosecute its claim was based on political reasons"; and (e) the distinction drawn by the law among perpetrators of the same offence on the basis of the State's reason for prosecuting such offences violated the prohibition of arbitrariness under Art. 54 (1) and equal protection of citizens under Art. 70/A (1).

IN THE NAME OF THE REPUBLIC OF HUNGARY!

Pursuant to the petition submitted by the President of the Republic seeking a preliminary review of the Act passed by Parliament but not yet promulgated, the Constitutional Court has made the following

DECISION

The Constitutional Court holds that the Act passed during the 4 November 1991 parliamentary session concerning the Prosecution of Serious Criminal Offences Committed between 21 December 1944 and 2 May 1990 that had not been previously prosecuted for Political Reasons (hereinafter the Act) is unconstitutional.

The Act violates the principle of legal certainty by reason of vagueness and ambiguity in definition.

The Act violates the requirement of constitutional criminal law that the statute of limitations—including the interruption and tolling of the statute of limitations—must be governed by the law in effect at the time of the commission of the crime except that if during the running of the statute of limitations, laws more favourable to the defendant came into force.

REASONING

Justice Szabó (Parts I. II and IV) and President Solyóm (Parts III and V), delivering the Opinion of the Court:

The substance of the [constitutional] concern is whether s. 1 of the Act violates the principle of the rule of law contained in Art. 2 (1) of the Constitution: ["The Republic of Hungary is an independent, democratic constitutional state."] * * *

The Act under review illustrates with unusual sharpness the relationship between the law of the preceding political systems and the principle of the rule of law declared by the new Constitution.

1. With the enactment of the constitutional amendment of 23 October 1989, in fact, a new Constitution came into force, which, with its declaration that "the Republic of Hungary is an independent democratic state under the rule of law," conferred on the State its law and the political system a new quality, fundamentally different from that of the previous, regime. In the constitutional law sense, this is the substance of the political category of the "change of system" or "transition." Accordingly, any evaluation of state actions necessitated by the transition cannot be separated from the requirements of the rule of law as crystallized during the history of constitutional democracies and also

considered by the 1989 Hungarian constitutional revision. The Constitution provides for the basic institutions of the state under the rule of law and defines the human and civil rights together with their basic guarantees.

2. That Hungary is a state under the rule of law is both a statement of fact and a statement of policy. A state under the rule of law becomes a reality when the Constitution is truly and unconditionally given effect. For the legal system the change of system means, and the change of the legal system is possible only in that sense, that the whole body of law must be brought into harmony—and new legislation must be kept in harmony—with the new Constitution. Not only must the legal provisions and the operation of state organs comply strictly with the Constitution but the Constitution's values and its conceptual culture must permeate the whole of society. This is the rule of law, and this is how the Constitution becomes a reality. The realization of the rule of law is a continuous process. For the organs of the State participation in this process is a constitutional duty * * *.

3. The change of system has been carried out on the basis of legality. The principle of legality imposes on the state under the rule of law the requirement that legal regulations regarding the legal system itself should be abided by unconditionally. The politically revolutionary changes adopted by the Constitution and all the new fundamental laws were enacted in full compliance with the old legal system's procedural laws on legislation, thereby gaining their binding force. The old law retained its validity. With respect to its validity, there is no distinction between "pre-Constitution" and "post-Constitution" law * * *. Irrespective of its date of enactment, each valid legal rule must conform with the new Constitution. Likewise, constitutional review does not admit two different standards for the review of laws. The date of enactment can be important insofar as previous laws may have become unconstitutional when the new Constitution entered into force * * *.

A fundamental principle of the rule of law is legal certainty. Legal certainty demands, inter alia, the protection of vested rights, non-interference with legal relations already executed or concluded and limiting the possibility of modifying existing long-term legal relations. As the Constitutional Court held in *Dec. 10/1992 (11.25) AB* (MK 1992/19 ABH 1992.72) the consequences of the unconstitutionality of a law must be evaluated primarily with reference to their impact on legal certainty. This is the guiding principle for determining the date of invalidation for an unconstitutional law and especially for the invalidation of the legal relations arising therefrom. This is so because the individual legal relations and legal facts become independent of the statutory sources from which they emerge and do not automatically share their fate. Were this otherwise, a change in the law would necessitate in every instance a review of the whole body of legal relations. Thus, from the principle of legal certainty, it follows that already executed or concluded legal relations cannot be altered constitutionally by enactment of a law or by invalidation of a law by either the legislature or the Constitutional Court.

An exception to this principle is permissible only if a constitutional principle competing with legal certainty renders this outcome unavoidable and provided that in fulfilling its objectives it does not impose a disproportionate harm. The review of a final criminal court decision, if the decision had been based upon a law which was subsequently declared, unconstitutional, is an example of such an exception. A constitutional criminal justice system demands this exception. However, the unjust result of legal relations does not constitute an argument against the principle of legal certainty. As the Constitutional Court's Decision *(9/1992 (1.30) AB.)* stated: "[T]he requirement of the rule of law as to substantive justice may be attained within the institutions and guarantees ensuring legal certainty. The Constitution does not and cannot confer a right for substantive justice."

As far as the protection afforded to already concluded legal relations is concerned, no distinction can be made according to the time of and reasons for striking down a law as unconstitutional. With respect to every legal relation, the legislature is constrained by the restrictions imposed on retroactive legislation: the Constitutional Court is even further constrained as it cannot even establish the unconstitutionality of the substance of norms with effect for the time before the entry into the force of the new Constitution

Retroactive modification of the law and legal relations is permitted only within very narrow limits. * * *

5. It is to be decided whether the unique historical circumstances of the transition should be considered in reviewing the constitutionality of new laws pertaining to the unconstitutional acts and measures of the former regime.

Within the framework of the rule of law, and in order to further its development, the given historical situation can be taken into consideration. However, the basic guarantees of the rule of law cannot be set aside by reference to historical situations and to justice as a requirement of the state under the rule of law. A state under the rule of law cannot be created by undermining the rule of law. Legal certainty based on formal and objective principles is more important than necessarily partial and subjective justice. In its practice, the Constitutional Court has already given effect to this principle.

The Constitutional Court cannot ignore history since it has to fulfill its task embedded in history. The Constitutional Court is the repository of the paradox of the "revolution under the rule of law" in the process of the peaceful transition, beginning with the new Constitution, the Constitutional Court must, within its competence in all cases unconditionally guarantee the conformity of the legislative power with the Constitution.

IV. In the Constitutional Court's opinion, in a state under the rule of law the violation of rights can only be remedied by upholding the rule of the law. The legal system of a state under the rule of law cannot deprive anyone of legal guarantees. * * *

1. * * * [T]he principle of the rule of law, in comparison with the specific constitutional provisions, is not a mere auxiliary rule, nor a mere

declaration, but an independent constitutional norm, the violation of which is itself a ground for declaring a law unconstitutional. In the Constitutional Court's practice, legal certainty is closely interconnected with the constitutional law principle of the rule of law.

Conviction (declaration of guilt) and punishment can only proceed according to the law that was in effect at the time of the commission of' the crime. This requirement is imposed by Art. 57(4) of the Constitution echoed by the Criminal Code's prohibition of retroactivity (art. 2). The court must judge (determine criminal liability, convict and pass sentence for), the offence in accordance with the law in force at the time of its commission, and the punishment is also so determined unless a new law is passed subsequent to the of fence which prescribes a more lenient punishment or decriminalizes the act, thus making the action nonpunishable by criminal law. This is the necessary result of the prohibition of retroactivity embodied in the principle of legal certainty (foreseeability and predictability), which, in turn, stems from the principle of the rule of law. * * *

V. I. The re-imposition of criminal punishability for a crime for the prosecution of which the statute of limitations had already expired violates the Constitution.

With the expiration of the statute of limitations, the criminal punishability of the offender is irrevocably extinguished. * * *

5. and 6. The statute of limitations for the punishability of the criminal offences set out in the Act under review recommences "if the State's failure to prosecute its claim to punish was based on political reasons." This condition is unconstitutional per se.

Legal certainty demands the clear and unambiguous formulation of legal rules. * * * Not even with the knowledge of the special purpose of this Act can the meaning of "failure to prosecute its claim to punish" be determined with sufficient certainty. Failure to initiate proceedings and termination of criminal proceedings in the absence of legal justifications fall within the ambit of this concept, but so does, for instance, the conclusion of proceedings with an unlawfully lenient punishment such as a warning. Likewise, what constitutes "political reasons" and what criteria are to be applied cannot be determined unequivocally especially in light of the political changes which have taken place during the long period of time covered by this Act. * * *

Notes and Questions

1. On the surface, at least, the GFCC links the rule of law with justice, whereas the Hungarian Constitutional Court (HCC) specifically refuses to equate rule of law with justice, stressing that, consistent with constitutionalism, it is paramount to regard the rule of law as requiring predictability and legal certainty. Are these two positions inconsistent? Or do they merely reflect the fact that the cases involve very distinct issues and arise under different circumstances?

Both Germany and Hungary went through a transition from authoritarian dictatorial regimes to constitutional democracy, in the interval between enactment of the underlying law at stake in the relevant controversy and consideration of that controversy by the country's constitutional court. Although issues relating to such transition were crucial in the Hungarian case, they played no discernible role in the German one. Indeed, whether to provide a private tort remedy under the Civil Code for invasion of privacy seems much more a public-policy issue than one closely linked to the difference between authoritarianism and constitutional democracy. In contrast, the issue of dispensing justice for the abuses perpetrated by the previous nondemocratic regime, which led the Hungarian Parliament to retroactively extend the statute of limitations for particularly reprehensible crimes, such as murder and torture, was certainly important in the context of Hungary's transition from communism to constitutional democracy as it has been in other transitions from abusive authoritarian regimes, such as those in Argentina and South Africa.

2.   Did the HCC sacrifice justice to an overly formalistic conception of the rule of law? Or was it compelled to act as it did because the "rule of law" was specifically enshrined in Hungary's amended postcommunist Constitution? What about the Court's stress on the importance to abide by a strict conception of legality as a paramount attribute of postcommunist constitutionalism, distinguishing the latter from the communist regime's disregard for the rule of law?

An added reason for not giving in too easily to claims of justice at the expense of strict adherence to legality in the aftermath of a transition to constitutional democracy is that the line between claims for justice and thirst for revenge is often opaque. See András Sajó and Vera Losonci, *Rule by Law in East Central Europe*, in *Constitutionalism and Democracy: Transitions in the Contemporary World*, above, at 321.

3.   Although the HCC rejected the retroactive tolling of statutes of limitation as unconstitutional, it declared it permissible to prosecute those crimes that qualified as "crimes against humanity." See *Retroactivity II Case*, Decision No. 53/1993 (X.13.) AB hat. The basis for this exception was Hungary's ratification (during its communist period and prior to the expiration of the relevant statutes of limitation) of international covenants providing for prosecution of "crimes against humanity," which are not subjected to any statute-of-limitation constraints. Is that consistent with the strict standards of legality articulated in the Court's *Retroactive Criminal Legislation Case*?

4.   The protection against retroactive laws looms as an important feature of the rule of law and of constitutionalism in general. But how far should the protection against retroactive laws go? Should it be absolute? Or should it be balanced against considerations of justice and public policy?

Article I, § 9 of the U.S. Constitution contains a prohibition against "ex post facto" laws. Yet since the eighteenth century, this prohibition has been interpreted as applying to criminal but not civil laws. See *Calder v. Bull*, 3 U.S. 386 (1798). Whereas the criminal law may provide for loss of life through capital punishment or loss of liberty through imprisonment, civil law, by and large, exposes citizens only to losses of property. Does that justify the difference? What about the fact that a retroactive law imposing a minimal criminal fine would be prohibited but not a retroactive civil law exposing citizens to huge monetary liability for acts that were entirely legal when performed? Can the distinction drawn pursuant to the U.S. Constitution be justified in terms of adherence to the rule of law? See Chapter 9, Section J.

D. CONSTITUTIONAL MODELS

Constitutions are structured in different ways, implemented through various means and imposed on those subjected to their prescriptions through distinct devices. Beyond that, the importance of a constitution can vary significantly from one setting to another. In some countries, like the U.S., the constitution plays a central role in the definition of the nation's identity, while in others it is a minor factor. See Mark V. Tushnet, *The Possibilities of Comparative Constitutional Law,* 108 Yale L.J. 1225, 1270–71 (1999). Consequently, varying constitutional models and the different relationships between a constitution and the society in which it is embedded are bound to affect the nexus between constitutional and extraconstitutional norms. These issues are examined in this section, primarily through a focus on ways in which constitutional order has been structured and on how some prominent constitutional systems have integrated into their larger social and political milieu.

D.1. WRITTEN VS. UNWRITTEN CONSTITUTIONS

Eighteenth-century France and the U.S. provide the model for modern constitutions. Both adopted written constitutions after the violent overthrow of their previous regimes. Though many constitutions witnessed no prior violent revolutions, today most countries have constitutions, and most are written.

The United Kingdom, New Zealand, and Israel possess no written constitutions but are nonetheless considered constitutional democracies subjected to "unwritten" constitutions. See Colin Turpin, *British Government and the Constitutions: Text, Cases and Materials* ch 1 (1999); *New Zealand: The Development of its Laws and Constitution* 1–39 (J. L. Robson ed., 1967); Gary J. Jacobsohn, *Apple of Gold: Constitutionalism in Israel and the United States* 4–9 (1993). It has often been a matter of dispute whether countries deemed as having an "unwritten constitution" actually have one. Cf. Thomas Paine, *The Rights of Man*, Part the Second, ch 4 (1792); Alexis de Tocqueville, *Democracy in America,* Vol. 1, pt. 1 ch 6 (1835) (asserting that England lacks a constitution). Does asserting that a country has an "unwritten constitution" amount to claiming that its government comports with the essential dictates of constitutionalism without relying on a formal constitution? In other words, does constitutionalism exist without a constitution in such countries? Consider the following excerpts.

Giovanni Sartori, CONSTITUTIONALISM: A PRELIMINARY DISCUSSION

56 American Political Science Review 853, 853–857, 861–862 (1962).

* * *

[T]he United Kingdom has a difficult and *sui generis* constitution, deriving from a tortuous sedimentation of common law, acts and conventional usage, partly legal and partly extra-legal, and despite the fact that, when one reads the British constitutional lawyers, one is often reminded of what was said in a review of Stirling's book, *The Secret of Hegel:* "never has a secret been better kept."

For one thing, English constitutional lawyers appear to take a particular pleasure in pointing out to foreign jurists and political thinkers (beginning with Montesquieu) that their understanding of the English system is quite wrong. To be sure, this has been and still is very often the case. But one remains with a feeling that the British find a special gratification in confounding alien scholars: there is an element of polemic coquetry in the emphasis they lay on the principle of the supremacy of Parliament (exhibited as being unlimited, arbitrary, omnipotent, *supra* and *contra legem,* etc); in the somewhat provocative and bold statement that, according to the American and French meaning of the term, the United Kingdom does not have a constitution[;] in the point that the British system is based not on the "division" but on the "fusion" of powers; or in the way in which Sir Ivor Jennings puts forward that, "Since Great Britain has no written constitution, there is no special protection for fundamental rights."[4] And one could quote at length.

All these statements are, to be sure, true. But they are "literally true," and one is brought to wonder why the emphasis is laid on the *letter* so much more than on the *spirit* of the law of the constitution.
* * *

[T]ake, for instance, the principle of the supremacy of Parliament. Would it be far from the mark to say that if the principle is related to the historical circumstances of its establishment, it hardly carries with it the dangerous implications that British scholars somewhat proudly expound? Parliament, in the English terminology, means the King, the Lords and the Commons acting together as the supreme governing body of the realm. Thus, if the principle of the supremacy of Parliament is translated into continental terminology, it amounts to what is otherwise called the "sovereignty of the State." * * * [W]hat it really meant * * * was that the King had no power *outside* of Parliament, that his prerogatives could only be exercised according to the formula of the King *in* Parliament. If this be so, would it be very wrong to conclude * * * that parliamentary sovereignty in England actually contradicts the idea of a "higher law" no more than any flexible constitution does, and that the

4. *The Law and the Constitution,* 5th ed. (London, University of London Press, 1959), p. 40.

conventions of the constitution hardly allow a parliamentary majority to pass any law whatever? * * *

* * *

[I]n the 19th century, all over Europe as well as in the United States, a general agreement prevailed as to the basic meaning of the term "constitution" * * * If, in England, "constitution" meant the system of British liberties, *mutatis mutandis* the Europeans wanted exactly the same thing: a system of protected freedom for the individual, which—according to the American usage of the English vocabulary— they called a "constitutional system" * * * [They] wanted a written document, a charter, which would firmly establish the overall supreme law of the land. The British too, however, had, from time to time, relied on particularly solemn written documents: the Magna Charta, the Con- firmation Acts, the 1610–1628 Petition of Rights, the Habeas Corpus Act of 1679, the Bill of Rights, the Act of Settlement, etc. The circumstance that these British "supreme laws" are not collected in a single document does not really mean that England has an unwritten constitution. I would rather say that the English do not have a codified constitution, *i.e.,* that Britain has a constitution which is written only in part (or, even better, unwritten to a much greater extent than "written" constitutions are), in a piecemeal fashion, and scattered in a variety of sources.

However * * * this question is of secondary importance. I mean that the written, complete document is only a means. What really matters is the end, the *telos*. And the purpose, the *telos,* of English, American and European constitutionalism was, from the outset, identical. * * * [T]his common purpose could be expressed and synthesized by just one word: the French (and Italian) term *garantisme*. In other terms, all over the Western area people requested, or cherished, "the constitution," because this term meant to them a fundamental law, or a fundamental set of principles, and a correlative institutional arrangement, which would restrict arbitrary power and ensure a "limited government." * * *

[According to] Weare's definition * * * the English constitution is "the collection of legal rules and non-legal rules which govern the government in Britain." Or allow me to quote, as another instance, Jennings' definition, according to which a constitution is "the document in which are set out the rules governing the composition, powers and methods of operation of the main institutions of government."[14] The peculiar feature of these definitions is * * * the silence which covers the *telos* of constitutionalism. Actually they are purely "formal" definitions, in the sense that they can be filled with any content whatever. We are thus faced, nowadays, with this puzzling situation: that the very inven- tors of the constitutional solution provide us with a definition which amounts to saying that any instrument of government, any "traffic rule," is a constitution. * * *

[I]f a constitution is defined as "any way of giving form to any State whatever," then the question "What is the role of a constitution in a political system?" either cannot be answered, or can be answered only

14. [ ] *The Law and the Constitution,* pp. 33, 36.

country by country, and even then in a very uninteresting and banal way. For in this case the answer is that the constitution plays no role, properly speaking: It is only a shorthand report which may describe * * * the formalization of the power structure of the given country. * * *

[We need] a convincing answer to the question, "What is a constitution?" * * *

Basically we are confronted with three possibilities: (i) *garantiste* constitution (constitution, proper); (ii) nominal constitution; (iii) façade constitution (or fake constitution).

    * * *

I call "nominal" the constitutions that * * * bear the "name" constitution. This amounts to saying that nominal constitutions are merely organizational constitutions, *i.e.,* the collection of rules which organize but do not restrain the exercise of political power in a given polity. Actually, nominal constitutions do not really pretend to be "real constitutions." They frankly describe a system of limitless, unchecked power. * * *

The façade constitutions are different from the nominal ones in that they take the appearance of "true constitutions." What makes them untrue is that they are disregarded (at least in their essential *garantiste* features). Actually they are "trap-constitutions." As far as the techniques of liberty and the rights of the power addressees are concerned, they are a dead letter. * * *

There is often a considerable overlapping between nominal and façade constitutions. The distinction is nevertheless basic, for the two cases are indeed very different. Nominal constitutions actually describe the working of the political system (they do not abide by the *telos* of constitutionalism, but they are sincere reports), while the façade constitutions give us no reliable information about the real governmental process. In most cases one can clearly perceive * * * which is the prevalent aspect: I mean, whether a constitution is basically nominal or basically a disguise. At any rate * * * the distinction is serviceable for analytical purposes, that is, for dissecting the component parts of a "mixed type" (partly nominal and partly fake) of pseudo-constitution. * * *

Some troublesome problems arise when one focuses further attention on: (i) the decalage between the written and the living constitution, and on (ii) the frequent disregard of some of the constitutional provisions. In this connection the point can be made that a clear-cut distinction between real constitutions and façade constitutions is hardly realistic, since the real ones too come to differ widely, in practice, from their original formalization, or may not be fully activated (the former being usually the case with old constitutions, and the latter with recent ones).

Personally I am not dismayed by the first indictment. If a constitution is written, then, with the passing of time, the formal document and the living constitution inevitably come to be related much as the past is related to the present. (In this sense, then, written constitutions too become, in part, non-written.) However, as long as the spirit and the *telos* of the original document are maintained in the new circumstances, the *decalage* only affects the myth of a "fixed constitution"; and the American experience goes to show, if anything, that written constitutions can endure despite the anti-historical assumption upon which they have been conceived. * * *

The thorny point is instead the non-fulfillment of constitutional provisions not because of the time factor, because they have gradually become outdated, but with reference to norms that have never been activated owing to the unwillingness of the executive or of the legislative body to give them life. This problem cannot be dismissed lightly, if we consider that "delinquencies in the application" of the constitution (as Loewenstein calls them) are rather frequent in most countries. It is safe to ask: "Why?" Is it because the constitutional spirit * * * is withering away? Or is it because of other reasons?

It is well to remind ourselves that most countries have a recent constitution, either because they have re-written their previous charters, or because they have started anew. And contemporary constitutions are, as a rule, bad constitutions—technically speaking. They have come to include unrealistic promises and glamorous professions of faith on the one hand, and numberless frivolous details on the other. * * *

Eric Barendt, AN INTRODUCTION TO CONSTITUTIONAL LAW

26–34 (1998).

DOES THE UNITED KINGDOM HAVE A CONSTITUTION?

There is no document in the United Kingdom equivalent, say, to the United States Constitution of 1787 or to the Constitution of the Fifth Republic in France approved in September 1958. Nor, for that matter, is there a set of statutes clearly indicated by their titles as 'Constitutional' or 'Basic laws'.[1] Yet judges, politicians, and commentators in the United Kingdom often refer in general terms to its constitution, and they describe various rules and principles as 'constitutional'. * * *

[F]or example, * * * Law Lords and other judges sometimes state that cases raise issues of 'constitutional importance'; in one case Lords Diplock and Scarman specifically claimed that the constitution is based on the separation of powers.[2] Or, to take another topic, some commentators have argued that it is unconstitutional for a Prime Minister in effect to be elected by a vote of Members of Parliament from the majority party, as happened when John Major replaced Mrs. Thatcher as leader of the Conservative Party, and hence as Prime Minister, in November 1990. In fact that step was perfectly proper, and certainly lawful, under present constitutional arrangements. What is interesting is that the constitutional propriety of the election procedure was even debated.

---

1. New Zealand has a Constitution Act 1986, bringing together a number of earlier statutes, while the uncodified Israeli Constitution consists of a number of Basic Laws.

2. *Duport Steels* v. *Sirs* [1980] 1 WLR 142, 157, 169.

There is, therefore, a widespread assumption that the United Kingdom does have a constitution. But is that assumption justified? * * *

[Some believe] that it is appropriate to use the term 'constitution' only to refer to a higher set of rules, superior to ordinary laws. One characteristic of such higher rules is that they cannot be amended or repealed by the normal legislative process, so that a constitution is necessarily rigid. Acceptance of that claim would certainly mean that the United Kingdom does not have one. Leaving aside conflicts between its enactments and some rules of European Community law, the Westminster Parliament has been legally free to enact whatever legislation it chooses from one year to the next; it has not been limited in its freedom by any higher rules of law contained in an authoritative text. That is what is meant when it is said that Parliament is sovereign. (This position is not affected by the Human Rights Act 1998 * * *). As a result, although Magna Carta 1215 and the European Communities Act 1972 are in one sense fundamental laws, they can be as easily repealed as, say, the Animals Act 1971 or the Estate Agents Act 1979.

The view * * * that only a set of higher laws can qualify as a constitution is too restrictive. It is surely preferable to conclude that the United Kingdom does have a constitution, or at least some laws and arrangements which have that character. But in contrast to almost every other constitution it lacks any authoritative text or document. Moreover, it is flexible, in that it may be amended without recourse to any special procedure for the introduction of constitutional laws. * * *

There is no * * * simple criterion for what counts as constitutional law in the United Kingdom. Any test has to be substantive rather than formal. We must first formulate some ideas about what types of rule or principle should count as constitutional *in substance* before determining whether a particular or court belongs to constitutional law rather than some other branch of law. * * *

Uncertainty about the contours of the constitution does not * * * affect only the contents of constitutional law books. It also affects the tone of public debate. Opponents of a particular Bill or other development often argue that it is of constitutional significance. Such claims may have the effect of raising the temperature of the debate; constitutional disputes tend to become particularly heated. The extension of the right to vote and the introduction of the secret ballot were controversial 100 years ago for this reason; conservatives resisting change argued that these developments altered the constitution. Now opponents of devolution to Scotland and Wales, and of United Kingdom participation in Economic and Monetary Union, make the same argument. The point is that in the absence of an authoritative text (or of a constitutional court with final authority to rule on its interpretation) it is often difficult to substantiate or repudiate claims that a development has constitutional significance, let alone to resolve its merits.

Conversely, in the absence of a codified constitution, it is very difficult for judges in the United Kingdom to rule plainly that government conduct is unconstitutional. Of course, under the fundamental principle of parliamentary sovereignty or legislative supremacy * * * they have not been able to rule that an Act of Parliament is invalid. On the other hand, courts are prepared to hold executive action unlawful, if it is outside the powers conferred on the minister, government agency, or other administrative body by the relevant legislation. But in these circumstances, a court simply rules that the action is unlawful or unauthorized. It is unusual for judges to state that such conduct is unconstitutional. This reluctance may be attributable to a fear that use of the term would make the ruling more controversial. The effect of this reluctance is to make it more difficult in the United Kingdom than in other countries to see what are the principles of the constitution.

Even in those cases when there is a clear constitutional issue, judges prefer to minimize its significance. When, for instance, there was a challenge to the constitutionality of accession to the European Community in 1971, the Court of Appeal rejected it on the ground that it was no business of the courts to question how the Crown, in effect the government, exercised its prerogative power to enter into treaties, in this case the Treaty of Rome.[12] The decision was correct on traditional principles; the point is, however, that the judges refused to consider the argument that accession to the Community entailed the surrender of parliamentary sovereignty. In a later case, involving an unsuccessful attempt to question the legality of ratification of the Maastricht Treaty, on the ground that it involved the transfer of power over foreign policy, the court considered the constitutional arguments exaggerated.[14] In the absence of a codified constitutional text, it was difficult for the English courts in these cases to do full justice to constitutional arguments about loss of sovereignty. In comparison, both the French Constitutional Council and the German Constitutional Court have reviewed at length the constitutionality of accession to the Maastricht Treaty. * * * [See Subsection D.3. below.]

2.   THE CHARACTER OF THE UNITED KINGDOM CONSTITUTION

According to Dicey, the United Kingdom has an unwritten, or partly unwritten, constitution. That proposition is acceptable inasmuch as it is another way of stating that there is no single authoritative text. But it is quite inaccurate if it is taken to mean that there is no *written* constitutional law. For much of the constitution, and certainly all constitutional *law,* is written. There are in the first place many important statutes. They include the Bill of Rights 1689, enacted after the Glorious Revolution; it established the illegality of levying taxation without the consent of Parliament and curtailed other powers of the Crown. Other important statutes are the Act of Settlement 1701 which regulates the succession to the throne and guarantees the independence of the judiciary, the Parliament Acts 1911–49 which limit the legislative power of the House of Lords, and the European Communities Act 1972 which gives effect in the United Kingdom to Community law and which establishes its supremacy

---

12. *Blackburn* v. *Attorney-General* [1971] 1 WLR 1047.

14. *R.* v. *Secretary of State for Foreign and Commonwealth Affairs, ex parte Rees-Mogg* [1994] QB 552.

over domestic law. To this list should now be added the Human Rights Act 1998 and the enactments devolving power to Scotland and to Wales.

Secondly, of course, court decisions are written. There are for instance the great cases of the eighteenth century establishing that the Crown cannot issue general search warrants,[17] the recent ruling of the House of Lords to the effect that ministers may be in contempt of court if they do not comply with court orders,[18] and rulings on the scope of the Crown's non-statutory or prerogative powers. Indeed, the fundamental constitutional principle of parliamentary legislative supremacy has been gradually formulated and refined in judgments of the courts.

Perhaps the only unwritten parts of the constitution are conventions, that is the non-legal rules, for instance, obliging the Monarch to assent to Bills which have passed Parliament and requiring her in almost all circumstances to act on the advice of the government. * * * Even conventions may be expressed in writing, perhaps in the letters page of *The Times*. That happened in 1950 when there was a long correspondence, including a letter from George VI's Private Secretary, concerning the King's right to refuse a request from the Prime Minister to dissolve Parliament for a general election. But it is rare for conventions to be formulated clearly in a single authoritative text, equivalent to a statute or the judgment of a court.

The constitution is therefore very largely a written one. The point is that it is *uncodified*. It is a jumble of diffuse statutes and court rulings, supplemented by extra-legal conventions and practices. It has also been described as a *common law* constitution. There is a connection between these two descriptions. The common law consists of court rulings, modified or partly replaced by statutory rules, which must then be interpreted by the courts. Under the common law constitution of the United Kingdom it is the courts, rather than a constitutional text, which lay down its fundamental principles, although these may in their turn be reformulated by statutes. This general statement is best exemplified by reference to the most fundamental of these principles, that of parliamentary legislative supremacy. This is a common law principle, as is evidenced by the number of court decisions upholding the unlimited right of Parliament to enact any legislation it likes. But what counts as parliamentary legislation has been modified by the Parliament Acts 1911–49 reducing the powers of the House of Lords. Further, the principle of legislative supremacy has been compromised by another statute, the European Communities Act 1972. According to the courts, that legislation indicates that European Community law should in some circumstances prevail over inconsistent statutes. It is appropriate to describe the uncodified arrangements in the United Kingdom as a common law constitution, because it is the courts which have hitherto permitted Parliament to legislate without restraint. The authority of Parliament rests on case law, rather than on any codified constitution. * * *

---

17. E.g., *Entick v. Carrington* (1765) 19 St. Tr. 1030; *Wilkes v. Wood* (1763) 19 St. Tr. 1153.

18. *M* v. *Home Office* [1994] 1 AC 337.

The constitution is therefore uncodified, common law, and political in character. It is flexible, in the sense that even the most important laws can be amended or repealed by the ordinary legislative process. * * *

Notes and Questions

1.   Consistent with Professor Barendt's views, it is a misnomer to refer to the British Constitution as being "unwritten." It is, rather, "uncodified," although it is "written" in many different places. Similarly, Professor Sartori seems to downplay the difference between written and unwritten constitutions. What is much more important, according to him, is whether a constitution provides actual guarantees or is a mere façade. Furthermore, he draws attention to the fact that the "living" constitution may be very different than the written one. See Thomas Grey, *Do We Have an Unwritten Constitution?*, 27 Stanford L. Rev. 703 (1975) (arguing that it is legitimate for courts to enshrine as constitutional fundamental norms not explicitly found in the written constitution). Do you agree that there may be little difference between written and unwritten constitutions? That what counts most is a polity's attitude toward the constitution, which will, in the end, determine whether the constitution will promote guarantees or end up as a mere façade? Can the difference between a written constitution and an "unwritten" or an evolving uncodified one be made to count by requiring a more "literal" interpretation of the written text? Cf. Henry P. Monaghan, *Our Perfect Constitution,* 56 N.Y.U.L. Rev. 353 (1981) (asserting that judges should hold to the text of the written constitution rather than aiming to perfect it). For an extended discussion on issues of constitutional interpretation, see Chapter 2.

2.   Does a written constitution necessarily lead to greater certainty and predictability in constitutional law than an unwritten one that draws on customs, conventions, and evolving legal doctrines? Or does such certainty and predictability depend more on the existence of a broad consensus in the particular culture where the relevant constitution is in force? Consider that the U.S. Constitution is silent on the issue of abortion, and yet the USSC upheld a constitutional right to abortion in *Roe v. Wade,* 410 U.S. 113 (1973). See Chapter 5, Subsection C.1. The seven justices in the majority in *Roe* indeed linked the right to abortion to various provisions of the U.S.'s written Constitution. Critics, however, have vehemently condemned the decision, though they generally share the view that the U.S. Constitution protects the liberty and privacy rights upon which the Court's majority relied in the course of constitutionalizing the right to abortion. Would a country with an unwritten constitution but a strong consensus on abortion have reached a more predictable result when confronted by the issue raised in *Roe*? Is it not reasonable to assume, for example, that a culture with a strong antiabortion tradition and mores would have rejected the constitutionalization of abortion rights as a matter of course?

3.   Professor Barendt draws a distinction between a "rigid" constitution and a "flexible" one, like the British Constitution. A rigid constitution is one that is difficult to change; while a flexible one can be easily altered. Whether a constitution is flexible or rigid largely depends on the ease with which it can be amended. See Section E., below, for a discussion on constitutional amendments. To the extent that the British Parliament can

change the constitution through ordinary lawmaking, the British Constitution is so flexible as to afford little protection against the will of the majority. Would you agree, therefore, that it is its flexibility—rather than its "unwritten" or uncodified form—that accounts for the impression that the British Constitution is largely nominal?

4.   What accounts for the UK's unwritten constitution? Consider the following observation from Colin R. Munro, *Studies in Constitutional Law* 3–4 (2d ed. 1999):

> It is easy to understand why in many countries the fundamental framework for government has been set forth in a document. What was more natural in Soviet Russia, after the revolution in 1918, or newly independent India in 1950, or the new Czech Republic, freed from a totalitarian regime and then peacefully separated from Slovakia, in 1992? When there is a break with the past, and the institutions or the principles of government are altered, a formal embodiment of the new arrangements seems appropriate. The births of new nations and the unions or the divorces of partners are aptly marked by rites of passage in the form of documents to which a special significance is attached. If later, in a state which has had such a constitution, it is desired to change some fundamentals, as in Spain in 1978 following its return to democracy (and monarchy) after the death of the dictator Franco, or in post-apartheid South Africa in 1996, then a document is likely to be employed, for symbolic reasons and as a badge of legitimacy.

> The circumstances which have led to the making of constitutions in other countries have largely been absent in Britain. The British have not suffered conquest, or the loss of a major war, or revolution, for several hundred years.

5.   Lacking a break with the past may account for Britain's unwritten constitution, but this can hardly do for Israel. Israel is a new nation, born in 1948, whose Declaration of Independence both embodies human rights and affirms that "the state of Israel is the state of the Jewish people, established by * * * Zionists." Moshe Landau, *The Limits of Constitutions and Judicial Review*, cited in Jacobsohn, *op. cit.* at 120–21. Justice Landau further notes: "How to bridge this tension between these two parts of the declaration is, of course, a question which has been with us for a long time and will continue to be with us for a long time to come * * *." *Id*. The first Israeli Parliament was supposed to function as a constituent assembly, but that never occurred; and although the Israeli Supreme Court has protected basic civil rights, the country never adopted a formal written constitution. See Jacobsohn, *op. cit.* at 10. This is due, in part, to the fact that ultra-Orthodox Jews maintain "that Israel ha[s] no need for *another* constitution, the Torah being a more than fundamental law." *Id*. at 102. In short, the absence of a written constitution in Israel may be due less to tradition than to the lack of sufficient consensus between its secular and religious citizens concerning fundamental norms.

D.2. MAJOR TYPES OF CONTEMPORARY CONSTITUTIONAL SYSTEMS

Even if we discard largely sham constitutions, like those of the former Soviet Union, we are bound to find that constitutions and constitutional systems can vary significantly from one setting to another. Differences among constitutions depend on history, tradition, and ideology, as well as physical, economic, and social conditions. Beyond that, how central or peripheral a constitution is in daily life is a function of the prevailing constitutional culture. In some countries, like the U.S., the constitution plays a central role in the political arena and in the definition and consolidation of national identity. In other countries, in contrast, the constitution plays a more restricted political role and is peripheral to shaping national identity. Accordingly, there are several different constitutional models, and similar constitutional norms within closely resembling constitutional models may have divergent impacts.

Until recently, constitutions emerged only in the context of the nation-state or in a subnational unit, such as an American state. See Subsection D.3., below, for a discussion of the viability of constitutions beyond the bounds of the nation-state. Several key questions arise: What ought to be included in a constitution? How should a constitution be linked to the law, society, and democracy? What is the role of a constitution in mediating between society and the state? Should a constitution be confined to the relationships among citizens and the state, or should it also regulate certain relationships *among* citizens?

Ulrich K. Preuss, PATTERNS OF CONSTITUTIONAL EVOLUTION AND CHANGE IN EASTERN EUROPE, in CONSTITUTIONAL POLICY AND CHANGE IN EUROPE

95, 101–103 (Joachim J. Hesse and Nevil Johnson eds., 1995).

[Professor Preuss asserts that modern constitutions have both a *legitimating* function, as they purport to justify political authority, and an *integrative* function, inasmuch as they embody common goals, aspirations, values, and beliefs that bind together the members of the polity.]

* * *

Generally speaking * * * constitutions which are very much concerned with the problem of social integration tend to weaken their legitimizing function, in that they rely more on the integrating and beneficial effects of constitutional pledges and the ensuing policies which they envision than on the purely procedural rights of citizens to participate in the democratic process of will-formation. In a country with a long history of constitutionalism which is deeply rooted in its political culture—such as Britain or the USA—the tensions between the different functions of a constitution are of minor importance. There is a gradual progression of consecutive steps which include the formation of the modern state, the emergence of a civil society, the privatization/marketization of the economy, the establishment of a constitution which safeguards rights to freedom (later also rights to political participation), and, finally, the generation of the welfare state, with its bundle of legal rights to social benefits. * * *

In contrast to these ingrained constitutional democracies, both the Weimar Constitution contained and the Basic Law contains welfare state pledges and guarantees. Whereas the Weimar Constitution was fairly specific, the Basic Law contented itself with the general clause of the 'social state'. But this state goal has a prominent place in the constitution, in that it is associated with the fundamental principles of rule of law, democracy, and federalism (Article 20). * * * Interestingly enough, Germany has a somewhat shady record with respect to its constitutional history. There are good reasons for Germany to be less certain of the compatibility of its political culture with the principles of constitutionalism and of the robustness of its political institutions than, for example, Britain or the USA. As a 'belated nation' the processes of nation-building, of constitution-building (including institution-building), and of the marketization of the economy not only did not always harmonize, but were opposed to each other for long periods. * * * [Accordingly, Germany's integrating constitutional formula had to compensate] for the lack of a continual and consecutive * * * formation of a nation-state and of a democratic constitution.

[T]he situation of many of the post-communist countries of Eastern and Central Europe is even worse. Given the fact that many of them are either internally or externally heterogeneous—i.e., * * * they contain either non-negligible numbers of members of several peoples, or they have one dominant people, and non-negligible numbers of that people who live outside their borders—their existence as a nation-state is highly disputed. As a consequence, they have to accomplish the separate processes of marketization of the economy, nation-building, and establishing constitutional democracy, for which other countries needed centuries or at least decades, at the same time.

An inquiry into their constitutions * * * shows a strong inclination to determine particular constitutional pledges, such as the right to safe and healthy working conditions, to annual paid leave, to social security in case of sickness, invalidity, old age, and unemployment, * * * the right to education, and the 'right to a healthy and favourable environment * * *.'[19] There seems to be a significant correlation between the dearth of a long-standing and firm constitutional tradition and the preference for teleological constitutions. Thus we can point to three categories of constitutional states: those with a long and continuous tradition like Britain and the USA; a country with an erratic constitutional development like Germany; and finally the post-communist countries of East and Central Europe which have to achieve the nation-state, a civil society with a private economy, and democratic structures at the same time. If a rough comparison of them is made, it is striking that the number of pledges—be they state goals or social rights—increases in inverse proportion to the extent that these countries are able and prepared to establish a welfare state and a standard of environmental protection which could compare * * * with [that of] * * * West European * * * states.

---

19. Art. 70/B–70/F, Constitution of Hungary; arts. 15, 48, 51–3, 55, Constitu- tion of the Republic of Bulgaria, effective 12 July 1991.

Professor Preuss's conclusion suggests a paradox. The greater the constitutional tradition the more the constitutional system may rely on procedural guarantees and ignore common goals. Conversely, the lesser the constitutional tradition the more the viability of the constitutional system would seem to depend on the constitutionalization of common goals. But does not the very lack of a common tradition make it less likely to reach a workable agreement on common goals? In thinking about this apparent paradox, consider that constitutional systems depend not only on issues of integration but also on issues of identity.

Michel Rosenfeld, CONSTITUTION-MAKING, IDENTITY BUILDING, AND PEACEFUL TRANSITION TO DEMOCRACY: THEORETICAL REFLECTIONS INSPIRED BY THE SPANISH EXAMPLE

19 Cardozo L. Rev. 1891, 1897–1899, 1917, 1919 (1998).

[Traditionally, three distinct constitutional models emerged,] each leading to a different constitutional identity. These three models are the German, the French, and the American * * *. [T]hese constitutional models differ from one another in the ways in which they conceive the relationship between nation and state and between constitutional identity and other critical identities such as ethnic, cultural or national identity.

The principal difference between the German and French models can be traced back to their contrasting conceptions of the nation. As Ulrich Preuss notes: "Whereas in the French concept the nation is the entirety of the *demos,* in the German and East European concept the nation is a group defined in terms of ethnicity—the nation is the *ethnos.*"[29] Accordingly, the French model envisions a nation founded on equal citizenship rooted in the social contract and operating through the principle of democratic sovereignty. Within this model, each citizen enjoys universal rights and the polity's destiny is shaped by the general will as conceived in Jean–Jacques Rousseau's political philosophy. Within the French model, moreover, it is the task of the constitution-makers to give birth to a democratic nation united through equal citizenship, a political framework suited to give an effective voice to the people as a whole, and a constitutional regime designed to safeguard the rights of citizens. Consistent with Sieyès's conception of a nation as "a body of associates living under common laws and *represented* by the same *legislative assembly,*"[32] the constitution-makers of the Revolution created the French nation. Indeed, although the French Monarchy already claimed to embody the French nation, it did so only in contrast to the particularism of the powers of feudalism above which it rose * * *. [T]he

29. [See Ulrich K.] Preuss, [*Constitutional Powermaking for the New Polity: Some Deliberations on the Relations Between Constituent Power and the Constitution,* in *Constitutionalism, Identity, Difference and Legitimacy* (Michel Rosenfeld ed., 1994)] at 150.

32. [See Emmanuel Joseph] Sieyès, [*What is the Third Estate?* 58 (S.E. Finer ed. and M. Blondel trans., 1963) (1789)] at 58.

constitution-makers of the Revolution transformed the disparate population previously subjected to the French Monarchy into a democratic nation-state governed by the ideals of reason, equality, and universality.

In sharp contrast to its French counterpart, the German model places *ethnos* above *demos* and thus gives the prepolitical bonds, cemented through a common language culture, ethnicity, or religion, clear priority. Unlike the French model where the nation must be constructed within the newly instituted constitutional order, the German model does not depend on a constitution because the nation as an indivisible ethnic, linguistic, cultural, etc., group is already fully formed. Accordingly, in the German model, constitution-making is important to enable an already existing nation to give expression to its will and to fulfill its own destiny through the instrumentalities of a full functioning state * * *. Consistent with this, and as envisioned by the German model's foremost constitutional theorist, Carl Schmitt, democracy must be reinterpreted in ethnicist terms * * * [T]he constitution-makers must produce an institutional framework capable of affording political expression to the nation's unique culture and character as distinguished from both the culture of the other ethnic groups and from the liberal-universalist aspirations inherent in the French model. Within this perspective, as elaborated by Schmitt, true democracy provides authentic expression to the unified pre-political identity of the ethnically defined people.

[Unlike] [i]n the French and German models, [where] the nation is in place prior to the exercise of constituent power designed to lead to the institution of a constitutional democracy * * * in the making of the American Constitution, the state preceded the nation. Indeed, in the United States, the Constitution provided a framework for the deployment of a full-fledged state prior to the formation and consolidation of an American nation through an extended absorption and integration of large waves of immigration coming from a multitude of different nations and diverse cultures. Under the German model, the identity of the nation is not supposed to be changed through constitution-making, and under the French model an existing nation's identity is supposed to be transformed, while under the American model, the constitution not only antedates the nation but it also predetermines to a significant extent the kind of nation that may emerge and grow within the institutional framework it circumscribes. In short, in the German model the constitution is supposed to give expression to a prevailing national identity; in the French, to transform and redirect an existing national identity; and in the American, to lay down the essential characteristics of the identity of a nation that is yet to be formed.

* * *

[The Spanish Constitution, adopted in 1978, can be seen as giving rise to a new constitutional model, which has influenced recent transitions to constitutional democracy, such as those that occurred in East and Central Europe after 1989. This new model does not] fit within any of the three constitutional models thus far encountered. It does not fit within the German model since one of its chief characteristics is the move away from ethnocentrism—or, more precisely, from the linguistic and cultural hegemony pursued throughout the Franco dictatorship. Likewise, the Spanish experience cannot be satisfactorily incorporated within the French model to the extent that the latter is predicated on the indivisibility of the *demos* and the general will, and that it gives recognition to the individual as the embodiment of the ideal of universal equal citizenship to the exclusion of any consideration of group affiliation or allegiance. Finally, the Spanish transition to constitutional democracy cannot be subsumed under the American model, for Spain's constitution clearly did not establish the framework for a new nation, but rather carved out a new identity and a new set of institutions designed to mediate among various, often antagonistic, visions of the nation, and to preserve the polity's unity while affording sufficient space for meaningful expression of its diversity.

The Spanish experience suggests the emergence of a fourth constitutional model, the Spanish model * * * revolv[ing] around a twofold transformation of the relationship between the nation and the state that is motivated, in part by external factors, and, in part, by internal ones. Moreover, the transformation in question consists of the reframing of the relationship between the nation and the state in terms of the broader perspective projected by political actors engaged in a common supra-national project, such as the European [Union] and of a movement toward a more supple, nuanced, and complex relationship between nation and state, designed to include and accommodate national diversity without thereby threatening the integrity or viability of the nation as a whole.

* * *

The Spanish constitutional model is shaped by the convergence of internal and external trends and it emerges out of negotiations among various political actors who pursue divergent objectives but are (or perceive themselves to be) too weak to impose their will on their antagonists. Within this model, the constitution is much more likely to be the product of consensus than majority politics. Moreover, such a consensus-based constitution is likely to remain ambiguous in significant respects, and adherence to it notwithstanding strong disagreements concerning its ambiguous provisions—in the case of Spain, the provisions regarding regional autonomy—is likely to be buttressed both by fear of violence and by transnational aspirations.

Notes and Questions

1. The four constitutional models discussed above should be regarded as prototypes. As countries change constitutions or as their constitutions evolve, they may deviate significantly or even abandon their original models. Thus, for example, Germany's post-World War Two Constitution has departed from Schmitt's conception of a constitutional order predicated exclusively on *ethnos*. Cf. Bernhard Schlink, *Why Carl Schmitt?*, 2 Constellations 429, 435 (1996) (stressing that the legal culture of postwar West Germany disavowed Schmitt's views in order to ground the new legal system on the concept of right and just law). Germany's current Constitution, the *Grundgesetz* (Basic Law), thus does not conform to the original model, in as much

as it requires a filtering of the expression of ethnic identity through certain fundamental constraints, such as the preservation of "militant democracy." See Basic Law, Arts. 18, 20; Donald P. Kommers, *The Constitutional Jurisprudence of the Federal Republic of Germany* 37–38 (2d ed. 1997); and respect for human dignity, see the Basic Law Art. 1 (1). In spite of these changes, the Basic Law continues to be influenced by the German model. For example, as contrasted to the U.S., Germany continues to have a strongly ethnocentric constitutional conception of citizenship. See Ulrich K. Preuss, *Patterns of Constitutional Evolution and Change in Eastern Europe*, above, at 115.

2. The four constitutional models, including the Spanish one, are meant for constitutional ordering within the nation-state. All but the German model incorporate norms that purport to be more than nationalistic in scope. The French and American models embrace norms, such as liberty, equality, and democracy, that are envisioned as universal in scope and thus enlist the constitution as a vehicle for the adaptation of universal values within the nation-state. On the other hand the Spanish model incorporates norms originating beyond the borders of the relevant constitutional polity, not so much because they are universal as because they are desirable to a nation-state's transnational objectives. In the case of post-Franco Spain, the transnational objective was membership in what is now the European Union. See Juan J. Linz and Alfred Stepan, *Problems of Democratic Transition and Consolidation* 113 (1996). Similar transnational concerns played a significant role in shaping the postcommunist constitutions in countries in East and Central Europe. See Eric Stein, *International Law in Internal Law: Toward Internationalization of Central–Eastern European Constitutions?*, 88 A.J.I.L. 427, 448 (1994):

> The international arena has undergone profound modifications whose import could escape the attention of only the most parochial of the constitution makers: the massive proliferation of international agreements after World War II, including novel types of lawmaking conventions and treaties specifically designed to affect internal legal orders; the unprecedented growth of international regimes, some with prescriptive authority; and the intensified common security interest in moderating the unilateral use of state military power. The pervasive normative changes correspond also to the globalization of the economy and communications. Even the traditional rules of recognition of states and governments appear to be changing, in that observance of basic human rights is increasingly required as an additional precondition to recognition. The two developments specifically relevant to post-Communist Central and Eastern European governments with totalitarian histories are the emerging status of the individual in international law and the integration of Western Europe, in which these governments propose to participate.

3. Do constitutions merely reflect a people's identity, or can they help transform it? Consider the case of Japan as presented by Lawrence W. Beer and Hiroshi Itoh in *The Constitutional Case Law of Japan, 1970 through 1990*, at 3, 7, 10 (1996):

> The barbarism of the Second World War ended with Emperor Hirohito's announcement of surrender on August 15, 1945; Japan has fought in no war since, despite the Cold War environment and the wars of Asian

geopolitics. That is part of the remarkable story of constitutional transformation which began under the United State-led Occupation (September 2, 1945–April 28, 1952) and continues on today. Peacefulness has replaced myopic nationalism and militarism at home and abroad; capricious authoritarianism in the name of the emperor is gone and a revolution for human rights, more democratic choice of leaders, and a responsible government of limited and divided powers has been institutionalized.

The Constitution of Japan was drafted, debated, approved by parliament, and promulgated by the emperor between February and November, 1946, in the form of a revision of the 1889 Constitution of the Empire of Japan (the so-called "Meiji Constitution"); it came into effect on May 3, 1947. However, radical systemic changes began in the fall of 1945 when personnel working in the General Headquarters (GHQ) of "SCAP" (Supreme Commander for the Allied Powers), General Douglas MacArthur, disassembled the old order and served as the catalyst for the new democratic order required by Japan's acceptance of the Potsdam Declaration. * * *

* * *

Japan's constitutional revolution since 1945 has fundamentally altered the status of the emperor (*tennō*), ordinary people and their rights, the military, the courts, and local government under the "new" constitution. By "Constitutional revolution" I mean a basic change in the primary public values legitimized and served by law and constitution, values diffused throughout a nation's culture by public and private community means of education, persuasion, and coercion such as schools, religious institutions, the mass media, and administrative policies and processes. At the outset of Japan's revolution between 1945 and 1948 the primacy of the emperor and his state was replaced by the primacy of popular sovereignty, the individual person, and human rights, what I would call "human rights constitutionalism." As theory, "human rights constitutionalism" grounds government and law in recognition of the equal inherent dignity of each human and thus in a comprehensive notion of human rights and community responsibility to honor those rights.

* * *

What to do with the emperor may have been the most controversial question in 1946: Arrest him as a war criminal? Replace him with his young son Akihito? Abolish the imperial institution? Leave the emperor with some, most or none of this formal prerogatives under the Meiji Constitution? Or render him virtually powerless in real as well as formal terms, but preserve the dynasty; and in return require his support for a transition to a new and demilitarized democratic order? The latter option was chosen by Occupation policy makers to optimize chances for political stability in the challenging tumult of the early Occupation years.

* * *

Unique [to Japan's Constitution] is Chapter 2, "Renunciation of War," which consists of one provision, Article 9. Article 9 renounces war, military power, and "the threat or use of force as a means of settling international disputes." The presence of military officers in the Cabinet is also prohibited

(Article 66, 2); in practice, the military is totally subordinate to civilian leaders, in contrast to its privileged status in pre–1945 modern Japan. In 1928 war was outlawed by the Kellogg–Briand Pact ratified by Japan, the United States, Germany, the United Kingdom, the Soviet Union and other countries. Although technically never revoked, the treaty was disregarded when the Second World War erupted in the 1930s. Particularly since the mid–1950s, Japan has gradually developed a modest military capacity, but as James Auer notes, Japan "simultaneously has attempted to live up to the ideals of the Constitution to a degree that the other signatories of the Kellogg–Briand Pact never have."

4.   In addition to conforming to the requirements of constitutionalism and fulfilling the proper legitimating, integrative, and identity-related functions, a working constitution can thrive only so long as certain basic sociopolitical and material conditions prevail. Linz and Stepan include among these, a "free and lively civil society," the existence of a state bureaucracy usable by democratic government for the implementation of policy, and the presence of an "institutionalized economic society"—i.e., one that mediates between state and market, as the authors assert that neither a state command economy nor a pure market economy is compatible with a consolidated constitutional democracy. See Linz and Stepan, *op. cit.* at 7–8, 56. Do you agree? Are there differences among the various models mentioned above? Compare the views of Professor H.W.O. Okoth–Ogendo relating to Africa, discussed above in Section B., Notes and Questions.

D.3.   CONSTITUTIONS BEYOND THE NATION–STATE?

As indicated in Section A., since the end of World War Two, a trend has developed toward the internationalization of fundamental rights, on both a global and regional scale. Many of these rights very much resemble constitutional rights, and in some cases—such as in the European HR Convention—are judicially enforced much as constitutional rights under national constitutions. If to this is added the EU with its supranational governmental institutions, such as the European Parliament, the European Commission, and the European Council, the question arises whether constitutions can be viable beyond the borders of the nation-state. Strictly speaking, supranational norms do not arise out of constitutions but out of international treaties and covenants.[d] The question is not so much how they originate, however, but rather how they function. Do they—or can they—function as constitutions?

For example, the EU lacks the power over the military and foreign affairs that its members possess as nation-states. Also, the EU is widely perceived as experiencing a "democratic deficit" because its most democratic institution, the European Parliament, has little power compared with the Commission and the Council, which depend on the will of the member-states rather than their peoples. See Joseph H.H. Weiler, *Does Europe Need a Constitution? Reflections on Demos, Telos and the Ger-*

d. At this writing, however, the EU has established a European Convention charged with drafting a "constitutional treaty" for the Union. If this constitution-making pro- ject is successfully completed, the Union will have the first full-fledged supranational constitution.

man Maastricht Decision, 1 European Law Journal 219, 232–35 (1995). Finally, the EU and other supranational entities tend to lack the kind of common culture and national identity that appear to provide a unified framework and an important source of legitimacy to national constitutions.

Whether the EU has (or is evolving toward) a constitution, its legal regime has a substantial impact on the constitutional order of its member-states. Moreover, this substantial impact derives not only from implementation of EU norms but also from other regional and international conventions, such as the European HR Convention. These developments have altered traditional conceptions of the sovereignty of the nation-state. See, generally, Neil MacCormick, *Questioning Sovereignty: Law, State, and Nation in the European Commonwealth* (1999). Unlike federalism, which can be said to split the atom of sovereignty but does so within the confines of a single constitutional order (see Chapter 4), supranational constitutions (or legal regimes with quasi-constitutional functions) seemingly fragment sovereignty. Does this ultimately reinforce or weaken constitutionalism and the spread of constitutional norms?

How do legal rights and obligations arising out of a treaty among nation-states extend rights to private parties? In the case of the Treaty of Rome, establishing on the longer run the European Community (which has become the European Union), member-states argued that its provisions did not explicitly provide for such rights. If a nation-state's constitution made a tariff unconstitutional and the state nonetheless imposed it by law on its citizens, the latter would be justified in claiming that the state should not subject them to unconstitutional laws. A similar argument was made in the context of *Van Gend & Loos v. Netherland Inland Revenue Service*, European Court of Justice 163 E.C.R. 1, 2 C.M.L.R. 105 (1963). In this case the Dutch authorities, in conformity with the Dutch Constitution, imposed a duty in conflict with a prohibition of the Treaty. The European Court of Justice (ECJ) held:

> The conclusion to be drawn from this is that the Community constitutes a new legal order of international law for the benefit of which the states have limited their sovereign rights, albeit within limited fields, and the subjects of which comprise not only Member States but also their nationals. Independently of the legislation of Member States, Community law therefore not only imposes obligations on individuals but is also intended to confer upon them rights which become part of their legal heritage. These rights arrive not only where they are expressly granted by the Treaty but also by reason of obligations which the Treaty imposes in a clearly defined way upon individuals as well as upon the Member States and upon the institutions of the Community.
>
> * * *
>
> The wording of Article 12 [of the Treaty] contains a clear and unconditional prohibition which is not a positive but a negative obligation. This obligation, moreover, is not qualified by any reservation on the part of states which would make its implementation conditional upon a positive legislative measure enacted under national law. The very nature of this

prohibition makes it ideally adapted to produce direct effects in the legal relationship between Member States and their subjects.

The implementation of Article 12 does not require any legislative intervention on the part of the states. The fact that under this Article it is the Member States who are made subject to the negative obligation does not imply that their nationals cannot benefit from this obligation.

* * *

The vigilance of individuals concerned to protect their rights amounts to an effective supervision in addition to the supervision entrusted by Articles 169 and 170 to the diligence of the Commission and of the Member States.

It follows from the foregoing considerations that, according to the spirit, the general scheme and the wording of the Treaty, Article 12 must be interpreted as producing direct effects and creating individual rights which national courts must protect.

Does the fact that the ECJ held that the tariff prohibition resulted in rights for private parties suggest that the prohibition in question ought to be regarded as a constitutional norm?

The second question raised in *Van Gend* concerns whether, or to what degree, the ECJ ought to defer to national courts when interpreting and applying European treaty provisions. The answer depends, in part, on interpretation of national law or regulation. In addition to interpretation of the relevant European treaty provisions, the tariff issue in *Van Gend* involved a determination of the nature and origin of certain tariffs arising under national law. The Court asserted that it lacked competence to interpret national law. Does that signify that it is unlike a constitutional court (or any court exercising constitutional review) in a nation-state? In thinking about this question, consider that in a federal constitutional republic, such as the U.S., federal courts are bound by the highest state court's interpretation of its own law. See, e.g., *Bush v. Gore*, 531 U.S. 98 (2000). Thus, while a state law is invalid if it violates the federal constitution, if its unconstitutionality depends on how it is interpreted, its interpretation by state courts may bear on its validity. Does this mean that the situation at the supranational level is equivalent to the national one? Note further that as to the interpretation of EU law (including the law created by the organs of the EU), the interpretation of the ECJ prevails. Is EU law the equivalent of federal law? See Chapter 4.

Community law arguably incorporates certain constitutional precepts enshrined in each member-state's national constitution. Advocate–General Roemer stated in *Erich Stauder v. City of Ulm*, European Court of Justice, [1969] E.C.R. 419, [1970] C.M.L.R. 112[e]:

e. A European Commission decision authorized the sale of butter at a reduced price to certain consumers eligible for certain social-welfare benefits and whose income left them unable to buy butter at market prices. To avoid fraud, those eligible had to present a coupon that had to include the person's name, according to the German version of the decision, but which had only to be "individualized," according to the French and Italian versions. Plaintiff, a German disabled war veteran entitled to the price reduction, brought an action in the German courts, claiming that the requirement that his coupon bear his name violated Arts. 1 (right to human dignity) and 3 (right to equality) of the German Basic Law. The German court (the

In the present case the Court is not, contrary to what one might think at first sight, being asked about the compatibility of a Community measure with national constitutional law. In fact in view of your previous case-law examination of such a question would be impossible. The court making the reference is asking for a decision on the legal validity of the Commission's decision in the light of 'the general legal principles of Community law in force'. As the ground of the order making the reference shows, the Verwaltungsgericht thus thinks that it must be guided by reference to the fundamental principles of national law. This is in line with the view taken by many writers that general qualitative concepts of national constitutional law, in particular fundamental rights recognized by national law, must be ascertained by means of a comparative evaluation of laws, and that such concepts, which form an unwritten constituent part of Community law, must be observed in making secondary Community law.[f] Applying this test, there is accordingly every justification for seeking to test the validity of a Commission decision.

Does this make the EU more of a constitutional regime or less than one, inasmuch as it seems partly dependent on the member-states' constitutions for its own fundamental law?

In a federal system, such as the U.S., if a state law (or for that matter a state constitutional provision), see *Romer v. Evans*, 517 U.S. 620 (1996), chapter 6, below, violates the federal constitution, it is invalid. Moreover, such a state law's validity does not depend on which state law is involved or where it is located. For example, if a state law banning flag burning is unconstitutional, an identical law in another state is equally unconstitutional. The European HR Convention (1950) grants jurisdiction to the ECHR (Strasbourg) to consider whether the application of national law violates the Convention obligations of the member-states, in the sense of violation of human rights of individuals under the jurisdiction of a member-state. In *Handyside v. United Kingdom*, European Court of Human Rights (1979) 1 E.H.R.R. 737, [1976] ECHR 5493/72,[g] the ECHR held:

> 48.   The Court points out that the machinery of protection established by the Convention is subsidiary to the national systems safeguarding human rights (judgment of 23 July 1968 on the merits of the "Belgian Linguistic" case, Series A no. 6, p. 35, para. 10 in fine). The Convention leaves to each Contracting State, in the first place, the task of securing the rights and liberties it enshrines. The institutions created by it make

Verwaltungsgerichtshof of Stuttgart) referred the case to the ECJ, asking it to determine whether the Commission decision was contrary to the general principles of Community law. The ECJ decided there was no violation as it interpreted the Commission's decision as not requiring the name of an eligible beneficiary to be included on the requisite coupon.

f. Secondary Community law is that part of the Community (now Union) law that is enacted on the basis of the constituent treaties by the appropriate organs of

the Community, on the basis of competences conferred by the treaties.

g. Handyside published a book in the UK titled *The Little Red School Book*, written by Danish authors and previously published in other countries. After several complaints, British authorities prosecuted Handyside for having violated domestic antiobscenity law. Handyside was convicted, and copies of the book were ordered destroyed. Handyside brought a complaint, alleging that the conviction violated his Art. 10 (free speech) rights.

their own contributions to this task but they become involved only through contentious proceedings and once all domestic remedies have been exhausted (art. 26).

These observations apply, notably, to Article 10(2). In particular, it is not possible to find in the domestic law of the various Contracting States a uniform European Conception of morals. The view taken by their respective laws of the requirements of morals varies from time to time and from place to place, especially in our era which is characterised by a rapid and far-reaching evolution of opinions on the subject. By reason of their direct and continuous contact with the vital forces of their countries, State authorities are in principle in a better position than the international judge to give an opinion on the exact content of these requirements as well was on the "necessity" of a "restriction" or "penalty" intended to meet them. The Court notes at this juncture that, whilst the adjective "necessary", within the meaning of Article 10(2), is not synonymous with "indispensable"(cf., in Articles 2(2) and 6(1), the words "absolutely necessary" and "strictly necessary" and, in Article 15(1), the phrase "to the extent strictly required by the exigencies of the situation"), neither has it the flexibility of such expressions as "admissible", "ordinary" (cf. Article 4(3)), "useful" (cf. The French text of the first para. Of Article 1 of Protocol No. 1), "reasonable" (cf. Articles 5(3) and 6(1)) or "desirable". Nevertheless, it is for the national authorities to make the initial assessment of the reality of the pressing social need implied by the notion of "necessity" in this context.

Consequently, Article 10(2) leaves to the Contracting States a margin of appreciation. This margin is given both to the domestic legislator ("prescribed by law") and to the bodies, judicial amongst others, that are called upon to interpret and apply the laws in force. * * *

49.   Nevertheless, Article 10(2) does not give the Contracting States an unlimited power of appreciation. The Court, which, with the Commission, is responsible for ensuring the observance of those States' engagements (art. 19), is empowered to give the final ruling on whether a "restriction" or "penalty" is reconcilable with freedom of expression as protected by Article 10. The domestic margin of appreciation thus goes hand in hand with a European supervision. Such supervision concerns both the aim of the measure challenged and its "necessity", it covers not only the basic legislation but also the decision applying it, even one given by an independent court.

50.   It follows from this that it is in no way the Court's task to take the place of the competent national courts but rather to review under Article 10 the decisions they delivered in the exercise of their power of appreciation.

However, the Court's supervision would generally prove illusory if it did no more than examine these decisions in isolation; it must view them in the light of the case as a whole, including the publication in question and the arguments and evidence adduced by the applicant in the domestic legal system and then at the international level. The Court must decide, on the basis of the different date available to it, whether the reasons given by the national authorities to justify the actual measures of "interference" they take are relevant and sufficient under Article 10(2).

Note, however, that as the *Socialist Reich Party Case* (see Chapter 11, Subsection A.3.) indicates, this margin of appreciation does not rule out a common European minimum standard that is to be defined by the ECHR. See *Ceylan v. Turkey* in Chapter 7. Does allowance for a "margin of appreciation" therefore undermine the notion that protection of fundamental rights under the European HR Convention is akin to protection of such rights under a national constitution? Or does allowance for a "margin of appreciation" merely permit circumscribed variations in the interpretation of the same principle; thus *essentially* affording the same constitutional protection to all citizens whose countries have ratified the European HR Convention? Cf. *Miller v. California*, 413 U.S. 15 (1973), (making obscenity depend inter alia on whether sexually explicit material is offensive to community standards of the locality where prosecution takes place rather than to national standards). Accordingly, the same movie could be constitutionally protected in New York City but not in many small cities or rural communities. Cf. *Jenkins v. Georgia*, 418 U.S. 153 (1974), (the state of Georgia labeling a mainstream Hollywood movie as obscene held beyond local communities' power to set obscenity standards).

In *Handyside* the ECHR upheld the UK obscenity conviction, and in both *Van Gend* and *Stauder* the ECJ ruled in ways that avoided conflict with the national laws and regulations involved. In *Van Gend* the Court did so by refusing to interpret Dutch law and in *Stauder* by interpreting Community law in a way that obviated the potential for conflict with German constitutional law. But what about when such conflicts cannot be avoided? The ECHR has ruled against nations party to the European HR Convention. See, e.g., *Lingens* and *Ceylan* in Chapter 7.

Determining whether supranational norms are akin to constitutional norms depends, also, on how they are treated in the member-states. In *Stauder* the ECJ avoided the conflict in the course of interpreting Community law at the request of a German court. But what about a national court confronting an allegation of conflict between Community law and its own constitution?

INTERNATIONALE HANDELSGESELLSCHAFT MBH v. EINFUHR–UND VORRATSSTELLE FÜR GETREIDE UND FUTTERMITTEL [ALSO KNOWN AS SOLANGE I]

Federal Constitutional Court (Germany).
37 BVerfGE 271 (1974).

[A German company that had forfeited a deposit related to an export license pursuant to European Community regulations challenged such regulations as violative of fundamental rights protected under the German Basic Law.]

Judgement of the Second Senate:

* * *

[18]   1. An essential preliminary for this ruling is the determination of the relationship between the constitutional law of the Federal Repub-

lic of Germany and European Community law, which has come into being on the basis of the Treaty establishing the European Economic Community (hereinafter referred to as 'Community law'). The present case demands only the clarification of the relationship between the guarantees of fundamental rights in the Constitution and the rules of secondary Community law of the EEC, the execution of which is in the hands of administrative authorities in the Federal Republic of Germany. For there is at the moment nothing to support the view that rules of the Treaty establishing the EEC, that is, primary Community law, could be in conflict with provisions of the Constitution of the Federal Republic of Germany. It can equally remain open whether the same considerations apply to the relationship between the law of the Constitution *outside* its catalogue of fundamental rights, and Community law, as applied, according to the following reasoning, to the relationship between the guarantees of fundamental rights in the Constitution and secondary Community law.

[19] 2. This Court—in this respect in agreement with the law developed by the European Court of Justice—adheres to its settled view that Community law is neither a component part of the national legal system nor international law, but forms an independent system of law flowing from an autonomous legal source; for the Community is not a State, in particular not a federal State, but 'a *sui generis* community in the process of progressive integration', an 'inter-State institution' within the meaning of Article 24 (1) of the Constitution.

[20] It follows from this that, in principle, the two legal spheres stand independent of and side by side one another in their validity, and that, in particular, the competent Community organs, including the European Court of Justice, have to rule on the binding force, construction and observance of Community law, and the competent national organs on the binding force, construction and observance of the constitutional law of the Federal Republic of Germany. The European Court of Justice cannot with binding effect rule on whether a rule of Community law is compatible with the Constitution, nor can [the GFCC] rule on whether, and with what implications, a rule of secondary Community law is compatible with primary Community law. This does not lead to any difficulties as long as the two systems of law do not come into conflict with one another in their substance. There therefore grows forth from the special relationship which has arisen between the Community and its members by the establishment of the Community first and foremost the duty for the competent organs, in particular for the two courts charged with reviewing law—the European Court of Justice and the German Constitutional Court to concern themselves in their decisions with the concordance of the two systems of law. Only in so far as this is unsuccessful can there arise the conflict which demands the drawing of conclusions from the relationship of principle between the two legal spheres set out above.

[21] For, in this case, it is not enough simply to speak of the 'precedence' of Community law over national constitutional law, in order to justify the conclusion that Community law must always prevail over national constitutional law because, otherwise, the Community would be

put in question. Community law is just as little put in question when, exceptionally, Community law is not permitted to prevail over entrenched constitutional law, as international law is put in question by Article 25 of the Constitution when it provides that the general rules of international law only take precedence over simple federal law, and as another (foreign) system of law is put in question when it is ousted by the public policy of the Federal Republic of Germany. The binding of the Federal Republic of Germany (and of all member-States) by the Treaty is not, according to the meaning and spirit of the Treaties, one-sided, but also binds the Community which they establish to carry out its part in order to resolve the conflict here assumed, that is, to seek a system which is compatible with an entrenched precept of the constitutional law of the Federal Republic of Germany. Invoking such a conflict is therefore not in itself a violation of the Treaty, but sets in motion inside the European organs the Treaty mechanism which resolves the conflict on a political level.

[22]   3. Article 24 of the Constitution deals with the transfer of sovereign rights to inter-State institutions. This cannot be taken literally. Like every constitutional provision of a similar fundamental nature, Article 24 of the Constitution must be understood and construed in the overall context of the whole Constitution. That is, it does not open the way to amending the basic structure of the Constitution, which forms the basis of its identity, without a formal amendment to the Constitution, that is, it does not open any such way through the legislation of the inter-State institution. Certainly, the competent Community organs can make law which the competent German constitutional organs could not make under the law of the Constitution and which is nonetheless valid and is to be applied directly in the Federal Republic of Germany. But Article 24 of the Constitution limits this possibility in that it nullifies any amendment of the Treaty which would destroy the identity of the valid Constitution of the Federal Republic of Germany by encroaching on the structures which go to make it up. And the same would apply to rules of secondary Community law made on the basis of a corresponding interpretation of the valid Treaty and in the same way affecting the structures essential to the Constitution. Article 24 does not actually give authority to transfer sovereign rights, but opens up the national legal system (within the limitations indicated) in such a way that the Federal Republic of Germany's exclusive claim to rule is taken back in the sphere of validity of the Constitution and room is given, within the State's sphere of rule, to the direct effect and applicability of law, from another source.

[23]   4. The part of the Constitution dealing with fundamental rights is an inalienable essential feature of the valid Constitution of the Federal Republic of Germany and one which forms part of the constitutional structure of the Constitution. Article 24 of the Constitution does not without reservation allow it to be subjected to qualifications. In this, the present state of integration of the Community is of crucial importance. The Community still lacks a democratically legitimated parliament directly elected by general suffrage which possesses legislative powers and to which the Community organs empowered to legislate are

fully responsible on a political level; it still lacks in particular a codified catalogue of fundamental rights, the substance of which is reliably and unambiguously fixed for the future in the same way as the substance of the Constitution and therefore allows a comparison and a decision as to whether, at the time in question, the Community law standard with regard to fundamental rights generally binding in the Community is adequate in the long term measured by the standard of the Constitution with regard to fundamental rights (without prejudice to possible amendments) in such a way that there is no exceeding the limitation indicated, set by Article 24 of the Constitution. As long as this legal certainty, which is not guaranteed merely by the decisions of the European Court of Justice, favourable though these have been to fundamental rights, is not achieved in the course of the further integration of the Community, the reservation derived from Article 24 of the Constitution applies. What is involved is, therefore, a legal difficulty arising exclusively from the Community's continuing integration process, which is still in flux and which will end with the present transitional phase.

[24]   Provisionally, therefore, in the hypothetical case of a conflict between Community law and a part of national constitutional law or, more precisely, of the guarantees of fundamental rights in the Constitution, there arises the question of which system of law takes precedence, that is, ousts the other. In this conflict of norms, the guarantee of fundamental rights in the Constitution prevails as long as the competent organs of the Community have not removed the conflict of norms in accordance with the Treaty mechanism.

RE THE APPLICATION OF WUNSCHE HANDELSGESLLSCHAFT [ALSO KNOWN AS SOLANGE II]

Federal Constitutional Court (Germany).
73 BVerfGE 339 (1986).

[In this case, involving another challenge to European Community import-duty regulations and to adjudication regarding such regulation by the ECJ, the GFCC overruled its previous position concerning the validity of European norms from the standpoint of German constitutional law.]

Judgement of the Second Senate:

* * *

[33]   (c) This Court explained in its judgment of 29 May 1974 that having regard to the state of integration which had been reached at that time the standard of fundamental rights under Community law generally binding within the European Communities did not yet show the level of legal certainty for the Court to conclude that that standard would permanently satisfy the fundamental rights standards of the Constitution. It said that the Community still lacked a parliament legitimized by direct democratic means and established by general suffrage, which possessed legislative powers and to which the Community institutions competent to issue legislation were politically fully responsible; in partic-

ular the Community still lacked a codified catalogue of fundamental rights)

* * *

[35]   (d) In the judgment of this Chamber a measure of protection of fundamental rights has been established in the meantime within the sovereign jurisdiction of the European Communities which in its conception, substance and manner of implementation is essentially comparable with the standards of fundamental rights provided for in the Constitution. All the main institutions of the Community have since acknowledged in a legally significant manner that in the exercise of their powers and the pursuit of the objectives of the Community they will be guided as a legal duty by respect for fundamental rights, in particular as established by the *constitutions of member-States and by the European Convention on Human Rights*. There are no decisive factors to lead one to conclude that the standard of fundamental rights which has been achieved under Community law is not adequately consolidated and is only of a transitory nature.

[36]   (aa) This standard of fundamental rights has in the meantime, particularly through the decisions of the European Court, been formulated in content, consolidated and adequately guaranteed.

[37]   In the early years the European Court refused to investigate accusations by parties that decisions of the High Authority had infringed principles of German constitutional law and in particular Articles 2 and 12 of the Constitution; it stated that it had no authority to ensure respect for rules of internal law in force in one or other member-State, even if they involved principles of constitutional law, and explained that 'Community law as it arises under the European Coal and Steel Community Treaty does not contain any general principle, express or otherwise, guaranteeing the maintenance of vested rights. In the following period the European Court made it clear that the general principles of Community law, the maintenance of which it was bound to protect, included the fundamental rights of the individual. It is true that in the [*Solange I*] case it held that the validity of a Community measure or its effect within a particular member-State could not be affected by an allegation that it ran counter to fundamental rights as formulated by the constitution of the member-State or to the principles of its constitutional structure.

[38]   The European Court took the essential step (from the viewpoint of the Constitution) in its judgment in the *Nold* case[1] where it stated that in relation to the safeguarding of fundamental rights it had to start from the common constitutional traditions of the member-States: 'it cannot therefore allow measures which are incompatible with fundamental rights recognized and guaranteed by the constitutions of those States'.

[39]   On the legal basis of the general principles of Community law thus defined and given that content, the European Court in the period

---

1. J. Nold KG v. E.C. Commission   C.M.L.R. 338 at 354.
(4/73): [1974] E.C.R. 491 at 507, [1974] 2

that followed cited fundamental rights as recognized in the constitutions of member-States as obligatory standards for reviewing measures of Community organs taken within their spheres of jurisdiction. Side by side with the express guarantees of liberties contained in the Community Treaties themselves the foreground was occupied naturally by the fundamental rights and freedoms relating to economic activities, such as the right to property and freedom to pursue economic activities. In addition to that it cited other basic rights, such as freedom of association, the general principle of equal treatment and the prohibition on arbitrary acts, religious freedom or the protection of the family, as standards of assessment.

[40]   The European Court has generally recognized and consistently applied in its decisions the principles, which follow from the rule of law, of the prohibition of excessive action and of proportionality as general legal principles in reaching a balance between the common-interest objectives of the Community legal system and the safeguarding of the essential content of fundamental rights * * *

[44]   (e) Compared with the standard of fundamental rights under the Constitution it may be that the guarantees for the protection of such rights established thus far by the decisions of the European Court, since they have naturally been developed case by case, still contain gaps in so far as specific legal principles recognized by the Constitution or the nature, content or extent of a fundamental right have not individually been the object of a judgment delivered by the Court. What is decisive nevertheless is the attitude of principle which the Court maintains at this stage towards the Community's obligations in respect of fundamental rights, to the incorporation of fundamental rights in Community law under legal rules and the legal connection of that law (to that extent) with the constitutions of member-States and with the European Human Rights Convention, as is also the practical significance which has been achieved by the *protection* of fundamental rights in the meantime in the Court's application of Community law.

[45]   By virtue of the connection through legal rules as explained above of the guarantees of fundamental rights contained in the constitutions of member-State and in the European Human Rights Convention with the general principles of Community law, the requirement of a catalogue of fundamental rights decreed by a parliament, which was regarded as necessary by this Chamber in its judgment of 29 May, has also been satisfied in all the circumstances. In the first place, since 1974 all the original member-States of the Community (like those which acceded later) have acceded to the European Human Rights Convention, and their respective parliaments have approved their accession; in the second place the common declaration of 5 April 1977, which was also adopted by the European Parliament, can be judged from the viewpoint of the requirement to be sufficient parliamentary recognition of a formulated catalogue of effectively operating fundamental rights. Whilst this Chamber in its [*Solange I*] judgment of 29 May 1974 observed that the Community lacked a parliament legitimized by direct and democratic means and established by general suffrage which possessed legislative powers and to which the institutions competent to issue legislation were

politically fully responsible, that was an element in the description of the state of integration as it appeared at that time; the basis for that finding was clearly the consideration that protection of fundamental rights has to begin as early as the stage of law-making and parliamentary responsibility provides a suitable protective arrangement for that purpose. Thee was no intention however of laying down a constitutional requirement that such a position must have prevailed before there could be any possibility of the withdrawal of the Federal Constitutional Court's jurisdiction over derived community law in proceedings by way of review of legislation under Article 100 (1) of the Constitution.

* * *

[47] The fact that at the Community level questions of a different nature arise in certain circumstances in connection with the regulation of fundamental rights or the practical definition of the extent to which they are protected does not in general impair the adequacy of the protection of fundamental rights provided by Community law from the point of view of the Constitution. In regard especially to the objectives laid down in the Community Treaties, which for their part are compatible with the Constitution, questions of balance will arise in this connection involving Treaty and common-interest objectives of the Community which will not arise, at least directly, in the same way at member-State level. Furthermore, the fundamental rights safeguarded by the Constitution take their place in a constitutional framework as a body of rules representing a unified purpose and are accordingly to be interpreted and applied in harmony and co-ordination with other legal interests conferred or recognized thereby. They include the belief, expressed in the preamble forms of supranational co-operation made possible under Article 24 (1). Under the Constitution therefore it is also possible to have legal provisions at Community level which protect fundamental rights in accordance with the objectives and special structures of the Community; the substantive content of the fundamental rights and indeed of human rights on the other hand is unconditional and must continue in existence in face of the sovereign powers of the Community as well. This Chamber holds that requirement to be adequately guaranteed in general at the present stage at Community level.

[48] (f) In view of those developments it must be held that, so long as the European Communities, and in particular in the case law of the European Court, generally ensure an effective protection of fundamental rights as against the sovereign powers of the Communities which is to be regarded as substantially similar to the protection of fundamental rights required unconditionally by the Constitution, and in so far as they generally safeguard the essential content of fundamental rights, the Federal Constitutional Court will no longer exercise its jurisdiction to decide on the applicability of secondary Community legislation cited as the legal basis for any acts of German courts or authorities within the sovereign jurisdiction of the Federal Republic of Germany, and it will no longer review such legislation by the standard of the fundamental rights contained in the Constitution.

MAASTRICHT TREATY CASE

Federal Constitutional Court (Germany).
89 BVerfGE 155 (1993).

[The German federal government signed the amendments of the European treaties and legal instruments at Maastricht in 1992, in order to achieve further integration on the social, monetary, and political levels of the European Community in a then-to-be European Union. Professors and politicians brought constitutional challenges to Germany's participation in the EU under the German Basic Law.]

* * *

[The constitutional right to vote] forbids the weakening * * * of the legitimation of State power gained through an election, and of the influence on the exercise of such power, by means of a transfer of duties and responsibilities of the Federal Parliament, to the extent that the principle of democracy [is] violated.

The principle of democracy does not prevent the Federal Republic of Germany from becoming a member of an inter-governmental community which is organised on a supranational basis. However, it is a precondition of membership that the legitimation and influence which derives from the people will be preserved within an alliance of States.

If a community of States assumes sovereign responsibilities and thereby exercises sovereign powers, the peoples of the Member States must legitimate this process through their national parliaments. Democratic legitimation derives from the link between the actions of European governmental entities and the parliaments of the Member States. To an increasing extent in view of the degree to which the nations of Europe are growing together, the transmission of democratic legitimation within the institutional structure of the European Union by the European Parliament elected by the citizens of the Member States must also be taken into consideration.

The important factor is that the democratic foundations upon which the Union is based are extended concurrent with integration, and that a living democracy is maintained in the Member States while integration proceeds.

If the peoples of the individual States (as is true at present) convey democratic legitimation via the national parliaments, then limits are imposed, by the principle of democracy, on an extension of the functions and powers of the European Communities. The German Federal Parliament must retain functions and powers of substantial import.

[The reasons for this are the following. Political rights are] violated if a law which subjects the German legal system to the direct validity and application of the law of the supranational European Communities does not give a sufficiently precise specification of the assigned rights to be exercised and of the proposed program of integration. This also means that any subsequent substantial amendments to that program of integration provided for by the Maastricht Treaty or to its authorizations to act are no longer covered by the Act of Accession to this Treaty. The German Federal Constitutional Court must examine the question of whether or not legal instruments of European institutions and governmental entities may be considered to remain within the bounds of the sovereign rights accorded to them, or whether they may be considered to exceed those bounds.

Acts of the particular public power of a supranational organisation which is separate from the State power of the Member States may also affect those persons protected by basic rights in Germany. Such acts therefore affect the guarantees provided under the Basic Law and the duties of the Federal Constitutional Court, which include the protection of basic rights in Germany, and not only in respect of German governmental institutions). However, the Federal Constitutional Court exercises its jurisdiction regarding the applicability of derivative Community law in Germany in a "cooperative relationship" with the European Court of Justice.

[The] Federal Republic of Germany is not, by ratifying the Maastricht Treaty, subjecting itself to an uncontrollable, unforeseeable process which will lead inexorably towards monetary union; the Maastricht Treaty simply paves the way for gradual further integration of the European Community as a community of laws. Every further step along this way is dependent either upon conditions being fulfilled by the parliament which can already be foreseen, or upon further consent from the Federal Government, which consent is subject to parliamentary influence.

1. The right granted [in the Constitution] to participate, by means of elections, in the legitimation of State power and to influence the implementation of that power, precludes, within the scope of application of [the constitutional provision on European integration], such right being weakened by reassignment of the functions and the authority of the Federal Parliament in such a way that the principle of democracy declared inviolable * * * is infringed.

2. [It] is an inviolable element of the principle of democracy that the performance of State functions and the exercise of State power derive from the people of the State and that they must, in principle, be justified to that people. This sequence of responsibility may be created in various ways, not just in a single specific way. The crucial factor is that a sufficient proportion of democratic legitimation, a specific level of legitimation, is achieved.

a) If the Federal Republic of Germany becomes a member of a community of States which is entitled to take sovereign action in its own right, and if that community of States is entrusted with the exercise of independent sovereign power (both of which the German Constitution expressly permits for the realisation of a unified Europe * * *), then democratic legitimation cannot be effected in the same way as it can within a State regime which is governed uniformly and conclusively by a State constitution. If sovereign rights are granted to supranational organisations, then the representative body elected by the people, i.e., the German Federal Parliament, and with it the enfranchised citizen, necessarily lose some of their influence upon the processes of decision-making and the formation of political will. Accession to an inter-governmental community has the consequence that any individual member of that community is bound by decisions made by it. Of course, a State, and with it its citizens, which is a member of such a community also gains opportunities to exert influence as a consequence of its participation in the process of forming political will within the community for the purpose of pursuing common (and with those, individual) goals. The fact that the outcome of these goals is binding upon all Member States necessarily assumes that each Member State acknowledges the fact that it is bound.

* * *

b) The principle of democracy does not, therefore, prevent the Federal Republic of Germany from becoming a member of an inter-governmental community which is organised on a supranational basis. However, it is a precondition of membership that the legitimation and influence which derives from the people will be preserved within an alliance of States.

* * * As the functions and powers of the Community are extended, the need will increase for representation of the peoples of the individual States by a European Parliament that exceeds the democratic legitimation and influence secured via the national parliaments, and which will form the basis for democratic support for the policies of the European Union. The common Union citizenship established by the Maastricht Treaty forms a legal bond between the citizens of the individual Member States which is designed to be lasting; it is not characterised by an intensity comparable to that which follows from common membership in a single State, but it does lend legally binding expression to that level of existential community which already exists. The influence which derives from the citizens of the Community may develop into democratic legitimation of European institutions, to the extent that the following conditions for such legitimation are fulfilled by the peoples of the European Union:

If democracy is not to remain a formal principle of accountability, it is dependent upon the existence of specific privileged conditions, such as ongoing free interaction of social forces, interests, and ideas, in the course of which political objectives are also clarified and modified, and as a result of which public opinion moulds political policy. For this to be achieved, it is essential that both the decision-making process amongst those institutions which implement sovereign power and the political objectives in each case should be clear and comprehensible to all, and also that the enfranchised citizen should be able to use its own language in communicating with the sovereign power to which it is subject.

* * * State power in each of the States emanates from the people of that State. The States require sufficient areas of significant responsibility of their own, areas in which the people of the State concerned may develop and express itself within a process of forming political will which it legitimates and controls, in order to give legal expression to those matters which concern that people on a relatively homogenous basis spiritually, socially, and politically.

All of this leads to the conclusion that the German Federal Parliament must retain functions and powers of substantial import. * * *

MAASTRICHT I DECISION

Constitutional Council (France).
92–308 DC of 9 April 1992.

[Under Art. 54 of the French Constitution, a treaty declared unconstitutional by the Constitutional Council cannot be ratified without first revising the Constitution so as to eliminate the conflict between the treaty and the Constitution. The Constitutional Council found that the Maastricht Treaty violated the French Constitution because its provisions regarding Union citizenship, a single European currency, and the right of non-French nationals to vote in French municipal elections impinged on maintenance of "the essential conditions for the exercise of [national] sovereignty." Of the three subjects addressed by the Treaty, the one concerning foreign citizens voting in French municipal elections seemed to pose the most serious threat as it affected not only French sovereignty but also French democracy.]

    * * *

14.   * * * [S]hould an international agreement entered into involve a clause conflicting with the Constitution or jeopardizing the essential conditions for the exercise of national sovereignty, authorization to ratify would require prior amendment of the Constitution.

    * * *

20.   The rights enjoyed by Union citizens include the right conferred by Article 8b of the Treaty establishing the European Community to vote and stand as a candidate at both municipal elections and elections to the European Parliament in the Member State in which they reside.

    * * *

24.   The first paragraph of article 3 of the Constitution provides that 'national sovereignty shall belong to the people, who shall exercise it through their representatives and by means of referendum'; the third paragraph of that article provides that 'suffrage may be direct or indirect as provided by the Constitution. It shall always be universal, equal and secret'; the fourth paragraph provides that 'All French citizens of either sex who have reached their majority and are in possession of their civil and political rights may vote as provided by statute'.

25.   By article 24 of the Constitution the Senate, which is elected by indirect suffrage, represents the territorial units of the Republic, by the first paragraph of article 72 of the Constitution, 'the territorial units of the Republic shall be the communes, the departments and the overseas territories. Any other territorial unit shall be created by statute'; by the second paragraph of the latter article, 'these units shall be self-governing through elected councils and in the manner provided by statute'.

26. It follows from all these provisions that the decision-making body of a territorial unit of the Republic may come into being only after an election by universal suffrage; the Senate, which is to represent the territorial units of the Republic, must be elected by an electorate that itself is an emanation of these units; the designation of municipal councillors thus has an impact on the election of Senators; the Senate, as a House of Parliament, takes part in the exercise of national authority; the fourth paragraph of article 3 of the Constitution implies that only 'French citizens' are entitled to vote and stand as candidates at elections to decision-making bodies of territorial subdivisions of the Republic, and in particular municipal councils and the Council of Paris.

27. This being so, Article 8b (*l*) inserted in the Treaty establishing the European Community by Article G of the international agreement referred to the Constitutional Council is unconstitutional.

MAASTRICHT II DECISION

Constitutional Council (France).
92–312 DC of 2 Sept. 1992.

[After France amended its Constitution to eliminate conflicts between the Constitution and the Maastricht Treaty, a new challenge was brought before the Constitutional Council.]

* * *

16. Section 5 of the Constitutional Act of 9 April 1992 inserted in the Constitution a new article 88–3 worded as follows: 'On condition of reciprocity and according to the terms and conditions laid down in the Treaty on European Union signed on 7 February 1992, the right to vote and the conditions of eligibility in local elections may be granted to those citizens of the European Union who are resident in France. These citizens may not exercise the function of Mayor or Deputy Mayor, nor may they participate either in the nomination of those to elect senators or directly in the election of senators. An institutional statute passed in identical terms by the two Houses of Parliament shall lay down the conditions for application of this article'.

* * *

19. Subject to the provisions governing the periods in which the Constitution cannot be revised (articles 7 and 16 and the fourth paragraph of article 89) and to compliance with the fifth paragraph of article 89 ('No amendment shall be passed that affects the Republican form of government'), the constituent authority is sovereign; it has the power to repeal, amend or amplify constitutional provisions in such manner as it sees fit; there is accordingly no objection to insertion in the Constitution of new provisions which derogate from a constitutional rule or principle; the derogation may be express or implied.

20. By the first sentence of article 88–3 of the Constitution, 'On condition of reciprocity and according to the terms and conditions laid down in the Treaty on European Union signed on 7 February 1992, the right to vote and the conditions of eligibility in local elections may be granted to those citizens of the European Union who are resident in

France'; it cannot therefore be validly argued that article 8b(l) inserted in the Treaty establishing the European Community by article G of the Treaty on European Union is contrary to article 3 of the Constitution.

2I. The authors of the referral argue that, since the designation of municipal councilors has an impact on the election of senators, the recognition of the right on non-nationals to vote and stand as candidates at municipal elections requires prior amendment of article 24 of the Constitution; it is true that by the second sentence of article 88–3, nationals of other Member States of the European Union 'may not exercise the functions of Mayor or Deputy Mayor, nor may they participate either in the nomination of those to elect senators or directly in the election of senators', but they can elect municipal councilors; their participation in such elections has an impact on the election of senators through the designation of senatorial delegates.

22.   There is no doubt that the combined effect of articles 3, 24 and 72 of the Constitution is that the Senate, elected by indirect universal suffrage, represents the territorial subdivisions of the Republic, whose decision-making bodies are themselves elected by universal suffrage; the designation of the decision-making body of a territorial subdivision is thus liable to have an impact on the election of senators via the multistage indirect suffrage system.

23.   But, as has been seen, the first sentence of article 88–3 of the Constitution provides for recognition of the right to vote and the conditions of eligibility in local elections of those citizens of the European Union who are resident in France but do not have French nationality, on the terms laid down by the Treaty on European Union; this necessarily entails a derogation from articles 3, 24 and 72 of the Constitution, with which Article 8b(1) was in conflict; the second sentence of article 88–3, whereby nationals of other Member States of the European Union 'may not participate either in the nomination of those to elect senators or directly in the election of senators', implies that Union nationals other than French nationals cannot as municipal councilors take part in subsequent stages of the process of electing senators within the meaning of article 59 of the Constitution.

24.   It follows that Article 8b(1) is in no way contrary to article 24 of the Constitution.

TREATY OF AMSTERDAM DECISION
Constitutional Council (France).
97–394 DC of 31 Dec. 1997.

[The 1997 Amsterdam Treaty sought to further integrate the EU. It provided for, among others, Union regulation of border crossing by persons, involving both borders among member-states (internal borders) and between Union countries and countries outside the Union (external borders.) This could affect "the conditions essential for the exercise of national sovereignty." But what was even more important was that after a transition of five years, the Treaty contemplated that Union regulation in the area of border crossing could be achieved with less than unanimous approval by the member-states.]

* * *

27.   In its decision of 2 September 1992 the Constitutional Council stated that article 100c of the Treaty establishing the European Community concerning the list of non-member countries whose nationals require a visa and the model of such visa was compatible with the Constitution, and in particular article 88–2. The status of *res judicata* of the Constitutional Council's decision precludes questions as to the validity of provisions of the Treaty of Amsterdam concerning the rules relating to the list of non-member countries whose nationals require a short-term visa and the model of such visa, which merely reproduce the decision-making rules of article 100c;

28.   The automatic changeover from unanimity to qualified majority voting and to the codecision procedure after a five-year period following the entry into force of the Treaty of Amsterdam for the determination of procedures and conditions for the issuance of short-term visas by the Member States and the rules governing the uniform visa, provided for by the fourth paragraph of article 73o, is, for the purposes of the Treaty on European Union, a new form of transfer of powers in matters where national sovereignty is at stake; the changeover to qualified majority voting and to the codecision procedure in these matters could have the effect of affecting the essential conditions for the exercise of national sovereignty;

29.   It follows that the fourth paragraph of article 73o, inserted in the Treaty establishing the European Community by article 2 of the Treaty of Amsterdam, is accordingly unconstitutional;

30.   The changeover to qualified majority voting and to the codecision procedure by simple Council decision, in accordance with the procedure provided for by the second paragraph of article 73o, as regards the measures provided for by point (a) of the second paragraph of article 73j, which are to determine the rules and procedures to be followed by the Member States for controls on persons crossing external borders jeopardizes the essential conditions for the exercise of national sovereignty; the second paragraph of article 73o, as regards the measures provided for by point (a) of the second paragraph of article 73j; is accordingly unconstitutional;

Notes and Questions

1.   After the decision of the French Constitutional Council in *Treaty of Amsterdam*, France amended its Constitution, on January 18, 1999, and then both the National Assembly and the Senate ratified the Treaty, in March 1999. For further discussion, see *Le traité d'Amsterdam face aux constitutions nationales* (Didier Maus and Olivier Passelecq eds., 1998); Dietmar Nickel, *The Amsterdam Treaty: A Shift in the Balance Between the Institutions?* Jean Monet Chair Working Papers Series, No. 14, Harvard Law School (1998); Alec Stone Sweet and W. Standholtz, *Integration, Supranational Governance, and Institutionalization of the European Polity,* in *European Integration and Supranational Governance* 1–26 (W. Standholtz and Alec Stone Sweet eds., 1998).

2.   The German Basic Law presents, potentially, greater national obstacles to further integration of the EU under a common constitution than the

French Constitution. The German Basic Law comprises unamendable provisions, whereas the French Constitution does not, provided a republican form of government is maintained. In theory, at least, the Union is not entirely free to shape it own constitutional order so long as Germany remains a member-state, given that any Union legal norm that contravenes an unamendable constitutional norm under the German Basic Law could not be enforced in Germany. Does that preclude the possibility of a full-blown constitution for the Union? Or can the Union avoid this problem by ensuring that its constitutional norms do not conflict with unamendable norms found in the member-states' national constitutions?

3. As European integration progresses, the potential clashes between the EU "constitution" and those of the member-states seem to shift. Viewed from the standpoint of the states, the potential difficulties stemming from EU treaties and regulations fall broadly into two categories: conflicts with fundamental rights protections guaranteed by national constitutions; and undue curtailment of sovereign power protected by national constitutions or unacceptable disruptions of allocations of governmental powers under such constitutions. As the EU evolves, the danger of fundamental rights conflicts diminishes, whereas that regarding allocations of governmental power seems to increase. Thus in *Solange I* the GFCC was concerned about the then-existing European protections of fundamental rights—a concern dispelled a decade later in the *Solange II* decision. Since then, the Union has moved even further on the fundamental rights front, agreeing in the Treaty of Nice, in 2000, to adopt the *Charter of Fundamental Rights of the European Union.*

On the other hand the increasing sovereignty and allocation-of-powers concerns exacerbate the issue of the "democratic deficit" of the EU. See Joseph H.H. Weiler, *Does Europe Need a Constitution? Reflection on Demos, Telos and the German Maastricht Decision,* above. To the extent that constitutions and laws are ultimately dependent on broad democratic backing for their legitimacy, that the bulk of the Union's powers resides in its least democratic institutions presents a serious problem of its own. Given these difficulties, what are the prospects of a full-blown European constitution that does not seriously conflict with those of the member-states? See Joseph H.H. Weiler, *The Constitution of Europe: Do the New Clothes Have an Emperor? And Other Essays on European Integration* (1999).

D.4. THE DEBATE OVER "CONSTITUTIONAL PATRIOTISM"

In addition to raising structural, institutional, and political issues, supranational constitutionalism also puts in question important "identity" issues. Within the nation-state, the constitutional order is embedded in, and to a significant extent dependent on, a common identity forged by language, culture, and history. This common identity is absent at the supranational level, thus prompting the debate excerpted below, between the German philosopher and social theorist, Jürgen Habermas, and the former Justice of the German Constitutional Court, Dieter Grimm, over "constitutional patriotism" as a plausible substitute for national identity. See Jürgen Habermas, *Between Facts and Norms: Contribution to a Discourse Theory of Law and Democracy* 465–66, 499–500 (William Rehg trans., 1996) (defining "constitutional patriotism" and placing it in context).

Dieter Grimm, DOES EUROPE NEED A CONSTITUTION?

1 European Law Journal 282, 292–297 (1995).

Democracies are characterized by having political rule in them legitimated not transcendentally, traditionally or through elites, but consensually. State power derives from the people and is exercised on their behalf by special agencies in turn answerable before the people for that exercise. The people are certainly not some community whose unity and will are pre-given, just needing to be given expression through the State bodies. They are instead permeated by divergences of opinion and interests, out of which negotiation or majority decision in the political process must first create unity, which can of course change. The key problem of this sort of system, in which possession and exercise of State power are separated, is mediation between people and institutions, and the biggest danger comes from the latter's tendency to become independent. The constitutional solution to this problem lay in periodic election of a representative body in which the various social positions were present and strove for compromise, to be embodied in laws by which in turn the State's executive was bound. On top of this came the constitutional guarantee of free communication, without which the elections could not work.

Democracy ought not, however, to be equated with parliamentarism. * * * [T]he parliamentary process does not by itself guarantee democratic structures. On the one hand, voters' individual preferences are no longer adequately expressed in the highly generalized electoral option between vaguely defined parties. The individual is instead thrown back on additional organizations and channels of influence in order to assert his views and his interests. On the other hand, a party-recruited parliament cannot adequately reflect and process the multiplicity of social views and interests. The parliamentary process instead builds on a social process of interest mediation and conflict control that partly eases the burden on parliamentary decision and partly patterns it. The links between the individual, social associations and the State bodies are maintained chiefly by the communication media, which create the public needed for any general opinion forming and democratic participation at all. * * *

[T]he success of democratic constitutions depends not just on the intrinsic excellence of their regulations, but equally on the external conditions for their effectiveness. This also applies to the central institution of democratic States, the Parliament. The democratic nature of a political system is attested not so much by the existence of elected parliaments, which is today guaranteed almost everywhere, as by the pluralism, internal representativity, freedom and capacity for compromise of the immediate area of parties, associations, citizens' movements and communication media. Where a parliament does not rest on such a structure, which guarantees constant interaction between people and State, democratic substance is lacking even if democratic forms are present. * * *

At European level, though, even the prerequisites are largely lacking. Mediatory structures have hardly even been formed here yet. There is no Europeanised party system, just European groups in the Strasbourg parliament, and apart from that, loose cooperation among programmatically related parties. This does not bring any integration of the European population, even at the moment of European elections. Nor have European associations or citizens' movements arisen, even though cooperation among national associations is further advanced than with parties. A search for European media, whether in print or broadcast, would be completely fruitless. * * *

The prerequisites cannot simply be created. It can admittedly be expected that advancing parliamentarisation of the European Union would also enhance the pressure to Europeanize the party system. A similar development could be expected with interest groups. It can certainly be taken that there would be Europeanisation at the level of leaderships and officials, while the levels of membership, because of lesser communicatory competences, would continue to be defined nationally. The distance between elite and rank and file, which in view of the professionalisation of politics is already a democracy problem nationally, would accordingly increase still further in a European context * * *.

Prospects for Europeanisation of the communication system are absolutely nonexistent. A Europeanised communications system ought not to be confused with increased reporting on European topics in national media. These are directed at a national public and remain attached to national viewpoints and communication habits. They can accordingly not create any European public nor establish any European discourse. Europeanisation in the communications sector would by contrast mean that there would be newspapers and periodicals, radio and television programmes, offered and demanded on a European market and thus creating a nation-transcending communicative context. But such a market would presuppose a public with language skills enabling it to utilize European media. * * *

In the European Union there are now eleven languages, none of which covers a majority of the population. Even English and French are each foreign languages to over 80% of the Union population. * * *

* * * [T]he absence of a European communication system, due chiefly to language diversity, has the consequence that for foreseeable future there will be neither a European public nor a European political discourse. Public discourse instead remains for the time being bound by national frontiers, while the European sphere will remain dominated by professional and interest discourses conducted remotely from the public. European decisional processes are accordingly not under public observation in the same way as national ones. The European level of politics lacks a matching public. The feedback to European officials and representatives is therefore only weakly developed, while national politicians orient themselves even in the case of Council decisions to their national publics, because effective sanctions can come only from them. * * *

The European Parliament does not meet with any European mediatory structure in being; still less does it constitute a European popular representative body, since there is as yet no European people. * * *
* * *

[Any] suspicion that this assessment is a front for the idea that democracy is possible only on the basis of a homogeneous *'Volksgemeinschaft'* [ethnic community] is, * * * baseless. The requirements for democracy are here developed not out of the people, but out of the society that wants to constitute itself as a political unit. It is true that this requires a collective identity, if it wants to settle its conflicts nonviolently, accept majority rule and practice solidarity. But this identity need by no means be rooted in ethnic origin, but may also have other bases. All that is necessary is for the society to have formed all awareness of belonging together that can support majority decisions and solidarity efforts: and for it to have the capacity to communicate about its goals and problems discursively. What obstructs democracy is accordingly not the lack of cohesion of Union citizens as a people, but their weakly developed collective identity and low capacity for transnational discourse. This certainly means that the European democracy deficit is structurally determined. It can therefore not be removed by institutional reforms in any short term. The achievement of the democratic constitutional State can for the time being be adequately realized only in the national framework.

Jürgen Habermas, REMARKS ON DIETER GRIMM'S 'DOES EUROPE NEED A CONSTITUTION?'

1 European Law Journal 303, 305–307 (1995).

I basically agree with Dieter Grimm's diagnosis; however, an analysis of its presuppositions leads me to a different political conclusion.
* * *

Grimm rejects a European constitution 'because there is as yet no European people'. This would on first glance seem founded upon the same premise that informed the tenor of the German Constitutional Court's Maastricht judgment: namely, the view that the basis of the state's democratic legitimation requires a certain homogeneity of the state-constituting people. However Grimm immediately distances himself from a Schmittian kind of definition of *völkischen* homogeneity * * *. This * * * leaves open the question of how the called-for collective identity is to be understood. I see the nub of republicanism in the fact that the forms and procedures of the constitutional state together with the democratic mode of legitimation simultaneously forge a new level of social integration. Democratic citizenship establishes an abstract, legally mediated solidarity among strangers. This form of social integration which first emerges with the nation-state is realised in the form of a politically socializing *communicative context*. Indeed this is dependent upon the satisfaction of certain important functional requirements that cannot be fulfilled by administrative means. To these belong conditions in which an ethical-political self-understanding of citizens can communicatively develop and likewise be reproduced—but in no way a collective identity that is *independent of the democratic process itself* and as such existing prior to that process. What unites a nation of citizens as opposed to a *Volksnation* is not some primordial substrate but rather an intersubjectively shared context of possible understanding.

It is therefore crucial in this context whether one uses the term 'people' in the juristically neutral sense of 'state-constituting people', or whether one associates the term with notions of identity of some other kind. In Grimm's view the identity of a nation of citizens 'need not' be 'rooted in ethnic origin, but may also have other bases'. I think on the contrary that it *must* have another basis if the democratic process is to finally guarantee the social integration of a differentiated—and today increasingly differentiating society. This burden must not be shifted from the levels of political will-formation to pre-political, pre-supposed substrates because the constitutional state guarantees that it will foster necessary social integration in the legally abstract from of political participation and that it will actually secure the status of citizenship in democratic ways. The examples of culturally and ideologically pluralistic societies only serve to emphasize this normative point. The multicultural self-understanding of the nations of citizens formed in classical countries of immigration like the USA is more instructive in this respect than that derived from the assimilationist French model. If in the same democratic political community various cultural, religious and ethnic forms of life are to exist among and with each other then the majority culture must be sufficiently detached from its traditional fusion with the *political* culture shared by all citizens.

To be sure, a politically constituted context of solidarity among citizens who despite remaining strangers to one another are supposed to stand up for each other is a communicative context *rich in prerequisites*. On this point there is no dissent. The core is formed by a political public sphere which enables citizens to take positions at the same time on the same topics of the same relevance. This public sphere must be deformed neither through external nor internal coercion. It must be embedded in the context of a freedom-valuing political culture and be supported by a liberal associational structure of a civil society. Socially relevant experience from still-intact private spheres must flow into such a civil society so that they may be processed there for public treatment. The political parties—not state-dependent—must remain rooted in this complex so as to mediate between the spheres of informal public communication, on the one hand, and the institutionalized deliberation and decision processes, on the other. Accordingly, from a normative perspective, there can be no European Federal state worthy of the name of a democratic Europe unless a European-wide, integrated public sphere develops in the ambit of a common political culture: a civil society with interest associations; non-governmental organizations; citizens' movements, etc.; and naturally a party system appropriate to a European arena. In short, this entails public communication that transcends the boundaries of the until now limited national public spheres.

Certainly, the ambitious functional requirements of democratic will-formation can scarcely be fulfilled in the nation-state framework; this is all the more true for Europe. What concerns me, however, is the perspective from which these functional prerequisites are normatively justified; for this, as it were, prejudices the empirical evaluation of the present difficulties. These must, for the time being, seem insuperable if a pre-political collective identity is regarded as necessary, that is an independent cultural substrate which is *articulated only* in the fulfillment of the said functional requirements. But a communications-theoretical understanding of democracy, one that Grimm also seems to favor, can no longer rest upon such a concretistic understanding of 'the people'. This notion falsely pretends homogeneity, where in fact something still quite heterogeneous is met.

The ethical-political self-understanding of citizens in a democratic community must not be taken as an historical-cultural *a priori* that makes democratic will-formation possible, but rather as the flowing contents of a circulatory process that is generated through the legal institutionalization of citizens' communication. This is precisely how national identities were formed in modern Europe. Therefore it is to be expected that the political institutions to be created by a European constitution would have an inducing effect. Europe has been integrating economically, socially and administratively for some time and in addition can base itself on a common cultural background and the shared historical experience of having happily overcome nationalism. Given the political will, there is no *a priori* reason why it cannot subsequently create the politically necessary communicative context as soon as it is constitutionally *prepared* to do so. Even the requirement of a common language— English as a second first language—ought not to be an insurmountable obstacle with the existing level of formal schooling. European identity can in any case mean nothing other than unity in national diversity. And perhaps German Federalism, as it developed after Prussia was shattered and the confessional division overcome, might not be the worst model.

E. THE BIRTH, ALTERATION AND REVISION OF THE CONSTITUTION: PERSPECTIVES ON CONSTITUTION–MAKING AND CONSTITUTIONAL AMENDMENTS

In the words of Ulrich Preuss:

The power to make a constitution is the power to create a political order *ex nihilo*. Of course, in reality there is no such thing as a *nihil*, therefore new constitutions are empirically instituted on the ruins of an order which has collapsed after a revolution, a lost war, or a similar catastrophic event. In modern terms, constitution means the active making of a new order, as opposed to its gradual emergence in the course of continual historical development. Constitution making involves the idea of an authority and an author whose will power is the ultimate cause of the polity.

Ulrich K. Preuss, *Constitutional Powermaking for the New Polity: Some Deliberations on the Relation Between Constituent Power and the Constitution*, in *Constitutionalism, Identity, Difference and Legitimacy: Theoretical Perspectives* 143 (Michel Rosenfeld ed., 1994).

To generate a new order, constitution-making must therefore make a clear break with the past, such as that brought about by a revolution. Thus the constituent power (*pouvoir constituant*) presumably must achieve independence from the order preceding the new constitution. Moreover, after the constituent power has completed its task, the resulting constitutional power must emerge as a legitimate and binding constituted power (*pouvoir constitué*). To the extent that the constituent power must break with the past but bind the future in order to achieve a genuine constituted power, constitution-making apparently requires a "bootstrapping" process. See Jon Elster, *Constitutional Bootstrapping in Philadelphia and Paris*, in *id*. at 57. As we shall see in the materials below, successful constitution-making may depend on how the constituent power deals with revolution or on whether genuine constitution-making can occur without revolution.

Constitution-making amounts to higher-order lawmaking and as such requires greater consensus or some other greater authoritative imprint than ordinary lawmaking. Viewed from this perspective, moreover, constitutional revision and constitutional amendment could be regarded as some species of constitution-making or at least as involving adaptations or changes that should not be as easily brought about as ordinary legislation.

E.1. CONSTITUTION–MAKING IN HISTORICAL PERSPECTIVE

In general terms four different models of constitution-making have emerged since the eighteenth century. The first, which arose in the context of the birth of modern constitutions in France and the U.S., involves a close connection between violent revolution and constitution-making. Both the American Revolution—which strictly speaking was rather a war of liberation, see Daniel Farber and Suzanna Sherry, *A History of the American Constitution* 9–13 (1990)—and the 1789 French Revolution put a violent end to regimes regarded as oppressive, thus clearing the way for new constitutional orders. Although both involved a break with the past, the break in France was much more radical, with important consequences for the success of the ensuing constitutional order.

The second model of constitution-making also involves violence and consists of constitution-making initiated or directed, at least in part, by foreign occupiers in the aftermath of complete military defeats, as in Germany and Japan at the conclusion of World War Two. See generally Peter Young, *World War 1939–1945*, at 393–416 (1980). While military defeat and submission to foreign occupation eliminates previously entrenched domestic impediments to genuine constitution-making, the success of foreign-initiated constitutions seems dependent on the extent to which the defeated polity embraces the new constitutional project as its own. For example, speaking of Japan's constitutional revolution, "[t]he catalytic influence of the United States at the outset seems to have been essential for Japan's metamorphosis [after 1945]; it seems improbable that Japan would have evolved peacefully into a democracy on its own." Lawrence W. Beer, *Constitutionalism and Rights in Japan and Korea*, in *Constitutionalism and Rights*, above, at 225, 230. See also Helmut Steinberger, *American Constitutionalism and German Constitutional Development*, in *id.* at 199, 212 (American influence on, and West German acceptance of, post-World War Two constitutional order embodied in the 1949 German Basic Law).

The third model of constitution-making is a peaceful transition from authoritarianism to constitutional democracy, exemplified by Spain's post-Franco 1978 Constitution, see Franciso Rubio Llorente, *The Writing of the Constitution of Spain,* in *Constitution Makers on Constitution–Making* 239 (Robert A. Goldwin and Art Kaufman eds., 1988), and subsequently replicated in many different locations, ranging from Eastern Europe to South Africa. See, e.g., Robert C. Johansen, *Towards a New Code of International Conduct: War, Peacekeeping and Global Constitutionalism*, in *The Constitutional Foundations of World Peace* 39 (Richard Falk et al. eds., 1993).

A fourth model of constitution-making relates to emergence from colonial rule and involves nation-state building. The path to sovereignty through independence from colonial rule requires that the new state have a constitution. This requirement is particularly important in the context of the twentieth-century emergence from colonialism in Africa and Asia as well as in that of certain states coming out of Soviet domination. The new constitution may draw on colonial institutions, but in the majority of cases it reflects the concerns of the liberating forces or it involves state-building in line with the legal traditions of the colonizing power. See András Sajó, *Preferred Generations: A Paradox of Restoration Constitutions*, below, for a discussion of constitutions as counter-revolutionary instruments.

The key to successful constitution-making seems to depend on achieving a break with the past that is neither too great nor too modest. Consider the following excerpts.

Hannah Arendt, ON REVOLUTION
165–166 (1965).

The great and fateful misfortune of the French Revolution was that none of the constituent assemblies could command enough authority to lay down the law of the land; the reproach rightly leveled against them was always the same: they lacked the power to constitute by definition; they themselves were unconstitutional. Theoretically, the fateful blunder of the men of the French Revolution consisted in their almost automatic, uncritical belief that power and law spring from the selfsame source. Conversely, the great good fortune of the American Revolution was that the people of the colonies, prior to their conflict with England, were organized in self-governing bodies, that the revolution—to speak the language of the eighteenth century—did not throw them into a state of nature, that there never was any serious questioning of the *pouvoir constituant* of those who framed the state constitutions and, eventually, the Constitution of the United States. What Madison proposed with respect to the American Constitution, namely, to derive its 'general authority * * * entirely from the subordinate authorities',[43] repeated only on a national scale what had been done by the colonies themselves when they constituted their state governments. The delegates to the provincial congresses or popular conventions which drafted the constitutions for state governments had derived their authority from a number of subordinate, duly authorized bodies—districts, counties, townships; to preserve these bodies unimpaired in their power was to preserve the source of their own authority intact. Had the Federal Convention, instead of creating and constituting the new federal power, chosen to curtail and abolish state powers, the founders would have met immediately the perplexities of their French colleagues; they would have lost their *pouvoir constituant*—and this, probably, was one of the reasons why even the most convinced supporters of a strong central government did not want to abolish the powers of state governments altogether. Not only was the federal system the sole alternative to the nation-state principle; it was also the only way not to be trapped in the vicious circle of *pouvoir constituant* and *pouvoir constitué*.

Jon Elster, CONSTITUTIONAL BOOTSTRAPPING IN PHILADELPHIA AND PARIS, in CONSTITUTIONALISM, IDENTITY, DIFFERENCE AND LEGITIMACY: THEORETICAL PERSPECTIVES

66–67 (Michel Rosenfeld ed., 1994).

A number of decisions have to be made in the convocation and constitution of a constituent assembly. First, the assembly must be convoked. Second, a procedure for selecting or electing delegates must be adopted. Third, the mandate of the assembly and of the delegates must be defined in terms of constraints on what needs to be included, and what cannot be included, in the final document. Fourth, once the delegates meet, their credentials have to be verified so that the assembly can be formally constituted. Fifth, an internal decision-making procedure of the assembly must be specified. Sixth and finally, a mode of ratifying the constitution must be established.

These decisions flow either from an external authority or from the assembly itself. The first two decisions must clearly be taken by outside agents. The decision to convene the assembly must be made by preexisting authorities, which, in our two cases, are the Continental Congress and the King of France.[45] The mechanism by which delegates are elected

---

43. [Madison, i]n a letter to Jefferson of October 24, 1787 [in Max Farrand, *Records of the Federal Convention of 1787,* New Haven, 1937, vol. 3, p. 137].

45. That authority could be the constitution itself, if calling for periodical constitutional conventions, an occupying power, as in Japan or West Germany after World War II, a provisional government, as in France in 1848, or Round Table Talks between the old regime and the opposition, such as in Poland, Hungary, and Bulgaria

in 1989–90. Although a self-convening assembly is a logical impossibility, the Frankfurt Parliament of 1848 does, to some extent, fit that description. On March 5, 1848, 51 self-selected leaders of the public met in Heidelberg to discuss Germany's future. They convened a *Vorparlament* that met in Frankfurt on March 31, 1848. That body voted for elections to a constituent assembly and set up a committee to help administer them. The assembly then met on May

or selected also must be in existence prior to the Assembly itself. In the cases concerned here, and in most others of interest, these two outside authorities do not coincide.[46] Although Louis XVI decided the convocation of the Estates General, he could not pick the delegates. When he tried to obtain the power to verify their credentials, he was rebuffed. In America, whereas the Continental Congress made the decision to convene the Federal Convention, the state legislatures chose the delegates.[47]

The assembly is obviously incapable of deciding the initial convocation and delegation. It can, however, arrogate to itself the power to control all other decisions. To varying degrees this is what happened in the two eighteenth-century assemblies. Those assemblies verified their own credentials, and set many of their own rules, sometimes overruling their instructions, sometimes supplementing them. The tension between the assemblies and their conveners—between the creature and its creator—was at the heart of both processes. The state legislatures in Philadelphia, the source of the authority of the delegates, were perceived by many as a major obstacle to the assemblies' efforts. There was a somewhat similar relationship in Paris between the King and the Assembly. The general form of the paradox is simple. On one hand, it seems to be a general principle that if X brings Y into being, then X has an authority superior to that of Y. On the other hand, if Y is brought into being to regulate, among other things, the activities of X, Y would seem to be superior. The paradox can also be summarized in two opposing slogans: "Let the kingmaker beware of the king" and "Let the king beware of the kingmaker." These relationships exist both between the assembly and its convener, and between the delegates and their constituencies. Collectively, the delegates owe their existence to one institution; individually, to another. These facts are crucial to understanding the debates in both assemblies.

In both cases, the delegates at the Federal Convention succeeded in replacing the state legislatures with special conventions as the ratifying bodies. Also, the delegates implicitly overruled Congress when they demanded ratification by nine of the thirteen states instead of the unanimity that governed changes in the Articles of Confederation. The French delegates changed the King's veto *in* the constitution into a merely suspensive one, and his veto *over* the constitution into a mere formality.[49] The French delegates also ignored the instructions of their

18, 1848. J.J. SHEEHAN, GERMAN HISTORY 1770–1866, at 674–83 (1989).

46. Such coincidence would indicate that we are dealing with a mere puppet assembly, with no will of its own. An example of such an assembly is the body of 66 men convened in China by Yuan Shikai, (who was President of China from 1912 to 1916, and served in 1916 as Emperor) in 1914 to give his rule a semblance of legality through a "constitutional compact".

47. I am not denying the close ties between the legislatures and Congress. However legislatures' acting collectively through Congress to call a convention should not be confused with their individual power to select delegates.

49. This kind of outcome is generally obtained. Whenever the assembly is more than a mere puppet body, the convoking authorities rarely succeed in imposing their will on it. The Japanese constitution of 1946 is the only clear case of this situation that comes to my mind. See KYOKO INOQUE, MACARTHUR'S JAPANESE CONSTITUTION (1991). The Western occupying powers had Some influence on the West German constitution of 1948, but substantially less than they had hoped for. See [Peter Merkel, *The Origin of the West Ger-*

constituents on several crucial issues. This outcome is not surprising. Almost by definition, the old regime is part of the problem to be solved by a constituent assembly. If the regime is flawed, however, why should the assembly respect its instructions?

Michel Rosenfeld, CONSTITUTION-MAKING, IDENTITY BUILDING, AND PEACEFUL TRANSITION TO DEMOCRACY: THEORETICAL REFLECTIONS INSPIRED BY THE SPANISH EXAMPLE

19 Cardozo L. Rev. 1891, 1893, 1903–1905, 1907–1913, 1919–1920 (1998).

Spain's peaceful transition from the Franco dictatorship to constitutional democracy in the mid–1970s and its ability to develop a vibrant constitutional culture in the subsequent two decades is truly remarkable. Moreover, the Spanish case is all the more striking because it hardly qualifies as an anomaly. Instead, it marks a turning point towards peaceful transitions to constitutional democracy which has reached global proportions since the 1980s. In the last two decades * * * a majority of the transitions involved—in Eastern and Central Europe, Latin America, or South Africa—have been peaceful. * * *

Spain's transition to constitutional democracy is remarkable in several key respects. Above all, not only did the transition in question avoid violence, but it also managed to proceed from beginning to end without any break in legality * * *.

Ironically, the Spanish transition might well not have been peaceful were it not for the fact that both the political heirs of Franco and those who wished to institute a democracy proved too weak to take the country's destiny into their own hands. * * *

Franco's regime has been characterized as a "kingdom without a king." Drawing from fascism as well as from tradition, Franco shaped the state according to three fundamental principles. First, "subordination of the individual to the communal interests of the nation;"[79] second, rejection of capitalism and Marxism in favor of a corporatist economy designed to harmonize the interests of business and labor;[80] and third, "concentration of political power in a charismatic leader" only answerable to "God and History."[81] * * *

The above mentioned identity stands in sharp contrast to that forged in the wake of the Spanish transition to constitutional democracy. Not only has Spain become a typical Western constitutional parliamentary democracy, but it has also abandoned corporatism, collectivism and the close nexus between church and state, in favor of a pluralistic and secular political society that has institutionalized a large degree of regional autonomy within its new constitutional framework. This raises

man Republic] at 103, 117, 120–21, 123. When the assembly is convened by an internal authority, and not a foreign power, the assembly is even less likely to listen to dictates.

79. [See Rubio Llorente, *The Writing of the Constitution of Spain*, in *Constitution*

Makers on Constitution–Making (Robert A. Goldwin and Art Kaufman eds., 1988)] at 241.

80. *See id.*

81. *Id.*

the question of what accounts for these dramatic changes in identity between Francoist and post-Francoist Spain. * * *

[O]ne key factor that played a major role in leading to a peaceful transition was * * * the cultural reconstruction—over the course of the last two decades of Franco's regime—of the historical memory of the civil war in a way that transformed what had been a deep tear within the very fabric of the Spanish polity into a building block on the path to democracy. * * * [T]he severe wound that Spain's bloody civil war inflicted on the nation's self-image had to be healed before it could forge ahead towards democracy. And this was accomplished through cultural reconstruction of the country's historical identity so as to emphasize the commonalities among all Spaniards rather than the irreconcilable differences that led to fratricidal strife. * * *

Although the Spanish transition was not itself violent * * * it was surrounded by violence. At the time the transition was about to begin, violence, the threat of violence, and the memory of violence were all very much present * * * Moreover, Basque terrorism would continue throughout the transition and thereafter, but would also become increasingly politically isolated. By all indications, Basque terrorism did not shape the transition but it remained ever present within the political landscape * * *.

The situation was precarious, but remarkably * * * the path towards a working democracy [was completed] without ever exceeding the bounds of legality. The task was formidable as, to remain within the realm of legality, Suarez [the Prime Minister who led the transition] could only count on Francoist law and had to work together with the Cortes—the corporatist legislature created by Franco and whose membership comprised a significant number of his appointees. Insisting on the importance of adhering to the rule of law, and adroitly navigating in treacherous political waters * * * Suarez managed to have the Cortes enact two crucial pieces of legislation in 1976. The first of these legalized political association and paved the way for the establishment of full-fledged non-Francoist political parties. The second—which was even more remarkable, because in enacting it the Cortes were in effect voting themselves out of office—provided for political reform and called for free elections.

For his part, the King made full use of the powers awarded him by the dictatorship, but did so not in furtherance of authoritarianism but with a view toward breaking away from it * * *. [A]fter the first elections which took place in June 1977, the King declared at the opening of the new Parliament in July 1977 that it was the Spanish people who were sovereign and that as a constitutional monarch he would take no role in fashioning a political program for Spain. From that moment on, the King rose above politics and became a symbol of national unity as the vexing and delicate process of constitution-making was about to commence. * * *

The June 1977 elections were carried out without significant problems and gave Suarez's centrist party the largest number of seats in the Parliament. * * * Socialists, * * * Communists, Basques, and Catalans all managed to achieve significant representation. Accordingly, the Parliament had broad enough representation for most concerned to regard it as a legitimate constituent assembly.

Prior to launching in a full-fledged process of constitution-making, several key actions essential for purposes of facilitating the task ahead were undertaken by the Suarez government and by Parliament. * * * [T]wo * * * are worthy of mention. The first is the Amnesty Act of 1977 * * * designed to lift all sanctions going as far back as 1936—the beginning of the civil war—imposed for politically motivated acts, including some of those perpetrated by ETA, the Basque organization responsible for many terrorist incidents. The purpose of the Amnesty Act was to eliminate restrictions on political activity imposed by Franco's dictatorship, and its broad scope was well suited to promote a break away from the past without emphasis on account settling.

The second action undertaken by the Suarez government was as bold as it was crucial to the success of the constitution-making process. * * * [It] provisionally granted autonomous rule to Catalonia and the Basque region and to all other regions of Spain even though the latter were not particularly interested in such rule. Suarez's strategy was to accommodate the Basque and Catalan quest for autonomy while underplaying their uniqueness. * * *

The constitution-making process took place between September 1977 and October 1978, and the constitution that emerged from it was approved by a nationwide referendum on December 6, 1978. * * *

The Spanish Constitution of 1978 opts, in stark contrast to the preceding dictatorship, for a federal or quasi-federal system headed by a constitutional monarch and comprised of a national bicameral parliament, as well as broadly and vaguely spelled out autonomous communities with certain enumerated powers. Moreover, the constitution provides for a political life dominated by political parties and guarantees rights and liberties that are standard throughout Western Europe.

The determinative features that loom as crucial to the success of the Spanish constitution-making experience can, in turn, be encapsulated in the following three words: delegation, ambiguity, and consensus. Delegation of the initial drafting of the constitution to a group of lawyers and legal academics, who worked largely in secret, made it possible to deal with divisive issues such as the aspirations to autonomy of Basques and Catalans without alienating a large segment of the population. Furthermore, the seven drafters of the constitution were representatives of the major parties, and each of them was responsible to his own party. The parties represented * * * [included] the Catalan party, whose representative also took into account the Basque point of view.

* * *

The peaceful type of transition that occurred in Spain and the kind of constitutional model to which it gave rise seem above all the products of an internal erosion of authoritarianism, concurrent with a gradual strengthening of democratically inspired opposition, coupled with increased influence or pressure coming from abroad. [A] large number of the transitions to constitutional democracy that took place after Spain's have been peaceful in kind. To what extent these transitions ought to be considered to be of the same kind as Spain's * * * [is an] open question that require[s] further examination. Nevertheless, it appears that many of the more recent transitions bear significant similarities to Spain's * * * [such as the] pacted transitions * * * in Hungary and in Poland, which arose as a consequence of roundtable negotiations between weakened communist governments and rapidly emerging movements committed to democracy. * * *

András Sajó, PREFERRED GENERATIONS: A PARADOX OF RESTORATION CONSTITUTIONS, in CONSTITUTIONALISM, IDENTITY, DIFFERENCE AND LEGITIMACY: THEORETICAL PERSPECTIVES

335, 341–346, 351 (Michel Rosenfeld ed., 1994).

What is the impact of the counterrevolutionary nature of the political and perhaps social, transition on emerging constitutions, particularly in East–Central Europe and Hungary?

* * *

Counterrevolutionary (or more properly restoration) constitutions may well constitute the majority of constitutions, but the idea of modern constitution is eminently a revolutionary idea, revolutionary in the sense of being a revolution's creation. Modern revolutionary constitutions are intended to be blueprints for the future. Restoration constitutions represent a return to the past while avoiding the possibility that what happened will "unhappen." After a major revolution, there is neither serious willingness nor any real possibility to return to the status quo ante, and, for example, reinstate the pre-Revolutionary constitution. There are a number of reasons for this. Time has elapsed. New social and political relations have emerged which make impossible a total restoration. Moreover, the original imperfection of the ex ante *constitution* cannot be denied anymore. Revolutionary changes in the constitution occur when fundamental flaws in the constitutional arrangements prevent a more "organic" development.

One may argue that all this is irrelevant in East–Central Europe, where the revolution and the Communist constitutions were imposed by the Red Army. This is not to say, however, that the pre-Communist constitutions were adequate. A return to those constitutions in terms of their direct application was not a serious option in any of the region's countries. Even a return to the quite advanced Masaryk Constitution in Czechoslovakia seems impossible in view of Slovak and other minority concerns. If there is anything "revolutionary" in the present post-Communist situation, it is the belief of the emerging elite that they are really *constituting* a new fabric of politics.

Constitution making includes the power, legitimation, and mandate to restructure the political sphere and, in particular, to create a new structure of powers which is intended to serve, as usual, those who happen to be the framers.[17]

* * *

An unconditional return to the past was impossible in East–Central Europe in 1989. Even today it seems impossible. There were and are reasons and forces which make some kind of restoration after the collapse of communism attractive and compelling. First, one of the most important sources of intellectual resistance to communism was a "glorious past"-oriented nationalism. During the Hungarian round table talks of 1989, the 1946 system of "weak" presidency was used as a model and as a compelling argument. The 1946 model represented both national tradition and sufficient return to the denied past. This was compelling enough to make it legitimate for Communist government and opposition groups alike. In Poland there is continuous reference to Pilsudski's Constitution (or to Pilsudski's reaction to the 1920 Constitution) and to the United States Constitution. The move for a *return* to the monarchy is gaining popularity in Romania, as well as in Serbia and Russia.

The second reason that restoration or past-oriented constitutional thinking seems attractive is related to the semi-modernized nature of these societies. A partial return to past constitutional structures makes the modernization of political, and perhaps social, structures of these countries less compelling; it offers legitimate protection from menacing modernization. The simple transplant or adaptation of the constitution of an existing Western democracy seems to be unacceptable to those who fear modernization. These status quo interests, supported by nationalist concepts, have no other choice but to turn to ideas such as organic development and national character, and, inevitably, to models of the past. Nationalistic traditionalism serves, of course, as legitimation and justification for a nationalistic-exclusive, or national-constitutional system (as opposed to universalistic constitutionalism). However, nationalism, with its own irrationality, is not simply an ideological outcome of antimodernization. It has its own compelling force. Nationalism is a highly respected, nearly uncontested value of the community. (Or at least it is generally believed to have this status.) Nationalistic concerns may have a conservative impact of their own on forces which may otherwise be interested in "Western-type" modernization.

* * *

The post-Communist era is considered an exceptional period in which the application of universal criteria may help the former Communists and other malefactors. Therefore, the constitution makers have a special obligation (or justification): They have to remedy the Communist

17. The lack of a stable constitutional arrangement or the delay in creating constitutions is due to the struggle to control the constitution-making process. However, in Hungary, where there is a more established uncontested conservative power monopoly, the conservatives prefer to make subconstitutional changes in the political structure slowly; this will increase their power to the extent that they can dictate a constitution at a latter stage. Therefore, while in all the other countries there is an open political struggle to create a constitution, open constitutional amendments are not discussed in Hungary. Human and political (individual) rights are less subject to the power struggle, partly because most political forces and parties currently need the degree of credibility associated with being Europeans.

past. Thus, universal rules apply only to the extent that they do not undermine the special constitutional mandate of the framers to undo communism. A restoration constitution of a post-Communist regime has to be a combination of universal neutral constitutionalist rules and special rules (exceptions) and institutional settings which are intended to make a break with the past.

A crucial element in the determination of the constitutional self under these conditions of restoration is the issue of the relevant genera-tion: Is the present generation the point of reference or is it the constitutional self of the past, a quasi-imaginary, or past self of a semi-retired generation? * * * At least in Hungary, there is a clear conflict over who should pay the costs of reprivatization and compensation: A past generation (including former owners, victims of communism, and established churches) with previously strong economic and political power or a younger, propertyless generation. The result is a conflict of generations, although it can be interpreted as a conflict between expropriated owners and propertyless classes.

The creation of a constitutional self which refers to past generations (and inclusion rules as practiced by those unspecified generations) is not limited strictly to property issues. Restoration of church privileges is another element of this struggle, although once again the problem is primarily conceived of as a restoration issue.

　　　* * *

Of course, the language of the present debate is not predominantly generational. The debate deals with reprivatization and compensation, with punishing politicians and others who are considered responsible for Communist sins and mistakes. The constitutional issues are takings, government liabilities, and governmental power to allocate government property. In the political justice cases, the primary constitutional issue is retroactivity. In the case of church reprivatization-compensation, the separation of church and state and the right to education is constitution-ally arguable. Reference in these issues is made mostly to the constitu-tion in effect, although, in a discreet way, it is inevitable to discuss and measure constitutionality in terms of the past constitution. The govern-ment, at least in Hungary, seems to interpret its constitutional duties of legislation as being related to the past. Past injustices are to be remedied and the measure of those injustices is to be found in the imaginary constitution of past values and hierarchies. One cannot avoid that kind of reference to a past, or imaginary, constitution and to its constitutional self—a semi-past generation with its traditional values, if restoration and continuation or at least *constitutional complicity* with the past is what is desired. If the constitutional debate concerns pre-Communist nationalizations, it is nearly inevitable that sooner or later one must evaluate the constitutionality of those takings in light of the constitution under which they occurred. * * *

It is well known how vehemently Thomas Jefferson and Thomas Paine objected to the privileges of the generation which has created a constitution: "The vanity and presumption of government beyond the grave, is the most ridiculous and insolent of tyrannies."[45] According to Hannah Arendt, Jefferson's insistence on granting every generation the right to choose the form of government it believes to be most promotive of its happiness reflects Jefferson's interest in maintaining a scheme which enables the people to engage in the peaceful expression of opinion. In this light, the present desire to create constitutional arrangements which *ab initio* govern from the grave is nothing but an attempt to exclude the public from that discourse.

———————

The transition in South Africa, during the 1990s, from an apartheid regime to a full-fledged constitutional democracy with equal rights for all, offers a unique and remarkable example of pacted constitution-making. Due to external pressure and internal changes, the white government negotiated a transition to a constitutional democracy that would enfranchise the country's nonwhite majority. The main negotiating partner of the government was the African National Congress (ANC), under the leadership of the then-recently freed Nelson Mandela. In 1993, the negotiating parties drafted an interim constitution. In 1994, an interim constitution was adopted, and Nelson Mandela was elected President of South Africa. In 1996, a new constitution was adopted and submitted to the South African Constitutional Court (SACC) for approval. In a lengthy opinion the Court refused to approve the new constitution. The following excerpts from that opinion provide background to the SACC's intervention, and the subsequent summary provides an overview of the Court's reasons for refusing to accept the new constitution.

CERTIFICATION OF THE CONSTITUTION OF THE REPUBLIC OF SOUTH AFRICA[h]

Constitutional Court (South Africa).
1996 (4) SALR 744 (CC).

JUDGEMENT

* * *

* * * [R]emarkably and in the course of but a few years, the country's political leaders managed to avoid a cataclysm by negotiating a largely peaceful transition from the rigidly controlled minority regime to a wholly democratic constitutional dispensation.

After a long history of "deep conflict between a minority which reserved for itself all control over the political instruments of the state and a majority who sought to resist that domination", the overwhelming majority of South Africans across the political divide realised that the country had to be urgently rescued from imminent disaster by a negotiated commitment to a fundamentally new constitutional order premised upon open and democratic government and the universal enjoyment of

45. Thomas Paine, The Rights of Man 63 (Henry Collins ed., Penguin 1969) (1791).

h. Further excerpts from this decision are presented in Chapter 4, subsections C.2.1 and C.2.2.b.

fundamental human rights. That commitment is expressed in the preamble to the Interim Constitution [IC] by an acknowledgement of the

" * * * need to create a new order in which all South Africans will be entitled to a common South African citizenship in a sovereign and democratic constitutional state in which there is equality between men and women and people of all races so that all citizens shall be able to enjoy and exercise their fundamental rights and freedoms".

With this end in view the [Interim Constitution]

" * * * provides a historic bridge between the past of a deeply divided society characterized by strife, conflict, untold suffering and injustice, and a future founded on the recognition of human rights, democracy and peaceful co-existence and development opportunities for all South Africans, irrespective of color, race, class, belief or sex."

[11]   Following upon exploratory and confidential talks across the divide, the transitional process was formally inaugurated in February 1990, when the then government of the Republic of South Africa announced its willingness to engage in negotiations with the liberation movements. Negotiations duly ensued and persevered, despite many apparent deadlocks. Some of the "independent homeland" governments gave their support to the negotiation process. Others did not but were overtaken by the momentum of the ensuing political developments and became part of the overall transition, unwillingly or by default.

[12]   One of the deadlocks, a crucial one on which the negotiations all but foundered, related to the formulation of a new constitution for the country. All were agreed that such an instrument was necessary and would have to contain certain basic provisions. Those who negotiated this commitment were confronted, however, with two problems. The first arose from the fact that they were not elected to their positions in consequence of any free and verifiable elections and that it was therefore necessary to have this commitment articulated in a final constitution adopted by a credible body properly mandated to do so in consequence of free and fair elections based on universal adult suffrage. The second problem was the fear in some quarters that the constitution eventually favored by such a body of elected representatives might not sufficiently address the anxieties and the insecurities of such constituencies and might therefore subvert the objectives of a negotiated settlement. The government and other minority groups were prepared to relinquish power to the majority but were determined to have a hand in drawing the framework for the future governance of the country. The liberation movements on the opposition side were equally adamant that only democratically elected representatives of the people could legitimately engage in forging a constitution: neither they, and certainly not the government of the day, had any claim to the requisite mandate from the electorate.

[13]   The impasse was resolved by a compromise which enabled both sides to attain their basic goals without sacrificing principle. What was no less important in the political climate of the time was that it enabled them to keep faith with their respective constituencies: those who feared engulfment by a black majority and those who were deter-

mined to eradicate apartheid once and for all. In essence the settlement was quite simple. Instead of an outright transmission of power from the old order to the new, there would be a programmed two-stage transition. An interim government, established and functioning under an interim constitution agreed to by the negotiating parties, would govern the country on a coalition basis while a final constitution was being drafted. A national legislature, elected (directly and indirectly) by universal adult suffrage, would double as the constitution-making body and would draft the new constitution within a given time. But—and herein lies the key to the resolution of the deadlock—that text would have to comply with certain guidelines agreed upon in advance by the negotiating parties. What is more, an independent arbiter would have to ascertain and declare whether the new constitution indeed complied with the guidelines before it could come into force.

* * *

Summary of the Court's Decision[i]

Since 27 April 1994 South Africa has functioned under an interim constitution, the Constitution of the Republic of South Africa, 1993. The negotiating parties designed the Interim Constitution as a bridge between the old order and the new, to regulate the governance of the country under a government of national unity while a popularly mandated Constitutional Assembly (CA) drafted a new constitution. The Interim Constitution also served to mark out the further transitional steps to be taken.

One of these steps was that the CA had to adopt the new draft constitution within a period of two years and by a majority of at least two-thirds of the CA's members. A second requirement was that the constitutional text had to comply with a set of Constitutional Principles agreed to by the negotiating parties and set out in Schedule 4 to the Interim Constitution. A third requirement of the Interim Constitution was that the constitutional text has no legal force unless the Constitutional Court certifies that all the provisions of the text comply with the Constitutional Principles. The Court must determine whether every requirement of the Principles has been satisfied by the provisions of the text and whether any provision in the text conflicts with the CPs. The Court's powers and functions in regard to certification of the text are confined to this determination.

The CA adopted the new constitutional text, the Constitution of the Republic of South Africa 1996, timorously and with the requisite majority. The Chairperson of the CA then transmitted the text to the Court for certification. The CA and all political parties represented in the CA were entitled to present oral argument to the Court. In addition the public at large was invited to submit representations relevant to the question of certification of the text. Many written submissions were received and over a period of nine days the CA, five political parties and certain other bodies and persons who had filed relevant submissions were afforded an opportunity to advance oral argument to the Court.

i. As provided on the Court's website at
<www.concourt.gvt.za>.

The Court's judgment is divided into eight chapters, *each* dealing with a particular main topic under various subheadings. Having sketched the background and context of the certification exercise, the judgment explains the Court's approach to its task and then deals with each identified issue bearing on the question of certification. In the main, these relate to the provisions in the Bill of Rights and their entrenchment; to the separation of powers between the executive, legislative and judicial branches of the state, including the independence of the judiciary; to the relationship between the legislative and executive tiers of government at the national, provincial and local levels, with special reference to the individual and collective powers and functions of the provinces; to the position of traditional leadership and customary law; and to the functions and independence of 'watchdog' institutions of state. * * *

The Court's ultimate finding was that the constitutional text cannot be certified as complying fully with the Constitutional Principles [CP]. The following instances of non-compliance were identified; [among others]:

CP XV in that certain amendments * * * Do not require special procedures involving special majorities and

CP II in that the fundamental rights, freedoms and civil liberties protected in the NT are not entrenched.

* * *

Section 194, which fails in respect of the Public Protector and the Auditor–General to comply with CP XXIX in that it does not adequately provide for and safeguard the independence and impartiality of these institutions.

* * *

Chapter 7, which fails to comply with

CP XXIV in that it does not provide a 'framework for the structures' of local government;

CP XXV in that it does not provide for appropriate fiscal powers and functions for local government; and

CP X in that it does not provide for formal legislative procedures to be adhered to by legislatures at local government level.

* * *

The Court emphasized that the constitutional text represents a monumental achievement.

The basic structure of the proposed constitution is sound and the overwhelming majority of the requirements of the Constitutional Principles have been satisfied. The instances of non-compliance that have been identified should present no significant obstacle to the CA in formulating a text which complies fully with those requirements.

In addition to constitution-making under the varying sets of circumstances discussed above, instances of constitution-making have occurred in the context of impending counterrevolution and civil war. In one such situation Charles de Gaulle came to power in France, in 1958, leading to the adoption of the Fifth Republic's Constitution that year.

John Bell, FRENCH CONSTITUTIONAL LAW
11–13 (1992).

The Fourth Republic [established in 1946] was ill-fated from the start.

* * *

* * * Like Britain, France did not leave its colonies without putting up significant military resistance. The military activities of the period were marked by notable defeats, leading to recriminations between the military leadership and the politicians at home. * * * Although politicians often felt obliged to defend military actions after the event, they preferred other policies that were not appreciated by the military. For example, the Government put an end to martial law in Algeria in March 1958, against the advice of military commanders and just at the time when the latter claimed that this policy was beginning to reduce the number of terrorist incidents.

Domestically, there were also problems with the police, who in March 1958 staged an anti-parliamentary, anti-Semitic demonstration outside the National Assembly.

The Transition to the Fifth Republic. These problems came to a head on 13 May 1958, when the army occupied Government House in Algiers and set up a Committee of Public Safety, warning the President not to sell out to the liberation movements on Algerian independence. * * * There was clearly the danger of a military coup that would spread to the mainland. The rebels threatened that 'Operation Resurrection' would be launched unless de Gaulle formed a Government. The centre-right coalition collapsed on 28 May, and the President warned that he would resign unless Parliament accepted de Gaulle, which many parliamentary leaders were prepared to do. On 1 June the President invited de Gaulle to head a Government. The General agreed, on condition that he could draw up a new Constitution. A *Loi* of 3 June 1958 gave his Government powers to make decrees on whatever matters it thought necessary for six months, while it prepared a draft of a Constitution to be put to the people by referendum.

The crisis atmosphere, and the limited time for the exercise, ensured that the writing of the Constitution was not going to be a slow process of reflection and discussion. The Government began work on a draft in July. This was submitted to the Comité consultatif constitutionnel, which met for eighteen sessions between 29 July and 14 August. The draft was then presented to the Conseil d'État at the end of August, and was voted by referendum on 28 September 1958. The majority in favour was substantial (80.1 per cent of those voting, constituting 66.4 per cent of the electorate), even though some Socialists and the Communists were against it.

Clearly, given the time-scale, there was no room for enormous originality. In its delegation of full powers to de Gaulle, Parliament had isolated five principles that the new Constitution had to reflect: (i) universal suffrage as the sole source of political power; (ii) the separation of legislative and executive powers so that each was assured the full exercise of its proper functions; (iii) the answerability of Government to Parliament; (iv) the independence of the judiciary; and (v) a relationship between the Republic and associated peoples.

———————

Another example of constitution-making in the context of impending civil war and potential counterrevolution is the 1993 Russian Constitution.

Rett R. Ludwikowski, CONSTITUTION-MAKING IN THE REGION OF FORMER SOVIET DOMINANCE
59–60 (1996).

[In 1993, Russian President Boris Yeltsin was locked in a political struggle with Parliament over a new constitution and apportionment of powers between the legislature and the presidency.]

Realizing the futility of his negotiations with the congress, Yeltsin convened a constitutional assembly composed of seven hundred regional and state officials and interest group leaders to revise the presidential draft constitution. Given ten days to make changes to Yeltsin's draft, the delegates proposed more than five thousand amendments, but they were unable to reach any final agreement. Because of this situation, the task of preparing a new draft was given to a sixty-member conciliatory commission. The commission submitted its proposal to the convention, which approved the draft by two-thirds majority on July 12, 1993. In response, four days later the congress denounced the convention as illegal and passed a resolution on the Procedure of Adopting the Constitution of the Russian Federation. The resolution provided for two alternative methods of adopting a new constitution, one by the two-thirds vote of the registered deputies of the congress and the other by a referendum. For the referendum to be valid, the qualified majority of two-thirds would have to cast an affirmative vote with a majority of voters participating, including an absolute majority of voters in each component of the federation. As Dwight Semler commented, "These requirements practically ensure that the Congress will remain the only body authorized to adopt a new constitution."[94]

As of September 1, 1993 two draft constitutions existed, one by the constitutional commission, the other by the constitutional convention.

94. [Dwight Semler, *Special Reports, Summer in Russia Brings No Real Political Progress*, E. Eur. Const. Rev., vol. 2, no. 3 (1993) at] 21.

Also, at that time it was obvious to all Western observers that constitutional progress would reach a standstill until the political crisis was resolved.

On September 21, 1993, Yeltsin dissolved parliament, thereby creating a diarchy in Russia. In response to this move, parliament, under the leadership of Ruslan Khasbulatov, voted to depose Yeltsin and name Vice President Aleksander Rutskoi as acting president. The result of these actions was a virtual standoff, pitting Yeltsin and his supporters against Khasbulatov and Rutskoi and their supporters. Finally, on October 4, 1993, military forces, loyal to Yeltsin, attacked the parliament building and arrested militant deputies, including Rutskoi and Khasbulatov. Moreover, Yeltsin banned opposition parties and newspapers, disbanded local soviets or councils, and suspended Russia's constitutional court. Thus, the constitution-making process was immediately accelerated, yet the democratic character of this process was undermined, and Yeltsin's autocratic inclinations were immediately boosted.

On November 10, 1993, Yeltsin unveiled a draft of a new constitution. Despite a campaign against the constitution as "a granted" charter rather than a democratically adopted one, the draft was submitted to a nationwide vote on December 12, the same day that Russia held elections for a new legislature. The referendum resulted in 58.4 percent of the voters in favor of adopting the constitution, and, after its approval, the constitution was immediately signed.

Notes and Questions

1. The success of a new constitution seems to depend on achieving a break with the past that is neither too great nor too small. Does it make any difference which model of constitution-making is involved? Or are the social, economic, and political conditions that prevail at the time of the constitution-making endeavor key to determining the kind of constitution that may be instituted and its likelihood of success? For example, the 1978 Spanish Constitution, the transitions to constitutional democracy in Hungary and Poland after the fall of communism, and the postapartheid constitution-making in South Africa, all involved pacted, peaceful transitions. The circumstances surrounding these transitions were quite different, however. Spain had a robust, functioning market economy; Poland and Hungary did not. South Africa's white-minority government was under intense pressure both from within and from the international community. Cf. Linz and Stepan, *op. cit.* at 7–11 (arguing that the presence of a working civil society are, among other factors, preconditions to establishment of a working constitutional democracy).

2. The constitution-making process in South Africa was unique in that it granted an important role to that country's Constitutional Court. The passage from an interim constitution to a constitution that satisfied 34 recently adopted constitutional principles was necessitated by the aim to achieve rapid transition from the apartheid system and the adoption of a constitution enjoying broad-based democratic legitimacy. In entrusting the SACC with the task of determining whether the proposed constitution was consistent with the constitutional principles, South African constitution-makers relied heavily on a postapartheid institution with a high level of

public trust. By ordering that changes be made to the proposed constitution, arguably the SACC blurred the distinction between constitution-making and amending a constitution. In any event, shortly after the decision, the Constitution was revised to address the Court's objections and then approved by the Court, in late 1996. See *In re Certification of the Amendment Text of the Constitution of the Republic of South Africa,* 1996 (2), SALR 97 (CC). The Constitution entered into force on February 4, 1997.

3.   The 1958 French Constitution was adopted during a national crisis brought about by the Algerian war. See Didier Maus, *Études sur la constitution de la Ve République* 139–64 (1990). Not only were the prevailing governmental institutions under the 1946 French Constitution inadequate in the face of that war, but there was also the danger of a military coup. Under these circumstances, De Gaulle's ascent to power and adoption of his 1958 Constitution instituting a strong presidency may have saved French democracy. Moreover, though the transition from parliamentary democracy to a presidential or semipresidential regime represents a major change, the nature of that change cannot be equated to a transition from an authoritarian regime to a constitutional democracy. Indeed the 1958 French Constitution retained many features of its 1946 predecessor and earlier French constitutions, including the incorporation by reference of the 1789 Declaration of the Rights of Man and of the Citizen, which encompasses France's most enduring constitutional values. See Bell, *op. cit.* at 64–68. Although France's 1958 Constitution is undoubtedly a newly made one from a formal standpoint, does it amount to a new constitution or to an amended one from a functional perspective?

4.   Conversely, the transitions to constitutional democracy in Hungary and Poland after the fall of communism in Eastern and Central Europe appear to involve constitution-making functionally, but they were achieved in large measure through what formally are constitutional amendments. In Hungary, the changes were accomplished through comprehensive amendments to the 1949 constitution. Pursuant to 1989 amendments, Hungary was transformed from a socialist state led by a Marxist–Leninist party to a multiparty parliamentary democracy with a market economy. See Rett R. Ludwikowski, *Constitution-Making in the Region of Former Soviet Dominance* 180 (1996). Similarly, in Poland, constitutional reforms were first institutionalized through amendments to the 1952 constitution. *Id.* at 155. While Hungary has yet to adopt a new constitution, in 1992 Poland adopted the "Little Constitution," after failing to agree on a permanent constitution, and had to wait until 1997 for adoption of a new postcommunist constitution. See Wiktor Osiatynski, *A Brief History of the Constitution*, E. Eur. Const. Rev., vol. 6, nos. 2–3 at 66 (1997).

E.2.   AMENDING THE CONSTITUTION

While it is not always easy to draw a firm line between constitution-making and amending the constitution, from a formal standpoint constitutional amendments are readily identifiable inasmuch as the constitution itself prescribes how it may be amended. For example, Art. V of the U.S. Constitution specifies the required procedures to enact amendments. Even with a provision such as this, questions may remain concerning what ought to count as a genuine amendment. For one thing, the relevant provision arguably may not be exclusive. Bruce Ackerman has maintained the view that certain transformative decisions of the USSC have resulted in structural amendments to the Constitution without use or invocation of Art. V. See Bruce A. Ackerman, *We the People: Foundations* (1991). There are even instances of formal amendments adopted in contravention to a constitution's prescriptions for valid amendments, such as De Gaulle's 1962 amendment to the 1958 French Constitution, establishing universal suffrage for the election of the French President. De Gaulle submitted his proposed amendment to a popular referendum, ignoring the Constitution's amendment provisions. After the amendment was approved by French voters, the French Constitutional Council, notwithstanding the failure to comply with constitutional prescriptions, upheld it (see the decision reproduced below).

Conceptually, an "amendment" can be distinguished from a "revision." In Professor Walter Murphy's words:

> The word *amend*, which comes from the Latin *emendere*, means to correct or improve; amend does not mean "to deconstitute and reconstitute," to replace one system with another or abandon its primary principles. Thus changes that would make a polity into another kind of political system would not be amendments at all, but revisions or transformations. In sum, valid amendments can operate only within the existing political system; they cannot deconstitute, reconstitute, or replace the polity; Most constitutional texts authorize only amendments, though a few others, like those of Spain and some American states, also provide for revision and the German Basic Law [Art. 146] allows for its own replacement by a new text.
>
> Walter F. Murphy, *Merlin's Memory*: *The Past and Future Imperfect of the Once and Future Polity*, in *Responding to Imperfection: The Theory and Practice of Constitutional Amendment* 163, 177 (Sanford Levinson ed., 1995).

Consistent with Murphy's definition, the amendments to the Hungarian Constitution, discussed above, transforming that country from a socialist society to a democratic free-market one, conceptually would be "revisions" if not "constitution-making," rather than "amendments." Consider the view of Professors Holmes and Sunstein:

> Western observers have been tempted to condemn easy paths to constitutional modification in Eastern Europe * * * and to denounce more generally the "confusion" between constitutional politics and ordinary politics characteristic of every post-Communist society * * *.
>
> There is something to be said for this view * * *. But the view is far too simple * * *. Not only does social turbulence demand a good deal of flexibility and "ad hockery," but *the very creation of a constitutional culture in post-Communist societies depends upon a willingness to mix constitutional politics and ordinary politics.* * * * To change a communist constitution into a liberal-democratic one required something more drastic than modification, revision, or amendment. It required the wholesale destruction of the old and the creation, from ground zero, of the new. It required a *constitutional revolution,* or new founding. * * *
>
> More precisely, they are constitutional revolutions *cloaked* as constitutional revisions. Most striking, from this perspective, is the discordance

of content and form. A wholesale constitutional replacement was presented to domestic publics and the world at large as an act of constitutional tinkering. One of the most revolutionary changes of modern times was symbolically de-revolutionized. A total rupture with the past, all aspects of society being reformed simultaneously, was packaged as a piecemeal reform.

Stephen Holmes and Cass R. Sunstein, *The Politics of Constitutional Revision in Eastern Europe*, in *id.* at 275, 278–80, 282–90, 294–97.

The degree of difficulty involved in amending a constitution varies from country to country. At one end of the spectrum, the constitution is nearly as easy to amend as it is to enact ordinary legislation. In Hungary, for example, a constitutional amendment requires only a two-thirds majority in the Parliament. At the other end, amendment of the constitution is so difficult as to be practically impossible short of nation-wide consensus. Among the most difficult constitutions to amend are those of the U.S. and Australia. The U.S. requires passage by a two-thirds majority in each chamber of the federal Congress, followed by ratification by three-quarters of the 50 state legislatures. Since 49 of the 50 states are bicameral and ratification in bicameral states requires a majority vote in both chambers, a negative vote by as few as 13 of the country's 99 state legislative chambers is sufficient to defeat a proposed amendment. In Australia, some amendments require approval by both chambers of Parliament (or by one chamber twice), followed by ratification by a majority of the voters nationwide and a majority of the voters in each of the country's six states (although most amendments can still be ratified if the majority of voters in two of the six states refuse to ratify).

The consequences of the difficulty in amending the constitutions in these two countries are quite different. In the U.S., the near impossibility of adopting significant amendments is mitigated by the breadth and flexibility of the Supreme Court's powers of interpretation in constitutional cases. For example, in 1954 the constitutionality of state-sponsored racial segregation in public education was abolished not by a constitutional amendment but by a unanimous Supreme Court decision reversing nearly 60 years of contrary interpretation. See *Brown v. Board of Education*, 347 U.S. 483 (1954) (in Chapter 6). In contrast, the Australian High Court has steadfastly refused to engage in expansive constitutional interpretation. This has led to widespread dissatisfaction among Australians. See Donald Lutz, *Towards a Theory of Constitutional Amendment*, in *Responding to Imperfection: The Theory and Practice of Constitutional Amendment*, above at 237, 266 n.12. Accordingly, although from a formal standpoint both constitutions seem too rigid, because of the outlet provided by expansive judicial interpretation, the U.S. Constitution is more adaptable to changing conditions than its Australian counterpart. Professors Holmes and Sunstein argue:

Amendability suggests, to put it crudely, that basic rights are ultimately at the mercy of interest-group politics, if some arbitrary electoral threshold is surpassed and amenders play by the book. Is this a correct way of understanding liberal democracy? Does Article V of the U.S. Constitution imply the triumph of procedure over substance, formal rules over moral norms? Are there no fundamental rights beyond the reach of politics? Are there no goods that are protected absolutely, rather than depending on percentage of votes?

* * * Every functioning liberal democracy depends on a variety of techniques for introducing flexibility into the constitutional framework. The two usual methods are, first, amendment and, second, judicial interpretation in the light of evolving circumstances and social norms. There are intriguing or mutual compensation effects of constitutional amendment and constitutional interpretation, and these can help us understand better the relationship between the judiciary and the political branches. Both parliaments and courts can actually benefit from a stringent amending procedure. If amendments are relatively difficult, the legislature has a ready alibi for failure to give in to the electorate, and the court, in turn, will gain in prestige because it can pose as the guardian of the ark of the covenant. * * *

The free availability of amendment may have a range of diverse effects on the courts. If it is easy to amend the Constitution, the stakes of constitutional decision are lowered, for an erroneous or unpopular judicial decision can be overridden. Moreover, the availability of the amendment option may embolden the court, since the judges will know that mistaken decisions can be corrected.

* * * Constitutionalists tend to favor a system of deep entrenchment of constitutional provisions (i.e., a stringent amending formula) and recourse to popular referenda. This may be desirable in Western democracies, but it is inappropriate, we argue, in Eastern Europe. The amending formula should be relatively lax, and it should be virtually monopolized by parliament, with no recourse to referenda. * * * The "deep entrenchment" of constitutional provisions, on the other hand, and the availability referenda in south-eastern Europe, result from the dominance of ex-Communists, eager to "lock in" their privileges, over the constitution-drafting process there.

Holmes and Sunstein, *op. cit.* at 275.

Some constitutions provide that various provisions are altogether unamendable. Thus Art. 79 (3) of the German Basic Law forbids amendments that would be counter to upholding the "dignity of man" constitutionalized in Art. I or that would undermine the democratic or federal nature of the German state. Similarly, Art. 139 of the Italian Constitution makes the requirement of a republican form of government unamendable. Unamendable constitutional provisions give rise to the problem of the unconstitutional amendment, as illustrated by the following German case.

PRIVACY OF COMMUNICATIONS CASE

[ALSO KNOWN AS THE KLASS CASE]
Federal Constitutional Court (Germany).
30 BVerfGE 1 (1970).

[Originally, Art. 10 of the Basic Law provided that "Secrecy of the mail and secrecy of posts and telecommunications shall be inviolable. Restrictions may be ordered only pursuant to law." Pursuant to certain of Germany's treaty obligations, Art. 10 was amended to allow for broader surveillance without notifying the person affected and to allow certain substitutions of administrative supervision for judicial ones. This amendment was meant to address serious espionage problems and was followed by enactment of a statute designed to implement the broader powers authorized by the amendment.]

Judgement of the Second Senate:

1. Constitutional provisions must not be interpreted in isolation, but rather so that they are consistent with the Basic Law's fundamental principles and its system of values * * *. In the context of this case, it is especially significant that the Constitution * * * has decided in favor of a "militant democracy" that does not submit to abuse of basic rights for an attack on the liberal order of the state. Enemies of the Constitution must not be allowed to endanger, impair, or destroy the existence of the state while claiming protection of rights granted by the Basic Law (cf. Art. 9 par. 2, Arts. 18 and 21). * * *

Of no lesser importance is the Basic Law's fundamental decision authorizing limits on basic rights in order to protect the common welfare and paramount legal interests (cf., e.g., Art. 2, par. 1.). "The concept of man in the Basic Law is not that of an isolated, sovereign individual; rather, the Basic Law has decided in favor of a relationship between individual and community in the sense of a person's dependence on and commitment to the community, without infringing upon a person's individual value. This choice becomes clear in particular if one considers Arts. 1, 2, 12, 14, 15, 19, and 20 together. This choice also requires an individual to submit to those restrictions on his freedom that the legislator sets for cultivation and furthermore of the social community * * * provided that in doing so a person's independence is maintained".

From a third fundamental decision made in the Basic Law—the principle of the rule of law—the Federal Constitutional Court has derived the principle of proportionality. This principle demands that, where basic rights are restricted, a law may provide for only that * * * which is absolutely necessary for protection of the legal interest recognized by the Basic Law—in this case the existence of the state and its constitutional order. It also follows from the principle of the rule of law that any governmental encroachment upon a citizen's freedom or property must at least be subject to effective judicial control * * *. [This goes to proportionality. See Chapter 2.]

2. The interpretation of Art. 79, par. 3, has the following result:

a. The purpose of Art. 79, par. 3, as a check on the legislator's amending the Constitution is to prevent both abolition of the substance or basis of the existing constitutional order, by the formal legal means of amendment * * * and abuse of the Constitution to legalize a totalitarian regime. This provision thus prohibits a fundamental abandonment of the principles mentioned therein. Principles are from the very beginning not "affected" as "principles" if they are in general taken into consideration and are only modified for evidently pertinent reasons for a special case according to its peculiar character * * *.

b. It is also of importance that Art. 79, par. 3, mentions as inviolable, apart from the principles of division of the Federation into *Länder* and participation on principle of the *Länder* in legislation, "the principles laid down in Arts. 1 and 20." * * * More principles than just that of respect for the dignity of man are "laid down" in Art. 1. Art. 20 also contains several principles. The general "principle of the rule of law," however, is not "laid down" there, but only certain very specific maxims of that principle: in par. 2 the principle of separation of powers and in par. 3 the principle of legislation being subject to the constitutional order, and of the executive and judiciary being bound by law and justice. More than the legal principles of Art. 20 referred to in Art. 79, par. 3, can be deduced from the principle of the rule of law, and the Federal Constitutional Court has established such legal principles (e.g., prohibition of ex *post facto* laws, the rule of * * * the principle of a maximum of legal protection). *Restriction* on the legislator's amending the Constitution * * * must not, however, prevent the legislator from modifying by constitutional amendment even basic constitutional principles in a system-immanent manner. From this point of view, the subsidiary principle derived from the principle of the rule of law, that a maximum of *judicial* protection must be available to the citizen, does not belong among the principles laid down" in Art. 20; it is nowhere mentioned in Art 20. The guarantee of recourse to the courts is located in Art. 19, par. 4; thus Art. 79, par. 3, does not exempt this right from * * * modification by constitutional amendment.

c. Art. 79, par. 3, does exempt from possible amendment the protection afforded by Art. I to the dignity of man. But whether a constitutional amendment violates human dignity can only be decided in the context of a specific situation. Overarching rules can only indicate general directions here * * *. Art. I forbids treatment which on principle jeopardizes a citizen's personality as an individual or treats him in a manner that expresses contempt for his inherent value as a human being.

II.   Art. 10. par. 2, sent 2 * * * is compatible with Art. 79, par. 3 * * *

3.   Nor does substitution of recourse to the law by some other judicial control as provided for in Art. 10. par. 2, sent. 2. violate the principle of separation of powers * * *. For this principle does not demand a strict separation of powers, but in exceptional cases permits legislative functions to exercised by governmental and administrative bodies or government and administration to be exercised by legislative bodies. In exceptional cases, the principle of separation of powers also permits legal protection against acts of the executive to be furnished not by courts, but by independent institutions, appointed or established by Parliament and operating within the framework of the executive department. The essential point is that the rationale for separation of powers, namely reciprocal restriction and control of state is still fulfilled. * * *

Substitution of recourse to the courts by independent legal control of a different kind * * * and limited absence of notification * * * do not contravene the principle of the rule of law * * *. The executive is bound by law and justice * * *.

Dissenting opinion by Justices Geller, Dr. V. Schlabrendorff, and Prof. Dr. Rupp * * *

When examining the constitutionality of the amendment, one cannot interpret it on the basis of principles which are valid for interpretation of constitutional standards for the precise question is whether Art. 10. par. 2, sent. 2, is a valid constitutional standard. In applying the standard of Art. 79, par. 3, it is of decisive importance how an amendment must be understood in its wording, context, and purpose. * * *

Considering these factors, it becomes clear that Art. 10, par, 2. cannot be interpreted as "in conformity with the Basic Law." * * *

The guarantee of recourse to the courts laid down in Art. 19. par. 4. serves the purpose of legal protection for the individual * * *. The essential aspect of this constitutional provision is that legal protection is furnished by a materially and personally independent body, separate from the executive and legislative and therefore neutral * * *. If the Constitution is amended so that "recourse to the courts" is "replaced by a review of the case by bodies and auxiliary bodies appointed by parliament." then the entire system of legal protection is replaced * * *.

Furthermore, one cannot infer from the constitutional amendment any tangible limitation on the number of people who may be kept under surveillance. Restrictions on privacy may be ordered in a very general manner, whenever they serve to protect the free democratic basic order or the existence or security of the Federation or a Land * * *.

* * * a) Art. 79, par 3, declares inviolable certain principles laid down in the Constitution. The Basic Law also * * * limits constitutional amendments. Such an important, far-reaching, and exceptional provision must certainly not be interpreted in an extensive manner. But it would be a complete misunderstanding of its meaning to assume that its main purpose was only to prevent misuse of the formal legal means of a constitutional amendment to legitimize a totalitarian regime * * * Art. 79, par. 3, means more: Certain fundamental decisions of the Basic Law maker are inviolable * * *.

According to Art. 79, par. 3, the fundamental decisions which should not be altered are those * * * manifested in Arts. 1 and 20. Regardless of how widely or narrowly the principles of Arts. 1 and 20 are defined, they form * * * the cornerstones of the Basic Law.

b) According to decisions of the Federal Constitutional Court, Art. 1 is one of the "governing constitutional principles" which permeate all provisions contained in the Basic Law. The Basic Law considers free human personality and its dignity as the highest legal value. When answering the question what the "dignity of man" means, one must be careful not to understand the expression exclusively in its highest meaning, for instance, by proceeding from the assumption that the dignity of man is violated only if the treatment "expresses contempt for his inherent value as a human being." * * * Such a restricted interpretation does not do justice to the spirit of the Basic Law * * *. By giving first priority to the free human personality, the Basic Law recognizes the individual's value and independence * * *. He must not be treated in an "impersonal" manner, like an object * * *. The First Senate of this Court has ruled that it violates the dignity of man to treat him as a mere subject of state activity [citations omitted]. * * *

The question whether the "principle of the rule of law" as such or only very specific maxims of that principle are "laid down" in Art. 20 * * * need not be discussed * * *. What is essential is that Art. 20 contains the principle of lawfulness and the principle of separation of powers; both are principles based on the rule of law. It follows from them that the Basic Law not only accords man a privilege place in its hierarchy of values, but that it also protects him. As a matter of fact, individual freedom and rights would be meaningless without constitutionally guaranteed, effective judicial protection. The principle of lawfulness embodied in Art. 20, par. 3, binds state officials and institutions-to the constitutional order, law, and justice, and thus often objective protection. If that protection is to be effective, a citizen must also be able to defend himself against an encroachment by state authorities and to have the lawfulness of their action evaluated. This protection is guaranteed in the form of a judiciary which, pursuant to Art. 20, par. 2, is separate from the legislative and the executive * * *. Consequently, Art. 20, par. 2, contains the rule-of-law principle of individual judicial protection * * *.

The Federal Constitutional Court has repeatedly spoken of the "rule of law requiring a maximum of judicial protection against infringement upon an individual's rights by public authority" [citation omitted]. * * * The requirement of a *maximum of* legal protection is not relative, but absolute.

On the basis of these considerations we conclude: the principle based upon Art. 1 that man must not be treated as a mere object of the state and that his rights must not summarily be disposed of by authorities and Art. 20's constitutional call for a maximum of individual legal protection are among the "principles laid down in Arts. 1 and 20." These two principles contain fundamental decisions of the Basic Law that decisively shape the image of a state based upon the rule of law * * *. Art. 79, par. 3, specifies that these constituent elements shall be irrevocable.

c) The constitutional amendment "affects" the principles laid down in Arts. 1 and 20.

The wording and meaning of Art. 79, par. 3, do not merely forbid complete abolition of all or one of the principles. The word "affect" means less * * *. The constituent elements are also * * * to be protected against a gradual process of disintegration. * * *

Secret encroachment upon a citizen's private sector while eliminating recourse to the courts * * * may affect not only enemies of the Constitution and [foreign] agents, but also unsuspected and uninvolved persons * * *. Such treatment means * * * that an individual's right to respect for his private sphere is disposed of "summarily by public authority," that the citizen is treated as an object of the authority * * *.

ON CONSTITUTIONAL AMENDMENT
ADOPTED BY REFERENDUM

Constitutional Council (France).
62–20 DC of 6 Nov. 1962.

[The circumstances surrounding this case are summarized by John Bell in *French Constitutional Law* 133–34 (1992):

After the assassination attempt at Petit–Clamart on 22 August 1962, General de Gaulle announced at the Council of Ministers on 12 September that he was going to seek to change the Constitution's method of appointing a President of the Republic and to introduce popular, rather than indirect, election. The procedure he adopted was that for amending the Constitution provided for in article 89, which involves a bill being passed by both chambers. The Pompidou Government was already facing problems in Parliament, so that such a bill was unlikely to pass. Drawing on * * * his success in the referendum of April 1962 that put an end to the Algerian crisis, the President relied on article 11, which enables the President to put a bill 'concerning the organization of public authorities' to a referendum, 'on the recommendation of the Government'. The President of the Senate and the opposition criticized the Government for this 'outrageous breach of the Constitution', and it was defeated in a confidence motion on 5 October 1962. Parliamentary elections were called on 9 October, and fixed for 18 and 25 November. In the meantime, the President decided by a decree of 2 October to submit the proposed law in relation to the election of the President to a referendum on 28 October. * * *

De Gaulle was successful in the referendum, but the President of the Senate, the Socialist Gaston Monnerville (later to be member of the Conseil constitutionnel) referred the [matter] to the Conseil constiution-nel as unconstitutional.]

DECISION

1. Considering that the competence of the Conseil constitutionnel is strictly limited by the Constitution, as well as by the provisions of the organic law of 7 November 1958 on the Conseil constitutionnel * * * that the Conseil constitutionnel cannot be called upon to rule on matters other than the limited number for which those texts provide;

2. Considering that, even if article 61 of the Constitution gives the Conseil constitutionnel the task of assessing the compatibility with the Constitution of organic laws and ordinary laws, which, respectively, must be submitted to it for scrutiny, without stating whether this competence extends to all texts of legislative character, be they adopted by the people after a referendum or passed by Parliament, or whether, on the contrary, it is limited only to the latter category, it follows from the spirit of the Constitution, which made the Conseil constitutionnel a body regulating the activity of public authorities, that the laws to which the Constitution intended to refer in article 61 are only those *lois* passed by Parliament, and not those which, adopted by the people after a referendum, constitute a direct expression of national sovereignty;

* * *

5. Considering that it follows from what has been said that none of the provisions of the Constitution, nor of the above-mentioned organic law applying it, gives the Conseil constitutionnel the competence to rule on the request submitted by the President of the Senate, that it consider whether the bill adopted by the French people by way of referendum on 28 October 1962 is compatible with the Constitution. [The referral was rejected.]

Notes and Questions

1. Compare the SACC's role in its decision in the 1996 *Certification of the Constitution Case*, above, with the GFCC's decision in the *Privacy of Communications Case*. Formally, the South African case involved constitution-making, whereas the German one related to a constitutional amendment. However, are not the constitutional principles functionally and structurally equivalent in the two cases? Consider, further the Indian doctrine of unamendable "basic structure" in *Kesavananda* (see Chapter 10).

2. The majority and dissent in the *Klass Case* had very different conceptions of the German Basic Law's constraints on legitimate constitutional amendments. Does this discrepancy suggest that German constitutional judges have very broad power to approve or block constitutional amendments? If they do, is this power more objectionable for constitutional amendments than in interpretation of other constitutional provisions? See Chapter 2 for further discussion of constitutional interpretation in general. The *Klass* decision was reviewed by the ECHR (see *Klass v. Germany* in Chapter 9).

3. Professors Holmes and Sunstein argue for ease of constitutional amendment in Eastern Europe because they view the constitutional projects in the region as protracted works in progress. They suggest that amendments in Eastern Europe play a role much more akin to constitution-making than they do in other constitutional democracies, such as Germany or the U.S. Do you agree? Furthermore, the authors argue that ease of amendment is important because, among other reasons, democracy in Eastern Europe is fragile and party-based political representation unsettled. Is this not paradoxical? Because the constitution is supposed to embody the will of the people, does it not make sense to allow for more-flexible amendment procedures in a settled democracy with stable and well-defined political-party representation?

Chapter 2

JUDICIAL ENFORCEMENT OF THE CONSTITUTION AND MODELS OF CONSTITUTIONAL ADJUDICATION

A written constitution,[a] which creates legal rights and obligations, is bound to raise questions of interpretation and enforcement much like any ordinary law. Moreover, as constitutional provisions are often more general and open-ended than typical statutory provisions, arguably they allow far greater interpretive latitude than do their statutory counterparts. Indeed, as the readings in the relevant chapters below clearly demonstrate, generally stated constitutional rights to privacy and equality and freedoms of speech and religion are open to multiple and often contradictory interpretations. This raises the following basic questions: Who is (or ought to be) the authoritative interpreter of the constitution? And, what are the proper canons and limits of constitutional interpretation?

These questions are particularly crucial in the context of constitutions that are difficult to amend. As noted in the discussion on constitutional amendments in Chapter 1, innovative and far-reaching constitutional interpretations by courts may well have the same consequences as a formal amendment to a constitution. Unlike in the case of statutory interpretation, where a parliament may deal with judicial interpretations it disagrees with through further legislation, a parliament with no control over the adoption of constitutional amendments seems largely helpless in the face of constitutional adjudications with which it disagrees.

Given these dangers, is it wise to entrust enforcement of the constitution to courts? Or is it best to apportion that task among various different powers? Or should courts be deprived of the power of having the last word? Section A. deals with these issues and focuses on whether a working constitutional order can be maintained without constitutional adjudication; whether, where courts have a role in constitutional enforcement and adjudication, they should be given sole or ultimate authority;

a. Unwritten constitutions are also bound to require interpretation but may raise certain issues of their own. See *United Mizrahi Bank, Ltd. v. Migdal Village* below.

99

and whether the legitimacy of constitutional adjudication depends on granting finality to such adjudication. Section B. reviews the principal models of constitutional adjudication and concentrates on the contrast between centralized and decentralized constitutional review and on whether centralized review by specialized bodies is genuinely judicial in nature. Next, the section deals with issues concerning the independence of the constitutional adjudicator, by focusing on methods and criteria of appointment, composition of the relevant court, and its relation to the other branches of government. Section B. asks several questions: *Who* can trigger the process of constitutional adjudication?; *What* is properly subject to constitutional adjudication?; and *Who* is bound by it and to what extent? Section C., the final section, is devoted to salient issues relating to theories and practices of constitutional interpretation in various constitutional systems.

A. THE PLACE OF CONSTITUTIONAL ADJUDICATION IN A WORKING CONSTITUTIONAL ORDER

Disputes concerning ordinary legal rights and obligations are customarily resolved by courts. Similarly, to the extent that constitutions grant legally enforceable rights and impose legally binding obligations, it seems logical to submit constitutional disputes to judicial resolution. Most countries with written constitutions provide for constitutional adjudication by courts or court-like institutions; but some do not. One such constitutional democracy is The Netherlands.

Even in countries in which courts can adjudicate cases involving constitutional issues, questions may arise concerning whether such courts may invalidate ordinary laws conflicting with the constitution but enacted after the constitution's adoption; whether constitutional interpretations rendered in the course of adjudications are authoritative and binding on other branches of the government, such as the legislative or executive branch; and whether courts ought to have the final word when it comes to interpreting the constitution.

The United States Constitution does not designate an authoritative interpreter of the Constitution. It also does not specify whether courts can invalidate ordinary federal laws that are in conflict with the Constitution. Article III Sec. 2 of the Constitution does provide, however, that "The judicial Power shall extend to all Cases * * * arising under this Constitution * * *." The U.S. Supreme Court (USSC) addressed these crucial questions, left open by the Constitution, in the following landmark decision.

MARBURY v. MADISON

Supreme Court (United States).
5 U.S. 137 (1803).

[William Marbury was nominated to be a federal judge by President Adams and confirmed by the U.S. Senate on the very last day of the

Adams Administration. In order to assume his duties as a judge, Marbury had to receive his commission, which was to be delivered by the Secretary of State. The incoming President, Thomas Jefferson, refused to have Marbury and other so called midnight judges appointed at the very end of the preceding Administration serve as judges and instructed his Secretary of State, James Madison, not to deliver the requisite commissions. Marbury sued to request that the Court instruct Madison to deliver the commission. In the course of adjudicating the dispute, the Supreme Court had to decide how to deal with a contradiction between the Judiciary Act of 1789, adopted by the U.S. Congress, and Article III of the 1787 Constitution.]

The opinion of the Court was delivered by Chief Justice Marshall:

* * *

The Constitution vests the whole judicial power of the United States in one Supreme Court, and such inferior courts as Congress shall, from time to time, ordain and establish. This power is expressly extended to all cases arising under the laws of the United States; and, consequently, in some form, may be exercised over the present case; because the right claimed is given by a law of the United States.

The question, whether an act, repugnant to the Constitution, can become the law of the land, is a question deeply interesting to the United States; but, happily, not of an intricacy proportioned to its interest. It seems only necessary to recognize certain principles, supposed to have been long and well established, to decide it.

That the people have an original right to establish, for their future government, such principles as, in their opinion, shall most conduce to their own happiness, is the basis on which the whole American fabric has been erected. The exercise of this original right is a very great exertion: nor can it, nor ought it, to be frequently repeated. The principles, therefore, so established, are deemed fundamental. And as the authority from which they proceed is supreme, and can seldom act, they are designed to be permanent.

This original and supreme will organizes the government, and assigns to different departments their respective powers. It may either stop here, or establish certain limits not to be transcended by those departments. The government of the United States is of the latter description. The powers of the legislature are defined and limited; and that those limits may not be mistaken, or forgotten, the constitution is written. To what purpose are powers limited, and to what purpose is that limitation committed to writing, if these limits may, at any time, be passed by those intended to be restrained? The distinction between a government with limited and unlimited powers is abolished, if those limits do not confine the persons on whom they are imposed, and if acts prohibited and acts allowed, are of equal obligation. It is a proposition too plain to be contested, that the constitution controls any legislative acts repugnant to it; or, that the legislature may alter the constitution by an ordinary act.

Between these alternatives there is no middle ground. The constitution is either a superior, paramount law, unchangeable by ordinary means, or it is on a level with ordinary legislative acts, and, like other acts, is alterable when the legislature shall please to alter it.

If the former part of the alternative be true, then a legislative act contrary to the constitution is not law: if the latter part be true, then written constitutions are absurd attempts, on the part of the people, to limit a power in its own nature illimitable.

Certainly all those who have framed written constitutions contemplate them as forming the fundamental and paramount law of the nation, and consequently, the theory of every such government must be, that an act of the legislature, repugnant to the constitution, is void.

This theory is essentially attached to a written constitution, and is; consequently, to be considered, by this court, as one of the fundamental principles of our society. It is not therefore to be lost sight of in the further consideration of this subject. If an act of the legislature, repugnant to the constitution, is void, does it, notwithstanding its invalidity, bind the courts, and oblige them to give it effect? Or, in other words, though it be not law, does it constitute a rule as operative as if' it was a law? This would be to overthrow in fact what was established in theory; and would seem, at first view, an absurdity too gross to be insisted on. It shall, however, receive a more attentive consideration.

It is emphatically the province and duty of the judicial department to say what the law is. Those who apply the rule to particular cases, must of necessity expound and interpret that rule. If two laws conflict with each other, the courts must decide on the operation of each.

So if a law be in opposition to the constitution; if both the law and the constitution apply to a particular case, so that the court must either decide that case conformably to the law, disregarding the constitution; or conformably to the constitution, disregarding the law; the court must determine which of these conflicting rules governs the case. This is of the very essence of judicial duty.

If, then, the courts are to regard the constitution, and the constitution is superior to any ordinary act of the legislature, the constitution, and not such ordinary act, must govern the case to which they both apply.

Those then who controvert the principle that the constitution is to be considered, in court, as a paramount law, are reduced to the necessity of maintaining that courts must close their eyes on the constitution, and see only the law * * *

The judicial power of the United States is extended to all cases arising under the constitution. Could it be the intention of those who gave this power, to say that in using it the constitution should not be looked into? That a case arising under the constitution should be decided without examining the instrument under which it arises? This is too extravagant to be maintained.

In some cases, then, the constitution must be looked into by the judges. And if they can open it at all, what part of it are they forbidden to read or to obey? There are many other parts of the constitution, which serve to illustrate this subject. It declared that "no tax or duty shall be laid on articles exported from any state." Suppose a duty on the export of cotton, of tobacco, or of flour; and a suit instituted to recover it ought judgment to be rendered in such a case? Ought the judges to close their eyes on the constitution, and only see the law? * * *

From [this], and many other selections, which might be made, it is apparent, that the framers of the constitution contemplated that instrument as a rule for the government of *courts,* as well as of the legislature. Why otherwise does it direct the judges to take an oath to support it? This oath certainly applies, in an especial manner, to their conduct in their official character. How immoral to impose it on them, if they were to be used as the instruments, and the knowing instruments, for violating what they swear to support! * * *

It is also not entirely unworthy of observation that in declaring what shall be the *supreme* law of the land, the *constitution* itself is first mentioned; and not the laws of the United States generally, but those only which shall be made in *pursuance* of the constitution, have that rank. Thus, the particular phraseology of the constitution of the United States confirms and strengthens the principle, supposed to be essential to all written constitutions, that a law repugnant to the constitution is void; and that *courts,* as well as other departments, are bound by that instrument.

If the legitimacy of constitutional adjudication can be vexing in certain countries with written constitutions, like the U.S., it seems fraught with greater difficulties in countries with no written constitution. Indeed, in the absence of a written text it may prove difficult to distinguish between constitutional and infraconstitutional legal norms or to account for constitutional changes, let alone to determine whether courts can invalidate laws on ill-defined or fragile and changing constitutional grounds. Nevertheless, in a landmark decision excerpted below, the Supreme Court of Israel confronted the issue of constitutional review in a broad-based decision that addresses not only the issue of judicial invalidation of laws contrary to the Constitution but also involves the Court in shaping the constitutional order in a way that apparently blurs the boundary between constitution-making and interpreting and applying the constitution.

UNITED MIZRAHI BANK LTD. v. MIGDAL VILLAGE

Supreme Court (Israel).
C.A. 6821/93,
49(4)P.D.221 (1995).

[In this case, the Supreme Court of Israel decided not only whether it had the authority to interpret the country's "Basic Laws" and to determine that legislation incompatible with a Basic Law is invalid, but also whether the Basic Laws in question had constitutional status. This latter question was quite important because, if answered in the affirmative, it would follow that all ordinary legislation incompatible with Israel's Basic Laws could be struck down as unconstitutional.

[Upon creation of the State of Israel, in 1948, the country's Parliament, the Knesset, was constituted both as a constituent assembly and as a legislature. The Knesset failed to adopt a constitution, but in later years it has enacted various Basic Laws, which can be repealed by absolute majority only (as opposed to ordinary legislation, which can be repealed by a majority of those present, provided there is a quorum). The two Basic Law Chapters at stake in this case, namely, that on "Freedom of Occupation" and that on "Human Dignity and Freedom," were enacted in 1994. The specific issue raised in the case was whether legislation affecting property in the "familial agricultural sector" violated rights to property enshrined in the aforementioned Basic Laws.]

Chief Justice A. Barak:

* * *

6.   *Judicial Precedent of the Supreme Court*

55.   The Supreme Court recognized the power of the Knesset to entrench the provisions of a Basic Law against regular legislation, as set forth in four decisions rendered before the March 1992 enactment of the Basic Laws as to human rights * * *

In the *Tenuat Le Or* case I noted as follows:

> A law of the Knesset—whether a 'regular' law or a basic law—that seeks to change an 'entrenched' provision without having been adopted by the necessary majority contradicts the entrenchment provision of the Basic Law. In light of its legal effect the 'entrenchment' provision takes precedence. In this clash between the entrenchment provision and the provision that seeks to change it without meeting the necessary majority requirement we do not apply the standard rules of construction, according to which a later enacted law invalidates an earlier enacted law. In this clash we apply the principle that gives normative precedence to the entrenched Basic Law. (H.C.J. 142/89 *supra* at p. 539).

Thus the Court has recognized the Knesset's power to "entrench" the Basic Laws against change or infringement * * * This primacy is certainly consistent * * * with the constituent authority of the Knesset, empowered to enact a constitution for the State. In * * * the *Tenuat Le Or case*, I discussed the Knesset's status as a constituent authority, noting as follows:

> This 'entrenchment' applies in our system, for we recognize the Knesset's power to function as a constituent authority and to prepare Basic Laws that will constitute the various chapters of the State constitution. (p. 539).

36.   Since the enactment of Basic Law: Freedom of Occupation and Basic Law: Human Dignity and Freedom

The question of the normative status of these Basic Laws has arisen incidentally in the decisions of the Supreme Court. The Supreme Court has taken the position that these two Basic Laws enjoy constitutional supra-legislative status. Justice D. Levin concluded that this was so in the first decision to deal with the constitutionality of Basic Law: Freedom of Occupation. Justice Levin wrote:

> When these two Basic Laws came into being they erected, by their own force and in conjunction with various basic rights that had been scattered here and there throughout our caselaw, the foundations and walls of' the Israeli constitutional edifice. This construction has not, however, been completed, and there remains more to be drafted and enacted so that the constitution may stand in its full glory, radiating its light on the institutions of government and law in Israel. Nonetheless, the work that has been done is the construction of a stable constitutional structure, protected by the mantle of the principle and values anchored in the Declaration of' Independence.

6.   The Knesset as Exercising Constituent Authority Conclusions.

38.   The social-historical journey has concluded. This journey is necessary. Constitutionality and the constitution are not mere formal documents. They are not mere law. They are the fruit of the national experience. They are society and culture. Indeed the constitution is the reflection of the national experience. The words of Justice Agranat still resonate:

> For it is a well-known axiom that to study the law of a people one may look through the prism of its system of national life.

Our system of national life, our national experience, from the establishment of the State until today, is that the Knesset is seen in our national consciousness as the body authorized to enact a constitution for Israel. This consciousness originated before the establishment of the State and the preparation for the giving of the constitution. This consciousness was crystallized in the Declaration of Independence. It took on real form in the elections for the Constituent Assembly. It was consolidated in the social-legal understanding that the Knesset is endowed with constituent authority and is empowered to enact a constitution for Israel. The rhetoric of constituent authority and constituent power was particularly strong during the first years after establishment of the State. This rhetoric weakened with the passage of time. That is natural. Nonetheless, the basic understanding that the Knesset is endowed not only with regular legislative authority but also with constituent authority accompanied the Knesset from its inception * * * The renewed rhetorical reference to the Knesset as endowed with constituent authority in the context of the enactment of Basic Law: Freedom of Occupation in 1994 shows this as well. Indeed, the view that the Knesset is authorized to enact a constitution is deeply embedded in the social and legal consciousness of the Israeli community. This is part of our political culture. On the basis of this view, we, the judges of Israel are entitled to declare today that according to the rule of recognition of the State of Israel the Knesset is endowed with legislative and constituent authority and that the Knesset may, in exercising its constituent authority, limit the exercise of legislative authority. In truth, the rule of recognition at the outset of the Second Knesset might have been different had the Supreme Court determined that constitutional continuity was cut off. But this did not happen. In my opinion this would not have happened even had the question arisen before the Court at that time. In any event, today's social-legal reality enables the Supreme Court—in whose hands rests consolidation of the rule of recognition—(see H.L.A., Hart, *The Concept of Law* 147–154 (2nd ed. (1994)) to identify and declare that our Knesset is endowed with both constituent and legislative authority: that it wears two "hats," that in enacting the constitution it may limit its regular legislative power, that its constituent actions stand above its legislative actions. Of course while the Knesset's lawmaking power (its "legislative hat") is continuous and everlasting, its power to enact a constitution (its "constituent hat") is temporary and will terminate when the Knesset, as a constituent authority, determines that the constitutional undertaking has been completed. The constitution itself will set forth the means by which it may be revised and corrected. This conclusion—the fruit of the recognition—is also the best explanation for our social-legal history from the establishment of the State until today.

39.   * * * [T]he constituent authority of the Knesset is always in the hands of the people. Indeed a constitution is not the act of a Government which endows its people with a constitution. The constitution is the act of people, which creates the government. It is the people that determines—according to its social viewpoint during the course of its history—in whose hands rests the highest authority of the State, and what is its rule of recognition. The Court gives expression to this social determination. The Court is the faithful interpreter of the people's will as expressed in the constitution. The Court attempts to give the best possible interpretation for the entire national experience. The existence of a constitution is not a logical matter but a social phenomenon. The Court interprets the "social facts" and concludes from them as to the constituent power of the Knesset. This interpretation is not the result of intellectual construction. It is the expression of the social reality. * * *

[I]t is well accepted for courts to test the constitutionality of amendments. More than one such amendment has been invalidated as unconstitutional, and this has been not only for "formal" reasons (such a failure to meet majority requirements) but for substantive reasons as well (see the opinion of the Supreme Court of India in the case of *Kesavananda v. State of Kerala*, A.I.R. 1973 S.C. 146 [see Chapter 10, Section A.]). Consider, in this regard, the following words of the Constitutional Court of Germany:

> Laws are not constitutional merely because they have been passed, in conformity with procedural provisions * * * They must be substantively compatible with the highest values of a free and democratic order, i.e., the constitutional order of values, and must also conform to unwritten fundamental constitutional principles as well as the fundamental decisions of the Basic Law. (6 BVerfGE 32 (1957)).
>
> * * *

[W]hen a judge must ask himself—while taking into account the entire picture—what is the look of today's Israeli community, against the background of the multi-faceted constitutional enterprise undertaken since the establishment of the State, and in light of the two latest Basic Laws and the reactions to them, my answer is that the Israeli Knesset is endowed with constituent authority. Indeed the judge's task is to give our legal and social history the explanation that best accords with the legal and social data.

III.   Judicial Review of Constitutionality

A.   Constitutional Supremacy and Judicial Review

The constitution is the supreme norm of the legal system. A regular law may be permitted to conflict with the provisions of the constitution only if it meets the *criteria* provided in the constitution itself. What is the fate of a law that does not meet these criteria? What is the remedy for unconstitutional law? The answer to these questions depends first and foremost upon the provisions of the constitution itself. Often the constitution sets forth—and is empowered to set forth—the legal sanctions imposed upon an unconstitutional law. Thus, for example, the "Supremacy Clause" of the Canadian Charter of Rights and Freedoms (Section (1)52) invalidates conflicting legislation that does not meet the requirements of the Constitution as follows:

> "The Constitution of Canada is the supreme law of Canada, and any law that is inconsistent with the provisions of the Constitution is to the extent of the inconsistency, of no force or effect."

Similar provisions are found in many modern constitutions, particularly those of European countries after the First World War. Such provisions proliferated in the constitutions of European countries after the Second World War and the victory over the Nazis. One of the lessons of the Second World War was that constitutional supremacy and judicial review of constitutionality are potent weapons against the enemies of democracy. But what is the rule when the constitution is silent in this matter? The answer to this question depends upon the culture and tradition of the legal system. It is determined by the adjudication rule of the particular legal system. (See H.L.A. Hart, *The Concept of Law* p. 96). Thus, for example, it may be recognized—as was the tradition in nineteenth century Europe—that the constitution binds the institutions of the government. However, noncompliance with a constitutional directive does not lead to invalidation of the law, and the court is not empowered to impose the sanction of voiding such legislation. According to this view, the obligation to ensure compliance with the constitution rests with the government institutions themselves, and if they violate this obligation, the sanctions are in the hands of the public on election day. But this is not the only view, nor is it the most widely held. Today this is the minority view. Indeed, a particular legal tradition and culture are likely to lead to the conclusion that constitutional science in this matter should be interpreted as calling for the invalidation of conflicting legislation and to the concomitant conclusion that the determination of whether such a conflict exists rests not with the legislature but with the court. Under this view, constitutional silence requires judicial review and authorizes the Court to declare unconstitutional legislation void. [This point is buttressed by a discussion of *Marbury v. Madison* above.]

D.   Judicial Review of Constitutionality in Israel

77.   * * * The two Basic Laws contain no "supremacy clause." What is the law in this situation? It seems to me that our legal tradition requires us to conclude that the remedy for an unconstitutional law is its invalidation and that the courts have been endowed with the authority to declare it so. Just as a regulation that conflicts with a statute is void and may be declared as such by the court, so also should be the case when a regular law conflicts with a Basic Law; the law is void and the court is empowered to declare it so.

E.   The Rationale for Judicial Review of Constitutionality

(1)   Judicial Review and the Rule of Law

78.   The doctrine of judicial review of constitutionality is based upon the "rule of law", or, more correctly, the rule of the constitution * * * The central role of the court in a democratic society is "to protect the rule of law. This means, inter alia, that it must enforce the law in the institutions of the government and it must ensure that the government acts according to the law". When a given legal system includes a constitution, the "rule of law" requires that the sovereignty of the constitution be protected. Thus the Knesset, in using its constituent authority endowed the State with Basic Laws. In the normative hierarchy the Basic Laws are paramount. In order to fulfill the Knesset's directives, regular legislation that conflicts with a Basic Law must be invalidated * * *

* * *

(3)   Judicial Review and Democracy

80.   But is judicial review democratic? Is it democratic that the court—whose judges, are not elected by the people and do not represent a social and political platform—be empowered to invalidate a law enacted by elected officials? The formal answer is simple. The court in its judicial review of the constitutionality of law gives effect to the constitution and the Basic Law. Hamilton addressed this point over two hundred years ago, (in *The Federalist* No. 78).

In a similar spirit Rawls stated the following:

"A supreme court fits into this idea of dualist constitutional democracy as one of the institutional devices to protect the higher law. By applying public reason the court is to prevent that law from being eroded by the legislation of transient majorities, or more likely, by organized and well-situated narrow interests skilled at getting their way. If the court assumes this role and effectively carries it out, it is incorrect to say that it is straightforwardly antidemocratic. It is indeed antimajoritarian with respect to ordinary law, for a court with judicial review can hold such law unconstitutional. Nevertheless, the higher authority of the people supports that. The court is not antimajoritarian with respect to higher law when its decisions reasonably accord with the constitution itself and with its amendments and politically mandated interpretations." (J. Rawls, *Political Liberalism*, 233 (1993)).

However, the formal answer alone is not sufficient.

In fact when the majority strips the minority of its human rights, democracy is impaired. (See J. Ely, *Democracy and Distrust: A Theory of*

Judicial Review (1980)). Judicial review of constitutionality therefore prevails over what is known as the "counter-majoritarian dilemma." One way to accomplish this is by emphasizing that when judges interpret the constitution and invalidate contradictory laws they give expression to the fundamental values of society that have developed over time. Thus the court safeguards constitutional democracy and maintains the delicate balance upon which it is based. Remove majority rule from constitutional democracy and its essence is harmed. Remove the sovereignty of fundamental values from constitutional democracy and its existence is called into question. Judicial review of constitutionality enables the society to be true to itself and to honor its basic conceptions. This is the basis for the substantive legitimacy of judicial review. This is also the true basis for the principle of constitutionality itself. We are bound by the constitution that was enacted in the past because it expresses the fundamental outlook of modern society. It may therefore be said that each generation enacts the constitution anew. By means of judicial review we are loyal to the fundamental values that we took upon ourselves in the past, that reflect our essence in the present and that will direct our national development as a society in the future. It is therefore no wonder that judicial review is now developing. The majority of enlightened democratic states have judicial review. It is difficult to imagine the United States, Canada, Germany, Japan, Spain, Italy, and many other nations without judicial review of constitutionality. The Twentieth Century is the century of judicial review.

* * *

(4) *Judicial Review and Judicial Objectivity*

81. Judicial review expresses the values of the constitution. By means of judicial *review* the judge makes manifest the ideals of the society in which he lives. He expresses the fundamental conceptions of society as it moves through the shifting sands of history. The judge in particular—who does not face election—and therefore benefits from judicial independence, is worthy of this task. It is because the judge is not elected by the people and does not present before them a social and political platform that he is qualified to express the deepest perceptions of society without being influenced by the needs of the moment. For this purpose he must operate with judicial objectivity. He must express the outlook of society even if it is not his personal outlook. * * *

Declaring a law unconstitutional is a serious matter. Such a declaration would seem to undermine the will of today's majority. It may be justified by the supremacy of the constitution and its values. The justification applies when the judiciary, gives expression to the values of society as they are understood by the culture and tradition of the people as they move forward through history. This justification does not, however operate when the judge expresses his subjective beliefs. Indeed judicial objectivity is part and parcel of the basis of judicial review of constitutionality. In granting weight to different considerations the judge aspires to the best of his ability to achieve judicial objectivity. He reflects neither his personal values nor his personal considerations. The judge reflects "the values of the State of Israel as a Jewish democratic state." (*Eisenberg v. Housing Ministry,* 47(2) P.D. 229 (1993)). Indeed, this most difficult task can be achieved only by the professional judge, who has absorbed through years of experience the need to guarantee judicial objectivity, and benefits from total independence.

Notes and Questions

1. Contrast the respective approaches of Chief Justice Marshall in *Marbury* and Chief Justice Barak in *Migdal.* Whereas the former's opinion is circumspect and open to different interpretations, the latter appears much more forceful and unequivocal. Both opinions agree that the constitution is hierarchically superior to ordinary laws, a position generally shared by all constitutional regimes that regard the constitution as legally binding rather than merely as a political blueprint. Beyond that, however, whereas *Marbury* asserts that judges are empowered to adjudicate constitutional claims as part of their mandate to decide legal disputes, *Migdal* suggests that the very logic and cogency of a constitutional system based on the rule of law requires that judges be responsible for interpreting the constitution and for invalidating laws they deem incompatible with it. Do you agree? And assuming you do, is it nonetheless advisable for judges to step into that role without express authorization granted by the constitution itself?

2. *Marbury* established that the USSC could adjudicate constitutional claims and that its decisions were binding on the parties before it. This has been generally accepted ever since, but the broader implications of *Marbury* are still a matter of dispute. Thus, for example, if a local police officer arrests a citizen for criticizing the government and if the Court decrees that the arrest in question was in violation of the citizen's freedom of speech, then it is clear that the local government and citizen involved are bound by the decision. But what about another local government and another citizen in a similar case? See *Cooper v. Aaron,* 358 U.S. 1 (1958) (governor of Arkansas argued that the USSC decision holding Kansas's law mandating racial segregation in public schools to be unconstitutional was not applicable to Arkansas as it was not a party to the Kansas litigation). In rejecting the governor's argument, a unanimous USSC stressed that *Marbury* had established "the principle that the Federal judiciary is supreme in the exposition of the law of the Constitution, and that principle has ever since been respected by this court and the country as a permanent and indispensable feature of our constitutional system." Some scholars, however, have criticized this last statement as confusing *Marbury*'s "assertion of judicial *authority* to interpret the Constitution with judicial *exclusiveness*." Gerald Gunther, *The Subtle Vices of the "Passive Virtues"—A Comment on Principle and Expedience in Judicial Review,* 64 Colum. L. Rev. 1, 25 n.155 (1964) (emphasis added). In spite of the Court's broad statement in *Cooper v. Aaron,* the issue of exclusiveness of judicial review is still heatedly debated. See, e.g., Edwin Meese III, *The Law of the Constitution,* 61 Tulane L. Rev. 979 (1987) (arguing that since the three branches of the national government are co-equal, the U.S. President and the Congress are as authoritative interpreters of the Constitution as is the Supreme Court, and drawing a distinction between "the Constitution"—to which all branches of government are equally bound—and "constitutional law," i.e., the law that emerges in judicial interpretations of the Constitution—which is binding on the parties before the courts but not on the other branches of the national

government). Does the distinction drawn by Professor Meese (who was the U.S. Attorney General during the Reagan presidency) strike you as sound and helpful? For a more general discussion of who is bound by constitutional adjudication in various different systems of constitutional review, see Section B. below. Finally, contrast the issues left open in the U.S. with the precise prescriptions concerning constitutional review and the authoritativeness of such review under many more-recent constitutions, such as the German Basic Law (Art. 93) and the French 1958 Constitution, Art. 62 (2): "The decisions of the Constitutional Council shall be binding on the governmental authorities and all administrative and jurisdictional authorities."

3.   Lacking a textual constitutional provision on which to rely, Chief Justice Barak bases his conclusion that the Supreme Court of Israel is the authoritative interpreter of claims arising under that country's Basic Laws on two principal considerations. The first focuses on the "culture and tradition of the legal system involved" in general and its "adjudication rule" in particular. The second focuses on the very logic of constitutional government and refers to the seminal work of Hans Kelsen.

Kelsen's views were particularly influential in Europe as he was instrumental in introducing judicial review of the constitution there in the early part of the twentieth century, starting with Austria in 1920. European judicial review, as launched in Europe by Kelsen, relies on a specialized constitutional court and stands in sharp contrast with the older American approach. See Hans Kelsen, *Judicial Review of Legislation: A Comparative Study of the Austrian and the American Constitution,* 4 Journal of Politics 183 (1942). This contrast is further examined in the articles by Louis Favoreu and Alec Stone Sweet excerpted below. Moreover, whereas Kelsen's general theory of the constitution and of the need for judicial review is largely compatible with different systems of constitutional adjudication, its conceptual underpinnings are steeped in the European model.

In the broadest terms Kelsen conceives a valid legal system as involving a hierarchy of norms shaped as a pyramid, with the constitution to which he also refers as the *gründnorm* (the basic norm)—standing at the very top. See Hans Kelsen, *General Theory of Law and State* 124 (Anders Wedberg trans., 1961). Moreover, for Kelsen, the constitution both sets the procedures for adoption of legitimate infraconstitutional laws and imposes substantial constraints on the subject matter or content of valid legislation.

With parliamentary democracy in mind, Kelsen argues that adherence to the requisite hierarchy emanating from the constitution requires a check on the laws passed by the legislature. That check must be provided by an independent institution; and since traditionally the judicial power in Europe was not sufficiently independent from the other branches of government, ordinary judges could not be entrusted with the task. The institution recommended by Kelsen, and later developed throughout Europe and beyond, is the constitutional court, a specialized body made up of independent judges who do not ordinarily come from the ranks of the judiciary. While the constitutional court is an institution designed to check the legislature and control that the latter's enactments are constitutional, it is unclear whether its function is ultimately legislative rather than judicial. In discussing the constitutional court, Kelsen asserts that "[t]he annulment of a law is a legislative function, an act—so to speak—of negative legislation. A court which is competent to abolish laws—individually or generally—functions as a negative legislator." *Id.* at 268. Particularly, after reviewing the materials on judicial interpretation of the constitution below, do you agree that judicial review of constitutional issues is akin to negative legislation? Or do courts also, for all practical purposes, engage in positive legislation when they provide certain interpretive glosses on statutes they evaluate in terms of compatibility with the constitution? Or else, is judicial interpretation altogether different than legislation?

4.   Inasmuch as constitutional review may be more akin to legislation—albeit negative legislation—than to mere application of objective rules and standards, it may seem prone to undermining democracy. Thus a statute adopted by a large majority in a democratically elected parliament may be struck down as unconstitutional by a small number of unelected judges serving on the constitutional court. This raises the vexing problems of democratic legitimacy of judicial review and constitutional interpretation leading to invalidation or to what amounts to a "rewriting" of popular laws. In the U.S., the problem in question is known as the "countermajoritarian" difficulty, and it has generated an immense literature. See, e.g., Alexander Bickel, *The Least Dangerous Branch* (2d ed. 1986) (justifying judicial review notwithstanding that it is countermajoritarian); and John Hart Ely, *Democracy and Distrust* (1980) (defending judicial review inasmuch as it buttresses, and makes up for flaws in, the democratic process). Chief Justice Barak acknowledges that judicial review is countermajoritarian but emphasizes that democracy should not be reduced to majoritarianism. Instead, according to him, legitimate democracy depends as much on adherence to fundamental rights and the rule of law as on reliance on majoritarian legislation. In spite of Chief Justice Barak's justification of judicial review in terms of Israel's legal tradition, logic, and democracy, the sweeping powers of constitutional review established in *Migdal* have led to an undermining of the Court's legitimacy as a large segment of the Israeli population increasingly regards the Court in general, and its Chief Justice in particular, as furthering a contested and divisive political agenda rather than merely upholding entrenched constitutional norms. As a result of this ongoing controversy, the Court has retrenched somewhat from the activism manifest in the *Migdal* decision.

Do the Israeli Supreme Court's legitimacy problems stem from a lack of precise delimitation of the powers of judicial review or, rather, from the lack of a written constitution? In contrast to Israel, the U.S. enjoys both a written constitution and broad consensus concerning the legitimacy of judicial review as such if not on the exclusiveness or scope of such review. Nonetheless, the USSC is by no means immune from attacks on the grounds that it is too political. Unlike in Israel, however, in the U.S. the controversy is much less over judicial review itself than over its scope and over the proper cannons of constitutional interpretation. Could that latter controversy be altogether eliminated or significantly reduced by means of detailed constitutional provisions regarding the powers, scope, and extent of judicial review of constitutional claims? Even in Germany, where the Constitution explicitly institutes the Federal Constitutional Court as its authoritative interpreter and where the scope of judicial review is precisely delimited (See German Basic Law, Art. 93), the Court is not immune to the charge that it unduly impacts on democratic politics. Indeed the combination of the powers of parliamentary minorities to challenge laws they oppose as unconstitutional before the Constitutional Court and the latter's broad conception of its powers of interpretation have led to the perception that frustrated legislative minorities often get a second chance at defeating legislation they unsuccessfully opposed in Parliament by persuading the Court to declare such legislation unconstitutional. Does this mean that ultimately it makes little difference whether the constitution is precise, vague, or silent regarding judicial review?

5.   One way of dealing with the problem of democratic legitimacy of judicial review is by denying such review irrevocable finality. In most constitutional democracies, the constraints imposed as a result of judicial interpretation of the constitution cannot be altered except by means of constitutional amendments. In Canada, however, the Constitution allows for parliamentary override of specific provisions of the Charter of Rights and Freedoms and, by extension, of judicial interpretations of such provisions. See the Canada Constitution Act of 1982, Sec 33. According to this override provision, the federal Parliament or a provincial legislature may declare by a simple majority that legislation contrary to a judicial interpretation of a right protected by the Constitution will be valid notwithstanding the conflict. The override involved cannot be extended to those rights that are essential to the democratic process itself, and it expires automatically after five years, though it can be extended by new legislation at that time. Although the override provision has been sometimes used by the Quebec legislature, it has had little impact in the rest of Canada. Is it significant, in this respect, that Quebec has not ratified the 1982 Constitution Act while the rest of the country has? It has been argued that availability of the override provision has both afforded greater latitude to the Canadian Supreme Court and infused its decisions with greater legitimacy. Indeed the Court need not worry as much as it would have absent any override because it knows that if its decisions run deeply counter to the prevailing consensus, the legislature can act to remedy the situation. On the other hand legislatures (outside Quebec) are reluctant to trigger the override as they run the risk of being perceived as lacking respect for the fundamental rights enshrined in the Constitution. See Peter W. Hogg, *Constitutional Law of Canada* 914–17 (4th ed. 1997). Do you agree that existence of an override provision paradoxically enhances the legitimacy of judicial review and reinforces its finality? Or do you suspect that the reason for stability in Canada is that, outside of Quebec, there is broad consensus on constitutional rights?

B.   PRINCIPAL MODELS OF CONSTITUTIONAL ADJUDICATION

B.1.   THE CENTRALIZED vs. DECENTRALIZED MODEL: ABSTRACT vs. CONCRETE REVIEW

As to the structure of the courts dealing with constitutional review, there are two principal models of judicial review relating to the constitution: the centralized model, which originated in Europe, and the decentralized one, first established in the U.S. In terms of subject matter,

[t]here are three basic types of review jurisdiction: abstract review, concrete review, and the individual constitutional complaint procedure.

Abstract review is 'abstract' because the review of legislation takes place in the absence of litigation, in American parlance, in the absence of a concrete case or controversy. Concrete review is 'concrete' because the review of legislation, or other public act, constitutes a separate stage in an ongoing judicial process (litigation in the ordinary courts). In individual complaints, a private individual alleges the violation of a constitutional right by a public act or governmental official, and requests redress from the court for this violation.

Abstract review processes result in decision's on the constitutionality of legislation that has been adopted by parliament but has not yet entered into force (France), or that has been adopted and promulgated, but not yet applied (Germany, Italy, Spain).

Alec Stone Sweet, *Governing with Judges: Constitutional Politics in Europe* 44–45 (2000).

Louis Favoreu, CONSTITUTIONAL REVIEW IN EUROPE, in CONSTITUTIONALISM AND RIGHTS: THE INFLUENCE OF THE UNITED STATES CONSTITUTION ABROAD

38, 40–42, 44–46, 51–56, 58–59 (Louis Henkin and Albert J. Rosenthal eds., 1990)

* * *

TWO MODELS OF CONSTITUTIONAL REVIEW

European and American models of constitutional review differ principally in how the system of constitutional review is organized. The difference between the two models has been summarized as follows:

One might distinguish two broad types of judicial control over the constitutionality of legislation: (a) the "decentralized" type gives the power of control to *all the judicial organs* of a given legal system. This has also been called the "American" system of control * * * (b) the "centralized" type of control confines the power of review to *one single judicial organ*. By analogy, the "centralized" type may be referred to as "Austrian."[6]

In the American system, constitutional review is lodged in the judicial system as a whole, and is not distinct from the administration of justice generally. All disputes, whatever their nature, are decided by the same courts, by the same procedures, in essentially similar circumstances. Constitutional matters may be found in any case and do not receive special treatment. At bottom, then, there is no particular "constitutional litigation," anymore than there is administrative litigation; there is no reason to distinguish among cases or controversies raised before the same court. Moreover, in de Tocqueville's words, "An American court can only adjudicate when there is litigation; it deals only with a particular case, and it cannot act until its jurisdiction is invoked."[7] Review by the court, therefore, leads to a judgment limited in principle to the case decided, although a decision by the Supreme Court has general authority for the lower courts.

---

6. Cappelletti and Cohen, *Comparative Constitutional Law*, p. 14.

7. [Alexis de Tocqueville, *De la démocratie en Amerique* 78 (1835) (1963).]

In the European system, constitutional review is organized differently. It is common in Europe to differentiate among categories of litigation (administrative, civil, commercial, social, or criminal) and to have them decided by different courts. Constitutional litigation, too, is distinguished from other litigation and is dealt with separately. Constitutional issues are decided by a court specially established for this purpose and enjoying a monopoly on constitutional litigation. That means that, unlike United States courts, the ordinary German, Austrian, Italian, Spanish, or French courts cannot decide constitutional issues. At most they can refer an issue to the constitutional court for a decision; the decision of the constitutional court will be binding on the ordinary courts.

In Europe, moreover, in general, the constitutionality of a law is examined in the abstract, not, as in the United States, in the context of a specific case; therefore the lawfulness of legislation is considered in general, without taking into account the precise circumstances of any particular case. This is because in Europe constitutional issues are generally raised by a public authority (the government, members of Parliament, courts) and not by individuals.

As a consequence, the effect of the decision is *erga omnes,* i.e., applicable to all, absolute. When a European constitutional judge declares an act unconstitutional, his declaration has the effect of annulling the act, of making it disappear from the legal order. It is no longer in force, it has no further legal effect for anybody, and sometimes the ruling of unconstitutionality operates retroactively. Kelsen characterized the constitutional court as a "negative legislator," as distinguished from the "positive legislator," the parliament.

The United States model and the European model, however, are two means to the same end. Both have to fulfill the same tasks:

- Above all, the United States and the European systems protect fundamental rights against infringement by governmental authority, particularly the legislature. The means are different, but the ends are the same and the results similar

- Both systems generally try to maintain a balance between the state and the entities of which it is composed. In a federal state, constitutional review serves that function whether the system of review follows the United States model or the European one. The United States Supreme Court and the German Constitutional Tribunal play a similar role in maintaining the balance between the federal government and the member states.

- United States and European constitutional courts perform the same tasks, as contemplated by their respective constitutions, when they protect the separation of powers—the division of authority between various organs of the state, whether between the executive and the legislature, or between the chambers of Parliament * * *

The United States Model in Europe Between the Wars

A different model of constitutional review emerged in Europe because in various European countries the United States model could not strike root. At the beginning of the twentieth century, several European states wished to adopt the American model, but despite numerous efforts, the "graft" proved unsuccessful. * * *

Why the Graft Failed to Work

The graft of the United States system onto the European legal and political order was not successful * * * [One reason for that failure is that i]n Europe, the law is identified with legislation, whereas in the United States there is still a substantial common law and, in the past at least, legislation was seen as an exception to the common law. In Europe, courts cannot interpret the constitution and apply their interpretation to legislation, whereas in the United States the opposite attitude was established at the beginning by Chief Justice Marshall.

In the United States, the Constitution is sacred. In Europe, "the law"—legislation is sacred.

A second reason for the failure of the graft is the inability of the ordinary European judge to exercise constitutional review. As Mauro Capelletti stressed,

> The bulk of Europe's judiciary seems psychologically incapable of the value-oriented, quasi-political functions involved in judicial review. It should be borne in mind that continental judges usually are "career" judges who enter the judiciary at a very early age and are promoted to the higher courts largely on the basis of seniority. Their professional training develops skills in technical rather than policy-oriented application of statutes. The exercise of judicial review, however, is rather different from [the] usual judicial function of applying the law is * * * [T]he task of fulfilling the Constitution often demands a higher sense of discretion than the task of interpreting ordinary statutes. That is certainly one reason why Kelsen, * * * considered it to be a legislative rather than a purely judicial activity.[17]
>
> * * *

Another reason why the United States model was rejected by some European countries between the two world wars was that constitutions, in those countries at that time, were not in fact supreme and binding on parliaments. This was clear with respect to France during the Third Republic:

> In America, a court decision declaring a law unconstitutional has the effect of raising an impassable barrier since the legislature is powerless by itself to modify the constitution * * * In France, on the contrary, the Parliament, if confronted with a court decision of unconstitutionality, could rather easily overcome the resistance of the court: the parliamentary majorities that adopted the law paralyzed by the judicial action have only to reaffirm their original measure by a simple majority in order to make their will prevail * * * *In such circumstances, it is likely that the judiciary would hesitate to refuse to apply a law on grounds of its unconstitutionality.*

17. [Mauro Capelletti, *Judicial Review in the Contemporary World* 45 (1971).]

Similarly, in Germany under the Weimar Constitution, laws passed with the special majority provided for in Article 76 of the Constitution could "materially depart" from the Constitution to the prejudice of fundamental rights.

Models of Review in Contemporary Europe

After World War II, Western European countries rebuilt their political institutions, with particular concern to assure respect for fundamental rights. Inevitably, the influence of the United States was strongly felt, both for reasons of international politics and because the success of its constitutional system was commonly recognized. The influence of the ideas that the United States and France had developed and helped spread was reflected in new national constitutions and in international instruments—the Universal Declaration of Human Rights, and, in Europe, the European Convention on Human Rights. New European constitutions reflected also the appeal of United States institutions, especially judicial review. In time, countries of western and northern Europe (except Great Britain, the Netherlands, Finland, and Luxembourg) moved toward some system of constitutional review. Some—the Scandinavian countries, Greece, and Switzerland—adopted the United States model; others—Austria, the Federal Republic of Germany, Italy, and France—opted for the European model.

* * *

The European Model

"It is impossible * * * to propose a uniform solution for all possible constitutions: constitutional review will have to be organized according to the specific characteristics of each of them."[35] Kelsen's wise warning was followed by countries establishing systems of constitutional review. Although many countries have followed the European model, each has tailored its system to its own needs and circumstances.

Countries that have adopted the European model include Austria (since 1920), the Federal Republic of Germany (1951), Italy (1956), France (1958), Cyprus (1960), Turkey (1961), Yugoslavia (1963), Portugal (1976 and 1983), Spain (1980), Belgium (1984), and Poland (1985). I consider the principal examples.

Austria

The Austrian High Constitutional Court, the oldest in Europe, was established in 1920 according to a plan developed by Hans Kelsen, who was a member of the Court and its general reporter until 1929. The Court was suppressed on March 13, 1938, when Germany invaded Austria, but was reestablished in the constitutional law of October 12, 1945.

The Court has jurisdiction over several matters: elections, conflicts between courts, and litigation between the federal state and the *Länder* (states). It acts as an administrative court to review administrative acts alleged to violate rights guaranteed by the constitution. It acts also as a

---

35. [Hans Kelsen, *La garantie juridictionnelle de la Constitution*, 45 Revue du droit public et de la science politique 201 (1928).]

high court of justice to bring to trial the head of state or ministers accused by the house of Parliament.

The Court can exercise judicial review at the request of any of the following: a *Land* government, higher courts, a third of the members of the National Council (or a third of the members of a *Land* legislature), or, under some conditions, individuals. The Court may also raise constitutional issues on its own initiative. The Court's case law, developed over the last sixty years, is extensive, particularly in relation to fundamental rights. The impact of its decisions on the legal and political system is strong even though the Court's decisions are not binding on ordinary courts, unlike the decisions of the German and Spanish high courts.

About 90 percent of the registered or decided cases of the Court in 1982 dealt with the constitutionality of administrative acts. This is probably due to the fact that it is easier to challenge the constitutionality of an administrative act than to bring a case by direct petition.

The Federal Republic of Germany

[See the discussion by Wolfgang Zeidler below.]

Italy

The Italian Constitutional Court was established by the 1947 Constitution, and came into the force in 1956. The Court is composed of fifteen judges appointed equally by the Parliament, the President of the Republic, and the Supreme Courts (the Council of State, the Court of Cassation, and the Court of Auditors).

The Constitutional Court has jurisdiction over conflicts of jurisdiction between various state authorities and between regions; over allegations against the President of the Republic, the President of the Council of Ministers, and the ministers; the acceptance of abrogative referendums; and the constitutional review of laws. This last area of jurisdiction is by far the most important. Constitutional issues regarding laws are referred to the Court by the ordinary civil, administrative, and commercial courts that would have had to apply to them.

The number of cases submitted to the Court is noteworthy. In 1983, 1,100 issues were referred to the Court, which made 400 decisions as to the constitutionality of laws. In 1984, out of 1,489 cases registered, 1,384 (93 percent) were referred to the Court by ordinary courts. The other areas of jurisdiction appear less important. Since ordinary courts have a tendency to refer difficult cases to the Constitutional Court, the Court has been increasingly overwhelmed by these issues.

Clearly, the Court plays a large legal and political role.

France

[See the discussion by John Bell below.]

Spain

The Spanish Constitutional Tribunal was established by the 1978 Constitution, and started its work in 1980. It is composed of twelve judges appointed by the king, four upon nomination by Congress, four by

Senate, two by the government, and two by the General Council of the Judicial Power.

The Constitutional Tribunal has jurisdiction over conflicts between state authorities; the petition of *amparo* against administrative acts and court decisions interfering with fundamental rights; the lawfulness of treaties in the light of the Constitution; and the constitutionality of laws. In this last category, issues can be raised by the President of the Government, by fifty deputies or fifty senators, by the authorities of autonomous communities, or by the people's defender (*defensor del pueblo*). Constitutional issues can be raised by courts when they are confronted with them during litigation. The Constitutional Tribunal's role already appears important, particularly concerning respect for the balance between the state and the autonomous communities.

The writ of *amparo*, the origins of which go back to the Kingdom of Aragon, is an institution that has been used since the nineteenth century in Latin America and was adopted in the Spanish Constitution of 1931. Under the present Spanish Constitution, an individual may invoke this writ to request the Constitutional Tribunal to assure the protection of his or her fundamental rights against an administrative act or a judgment of a court, when the ordinary courts have not provided such protection. (In fact, the writ of *amparo* is invoked particularly against judicial acts.) *Amparo* cannot be invoked directly for review of the constitutionality of a statute (unlike constitutional review in the Federal Republic of Germany), but the chamber of the Constitutional Tribunal that reviews writs of *amparo* may refer questions on the constitutionality of an underlying statute to the full court. The petition of *amparo* is the basis of 90 percent of the registered cases. This action is popular because claimants doubt the ability of ordinary courts to formulate proper constitutional principles.

* * *

The Significance of the Differences Between the Two Models

Differences between the United States and European models of constitutional review are mostly clearly seen in the way such review is organized, which can be explained by differences in the institutions and political culture of the different countries. Are these differences merely technical, or do they have theoretical significance? Have they made a difference in practice? Are there convergences between the two systems? There has been no thorough study of these questions, but some preliminary observations are now in order.

The fact and the form of constitutional review pose the fundamental question—first addressed and resolved by the United States—of how to limit power, executive as well as legislative, and reduce confrontation between judge and legislature. The United States has resolved these problems in its own way by a diffused, or decentralized, system of constitutional review. Europe, unable to adopt the American system, has provided a solution by creating constitutional review that is concentrated or centralized. From a theoretical perspective, differences between the two systems may reflect different conceptions of the separation of powers. In the American model, limitations on executive and legislative power have been achieved by the progressive recognition of a third power, the judiciary, described as "the least dangerous branch." That third power does not exist in most European countries. European constitutional theory acknowledges only executive and legislative power. There is no recognition of a "judicial power" and judges do not enjoy the legitimacy and authority of their American counterparts.

It was therefore necessary to build—following Kelsen—a system in which constitutional review, entrusted to a single court, constitutes not a third parallel power but one above the others that is charged with monitoring the three essential functions of the state (executive, legislative, and judicial) to ensure that they are exercised within the limits set by the Constitution. That has been clearly explained with the reference to the Italian Constitutional Court:[43]

[The Court] is neither part of the judicial order, nor part of the judicial organization in its widest sense: * * * the Constitutional Court remains outside the traditional categories of state power. It is an independent power whose functions consist in insuring that the Constitution is respected in all areas.

* * *

Conclusion: Does Constitutionalism "Work Well" in Europe?

Is constitutionalism, the doctrine of constitutional supremacy which owes so much to the United States, well established in Europe—thanks, notably, to constitutional review?

One can say that constitutionalism has made great progress in countries that have established constitutional courts. Because of their decisions, constitutional courts have engendered respect for constitutions and for fundamental rights that did not exist previously and that are still absent in countries that lack an efficient system of constitutional review (e.g., the Scandinavian countries), even though these countries proclaim the supremacy of their constitutions. The recent Spanish, Portuguese, and Greek constitutions show that modern constitutions in democratic countries necessarily include constitutional supremacy and constitutional review. The effective supremacy of the constitution is always affirmed. It is a fundamental change from the situation that prevailed before World War II; one that cannot be reversed. The constitution has finally become "holy writ" in Europe as it is in the United States.

Can one compare the results of the American and European systems of judicial review? It is difficult, since their contexts are so different. * * *

Comparing the systems nevertheless suggests some conclusions. First, the European system seems to have the advantage of isolating important constitutional issues for decision by a specialized court, which is free from other duties and can devote the time required for this delicate task. The constitutionality of a national law is taken immediate-

---

43. Vezio Crisafulli, "Le système de contrôle de constitutionnalité des lois en   Italie," R.D.P. (1968), No. 84, p. 130.

ly to the constitutional court and does not have to go through the various steps of the jurisdictional ladder * * *

On the other hand, one might ask whether—with a view to strengthening constitutionalism—the European system is as successful as is the American system in spreading constitutional rules throughout the various branches of law. In the European system the ordinary judge is excluded from the process of constitutional review, although he can sometimes set the process in motion (as in Italy, Spain, or Germany). If the judge later has to apply the decision of a constitutional court and follow its interpretation, he is not in the same position as are the lower courts in the United States in relation to the Supreme Court. In the European system, constitutional courts cannot even impose sanctions if their decisions are disregarded * * *

Notes and Questions

1. Of the European constitutional courts discussed above, the French Constitutional Council seems by far the most political. Its function under France's 1958 Constitution was to ensure, above all, that Parliament not infringe on the newly expanded powers of the executive concentrated in the strong presidency crafted for the Fifth Republic's principal architect, Charles de Gaulle. As Professor Alec Stone Sweet notes in *Governing with Judges: Constitutional Politics in Europe* 41 (2000):

> the new constitutionalism emerged [in France] by a * * * circuitous route. * * * The Gaullists replaced France's traditional, British-style, parliamentary system with a 'mixed presidential-parliamentary' one, strengthening the executive. The constitution established a Constitutional Council, but its purpose was to guarantee the dominance of the executive (the government) over a weak parliament. Beginning in 1971, however, the Council began to assert its independence. In that year, for the first time, it declared a government-sponsored law unconstitutional on the grounds that the law violated constitutional rights. This decision paved the way for the incorporation of a charter of rights into the 1958 constitution, a charter that the Council has taken upon itself to enforce. Thus, for the first time, and against the wishes of de Gaulle, his agents, and the other political parties in 1958, France has both an effective bill of rights and an effective constitutional court. [However, in France there is abstract review only; the jurisdiction of the Constitutional Council is limited to Acts of Parliament and only before the promulgation of the law (preliminary review).]

Alec Stone Sweet specifies:

> [A]lthough its rule in reviewing legislation was that of a referee engaged in settling conflicts between the executive and the legislature, *the Council was not meant to be a fair or impartial referee* (any more than the constitution was designed to be fair or impartial). Its field of play was to be exclusively parliamentary space; it was to have jurisdiction only over legislative and *not* executive acts; and a proposal to balance the equation—to allow legislative authorities to refer executive acts to the Council—was not seriously considered. Moreover, the mode of recruitment proposed all but guaranteed that a majority of the Council's members would be active supporters of the government. Indeed, the

government's working draft (as well as the final product) strictly limited access to the institution for rulings on constitutionality of proposed legislation to four officials—the president of the Republic, the prime minister, the president of the Senate, and the president of the National Assembly * * *.

Alec Stone Sweet, *The Birth of Judicial Politics in France* 48 (1992).

2.   Professor Stone Sweet further observes that:

1.   Constitutional adjudication * * * is implicated in the exercise of legislative power. If in exercising review authority, the judges simply controlled the integrity of parliamentary procedures, and not the substance of legislation, the judges would be relatively minor policy-makers (akin to Kelsen's 'negative legislator'). But the judges possess jurisdiction over rights which are, by definition, substantive constraints on law-making powers. The political parties thus transferred their own entirely unresolved problem—what is the nature and purpose of any given rights provision, and what is the normative relationship of that provision to the rest of the constitutional text?—to judges. This transfer constitutes a massive, virtually open-ended delegation of policy-making authority. Similarly, review jurisdiction organizes the elaboration of higher law rules governing federalism and regional autonomy in Germany, Italy, and Spain. To the extent that it is costly or difficult to activate constitutional review of legislation, the importance of review within policy processes, and the authority of judges over outcomes, would be mitigated. But initiating abstract review is virtually without cost for oppositions; concrete review procedures entail delays for the litigants, but other costs are essentially borne by the state; and individual complaints can be scribbled by anyone on notebook paper. If it were relatively easy for the governing majority to overturn the case law of the court, or to curb the judges' powers, the court's authority over the legislature might be fleeting * * *. [However, the only direct control over constitutional judges is thorough constitutional amendment, which in most cases is not within the exclusive purview of the Parliament.]

Alec Stone Sweet, *Governing With Judges,* above, at 48.

What implications derive from this?

3.   The role of the Constitutional Council changed dramatically, however, as a consequence of its landmark 1971 *Associations Law Decision*, 71–41 DC of 16 July 1971 (as summarized and translated in John Bell, *French Constitutional Law* 272–73 (1992)):

Background: This is the first decision of the Conseil constitutionnel that struck down a provision of a *loi* for breach of fundamental rights. Its justification appealed to the Preamble of the 1958 Constitution and to a fundamental principle recognized by the laws of the Republic, to be found in the *loi* of 1 July 1901 on associations. That *loi* provides that, before an association may be recognized as having legal status, it must file certain particulars with the prefect, who must then issue a certificate of registration.

In this case the National Assembly sought, against the opposition of the Senate, to pass a *loi* that would empower the prefect to refuse registration pending a reference to the courts over the legality of the objectives of a proposed association. The President of the Senate referred the *loi* to the Conseil. The principal issue was the constitutionality of prior restraint of the freedom of association.

DECISION

* * * In the light of the *ordonnance* of 7 November 1958 creating the organic law on the Conseil constitutionnel, especially chapter 2 of title II of the said *ordonnance;*

In the light of the *loi* 1 July 1901 (as amended) relating to associations;

In the light of the *loi* of 10 January 1936 relating to combat groups and private militias;

1. Considering that the *loi* referred for scrutiny by the Conseil constitutionnel was put to the vote in both chambers, following one of the procedures provided for in the Constitution, during the parliamentary session beginning on 2 April 1971;

2. Considering that, among the fundamental principles recognized by the laws of the republic and solemnly reaffirmed by the Constitution, is to be found the freedom of association; that this principle underlines the general provisions of the *loi* of 1 July 1901; that, by virtue of this principle, associations may be formed freely and can be registered simply on condition of the deposition of a prior declaration; that, thus, with the exception of measures that may be taken against certain types of association, the validity of the creation of an association cannot be subordinated to the prior intervention of an administrative or judicial authority, even where the association appears to be invalid or to have an illegal purpose. * * *

From a purely formal standpoint, this decision falls within the powers explicitly granted to the Constitutional Council by the 1958 Constitution. See the excerpt by Alec Stone Sweet above. From a substantive standpoint, in contrast, this decision is truly a transformative one as it paves the way for the Council to evolve from a narrowly confined arbiter of the boundary between executive and legislative powers to a guardian of fundamental individual rights against legislative infringement.

As Professor Morton observes:

In the 1970's, two events transformed the *Counseil Constitutionnel* from a secondary and relatively unimportant institution to a central agent in the governing process. [Because of the *Associations Law Decision* above,] *Parlement's* freedom to legislate was suddenly fenced in by the full panoply of liberal rights and freedoms. Subsequent decisions incorporated additional rights declared in previous French laws and constitutions. By 1987, "fundamental rights" accounted for forty percent of the Conseil's annulment of ordinary laws.

The second catalyst of the *Conseil's* rise to political prominence was the 1974 reform that extended its authority to rule on the constitutionality of a law upon petition by any sixty members of the National Assembly or the Senate. * * * The 1974 reform conferred th[e] power of reference on opposition parties (providing they could muster sixty signatures), who immediately seized this opportunity as a way to obstruct, at least temporarily, new government policies. By 1987, parliamentary references accounted for eighty percent of all decisions dealing with ordinary laws. Even more striking—since 1979, forty-six of the forty-eight deci-

sions nullifying laws have been initiated by members of *Parlement*.
* * *

It is now common practice for all major government bills to be challenged * * * by the opposition. The more important the bill, the more likely the challenge. Combined with the vastly expanded scope of constitutional restrictions imposed by the Declaration of the Rights of Man and other implied liberties, this new procedure has thrust the *Conseil Constitutionnel* to the center of the policy-making process. It is now a "hurdle" that every major piece of legislation must clear before becoming law.

F. L. Morton, *Judicial Review in France: A Comparative Analysis*, 36 Am. J. of Comp. Law 89, 90–92 (1988).

While there is an ongoing debate as to whether it is a true court, see *id.* at 106, by examining legislation to test the latter's compatibility with constitutionally protected individual rights, the Constitutional Council performs essentially the same task as other constitutional courts or as the U.S. courts when they adjudicate constitutional claims. Does that mean that, beginning in 1971, the Council has become a genuine court? Or does the fact that only politicians can raise issues before it and that they can do so only before a law goes into effect relegate the Council to a mere extension of the legislature, thus making it a political body rather than a judicial one?

4. From the accounts provided above, it seems that the various European constitutional courts discussed here are to varying degree political rather than merely judicial bodies. Is this the result of their structure and place in the parliamentary systems in which they are embedded? Or does this stem from the very nature of constitutional review? In this connection it may be useful to focus on the salient features of the decentralized system of constitutional review based on the American model. In the U.S., both federal and state courts are empowered to adjudicate constitutional claims that arise in the course of ordinary litigation. Article III of the U.S. Constitution confines the jurisdiction of federal courts to "cases or controversies," precluding abstract review or advisory opinions. Because of this, constitutional adjudication is concrete, spread out, and piecemeal. American courts, moreover, are not supposed to adjudicate constitutional claims raised in cases before them unless the particular case at stake cannot be resolved without deciding the constitutional claim(s) involved. Thus, for example, if a plaintiff seeks a judgment on both statutory and constitutional grounds, a determination that such plaintiff should prevail on statutory grounds obviates the need for the court involved to consider the constitutional claim. See, e.g., *Regents of the University of California v. Bakke*, 438 U.S. 265 (1978), in Chapter 6, Section D. (four of the nine justices held that the case could be decided on statutory grounds obviating the need to adjudicate the constitutional issues raised by plaintiff). Furthermore, as a consequence of decentralization, different courts may well adjudicate similar claims in diametrically opposed ways. Unity within the system is eventually achieved through adjudication by the USSC, which binds all courts within the country. Whereas all decisions of the highest state courts and of the federal courts of appeals relating to constitutional issues may be appealed to the USSC, since 1988 the latter enjoys virtually unlimited discretion in the selection of cases for review. See 28 U.S.C. § 1257 (1988). Indeed the USSC can agree to entertain an appeal by granting a *writ of certiorari*, which requires an affirmative vote

of four of the nine justices. Often, in the context of a controversial issue, the USSC awaits the development of different, at times contradictory, jurisprudences among various lower courts before agreeing to tackle such issue, to bring unity within the system. Presumably, the Court does so to be in a better position to evaluate the relative merits and drawbacks of the clashing approaches reflected in the decisions below it. The reason for this is to allow the Court to benefit from the experience accumulated regarding plausible approaches to important constitutional issues. Does this way of proceeding render the American approach less prone than its European counterparts to being coopted by politics?

5. The Kelsenian objective of setting constitutional courts as "negative legislators" is compromised when such courts evaluate legislation in terms of compatibility with fundamental rights. Indeed, given the generality of rights, such as free speech, equality, privacy, and the like, and given their amenability to a variety of interpretations, constitutional courts charged with enforcing these rights seem bound to enjoy great latitude to set public policy, thus becoming "positive legislators" while lacking the democratic legitimacy enjoyed by members of parliament. Whether constitutional adjudicators are more like legislators than like judges depends significantly on the nature, scope, and limits of constitutional interpretation, which are addressed below. To some extent, however, the functioning of a constitutional court as a positive legislator seems to depend on institutional factors, as indicated by the above discussion of the French Constitutional Council. In this respect the German Federal Constitutional Court (GFCC) provides an interesting example, inasmuch as it falls somewhere between the French Council and the USSC in that it engages in abstract as well as concrete review and deals with matters initiated by members of Parliament as well as with claims brought by individuals. Consider the following description of the GFCC's jurisdiction.

Wolfgang Zeidler, THE FEDERAL CONSTITUTIONAL COURT OF THE FEDERAL REPUBLIC OF GERMANY: DECISIONS ON THE CONSTITUTIONALITY OF LEGAL NORMS

62 Notre Dame L. Rev. 504, 504–507 (1987).

In the Federal Republic of Germany, the Federal Constitutional Court is the principal body of constitutional jurisdiction. The Court's exclusive jurisdiction is to decide constitutional questions arising under the Federal Republic's Constitution, the Basic Law (das Grundgesetz). A constitution, particularly one that contains an extensive catalogue of basic rights binding on all public authority, will necessitate a greater degree of interpretation than other legal norms. Unlike other courts of last resort, access to the Federal Constitutional Court is limited, except in the case of constitutional complaints, to state and federal governments, state and federal courts, and parliamentary groups such as party factions and minorities in national and state legislatures. * * *

I.   Categories of Disputes

Nearly all of the Federal Constitutional Court's jurisdiction, covering fourteen types of disputes, is defined in the Basic Law.[b] The most significant areas of review involve abstract and concrete judicial review and constitutional complaints. There are no statutory provisions for a preventative or an advisory judicial review of legal norms. The Law Concerning the Federal Constitutional Court originally provided for the possibility of obtaining advisory opinions. The provision was soon dropped, however, in view of the difficulties that arose in conjunction with the binding nature of such decisions.

A.   Abstract Judicial Review

The federal government, a state government, or one-third of the Bundestag may require the Federal Constitutional Court to determine the compatibility of federal or state law with the Basic Law as well as the compatibility of state law with any other federal law. All legal norms, including laws properly passed by Parliament, statutory orders, by-laws adopted by municipalities or other types of corporate bodies may be subjected to this review. This procedure may also be used to ascertain the validity of a norm after a court of law, an administrative authority, any body of the Federal Republic or a state has refused to implement the law because it was not compatible with the Basic Law. In practice, the party requesting an abstract judicial review is frequently the political opposition in the Bundestag or a state government ruled by the opposition party. Commentators critically note that it is only the political disputes which were unsuccessfully resolved in the Bundestag that are continued in the courtroom. Because an abstract judicial review forces the Federal Constitutional Court to decide the constitutionality of a legal norm without access to sufficient information regarding the implementation of the norm or its implications, this review procedure has been subject to criticism.

B.   Concrete Judicial Review

Any court that employs a legal norm, upon which its decision depends, must first examine the compatibility of this norm with a higher norm, especially the Basic Law. If a court reaches the conclusion, mere doubts will not suffice, that a law passed by Parliament, a formal law, is not compatible with the Basic Law then the court must discontinue the proceedings and certify the question of compatibility to the Federal Constitutional Court. The Court will only decide whether or not the submitted legal norm is compatible with the Basic Law. Subsequently, a concrete ruling on the matter must be made by the proper specialized court. The exclusive power of the Federal Constitutional Court to proclaim a formal law unconstitutional is intended to foreclose a lower court from bypassing the will of the democratic legislature by means of declaring a law unconstitutional.

C.   Constitutional Complaints

Unlike the other methods of judicial review, a constitutional complaint can be lodged by any person asserting a violation by a public authority of either basic rights or certain other constitutional rights

b. The GFCC decided 82,516 cases between 1951 and 1994.

(such as the right to be heard). The constitutional complaint can be lodged against any act of public authority, including measures taken by administrative agencies or court decisions. However, available legal recourse must be exhausted prior to any such review by the Federal Constitutional Court. * * *

Regardless of the context of the constitutional complaint, the Federal Constitutional Court examines the constitutionality of the legal norms, whether express or implied. As a result, numerous decisions of the court on constitutional complaints concern the compatibility of laws or other legal norms with the Basic Law. One must note here, however, that a review of the constitutionality of a norm, within the framework of a constitutional complaint proceeding, would be precluded when there remains no question whatsoever about the subjective legal position of the complainant but only about other objective rules and regulations of constitutional law. The practical impact of this limitation is curtailed by the fact that the Federal Constitutional Court interprets the Basic Law to include not only the grant of a general freedom to develop one's personality but also as to incorporate the constitutional right to remain unencumbered by public authority exercised with no constitutional basis. As such, one must also examine within the framework of a constitutional complaint objections claiming a deficiency of legislative authority of the Federal Republic or citing a faulty drafting process.

D.   Other Methods of Procedure

The incidental review of legal norms has arisen in the context of judicial disputes between public bodies concerning the respective rights and duties of not only the highest federal bodies but also of parliamentary groups and parties as well. For example, the authority of the Federal Constitutional Court to rule on complaints against decisions by the Bundestag pertaining to the validity of elections led to a review of the constitutionality of the Federal Election Laws.

E.   Legislative Omissions

Legislative omissions can also be the subject of a ruling by the Federal Constitutional Court. Such cases pose many problems, including the determination of the unconstitutionality of a present legal condition and appeals to the legislature. Although not intended to be exhaustive, the following examples may serve as illustrative: Constitutionally required mandates, the constitutional duty to regulate by law the basic rights and duties of a certain group of people, the constitutional duty of the legislature to take into consideration changes in actual conditions, as well as disparities which are incompatible with the principle of equality. These examples range from cases involving genuine omission (the legislature does not act in defiance of a specific constitutional mandate) and lack of implementation (the legislature has not acted for a long time) to discrimination (the legislature acted, but failed to consider a certain group).

John Bell, JURISDICTION OF THE FRENCH CONSTITUTIONAL COUNCIL, IN FRENCH CONSTITUTIONAL LAW

30–33 (1992).

First, the Conseil is an election court * * * The caseload is quite considerable. As a result of the parliamentary elections of June 1988, some eighty-five decisions on electoral matters are reported in the annual *Recueil* of decisions of the Conseil constitutionnel. * * *

* * *

Secondly, the Conseil also advises the President both when he seeks to use emergency powers under article 16 and on the rules made thereunder. Such advice is not binding, but it is of considerable authority all the same. * * *

Thirdly, the Conseil may also be asked to rule on the constitutionality of treaties. Treaties are signed by the President, but require parliamentary legislation in most cases before they can be ratified. Once ratified, they have a status superior to *lois* (article 55). Although the Conseil constitutionnel will not strike down a *loi* for incompatibility with a treaty, other courts may refuse to apply it in such a case. Prior examination of the compatibility of a treaty and the Constitution is thus desirable. [See the *Amsterdam Treaty* decision in Chapter 1.]

* * *

Fourthly, the Conseil also examines the constitutionality of organic laws and parliamentary standing orders. Both are subject to compulsory review by the review by the Conseil before they are promulgated (article 61 § 1).

* * *

Fifthly, the Conseil had, as its primary original function, to police the boundaries of the legislative competence of Parliament and of the executive. * * *

* * *

(3) Once a *loi* has been passed by Parliament, the Conseil has jurisdiction to rule on its constitutionality * * *

Although originally designed to keep Parliament within the competence set out in article 34, the reference of enacted *lois* to the Conseil has become a procedure for challenging them on wider, substantive grounds, particularly for breach of fundamental rights. * * *

The Conseil only has jurisdiction to challenge a *loi* before it has been promulgated. In early decisions it stated that references cannot be used to challenge the validity of previously promulgated *lois*. But in 1985 the Conseil declared *obiter:* 'though the validity with respect to the Constitution of a promulgated *loi* may properly be contested on the occasion of an examination of legislative provisions that amend it, complement it, or affect its scope, this is not the case when it is a matter of simply applying such a *loi*.' [CC decision no. 85–187 DC of 25 Jan. 1985, *Urgency in New Caledonia*, D. 1986, 361, note *Luchaire*.]

Notes and Questions

1. It is argued that the notion that abstract review initiated by officials in the various branches of government is what renders a constitutional court more akin to a political body than to a judicial one. Do you agree?

2. Are the distinctions between the "negative" and "positive" legislator and "abstract" and "concrete" review that important in terms of whether constitutional courts are ultimately political rather than judicial bodies? On the surface a "negative" legislator has much less power than a "positive" one, in that the former can only block legislation while the latter can also reshape it. Nevertheless, to the extent that they both enjoy a significant degree of interpretive discretion, is it not as political and as antimajoritarian to strike down popular legislation at the behest of a small legislative minority (e.g., the 60 members of the National Assembly, who can challenge a law before it is promulgated before the French Constitutional Council, represent barely more than 10 percent of the Assembly's deputies) as it is for constitutional judges essentially to rewrite it?

In theory abstract review affords greater discretion to the constitutional judge than concrete review. This is presumably because, in the case of concrete review, the judge is constrained by the facts of the case at hand, over which the judge in question has no control. Upon closer scrutiny, however, this distinction may be less important than it seems initially as other factors may have a far greater impact on the discretion of the constitutional judge. For example, in the U.S., the prevailing common law tradition has long given judges fairly broad powers to shape the law by enabling them to develop and adapt legal rules through interpretation, expansion, or limitation of precedents. Furthermore, concrete review can certainly be cast very narrowly to address nothing more than the actual dispute before the Court when adjudicating constitutional issues. Such narrow casting, however, may be undesirable in constitutional cases as it would offer too little guidance for future enforcement of the constitution. Consistent with this, although limited to concrete review by the "case-or-controversy" requirement, the USSC had tended to cast its opinions in broader strokes than strictly necessary to resolve the concrete conflicts before it. For example, in its landmark abortion decision, *Roe v. Wade*, 410 U.S. 113 (1973), in Chapter 5, the Court had before it a challenge by a woman seeking an abortion against a Texas law that made abortion a crime, except if necessary to save the life of the mother. The woman who contested the law in question did not claim that her life would be in danger if she did not abort. Accordingly, the Court, strictly speaking, should have limited its decision to a determination of whether the Texas abortion law was unconstitutional as applied against a woman in the circumstances of the woman who raised the challenge. Instead, however, the Court divided pregnancy into three trimesters and provided standards for when abortions could or could not be criminalized. See Chapter 5, Subsection C.1. Is this more akin to judicial lawmaking than to straightforward adjudication?

B.2. THE INDEPENDENCE OF THE CONSTITUTIONAL ADJUDICATOR: APPOINTMENTS, COURT COMPOSITION, AND RELATIONS WITH THE OTHER BRANCHES OF GOVERNMENT

The independence of the constitutional adjudicator depends on many factors, including *inter alia*, the legal and political culture and traditions. For example, as noted above, ordinary judges in civil law systems did not enjoy the tradition of independence of their common law counterparts, and that figured prominently in the need for constitutional courts. Beyond this, independence also depends on the mode of appointment, the terms and conditions of service of adjudicators, the composition of the adjudicatory body, and its relation to the other branches of government. We consider these issues here in the context of constitutional adjudication. For further discussion of judicial independence in the context of separation of powers, see Chapter 3, Section D.

Appointments to the French Constitutional Council are made one-third by the President of the Republic, one-third by the President of the National Assembly, and one-third by the President of the Senate. There are nine members of the Council who serve for a single nine-year term, and as the terms on the Council are staggered (every three years there are three new appointees), each of the three persons with appointment power can make one appointment every three years. Given that many of the appointees have a political rather than legal background and that appointments are political—inasmuch as those who appoint choose persons within their own political party or with clear ties to their party— the Council is certainly in many respects a political body. In other respects, however, the Council functions more as a judicial body, in large part due to the role it assumed in the *Associations Law Decision*, 71–41 DC of 16 July 1971, see above, namely, that of an institutional guardian of fundamental rights against infringement by challenged legislation. Finally, the degree to which the Council functions as a judicial rather than a political body depends in significant measure on the institutional vision of its members. Thus, under the presidency of Robert Badinter (1986–1995), a noted jurist and former Minister of Justice, the Council enhanced its profile as a judicial body. In contrast, the Council's current President, Yves Guéna, a former president of the French Senate and close collaborator of Charles De Gaulle, regards the proper role of the Council more in terms of its original mission, as mediator between the legislature and executive, than as an activist constitutional court.

Although there is a significant overlap of functions between their respective institutional roles, the GFCC differs in many key respects from the French Constitutional Council.

Alec Stone Sweet, CONSTITUTIONAL ADJUDICA-TION AND PARLIAMENTARY DEMOCRACY, in GOVERNING WITH JUDGES: CONSTITUTIONAL POLITICS IN EUROPE

31, 46–49 (2000).

Composition

[Based on the rules governing the recruitment of constitutional judges in France, Germany, Italy, and Spain, two] modes of appointment exist—nomination and election. Where nomination procedures are used, the appointing authority simply names a judge or a slate of judges; no countervailing confirmation or veto procedures exist. Such is the case of France, where all constitutional judges are named by political authorities. Italy and Spain have mixed nomination and election systems. Where election systems are used, a qualified, or super, majority (a 2/3 or 3/5 vote) within a parliamentary body is necessary for appointment. Because the German, Italian, and Spanish polities are multi-party systems, and because no single party has ever possessed a super-majority on its own, the qualified majority requirement effectively necessitates the parties to negotiate with each other in order to achieve consensus on a slate of candidates. This bargaining process occurs in intense, behind-closed-doors negotiations. In practice, these negotiations determine which party will fill vacancies on the court, with allocations usually roughly proportionate to relative parliamentary strength.

Table 2.3 also indicates who may serve as a constitutional judge. All German, Italian, and Spanish judges must have had advanced legal training, as well as professional experience in some domain of law. The constitution may also contain precise quotas, guaranteeing a minimal number of professional judges drawn from the ordinary courts. In Germany, the sixteen-member court must always contain at least six federal judges; in Italy, representatives of the judiciary control the appointment of 5/15 seats; and in Spain, they control 2/12. In France, no legal training is required. Perhaps in consequence, a majority of the French Council has always been made up of former ministers and parliamentarians, although many of these have studied or practiced some law. Several influential law professors and a few former ordinary judges have served on the French Council, but far fewer than in the other countries. In Germany, Italy, and Spain, law professors make up the largest group of appointees, followed by former ordinary judges and lawyers * * *

In France and Italy, decisions are presented as unanimous, and publication of votes and dissents are prohibited by law. In Germany and Spain dissents are permitted but rare. In all cases, internal deliberations are, by law, secret * * *

Table 2.3 Recruitment and composition of European constitutional courts

	France	Germany	Italy	Spain
Number of members	9	16	15	12
Recruiting authorities	*Named by:* President (3) Pres. Assembly (3) Pres. Senate (3)	*Elected by:* Bundestag (8) Bundesrat (8) (by 2/3 majority)	*Named by:* National Govt (5) Judiciary (5) *Elected by:* Parliament (5) (2/3 majority of joint session)	*Named by:* National Govt (2) Judiciary (2) *Elected by:* Congress (4) Senate (4) (by 3/5 majority)
Length of term	9 years	12 years	9 years	9 years
Age limit	None	40 year min. 68 year max.	None	None
Requisite qualifications	None	6/16 must be federal judges; all must be qualified to be federal judges	All must be judges with 20 years in practice, or tenured law professors	May be judges, law professors, lawyers, or civil servants, with at least 15 years experience, and whose 'judicial competence' is well known

Note on Appointment to the U.S. Supreme Court

In the U.S., Article II. Sec. 2 of the Constitution provides that the President nominates justices to the Supreme Court and that such nominees are appointed upon the "advice and consent" of the Senate, i.e., upon the affirmative vote of a majority of Senators. Appointments are for life, and justices can be removed only through impeachment for violation of the standard of "good behavior" set by Article III, Sec. I of the Constitution. To date, no justice of the Supreme Court has been removed by impeachment, but proceedings were brought in 1805 against Justice Samuel Chase, who had been nominated to the Court by George Washington and who was eventually acquitted in a trial in the U.S. Senate.

The Senate has by no means rubber stamped presidential nominations to the high court. Approximately a quarter of the nominations have been rejected. The Constitution does not set qualifications for justices, but the Senate's confirmation process has been used in certain cases to weed out mediocre candidates.

While the debate goes on, albeit with less intensity, Supreme Court nominations remain highly political, a fact that is particularly evident when control of the Senate is in a different political party than the presidency. As for the proper role of the Senate, in the words of one of the country's most prominent constitutionalists: "In an appointment to the United States Supreme Court the Senate comes second, but is not secondary. The standards the Senate should apply are the same as those that should govern the President: what would serve the national interest." Louis Henkin, *"Ideology" Is a Central Consideration*, N.Y. Times Sept 11, 1987, at A31, col. 2.

Once on the Court, justices, by and large, have demonstrated great independence from the other branches of government. Moreover, in many cases a justice has disappointed the expectations of the President who nominated him or her. One notorious case is that of Justice William Brennan, nominated to the Court by President Eisenhower, in 1956, and serving with great distinction until his retirement, in 1990, as the most prominent member of the Court's liberal wing.

B.3.   WHO? WHAT? AND WHOM?: STANDING, JUSTICIABILITY AND THE BINDING EFFECT OF CONSTITUTIONAL ADJUDICATION

Constitutions typically allocate rights and duties, and constitutional adjudication is generally meant to be used for vindication of the rights, and enforcement of the duties, involved. Rules concerning *who* has standing to raise a constitutional claim for adjudication, concerning *what* constitutional claims are justifiable, and concerning *whom* does a constitutional adjudication bind, can shape and constrain the scope of constitutional justice. Thus in many constitutional regimes not everyone can submit constitutional claims for adjudication; not all such claims are justiciable; and not all equally situated citizens may be able to benefit from adjudication in favor of some among them.

B.3.1.   STANDING

Rules of standing vary from the extremely restrictive to the virtually unconstrained. As noted above, before 1974 only four persons—the President, the Prime Minister, the President of the National Assembly, and the President of the Senate—could challenge the constitutionality of a law voted by the French Parliament before the Constitutional Council. At the other end of the spectrum, in contrast, virtually everyone in the world, even foreigners with no links to the country, can raise a constitutional claim before the Hungarian Constitutional Court (HCC). Moreover, standing is based on status in some countries. For example, in France, only those in the four positions just mentioned as well as groups of 60 or more parliamentarians have standing. In other countries, such as the U.S., standing does not depend on status but on the party who brings a constitutional claim being able to allege an individualized injury caused by the governmental entity being sued. For example, whereas 60 French parliamentarians can challenge a law as unconstitutional on any ground, such as for example that it violates private property rights, see 82–139 DC of 11 Feb. 1982, the members of the U.S. Congress have no standing under such circumstances. Conversely, whereas a person who has lost private property as a consequence of application of a U.S. law can sue to have such law declared unconstitutional, if a French law is promulgated unchallenged, then no one has standing to challenge its constitutionality under similar circumstances.

Because of the "case-or-controversy" requirement of Article III of the U.S. Constitution, to have standing, a party must meet the following requirements articulated by the USSC in its decision in *Lujan v. Defenders of Wildlife,* 504 U.S. 555 (1992):

> Over the years, our cases have established that the irreducible constitutional minimum of standing contains three elements: First the plaintiff must have suffered an 'injury-in-fact'—an invasion of a legally protected interest which is (a) concrete and particularized, and (b) actual or imminent, not 'conjectural' or 'hypothetical'. Second, there must be a causal connection between the injury and the conduct complained of— the conduct has to be fairly traceable to the challenged action of the defendant, and not the result of the independent action of some third party not before the court. Third, it must be 'likely' as opposed to merely 'speculative', that the injury will be redressed by a favorable decision.

To satisfy the "injury-in-fact" requirement, a plaintiff must allege a particularized injury suffered individually. Such injury is most often a monetary one, but it need not be. Thus in *Lujan* the Court recognized that a plaintiff who enjoyed observing the natural habitat of endangered species, such as the Nile crocodile or the Asian elephant, would suffer an "injury-in-fact" if unconstitutional government conduct led to the extinction of the species involved. Nevertheless, in *Lujan* the Court denied standing because the individuals claiming injury had not recently visited the relevant habitats and did not have concrete plans to do so in the near future. But see *Friends of the Earth v. Laidlaw Environmental Services,* 528 U.S. 167 (2000) (injury-in-fact requirement satisfied by environmentalists asserting that discharges of pollutants into a river had deterred them from fishing, camping, bird-watching, etc. in or near that river).

The "injury-in-fact" and "causation" requirements for standing have not always been used clearly or consistently by the USSC, leading to criticisms to the effect that the Court sometimes uses standing to reach a result impermissibly influenced by its leanings on the merits of the case. (For standing purposes, allegations made in a complaint must be taken at face value regardless of their merit. For example, if a plaintiff alleges loss of income because of unconstitutional government censorship, then he or she has standing regardless of whether the claim of loss of income turns out to be true.) In *Allen v. Wright,* 468 U.S. 737 (1984), parents of black children in public schools sued, alleging that government tax subsidies to private schools that were for white students only violated their constitutional right to racially integrated public schools. In the context of white resistance to constitutionally mandated racial integration through withdrawing children from public schools, the plaintiffs alleged that the government tax subsidy to private schools, including those that practiced racial segregation, injured them by stigmatizing them on account of their race. Furthermore, the plaintiff alleged that the tax subsidy, by making private school affordable for many white families who would not otherwise have the option of taking their children out of tuition-free public schools, was in significant measure responsible for the public schools attended by their children remaining virtually exclusively black.

The Court's majority held that the plaintiffs lacked standing, both because they had not suffered an injury-in-fact and because the tax subsidies complained off could not be properly considered as the direct cause of the continuing segregation in the public schools. Justice O'Connor's opinion for the majority found the "abstract stigmatic injury" to be insufficient to meet the constitutional requirement, and while she recognized that being forced to attend a still-segregated public school was a cognizable injury, she concluded that it was at best speculative to consider that elimination of the tax subsidy at issue would lead to greater integration. While the lack of subsidy would make the private school more expensive, it would still be possible for the white families to pay more for private education or for the private school to seek alternative funds. Accordingly, the tax subsidies could not be viewed as the direct cause for the continuing segregation. The four dissenting justices angrily accused the majority of misusing the standing issue. In Justice Brennan's view, "the causation components of the Court's standing inquiry is no more than a poor disguise for the Court's view of the merits of the underlying claims."

Even when causation is not an issue, there are cases where no one has standing to challenge a constitutional violation. A case in point is *Valley Forge Christian College v. Americans United*, 454 U.S. 464 (1982). Citizens and taxpayers challenged the gift of real estate by the federal government to a private Christian university under the supervision of a religious order as in violation of the "Establishment Clause," which requires separation between church and state (see Chapter 8) and prohibits government from favoring one religion over others. Although the gift in question clearly appeared in violation of the Constitution, the Court refused to entertain the case, finding that the plaintiffs had not suffered any "injury-in-fact," no matter how offended they may have been by government subsidy of a religion other than their own.

Both in France and the U.S., standing restrictions may frustrate adjudication of constitutional claims that are in all likelihood valid on the merits. In contrast, in some countries, like Hungary, there are virtually no standing barriers to the filing of constitutional complaints. In Hungary, any person who claims that the state has violated one or more of his or her rights under the Constitution may file a constitutional complaint in the Constitutional Court. Moreover, the procedure for filing such complaints is simple and inexpensive. As a result, the Constitutional Court has been flooded with complaints. A similar trend emerged in Germany, and, consequently, the GFCC has established a filtering process, leading to summary disposition of 99 percent of such complaints. Does it make any significant difference whether one's claim is rejected because of standing barriers or whether it is summarily disposed of in a screening proceeding?

For a stark contrast with the handling of the standing issue as it arises in the above-mentioned countries, consider the decision in *Rev. Christopher Mtikila v. the Attorney General*, Civil Case No. 5 of 1993, High Court of Tanzania:

* * *

The notion of personal interest, personal injury or sufficient interest over and above the interest of the general public has more to do with private law as distinct from public law. In matters of public interest litigation this Court will not deny standing to a genuine and bona fide litigant even where he has no personal interest in the matter. This position also accords with the decision in *Benazir Bhutto v. Federation of Pakistan*, PLD 1988 SC 46, where it was held by the Supreme Court that the traditional rule of locus standi can be dispensed with and procedure available in public interest litigation can be made use of if the petition is brought to the court by a person acting bona fide.

The relevance of public interest litigation in Tanzania cannot be overemphasized. Having regard to our socio-economic conditions, this development promises more hope to our people than any other strategy currently in place. First of all, illiteracy is still rampant. We were recently told that Tanzania is second in Africa in wiping out illiteracy but that is statistical juggling which is not reflected on the ground. If we were that literate it would have been unnecessary for Hanang District Council to pass bylaws for compulsory adult education which were recently published as Government Notice No. 191 of 1994. By reason of this illiteracy a greater part of the population is unaware of their rights, let alone how the same can be realised. Secondly, Tanzanians are massively poor. Our ranking in the world on the basis of per capita income has persistently been the source of embarrassment. Public interest litigation is a sophisticated mechanism which requires professional handling. By reason of limited resources the vast majority of our people cannot afford to engage lawyers even where they were aware of the infringement of their rights and the perversion of the Constitution. Other factors could be listed but perhaps the most painful of all is that over the years since independence Tanzanians have developed a culture of apathy and silence. This, in large measure, is a product of institutionalized mono-party politics which in its repressive dimension, like detention without trial, supped up initiative and guts. The people found contentment in being receivers without being seekers. Our leaders very well recognise this, and with the emergence of transparency in governance they have not hesitated to affirm it.

* * *

Given all these and other circumstances, if there should spring up a public-spirited individual [who] seek[s] the Court's intervention against legislation or actions that pervert the Constitution, the Court, as guardian and trustee of the Constitution and what it stands for, is under an obligation to rise up to the occasion and grant him standing.

Note on the U.S. Political Question Doctrine and Other Limits on Constitutional Adjudication

In the U.S., there is one important limitation on the justiciability of constitutional claims, namely, that provided by the "political question doctrine." Although the contours of the doctrine are hardly clear and certain scholars have strongly criticized its coherence, see, e.g., Louis Henkin, *Is There a Political Question Doctrine?*, 85 Yale L. J. 597 (1976), the political question doctrine has been regularly invoked by courts to refuse adjudicating certain types of constitutional claims. It must be emphasized that the doctrine is not meant to inhibit adjudication of politically charged constitutional issues. For example, the constitutional issues surrounding abortion have been highly politicized for a number of decades in the U.S. (see Chapter 5), but they are justiciable in the same way as all other individual rights issues arising under the Constitution. Instead the "political question doctrine" must be understood in a more technical sense as defined by its many pronged nature. As the Court stated in *Baker v. Carr,* 369 U.S. 186, 217 (1962):

> Prominent on the surface of any case held to involve a political question is found a textually demonstrable constitutional commitment of the issue to a coordinate political department; or a lack of judicially discoverable and manageable standards for resolving it; or the impossibility of deciding without an initial policy determination of a kind clearly for nonjudicial discretion; or the impossibility of a court's undertaking independent resolution without expressing lack of the respect due coordinate branches of government; or an unusual need for unquestioning adherence to a political decision already made; or the potentiality of embarrassment from multifarious pronouncements by various departments on one question.

The first of these prongs, "commitment to a coordinate branch," stems from a separation of powers concern (see generally Chapter 3) and appears rather straight forward. For example, where the Constitution assigns a matter to another branch of government, such as the executive or the legislative branch, the courts lack justiciability. See, e.g., *Nixon v. United States,* 506 U.S. 224 (1993) (impeachment trial of federal judge entrusted by the Constitution to the Senate and hence whether presentation of evidence to a Senate Committee rather than the full Senate constitutes a "trial" is a nonjusticiable political question). But see *Bush v. Gore,* 531 U.S. 98 (2000), in Chapter 6 (Supreme Court puts an end to disputed Florida presidential election notwithstanding that the Twelfth Amendment of the U.S. Constitution provides for resolution of contested presidential elections in the Congress). For wide-ranging views on *Bush v. Gore* and a comparison of the handling of contested elections in the U.S., France, Germany, Israel, and Italy, see *The Longest Night: Polemics and Perspectives on Election 2000* (Arthur J. Jacobson and Michel Rosenfeld eds., 2002).

The last prongs of the "political question doctrine," dealing with "embarrassment," "need to adhere to a decision already made," and "lack of respect to a coordinate branch," seem to mark the boundary between law and politics but remain particularly nebulous and open-ended. The Court's jurisprudence relating to these prongs, moreover, is far from clear or consistent. See, e.g., *Goldwater v. Carter,* 444 U.S. 996 (1979) (concerning the question of whether the President can abolish a treaty without the participation of the Senate although the latter must ratify treaties by a two-thirds majority, some justices opine that this involves a political question and is hence nonjusticiable, while other justices affirm that the question raises an ordinary constitutional issue that the Court ought to resolve).

Limitations on justiciability can also be used for other purposes besides marking the boundary between the legal and the political. In Spain, for instance, constitutional adjudication does not extend to certain welfare rights. See Javier Perez Royo, *Curso De Derecho Constitucional* 363–64 (3d ed. 1996). This limitation allows for drawing a clear line between judicially enforceable constitutional rights and constitutionally grounded goals. Many European courts, however, have power to review even the standing rules and certain procedural decisions of their respective parliaments (see Chapter 3).

In the last analysis, flexible standards regarding standing and justiciability rules seem to enhance the discretion of the constitutional adjudicator. However, limitations on standing and justiciability are but some of the many different factors that influence the scope of judicial review of constitutional claims. In France, standing is much more restricted than in Germany or the U.S., but justiciability is precisely defined, and the Constitutional Council has no discretion to turn down claims properly brought before it. In contrast, although both Germany and the U.S. have more-sweeping standing standards, among the availability of summary dispositions, freedom to chose cases, and rather vague and malleable justiciability standards, the GFCC and even more the USSC seem to enjoy broad latitude in choosing constitutional cases or issues for full-fledged adjudication. Is flexibility preferable? Or is it inherently problematic?

B.3.2. BINDING EFFECTS OF CONSTITUTIONAL ADJUDICATION

As already indicated in the context of abstract review, the decisions of constitutional courts under the European model are *erga omnes* (binding on everyone), whereas those by the USSC are most certainly binding on the parties to the decided case. Beyond that, however, there is no unanimity. As a practical matter, because of adherence to the doctrine of *stare decisis*, or precedent, prior decisions are dispositive of similar subsequent cases not because the parties to the subsequent case are bound by the prior decision but because the judge in the new case is bound by the *ratio decidendi* of the prior case. Moreover, in the case of the European model the situation is not entirely clear in relation to certain instances involving concrete review. Finally, in the case of France, because the Constitutional Council cannot adjudicate issues arising in other courts, some of its decisions may not in fact be *erga omnes*. See, e.g., the *Schiavon Decision* by the Court of Cassation of February 26, 1974.

Another question is, what happens to a law after it has been declared unconstitutional by the constitutional adjudicator? The answer varies from one setting to another, with France and the U.S. occupying opposite ends of the spectrum. In France, where laws can be challenged only before the Constitutional Council before they become effective, a decision that a law is unconstitutional means that the law at stake can never be promulgated, and it thus never sees the light of day. In the U.S., in contrast, a USSC decision declaring that an existing law is unconstitutional results in the subsequent nonenforcement of that law but not in its abolition or repeal. Thus if the Court reverses its jurisprudence after a number of years, the invalidated law can be implemented anew without any need for a reenactment. Thus, for example, the Court held a minimum-wage law unconstitutional in *Adkins v. Children's Hospital,* 261 U.S. 525 (1923), a decision which it overruled in *West Coast Hotel v. Parrish,* 300 U.S. 379 (1937). In 1937, the Attorney General advised President Roosevelt that the minimum-wage law in question never repealed after 1923 was again applicable. The Attorney General opined that the 1923 decision had simply "suspended" the law and explained that "the courts have no power to repeal or abolish a statute, and that notwithstanding a decision holding it unconstitutional, a statute continues to remain on the statute book." 39 Ops. Atty. Gen. 22 (1937). Do you agree with the Attorney General, or do you think that democratic lawmaking should require reenacting a law not enforced for many years because it had been adjudged unconstitutional?

C.   CONSTITUTIONAL INTERPRETATION

Constitutional adjudicators can have their greatest impact on shaping a constitutional regime through interpretation of the constitution. Recall, for example, the French Constitutional Council's decision of July 16, 1971, above, in which by interpreting the incorporation by reference of the 1789 Declaration of the Rights of Man into the 1958 French Constitution, it arrogated to itself broad powers to invalidate laws infringing on fundamental rights not contemplated by the Constitution's framers. Inasmuch as constitutional texts are often general and open ended, and as constitutions may be difficult to amend, the constitutional adjudicator may enjoy great latitude in shaping constitutional law for a long time to come. This great power is not easily submitted to democratic control and seems prone to abuse unless the constitutional adjudicator can be subjected to widely accepted interpretive constraints. This section begins with a comparative account of typologies of constitutional arguments and then explores dilemmas of constitutional interpretation, followed by a review of fundamental interpretative doctrines.

C.1. TYPOLOGY OF CONSTITUTIONAL ARGUMENTS

C.1.1. UNITED STATES

Richard H. Fallon, Jr., A CONSTRUCTIVIST COHERENCE THEORY OF CONSTITU-TIONAL INTERPRETATION

100 Harv. L. Rev. 1189, 1189–1190, 1195–1196,
1198–1202, 1204–1206, 1208–1209 (1987).

Introduction

[M]ost judges, lawyers, and commentators recognize the relevance of at least five kinds of constitutional argument: arguments from the plain, necessary, or historical meaning of the constitutional text; arguments about the intent of the framers; arguments of constitutional theory that reason from the hypothesized purposes that best explain either particular constitutional provisions or the constitutional text as a whole; arguments based on judicial precedent; and value arguments that assert claims about justice or social policy.

* * *

A. Arguments from Text

Arguments from text play a universally accepted role in constitutional debate. If there is any surprise, it is how seldom the text is relied on directly, in comparison with arguments based on historical intent, precedent, and social policy or moral principle. But perhaps this situation only emphasizes the text's importance. The text, and its plain language, are taken for granted. Where the text speaks clearly and unambiguously—for example, when it says that the President must be at least thirty-five years old—its plain meaning is dispositive. Where the text is ambiguous or vague, other sources are consulted as guides to textual meaning.

If this account is accurate—as I believe that generally it is—then it will be helpful to recognize an important distinction between arguments *about* the text and arguments *from* the text. In one sense, all constitutional arguments—including, for example, arguments concerning precedent and the intent of the framers—are about the text and what it should be held to mean. It is, after all, a constitution we are interpreting. From arguments that are merely about the meaning of the text, we can distinguish arguments from the text: arguments that purport to resolve a question by direct appeal to the Constitution's plain language. These are arguments that the plain language of the Constitution either requires or forbids a certain conclusion, irrespective of what might be said about that conclusion on other grounds.

One reason we see relatively few arguments from the text is that the language of the Constitution, considered as a factor independent from the other kinds of argument familiar in constitutional debate, resolves so few hard questions. Nonetheless, arguments from text can fulfill three functions. Occasionally, an argument from text will require a unique conclusion—for example, that the President must be at least thirty-five years old. More commonly, arguments from the text achieve the somewhat weaker but nontrivial result of excluding one or more positions that might be argued for on nontextual grounds. Thus, although the text of the eighth amendment may not tell us precisely what "cruel and unusual punishments" are, the language does require that the amendment's prohibition apply only to actions that can plausibly be described as "punishments." Finally, among the meanings that are not excluded by arguments from text, a narrowly text-focused reading will sometimes yield the conclusion that some are more plausible than others * * *

B. Arguments about the Framers' Intent

Searches for the meaning of a constitutional provision frequently involve inquiries into the intent of the framers and ratifiers. Controversy abounds concerning the weight that intent ought to have. Although "interpretivists" view the intent of the framers as controlling, most other constitutional lawyers regard intent as entitled to only some, not very clearly specified, weight. Moreover, several important scholars have recently argued that the intent of the framers generally has no justifiable place in constitutional argument. But this form of nonintentionalism is more plausibly viewed as a prescriptive proposal than as an account of existing practice. It is relatively uncontroversial that the Supreme Court regards the framers' intent as an important factor in constitutional adjudication.

Notoriously, searches for intent divide into several types. One helpful division distinguishes between "specific" or "concrete" and "general" or "abstract" intent. Specific intent involves the relatively precise intent of the framers to control the outcomes of particular types of cases * * * Abstract intent refers to aims that are defined at a higher level of generality, sometimes entailing consequences that the drafters did not specifically consider and that they might even have disapproved * * * It clearly is an interesting and important question how the choice is and ought to be made between the types of intent—especially between specific and abstract intent—that sometimes are resorted to in constitutional argument. * * *

C. Arguments of Constitutional Theory

A third familiar kind of argument involves the purposes, described in a general, functional, or theoretical sense, of the Constitution as a whole or of its provisions individually. Arguments of this kind push beyond what could plausibly be considered the plain meaning of constitutional language. Instead, they claim to understand the Constitution as a whole, or a particular provision of it, by providing an account of the values, purposes, or political theory in light of which the Constitution or certain elements of its language and structure are most intelligible. Arguments asserting that particular values or principles enjoy constitutional status because of their role in a theory of this kind I shall refer to as arguments of constitutional theory.

This category is, admittedly, rather loosely defined * * * A famous example of structural argument comes from Chief Justice Marshall's opinion in *McCulloch v. Maryland,* [see Chapter 4] forbidding state taxation of federal entities on the ground that the power to tax is the power to destroy. With the state and national governments structured as they were under the Constitution, it would make no sense, Marshall reasoned, for the states to be able to frustrate constitutionally legitimate federal policies. Arguments of this kind can be viewed as ones of constitutional theory because, although they do not rely on either the precise linguistic meaning of particular constitutional provisions or on the historically identifiable intent of the framers, they are text focused * * *

D.   Arguments from Precedent

Constitutional disputes frequently abound with analysis of the meanings of judicial precedents. Indeed, constitutional arguments sometimes address themselves almost entirely to the meanings of previously decided cases: read one way, precedent indicates one result * * * whereas if read another, it leads to a different conclusion. More commonly, however, prior judicial decisions form a patchwork into which a current problem must be fitted through a combination of analytical, analogical, and theoretical reasoning * * *

E.   Value Arguments

Sometimes openly, sometimes guardedly, judges and lawyers make arguments that appeal directly to moral, political, or social values or policies. Every now and then, of course, courts assert that value choices are never for them to make but are solely the domain of the political branches. However, protestations of this kind are simply not credible. Indeed, at least occasionally they signal that the court is about to implement a value choice so controversial that denial is easier than explanation. Value arguments are even more prominent; indeed, they enjoy almost total predominance, in much of the most respected modern constitutional scholarship.

Although various other definitions would be possible, I shall use the term "value argument" to refer only to claims about the moral or political significance of facts or about the normative desirability of outcomes. Defined in this way, value arguments assert claims about what is good or bad, desirable or undesirable, as measured against some standard that is independent of what the constitutional text requires. Value arguments do not claim that the particular value judgments they assert are necessarily ones that the framers intended to constitutionalize, or that they express the best constitutional theory. Rather, value arguments advance conclusions about what is morally or politically correct, desirable, or expedient as measured against some standard.

To make these claims somewhat more concrete, it may help to posit a provisional distinction between two kinds of cases in which value arguments have a conventionally accepted role. One involves constitutional language whose meaning has a normative or evaluative component. Examples include the due process clauses, the equal protection clause, the fourth amendment's prohibition of "unreasonable" searches and seizures, and the eighth amendment's guarantee against "cruel and unusual punishments." These phrases constitutionalize particular concepts or values. But those values or concepts are, in the idiom of ordinary language philosophy, "essentially contestable." Although the evaluative judgments that the concepts are used to express are wholly intelligible even to those who disagree with them, consensus breaks down over the proper criteria for determining when such labels as "procedurally fair" or "unfair," "equal" or "unequal," "reasonable" or "unreasonable," and "cruel and unusual" are apt. Different people apply the terms differently, not because some misuse the language, but because the full meaning of each term depends upon a background network of philosophical values and assumptions that is itself disputable. To decide when an essentially contestable concept "properly" applies therefore requires the conscious or unconscious undertaking of moral and political commitments * * *

Within the category of arguments of value, a final distinction will prove helpful. It involves the sources of values to which a judge might appeal. One kind of value argument refers to some repository of values, outside of herself, that a judge or lawyer believes to be a legitimate source of authority in constitutional interpretation. That source might be traditional morality, consensus values, natural law, economic efficiency, or the original position liberal methodology of John Rawls. Another imaginable kind of value argument would be one in which a judge or theorist simply asserts her own values and claims their entitlement to constitutional weight. This second sort of argument may never be made explicitly, but critics frequently claim to find it only barely concealed in invocations of such sources of authority as traditional morality and natural law.

C.1.2. GERMANY

Winfried Brugger, LEGAL INTERPRETATION, SCHOOLS OF JURISPRUDENCE, AND ANTHRO-POLOGY: SOME REMARKS FROM A GERMAN POINT OF VIEW

42 Am. J. Comp. L. 395, 396–401, 410–411, 415–416 (1994).

* * *

I. The Canon of Interpretation in German Law

The classic method of interpretation in Germany was established by the founder of the 'historical school of jurisprudence', Friedrich Carl von Savigny, in an 1840 treatise on Roman law. Savigny distinguished, in modern parlance, textual, verbal or grammatical interpretation, systematic, structural or contextual interpretation, and historical interpretation. Later on, a fourth perspective was added: teleological interpretation, which might also be termed purposive interpretation.

In verbal or grammatical interpretation, philological methods are used to analyze the meaning of a particular word or sentence. In systematic interpretation, one attempts to clarify the meaning of a legal provision by reading it in conjunction with other, related provisions of the same section, or title, of the legal text, or even other texts within or outside the given legal system; thus, this method relies upon the unity, or at least the consistency, of the legal world. In historical analysis, the interpreter attempts to identify what the founders of a legal document wanted to regulate when they used certain words and sentences; here, both the specific and the general declarations of intent are of crucial importance. In teleological analysis, the historical will of the framers is devalued: Instead of being accorded critical emphasis as to what was then willed, their declarations of intent are only deemed indicative, not determinative, of the contemporaneous purpose of the legal provision or document. The same holds for the weight of textual and systematic interpretation in teleological analysis: These methods suggest an outcome or a certain range of outcomes, but the decisive point of reference is the interpreter's notion of a result that, according to the "independent function"[3] or value of the pertinent legal provision, must be the correct one.

These four methods constitute the classic catalog of statutory interpretation in Germany. They also comprise the core of constitutional interpretation, as is evidenced by many cases decided by the Federal Constitutional Court (and, in the United States, by the Supreme Court.) * * *

The prevailing view holds that the Constitution differs from statutes in that it is more political, more open-ended, and less complete. From that it follows, according to this view, that vague constitutional provisions cannot be 'construed' (*ausgelegt*) but must be 'actualized' (*aktualisiert*) or 'concretized' (*konkretisiert*); the difference being that a strict 'construction' reveals a solution already inherent in the text, whereas an 'actualization' or 'concretization' entails a dialectic process of creatively determining results in conformity with, but not determinable by, the Constitution. According to the most influential proponent of this view, Konrad Hesse, the goal of creating constitutional law while respecting the Constitution may be reached through adherence to five points of reference for constitutional interpretation, in addition to, and relativization of, the four classic methods of statutory interpretation: (1) Each interpretation must support the unity of the constitution. (2) In cases of tension or conflict, the principle of practical concordance (*praktische Konkordanz*) must be employed to harmonize conflicting provisions. (3) All governmental organs must respect the functional differentiation of the Constitution, that is, their respective tasks and powers in the separation of powers scheme. (4) Each interpretation must try to create an integrative effect with regard to both the various parties of a constitutional dispute as well as to social and political cohesion. (5) These points together lead to the legitimating function of the Constitution: Each interpretation shall attempt to optimize all the aforementioned elements.

* * *

3. This expression, taken from Justice Frankfurter's concurring opinion in *Adamson v. California*, 332 U.S. 46, 67 (1947), aptly captures the main characteristic of teleological interpretation.

Even if one assumes that the dissimilarities between the German Constitution and German legislation in general are so substantial as to create a qualitative difference between these two kinds of legal texts, one can argue that the additional methods of constitutional interpretation proposed by Konrad Hesse form a part of or can be viewed as an annex to the classic canon of statutory interpretation, especially the systematic and teleological perspectives: (1) It is the goal of systematic, respectively structural or contextual interpretation to clarify the meaning of a rule by reference to other related provisions, but this reference presupposes the unity or consistency of the legal order and implies (2) that if tensions arise, they may be alleviated by a reasonable accommodation of the pertinent provisions. (4) If one of the overarching aims of the legal system is the integration of the political community, then teleological interpretation clearly permits inclusion of this goal. Within the same approach it is also possible and perfectly reasonable to advocate the view that in order to (5) further the normative force of the legal text at hand, one must attempt to optimize all the aforementioned points. The only reference point remaining, then, is (3) adherence to the functional differentiation of the Constitution—meaning that judges should adjudicate, while legislators should adopt and administrators execute the law. This point, admittedly, plays a stronger role in constitutional adjudication than in statutory interpretation, but in the process of the former, respect for separation of powers concerns falls clearly under the auspices of a contextual analysis of the text of the Constitution.

* * *

First, each interpretation must respect the outer bounds of grammatical analysis. For example, if the constitutionality of a legal provision is in doubt, the judge should construe it in a way compatible with the constitutional command; however, this is not a license to manipulate the ordinary meaning of the language. Yet, with a closer look, one can identify decisions in which the courts have used systematic and teleological arguments in order to disregard the wording of a rule; usually these are instances in which the result reached by textual analysis is considered by the judges to be irrational or unjust.

Second, more importance must be placed on the 'objective' textual, systematic, and teleological methods than on the 'subjective' historical method.[12] Historical analysis, indeed, generally serves only as a secondary, supplementary way of clarifying a rule's meaning. But in some cases, courts place great emphasis on this type of argument, and it is the other methods which seem to be supplementary.

The designation of the textual, systematic, and teleological analyses as objective is meant to express the view that the text of the provision is used as an independent starting point. Once a law is adopted, according to German understanding, it becomes an independent entity, and is supposed to regulate not only the present, but the future as well. What the adopters said is paramount to what they willed. * * *

* * *

12.   See 11 BVerfGE 126, 129–30 (1960)   * * *.

Gerhard Leibholz, an influential former Justice of the German Federal Constitutional Court, has expressed this master ideal of interpretation as follows:

"If the world as it is, i.e., political reality, is left out of account by the law, the lawyer becomes detached from life, from reality, and so from the law itself. If the value of the legal rule is overlooked because of an uncritically extended theory of the normative force of fact, the choice in favour of the ever-changing forces behind constitutional reality destroys the dignity and authority of the law. It must be the task of the constitutional lawyer to reconcile rules of law and constitutional reality in such a way that the existing dialectical conflict between rule and reality can be removed as far as possible by creative interpretation of the constitution without doing violence thereby either to reality in favour of the rule, or to the rule in favour of reality."[37]

Karl Llewellyn summarizes the same point as follows:

"Thus it is ABC stuff that our appellate courts are interested in and do feel a duty to the production of a result that satisfies, placed upon a ground which also satisfies. One can indicate this crudely as the presence of a felt duty to Justice, a felt duty to The Law, and a third felt duty to satisfy both of the first two at once, if that be possible."[38]

* * *

Legal interpretation is the act of judging in a structured context. This structure stems from constitutional, statutory, and judicial pronouncements of law which, in each hard case, pose problems of indeterminacy. The starting point is the analysis of the relevant provision and its legal context. However, the interpretive result of this first step, in every hard case, must be affirmed or qualified—that is, broadened or narrowed—by taking additional reflective steps. These can be directed forward, backward, upward, and/or downward. Upward arguments rely upon either explicit or implicit constitutional ideals of the political community, such as 'justice for all.' Downward arguments are based on the perceived urgency of needs and interests. Or, to put it more crudely: Looking downward, what we want is what counts, while looking upwards, what we legitimately can and should expect or do is of greatest weight. These perspectives are intertwined with the backward and forward relationship of legal interpretation: The meaning of text and context always expresses past experiences of which the words themselves form a part; the past is constantly present in the meaning of the words. The past, however, does not necessarily determine and constrict their essence. Words possess open-ended significance; contemporary developments in the real or ideal world shape their past purport so that the traditional understanding of the word is affirmed, broadened or narrowed. These new speech conventions then in time become part of the modern 'tradition' of the words' meaning. This is the forward-looking perspective, in which contemporary goals and purposes become primary

37. Gerhard Leibholz, "Constitutional Law and Constitutional Reality," in Festschrift für Karl Loewenstein 305, 308 (Henry Steele Commager et al., eds. 1971).

38. Karl Llewellyn, The Common Law Tradition. Deciding Appeals (1960) at 59.

roots of reference. These four perspectives are critical to legal interpretation.

Any random reading of American legal literature confirms this statement: "[I]n a going life-situation, fairness, rightness, minimum decency, injustice look not only back but forward as well, and so infuse themselves not only with past practice but with good practice, right practice, right guidance of practice, i.e., with felt net values in and for the type of situation, and with policy for legal rules."[51] * * *

Wolfgang Zeidler, THE FEDERAL CONSTITUTIONAL COURT OF THE FEDERAL REPUBLIC OF GERMANY: DECISIONS ON THE CONSTITUTIONALITY OF LEGAL NORMS,

62 Notre Dame L. Rev. 504, 509–11 (1987).

* * *

C. Interpretations which Conform with the Constitution

* * *

If the wording of a law permits several interpretations, then the Federal Constitutional Court must choose the one which produces results harmonious with the Basic Law. There is no room for any interpretation that would lead to an unconstitutional result.[30] The constitutionally acceptable interpretation also must not conflict with the wording and the clearly expressed intent of the legislature. Accordingly, the normative content of the law to be interpreted must not be determined anew and the essential legislative goals must not be missed in the process. Admittedly, this applies only to those basic principles, determinations of value and regulative purpose, which are recognizably expressed by the law.

The statements by legislative committees or individual members of the legislative bodies concerning the significance of a normative component or concept (or scope of an individual provision), its handling, and result do not constitute binding guidelines for the courts, no matter how illuminating they might be in determining meaning. The existence of adverse legislative history, however, occasionally proves problematic. In 1980, such a quandary resulted in a fairly rare decision by the plenum session of the Federal Constitutional Court.[32] Rather briefly, the full

---

51. Llewellyn, *supra* n. 38, at 60.

30. One must distinguish from this the duty of all courts and appliers of the law to lend in a given case the greatest possible force to the fundamental rights established by the constitution. For example, courts must enforce freedom of speech while interpreting rules concerning civil law and professional rules and regulations. Occasionally, this is referred to as an interpretation which takes its cues from the constitution. See, e.g., Simon, in GENERAL REPORT

FOR THE 2ND CONFERENCE, 1974 EuGRZ 85, 86.

32. The Federal Constitutional Court is divided into two chambers, called senates, which have exclusive memberships and exclusive jurisdiction over certain constitutional cases. The plenum, an en banc session of the Court, meets only to address matters concerning the internal administration of the Court as a whole, the disputes arising out of the wish of one senate to depart from a formal ruling by the other, or

court found that restricting the language of a statutory provision which revised the legal recourse to the Federal High Court of Justice in its function in civil matters as a Court of Appeals was proper, in light of the de minimus restriction on legislative intent.[33]

In another decision, the Federal Constitutional Court interpreted as constitutionally conforming, a provision in the tax laws which afforded unwed mothers and foster parents certain special benefits. The Court concluded that fathers of illegitimate children—who are not specifically covered by the wording of the law—could, in certain circumstances,[34] be considered " 'foster parents,' " in view of the constitutional requirement of equality of illegitimate children.[35] The Court premised its decision on the assumption that the legislature would have augmented the provision accordingly if it had recognized the omission.

By comparison, the Federal Constitutional Court rejected as an interpretation which did not conform with the constitution, a National Socialist administrative order—that is, an order that reflected a totalitarian administrative philosophy—which did not meet the constitutional requirement of definiteness. It was deemed impossible to reinterpret such a vague regulation without simultaneously examining whether the subsequent effect agreed at all with the intentions of the democratic legislature. A constitutionally conforming interpretation would have essentially redefined the normative content, and to do so would not have been within the purview of the Federal Constitutional Court.[36] Indeed, by employing a constitutionally acceptable interpretation one must not disregard the danger of shouldering the legislature with results it did not intend.

Equally, and only slightly less problematical, is the functional relationship between the Federal Constitutional Court and the specialized courts, especially the highest. In certain instances, the Federal Constitutional Court may prescribe a constitutionally conforming interpretation of a provision which a specialized court did not support in an earlier decision despite careful deliberations. Furthermore, the Federal Constitutional Court's specific mission authorizes it only to proclaim that a certain interpretation is incompatible with the Basic Law. To do so, the Court must demonstrate that an interpretation which is different from the one held unconstitutional is indeed possible. The Court, however, must leave undecided whether only the specified interpretation is possible or whether there is the possibility for additional constitutional interpretations. Also, the Federal Constitutional Court is not authorized to decide for the specialized courts whether only one of several differing interpretations is legitimate.

the transfer of jurisdiction from one senate to another.

33. 54 BVerfGE 277, 298.

34. 36 BVerfGE 126.

35. GRUNDGESETZ [Basic Law] art. 6(V).

36. 8 BVerfGE 71. See also 20 BVerfGE 150, 160.

Bernhard Schlink, GERMAN CONSTITUTIONAL CULTURE IN TRANSITION, in CONSTITUTIONALISM, IDENTITY, DIFFERENCE, AND LEGITIMACY: THEORETICAL PERSPECTIVES

197, 199–201, 203, 204–06, 211–12 (Michel Rosenfeld ed., 1994).

* * *

Before we can describe and analyze the change in the view of fundamental rights as rights to the view of them as principles, we must ask what rights and principles are and what distinguishes them from each other. There are two answers in legal precedent and jurisprudence. On the one hand, we speak of subjective rights in contrast to objective principles, and, on the other hand, of rights as determinations, in contrast to principles as rules of optimization.[2]

The phrase "fundamental rights as subjective rights" means the characterization of fundamental rights as entitlements of the individual subject, the individual citizen, to be respected by the state in his individual freedoms, to participate as an individual in the practice of state power, or to be considered in the distribution of positions, means, and opportunities. On the other hand, when described as "objective principles," fundamental rights are maxims according to which social relationships, as well as the relationship between state and society, are to be ordered.

Freedom of the press and of broadcasting may illustrate the difference. As a subjective right, freedom of the press guarantees the individual citizen the freedom to print and publish, while freedom of broadcasting guarantees the right to run radio and television stations. As an objective principle, freedom of the press and freedom of broadcasting demand that the legislature regulate publications, radio, and television so as to allow as many citizens as possible to express, or see expressed, their opinions and inclinations, and to satisfy their need for information. In other words, freedom of the press and of broadcasting, as an objective principle, demands a system of press, radio, and television characterized by varied content and diverse supply?

The freedoms of the press and broadcasting can coexist harmoniously as a subjective right and an objective principle. If many make use of their subjective rights, the diversity of content that the principle demands can emerge by itself. However, the subjective right and objective principle can also conflict with one another. For example, diversity of content may only be achievable through the imposition of some limits on individual rights, such as regulation and control of the press and broadcasting markets. This might involve the breaking up of monopolies, the closing off of access to some citizens, the promoting of access to others, and perhaps the use of subsidies.

The other view of the difference between rights and principles differentiates fundamental rights as determinations from fundamental

---

2. ROBERT ALEXY, THEORIE DER GRUNDRECHTE 71–104 (1986); Robert Alexy, *Grundrechte als subjektive Rechte und als objektive Normen*, 29 STAAT 49 (1990).

rights as rules of optimization, and thereby juxtaposes a strict and a relative conception of fundamental rights? Viewing fundamental rights as determinations means that the citizen is entitled to have his freedom respected and to participate in the practice of state power and distribution of positions, means, and opportunities, although the entitlement may be denied to him in exceptional cases. The rule is that the citizen is entitled; the exception lies in the denial of the citizen's entitlements. The exception must be expressly admitted and must be particularly justified, as, for example, when one citizen's claim to his fundamental right conflicts with other citizens' claims to their fundamental rights, or when conflicts arise between fundamental rights and state interests and cannot be settled in any other way.

On the other hand, as rules of optimization, fundamental rights from the outset guarantee the citizen entitlements only in accordance with what is legally and actually possible. In this view, because conflicts are unavoidable among fundamental rights, as well as between fundamental rights and state interests, the entitlement to a fundamental right does not go beyond its enforcement in the conflict. The degree of enforcement will be more in one conflict, less in another; it is as much as possible and, to the extent possible, the optimum.

This second difference can also be illustrated with an example. Most constitutions, including the German Grundgesetz, guarantee each citizen a fundamental right to his dwelling; that is, the dwelling may not be entered and searched by state organs unless certain prerequisites are fulfilled, ranging from a judge's decree to the existence of certain clearly defined dangers. When the Bundesverfassungsgericht faced the question of whether protection of the fight to a dwelling included not only the home but also business premises, it answered positively. At the same time, for practical reasons, it permitted state entry onto business premises under conditions less strict than those for entry into the dwelling as specified in the Grundgesetz.

* * *

The two methods of characterizing the different conceptions of fundamental rights each employ differing sets of criteria. The rights/principles model uses a subjective/objective pair of criteria, while the determination/rule of optimization model uses a strict/relative pair of criteria. But they are related to each other from a practical point of view.

* * * When one speaks of fundamental rights as rights, in contrast to fundamental rights as principles, this does not mean that an interpretation of fundamental rights as rights would be possible without considerations of principle. It means that fundamental rights are not *themselves* principles. However, considerations of principle must be recognized in discussing how far protection of a fundamental right can reach and how intrusions in exceptional cases may be justified.

Let us take once again the right to a dwelling as an example. Whether business premises fall under the term "dwelling," and are therefore encompassed by the fundamental right to a dwelling and its protections, is a question that creates issues of principle involving the function of the fundamental right to a dwelling, the relationship between social and spatial privacy, and the separation and categorization of privacy and the public sphere? In the German tradition of public law, whether or not an intrusion is actually permitted upon the fundamental right to a dwelling, whether narrowly or broadly defined, depends not only on the actual existence of the dangers listed in the constitution as conditions for an intrusion, but also on whether the intrusion is necessary and proper to repel the danger. It must be a means related to the ends sought—this principle of proportionality is decisive in the interpretation and treatment of fundamental rights. However, fundamental rights themselves do not need to become principles. They can remain subjective rights in the strict sense.

II

The consequences of interpreting and treating fundamental rights as rights or as principles become clear when one views the development of decision making by the Bundesverfassungsgericht. * * *

The cases themselves speak of fundamental rights as values and value decisions, as fundamental value-determining norms, objective fundamental rights—fundamental rights as objective principles.

* * *

[One of the issues] that furthered development from the subjective rights view to the objective principles view was the role of government in protecting fundamental rights: whether fundamental rights required the government to take only a passive role in protecting freedoms by not intruding on them, as per the traditional view, or whether the government had a duty to take an active role in protecting freedoms against intrusions by others. The issue arose during the 1970s in the struggle over the criminal treatment of abortion. The legislature had created a scheme that unconditionally legalized abortion in the first trimester, and then legalized it during the following months if certain indicators were present. The Bundesverfassungsgericht considered this insufficient protection of the unborn, who, according to the Court, were better protected by an indicator requirement that applied from the start of pregnancy. The Court considered this increased protection necessary to insure fundamental rights—the fundamental right to life, as a value-determinative fundamental norm and objective principle. Defined as such, this fundamental right required the government not only to refrain from intrusions, but also to support and protect life. Thus, the Court rejected the legislature's arrangement and obliged it to promulgate legislation that applied the criminally stricter indicator arrangement from the start of pregnancy. Two dissenting judges strongly criticized the decision and rejected the objective principle characterization of fundamental rights as a heading under which fundamental rights changed from individual freedoms to a governmental duty of punishment.

The Bundesverfassungsgericht has never again inferred a duty of punishment from a fundamental right. However, it also has never had another opportunity to do so.

* * *

In order to fulfill its activist role, the Bundesverfassungsgericht has driven forward the development from the understanding of fundamental rights as subjective rights to the understanding of them as objective principles. Has this been a negative development? What are, in fact, the fundamental rights of the Grundgesetz: subjective rights or objective principles?

Beyond question, the authors of the Grundgesetz considered its fundamental rights to be subjective rights—protections of personal freedoms through repulsion of state intrusions. After the unfortunate experience with the Weimar Constitution's programmatically broad fundamental rights, which tried and failed not only to secure freedoms through defense against intrusions but also to guarantee government services and the structuring of social relations, the creators of the Grundgesetz consciously limited themselves to guaranteeing fundamental freedoms. Naturally they were guided by principles—that is, maxims—for ordering social relations and the relationship between state and society. However, rather than principles, the Grundgesetz's authors considered fundamental rights to be guarantees of specific freedoms of citizens from specific state intrusions. They considered fundamental rights as necessary, but not sufficient, conditions for a satisfactory ordering of social relations.

Thus if it were simply a question of the authors' original intent, the question asked above would be easy to answer: Fundamental rights are not actually objective principles, but subjective rights. However, as the authors themselves know, original intent is only of relative significance. They know that their legal texts are introduced into a legal process where interpretations and reinterpretations, and constructions and deconstructions, alternate with one another. The outcome is open, constantly changing, and never more than temporary. The authors' awareness of this legal process overcomes their original intent. Thus, original intent cannot be contrary to textual interpretation because it has anticipated this interpretation. In other words, the authors know what they intend, but they also know that their original intent can only offer the limited authority conveyed by the text; they intend as much of their intentions as the text conveys.

So what does the text of the fundamental rights convey? The answer—and how could it be otherwise?—is ambiguous. According to traditional formulations, nearly all fundamental rights are formulated to repel government intrusions upon freedoms. However, the text of these fundamental rights includes formulations that are concerned not only with freedoms as attached to individuals, but with the freedoms themselves. "Each person has the right . . . freely to express and make known his opinion" [Basic Law, art. 5, para. 1, cl. 1]—this is a subjective rights formulation. "Freedom of the press and freedom of broadcasting . . . are guaranteed" [Basic Law, art. 5, para. 1, cl. 2.]—this can be understood as an objective principle formulation. * * *

C.1.3. FRANCE

Dominique   Rousseau,   THE   CONSTITUTIONAL
JUDGE: MASTER OR SLAVE OF THE CONSTITU-
TION?, in CONSTITUTIONALISM, IDENTITY,
DIFFERENCE AND LEGITIMACY: THEORETI-
CAL PERSPECTIVES

261, 263–67 (Michel Rosenfeld ed., 1994).

* * *

*1. THE CONSTITUTIONAL JUDGE'S INTERPRETATION AS
THE PRODUCT OF MULTIPLE, COMPLEX INTERACTION*

A. *The Techniques of Interpretation*

The main means of constitutional control is textual interpretation.
When a statute is challenged in court, claimants always allege that the
legislator misinterpreted constitutional principles and that the purpose
or effects of the law, as interpreted by those who bring the action, are
unconstitutional. In order to respond to these challenges, in a word to
declare that a law is or is not consistent with a given constitutional
principle, the Council must determine both the meaning of the right or
liberty in question and the correct meaning of the disputed law. The
interpretation of texts is thus a stake in a constitutional contest in which
the interpretations of Parliament, of those bringing the action, and of
the Council vie with one another. For the Council, interpretation is an
inherently intellectual operation that is indispensable for its exercise of
control. Thanks to constitutional interpretation and a meticulous analysis of the content of the statute, the Council can speak out about the
consistency of its constitutional rulings. In order to accomplish this task,
the Council has gradually evolved three specific interpretive techniques.

1. The Three Techniques of Interpretation

The first, the *limiting interpretation*, involves the Council's removing juridical effect from disputable legislative provisions or excluding
from among possible interpretations those that would make it contradict
the Constitution. Thus, for example, where, a claimant takes issue with
certain provisions of a statute, the Council may reason that the "provisions are devoid of any legal effect"; by rendering the provisions inoperative, "there are no grounds to declare them inconsistent with the
Constitution. Or, the Council may decide that a statute could not
possibly have the unconstitutional effect ascribed to it by the claimants.

The second technique is *constructive interpretation,* in which the
Council no longer curtails but adds provisions to the law that are
designed to make it consistent with the Constitution or make a legal
clause convey more meaning than is expressly provided in the text. Thus,
when article twenty-nine of the law concerning the prevention of lay-off
orders [provides] only that the labor union bringing suit on behalf of a
wage-earner must give him notice "in a registered letter with acknowledgement of receipt," the Council assumes that this provision

"implies that the letter must contain all relevant details about the nature and purpose of the current lawsuit, about the full implication of his acceptance, and about his acknowledged right to stop the suit at any point * * * and that the tacit acceptance of the wage-earner may be considered granted only when the union can prove when it brings the suit that the wage-earner personally had thorough knowledge of the letter including the details mentioned above." [CC decision no. 89–257 of 25 July 1989.]

None of these specifications is delineated in the text of the law; the Council, through the task of interpretation, added them so that the law may be deemed consistent with the Constitution.

The third technique, *guideline interpretation,* consists of the Council defining and specifying for those authorities responsible for implementing the law, the modes of application necessary for conformity with the Constitution. Thus, in its decision issued on July 28, 1989, the Council first specified the rules of application in a case where several financial and penal sanctions could obtain against the perpetrators of stock exchange misdemeanors, by providing that the total amount of sanctions must not in these cases exceed "the highest amount of one of the sanctions incurred." The Council immediately added a directive of application by asking, "the competent administrative and legal authorities to pay careful heed to the fulfillment of his demand in the implementation of these provisions."

Whatever the technique, the Constitutional Council does exert its control through an interpretation of the statutes whose scope it limits, whose provisions it completes, and whose modes of application it specifies. Because of its judicial and political implications, this means of control raises many problems.

2. *The Clear Error* (l'erreur manifeste) *Standard*

The Council's use of "clear error" as a standard for control over the legislator's awareness of the facts, circumstances or situations forming the bases of a statute, appears for the first time implicitly in its decision issued on January 19–20, 1981 and explicitly in its decision issued on January 16, 1982: "[T]he legislator's assessment of the necessity of nationalizations decided by the law which is under examination by the Constitutional Council could not be challenged *in the absence of unmistakable error*". [CC decision no. 86–215.]

Since that decision, the Council has regularly used this means of control of facts both to underscore the legislator's awareness of the severity and need for disciplinary measures regarding the unacceptable features and the length of time during which valid provisions remain temporarily applicable; this means also helps the Council to find out whether Parlement has made an error in its weighing of contextual distinctions that might justify an infringement on the principle of equality. The Council ensures that decisions, such as where the threshold from which professional property is exempt from the surtax on great wealth belongs, or regarding the setting of different age limits for various classes of civil servants do not arise from obviously flawed judgments * * *

With the clear error standard, the Council thus introduces control of proportionality in disputed constitutional claims. This clearly springs from the wording of recent decisions in which the Council examined in turn whether statutes set up "an *obvious disproportion* between the offense and the punishment incurred," [CC decision no. 86–215] or create *excessively disproportionate* gaps in representation between election districts * * *

* * * As a general rule, the Council always ascertains whether the legislator's threats to a constitutional right are not so severe that its meaning and implication would be distorted. In other words, the clear error standard allows the Council to weigh, on one hand, the common interest sought by the statute and on the other hand, the threats to a given constitutional principle; depending on the result, whether or not the Council judges the threats to be disproportionate or excessive with respect to the interest sought by the legislator, the statute will be declared consistent or inconsistent with the Constitution * * *

With the evolution of such a method, isn't the control of constitutionality constrained by political exigencies?

Notes and Questions

1. With the exception of arguments from precedent, which have no place in German constitutional interpretation, the different types of constitutional arguments prevalent in the U.S. and Germany seem largely similar.

United States	Germany
Arguments from the text	Grammatical arguments
Arguments from framers' intent	Historical arguments
Arguments from constitutional theory	Systematic arguments
Value arguments	Teleological arguments

Furthermore, even though precedents do not figure in the German system of constitutional interpretation, functionally the GFCC's concern with institutional consistency and integrity leads it to treat its own past decisions as if they had the force of precedent. Both the USSC and the GFCC have occasionally deviated from past decisions, but the latter does not appear to have done so more freely or more frequently because it is unconstrained by precedents.

On the other hand the similarities noted above do not preclude important differences concerning the relative force or context of the respective types of arguments involved. Historical arguments, in Germany, do not have nearly the same importance as framers' intent arguments in the U.S. Is this because the German Basic Law is much younger than the U.S. Constitution? Or does it have more to do with the respective histories of constitution-making and ideologies of the two countries?

There also seem to be important differences between value arguments in the U.S. and teleological arguments in Germany. The principal differences are that whereas value arguments appear to be external to the U.S. Constitution, teleological arguments loom as internal to the German Basic Law. For example, as there is no explicit reference to abortion in the U.S.

Constitution, value arguments both in favor and against abortion rights tend to refer to general moral precepts debated within American society at large rather than clearly embedded in the U.S. Constitution. In Germany, in contrast, specific values, such as the paramountcy of human dignity enshrined in Article I of the Basic Law, provide a teleological framework for the Constitution taken as a whole. Accordingly, teleological arguments are supposed to guide the constitutional adjudicator toward vindication of the values and normative purposes explicitly embraced by the Basic Law. Does this make teleological arguments inherently different than value arguments? And, more generally, does the type or argument involved matter less than the institutional and ideological setting in which it is inserted?

2.   The techniques of interpretation used by the French Constitutional Council described by Professor Rousseau seem altogether different than the types of arguments prevalent in Germany or the U.S. The French techniques appear less concerned with providing meaning to the constitutional text than with reshaping the challenged statutory text to make it consistent with the Constitution. Thus in "limiting interpretation," the Council weakens or renders ineffective statutory provisions; in "constructive interpretation," the Council adds to the statute; and in "guideline interpretation," the Council instructs the authorities on how to implement the statute. Does the French approach make the constitutional adjudicator more like a legislator than does the German or U.S. approach? Note, however, that, as Chief Justice Zeidler indicates, courts tend to provide the statutory text under review with constitution-conforming meaning. In *Ashwander v. T.V.A.*, 297 U.S. 288 (1936), Justice Brandeis gave a whole catalogue of techniques for avoiding unnecessary constitutional decisions. A similar attitude is present in Canada in the "reading-down" technique.

3.   In contrast to the approaches discussed so far, the Supreme Court of India has advocated a far more sweeping and self-consciously more ideological way of engaging in constitutional adjudication. As stated in Jamie Cassels, *Judicial Activism and Public Interest Litigation in India: Attempting the Impossible?*, 37 Am. J. Comp. L. 495, 502 (1989):

> The former Chief Justice of the Supreme Court, writing in both the popular press and the academic journals, made quite clear his rejection of the "bureaucratic tradition" of mechanical and rule-bound adjudication.[36] He suggested that positivism is a myth, "deliberately constructed to insulate judges against vulnerability to public criticism, and to preserve their image of neutrality * * * It also helps judges to escape accountability for what they decide, because they can always plead helplessness." In interpreting the Constitution, the Supreme Court is neither bound by doctrines of literal meaning or original intent, nor constrained to read into it only formal rights and liberties. Instead, the text can be read as one which is "vibrant with a socio-economic ideology geared to the goal of social justice" and can be infused with principles that transcend mere equality, and transform legal rights into positive social entitlements.
>
> The judges in India have asked themselves the question: can judges really escape addressing themselves to substantial questions of social

36. Bhagwati, "Bureaucrats? Photographers? Creators?" The *Times of India*, 21–   23 September 1986.

justice? Can they * * * simply follow the legal text when they are aware that their actions will perpetuate inequality and injustice? Can they restrict their inquiry into law and life within the narrow confines of a narrowly defined rule of law?[38]

Is the approach in India more political and hence more objectionable than the other approaches discussed above? Or is it rather more open and honest? Does the answer depend on whether there can be objective interpretations of texts? Compare Frederick Schauer, *Easy Cases*, 58 S. Cal. L. Rev. 399 (1985) (arguing that some constitutional cases lead to a single obvious solution) with Michel Rosenfeld, *Just Interpretations: Law Between Ethics and Politics,* ch I (1998) (arguing that texts do not speak for themselves and that all interpretations are intersubjective and open-ended). Or, on whether the framers' intent can be established fully and unequivocally? See the discussion on originalism below.

C.2. DILEMMAS OF CONSTITUTIONAL INTERPRETATION

C.2.1. TEXTUALISM AND BEYOND

Can the text of a constitution ever be determinative in any but the simplest of cases? In the U.S., the most often cited example of a straightforward constitutional provision making for a simple textual solution is that in Art II, Sec. 1, which requires, in part, that no person shall "be eligible to [the] office [of President] who shall not have attained the age of thirty five years." It is clear that if a fourteen-year-old were elected President he or she would not be constitutionally eligible to hold that office. But what about someone who had his or her thirty fifth birthday sometime between election day in November and inauguration in January of the next year? And what about a candidate who turns thirty five three months after the day of inauguration, but argues that age should be counted from conception, as it is in certain cultures, rather than from birth, as it is customarily done in the U.S.? Is there a textual solution to these last two hypothetical cases? More generally, consider the following cases.

AUSTRALIAN CAPITAL TELEVISION v. THE COMMONWEALTH OF AUSTRALIA

High Court (Australia).
(1992) 177 C.L.R. 106.

[The Political Broadcasts and Political Disclosures Act 1991, Part IIID introduced rules regarding the allocation of free television time in electoral campaigns, providing advantages to certain incumbent political parties. It also prohibited paid political advertisements during the run-up to state and federal elections.]

Mr. Justice Mason * * *

14. The effect of Pt IIID [of the statute] is, as the plaintiffs submit, to exclude the use of radio and television during election periods as a

---

38. Bhagwati, "Bureaucrats," *supra* n. 36.

medium of political campaigning and even as a medium for the dissemination of political information, comment and argument and as a forum of discussion except in so far as (a) s.95A permits the broadcasting of news and current affairs items and talkback radio programmes; (b) Div. 3 permits free election broadcasts; and (c) Div. 4 permits the broadcasting of policy launches.

* * *

16.   The consequence is that Pt IIID severely impairs the freedoms previously enjoyed by citizens to discuss public and political affairs and to criticize federal institutions. Part IIID impairs those freedoms by restricting the broadcasters' freedom to broadcast and by restricting the access of political parties, groups, candidates and persons generally to express views with respect to public and political affairs on radio and television.

17.   The Commonwealth's response is that the evident and principal purpose of Pt IIID is to safeguard the integrity of the political system by reducing, if not eliminating, pressure on political parties and candidates to raise substantial sums of money in order to engage in political campaigning on television and radio, a pressure which renders them vulnerable to corruption and to undue influence by those who donate to political campaign funds.

* * *

22.   [The Court reviewed election-related speech restrictions in democracies but found that] the overseas experience does not refute the proposition that Pt IIID impairs freedom of discussion of public and political affairs and freedom to criticize federal institutions in the respects previously mentioned. * * * [T]he provisions regulating the allocation of free time allow no scope for participation in the election campaign by persons who are not candidates or by groups who are not putting forward candidates for election.

* * *

The Implication of Fundamental Rights

31.   The adoption by the framers of the Constitution of the principle of responsible government was perhaps the major reason for their disinclination to incorporate in the Constitution comprehensive guarantees of individual rights, "(T)he Australian Constitution is built upon confidence in a system of parliamentary Government with ministerial responsibility": Attorney–General (Cth); Ex rel. *McKinlay v. The Commonwealth* (1975) 135 CLR 1, per Barwick C.J. at p. 24. They refused to adopt a counterpart to the Fourteenth Amendment to the Constitution of the United States. * * * The framers of the Constitution accepted, in accordance with prevailing English thinking, that the citizen's rights were best left to the protection of the common law in association with the doctrine of parliamentary supremacy.

* * *

33.   In the light of this well recognized background, it is difficult, if not impossible, to establish a foundation for the implication of general

guarantees of fundamental rights and freedoms. To make such an implication would run counter to the prevailing sentiment of the framers that there was no need to incorporate a comprehensive Bill of Rights in order to protect the rights and freedoms of citizens. That sentiment was one of the unexpressed assumptions on which the Constitution was drafted.

34. However, the existence of that sentiment when the Constitution was adopted and the influence which it had on the shaping of the Constitution are no answer to the case which the plaintiffs now present. Their case is that a guarantee of freedom of expression in relation to public and political affairs must necessarily be implied from the provision which the Constitution makes for a system of representative government. The plaintiffs say that, because such a freedom is an essential concomitant of representative government, it is necessarily implied in the prescription of that system.

Representative Government

* * *

37. The very concept of representative government and representative democracy signifies government by the people through their representatives. Translated into constitutional terms, it denotes that the sovereign power which resides in the people is exercised on their behalf by their representatives. * * *

* * *

The point is that the representatives who are members of Parliament and Ministers of State are not only chosen by the people but exercise their legislative and executive powers as representatives of the people. And in the exercise of those powers the representatives of necessity are accountable to the people for what they do and have a responsibility to take account of the views of the people on whose behalf they act.

Freedom of Communication as an Indispensable Element in Representative Government

38. Indispensable to that accountability and that responsibility is freedom of communication, at least in relation to public affairs and political discussion. Only by exercising that freedom can the citizen communicate his or her views on the wide range of matters that may call for, or are relevant to, political action or decision. Only by exercising that freedom can the citizen criticize government decisions and actions, seek to bring about change, call for action where none has been taken and in this way influence the elected representatives. By these means the elected representatives are equipped to discharge their role so that they may take account of and respond to the will of the people. Communication in the exercise of the freedom is by no means a one-way traffic, for the elected representatives have a responsibility not only to ascertain the views of the electorate but also to explain and account for their decisions and actions in government and to inform the people so that they may make informed judgments on relevant matters. Absent such a freedom of communication, representative government would fail to

achieve its purpose, namely, government by the people through their elected representatives; government would cease to be responsive to the needs and wishes of the people and, in that sense, would cease to be truly representative.

39.   Freedom of communication in relation to public affairs and political discussion cannot be confined to communications between elected representatives and candidates for election on the one hand and the electorate on the other. The efficacy of representative government depends also upon free communication on such matters between all persons, groups and other bodies in the community. That is because individual judgment, whether that of the elector, the representative or the candidate, on so many issues turns upon free public discussion in the media of the views of all interested persons, groups and bodies and on public participation in, and access to, that discussion. In truth, in a representative democracy, public participation in political discussion is a central element of the political process.

* * *

[Justice Mason accepted that the need to "safeguard the integrity of the political process" might be a legitimate ground for Parliament to limit politicians' use of paid advertisement. Free speech is not absolute. The solution of the Act, however, was in violation of the implied constitutional right to speech as it was sweeping in scope and discriminatory in nature.][c]

SPINAL TAP CASE

Federal Constitutional Court (Germany).
16 BVerfGE 194 (1963).

[Complainant was the manager of an enterprise associated with the Central Chamber of the Munich Knitting Goods Company. He and his eighty-year-old mother, with whom he lived, owned a small number of shares in the parent company. He refused to properly fill out a Board of Trade questionnaire relating to his business, as he was legally required to do. Instead, he returned the questionnaire with a number of frivolous and nonsensical comments on it, whereupon the Board of Trade fined him DM 500 for his failure to cooperate. He refused to pay the fine, claiming that the board lacked jurisdiction over his business. In an action to collect the fine, a district court judge, suspecting a disorder of the complainant's central nervous system, ordered him to undergo a medical test requiring the withdrawal of body fluid for the purpose of determining his mental condition pursuant to section 81a of the Code of Criminal Procedure. The court of appeals sustained the order. The complainant challenged these court orders as violative of his right to a hearing in accordance with law under Article 103(1) and personal inviolability under Article 2 (2) of the Constitution.]

Judgment of the First Senate * * *

c. For a critical examination, see K. D.   *Australia*, Public Law 256 (1993). Ewing, *New Constitutional Constraints in*

The district court decision of September 11, 1958, and the superior court decision of October 14, 1958, violate the complainant's basic right under Article 2 (2) of the Constitution. They are quashed and the case is remanded to the Munich District Court * * *

B. We need not decide whether the court of appeals ruling violates Article 103 (I). The constitutional complaint is sustained because the ruling violates the basic right to physical inviolability (Article 2[2]).

The extraction of cerebral and spinal fluid by means of a cannula is not an insignificant surgical invasion of bodily integrity within the meaning of Article 2(2) of the Constitution. When conducted in accordance with the standards of modern medicine this procedure is not normally dangerous; yet severe pain and nausea are possible. In fact, according to a report submitted by the court-appointed expert, approximately 10 percent of the persons undergoing spinal taps experience such severe effects. The extraction of fluids may also lead to serious complications in certain cases * * *

The right to physical inviolability can be limited only by general law (Article 2(2)[3]). Section 81a of the Criminal Procedure Code formally satisfies this requirement * * *

[In this part of the opinion the Court sustained the validity of section 81a over objections that the statute is unduly vague and violates the principle of presumption of innocence. Section 81a authorizes a judge to order a criminal defendant, against his consent, to undergo blood tests and other bodily penetrations if such evidence is necessary in a criminal proceeding. The physical examination can be performed only "by a physician pursuant to the rules of medical science" and only if "no resulting detriment to [the defendant's] health is to be feared." The Court pointed out that section 81a could be reasonably construed to require judges to apply the principle of proportionality before authorizing such an examination. Judges must be mindful of constitutional values in the application of this provision.]

(c) When ruling on cases involving the compulsory extraction of body fluids, the judge must—as in all cases involving government encroachment on the sphere of freedom—observe the principle of proportionality relative to ends and means. While the public interest in solving crimes—an interest based on the especially important principle of legality—ordinarily justifies even encroachments on the freedom of the accused, this general interest suffices less the more severe infringement of freedom. Thus, in order properly to evaluate the relationship between means and end, one must also consider the severity of the criminal offense. This is especially to be considered when determining criminal responsibility pursuant to the serious procedures under sections 81 and 81a of the Criminal Code. An application of the law in the light of the meaning of the basic rights requires that the proposed measure be proportionate to the seriousness of the offenses, so that the consequences connected with the detection of the crime will not encumber the criminal more than the expected punishment. The judge therefore, has the constitutional duty to weigh an encroachment, in itself legally permissible, against the ban on its excess * * * The Federal Constitutional Court has repeatedly applied this principle to the process of investigative custody. Therefore an interpretation of section 81a which conforms to the Constitution demands the application of the principle of proportionality consistent with the approach the courts have previously taken.

3.   The courts disregarded these principles in the present case * * * All in all, the matter is a minor offense that might lead to only a light sentence, possibly even an acquittal on account of its insignificance. By comparison, the extraction of fluid is not an insignificant physical procedure. There is no justification for submitting the accused to such a surgical procedure against his will. Because the courts disregarded the principle of proportionality by misunderstanding the range of the basic right provided for by Article 2(2), [we] will not set aside the contested decisions. [Instead, we will] remand the case to the district court.

GRISWOLD v. CONNECTICUT

Supreme Court (United States).
381 U.S. 479 (1965).

Mr. Justice Douglas delivered the opinion of the Court.

Appellant, [a director of Planned Parenthood and a physician were convicted for having advised married couples to use contraceptives in violation of a Connecticut criminal statute].

The statutes whose constitutionality is involved in this appeal are ss 53–32 and 54–196 of the General Statutes of Connecticut (1958 rev.). The former provides:

'Any person who uses any drug, medicinal article or instrument for the purpose of preventing conception shall be fined not less than fifty dollars or imprisoned not less than sixty days nor more than one year or be both fined and imprisoned.'

Section 54–196 provides:

'Any person who assists, abets, counsels, causes, hires or commands another to commit any offense may be prosecuted and punished as if he were the principal offender.'

The appellants were found guilty as accessories and fined $100 each, against the claim that the accessory statute as so applied violated the Fourteenth Amendment.

* * *

Coming to the merits, we are met with a wide range of questions that implicate the Due Process Clause of the Fourteenth Amendment. Overtones of some arguments suggest that *Lochner v. State. of New York*, 198 U.S. 45 [1905], should be our guide. But we decline that invitation as we did in *West Coast Hotel Co. v. Parrish*, 300 U.S. 379 [1937]. We do not sit as a super-legislature to determine the wisdom, need, and propriety of laws that touch economic problems, business affairs, or social conditions. This law, however, operates directly on an intimate relation of husband and wife and their physician's role in one aspect of that relation.

The association of people is not mentioned in the Constitution nor in the Bill of Rights. The right to educate a child in a school of the parents' choice—whether public or private or parochial—is also not mentioned. Nor is the right to study any particular subject or any foreign language. Yet the First Amendment has been construed to include certain of those rights.

By *Pierce v. Society of Sisters*, [268 U.S. 510 (1925)] the right to educate one's children as one chooses is made applicable to the States by the force of the First and Fourteenth Amendments. By *Meyer v. State of Nebraska*, [262 U.S. 390 (1923)] the same dignity is given the right to study the German language in a private school. In other words, the State may not, consistently with the spirit of the First Amendment, contract the spectrum of available knowledge. * * *

[The Constitution does not explicitly guarantee a right to privacy, but precedents] suggest that specific guarantees in the Bill of Rights have penumbras, formed by emanations from those guarantees that help give them life and substance. Various guarantees create zones of privacy. The right of association contained in the penumbra of the First Amendment is one, * * *. The Third Amendment in its prohibition against the quartering of soldiers 'in any house' in time of peace without the consent of the owner is another facet of that privacy. The Fourth Amendment explicitly affirms the 'right of the people to be secure in their persons, houses, papers, and effects, against unreasonable searches and seizures.' The Fifth Amendment in its Self–Incrimination Clause enables the citizen to create a zone of privacy which government may not force him to surrender to his detriment. The Ninth Amendment provides: 'The enumeration in the Constitution, of certain rights, shall not be construed to deny or disparage others retained by the people.'

The Fourth and Fifth Amendments were described in *Boyd v. United States,* 116 U.S. 616, 630 [ ] as protection against all governmental invasions 'of the sanctity of a man's home and the privacies of life. 'We recently referred in *Mapp v. Ohio*, 367 U.S. 643, 656 [1961] to the Fourth Amendment as creating a 'right to privacy, no less important than any other right carefully and particularly reserved to the people.'

We have had many controversies over these penumbral rights of 'privacy and repose.' Our cases bear witness that the right of privacy which presses for recognition here is a legitimate one.

The present case, then, concerns a relationship lying within the zone of privacy created by several fundamental constitutional guarantees. And it concerns a law which, in forbidding the use of contraceptives rather than regulating their manufacture or sale, seeks to achieve its goals by means having a maximum destructive impact upon that relationship * * * Would we allow the police to search the sacred precincts of marital bedrooms for telltale signs of the use of contraceptives? The very idea is repulsive to the notions of privacy surrounding the marriage relationship.

We deal with a right of privacy older than the Bill of Rights—older than our political parties, older than our school system. Marriage is a coming together for better or for worse, hopefully enduring, and intimate to the degree of being sacred. It is an association that promotes a way of life, not causes; a harmony in living, not political faiths; a bilateral loyalty, not commercial or social projects. Yet it is an association for as noble a purpose as any involved in our prior decisions.

Reversed.

Mr. Justice Black, with whom Mr. Justice Stewart joins, dissenting.

* * * I do not to any extent whatever base my view that this Connecticut law is constitutional on a belief that the law is wise or that its policy is a good one. In order that there may be no room at all to doubt why I vote as I do, I feel constrained to add that the law is every bit as offensive to me as it is to my Brethren of the majority * * * who, reciting reasons why it is offensive to them, hold it unconstitutional. [I agree with all their critical remarks,] except their conclusion that the evil qualities they see in the law make it unconstitutional.

The Court talks about a constitutional 'right of privacy' as though there is some constitutional provision or provisions forbidding any law ever to be passed which might abridge the 'privacy' of individuals. But there is not. There are, of course, guarantees in certain specific constitutional provisions which are designed in part to protect privacy at certain times and places with respect to certain activities. Such, for example, is the Fourth Amendment's guarantee against 'unreasonable searches and seizures.' But I think it belittles that Amendment to talk about it as though it protects nothing but 'privacy.' To treat it that way is to give it a niggardly interpretation, not the kind of liberal reading I think any Bill of Rights provision should be given * * *

One of the most effective ways of diluting or expanding a constitutionally guaranteed right is to substitute for the crucial word or words of a constitutional guarantee another word or words, more or less flexible and more or less restricted in meaning. This fact is well illustrated by the use of the term 'right of privacy' as a comprehensive substitute for the Fourth Amendment's guarantee against 'unreasonable searches and seizures * * * 'Privacy is a broad, abstract and ambiguous concept which can easily be shrunken in meaning but which can also, on the other hand, easily be interpreted as a constitutional ban against many things other than searches and seizures. I like my privacy as well as the next one, but I am nevertheless compelled to admit that government has a right to invade it unless prohibited by some specific constitutional provision. For these reasons I cannot agree with the Court's judgment and the reasons it gives for holding this Connecticut law unconstitutional.

* * * While I completely subscribe to the holding of *Marbury v. Madison* and subsequent cases, that our Court has constitutional power to strike down statutes, state or federal, that violate commands of the Federal Constitution, I do not believe that we are granted power by the Constitution to measure constitutionality by our belief that legislation is arbitrary, capricious or unreasonable, or accomplishes no justifiable purpose, or is offensive to our own notions of 'civilized standards of conduct'. Such an appraisal of the wisdom of legislation is an attribute of the power to make laws, not of the power to interpret them. The use by

federal courts of such a formula or doctrine or whatnot to veto federal or state laws simply takes away from Congress and States the power to make laws based on their own judgment of fairness and wisdom and transfers that power to this Court for ultimate determination—a power which was specifically denied to federal courts by the convention that framed the Constitution.

I repeat so as not to be misunderstood that this Court does have power, which it should exercise, to hold laws unconstitutional where they are forbidden by the Federal Constitution. My point is that there is no provision of the Constitution which either expressly or impliedly vests power in this Court to sit as a supervisory agency over acts of duly constituted legislative bodies and set aside their laws because of the Court's belief that the legislative policies adopted are unreasonable, unwise, arbitrary, capricious or irrational. The adoption of such a loose, flexible, uncontrolled standard for holding laws unconstitutional, if ever it is finally achieved, will amount to a great unconstitutional shift of power to the courts which I believe and am constrained to say will be bad for the courts and worse for the country. Subjecting federal and state laws to such an unrestrained and unrestrainable judicial control as to the wisdom of legislative enactments would, I fear, jeopardize the separation of governmental powers that the Framers set up * * *

I realize that many good and able men have eloquently spoken and written, sometimes in rhapsodical strains, about the duty of this Court to keep the Constitution in tune with the times. The idea is that the Constitution must be changed from time to time and that this Court is charged with a duty to make those changes. For myself, I must with all deferences reject that philosophy. The Constitution makers knew the need for change and provided for it. Amendments suggested by the people's elected representatives can be submitted to the people or their selected agents for ratification. That method of change was good for our Fathers, and being somewhat old-fashioned I must add it is good enough for me. And so, I cannot rely on * * * any mysterious and uncertain natural law concept as a reason for striking down this state law.

* * * The practice has been firmly established for better or worse, that courts can strike down legislative enactment's which violate the Constitution. This process, of course, involves interpretation, and since words can have many meanings, interpretation obviously may result in contraction or extension of the original purpose of a constitutional provision thereby affecting policy. But to pass upon the constitutionality of statutes by looking to the particular standards enumerated in the Bill of Rights and other parts of the Constitution is one thing; to invalidate statutes because of application of 'natural law' deemed to be above and undefined by the Constitution is another. 'In the one instance, courts proceeding within clearly marked constitutional boundaries seek to execute policies written into the Constitution; in the other they roam at will in the limitless area of their own beliefs as to reasonableness and actually select policies, a responsibility which the Constitution entrusts to the legislative representatives of the people.'

The late Judge Learned Hand, after emphasizing his view that judges should not use the Constitution to invalidate legislation offensive to their 'personal preferences,' made the statement, with which I fully agree, that:

'For myself it would be most irksome to be ruled by a bevy of Platonic Guardians, even if I knew how to choose them, which I assuredly do not.'

So far as I am concerned, Connecticut's law as applied here is not forbidden by any provision of the Federal Constitution as that Constitution was written, and I would therefore affirm.

REFERENCE RE SECESSION OF QUEBEC

Supreme Court (Canada).
[1998] 2 S.C.R. 217.

REFERENCE BY GOVERNOR IN COUNCIL

THE COURT—

I. Introduction

1. This Reference requires us to consider momentous questions that go to the heart of our system of constitutional government. * * * In our view, it is not possible to answer the questions that have been put to us without a consideration of a number of underlying principles. An exploration of the meaning and nature of these underlying principles is not merely of academic interest. On the contrary, such an exploration is of immense practical utility. Only once those underlying principles have been examined and delineated may a considered response to the questions we are required to answer emerge.

2. The [first] question [ ] posed by the Governor in Council by way of Order in Council P.C. 1996–1497, dated September 30, 1996, reads as follows:

1. Under the Constitution of Canada, can the National Assembly, legislature or government of Quebec effect the secession of Quebec from Canada unilaterally? * * *

[Questions 2 and 3 concerning international law and its relation to domestic law are omitted.]

[Preliminary objections on jurisdiction and justiciability omitted.]

III. Reference Questions

A. *Question 1*

Under the Constitution of Canada, can the National Assembly, legislature or government of Quebec effect the secession of Quebec from Canada unilaterally?

(1) Introduction

32. As we confirmed in Reference re Objection by Quebec to a Resolution to amend the Constitution, [1982] 2 S.C.R. 793, at p. 806, "The Constitution Act, 1982 is now in force. Its legality is neither challenged nor assailable." The "Constitution of Canada" certainly

includes the constitutional texts enumerated in s. 52(2) of the Constitution Act, 1982. Although these texts have a primary place in determining constitutional rules, they are not exhaustive. The Constitution also "embraces unwritten, as well as written rules" * * * Finally, * * * the Constitution of Canada includes the global system of rules and principles which govern the exercise of constitutional authority in the whole and in every part of the Canadian state.

These supporting principles and rules, which include constitutional conventions and the workings of Parliament, are a necessary part of our Constitution because problems or situations may arise which are not expressly dealt with by the text of the Constitution. In order to endure over time, a constitution must contain a comprehensive set of rules and principles which are capable of providing an exhaustive legal framework for our system of government. Such principles and rules emerge from an understanding of the constitutional text itself, the historical context, and previous judicial interpretations of constitutional meaning. In our view, there are four fundamental and organizing principles of the Constitution which are relevant to addressing the question before us (although this enumeration is by no means exhaustive): federalism; democracy; constitutionalism and the rule of law; and respect for minorities. The foundation and substance of these principles are addressed in the following paragraphs. We will then turn to their specific application to the first reference question before us.

3) Analysis of the Constitutional Principles

(a) Nature of the Principles

49. What are those underlying principles? Our Constitution is primarily a written one, the product of 131 years of evolution. Behind the written word is an historical lineage stretching back through the ages, which aids in the consideration of the underlying constitutional principles. These principles inform and sustain the constitutional text: they are the vital unstated assumptions upon which the text is based. The following discussion addresses the four foundational constitutional principles that are most germane for resolution of this Reference: federalism, democracy, constitutionalism and the rule of law, and respect for minority rights. These defining principles function in symbiosis. No single principle can be defined in isolation from the others, nor does any one principle trump or exclude the operation of any other.

(b) Federalism

55. It is undisputed that Canada is a federal state. * * *

58. The principle of federalism recognizes the diversity of the component parts of Confederation, and the autonomy of provincial governments to develop their societies within their respective spheres of jurisdiction. The federal structure of our country also facilitates democratic participation by distributing power to the government thought to be most suited to achieving the particular societal objective having regard to this diversity. The scheme of the Constitution Act, 1867, it was said in Re the Initiative and Referendum Act, [1919] A.C. 935 (P.C.), at p. 942, was not to weld the Provinces into one, nor to subordinate

Provincial Governments to a central authority, but to establish a central government in which these Provinces should be represented, entrusted with exclusive authority only in affairs in which they had a common interest. Subject to this each Province was to retain its independence and autonomy and to be directly under the Crown as its head.

59.   The principle of federalism facilitates the pursuit of collective goals by cultural and linguistic minorities which form the majority within a particular province. This is the case in Quebec, where the majority of the population is French-speaking, and which possesses a distinct culture. This is not merely the result of chance. The social and demographic reality of Quebec explains the existence of the province of Quebec as a political unit and indeed, was one of the essential reasons for establishing a federal structure for the Canadian union in 1867. The experience of both Canada East and Canada West under the Union Act, 1840 (U.K.), 3–4 Vict., c. 35, had not been satisfactory. The federal structure adopted at Confederation enabled French-speaking Canadians to form a numerical majority in the province of Quebec, and so exercise the considerable provincial powers conferred by the Constitution Act, 1867 in such a way as to promote their language and culture. It also made provision for certain guaranteed representation within the federal Parliament itself. * * *

(c) Democracy

61.   Democracy is a fundamental value in our constitutional law and political culture. While it has both an institutional and an individual aspect, the democratic principle was also argued before us in the sense of the supremacy of the sovereign will of a people, in this case potentially to be expressed by Quebecers in support of unilateral secession. It is useful to explore in a summary way these different aspects of the democratic principle.

62.   The principle of democracy has always informed the design of our constitutional structure, and continues to act as an essential interpretive consideration to this day. A majority of this Court in *OPSEU v. Ontario*, [[1987] 2 S.C.R. 2 (S.C.C.)], at p. 57, confirmed that "the basic structure of our Constitution, as established by the Constitution Act, 1867, contemplates the existence of certain political institutions, including freely elected legislative bodies at the federal and provincial levels". As is apparent from an earlier line of decisions emanating from this Court,* * * the democracy principle can best be understood as a sort of baseline against which the framers of our Constitution, and subsequently, our elected representatives under it, have always operated. It is perhaps for this reason that the principle was not explicitly identified in the text of the Constitution Act, 1867 itself. To have done so might have appeared redundant, even silly, to the framers. As explained in the Provincial Judges Reference, [*R. v. Campbell*, [1997] 3 S.C.R. 3,] at para. 100, it is evident that our Constitution contemplates that Canada shall be a constitutional democracy. Yet this merely demonstrates the importance of underlying constitutional principles that are nowhere explicitly described in our constitutional texts. The representative and democratic nature of our political institutions was simply assumed.

63. Democracy is commonly understood as being a political system of majority rule. It is essential to be clear what this means. The evolution of our democratic tradition can be traced back to the Magna Carta (1215) and before, through the long struggle for Parliamentary supremacy which culminated in the English Bill of Rights of 1689, the emergence of representative political institutions in the colonial era, the development of responsible government in the 19th century, and eventually, the achievement of Confederation itself in 1867. "[T]he Canadian tradition", the majority of this Court held in Reference re Provincial Electoral Boundaries (Sask.), [1991] 2 S.C.R. 158, at p. 186, is "one of evolutionary democracy moving in uneven steps toward the goal of universal suffrage and more effective representation". Since Confederation, efforts to extend the franchise to those unjustly excluded from participation in our political system—such as women, minorities, and aboriginal peoples—have continued, with some success, to the present day.

64. Democracy is not simply concerned with the process of government. On the contrary, democracy is fundamentally connected to substantive goals, most importantly, the promotion of self-government. Democracy accommodates cultural and group identities. Put another way, a sovereign people exercises its right to self-government through the democratic process. In considering the scope and purpose of the Charter, the Court in *R. v. Oakes*, [1986] 1 S.C.R. 103, articulated some of the values inherent in the notion of democracy (at p. 136):

> The Court must be guided by the values and principles essential to a free and democratic society which I believe to embody, to name but a few, respect for the inherent dignity of the human person, commitment to social justice and equality, accommodation of a wide variety of beliefs, respect for cultural and group identity, and faith in social and political institutions which enhance the participation of individuals and groups in society.

65. In institutional terms, democracy means that each of the provincial legislatures and the federal Parliament is elected by popular franchise. These legislatures, we have said, are "at the core of the system of representative government": *New Brunswick Broadcasting*, [[1991] 2 S.C.R. 158 (S.C.C.),] at p. 387. In individual terms, the right to vote in elections to the House of Commons and the provincial legislatures, and to be candidates in those elections, is guaranteed to "Every citizen of Canada" by virtue of s. 3 of the Charter. Historically, this Court has interpreted democracy to mean the process of representative and responsible government and the right of citizens to participate in the political process as voters (Reference re Provincial Electoral Boundaries, supra) and as candidates (*Harvey v. New Brunswick (Attorney General)*, [1996] 2 S.C.R. 876). In addition, the effect of s. 4 of the Charter is to oblige the House of Commons and the provincial legislatures to hold regular elections and to permit citizens to elect representatives to their political institutions. The democratic principle is affirmed with particular clarity in that s. 4 is not subject to the notwithstanding power contained in s. 33.

66. It is, of course, true that democracy expresses the sovereign will of the people. Yet this expression, too, must be taken in the context of the other institutional values we have identified as pertinent to this Reference. The relationship between democracy and federalism means, for example, that in Canada there may be different and equally legitimate majorities in different provinces and territories and at the federal level. No one majority is more or less "legitimate" than the others as an expression of democratic opinion, although, of course, the consequences will vary with the subject matter. A federal system of government enables different provinces to pursue policies responsive to the particular concerns and interests of people in that province. At the same time, Canada as a whole is also a democratic community in which citizens construct and achieve goals on a national scale through a federal government acting within the limits of its jurisdiction. The function of federalism is to enable citizens to participate concurrently in different collectivities and to pursue goals at both a provincial and a federal level.

67. The consent of the governed is a value that is basic to our understanding of a free and democratic society. Yet democracy in any real sense of the word cannot exist without the rule of law. It is the law that creates the framework within which the "sovereign will" is to be ascertained and implemented. To be accorded legitimacy, democratic institutions must rest, ultimately, on a legal foundation. That is, they must allow for the participation of, and accountability to, the people, through public institutions created under the Constitution. Equally, however, a system of government cannot survive through adherence to the law alone. A political system must also possess legitimacy, and in our political culture, that requires an interaction between the rule of law and the democratic principle. The system must be capable of reflecting the aspirations of the people. But there is more. Our law's claim to legitimacy also rests on an appeal to moral values, many of which are imbedded in our constitutional structure. It would be a grave mistake to equate legitimacy with the "sovereign will" or majority rule alone, to the exclusion of other constitutional values.

68. Finally, we highlight that a functioning democracy requires a continuous process of discussion. The Constitution mandates government by democratic legislatures, and an executive accountable to them, "resting ultimately on public opinion reached by discussion and the interplay of ideas" (*Saumur v. City of Quebec*, [[1953] 2 S.C.R. 299 (S.C.C.),] at p. 330). At both the federal and provincial level, by its very nature, the need to build majorities necessitates compromise, negotiation, and deliberation. No one has a monopoly on truth, and our system is predicated on the faith that in the marketplace of ideas, the best solutions to public problems will rise to the top. Inevitably, there will be dissenting voices. A democratic system of government is committed to considering those dissenting voices, and seeking to acknowledge and address those voices in the laws by which all in the community must live.

69. The Constitution Act, 1982 gives expression to this principle, by conferring a right to initiate constitutional change on each participant in Confederation. In our view, the existence of this right imposes a corresponding duty on the participants in Confederation to engage in

constitutional discussions in order to acknowledge and address democratic expressions of a desire for change in other provinces. This duty is inherent in the democratic principle which is a fundamental predicate of our system of governance.

(d) Constitutionalism and the Rule of Law

70. The principles of constitutionalism and the rule of law lie at the root of our system of government. * * * At its most basic level, the rule of law vouchsafes to the citizens and residents of the country a stable, predictable and ordered society in which to conduct their affairs. It provides a shield for individuals from arbitrary state action.

72. The constitutionalism principle bears considerable similarity to the rule of law, although they are not identical. The essence of constitutionalism in Canada is embodied in s. 52(1) of the Constitution Act, 1982, which provides that "[t]he Constitution of Canada is the supreme law of Canada, and any law that is inconsistent with the provisions of the Constitution is, to the extent of the inconsistency, of no force or effect." Simply put, the constitutionalism principle requires that all government action comply with the Constitution. The rule of law principle requires that all government action must comply with the law, including the Constitution. * * *

74. First, a constitution may provide an added safeguard for fundamental human rights and individual freedoms which might otherwise be susceptible to government interference. Although democratic government is generally solicitous of those rights, there are occasions when the majority will be tempted to ignore fundamental rights in order to accomplish collective goals more easily or effectively. Constitutional entrenchment ensures that those rights will be given due regard and protection. Second, a constitution may seek to ensure that vulnerable minority groups are endowed with the institutions and rights necessary to maintain and promote their identities against the assimilative pressures of the majority. And third, a constitution may provide for a division of political power that allocates political power amongst different levels of government. That purpose would be defeated if one of those democratically elected levels of government could usurp the powers of the other simply by exercising its legislative power to allocate additional political power to itself unilaterally.

75. The argument that the Constitution may be legitimately circumvented by resort to a majority vote in a province-wide referendum is superficially persuasive, in large measure because it seems to appeal to some of the same principles that underlie the legitimacy of the Constitution itself, namely, democracy and self-government. In short, it is suggested that as the notion of popular sovereignty underlies the legitimacy of our existing constitutional arrangements, so the same popular sovereignty that originally led to the present Constitution must (it is argued) also permit "the people" in their exercise of popular sovereignty to secede by majority vote alone. However, closer analysis reveals that this argument is unsound, because it misunderstands the meaning of popular sovereignty and the essence of a constitutional democracy.

76.   Canadians have never accepted that ours is a system of simple majority rule. Our principle of democracy, taken in conjunction with the other constitutional principles discussed here, is richer. Constitutional government is necessarily predicated on the idea that the political representatives of the people of a province have the capacity and the power to commit the province to be bound into the future by the constitutional rules being adopted. These rules are "binding" not in the sense of frustrating the will of a majority of a province, but as defining the majority which must be consulted in order to alter the fundamental balances of political power (including the spheres of autonomy guaranteed by the principle of federalism), individual rights, and minority rights in our society. Of course, those constitutional rules are themselves amenable to amendment, but only through a process of negotiation which ensures that there is an opportunity for the constitutionally defined rights of all the parties to be respected and reconciled.

77.   In this way, our belief in democracy may be harmonized with our belief in constitutionalism. Constitutional amendment often requires some form of substantial consensus precisely because the content of the underlying principles of our Constitution demand it. By requiring broad support in the form of an "enhanced majority" to achieve constitutional change, the Constitution ensures that minority interests must be addressed before proposed changes which would affect them may be enacted.

78.   It might be objected, then, that constitutionalism is therefore incompatible with democratic government. This would be an erroneous view. Constitutionalism facilitates—indeed, makes possible—a democratic political system by creating an orderly framework within which people may make political decisions. Viewed correctly, constitutionalism and the rule of law are not in conflict with democracy; rather, they are essential to it. Without that relationship, the political will upon which democratic decisions are taken would itself be undermined.

(e) Protection of Minorities

79.   The fourth underlying constitutional principle we address here concerns the protection of minorities. There are a number of specific constitutional provisions protecting minority language, religion and education rights. * * * In the absence of such protection, it was felt that the minorities in what was then Canada East and Canada West would be submerged and assimilated. * * *

80.   However, we highlight that even though those provisions were the product of negotiation and political compromise, that does not render them unprincipled. Rather, such a concern reflects a broader principle related to the protection of minority rights. Undoubtedly, the three other constitutional principles inform the scope and operation of the specific provisions that protect the rights of minorities.

81.   The concern of our courts and governments to protect minorities has been prominent in recent years, particularly following the enactment of the Charter. Undoubtedly, one of the key considerations motivating the enactment of the Charter, and the process of constitutional judicial review that it entails, is the protection of minorities.

However, it should not be forgotten that the protection of minority rights had a long history before the enactment of the Charter. Indeed, the protection of minority rights was clearly an essential consideration in the design of our constitutional structure even at the time of Confederation. Although Canada's record of upholding the rights of minorities is not a spotless one, that goal is one towards which Canadians have been striving since Confederation, and the process has not been without successes. The principle of protecting minority rights continues to exercise influence in the operation and interpretation of our Constitution.
* * *

(4) The Operation of the Constitutional Principles in the Secession Context

83.   Secession is the effort of a group or section of a state to withdraw itself from the political and constitutional authority of that state, with a view to achieving statehood for a new territorial unit on the international plane. In a federal state, secession typically takes the form of a territorial unit seeking to withdraw from the federation. Secession is a legal act as much as a political one. By the terms of Question 1 of this Reference, we are asked to rule on the legality of unilateral secession "[u]nder the Constitution of Canada". This is an appropriate question, as the legality of unilateral secession must be evaluated, at least in the first instance, from the perspective of the domestic legal order of the state from which the unit seeks to withdraw. As we shall see below, it is also argued that international law is a relevant standard by which the legality of a purported act of secession may be measured.

84.   The secession of a province from Canada must be considered, in legal terms, to require an amendment to the Constitution, which perforce requires negotiation. The amendments necessary to achieve a secession could be radical and extensive. Some commentators have suggested that secession could be a change of such a magnitude that it could not be considered to be merely an amendment to the Constitution. We are not persuaded by this contention. It is of course true that the Constitution is silent as to the ability of a province to secede from Confederation but, although the Constitution neither expressly authorizes nor prohibits secession, an act of secession would purport to alter the governance of Canadian territory in a manner which undoubtedly is inconsistent with our current constitutional arrangements. The fact that those changes would be profound, or that they would purport to have significance with respect to international law, does not negate their nature as amendments to the Constitution of Canada.

85.   The Constitution is the expression of the sovereignty of the people of Canada. It lies within the power of the people of Canada, acting through their various governments duly elected and recognized under the Constitution, to effect whatever constitutional arrangements are desired within Canadian territory, including, should it be so desired, the secession of Quebec from Canada. As this Court held in the *Manitoba Language Rights Reference*, [[1985] 1 S.C.R. 721,] at p. 745, "[t]he Constitution of a country is a statement of the will of the people to be governed in accordance with certain principles held as fundamental and

certain prescriptions restrictive of the powers of the legislature and government". The manner in which such a political will could be formed and mobilized is a somewhat speculative exercise, though we are asked to assume the existence of such a political will for the purpose of answering the question before us. By the terms of this Reference, we have been asked to consider whether it would be constitutional in such a circumstance for the National Assembly, legislature or government of Quebec to effect the secession of Quebec from Canada unilaterally.

86. The "unilateral" nature of the act is of cardinal importance and we must be clear as to what is understood by this term. In one sense, any step towards a constitutional amendment initiated by a single actor on the constitutional stage is "unilateral". We do not believe that this is the meaning contemplated by Question 1, nor is this the sense in which the term has been used in argument before us. Rather, what is claimed by a right to secede "unilaterally" is the right to effectuate secession without prior negotiations with the other provinces and the federal government. At issue is not the legality of the first step but the legality of the final act of purported unilateral secession. The supposed juridical basis for such an act is said to be a clear expression of democratic will in a referendum in the province of Quebec. This claim requires us to examine the possible juridical impact, if any, of such a referendum on the functioning of our Constitution, and on the claimed legality of a unilateral act of secession.

87. Although the Constitution does not itself address the use of a referendum procedure, and the results of a referendum have no direct role or legal effect in our constitutional scheme, a referendum undoubtedly may provide a democratic method of ascertaining the views of the electorate on important political questions on a particular occasion. The democratic principle identified above would demand that considerable weight be given to a clear expression by the people of Quebec of their will to secede from Canada, even though a referendum, in itself and without more, has no direct legal effect, and could not in itself bring about unilateral secession. Our political institutions are premised on the democratic principle, and so an expression of the democratic will of the people of a province carries weight, in that it would confer legitimacy on the efforts of the government of Quebec to initiate the Constitution's amendment process in order to secede by constitutional means. In this context, we refer to a "clear" majority as a qualitative evaluation. The referendum result, if it is to be taken as an expression of the democratic will, must be free of ambiguity both in terms of the question asked and in terms of the support it achieves.

88. The federalism principle, in conjunction with the democratic principle, dictates that the clear repudiation of the existing constitutional order and the clear expression of the desire to pursue secession by the population of a province would give rise to a reciprocal obligation on all parties to Confederation to negotiate constitutional changes to respond to that desire. The amendment of the Constitution begins with a political process undertaken pursuant to the Constitution itself. In Canada, the initiative for constitutional amendment is the responsibility of democratically elected representatives of the participants in Confederation. Those

representatives may, of course, take their cue from a referendum, but in legal terms, constitution-making in Canada, as in many countries, is undertaken by the democratically elected representatives of the people. The corollary of a legitimate attempt by one participant in Confederation to seek an amendment to the Constitution is an obligation on all parties to come to the negotiating table. The clear repudiation by the people of Quebec of the existing constitutional order would confer legitimacy on demands for secession, and place an obligation on the other provinces and the federal government to acknowledge and respect that expression of democratic will by entering into negotiations and conducting them in accordance with the underlying constitutional principles already discussed. * * *

[Thereafter, the Supreme Court discussed the contents of the "obligation to negotiate."]

95.   Refusal of a party to conduct negotiations in a manner consistent with constitutional principles and values would seriously put at risk the legitimacy of that party's assertion of its rights, and perhaps the negotiation process as a whole. Those who quite legitimately insist upon the importance of upholding the rule of law cannot at the same time be oblivious to the need to act in conformity with constitutional principles and values, and so do their part to contribute to the maintenance and promotion of an environment in which the rule of law may flourish.

96.   No one can predict the course that such negotiations might take. The possibility that they might not lead to an agreement amongst the parties must be recognized. Negotiations following a referendum vote in favor of seeking secession would inevitably address a wide range of issues, many of great import. After 131 years of Confederation, there exists, inevitably, a high level of integration in economic, political and social institutions across Canada. The vision of those who brought about Confederation was to create a unified country, not a loose alliance of autonomous provinces. Accordingly, while there are regional economic interests, which sometimes coincide with provincial boundaries, there are also national interests and enterprises (both public and private) that would face potential dismemberment. There is a national economy and a national debt. Arguments were raised before us regarding boundary issues. There are linguistic and cultural minorities, including aboriginal peoples, unevenly distributed across the country who look to the Constitution of Canada for the protection of their rights. Of course, secession would give rise to many issues of great complexity and difficulty. These would have to be resolved within the overall framework of the rule of law, thereby assuring Canadians resident in Quebec and elsewhere a measure of stability in what would likely be a period of considerable upheaval and uncertainty. Nobody seriously suggests that our national existence, seamless in so many aspects, could be effortlessly separated along what are now the provincial boundaries of Quebec. As the Attorney General of Saskatchewan put it in his oral submission:

A nation is built when the communities that comprise it make commitments to it, when they forego choices and opportunities on behalf of a nation, * * * when the communities that comprise it make compromises, when they offer each other guarantees, when they make transfers and perhaps most pointedly, when they receive from others the benefits of national solidarity. The threads of a thousand acts of accommodation are the fabric of a nation * * *

97.   In the circumstances, negotiations following such a referendum would undoubtedly be difficult. While the negotiators would have to contemplate the possibility of secession, there would be no absolute legal entitlement to it and no assumption that an agreement reconciling all relevant rights and obligations would actually be reached. It is foreseeable that even negotiations carried out in conformity with the underlying constitutional principles could reach an impasse. We need not speculate here as to what would then transpire. Under the Constitution, secession requires that an amendment be negotiated.

101.   If the circumstances giving rise to the duty to negotiate were to arise, the distinction between the strong defence of legitimate interests and the taking of positions which, in fact, ignore the legitimate interests of others is one that also defies legal analysis. The Court would not have access to all of the information available to the political actors, and the methods appropriate for the search for truth in a court of law are ill suited to getting to the bottom of constitutional negotiations. To the extent that the questions are political in nature, it is not the role of the judiciary to interpose its own views on the different negotiating positions of the parties, even were it invited to do so. Rather, it is the obligation of the elected representatives to give concrete form to the discharge of their constitutional obligations which only they and their electors can ultimately assess. The reconciliation of the various legitimate constitutional interests outlined above is necessarily committed to the political rather than the judicial realm, precisely because that reconciliation can only be achieved through the give and take of the negotiation process. Having established the legal framework, it would be for the democratically elected leadership of the various participants to resolve their differences.

[The Court went on to specify that constitutional prerequisites to secession did not depend on whether they would likely be effective or on whether Quebec could in fact successfully secede unilaterally and become accepted as a new nation by the international community.]

IV.   Summary of Conclusions

[Quebec has no constitutional right to unilateral secession. But if a clear majority of its citizens vote in favor of a clearly phrased proposal for independence, then Quebec and the remaining provinces have a duty to negotiate Quebec's proposed secession in good faith and mindful of each other's interests.]

　　　* * *

153.   The task of the Court has been to clarify the legal framework within which political decisions are to be taken "under the Constitution", not to usurp the prerogatives of the political forces that operate within that framework. The obligations we have identified are binding obligations under the Constitution of Canada. However, it will be for the

political actors to determine what constitutes "a clear majority on a clear question" in the circumstances under which a future referendum vote may be taken. Equally, in the event of demonstrated majority support for Quebec secession, the content and process of the negotiations will be for the political actors to settle. The reconciliation of the various legitimate constitutional interests is necessarily committed to the political rather than the judicial realm precisely because that reconciliation can only be achieved through the give and take of political negotiations. To the extent issues addressed in the course of negotiation are political, the courts, appreciating their proper role in the constitutional scheme, would have no supervisory role.

* * *

PENSIONS CASE

Constitutional Tribunal (Poland).
Decision dated 11 February 1992 (K. 14/91).

[As the country was experiencing serious economic difficulties, the Polish Parliament revised its retirement and disabilities pensions law inherited from communism, setting lower benefits for present and future beneficiaries. The changes in question, which were to cause reductions in present and future benefits, were challenged under various provisions of the Polish Constitution.]

* * *

IV

* * * Prior to undertaking any decision regarding the nonconformity of the regulations of the Act dated 17 October 1991 on the Revaluation of Retirement and Disability Pensions as listed in Items 1 and 2 of this Decision with the Constitution, the Constitutional Tribunal conducted an interpretation of that part of article 1 pertaining to the rule of law as well as of article 70, sections 1 and 2, sub-section 1 of the Constitution.

As to the interpretation of article 1 of the Constitution in the section pertaining to the rule of law with respect to social security law within the scope of these proceedings, the Constitutional Tribunal lays it down in the form of the hypotheses listed below. The Constitutional Tribunal also makes reference to its jurisprudence as well as to legal doctrine.

1. The rule of law embodies maintaining the confidence of citizens in the State; the protection of acquired rights (also the non-retroactive effect of law) is tied to the foregoing according to the principle of instrumental links.

2. Maintaining confidence is the guiding principle serving as the basis of the social security relationship as it is based on the legal structure of maintaining confidence and on the conviction of the insured that upon the performance of defined terms (work, premiums) and upon the elapse of a defined period of time (achievement of the required age) or the occurrence of some other insurance risk (disability), the insured shall receive defined benefits—in principle greater as work effort in-

creases—which , put simply, means that this will be taken on by the social security system. Thus, the social security system takes on the form of a unique type of social contract governed by the principle of *pacta sunt servanda*.

3. Equitably (justly) acquired rights, including rights acquired within the framework of the social security system, fit within the binding scope of the protection of acquired rights. Thus, only limited protection of acquired rights exists. In principle, there is no reason to assume—if there is no justified basis for such an assumption—that retirement and disability pension rights, inclusive of the level of such benefits, as stemming from the rules by which they are determined, are acquired inequitably * * *

4. The protection of acquired rights encompasses both the rights acquired by way of a concrete final decision granting benefits and the rights acquired in *abstracto* pursuant to legislation prior to the submission of an application regarding the award thereof. As to expected rights, the need for their protection, by their very nature, stems from the social security system, which is based on the assumption that in exchange for premiums—work input—guaranties of future, gradually increasing rights are created.

The Constitutional Tribunal, in spite of all the difficulties emerging at this point, has taken the stand of protecting expected rights to their maximum extent * * *

It is this stand of the Constitutional Tribunal that should be used to explain the decision that article 26 of the Act dated 17 October 1991 on the Revaluation of Retirement and Disability Pensions is inconsistent with article 1 of the Constitution within the scope defined in Item 2 of this Decision.

5. The primary assumption applied by the Constitutional Tribunal was that retirement and disability pension benefits are subject to strong legal protection. They guarantee a minimum of social security to the beneficiaries * * *

6. * * * The foregoing statements do not imply that all modifications or restrictions whatsoever to equitably acquired retirement and disability pension rights are impermissible * * * This is particularly pertinent in the case of the reform of retirement and disability pension rights during an economic crisis in the State and the poor financial state of the social security system. * * * What is more, the velocity of change within the realm of economic and social relations, especially over a period of basic transformations in these relations as is the case at present * * * demands that the lawmaker be given a relatively broad range of freedom in molding the law.

* * * [T]he concepts of social equality and justice signify that "the weight of economic crisis should encumber all social strata and not specifically affect only certain strata or groups" especially if these were to have been pensioners.

7. In the event that sufficient justification is found to restrict acquired retirement and disability pension rights, the lawmaker should

apply maximum effort so that the new, less advantageous legal regulations are undertaken maintaining democratic procedures as stemming from the rule of law and the binding provisions of law. It follows from the above that the new regulations should be ratified in the wake of negotiations with the interested parties of their representatives.

Secondly, the lawmaker should create a maximum of legal security, under the given circumstances, for persons encompassed by the new legal regulations. Since the citizens of the land ruled by legality should not be suddenly surprised by regulations that are to their disadvantage, the lawmaker, in order to preserve safety, should use techniques such as transitory regulations phasing in the reduction of benefits over time, or the suitable adjustment period should be long enough to permit the interested parties to adapt to the changed legal situation to the best of their ability. The absence of a suitable adjustment period is a violation of article 1 of the Constitution if it infringes on acquired rights or expectations thereof * * *

No such guaranties of legal and social security were created by the Act in question with respect to the persons whose rights were affected by the provisions of the Act dated 17 October 1991 on the Revaluation of Retirement and Disability Pensions when considering the entirety of the technique of direct action applied by the new Act * * * This technique * * * leads to changes, as is the case here that surprised those insured and infringed upon their confidence in the law. It is difficult to reconcile this technique with the requirements of the rule of law in a matter of social import as significant to the individual as social security. It is for this reason * * * that the provisions discussed * * * contravene article 1 of the Constitution.

V

* * * The principle of social justice claimed by certain Applicants (* * *) is the primary assumption of the social security system. It primarily appears in the form of a formula for granting benefits in line with work (mainly in the case of pensioners), but also distribution in line with needs (especially in relation to people collecting disability pensions, family pensions, and accident pensions). From the point of view of all evaluation of the challenged provisions of the Act, the Constitutional Tribunal considers the following to be significant components of justice:

* * *

2. Social justice is realized in the social security system bearing in mind its redistributive function. Put most simply, redistribution is based on a defined flattening of the level of benefits to the advantage of people with a low benefit base and to the disadvantage of those with a high base. Social solidarity is the justification of social security's function of redistribution forcing the distribution of the burden of benefits over a wider group of people encompassed by social security.

The attenuation in the level of benefits with respect to persons with a high base necessitates that the proportionality between the level of benefits and premiums be kept in mind—i.e., the insured's share in accumulating the insurance fund. Concurring with the experts, the

Constitutional Tribunal has accepted the premise that the level of benefits should be approximately appropriate with respect to the insured's personal share in the creation of the insurance fund, and in no case should it deviate from that share excessively. The principle of Proportionality is thus in harmony with justice in the formula assuming distribution by merit and it is here that it finds its justification. This has also been expressed in ILO conventions, including those ratified by Poland—Number 35 (article 7), Number 37 (article 7), and Number 39 (article 9).

3.   Social justice demands that prescribed preferences be awarded to those insured parties who were employed under extremely difficult working conditions or in some specific nature if their work input could not have been appropriately taken into account in the form of a higher benefit base dependent on the level of remuneration (income) * * *

Social justice was the basis for reviewing the constitutionality of the Act in Question * * * along with equality (article 67, section 2 of the Constitution). In keeping with its jurisprudence the Constitutional Tribunal understands it as an injunction to treat legal entities under identical circumstances, including the realm of social security law, without applying any solutions that are discriminatory or marked by favoritism. The interdiction against favoring certain categories (groups) of entities is not inconsistent with objectively justified social preferences based on justice * * *.

* * * [T]he constitutional assumptions of molding the level of benefits should be approximately proportional to the level of premiums channeled into the insurance fund. This principle maintains its value as a characteristic quality of the insurance relationship in spite of the State's defined share in supplementing the fund because *that* share—as the experts asserted—is not excessive. The principle of mutuality and proportionality of benefits as the premise of social security therefore generally defines the *statutory* rules for setting the amounts of benefits and is subject to protection by the power of article 70 sections I and 2, sub-section I of *the Constitution.*

For this reason the Constitutional Tribunal held that article 7, section 6 of the challenged statute, which excessively flattens benefits in relation to those persons who paid an appropriately high premium, is at odds with the mutuality and proportionality of benefits and premiums and is therefore inconsistent not only with the protection of acquired rights (article 1 of the Constitution) but also with article 70, sections 1 and 2, sub-section 1 of the Constitution * * *

CUNNINGHAM v. CANADA

Supreme Court (Canada).
[1993] 2 S.C.R. 143.

Appeal from judgment of Ontario Court of Appeal affirming judgment of SMITH J. dismissing prisoner's application for habeas corpus.

The judgment of the court was delivered by McLachlin J.

Cunningham was sentenced to 12 years in prison upon conviction for a brutal slaying in 1981. Under the Parole Act in force at the time of his sentencing, he was entitled to be released on mandatory supervision after serving approximately two-thirds of his sentence, on April 8, 1989, provided that he was of good behaviour.

2. In 1986 the Parole Act was amended to allow the Commissioner of Corrections, within six months of the "presumptive release date", to refer a case to the National Parole Board where he has reason to believe, on the basis of information obtained within those six months, that the inmate is likely, prior to the expiration of his sentence, to commit an offence causing death or serious harm. The Parole Board may, if it sees fit, deny release of the inmate.

3. The appellant had maintained a good behaviour record in prison. In 1988, his parole officer recommended him for parole and requested a community assessment, since the appellant had indicated he would be returning to his home community, not far from the scene of the crime. The appellant expected to be released on April 8, 1989.

4. This, however, was not to be. Shortly before his release date, the appellant received a notice that the Commissioner had decided to seek the continued detention of the appellant under the 1986 amendments to the Parole Act. His community alerted to his release by the community assessment, evinced concern at his early release given the violence of the crime. * * *

5. Following a detention hearing, the appellant was ordered to be detained until his sentence expired on February 13, 1993, subject to annual reviews. The appellant brought an action to the Supreme Court of Ontario for a writ of habeas corpus. The application was refused. The appellant appealed to the Court of Appeal for Ontario, but his appeal was dismissed. The appellant now appeals to this court.

6. [The following] issue[ ] arise[s] before us:

Does the 1986 amendment to the Parole Act changing the conditions for release on mandatory supervision amount to a denial of the appellant's liberty contrary to the principles of fundamental justice under s. 7 of the Canadian Charter of Rights and Freedoms? * * *

7. In order for the appellant to succeed in this argument, he must establish two things:

(1) that he was deprived of his liberty by the amendment to the Parole Act which resulted in denial of his release on mandatory supervision; and

(2) that the deprivation of his liberty was contrary to the fundamental interests of justice.

8. My conclusion is that while the appellant's liberty may be said to have been adversely affected by the changes to the Parole Act, the deprivation was not contrary to the principles of fundamental justice.

10. In my view, the appellant has shown that he has been deprived of liberty * * *

13. In the case at bar, the appellant was sentenced to twelve years and was required under his warrant of committal, both before and after the amendment of the Parole Act, to serve that sentence in its entirety.

Thus the duration of the restriction of his liberty interest has not been affected * * *

14. However the manner in which he may serve a part of that sentence, [a liberty interest identified by Justice Lamer in *Dumas*] has been affected. One has "more" liberty, or a better quality of liberty, when one is serving time on mandatory supervision than when one is serving time in prison. The appellant had a high expectation, contingent on his good behaviour, that he would be released on mandatory supervision on April 8, 1989, had the Parole Act not been amended; indeed, he would automatically have been released on mandatory supervision given his good behaviour. The effect of the 1986 amendment of the Parole Act was to reduce that expectation of liberty, in the sense that it curtailed the probability of his release on mandatory supervision * * *

15. I conclude that the appellant has suffered [a substantial] deprivation of liberty * * *

17. Having concluded that the appellant has been deprived of a liberty interest protected by s. 7 of the Charter, we must determine whether this is contrary to the principles of fundamental justice under s. 7 of the Charter. In my view, while the amendment of the Parole Act to eliminate automatic release on mandatory supervision restricted the appellant's liberty interest, it did not violate the principles of fundamental justice. The principles of fundamental justice are concerned not only with the interest of the person who claims his liberty has been limited, but with the protection of society. Fundamental justice requires that a fair balance be struck between these interests, both substantively and procedurally. In my view the balance struck in this case conforms to this requirement.

* * *

19. The balance is struck by qualifying the prisoner's expectation regarding the form in which the sentence would be served. The expectation of mandatory release is modified by the amendment permitting a discretion to prevent early release where society's interests are endangered.

20. The next question is whether the nature of this particular change in the rules as to the form in which the sentence would be served violates the Charter. In my view, it does not. The change is directly related to the public interest in protecting society from persons who may commit serious harm if released on mandatory supervision. It is difficult to dispute that it is just to afford a limited discretion for the review of parole applicants who may commit an offence causing serious harm or death. Substantively, the balance is fairly struck.

21. Nor does the procedure established under the Act and regulations violate the principles of fundamental justice. The change was made by law. The new procedure provides for a hearing to consider whether the expectation of release on mandatory supervision was warranted. The prisoner is entitled to representation throughout. * * *

Appeal dismissed.

RE B.C. MOTOR VEHICLE ACT

Supreme Court (Canada).
[1985] 2 S.C.R. 486.

The judgment of Dickson C.J. and Beetz, Chouinard, Lamer and Le Dain JJ. was delivered by

Lamer J.—

Introduction

A law that has the potential to convict a person who has not really done anything wrong offends the principles of fundamental justice and, if imprisonment is available as a penalty, such a law then violates a person's right to liberty under s. 7 of the *Charter of Rights and Freedoms* (*Constitution Act, 1982*, as enacted by the *Canada Act, 1982*, 1982 (U.K.), c. 11).

In other words, absolute liability and imprisonment cannot be combined.

The Legislation

Motor Vehicle Act, R.S.B.C. 1979, c. 288, s. 94, as amended by the *Motor Vehicle Amendment Act, 1982*, 1982 (B.C.), c. 36, s. 19:

94. (1) A person who drives a motor vehicle on a highway or industrial road while

(a) he is prohibited from driving a motor vehicle under sections 90, 91, 92 or 92.1, or

(b) his driver's license or his right to apply for or obtain a driver's licence is suspended under section 82 or 92 as it was before its repeal and replacement came into force pursuant to the *Motor Vehicle Amendment Act, 1982*, commits an offence * * *

(2) Subsection (1) creates an absolute liability offence in which guilt is established by proof of driving, whether or not the defendant knew of the prohibition or suspension.

Canadian Charter of Rights and Freedoms; Constitution Act, 1982:

1. The *Canadian Charter of Rights and Freedoms* guarantees the rights and freedoms set out in it subject only to such reasonable limits prescribed by law as can be demonstrably justified in a free and democratic society.

7. Everyone has the right to life, liberty and security of the person and the right not to be deprived thereof except in accordance with the principles of fundamental justice.

11. Any person charged with an offence has the right

(*d*) to be presumed innocent until proven guilty according to law in a fair and public hearing by an independent and impartial tribunal * * *

1 Introduction

The issue in this case raises fundamental questions of constitutional theory, including the nature and the very legitimacy of constitutional adjudication under the *Charter* as well as the appropriateness of various techniques of constitutional interpretation. I shall deal first with these questions of a more general and theoretical nature as they underlie and have shaped much of the discussion surrounding s. 7.

2. *The Nature and Legitimacy of Constitutional Adjudication Under the Charter*

[C]ourts [have not] been enabled to decide upon the appropriateness of policies underlying legislative enactments. * * * [H]owever, the courts are empowered, indeed required, to measure the content of legislation against the guarantees of the Constitution. * * *

In this respect, s. 7 is no different than other *Charter* provisions. As the Attorney General for Ontario has noted in his factum:

* * * Yet, in the context of s. 7, and in particular, of the interpretation of "principles of fundamental justice", there has prevailed in certain quarters an assumption that all but a narrow construction of s. 7 will inexorably lead the courts to "question the wisdom of enactments", to adjudicate upon the merits of public policy.

From this have sprung warnings of the dangers of a judicial "super-legislature" beyond the reach of Parliament, the provincial legislatures and the electorate * * *

The concerns with the bounds of constitutional adjudication explain the characterization of the issue in a narrow and restrictive fashion, *i.e.*, whether the term "principles of fundamental justice" has a substantive or merely procedural content. In my view, the characterization of the issue in such fashion preempts an open-minded approach to determining the meaning of "principles of fundamental justice".

The task of the Court is not to choose between substantive or procedural content *per se* but to secure for persons "the full benefit of the *Charter*'s protection" under s. 7, while avoiding adjudication of the merits of public policy. This can only be accomplished by a purposive analysis and the articulation of "objective and manageable standards" for the operation of the section within such a framework.

* * *

In my view this analysis is to be undertaken, and the purpose of the right or freedom in question is to be sought by reference to the character and the larger objects of the *Charter* itself, to the language chosen to articulate the specific right or freedom, to the historical origins of the concepts enshrined, and where applicable, to the meaning and purpose of the other specific rights and freedoms with which it is associated within the text of the *Charter*. The interpretation should be, as the judgment in *Southam* emphasizes, a generous rather than a legalistic one, aimed at fulfilling the purpose of the guarantee and securing for individuals the full benefit of the *Charter*'s protection.

3. *The Principles of Fundamental Justice*

* * *

In the framework of a purposive analysis * * * it is clear to me that the interests which are meant to be protected by the words "and the right not to be deprived thereof except in accordance with the principles of fundamental justice" of s. 7 are the life, liberty and security of the person. The principles of fundamental justice, on the other hand, are not a protected interest, but rather a qualifier of the right not to be deprived of life, liberty and security of the person.

* * * [T]he narrower the meaning given to "principles of fundamental justice" the greater will be the possibility that individuals may be deprived of these most basic rights. This latter result is to be avoided given that the rights involved are as fundamental as those which pertain to the life, liberty and security of the person, the deprivation of which "has the most severe consequences upon an individual."

For these reasons, I am of the view that it would be wrong to interpret the term "fundamental justice" as being synonymous with natural justice * * * To do so would strip the protected interests of much, if not most, of their content and leave the "right" to life, liberty and security of the person in a sorely emaciated state. Such a result would be inconsistent with the broad, affirmative language in which those rights are expressed and equally inconsistent with the approach adopted by this Court toward the interpretation of *Charter* rights * * *

It would mean that the right to liberty would be narrower than the right not to be arbitrarily detained or imprisoned (s. 9), that the right to security of the person would have less content than the right to be secure against unreasonable search or seizure (s. 8). Such an interpretation would give the specific expressions of the "right to life, liberty and security of the person" which are set forth in ss. 8 to 14 greater content than the general concept from which they originate.

Sections 8 to 14, in other words, address specific deprivations of the "right" to life, liberty and security of the person in breach of the principles of fundamental justice, and as such, violations of s. 7. * * *

Thus, ss. 8 to 14 provides an invaluable key to the meaning of "principles of fundamental justice". Many have been developed over time as presumptions of the common law; others have found expression in the international conventions on human rights. All have been recognized as essential elements of a system for the administration of justice which is founded upon a belief in "the dignity and worth of the human person" (preamble to the *Canadian Bill of Rights*, R.S.C. 1970, App. III) and on "the rule of law" (preamble to the *Canadian Charter of Rights and Freedoms*).

It is this common thread which, in my view, must guide us in determining the scope and content of "principles of fundamental justice". In other words, the principles of fundamental justice are to be found in the basic tenets of our legal system. They do not lie in the realm of general public policy but in the inherent domain of the judiciary as guardian of the justice system. * * *

4. Proceedings and Evidence of the Special Joint Committee of the Senate and of the House of Commons on the Constitution of Canada

* * *

Were this Court to accord any significant weight to this testimony of the Committee Record, it would in effect be assuming a fact which is nearly impossible of proof, *i.e.*, the intention of the legislative bodies which adopted the *Charter*. In view of the indeterminate nature of the data, it would in my view be erroneous to give these materials anything but minimal weight.

* * * Narrow and technical interpretation, if not modulated by a sense of the unknowns of the future, can stunt the growth of the law and hence the community it serves * * * With the *Constitution Act, 1982* comes a new dimension, a new yardstick of reconciliation between the individual and the community and their respective rights, a dimension which, like the balance of the Constitution, remains to be interpreted and applied by the Court.

* * *

* * * [T]he principles of fundamental justice are to be found in the basic tenets and principles, not only of our judicial process, but also of the other components of our legal system.

* * *

Absolute Liability and Fundamental Justice in Penal Law
* * *

It is submitted that if S. 94(2) is inconsistent with one of the above-noted provisions of the Charter, then S. 94(2) contains a 'reasonable limit, etc.' within the meaning of S. 1 of the Charter.

I do not take issue with the fact that it is highly desirable that "bad drivers" be kept off the road. I do not take issue either with the desirability of punishing severely bad drivers who are in contempt of prohibitions against driving. The bottom line of the question to be addressed here is: whether the Government of British Columbia has demonstrated as justifiable that the risk of imprisonment of a few innocent is, given the desirability of ridding the roads of British Columbia of bad drivers, a reasonable limit in a free and democratic society. That result is to be measured against the offence being one of strict liability open to a defence of due diligence, the success of which does nothing more than let those few who did nothing wrong remain free.

As did the Court of Appeal, I find that this demonstration has not been satisfied, indeed, not in the least.

Notes and Questions

1. Perhaps the most striking feature that all the above cases share in common is that none of them is resolved by an argument based exclusively on the relevant constitutional text. Is that surprising? None of the above cases qualifies as an "easy case." See Schauer, *op. cit.* While arguably there are no easy cases as language is rarely if ever amenable to only one interpretation (cf. the example of the age requirement for the office of president under the U.S. Constitution above), the text matters. As Professor Schauer notes: "The focus of constitutional litigation on certain substantive areas is importantly, although certainly not exclusively, a product of linguis-

tic design, in which relatively precise language forestalls with respect even to matters of great moment, while relatively vague language encourages litigation, even as to matters that are comparatively trivial." Schauer, *op. cit.* at 404. Thus it may be that "easy cases" are routinely resolved on the basis of arguments from the text, and precisely because of that, they are rarely brought before the constitutional adjudicator. The more difficult question is, even admitting that the text constrains, how important are its constraints, given that in all the above cases the relevant textual constraints involved appear to have been by no means outcome determinative?

2. In *Australian Capital Television* the Court struck down a restraint on political speech while emphasizing that the Australian Constitution, relying on English common law, does not purport to establish judicial oversight of individual rights. The Court justified its speech-rights-creating decision based on the Australian Constitution's provisions designed to guarantee a representative government. Is the Court's decision grounded, accordingly, on an argument from constitutional theory or on a value argument? Does it matter whether it is one or the other or both?

3. Assuming that a value argument is involved, does it matter whether the value in question is enshrined in the constitution? As already indicated, some constitutions, such as the German, enshrine particular values—e.g., "human dignity"—while others do not. For example, the dissenting opinion in *Griswold* appears to treat constitutional rights as specific limitations on legislative discretion. Since the U.S. Constitution has no provision that explicitly protects privacy as such, the dissenting justices regarded the prohibition against the use of contraceptives as legitimate even if contrary to prevailing values or to values implicit in other explicitly protected constitutional rights. Consistent with this, are decisions based on value arguments, such as that in the *Princess Soraya Case* (see above), legitimate in the context of the German Constitution but not in that of the U.S. Constitution (at least as conceived by the *Griswold* dissenters)? What if the U.S. Constitution had an explicit provision protecting privacy but was silent on contraception? Would value arguments then be legitimate to determine whether constitutionally guaranteed privacy encompassed freedom to use contraceptives? On the dignity–privacy relation in comparative perspective, see Chapter 5.

4. The majority opinion in *Griswold* infers a right to privacy from aspects of such right encompassed within other constitutional rights that are explicitly protected—e.g., right against unreasonable searches and seizures, right against self-incrimination—and from "penumbras" emanating from explicitly protected rights. Many commentators have criticized the Court's majority, accusing it of having ventured well beyond the bounds of legitimate constitutional interpretation. See, e.g., Robert H. Bork, *Neutral Principles and Some First Amendment Problems*, 47, Ind. L.J. 1 (1971). The concurring opinion relies on the U.S. Constitution's Ninth Amendment—which provides that "the enumeration in the Constitution of certain rights, shall not be construed to deny or disparage others retained by the people"—to recognize a constitutional right to privacy. Does that provide a better basis for recognizing such a constitutional right? Or at least, does it justify claiming that the absence of an explicit reference to such right should not be construed as evidence against its protection by the Constitution? For an argument in favor of the decision in *Griswold*, see Thomas Grey, *Do We Have an Unwritten Constitution?* 27 Stan. L. Rev. 703 (1975) (arguing that

the Ninth Amendment justifies adapting constitutional rights to the needs of contemporary society).

5.   The Canadian Supreme Court's opinion in *Re Secession of Quebec* does not seem to have any more of a textual basis than the USSC's endorsement of a privacy right in *Griswold*. Are the two decisions equivalent or is the Canadian one less justifiable inasmuch as arguably some elements of privacy can be inferred from the U.S. Bill of Rights while no mention whatever of secession can be found in the Canadian Constitution? Is *Re Secession of Quebec* more like *Migdal*, above, in that the courts in both cases seem to engage in constitution-making rather than in interpreting their respective constitutions? Or is *Re Secession of Quebec* different, given that Canada has a written constitution whereas Israel does not? *Re Secession of Quebec* is arguably justified as a structural and functional interpretation of the Canadian Constitution. In other words, given the Canadian Constitution's provisions relating to federalism, democracy, and minority rights, the most logical way to deal with the issue of secession is that provided by the Court in *Re Secession of Quebec*. Is that argument persuasive?

6.   The Polish *Pensions Case* gives interpretive shape to "the rule of law" (see discussion in Chapter 1) as a constitutional principle. The "rule of law" is commonly associated with nonretroactivity and protection of legally generated expectations. In view of this, is the Polish Constitutional Court's conclusion that reduction of pension benefits as a consequence of Poland's serious economic difficulties is contrary to the Constitution compelled by its rule-of-law provision? Would it have been plausible and legitimate for the Court to have ruled instead that the reasonable expectation created by the previous law was that pension benefits would not be reduced so long as the country did not face serious economic difficulties? Is not the decision about *future* pension benefits primarily a political one? Does the "rule of law" carry particular substantive implications? Or is the controversy over the level of pension benefits an acutely political one in a country that had recently achieved a transition from socialism to capitalism, pitting those who would accelerate the completion of the switch against those who would temper it to avoid certain unpalatable social costs? Cf. the contrast between the *Princess Soraya Case* (imposing unexpected liability on account of justice and the rule of law) and the Hungarian *Retroactive Justice* decision (affirming nonretroactivity as essential for upholding the rule of law in the context of compelling calls for justice against politically motivated murder and torture), excerpted in Chapter 1.

7.   Both the *Cunningham* and *B.C. Motor Vehicle* cases, decided by the Canadian Supreme Court, involve issues of proportionality and balancing (see the discussion in Subsection C.2.3. below) in relation to the principles of fundamental justice. In both cases the Court was confronted with a conflict between individual liberty rights and society's interest in protecting life. Are the results in the two cases consistent? Does *B.C. Motor Vehicle* even turn on any kind of balancing? Or does the presumption of innocence trump all other considerations? Can any principles of judicial interpretation be derived from these two decisions? Note that the drafters of S.7 of the Canadian Charter intended to come up with a clause that would not give rise to a substantive due process principle along the lines developed by the USSC. Although this intention was clearly expressed, the Canadian Court obviously disregards it. Likewise, the founding fathers of the Indian Constitution, following the

advice of Justice Frankfurter of the USSC, avoided an American-type due process clause.

8. Consider Professor Schlink's description of the German approach to providing institutional protection to rights (for a specific example, see the German abortion decision in Chapter 5). Is there a textual basis for such activism?

C.2.2. ORIGINALISM

Note on the Debate over Originalism in the United States

There has been a heated debate in the U.S. over the role of "originalism" in constitutional interpretation. Originalists maintain that legitimate judicial interpretation of the Constitution should be confined to the understanding of the Constitution as it stood at the time of its drafting. Originalists differ, according to whether they rely on the intent of the framers of the Constitution, the intent of its ratifiers, or on the original meaning of the constitutional text as measured by how such text would have been understood by the contemporaries of the framers and ratifiers.

Proponents of originalism maintain that unless judges interpreting the Constitution adhere to its original meaning, they would inevitably distort the nature and scope of constitutional rights, thus undermining both the Constitution and democracy. Judge Robert H. Bork, a strong proponent of constraining judicial interpretation to its original meaning, maintains that the individual rights protected by the Constitution are essentially antimajoritarian. Moreover, in Bork's view, the Constitution provides for majority rule except for those rights and freedoms it explicitly protects, thus placing them beyond the powers of legislative majorities. Accordingly, unless judges are bound by the original meaning, they will inevitably shape constitutional rights according to their own values, thus both upsetting the Constitution's design for apportioning antimajoritarian rights and majoritarian policies and rendering judge-made value choices immune to democratic control or reversal. As Bork specifies,

> * * * The Court can act as a legal rather than a political institution only if it is neutral * * * in the way it derives and defines the principles it applies. If the Court is free to choose any principle that it will subsequently apply neutrally, it is free to legislate just as a political body would * * * Similarly, if the Court is free to define the scope of the principle as it sees fit, it may, by manipulating the principle's breadth, make things come out the way it wishes on grounds that are not contained in the principle it purports to apply * * * The philosophy of original understanding is capable of supplying neutrality in all three respects—in deriving, defining, and applying principle. * * *

> When a judge finds his principle in the Constitution as originally understood, the problem of the neutral derivation of principle is solved. The judge accepts the ratifiers' definition of the appropriate ranges of majority and minority freedom. The [issue] is resolved in the way that the founders resolved it, and the judge accepts the fact that he is bound by that resolution as law. He need not, and must not, make unguided value judgements of his own.

Robert H. Bork, *The Tempting of America* 146 (1990).

Furthermore, Bork argues that neutrality in defining and applying principles derived from the Constitution can also be secured through adherence to the original meaning or understanding. Some rights protected by the Constitution, such as the right to "due process" or "equal protection," are stated at such a high level of generality that they seem susceptible to widely differing interpretations and hence to a broad range of diverse or even contradictory applications. For example, the Fourteenth Amendment of the U.S. Constitution guarantees to all persons "the equal protection of the laws." Does that allow or prohibit affirmative action? Does it mandate equal treatment of men and women, homosexuals and heterosexuals, and the like?

These issues have generated much debate on and off the Bench (see Chapter 6), but Bork forcefully insists that neutrality in definition and application of equal protection rights can be achieved by adhering to the levels of generality and abstraction found in the original understanding. *Id.* at 143–160.

Originalism has been widely attacked by many American judges and scholars. One of the best known attacks is by Paul Brest, *The Misconceived Quest for the Original Understanding*, 60 B.U. L. Rev. 204 (1980). Professor Brest rejects originalism on two principal counts: it is unworkable, and it fails to account for much American constitutional jurisprudence.

Brest divides originalists into textualists and intentionalists and draws a further distinction between "strict" textualists and intentionalists on the one hand and "moderate" ones on the other. His main thesis is that in its "strict" versions originalism is unworkable, whereas in its "moderate" ones it is so general and vague as to become difficult to distinguish from nonoriginalism. Textualists are concerned with the "plain meaning" of a text. As Brest specifies,

> The plain meaning of a text is the meaning that it would have for a "normal speaker of English" under the circumstances in which it is used. Two kinds of circumstances seem relevant: the linguistic and the social contexts. The linguistic context refers to vocabulary and syntax. The social context refers to a shared understanding of the purposes the provision might plausibly serve. A tenable version of the plain meaning rule must take account of both of these contexts. The alternative, of applying a provision according to the literal meanings of its component words, misconceives the conventions that govern the use of language
> * * *

Id. at 206.

Even if we assume that textualism was perfectly workable for the framers' generation—inasmuch as they had uniformly internalized the relevant linguistic and social conventions—the same is highly unlikely for those living one or two hundred years later. Even if linguistic conventions were deemed to have remained largely unchanged, the social context has become so different that the contemporary interpreter could not be a genuine textualist without shedding his or her own social context for that of distant ancestors. Moreover, even if that were possible, in many cases the relevant past social context cannot be recovered with the requisite amount of determinacy through historical research and analysis. Accordingly, "strict" textualism is most often impossible. On the other hand, if a social context is framed in broad general terms rather than with historic specificity, then past social contexts might well be easily linked to contemporary ones. That would allow for "moderate" textualism but would so dilute the social context as to allow us to project our own into the past, thus in effect undermining originalism.

Brest's attack on intentionalist originalism proceeds along similar lines. If, consistent with "strict" intentionalism, interpretation must be consistent with the specific intent of the framers, then there are insurmountable historical hurdles in ascertaining what that intent was in a vast number of cases. Moreover, even if the intent of individual framers could be ascertained, how could their collective intent be established where diverse, and to some extent contradictory, intents may have led to the same constitutional provision? Again, this problem can be avoided if "moderate" rather than "strict" intent is involved. But "moderate" intent may be cast in such general and abstract terms as to ultimately belie the specific intent of the framers. At that point, originalism would simply collapse into nonoriginalism.

Even without reliance on originalism it may be possible to ground judicial interpretation of the Constitution on principle and to insulate it from the vicissitudes of ordinary politics. This is the position advanced in Herbert Wechsler, *Toward Neutral Principles of Constitutional Law*, 73 Harv. L. Rev. 1 (1959). Professor Wechsler's theory is that judges may not be able to avoid making value-choices, but they may nonetheless remain above the political fray so long as they adhere to "neutral principles." Constitutional provisions may be so open-ended as to allow for a multiplicity of interpretations, each of which is backed by a different value choice. Accordingly, judicial interpretation cannot be value-free, but it can remain "neutral" in Wechsler's sense of the term if a judge can justify it in terms of general principles that he or she is prepared to follow in future cases without regard for the actual result to which application of the relevant principle may lead. For example, in deciding an "equal protection" claim, a judge may have to decide whether the Constitution requires equal treatment or whether it prohibits disadvantaging oppressed minorities. In a case involving a law that disadvantages an oppressed minority a judge may hold the law in question unconstitutional under either of the two above alternatives. However, if the judge justifies the decision in terms of the principle of equal treatment, he or she would be precluded from upholding affirmative action in favor of oppressed minorities that might disadvantage members of a privileged majority in a subsequent case. In short, Wechsler's commitment to neutral principles boils down to two requirements: (1) if a judge cannot offer a principled reason for constitutional invalidation of a democratically generated law, he or she should refuse to strike it down; and (2) in using principles to adjudicate constitutional claims, judges should remain neutral by applying the principles in question in ways that "transcend any immediate result that is involved." *Id*. at 19.

Bork's use of neutrality may be viewed as a generalization of Wechsler's theory and as an adaptation of it in the service of originalism. Professor Mark V. Tushnet has attacked both Wechsler's and Bork's theories of neutrality as ultimately incoherent and as lacking determinate applicability in his *Following the Rules Laid Down: A Critique of Interpretivism and Neutral Principles*, 96 Harv. L. Rev. 781 (1983). Tushnet points out that neutrality is attractive because it seems to promote the liberal conception of the rule of law, according to which judges should be prevented from exercising arbitrary power. Tushnet observes further that neutrality constraints have been elaborated variously as either substantive or methodological. He concludes, however, that they fail in either case. Substantive neutrality, in Tushnet's view, is ultimately parasitic on substantive values, and the results to which it leads can be traced back to such values, thus making it superfluous. Methodological neutrality, on the other hand, is reducible to prevailing but contingent social practices and thus undermines liberalism's assumptions about society and the rule of law.

Substantive neutrality depends on neutral application of a set of substantive principles, such as, for example, those prescribed by a particular moral philosophy. Tushnet's argument is that in that case, judges would be obligated to faithfully apply the moral principles involved, but that any reference to neutrality in that context would be merely vacuous.

That leaves methodological neutrality, that is, neutrality in the selection, justification, and application of principles, rather than neutrality in the principles themselves. Tushnet maintains, however, that such neutrality is impossible for both institutional and conceptual reasons. From an institutional standpoint, Wechsler's conception of judicial neutrality is often impossible to achieve because the USSC is a collective body subjected to majority rule. Different justices on the Court may be inclined to adhere to different principles, and if each were obligated to adhere to neutrality over time, the Court would become paralyzed. Accordingly, the institutional constraints favoring compromise undermine the viability of neutrality.

From a conceptual standpoint, Wechsler's neutral principles are prospective as they must be measured by the handling of subsequent cases. Tushnet argues, however, that judges are unlikely to fully elaborate a principle for future application to changing and unforeseen circumstances the first time they invoke it. For example, judges confronted with whether constitutional equality precludes racially segregated public schools are unlikely to anticipate which principles would also be best suited to deal with sex-equality or affirmative-action claims. Accordingly, either neutral principles unduly constrain judges in that overly narrow ones are chosen because of lack of foresight or imagination, or they remain underdetermined as the full implications of a principle underlying a past decision do not become obvious until further elaboration in a subsequent case. Cf. Michel Rosenfeld, *The Rule of Law and the Legitimacy of Constitutional Democracy*, in Chapter 1. Furthermore, Tushnet observes that when looking at what appears to be relevant precedents, a judge may derive more than one principle capable of linking past cases with a present one. Under such circumstances neutrality would hardly be meaningful.

For Tushnet, in the last analysis, it is law and judging as a social practice prevalent in a liberal capitalist society rather than neutrality that frame and constrain judicial interpretation. That means, however, that constitutional adjudication is ultimately ideological and political. And this contradicts the liberal ideal of a rule of law that transcends arbitrariness.

In *The Forum of Principle*, 56 N.Y.U. L. Rev. 469 (1981), Professor Ronald Dworkin argues that neither originalism nor an alternative theory based on democratic process can succeed in their common aim to render constitutional adjudication apolitical. Dworkin maintains that constitutional interpretation cannot avoid reliance on political theory and moral philosophy but asserts that it need not thereby sink into mere politics. Drawing on the distinction between policy and principle, Dworkin concludes that constitutional interpretation can remain above the political fray if it faithfully adheres to principle.

For Dworkin, originalism, and for that matter all forms of intentionalism, cannot be intelligible or usable unless embedded in a particular theory of legal practice that must itself be grounded in a given political vision. For example, when searching for the original intent of the framers of the "equal protection" provision, we can all agree that they sought to constitutionalize equality, but that does not afford sufficient guidance to decide concrete cases. As Dworkin observes:

> We agree on [the] general proposition, and this agreement gives us what we might call the *concept* of a constitutional intention. But we disagree about how the blanks in the proposition should be filled in. We disagree in which sense some purpose must have been in the minds of particular people, in which sense these people must have been connected with the adoption of the constitutional provision, and so forth.

> Different *conceptions* of constitutional intention give different answers to these questions * * * [It] is a matter of filling in the blanks provided by the common concept through making political choices, not a matter of best capturing what a group intention, considered as a complex psychological fact really is. There is no stubborn fact of the matter—no "real" intention fixed in history independent of our opinions about proper legal or constitutional practice—against which the conceptions we construct can be tested for accuracy. The idea of an original constitutional understanding therefore cannot be the start or the ground of a theory of judicial review. At best it can be the middle of such a theory, and the part that has gone before is not philosophical analysis of the idea of intention, and still less detailed historical research. It is substantive—and controversial—political morality.

Id. at 477–78.

The democratic-process theory of constitutional adjudication was elaborated in John Hart Ely's *Democracy and Distrust* (1980). According to Professor Ely, for the most part judicial interpretation of the Constitution can be justified as a means to safeguard the integrity of the democratic process. In Ely's view, most legitimate adjudication under the Bill of Rights, such as that relating to freedom of speech or the rights of criminal defendants, is process oriented. Thus, for example, a working democracy requires freedom of speech to debate political alternatives and allow the electorate to make informed choices. Accordingly, when judges decide free speech cases, they do not engage in substantive policymaking, but, rather, they secure the means to genuine democratic decisionmaking.

It seems more difficult to subsume equality cases under democratic-process theory, but Ely argues that equal protection cases can indeed be decided consistent with that theory. In the context of the massive and systematic segregation and discrimination of African Americans, they have been cast as a "discrete and insular minority" singularly targeted for unfavorable treatment. This for Ely amounts to a distortion of the democratic process inasmuch as white racists depart from competition over diverse policies in order to focus on oppressing African–Americans. In other words, racist lawmaking is less about securing a particular vision of the political good than about disenfranchising and humiliating a particular racial minority. Accordingly, in Ely's view, when judges hold racially discriminatory laws to be unconstitutional, they are not imposing a substantive view. On the contrary, they are restoring the democratic process.

Dworkin thoroughly disagrees with Ely's analysis. Dworkin raises two principal objections against Ely's theory. First, Dworkin points out that there is not a single neutral conception of democratic process but rather a plurality of conceptions of democracy, some of them substantive and others mainly procedural. All of these, however, are ultimately grounded on some contested substantive political vision. For example, for some, democracy is inextricably linked to the protection of fundamental rights or the maintenance of a certain minimum standard of living for all. For others, it is mainly defined in terms of adherence to majoritarian decisionmaking.

Second, Dworkin insists that even if everyone accepted a purely process-based conception of democracy, Ely's conclusions would still be unacceptable. Suppose, for example, argues Dworkin, that we share a utilitarian view of the justification for process-based democracy. Under that view every person counts as an equal, in that everyone's preferences are given equal weight, and policies depend on the democratic process inasmuch as they result from the expression of the greater preferences of the greatest number. Under such a system a policy of racial segregation can be justified not because of animus against a racial minority but as a consequence of the white majority expressing through democratic channels a genuine preference for living among themselves, separate from those whom they do not regard as alike. Far from being a distortion of the majoritarian process, racial segregation thus becomes a genuine expression of it. Consistent with this, Dworkin concludes, judicial invalidation of racial segregation as incompatible with equal protection ultimately must be grounded on some substantive conception of equality.

Dworkin's own alternative to originalism and democratic-process theory is based on the distinction between principle and policy. Policy is related to the pursuit of interests, and to the extent that particular policies promote certain interests at the expense of others, they are inevitably partisan. Principle, on the other hand, is based on values, such as moral values. For example, constitutional equality may be based on the principle of equal worth, equal concern, and equal respect for all persons. Consistent with this distinction, Dworkin concludes that judges interpreting the Constitution cannot avoid substance or political or moral theory, but they can avoid politics if they are guided in their decisions by principle rather than policy.

Notes and Questions

1.   The debate over originalism is a peculiarly American phenomenon. To be sure, certain other constitutional adjudicators look to the intent of the constitution-makers in the course of interpreting constitutional provisions— e.g, the GFCC, as noted above, considers historic arguments as well as several others when interpreting the Basic Law—but its judges do not ascribe the prominence or near-exclusiveness to originalism that many American judges and scholars, such as Bork, do. Is it not paradoxical that Americans rely on originalism even though their Constitution is more than two hundred years old, whereas constitutional adjudicators in countries with much more recent constitutions do not, even when they belong to the same generation as the framers? If originalism is defended, as does Bork, on the

grounds that it is consistent with democracy—one could even say doubly consistent with democracy to the extent that the framers' Constitution was, on the one hand, ratified by the people, and, on the other, it is meant to narrowly constrain the power of judges to invalidate democratically enacted laws—does not such originalism become self-defeating with the passage of time? Arguably, the framers' generation gave its consent to the Constitution. But what about generations more than two centuries later? Does it make any sense to claim that these latter generations should be deemed to have consented to the framers' Constitution?

2. American proclivities toward originalism may have much less to do with democracy than with the fact that, as some have suggested, the Constitution in the U.S. figures as the centerpiece of a nearly universally shared civil religion. See Sanford Levinson, *"The Constitution" in American Civil Religion*, 1979 Sup. Ct. Rev. 123. If the framers are perceived as superhuman beings with quasi-divine insights, then it makes sense to stick to originalism rather than deferring to mere mortals belonging to succeeding generations. Do you agree?

3. Is originalism—whether understood in terms of original intent or original meaning—inherently conservative? Cf. Thomas Grey, *Do We Have an Unwritten Constitution?*, 27 Stan. L. Rev. 703 (1975) (rejecting originalism in view of the need to interpret the Constitution so as to meet the evolving needs of successive generations). In considering this question, note that both the political Right and the political Left have embraced originalism at different times in the history of the U.S. Constitution. In *Lochner v. New York*, 198 U.S. 45 (1905), (see Chapter 10), the proponents of social and economic regulation invoked originalism against the Court's natural rights approach. In contrast, in the 1960s and 1970s, after the Court's decision in *Griswold*, above, and in *Roe v. Wade*, 410 U.S. 113 (1973) (see Chapter 5), recognizing a constitutional right to an abortion, conservatives resorted to originalism to counter what they regarded as the Court's undermining of traditional morality.

4. Does it matter what the framers and the framers' generation thought about original intent? What if they believed that their own intent should be given little weight in the context of constitutional interpretation? See H. Jefferson Powell, *The Original Understanding of Original Intent*, 98 Harv. L. Rev. 885 (1985) (arguing that while the framers were textualists, they were not originalists; rather, they expected subsequent generations to adapt the Constitution to their own needs). Arguably, the framers' conception of the importance of their own intent should be irrelevant as the democratic legitimacy of the original Constitution stems from the people that ratified the Constitution rather than the framers. Accordingly, it is the original intent as understood by the ratifiers that ought to be binding. Do you agree?

5. As noted above, originalism is largely an American phenomenon. Should constitutional adjudicators from other countries take a closer look at originalism and embrace it in some form? Does it make a difference whether the text of the relevant constitution is deemed to provide outcome-determinative guidance? Or whether the constitution in question is easy to amend? On the other hand perhaps the reason why originalism is not much of an issue in the context of recent constitutions is that there is a commonly

shared sense of understanding between the constitution-makers and those coming under it. Does that sound plausible?

6. At some level the theory of "neutral principles" advocated by Wechsler seems obvious. For example, most would undoubtedly agree that a judge should not be inconsistent in his or her adjudications so as to favor one litigant over another. In a broader sense, however, the very plausibility of neutral principles is challenged by both Professors Dworkin and Tushnet. Both, moreover, seem to think that neutrality is not possible because adjudication requires commitment to extralegal substantive values. However, Tushnet seems to draw a conclusion that is diametrically opposed to Dworkin's. According to Tushnet, there is no way for judges to avoid recourse to political values, and judges cannot—at least in practice—anticipate which rule they will endorse in subsequent rulings. Accordingly, not only are neutral principles impossible, but there can be no coherent liberal rule of law. For Dworkin, on the other hand, commitment to liberal values and embrace of the moral norms associated with them lead to principled judicial interpretation in constitutional cases, including hard ones. Far from undermining the rule of law, therefore, recourse to liberalism is a necessary adjunct to it. See Ronald Dworkin, *Taking Rights Seriously* (1977). Are Dworkin and Tushnet in fundamental disagreement concerning principled adjudication, or do they merely disagree on the merits of liberalism? Furthermore, Dworkin asserts that the U.S. Constitution happens to enshrine fundamental liberal rights as legally binding constitutional rights. See *id.* at 184–205. Does that make it particularly convenient for American judges to be principled? Is Dworkin's justification of principled constitutional adjudication therefore contingent on a peculiar fact about the U.S.? Or are all contemporary constitutional democracies fundamentally bound to the essential normative tenets of liberalism, thus making Dworkin's views on constitutional adjudication universally relevant? For a more extensive account of Dworkin's theory of judicial interpretation, including constitutional interpretation, see his *Law's Empire* (1986).

C.2.3. FUNDAMENTAL INTERPRETIVE DOCTRINES AND TECHNIQUES

C.2.3.a. CONSTITUTIONAL INTERPRETATION AND BALANCING

One method of constitutional interpretation used frequently by the USSC is that of balancing. Balancing involves "identification, valuation, and comparison of competing interests." T. Alexander Aleinikoff, *Constitutional Law in the Age of Balancing*, 96 Yale L.J. 943, 945 (1987). Balancing in the course of adjudicating a constitutional claim typically consists in identifying competing interests at stake, ascribing each of them a value, and assessing their relative weight. The more weighty among competing interests should prevail, and the balancing process from which it emerges should thus shape the ensuing constitutional jurisprudence. For example, if the free speech interests of one who utters distasteful statements is deemed to outweigh society's interests in remaining free from such statements, then the constitutional right to free speech ought to be interpreted as extending to distasteful utterances. In this example a constitutional right is weighed against a societal interest, and that occurs frequently in balancing cases. Other balancing cases may result from the application of a constitutional rule that requires balancing between nonconstitutional interests. For example, under U.S. federalism balancing is used to determine whether a state law that burdens national commerce is constitutional. Thus a state health law that imposes a burden on the free flow of goods would be constitutional only if the benefits it confers outweigh the burdens it imposes on national commerce. See the discussion on U.S. federalism in Chapter 4.

Professor Aleinikoff has criticized the use of balancing as a method of constitutional interpretation on several grounds. His chief criticisms are that balancing is prone to being incomplete, arbitrary, and unsuited for judicial enforcement of the Constitution. See Aleinikoff, *op. cit.* According to Aleinikoff, balancing is frequently incomplete as the courts weigh certain factors while ignoring others that are at least as important for purposes of the case at hand. On the other hand balancing can be arbitrary in its typical weighing of individual rights against societal interests. For example, free speech cases are often treated as requiring a balance between an individual right and a societal interest. Casting free speech rights as individual ones, however, is arbitrary, inasmuch as it is equally plausible to regard the individual's right of expression as a societal interest in vigorous public debate. Finally, and this is perhaps the most stinging criticism, balancing requires judges to engage in cost-benefit analysis—a task that is the very essence of the legislative function. Moreover, that not only forces judges to assume the role of policymakers, but it also tends to devalue constitutional rights by casting them as interests similar to all others rather than as genuine rights that for the most part trump societal interests.

Aleinikoff's views on balancing are by no means unanimously shared. For a defense of balancing, see Frank M. Coffin, *Judicial Balancing: The Protean Scales of Justices*, in *The Evolving Constitution: Essays on the Bill of Rights and the U.S. Supreme Court* 271 (Norman Dorsen ed., 1989). While acknowledging that balancing can have pitfalls, Judge Coffin emphasizes that it also has virtues and that it allows judges, if properly used, to perform their tasks with greater fairness and greater competence. Coffin maintains that balancing prompts judges to be more open and more careful since they must assess all facts, arguments, and interests before reaching a decision, thus minimizing the chances of being trapped by formulaic slogans or personal prejudices. As Coffin states: "Open balancing restrains the judge and minimizes hidden or improper preference by revealing every step in the thought process; it maximizes the possibility of attaining collegial consensus by responding to every relevant concern of disagreeing colleagues; and it offers a full account of the decision-making process for subsequent professional assessment and public appraisal." *Id.* at 280.

In short, from this standpoint the principal virtue of balancing is that it calls for dialogue and for taking into account various competing perspectives. In the words of Professor Michelman: "[A]doption of the balancing standard commits [judges] to the [Supreme] Court's and the country's project of resolving normative disputes by conversation * * * as opposed to self-justifying impulse and *ipse dixit* * * *. The balancing test, with its contextual focus, solicits future conversation, by allowing for resolution of this case without predetermining so many others that one 'side' experiences large-scale victory or defeat." Frank I. Michelman, *The Supreme Court 1985, Term–Foreword: Traces of Self–Government*, 100 Harv. L. Rev. 4, 34 (1986). (On balancing in the context of free speech, see Chapter 7.)

C.2.3.b. PROPORTIONALITY

BUITONI SA v. FONDS D'ORIENTATION ET DE REGULARISATION DES MARCHES AGRICOLES

European Court of Justice.
[1977] E.C.R. 677, 20 Feb. 1979.

Before the Court of Justice of the European Communities

Reference by the Tribunal Administratif, Paris, under Article 177 EEC.

[A French importer of tomatoes from a country not a member of the European Community forfeited his entire security deposit pursuant to Art. 3 of EEC Commission Regulation 499/79, for failure to report to the appropriate agency the completion of imports within the period covered by the importer's valid import license. As forfeiture of the security deposit was the penalty for failure to import during the period of validity of the import license as well as for mere failure to report imports completed within the period of the license's validity, the importer challenged his forfeiture under the above-mentioned regulation before the European Court of Justice as being disproportionate.]

* * *

Judgement.

[11]   The plaintiff * * * has claimed * * * that it is contrary to the principle of proportionality to apply the same penalty for failure to fulfill the obligation to import, which the security is intended to guarantee, and for mere delay in submission of the proofs of fulfillment of the obligation, which has been discharged correctly and within the prescribed period.

[12]   In its written observations the Commission maintains that Article 3 of Regulation 499/79 is justified by the fact that before its introduction the forfeiture of securities occurred on the expiry of different periods from one member-State to another, which led both to discriminatory treatment for traders and distortion of the system of securities, the purpose of that system being to enable the Community to have precise knowledge of the market situation.

[13]   There was, in addition, the need, at the administrative level, to set a period for the definitive closure of files.

[14]   However, the Commission also emphasized, during the oral procedure, the importance, within the system of import and export

licenses, of the informational role played by the submission by traders to the competent national agencies of the proofs, in the form of Copy No. 1 of the license endorsed by the office where the customs formalities were completed, of completion of the import or export transactions.

[15] In its submission, indeed, it is only by that means that the national agencies and, through them, the Community authorities, can obtain exact knowledge of the number of transactions actually effected on the basis of the licenses.

[16] As regards the problem of proportionality, it should be examined whether the penalty laid down in Article 3 of Regulation 499/76 for failure to comply with the period for presentation of the proofs prescribed by that provision exceeds what is appropriate and necessary to attain the objective sought.

[17] In this respect it should be recalled, on the one hand, as appears from the sixth recital in the preamble to Regulation 193/75, that the system of securities is intended to guarantee that the obligation to import or export, which has been voluntarily undertaken, will be fulfilled during the period of validity of the license issued for that purpose.

[18] * * * [P]ursuant to Article 18 (2) and (3) of that regulation the penalty laid down in case of failure to fulfill the obligation is, in essence, proportionate to the degree of that failure.

[19] On the other hand, the provisions of Article 3 of Regulation 499/76, prompted by 'administrative reasons', provide not only for a period within which those proofs must be furnished but also the loss of the whole of the security in the event of failure to comply with that period.

[20] That fixed penalty, which is applied to an infringement which is considerably less serious than that of failure to fulfill the obligation which the security itself is intended to guarantee, which is sanctioned by an essentially proportionate penalty, must therefore be held to be excessively severe in relation to the objectives of administrative efficiency in the context of the system of import and export licenses.

[21] Although, in view of the inconvenience caused by the belated production of proofs, the Commission was entitled to introduce the period laid down in Article 3 of Regulation 499/76 for the furnishing of proof, it should have sanctioned failure to comply with that period only with a penalty considerably less onerous for those concerned than that prescribing the loss of the whole of security and more closely allied to the practical effects of such an omission.

[22] Indeed, even if administrative efficiency requires that files should not remain open indefinitely, it must, however, be noted that failure to comply with such a period will be exceptional in nature in that it is contrary to the very interests of the exporter or importer concerned, who will normally seek release of his security as soon as possible.

[23] * * * [A]ccordingly * * * Article 3 of Regulation 499/76 is invalid.

PHARMACY CASE

Federal Constitutional Court (Germany).
7 BVerfGE 377 (1958).

[This case is presented in Chapter 10.]

LISELOTTE HAUER v. LAND RHEINLAND–PFALZ

European Court of Justice.
[1979] E.C.R. 3727, 13 Dec. 1979.

[European Community regulation imposing a two-year moratorium on new planting of vines to curtail wine production surpluses and stabilize the wine market challenged by plaintiff as violative inter alia of her right to property.]

* * *

The Question of the Right to Property

17.   The right to property is guaranteed in the Community legal order in accordance with the ideas common to the constitutions of the Member States, which are also reflected in the first Protocol to the European Convention for the Protection of Human Rights.

18.   Article 1 of that Protocol provides as follows:

"every natural or legal person is entitled to the peaceful enjoyment of his possessions. No one shall be deprived of his possessions except in the public interest and subject to the conditions provided for by law and by the general principles of international law."

The preceding provisions shall not, however, in any way impair the right of a state to enforce such laws as it deems necessary to control the use of property in accordance with the general interest or to secure the payment of taxes or other contributions or penalties."

19.   Having declared that persons are entitled to the peaceful enjoyment of their property, that provision envisages two ways in which the rights of a property owner may be impaired, according as the impairment is intended to deprive the owner of his right or to restrict the exercise thereof. In this case it is incontestable that the prohibition on new planting cannot be considered to be an act depriving the owner of his property, since he remains free to dispose of it or to put it to other uses which are not prohibited. On the other hand, there is no doubt that that prohibition restricts the use of the property. In this regard, the second paragraph of Article 1 of the Protocol provides an important indication in so far as it recognizes the right of a state "to enforce such laws as it deems necessary to control the use of property in accordance with the general interest." Thus the Protocol accepts in principle the legality of restrictions upon the use of property, whilst at the same time limiting those restrictions to the extent to which they are deemed "necessary" by a state for the protection of the "general interest". However, that provision does not, enable a sufficiently precise answer to be given to the question [raised here].

20. Therefore, in order to be able to answer that question, it is necessary to consider also the indications provided by the constitutional rules and practices of the nine Member States. One of the first points to emerge in this regard is that those rules and practices permit the legislature to control the use of private property in accordance with the general interest. Thus some constitutions refer to the obligations arising out of the ownership of property (German Grundgesetz, Article 14 (2), first sentence), to its social function (Italian constitution, Article 42 (2)), to the subordination of its use to the requirements of the common good (German Grundgesetz, Article 14 (2), second sentence, and the Irish constitution, Article 43.2.2*), or of social justice (Irish constitution, Article 43.2.1*). In all the Member States, numerous legislative measures have given concrete expression to that social function of the right to property. Thus in all the Member States there is legislation on agriculture and forestry, the water supply, the protection of the environment and town and country planning, which imposes restrictions, sometimes appreciable, on the use of real property.

21. More particularly, all the wine-producing countries of the Community have restrictive legislation, albeit of differing severity, concerning the planting of vines, the selection of varieties and the methods of cultivation. In none of the countries concerned are those provisions considered to be incompatible in principle with the regard due to the right to property.

22. Thus it may be stated, taking into account the constitutional precepts common to the Member States and consistent legislative practices, in widely varying spheres, that the fact that Regulation no 1162/76 imposed restrictions on the new planting of vines cannot be challenged in principle. It is a type of restriction which is known and accepted as lawful, in identical or similar forms, in the constitutional structure of all the Member States.

23. However, that finding does not deal completely with the problem raised [here]. Even if it is not possible to dispute in principle the Community's ability to restrict the exercise of the right to property in the context of a common organization of the market and for the purposes of a structural policy, it is still necessary to examine whether the restrictions introduced by the provisions in dispute in fact correspond to objectives of general interest pursued by the Community or whether, with regard to the aim pursued, they constitute a disproportionate and intolerable interference with the rights of the owner, impinging upon the very substance of the right to property. Such in fact is the plea submitted by the plaintiff in the main action, who considers that only the pursuit of a qualitative policy would permit the legislature to restrict the use of wine-growing property, with the result that she possesses an unassailable right from the moment that it is recognized that her land is suitable for wine growing. It is therefore necessary to identify the aim pursued by the disputed Regulation and to determine whether there exists a reasonable relationship between the measures provided for by the Regulation and the aim pursued by the Community in this case.

24.   The provisions of Regulation no 1162/76 must be considered in the context of the common organization of the market in wine which is closely linked to the structural policy envisaged by the Community in the area in question * * *

25.   [T]he policy initiated and partially implemented by the Community consists of a common organization of the market in conjunction with a structural improvement in the wine-producing sector. Within the framework of the guidelines laid down by Article 39 of the EEC Treaty that action seeks to achieve a double objective, namely, on the one hand, to establish a lasting balance on the wine market at a price level which is profitable for producers and fair to consumers and, secondly, to obtain an improvement in the quality of wines marketed. In order to attain that double objective of quantitative balance and qualitative improvement, the Community rules relating to the market in wine provide for an extensive range of measures which apply both at the production stage and at the marketing stage for wine.

27.   It is in this context that Regulation no 1162/76 was adopted. It is apparent from the preamble to that Regulation and from the economic circumstances in which it was adopted, a feature of which was the formation as from the 1974 harvest of permanent production surpluses, that that Regulation fulfils a double function: on the one hand, it must enable an immediate brake to be put on the continued increase in the surpluses; on the other hand, it must win for the Community institutions the time necessary for the implementation of a structural policy designed to encourage high-quality production, whilst respecting the individual characteristics and needs of the different wine-producing regions of the Community, through the selection of land for grape growing and the selection of grape varieties, and through the Regulation of production methods.

28.   It was in order to fulfil that twofold purpose that the Council introduced by Regulation no 1162/76 a general prohibition on new plantings, without making any distinction, apart from certain narrowly defined exceptions, according to the quality of the land. It should be noted that, as regards its sweeping scope, the measure introduced by the Council is of a temporary nature. It is designed to deal immediately with a conjunctural situation characterized by surpluses, whilst at the same time preparing permanent structural measures.

29.   Seen in this light, the measure criticized does not entail any undue limitation upon the exercise of the right to property. Indeed, the cultivation of new vineyards in a situation of continuous over-production would not have any effect, from the economic point of view, apart from increasing the volume of the surpluses; further, such an extension at that stage would entail the risk of making more difficult the implementation of a structural policy at the Community level in the event of such a policy resting on the application of criteria more stringent than the current provisions of national legislation concerning the selection of land accepted for wine-growing.

30.   Therefore it is necessary to conclude that the restriction imposed upon the use of property by the prohibition on the new planting of

vines introduced for a limited period by Regulation no 1162/76 is justified by the objectives of general interest pursued by the Community and does not infringe the substance of the right to property in the form in which it is recognized and protected in the Community legal order.

R. v. OAKES

Supreme Court (Canada).
[1986] 1 S.C.R. 103.

Dickson C.J.C. (Chouinard, Lamer, Wilson and Le Dain JJ., concurring)

This appeal * * * concerns the constitutionality of s. 8 of the Narcotic Control Act, R.S.C. 1970, c. N–1. The section provides, in brief, that if the court finds the accused in possession of a narcotic he is presumed to be in possession for the purpose of trafficking. Unless the accused can establish the contrary, he must be convicted of trafficking. The Ontario Court of Appeal held that this provision constitutes a "reverse onus" clause and is unconstitutional because it violates one of the core values of our criminal justice system, the presumption of innocence, now entrenched in s. 11(d) of the Canadian Charter of Rights and Freedoms. The Crown has appealed.

* * *

II.   Facts

The respondent, David Edwin Oakes, was charged with unlawful possession of a narcotic for the purpose of trafficking, contrary to s. 4(2) of the Narcotic Control Act. He elected trial by magistrate without a jury. At trial, the Crown adduced evidence to establish that Mr. Oakes was found in possession of eight 1–gram vials of cannabis resin in the form of hashish oil. Upon a further search conducted at the police station, $619.45 was located. Mr. Oakes told the police that he had bought ten vials of hashish oil for $150 for his own use, and that the $619.45 was from a workers' compensation cheque. He elected not to call evidence as to possession of the narcotic. Pursuant to the procedural provisions of s. 8 of the Narcotic Control Act, the trial judge proceeded to make a finding that it was beyond a reasonable doubt that Mr. Oakes was in possession of the narcotic.

Following this finding, Mr. Oakes brought a motion to challenge the constitutional validity of s. 8 of the Narcotic Control Act, which he maintained imposes a burden on an accused to prove that he or she was not in possession for the purpose of trafficking. He argued that s. 8 violates the presumption of innocence contained in s. 11(d) of the Charter. * * *

IV.   The Issues

The constitutional question in this appeal is stated as follows: Is s. 8 of the Narcotic Control Act inconsistent with s. 11(d) of the Canadian Charter of Rights and Freedoms and thus of no force and effect? Two specific questions are raised by this general question: (1) Does s. 8 of the Narcotic Control Act violate s. 11(d) of the Charter?; and (2) If it does, is

s. 8 a reasonable limit prescribed by law as can be demonstrably justified in a free and democratic society for the purpose of s. 1 of the Charter? If the answer to Q. 1 is affirmative and the answer to Q. 2 negative, then the constitutional question must be answered in the affirmative.

V. Does S. 8 of the Narcotic Control Act Violate S. 11(d) of the Charter?

[The Court concluded that imposing on the accused the burden of proving that the drugs he was convicted beyond a reasonable doubt of possessing were meant for personal consumption rather than trafficking violated the presumption of innocence protected by s. 11(d) of the Charter.]

* * *

V. Is S. 8 of the Narcotic Control Act a Reasonable and Demonstrably Justified Limit Pursuant to S. 1 of the Charter?

The Crown submits that, even if s. 8 of the Narcotic Control Act violates s. 11(d) of the Charter, it can still be upheld as a reasonable limit under s. 1 which, * * * provides: "The Canadian Charter of Rights and Freedoms guarantees the rights and freedoms set out in it subject only to such reasonable limits prescribed by law as can be demonstrably justified in a free and democratic society." The question whether the limit is "prescribed by law" is not contentious in the present case, since s. 8 of the Narcotic Control Act is a duly-enacted legislative provision. It is, however, necessary to determine if the limit on Mr. Oakes' right, as guaranteed by s. 11(d) of the Charter, is "reasonable" and "demonstrably justified in a free and democratic society" for the purpose of s. 1 of the Charter, and thereby saved from inconsistency with the Constitution * * *

It is important to observe at the outset that s. 1 has two functions: first, it constitutionally guarantees the rights and freedoms set out in the provisions which follow; and second, it states explicitly the exclusive justificatory criteria (outside of s. 33 of the Constitution Act, 1982) against which limitations on those rights and freedoms must be measured. Accordingly, any s. 1 inquiry must be premised on an understanding that the impugned limit violates constitutional rights and freedoms—rights and freedoms which are part of the supreme law of Canada * * *

A second contextual element of interpretation of s. 1 is provided by the words "free and democratic society". Inclusion of these words as the final standard of justification for limits on rights and freedoms refers the court to the very purpose for which the Charter was originally entrenched in the Constitution: Canadian society is to be free and democratic. The court must be guided by the values and principles essential to a free and democratic society, which I believe embody, to name but a few, respect for the inherent dignity of the human person, commitment to social justice and equality, accommodation of a wide variety of beliefs, respect for cultural and group identity, and faith in social and political institutions which enhance the participation of individuals and groups in society. The underlying values and principles of a free and democratic society are the genesis of the rights and freedoms guaranteed by the

Charter and the ultimate standard against which a limit on a right or freedom must be shown, despite its effect, to be reasonable and demonstrably justified.

The rights and freedoms guaranteed by the Charter are not, however, absolute. It may become necessary to limit rights and freedoms in circumstances where their exercise would be inimical to the realization of collective goals of fundamental importance. For this reason, s. 1 provides criteria of justification for limits on the rights and freedoms guaranteed by the Charter.

    * * *

To establish that a limit is reasonable and demonstrably justified in a free and democratic society, two central criteria must be satisfied. First, the objective, which the measures responsible for a limit on a Charter right or freedom are designed to serve, must be "of sufficient importance to warrant overriding a constitutionally protected right or freedom". The standard must be high in order to ensure that objectives which are trivial or discordant with the principles integral to a free and democratic society do not gain s. 1 protection. It is necessary, at a minimum, that an objective relate to concerns which are pressing and substantial in a free and democratic society before it can be characterized as sufficiently important.

Second, once a sufficiently significant objective is recognized, then the party invoking s. 1 must show that the means chosen are reasonable and demonstrably justified. This involves "a form of proportionality test". Although the nature of the proportionality test will vary depending on the circumstances, in each case courts will be required to balance the interests of society with those of individuals and groups. There are, in my view, three important components of a proportionality test. First, the measures adopted must be carefully designed to achieve the objective in question. They must not be arbitrary, unfair or based on irrational considerations. In short, they must be rationally connected to the objective. Second, the means, even if rationally connected to the objective in this first sense, should impair "as little as possible" the right or freedom in question. Third, there must be a proportionality between the effects of the measures which are responsible for limiting the Charter right or freedom and the objective which has been identified as of "sufficient importance".

With respect to the third component, it is clear that the general effect of any measure impugned under s. 1 will be the infringement of a right or freedom guaranteed by the Charter; this is the reason why resort to s. 1 is necessary. The inquiry into effects must, however, go further. A wide range of rights and freedoms are guaranteed by the Charter, and an almost infinite number of factual situations may arise in respect of these. Some limits on rights and freedoms protected by the Charter will be more serious than others in terms of the nature of the right or freedom violated, the extent of the violation, and the degree to which the measures which impose the limit trench upon the integral principles of a free and democratic society. Even if an objective is of sufficient importance, and the first two elements of the proportionality test are satisfied, it is still possible that, because of the severity of the deleterious effects of a measure on individuals or groups, the measure will not be justified by the purposes it is intended to serve. The more severe the deleterious effects of a measure, the more important the objective must be if the measure is to be reasonable and demonstrably justified in a free and democratic society.

Having outlined the general principles of a s. 1 inquiry, we must apply them to s. 8 of the Narcotic Control Act. Is the reverse onus provision in s. 8 a reasonable limit on the right to be presumed innocent until proven guilty beyond a reasonable doubt as can be demonstrably justified in a free and democratic society?

The starting point for formulating a response to this question is, as stated above, the nature of Parliament's interest or objective which accounts for the passage of s. 8 of the Narcotic Control Act * * * In my opinion, Parliament's concern that drug trafficking be decreased can be characterized as substantial and pressing. The problem of drug trafficking has been increasing since the 1950s, at which time there was already considerable concern. Throughout this period, numerous measures were adopted by free and democratic societies, at both the international and national levels.

The objective of protecting our society from the grave ills associated with drug trafficking is, in my view, one of sufficient importance to warrant overriding a constitutionally-protected right or freedom in certain cases. Moreover, the degree of seriousness of drug trafficking makes its acknowledgement as a sufficiently important objective for the purposes of. s. 1 to a large extent self-evident. The first criterion of a s. 1 inquiry, therefore, has been satisfied by the Crown.

The next stage of inquiry is a consideration of the means chosen by Parliament to achieve its objective. The means must be reasonable and demonstrably justified in a free and democratic society. As outlined above, this proportionality test should begin with a consideration of the rationality of the provision: Is the reverse onus clause in s. 8 rationally related to the objective of curbing drug trafficking? At a minimum, this requires that s. 8 be internally rational; there must be a rational connection between the basic fact of possession and the presumed fact of possession for the purpose of trafficking. Otherwise the reverse onus clause could give rise to unjustified and erroneous convictions for drug trafficking of persons guilty only of possession of narcotics.

In my view, s. 8 does not survive this rational connection test * * * [P]ossession of a small or negligible quantity of narcotics does not support the inference of trafficking. In other words, it would be irrational to infer that a person had an intent to traffic on the basis of his or her possession of a very small quantity of narcotics. The presumption required under s. 8 of the Narcotic Control Act is overinclusive and could lead to results in certain cases which would defy both rationality and fairness. In light of the seriousness of the offence in question, which carries with it the possibility of imprisonment for life, I am further convinced that the first component of the proportionality test has not been satisfied by the Crown.

As I have concluded that s. 8 does not satisfy this first component of proportionality, it is unnecessary to consider the other two components.

VI.   Conclusion

* * *

I would therefore dismiss the appeal.

C.2.3.c.   THE INTERPRETIVE USES OF FOREIGN AND COMPARATIVE MATERIALS

S. v. MAKWANYANE AND ANOTHER

[SOUTH AFRICA DEATH PENALTY CASE]
Constitutional Court (South Africa).
1995 (3) SALR 391 (CC).

[This case is presented in Chapter 5.]

PRINTZ v. UNITED STATES

Supreme Court (United States).
521 U.S. 898 (1997).

[This case is presented in Chapter 4.]

C.2.3.d.   LAW MAKING BY THE JUDICIARY AS CONSTITUTIONAL INTERPRETATION

PRINCESS SORAYA CASE

Federal Constitutional Court (Germany).
34 BVerfGE 269 (1973).

[This case is presented in Chapter 1.]

Notes and Questions

1.   Unlike textualism or originalism, balancing, the principle of proportionality, and that of subsidiarity (see Note 4 below), do not seem as much concerned with discovery of the meaning of the constitution as with elaborating and developing constitutional doctrine. Balancing and proportionality analysis seem particularly focused on establishing the boundaries between the realm of the constitution and that of legislative policymaking. Subsidiarity, in turn, seems to be primarily a tool for constitutional construction, inasmuch as it is suited to specify and monitor the apportionment of powers among more-remote and more-local governmental units. In short, are balancing, proportionality, and subsidiarity the instruments of constitution-making rather than those of constitutional interpretation? Does an affirmative answer depend on a conception of textualism and originalism as largely fixed and transparent? What if the text is open to many different meanings and thus not outcome determinative and if originalism yields largely contested glimpses into the founding generation that cannot be reasonably pinned down?

2. Professor Aleinikoff criticizes balancing because courts tend to weigh interests that are incommensurable and because they become involved in the paradigmatically legislative task of comparing "costs" and "benefits." Is balancing altogether inappropriate in constitutional as opposed to statutory interpretation, given that balancing may be suitable for purposes of weighing and comparing competing interests but constitutional *rights* should not be treated as mere interests. For example, my interest in keeping everyone off my huge landholdings would be clearly outweighed by the need of dozens of children from the surrounding community for recreation in nature at the very end of my property where I can neither see them nor hear them. However, if we address this matter from the standpoint of my constitutional right to property, then arguably any weighing of the respective interests involved would be inappropriate. Do you agree?

What if, on the other hand, we are dealing with constitutional rights subject to limitations, such as those allowed by Section 1 of the Canadian Constitution, namely, those that are "reasonable" and "justified in a free and democratic society." Does that mean that it ought to be legitimate to weigh constitutional rights against those interests—but only those—that help promote and sustain "a free and democratic society." Consider the following analysis:

> This test of proportionality is used in a wide range of Canadian constitutional adjudications that take place under a constitutional delegation to the courts essentially to strike a balance between the protection of Charter-identified rights and freedoms, on the one hand, and the "demonstrably justified" claims of the government consistent with a "free" and "democratic" society, on the other. [Section 1's provisions] were fairly widely understood to invite the Court to make "moral and political" inquiries and judgments in resolving constitutional questions.
>
> A significant number of cases in Canada apply the *Oakes* test of proportionality to determine whether to uphold a law even though it trenches in some way on basic rights and freedoms. The test does not seem to be particularly associated with outcomes in favor of or against the government position, unlike the "compelling interest" test of U.S. equal protection jurisprudence. Some famous cases, like *Oakes* itself (dealing with the presumption of innocence), the Canadian abortion decision, [*Morgenthaler*, see Chapter 5] and a recent decision concerning a national ban on tobacco advertising, have struck down laws that the government argued were sustainable under the proportionality test. In other areas, the Canadian Court has sustained challenged statutes under the *Oakes* test, including the hate speech statute challenged in *Keegstra* [see Chapter 7], a mandatory retirement age, a ban on advertising directed at children, and a "secular" one-day-a-week closing law. [See Chapter 8.]
>
> Vicki C. Jackson, *Ambivalent Resistance and Comparative Constitutionalism: Opening up the Conversation on "Proportionality," Rights and Federalism*, 1 U. Pa. J. Const. L. 583, 607 (1999).

Under the *Oakes* test the first issue concerns the purpose of the challenged legislation, namely, whether the purpose is legitimate and sufficiently important. Is this analysis persuasive, given a proper division of labor between courts and the legislature?

What about balancing when competing rights are at stake—such as, e.g., the free speech rights of those lawfully on a shopping mall and the property rights of the mall owner. Compare *Amalgamated Food Employees v. Logan Valley Plaza*, 391 U.S. 308 (1968) (free speech right of labor union picketing a store within shopping center treated as outweighing property right of center's owner to exclude protesters) with *Lloyd Corp. v. Tanner*, 407 U.S. 551 (1972) (shopping center owner's property rights considered as outweighing antiwar demonstrators' free speech rights). Subsequently, in *Hudgens v. N.L.R.B.*, 424 U.S. 507 (1976), the Court overruled *Logan Plaza* and held that labor picketing violated the property rights of the shopping center. The Court reasoned that since antiwar protests violated such property rights, analogously, so should labor protests, thus seemingly replacing balancing with a hierarchy among conflicting rights. Would maintaining balancing have been preferable? Can balancing under such circumstances be principled? Do the arguments advanced by Judge Coffin and Professor Michelman shed further light on this question? The issue in all these cases is whether a private property owner who invites the public to his or her property to gather, socialize, and shop (the American suburban shopping mall having become the equivalent of the shopping streets in a city) ought to be free to exclude peaceful protesters who may distract or dissuade potential shoppers. It is noteworthy that both *Logan Valley* and *Lloyd Corp.* were 5–4 decisions.

3. Is the principle of proportionality distinct and coherent, or does it tend to collapse, on the one hand, into balancing, and, on the other, into the equivalent of a rationality requirement as suggested in *Council of Civil Service Unions* (in Chapter 3)? Certain regulations seem to be objectionably disproportionate either because they tend to be irrational or palpably unfair. Thus a law that would ban all driving as a means to get all drunk drivers off the roads would fail proportionality analysis and so would a law that imposed the same penalty for petty theft and for murder. In murkier cases, however, is proportionality largely a cover for something else? Is it inherently subjective?

Consider the *Pharmacy Case*, where the GFCC determined that constraints on the choice of a profession can only satisfy the proportionality requirement if they are meant to promote a compelling state interest, whereas constraints on the practice of a profession may be proportional if they are reasonably suited to promote a rational state interest. What accounts for that difference? Does proportionality itself provide any insight into the difference between choice and practice in the context of this case? Does not the case ultimately turn on the determination that it is unfair and may be also inefficient to deprive an East German refugee of his right to pursue his livelihood, to uphold protection of existing pharmacists against competition? For a discussion of the nature and scope of proportionality in the context of constitutional equality cases in Germany, see Susanne Baer, *Constitutional Equality: The Jurisprudence of the German Constitutional Court*, in Chapter 6.

In both *Hauer* and *Oakes* proportionality seems to stand for something else. In *Hauer* it is for balancing as the issue boils down to a balancing between the individual's interest in using her property as she chooses and the state's interest in stabilizing wine markets; in *Oakes* it is for the virtual inalienability of a fundamental right and for fairness as the presumption of innocence is a right that trumps all—or at least all but the most compelling—interests, and as it is unfair to infer as a matter of law from the mere possession of illegal drugs an intent to sell. If this view is accurate, is the recourse to proportionality useful in these cases? Consider that the ECHR systematically uses proportionality to determine whether particular restrictions on fundamental rights are necessary in a democratic society. See, e.g., *Handyside v. United Kingdom* in Chapter 1 and *Lingens v. Austria* in Chapter 7.

4. The principle of subsidiarity, which has played a prominent role in the EU, establishes that the Union should not regulate areas that can be as, or more, effectively regulated by the member-states. See generally, George A. Bermann, *Taking Subsidiarity Seriously: Federalism in the European Community and the United States*, 94 Colum. L. Rev. 332 (1994). Subsidiarity is a tool of federalism, which, from an interpretive standpoint, is supposed to allow the constitutional adjudicator to decide which matters ought to be left to local government and which to regional, national, or supranational ones. Subsidiarity has been used in the context of national constitutions as well as in that of supranational entities, such as the EU. See Donald P. Kommers, *The Constitutional Jurisprudence of the Federal Republic of Germany* 112–13 (2d ed. 1997). The GFCC resorted to subsidiarity to decide that the state can intervene in the care of children only when "the smaller community" (i.e., the family) cannot. *Id.* The principle of subsidiarity has its origins in Catholic social thought, which "affirms that there is nothing done by a higher or larger organization that cannot be done as well by a lower or smaller one." Judith A. Dwyer, *The New Dictionary of Catholic Social Thought* 927 (1994).

There is a serious question whether the principle of subsidiarity is suited for judicial use as an interpretive tool. Of course, there are certain clear cases. Suppose parents abandon their children; then it seems obvious that state intervention would be proper. But what if parental care is somewhat adequate and somewhat inadequate, or if parents neglect certain aspects of a child's development that the state considers important but over which there is significant disagreement in the society at large. Are not those issues more properly entrusted to legislatures than to judges? Cf. George Bermann, *op. cit.* at 336 (arguing in the context of the EU that subsidiarity is more suited for policymakers than for judges and advocating that judges use it in a procedural or supervisory manner rather than in a substantive one).

Even admitting that subsidiarity is a proper judicial interpretive tool, arguably it can be in serious tension with proportionality. Referring again to the EU context, Professor Bermann has argued that subsidiarity may run counter to the requirement derived from proportionality that the legislator choose the least burdensome means available to achieve the legislative aims at hand. See Bermann, *op. cit.* at 386–88. In other words, it may be entirely possible for member-states to regulate a particular area but nonetheless more efficient for the Union to take charge. Does that make subsidiarity an unmanageable interpretive tool? Or is it merely another case of competing norms that the judiciary is called upon to reconcile as best it can?

5. To put in context the uses of foreign materials in constitutional adjudication, see Chapter 1 and Section A. above. Concerning the *Princess Soraya Case*, is what the Court doing—namely, creating a new legal right based on constitutionally implicit notions of justice—interpretation, or is it simply blatant legislation? To put the matter in Kelsenian terms, is the

problem that the Court appears to act as a positive legislator rather than as a merely negative one? Thus, for example, would it be equally objectionable if the German Civil Code provided for a civil monetary remedy and the Court invalidated it as unconstitutional, interpreting the addition of a civil remedy to criminal liability as exceeding the bounds of constitutional justice? Or is the difficulty that, by enshrining justice as a constitutional norm, license is granted to judges to make sweeping and largely unconstrained interpretations? And if the latter is the problem, is it not irrelevant whether the Court mandates a law or whether it invalidates one? Finally, it is exceedingly rare for the GFCC to mandate a law based on its conception of constitutional justice. Does that make the decision in the *Princess Soraya Case* more defensible?

Chapter 3

STRIKING A BALANCE AMONG THE BRANCHES OF GOVERNMENT: HORIZONTAL SEPARATION OF POWERS

It is widely accepted that government power must be divided to prevent any concentration that inevitably would lead to tyranny. This is asserted as a revolutionary proposition in Art. 16 of the French Declaration of the Rights of Man and of the Citizen of 1789: "Any society in which the safeguarding of rights is not assured, and the separation of powers is not established, has no constitution"—that is, no constitutional regime exists absent separation of powers. James Madison identified one of the reasons for avoiding power's concentration: "But the great security against a gradual concentration of the several powers in the same department consists in giving those who administer each department the necessary constitutional means and personal motives to resist encroachments of the others. * * * Ambition must be made to counteract ambition." *The Federalist* No. 51, at 321–22. (James Madison) (Clinton Rossiter ed., 1961).

In this chapter we discuss relations among the branches of government and the various levels of judicial involvement in the conflicts among them. American terminology uses the expression "separation of powers" for the constitutionally desirable checks and balances of government authority. In England, checks and balances refer to a parliamentary system. "Separation," if complete, refers to a situation where each branch possesses exclusive jurisdiction to carry out its mandate. Contemporary constitutional arrangements depart from the "clean" models primarily because the role of—and, consequently, the power of—the executive has dramatically increased in the modern administrative state. On the other hand the traditional legitimation of representative government continues to exist; hence legislatures have the legitimacy to balance the executive. Efforts to check the executive are also supported to a limited extent by judicial review, which strives to maintain a constitutional balance. American courts, for example, are concerned with government aggrandizement. But concepts concerning the acceptable balance are fluid and variable. After all, government is not exclusively about a negative virtue, that is, avoidance of tyranny. Governments must be effective, they must perform, and this requires the efficient use of power.

Section A. addresses fundamental issues of government power—sovereignty and citizenship—and scrutinizes various separation-of-powers models. The respective functions of the three branches of government, including cases dealing with their structures and powers, are presented in sections B., C., and D. Conflicts arise when one branch seeks to intervene in the affairs of another, although in most systems no branch seems to command exclusive power in matters that primarily pertain to it. The tensions that emerge among the branches are seen as being part of the ordinary workings of democratic government and can be managed by the standard operating procedures of constitutional decisionmaking. From time to time, however, democracies face challenges to the established divisions and cooperation among the branches. War and internal factionalism, as well as attempts to overthrow the democratic constitutional order, present special problems to the constitutional order. In Section E., we look at emergency situations.

A. SEPARATION VS. CHECKS AND BALANCES (PRESIDENTIALISM AND PARLIAMENTARISM)

First we present several views on separation of powers to indicate that the notion is merely shorthand to refer to various and changing arrangements.

Bruce A. Ackerman, THE NEW SEPARATION OF POWERS

113 Harv. L. Rev. 633, 633–729 (2000).

* * * [T]he Federalist Constitution has proved to be a brilliant success, which unitary nation states and parliamentary democracies all over the world would do well to copy. I give it most of the credit for the fact that ours is the wealthiest, most technologically advanced, and most socially just society in human history, not to mention the fact that we have with ease become a military superpower. * * * The rest of the world is quite rightly impressed with us, and it is thus no accident that the United States of America has become the biggest single exporter of public law in the history of humankind.[1]

Perhaps Steven Calabresi's triumphalism is typical today, but it contrasts sharply with previous American attitudes. A half-century ago this country stood even taller in the world than it does now. As the only great power escaping massive destruction during World War II, America's moralistic pretensions were at their apogee. Yet its constitutional prescriptions were a good deal more discriminating. To be sure, the

---

1. Steven G. Calabresi, An Agenda for Constitutional Reform, in Constitutional Stupidities, Constitutional Tragedies 22, 22 (William N. Eskridge, Jr. & Sanford Levinson eds., 1998).

United States supported written constitutions, bills of rights, judicial review—and, on occasion, federalism. But the separation of powers?

American influence reached its zenith in post-war Japan—with General MacArthur's legal staff presenting a draft constitution to the Japanese within a ridiculously short space of time. For all the rush, the draftsmen did not propose an American-style separation of powers. * * *

Nor did the Americans impose a strongly bicameral legislature—featuring an upper house checking and balancing the lower with full Madisonian vigor. The Japanese House of Representatives plays the dominant role in selecting the Cabinet. Although the upper House of Councillors has significant powers, it is not the constitutional equal of the lower House.[5] Call this the "one-and-a-half house solution."

The story is the same in Germany—constrained parliamentarianism, with a one-and-a-half house solution.[7]

* * * [There are alternatives to American separation of powers. In the elections of the Westminster democracy] each voter casts a single ballot—he cannot vote, say, for a Labor Member of Parliament and a Tory Prime Minister. The only way a voter can assure his party's choice for PM is to vote for his party's choice for MP. This basic point ties each MP's fate to his party's leadership in ways that are unknown in separated systems. * * * Given these overwhelming electoral incentives to support the government of the day, the Westminster model is not only constitutionally committed to rule by the last majority in a strictly legal sense. * * *

Another key feature is the PM's ability to determine the time of the next election (with only a five-year deadline constraining this decision). * * * The majority not only rules, but it also has a fair chance to put its program into action before returning to the people for collective judgment.

1. The Separationist Response—There is much more to be said, but this simple model allows us to frame some basic issues raised by the "separation of powers." When considered as a doctrine of political legitimacy, its proponents are united around a single key normative proposition. They deny that a single electoral victory is sufficient to vest plenary lawmaking authority in the victorious political movement. This proposition yields one of the most distinctive features of the separation of powers: the fact that the different lawmaking powers often operate on a staggered electoral schedule. Even if party A wins big at time one, it

5. The House of Representatives has the power to choose the Prime Minister unilaterally when the two houses disagree. See Japan Const. art. 67. It also has the exclusive power to remove the government through a vote of no-confidence, see id. art. 69, and to pass a budget over the opposition of the House of Councillors, see id. art. 60. * * *

7. The Weimar Constitution of 1919 created a strong, directly elected president who was independent of parliamentary control. This came to be regarded as a "major er-

ror" after Hindenburg's appointment of Hitler as Chancellor. David P. Conradt, The German Polity 182–83 (6th ed. 1996). The post-war draftsmen of the German Basic Law established a Bundestag that "no longer had to compete with an executive over which it had no direct control." Id. at 183. The Basic Law was unprecedented in German constitutional history because it "assigned sole control over government and bureaucracy to the parliament." Id.

may have to win n times more before it can gain plenary lawmaking authority.

Within this normative framework many things are possible, and the current American system is very much a special, and specially complicated, case.

* * * Linz argues that the separation of powers has been one of America's most dangerous exports, especially south of the border.[19] Generations of Latin liberals have taken Montesquieu's dicta, together with America's example, as an inspiration to create constitutional governments that divide lawmaking power between elected presidents and elected congresses—only to see their constitutions exploded by frustrated presidents as they disband intransigent congresses and install themselves as caudillos with the aid of the military and/or extraconstitutional plebiscites. From a comparative point of view, the results are quite stunning. There are about thirty countries, mostly in Latin America, that have adopted American-style systems. All of them, without exception, have succumbed to the Linzian nightmare at one time or another, often repeatedly. * * *

It is possible, of course, to avoid the Linzian nightmare without redeeming the Madisonian hope. Rather than all out war, president and house may merely indulge a taste for endless backbiting, mutual recrimination, and partisan deadlock. Worse yet, the contending powers may use the constitutional tools at their disposal to make life miserable for each other: the house will harass the executive, and the president will engage in unilateral action whenever he can get away with it. I call this scenario the "crisis in governability."

Once the crisis begins, it gives rise to a vicious cycle. Presidents break legislative impasses by "solving" pressing problems with unilateral decrees that often go well beyond their formal constitutional authority; rather than protesting, representatives are relieved that they can evade political responsibility for making hard decisions; subsequent presidents use these precedents to expand their decree power further; the emerging practice may even be codified by later constitutional amendments. Increasingly, the house is reduced to a forum for demagogic posturing, while the president makes the tough decisions unilaterally without considering the interests and ideologies represented by the leading political parties in congress. This dismal cycle is already visible in countries like Argentina and Brazil, which have only recently emerged from military dictatorships. A less pathological version is visible in the homeland of presidentialism, the United States.

* * * (b) Full Authority—I have been considering separation of powers in its impasse mode, when no political party has won often enough to satisfy the system's criteria for plenary lawmaking power. But there is an obvious alternative: the same party wins enough elections in a row to take control of all the relevant powers. I call this the mode of full authority.

---

19. Linz presents his arguments most comprehensively in Juan J. Linz, Presidential or Parliamentary Democracy: Does It Make A Difference?, in 1 The Failure of Presidential Democracy 3 (Juan J. Linz & Arturo Valenzuela eds., 1994).

* * * Under the French system, the President is directly elected for a fixed term of seven years but is obliged to appoint a Premier who has majority support in the National Assembly. Because the Assembly's electoral mandate must be renewed within a five-year interval, the Constitution contemplates a system of staggered elections—with the relationship between the President and the Premier depending on the outcome of the most recent election to the Assembly. When voters elect an Assembly majority that supports the President, he operates (more or less)[26] in the mode of full authority, and his Premier functions as his principal subordinate. But when the Assembly is dominated by the President's opponents, he confronts a problem broadly analogous to the one prevailing when an American President * * * confronts a hostile Speaker of the House. * * * Up to the present time, the French have managed these tension-filled periods with Madisonian panache. Although the constitutional text is not much help in defining the terms of competition/cooperation between "cohabiting" powers, the two sides have generally cooperated without pathological conflict. Nonetheless, the potential for an ongoing crisis in governability is certainly present.

When judged by American standards, French separation seems relatively weak. On the political side, the French President must worry mostly about hostility from the National Assembly, since the French Senate is not very powerful. Moreover, the President can try to regain full authority by calling a new Assembly election at a time of his own choosing. In contrast, the American system of fixed and staggered two-, four-, and six-year terms for House, President, and Senate is much more exigent, requiring more elections before a rising political movement is in solid control of full lawmaking power.

* * * Beyond the Westminster Tradition—I have been using a simplified version of the familiar Westminster system as a foil for an initial foray into the separation of powers. But perhaps I have been using the wrong benchmark. After all, there are many parliamentary systems in which cabinets do not have the staying power of the British type. Between 1945 and 1996, the average Italian Cabinet lasted 1.28 years before it was displaced by the next governing coalition, and Cabinets turned over even more quickly during the last years of the Fourth French Republic. If this Italo–French model had been made the salient point of contrast, wouldn't an American-style system look better?

Yes, but the weakness of the Italo–French model is not due to unseparated power but to the system of proportional representation through which MPs are selected. * * * Although individual cabinets may come and go, many of the same ministers and parties remain in government for many years, thereby providing a longer-term perspective on policy.

* * * [Constitutional engineering may improve the system.] [O]ne obvious step is to deny splinter parties entrance into parliament. Many

---

26. When the President's party dominates the governing coalition, his power is at a maximum, as in the [case] of Charles de Gaulle between 1962 and 1969. * * * If the governing coalition is favorable to the President but the President is not in direct control of the dominant party of the coalition, his Prime Minister exercises greater autonomy. * * *

PR systems require parties to leap over a substantial threshold of popular support—say four or five percent—before they may become cabinet makers or breakers. This requirement reduces cabinet instability by reducing the number of potential bargaining partners who can make offers that disrupt the existing coalition.

Another stabilizing measure is the "constructive vote of no confidence." Under this system, the parliamentary opposition cannot throw out the cabinet simply because it does not like what it is doing. Instead, the opposition must affirmatively select a new government before the old prime minister can be ousted. This is a much tougher job because it is easier for the extreme Left and Right to vote against a centrist cabinet than to agree affirmatively on a successor. This technique is also quite common nowadays.[46]

Constitutions that combine these two techniques have had substantial success in curbing incessant cabinet shuffles. Most notably, the modern German Constitution, which endorses both, has provided the Chancellor and his governing coalition with an average life expectancy of 3.6 years since the war. * * *

Notes and Questions

1. Separation of powers is subject to historical changes. In the United States, accepted practices developed in relation to the increased powers of the executive to steer the country. In *Industrial Union Department, AFL–CIO v. American Petroleum Institute*, 448 U.S. 607, 674 (1980), Justice Rehnquist (concurring in the judgment) summarized these developments:

> The Framers of the Constitution were practical statesmen, who saw that the doctrine of separation of powers was a two-sided coin. James Madison, in Federalist Paper No. 48, for example, recognized that while the division of authority among the various branches of government was a useful principle, 'the degree of separation which the maxim requires, as essential to a free government, can never in practice be duly maintained.' The Federalist No. 48, at 308 (James Madison) (Henry Cabot Lodge ed., 1888).

> This [U.S. Supreme] Court also has recognized that a hermetic sealing-off of the three branches of government from one another could easily frustrate the establishment of a national government capable of effectively exercising the substantive powers granted to the various branches by the Constitution. Chief Justice Taft, writing for the Court in *J. W. Hampton & Co. v. United States*, 276 U.S. 394 (1928), noted the practicalities of the balance that has to be struck:

> > [T]he rule is that in the actual administration of the government Congress or the Legislature should exercise the legislative power, the President or the State executive, the Governor, the executive power, and the Courts or the judiciary the judicial power, and in carrying out that constitutional division into three branches it is a breach of the National fundamental law if Congress gives up its

46. Among relatively stable democracies, Spain, Papua New Guinea, and Belgium have adopted the technique. See [Arend Lijphart, *Patterns of Democracy* 101 (1999)]. Newly emerging democracies in Hungary and Poland have also adopted it. * * *

legislative power and transfers it to the President, or to the Judicial branch, or if by law it attempts to invest itself or its members with either executive power or judicial power. This is not to say that the three branches are not co-ordinate parts of one government and that each in the field of its duties may not invoke the action of the two other branches in so far as the action invoked shall not be an assumption of the constitutional field of action of another branch. In determining what it may do in seeking assistance from another branch, the extent and character of that assistance must be fixed according to common sense and the inherent necessities of the governmental co-ordination. *Id.* at 406.

Is this to say that the branches are separate *and* coordinate? Compare with the position of Justice Blackmun in *Mistretta v. United States*, 488 U.S. 361, 381 (1989):

In adopting this flexible understanding of separation of powers, we simply have recognized Madison's teaching that the greatest security against tyranny—the accumulation of excessive authority in a single branch—lies not in a hermetic division between the Branches, but in a carefully crafted system of checked and balanced power within each Branch. "[T]he greatest security," wrote Madison, "against a gradual concentration of the several powers in the same department, consists in giving to those who administer each department, the necessary constitutional means, and personal motives, to resist encroachments of the others." The Federalist No. 51, p. 349 (J. Cooke ed. 1961). Accordingly, as we have noted many times, the Framers "built into the tripartite Federal Government ... a self-executing safeguard against the encroachment or aggrandizement of one branch at the expense of the other." *Buckley v. Valeo*, 424 U.S., at 122. See also *INS v. Chadha*, 462 U.S. 919, 951 (1983).

It is this concern of encroachment and aggrandizement that has animated our separation-of-powers jurisprudence and aroused our vigilance against the "hydraulic pressure inherent within each of the separate Branches to exceed the outer limits of its power." *Ibid.*

2. To be sure, the rejection of strict separationism may go exceptionally far:

The doctrine, as propounded by Montesquieu and his followers, may be stated briefly as follows.

1. There are three main classes of governmental functions: the legislative, the executive and the judicial.

2. There are (or should be) three main organs of government in a State: the Legislature, the Executive and the Judiciary.

3. To concentrate more than one class of function in any one person or organ of government is a threat to individual liberty. For example, the Executive should not be allowed to make laws or adjudicate on alleged breaches of the law; it should be confined to the executive functions of making and applying policy and general administration.

Even if one accepts the first two propositions, one is not obliged to accept the third. To concentrate a large quantity of power in the hands of one person, in the absence of proper safeguards, is surely more dangerous than to combine a few powers analytically different in quality in the same hands, if adequate safeguards exist. And a rigorous segregation of functions may be highly inconvenient. In many countries subscribing to versions of the separation of powers doctrine, rulemaking powers have been vested in the Executive because it is manifestly impracticable to repose such powers exclusively in the Legislature. The third proposition stated above is therefore both extreme and doctrinaire, and is not taken literally by all proponents of the theory.

One of the implications commonly read into the separation of powers doctrine is that the three branches of government ought to be composed of different persons. In the United States, for instance, the President and his Cabinet cannot be members of Congress (although the Vice-President presides over the Senate). It does not inevitably follow that the one branch of government should not be in a position to dominate others. Matters may be so designed that each branch operates as a check on the others.

Stanley de Smith and Rodney Brazier, *Constitutional and Administrative Law* 19–20 (6th ed. 1989).

The same personnel in the branches may increase the domination of one branch over the other (for example, the British cabinet).

3. The parliamentary system is based, in principle, on some kind of "primacy" of the legislature, which follows from the representative nature of the legislative body. Legislation predetermines executive action. The executive's subordination, however, does not accurately reflect the importance of the executive, which controls public administration.[a] The German Federal Constitutional Court (GFCC) confirmed the autonomous position of the executive vis-à-vis Parliament in the *Kalkar I Case*, 49 BVerfGE 89 (1978):

> The Basic Law does not confer on parliament total priority in fundamental decision-making. By insisting upon separation of powers it imposes limits on parliament's authority. The Basic Law relegates far-reaching decisions, particularly those of a political nature, to other supreme constitutional organs. Examples include the chancellor's power to determine general policy guidelines (Article 65 [1]) and the president's authority to dissolve the Bundestag (Article 68) and declare a state of legislative emergency (Article 81). * * * The Bundestag may check the exercise of such powers by electing a new chancellor and bringing down the federal government. * * * A monistic theory of power, incorrectly deduced from the principle of democracy, which would confer a monopoly of decision-making power on parliament must not undermine the concrete distribution and balance of political power guaranteed by the Basic Law. Other institutions and organs of political authority do not lack democratic legitimacy [merely] because of parliamentary delegates are the only officials elected by direct popular vote. Legislative, executive, and judicial organs derive their institutional and functional democratic legitimacy from Article 20 (2) of the Basic Law. * * * Nevertheless, we are able to deduce from the principle of parliamentary democracy that parliament and its decisions do have priority

---

a. Subordination is exceedingly complex in Germany. The aggressive imperialism of Prussia's centralized administration was very much in the minds of the drafters of the Basic Law. Hence in most issues civil servants act as employees of the *Land*, and the central government relies on the *Länder* to carry out its administrative tasks.

vis-à-vis other branches [of government]. We hold this to be a principle of interpretation transcending all concrete allocations of authority.

Are parliamentary systems moving toward a form of stronger separation, allowing for the constitutional legitimization of an autonomously acting cabinet to counter popular representation in the legislature? Consider the following position on the current constitutional arrangement in India: "The executive function comprises both the determination of the policy as well as carrying it into execution. This evidently includes the initiation of legislation, the maintenance of order, the promotion of social and economic welfare, the direction of foreign policy, in fact the carrying on or supervision of the general administration of the State." *R.S. Ram Jawaya Kapur v. State of Punjab*, (1955) 2 S.C.R. 225, 236. The Indian government was shaped by British parliamentary concepts. Is there a hidden tension here between constitutionalism and democratic representation? The following excerpt captures how the German position tends to diminish the importance of strict separation:

> The separation of powers is a fundamental constitutional principle for the organization and function [of the state]. The Basic Law provides for a distribution of political power, the harmonious cooperation of the three branches, and the moderation of political rule which will result from it. The principle of separation of powers is not, however, realized in pure form in the federal arena. Numerous interconnections and balances of power exist. It is not an absolute separation of powers which we must glean from the constitutional design of the Basic Law but [rather] mutual control, restraint, and moderation.

> [Even] if the separation of powers cannot be understood as meaning a clear-cut separation of the functions of political power, [we] must retain the distribution of weight among the three powers as outlined by the Constitution. No branch may obtain a predominance not intended by the Constitution over another power. Nor may [one branch] deprive another of the authority needed to fulfill its constitutional tasks. The core functions of the different governmental branches cannot be altered. This precludes one of the powers from relinquishing tasks which—according to the Constitution—are typically within its purview.

Judicial Qualification Case, 34 BVerfGE 52 (1972).

4. For now it is more important to recognize that the U.S. is exceptional in its relatively benign experience with its familiar form of separation. Despite its present military and cultural hegemony, we should be reluctant to hold the American system as an ideal for aspiring democracies. Yet the contrary is seemingly unfolding: "[I]n the 1980s and 1990s, all the new aspirant democracies in Latin America and Asia (Korea and the Philippines) have chosen pure presidentialism. * * * [O]f the approximately twenty-five countries that now constitute Eastern Europe and the former Soviet Union, only three—Hungary, the new Czech Republic, and Slovakia—have chosen pure parliamentarism." Alfred Stepan and Cindy Skach, *Presidentialism and Parliamentarism in Comparative Perspective*, in *The Failure of Presidential Democracy* 120 n.19 (Juan Linz and Arturo Valenzuela eds., 1994). "Rather than praising this development [that most emerging democracies choose presidentialism] as a latter-day vindication of the eternal truths first glimpsed by Montesquieu and the American Founders, we should view it with anxious concern. Are we beginning yet another round of Latin Amer-

ica's disastrous nineteenth[-]century experience with the North American model, but this time on a global scale?" Ackerman, *op. cit.* at 729.

Professor Ackerman agrees that the "Westminster system is no bar to the rise of dictatorship. But there will be many fewer crises in governability during more normal times." Ackerman, *op. cit.* at 648. Many observers speak of Chancellor dictatorship in regard to Germany and of elected dictatorship in England. Is it true that normalized dictatorships are likely to emerge in the absence of stronger versions of separation? Rousseau wrote that the English were free only for a day—when they elected the Parliament. On the other hand, who should be the protector of the constitution against a parliamentary majority that is guided by a "winner-take-all" mentality?

Presidential systems may have built-in balances, or they might mobilize self-limiting mechanisms to the extent that Professor Ackerman's fears will not materialize. Although the Romanian Constitution was written under the strong cultural influence of France, the President never possessed exclusive power over the executive. In Poland, the 1997 Constitution removed some of the presidential powers that were the source of conflicts among the branches in the early postcommunist years. In Bulgaria, the popularly elected yet powerless President was instrumental in solving a major constitutional crisis driven by parliamentary majorities. In the context of the President's appointment powers, the Bulgarian Constitutional Court has discussed separation of powers in a parliamentary system:

> There is some degree of relativity in the term "separation of powers" * * * but today it is used in a tradition that evolved out of definite historical and political factors. The legal and political content of the term "separation of powers" is that three basic spheres are identified in state power and handed for exercise to the three basic systems of bodies that are relatively independent of one another and function in definite interrelation. * * * This concept sees the separation of powers as a method of the optimum functioning of supreme state power and an instrument to prevent any possible arbitrary action on the part of the other state bodies affecting the citizens' rights.

Bulgarian Constitutional Court, Decision No. 6. April 22, 1993.

5. Contemporary approaches to separation often stress the constitutional duty of interbranch cooperation. This is hardly surprising as even separationist constitutional regimes leave important decisions to joint action of the branches, expressly or implicitly. But the judicial emphasis on cooperation offers little guidance about the specific procedures to follow. As the Italian *Judicial Nomination Case* (see Section D. below) indicates, it may leave a dispute undecided. During grave conflicts between Prime Minister Meciar and the President of Slovakia, the government requested an abstract interpretation of the Slovak Constitution regarding a dispute between the President and Prime Minister. The Slovak Parliament elects the President by a simple-majority vote. The Slovak Constitution states that the President has the right to preside at meetings of the Council of Ministers and to request reports from both the government and ministers and, also, that the government is the supreme executive power. The President sought to make use of his powers to request reports. The government claimed that the President, in making such requests, would subordinate the government to the President. The Slovak Constitutional Court found that the President could not determine the procedure or manner of reporting to him, nor could

he set time limits for reporting. Where no time limit is enunciated by the Constitution, the relation between governmental bodies is based solely on the principle of cooperation. (I. ÚS 7/96, C. 12–96). The Slovak Constitutional Court reads its Constitution very closely: only what is prescribed will be the rule. The Italian Constitutional Court (ICC), however, takes the position that what is not prohibited is possible, especially in combination with an additional provision. Is there a constitutional theory behind the two approaches, or do the courts simply acquiesce in what actually occurs, given power relations, and thus the extreme difference in their interpretations is simple happenstance?

6.   In another postcommunist system the emphasis has been more on the independence of the branches. The Russian Constitutional Court (RCC), in its *Ruling On the Constitutionality of Certain Provisions of the Basic Law of the Altai Territory*, Decision 2–P of 18 January 1996, stated:

> Separation of powers is stipulated in the RF [Russian Federation] Constitution as one of the fundamentals of the constitutional system of the RF as a whole, that is, not only on the federal level, but also on the level of government of the RF subjects.

> Separation of powers into legislative, executive, and judicial branches contemplates the system of legal guarantees, checks and balances that exclude the possibility of concentration of power by one of the branches, ensures the independent functioning of all branches, and at the same time provides for cooperation between the branches.

> Within the limits of their competencies, legislative and executive branches function independently of each other. Either branch is formed independently, and the power of one branch to end the activities of the other is permissible only on condition of balancing such power, as laid down in the law.

In this instance the strong emphasis on the independence of the branches had to do with the attempt of procommunist and other authoritarian forces to create parliamentary supremacy. The constituent entities of the Russian Federation (called "subjects of the Federation") have their own constitutions and charters. These fundamental laws were enacted by the respective legislatures of these entities. In many constituent entities, various procommunist groups were in the majority when these basic laws were drafted. Partly following the Leninist tradition of the supremacy of the representative–legislative body and partly to guarantee their powers vis-à-vis the local executive, which was likely to fall under the spell of the President of the Russian Federation, they experimented with various division-of-powers arrangements. As the *Altai Territory Case* indicates, the separation arrangement in the Russian Federation Constitution became the model for the RCC (see Chapter 4). For a contrary Indian approach, see *S.R. Bommai*, paras. 22–23, in Chapter 4.

B.   THE LEGISLATIVE BRANCH

The importance of the legislative branch is related to the historical fact that it was seen, in modern democracies, as the quintessential form of representative government. The original concept of the U.S. Constitution presupposed a president not popularly elected. The British tradition of parliamentary sovereignty and the Rousseauist idea that the people's will is supreme—hence legislation expressing that will is also supreme—enhanced the recognition of Parliament's special position in constitutional systems. The communist constitutions expressly confirmed the "conception of unlimited and limitless parliamentary power." Postcommunist constitutions were keen to substitute "a distribution of power based on a separation of the branches, creating such a model of the system of governance based on checks and balances in which the separate branches appear primarily as one another's limitations." As the Hungarian Constitutional Court (HCC) stated:

> [A]ccordingly, the Parliament no longer exercises 'all the rights arising from popular sovereignty,' and it cannot rescind the other branches' rights—including the executive branch. * * * In light of the aforementioned, parliamentary democracy in the system of governance of the Republic of Hungary is not identical with the unlimited power of the existing parliamentary majority since the latter—in addition to the constitutionally distributed spheres of duties—is limited by [a number of specific limiting provisions] a two-thirds majority requirement for a constitutional amendment; a two-thirds majority requirement for the enactment of certain Acts; a two-thirds majority requirement to initiate a proceeding to hold the President of the Republic accountable; the jurisdiction of the Constitutional Court; the President's sphere of authority, albeit to a limited extent.

Presidential Appointments Case, Decision 36/1992 (VI.10.) AB hat.

B.1. PARLIAMENT

Even minimally democratic constitutions contain some guarantees for the independent functioning of the legislature to facilitate the operation of the institution and enable individual members to carry out their mandate. Beginning in the twentieth century, parliaments grew increasingly incapable of functioning, partly because they abused their independence. Some contemporary constitutions provide for the "rationalized" operation of parliament, in an effort to enhance performance and minimize instability. A rationalized parliament limits the powers of its members (e.g., in terms of speech, motions, crossing the floor, etc.) and tends to increase the importance of factions and political parties behind the factions. These measures are understandable reactions to the historical difficulties of parliamentary democracy, but they result in new problems of abuse of power and privilege. In many countries, owing to changes in the understanding of constitutionalism, constitutional oversight was extended to the activities of their parliaments, at least to some extent. Other countries, e.g., the U.S. (see political question doctrine in Chapter 2, Subsection B.3.1.) and the UK, are reluctant to allow the other branches to probe into the activities of the legislature.

Notes on Parliamentary Sovereignty and Autonomy

1. Parliamentarism has no fixed set of rules. In the nineteenth century, the leading authority on the British Constitution found that the sover-

eignty of the Parliament was "the dominant characteristic of our political institutions * * *." It follows from that doctrine that "[a]ny Act of Parliament, or any part of an Act of Parliament, which makes a new law, or repeals or modifies an existing law, will be obeyed by the courts." A. V. Dicey, *Introduction to the Study of the Law of the Constitution* 37–38 (7th ed. 2000). According to Dicey, parliamentary sovereignty consists of three prevalent traits: "first, the power of the legislature to alter any law, fundamental or otherwise, as freely and in the same manner as other laws; secondly, the absence of any legal distinction between constitutional and other laws; thirdly, the inability of any judicial or other authority to nullify an Act of Parliament, or to treat it as void or unconstitutional." *Id.* at 87.

Even where Westminster served as a model, parliamentarism might have moved away from this understanding, as the example of India suggests:

> Although our Constitution is federal in its structure it provides a system modelled on the British parliamentary system. It is the executive that has the main responsibility for formulating the governmental policy by 'transmitting it into law' whenever necessary. * * * [T]he doctrine of parliamentary sovereignty as it obtains in England does not prevail here except to the extent provided by the Constitution. * * * Under our Constitution none of the three great departments of the State is supreme and it is only the Constitution which is supreme and which provides for a government of laws and not of men.

Kesavananda v. Kerala, (1973) Supp. S.C.R. 1, 221, 277. (Justices Shelat and Grover).

2. The traditional doctrine of parliamentary sovereignty dictates that Parliament alone determines all matters regarding its functions. (See the political question doctrine and nonjusticiability issues in Chapter 2.) Thus the nineteenth-century idea of sovereignty entailed that Parliament itself decided its elections and membership issues. In the twentieth century, increasingly the concept of constitutional oversight challenged this traditional position. More and more election-related contests have been adjudicated by courts, including special courts and constitutional courts. The desire to protect individual fundamental rights affected even the affairs of legislative bodies.

In deliberate defiance to the traditional understanding of internal autonomy and self-determination of legislative bodies, the 1958 French Constitution contains rules that affect the internal organization of the National Assembly and Senate. In addition, it prescribes that the Internal Rules (Standing Orders) of the two chambers be submitted to the Constitutional Council for mandatory scrutiny. Moreover, to preclude the continuation of the parliamentary practices of the Fourth Republic, the National Assembly wrote a new standing order to conform with the new Constitution and limited the period of speaking time in parliamentary debate. The Council found that providing the government and deputies equal time for speech during debates violated the Constitution, which permits members of the government to be heard at their request.[b] The Council had no difficulty with time limits and other speech limits imposed on parliamentarians by the Standing Orders. Compare this position with the speech-restriction concerns

b. The same decision of the Constitutional Council prohibited the use of parliamentary resolutions to guide the Cabinet (see below), 59–2 DC of 17, 18, 24 June 1959.

of the Indian Supreme Court (ISC) in *Kihoto Hollohan v. Zachillhu*, (1992) 1 S.C.R. 686.

Owing to the limits on the initiation of the review procedure in the French system (see judicial review in Chapter 2), the Constitutional Council cannot intervene in instances of unconstitutional parliamentary practices if all the political parties involved in the procedure agree in their unconstitutional convention. It is common practice to vote by proxy (by providing duplicate keys that are used in electronic voting). The Constitution prohibits this practice, yet the potential parties do not challenge it. But if an irregularity occurred in vote counting, an injured party could use the irregularity of the procedure to challenge the constitutionality of the law. Parliamentary fairness blooms in the shadow of irregularity.

3. The GFCC claims that it respects the internal matters and procedures of the legislature. The Polish Constitutional Tribunal is also of the opinion that only Parliament's autonomy is to be respected. The GFCC reviews Standing Orders and procedures only if they affect third parties. The German Parliament is not sovereign in the British sense, and, to the extent that Parliament carries out a constitutional mandate or its functioning affects a constitutional value, such as representative democracy, it is subject to constitutional review. The GFCC took positions regarding the right of a parliamentary minority to create investigative committees (with an agenda specified by the initiating minority). Investigative committees are a pertinent part of parliamentary democracy and serve constitutional parliamentary control over the executive. "In a parliamentary democracy the majority [party] normally dominates the parliament. Today, this relationship is characterized by the political tension between the government and the parliamentary fractions supporting it, on the one hand, and the opposition [party or parties] on the other hand. In a parliamentary system of government [therefore] the majority does not primarily watch over the government. This is rather the task of the opposition * * *." *Schleswig-Holstein Investigative Committee Case*, 49 BVerfGE 70 (1978). In the *Green Party Exclusion Case*, 70 BVerfGE 324 (1986), however, the GFCC found no violation of parliamentary-minority protection when no member of the Green fraction was elected to the budget subcommittee dealing with the finances of the Secret Services.[c] The GFCC found that because opposition members were on the subcommittee and it was important in security matters to have the personal confidence of the majority, the Greens' exclusion was not an abuse dictated by political persuasion. Justice Böckenförde argued in his dissent what is otherwise the generally held contrary view of the Court: "every individual representative is called upon to represent the people and to participate in the parliament's negotiations and decisions. He has a specific and equal right to such participation." (See further, Chapter 11, Subsection C.1.)

4. Contrary to all eighteenth-century myths about the popular mandate of individual representatives, contemporary rules enhance parliamentary stability to the detriment of members' rights. Standing rules often impose, among others, certain sanctions on any member defecting his faction. This is the case, in India, in *Kihoto Hollohan v. Zachillhu*, (1992) 1 S.C.R. 686:

---

c. In 1983, when the Greens were first elected to the Bundestag, the established parties perceived them as a flamboyant, nonconstructive ecological–feminist group.

[B]y the Constitution (Fifty–Second Amendment) Act, 1985 (popularly known as the Anti-defection law) a provision was inserted in the constitution of India providing for disqualification of a Member of either House of Parliament or of a State Legislature found to have defected from continuing as a Member of the House. Paragraph 2 of the Tenth Schedule states that a Member of a House would incur disqualification if he voluntarily gives up his membership of the party by which he was set up as a candidate at the election, or if he without obtaining prior permission of the political party to which he belongs votes or abstains from voting in the House contrary to "any direction" issued by such political party, or joins another party. The question of disqualification shall be referred for decision of the chairmen/Speaker of the House and his decision shall be final. * * * The Statement of Objects and Reasons appended to the Bill which was adopted as the Constitution (Fifty–Second Amendment) Act, 1985 says:

> The evil of political defections has been a matter of national concern. If it is not combated, it is likely to undermine the very foundation of our democracy and the principles which sustain it. With this object, an assurance was given in the Address by the President to Parliament that the Government intended to introduce in the current session of Parliament an anti-defection.

The Supreme Court deferred "to this legislative wisdom and perception" but found that the denial of judicial review violates the basic structure of the Indian Constitution.

The prohibition on changing parties was incorporated into the Constitution of Pakistan by the Fourteenth Amendment, in 1997. As in India, this was driven by concerns that parliamentary-faction defections would lead to nongovernability. The amendment was challenged in *Wukala Mahaz Barai Tahafaz Dastoor v. Federation of Pakistan*, P.L.D. 1998 S.C. 1263. The Supreme Court of Pakistan refused to consider the applicability of the Indian basic-structure theory[d] as the three alleged basic structures of the Pakistan Constitution, namely, the representative form of government, the Islamic concept of democracy, and the independence of the judiciary, were not violated. "The impugned Article will bring stability in the polity of the country * * * It is also in consonance with the tenets of Islam and Sunnah as the same enjoined its believers to honour their commitments if the same are not in conflict with the teachings of Islam and Sunnah." *Id.* at 1314 (Chief Justice Ajmal Mian). Disqualification of a member of a parliamentary party on grounds of defection is a constitutional provision; the Supreme Court found it necessary to clarify that the rule was to be read in conjunction with the "Explanation to the Article." It follows that the breach complained of occurred within the House and that the member's right to speech was observed. (Only a vote as defined in Art. 63/A(1)(b) or (c) is considered floor-crossing.)

---

d. Note, however, according to Chief Justice Ajmal Mian: "[I]n Pakistan instead of adopting the basic structure theory or declaring a provision of the Constitution as ultra vires to any of the Fundamental Rights, this Court has pressed into service the rule of interpretation that if there is a conflict between the two provisions of the Constitution which is not reconcilable, the provision which contains lesser right must yield in favour of a provision which provides higher rights." *Id.* at 1315.

PARLIAMENTARY DISSOLUTION CASE
Federal Constitutional Court (Germany).
62 BVerfGE 1 (1984).

[Reacting to the parliamentary instability of the Weimar Constitution, the Basic Law leaves the President with no authority to dissolve Parliament at his pleasure. On the other hand the Chancellor cannot be removed by a simple no-confidence vote. The Chancellor can be removed in a process of constructive vote of no confidence, when his or her successor is simultaneously elected. The *Bundestag* is dissolved by the President only if the vote of confidence requested by the Chancellor fails and the Chancellor requests a dissolution. (The *Bundestag* can also be dissolved if it fails to elect a new Chancellor in case of vacancy, after repeated unsuccessful election rounds.) The Basic Law does not authorize the *Bundestag* to dissolve itself. Only on two occasions, in 1972 and 1982, has the Chancellor called a vote of confidence against himself, which was deliberately lost so that the he could ask the President to dissolve the *Bundestag* and schedule early elections. In December 1982, Chancellor Kohl, who enjoyed substantial political support, reached an arrangement with all the parties not to vote confidence in him, allowing the President an early dissolution of Parliament. Some delegates, arguing they had a popular binding mandate, initiated an *Organstreit* proceeding. The delegates claimed that the term of the *Bundestag* was fixed (four years) in order to stabilize the system and that the Chancellor, together with the President and parliamentary parties, sought to manipulate the Constitution.

[The fundamental legal issues were whether the Chancellor could call for a vote of no-confidence when he commanded the support of a parliamentary majority and whether the President could dissolve the *Bundestag*, pursuant to the Chancellor's request, if his loss was a mere contrivance.

[The following summary was prepared by the Court.]

* * *

2. An order to dissolve the federal parliament or the refusal to do so pursuant to Article 68 of the Basic Law is a political decision within the lawful discretion of the federal president. The president may exercise his discretionary authority under Article 68 (I) only when the constitutional prerequisites are fulfilled at the time of his decision.

* * *

5. In the tradition of German constitutional history, the term "confidence" within the meaning of Article 68 refers to parliament's official approval—manifested in the act of voting—of the chancellor's programs with respect to personnel and substantive issues.

6. Under Article 68, the chancellor may try to dissolve the *Bundestag* only when he finds that it is no longer politically possible to govern with the prevailing configuration of parliamentary votes. This configuration must so severely cripple or impair the capacity to govern that the chancellor can no longer expect to advance his political program in a meaningful way and [at the same time] secure the continuing support of

the parliamentary majority. This principle is part of the unwritten [text] of Article 68 (I).

7. Article 68 (I) cannot be construed to allow a chancellor who is certain of receiving a parliamentary majority in support of his program to request a no confidence vote merely because he thinks it would be convenient [to hold new elections].

8. (a) Before the chancellor asks for a vote of no confidence for the purpose of requesting the president to dissolve parliament, he must determine whether there is still a good chance that a majority will endorse his policy and do so with continuing confidence.

(b) When deciding whether the chancellor's petition (for a confidence vote) and proposal [to dissolve parliament] are constitutional under Article 68, the president must * * * respect the chancellor's authority to judge and evaluate the (political situation) unless some other [valid] assessment of the situation would clearly forbid parliament's dissolution.

(c) The unanimous decision of the (political) parties represented in parliament to bring about new elections should not serve as a limit on the president's discretion; he may construe such unanimity as an additional indication that the dissolution of parliament would produce a result closer to the intent of Article 68 than a decision against dissolution.

      * * *

12. The three highest constitutional organs (i.e., president, chancellor, and *Bundestag*) enjoy (considerable) latitude in judging, evaluating, and making political decisions (under Article 68 (I)). Thus, in interpreting Article 68, the standard of (judicial) review is narrower than would be the case in assessing the validity of (ordinary) legislation and its implementation. Here the Basic Law relies mainly on the internal system of checks and balances between the highest constitutional organs mentioned in Article 68. The Federal Constitutional Court may find a constitutional violation here only when standards expressly laid down in the Basic Law have been ignored. [The majority of the Second Senate found that the dissolution was constitutional as all three constitutional actors had reason to believe independently that there would be no stable majority.]

MUHAMMAD NAWAZ SHARIF v. FEDERATION OF PAKISTAN

Supreme Court (Pakistan).
P.L.D. 1993 S.C. 473.

Nasim Hasan Shah, C.J.

On the evening of 17th April, 1993, Mian Muhammad Nawaz Sharif, Prime Minister of Pakistan addressed the Nation on the National Radio and Television Networks. It was an emotional address wherein he alleged, inter alia, that disgruntled political elements were working against his Government, hatching conspiracies to destabilise it and trying to undo all the good work he was trying to do. All this, he alleged, was being done under the patronage of the President of Pakistan. He ended his speech with the following challenging words: "I will not resign; I will not dissolve the National Assembly; and I will not be dictated."

* * * [T]he President of Pakistan * * * declared that the speech of the Prime Minister of the previous evening and other acts of his Government had convinced him that the Government of the Federation could not be carried on in accordance with the provisions of the Constitution. He had, accordingly, in exercise of the powers conferred on him under Article 58(2)(b) of the Constitution, ordered the dissolution of the National Assembly, dismissed the Prime Minister and his Cabinet and called for General Elections in the country. A Care-taker Cabinet was immediately sworn in the same evening, which was later expanded to include 62 Ministers.

* * * Two questions in the main arise for decision in this case, namely:—

(1) Is this petition under Article 184(3) of the Constitution maintainable?

and

(2) If so, has the President exceeded the powers conferred on him under clause (b) of Article 58(2) of the Constitution in ordering the dissolution of the National Assembly?

* * * Article 184(3) of the Constitution, which has been invoked by the petitioner, lays down:

" * * * (3) Without prejudice to the provisions of Article 199, the Supreme Court shall, if it considers that a question of public importance with reference to the enforcement of any of the Fundamental Rights conferred by the Chapter 1 of Part II is involved, have the power to make an order of the nature mentioned in the said Article."

[The Court rejected the preliminary objection that Sharif had no standing under Fundamental Right 17, which guarantees the right to form a political party and the right to be a member of only one political party and no more. The provision was interpreted as "a basic guarantee to the citizen against usurpation of his will to freely participate in the affairs and governance of Pakistan through political activity relating thereto." Because the Constitution guarantees democratic government, it guarantees it through a party system that "converts the results of a Parliamentary election into a Government." The Court found that the fundamental political right under Art. 17(2) includes the right to form a government. Standing was granted to the deposed Prime Minister.]

* * * Article 58 provides:

"58. (1) The President shall dissolve the National Assembly if so advised by the Prime Minister; and the National Assembly shall, unless sooner dissolved, stand dissolved at the expiration of forty-eight hours after the Prime Minister has so advised.

(2) Notwithstanding anything contained in clause (2) of Article 48, the President may also dissolve the National Assembly in his discretion where, in his opinion:

> * * * (b) a situation has arisen in which the Government of the Federation cannot be carried on in accordance with the provisions of the Constitution and an appeal to the electorate is necessary."

* * * This Court in the case of Haji Muhammad Saifullah P.L.D. 1989 S.C. 166 has held that the grounds and material which form the basis of the of dissolution are open to scrutiny and judicially reviewable, observing in this connection:

> "The discretion conferred by Article 58(2)(b) of the Constitution on the President cannot, therefore, be regarded to be an absolute one, but is to be deemed to be qualified one, in the sense that it is circumscribed by the object of the law that confers it.

> It must further be noted that the reading of the provisions of Articles 48(2) and 58(2) shows that the President has to first form his opinion, objectively and then, it is open to him to exercise his discretion one way or the other i.e. either to dissolve the Assembly or to decline to dissolve it."

* * * On March 7, 1977, general elections were held in the country. However, as soon as the results of the elections were announced practically the whole country rose in protest against them, being convinced that they were manipulated and the outcome of massive rigging. The working of the Government came to a standstill. The main demands of the opposition parties involved in the agitation were that the Prime Minister should go, the National Assembly should be dissolved and fair and free elections be held afresh. The Prime Minister was not, however, prepared to dissolve the National Assembly and under the [1973] Constitution [then in force] it was he and he alone who could get the National Assembly dissolved. To overcome this impasse and to remedy the situation the Army decided to intervene and on 5th of July, 1977 imposed Martial Law. This intervention ostensibly was for a temporary period (for the limited purpose of arranging free and fair elections, so as to enable the country to return to a democratic way of life but, in point of fact, lasted for 8-1/2 years). This tragedy, many people thought, could have been avoided if the President had also been vested, in exceptional circumstances, with the power of dissolving the National Assembly.

Accordingly, this deficiency, amongst others, was sought to be remedied when the 1973 Constitution (which was suspended on the imposition of Martial Law) was being revived in 1985 and to this end clause (2) added to Article 58 by the Constitution (Eight Amendment) Act, 1985.

* * * This Court, in Haji Muhammad Saifullah's case (P.L.D. 1989 S.C. 166) after a close analysis of [the *non obstante* clause contained in sub-Article (2) of Article 58], in the light of the relevant background, held that if it could be shown that no grounds existed on the basis of which an honest opinion could be formed "that a situation had arisen in which the Government of the Federation cannot be carried on in accordance with the provisions of the Constitution and an appeal to the

electorate is necessary" the exercise of the power would be unconstitutional and open to correction through judicial review. As the examination of the grounds of the order of dissolution passed by the President on 29th May, 1988 revealed that the prerequisites prescribed for the exercise of the powers conferred by Article 58(2)(b) did not exist, the said action was found to be unlawful.

However, despite the above finding, the consequential relief of restoration of the National Assembly was not granted. It was observed that "the writ jurisdiction is discretionary in nature and even if the Court finds that a party has a good case, it may refrain from giving him the relief if greater harm is likely to be caused thereby that the one sought to be remedied." * * *

* * * On hindsight, I now think that after having found the action of dissolution of the National Assembly was not sustainable in law, the Court should not have denied the consequential relief and ought to have restored the National Assembly.

* * * [In the case of Kh. Ahmad Tariq Rahim (P.L.D. 1992 S.C. 646)] the Court * * * found the order of dissolution passed by the President * * * to be valid and upheld it.

* * * In view of these newly-added provisions, it was argued that a preeminent role had been assigned to the President. He was not now merely the Constitutional Head of the State simply enjoying a high ceremonial office but had, in fact, become a full partner in the governance of the country and indeed the more important partner.

* * * Unfortunately, this belief that he enjoys some inherent or implied powers besides these specifically conferred on him under Articles 46, 48(6), 101, 242(1A) and 243(2)(c) is a mistaken one. In a Constitution contained in a written document wherein the powers and duties of the various agencies established by it are formulated with precision, it is the wording of the Constitution itself that is enforced and applied and this wording can never be overridden or supplemented by extraneous principles or non-specified enabling powers not explicitly incorporated in the Constitution itself. In view of the express provisions of our written Constitution detailing with fullness, the powers and duties of the various agencies of the Government that it holds in balance there is no room of any residual or enabling powers inhering in any authority established by it besides those conferred upon it by specific words.

* * * [T]he President cannot remove [the Prime Minister] from his office as long as he commands the confidence of the majority of the members of the National Assembly.

* * * Undoubtedly, the President may require the Cabinet or the Prime Minister, as the case may be, to reconsider any advice tendered to him but the President is bound to act on the advice tendered, even if it be the same, after consideration. Undoubtedly, both are expected to work in harmony and in close collaborations for the efficient running of the affairs of the State but as their roles in the Constitution are defined, which do not overlap, both can exercise their respective functions unhin-

dered and without bringing the machinery of the Government to a standstill.

* * *

According to the learned Attorney–General the said speech and conduct of the Prime Minister amounted, inter alia, to "subversion of the Constitution" and, therefore, was by itself a sufficient ground for dissolving the National Assembly under Article 58(2)(b).

The words "situation has arisen in which the Government of the Federation cannot be carried on in accordance with the provisions of the Constitution, [sic] in which situation alone the President is empowered to dissolve the National Assembly also came up for interpretation by this Court in the case of Haji Muhammad Saifullah (P.L.D. 1989 S.C. 166) and these words were explained by me to mean:

> "Thus, the intention of the law-makers, as evidenced from their speeches and the terms in which the law was enacted, shows that any order of dissolution by the President can be passed and an appeal to the electorate made only when the machinery of Government has broken down completely, its authority eroded and the Government cannot be carried on in accordance with the provisions of the Constitution."

* * * In the present case, the breakdown of the machinery of the Government is said to have occurred because of the Prime Minister's speech as it made it impossible thereafter for these two pillars of the State to co-exist.

* * * No one man how high so ever can, therefore, destroy an organ consisting of chosen representatives of the people unless cogent, proper and sufficient cause exists for taking such a grave action. Article 58(2)(b), no doubt, empowers the President to take this action but only where it is shown that "a situation has arisen in which the Government of the Federation cannot be carried on in accordance with the provisions of the Constitution."

* * * The action taken did not fall within the ambit of this provision. [The Supreme Court ordered the reinstatement of the Prime Minister and declared the Parliament not dissolved.]

Notes and Questions

1.   The prohibition on the dissolution of a legislative body is one of the strongest elements of legislative independence.

> A parliamentary body may cease to function before the end of its term, and under certain conditions it can dissolve itself or be dissolved. The relevant constitutional regulations provide room for a number of solutions. Generally, in a parliamentary system where the ministers lose a vote of confidence, it can be dissolved. Often this is a matter of tradition, and if dissolution is a possibility at all, the final decision may rest with the executive. The majority of the day or the majority-party leadership may wish to form a new government, or it may decide to go to the country, that is, it may ask the head of state (president or king) to dissolve the parliament and call new elections. How dissolution opportu-

nities are used—if this is a choice—is again a matter of political tradition. In Holland, where the system is built on wide-scale consensus building through political bargaining, since 1815 the monarch has dissolved the lower house only eleven and the upper house three times. Tradition or the constitution may set limits to dissolution (probably linked to popular sovereignty); as a rule parliament cannot be twice dissolved for the same reason. (In the Netherlands this tradition has prevailed since 1868, while the Weimar Constitution explicitly mentions the point in Art. 25.).

* * *

It is constitutionally acceptable both that the elected body itself decides as to dissolution or that it can be dissolved only by someone else (including the executive power), or it cannot be dissolved at all. In eighteenth-century England, the monarch had the right to dissolve the parliament whenever he wanted. In reaction, the U.S. approach is the complete reverse of this practice. Congress cannot be dissolved (not by itself or by any other person), and it is elected for a determined period. Modern English parliamentarism, in theory, rests on the assumption that both the executive and the legislative powers have the right to "dissolve" each other. Dissolution and the vote of no-confidence threaten the position of the people in the "other" power; and this is how the system of checks and balances becomes complete. In the case of separation in the U. S., the powers cannot affect each other's existence. The German Basic Law knows no opportunity for the Bundestag to dissolve itself; with the complicity of all the members, in 1982 it managed nevertheless to do so.[e]

[T]he Dutch Constitution [is] exactly the reverse, namely, the king (that is, the government) could dissolve the parliament without any restrictions. Since 1958, however, Dutch public opinion holds that the government has no right (to initiate) dissolution. * * * [A]ll the majority parties must give support before the government can ask the king to act.

* * *

In the newly independent republics of the former Soviet Union, the parliaments are divided, paralyzed, and chaotic, as if attempting to demonstrate in practice the Marxist–Leninist tenet of the impotence of "Western parliamentarism." Disillusionment came to a head when the building of the Russian Parliament was bombarded. In response to the dissatisfaction, parliament's powers were restricted in a number of constitutions. The presidents of many post-Soviet republics were granted almost unlimited power to dissolve their parliaments. The often and worldwide heard explanation was that it was unacceptable that discord and sloth paralyze the life of the country, especially in "hard times like these." If the members of parliament do not work for their pay, they

---

e. By an agreement among the various parties, since the Federal Assembly did not nominate a new Chancellor to replace the Chancellor who was voted out, President Carstens called new elections. The GFCC found the action in keeping with the Basic Law, 62 BVerfGE 1 (1984) (above), because, while the arrangement went against the Constitution in forcing an election by abus-ing the provisions of the constructive no-confidence, the consensus among the branches of power rendered revision by the Court impossible in a political issue. This suggests that a constitution is not omnipotent, even in the eyes of its guardians, especially if the entire political elite agree on an anticonstitutional interpretation.

must be fired. The great example followed in matters pertaining to presidential dissolution powers is that of the Fifth French Republic, where the president of the republic, after some consultations, may call new elections whenever he wishes.

* * *

The fact that parliament may be dissolved involves undeniable dangers to constitutionalism. In the Weimar Republic in 1932, Hindenburg repeatedly dissolved the parliament, and in the ensuing interim, he governed the country with presidential decrees. These dissolutions contributed to the process that led to Hitler's rule. Constitutional considerations would then require the dissolution of parliament to be subjected to specific conditions. In a rule-of-law state the laws are predictable, in other words, it is important to define, if possible, in concrete terms, when parliament can be dissolved. If such limits restrict self-dissolution, it would affect parliament's sovereignty; however, if the right of dissolution by another branch becomes subject to specific nondiscretionary conditions, parliament's position improves.

András Sajó, *Limiting Government: An Introduction to Constitutionalism* 126–29 (1999).

2. The German Basic Law's concerns regarding parliamentary and governmental stability had considerable influence in the emerging Central European democracies. The Czech Constitution (like the Hungarian until 1997 and the Slovak ones) is very reluctant to grant dissolution powers to the Assembly or the executive. After the collapse of Václav Klaus's majority coalition, in 1997, a caretaker government was charged with calling new elections, to which most of the parties agreed. The Czech Constitution (Art. 35.1.b.), however, allows dissolution of the Assembly only if it "fails, within three months, to reach a decision on a government bill, to the consideration of which the government has joined the issue of confidence." (The French motion of censure is comparable to this solution, but it results in the resignation of the Council of Ministers.) In light of the government-stability concerns, is the use of the vote of confidence for purposes of dissolution constitutional? Is honesty a constitutional value? Had the procedure in Art. 35 been applied, MPs would have lost their salaries for two months. Party leaders, therefore, preferred a new constitutional act, shortening the electoral term. The act that limited the term of Parliament was a one-time amendment to the Constitution. Only the term of the then-current legislature was shortened. Is this compatible with the nonretroactivity requirement of the rule-of-law state? Both Houses provided the necessary majorities, and since the President of the Republic has no veto power in matters of constitutional acts, the Act never saw the scrutiny of constitutional review.

3. After the unconstitutional presidential order of 1993 (discussed above), the President of Pakistan ordered another dissolution of Parliament, on October 11, 1996. The President accused the Prime Minister and her party of being incapable of putting an end to the killing of thousands of people, including extrajudicial killings. Three days prior to scheduled elections, the Supreme Court found that the President acted lawfully. In *Benazir Bhutto v. President of Pakistan*, P.L.D. 1998 S.C. 388, 429–30, the Court said:

[W]e do not accept the contention * * * that the President can invoke Article 58(2)(b) to dissolve the National Assembly only in such a grave situation in which Martial Law can be imposed as in 1977 and there is complete breakdown of Constitutional machinery. * * * [T]he President in his discretion may dissolve the National Assembly where he forms opinion on the basis of material before him having nexus with the dissolution order * * * that situation has arisen in which the Government of the Federation cannot be carried on * * * and appeal to the electorate is necessary. * * * There may be occasion for the exercise of such power where there takes place extensive, continued and pervasive failure to observe no one but numerous provisions of the Constitution, creating the impression that the country is governed not so mush by the Constitution but by methods extra-Constitutional.

In *Bhutto* the Supreme Court of Pakistan found that the petitioner ridiculed the Court in the National Assembly and only belatedly appointed judges. Indeed the President relied heavily on this behavior in his dissolution order, while the Court held the dissolution order constitutional on the basis, among others, of the *Appointment of Judges Case* (see below).

4.   In Poland, under the 1992 Amendments of the Constitution (the so-called Little Constitution), the President had the authority to dissolve Parliament if a budget was not adopted within three months of its tabling in Parliament. President Walesa argued that the three-month deadline included the period during which he was authorized to sign the budget bill. In withholding his signature beyond the three-month requirement, Walesa sought to increase his presidential dissolution powers by not exercising his own powers. His action was in conformity with the language of the constitutional text, but the dissolution power clearly was enacted to solve any impasse related to the non-enactment of a budget, which was not the case under the circumstances. The legalistic approach of the President provoked a major political crisis, in 1995. The Polish Constitutional Tribunal (11 April 1995, W.2/95) found the President's interpretation unconstitutional.

B.2.   LEGISLATIVE FUNCTIONS, DELEGATED LEGISLATION

A legislature's primary function is to legislate. Nevertheless, legislative bodies tend to share this constitutionally mandated power with the executive. Realizing the political dangers and alleged unconstitutionality of delegation, a number of constitutions expressly authorize delegation, attempting to set limits on it and allowing ultimate legislative control over executive "legislation." The 1958 French Constitution went even further, transferring the power of original legislation in certain domains to the executive. A second standard problem of legislation concerns the abuse of legislative powers by legislating ultra vires; for example, where the legislature violates its enumerated legislative powers. This problem is common in federal systems (see Chapter 4). (Here we do not discuss other important functions that are often only incompletely constitutionalized, like taxation and spending powers.) Certain attempts of parliaments to control and supervise the other branches are considered in Section C. below.

INDUSTRIAL UNION DEPARTMENT, AFL–CIO
v. AMERICAN PETROLEUM INSTITUTE

Supreme Court (United States).
448 U.S. 607 (1980).

[Under the authority of an Act of Congress, the Secretary of Labor regulated workplace air quality without regard to the significance of the risks. The Congressional authorization might have been unconstitutional, but the Court interpreted the statute as requiring the Secretary to regulate only significant risks.]

Mr. Justice Rehnquist, concurring in the judgment.

The statutory provision at the center of the present controversy, § 6(b)(5) of the Occupational Safety and Health Act of 1970, states, in relevant part, that the Secretary of Labor

" * * * in promulgating standards dealing with toxic materials or harmful physical agents * * * shall set the standard which most adequately assures, *to the extent feasible,* on the basis of the best available evidence, that no employee will suffer material impairment of health or functional capacity even if such employee has regular exposure to the hazard dealt with by such standard for the period of his working life." 84 Stat. 1594, 29 U.S.C. § 655(b)(5).

According to the Secretary, who is one of the petitioners herein, § 6(b)(5) imposes upon him an absolute duty, in regulating harmful substances like benzene for which no safe level is known, to set the standard for permissible exposure at the lowest level that "can be achieved at bearable cost with available technology." While the Secretary does not attempt to refine the concept of "bearable cost," he apparently believes that a proposed standard is economically feasible so long as its impact "will not be such as to threaten the financial welfare of the affected firms or the general economy." 43 Fed. Reg. 5939 (1978).

Respondents reply, and the lower court agreed, that § 6(b)(5) must be read in light of another provision in the same Act, § 3(8), which defines an "occupational health and safety standard" as " * * * a standard which requires conditions, or the adoption or use of one or more practices, means, methods, operations, or processes, reasonably necessary or appropriate to provide safe or healthful employment and places of employment."According to respondents, § 6(b)(5), as tempered by § 3(8), requires the Secretary to demonstrate that any particular health standard is justifiable on the basis of a rough balancing of costs and benefits.

* * * I would * * * suggest * * * that Congress, the governmental body best suited and most obligated to make the choice confronting us in this litigation, has improperly delegated that choice to the Secretary of Labor and, derivatively, to this Court.

I

In his Second Treatise of Civil Government [J. Locke, *Second Treatise of Civil Government, in the Tradition of Freedom,* ¶ 141, p. 244

(M. Mayer ed., 1957)], published in 1690, John Locke wrote that "[t]he power of the legislative, being derived from the people by a positive voluntary grant and institution, can be no other than what that positive grant conveyed, which being only to make laws, and not to make legislators, the legislative can have no power to transfer their authority of making laws and place it in other hands."[1] Two hundred years later, this Court expressly recognized the existence of and the necessity for limits on Congress' ability to delegate its authority to representatives of the Executive Branch: "That Congress cannot delegate legislative power to the president is a principle universally recognized as vital to the integrity and maintenance of the system of government ordained by the Constitution." *Field v. Clark*, 143 U.S. 649, 692 (1892).

The rule against delegation of legislative power is not, however, so cardinal of principle as to allow for no exception.

* * * During the third and fourth decades of this century, this Court within a relatively short period of time struck down several Acts of Congress on the grounds that they exceeded the authority of Congress under the Commerce Clause or under the nondelegation principle of separation of powers, and at the same time struck down state statutes because they violated "substantive" due process or interfered with interstate commerce. When many of these decisions were later overruled, the principle that Congress could not simply transfer its legislative authority to the Executive fell under a cloud. Yet in my opinion decisions such as *Panama Refining Co. v. Ryan*, 293 U.S. 388 (1935), suffer from none of the excesses of judicial policymaking that plagued some of the other decisions of that era. The many later decisions that have upheld congressional delegations of authority to the Executive Branch have done so largely on the theory that Congress may wish to exercise its authority in a particular field, but because the field is sufficiently technical, the ground to be covered sufficiently large, and the Members of Congress themselves not necessarily expert in the area in which they choose to legislate, the most that may be asked under the separation-of-powers doctrine is that Congress lay down the general policy and standards that animate the law, leaving the agency to refine those standards, "fill in the blanks," or apply the standards to particular cases. * * *

Viewing the legislation at issue here in light of these principles, I believe that it fails to pass muster. Read literally, the relevant portion of § 6(b)(5) is completely precatory, admonishing the Secretary to adopt the most protective standard if he can, but excusing him from that duty if he cannot. In the case of a hazardous substance for which a "safe" level is either unknown or impractical, the language of § 6(b)(5) gives the Secretary absolutely no indication where on the continuum of relative safety he should draw his line. * * *

* * *

---

1. * * * In the same treatise, Locke also wrote that "[t]he legislative cannot transfer the power of making laws to any other hands; for it being but a delegated power from the people, they who have it cannot pass it over to others." *Id.*

IV

As formulated and enforced by this Court, the nondelegation doctrine serves three important functions. First, and most abstractly, it ensures to the extent consistent with orderly governmental administration that important choices of social policy are made by Congress, the branch of our Government most responsive to the popular will. Second, the doctrine guarantees that, to the extent Congress finds it necessary to delegate authority, it provides the recipient of that authority with an "intelligible principle" to guide the exercise of the delegated discretion. Third, and derivative of the second, the doctrine ensures that courts charged with reviewing the exercise of delegated legislative discretion will be able to test that exercise against ascertainable standard.

I believe the legislation at issue here fails on all three counts. * * *

We ought not to shy away from our judicial duty to invalidate unconstitutional delegations of legislative authority solely out of concern that we should thereby reinvigorate discredited constitutional doctrines of the pre-New Deal era.

* * * It is the hard choices, and not the filling in of the blanks, which must be made by the elected representatives of the people. When fundamental policy decisions underlying important legislation about to be enacted are to be made, the buck stops with Congress and the President insofar as he exercises his constitutional role in the legislative process.

Notes and Questions

1. D. L. Keir and F. H. Lawson, *Cases in Constitutional Law* 35 (5th ed. 1967).

> It might then have been the task of the courts to consider whether the subordinate legislation was legally appropriate to the statute, and perhaps a body of common law doctrine might have arisen from the decisions in difficult cases. Subordinate legislation would have been seen to be—what it assuredly is—a natural function of executive government. However, this did not happen: English law insisted that the authority of non-parliamentary bodies to legislate must, apart from the very narrow scope left to the prerogative, be derived from Parliament itself. But now that governments can to all intents and purposes obtain from Parliament all the powers they need, this hardly represents a check on the enactment of subordinate legislation.

Under the influence of the American doctrine, the ISC exercised substantive review powers, which prevailed until the 1970s. In *M/s. Dwarka Prasad Laxmi Narain v. Uttar Pradesh*, (1954) 1 S.C.R. 674, 682 (Justice Mahajan), the Court said: "[I]n order to decide whether a particular legislative measure contravenes any of the provisions of Part III of the Constitution it is necessary to examine with some strictness the substance of the legislation in order to decide what the legislature has really done. Of course, the legislature cannot bypass such constitutional prohibition by employing indirect methods and therefore the Court has to look behind the form and appearance to discover the true character and nature of the legislation." Later, in *Hamdard Dawakhana (WAKF) Lal Kuan v. Union of India*, (1960) 2 S.C.R. 671, 678, 696 (Justice Kapur), the Court said:

* * * [W]hen the delegate is given the power of making rules and regulations in order to fill in the details to carry out and subserve the purposes of the legislation the manner in which the requirements of the statute are to be met and the rights therein created to be enjoyed it is an exercise of delegated legislation. But when the legislation is complete in itself and the legislature has itself made the law and the only function left to the delegate is to apply the law to an area or to determine the time and manner of carrying it into effect, it is conditional legislation. To put it in the language of another American case:

> "The legislature cannot delegate its power to make a law, but it can make a law to delegate a power to determine some fact or state of things upon which the law makes or intends to make its own action depend." (In *Lockes Appeal*, 72 Pa. St. 491; *Field v. Clark*, 143 U.S. 649.) But the discretion should not be so wide that it is impossible to discern its limits. There must instead be definite boundaries within which the powers of the administrative authority are exercisable."

Compare the Indian doctrine with the constitutional conditions of delegation in Germany. Note that the apparently defunct nondelegation doctrine is used in the U.S. to curtail administrative discretion. In *American Trucking Associations, Inc. v. United States Environmental Protection Agency* [EPA], 195 F.3d 4 (D.C.Cir.1999), the EPA claimed regulatory authority, under the Clean Air Act, to take any measure to protect public health. The court found that the EPA's reach for authority was based on an unconstitutional interpretation of the Constitution as it violated the nondelegation doctrine. An acceptable interpretation of the Act would have required the Agency to establish its own standards, which would have limited discretion. *Id.* at 7–8.

KALKAR I CASE

Federal Constitutional Court (Germany).
49 BVerfGE 89 (1978).

[Section 7 (1) of the Atomic Energy Act provides that any person who constructs or operates an installation for the production or fission of nuclear fuel requires a license. Authorities may grant such a license under sec. 7 (2) only if "he takes every necessary precaution in the light of existing scientific knowledge and technology to prevent damage resulting from the construction and operation of the installation." On December 18, 1972, licensing authorities granted a first, partial-construction permit for the SNR–300 fast-breeder nuclear-power station, in Kalkar.

[The owner of a farm within a mile of the station sued to have the license revoked. * * * In view of the awesome implications for public safety and the rights of citizens involved in the production and recycling of plutonium, however, the North Rhine–Westphalia Administrative Court felt that Parliament had a duty to establish more concrete criteria for the construction of fast-breeder reactors than those provided in the Atomic Energy Act. The Court of Appeals referred this question to the Constitutional Court.]

Judgment of the Second Senate:

* * * B. II. Section 7, paragraphs 1 and 2, of the Atomic Energy Act are compatible with the Basic Law.

* * * 1. b) The case at bar deals with legislation, an area where the Basic Law specifically allocates authority to the *Bundestag*. It follows from the principle of legality that executive acts which significantly affect the freedom and equality of citizens must be based on law.

2. Section 7, paragraphs one and two, of the Atomic Energy Act do not violate this principle. * * *

(a) Separation of powers is not specifically mentioned in the Basic Law. Its validity, however, follows from the terms of Article 20 (3). The interpretation of this principle has undergone change in recent years, especially in the light of its democratic component. Today our established case law makes clear that the legislature is obligated * * * to make all crucial decisions in fundamental normative areas, especially in those cases where basic rights become subject to governmental regulation. * * * To determine those areas in which governmental acts require a basis in law, [one must] consider the subject matter and "intensity" of the planned or enacted regulation, particularly taking into account the fundamental rights granted by the Basic Law.

[One] must also use similar criteria to judge whether the legislature has established the essential legal standards for the matter to be regulated as the constitutional requirement of a specific enactment mandates and not left this for the administration to determine. [The principle of constitutional requirement of a specific enactment (*Gesetzesvorbehalt*) means that only the legislature may enact statutory restraints upon fundamental rights contained in the Basic Law where the language of the Basic Law expressly provides for such restraints.]

(b) The normative decision whether to permit the peaceful uses of nuclear energy in the Federal Republic of Germany is a fundamental and essential decision in the sense that a specific enactment is constitutionally required. * * *

Contrary to the opinion of the court below, the legislature was not bound to include in the Act a provision declaring that it was ready to accept the risks possibly resulting from such a reactor. The legislature bears the political responsibility for the consequences of its decision. * * *

[The provisions of the Act regulate all essential and fundamental questions of the licensing procedure and fix with sufficient precision the requirements for the construction, operation, and modification of nuclear installations, including fast-breeder reactors.] * * *

(c) * * * [We] cannot now foresee whether the court below is correct in assuming that the industrial use of the fast breeder may lead to dangerous constraints and consequences. * * * Only the future will show whether this decision to implement breeder technology will be useful or harmful. In this necessarily uncertain situation the legislature and the government primarily have the political responsibility for making what they consider pragmatic decisions within the confines of their respective authority. Under these circumstances, it is not the function of the courts to substitute their judgment for that of the political branches when assessing the situation since legal criteria for such decisions do not exist.[f]

3. Section 7 (1) and 7 (2) of the Atomic Energy Act do not violate the constitutional requirement that laws be drafted with sufficient precision. * * *

b) * * * The provisions of the statute in question make use of undefined legal terms such as "reliability" and "necessary knowledge" [*unbestimmte Rechtsbegriffe*—terms that are] not precisely defined. The use of these terms is constitutionally permissible. The degree of precision required depends on the nature of the matter to be regulated and the intensity of the regulation. * * * [In any case such terminology] has been traditionally subject to interpretation by the legislature, executive and judiciary. * * *

When fixing norms, which keep abreast of scientific and technological developments, the legislature has a number of options available for making these developments legally binding. These norms have one common feature: by using undefined legal terms [the legislature] shifts the difficulties involved in giving these terms specific, binding content and adjusting them to scientific and technological developments to the administrative and—should litigation arise—to the judicial level. Thus,

---

f. Compare with the dissenting opinion of Justice Marshall in *Industrial Union Department, AFL–CIO v. American Petroleum Institute*, 448 U.S. 607, 688, 690–91, 693, 706 (1980):

Unlike the plurality, I do not purport to know whether the actions taken by Congress and its delegates to ensure occupational safety represent sound or unsound regulatory policy. The critical problem in cases like the ones at bar is scientific uncertainty. While science has determined that exposure to benzene at levels above 1 ppm creates a definite risk of health impairment, the magnitude of the risk cannot be quantified at the present time. The risk at issue has hardly been shown to be insignificant; indeed, future research may reveal that the risk is in fact considerable. But the existing evidence may frequently be inadequate to enable the Secretary to make the threshold finding of "significance" that the Court requires today. If so, the consequence of the plurality's approach would be to subject American workers to a continuing risk of cancer and other fatal diseases, and to render the Federal Government powerless to take protective action on their behalf. Such an approach would place the burden of medical uncertainty squarely on the shoulders of the American worker, the intended beneficiary of the Occupational Safety and Health Act. It is fortunate indeed that at least a majority of the Justices reject the view

that the Secretary is prevented from taking regulatory action when the magnitude of a health risk cannot be quantified on the basis of current techniques. * * *

[T]he requirement that the Secretary act on the basis of "the best *available* evidence" was intended to ensure that the standard-setting process would not be destroyed by the uncertainty of scientific views. Recognizing that existing knowledge may be inadequate, Congress did not require the Secretary to wait until definitive information could be obtained. Thus "it is not intended that the Secretary be paralyzed by debate surrounding diverse medical opinions." * * *

The decision to take action in conditions of uncertainty bears little resemblance to the sort of empirically verifiable factual conclusions to which the substantial evidence test is normally applied. Such decisions were not intended to be unreviewable; they too must be scrutinized to ensure that the Secretary has acted reasonably and within the boundaries set by Congress. But a reviewing court must be mindful of the limited nature of its role. See *Vermont Yankee Nuclear Power Corp. v. NRDC*, 435 U.S. 519 (1978). It must recognize that the ultimate decision cannot be based solely on determinations of fact, and that those factual conclusions that have been reached are ones which the courts are ill-equipped to resolve on their own.

administrative authorities and courts have to make up the "regulatory deficit" incurred by the legislature. * * *

Section 7 (2), no. 3, of the Atomic Energy Act goes a step further by referring to "existing scientific knowledge," which requires the legislature to make even stronger efforts to keep regulations abreast of scientific and technological developments.

It is within the legislature's discretion to use either undefined legal terms or precise terminology. Good reasons support the use of undefined legal terms in sec. 7 (2), no. 3. The wording of sec. 7 (2), no. 3, of the Atomic Energy Act, which is open to future developments, serves as a dynamic protection of fundamental rights. It furthers the protective purpose of sec. 1, no. 2, of the Atomic Energy Act in the best possible way currently available. To fix a safety standard by establishing rigid rules, if that is even possible, would impede rather than promote technical development and adequate safeguards for fundamental rights. * * * By referring to existing scientific knowledge and technology the law forces the executive [agency] to observe the principle of the best possible protection against dangers and risks. The legislature was not bound, however, to define with precision the possible kinds and factors of risk ... The assessment of risks resulting from a nuclear installation depends upon a multitude of circumstances many of which are constantly evolving. * * * In the interest of flexible protection of life and property the executive must assess and constantly adjust safety measures—a task which it is better equipped to perform than the legislature. The unavoidable degree of uncertainty in assessing such risks resides in the nature of human knowledge.

Notes and Questions

1. The Basic Law attempts to restrain delegation and excludes the possibility of original executive legislation. This detailed provision is a reaction to the Weimar Republic's abuses of legislation by executive order. (The technical basis of Hitler's rule was that an enabling law authorized the Chancellor to enact decrees with the force of statutes.) Today, the executive must demonstrate that its acts are based on statutes. The issue centers on how close the relationship should be. And not only separation-of-powers concerns are applicable; the Basic Law requires also that the democratic component of legislation be observed. In particular, as fundamental rights can be restrained by statute only, the legislature cannot delegate this responsibility. The principle applies to the realization of rights by the state. "The principle of the rule of law and the precept of democracy place upon the legislature the duty of formulating essentially by itself those regulations that are decisive for realization of basic rights—and of not leaving this to activity and decision-making authority of the executive." *Mützenbacher Case,* 83 BVerfGE 130 (1990). The level of precision in the legislative determination depends on the extent to which it affects fundamental rights. One might say that this goal was achieved in *Kalkar I* by downplaying the rights restriction (the risk to the right to life). But even in areas not affecting rights,

> to the extent that [a statute] delegates the authority to issue regulations to the executive, the legislative intent must provide * * * a guide for the content of the regulation. The statute must give expression to the

legislative intent. It must be clear whether or not the executive confined itself to the express limits [of the delegating statute] in issuing the regulation. If the content [of the regulation] goes beyond the legislative intent, then the issuer of the regulation overstepped the boundaries of its delegated power. The regulation is then invalid because it has insufficient legal basis. It is not within the Federal Constitutional Court's authority to decide this case, which falls within the procedur[al] [provisions] of Article 100 (I). But it is within this court's authority to decide if the statutory delegation is compatible with the aforementioned principles.

Judicial Qualification Case, 34 BVerfGE 52 (1972).

2. The use of scientific expertise and research may challenge the relations of the branches of power. In light of a 1999 decision of the ICC, the branch of power that controls the use of scientific evidence may gain additional powers. This may result in the usurpation of the power of another state organ as a result of the "intrinsic nature of the claims" of the first state organ. The ICC (in the second *Di Bella Treatment Case*, 121/1999) found that a local court was not entitled, on its initiative, to ask for scientific evidence regarding the assessment of a controversial multidrug cancer treatment (see Chapter 10). The local court's request was seen as an abuse of the powers of the executive branch. The court ordered the Ministry of Health to provide it with a list of the patients taking the drug (other than those who had participated in the controlled clinical experiment). The court's attempt to evaluate the drug trial, which was required by the legislative decree that created the whole trial, was seen as an act outside the judiciary's competence and an incursion into the competence of medical bodies. (The action of the local magistrate had to do with allegations that financial abuses had occurred in the heavy promotion of an ineffective drug.) Note that in the U.S. cases above, it is in the context of scientific uncertainty that executive regulation is challenged on nondelegation grounds. Will legislatures, as we know them, be capable of deliberating when they must decide complex matters generated by scientific research where risks remain unknown?

ECONOMIC AUTHORIZATION CASE

[ON THE LAW AUTHORIZING GOVERNMENT TO TAKE
DIVERSE MEASURES CONCERNING THE ECONOMIC AND SOCIAL ORDER]
Constitutional Council (France).
86–207 DC of 25, 26 June 1986.

[The constitutionally permissible level of delegated legislation continues to generate tensions in relations between the executive and legislative branches. The traditional doctrine of Locke (above) and Rousseau advocates that primary legislation is exclusively within the powers of the legislature and cannot be delegated. The French Constitution of 1791 states: "There is no authority in France higher than the *loi* [an enactment of the National Assembly]." "The executive power cannot make *lois*, even provisionally, but only proclamations consistent with *lois* for the purpose of ordering or encouraging their execution." In reaction to legislative paralysis and dissatisfaction with executive legislation, widespread in the Third French Republic (1875–1946), Art. 13 of the

French Constitution of 1946 expressly prohibited the delegation of legislation to the executive. Within a few years, the practice of delegation was recognized by the Council of State. "One of the principal criticisms made by the authors of the Constitution [of 1958] was that Parliament had, in the recent past, been too keen to intervene, making the task of governing difficult, if not impossible. The Fifth Republic set out to remedy this. Both De Gaulle and Debré considered that a clearer division of labour between Government and Parliament was necessary. This is carried out by a separation of both functions and of personnel." John Bell, *French Constitutional Law* 16 (1992). The Fifth Republic not only recognized delegation (granting reserved legislative powers to the government, which can enact in this case an *ordonnance* and may repeal or amend acts of Parliament), it also restricted the legislative competence of Parliament to specifically named areas, granting original legislation to the executive in all other matters.[g] (In addition, the executive has the power to regulate, in order to complement legislative rules,[h] and determine details where legislation is enabled to determine fundamental principles.) Delegation is authorized by a special enabling act of Parliament, upon the government's request. Although there are no specific substantive criteria in regard to enabling legislation in the text of the Constitution, these enabling acts were subject to constitutional review, among others, when, in circumstances of cohabitation, the President was reluctant to sign laws and the government tried to bypass him through *ordonnances*.

[In 1986, by "letting the public sector breathe" (*la respiration du secteur public*), the Right put forward a five-year program to privatize a total of 65 companies, those nationalized by the Socialists in 1982 as well as those by earlier administrations as far back as the Liberation of 1944.]

[The Reference by Deputies to the French Constitutional Council (J.O. 27 June 1986: 7984–5) is as follows]:

Mr. President, Messrs, Counsellors: In accordance with paragraph 2 of article 61 of the Constitution, we have pleasure in referring to the Conseil constitutionnel the text of the *loi* enabling the Government to take miscellaneous economic and social measures, in the form that has been finally adopted by Parliament. * * *

Concerning article 1 of the loi[i]

Since, in the first place, it concerns competition law, the delegation of power granted obviously exceeds the limits permitted by article 38. In

g. Jean Rivero argued that the new distribution of legislative powers saw no fundamental change in the way the country was governed. *Le Domaine de la loi et du réglement* 261 (2d ed. 1981).

h. "Even if the Constitution * * * reserves to the legislature the fixing of the rules [on voting] * * * it leaves to the regulatory power, by virtue of article 37, the task of laying down measures for their application." 76–94 DC of 2 Dec. 1976., Rec. 67.

i. To assure businesses greater freedom of operation and to define a new competition law, the government is authorized, within six months of the publication of the present *loi* and under the terms provided for in Art. 38 of the Constitution, to amend or repeal certain provisions of economic legislation concerning prices and competition, especially those of *ordonnances* no. 45–1483 of 30 June 1945 on prices and no. 45–1484 of 30 June 1945 on the determination, prosecution, and punishment of economic offences. The new competition law provides safeguards for economic actors in the exercise of the powers given to public authorities and ensures rights to a hearing in their procedures.

its decision no. 76–72 DC of 12 January 1977, the Conseil Constitution-nel emphasized the obligation imposed on the Government to indicate with precision to Parliament, when the enabling bill is presented, the objective of the measures that it proposes to take. Naturally, this is not a simple act of courtesy with regard to Parliament, no more is it an exclusively political obligation, but rather it is a condition on which the constitutionality of the enabling bill depends. Moreover, it is this re-quirement of precision on the objectives that makes all the difference between an enabling law and a law granting full power [to do whatever the Government wants]. The Constitution of the Fifth Republic only permits the first, and excludes the second.

Now, this condition is obviously not satisfied in this case. Moreover, implicitly, but inevitably, the text of the *loi* recognizes this, not without a degree of *candour*. In fact, the use of the verb 'define' suffices to demonstrate that it is impossible for Parliament to know and assess the objectives of the measures that the Government proposes to take in the area of competition law.

In vain is the second paragraph of article 1 [of the *loi*] cited. This cannot be seriously considered as providing the indispensable details (and, in any case, such details are the opposite of the notion of a definition in the future). At most, it provides superfluous verbiage in a measure in which the prescription that it lays down are necessary in any case, because they follow from constitutional requirements, and their inclusion in the *loi* does not add anything to their binding force, just as their omission would not detract from that force.

* * *

Since, in second place, it concerns "the freedom of operation of businesses," article 1 pursues the objective of the repeal of *ordonnance* no. 45–1483 of 30 June 1945 relating to prices. It is not simply a matter of a mere possibility, but rather of a clearly stated intention * * *

* * *

In truth, the repeal of the ordonnance of 1945 relating to prices would leave the State completely defenseless in a serious economic crisis. * * *

* * *

DECISION

On the substance of the loi

13. Considering that, since it is specified in article 38 § 1, cited above, that it is for the implementation of its programme that the Government is given the possibility of asking Parliament for authority to take measures that are normally within the province of *loi* by *ordon-nance* for a limited period, this text should be understood as requiring the Government to indicate with precision to Parliament the objective of the measures that it proposes to take, and the areas in which they will intervene;

14.   Considering that the provisions of an enabling law cannot have as either a purpose or a consequence to dispense the Government from respecting rules and principles of constitutional value[j] when it is exercising the powers conferred on it in application of article 38 of the Constitution;

15.   Considering that it is up to the Conseil Constitutionnel on the one hand to verify that the enabling law does not contain any provision that permits a breach of those rules and principles, and, on the other hand, not to accept an enabling law as being consistent with the Constitution except on the express condition that it is interpreted and applied with strict respect for the constitution;

16.   Considering that the authors of both references raise complaints of unconstitutionality against each of the articles 1 to 7 of the *loi*;

* * *

Concerning the argument that the terms of the authorization are insufficiently precise

21.   Considering that, even if the Government has to define precisely the objectives of the authorization that it requests in order to achieve its programme, it is not bound to make known the content of the *ordonnances* that it will make by virtue of authorization, and it is not impermissible for it to make their content depend upon the results of work and studies of which it will only know the details later;

22.   Considering that, if article 1 of the *loi* designates as the objective of the *ordonnances* that it authorizes the Government to make the definition of a new competition law and the search for greater freedom of operation for businesses, it does not authorize the Government thereby to amend or repeal the totality of the rules of civil, commercial, criminal, administrative, and social law affecting economic life; that it follows from its terms, clarified by the *travaux préparatoires* and especially, by the statements of the Government to Parliament, that the authority thus sought involves the amendment or repeal of specific provisions of economic legislation relating to the control of combinations, to competition, and to prices, as well as to the punishment of economic offences contained in the *ordonnances* of 30 June 1945, in *loi* no. 77–806 of 19 July 1977, and in special legislative provisions on prices; that, within these limits, the authority granted by article 1 is not contrary to the terms of article 38 of the Constitution;

23.   Considering that the clarification provided by paragraph 2 of article 1 on the safeguards for economic actors and on the observance of rights to a hearing in procedures should not be understood as excluding other safeguards resulting from the principles and rules of constitutional value, and, in particular, the right to judicial review and rights of due process; that, furthermore, they should not be understood as excluding

j.   "Principles of constitutional value" is a concept used by the Constitutional Council. The term refers to certain values found in the text of the Preamble of the 1946 Constitution and the 1789 Declaration. These "principles" (like dignity) may justify limits to fundamental constitutional rights and liberties.

the safeguards for human or legal persons not having the status of economic actors;

* * *

Concerning the possible repeal of the ordonnances *of 30 June 1945 relating to prices*

25. Considering that no principle or rule of constitutional value requires the legislature to enact texts of permanent force conferring special powers on the Government in case of possible eventualities; that, moreover, article 1 of the *loi*, even if it authorizes the amendment or repeal of the *ordonnances* of 30 June 1945 relating to prices, does not permit the amendment or repeal of the rules or principles currently in force giving power to the Government or to agents of a public authority in the case of crisis, exceptional circumstances, or national disaster;

Concerning the whole of article 1

26. Considering that, within the limits of, and conditional upon, the interpretation that has just been given, article 1 is not contrary to the Constitution * * *

Notes and Questions

1. According to the French Constitution, the restriction of constitutional rights and freedoms resides in the domain of the *loi*. Note that the restriction of fundamental rights by parliamentary enactments is an idea originating in Art. 4 of the Declaration of the Rights of Man and of the Citizen of 1789: " * * * the only limits on the exercise of the natural rights of each man shall be those that ensure the enjoyment of the same rights by other members of society. Such limits may only be established by law [*loi*]." The concept is accepted in many constitutions, including the German Basic Law (*Gesetzesvorbehalt*), various posttotalitarian constitutions, following the German example (e.g., Spain, Hungary, and, arguably, Russia),[k] and the European Convention for the Protection of Human Rights and Fundamental Freedoms (hereafter, European HR Convention). In principle the democratic and open process of legislation is itself a safeguard of rights. In addition, in cases of *loi* there is always the possibility of additional protection by the Constitutional Council.

The relevance is illustrated by a debate regarding the regulation of punishments. Article 8 of the 1789 French Declaration asserts that no one can be punished except according to *loi*. The 1958 Constitution classifies the determination of *crimes et délits* as pertaining to the domain of *loi*. A third

k. The Spanish Constitutional Tribunal gave the following definition in its *Pharmacy Case* (83/1984) (see Chapter 10): "The principle of the reservation of laws is an essential guarantee of our State of law. * * * Its importance is * * * that it safeguards that the regulation of citizens' liberties be exclusively dependent on the will of citizens' representatives * * * The principle does not exclude the possibility that the laws contain delegations to regulatory norms but such delegations make impossi-ble an independent regulation and one that is not subordinated to law." In Russia, the Constitution allows the restriction of fundamental rights only by federal law. The Russian scholarly position, however, is that the word *law* means "all enactments." See *Konstitutsiia Rossiiskoi Federatsii Entsiklopedicheskii Slovar* 68 (The Constitution of the Russian Federation. An Encyclopedic Dictionary) (Vladimir A. Toumanov et al. eds., 1997).

form of sanction in French law is known as contravention. Police fines are a typical contravention. However, the police may administer custodial (*detentive*) penalties, which in 1958 were extended to two months by executive legislation (*réglement*). At a later time, revisions in executive (administrative) orders resulted in changes to the content of criminal law. For example, changes in price controls and in the Law on Buildings affected the criminal law, which sanctioned the violation of the administrative prescription. In 1969, the Constitutional Council amended its original position and found that such administrative provisions sanctioned by criminal law should be determined by *loi* because they determine a *délit*. 69–55 DC of 26 June 1969 (Protection of Scenic Sites—change in the period of notice by owners of natural beauty (scenic) sites to prefects, before the commencement of major alterations to sites, where the breach of notice constitutes a *délit*). In 1973, the Council found that even a brief imprisonment applied as a sanction for a contravention should be determined by *loi*. However, the ordinary courts and the Conseil d'État reinterpreted the ruling, stating that the requirement did not affect the jurisdiction of the executive to determine the content of a contravention. The main pragmatic reason for such a position was that this would have left an inordinate number of punishments, originating from violations of traffic rules, public-health codes, etc., subject to challenge. The Council has retreated in more recent decisions, allowing the practice of custodial imprisonment for fines to continue. Note there was no direct confrontation among the various courts.

2.   Tension among the branches in matters of legislation might be particularly tenuous in the formative years of a new constitutional regime, until certain constitutional practices and conventions consolidate. After the Constitution of 1993 came into force in Russia, politically motivated conflicts swirled endlessly between the Parliament and President. The Constitution, in Art. 90(3), states that presidential decrees and orders cannot contravene the Constitution and federal laws. In the *Chechnya Case* (see Section E. below), however, the RCC found legislative powers in the President's role as the "protector of the Constitution." Consider the denial of legislative power to the executive in *Youngstown Sheet & Tube Co. v. Sawyer*, 343 U.S. 579 (1952), in Subsection C.2. below. On the other hand the concept of royal privilege in England and the French doctrine, which probably dates back to the prerogative, allow for executive legislation where Parliament does not legislate. Such is the case in France even in matters that are reserved for exclusive parliamentary legislation. The RCC, however, did not allow the transfer of tax legislation to the executive in a case where certain fees were to be determined under delegated powers relating to the amount of a fee concerning frontier matters. Delegating the determination of the fee (which was qualified as a tax) was held to violate the separation of powers. (*National Frontier of the Russian Federation Case*, Decision of November 11, 1997 No. 16–P, *On Determining the Constitutionality of Art. 11 of the Law of the Russian Federation of April 1, 1993, "On the National Frontier of the Russian Federation"* in the Redaction of July 17, 1997.) The French Constitutional Council, too, became increasingly concerned about delegation where the matter is otherwise within the domain of legislation. In 1986, the Council found unconstitutional an amendment of the tax code that left the implementing decree to determine the amendment's entry into force without specifying the conditions for determining its entry into force. (The amendment concerned the abolition of certain certificates that were required from

fruit transporters for tax-inspection purposes. 86–223 DC of 29 Dec. 1986.) Such concerns over delegation, discussed in terms of legislative powers, might find scrutiny in other jurisdictions in terms of the rule of law, where the solutions are found wanting for lack of legal certainty.

3. *Constitutional duty to legislate (constitutional omission).* Separation of powers requires that legislation should remain within the domain of the legislative branch. What happens if the legislature fails to legislate, especially when a constitution requires the enactment of specific legislation? This problem is further complicated where there is no specific language regarding a duty to legislate or where a court finds that a constitutional provision is not self-executing. (See *Santiago v. Commission on Elections* below.) Is the legislative branch required to legislate where the constitution is found to lack self-execution? Or is it the constitutional intent in such cases to leave the matter to the discretion of the legislature?

Some courts in Europe and on the Indian subcontinent condemn their legislatures for failing to act. This is somewhat problematic under certain constitutional theories, given the legislative supremacy of Parliament. Condemnations of Parliament for omission pose practical problems, too, as there is no way to force it to act. Declarations of omission provide no practical solutions.[1] Parliaments are often hampered not by a lack of will but by paralysis caused by insufficient majorities. The European Court of Justice (ECJ), in particular, faces such problems as hundreds of Union directives remain unimplemented by the member-states. The ECJ holds the member-states liable for damages to private parties who are affected by the member-states' failures to implement EU directives. An amendment to the governing EU Treaty allows the Court to impose fines on member-states in breach. Nevertheless, unconstitutional legislative omissions—especially continued nonaction—may undermine the Court.

Matters of equality have spawned a specific form of constitutional omission. The ICC has often found that an omitted reference to one gender is solved simply by reading the other gender into the text of the law. Otherwise, laws that fail to include certain groups would be held unconstitutional. "Reading in" might be a proactive solution that satisfies the demand of constitutional interpretation. But there is a precondition; namely, that there is some kind of law on the matter that requires regulation according to the constitution.

Legislative omission in the equality context is illustrated by *Eldridge v. Attorney General of British Columbia*, [1997] 3 S.C.R. 624 (Justice La Forest). The Supreme Court of Canada found that the legislature of British Columbia failed to satisfy the Canadian Charter's antidiscrimination obligations in its neglect of funding sign-language interpreters for the deaf when they receive medical treatment. (The Charter requires that laws be provided without discrimination based on physical disability.) (See *Egan* in Chapter 6.) In some jurisdictions, government provision of services creates additional legislative or executive obligations. In India, when 15 poor harijans[m] ("un-

---

l. The finding of legislative omission may result in a denial of remedy. In 31/96, Cour d'Arbitrage (1996) BCCL 1996, 183 (above), the Court of Arbitration found that the unconstitutional situation was the consequence of a loophole in the law and ruled that it could not provide remedy because such remedy could be provided by relevant legislation.

m. The harijans are afforded special protection in the Indian Constitution and not only in the directive principles. It was argued in the case that they were shut off

touchables") protested the discontinuation of a state-constructed road to the High Court, it ordered the construction to continue, with the state government bearing the expense. The ISC found there was state inaction because there was a positive constitutional obligation to satisfy a constitutional right; namely, to provide residents in hilly areas the means to communicate. This right was part of the right to life (as livelihood), which is to be protected to the extent feasible. As state funds were partially allocated and the road partly built, the obligation existed. Where there are no preestablished priorities or where specific expertise is involved, the Court cannot make an affirmative directive. The Court's position regarding affirmative duties may have been prompted by the especially vulnerable position of the petitioners. *Himachal Pradesh v. Umed Ram Sharma*, (1986) 1 S.C.R. 251. To resist the temptation of reading into the law what was left out on grounds of equality, the French Constitutional Council had to specify that the principle of equality does not require legislation to correct all the disparities in a given domain, if it attempts to correct some of them (99–419 DC).

Spending decisions (tax exemptions, subsidies, etc.) are rarely challenged on grounds of legislative omission: granting selective tax benefits to groups or constituencies is generally held constitutional. See for the U.S., e.g., *Regan v. Taxation With Representation*, 461 U.S. 540 (1983) (Justice Rehnquist).

Given concepts of parliamentary sovereignty, among others, it is unlikely that the legislative body will be called to account for unconstitutional acts and omissions, except through the political process. Courts have no means to compel legislation to carry out its constitutional mandate. (Directive principles and state goals are expressly written to deny judicial enforcement.) Indirect remedies were developed in the EU in case a member-state fails to implement Union legislation, including damages that are to be paid to those whose rights were affected by the lack of applicable law. In Japan, an attempt was made to apply the State Compensation Law to the Diet and its members (being public officials) in a case of legislative inaction.[n] In *Japan v. Sato*, Sapporo High Court (1978), the issue was whether proven inactivity of the Diet was unconstitutional. The immunity for decisions of members bars

from the rest of the world as there was no possibility of communication whatsoever. It was further alleged that the authorities and landowners colluded to stop the road construction at the adjacent village.

n. See Lawrence Beer and Hiroshi Itoh, *The Constitutional Case Law of Japan, 1970 through 1990*, at 69 (1996). *Japan v. Sato* (1978) (quoting from the editorial note):

On August 16, 1952, the Diet partially amended the Public Offices Election Law to eliminate various abuses which had been observed in previous elections. The amendment abolished a system of absentee voting which had allowed handicapped people to vote in their own homes. The law came into force on September 1, 1952; from that date until the law was amended on January 20, 1975, to allow severely handicapped people to vote by

mail, handicapped people in Japan were required to vote in person at a polling place or not to vote at all. In 1967 a petition was presented to the Diet demanding an amendment of the law to restore the voting rights of handicapped people. The Diet failed to act on this petition prior to December 10, 1972. The high court found that over one million handicapped people had lost their ability to vote because of the change in 1952.

* * *

* * * [T]he court also considered whether the failure to reinstitute the absentee system between 1952 and 1975 was unconstitutional legislative inaction, and whether an action for damages under the State Compensation Law could be brought against Diet members for such inactivity.

responsibility, but the nation or a public body may be held responsible for the members' inaction for compensation purposes.

The guarantees of equality of exercise of rights, including voting rights, must be realized by legislation, [although] * * * there may be rational and justifiable reasons in the interests of fairness and the freedom of elections which may modify that right.

From the above, it may be said that a law which sets up methods for voting must protect and guarantee the mechanisms of voting for all electors. It follows that in a voting system law, the Diet has a legislative duty, fully grounded in the Constitution, to establish and protect a voting machinery for a group of people with the right to vote whose right there is no good reason to limit, and to amend the laws on the methods of voting if necessary to protect their right.

* * *

* * * [T]he Diet has discretion on whether or not to enact certain legislation and to determine the timing and the kind of legislation it will adopt. * * *

* * * In light of the fact that the Constitution is the nation's supreme law (Article 98), the legislation of the Diet and the right of members of the Diet to introduce bills and to debate cannot be considered matters entrusted to an absolute, unconditional, free discretion. * * *

* * *

If an occasion arises in which the Diet has not enacted legislation required by the Constitution after a not inconsiderable time, it goes without saying that both Houses of the Diet must have mad a decision. However, it is not absolutely necessary that the decision take the form of voting against a bill * * *.

Lawrence W. Beer and Hiroshi Itoh, *The Constitutional Case Law of Japan, 1970 through 1990*, at 76–78 (1996).

Notwithstanding the finding of illegal inaction, Sato could not establish the negligent infliction of injury in the case. Note that beyond the equality argument, here there is a related duty of the state to promote a right; the right to vote, of course, is a fundamental right that is enabled through electoral laws in all democracies. Consider the following modified application of Hohfeld's distinction between a right and a liberty. Wesley Newcomb Hohfeld, *Fundamental Legal Conceptions as Applied in Judicial Reasoning* (Walter Wheeler Cook ed., 1919). A liberty allows someone to do what one pleases. If a person acts under a legal right, he or she will have submitted to scrutiny the *use* of the right. One is at liberty to hire or not hire a new employee. But when one determines to use the right to dismiss the employee, that right is subject to conditions and review. In some respects the state's constitutional goals and policies are its liberties; however, once the state engages in an action to realize a goal, the action is subject to constitutional scrutiny. Ironically, liberty triggers lesser scrutiny.

B.3.   REFERENDUM: THE LEGISLATIVE AND CONSTITUENT POWERS OF THE PEOPLE

An important democratic tradition in liberal democracies emphasizes that the people are the source of state power, and they are the only source of sovereign rule that should determine legislation, directly and indirectly. Such is the position of the French Constitution, although it limits referenda to institutional matters. Referenda are also resorted to for practical reasons; for instance, in the event of shortcomings of legislation enacted by representative bodies. The U.S. and Germany oppose the institution at the federal level, probably for fear that constitutional structures will suffer. Elsewhere (Switzerland and Italy), there is more reliance on this most robust form of popular democracy: in this context the constitutional law problems concern the admissibility of particular questions. Certain experiences with, and concerns about, the abuse of direct democracy have discredited the referendum as a constitutional means of the people's exercise of power in some democracies. This is the case in Germany, where the referendum is not recognized as a form of federal legislation—except in matters of territorial reorganization. But a considerable number of scholars believe that even a constitutional amendment allowing federal legislative referenda would be unconstitutional, contradicting basic, unamendable provisions of parliamentary democracy. The German attitude is understandable in view of Hitler's abuse of referenda. In matters of exclusive federal jurisdiction, the GFCC found unconstitutional the use of *Land* referenda intended to express public opinion only.[o]

In Eastern Europe, most postcommunist countries disregarded the German position. The foremost criticism of communist rule was that it prohibited the people from expressing their genuine will. Owing to this strong democratic concern, legislation by popular initiative and referendum were made constitutional, and constitutional amendments via referenda are permitted if authorized by the constitution. On the other hand the political conflicts that have arisen because of referenda in postcommunist East Europe indicate how destabilizing prolonged and improperly prepared referenda can be. Without judicial control, minorities and their fundamental rights might be imperiled by referenda. In the U.S., this is made clear, among others, in *Romer v. Evans*, 517 U.S. 620 (1996) (see Chapter 6). Notwithstanding the abuse of referenda by demagogues, given the insufficiencies and stalemates in legislation and the prevalence of parochial interests in legislation, one should not disregard the referendum alternative. This is made clear in the following case.

o. *Atomic Weapons Referenda Case I*, 8 BVerfGE 104 (1958) (Social Democrats, the minority in the Bundestag, seek to organize referenda at the *Land* level against the placement of nuclear weapons on German soil). "The clear goal of these two referenda—to force the competent constitutional organs of the federation to change a decision of about a matter of defense that these organs consider right—represent an attempted infringement upon the exclusive jurisdiction of the federation."

SANTIAGO v. COMMISSION ON ELECTIONS

Supreme Court (the Philippines).
270 S.C.R.A. 106 (1997).

[The collapse of the Marcos dictatorship, in the Philippines, was the result of significant popular discontent. While the Constitutional Commission worked on amendments to the Constitution, the reliance on people's power continued. The public relied extensively on referenda in cases where the elected political powers betrayed their mandate and the people. However, the post-Marcos legislature and judiciary sought to curtail a popular initiative that attempted to address legislative (and institutional) corruption. When President Ramos's term as president neared expiration, his supporters set out to amend the Constitution, in an attempt to secure him a second term in office. (The President was precluded by a term-limit provision from running a second time.) Ramos's supporters collected more than six million signatures, satisfying the conditions of the initiative.[p]]

Davide, Jr., J.

The heart of this controversy * * * is the right of the people to directly propose amendments to the Constitution through the system of initiative under Section 2 of Article XVII of the 1987 Constitution. * * * The 1986 Constitutional Commission itself, through the original proponent and the main sponsor of the proposed Article on Amendments or Revision of the Constitution, characterized this system as "innovative."

* * * On 6 December 1996, private respondent Atty. Jesus S. Delfin filed with public respondent Commission on Elections (hereafter, COMELEC) a "Petition to Amend the Constitution, to Lift Term Limits of Elective Officials, by People's Initiative" (hereafter, Delfin Petition) wherein Delfin asked the COMELEC for an order:

1. Fixing the time and dates for signature gathering all over the country. * * *

Delfin alleged in his petition that he is a founding member of the Movement for People's Initiative, a group of citizens desirous to avail of the system intended to institutionalize people power; that he and the members of the Movement and other volunteers intend to exercise the power to directly propose amendments to the Constitution granted under Section 2, Article XVII of the Constitution. * * *

[T]he petitioners herein—Senator Miriam Defensor Santiago, [raised] the following arguments:

1. The constitutional provision on people's initiative to amend the Constitution can only be implemented by law to be passed by Congress. No such law has been passed. * * *

p. Article XVII Sec. 2 of the 1987 Constitution reads: "Amendments to this Constitution may likewise be directly proposed by the people through initiative upon a petition of at least twelve per centum of the total number of registered voters, of which every legislative district must be represented by at least three per centum of the registered votes therein. No amendment under this section shall be authorized within five years following the ratification of this Constitution nor oftener than once every five years thereafter."

5. The people's initiative is limited to amendments to the Constitution, not to revision thereof. Extending or lifting of term limits constitutes a revision and is, therefore, outside the power of the people's initiative. * * *

II.

Section 2 of Article XVII of the Constitution provides:

Sec. 2. Amendments to this Constitution may likewise be directly proposed by the people through initiative upon a petition of at least twelve per centum of the total number of registered voters, of which every legislative district must be represented by at least three per centum of the registered voters therein. No amendment under this section shall be authorized within five years following the ratification of this Constitution nor oftener than once every five years thereafter.

The Congress shall provide for the implementation of the exercise of this right.

This provision is not self-executory. * * *

Bluntly stated, the right of the people to directly propose amendments to the Constitution through the system of initiative would remain entombed in the cold niche of the Constitution until Congress provides for its implementation. Stated otherwise, while the Constitution has recognised or granted that right, the people cannot exercise it if Congress, for whatever reason, does not provide for its implementation. * * *

We agree that R.A. No. 6735 [the Act regulating popular initiative] was, as its history reveals, intended to cover initiative to propose amendments to the Constitution. * * *

But is R.A. No. 6735 a full compliance with the power and duty of Congress to "provide for the implementation of the exercise of the right?"

A careful scrutiny of the Act yields a negative answer.

First * * * Section 2 of the Act does not suggest an initiative on amendments to the Constitution. The said section reads:

"Section 2. The power of the people under a system of initiative and referendum to directly propose, enact, approve or reject, in whole or in part, the Constitution, laws, ordinances, or resolutions passed by any legislative body upon compliance with the requirements of this Act is hereby affirmed, recognized and guaranteed."

The inclusion of the word "Constitution" therein was a delayed afterthought. The word is neither germane nor relevant to said section, which exclusively relates to initiative and referendum on national laws and local laws, ordinances, and resolutions. That section is silent as to amendments on the Constitution. As pointed out earlier, initiative on the Constitution is confined only to proposals to amend. The people are not accorded the power to "directly propose, enact, approve, or reject, in whole or in part, the Constitution" through the system of initiative. They can only do so with respect to "laws, ordinances, or resolutions."
* * *

Second. It is true that Section 3 (Definition of Terms) of the Act defines initiative on amendments to the Constitution and mentions it as one of the three systems of initiative, and that Section 5 (Requirements) restates the constitutional requirements as to the percentage of the registered voters who must submit the proposal. But unlike in the case of the other systems of initiative, the Act does not provide for the contents of a petition for initiative on the Constitution. * * *

Third. * * * If Congress intended R.A. No. 6735 to fully provide for the implementation of the initiative on amendments to the Constitution, it could have provided for a subtitle therefor, considering that in the order of things, the primacy of interest, or hierarchy of values, the right of the people to directly propose amendments to the Constitution is far more important that the initiative on national and local laws.

* * * Curiously, too, while R.A. No. 6735 exerted utmost diligence and care in providing for the details in the implementation of initiative and referendum on national and local legislation thereby giving them special attention, it failed, rather intentionally, to do so on the system of initiative on amendments to the Constitution. * * *

* * * There was, therefore, an obvious downgrading of the more important or the paramount system of initiative. R.A. No. 6735 thus delivered a humiliating blow to the system of initiative on amendments to the Constitution by merely paying it a reluctant lip service.

The foregoing brings us to the conclusion that R.A. No. 6735 is incomplete, inadequate, or wanting in essential terms and conditions insofar as initiative on amendments to the Constitution is concerned.

* * * We feel, however, the system of initiative to propose amendments to the Constitution should no longer be kept in the cold; it should be given flesh and blood, energy and strength. Congress should not tarry any longer in complying with the constitutional mandate to provide for the implementation of the right of the people under that system.

Wherefore, judgement is hereby rendered * * *

b) Declaring R.A. No. 6735 inadequate to cover the system of initiative on amendments to the Constitution, and to have failed to provide sufficient standard for subordinate legislation. * * *

Concurring and Dissenting Opinion

Puno, J.

* * * First, I submit that R.A. No. 6735 sufficiently implements the right of the people to initiate amendments to the Constitution through initiative. Our effort to discover the meaning of R.A. No. 6735 should start with the search of the intent of our lawmakers. * * * [I]ntent is the essence of the law, the spirit which gives life to its enactment.

Significantly, the majority decision concedes that " * * * R.A. No. 6735 was intended to cover initiative to propose amendments to the Constitution." It ought to be so for this intent is crystal clear from the history of the law which was a consolidation of House Bill No. 21505 and Senate Bill No. 17. * * *

Since it is crystalline that the intent of R.A. No. 6735 is to implement the people's initiative to amend the Constitution, it is our bounden duty to interpret the law as it was intended by the legislature. We have ruled that once intent is ascertained, it must be enforced even if it may not be consistent with the strict letter of the law and this ruling is as old as the mountain. We have also held that where a law is susceptible of more than one interpretation, that interpretation which will most tend to effectuate the manifest intent of the legislature will be adopted.

The text of R.A. No. 6735 should therefore be reasonably construed to effectuate its intent to implement the people's initiative to amend the Constitution.

* * * COMELEC Resolution No. 2300 * * * spelled out the procedure on how to exercise the people's initiative to amend the Constitution. This is in accord with the delegated power granted by Section 20 of R.A. No. 6735 to the COMELEC which expressly states: "The Commission is hereby empowered to promulgate such rules and regulations as may be necessary to carry out the purposes of this Act." By no means can this delegation of power be assailed as infirmed. In the benchmark case of *Pelaez v. Auditor General*, [15 S.C.R.A. 569 (1965)] this Court, through former Chief Justice Roberto Concepcion laid down the test to determinate whether there is undue delegation of legislative power, *viz*:

> Although Congress may delegate to another branch of the Government the power to fill details in the execution, enforcement or administration of law, it is essential, to forestall a violation of the principle of separation of powers, that said law: a) be complete in itself—it must set forth therein the policy to be executed, carried out or implemented by the delegate—and b) to fix a standard—the limits of which are sufficiently determine or determinable—to which the delegate must conform in the performance of his functions. Indeed, without a statutory declaration of policy, which is the essence of every law, and, without the aforementioned standard, there would be no means to determine, with reasonable certainty, whether the delegate has acted within or beyond the scope of his authority. Hence, he could thereby arrogate upon himself the power, not only to make the law, but, also—and this is worse—to unmake it by adopting measures inconsistent with the end sought to be attained by the Act of Congress.* * *

OPINION ON THE CONSTITUTIONAL REFERENDUM IN UKRAINE

European Commission for Democracy through Law (Venice Commission).
42nd Plenary Session, Venice, 31 March 2000
Cdl (2000) 4 Rev.

[After having obtained more than three million signatures requesting a referendum to amend the Constitution, the President of Ukraine, upon announcing an All–Ukraine referendum on the People's Initiative, adopted a decree. A couple of weeks before the planned referendum, upon a petition by the Communist Party, the Constitutional Court of Ukraine ruled most questions admissible. The no-confidence initiative, directed against the Verkhovna Rada (Parliament), was found unconstitutional because Ukraine's Constitution does not stipulate that such a vote—whose result could suspend the activities of a state body—can be held via a referendum. Likewise, the question regarding the adoption of a new constitution by popular plebiscite was found unconstitutional. A few days later, an independent expert commission of the Council of Europe evaluated the presidential decree.

[Amendments to most parts of the Constitution require a qualified majority of the Verkhovna Rada, while certain parts, like the General Principles and the Referendum chapters, require, in addition, an approval in referendum.]

8.   Law No. 1286–XII on All–Ukraine and Local Referendums of 3 July 1991 was adopted before Ukraine became an independent state. * * * The law was never brought into conformity with the Constitution of Ukraine adopted on 28 June 1996. Its applicability is therefore governed by the transitional provisions of the Ukrainian Constitution:

Chapter XV

Transitional Provisions

Laws and other normative acts, adopted prior to this Constitution entering into force, are in force in the part that does not contradict the Constitution of Ukraine.

9.   On 11 January 2000 the Parliament of Ukraine adopted a law (Law No. 1356–XIV) introducing a ban on all referendums due to the fact that there "was a difficult socio-economic situation in the country and no sufficient legislative basis for organising a referendum." The President refused to sign this law and returned it to the Parliament on 26 January 2000. In his reply to the Parliament the Head of State said that referendum is a sovereign right of the people of Ukraine that cannot be restricted.

III.   The developments in Ukraine leading to the referendum

11.   The proposed referendum can only be understood in the context of the current political conflicts in Ukraine. The Parliament (the Verkhovna Rada) has been perceived by many as not being able or willing to adopt the legislation necessary to implement reforms in the country. It has recently split into two parts, a majority broadly favourable to the President and the government and a minority headed by the previously elected speaker. Both parts of the parliament have even held separate sessions and the question whether the election of a new speaker by the new majority is valid or not is contested between both sides.

IV.   The legal nature of the referendum

12.   In general, two main types of referendums can be distinguished: consultative or binding. The binding referendum can relate to the Constitution or to legislation. With respect to the referendum on popular initiative, the Ukrainian Constitution unfortunately is silent as to its legal nature. * * *

13.   The present referendum relates to the Constitution and not to legislation. It is less clear whether it is binding or not. * * *

14. The text of the presidential decree is not absolutely clear in this respect. * * * With respect to the various questions, it is clear that question 5 on the introduction of a bicameral parliament cannot be directly binding since no detail is given as to the composition and powers of such a second chamber. By contrast, other questions contain the precise text of an amendment to the constitution.

18. Chapter XIII on introducing amendments to the Constitution of Ukraine contains detailed provisions on the procedures required for amending the Constitution. These procedures clearly reflect the conviction of the authors of the Constitution that the Ukrainian Constitution should be a rigid constitution which cannot be amended very easily but only on the basis of procedures implying sufficient guarantees. Article 156 mentions the possibility of constitutional referendums, but only with respect to certain chapters of the Constitution and only to confirm a decision already taken by the Verkhovna Rada by a two-thirds majority in favour of a constitutional change.

20. Under the Constitution of Ukraine, it is therefore not possible to give the present referendum a legally binding character. The referendum does not have, and may not have, the character of a binding constitutional referendum.

21. A consultative referendum is not legally irrelevant. By giving the people the possibility to express their opinion, pressure is put on the elected bodies to abide by the will of the people. * * *

22. * * * A consultative referendum makes sense if the State organ, be it the President, the government or the Parliament, asks the population to give its opinion on a specific issue. Here the referendum was not initiated by a State organ but by the population itself. It would appear highly unusual and would probably be without precedent elsewhere if the result of an initiative by the people would only be that the people have to be consulted and cannot decide directly.

VI. Constitutionality of the proposals submitted to referendum and their compatibility with international standards

29. * * * [After amending the Constitution], the issue remains whether such proposals are compatible with international standards, in particular whether a sufficient balance of powers would remain if the proposals were adopted.

[Referendum] Question 1

["Are you in favor of expressing no confidence in the XIVth sitting of the Verkhovna Rada of Ukraine and of introducing a corresponding amendment to Article 90 of the Constitution of Ukraine with the following content: in the case of a vote of no confidence in the Verkhovna Rada expressed at all-Ukraine referendum the President of Ukraine is empowered to dissolve the Verkhovna Rada of Ukraine?"]

30. The first question contains in reality two questions. Citizens are asked to pronounce themselves at the same time

—on the question whether the present Verkhovna Rada enjoys their confidence;

—on a proposal to amend the Constitution introducing the possibility for the President of Ukraine to dissolve the Verkhovna Rada in the case of such a vote of no confidence.

31.   To combine two questions in this way is in contradiction with a principle of referendum law known for example in Switzerland or Italy as the unity of subject matter. It may well be that a citizen of Ukraine wishes to have in general the right to express his lack of confidence in parliament without at the same time doing so with respect to the Verkhovna Rada presently in office. The present wording of the question deprives him of this possibility to give different replies to the two questions.

32.   The first part of the question is clearly unconstitutional. The Constitution of Ukraine contains no legal basis for a vote of no confidence by the people in the Verkhovna Rada. * * * The possibility of a vote of no confidence by the people in Parliament is alien to the Western concept of representative democracy and can in no way be presumed in the absence of an express constitutional authorisation. * * *

35.   As regards the second part of the question * * * [t]he possibility to hold such referendums would be a permanent source of instability. To provide it with respect to one of the State organs, the Verkhovna Rada elected by the people, would seriously undermine the balance of powers between Parliament and President by giving the President the possibility to appeal to the people in the case of conflict between him and Parliament without giving a similar possibility to Parliament. * * *

[Referendum] Question 5

["Do you agree that it is necessary to create a two-chamber parliament, where one of the chambers would represent interests of the Ukrainian regions, and to introduce the corresponding changes to the Constitution of Ukraine and legislation on elections?"]

43.   This question cannot be directly binding. It would require amendments to the Constitution which are however not spelt out. Even as a consultative question it thus appears highly problematic since the elements provided in the question do not enable the voters to make an informed judgment on the advisability of the proposed reform. Nothing is said with respect to the powers of the suggested second chamber and information on its composition is limited to the statement that it would represent interests of the Ukrainian regions.

Notes and Questions

1.   In its opinion on the Ukrainian referendum the Council of Europe's Venice Commission found that granting the power to the people to have a completely new constitution by referendum would disregard important constitutional safeguards. What is wrong with such powers? Should there be inherent constitutional limits to people's constituent power through referenda? "[O]n April 16, Ukrainians (who typically do not hold their politicians in high esteem) turned out in high numbers to approve the four questions put before them. [The proposals received overwhelming support from the people.] The looming question is, what happens now that the people have

spoken?" *Ukraine Update*, E. Eur. Const. Rev., vol. 9, nos. 1–2, at 43 (2000). The Rada never implemented the changes.

In Moldova, the use of a referendum to change the form of government in favor of the President brought a constitutional crisis. The President initiated a consultative referendum on May 23, 1999, notwithstanding the opposition of Parliament, which claimed that the referendum was scheduled at a time when there could be no referendum, since the Electoral Code stipulates that no nationwide referendum can be organized 120 days before or after elections. However, presidential advisers countered that the Code read that if a referendum occurred at the same time as an election, all the electoral councils that were established for the election automatically acted as councils for the referendum; thus providing the procedure for holding a referendum alongside a local ballot. The Central Electoral Commission found that the referendum could be held. Later, it found that the results were valid, although the statutorily required minimum level of voter participation had not been achieved. The voters overwhelmingly endorsed the positions of the President. The Constitutional Court of Moldova, in line with the French Constitutional Council's decision of 1962, found that it had no jurisdiction as the presidential decree requesting the referendum had achieved its objective. The Constitutional Court declared at the same time that the consultative referendum had no binding force. A few months later, the Parliament declared the referendum unconstitutional, an action that the Court found unconstitutional. Further, during the same year, the Court was obligated to certify both presidential and parliamentary draft amendments to the Constitution. On July 5, a compromise constitutional amendment was adopted that followed the suggestions of the Council of Europe's Venice Commission. The resulting scheme required that the President be elected by Parliament. But Parliament was unable to elect a new president; this enabled the president then in office to dissolve Parliament (dissolution was a new power created by the amendment), which he had always intended to do. The new elections ushered in a communist majority.

2.   Referenda allow for interactions between the legislative branch and the people, as well as between the political parties inside and outside Parliament. The political relevance of the referendum in Switzerland, where its various forms are an ordinary part of political decisionmaking, is due partly to the fact that the ability to call for a referendum (even if only to delay the legislative process) increases the power of minority parties. The majority becomes more ready to seek compromise, knowing that opposition parties may mobilize their constituencies to call a referendum by popular initiative. The Latvian Constitution of 1922 (as reinstated in 1993, two years after independence was regained) followed the Swiss and Weimar constitutions. If one-third of the members of the Saeima (Parliament) so request or if the President refuses to sign a bill into law for more than two months and one-tenth of the electorate request, a national referendum on the bill is held. In 1999, the opposition forced a referendum on the Law on State Pensions. The majority in Parliament "softened" the law before it was submitted to referendum, and in consequence less than half of the electorate participated in the vote, which had the effect of upholding the softer law. (The Latvian law follows the Swiss referendum solutions of the nineteenth century, originating in the French system of the postrevolutionary Directorate.)

3.   *Constitutional Referenda in Hungary.* At the time of the collapse of communism, the prevailing doctrine of the emerging democracies empha-

sized people's power exercised through referenda. Referenda had been used successfully against the communists in Hungary, including rejection of the direct election of the President. The idea of referendum gains appeal when a democracy is created by popular antidictatorial movements, as in the Philippines. Once the parliamentary system established itself in Eastern Europe and then quickly lost its credibility, the political system was challenged by referenda initiatives. Sometimes parliamentary oppositions used it; sometimes it served the goals of extraparliamentary forces. In Belarus, a referendum approved an amendment to the Constitution that enabled President Lukashenko to win overwhelming powers over Parliament. Contrary to the Ukrainian Court, the HCC sought to restrict and streamline referenda. Among other things, it found that a popular initiative for a referendum to dissolve the Parliament (resulting in new elections) was unconstitutional as the Constitution did not contemplate the possibility of dissolution via referendum (Decision 2/1993 (I.22.) AB hat.).

4. Referenda initiatives give rise to important constitutional issues. (1) Attempts at secession and devolution (or to stop such initiatives) raise questions about territorial integrity and sovereignty. (2) Direct challenges to the powers of Parliament, especially in terms of its existence, bring up issues of constitutionalism as a limit against popular self-determination. (3) A popular initiative may attempt to change fundamental rights provisions. Some constitutions expressly prohibit referenda regarding fundamental rights or the enlargement of the scope of rights.

5. "It is of great importance in a republic not only to guard the society against the oppression of its rulers, but to guard one part of the society against the injustice of the other part." *The Federalist* No. 51[, at 313] (James Madison) (Clinton Rossiter ed., 1961). This is perhaps the underlying fear that motivates restrictions on, and prohibitions of, referenda in some constitutions, especially at the federal level. But even in countries where this is the case, there might be widespread use of referenda at the member-states level. In the U.S., the Supreme Court upheld the constitutionality of the institution of the referendum at the state level. If a referendum is the direct expression of the will of the people, in places where referenda are inadmissible is the legislature an adequate body to express such will? Is one or the other institution more reliable to protect the fundamental rights of people?

6. Notwithstanding the lack of constitutional rules in the federal constitution, the Supreme Court of Canada held the following in *Reference Re Secession of Quebec*, [1998] 2 S.C.R. 217, 265 (see Chapter 2):

> Although the Constitution does not itself address the use of a referendum procedure, and the results of a referendum have no direct role or legal effect in our constitutional scheme, a referendum undoubtedly may provide a democratic method of ascertaining the views of the electorate on important political questions on a particular occasion. The democratic principle identified above would demand that considerable weight be given to a clear expression by the people of Quebec of their will to secede from Canada, even though a referendum, in itself and without more, has no direct legal effect, and could not in itself bring about unilateral secession. Our political institutions are premised on the democratic principle, and so an expression of the democratic will of the people of a

province carries weight, in that it would confer legitimacy on the efforts of the government of Quebec to initiate the Constitution's amendment process in order to secede by constitutional means. In this context, we refer to a "clear" majority as a qualitative evaluation. The referendum result, if it is to be taken as an expression of the democratic will, must be free of ambiguity both in terms of the question asked and in terms of the support it achieves.

Consider the Ukrainian referendum questions in light of the Canadian requirements. In an effort to satisfy the conditions set by the Supreme Court of Canada, the Parliament enacted the Clarity Act, 2000. The Act provides that in the event of a secession initiative, the House of Commons "shall consider whether the question would result in a clear expression of the will of the population of a province." Likewise, it is up to the Commons to determine whether a referendum result has been a clear expression of the will of the population. The Act does not preordain the quorum or majority required for validity. Is this solution satisfactory in view of popular sovereignty and the rule of law?

C.   EXECUTIVE POWER

First we discuss constitutionally adjudicated cases concerning the formation of the executive power, primarily in parliamentary systems.[q] Here the nomination of the Prime Minister and relations between the Cabinet and the President (or the ruler) are particularly dramatic. A much more common question for judicial review concerns the competence of the executive, that is: When does it improperly assume the powers of the legislative branch? These cases are equally relevant in terms of the limits of the power of the legislative branch. The third subsection is dedicated to judicial accountability of the executive, including doctrines that make the executive immune to parliamentary or judicial questioning.

C.1.   THE MAKING OF THE EXECUTIVE

The following cases deal with prime ministerial appointments as well as appointments to public positions (not necessarily of an executive nature) that require some co-decision with the executive.

COMPETENCE DISPUTE BETWEEN THE PRESI-DENT OF THE REPUBLIC AND MEMBERS OF THE NATIONAL ASSEMBLY [OF SOUTH KOREA]

Constitutional Court (South Korea).
29 KCCG 583, 98 HunRa 1, July 14, 1998.[r]

Facts

[Summary by the Court]

[Dae–Jung Kim was popularly elected to become the President of South Korea. At the time of the election, the majority in the National

---

q. The USSC adjudicated a similarly dramatic contest in a presidential election matter. See *Bush v. Gore*, 531 U.S. 98 (2000), in Chapter 6.

r. Available at <www.ccourt.go.kr/english/case60.html>.

Assembly represented parties that supported Kim's rival.] President Kim sought the consent of the National Assembly on the appointment of Jong–Pil Kim as the Prime Minister on his inauguration day, pursuant to Article 86 (1) of the Constitution. The Speaker of the National Assembly convened the 189th extraordinary session to vote on the President's appointment. During the session, a disagreement on the voting procedure arose between the majority party and the minority (then-ruling) parties, and the National Assembly session ended without making a decision on the appointment. Nevertheless the President appointed Jong–Pil Kim as the Acting Prime Minister without the National Assembly's consent. Thereupon, the petitioners, one hundred fifty (150) Assemblymen who belonged to the majority party, submitted this competence dispute with this Court contending that the President infringed upon the National Assembly's consent powers.

Issues

The issues were (A) whether the petitioners had standing to submit a competence dispute on behalf of the National Assembly; (B) whether the President's appointment of the Prime Minister without the National Assembly's consent infringes upon the National Assembly's and the petitioners' right to consent; and (C) consequently, whether the appointment was valid.

Decision

In five separate opinions, five Justices agreed to dismiss the case.

Rationale

Opinion of President Yong–Joon Kim:

When the National Assembly is unable to file a competence dispute based on the administration's ultra vires acts because the majority decides not to, the minority of the National Assembly has standing to bring the suit because the Constitutional Court must protect the rights of the minority. However, in this case, because the petitioners constituted the majority of the Assembly, they could have voted for the filing of a suit in the name of the National Assembly or could have redressed the alleged ultra vires act through a legislative vote.[s] Therefore, the individual petitioners do not have standing.

Opinion of Justices Seung–Hyung Cho and Joong–Suk Koh:

If the President had appointed the Prime Minister without seeking the National Assembly's consent or if the appointment had been made despite the National Assembly's opposition, this Court would have decided the case differently. However, in this case, the President submitted the request, but the National Assembly was unable to decide on the appointment. To avoid having a vacancy and the possibility of subsequent disorder, the President appointed Jong–Pil Kim as the Acting

---

s. Article 62 (1) 1 of the South Korean Constitutional Court Act states only that the Court adjudicates competence disputes between the National Assembly and the executive.

Prime Minister in the interim in a provisional effort, pursuant to Article 23 of the Government Organization Act. Therefore, the President's course of action did not infringe upon the petitioners' right to consent to the appointment of the Prime Minister. In addition, the petitioners, constituting the majority of the Assembly, could resolve the dispute on their own through a legislative vote. Because they failed to exhaust all the available remedial avenues, this Court could not adjudicate the matter.

Opinion of Justices Kyung–Sik Chung, Chang–On Shin:

A state agency which is not enumerated in Article 62 (1) of the Constitutional Court Act cannot be a party in a competence dispute. Furthermore, an intra-agency dispute within an enumerated agency cannot be the subject of a competence dispute. Therefore, only the National Assembly can be a party in this competence dispute, and neither Assemblymen nor any political parties have standing to bring the suit.

Dissenting opinion of Justices Moon–Hee Kim, Jae–Hwa Lee, and Dae–Hyun Han:

The National Assembly's right to consent to the appointment of the Prime Minister cannot be viewed separately from the National Assembly members' voting rights.

Therefore, the petitioners should have standing to file a competence dispute.

Whether the petitioners would be able to veto the President's designation was not a material issue in this case. Article 86 (1) of the Constitution leaves no room for an interpretation other than that the National Assembly's prior consent must be acquired before the appointment of the Prime Minister. If the appointment is made without the National Assembly's consent, it clearly violated the Constitution, regardless of whether the title "Acting Prime Minister" is used.

Dissenting opinion of Justice Young–Mo Lee:

The founders of the Constitution did not foresee a case where the National Assembly would be unable to decide on the appointment of a Prime Minister. In consideration of the absence of relevant law and the urgency of the situation (the resignation of the incumbent Prime Minister and the resultant inability of the new President to appoint the new executive cabinet), the President's temporary appointment of a Prime Minister is constitutional.

RUSSIAN PRIME MINISTERIAL
APPOINTMENT CASE

[DECISION CONCERNING THE INTERPRETATION OF PROVISIONS
OF ARTICLE 111, PARA 4, OF THE RF CONSTITUTION]
Constitutional Court (Russia).
Decision 28–P of 11 Dec. 1998.

[In 1998, Russian President Boris Yeltsin sacked the then-Prime Minister and proposed a new candidate to the Duma. Yeltsin's supporters in the Duma were in the minority, and the candidate was rejected. Yeltsin twice repeated the nomination, threatening the Duma that members' privileges, provided by the executive, would be cut back and that he would act pursuant to Art. 111, para. 4, of the RF Constitution: "After the President's nomination for the post of the Prime Minister of the RF Government is rejected three times by the State Duma, the President appoints the Prime Minister, dissolves the State Duma, and calls for the new election." The repeated nomination was seen as a test of the extent of presidential powers.]

The State Duma has requested interpretation of this constitutional provision; namely, it has asked to clarify whether the President may nominate the same candidate again after rejection by the State Duma, and what legal consequences are following the third rejection by the State Duma of the same nominee.

* * * 2. The wording of Article 111 of the RF Constitution does not exclude either of the two possibilities.

* * * The legal logic of Article 111 consists of preventing the situation, when separate branches of power—legislative, executive, and judicial—struggle against one another. This would run counter to the very principle that all state power takes inspiration from the multinational people of the RF as the bearer of sovereignty.

It follows from this fundamental constitutional principle—the basis of state power in a democratic rule-of-law state—that the consent of the State Duma is required to the President's nomination for the post of the Prime Minister.

Also, determining the conditions and procedures for appointment of the Prime Minister, the RF Constitution provides for the means to overcome possible disagreements between the branches, so to prevent unreasonable delays with forming the Government and consequent blocking of activities of the RF Government, which is one of the institutional elements of the RF constitutional system (Article 111, para. 3).

* * * 3. In accordance with the RF Constitution (Article 80, part 1), the RF President is the Head of the State. Hence his competencies to form the RF Government, to determine its program, and to exercise control over its activities, as well as constitutional responsibility of the RF President for the activities of the Government. Hence the key role of the President in determining individuals to serve on the cabinet.

In conjunction with other constitutional provisions, pertaining to the status of the Head of the State, it follows from Article 111, para. 4, of the RF Constitution that the choice of the candidate for the post of the Prime Minister, presented for approval to the State Duma, is a prerogative of the RF President. The RF Constitution, without limiting this prerogative, permits the President to determine a concrete method of realization of this prerogative: to nominate the same candidate twice or thrice, or to nominate a new candidate each time.

In turn, the State Duma partakes in appointment of the Prime–Minister by confirming or rejecting the nominee. The constitution does not stipulate any presidential restrictions on powers of the actors in this process.

4. The Preamble to the RF Constitution declares the objective of civil peace and accord, which requires coordination and cooperation of activities of the power bodies. Such coordination and cooperation is ensured by the RF President (Article 80, para. 2). Anything else does not conform to the principal purpose of state power, and would threaten stability of the RF constitutional system as a democratic rule-of-law state.

It also follows from Article 111 that there is a need to coordinate the activities of the President and the State Duma in realization of their powers in the appointment of the Prime Minister. Hence the procedure suggests that consensus must be sought between them in order to eliminate arising disagreement as to the candidacy for the post of the Prime Minister. Consensus is possible on the basis of provided in the RF Constitution forms of cooperation, or on the basis of procedures that emerge in process of realization of the powers of the Head of the State and in parliamentary practice.

* * * 5. From Article 111, part 4, of the RF Constitution it follows that, regardless which method of nomination was used, after the third rejection by the State Duma of the President's nominee for the post of the Prime Minister a mandatory consequence is appointment of the Prime Minister by the President, dissolution of the State Duma, and the new election. This constitutional means of overcoming disagreements between the President and the State Duma, using the mechanism of free elections, conforms to the fundamentals of the constitutional system of the Russian Federation as a democratic, rule-of-law state. * * *

Decided: * * * After the President's nomination for the post of the Prime Minister is rejected by the State Duma three time—regardless of whether there were different nominees each time, or whether one and the same candidate was nominated twice or thrice—the State Duma is subject to dissolution. * * *

Separate Opinion of Justice Vitruk

* * * The RF President, as the Head of the State and guarantor of the RF Constitution, ensures in accordance with the Constitution cooperation and coordinated functioning of all branches (Article 80, part 2).

The State Duma's consent to the President's nomination for the post of the Prime Minister serves as a check and balance. However, the State Duma cannot be a means of coercion, hence the number of rejections by the State Duma is limited.

The President, nominating the candidate for the post of the Prime Minister, must seek and obtain the consent of the State Duma in finding an appropriate candidate. The means of finding consensus may be different. This is why the RF Constitution provides for specific time limits for both the President and the State Duma to ensure their prompt cooperation (Article 111, parts 2 and 3).

Based on literal meaning of Article 111, in conjunction with other constitutional provisions, a general rule follows that the RF President must each time, after rejection by the State Duma, nominate a new candidate for the post of the Prime Minister.

If the State Duma withholds its consent, it is essential to continue the dialogue between the President and the State Duma as regards new nomination. The procedures for seeking consensus on the nominee for the post of the Prime Minister may eventually result in a constitutional custom (convention) that would have force of a constitutional norm.

Specific procedures of consulting the President as to an appropriate candidate for the post of the Prime Minister may be fixed in a federal law, or in the *Reglament* [Standing Rules] of the State Duma.

When the RF President nominates one and the same candidate twice and especially thrice then, as rightly pointed out by the representative of the State Duma in judicial proceedings, the State Duma is deprived of its right of independent choice, guaranteed in Articles 10 and 111 of the RF Constitution, and is reduced to a means of transmission of the will of the Head of the State.

Nominating the same candidate for the second time (at the same time barring the same nomination for the third time) in world practice is regarded as an exception to the general rule, and is fixed in the national Constitutions (Basic Laws). The same approach is observed in practice of constitutional regulation of the appointment to the post of the Prime Minister in the Subjects of the Russian Federation.

* * * 1. Neither the RF Constitution, nor any special law offer clarification concerning nomination of the same candidate for the post of the Prime Minister. Hence the State Duma has laid down the procedure for nominating the candidate for the post of the Prime Minister by the RF President, and for rendering consent by the State Duma. This procedure provides for nomination a new candidate after rejection of the earlier nominee.

We cannot agree with the opinion that the *Reglament* of the State Duma is non-binding upon the RF President. The *Reglament* is a legal act of the State Duma. * * *

PRESIDENTIAL APPOINTMENTS CASE

Constitutional Court (Hungary).
Decision 36/1992 (VI.10.) AB hat.

[After the collapse of communism, the first freely elected Hungarian Parliament, in conformity with the Constitution, elected the President. The Hungarian system is a nonfederal version of the German Chancellor-led parliamentary system. Nevertheless, serious conflicts emerged between the President and the Prime Minister, first regarding the powers of the President as commander in chief of the Army (resulting, in 1991, in the "First Decision" of the Constitutional Court)[t] and, later,

---

t. A similar conflict occurred in Bulgaria: the President is popularly elected, and yet the powers of the office are described in the Bulgarian Constitution in terms similar to those in the Hungarian one. In 1992, the Bulgarian Cabinet asked the Court in a referral to determine whether or not the President is the commander in chief in peacetime. The new Cabinet withdrew the referral.

over appointment-related issues. The conflict in this case was part of the so-called media war. In 1991–92, Hungary had but one national television station (a public one). The government concluded that the station was not particularly sympathetic toward, or supportive of, the government. The President was asked to agree with a proposal of the Prime Minister and dismiss the chairman of National Television. The action would have resulted in the de facto chairmanship of the vice-chairman of National Television, who was acceptable to the government but criticized by the opposition for being a government partisan. The Law on the Appointment of the Chairman of National Television required a two-thirds parliamentary majority, that is, a consensus between the majority and minority. Such agreement was out of the question. The President refused the Prime Minister's proposal to dismiss the chairman, and in the meantime, the Prime Minister asked for an abstract interpretation (advisory opinion) of the Constitution regarding the appointment (in this instance, dismissal) powers of the President.]

I.

* * *

The President expressed his views in writing concerning the questions raised in the petition. The essence of his position may be stated summarily as follows:

1. The system of governance functions democratically if the democratic rule of law and the maintenance and functioning of the related constitutional order embodies as a fundamental requirement the respect and protection of the rights of liberty. A violation of a right of liberty may constitute as grave a reason for determining the disruption of the democratic functioning of the system of governance as the activities of its institutions coming to a standstill.

2. The President, the "guardian" of the democratic functioning of the system of governance according to Art. 29(1) of the Constitution, integrates into the functioning of the system of governance as a check, counterweight or "resolver of a deadlock". The discharge of the President's duties within his authority of guarding constitutionalism is effected at different times, through different means and in different areas than the constitutional or right protective activities of the other branches of the government. The existence of the president's constitutional protective guardian role is legitimated precisely by the fact that even lawful activities may be contrary to one of the constitutionally enumerated democratic basic values. For this reason the scope of the President's duties includes the weighing of whether the functioning system of governance is in conflict with constitutional principles, as well as to give effect to those principles by his political decisions.

* * * II.

The President of the Republic stands outside the executive power and has an independent scope of authority as head of state. No construction may be derived from the Constitution according to which the Government and the President of the Republic jointly head the executive branch, making consensus-based decisions in a mutually limiting and counterbalancing manner with only the administrative decision-making falling exclusively within the Government's scope of authority.

* * * According to Art. 29(1) of the Constitution, the President manifests the unity of the nation and safeguards the democratic functioning of the system of governance. * * *

III.

First Question

"The grave disruption of the democratic functioning of the system of governance" criterion originates from two sources. One is Art. 29 of the Constitution, according to which the President manifests the unity of the nation and is the guardian of the democratic functioning of the system of governance. The second source is an analysis of independent political decisions contained in the Constitution of which the common feature is that they are called upon when a grave disruption to the system of governance arises.

* * * 2. The characteristics of an independent political decision may be deduced from the cases expressly regulated by the Constitution.

* * * In both cases the Constitution expressly defines the requirements which must be fulfilled for the President to have the opportunity to make independent political decisions.

(a) These are objectively dangerous situations concerning the democratic functioning of the system of governance whose existence or classification is not dependent on the President's assessment. He may only weigh the necessity of his own intervention. He must restore the Parliament's ability to function with the following step: he must arrange for a new Parliament to be formed or in an extraordinary situation must ensure the continued operation of the dissolved Parliament by its reconvocation. Thus, the issue is not that the Parliament has failed substantively to satisfy some constitutional requirement but a preliminary question—namely its own functioning—is at stake.

(b) If also follows from the position authorizing the independent political decision that no branch may appropriately take over the President's political accountability.

3. According to the first Constitutional Court Decision, the refusal to appoint for a substantive reason is an independent political decision, a dispositive and unreviewable decision for which no one bears political responsibility.

* * * [T]he right of refusal to appoint has been inferred by the Constitutional Court's interpretation that the power of appointment may not be precluded from the "guardian function" derived from Art. 29 of the Constitution.

* * * The Constitutional Court specifies the criterion of the grave disruption to the democratic functioning of the system of governance as a situation in which compliance with the recommendation of a person gives rise to a grave incapacitation of the basic functions of an implicated organ of such a nature with respect to which the Constitution confers on

the President of the Republic the power to make a political decision independent of the Parliament. Thus, what is at issue is not that the functioning of an organ (or its results) would fail to satisfy a certain political requirement but that the organ could not fulfil its basic function. * * *

Fourth Question

The refusal to comply with the request for an appointment (dismissal) must contain the reasons for the refusal.

* * * [A] duty of cooperation exists with respect to a refusal based on substantive grounds. If the President refuses to appoint on substantive grounds, the decision must contain an enumeration of those facts from which the President inferred on a well-grounded basis that complying with the request would have led to a grave disruption of the democratic functioning of the system of governance. The organ submitting the nomination needs that information for its own functioning: it must know for a future nomination what kind of mistakes it committed in the past, and the President's reasoning may be required for the determination of the accountability of the nominating party.

Finally, such information is also required for the determination of the President's potential accountability. * * *

Notes and Questions

1. Korea has a mixed parliamentary system, while the Russian Constitution follows, to some extent, the French system, although the Russian Prime Minister must obtain the support of the Duma. In the event that the President's choice of Prime Minister fails to win Duma support in three rounds of voting, the President can appoint his Prime Minister and dissolve the Duma. The Prime Minister continues in office regardless of whatever new majority takes shape in the Duma. A vote of no-confidence does not result in the resignation of the government.

Both the Korean and Russian presidents have sought to appoint prime ministers who did not command majority support in their respective parliaments. The Korean National Assembly failed to reject the candidate, probably because of changes in popular sentiment after the presidential election. The Russian Duma systematically voted against the candidate. In both cases the judicial response upheld each President's action. Might the Korean Court have been influenced by the recent expression of popular will? Parliament–President relations in the Russian and Korean cases described above are what the French call "cohabitation." In France, cohabitation is governed by a convention that requires the President to respect the parliamentary majority. In other words, beginning in the 1970s, France moved toward a convention of parliamentarism. When Mitterand, a socialist, was elected President of France in 1981, he immediately appointed a new prime minister and dissolved the National Assembly, which was controlled by conservatives. However, if an election turns in a majority that is opposed to the President, the President will try to work with the governmental choice of the new majority. Professor Linz (see Section A. above) finds that dual popular legitimation (both the President and Parliament are popularly elected) is a source of instability in the presidential system.

2. The President of Hungary refused to sign the dismissal of the chairman of National Television initiated by the Prime Minister. Additional legal harassment by the executive followed, and the chairman resigned. See Andrew Arato, *The Hungarian Constitutional Court in the Media War: Interpretations of Separation of Powers and Models of Democracy*, in *Rights of Access to the Media* (András Sajó and Monroe Price eds., 1996). As in Hungary, the 1992 Polish Law on Radio and Television was silent regarding the dismissal of the chairman of the Committee for the Supervision over Radio and Television (CSRT).[u] Polish President Walesa's decision to dismiss the CSRT chairman, who was his appointee, was challenged by the ombudsman. The Constitutional Tribunal ruled that the President could not dismiss the chairman, except for a judicially established gross violation of the law. The decision of the Tribunal was based on its doctrine of "the state governed by law" (rule of law), which dictates that a state body's powers must be expressly conferred by law. Decision of 10 May 1994 W. 7/94. President Walesa sought to skirt the ruling, claiming that it could not apply retroactively, i.e., for matters decided before the Tribunal developed its legal position. In 1995, the Tribunal ruled that its interpretations of law were applicable from the date of their enactment.

3. The HCC majority view in the *Presidential Appointments Case* was based on the assumption that the President of Hungary is not burdened by immediate political accountability. The lack of popular legitimacy was not raised. Why? Does the position of the President differ fundamentally from that of the Prime Minister, who can be censured in a constructive vote of no-confidence (a highly unlikely event)? In Andrew Arato's view, if the President is without political responsibility and, therefore, cannot make independent political decisions, "then the constitutional status of the Appointment Law should have been considered, because of the presumption that it incorporated a striving for consensus in the appointment of the leaders of the Hungarian media." Arato, *op. cit.* at 239. A delayed political accountability exists for the President, just as it does for members of Parliament: if the newly composed Parliament is dissatisfied with his performance, it should not reelect him. Compare the Indian and Hungarian positions: Are the positions of their presidents the same, and do they follow from general principles of governmental responsibility?

The Hungarian appointment dispute represents a characteristic uncertainty that occurs in parliamentary systems. The President's position and powers are unclear, and he is frequently in political conflict with the Prime Minister. Sometimes it is difficult to determine who heads the executive. Formal power and actual power may diverge: the President may claim to retain authority in his role as "protector of the Constitution" on the assumption that he has some kind of power as the head of state and, implicitly, is the depository of national sovereignty. The Indian Constitution vests executive power in the President. In *S.R. Bommai v. Union of India*, (1994) 2 S.C.R. 644, the ISC stated:

312.   * * * In [a parliamentary] democracy, the head of the State, be he the King or the President, remains a constitutional head of the State. He acts in accordance with the aid and advice tendered to him by the

u. The CSRT is an independent body overseeing the activities of broadcasters. Its members are appointed by the various branches of power. The body is expected to safeguard media independence. This type of independent-media supervisory body was developed, among others, in France.

Council of Ministers with the Prime Minister at its head. * * * The advice [of the Government] tendered on such reconsideration is made binding upon the President. * * *

318. * * * Any and every action taken by the President is really the action of his Ministers and subordinates. It is they who have to answer for, defend and justify any and every action taken by them in the name of the President, if such action is questioned in a court of law. The President cannot be called upon to answer for or justify the action. It is for the Council of Ministers to do so. * * *

319. * * * Even where he acts directly, the President has to act on the aid and advice of the Council of Ministers or the Minister concerned, as the case may be * * *.

Article 74(2) of the Indian Constitution states: "The question whether any, and if so what, advice was tendered by Ministers to the President shall not be inquired into in any Court." The British constitutional convention, which was adopted in several Commonwealth constitutions, is that the Crown is obliged to assent to a bill even if he or she personally disapproves. (The Belgian King declared himself incapacitated when he was supposed to sign a bill legalizing abortion. In the temporary regency the bill was signed by the authorized individual replacing the King.)

4. The Hungarian and Indian justices view their constitutions as if it would be unthinkable to have the powers of the executive divided. However, there are systems with dual executive power. One could argue that in a pure parliamentary system, such as Hungary, the President cannot have executive functions since he is elected by Parliament. Is this a credible argument? What happens if a new parliament is elected with a majority that differs politically from the one that elected the President? In Romania, the term of the popularly elected President coincides with that of the Parliament.

5. In parliamentary systems the traditional form of control over the executive is through the vote of no-confidence. In most systems which accept the concept of collective ministerial responsibility, lack of confidence affects the whole government; although some constitutions expressly allow for a motion of no-confidence directed against individual members of the cabinet. The German Basic Law expressly recognizes the individual responsibility of ministers, but it allows only a constructive vote of confidence against the Chancellor. The lack of confidence, however, affects the entire cabinet. In Italy, although the Constitution does not countenance a motion of no-confidence against an individual minister, the Italian Senate passed a vote of no-confidence against the Minister of Justice. In similar cases ministers have resigned. The Senate Rules of Procedure contained no specific rule on such motions. The minister brought an appeal against the Senate's no-confidence resolution, arguing not only that individual no-confidence was unknown but also that it contradicted the principle of the homogeneous nature of collective-government action. The ICC dismissed the appeal (Decision 7/1996), reasoning that executive activity was carried out in cooperation between the collective activity of the Council of Ministers and the discrete activity of individual ministers. Article 95 of the Constitution specifies that ministers are responsible for actions of the Council of Ministers and individually for acts of their own ministries. Can stable government exist with individual motions of no-confidence in inherently unstable parliamentary coalitions? What does ministerial responsibility mean if it is not related to no-confi-

dence? The Italian Constitution states that ministers are appointed by the President upon the recommendation of the Prime Minister.

6. What is the proper role of courts in political conflicts among the branches that arise out of personnel appointments? Are there intelligible constitutional principles in this context? In France, the Constitution leaves it to the President to appoint the Prime Minister and, upon the proposal of the Prime Minister, the members of the Council of Ministers. The Council can be forced to resign by the National Assembly only under very specific circumstances (primarily in the context of a procedure initiated by the Prime Minister). Nevertheless, when the President of the republic is of a political orientation that is different from that of the majority in the National Assembly (on cohabitation, see Ackerman, *op. cit.*), the President will appoint a Council of Ministers (as individuals) as requested by the majority. Some executive functions will pertain to the President and others to the Prime Minister and his ministers, forcing them to cooperate, for example, in foreign affairs. This is accepted by convention, and the Constitutional Council has no opportunity to intervene. Is this convention a recognition of parliamentarism and democratic values or mere acquiescence in the realities of power? Is this a betrayal of the structures and original intent of De Gaulle's Constitution?

C.2. THE SCOPE OF EXECUTIVE POWER

In theory the nature and extent of executive power is the most distinct feature of parliamentary and presidential systems of government. In parliamentary systems the Parliament is sovereign: it is the depository of people's power, and it can exercise decisive influence in the formation and actions of the executive. In presidential systems the President has his own popular legitimacy and is vested with elements of national sovereignty that provide additional powers not clearly specified in the constitution. The contemporary reality is that the executive branch prevails in both systems, irrespective of, and even against, constitutional arrangements of checks and balances. In both systems the actual source of power is that the executive controls public administration, which results in the acquisition of knowledge and personnel to carry out decisions determined by that knowledge. The social importance of the executive is based on the vitality of the public services it provides.

The executive is expected to carry out what is prescribed by legislation. The standard constitutional problem in this regard is the extent to which the executive has powers that are not derived from the legislature. Constitutions grant the legislature power to determine the scope of executive action through its laws. Tools of monitoring and control are also constitutional, like parliamentary questions, votes of confidence, and the budget. These attempts may result in incursions into the domain of the executive, but they cannot alter the prevailing domination of the executive over the other branches. Contemporary constitutional law offers only partial solutions to these dimensions of public power. The traditional constitutional doctrines, which were developed when excessive parliamentary power was the concern, continue to protect the domain of the executive, although other traditional doctrines, like the supremacy of law and the rule of law, offer a certain balance.

YOUNGSTOWN SHEET & TUBE CO. v. SAWYER

Supreme Court (United States).
343 U.S. 579 (1952).

Mr. Justice Black delivered the opinion of the Court.

We are asked to decide whether the President was acting within his constitutional power when he issued an order directing the Secretary of Commerce to take possession of and operate most of the Nation's steel mills. The mill owners argue that the President's order amounts to lawmaking, a legislative function which the Constitution has expressly confided to the Congress and not to the President. The Government's position is that the order was made on findings of the President that his action was necessary to avert a national catastrophe which would inevitably result from a stoppage of steel production, and that in meeting this grave emergency the President was acting within the aggregate of his constitutional powers as the Nation's Chief Executive and the Commander in Chief of the Armed Forces of the United States. The issue emerges here from the following series of events:

In the latter part of 1951, [during the Korean War] a dispute arose between the steel companies and their employees over terms and conditions that should be included in new collective bargaining agreements. Long-continued conferences failed to resolve the dispute. [As there was no settlement on April 4, 1952, the Union gave notice of a nationwide strike.] * * * The indispensability of steel as a component of substantially all weapons and other war materials led the President to believe that the proposed work stoppage would immediately jeopardize our national defense and that governmental seizure of the steel mills was necessary in order to assure the continued availability of steel. * * * [T]he President, a few hours before the strike was to begin, issued Executive Order 10340. * * * The order directed the Secretary of Commerce to take possession of most of the steel mills and keep them running. The Secretary immediately issued his own possessory orders, calling upon the presidents of the various seized companies to serve as operating managers for the United States.

[The President reported his action to Congress, which took no action. The managers of the companies had obeyed the Secretary's order under protest and brought suit.]

* * * The President's power, if any, to issue the order must stem either from an act of Congress or from the Constitution itself. There is no statute that expressly authorizes the President to take possession of property as he did here.

* * * Moreover, the use of the seizure technique to solve labor disputes in order to prevent work stoppages was not only unauthorized by any congressional enactment; prior to this controversy, Congress had refused to adopt that method of settling labor disputes.

* * * It is clear that if the President had authority to issue the order he did, it must be found in some provisions of the Constitution. And it is not claimed that express constitutional language grants this power to the President. The contention is that presidential power should be implied from the aggregate of his powers under the Constitution. Particular reliance is placed on provisions in Article II which say that "The executive Power shall be vested in a President * * * "; that "he shall take Care that the Laws be faithfully executed"; and that "he shall be Commander in Chief of the Army and Navy of the United States."

The order cannot properly be sustained as an exercise of the President's military power as Commander in Chief of the Armed Forces. The Government attempts to do so by citing a number of cases upholding broad powers in military commanders engaged in day-to-day fighting in a theater of war. Such cases need not concern us here. Even though "theater of war" be an expanding concept, we cannot with faithfulness to our constitutional system hold that the Commander in Chief of the Armed Forces has the ultimate power as such to take possession of private property in order to keep labor disputes from stopping production. This is a job for the Nation's lawmakers, not for its military authorities.

Nor can the seizure order be sustained because of the several constitutional provisions that grant executive power to the President. In the framework of our Constitution, the President's power to see that the laws are faithfully executed refutes the idea that he is to be a lawmaker. The Constitution limits his functions in the lawmaking process to the recommending of laws he thinks wise and the vetoing of laws he thinks bad. And the Constitution is neither silent nor equivocal about who shall make laws which the President is to execute. * * *

The President's order does not direct that a congressional policy be executed in a manner prescribed by Congress—it directs that a presidential policy be executed in a manner prescribed by the President. * * *

It is said that other Presidents without congressional authority have taken possession of private business enterprises in order to settle labor disputes. But even if this be true, Congress has not thereby lost its exclusive constitutional authority to make laws necessary and proper to carry out the powers vested by the Constitution "in the Government of the United States, or in any Department or Officer thereof."

The Founders of this Nation entrusted the law making power to the Congress alone in both good and bad times. It would do no good to recall the historical events, the fears of power and the hopes for freedom that lay behind their choice. Such a review would but confirm our holding that this seizure order cannot stand.

The judgment of the District Court is affirmed.

Mr. Justice Frankfurter, concurring

* * *

Not so long ago it was fashionable to find our system of checks and balances obstructive to effective government. It was easy to ridicule that system as outmoded—too easy. The experience through which the world has passed in our own day has made vivid the realization that the Framers of our Constitution were not inexperienced doctrinaires. * * * The accretion of dangerous power does not come in a day. It does come, however slowly, from the generative force of unchecked disregard of the restrictions that fence in even the most disinterested assertion of authority. * * *

Marshall's admonition that "it is a constitution we are expounding" [*McCulloch v. Maryland*, 4 Wheat. 316, 407 (1819)] is especially relevant when the Court is required to give legal sanctions to an underlying principle of the Constitution—that of separation of powers. "The great ordinances of the Constitution do not establish and divide fields of black and white." [*Springer v. Philippine Islands*, 277 U.S. 189, 209 (1928) (Justice Holmes, dissenting).] * * *

We must therefore put to one side consideration of what powers the President would have had if there had been no legislation whatever bearing on the authority asserted by the seizure, or if the seizure had been only for a short, explicitly temporary period, to be terminated automatically unless Congressional approval were given. * * *

The question before the Court comes in this setting. Congress has frequently—at least 16 times since 1916—specifically provided for executive seizure of production, transportation, communications, or storage facilities. In every case it has qualified this grant of power with limitations and safeguards. This body of enactments * * * demonstrates that Congress deemed seizure so drastic a power as to require that it be carefully circumscribed whenever the President was vested with this extraordinary authority. * * *

To be sure, the content of the three authorities of government is not to be derived from an abstract analysis. The areas are partly interacting, not wholly disjointed. * * * It is an inadmissibly narrow conception of American constitutional law to confine it to the words of the Constitution and to disregard the gloss which life has written upon them. In short, a systematic, unbroken, executive practice, long pursued to the knowledge of the Congress and never before questioned, engaged in by Presidents who have also sworn to uphold the Constitution, making as it were such exercise of power part of the structure of our government, may be treated as a gloss on 'executive Power' vested in the President by § 1 of Art. II. * * *

[The historical evidence indicates that there is no] long-continued acquiescence of Congress giving decisive weight to a construction by the Executive of its powers.

Mr. Justice Jackson, concurring in the judgment and opinion of the Court.

* * * While the Constitution diffuses power the better to secure liberty, it also contemplates that practice will integrate the dispersed powers into a workable government. It enjoins upon its branches separateness but interdependence, autonomy but reciprocity. Presidential powers are not fixed but fluctuate, depending upon their disjunction or conjunction with those of Congress. We may well begin by a somewhat

over-simplified grouping of practical situations in which a President may doubt, or others may challenge, his powers, and by distinguishing roughly the legal consequences of this factor of relativity.

1. When the President acts pursuant to an express or implied authorization of Congress, his authority is at its maximum, for it includes all that he possesses in his own right plus all that Congress can delegate. In these circumstances, and in these only, may he be said (for what it may be worth), to personify the federal sovereignty. If his act is held unconstitutional under these circumstances, it usually means that the Federal Government as an undivided whole lacks power. A seizure executed by the President pursuant to an Act of Congress would be supported by the strongest of presumptions and the widest latitude of judicial interpretation, and the burden of persuasion would rest heavily upon any who might attack it.

2. When the President acts in absence of either a congressional grant or denial of authority, he can only rely upon his own independent powers, but there is a zone of twilight in which he and Congress may have concurrent authority, or in which its distribution is uncertain. Therefore, congressional inertia, indifference or quiescence may sometimes, at least as a practical matter, enable, if not invite, measures on independent presidential responsibility. In this area, any actual test of power is likely to depend on the imperatives of events and contemporary imponderables rather than on abstract theories of law.

3. When the President takes measures incompatible with the expressed or implied will of Congress, his power is at its lowest ebb, for then he can rely only upon his own constitutional powers minus any constitutional powers of Congress over the matter. Courts can sustain exclusive Presidential control in such a case only by disabling the Congress from acting upon the subject. Presidential claim to a power at once so conclusive and preclusive must be scrutinized with caution, for what is at stake is the equilibrium established by our constitutional system.

[Justice Jackson finds only the severe tests under the third grouping applicable.]

The Solicitor General seeks the power of seizure in three clauses of the Executive Article, the first reading, "The executive Power shall be vested in a President of the United States of America." * * * I quote the interpretation which his brief puts upon it: "In our view, this clause constitutes a grant of all the executive powers of which the Government is capable." If that be true, it is difficult to see why the forefathers bothered to add several specific items, including some trifling ones.

The example of such unlimited executive power that must have most impressed the forefathers was the prerogative exercised by George III, and the description of its evils in the Declaration of Independence leads me to doubt that they were creating their new Executive in his image. * * *

The clause on which the Government next relies is that "The President shall be Commander in Chief of the Army and Navy of the United States" * * *

That seems to be the logic of an argument tendered at our bar—that the President having, on his own responsibility, sent American troops abroad derives from that act "affirmative power" to seize the means of producing a supply of steel for them. * * *

I cannot foresee all that it might entail if the Court should indorse this argument. Nothing in our Constitution is plainer than that declaration of a war is entrusted only to Congress. Of course, a state of war may in fact exist without a formal declaration. But no doctrine that the Court could promulgate would seem to me more sinister and alarming than that a President whose conduct of foreign affairs is so largely uncontrolled, and often even is unknown, can vastly enlarge his mastery over the internal affairs of the country by his own commitment of the Nation's armed forces to some foreign venture. I do not, however, find it necessary or appropriate to consider the legal status of the Korean enterprise to discountenance argument based on it.

* * * The third clause in which the Solicitor General finds seizure powers is that "he shall take Care that the Laws be faithfully executed. * * *" That authority must be matched against words of the Fifth Amendment that "No person shall be * * * deprived of life, liberty, or property, without due process of law." * * * One gives a governmental authority that reaches so far as there is law, the other gives a private right that authority shall go no farther. These signify about all there is of the principle that ours is a government of laws, not of men, and that we submit ourselves to rulers only if under rules.

* * * The claim of inherent and unrestricted presidential powers [the Solicitor General's last argument] has long been a persuasive dialectical weapon in political controversy. * * *

The appeal, however, that we declare the existence of inherent powers *ex necessitate* to meet an emergency asks us to do what many think would be wise, although it is something the forefathers omitted. They knew what emergencies were, knew the pressures they engender for authoritative action, knew, too, how they afford a ready pretext for usurpation. * * *

As to whether there is imperative necessity for such powers, it is relevant to note the gap that exists between the President's paper powers and his real powers. The Constitution does not disclose the measure of the actual controls wielded by the modern presidential office. That instrument must be understood as an Eighteenth–Century sketch of a government hoped for, not as a blueprint of the Government that is. Vast accretions of federal power, eroded from that reserved by the States, have magnified the scope of presidential activity. Subtle shifts take place in the centers of real power that do not show on the face of the Constitution.

Executive power has the advantage of concentration in a single head in whose choice the whole Nation has a part, making him the focus of public hopes and expectations. In drama, magnitude and finality his decisions so far overshadow any others that almost alone he fills the public eye and ear. No other personality in public life can begin to compete with him in access to the public mind through modern methods of communications. By his prestige as head of state and his influence upon public opinion he exerts a leverage upon those who are supposed to check and balance his power which often cancels their effectiveness.

Moreover, rise of the party system has made a significant extra-constitutional supplement to real executive power. No appraisal of his necessities is realistic which overlooks that he heads a political system as well as a legal system. Party loyalties and interests, sometimes more binding than law, extend his effective control into branches of government other than his own and he often may win, as a political leader, what he cannot command under the Constitution. * * *

Mr. Chief Justice Vinson, with whom Mr. Justice Reed and Mr. Justice Minton join, dissenting.

* * * Plaintiffs do not remotely suggest any basis for rejecting the President's finding that any stoppage of steel production would immediately place the Nation in peril. * * *

Under [the plaintiffs'] view, the President is left powerless at the very moment when the need for action may be most pressing and when no one, other than he, is immediately capable of action. Under this view, he is left powerless because a power not expressly given to Congress is nevertheless found to rest exclusively with Congress. * * *

[But the] whole of the "executive Power" is vested in the President. * * *

This comprehensive grant of the executive power to a single person was bestowed soon after the country had thrown the yoke of monarchy. Only by instilling initiative and vigor in all of the three departments of Government, declared Madison, could tyranny in any from be avoided. [*The Federalist* No. 48 (James Madison) (Clinton Rossiter ed., 1961).] * * * [It] is thus apparent that the Presidency was deliberately fashioned as an office of power and independence. Of course, the Framers created no autocrat capable of arrogating any power unto himself at any time. But neither did they create an automaton impotent to exercise the powers of Government at a time when the survival of the Republic itself may be at stake.

* * * With or without explicit statutory authorization, Presidents have at such times dealt with national emergencies by acting promptly and resolutely to enforce legislative programs, at least to save those programs until Congress could act. Congress and the courts have responded to such executive initiative with consistent approval. * * *

In an action furnishing a most apt precedent for this case, President Lincoln without statutory authority directed the seizure of rail and telegraph lines leading to Washington.

* * * In his autobiography, President Roosevelt expounded the "Stewardship Theory" of Presidential power, stating that "the executive is subject only to the people, and, under the Constitution, bound to serve

the people affirmatively in cases where the Constitution does not explicitly forbid him to render the service." * * *

Notes and Questions

1. In Great Britain, the executive, partly on the basis of its intimate relation to national sovereignty, can be granted nearly unchecked powers to legislate under the guise of execution. There might be some inherent powers for presidents under the U.S. Constitution, but in a constitutional system these remain bounded even in the absence of congressional constriction. For example, President Richard Nixon was held to have acted unconstitutionally when he purported by presidential proclamation to impose, without congressional authorization, a 10 percent surcharge on most goods imported into the U.S.[v] As *Youngstown* indicates, the U.S. Constitution offers no clear answer to executive legislation. To be sure, the President participates in legislation (in violation of a rigid separationist ideal) in the form of the veto, which can be overruled. In practice the executive office is the most important framer of legislation, though its bills are sponsored by members of Congress. The constitutional issue centers on the extent to which the President legislates "directly," i.e., without statutory authorization. Did a majority of the justices agree to the idea of emergency presidential action at least in the absence of a specific congressional negative?

2. In the French tradition the executive possessed inherent competencies under the Constitution. The 1958 Constitution has no specific provision on the matter, and courts held that the preexisting powers had not been withdrawn: "Considering that, even if article 34 of the Constitution has not withdrawn from the head of the Government the general policing functions that he used to exercise before, by virtue of his inherent powers and outside any specific legislative authorization, the creation of a special policing regime for hunting calls into question fundamental principles of property * * *." 87–149 DC of 20 Feb. 1987, in Bell, *op. cit.* at 96. The Constitutional Council recognizes the "inherited" preconstitutional powers. At the same time, it indicated that in new areas, previously not included in such powers, decision-making should not be left for original executive action. (The Council has limited powers to review such actions because its review powers are limited to *loi*.)

3. *Foreign Relations and Use of the Military.* Foreign relations remain an area of traditional conflict between the executive and legislative branches. At the dawn of the modern state, foreign relations were the exclusive domain of the absolute ruler. This included war and treatymaking powers, although the origins of the power of modern parliaments originate from a power related to war; namely, the funding of war efforts. Both the American and French revolutions claimed that war powers should pertain to the representatives of the nation, that is, to the legislature. But actual warfare remains the uncontested domain of the executive.

As a result of the separation from Great Britain by the colonies acting as a unit, the powers of external sovereignty passed from the Crown not to the colonies severally, but to the colonies in their collective and corpo-

v. *Yoshida International, Inc. v. United States*, 378 F.Supp. 1155 (Cust.Ct.1974), rev'd, 526 F.2d 560 (C.C.P.A.1975). See   Laurence H. Tribe, *American Constitutional Law* 221 (2d ed. 1988).

rate capacity as the United States of America. [Rulers] come and go; governments end and forms of government change; but sovereignty survives. A political society cannot endure without a supreme will somewhere. Sovereignty is never held in suspense. When, therefore, the external sovereignty of Great Britain in respect of the colonies ceased, it immediately passed to the Union. * * * It results that the investment of the federal government with the powers of external sovereignty did not depend upon the affirmative grants of the Constitution.

United States v. Curtiss–Wright Export Corp., 299 U.S. 304, 316 (1936) (Justice Sutherland).[w]

The President's prevailing powers are also justified by exigencies: "In this vast external realm, with its important, complicated, delicate and manifold problems, the President alone has the power to speak or listen as a representative of the nation. He makes treaties with the advice and consent of the Senate; but he alone negotiates. Into the field of negotiation the Senate cannot intrude; and Congress itself is powerless to invade it." *Id.* at 319.

4.   Collective-defense treaties became crucial in the last 50 years both for international relations and for domestic tranquillity. These treaty systems require at least some similarity in the domestic approach regarding military powers and the use of force as required by them. "These treaties, ratified by the President pursuant to the consent of the Senate, generally commit the United States to come to the aid of any signatory that is militarily attacked. Whether these treaties can serve as a predicate for executive deployment of military force has not been resolved." Laurence H. Tribe, *American Constitutional Law* 233 (2d ed. 1988).

While the U.S. Supreme Court (USSC) relied heavily on the political question doctrine to decline to review executive acts concerning foreign troop deployment and the use of force, courts of U.S. allies have taken a more proactive stance in requiring the executive to justify force. This is perhaps necessary in countries that have constitutions written with antiwar sentiments. After World War Two, the German and the Japanese constitutions were written with pronounced fears about rearmament. When the German government took steps to station nuclear missiles in Germany, as determined by NATO, opposition parties challenged the move, claiming that in the absence of statutory authority to do so, the federal government "indirectly infringed the rights of the Bundestag." In response, the Constitutional Court[x] noted that an act of executive assent taken within the framework of an existing treaty—here the NATO treaty—requires no new legislation under Article 59 (2).

---

w. A joint resolution of Congress, approved on May 28, 1934, authorized the President to ban arms sales as he saw fit for the maintenance of peace. In violation of a presidential proclamation, machine guns were sold. A year earlier, in *A.L.A. Schechter Poultry Corp. v. United States*, 295 U.S. 495 (1935) (Chief Justice Hughes), the nondelegation doctrine was upheld; in *Curtiss–Wright* the lower court found the resolution's delegation impermissible. Justice Sutherland had to distinguish the foreign-powers situation; he did so by finding that foreign relations were in large measure in the exclusive power of the President.

x. *Pershing 2 and Cruise Missile Case I*, 66 BVerfGE 39 (1983). In this instance the GFCC used a sort of political question doctrine. In a matter that requires political evaluation there are no justiciable criteria. See Chapter 2.

Further, in the *Pershing 2 and Cruise Missile Case II*, 68 BVerfGE 1 (1984), the GFCC ruled as follows: The challenged action would have survived constitutional review even if it had been taken independently of the treaty, for the assent granted here would have been classified neither as a 'political treaty' nor as a 'matter of federal legislation' under Article 59 (2). [In other words, the GFCC interpreted the powers of the legislature as limited to those areas that were expressly listed in the Basic Law].

* * * This strict demarcation of the powers allowed the legislative bodies under Article 59 (2) is an element in the separation of powers set up by the Basic Law. * * * But the concentration of political power which would lie in assigning the *Bundestag* central decision-making powers of an executive nature in foreign affairs beyond those assigned to it in the Basic Law would run counter to that structure of apportioning power, responsibility, and control laid down at present by the Basic Law. This is in no way changed by the fact that, at the federal level, only *Bundestag* members are directly elected by the people. The specific order of the apportionment and balancing of state power which the Basic Law wishes to see guaranteed must not be undermined by a monism of powers falsely derived from the democracy principle in the form of an all-embracing reservation on behalf of parliament. Again, the principle of parliamentary responsibility of the government necessarily presupposes a core area of the executive's own responsibility. The democracy constituted by the Basic Law is a democracy under the rule of law, and this means, in relation to the mutual relations of the organs of state, above all a democracy with separation of powers.

Pershing 2 and Cruise Missile Case I, 66 BVerfGE 39 (1983). See also *Kalkar I*, quoted in Section A., Notes and Questions, note 3.

The German approach indicates the intimate interrelations between foreign policy and military policy. Most constitutions limit the involvement of the legislature to declaration of war and peace. Modern warfare, however, is mostly carried out without formal declaration of war, or at least the hostilities resulting in formal conditions of war are authorized by the executive. Further, in an era of global alliances, the deployment and use of troops is determined within treaty regimes that enable the executive to take decisions, often without informing the other political branches. In military matters the German Basic Law (Art. 24) expressly authorizes the transfer of sovereignty to a system of collective security. Although the Basic Law (Art. 59) foresees the approval or participation of the legislature in treaties that regulate the political relations of the federation, the Second Senate of the GFCC found that the NATO Strategic Concept of 1999, which authorized the possibility of military-crisis intervention, did not violate the competencies of the legislature. The possible intervention, endorsed by the federal government, did not amount to undertaking any new international obligations (2 BvE 6/99, June 5, 2001). Earlier the *Bundestag* authorized the use of the Army in air strikes against Yugoslavia. The earlier military intervention in Bosnia–Hercegovina was a legitimate use of force under the authorization of the UN Security Council.[y] But the air strikes in Yugoslavia were NATO

y. During the 1991 Gulf War, the U.S. Congress authorized the President to use force against Iraq, in accordance with a UN Security Council resolution. Participation in the Gulf War resulted in heated debates in Japan and Germany on the meaning of

ordered. The claimants (the PDS faction of the *Bundestag*—the successor party of the East German communist party) argued that the use of the military was without constitutional basis and, therefore, illegitimate. The *Bundestag* resolution could not create new grounds for intervention. The GFCC (2 BvE 5/99 March 25, 1999) rejected the claim, arguing that a complaint could address the violation of a right, but the concerned state organs had no rights in the matter. The German position is that the consent of the *Bundestag* is needed for the deployment of the armed military (not only in case of war) (90 BVerfGE 286, 381). However, as the above cases indicate, military policymaking within the collective-security system limits the powers of the legislature.

The Basic Law relies on specific procedures to prevent the engagement of Germany in war. The Japanese Constitution has substantive prohibitions. Article 9 renounces war, stating that military forces and other war-making potential will never be maintained. Nevertheless, the Cabinet undertook measures related to the Self–Defense Forces that were upheld by the Japanese Supreme Court. The Court ruled that the building of a military base and the related contracts were a matter of private law and, therefore, not subject to constitutional review. See *Ishikuza et al. v. Japan et al.* (1989) (The *Hyakuri Air Base Case*); Lawrence W. Beer and Hiroshi Itoh, *The Constitutional Case Law of Japan, 1970 through 1990*, at 130–141 (1996). The Court found the US–Japan Security Treaty constitutional. The treaty was held to be a matter of a "highly political nature with an important relationship to the basis of our country's existence as a sovereign nation." In such matters "the judicial courts have need of circumspection; so long as that treaty is not deemed to be clearly contrary to provisions of the Constitution, it should not unnecessarily be held unconstitutional and invalid." *Japan v. Sakane*, 23 Keishū 5, 685 (Sup. Ct., Apr. 2, 1969) (*Court Worker Incitement Case*), reproduced in *The Constitutional Case Law of Japan: Selected Supreme Court Decisions, 1961–70*, at 103, 111 (Hiroshi Itoh and Lawrence W. Beer eds. and trans., 1978). Does the executive remain in control of military matters because of judicial deference? Are military matters so urgent and confidential that they should be left exclusively to the executive? Is ex post control over military matters sufficient for the protection of the constitutional order?

Note that both the German and the Japanese courts, though applying a different theory, found it necessary to counter the democratic legitimacy argument, which would have resulted in more parliamentary control over security, with a very strict conception of separation of powers. Should cooperation among the branches apply selectively, and is it less expedient in foreign and military affairs? Is the difference in judicial attitude (political question, in the US; review, in Germany and Japan) immaterial in view of the dictates of the treaty system, which means the supremacy of an internationalized executive? What is the appropriate arrangement to prevent war? Is democratic control the best arrangement? Is this the consideration that emerges from the above constitutional practices? If one accepts the compel-

their respective constitutions. In the aftermath of the Gulf debates, the Diet passed restrictive enabling legislation on Japanese participation in UN peace-keeping (in Cambodia). The 1994 GFCC decision required the participation of the legislature in decisions concerning UN peacekeeping. Later decisions, however, accepted that existing treaty obligations might determine the deployment of troops.

ling necessity of armed peace-keeping and humanitarian intervention, are the same kinds of democratic safeguards necessary?

Lawrence Lessig and Cass R. Sunstein, THE PRESIDENT AND THE ADMINISTRATION

94 Colum. L. Rev. 1, 5, 6, 8, 9, 22, 23, 28, 39–47, 84–85, 97–102 (1994).

* * * Whether the founders framed a strongly unitary executive, or whether we should continue to recognize what they framed, is not a new debate. Throughout our history the question has been the subject of intense controversy. * * * Before the late 1970s * * * [i]t was clear that "executive" functions must be performed by officers subject to the unlimited removal and broad supervisory power of the President.[9] But it was equally clear that Congress had the constitutional power to remove from the President's authority officers having "quasi-legislative" and "quasi-judicial" functions.[10] * * *

All this changed in the 1980s. Spurred by President Reagan's efforts to assert hierarchical control over the bureaucracy, the entire field experienced a minor revolution. * * * In several cases, the Supreme Court limited congressional efforts to insulate administration of the laws from presidential control.[12] These cases seemed to suggest that the whole idea of independent administration could no longer be sustained—a change in understanding that, if accepted, would dramatically alter the framework of American government.

* * * [I]n several more recent cases the Supreme Court unambiguously committed itself to the idea that Congress may, at least sometimes and at least to some extent, make administration independent of the President.[14] Indeed, the Court has allowed Congress to go beyond independent "quasi-legislators" and "quasi-judges" and create independent prosecutors[15]—an innovation from the previous cases that appears to expand congressional authority.

---

9. See [*Myers v. United States*, 272 U.S. 52, 161–64 (1926)]. The dispute in *Myers* involved President Wilson's power to remove a regional postmaster without first gaining the consent of the Senate as the statute required. The Court found unconstitutional the statutory provision limiting the President's removal authority. * * *

10. See *Humphrey's Executor v. United States*, 295 U.S. 602, 629 (1935). *Humphrey's* involved the power of President Roosevelt to remove a Commissioner from the Federal Trade Commission. The statute provided for removal by the President only for "inefficiency, neglect of duty, or malfeasance in office." The Court held that, because of the quasi-legislative and quasi-judicial nature of the Commission, these limitations on the removal power were constitutional.

12. See, e.g., *INS v. Chadha*, 462 U.S. 919, 965–67 (1983) (striking down the use of legislative veto); *Buckley v. Valeo*, 424

U.S. 1, 118–37 (1976) (holding that Congress does not have constitutional power to appoint members to Federal Election Commission, which is responsible for administration and enforcement of election laws).

14. In *Mistretta*, the Court upheld the constitutionality of the United States Sentencing Commission. See *Mistretta v. United States*, 488 U.S. 361, 408–12 (1989). The Commission consists of seven members, at least three of whom must be federal judges, and has the authority to promulgate binding sentencing guidelines. See id. at 368–70. Under the statute, the President may remove Commissioners only for "good cause." See id. at 368. In *Morrison*, the Court upheld a statute that allowed the President to remove an "independent prosecutor" only for "good cause." See *Morrison v. Olson*, 487 U.S. 654, 685–93 (1988).

15. See 487 U.S. at 685–93.

* * * No one denies that in some sense the framers created a unitary executive; the question is in what sense. Let us distinguish between a strong and a weak version. The strong version—held by those whom we will call the modern unitarians—contends that the President has plenary or unlimited power over the execution of administrative functions, understood broadly to mean all tasks of law-implementation. All officers with such functions must either be removable at the President's discretion or be subject to presidential countermand in the context of policy disagreements. The Constitution creates "a hierarchical unified executive department under the direct control of the President,"[21] * * * In the modern unitarian's view, the Constitution constitutionalizes a single organizational value—unitariness—at the expense of other possible governmental values—such as disinterestedness or independence. The conclusion is that any organizational structure that violates unitariness violates the Constitution.

The weak version offers a more unruly picture. It contends that there are functions over which the President has plenary powers; that these functions are the "executive" functions in the constitutional sense; but that in the founding vision, "executive" functions * * * are not coextensive with all the functions now (or then) exercised by the President.

* * * If the Constitution entrenches presidential control over all departments, we would expect the framers to have adopted a relatively uniform organizational structure—departments to be arranged hierarchically, all subordinate to the President and all answerable to him in the exercise of all discretionary functions. Congress may impose duties on departmental officers, but it may not "structure the executive department in ways that would deprive the President of his constitutional power to control that department."[97]

* * * [The framers] created a variety of structures, not a single one.

* * * Madison * * * stated and believed that Congress had considerable authority over entities that have "judicial qualities."[128] Many agencies, both executive and independent, are now engaged in adjudicative tasks. It appears to have been Madison's conviction that Congress has the authority to immunize such agencies from presidential control and indeed that Congress should exercise that authority.[129]

Madison's view was not shared by all. But at a minimum, we can say that the framers were not of one mind about the proper organizational structure and responsibility for these different departments.

* * * For most constitutionalists, resolving issues of what we call "executive" power means deciding two different sets of questions. The first set relates to who performs the political functions of an executive— the power to conduct foreign affairs, for example, or the power to act as

21. [Steven G. Calabresi and Kevin H. Rhodes, *The Structural Constitution: Unitary Executive, Plural Judiciary*, 105 Harv. L. Rev. 1153, 1165 (1992).]

97. Calabresi & Rhodes, supra [note 21], at 1168.

128. See 1 Annals of Cong. 636 (Gales & Seaton eds., 1834).

129. See id. at 636–37.

head of state. The second set of questions relates to who directs the administrative functions of an executive—in parliamentary systems, who controls the government.

Consider three possibilities:

(1) a constitution could vest control over all political and administrative functions in the executive;

(2) a constitution could vest control over just the political functions in the executive, and control over the administrative functions in the legislature; and

(3) a constitution could vest control over all political and some administrative functions in the executive, but leave to the legislature the power to decide how much of the balance of administrative power should be afforded the President.

Option two describes most existing constitutional systems; England is the most familiar example. Option one describes what most believe the framers created—a President with constitutional control over the administrative functions. But we believe that it is option three that describes best the original understanding of the framers' design. That is, we believe that the framers meant to constitutionalize just some of what we now think of as "the executive power," leaving the balance to Congress to structure as it thought proper. What follows from this is that if there were some functions that were not within the domain of what the framers were constitutionally vesting in the President when they vested "the executive power," then there are some functions over which the President need not, consistent with the original design, have plenary executive control.

* * * We believe that the framers wanted to constitutionalize just some of the array of power a constitution-maker must allocate, and as for the rest, the framers intended Congress (and posterity) to control as it saw fit.

* * * Now let us turn to the question of presidential authority. * * * First, we have to know whether "executive" power (in the constitutionally relevant sense) is at stake. Second, we have to know whether the limit on that power is both "necessary and proper" to carry into execution the President's power or other powers in the national government.

With respect to the first question, the issue is what the scope of the powers of the President will now be taken to be. Just as "commerce among the several States" took on a wider scope over time because of changes in the structure of the economy, so too might the executive power take on a wider scope because of changes in the structure of the national government itself. That is, it is possible that certain authority should now be deemed executive that was originally not so categorized, and precisely because of changed conditions and understandings.

With respect to this second question (whether a limitation on executive power is "necessary and proper"), the problem is more complex. What are the values against which Congress must test the administrative structures it establishes to determine whether they are "proper"?

Should Congress look only to the values of the framers when testing a particular executive structure? Can or must Congress look to contemporary institutions and even contemporary values when testing a particular executive structure? And what is the role of reviewing courts in assessing a claim that a particular structure is necessary and proper?

* * * From our focus on what the framers said and did, we can identify a number of values that bear on whether we categorize a particular institution as "executive" (and hence requiring plenary presidential control) and that affect whether a particular limit on presidential control is "proper." Unitariness was unquestionably one such value. As we have seen, the framers rejected a plural executive, and the Decision of 1789[z] shows that for some decisions, presidential control was indeed required. The framers believed that unitariness advanced the interests of coordination, accountability, and efficiency in the execution of the laws. All of these policies argued against a fragmented executive. In certain cases, it was critical that the executive be able to act with dispatch and without dissent. To account for those cases, the framers decided that the executive structure should be unitary.

* * * But it is equally certain that in some cases other values were relevant, and these values may at times constitutionally trump unitariness. On the founding view, efficiency not only justifies unitariness but also occasional legislative departures from that notion; it explains something of the relative independence of the district attorneys. So too does fear of executive and judicial aggrandizement.

* * * Accountability and avoidance of factionalism * * * are two central values of the framers' original executive. Let us focus now on two sorts of changes in the current constitutional context that may require accommodation to continue to preserve these two original values.

The first, and least controversial, type of change is in the functions of what we are calling administrative agencies. What agencies do—the nature of their power and the way that power is exercised—is very different now from what it was at the framing period. Lawmaking and law-interpreting authority is now concentrated in an extraordinary array of regulatory agencies. This development has ensured that domestic policymaking is often done, not at the state level or even through Congress, but through large national bureaucracies.

* * * Now consider the character of the modern presidency. In the aftermath of the New Deal, administrative agencies carry out a wide range of highly discretionary policymaking tasks in the domestic arena. Because of delegations of discretionary authority to administrative agencies, the functions of those who execute the law have dramatically altered. Because of this discretionary authority, these agencies are now principal national policymakers—in practice, crucial lawmakers, both

---

z. When the first Congress created the departments, in 1789, a major debate ensued over the President's powers of removal. In *Myers* Chief Justice Taft reconstruct- ed the Decision of 1789 as one in which there could be no limit of presidential control over the executive departments.

through regulation and interpretation. For example, control of the environment is in large measure a policy decision of the administrator of the Environmental Protection Agency. * * *

* * * In short, in a period in which administrators exercise a wide range of discretionary authority, the very meaning of immunizing them from presidential control changes dramatically. When fundamental policy decisions are made by administrators, immunizing them from presidential control would have two significant consequences: first, it would segment fundamental policy decisions from direct political accountability and thus the capacity for coordination and democratic control; and second, it would subject these institutions to the perverse incentives of factions, by removing the insulating arm of the President, and increasing the opportunity for influence by powerful private groups.

* * * In the last two centuries, there have been large-scale shifts in the nature of our understanding of what the administrators' power is. What was striking about the nineteenth century view was the faith in the ability of administrative bodies to stand impartial in some scientific search for the true (rather than best) policy judgment. This was the progressive faith in administrative expertise.

* * * In a world where administration is conceived as apolitical, granting administrators relatively independent authority could be thought to raise few constitutional issues. If the administrators are simply executing a technical skill, there is little reason to make their judgment subject to the review of the President. * * * The Supreme Court accepted this highly technocratic conception of administration in *Humphrey's Executor v. United States* [295 U.S. 602 (1935) (Justice Sutherland)], the heyday of the progressive model within the judiciary. * * *

But once this view of administration changes—once one sees the nature of administration as fundamentally political—new questions are raised about the extent to which courts may permit this power to be independent of the President.

* * * A structural argument for a unitary executive, then, comes down to this: Where the framers allocated a power that they thought of as political, that power was allocated to people who were themselves politically accountable. This was part of the fundamental commitments to accountability and avoidance of factionalism. At the founding period, the existence of a degree of independence in administration could not realistically have been thought to compromise these commitments. Today, by contrast, a strong presumption of unitariness is necessary in order to promote the original constitutional commitments. The legislative creation of domestic officials operating independently of the President but exercising important discretionary policymaking power now stands inconsistent with founding commitments.

TARIFF COUNCIL CASE

Constitutional Court (Latvia).
Decision No. 03–05 (1999).[a]

"On Conformity of Items 1 and 4 of the Saeima April 29, 1999 Resolution on the Telecommunications Tariff Council with Articles 1 and 57 of the Satversme (Constitution, 1921) of the Republic of Latvia and Other Laws."

[The Saeima (Parliament) established a Parliamentary Investigation Committee (henceforth, the Investigation Committee) on the tariff policy of the Telecommunications Tariff Council, with the requirements of the Law "On Telecommunications." On the basis of the inquiry, which found that the Tariff Council violated the Law "On Telecommunications," the Saeima passed a Resolution obliging the Cabinet of Ministers to dismiss the members of the Telecommunications Tariff Council.]

The representative of the Saeima denied that the disputable act could be considered a normative act. * * *

The Saeima representative expressed the viewpoint that, in conformity with the Rules of Procedure, the Saeima may adopt resolutions which are not of a normative nature. Evaluating several resolutions adopted by the Saeima from 1994–1996, he expressed a viewpoint that there existed a parliamentary tradition to assign different tasks to the Government in the above form. * * *

The Saeima representative emphasised that the disputable act was a political decision. It had been adopted to accomplish the Saeima controlling function. * * *

The Constitutional Court concluded:

1. Article 1 of the Satversme determines that "Latvia is an independent democratic republic." Several principles of a law-based state, including the principle of separation of power, follow from the Article.

The principle of separation of power manifests itself in division of the state power into legislative, executive and judicial power, which are being realised by independent and autonomous institutions. The above principle guarantees balance and mutual control among them. It favours moderation of power.

However, "in Western democracies the principle of separation of power is effective, but it is not implemented in strict conformity with an ideally typical model. Generally only the independence of judges from interference of the executive power is strictly protected. Yet the scheme of the division of power in the historical aspect does not exclude certain breach of the principal limits * * * Breaking of the above scheme does not mean that one power is just trying to influence another one—as in parliamentary control—but it also happens by one power accomplishing the functions of the other one * * * However, in spite of crossing of power, breakouts and disappearance of bounds, the main objective of the

a. Available at <www.satv.tie-sa.gov.lv/Eng/Spriedumi/03–05(99).htm>.

principle of separation of power is achieved if the state institutions of different groups effectively control one another". (R. Cepelius. A General Course on a State. Riga, 1998, pages 244–245).

Latvia is a parliamentary republic and, in compliance with Article 59 of the Satversme, the Government is accountable to the Saeima.

"The basis of the parliamentary responsibility is equal relations between the Parliament and the Government. If one institution had predominance over the other, the parliamentary responsibility institution would not be able to work efficiently and would be degraded to a simple formality. The viewpoint that the government is subordinated to the parliament and shall be regarded as its executive institution is wrong. * * *" (D.A. Lçbers, I. Biers. The Cabinet of Ministers. Riga, 1998, pages 111–112).

However, not long after the Satversme took effect the viewpoint was expressed that the Saeima shall realise a regulative function as well, because "in parliamentary states the government is dependent on the parliament and shall be accountable to it. Therefore it is only logical that the parliament not only controls the government but also puts forward both leading implications on general political directions and performance of separate departments. * * * Certainly, in any case and at any time the parliament may adopt specific resolutions with more or less expressed instructions to the government." (Dilers. Institutions of State Power and their Functions. Riga, 1925, page 90). * * *

The principle of separation of power resulting from the notion of a democratic republic included in Article 1 of the Satversme shall not be perceived dogmatically and formally. It has to be in proportion with the objective of preventing centralisation of power in one institution or official.

The fact that the Saeima with its decision has assigned a task to the Cabinet of Ministers does not contradict Article 1 of the Satversme as long as relations of mutual control and moderation are in balance and other principles of a law-based state are observed.

One of the principles—rule of law determines that the law and rights are binding to every state institution as well as to the legislator himself. Persons, exercising the power of legislation after they had assembled and passed laws under a certain procedure are subject to the effect of the laws. (See Two Treatises on Government, J. Locke. Collected Works in 3 volumes. Volume 3. Moscow, 1988, page 347).

In a democratic republic the parliament has to observe the Constitution and other laws, including those the parliament has passed itself.

Thus the Saeima is authorised to assign binding tasks to the Cabinet of Ministers, however the assignments shall not contradict the law.

* * *

2.1. After renewal of independence in Latvia, manifestation of the parliamentary regulative function has experienced several stages. The concept, predominating in the Soviet period, that the Council of Ministers was subordinated to the Supreme Soviet could be observed in relations between the Parliament of the Republic of Latvia (the Supreme Council) and the Government (the Council of Ministers) during the transitional period. * * *

[I]n May 1996 Amendments to the Rules of Procedure were elaborated and the third part of Article 117 reads that "except in the cases provided by law, it is not permitted to include Paragraphs of normative nature in the independent motion."

The viewpoint of the representatives of the Saeima and the Cabinet of Ministers that the disputable act does not contain paragraphs of normative nature is well founded. However, the fact that the disputable act is adopted under the procedure envisaged by the law does not mean that its contents may contradict the law.

2.2. The Saeima may adopt acts—independent motions—of different kind, even those that formulate attitude or viewpoint of the Saeima as a collective institution. The acts, formulating the attitude of the Saeima may be directed to both—a definite and indefinite scope of subjects. However, the acts may not be directed to creation, amendment, establishment or termination of rights, or assignment of fulfilling duties. [The Court found that the wording used in the Resolution ("obliged to revise") assigned duties, and, therefore, being normative, it was unconstitutional].

* * *

2.3. * * * In conformity with Article 57 of the Satversme "the relations between State institutions shall be as provided by law." In accordance with Article 13 of the Law "The Structure of the Cabinet of Ministers" "the Cabinet of Ministers shall discuss or resolve all issues which, in compliance with the Satversme and law, are within its competence." The Law "On Telecommunications" determines the right of the Cabinet of Ministers to establish the Tariff Council. Article 9 of the Law envisages that "the Telecommunications Tariff Council shall be appointed by the Republic of Latvia Government for a period of five years upon recommendation of the Minister of Transportation and shall be an independent body composed of seven experts." * * *

An unlawful act, adopted by the institution subordinated to the Cabinet of Ministers, may be abrogated under the procedure established by law. If the Saeima holds that the act of the above institution is illegal, it may submit a question or an interpellation, it may resolve to express a vote of no confidence to the Cabinet of Ministers, the Prime Minister or an individual minister, it may submit an application to initiate a case at the Constitutional Court. Thus, the Saeima may estimate compliance of the performance and acts of the Tariff Council with the law. But it may not pass a law, binding to the Cabinet of Ministers, on dissolution of the Tariff Council, it may not assign the Tariff Council with the task of revising an act.

Notes and Questions

1. Note the impact of the concept of Soviet parliamentary supremacy on the early practices of the post-Soviet Parliaments during their transition

to democracy. (See *Tariff Council Case*, above; cf. the RCC decision in the *Altai Territory Case* in Chapter 4). If Parliament has no power to interfere in administrative matters, how can it influence the executive? What would have been the constitutional procedure to force the Latvian Tariff Council to observe the law? Such control would be difficult in the U.S.: "In *Springer v. Philippine Islands* [277 U.S. 189 (1928)] the Supreme Court indicated that Congress may not control the law enforcement process by retaining a power to appoint the individual who will execute its laws." Tribe, *op. cit.* at 244. The American Constitution, however, has limits on the executive-appointment power of Congress, a provision that is somewhat unlikely in a parliamentary system. Imagine that the Saeima, after findings of illegality, enacted a new law terminating the powers of the Tariff Council and mandating a specific tariff. Would it be constitutional?

2. The Latvian Court referred to a 1925 commentary that argued in favor of at least some power to instruct the executive. A similar practice existed in France during the Fourth Republic. After the establishment of the Fifth Republic, the new 1959 Standing Orders of both the National Assembly and the Senate sought to maintain that approach. The Constitutional Council found that such powers of instruction contradicted Art. 20 of the 1958 Constitution as the determination and the conduct of national policy were entrusted to the government. Only the specific provisions on censure are recognized to call the government to account. On a more formal level, the Council found that the resolutions were functionally equivalent to members' legislative initiatives (private bills), and there was no ground for duplication of procedures (CC 59–2 and CC 59–3). In some cases, however, French legislation successfully required in various laws that the government take specific actions; but if the Premier Minister objects, claiming inadmissibility of the draft, the Council will strike down the rider, principally on grounds that specific policy actions fall outside the domain of legislation.

3. In *INS v. Chadha*, 462 U.S. 919 (1983) (Chief Justice Burger), the USSC rejected an attempt by the House of Representatives to usurp decisionmaking powers that pertain either to the judiciary or the executive. The matter is somewhat odd because it dealt with a practice that was used for decades. In principle the Court did not deny that Congress may, by proper legislation, determine naturalization or deportation of named individuals. In such a case, however, the executive could have its say through the Presentment Clause. Do such individualized acts conform to the idea of "general" legislation? Note that Congress is prohibited from enacting Bills of Attainder, which is a legislatively imposed and named punishment. What makes a deportation order different from a punishment? Are these differences substantial? Is the USSC of the opinion that only those unicameral decisionmaking processes that are named in the Constitution are permissible outside legislation proper?

The U.S. Constitution provides in Art. II. § 3. that the President "shall take Care that the Laws be faithfully executed." Is this to say that a similar responsibility of Congress is excluded? Some traditional parliamentary-control techniques (like question time) are unknown in the U.S., but ministerial responsibility is replaced by hearings in committees, strengthened by subpoena powers.

As Lessig and Sunstein indicate above, Congressional possibilities to influence and control the policies of the executive changed over time. The

Constitution itself allows for the intervention of Congress in the appointment of executive officers (a clear disregard of the separation principle; although certain conventions diminish the intervention of Congress in the appointment of executive officers). Further, beginning with the Federal Trade Commission, many important executive departments were established by legislation to carry out legislative mandates. The appointment of the heads of these bodies and their subordination remains somewhat contested. To the extent that these bodies are part of the executive, they should be responsible to the head of the executive. In practical terms the officials in a body that pertains, in principle, to the executive can be removed by the President, i.e., it depends on the President if the official is a "purely executive official." *Myers v. United States*, 272 U.S. 52 (1926), (Chief Justice Taft). Because some agencies and certain officers within these agencies may carry out nonexecutive functions and may exercise "quasi-legislative" or "quasi-judicial" functions, the USSC developed a different rule for such situations to satisfy the dictates of separation of powers. See *Humphrey's Executor v. United States*, 295 U.S. 602 (1935) (Justice Sutherland). Here the President does not dispose of an "illimitable power of removal." In the first case the locus of appointment prevailed, while in the second it was the nature of the function that determined the power of removal.

4. Compare the powers of Congress—a legislature technically separate from the executive that has criminal responsibility only in the form of impeachment—with the possibilities of the legislature in a parliamentary system to become involved in executive matters. In a Westminster-type Parliament, in principle there are no limits in determining the structure and policies of the administration. Further, government (ministerial) responsibility and parliamentary questions and inquiries seem to allow Parliament's involvement in executive activities or at least its influence through ulterior supervision. Departmental select committees in the UK shadow one or more governmental departments and examine their expenditures, administration, and policies. The committees have the authority to seize documents and invite witnesses to give evidence. Although refusal to testify may result in imprisonment by the House(!), the powers of the committees do not extend to ministers as they are members of the House, and, therefore, they are protected by privilege. Consequently, the impact of the reports of the committees (where the majority of the day prevails anyway) on the executive is no greater than that of questions in the House. These measures may mobilize public opinion—where public opinion is instrumental in shaping government behavior. "The evidence of the first two decades of their existence is, however, that the committees have not generally opted for the quiet, uncontroversial backwaters of public life. If anything, their work has created trouble for government rather than simply occupying the time of potential troublemakers." Paul Silk and R. H. Walteres, *How Parliament Works* 219 (4th ed. 1998). On the other hand committees could not take back power from the executive in cabinet dictatorships.

5. Note that courts are reluctant to give support to the efforts of Parliament to curb the executive by shaping administrative structures. In Spain, a new government swore in and established a new internal structure for the ministries by decree. Opposition MPs challenged the decree, arguing that the Constitution requires that only acts of Parliament regulate the internal structure of fundamental government institutions. The Constitutional Tribunal ruled for the government because the Constitution states

only that "important governmental structures are to be regulated by statute," but the structure of the ministries is not an exclusive legislative subject in the above sense. Government decrees may regulate matters of everyday life that do not have a prolonged effect on the rights of significant social groups. RTC 1986/60, 20 May 1986.

6.   The Polish Privatization Act of 1995 empowered the Sejm (the lower house) to express its consent, upon a motion of the Council of Ministers, regarding the privatization of specific sectors of industry. (Note the bicameralism argument of *Chadha* was not raised.) The Polish Constitutional Tribunal held that the Act was unconstitutional as it violated principles of separation of powers (November 22, 1995, K. 19/95). The Tribunal found that separation of powers is a Polish constitutional principle (the expression did not figure in the text). The involvement of the legislative branch in the decisionmaking of the executive was not per se a violation of the separation principle. Note that the Tribunal considered it a principle, that is, separation of powers was not assumed to be complete. Further, it was held that there was no need for some kind of equal powers among the branches.

The legislative branch may have preponderance over the executive as long as the functional dimensions of its powers are clearly established. In Poland, legislative encroachment into the executive was part of the interwar constitutional tradition. Cf. similar positions in Estonia and France. The preponderance of the legislature differs from the Soviet parliamentary-supremacy concept mentioned above: the Tribunal held that each of the branches represents the whole sovereign nation; hence the popular election of Parliament made no difference in this regard. The Tribunal found, however, that the Act was unconstitutional insofar as it did not make the functioning of the branches more efficient, as was required by the Preamble of the 1992 Constitutional Amendment. Was the Tribunal's decision in line with the understanding of separation of powers in the Latvian *Tariff Council Case* above? Note that Parliament's supervision of the executive's privatization decisions was inserted into the draft by the Peasant Party, a leftover from communism. The Council of Ministers' original draft excluded parliamentary involvement, arguably to speed the transition to a market economy. True, it is common in established democracies that legislation itself determines economic policies, e.g., it names industrial sectors or even the state-owned companies slated for privatization. The Polish Sejm, however, was merely participating in executive decisionmaking (a possibility expressly sanctioned in different matters in the German Basic Law). Note, also, that in the postcommunist privatizations the most strikingly corrupt transactions occurred after parliaments lost control over the process (as was predicted by the Peasant Party). The Latvian Constitutional Court found in 1997, No. 04–01 (97),[b] that privatization was of utmost importance, and its regulation fell within the competence of Parliament. The method of payment (in reality a scheme to pay less for national assets)—defined by a joint ministerial Interpretation on asset evaluations and accounting methods that were not established in the law—was held unconstitutional because it was executive legislation without delegation. The Interpretation, however, was enacted in 1993, before the Act on Government Powers of 1994. This was the objection of the concerned party, who used the payment scheme before 1994, but the Court held this point irrelevant. The Court argued that even without the Act

b.   Available   at<www.satv.tie-sa.gov.lv/Eng/Spriedumi/04–01(97).htm>.

and because Latvia was a democratic republic, the legislation only had the power to establish methods of payment in privatizations.

7. The USSC seemed to admit in *Youngstown* that certain governmental powers not specified in the Constitution may pertain to the various branches, including the executive. Most of these powers, however, are recognized as remnants of executive prerogative (see Subsection C.3. below) commonly applicable in foreign relations. Most powers are narrowly interpreted, at least in the sense that powers must be bounded not unlimited. In parliamentary systems the general understanding of the competencies of the President's powers is that only express powers pertain to the President. The Ukrainian Constitutional Court is also inclined to a narrow interpretation of powers. The Constitution provides in Art. 106.10 that the President appoints the heads of local state administration, while the composition of local state administration is formed by the heads of local state administration (Art. 118.3). It was held that the presidential appointment of deputy head administrators was unconstitutional, despite its preconstitutional practice, because there was no express provision in this regard. (The appointments made before the ruling remained in force, 3/690–97, 26.12. 1997. BCCL 1998. 145.) The Ukrainian Court is of the opinion that legislation cannot impose tasks on a constitutional institution in addition to those that are expressly stated in the Constitution. (The position is somewhat surprising to Americans schooled in a tradition where Congress can shape the institutions of the executive, which must faithfully execute laws. However, more recent constitutions themselves create institutions with apparently enumerated lists of powers. A standard clause at the end of such lists is that "other functions as established by law shall be carried out." Where there is no such clause the Ukrainian position would make sense.) When the Ukrainian Parliament extended the constitutionally mandated power of the Accounting Chamber to supervise expenditures other than state expenditures and the power to supervise certain income-generating ventures of the state, this law was held unconstitutional. By such extension the Rada had adopted a law that established the Accounting Chamber as an organ of Parliament and not as an organ of the Constitution. (The Ukrainian Constitution states, however, that the Chamber "exercises control over the use of finances of the State Budget on behalf of the Parliament of Ukraine," and the Parliament has express power over financial activities. Further, Art. 19.2 states: "Bodies of state power * * * are obliged to act only on the grounds * * * envisaged by the Constitution and the laws of Ukraine.") Further, the law created immunity for the officials of the Chamber. The Court ruled that the immunity was an extraordinary protection granted by the Constitution only. The Court found an additional violation of the separation-of-powers principle because the law granted executive powers to the Chamber by granting the power to oversee state incomes, although it could review only "costs" (the expenditures of the budget). The law grants investigative powers to the Chamber. In the first case the Parliament would exercise executive functions through its Accounting Chamber; in the second one it would have judicial powers (without the procedural restrictions that should apply in the administration of justice), 23.01.1997, 01/34–97, BCCL 1998. 143. Is it convincing that an institution established by the Constitution cannot be authorized by legislation to carry out tasks additional to its expressly mentioned functions as long as it does not violate separation of powers? Is there any specific

constitutional concern behind the Ukrainian Constitutional Court's decisions?

In *Bowsher v. Synar*, 478 U.S. 714 (1986) (Chief Justice Burger), the issue was whether Congress's assignment of certain functions, under the Balanced Budget and Emergency Deficit Control Act of 1985, to the Comptroller General violated the separation-of-powers principle. The Comptroller General heads the General Accounting Office, an agency created by Congress to investigate the receipt and disbursement of public funds. He is appointed by the President upon recommendation by the Speaker of the House and the President pro tempore of the Senate. He is removable only upon initiative of Congress. The Balanced Budget Act obligated the Comptroller General to report to the President in the event of certain deficits, and the President was required to issue "sequestration orders," mandating the spending reductions suggested by the Comptroller General. The Supreme Court found that these were executive functions that could not be carried out by an officer removable by Congress. Were the courts in Ukraine and the U.S. concerned by the fact that an apparently executive (though supervisory) body was under the control of the legislature? Do you agree with the characterization above of the Accounting Chamber? Accounting chambers and state audit offices in Europe are generally responsible to Parliament or are called "organs of Parliament," though sometimes, such as in the French tradition, they are quasi courts.

C.3.   EXECUTIVE IMMUNITIES AND PRIVILEGES

Immunities and privileges of the executive branch serve to protect it from unfounded incursions under the pretext of personal liability. In addition, they provide protection for the efficient operation of the executive branch, which requires, among others, the guarding of information. The personal immunity of the head of the executive power (king, president, etc.) originates in the sanctity of royalty. The 1791 French Constitution provided that the King had to be viewed as having abdicated if he failed to take the required oath or return to the country. In addition, it established ministerial responsibility in the sense that the ministers were held criminally accountable for all acts they signed; royal acts were invalid without such countersignatures. In Britain, however, certain powers of the executive (formally those of the Crown) are part of its prerogative and, therefore, beyond the control of the judiciary.

In this subsection we consider the extent to which the executive might act beyond the reach of the control of courts. Judicial control over the decisions and acts of members of the executive (including the chief executive officer) are crucial for rights protection. If the executive, at least in its exercise of discretionary powers, is not responsible before courts or may deny information to courts in the name of privilege, rights and the law might be violated with impunity. But there is a genuine public interest in not distracting the executive from its tasks by litigation; further, certain information should be protected in the interest of efficient policymaking and implementation. Courts in all democracies recognize this profound dilemma.

COUNCIL OF CIVIL SERVICE UNIONS v. MINISTER FOR THE CIVIL SERVICE

House of Lords (United Kingdom).
[1984] 3 All E.R. 935.

Lord Fraser of Tullybelton

My Lords, Government Communications Headquarters (GCHQ) is a branch of the public service under the Foreign and Commonwealth Office, the main functions of which are to ensure the security of the United Kingdom military and official communications, and to provide signals intelligence for the government. These functions are of great importance and they involve handling secret information which is vital to national security.

Since 1947, when GCHQ was established in its present form, all the staff employed there have been permitted, and indeed encouraged, to belong to national trade unions. * * * [U]ntil the events with which this appeal is concerned, there was a well-established practice of consultation between the official side and the trade union side about all important alterations in the terms and conditions of employment of the staff.

On 25 January 1984 all that was abruptly changed. The Secretary of State for Foreign and Commonwealth Affairs announced in the House of Commons that the government had decided to introduce with immediate effect new conditions of service for staff at GCHQ, the effect of which was that they would no longer be permitted to belong to national trade unions but would be permitted to belong only to a departmental staff association approved by the director. * * * The principal question raised in this appeal is whether the instruction by which the decision received effect, and which was issued orally on 22 December 1983 by the respondent, is valid and effective in accordance with art 4 of the Civil Service Order in Council 1982. The respondent [who is also the Prime Minister] maintains that it is. The appellants maintain that it is invalid because there was a procedural obligation on the respondent to act fairly by consulting the persons concerned before exercising her power under art 4 of the Order in Council, and she had failed to do so. Underlying that question, and logically preceding it, is the question whether the courts, and your Lordships' House in its judicial capacity, have power to review the instruction on the ground of a procedural irregularity, having regard particularly to the facts (a) that it was made in the exercise of a power conferred under the royal prerogative and not by statute and (b) that it concerned national security.

It is necessary to refer briefly to the events which led up to the decision on 22 December 1983. Between February 1979 and April 1981 industrial action was taken at GCHQ on seven occasions. * * * [In 1981,] according to Sir Robert Armstrong, the Secretary to the Cabinet, who made an affidavit in these proceedings, parts of the operations at GCHQ were virtually shut down. The appellants do not accept the respondent's view of the seriousness of the effects of industrial action on the work at GCHQ.

* * *

The mechanism on which the Minister for the Civil Service relied to alter the terms and conditions of service at GCHQ was an 'instruction' issued by her under art 4 of the 1982 Order in Council. That article, so far as relevant, provides as follows:

As regards Her Majesty's Home Civil Service—(a) the Minister for the Civil Service may from time to time make regulations or give instructions * * * (ii) for controlling the conduct of the Service, and providing for the classification of all persons employed therein and * * * the conditions of service of all such persons.* * *

The Order in Council was not issued under powers conferred by any Act of Parliament. Like the previous Orders in Council on the same subject it was issued by the sovereign by virtue of her prerogative, but of course on the advice of the government of the day. * * *

Starting with Blackstone's Commentaries * * * [it is agreed that] within the sphere of its prerogative powers, the Crown has an absolute discretion.* * *

As *De Keyser*'s case shows, the courts will inquire into whether a particular prerogative power exists or not and, if it does exist, into its extent. But once the existence and the extent of a power are established to the satisfaction of the court, the court cannot inquire into the propriety of its exercise. * * *

The issue here is not whether the minister's instruction was proper or fair or justifiable on its merits. These matters are not for the courts to determine. The sole issue is whether the decision on which the instruction was based was reached by a process that was fair to the staff at GCHQ. As Lord Brightman said in *Chief Constable of the North Wales Police v. Evans*, [1982] 3 All E.R. 141 at 154: "Judicial review is concerned, not with the decision, but with the decision-making process."

I have already explained my reasons for holding that, if no question of national security arose, the decision-making process in this case would have been unfair. * * *

The question is one of evidence. The decision on whether the requirements of national security outweigh the duty of fairness in any particular case is for the government and not for the courts; the government alone has access to the necessary information, and in any event the judicial process is unsuitable for reaching decisions on national security. But if the decision is successfully challenged, on the ground that it has been reached by a process which is unfair, then the government is under an obligation to produce evidence that the decision was in fact based on grounds of national security. Authority for both these points is found in *The Zamora*, [1916] 2 A.C. 77.

* * *

Lord Diplock

* * *

Judicial review, now regulated by RSC Ord 53, provides the means by which judicial control of administrative action is exercised. * * *

My Lords, I see no reason why simply because a decision-making power is derived from a common law and not a statutory source it should *for that reason only* be immune from judicial review. Judicial review has I think developed to a stage today when, without reiterating any analysis of the steps by which the development has come about, one can conveniently classify under three heads the grounds on which administrative action is subject to control by judicial review. The first ground I would call 'illegality', the second 'irrationality' and the third 'procedural impropriety.' That is not to say that further development on a case by case basis may not in course of time add further grounds. I have in mind particularly the possible adoption in the future of the principle of 'proportionality' which is recognised in the administrative law of several of our fellow members of the European Economic Community; but to dispose of the instant case the three already well-established heads that I have mentioned will suffice.

By 'illegality' as a ground for judicial review I mean that the decision-maker must understand correctly the law that regulates his decision-making power and must give effect to it. Whether he has or not is par excellence a justiciable question to be decided, in the event of dispute, by those persons, the judges, by whom the judicial power of the state is exercisable.

By 'irrationality' I mean what can by now be succinctly referred to as '*Wednesbury* unreasonableness' (see *Associated Provincial Picture Houses Ltd. v. Wednesbury Corp.*, [1947] 2 All E.R. 680). It applies to a decision which is so outrageous in its defiance of logic or of accepted moral standards that no sensible person who had applied his mind to the question to be decided could have arrived at it. Whether a decision falls within this category is a question that judges by their training and experience should be well equipped to answer, or else there would be something badly wrong with our judicial system. * * *

I have described the third head as 'procedural impropriety' rather than failure to observe basic rules of natural justice or failure to act with procedural fairness towards the person who will be affected by the decision. * * *

My Lords, that a decision of which the ultimate source of power to make it is not a statute but the common law (whether or not the common law is for this purpose given the label of 'the prerogative') may be the subject of judicial review on the ground of illegality is, I think, established * * * and extends to cases where the field of law to which the decision relates is national security. * * * While I see no a priori reason to rule out 'irrationality' as a ground for judicial review of a ministerial decision taken in the exercise of 'prerogative' powers, I find it difficult to envisage in any of the various fields in which the prerogative remains the only source of the relevant decision-making power a decision of a kind that would be open to attack through the judicial process on this ground. Such decisions will generally involve the application of government policy. The reasons for the decision-maker taking one course rather than another do not normally involve questions to which, if disputed, the judicial process is adapted to provide the right answer, by which I mean that the kind of evidence that is admissible under judicial procedures and the way in which it has to be adduced tend to exclude from the attention of the court competing policy considerations which, if the executive discretion is to be wisely exercised, need to be weighed against one another, a balancing exercise which judges by their upbringing and experience are ill-qualified to perform. So I leave this as an open question to be dealt with on a case to case basis if, indeed, the case should ever arise.

As respects 'procedural propriety,' I see no reason why it should not be a ground for judicial review of a decision made under powers of which the ultimate source is the prerogative. * * * [I]n any event what procedure will satisfy the public law requirement of procedural propriety depends on the subject matter of the decision, the executive functions of the decision-maker (if the decision is not that of an administrative tribunal) and the particular circumstances in which the decision came to be made.

      * * *

Prima facie, * * * civil servants employed at GCHQ who were members of national trade unions had, at best, in December 1983, a legitimate expectation that they would continue to enjoy the benefits of such membership and of representation by those trade unions in any consultations and negotiations with representatives of the management of that government department as to changes in any term of their employment. So, but again prima facie only, they were entitled, as a matter of public law under the head of 'procedural propriety', before administrative action was taken on a decision to withdraw that benefit, to have communicated to the national trade unions by which they had theretofore been represented the reason for such withdrawal, and for such unions to be given an opportunity to comment on it.

The reason why the Minister for the Civil Service decided on 22 December 1983 to withdraw this benefit was in the interests of national security. National security is the responsibility of the executive government; what action is needed to protect its interests is, * * * a matter on which those on whom the responsibility rests, and not the courts of justice, must have the last word. It is par excellence a non-justiciable question. The judicial process is totally inept to deal with the sort of problems which it involves.

      * * *

There was ample evidence to which reference is made by others of your Lordships that this was, indeed, a real risk; so the crucial point of law in this case is whether procedural propriety must give way to national security when there is conflict between (1) on the one hand, the prima facie rule of 'procedural propriety' in public law, applicable to a case of legitimate expectations that a benefit ought not to be withdrawn until the reason for its proposed withdrawal has been communicated to the person who has theretofore enjoyed that benefit and that person has been given an opportunity to comment on the reason, and (2) on the other hand, action that is needed to be taken in the interests of national security, for which the executive government bears the responsibility and alone has access to sources of information that qualify it to judge what the necessary action is.

To that there can, in my opinion, be only one sensible answer. That answer is Yes.

I agree with your Lordships that this appeal must be dismissed.

Notes and Questions

1. In sharp contrast to English judges' deference to executive affidavits and findings, only very rarely does the GFCC leave executive statements unquestioned. In the *Kramer Case*, 57 BVerfGE 250 (1981), it allowed the admissibility of security service officials' sworn statements about a German defector, where the information came from an Eastern defector whose life was allegedly in danger. The Court requires Cabinet-level certification in such cases and maintains its ability to independently assess the groundedness of government action.

2. The royal prerogative is the gradually diminishing residuum of customary authority, privilege and immunity, recognized at common law as belonging to the Crown, and the Crown alone. In the great *Case of Proclamations* (1611) the judges of the common-law courts emphatically asserted their right to determine the limits of the prerogative; and since the Revolution of 1688 this claim has not been contested by the Crown. Among the prerogatives still exercised by or in the name of the Crown are the appointment of Ministers, the dissolution of Parliament, the power of pardon and the award of honors and dignities; these powers must, as a matter of constitutional convention, normally be exercised on ministerial advice. The immunity of the monarch from prosecution in the courts is another aspect of the royal prerogative.

Stanley de Smith and Rodney Brazier, *Constitutional and Administrative Law* 24 (6th ed. 1989).

As the South African Constitutional Court (SACC) stated: "there has been a distinct movement in modern constitutional states (and, I include, for this purpose, England) in favour of recognising at least some power of review of what are or were prerogative powers of the head of state." *President of the Republic of South Africa v. Hugo*, 1997 (4) SALR 1, 17 (CC) (Justice Goldstone).

In the *S.R. Bommai v. Union of India*, (1994) 2 S.C.R. 644, B.P. Justice Jeevan Reddy (on behalf of Justice Agrawal and himself) stated that:

365. So far as India is concerned, there is no such thing as 'prerogative'. There is the executive power of the Government of India and there are the constitutional functions of the President. It is not suggested by the counsel for the respondents that all the orders passed and every action taken by the President or the Government of India is beyond judicial review. All that is suggested is that some of the powers of the President and the Government of India are immune. Shri Parasaran relies upon the opinion of Lord Roskill where certain prerogative powers are held not fit subject-matters for judicial scrutiny. They are the powers relating to entering of treaties with foreign power, defence of the realm, grant of pardon/mercy, conferring of honours, dissolution of Parliament and appointment of Ministers. We agree that broadly speak-

ing the above matters, because of their very nature, are outside the ken of courts and the courts would not, ordinarily speaking, interfere in matters relating to above subjects. But that is different from saying that all the President's action are immune. In fact, the main holding in this decision is that action taken in exercise of the prerogative power is not immune from judicial review apart from the clear enunciation of the grounds of judicial review. It is also held, of course, that in matters involving government policy, the ground of irrationality may not be an appropriate one.

The SACC found, in the context of a presidential pardon, that the prerogative powers of the executive were subject to judicial review:

[116] The power of the South African Head of State to pardon was originally derived from royal prerogatives. It does not, however, follow that the power given in NT [New Text of the Constitution under review] 84(2)(j) is identical in all respects to the ancient royal prerogatives. Regardless of the historical origins of the concept, the President derives this power not from antiquity but from the NT itself. It is that Constitution that proclaims its own supremacy. Should the exercise of the power in any particular instance be such as to undermine any provision of the NT, that conduct would be reviewable.

Certification of the Constitution of the Republic of South Africa (see Chapter 1).

3. In modern English law we have the following:

[I]t has become necessary [in 1992] to consider whether the judiciary has any and, if so, what power to enforce orders addressed to government departments or ministers. In particular it has been necessary to consider whether the prerogative remedies of habeas corpus (produce the body) which goes to the heart of individual liberty, mandamus (an order to do a particular thing) and prohibition (an order to refrain from doing a particular thing) when addressed to government departments or ministers are in law 'orders' or merely 'requests.'

* * *

[T]he day-to-day relationship between the judiciary and all governments and ministers in modern times has been based upon trust. In a sense the same is true of its relationship with all who resort to the courts for justice in civil disputes. The system would be put under intolerable strain and would be likely to break down if a significant number of citizens treated the courts' orders as mere requests which could be complied with or ignored as they thought appropriate.

M. v. Home Office, [1992] 4 All E.R. 97, 121–22 (C.A.) (Lord Donaldson).

The Court of Appeal's position in *M.* is a step toward making the administration judicially accountable for its actions through criminal law. It remains to be seen how the English courts will move toward a more substantive review of administrative decisions, notwithstanding the deferentialism of the *Wednesbury* rule. As we have seen in *Council of Civil Service Unions v. Minister for the Civil Service*, [1984] 3 All E.R. 935 (H.L.), Lord Diplock accepted irrationality of an official action as a basis for judicial review. "The significance of the statement lies perhaps in the fact that once irrationality is recognized as an independent ground of review, closer consideration may be given to developing, under the capacious concept of rationality, more exacting criteria of review." Dennis J. Galligan, *Discretionary Powers: A Legal Study of Official Discretion* 263 (1986).

Beginning in 2000, proportionality analysis was found applicable in cases decided under the Human Rights Act. But the House of Lords still found a distinction:

> [There is a] difference of function between the minister exercising his statutory powers, for the policy of which he is answerable to the legislature and ultimately to the electorate, and the court. What is required on the part of the latter is that there should be a sufficient review of the legality of the decisions and of the procedures followed. The common law has developed specific grounds of review of administrative acts and these have been reflected in the statutory provisions for judicial review. * * *

> It has long been established that if the Secretary of State misinterprets the legislation under which he purports to act, or if he takes into account matters irrelevant to his decision or refuses or fails to take account of matters relevant to his decision, or reaches a perverse decision, the court may set his decision aside. Even if he fails to follow necessary procedural steps—failing to give notice of a hearing or to allow an opportunity for evidence to be called or cross-examined, or for representations to be made or to take any step which fairness and natural justice requires, the court may interfere. The legality of the decision and the procedural steps must be subject to sufficient judicial control. * * *

> The European Court of Justice does of course apply the principle of proportionality when examining such acts and national judges must apply the same principle when dealing with Community law issues. There is a difference between that principle and the approach of the English courts in *Associated Provincial Picture Houses Ltd. v. Wednesbury Corp.*, [1947] 2 All E.R. 680. But the difference in practice is not as great as is sometimes supposed.

> *Regina v. Secretary of State for the Environment, Transport and the Regions (Alconbury)*, [2001] 2 All E.R. 929, 975–76 (H.L.) (Lord Slynn).

But in a subsequent case, dealing with a challenge concerning a new policy governing searches of prison cells, the House of Lords held:

> there is an overlap between the traditional grounds of review [i.e., *Wednesbury*] and the approach of proportionality. Most cases would be decided in the same way whichever approach is adopted. But the intensity of review is somewhat greater under the proportionality approach. Making due allowance for important structural differences between various convention rights, which I do not propose to discuss, a few generalisations are perhaps permissible. I would mention three concrete differences without suggesting that my statement is exhaustive. First, the doctrine of proportionality may require the reviewing court to assess the balance which the decision maker has struck, not merely whether it is within the range of rational or reasonable decisions. Secondly, the proportionality test may go further than the traditional grounds of review inasmuch as it may require attention to be directed to the relative weight accorded to interests and considerations. Thirdly, even the heightened scrutiny test developed in *R. v. Ministry of Defence*,

[1996] 1 All E.R. 257, 263 [gays in the military] is not necessarily appropriate to the protection of human rights. * * * [T]he intensity of the review, in similar cases, is guaranteed by the twin requirements that the limitation of the right was necessary in a democratic society, in the sense of meeting a pressing social need, and the question whether the interference was really proportionate to the legitimate aim being pursued.

The differences in approach between the traditional grounds of review and the proportionality approach may therefore sometimes yield different results.

R. v. Secretary of State for the Home Department (Daly), [2001] 3 All E.R. 433, 446 (H.L.) (Lord Steyn).

The policy provided, among others, that prisoners could not be present during search of their otherwise privileged legal correspondence. Daly, a long-term inmate, challenged the legality of the policy, arguing that it infringed his common law right to maintain the confidentiality of privileged legal correspondence, which is also protected under the European HR Convention. In his decision on the merits Lord Bingham of Cornhill wrote:

> Any prisoner who attempts to intimidate or disrupt a search of his cell, or whose past conduct shows that he is likely to do so, may properly be excluded even while his privileged correspondence is examined so as to ensure the efficacy of the search, but no justification is shown for routinely excluding all prisoners, whether intimidatory or disruptive or not, while that part of the search is conducted. * * * The infringement of prisoners' rights to maintain the confidentiality of their privileged legal correspondence is greater than is shown to be necessary to serve the legitimate public objectives already identified.

Id. at 443.

The House of Lords did not decide on the challenge based on the European HR Convention.

Does the difference in approach in *Alconbury* and *Daly* lay in the fact that *Alconbury* was a policy-planning decision while *Daly* was a rights case? In support of the *Alconbury* approach, it might be argued that courts will not review the merits of policy decisions. As for the merits, the minister is answerable to Parliament and to the electorate. According to Art. 3. (1) of the Human Rights Act: "So far as it is possible to do so, primary legislation and subordinate legislation must be read and given effect in a way which is compatible with the Convention rights." The definition of primary legislation in Art. 21 (1)(f)(i) covers "Orders in Council made in exercise of Her Majesty's Royal Prerogative."

UNITED STATES v. NIXON

Supreme Court (United States).
418 U.S. 683 (1974).

Mr. Chief Justice Burger delivered the opinion of the Court.

* * * On March 1, 1974, a grand jury of the United States District Court for the District of Columbia returned an indictment charging seven named individuals with various offenses, including conspiracy to

defraud the United States and to obstruct justice. Although he was not designated as such in the indictment, the grand jury named the President, among others, as an unindicted co-conspirator. * * * [A] subpoena * * * was issued * * * to the President by the United States District Court. * * * This subpoena required the production, in advance of the September 9 trial date, of certain tapes, memoranda, papers, transcripts, or other writings relating to certain precisely identified meetings between the President and others. * * * On May 1, 1974, the President's counsel filed a "special appearance" and a motion to quash the subpoena. * * * This motion was accompanied by a formal claim of privilege. * * *

On May 20, 1974, the District Court denied the motion to quash and * * * ordered "the President or any subordinate officer, official or employee with custody or control of the documents or objects subpoenaed," to deliver to the District Court, on or before May 31, 1974, the originals of all subpoenaed items. [The President sought review in the Court of Appeals, but the Supreme Court granted a writ of certiorari before that judgment.]

In the District Court, the President's counsel argued that the court lacked jurisdiction to issue the subpoena because the matter was an intra-branch dispute between a subordinate and superior officer of the Executive Branch and hence not subject to judicial resolution. * * * Since the Executive Branch has exclusive authority and absolute discretion to decide whether to prosecute a case, it is contended that a President's decision is final in determining what evidence is to be used in a given criminal case. * * *

[W]e turn to the claim that the subpoena should be quashed because it demands "confidential conversations between a President and his close advisors that it would be inconsistent with the public interest to produce." The first contention is a broad claim that the separation of powers doctrine precludes judicial review of a President's claim of absolute privilege, the court should hold as a matter of constitutional law that the privilege prevails over the subpoena. * * *

In the performance of assigned constitutional duties each branch of the Government must initially interpret the Constitution, and the interpretation of its powers by any branch is due great respect from the others. The President's counsel * * * reads the Constitution as providing an absolute privilege of confidentiality for all Presidential communications. Many decisions of this Court, however, have unequivocally reaffirmed the holding of *Marbury v. Madison*, that "[i]t is emphatically the province and duty of the judicial department to say what the law is."

No holding of the Court has defined the scope of judicial power specifically relating to the enforcement of a subpoena for confidential Presidential communications for use in a criminal prosecution, but other exercises of power by the Executive Branch and the Legislative Branch have been found invalid as in conflict with the Constitution. *Powell v. McCormack*, 395 U.S. 486 (1969); *Youngstown Sheet & Tube Co. v. Sawyer*, 343 U.S. 579 (1952). In a series of cases, the Court interpreted the explicit immunity conferred by express provisions of the Constitution on Members of the House and Senate by the Speech or Debate Clause. Since this Court has consistently exercised the power to construe and delineate claims arising under express powers, it must follow that the Court has authority to interpret claims with respect to powers alleged to derive from enumerated powers. * * *

In support of his claim of absolute privilege, the President's counsel urges two grounds, one of which is common to all governments and one of which is peculiar to our system of separation of powers. The first ground is the valid need for protection of communications between high Government officials and those who advise and assist them in the performance of their manifold duties; the importance of this confidentiality is too plain to require further discussion. Human experience teaches that those who expect public dissemination of their remarks may well temper candor with a concern for appearances and for their own interests to the detriment of the decisionmaking process. Whatever the nature of the privilege of confidentiality of Presidential communications in the exercise of Art. II powers, the privilege can be said to derive from the supremacy of each branch within its own assigned area of constitutional duties. * * *

The second ground asserted by the President's counsel in support of the claim of absolute privilege rests on the doctrine of separation of powers. Here it is argued that the independence of the Executive Branch within its own sphere insulates a President from a judicial subpoena in an ongoing criminal prosecution, and thereby protects confidential Presidential communications.

However, neither the doctrine of separation of powers, nor the need for confidentiality of high-level communications, without more, can sustain an absolute, unqualified Presidential privilege of immunity from judicial process under all circumstances. The President's need for complete candor and objectivity from advisers calls for great deference from the courts. However, when the privilege depends solely on the broad, undifferentiated claim of public interest in the confidentiality of such conversations, a confrontation with other values arises. Absent a claim of need to protect military, diplomatic, or sensitive national security secrets, we find it difficult to accept the argument that even the very important interest in confidentiality of Presidential communications is significantly diminished by production of such material for *in camera* inspection with all the protection that a district court will be obliged to provide. * * *

[T]he separate powers were not intended to operate with absolute independence.

Since we conclude that the legitimate needs of the judicial process may outweigh Presidential privilege, it is necessary to resolve those competing interests in a manner that preserves the essential functions of each branch. The right and indeed the duty to resolve that question does not free the Judiciary from according high respect to the representations made on behalf of the President.

The expectation of a President to the confidentiality of his conversations and correspondence, like the claim of confidentiality of judicial deliberation, for example, has all the values to which we accord deference for the privacy of all citizens and, added to those values, is the necessity for protection of the public interest in candid, objective, and even blunt or harsh opinions in Presidential decisionmaking. * * *

But this presumptive privilege must be considered in light of our historic commitment to the rule of law. This is nowhere more profoundly manifest than in our view that "the twofold aim [of criminal justice] is that guilt shall not escape or innocence suffer." * * *

In this case we must weigh the importance of the general privilege of confidentiality of Presidential communications in performance of the President's responsibilities against the inroads of such a privilege on the fair administration of criminal justice. The interest in preserving confidentiality is weighty indeed and entitled to great respect. However, we cannot conclude that advisers will be moved to temper the candor of their remarks by the infrequent occasions of disclosure because of the possibility that such conversations will be called for in the context of a criminal prosecution.

On the other hand, the allowance of the privilege to withhold evidence that is demonstrably relevant in a criminal trial would cut deeply into the guarantee of due process of law and gravely impair the basic function of the courts.

Notes and Questions

1. Paula Jones sued President Bill Clinton for damages for sexual harassment during his governorship in Arkansas. In *Clinton v. Jones*, 520 U.S. 681 (1997) (Justice Stevens), the Supreme Court found that presidential privilege, based on separation of powers, did not extend to civil damages litigation concerning conduct unrelated to official acts and specifically that the judicial action would not constitute a constitutionally impermissible impairment of the executive's ability to perform its constitutional duties. *Id.* at 701–06. The Court distinguished the case from *Nixon v. Fitzgerald*, 457 U.S. 731 (1982) (Justice Powell).

In *Nixon v. Fitzgerald* a then-former president was held to have absolute immunity from damages based on his official acts. What if the official acts are illegal? The divided Court applied the privilege to "acts within the 'outer perimeter' of his official responsibility." *Id.* at 756. What about President Pinochet, the Chilean dictator–president, who was accused of crimes against humanity, or President Milosevic of Yugoslavia? Justice White, dissenting, argued that the majority position was a return to the maxim "the King can do no wrong." *Id.* at 766. Should the same standard of absolute immunity apply to other executive officers? See *Harlow v. Fitzgerald*, 457 U.S. 800 (1982) (Justice Powell).[c] What is the constitutional or prudential basis for executive immunity? Is Congress prohibited from legislating ex post facto laws to establish criminal or torts responsibility for acts within the executive's official responsibility? What if a president authorizes assassination?

c. Fitzgerald was an Air Force management analyst who lost his job after his testimony before Congress about cost overruns, which embarrassed his superiors and President Nixon. He was later reinstated and sued the then-former President and his aides.

2.   The SACC held that the President of the republic is not above the law but that the presidency is a special office deserving of special protection and consideration. He can be called to testify in a civil case but only after balancing the interests of justice and the dignity of the presidency. The Court upheld presidential proclamations establishing an inquiry commission to investigate the affairs of the South African Rugby Football Union. (Rugby was the traditional game of whites in South Africa, and the Union was allegedly following racist policies.) The President has constitutional powers to form commissions of inquiry on matters that are of public concern. Rugby, however, was considered a matter of public concern as it both divided and united South Africans across racial lines. The Court also found that there were constitutional constraints on the President in the establishment of commissions of inquiry, but these requirements were not violated if those affected were not granted a hearing before appointment of the commission. *President of the Republic of South Africa v. South African Rugby Football Union*, 1999 (2) SALR 14 (CC).

D. THE JUDICIARY

The constitutional rules on the judiciary are intended, generally, to guarantee the independence and impartiality of judges. The fair and impartial administration of justice is a fundamental requirement of the rule of law, and as such, it is necessarily a high constitutional value. In addition, the integrity of the judiciary serves the protection of constitutional rights because access to impartial courts guarantees adequate protection of rights. What amounts to an independent court or judge or fair procedure? These issues are also discussed in Chapter 9.

The more the political branches can influence the composition or conditions of courts the more likely they will use such influence for narrow political purposes. The dangers of such dependence are obvious in regard to the constitutional role of the courts; and courts may become genuine defenders of the constitution only if they are separate from the other branches. Autonomy requires institutional guarantees. Some modern constitutions, following the Italian model, institutionalize self-governing bodies for the judiciary, avoiding, in principle, the involvement of the other branches in judicial matters. Popular election of judges and the civil service model are other applied techniques. Election, as in many U.S. states, is criticized for being too political; the civil-service model, used in Germany and elsewhere, allows for the intervention of the Ministry of Justice, which is allegedly an apolitical civil service but constitutionally a part of the executive. As Chapter 2 indicates, most supreme and constitutional courts are vulnerable to politicization, at least during the appointment process to these courts.

UNITED ENGINEERING WORKERS UNION v. DEVANAYAGAM

Privy Council (Ceylon).
[1967] 2 All E.R. 367.

[Appeal by special leave from a judgment and order of the Supreme Court of Ceylon.

[A labor tribunal in Ceylon ordered respondent to reinstate his former employee, a member of the appellant union.]

Viscount Dilhorne

* * *

Part VI of the Ceylon (Constitution) Order in Council, 1946, is headed "The Judicature." * * * Section 53 provides for the creation of a judicial service commission, which is to consist of the chief justice, a judge of the Supreme Court and one other person who is or has been a judge of the Supreme Court, and which by s. 55 is made responsible for the appointment, transfer, dismissal and disciplinary control of judicial officers. Section 55(5) defines a judicial officer as the holder of any judicial office. * * *

[I]t is apparent from the Order in Council that holders of judicial offices are to be regarded as members of the judicature and not of the civil service.

The presidents of labour tribunals have always been appointed by the Public Service Commission. If the majority of the Supreme Court of Ceylon are right in holding in this case that they are judicial officers and so should have been appointed by the Judicial Service Commission, then it follows that the acts and orders of the labour tribunals were without jurisdiction and so invalid.

* * *

Those discharging judicial functions in the courts of Ceylon are clearly holders of judicial offices, but it does not follow that they are the only holders of such offices for the legislature may create new ones. The Bribery Amendment Act, 1958, created bribery tribunals for the trials of person prosecuted for bribery, and in *The Bribery Comr. v. Ranasinghe* [[1964] All E.R. 785], it was held that the members of a bribery tribunal held judicial offices and that, as they had not been appointed by the Judicial Service Commission, they had no power to try a person accused of bribery and to sentence him to imprisonment.

There is no single test that can be applied to determine whether a particular office is a judicial one. In *Saskatchewan Labour Relations Board v. John East Iron Works Ltd.* [[1949] A.C. 134] the question was whether that labour relations board exercised judicial power and, if so, whether in that exercise it was a tribunal analogous to a superior, district or county court. Lord Simonds, delivering the judgment of the Board, * * * [said]:

> It is as good a test as another of 'analogy' to ask whether the subject-matter of the assumed justiciable issue makes it desirable that the judges should have the same qualifications as those which distinguish the judges of the superior or other courts. [*Id.* at 151.]

That test appears an appropriate one to apply in relation to the question now before the Board.

In *Shell Co. of Australia v. Federal Commissioner of Taxation* [[1930] All E.R. 671], the Board approved the definition of Griffiths, C.J.

in *Huddart Parker & Co. v. Moorehead* [(1909) 8 C.L.R. 330, 357], when he said:

> I am of opinion that the words 'judicial power' as used in s. 71 of the Constitution mean the power which every sovereign authority must of necessity have to decide controversies between its subjects, or between itself and its subjects, whether the rights relate to life, liberty or property. The exercise of this power does not begin until some tribunal which has power to give a binding and authoritative decision (whether subject to appeal or not) is called upon to take action.

[I]n relation to this, Lord Sankey, L.C., delivering the judgment of the Board, enumerated a number of negative propositions on this subject [[1930] All E.R. 671, 680]:

> 1. A tribunal is not necessarily a court in this strict sense because it gives a final decision. 2. Nor because it hears witnesses on oath. 3. Nor because two or more contending parties appear before it between whom it has to decide. 4. Nor because it gives decisions which affect the rights of subjects. 5. Nor because there is an appeal to a court. 6. Nor because it is a body to which a matter is referred by another body * * *

The holder of a judicial office exercises judicial power, but the fact that some judicial power is exercised does not establish that the office is judicial. * * *

To determine whether the office of president of a labour tribunal is a judicial office it is necessary to consider the powers, functions and duties entrusted to those tribunals. * * *

While the matter is not free from difficulty and, as has been said, no single test can be applied to determine whether an office is judicial, in their lordships' opinion the office of president of a labour tribunal is not a judicial office within the meaning of those words in the Constitution Order in Council. Their reasons for this conclusion may be summarised as follows:

> 1. Labour tribunals were established for the purposes of the Act of 1950, namely to provide for the prevention, investigation and settlement of industrial disputes. The Act making provision for them did not say that they were to perform the functions of a court in giving effect to the legal rights of workmen in connexion with their employment.
>
> 2. On a reference of an industrial dispute, a labour tribunal has the same powers and duties as an arbitrator under the Act. It was rightly held by the Supreme Court that when so acting, a labour tribunal was not acting judicially and that an arbitrator and a member of an industrial court did not hold judicial offices.
>
> 3. On an application, the powers and duties of a labour tribunal do not differ from those of an arbitrator and an industrial court or a labour tribunal on a reference in any material respect. A labour tribunal, an arbitrator and an industrial court are required to do what is just and equitable and it is expressly provided that a labour tribunal when dealing with an application is not restricted by the terms of the contract of employment in granting relief or redress.

In the course of hearing an application a tribunal may be informed of the terms of the contract, but it is not restricted to giving effect to legal rights.

4. The similarity of the powers and duties of a labour tribunal both in relation to a reference and to an application points strongly to the conclusion that its functions are not of a different character on an application to those on a reference or to those of an arbitrator or an industrial court.

5. * * * [F]ar from being established in substitution for or as an alternative to the ordinary courts, labour tribunals were created as part of the machinery for preventing and settling industrial disputes. It would indeed be novel if proceedings in a court of law were required by law to be suspended during discussions between the parties to those proceedings and if a court of law was required to have regard to awards made in respect of an industrial dispute by non-judicial persons, when making its order on an application; so novel, indeed, as to lead to the conclusion that labour tribunals were not intended to, are not required to and do not act as courts of law.

6. Applying the test adumbrated by Lord Simonds in the *Labour Relations Board* case [[1949] A.C. 134, 151], the matters with which a labour tribunal may be required to deal, both on a reference and on an application, do not make it desirable that presidents of labour tribunals should have the same qualifications as those which distinguish the judges of the superior or other courts.

Their lordships will, for the reasons stated, humbly advise Her Majesty that this appeal will be allowed and the case remitted to the Supreme Court of Ceylon to deal with the respondent's appeal to the court on questions of law. The respondent must pay the appellant's costs of this appeal except for the costs of the petition for special leave to appeal.

Lord Guest and Lord Devlin delivered the following dissenting judgment:

* * *

[Because of the increased power of trade unionism, the] law has * * * had to make a new entry into the field of industrial relations. It has had to start again from the beginning, and, as in the field of international relations, has had to make its way in by formulating methods of securing the peaceful settlement of disputes.

* * *

The Act of 1950 thus employed the known ways of settling the ordinary trade dispute. * * * A swift way of dealing with an individual grievance without calling out the whole force of trade unionism would certainly help to promote industrial peace.

* * *

Thus in our opinion the question whether a body is exercising judicial power is not to be determined by looking at its functions in conjunction with those of other bodies set up by the Act, and forming a general impression about whether they are judicial or administrative.

Nor is it to be answered by totting up and balancing resemblances between the labour tribunal and other judicial or administrative bodies. Judicial power is a concept that is capable of clear delineation. It has to be, since it is the basis of a constitutional requirement, and legislation which falls on the wrong side of the line can be completely avoided. It has been considered many times in relation to those constitutions, particularly the Australian, which provide for the separation of powers. We propose therefore to take the basic definition and consider whether or not the power of the labour tribunal falls within it. In the authorities there is also a discussion of a number of identifying marks distinguishing the judicial from the executive and legislative powers and we shall consider those that appear to us to be relevant.

The accepted definition of judicial power is that given by Griffiths, C.J., in *Huddart Parker & Co Proprietary v. Moorehead* [(1909) 8 C.L.R. 330, 357]. It is the power

> which every sovereign authority must of necessity have to decide controversies between its subjects, or between itself and its subjects, whether the rights relate to life, liberty, or property. The exercise of this power does not begin until some tribunal which has power to give a binding and authoritative decision (whether subject to appeal or not) is called upon to take action.

The power of the labour tribunal clearly falls within these general terms, but it is worth noting some particular aspects of it.

There must be a controversy about rights or, as it is sometimes put, a *lis*. Part IV A covers controversies between a workman and his employer about the rights arising out of that relationship. The power of the tribunal is that of giving a binding and authoritative decision. In this respect the procedure is to be distinguished from the conciliation procedures provided under the Act.

The power proceeds from the Sovereign, i.e., it is the judicial power of the State. In this respect it is to be distinguished from the power of an arbitrator whose authority is derived from the consent of the parties themselves. * * *

Another and essential characteristic of judicial power is that it should be exercised judicially. Put another way, judicial power is power limited by the obligation to act judicially. Administrative or executive power is not limited in that way. Judicial action requires as a minimum the observance of some rules of natural justice. * * * Whatever standard is adopted, Tucker, L.J., said [in *Russell v. Duke of Norfolk*, [1949] 1 All E.R. 109, 118], one essential is that the person concerned should have a reasonable opportunity of presenting his case. Lord Hodson in *Ridge v. Baldwin*, [[1963] 2 All E.R. 66, 114] after quoting Tucker, L.J.'s dictum added

> No one, I think, disputes that three features of natural justice stand out—(i) the right to be heard by an unbiased tribunal; (ii) the right to have notice of charges of misconduct; (iii) the right to be heard in answer to those charges.

These are not necessarily features of administrative decisions. The administrator is not required to be unbiased and his decision may often affect those who have no opportunity of presenting their views.

* * *

Finally, there is the principle that the judicial power must be exercised so as to do justice in the case that is being tried and the judge must not allow himself to be influenced by any other consideration at all. Considerations of policy or expediency, which are permissible for the administrator, must be altogether excluded by the judge.

MORRIS v. UNITED KINGDOM
European Court of Human Rights (Former Third Section).
(Application no. 38784/97) 26 February 2002[d].

[Applicant, a soldier in the British Army, went absent without leave. After court martial, no appeal was granted against the sentence. The European Court of Human Rights (ECHR) reviewed the British Court Martial system's conformity with the European HR Convention.]

B. The Court's assessment

58. The Court recalls that in order to establish whether a tribunal can be considered as "independent", regard must be had, *inter alia*, to the manner of appointment of its members and its term of office, the existence of guarantees against outside pressures and the question whether the body presents an appearance of independence.

As to the question of "impartiality," there are two aspects to this requirement. First, the tribunal must be subjectively free of personal prejudice or bias. Secondly, it must also be impartial from an objective viewpoint, that is, it must offer sufficient guarantees to exclude any legitimate doubt in this respect [see *Findlay v. United Kingdom*, Judgment of 25 February 1997, Reports 1997–I].

The concepts of independence and objective impartiality are closely linked and, as in the *Findlay* case, the Court will consider them together as they relate to the present case.

59. The Court notes that the practice of using courts staffed in whole or in part by the military to try members of the armed forces is deeply entrenched in the legal systems of many Member States.

It recalls its own case-law which illustrates that a military court can, in principle, constitute an "independent and impartial tribunal" for the purposes of Article 6 § 1 of the Convention. * * * However, the Convention will only tolerate such courts as long as sufficient safeguards are in place to guarantee their independence and impartiality.

60. In its above-mentioned *Findlay* judgment, the * * * Court's concerns centered around the multiple roles played in the proceedings by the "convening officer." That officer played a key prosecuting role, but at the same time appointed the members of the court martial, who were subordinate in rank to him and fell within his chain of command. He

d. Available at <www.echr.coe.int/Eng/Judgments.htm>.

also had the power to dissolve the court martial before or during the trial and acted as "confirming officer," with the result that the court martial's decision as to verdict and sentence was not effective until ratified by him. The Court held that these fundamental flaws were not remedied by the presence of safeguards, such as the involvement of the judge advocate, who was not himself a member of the court martial and whose advice to it was not made public (see §§ 74 to 78 of the Court's judgment).

* * *

64. [T]he question remains whether the members who heard the applicant's court martial collectively constituted an "independent and impartial tribunal," as those concepts have been explained in the case-law of the Court.

65. The Court recalls that, in the case of *Incal v. Turkey* (judgment of 9 June 1998, Reports 1998–IV, § 67), which concerned the criminal trial of a civilian before the Turkish National Security Court, it identified certain safeguards of independence and impartiality which existed in relation to the military judges who sat as members of that court. In particular, it noted that the military judges concerned underwent the same professional training as their civilian counterparts, that when sitting they enjoyed constitutional safeguards identical to those of civilian judges and that, according to the Turkish Constitution, they had to be independent and free from the instructions and influence of public authorities. However, it went on (at § 68) to identify other aspects of the military judges' status which made their independence questionable. In particular, they were servicemen who still belonged to the army, they remained subject to army discipline and assessment reports, decisions pertaining to their appointment were to a great extent taken by the administrative authorities and the army and their term of office was only four years and could be renewed.

66. Looking first at the manner of appointment in the present case, * * * [t]he fact that the head of the Court Martial Administration Office was appointed by the Defence Council does not of itself give reason to doubt the independence of the court martial because he was, in any event, adequately separated from those fulfilling prosecutory and adjudicatory roles at the court martial. * * *

67. Turning to the terms of office and the existence of safeguards against outside pressures, the Court considers that it is necessary to examine in turn the positions of the Permanent President and the two serving officers on the applicant's court martial. The applicant raises no objection as to the independence of the remaining member of the court martial, namely the judge advocate.

68. * * * The Court recalls that, although irremovability of judges during their terms of office must in general be considered as a corollary of their independence, the absence of a formal recognition of such irremovability in the law does not in itself imply a lack of independence, provided that it is recognised in fact and that other necessary guarantees are present (*Campbell and Fell v. the United Kingdom*, Judgment of 28 June 1984, Series A no. 80, § 80). * * *

72. However, the Court considers that the presence of * * * safeguards was insufficient to exclude the risk of outside pressure being brought to bear on the two relatively junior serving officers who sat on the applicant's court martial. In particular, it notes that those officers had no legal training, that they remained subject to army discipline and reports, and that there was no statutory or other bar to their being made subject to external army influence when sitting on the case. This is a matter of particular concern in a case such as the present where the offence charged directly involves a breach of military discipline. In this respect, the position of the military members of the court martial cannot generally be compared with that of a member of a civilian jury who is not open to the risk of such pressures.

73. In relation to the applicant's complaints about the role played by the "reviewing authority," the Court recalls that the power to give a binding decision which may not be altered by a non-judicial authority is inherent in the very notion of "tribunal." The principle can also be seen as a component of the "independence" required by Article 6 § 1 (see the above-mentioned *Findlay* case, § 77, and *Brumarescu v. Romania*, Judgment of 28 October 1999 [GC], no. 28342/95, § 61, ECHR 1999–VII). In the *Findlay* case, the role played by the "confirming officer" under the pre–1996 Act court martial system was found to be contrary to this well-established principle.

74. In the present case, the applicant's sentence and conviction were subject, under changes introduced by the 1996 Act, to automatic review by the "reviewing authority." The Court notes that the authority was empowered to quash the applicant's conviction and the sentence imposed by the court martial. More importantly, it had powers to reach any finding of guilt which could have been reached by the court martial and to substitute any sentence which would have been open to the court martial, not being in the authority's opinion more serious than that originally passed. Any substituted verdict or sentence was treated as if it had been reached or imposed by the court martial itself.

75. The Court considers that the very fact that the review was conducted by such a non-judicial authority as the "reviewing authority" is contrary to the principle cited at paragraph 73 above. The Court is particularly concerned by the fact that the decision whether any substituted sentence was more or less severe than that imposed by the court martial would have been left to the discretion of that authority. * * *

77. For all these reasons, the Court considers that the applicant's misgivings about the independence of the court martial and its status as a "tribunal" were objectively justified.

HINDS v. THE QUEEN

Privy Council (Jamaica).
[1977] A.C. 195.

On Appeal from the Court of Appeal of Jamaica

[In Jamaica, only members of the security forces were allowed to possess firearms; however, many people obtained guns illegally, and an eruption of gun-related crimes followed. The Gun Court Act of 1974 was enacted in response. By the Act, the Parliament of Jamaica established a new court, the Gun Court, to try "firearms offences." The Gun Court Act introduced a special-punishment regime with grave sanctions: the possession of a bullet could amount to indefinite detention—the actual term of a sentence, however, was not determined by the trial forum but by a "Review Board," whose members were not part of the judiciary. Applicants were sentenced by a subdivision of the Gun Court and appealed on the grounds that the Act was unconstitutional. See David P. Rowe, *Trial by Jury: Right or Privilege?*, 8 Univ. Miami Int'l & Comp. L. Rev. 115 (1999–2000).]

The majority judgment of their Lordships was delivered by Lord Diplock.

* * *

A written constitution, like any other written instrument affecting legal rights or obligations, falls to be construed in the light of its subject matter and of the surrounding circumstances with reference to which it was made. * * *

* * * It is taken for granted that the basic principle of separation of powers will apply to the exercise of their respective functions by these three organs of government. Thus the constitution does not normally contain any express prohibition upon the exercise of legislative powers by the executive or of judicial powers by either the executive or the legislature. As respects the judicature, particularly if it is intended that the previously existing courts shall continue to function, the constitution itself may even omit any express provision conferring judicial power upon the judicature. Nevertheless it is well established as a rule of construction applicable to constitutional instruments under which this governmental structure is adopted that the absence of express words to that effect does not prevent the legislative, the executive and the judicial powers of the new state being exercisable exclusively by the legislature, by the executive and by the judicature respectively.

* * * All Constitutions on the Westminster model deal under separate Chapter headings with the legislature, the executive and the judicature. The Chapter dealing with the judicature invariably contains provisions dealing with the method of appointment and security of tenure of the members of the judiciary which are designed to assure to them a degree of independence from the other two branches of government. It may, as in the case of the Constitution of Ceylon, contain nothing more. * * * What, however, is implicit in the very structure of a Constitution on the Westminster model is that judicial power, however it be distributed from time to time between various courts, is to continue to be vested in persons appointed to hold judicial office in the manner and on the terms laid down in the Chapter dealing with the judicature, even though this is not expressly stated in the Constitution: *Liyanage v. The Queen*, [1967] 1 A.C. 259, 287–288.

* * *

Where, under a constitution on the Westminster model, a law is made by the Parliament which purports to confer jurisdiction upon a court described by a new name, the question whether the law conflicts with the provisions of the constitution dealing with the exercise of the judicial power does not depend upon the label (in the instant case "The Gun Court") which the Parliament attaches to the judges when exercising the jurisdiction conferred upon them by the law whose constitutionality is impugned. It is the substance of the law that must be regarded, not the form. What is the nature of the jurisdiction to be exercised by the judges who are to compose the court to which the new label is attached? Does the method of their appointment and the security of their tenure conform to the requirements of the constitution applicable to judges who, at the time the constitution came into force, exercised jurisdiction of that nature? *Attorney-General for Australia v. The Queen*, [1957] A.C. 288, 309–310. * * *

     * * *

Turning now to the Gun Court Act 1974 * * *

Their Lordships understand the Attorney–General to concede that salaried judges of any new court that Parliament may establish by an ordinary law must be appointed in the manner and entitled to the security of tenure provided for members of the lower judiciary by section 112 of the Constitution. In their Lordships' view this concession was rightly made. To adopt the familiar words used by Viscount Simonds in *Attorney-General for Australia v. The Queen*, [1957] A.C. 288 it would make a mockery of the Constitution if Parliament could transfer the jurisdiction previously exercisable by holders of the judicial offices named in Chapter VII of the Constitution to holders of new judicial offices to which some different name was attached and to provide that persons holding the new judicial offices should not be appointed in the manner and upon the terms prescribed in Chapter VII for the appointment of members of the judicature. * * *

In the field of punishment for criminal offences, the application of the basis principle of separation of legislative, executive and judicial powers that is implicit in a constitution on the Westminster model makes it necessary to consider how the power to determine the length and character of a sentence which imposes restrictions on the personal liberty of the offender is distributed under these three heads of power. The power conferred upon the Parliament to make laws for the peace, order and good government of Jamaica enables it not only to define what conduct shall constitute a criminal offence but also to prescribe the punishment to be inflicted on those persons who have been found guilty of that conduct by an independent and impartial court established by law: see Constitution, Chapter III, section 20 (1). The carrying out of the punishment where it involves a deprivation of personal liberty is a function of the executive power; and, subject to any restrictions imposed by a law, it lies within the power of the executive to regulate the conditions under which the punishment is carried out. In the exercise of its legislative power, Parliament may, if it thinks fit, prescribe a fixed punishment to be inflicted upon all offenders found guilty of the defined offence—as, for example, capital punishment for the crime of murder. Or it may prescribe a range of punishments up to a maximum in severity, either with or, as is more common, without a minimum, leaving it to the court by which the individual is tried to determine what punishment falling within the range prescribed by Parliament is appropriate in the particular circumstances of his case.

Thus Parliament, in the exercise of its legislative power, may make a law imposing limits upon the discretion of the judges who preside over the courts by whom offences against that law are tried to inflict on an individual offender a custodial sentence the length of which reflects the judge's own assessment of the gravity of the offender's conduct in the particular circumstance of his case. What Parliament cannot do, consistently with the separation of powers, is to transfer from the judiciary to any executive body whose members are not appointed under Chapter VII of the Constitution, a discretion to determine the severity of the punishment to be inflicted upon an individual member of a class of offenders. Whilst none would suggest that a Review Board composed as is provided in section 22 of the Gun Court Act 1974 would not perform its duties responsibly and impartially, the fact remains that the majority of its members are not persons qualified by the Constitution to exercise judicial powers. * * * In this connection their Lordships would not seek to improve on what was said by the Supreme Court of Ireland in *Deaton v. Attorney–General and the Revenue Commissioners*, [1963] I.R. 170 , 182–183, a case which concerned a law in which the choice of alternative penalties was left to the executive.

> There is a clear distinction between the prescription of a fixed penalty and the selection of a penalty for a particular case. The prescription of a fixed penalty is the statement of a general rule, which is one of the characteristics of legislation; this is wholly different from the selection of a penalty to be imposed in a particular case. * * * The legislature does not prescribe the penalty to be imposed in an individual citizen's case; it states the general rule, and the application of that rule is for the courts * * * the selection of punishment is an integral part of the administration of justice and, as such, cannot be committed to the hands of the executive. * * *

This was said in relation to the Constitution of the Irish Republic [and] it applies with even greater force to constitutions on the Westminster model. [*Liyanage v. The Queen*, [1967] 1 A.C. 259.]

[In regard to the transfer of power from the judiciary to the Review Board, the majority of whose members were not qualified to exercise judicial powers, the Act was void.]

MISTRETTA v. UNITED STATES

Supreme Court (United States).
488 U.S. 361 (1989).

[The U.S. Sentencing Commission consists of seven members appointed by the President, of whom three must be federal judges. The statute creating the Commission states that it is "an independent commission located in the judicial branch." The Commission was created in response to concern that sentences for similar offenses and of similar offenders in the federal system varied too substantially to promote the goals of sentencing. Its role is to create mandatory sentencing guidelines, specifying rather narrow ranges of permissible sentences for different offenses and taking some account of the different circumstances under which different people commit crimes.]

Justice Blackmun delivered the opinion of the Court.

[Relying on the "intelligible-principle" test, a condition for constitutional delegation—see *Industrial Union Department, AFL–CIO v. American Petroleum Institute*, 448 U.S. 607 (1980)—was satisfied as Congress had given the Commission sufficiently detailed guidance.]

[The allocation of certain powers to the Sentencing Commission was found constitutional, in line with Justice Jackson's opinion in *Youngstown Sheet & Tube Co. v. Sawyer*, 343 U.S. 579 (1952)]. * * * Although the unique composition and responsibilities of the Sentencing Commission give rise to serious concerns about a disruption of the appropriate balance of governmental power among the coordinate branches, * * * petitioner's fears for the fundamental structural protections of the Constitution prove, at least in this case, to be "more smoke than fire." * * *

[The Court has] recognized significant exceptions to the general rule [that courts may not exercise executive and administrative duties of a nonjudicial nature]. In keeping with Justice Jackson's *Youngstown* admonition that the separation of powers contemplates the integration of dispersed powers into a workable government, we have recognized the constitutionality of a "twilight area" in which the activities of the separate Branches merge. * * *

That judicial rulemaking * * * falls within this twilight area is no longer an issue for dispute. * * *

[C]onsistent with the separation of powers, Congress may delegate nonadjudicatory functions that do not trench upon the prerogatives of another branch and that are appropriate to the central mission of the Judiciary. * * *

[The Sentencing Commission's location in the judicial branch] simply acknowledges the role that the Judiciary always has played, and continues to play, in sentencing. * * *

Just as the rules of procedure bind judges and courts in the proper management of the cases before them, so the Guidelines bind judges and courts in the exercise of their uncontested responsibility to pass sentence in criminal cases.* * *

[However,] the degree of political judgment about crime and criminality exercised by the Commission and the scope of the substantive effects of its work does to some extent set its rulemaking powers apart from prior judicial rulemaking. * * *

[T]he "practical consequences" of locating the Commission within the Judicial Branch pose no threat of undermining the integrity of the Judicial Branch or of expanding the powers of the Judiciary beyond constitutional bounds by uniting within the Branch the political or quasi-legislative power of the Commission with the judicial power of the courts.

[The Commission was not a court and was "fully accountable to Congress."]

[In] placing the Commission in the Judicial Branch, Congress cannot be said to have * * * deprived the Executive Branch of a power it once possessed. * * * And, since Congress did not unconstitutionally delegate its own authority, the Act does not unconstitutionally diminish Congress' authority. * * *

What Mistretta's argument comes down to, then, is that * * * [the judicial] Branch is inevitably weakened by its participation in policymaking. * * * [However, d]espite the substantive nature of its work, the Commission is not incongruous or inappropriate to the Branch. * * *

Although the Guidelines are intended to have substantive effects on public behavior * * *, they do not bind or regulate the primary conduct of the public or vest in the Judicial Branch the legislative responsibility for establishing minimum and maximum penalties for every crime. They do no more than fetter the discretion of sentencing judges to do what they have done for generations. * * * Given their limited reach, the special role of the Judicial Branch in the field of sentencing, and the fact that the guidelines are promulgated by an independent agency and not a court, it follows that as a matter of "practical consequences" the location of the Sentencing Commission within the Judicial Branch simply leaves with the Judiciary what long has belonged to it. * * *

[Three federal judges serve on the Commission. This was held "somewhat troublesome," but it was argued that t]he text of the Constitution contains no prohibition against the service of active federal judges on independent commissions. * * *

The judges serve on the Sentencing Commission not pursuant to their status and authority as Article III judges, but solely because of their appointment by the President. * * * Such power as these judges wield as Commissioners is not judicial power; it is administrative power. * * * [T]he Constitution * * * does not forbid judges from wearing two hats; it merely forbids them from wearing both hats at the same time. * * *

The ultimate inquiry remains whether a particular extrajudicial assignment undermines the integrity of the Judicial Branch. Because service by any particular judge on the Commission was voluntary, that service could not diminish the independence of the Judiciary. * * *

[The Court was] somewhat more troubled by [the] argument that the Judiciary's entanglement in the political work of the Commission undermines public confidence in the disinterestedness of the Judicial Branch. While the problem of individual bias is usually cured through recusal, no such mechanism can overcome the appearance of institutional partiality that may arise from judiciary involvement in the making of policy. * * *

Although it is a judgment that is not without difficulty, we conclude that the participation of federal judges on the Sentencing Commission does not threaten, either in fact or in appearance, the impartiality of the Judicial Branch. [This is in large part because the] Commission is devoted exclusively to the development of rules to rationalize a process that has been and will continue to be performed exclusively by the Judicial Branch. In our view, this is an essentially neutral endeavor and one in which judicial participation is peculiarly appropriate. * * *

We simply cannot imagine that federal judges will comport their actions to the wishes of the President for the purpose of receiving an appointment to the Sentencing Commission.

The President's removal power over Commission members poses similarly negligible threat to judicial independence. * * *

[S]ince the President has no power to affect the tenure or compensation of Article III judges, even if the Act authorized him to remove judges from the Commission at will, he would have no power to coerce the judges in the exercise of their judicial duties. * * *

Justice Scalia, dissenting.

* * *

[T]he decisions made by the Commission are far from technical, but are heavily laden * * * with value judgments and policy assessments. * * *

[The nondelegation principle] is not * * * readily enforceable by the courts. Once it is conceded, as it must be, that some judgments * * * involving policy considerations, must be left to the officers executing the law and to the judges applying it, the debate over unconstitutional delegation becomes a debate not over a point of principle but over a question of degree. * * * Since Congress is no less endowed with common sense than we are, and better equipped to inform itself of the "necessities" of government; and since the factors bearing on those necessities are both multifarious and (in the nonpartisan sense) highly political * * *, it is small wonder that we have almost never felt qualified to second-guess Congress regarding the permissible degree of policy judgment that can be left to those executing or applying the law. * * *

Precisely because the scope of delegation is largely uncontrollable by the courts, we must be particularly rigorous in preserving the Constitution's structural restrictions that deter excessive delegation. The major one * * * is that the power to make law cannot be exercised by anyone other than Congress, except in conjunction with the lawful exercise of executive or judicial power.

The whole theory of *lawful* congressional "delegation" is * * * that a certain degree of discretion, and thus of lawmaking, *inheres* in most executive or judicial action, and it is up to Congress, by the relative specificity or generality of its statutory commands, to determine * * * how small or how large that degree shall be. * * *

[Because whatever lawmaking occurs is ancillary to the exercise of executive or judicial power,] there is *no* acceptable delegation of legislative power. * * *

The lawmaking function of the Sentencing Commission is completely divorced from any responsibility for the execution of the law or adjudication of private rights under the law. * * *

The delegation of lawmaking authority to the Commission is * * * unsupported by any legitimating theory to explain why it is not a delegation of legislative power. To disregard structural legitimacy is wrong in itself—but since structure has purpose, the disregard also has adverse practical consequences. In this case, * * * the consequence is to facilitate and encourage judicially uncontrollable delegation. Until * * * *Morrison v. Olson*, 487 U.S. 654 (1988), it could have been said that Congress could delegate lawmaking authority only at the expense of increasing the power of either the President or the courts. Most often, as a practical matter, it would be the President, since the judicial process is unable to conduct the investigations and make the political assessments essential for most policymaking. Thus, the need for delegation would have to be important enough to induce Congress to aggrandize its primary competitor for political power, and the recipient of the policymaking authority, while not Congress itself, would at least be politically accountable. * * *

By reason of today's decision, I anticipate that Congress will find delegation of its lawmaking powers much more attractive in the future. If rulemaking can be entirely unrelated to the exercise of judicial or executive powers, I foresee all manner of "expert" bodies, insulated from the political process, to which Congress will delegate various portions of its lawmaking responsibility. How tempting to create an expert Medical Commission * * * to dispose of such thorny, "no-win" political issues as the withholding of life-support systems in federally funded hospitals or the use of fetal tissue for research. This is an undemocratic precedent that we set—not because of the scope of the delegated power, but because its recipient is not one of the three Branches of Congress. The only governmental power the Commission possesses is the power to make law; and it is not the Congress. * * *

I think the Court errs * * * not so much because it mistakes the degree of commingling [of the branches of government], but because it fails to recognize that this case is not about commingling, but about the creation of a new branch altogether, a sort of junior-varsity Congress. It may well be that in some circumstances such a branch would be desirable. * * * But there are many desirable dispositions that do not accord with the constitutional structure we live under.

Notes and Questions

1.   Independence of the judiciary is a fundamental requirement of any fair administration of justice in a liberal rule-of-law country. Clearly, separation of powers supports such independence and may contribute to judicial integrity. Nevertheless, the relationship remains nonspecific. Consider Ma-

hendra P. Singh, *Securing the Independence of the Judiciary—The Indian Experience*, 10 Ind. Int'l & Comp. L. Rev. 245, 246–48 (2000):

> The independence of the judiciary is not a new concept but its meaning is still imprecise. The starting and the central point of the concept is apparently the doctrine of the separation of powers. Therefore, primarily it means the independence of the judiciary from the executive and the legislature. But that amounts to only the independence of the judiciary as an institution from the other two institutions of the state without regard to the independence of judges in the exercise of their functions as judges. In that case it does not achieve much. The independence of the judiciary does not mean just the creation of an autonomous institution free from the control and influence of the executive and the legislature. The underlying purpose of the independence of the judiciary is that judges must be able to decide a dispute before them according to law, uninfluenced by any other factor. * * *
>
> The independence of the judiciary means and includes the independence of the judiciary as a collective body or organ of the government from its two other organs as well as independence of each and every member of the judiciary—the judges—in the performance of their roles as judges. Without the former the latter cannot be secured and without the latter the former does not serve much purpose.

2.   In the *Judicial Appointment Ruling Case*, 21 December 1999,[e] the Constitutional Court of the Republic of Lithuania had to determine the conditions of impartiality:

> The all-sufficiency and independence of the judiciary presupposes its self-government. The self-government of the judiciary also includes organisation of the work of courts and the activities of the professional corps of judges.
>
> The organisational independence of courts and their self-government are the main guarantees of actual independence of the judiciary. * * *
>
> The guarantee of the organisational independence of courts is one of essential conditions to ensure human rights.

Earlier, on 3 June 1999,[f] the Lithuanian Constitutional Court held that

> 'in cases when the powers of a concrete branch of power are directly established in the Constitution, then no institution may take over these powers, while an institution whose powers are defined by the Constitution may neither transfer nor refuse these powers. Such powers may neither be changed nor restricted by the law.'

The Lithuanian Court found that the powers of the Minister of Justice to appoint deputy chairpersons and court-division chairpersons of respective courts, decide on the number of judges, and determine the internal organization of courts violated the constitutional principle of the independence of judges and courts.

3.   Judicial self-governing bodies may result in constitutional conflict, if the executive feels that the judiciary is not conferring it support. Beginning in 1996, the Pakistani government failed to appoint five judges to the Supreme Court, as requested by the Chief Justice. In reaction the Court, in

---

e. Available at <www.lrkt.lt/1999/ n9a1221a.htm>.

f. Ruling available at <www.lrkt.lt/1999/n9a0603a.htm>.

Al-Jehad Trust v. Federation of Pakistan, P.L.D. 1997 S.C. 84 (Chief Justice Sajjad Ali Shah) (the *Appointment of Judges Case*), discussed the possibility of the nonimplementation of a judgment of the Supreme Court regarding judicial appointments. The Court found that in such case, where "[s]incere attempt is not being made to implement the judgment, then it will become the Constitutional duty of the President to see that judgment * * * is implemented. * * * If all the Executive and Judicial Authorities in Pakistan are unable to come in aid of the Supreme Court * * * then such situation would be open to be construed as impasse or deadlock * * * reflecting failure of Constitutional machinery and one would be justified [to find Art. 58(2)(b) applicable]." *Id.* at 147.

In a typical reaction of the executive to such conflicts, the government introduced a bill in Parliament that would have reduced the number of judges as well as the powers of the Supreme Court. The conflict was solved by a presidential dissolution of Parliament that was ordered, among others, for disobeying the Court's ruling on the appointment of judges. In this context the Pakistani Supreme Court came to the conclusion that final appointment orders were to be passed by the government within 30 days, and if this was not done, then it was to be deemed that the federal government and Prime Minister had no objection to the recommendations and steps could be taken by the President for final appointment. *Babar Awan v. Federation of Pakistan*, P.L.D. 1998 S.C. 45, 49 (Chief Justice Sajjad Ali Shah).

4. Similar conflicts occur when judges are appointed by a previous political regime or when they aim simply to follow their own convictions. In the 1950s, the German Parliament delayed appointments to the Constitutional Court until there were enough vacancies to give seats to the candidates of all the major political parties. In India, the Chief Justice failed to express views regarding his appointed successor, delaying the appointment process. President Roosevelt planned to appoint additional Associate Justices to the USSC, after certain rulings of the Court hampered his New Deal efforts. Congress objected to this court-packing plan, but due to unexpected death and a reversal of judicial position, Roosevelt achieved his aim without having to implement his plan. The U.S. Constitution is silent on the number of justices, which is determined by law, and until the twentieth century the number often changed.

5. The judicial appointment and removal systems have their origins in times before the separation of powers prevailed. Security of tenure developed as a reaction to arbitrary influences of the executive, especially from judicial decisions that favored the Crown. The Act of Settlement of 1701 (between England and Scotland) provided that judges of the superior courts held office *quamdiu se bene gesserit* (during good behavior), and their removal required a special address presented by both Houses of Parliament. The constitutions of Canada, Australia, and India have similar provisions regarding Supreme Court judges. (Compare with the U.S.: Is impeachment the equivalent of removal?)

Judicial appointments in India are formally left to the executive. Article 124 (2) of the Constitution states: "Every Judge of the Supreme Court shall be appointed by the President by warrant under his hand and seal after consultation with such of the Judges of the Supreme Court and of the High Courts in the States as the President may deem necessary for the purpose and shall hold office until he attains the age of sixty-five years: Provided that in the case of appointment of a Judge other than the Chief Justice, the Chief Justice of India shall always be consulted." The Supreme Court carved out a major role for the judiciary in judicial appointments (and transfers) in *Supreme Court Advocates-on-Record Association v. Union of India*, (1993) Supp. 2 S.C.R. 659. The Court interpreted "consultation" to mean "the power of consent"; moreover, the Supreme Court majority replaced the role of the Chief Justice with that of the Justices of the Court.

In November 1998, the President of India, abiding by the procedure elaborated by the Court, accepted nominations with the following observation:

> I would like to record my views that while recommending the appointment of Supreme Court judges, it would be consonant with constitutional principles and the nation's social objectives if persons belonging to weaker sections of society like SCs and STs, who comprise 25 per cent of the population, and women are given due consideration. * * * Eligible persons from these categories are available and their under-representation or non-representation would not be justifiable. Keeping vacancies unfilled is also not desirable given the need for representation of different sections of society and the volume of work the Supreme Court is required to handle.

> Mahendra P. Singh, *Securing the Independence of the Judiciary—The Indian Experience*, 10 Ind. Int'l & Comp. L. Rev. 245, 278 (2000).

The executive (or the legislature) may claim that by ignoring democratic representation on the Court, the composition and values of the judiciary become alienated from society. The Chief Justice of India responded that only merit should matter in judicial appointments. How strong is the representation argument? Is political appointment to constitutional courts the proper answer to the concerns of the Indian executive? (This is the case in Germany, while the other appointments are left exclusively to the executive on professional merit.) Consider paragraph 2.13 of the Universal Declaration on the Independence of Justice: "The process and standards of judicial selection shall give due consideration to ensuring a fair reflection by the judiciary of the society in all its aspects."

6. In an effort to avoid interference from other branches in appointment, tenure, etc., some constitutions attempt to make the judiciary a self-sustaining body. For example, a supreme judicial council is in charge of decisions regarding the judiciary, including the preparation and proposition of its budget. In Italy and France, such councils are composed partly (or overwhelmingly) by judges elected by their peers, and representatives of other branches often sit with the judges.

The Italian Minister of Justice could not agree with the Superior Council of the Magistracy on an appointment of a magistrate in charge of the administrative offices of the Appellate Court of Palermo. Four members of the Council were elected by the magistrates and two by Parliament. The administrative nature of the job was the reason for the participation of the Minister, who, under Art. 110 of the Constitution, had functions relating to the organization and functioning of judicial services. In an effort to guarantee the autonomy of the judiciary, the scheme was intended to exclude any determinative intervention of the executive power in the deliberations on the status of magistrates. It does not, however, prevent the existence of a collaborative effort between the Superior Council of the magistracy and the Ministry of Justice in the respective capacities attributed to each. Decision N. 80 of 1989 stated that

> 'there exists between the Superior Council and the Ministry of Justice, notwithstanding the individual safeguard of their reciprocal competencies, a specific duty of collaboration * * * Under the profile of honest cooperation and, in particular, under that of the correctness in reciprocal relations, the activity of harmonization must take place according to coherent and not contradictory behavior, as much in relation to the specific proposal to be formulated as well as previous ones regarding the magistrate or the office. The parties, in addition, cannot use dilatory, pretentious, incongruous or insufficiently motivated attitudes so that the comparison may occur on the basis of correctness and openness to the positions of others.'

In the *Judicial Nomination Case*, Judgment n. 379 of July 9, 1992, it was ruled that the duty of honest cooperation requires reasoned grounds for the position taken.

> [The Constitutional Court found that not all procedural steps were duly taken, and] it is up to the Minister of Justice not to give way to the deliberations of the Superior Council of the Magistracy on the appointment of court administration offices when an adequate activity of harmonization is lacking on behalf of the qualified commission. [However], it is not up to the Minister of Justice not to give course to the deliberations of the Superior Council of the Magistracy on the appointment of court administration offices when, notwithstanding the occurrence of an adequate activity of harmonization in the manner indicated in the previous paragraph, an agreement was not reached in a reasonable lapse of time between the commission and the Minister of the proposal to be formulated.

7.   A 1999 Bulgarian case indicates the level of politicization of judicial appointments, even when there is a judicial council. Article 130.4 of the Bulgarian Constitution provides that members of the Judicial Council are elected for five-year terms and cannot be dismissed prior to the end of their terms. In 1997, at the end of socialist rule in Parliament, the Council was renewed, and 11 of 25 members were elected by the parliamentary majority. Because of subsequent changes in the law, new appellate courts were created so that the 1997 composition of the Council did not correspond to the statutory quota reserved to various categories of judges. The new ruling party (the antisocialist UDF), which voted in the amendments establishing the new appellate courts, challenged the composition of the Council. The Constitutional Court agreed with the UDF complaint and approved the election of a new council despite the apparently clear rule prohibiting dismissal. Is this an appropriate judicial role? Consider: the socialists made their appointments in the last days of their rule, and, although the socialists were democratically elected, they were the successor party of the communists and their appointees guaranteed the continuity of a communist-appointed judiciary. (Is this story different from the appointment of the "midnight judges" by the outgoing Adams administration, which led to *Marbury v. Madison*?) Note that the old Judicial Council nominated a new prosecutor general to fill a vacancy only four days before it was to be

dissolved. The Bulgarian President vetoed the nomination, arguing that the outgoing (dissolved) Council should not have the power to nominate. Note further, in regard to the independence of the Judicial Council, the European Union suggested that, to satisfy accession to the Union, the Council's powers regarding the waiving of immunity of judges should be abolished in order to fight corruption! The competence of the Council was deemed to be used abusively, hampering investigations against corrupt judges. See *Bulgaria Update*, E. Eur. Const. Rev., vols. 7–9 (1998–2000).

8. As *Mistretta* and *Hinds* indicate, the judiciary might be compromised via the definition of its jurisdictional powers. Decisionmaking that would require independent judges is transferred to other branches (people controlled by other branches), or the judiciary is assigned functions that may not pertain to the judiciary, in particular functions that compromise the integrity of the judiciary. Stanley de Smith and Rodney Brazier, *Constitutional and Administrative Law* 19–20 (6th ed. 1989), offer the following summary of the problem:

> In Sri Lanka (Ceylon) the constitution [of 1972] did not allocate judicial powers in the same form, and it would be reasonable to infer that the separation of powers doctrine had no place in the constitutional jurisprudence of the island. But in a famous case [*Liyanage v. R.* [1967] 1 A.C. 259] the Judicial Committee of the Privy Council held that implicit in the constitution lay the principle that the province of the Judiciary was immune from the grosser kinds of encroachment by the Executive and the Legislature; hence, retroactive legislation designed to secure the conviction and punishment of particular persons for specified conduct was declared unconstitutional, for it approximated to a non-judicial judgment. One wonders how the War Damage Act 1965, which reversed a judicial decision of the House of Lords [*Burmah Oil Co. v. Lord Advocate* [1965] A.C. 75] with retroactive effect, would have fared if it had been measured against a written British constitution in which judicial review of the constitutionality of legislation was accepted.

There is no clear rule that would determine a priori what might pertain to the judiciary. In *Hinds v. The Queen*, [1977] A.C. 195, the Irish test of *Deaton v. Attorney General and the Revenue Commissioners*, [1963] I.R. 170, 182–83, was found to be evidently applicable. (*Deaton* concerned a law that left the choice of alternative penalties to the executive.) The *Deaton* court refused to open the door to the exercise of arbitrary power in criminal law: "There is a clear distinction between the prescription of a fixed penalty and the selection of a penalty for a particular case. The prescription of a fixed penalty is the statement of a general rule, which is one of the characteristics of legislation; this is wholly different from the selection of a penalty to be imposed in a particular case."

Does this position reflect parochial Anglo–American experiences? Consider fact-finding by the jury, which in other systems is a judicial function. Perhaps one cannot say more than what the High Court of Australia found: that powers wholly alien to the judiciary cannot be vested in "courts" where the constitution refers to courts. *Attorney-General for Australia v. The Queen*, [1957] A.C. 288 (P.C.) aff'g sub nom. *R. v. Kirby* (1956) 94 C.L.R. 254. There may be some incompatibility in the idea that judges participate in making rules that they will apply. Judicial functions are increasingly delegated to nonjudicial bodies that are under the control of the other branches, particularly the executive. In most countries, the public administration provides a considerable portion of the adjudicative services. Note that Art. 6 of the European HR Convention does not require a court of law but only an independent and impartial tribunal established by law: "1. In the determination of * * * any criminal charge against him, everyone is entitled to a fair and public hearing within a reasonable time by an independent and impartial tribunal established by law." Do the Privy Council and the European HR Convention use the term "tribunal" in the same sense?

E. STATE OF EMERGENCY

There are circumstances when the constitutional order and the state's existence are in danger; the government must act swiftly and efficiently. Such exigencies might require an extraordinary concentration of power. Viscount Haldane summarized such need in the following terms: "In the event of war, when the national life may require for its preservation the employment of very exceptional means, the provision of peace, order and good government for the country as a whole may involve effort on behalf of the whole nation, in which the interests of individuals may have to be subordinated to that of the community * * *." *Fort Frances Pulp and Paper Co. v. Manitoba Free Press Co.*, [1923] A.C. 695, 703–04 (P.C.), (appeal taken from Ontario).

There are democracies that constantly face problems that necessitate temporary use of emergency powers. As Justice Ahmadi in *S.R. Bommai v. Union of India*, (1994) 2 S.C.R. 644, 697, has stated, this is the case in India, where a complex system for declaring and withdrawing emergency exists:

11. In a country geographically vast, inhabited by over 850 million people belonging to different religions, castes and creeds, a majority of them living in villages under different social orders and in abject poverty, with a constant tug of war between the organised and the unorganised sectors, it is not surprising that problems crop up time and again requiring strong and at times drastic State action to preserve the unity and integrity of the country. Notwithstanding these problems arising from time to time on account of class conflicts, religious intolerance and socioeconomic imbalances, the fact remains that India has a reasonably stable democracy. The resilience of our Republic to face these challenges one after another has proved the people's faith in the political philosophy of socialism, secularism and democracy enshrined in the Preamble of our Constitution. Yet, the fact remains that the nation has had from time to time with increasing frequency to combat upheavals occasioned on account of militancy, communal and class conflicts, politico-religious turmoils, strikes, bandhs and the like occurring in one corner of the country or the other, at times assuming ugly proportions. We are a crisis-laden country; crisis situations created by both external and internal forces necessitating drastic State action to preserve the security, unity and integrity of the country. To deal with such extraordinarily difficult situations exercise of emergency powers becomes an imperative.

In India, the constitutionalization of peacetime emergency, in accordance with pre-independence British law, was intended to be a temporary and exceptional measure. These "hopes and assurances have been sadly belied. History has testified to the flagrant misuse of Art. 356[g] which has been invoked by the Centre so far about 100 times. Sadly every party at the Centre has succumbed to its fatal fascination." Soli J. Sorabjee, *Decision of the Supreme Court in* S.R. Bommai v. Union of India*: A Critique*, (1994) 3 S.C.C. 1.

War, civil unrest, natural disasters and epidemics, and economic crises are some of the events that necessitate extraordinary governmental measures, which may require temporary disregard of certain rights. Federal states, especially if they are forged of formerly independent units with secessionist potential, are particularly concerned about the maintenance of unity. The concern is present but hidden in the U.S. (see the constitutional requirement to guarantee "a republican form of government" to every state–Art. IV, Section 4.). "During a set of interviews in 1976, former President Richard Nixon maintained that only the president's judgment could fix the dividing line between constitutional and unconstitutional conduct when national security is at issue: when 'the President does it, that means that it is not illegal.' [Excerpts From Nixon's Responses to Senate Select Committee on Intelligence, N.Y. Times, Mar. 20, 1976, at A16.] Now, in the 1990s, executives from an eclectic combination of nations—Russia, Germany, Venezuela, and Brazil, among others—are claiming extraordinary powers." William C. Banks and Alejandro D. Carrió, *Presidential Systems in Stress: Emergency Powers in Argentina and the United States*, 15 Mich. J. Int'l L. 1, 2 (1993).

Both in India and Pakistan, detailed rules authorize the central government to declare emergency in the state governments that fail to carry out their duties.[h] Unfortunately, the fundamentals of civilian rule and individual rights might be disregarded in the name of the dictates of efficiency.[i] Crises will be exploited as a pretext to move from one

---

g. Article 356, "Provisions in case of failure of constitutional machinery in [the] States," reads as follows:

(1) If the President, on receipt of a report from the Governor of a State or otherwise, is satisfied that a situation has arisen in which the government of the State cannot be carried on in accordance with the provisions of this Constitution, the President may by Proclamation–

    a. assume to himself all or any of the functions of the Government of the State * * * other than the Legislature of the State;

    b. declare that the powers of the Legislature of the State shall be exercisable by or under the authority of Parliament [of the Union];

* * *

(3) Every Proclamation under this article shall be laid before each House of Parliament and shall, except where it is a Proclamation revoking a previous Proclamation, cease to operate at the expiration of

two months unless before the expiration of that period it has been approved by resolutions of both Houses of Parliament.

h. Part XVIII of the Indian Constitution carries the heading "Emergency Provisions." Article 352, the first article in this Part, empowers the President to proclaim emergency in the country or any part thereof if he is satisfied that a grave emergency exists whereby the security of India or any part thereof is threatened, whether by war, external aggression, or armed rebellion. By the 44th Amendment, the words "armed rebellion" replaced the words "internal disturbance." Article 355 imposes a duty upon the Union to protect the states against external aggression and armed rebellion and, also, to ensure that the governments of the states conduct their affairs in accordance with the Constitution.

i. See *The King v. Halliday*, [1917] A.C. 260, 292 (H.L.) (Lord Shaw of Dunfermline, dissenting):

The use of the Government itself as a Committee of Public Safety [the executive

dictatorship to the next. Constitutional regimes might be irreparably undermined in the name of emergency. The fate of the French Constitution of 1791 dramatically illustrates what occurs if the rules of the Constitution are disregarded in the name of the necessities of defense. Liberty was lost once most powers in the name of the country's defense were transferred to a small executive body that was not subject to the ordinary controls of the law and the legislature.

Emergency rules were applied in Weimar Germany, and Hitler ruled under emergency powers. The emergency rules of the Weimar Constitution were imperfect, and no legislation existed on the conditions for emergency power. This "technical" shortcoming led to abuses. On the other hand the 1958 French Constitution was adopted with the possibility of an imminent military coup d'état in mind. As a result, besides regulating the formal conditions of a state of siege,[j] the Constitution expressly authorizes presidential rule. According to Art. 16, in times of grave crises, when the institutions of the republic or its territorial integrity are threatened in a grave and immediate fashion, and the proper functioning of the public authorities has been interrupted, the President may take whatever measures are required by the circumstances, including the unlimited disregard of fundamental rights—but not amendment of the Constitution—without any external check. Is this an acceptable model for other countries or a quasi dictatorship? The National Assembly may sit under these circumstances, and thus it may at least criticize (and eventually initiate the "impeachment" of) the President. De Gaulle used Art. 16 powers during the 1961 military coup in Algeria.

Emergency rule is one of the greatest challenges to constitutional order. Israel's democracy is criticized for making use of its inherited British emergency rules. In India, certain applications of emergency were found politically and judicially unacceptable. Military regimes in Latin America, in the 1970s and 1980s, often claimed states of emergency. African countries move from one emergency rule to the next. For

committee in the French revolution that established Terror] has its conveniences, has its advantages. So had the Star Chamber. "The Star Chamber," says Maitland (Constitutional History of England, p. 263), "examining the accused, and making no use of the jury, probably succeeded in punishing many crimes which would otherwise have gone unpunished. But it was a tyrannical court, that it became more and more tyrannical, and under Charles I was guilty of great infamies, is still more indubitable." * * * [D]anger is found in an especial degree whenever the law is not the same for all, but the selection of the victim is left to the plenary discretion whether of a tyrant, a committee, a bureaucracy or any other depositary of despotic power.

j. See Andrew West et al., *The French Legal System: An Introduction* 153–54 (1992):

Art. 36 states that a state of siege may be declared by the Council of Ministers and it requires parliamentary authorization after 12 days. The Constitution does not specify the effects of the state of siege, namely that civil liberties are suspended and that the military authorities maintain public order. In addition "the Conseil d'Etat has developed the doctrine * * * that were there is a grave crisis, public authorities are to be recognised as having increased powers which are not subject to the normal principles of legality. * * * The doctrine states that where there are "exceptional circumstances," * * * public authorities may carry out acts required by the circumstances which would otherwise be illegal.

decades, partial emergency has defined life in Northern Ireland. Russia wages wars against Chechnya with claims that emergency rules apply.

The proper regulation of emergency situations is a significant challenge to constitutionalism. The constitutional regulation of emergency means that the constitution itself sets the conditions and procedures for declaring an emergency, and there are constitutional foundations and limits to any departure from the constitutional power (temporarily authorizing the executive and military to use the powers of the other branches). The constitutional order often attempts to set limits to rights restrictions. The main concerns are the scope of emergency and the judicial review of emergency declarations.

EX PARTE MILLIGAN

Supreme Court (United States).
71 U.S. (4 Wall.) 2 (1866).[k]

[The American Constitution contains no separate set of constitutional rules for emergency situations.][l]

Mr. Justice Davis delivered the opinion of the Court.

* * *

Time has proven the discernment of our ancestors; for even these provisions, expressed in such plain English words, that it would seem the ingenuity of man could not evade them, are now, after the lapse of more than seventy years, sought to be avoided. Those great and good men foresaw that troublous times would arise, when rulers and people would become restive under restraint, and seek by sharp and decisive measures to accomplish ends deemed just and proper; and that the principles of constitutional liberty would be in peril, unless established by irrepealable law. The history of the world had taught them that what was done in the past might be attempted in the future. The Constitution of the United States is a law for rulers and people, equally in war and in peace, and covers with the shield of its protection all classes of men, at all times, and under all circumstances. * * *

The proposition is this: that in a time of war the commander of an armed force (if in his opinion the exigencies of the country demand it, and of which he is to judge), has the power, within the lines of his

k. During the Civil War, "Milligan, not a resident of one of the rebellious states, or a prisoner of war, but a citizen of Indiana for twenty years past, and never in the military or naval service, is, while at his home, arrested by the military power of the United States, imprisoned, and, on certain criminal charges preferred against him, tried, convicted, and sentenced to be hanged by a military commission, organized under the direction of the military commander of the military district of Indiana. Had this tribunal the legal power and authority to try and punish this man?" *Ex Parte Milligan*, at 118. The military commander convicted Milligan based on powers conferred to him by the commander in chief—powers to be exercised in the theater of war.

l. The only emergency-like rules are that the writ of habeas corpus may be suspended in cases of rebellion or invasion (art. I, section 9, cl. 2), and Congress has the power to call the "militia" to suppress insurrections. When the legislature cannot be convened, the executive protects the states against domestic violence (art. IV, 4).

military district, to suspend all civil rights and their remedies, and subject citizens as well as soldiers to the rule of *his will*; and in the exercise of his lawful authority cannot be restrained, except by his superior officer or the President of the United States.

If this position is sound to the extent claimed, then when war exists, foreign or domestic, and the country is subdivided into military departments for mere convenience, the commander of one of them can, if he chooses, within his limits, on the plea of necessity, with the approval of the Executive, substitute military force for and to the exclusion of the laws, and punish all persons, as he thinks right and proper, without fixed or certain rules.

The statement of this proposition shows its importance; for, if true, republican government is a failure, and there is an end of liberty regulated by law. Martial law, established on such a basis, destroys every guarantee of the Constitution. * * *

But, it is insisted that the safety of the country in time of war demands that this broad claim for martial law shall be sustained. If this were true, it could be well said that a country, preserved at the sacrifice of all the cardinal principles of liberty, is not worth the cost of preservation. Happily, it is not so. * * *

––––––––––––

Notwithstanding the firm commitment to hold fast to this position, the Supreme Court (affirming the same principles) recognized that, during the Great Depression, "an emergency existed * * * which furnished a proper occasion for the exercise of the reserved power of the State to protect the vital interests of the community." *Home Building & Loan Ass'n v. Blaisdell*, 290 U.S. 398, 444 (1934). The Court found that a moratorium on mortgage (debt) was not an impairment of an obligation of contract (which would be prohibited by the Contracts Clause, which was written precisely to resist the dictates of an emergency debt crisis). *Id*. at 474–83. The *Japanese Internment* cases (see *Korematsu* in Chapter 6.) indicate the potential weakness of judicial review in times of crisis. Here the majority was too ready to accept the dictates of a military evaluation in the name of crisis management. Does this suggest the need for special rules for emergency situations to provide the best protection for liberty? In the British context, a different position was advocated in a famous dissent of Lord Atkin in the House of Lords, during World War Two. Lord Atkin emphasized that liberty would be guaranteed only if judges could not depart from the standard interpretation of the law in times of war.

LIVERSIDGE v. ANDERSON

House of Lords (United Kingdom).
[1941] 3 All E.R. 338.

[The facts of Liversidge offer a typical example of the situation where disregard of fundamental rights is enabled by regulations that are issued in a regulatory and decisionmaking process that departs from prevailing checks and balances. At the outbreak of World War Two, Parliament adopted an enabling act, allowing the Cabinet to take any necessary measures under the circumstances of the war.]

It was held uncontested that "it may be necessary in a time of great public danger to entrust great powers to His Majesty in Council, and that Parliament may do so feeling certain that such powers will be reasonably exercised." [*The King v. Halliday*, [1917] A.C. 260 (H.L.).[m]]

Viscount Maugham:

* * *

[By] the Emergency Powers (Defence) Act 1939, s. 1(1), it was provided that His Majesty by Order in Council:

* * * may make such regulations * * * as appear to him to be necessary or expedient for securing the public safety, the defence of the realm, the maintenance of public order and the efficient prosecution of any war in which His Majesty may be engaged, and for maintaining supplies and services essential to the life of the community.

By subsect. (2) it was enacted that:

* * * without prejudice to the generality of the powers conferred by the preceding subsection, defence regulations may, so far as appears to His Majesty in council to be necessary or expedient for any of the purposes mentioned in that subsection [make provision for a number of important purposes, including regulations] for the detention of persons whose detention appears to the Secretary of State to be expedient in the interests of the public safety or the defence of the realm. * * *

The Defence (General) Regulations 1939, reg 18B * * * is in the following terms:

If the Secretary of the State has reasonable cause to believe any person to be of hostile origin or associations or to have been recently concerned in acts prejudicial to the public safety or the defence of the realm or in the preparation or instigation of such acts and that by reason thereof it is necessary to exercise control over him, he may make an order against that person directing that he be detained.

* * *

[The Secretary of State claimed that he had "reasonable cause to believe" that Liversidge, a British subject, was a "person of hostile association" and ordered his detention, in 1940. Liversidge appealed, claiming that he was wrongfully detained. The House of Lords ruled that the legal basis of the detention order, reg 18B, authorized a departure

---

m. During World War One, the British Parliament delegated power to His Majesty in Council to enact regulations for securing the public safety. Zadig, "a person of hostile origin and associations," was interned; he appealed. It was argued on his behalf that "if the Legislature had intended to interfere with personal liberty it would have provided, as on previous occasions of national danger, for suspension of the rights of the subject as to a writ of habeas corpus. * * *

The Legislature has selected another way of achieving the same purpose." *The King v. Halliday*, [1917] A.C. 260, 267, 270 (H.L.) (Lord Finley, L.C.). In light of this disposition, it is even more remarkable that the U.S. Constitution, although it has no provisions on emergency, requires an Act of Congress to suspend habeas corpus. In light of the World War Two *Japanese Internment* cases, even this requirement is insufficient against abuses by the military.

from the standard requirement of judicial review of detention decisions. Lord Atkin, dissenting, argued that a fundamental right could not be disregarded and that the ordinary and unique meaning of the term "may make an order" should apply, which would subject the decision of the Secretary of State to review.]

Lord Atkin:

* * *

In [this country], amid the clash of arms, the laws are not silent. They may be changed, but they speak the same language in war as in peace. It has always been one of the pillars of freedom, one of the principles of liberty for which, on recent authority, we are now fighting, that the judges are no respecters of persons, and stand between the subject and any attempted encroachments on his liberty by the executive, alert to see that any coercive action is justified in law. * * *

I protest, even if I do it alone, against a strained construction put upon words, with the effect of giving an uncontrolled power of imprisonment to the Minister. To recapitulate, the words have only one meaning. They are used with that meaning in statements of the common law and in statutes. They have never been used in the sense now imputed to them. They are used in the Defence Regulations in the natural meaning, and, when it is intended to express the meaning now imputed to them, different and apt words are used in the Defence Regulations generally and in this regulation in particular. Even if it were relevant; which it is not, there is no absurdity, or no such degree of public mischief as would lead to a non-natural construction.

I know of only one authority which might justify the suggested method of construction. "When I use a word," Humpty Dumpty said in rather a scornful tone, "it means just what I choose it to mean, neither more nor less." "The question is," said Alice, "whether you can make words mean different things." "The question is," said Humpty Dumpty, "which is to be master—that's all." (*Alice Through the Looking Glass*, c vi).

TEH CHENG POH v. PUBLIC PROSECUTOR

Privy Council (Malaysia).
[1980] A.C. 458.

On appeal from the Federal Court of Malaysia.

The judgment of their Lordships was delivered by Lord Diplock.

[Modern written constitutions seek to limit abuse of emergency by establishing procedures for its declaration. The executive is generally entitled to take emergency measures only until the legislature can be convened, at which point the legislature may enable the executive to take legislative measures, disregarding some specified laws or all laws (within the limits of human rights protection), at least temporarily.

These considerations were adopted by the Privy Council (regarding emergency in Malaysia)."]

* * *

There are only two sources from which the Yang di-Pertuan Agong [the Head of State, elected by and among the Rulers] as such can acquire power to make written law, whatever label be attached to it: one is by a provision of the Constitution itself: the other is by the grant to him of subordinate legislative power by an Act passed by the Parliament of

n. An earlier decision, *Ningkan v. Gov't of Malaysia*, [1970] A.C. 379 (P.C.), was found relevant here. In *S.R. Bommai v. Union of India*, (1994) 2 S.C.R. 644, 838–40, Justice B.P. Jeevan Reddy gave the following summary of this case:

The appellant was the Chief Minister of Sarawak, an Estate in the Federation of Malaysia. On June 16, 1966, the Governor of Sarawak requested him to resign on the ground that he had ceased to command the confidence of the Council Negri. The appellant refused whereupon the Governor informed him on June 17, 1966 that he ceased to hold the office. The appellant approached the High Court of Kuching against the Governor's intimation. On September 7, 1966, the High Court upheld his plea and ruled that the Governor had no power to dismiss him. On September 14, 1966. His Majesty Yang di-Pertuan Agong (Head of the State of Malaysia) proclaimed a state of emergency throughout the territories of the State of Sarawak. The Proclamation was made under Article 150 of the Federal Constitution of Malaysia, which reads: "150. (1) If the Yang di-Pertuan Agong is satisfied that a grave emergency exists whereby the security or the economic life of the Federation or of any part thereof is threatened, he may issue a Proclamation or emergency."

The Article provided for such Proclamation being placed for approval before both the Houses of Parliament, who had the power to disapprove the same. Clause (5) of Article 150 empowered the Federal Parliament, during the period the Proclamation of emergency was in operation, to make laws with respect to any matter which it appeared to it as required by reason of the emergency. Such law, it was provided, shall be operative notwithstanding anything contained either in the Constitution of the Federation or the Constitution of the State of Sarawak, and will not be treated as amendment to the Constitution. Any such law was, however, to be in force only for the period of emergency. In exercise of the power conferred by clause (5) of Article 150, the Federation Parliament passed Emergency (Federal Constitution and Constitution of Sarawak) Act, 1966. Section 5 of this Act specifically empowered the Governor to dismiss the Chief Minister, in his absolute discretion, if, at any time, the Council Negri passed the resolution of no confidence in the Government by a majority and yet the Chief Minister failed to resign. On September 23, 1966, the Council Negri met and passed the resolution of no confidence in the Chief Minister (appellant). On the next day, the Governor dismissed the appellant under the new Act

* * *

The Privy Council (Lord MacDermott speaking for the Board) expressed the view in the first instance that it was "unsettled and debatable" whether a Proclamation made by the Supreme Head of the Federation of Malaysia under statutory powers could be challenged on some or other grounds but then *proceeded on the assumption* that the matter is justiciable. On that assumption, the Board proceeded to examine the further contentions of the appellant. It found that the Proclamation of emergency and the impugned Act were really designed to meet the constitutional deadlock that had arisen on account of the absence of provision empowering the Governor to dismiss the Chief Minister where the latter ceased to enjoy the confidence of the Council Negri. * * * The Privy Council observed further that "they can find, in the material presented, no ground for holding that the respondent Government was acting erroneously or in any way *malafide* in taking the view that there was a constitutional crisis in Sarawak, that it involved or threatened a breakdown of a State Government and amounted to an emergency calling for immediate action. Nor can their Lordships find any reason for saying that the emergency thus considered to exist was not grave and did not threaten the security of Sarawak. These were essential matters to be determined according to the judgment of the respondent-ministers in the light of their knowledge and experience * * * and that he (the appellant) failed to satisfy the Board that the steps taken by the Government including the Proclamation and the impugned Act, were in fraudem legis or otherwise unauthorised by the relevant legislation." The appeal was accordingly dismissed.

Malaysia * * * [A]fter Parliament has first sat * * * the only source from which he could derive such powers would be an Act of Parliament delegating them to him.

This is what had been done in the previous emergency. * * * Parliament on September 18, 1964, passed the Emergency (Essential Powers) Act 1964. * * * [I]t contained the declaration that the Act appeared to Parliament to be required by reason of that emergency. * * *

Because, unlike the No. 1 Ordinance, the Emergency (Essential Powers) Act 1964, was an Act of Parliament it was effective under the Constitution to delegate to the Yang di-Pertuan Agong wide powers exercisable throughout the duration of the emergency * * * to continue to make regulations having the force of law notwithstanding that Parliament had previously sat. * * * To the force of law notwithstanding that Parliament has sat, it suffers from the extent, however, that the No. 1 Ordinance purports to authorise the Yang di-Pertuan Agong to continue to make instruments having the fatal constitutional flaw that such exercise of legislative power by the ruler after Parliament has sat, is not authorised by the Constitution itself nor has it been delegated to him by Parliament in whom the legislative authority of the Federation is vested.

* * * [O]nce Parliament had sat on February 20, 1971, the Yang di-Pertuan Agong no longer had any power to make Essential Regulations having the force of law. The Essential (Security Cases) (Amendment) Regulations 1975 purport to alter in respect of security cases the mode of trial laid down by the Criminal Procedure Code. They are ultra vires the Constitution and for that reason void.

Notes and Questions

1. One of dangers of extending executive emergency powers is that they will be applied beyond the situation contemplated at their adoption, in particular, to the prolongation of the emergency situation itself. (For example, war powers have been used to break strikes in peacetime.) Hence the importance of judicial review or some other form of constitutional control. Are courts the appropriate body to intervene in the event of abuse of emergency powers? See the debate on the issue regarding the review of military decisions in *Korematsu* in Chapter 6. Consider the view of Justice Starke (dissenting) in *Adelaide Company of Jehovah's Witnesses Inc. v. The Commonwealth*, (1943) 67 C.L.R. 116, 152:[o] "The courts must not, of course, forget that those who are responsible for the national security must be the best judges of what the national security requires, but still in Australia

---

o. In this case the majority of the High Court of Australia found constitutional the dissolution order regarding a Jehovah's Witnesses organization that was incorporated, and, likewise, the ban on its teachings. The majority found that the National Security Act, which authorized such measures, did not violate the free exercise clause of the Commonwealth Constitution as that freedom is not absolute and, moreover, that the ban on the teachings of the Witnesses was justified as being "unlawful doctrine." ("It needs no argument to show that the doctrine that the Commonwealth is an organ of Satan is prejudicial to any defence of the Commonwealth against the enemy.") Note that, by 1943, many Witnesses perished in Nazi concentration camps for their beliefs. Note further that this case was an authority in the *Anti-witnesses* cases, in Singapore (see Chapter 8).

neither the Parliament nor the Governor–General in Council can transcend the Constitution." This position reserves an ultimate constitutional review power for the courts in states of emergency.

In the American separation-of-powers system Congress has very little authority to review the actions of the executive, except if it specifically resolves that the President should report about his actions taken under legislative authorization. In a parliamentary system, as the Malaysian Constitution demonstrates, Parliament may review executive action taken in emergency. Should there not be more judicial review of emergency powers in the U.S. than in England, given the difference in the powers of their respective legislatures?

2.   The cases below address certain attempts of the judiciary to review the use of emergency powers. Some observers are skeptical about the possibilities of resisting the executive:

> Despite important differences in history and traditions, Argentina and the United States each adopted a presidentialist system and then limited the president's constitutional powers, only to have those restrictions abused and often ignored in the last century through actions justified as necessary responses to emergency conditions. While presidents of both countries have frequently acted unilaterally, the judicial and legislative branches have also contributed to the ascendant presidencies. Over time, the legislatures of both countries have become close to impotent, calling into question the efficacy of the separation of powers and of the presidential systems. Instead of performing their constitutionally assigned role of checking executive abuses and protecting individual rights, the congresses and courts often have acquiesced in lawless presidential action, and at times have authorized or upheld presidential emergency powers.
>
> This comparative examination of presidential emergency powers in Argentina and the United States confirms Justice Jackson's warning that "emergency powers * * * tend to kindle emergencies." [*Youngstown Sheet & Tube Co. v. Sawyer*, 343 U.S. 579, 650 (1952), (Justice Jackson concurring).] As presidents have accrued ever greater discretion to act outside the bounds of rules for "ordinary" times, presidents who wish to act aggressively in implementing personal policy goals have found "emergency" conditions a convenient path for their actions. Unfortunately, excesses in the exercise of presidential emergency powers have exacerbated the growing disrespect that our citizens have for their governments and laws.
>
> Our constitutions could not have anticipated the growth in the real powers of the modern presidency in either Argentina or the United States. While constitutional changes may be needed in Argentina to control the excessive use of emergency powers by the president, a better strategy for strengthened constitutional government in both nations is to turn to the congresses and courts and seek structural and institutional change which would provide these two branches with the means for curbing executive power.

Banks and Carrió, *op. cit.* at 3–4.

"LAWLESS" CASE

European Court of Human Rights.
1 E.H.R.R. 1 (1961).

[One of the recurrent issues of emergency is the extent to which Parliament may authorize the executive to declare emergency or at least to determine, once emergency is declared, that certain people can be detained. With the Offences Against the State (Amendment) Act of 1940, the Republic of Ireland (living in a state of insurgency, given disagreements with the IRA) was probably the first modern democracy to enact legislation authorizing the government to use preventive detention.[p] The Act was referred to the Supreme Court of Ireland by the President. The Irish Constitution has no specific provisions on detention, although it requires trial of offences. In *Matter of Article 26 of the Constitution,* [1940] I.R. 470, the Irish Supreme Court held that the Act did not establish an offence; hence there was no need for trial, and the Constitution's requirement of habeas corpus was satisfied as one may have a judge to review whether the conditions of detention are satisfied.

[The Irish detention scheme was challenged in the ECHR. In this case a court (an international one) looked into the legitimacy of the finding of emergency. Once it is found that emergency is rightly proclaimed, the detention is legitimate. Article 15 of the European HR Convention expressly authorizes that "[i]n time of war or other public emergency threatening the life of the nation any High Contracting Party may take measures derogating from its obligations under this Convention to the extent strictly required by the exigencies of the situation" if the Secretary General of the Council of Europe is properly notified. In 1957, the Republic of Ireland sent a notification and used mass arrest

---

p. The Constitution of India constitutionalized peacetime detention in Art. 22. "Article 22 was initially taken to be the only safeguard against the legislature in respect of laws relating to deprivation of life and liberty protected by Article 21." Mahendra P. Singh, *V.N. Shukla's Constitution of India* 181 (9th ed. 1996). Detentions lasting longer than three months are reviewed by an advisory panel, with the participation of judges.

The Preventive Detention Act of 1950 was reviewed in *Gopalan v. State of Madras,* Supreme Court, (1950) 1 S.C.R. 88; the Court accepted the very restrictive regime of the Act, arguing that in the context of detention, the requirement that a deprivation of liberty be according to law is satisfied as it is not meant in the U.S. sense of due process. Justice Patanjali Sastri gave the following explanation: "This sinister-looking feature, so strangely out of place in a democratic Constitution * * * is doubtless designed to prevent the abuse of freedom by anti-social and subversive elements which might peril the national welfare of the infant republic." *Id.* at 208.

It is noteworthy how far the *Gopalan* position may take a court: in *Additional District Magistrate, Jabalpur v. S.S. Shukla,* (1976) Supp. S.C.R. 172, it was "held that in case enforcement of Article 21 was suspended by a presidential order under Article 359, the Court could not enquire whether the executive action depriving a person of his life or personal liberty was authorised by law. Soon after the emergency and all that was done in its name were rejected by the electorates in early 1977, the Supreme Court in *Maneka Gandhi v. Union of India* [(1978) 1 S.C.R. 248] changed this unfortunate position and gave a fundamental character to the right in Article 21." Singh, *op. cit.* at 170.

The Supreme Court of India moved toward the U.S. due process position—what the founders expressly wanted to avoid. While the propriety or reasonableness of the detention order cannot be raised in Court, the "courts, however, scrutinise whether the detention is for a purpose for which the Act authorised it." Singh, *op. cit.* at 198.

and detention to prevent the aggravation of armed unrest. Lawless, an Irish citizen, who earlier was several times arrested and prosecuted (unsuccessfully) for belonging to the IRA and possession of arms, was interned and detained for several months under the Offences against the State Act. He was not brought to a judge nor was he charged with any offense. The ECHR reviewed the legality of the derogation.]

* * *

29. [W]hereas the homicidal ambush on the night 3rd to 4th July 1957 in the territory of Northern Ireland near the border had brought to light, just before 12th July—a date, which, for historical reasons is particularly critical for the preservation of public peace and order—the imminent danger to the nation caused by the continuance of unlawful activities in Northern Ireland by the IRA and various associated groups, operating from the territory of the Republic of Ireland;

30. Whereas, in conclusion, the Irish Government were justified in declaring that there was a public emergency in the Republic of Ireland threatening the life of the nation and were hence entitled, applying the provisions of Article 15, paragraph 1 [Art. 15–1], of the Convention for the purposes for which those provisions were made, to take measures derogating from their obligations under the Convention;

* * *

36. Whereas, however, considering, in the judgment of the Court, that in 1957 the application of the ordinary law had proved unable to check the growing danger which threatened the Republic of Ireland; whereas the ordinary criminal courts, or even the special criminal courts or military courts, could not suffice to restore peace and order; whereas, in particular, the amassing of the necessary evidence to convict persons involved in activities of the IRA and its splinter groups was meeting with great difficulties caused by the military, secret and terrorist character of those groups and the fear they created among the population; whereas the fact that these groups operated mainly in Northern Ireland, their activities in the Republic of Ireland being virtually limited to the preparation of armed raids across the border was an additional impediment to the gathering of sufficient evidence; whereas the sealing of the border would have had extremely serious repercussions on the population as a whole, beyond the extent required by the exigencies of the emergency;

Whereas it follows from the foregoing that none of the above-mentioned means would have made it possible to deal with the situation existing in Ireland in 1957; whereas, therefore, the administrative detention—as instituted under the Act (Amendment) of 1940—of individuals suspected of intending to take part in terrorist activities, appeared, despite its gravity, to be a measure required by the circumstances. * * *

UNITED COMMUNIST PARTY
OF TURKEY v. TURKEY

European Court of Human Rights.
26 E.H.R.R. 121 (1998).

[Lawless was the first case ever decided by the ECHR. Once the ECHR established itself as an authority in the member-states of the Council of Europe, it developed a stricter standard to review emergency.]

* * *

10. On 16 July 1991 the Constitutional Court made an order dissolving the TBKP [United Communist Party of Turkey]. * * *

The [Turkish] Constitutional Court went on to hold that the mere fact that a political party included in its name a word prohibited by section 96(3) of Law no. 2820, as the TBKP had done in the present case, sufficed to trigger the application of that provision and consequently to entail the dissolution of the party concerned.

As to the allegation that the TBKP's constitution and programme contained statements likely to undermine the territorial integrity of the State and the unity of the nation, the Constitutional Court noted, *inter alia*, that those documents referred to two nations: the Kurdish nation and the Turkish nation. But it could not be accepted that there were two nations within the Republic of Turkey, whose citizens, whatever their ethnic origin, had Turkish nationality. * * *

[The Constitutional Court reiterated] that self-determination and regional autonomy were prohibited by the Constitution, the Constitutional Court said that the State was unitary, the country indivisible and that there was only one nation. [The Turkish government referred to security concerns related to the Kurdish party in the context of the armed separatist Kurdish movement. Reference was made to the German preventive ban on the Communist Party by the GFCC in the name of militant democracy. On militant democracy see Chapter 11.]

* * *

58. Admittedly, it cannot be ruled out that a party's political programme may conceal objectives and intentions different from the ones it proclaims. To verify that it does not, the content of the programme must be compared with the party's actions and the positions it defends. In the present case, the TBKP's programme could hardly have been belied by any practical action it took, since it was dissolved immediately after being formed and accordingly did not even have time to take any action. It was thus penalised for conduct relating solely to the exercise of freedom of expression.

59. The Court is also prepared to take into account the background of cases before it, in particular the difficulties associated with the fight against terrorism. In the present case, however, it finds no evidence to enable it to conclude, in the absence of any activity by the TBKP, that the party bore any responsibility for the problems which terrorism poses in Turkey.

S.R. BOMMAI v. UNION OF INDIA

Supreme Court (India).
(1994) 2 S.C.R. 644.

[In India, where (as mentioned above) the temporary use of emergency is seen as inevitable, given the heterogeneity and complexity of the country, the Supreme Court repeatedly reviewed declarations of emergency and established its power to review the President's emergency decisions. It has established that the power conferred on the President to declare emergency, according to Art. 356, is a conditioned power; it is not an absolute power to be exercised at the President's discretion. Soli J. Sorabjee writes: "After the demolition of the Babri mosque at Ayodhya[,] President's rule was imposed in the States of Uttar Pradesh, Rajasthan, Madhya Pradesh and Himachal Pradesh where the ruling party was the Bharatiya Janata Party (BJP). Imposition of President's rule in Madhya Pradesh, Rajasthan and Himachal Pradesh was assailed in the High Courts. The High Court of Madhya Pradesh held that imposition of President's rule in Madhya Pradesh was unconstitutional and there was no relevant material to justify the action [in] *Sunderlal Patwa v. Union of India*. The Union of India filed an appeal to the Supreme Court." Sorabjee, *op. cit.* at 7.]

B.P. Jeevan Reddy, J.

* * * 289. The question then arises at what stage should he exercise this power? To answer this query, we must turn to clause (3). Clause (3) says that every Proclamation issued under Article 356(1) shall be laid before both Houses of Parliament and shall cease to operate at the expiry of two months unless before the expiration of that period it has been approved by resolutions passed by both Houses. This is conceived both as a check upon the power and as a vindication of the principle of parliamentary supremacy over the Executive. The President's action—which is really the action of the Union Council of Ministers—is subject to approval of both Houses of Parliament. Unless approved by both Houses of Parliament, the Proclamation lapses at the end of two months and earlier if it is disapproved or declined to be approved by both the Houses of Parliament, as explained hereinafter. Having regard to the incongruity of the Executive (even though Union Executive) dissolving the Legislature (even if of a State), it would be consistent with the scheme and spirit of the Constitution—particularly in the absence of a specific provision in the Constitution expressly empowering the President to do so—to hold that this power of dissolution can be exercised by the President only after both Houses of Parliament approve the Proclamation and not before such approval.

* * * 330. Since it is not disputed by the counsel for the Union of India and other respondents that the Proclamation under Article 356 is amenable to judicial review, it is not necessary for us to dilate on that aspect. The power under Article 356(1) is a conditional power. In exercise of the power of judicial review, the court is entitled to examine whether the condition has been satisfied or not. In what circumstances the court would interfere is a different matter but the amenability of the

action to judicial review is beyond dispute. It would be sufficient to quote a passage from *State of Rajasthan* [*v. Union of India*, (1978) 1 S.C.R. 1, 80–81 (Justice Bhagwati)]:

> "So long as a question arises whether an authority under the Constitution has acted within the limits of its power or exceeded it, it can certainly be decided by the court. Indeed it would be its constitutional obligation to do so * * * this Court is the ultimate interpreter of the Constitution and to this Court is assigned the delicate task of determining what is the power conferred on each branch of Government, whether it is limited, and if so, what are the limits and whether any action of that branch transgresses such limits. It is for this Court to uphold the constitutional values and to enforce the constitutional limitations. That is the essence of the rule of law."

* * * 375. It is necessary to reiterate that the court must be conscious while examining the validity of the Proclamation that it is a power vested in the highest constitutional functionary of the Nation. The court will not lightly presume abuse or misuse. * * * But all this does not mean that the President and the Union Council of Ministers are the final arbiters in the matter or that their opinion is conclusive. The very fact that the Founding Fathers have chosen to provide for approval of the Proclamation by Parliament is itself a proof of the fact that the opinion or satisfaction of the President (which always means the Union Council of Ministers with the Prime Minister at its head) is not final or conclusive. It is well-known that in the parliamentary form of Government, where the party in power commands a majority in Parliament more often than not, approval of Parliament by a simple majority is not difficult to obtain. Probably, it is for this reason that the check created by clause (3) of Article 356 has not proved to be as effective in practice as it ought to have been.

* * * 410. In the elections held in February 1990, the BJP emerged as the majority party in the Assemblies of Uttar Pradesh, Madhya Pradesh, Rajasthan and Himachal Pradesh and formed the Government therein.

* * * 413. The demolition of the disputed mosque at Ayodhya on December 6, 1992, had serious repercussions all over the country as also in some neighbouring countries.* * * Serious disturbance to law and order occurred in various parts of the country resulting in considerable loss of lives and property. By an order dated December 10, 1992 issued under Section 3(1) of the Unlawful Activities (Prevention) Act, 1967 (37 of 1967), the Government of India banned several alleged communal organisations including RSS, VHP and Bajrang Dal. * * *

Madhya Pradesh:

414.   On December 8, 1992, the Governor of Madhya Pradesh sent a report to the President setting out the "fast deteriorating law and order situation in the State in the wake of widespread acts of violence, arson and looting." * * * [He] recommended "that there should not be any further delay in imposition of President's rule according to Article

356 of the Constitution of India''. [Similar events led to the dissolution of other BJP-led governments.]

* * *

433. Having given our earnest consideration to the matter, we are of the opinion that the situation which arose in these States consequent upon the demolition of the disputed structure is one which cannot be assessed properly by the court. * * * [W]hat happened on December 6, 1992 was no ordinary event, that it was the outcome of a sustained campaign carried out over a number of years throughout the country and that it was the result of the speeches, acts and deeds of several leaders of B.J.P. and other organisations. * * * The situation was an extraordinary one; its repercussions could not be foretold at that time. Nobody could say with definiteness what would happen and where? The situation was not only unpredictable, it was a fast-evolving one. The communal situation was tense. It could explode anywhere at any time. On the material placed before us, including the reports of the Governors, we cannot say that the President had no relevant material before him.[q] * * * The Governor of Rajasthan reported that the ban on R.S.S. and other organisations was not being implementeed [sic] because of the intimate connection between the members of the Government and those organisations. * * * If the President was satisfied that the faith of these B.J.P. government [sic] in the concept of secularism was suspect in view of the acts and conduct of the party controlling these governments and that in the volatile situation that developed pursuant to the demolition, the government of these States cannot be carried on in accordance with the provisions of the Constitution, we are not able to say that there was no relevant material upon which he could be so satisfied. * * * If the President was satisfied that the Governments, which have already acted contrary to one of the basic features of the Constitution, viz., secularism, cannot be trusted to do so in future, it is not possible to say that in the situation then obtaining, he was not justified in believing so. This is precisely the type of situation, which the court cannot judge for lack of judicially manageable standards. The court could be well advised to leave such complex issues to the President and the Union Council of Ministers to deal with. It was a situation full of many imponderables, nuances, implications and intricacies. There were too many ifs and buts which are not susceptible of judicial scrutiny. It is not correct to depict the said Proclamations as the outcome of political vendetta by the political party in power at the centre against the other political party in power in some States. Probably in such matters, the ultimate arbiter is the people. The appeal should be to the people and to people alone. The challenge to the Proclamation relating to these three States is, therefore, liable to fail.
* * *

[In regard to the dissolutions in other states, the Court found the proclamations unconstitutional.] [See further, in chapters 4 and 8.]

---

q. That the ban was later held to be unsustainable by the appropriate Tribunal was not relevant in judging the situation that unfolded in the days following the demolition.

Notes and Questions

1. Note the elaborate reliance on the checks and balances of the different branches of power in the use of emergency declarations in the Indian Constitution. Nevertheless, the Court finds insufficient the mere observance of the delicate intergovernmental procedure; hence the need for its intervention. The justices disagreed on the basis and the extent of their review power, especially regarding the correctness of the facts leading to the presidential proclamation. The intervention is nevertheless impressive, especially in view of what Carl Schmitt, a law professor and, for a season, Hitler's favorite jurist, argued: the sovereign declares emergency. (The power to declare an emergency makes one into a sovereign.) In India, the "sovereign" is limited by judicial review. Is the power of the Indian Court a "judicial" one as it reacts to emergency situations and not under an established emergency rule?

Soli J. Sorabjee argues that the ISC makes this clear:

Article 356 can be invoked only in cases where non-compliance with the Constitution is of such a nature that it results in situations which create an impasse and are not capable of being remedied and where governance of the State has become impossible.

It is respectfully submitted that the majority view is sound and well-founded. It gives effect to the intent of the Founding Fathers, takes into account the experience of the actual operation of Article 356 in our country, pays due regard to the principle of federalism and Centre–State relations and provides a salutary and much needed check on the deep potential for misuse of Article 356.

Sorabjee, *op. cit.* at 11.

Is a court, in reviewing the factual basis and perhaps even the wisdom of an emergency proclamation, violating the political question doctrine? Is emergency only a matter of political muscle? If judicial review of emergency is a constitutional exercise of judicial power, then perhaps a court is also entitled to find that the government failed to declare emergency. The Pakistani system allows the President to dissolve Parliament by declaring martial law, although new elections must be called. The Pakistani cases related to the Bhutto government (see above) indicate the limits of judicial review. In Pakistan, the Supreme Court's position was determined in 1998 by its long-standing conflict with the Prime Minister. Consider, however, the position of the South African Constitution. Article 34 authorizes any competent court to decide on the validity of a declaration of a state of emergency or on any legislation enacted, or other action taken, in consequence of a declaration of a state of emergency. Emergency was abused in the apartheid era, and the postapartheid Constitution contains one of the most elaborate system of guarantees against the repetition of that experience. Compare Art. 356 of the Indian Constitution with Art. 34 of the South African one. In India, the President plays a decisive role in declaring emergency, while in South Africa "a state of emergency may be declared only in terms of an Act of Parliament" and only for 21 days.

2. The activities and omissions of local authorities were at the heart of the problem in the case of the Indian emergency. The gravest form of such local disorder is the one where local, often democratically elected, authorities

or local movements attempt secession, endangering the territorial integrity of the state. (Of course, this might be justified in terms of self-determination.) This issue came up in the *Chechnya Case* (Resolution of July 31, 1995, No. 10, RCC). Chechnya is a republic of the Russian Federation ("subject of the federation"), having a mixed population of Muslim Chechens (an indigenous population decimated under Stalin) and Russians. The elected government ignored Russian laws and political requests, restricted federal authorities from operating in the republic, and contemplated some form of self-determination. The actions of the Chechen government (including an alleged military buildup) were considered mutinous by the central government. In 1994, President Yeltsin ordered Russian military intervention to impose an emergency regime in Chechnya. The action resulted in gross human rights violations and extensive fighting, without achieving the military's goals.

Yeltsin's decision to use military force came up for review in the RCC. The complaint argued that there was no legislation to implement the constitutional provisions regarding the protection of territorial integrity, a duty imposed on the President as determined by law. The repeated interventions of Russian federal authorities in Chechnya were presented by the central authorities as necessitated by such concerns as the federation's integrity, the systematic abuse of human rights, and acts of banditry. (Note that Russia inherited a self-contradictory legal system from the Soviet Union and that the Duma was unwilling to cooperate with the President to enact new legislation in conformity with the new 1993 Constitution.) The RCC found that the rules on deportation from the Chechen Republic of persons posing a threat to public security and citizens' personal safety and certain provisions on the accreditation of journalists working in the area of the military conflict violated specific provisions in the Constitution on residence and free speech. The Court's only sanction, however, was that damages be paid if such requests arose. The Court found that the presidential decree that authorized the use of military force to break the activity of illegally armed units was adopted within the scope of the constitutional powers of the President. The President had such legislative power, which established the basis for intervention, because under the Constitution, Art. 78 part 4, he "shall have power to exercise the authority of the federal state power throughout the territory." In Art. 80 para. 2 he is guarantor of the Constitution; in Art. 82 part 1 he takes an oath to protect the integrity of the state; and in Art. 90 part 3 he has decree-making powers. Note that the Constitution itself states that its rules are directly applicable and Art. 4 (3) states that the Russian Federation shall ensure the integrity and inviolability of its territory. Further, Art 13 (5) prohibits the activities of public associations whose aims are directed at violating the Russian Federation's territorial integrity. The Court said: "The preamble of Presidential Decree No. 2166 legitimately refers to article 13 (part 5) * * * However, outlawing such activities does not have legal consequence since it distorts the text of the constitutional norm and is not based on effective legislation."

One could argue that the President could not wait until public order had collapsed and the Chechen rebels had destroyed the territorial integrity of Russia. It was the Duma's omission that left legislation on the matter lacking; the President had to use his constitutional authority. (Note that the Weimar Constitution required that the legislature determine the conditions of emergency, but no law was ever enacted, and there were no limits on emergency declarations. This was the silence that enabled Hitler's use of emergency powers.)

The Court refrained from evaluating whether an actual danger to territorial integrity existed: "Pursuant to article 3 (part 2) of the Federal Constitutional Law 'On Constitutional Court of the Russian Federation,' the Constitutional Court of the Russian Federation will not consider the political expediency of decisions made, nor will it consider the adequacy of measures taken on the basis of such decisions." (Did the ISC go further in this regard?) Although the RCC was silent (for lack of competence) on the nature of the intervention, it tacitly admitted that such evaluation was part of the executive privilege that is based on the duties of the executive. In other respects the Court found that the decrees were issued on the basis of constitutional powers as these were measures to protect state security. It made use of the fundamental-rights-protection provisions. The Russian Constitution follows the trend of the European HR Convention and makes individual rights restrictions, e.g., deportation orders, conditional upon a formal declaration of a state of emergency, according to law and limited in time. These conditions, which are likely to be subject to judicial review, were not formally satisfied in the present case.

3. The ambitions of the executive and the incapacity of, or lack of a majority in, Parliament often invite emergency executive legislation. Constitutionally authorized constitutional courts sometimes tend to restrict such action, emphasizing the exceptional nature of emergency powers. The Romanian Constitutional Court declared in Decision 65/1995 that in order to establish the existence of exceptional circumstances and thus the constitutionality of an emergency order of the executive, it had to be shown that "because of exceptional circumstances, there is an urgent need to regulate a situation through the adoption of immediate measures in order to avoid serious harm to the public interest." Exceptional cases have an objective character, subject to judicial review, and are not simply a matter of government discretion.

4. A major danger to constitutionalism in Latin America is related to *decretismo*. The executive tends to rule through decrees that, in principle, are applicable only for a limited period of time; but the executive often possesses constitutional power to keep the decree in force through continuous extensions. In Argentina, the constitutional reform of 1994 introduced a concept of decree on the grounds of necessity and urgency (Art. 99.3). As the Supreme Court ruled, the measure was not intended to abolish separation of powers but to reduce presidentialism and strengthen the legislature. The decrees may be adopted in certain matters only, decided on by general agreement of the ministers (i.e., not the President), and are subject to submission to a bicameral committee of the national Congress. One of the following conditions must be met:

—it is impossible for the law to be passed in accordance with the ordinary procedure as laid down in the Constitution, e.g., if the Houses of the National Congress were prevented from sitting by force majeure, or

—the situation requiring legislation is of such urgency that a decision must be taken immediately, within a time frame which is incompatible with that of the normal legislative process.

The judiciary reviews the constitutionality of decrees issued on the grounds of necessity and urgency, including the assessment of facts. The Court has found that writing into a decree an agreement among the government, employees, and the employer associations, cutting back on welfare rights, is not a matter of urgency. 19.08.1999., V.916.XXXII, BCCL 1999. 344; see also Chapter 10.

5. The Italian Constitution (Art. 77.2–3) authorizes the government to issue law-decrees with the force of law in "exceptional" cases of urgency and necessity. The law-decrees are temporary; they must be submitted to Parliament on the day of their adoption. If the law-decree is not converted into law within 60 days, it loses its validity (as of the day of issuance). The Constitutional Court recognizes that reiterating law-decrees may have negative effects on the separation of powers, as do legal relations and secondary norms created under the law-decrees. The Court concluded that reiteration of law-decrees is implicitly prohibited and contrary to the intent of the framers. The reiteration is permissible only if an independent ground for necessity and urgency emerges. If the reiterated law-decree is converted into law, however, it is interpreted as full validation (Decision 360/1996).

6. *Emergency Powers and International Terrorism: The case of the United States After September 11, 2001.* On September 11, 2001, several commercial airlines hijacked by foreign nationals were flown into the two towers of the World Trade Center in New York City and the Pentagon in Washington, D.C., causing approximately 3,000 deaths. In reaction to these attacks, the President of the U.S. issued a Presidential Proclamation (No. 7463, 66 Fed. Reg. 48, 199, Sept. 14, 2001) declaring a national emergency by reason of the terrorist attacks. On September 18, 2001, the U.S. Congress authorized the President "to use all necessary and appropriate force against all nations, organizations, or persons he determines planned, authorized, committed, or aided the terrorist attacks" or "harbored such organizations or persons." Pub. L. No. 107–40, 115 Stat. 224 (2001). On October 26, 2001, the Congress enacted the so-called "USA Patriot Act," Pub. L. No. 107–56, 115 Stat. 272 (2002), which, among other things, allows for much broader surveillance and wiretapping of suspected terrorists; for detention of non-U.S. citizens suspected of terrorism without specific charges for up to one week; and which makes it illegal to knowingly harbor a terrorist. Furthermore, on November 13, 2001, President Bush issued an executive order instituting the use of military commissions to try suspected foreign terrorists, 66 Fed. Reg. 57, 883 (2001).

In what quickly became the most controversial measure in the aftermath of September 11, the President invoked his constitutional powers as Commander in Chief of the U.S. Armed Forces and the September 18 Congressional authorization cited above as the sources of his authority for creating special military tribunals. The President noted that international terrorists, including members of al Quaeda, had carried out terrorist acts against the U.S., that they were likely to carry out further attacks in the future causing massive death and placing "at risk the continuity of the operations of the United States Government," and that effective military actions against terrorism and prevention of planned terrorist acts makes it necessary for individuals subject to this order "to be tried for violations of the law of war and other applicable laws by military tribunals". The President concluded that national security in light of the emergency caused by terrorism precluded use of ordinary courts and the full panoply of constitutional guarantees afforded criminal defendants when bringing presumed foreign terrorists to justice. The Order specifies that only noncitizens, including members of al Quaeda who have engaged in or "aided or abetted or conspired to commit acts of international terrorism" and whose aim is to cause "adverse effects" on the U.S., "its citizens, national security, foreign policy or economy", can be tried by these special courts. The Order prescribes trial by military judges, allows conviction and sentencing, including imposition of the death sentence, by a vote of two-thirds of the military judges, lifts certain restrictions imposed by the rules of criminal procedure and evidence, and permits withholding relevant secret evidence from defendants. Finally, convictions by a Military Commission cannot be appealed to ordinary courts, the President having reserved for himself the right of final review. Procedures for trials by Military Commissions were set by the Secretary of Defense on March 21, 2002 (MCO No. 1), and introduced two important changes to the original Executive Order: 1) imposition of a death sentence requires the unanimous vote of the military judges; and 2) conviction shall be by "proof beyond a reasonable doubt" applicable in ordinary criminal trials rather than the more relaxed standard contemplated in the original Order.

At this writing, there have been no trials by military commission. But several actions, detentions, and trials since September 11, 2001, have sparked an animated constitutional debate and generated a number of judicial decisions by lower federal courts. After conducting a war in Afghanistan against the Taliban government and al Quaeda operatives in the fall of 2001, the U.S. captured several hundred prisoners and transported them to its naval base in Guantanamo, Cuba. These prisoners, all non-citizens, have been held there in detention and interrogated without charges against them being filed. Moreover, several persons, citizens and non-citizens, suspected of terrorism or of having relevant information relating to terrorism, have been incarcerated in the U.S. without charges and, in several cases, denied access to an attorney.

Two principal constitutional issues are raised by these developments: 1) whether creation of the Military Commissions amounts to an unwarranted extension of executive powers? and 2) whether a large number of the detentions in the U.S. and in Guantanamo are violations of individual rights protected by the Bill of Rights? Underlying these two issues is a seeming confusion succinctly articulated by Professor George Fletcher: "[T]he Bush team has been uncertain whether they are fighting a war or trying to arrest those who financed and organized the attacks of September 11. They cannot quite decide whether this was a collective crime of al-Quaeda and the Taliban, in which case a war is the proper response, or the individual crime of Osama bin Laden and others * * * in which case a criminal prosecution is the correct action." *American Prospect*, Jan. 1, 2002, p.26.

The Military Commissions may be unconstitutional under the criteria set in *Ex Parte Milligan,* above, but its proponents argue that it falls under the exceptions established in *Ex Parte Quirin*, 317 U.S. 1 (1942) In that case trials by military commission were held of seven German saboteurs who entered the U.S., hid their military uniforms, and were caught with explosives on the way to destroying U.S. facilities. The Supreme Court upheld their convictions, holding defendants to be "unlawful combatants" accused of violating the "laws of war" and hence subject to military courts notwithstanding that U.S. civilian courts were functioning normally. Opponents of the November 13, 2001 Order argue that *Quirin* is distinguishable because President Roosevelt unlike President Bush had Congressional authorization for military Commissions during World War II, and because the *Quirin* exception is limited to cases involving spying. On the other hand, Art. III of the U.S. Constitution grants Congress the power to create new inferior federal courts. Should that grant of power determine whether Bush's Military Commissions are constitutional?

Concerning alleged violations of constitutional rights of individuals detained for prolonged periods without charges, the Bush Administration has claimed that these are "enemy combatants" whose detention is necessary for "intelligence gathering" purposes. In *Hamdi v. Rumsfeld*, 296 F. 3d 278 (4th Cir. 2002), involving a U.S. citizen jailed for an indeterminate period and refused access to counsel, a federal appellate court held that the President had broad powers in military affairs and that an "enemy combatant" could be held at least until the "end of hostilities." The government had captured Hamdi during the hostilities in Afghanistan and argued that it had sole power to determine whether he was an "enemy combatant." The court refused to endorse this last argument—at least prior to final adjudication of Hamdi's claims on the merits. Should the courts become involved in determining who is an "enemy combatant"? Moreover, is detention until the "end of hostilities" an acceptable standard in the "war against terrorism" where the enemy is often invisible and the conduct of operations intermittent and without end in sight?

Detention of non-citizens outside the United States does not give rise to recognizable rights under U.S. constitutional law, and thus, presumably, use of Military Commissions beyond U.S. territory would not generate individual rights (as opposed to separation of powers) violations. *See Rasul v. Bush,* 215 F. Supp. 2d 55 (D.D.C.2002) (aliens held outside the sovereign territory of the U.S. cannot use U.S. courts to pursue claims under the U.S. Constitution. Guantanamo is not sovereign territory of U.S. as it is held pursuant to a lease agreement with Cuba). However, the Military Commissions and the treatment of aliens in Guantanamo may violate international law. *See* Christopher M. Evans, *Terrorism on Trial: The President's Constitutional Authority to Order the Prosecution of Suspected Terrorists By Military Commission,* 51 Duke L.J. 1831, 1851–54 (2002).

Chapter 4

FEDERALISM AND VERTICAL SEPARATION OF POWERS

Governmental powers can be apportioned vertically at different levels. Five levels of vertical government are distinguishable, moving from the purely local to the truly global: (1) local, i.e., municipal or citywide; (2) subnational–regional, i.e., state or provincial; (3) national, i.e., federal; (4) supranational, e.g., the European Union; and (5) global (arguably, the United Nations possesses some aspects of a global government, but no truly global government can be said to yet exist).

Vertical division of powers takes form either through federalism (federation or confederation) or through decentralization. Section A. compares various forms of federalism, whereas Section B. explores the ways in which decentralization is achieved in nonfederal states. Section C. focuses on the relation between the federal government and its federated entities. Specifically, Subsection C.1. explores the democratic tensions between federal sovereignty and federated-entity sovereignty. Subsection C.2. concentrates on conflicts concerning the apportionment of powers between the federation and its federated entities, including the relation between exclusive and concurrent powers, federal regulation of private conduct and federated-entity rights, federated-entity regulation and federation supremacy, and federal regulation of federated-entity activities. The chapter concludes with a note on the EU's supranational federalism.

A. FEDERALISM'S VARIOUS FORMS

There is a crucial distinction between federal states, such as the United States, Canada, Germany, Switzerland, and India, and unitary states, like France and Italy. Federal states maintain a constitutionally established vertical division of powers among federal and federated entities, while unitary states possess no such entrenched division of powers to apportion responsibilities among various levels of government. (See Section B., below, for a discussion on decentralization in unitary states.) Beyond this fundamental divide, federal systems exhibit considerable diversity. In this section we briefly examine some of the most important.

Federal systems may differ in their purpose, structure, and function. In general terms federalism can achieve two different purposes: (1) "distributive" purposes and (2) "identity-related" purposes. Distributive federalism is concerned primarily with apportioning political power among different levels of government. American federalism, for example, is embedded in a constitutional scheme designed to maintain a system of checks and balances that mitigates the threat of any "tyranny of the majority," through the layering and fragmenting of competing majorities. See *The Federalist* Nos. 10 and 51. In such a distributive scheme not only is democracy at the federal level limited by democracy at the state level, but in addition, the latter is apportioned among a multiplicity of individual states.

Identity-based federalism seeks primarily to preserve significant autonomy either for ethnic, religious, or linguistic groups. India is an example of identity-based federalism. Its multiethnic federalism saw the reorganizations of the states, in the 1950s, to mirror differences along linguistic lines. See S.D. Muni, *Ethnic Conflict, Federalism and Democracy in India*, in *Ethnicity and Power in the Contemporary World* ch. 10 (Kumar Rupesinghe and Valery A. Tishkov eds., 1996).[a] Similarly, Swiss cantons are divided along linguistic as well as religious lines. See Thomas Fleiner, *Switzerland: Constitution of the Federal State and the Cantons,* in *Federalism and Multiethnic States: The Case of Switzerland* 103–44 (Lidija R. Basta Fleiner and Thomas Fleiner eds., 2d ed. 2000). Furthermore, in Switzerland, linguistic identities predominate in certain instances—e.g., public education is conducted in the official language of some cantons—and religious identities predominate in others—e.g., some Catholic cantons long denied Protestant minorities certain privileges accorded Catholics. *Id.* at 104–05, 135–38.

While distributive-based and identity-based federalism are not mutually exclusive, they can be distinguished, according to whether political-autonomy concerns or identity concerns predominate. Moreover, some forms of federalism can be genuinely described as combining distributive-based and identity-based characteristics. Such is the case of Canadian federalism, which may be regarded as identity-based from the standpoint of French-speaking Quebec and distributive-based in the Anglophone provinces. See Katherine Swinton, *Federalism Under Fire: The Role of the Supreme Court of Canada*, 55 Law and Contemp. Probs. 121, 122 (1992).

In terms of structures the major distinction is found in the difference between federations and confederations. Although these terms are not always used consistently, in its technical sense a "confederation" is "a loose association of states in which the central government is subordinate to the states * * * [i.e.,] the central government is the delegate of the states [which assign it certain powers and which] retain the right to resume the delegated powers if they wish." Peter W. Hogg, *Constitutional Law of Canada* 106 (4th ed. 1997). In a federation, on the other hand,

a. Available at <www.unu.edu/unupress/unubooks/uu12ee/uu12ee00.htm>.

the federal government is independent from, and coordinate with or superior to, the states. In a democratic federation, the federal government is directly answerable to the national electorate rather than indirectly to the electorates of the several states. See *McCulloch v. Maryland*, 17 U.S. 316 (1819), below. A few years after its 1776 independence from the United Kingdom, the U.S. went from a confederation, under the 1781 Articles of Confederation, to a federation, under the 1787 Constitution. The foremost reason for this transformation was the failure of the confederation's weak central government to curb destructive economic competition among the American states. See Laurence Tribe, *American Constitutional Law* 32 n.7, 404 (2d ed. 1988). Finally, federative arrangements need not be purely federal or confederal. For example, although the EU has its roots in a limited-purpose confederation, arguably, it has grown to combine federal and confederal features. See "Note on Transnational Federalism: The Case of the European Union," at the conclusion of this chapter.

How a federal system functions is dependent on its structure, though structuring alone cannot account for all the significant differences in functions. Thus U.S. federalism is characterized by a legalistic approach, resulting in a clear separation of powers and rights between the federal government and the states, while Canada and Germany have developed versions of federalism marked by greater cooperation between levels of government and a greater blending of federal and federated institutions. Consider the following comparison between U.S. federalism and its Canadian counterpart.

Martha A. Field, THE DIFFERING FEDERALISMS OF CANADA AND THE UNITED STATES

55 Law and Contemp. Probs. 107, 108–110, 112–114, 118–119 (1992).

* * *

If anyone ever entertained the notion that there was a "normal" way for federalism to be structured, a comparison of the distribution of legislative power in the United States and Canada would dispel that notion. On one level, there are noticeable differences in where particular powers are lodged. Marriage and divorce and criminal law, for example, are governed by the central government in Canada but by the state governments in the United States, while labor law, nationalized in the United States, is an area jealously guarded by Canada's provincial governments. Moreover, Canadian provinces have much more exclusive power over local commerce * * *. The U.S. Congress, by comparison, has authority to regulate essentially all economic activity.

Even more basic than the different distribution of particular powers are the structural differences between the systems. In Canada, the federal and provincial governments are each assigned certain categories of legislation, to the exclusion of the other. If the government to which the subject has been entrusted does not act, therefore, the subject goes unregulated. In the United States, by contrast, the norm is that the nonexercise of federal power to regulate increases the area for state regulation; there are few if any separate spheres in which it is constitutionally permissible only for states to regulate.

* * *

In both countries the intent was that the government with the residual power would play the stronger role. The framers of the U.S. Constitution intended federal law to be supreme, but they also assumed that the subject matter of federal law would be limited, so that the [Tenth Amendment]—"The powers not delegated to the United States by the Constitution, nor prohibited by it to the States, are reserved to the States respectively, or the people"—would have some content. The general lawmaking power thus retained by states, including the basic police power functions of government, were thought to have some significant scope. But because in the U.S. governmental structure the tenth amendment was only a truism, granting to states only whatever power was not possessed by the federal government, expansions of federal power *ipso facto* cut down on what was reserved to the states. Eventually, federal powers in the United States were interpreted so broadly that little or nothing remained of the residuum.

The obvious example of broad interpretation of a federal power having this effect is the commerce clause, giving Congress power to regulate interstate commerce. The clause has been read to allow Congress to regulate any activity that could have any impact at all on interstate commerce, leaving Congress free to regulate any economic activity it wishes and displacing any separate sphere for state legislative control of the economy. The framers could not have foreseen the extent to which Congress would be empowered to control the economy.

In Canada, by contrast, the clause giving the central government control over trade and commerce has been interpreted to allow regulation on only international or interprovincial trade. That narrow interpretation of the commerce power is part of a more general cutback on the powers of the central government. Other legislative powers, most notably the power of the central government "to make laws for the Peace, Order and good Government of Canada" ("POGG"), were also narrowly read.

* * *

In the United States, the Constitution does not define the areas in which state law can operate; instead, it leaves that decision to be made primarily by Congress. While in comparison to the Canadian provinces the states are weak vis-à-vis the national legislature (except for their representation there), they are more insulated from national control in other ways. There is no predefined area in which state law can operate in the United States, but when it does operate, it is more autonomous and has more independent force than provincial law does in Canada.

In the United States, national courts sometimes apply state law, but they never claim to be its interpreter. State law is, by definition, what that state's Supreme Court says it is. However unreasonable a state's reading of its own law may appear to the U.S. Supreme Court, that law nonetheless governs unless the U.S. Supreme Court holds that the law, so interpreted, violates the U.S. Constitution.

* * *

Canada has a system of provincial courts, which are in fact the primary courts in Canada. When it reviews their decisions, however, the Canadian Supreme Court has the final word in deciding issues of common law and also in interpreting provincial enactments. Provincial law is not separated from national law or from the input of national judicial decisionmakers in the same way state law is in the United States.

* * *

In short, while the Canadian model recognizes much more of a separate and exclusive legislative sphere for provincial lawmaking than the U.S. model does for the states, it does not grant as much independence to the provincial law that is thus made; Canada has more centralized judicial control of provincial law, and provincial courts have less of a separate sphere than provincial legislatures do, or than the state judicial system does in the United States.

This may tell us something about federalism. It certainly suggests that there are varied ways for the different levels of government, which are the essence of federalism, to maintain their significance. It may be that one reason Canada does not need a separate, more independent provincial law is that the Canadian Constitution leaves for provinces important spheres of activity in which only provincial law can operate. Maybe as long as a nation has one of these forms of strong state or provincial power, it does not need others for there to be a strong intergovernmental relationship—strong enough to satisfy the demands of a viable federalism. Even powers as basic as a separate sphere of legislative competence or the ability to interpret one's own laws are not necessary in order for governments to retain significance if governments have other important powers.

The U.S. states and the Canadian provinces achieve their power through different mechanisms. In the United States, states remain significant units of government because they have the significant power of a separate and independent state law over which the state has the final word.[18] Moreover, there is a large area in which state law operates, although the area is not predefined or protected from possible future congressional encroachment.

In many ways, the *most* basic theme about Canadian governmental structure, including federalism, in relation to that of the United States, is that there is a less-felt need in Canada for separation of functions or clear definition of boundaries. While Canada's provinces do have a separate legislative sphere, in contrast to the states in the U.S. system, in all other ways the Canadian system has significantly less separation of

---

18. State law is subject to federal constitutional law, and in that sense is within the control of the federal judiciary, but unless the state law is held unconstitutional, the state, through its legislature, courts, or other agencies, can define what the law is and what it means.

functions than our own. Not only do national courts review provincial laws, but the central government participates in the appointment and compensation of most provincial judges. Provincial governors also are appointed by the national executive and are removable for cause by him or her. The Senate is also controlled by the Governor General through appointment of each senator and one speaker, a process that may affect the Senate's concern with national issues more than regional ones. Moreover, the Constitution gives the national government the power of disallowance, that is, the power to disallow any provincial legislation within a year of its passage, even legislation involving subjects delegated to the provinces. The power may exist in theory only (today it is not used), but its recognition in the Constitution shows a contemplation of intermixing functions, both between the judiciary and the other branches and between the provinces and the national government.

Moreover, the Canadian style of decisionmaking is more one of working things out through negotiation and compromise than one of finding the "right answer" to each problem or having one authoritative decisionmaker. Negotiation is a dominant form of the exercise power in Canada, including negotiation between the central and the provincial governments. This practice in some ways treats the provinces like separate sovereigns whose content must be obtained. Indeed, a primary forum for governmental decisionmaking in Canada is "executive federalism," whereby disputed issues are resolved through meetings and negotiations between the different levels of government.

Instead of dealing with economic problems on a nationwide basis through federal legislation, as the U.S. Congress does, Canada deals with these and other important and sensitive matters through negotiation, principally at federal-provincial conferences.

     * * *

In general, the Canadian attitude is that legalisms and legal analysis are less important than political flexibility, "cooperative federalism," negotiation and adjustment, and sharing of power. The United States resembles Canada in that it is not bound by the original understanding of its Constitution's composers. But unlike Canada, the U.S. power structure is based on legalisms, on a carefully worked-out hierarchy of rights, and not on practical stances like bargaining and compromise, to work out the bounds of central and state/provincial power.

Federalism can be used either to centralize disperse and largely unintegrated powers or to decentralize and divide concentrated powers. As seen by the transition from the Articles of Confederation to the 1787 Constitution, U.S. federalism was created initially to centralize dispersed powers that had proved inefficient. Post–World War Two German federalism, on the other hand, was adopted to ensure against any future kind of centralization of power achieved by Hitler during the Third Reich. Furthermore, to the extent that the creation of the EU can be viewed as a move toward federalism, clearly it seems to involve a centralizing federalism. By requiring transfers of powers from member-states to supranational institutions, however, the EU's integration fosters decentralization within the member-states. For example, the German states—the *Länder*—acquired new powers through amendment of the Basic Law, in an effort to allow for greater integration of Germany into the EU pursuant to the 1992 Maastricht Treaty. See Donald P. Kommers, *The Constitutional Jurisprudence of the Federal Republic of Germany* 107–08 (2d ed. 1997).

To better grasp how federalism can vary from one setting to the next, the following is a brief discussion of the respective federalism of the U.S., Germany, Switzerland, India, Canada, and Belgium.

A.1.   THE U.S.: PRAGMATIC AND ELASTIC FEDERALISM

As already noted, U.S. federalism relies on a federal government of limited and enumerated powers, with all remaining powers left to the states. This would seem to make for a weak central government and strong states, but the history of U.S. federalism reveals dramatic changes since the early nineteenth century. The central government, in fact, has since become much more powerful than the states, but the respective strengths of the two have been subject to ebbs and flows. Thus the federal government was most powerful in the period between 1937 and 1980, and state powers have slightly but steadily increased since that time, with a palpable acceleration after 1995.

McCULLOCH v. MARYLAND
Supreme Court (United States).
17 U.S. 316 (1819).

[The U.S. Congress chartered a federal bank that established a branch in Baltimore, Maryland. Maryland imposed taxes and fines on banks not incorporated in the state and on their cashiers. McCulloch, the cashier of the federal bank branch in Baltimore who was fined for failure to comply with applicable state law, appealed to the U.S. Supreme Court.]

Chief Justice Marshall delivered the opinion of the Court.

* * *

The first question made in the cause is—has congress power to incorporate a bank?

* * *

In discussing this question, the counsel for the state of Maryland have deemed it of some importance, in the construction of the constitution, to consider that instrument, not as emanating from the people, but as the act of sovereign and independent states. The powers of the general government, it has been said, are delegated by the states, who alone are truly sovereign; and must be exercised in subordination to the states, who alone possess supreme dominion.

It would be difficult to sustain this proposition. The convention which framed the constitution was indeed elected by the state legislatures. But the instrument, when it came from their hands, was a mere proposal, without obligation, or pretensions to it. It was reported to the then existing congress of the United States, with a request that it might 'be submitted to a convention of delegates, chosen in each state by the people thereof, under the recommendation of its legislature, for their assent and ratification.' This mode of proceeding was adopted; and by the convention, by congress, and by the state legislatures, the instrument was submitted to the *people*. They acted upon it in the only manner in which they can act safely, effectively and wisely, on such a subject, by assembling in convention. It is true, they assembled in their several states—and where else should they have assembled? No political dreamer was ever wild enough to think of breaking down the lines which separate the states, and of compounding the American people into one common mass. Of consequence, when they act, they act in their states. But the measures they adopt do not, on that account, cease to be the measures of the people themselves, or become the measures of the state governments.

From these conventions, the constitution derives its whole authority. The government proceeds directly from the people; is 'ordained and established,' in the name of the people; and is declared to be ordained, 'in order to form a more perfect union, establish justice, insure domestic tranquillity, and secure the blessings of liberty to themselves and to their posterity.' The assent of the states, in their sovereign capacity, is implied, in calling a convention, and thus submitting that instrument to the people. But the people were at perfect liberty to accept or reject it; and their act was final. It required not the affirmance, and could not be negatived, by the state governments. The constitution, when thus adopted, was of complete obligation, and bound the state sovereignties.
* * *

To the formation of a league, such as was the confederation, the state sovereignties were certainly competent. But when, 'in order to form a more perfect union,' it was deemed necessary to change this alliance into an effective government, possessing great and sovereign powers, and acting directly on the people, the necessity of referring it to the people, and of deriving its powers directly from them, was felt and acknowledged by all. The government of the Union, then (whatever may be the influence of this fact on the case), is, emphatically and truly, a government of the people. In form, and in substance, it emanates from them. Its powers are granted by them, and are to be exercised directly on them, and for their benefit.

This government is acknowledged by all, to be one of enumerated powers.
      * * *

[Moreover,] if any one proposition could command the universal assent of mankind, we might expect it would be this—that the government of the Union, though limited in its powers, is supreme within its sphere of action. This would seem to result, necessarily, from its nature.

It is the government of all; its powers are delegated by all; it represents all, and acts for all. Though any one state may be willing to control its operations, no state is willing to allow others to control them. The nation, on those subjects on which it can act, must necessarily bind its component parts. But this question is not left to mere reason: the people have, in express terms, decided it, by saying, 'this constitution, and the laws of the United States, which shall be made in pursuance thereof,' 'shall be the supreme law of the land,' and by requiring that the members of the state legislatures, and the officers of the executive and judicial departments of the states, shall take the oath of fidelity to it. The government of the United States, then, though limited in its powers, is supreme; and its laws, when made in pursuance of the constitution, form the supreme law of the land, 'anything in the constitution or laws of any state to the contrary notwithstanding.'

Among the enumerated powers, we do not find that of establishing a bank or creating a corporation. But there is no phrase in the instrument which * * * excludes incidental or implied powers * * *

Although, among the enumerated powers of government, we do not find the word 'bank' or 'incorporation,' we find the great powers, to lay and collect taxes; to borrow money; to regulate commerce; to declare and conduct a war; and to raise and support armies and navies. The sword and the purse, all the external relations, and no inconsiderable portion of the industry of the nation are entrusted to its government. * * * [A] government, entrusted with such ample powers, on the due execution of which the happiness and prosperity of the nation so vitally depends, must also be entrusted with ample means for their execution. The power being given, it is the interest of the nation to facilitate its execution. It can never be their interest, and cannot be presumed to have been their intention, to clog and embarrass its execution, by withholding the most appropriate means.

* * *

It is not denied, that the powers given to the government imply the ordinary means of execution. That, for example, of raising revenue, and applying it to national purposes, is admitted to imply the power of conveying money from place to place, as the exigencies of the nation may require, and of employing the usual means of conveyance. But it is denied, that the government has its choice of means; or, that it may employ the most convenient means, if, to employ them, it be necessary to erect a corporation.

The creation of a corporation, it is said, appertains to sovereignty. This is admitted. But to what portion of sovereignty does it appertain? Does it belong to one more than to another? In America, the powers of sovereignty are divided between the government of the Union, and those of the states. They are each sovereign, with respect to the objects committed to it, and neither sovereign, with respect to the objects committed to the other. * * * The power of creating a corporation, though appertaining to sovereignty, is not, like the power of making war, or levying taxes, or of regulating commerce, a great substantive and independent power, which cannot be implied as incidental to other powers, or used as a means of executing them. It is never the end for which other powers are exercised, but a means by which other objects are accomplished. * * *

[T]he constitution of the United States has not left the right of congress to employ the necessary means, for the execution of the powers conferred on the government, to general reasoning. To its enumeration of powers is added, that of making 'all laws which shall be necessary and proper, for carrying into execution the foregoing powers, and all other powers vested by this constitution, in the government of the United States, or in any department thereof.' * * *

Congress is not empowered * * * to make all laws, which may have relation to the powers conferred on the government, but such only as may be '*necessary and proper*' for carrying them into execution. The word '*necessary*' is considered as controlling the whole sentence, and as limiting the right to pass laws for the execution of the granted powers, to such as are indispensable, and without which the power would be nugatory. That it excludes the choice of means, and leaves to congress, in each case, that only which is most direct and simple.

Is it true, that this is the sense in which the word 'necessary' is always used? Does it always import an absolute physical necessity, so strong, that one thing to which another may be termed necessary, cannot exist without that other? We think it does not. If reference be had to its use, in the common affairs of the world, or in approved authors, we find that it frequently imports no more than that one thing is convenient, or useful, or essential to another. To employ the means necessary to an end, is generally understood as employing any means calculated to produce the end, and not as being confined to those single means, without which the end would be entirely unattainable. * * *

* * * [I]n the case under consideration, [t]he subject is the execution of those great powers on which the welfare of a nation essentially depends. It must have been the intention of those who gave these powers, to insure, so far as human prudence could insure, their beneficial execution. This could not be done, by confiding the choice of means to such narrow limits as not to leave it in the power of congress to adopt any which might be appropriate, and which were conducive to the end. This provision is made in a constitution, intended to endure for ages to come, and consequently, to be adapted to the various *crises* of human affairs. To have prescribed the means by which government should, in all future time, execute its powers, would have been to change, entirely, the character of the instrument, and give it the properties of a legal code. It would have been an unwise attempt to provide, by immutable rules, for exigencies which, if foreseen at all, must have been seen dimly, and which can be best provided for as they occur. To have declared, that the best means shall not be used, but those alone, without which the power given would be nugatory, would have been to deprive the legislature of the capacity to avail itself of experience, to exercise its reason, and to accommodate its legislation to circumstances.

* * *

We admit, as all must admit, that the powers of the government are limited, and that its limits are not to be transcended. But we think the sound construction of the constitution must allow to the national legislature that discretion, with respect to the means by which the powers it confers are to be carried into execution, which will enable that body to perform the high duties assigned to it, in the manner most beneficial to the people. Let the end be legitimate, let it be within the scope of the constitution, and all means which are appropriate, which are plainly adapted to that end, which are not prohibited, but consist with the letter and spirit of the constitution, are constitutional. * * *

After the most deliberate consideration, it is the unanimous and decided opinion of this court, that the act to incorporate the Bank of the United States is a law made in pursuance of the constitution, and is a part of the supreme law of the land.

[The second question decided by the Court is excerpted in Subsection C.1. below.]

Michel Rosenfeld, PRAGMATIC FEDERALISM, in THE FAILURES OF FEDERALISM IN THE UNITED STATES

1 Föderalismus-Studien 247, 247–249, 251–254, 259–260, 263, 265 (1993).

In light of its two-hundred-year history, the most striking feature of American federalism is its flexibility. This flexibility, which is predicated on the pragmatism that Americans bring to the interpretation and elaboration of constitutional norms, is the source of both the greatest strengths and the greatest weaknesses of American federalism. Indeed, the pragmatic approach to federalism can make it more responsive to changing circumstances, but by the same token, it can render it captive to intense but shortsighted interests.

In the short term, American federalism has tended to produce an ebb and flow in the importance of the powers of the federal government in relation to those of the states. But in the long run, American federalism has seen a dramatic reversal as the predominance of the states has given way to that of the federal government.

Two developments have been primarily responsible for the ascending predominance of the federal government: first, the nationalization of commerce, which emerged as a byproduct of the evolution of the United States towards a single economic market: and, second, the gradual nationalization of fundamental civil and political rights as a consequence of the implementation of the constitutional amendments adopted in connection with the abolition of slavery at the conclusion of the Civil War. In the face of the limited powers reserved to the federal government under the United States Constitution, the dramatic ascendance of the federal government in relation to the economic sphere was greatly facilitated on the one hand by the Supreme Court's increasingly broad conception of commerce and of the nexus between local economic activity and the economic welfare of the nation. On the other hand, the ascendance of the powers of the federal government has also been propelled by a dramatic surge in the importance of its spending power. Indeed, through its vast revenues collected through taxation, the federal government has reached a strong position from which it can successfully condition the grant of federal funds to states on terms that require the latter to make substantial concessions concerning their powers. Moreover, the nationalization of civil and political rights has also resulted in further significant curtailments of the states' sovereign powers. Thus, through the invocation of their federal constitutional civil and political rights, the citizens of a state may well succeed in securing a judicial invalidation of otherwise legitimate state laws, policies or practices. In other words, the uniformity generated as a consequence of the nationalization of civil and political constitutional rights materially constrains the state's legitimate potential for singularity and diversity.

The ascendance of the federal governments has resulted in a decrease of the powers of the state *relative* to those of the nation, but not in any absolute loss of state power. As a matter of fact, both the federal government and state governments are much more powerful, more broadly encompassing and more intrusive than they were at the beginning of the American republic.

* * *

The interplay between unity and diversity which animates American federalism is primarily structural in nature. Indeed, although the population of the United States is made up of a veritable mosaic of different racial, national, ethnic, religious and cultural groups, the allocation of various political powers to the individual states was neither meant to empower any such group nor had, by and large, the effect of enabling any such group to impose its identity on the socio-political order of any particular state. Rather, the juxtaposition of unity and diversity sought to be implanted by American federalism is one whose principal function is the division of power *per se* as a means to promote a brand of representative democracy capable of avoiding the dual pitfalls of excessive centralized detachment and disproportionate local passion and prejudice.

Given that the focal point of American federalism is structural in nature and that pragmatic concerns have generally played an important role in the context of American common law jurisprudence, it is not surprising that the actual boundaries between federal and state powers have shifted over the years in response to major economic, social and political changes. Furthermore, the plasticity of American federalism undoubtedly owes a fair amount to the open-ended nature of some of the constitutional provisions designed to regulate the relationship between the states and the federal government.[18] In spite of its flexibility and of the many changes which it has experienced throughout its history, however, American federalism has remained firmly anchored when it comes to several of the essential interests of the nation. Thus, the federal government has always maintained the power over such essential

---

18. *Cf. McCulloch v. Maryland,* 17 U.S. 316 (1819) (broad interpretation of the "necessary and proper" clause).

national concerns, as military and foreign affairs;[19] commerce with foreign nations;[20] and the coining of money.[21] Moreover, so long as the federal government remains within the scope of its enumerated powers, federal law is supreme and any inconsistent state law unconstitutional.[22]

* * *

[A] cogent assessment of the structural virtues of American federalism requires a consideration of the principal values which such federalism is supposedly meant to promote. These values include maintaining a system of "checks and balances" designed to prevent government abuses of power; increasing democratic participation by all citizens through greater involvement and through a greater voice in local and statewide affairs; making possible the proliferation of diverse cultural and political environments; and enhancing the possibilities for political experimentation and innovation through the spread of sovereign powers among a multitude of state governments.

Consistent with the preceding observations, the failures of American federalism [must be understood] in terms of significant departures from its functional mission of parsing out unity and diversity with a view to entrusting democratic decisionmaking to the appropriate constituency on the spectrum that spans between the local and statewide to the national.

* * *

The greatest failures of American federalism have included: frustrating highly desirable drives towards national unity; misusing diversity or squandering opportunities to produce genuine diversity; misallocating governmental powers in order to favor levels of government that seem least, rather than most, likely to foster protection of fundamental individual rights; exacerbating rather than minimizing government abuses; thwarting rather than promoting genuine democratic participation; fostering conformism rather than pluralism; and turning the channels of experimentation and innovation into a downward race towards the lowest conceivably acceptable standards.

* * *

As a general proposition, local majorities seem more intent on imposing conformism than national majorities, with the consequence that deference to state sovereignty often results in greater restrictions on antimajoritarian rights.[39] This is not to deny that federalism makes for greater diversity, but only to emphasize that such diversity may not be conducive to a greater toleration of non-conformity. Indeed, differences in the ethnic, religious, cultural and ideological make-ups of various states may lead to significant diversity *among* states without

---

19. See U.S. Const. Art. I and II.

20. U.S. Const. Art. I, § 8.

21. *Id.*

22. U.S. Const. Art. VI.

39. There are, of course, notable exceptions to these general propositions. Thus, for instance, [since the 1980s,] the United States Supreme Court has significantly retreated in its protection of antimajoritarian rights, with the result that some states now afford greater protection to such rights than does the federal government. If one considers the modern American jurisprudence on antimajoritarian rights in its entirety, however, the federal government clearly emerges as being more favorably disposed towards such rights than its state counterparts.

fostering any greater diversity *within* any of them. Moreover, a state's majority may feel particularly threatened by a sizeable minority.[40] * * *

The failures of American federalism regarding the allocation of powers over particular subjects to the level of government best suited to deal with them are best illustrated through focus on some of the highlights of the variegated and rich history surrounding the regulation of commerce. As the economy became increasingly integrated and national in scope, the need for uniform laws seemed more compelling, and the national government better suited than those of the several states to legislate consistently and uniformly in the context of a single nationwide economic market. Moreover, given the flexibility of the federalist framework established by the United States Constitution, suitable pragmatic adjustments to the relevant respective powers of the national and state governments were well within reach without requiring any stretch beyond widely accepted constitutional bounds. Yet the very flexibility of a constitutional practice steeped in the ebb and flow of a common law jurisprudence, which made American federalism particularly prone to success, by the same token, also made it highly vulnerable to failure. Thus, because of much judicial uncertainty and dispute concerning the proper scope of the term "commerce" and concerning the boundary between interstate and intrastate commerce, federalist constraints needlessly imperiled the massive federal effort to lift the United States out of the economic and social ravages of the Depression.[41] Actually, it was not until a major confrontation between President Roosevelt and the judiciary, which almost led to a serious constitutional crisis, that the Supreme Court retreated and reversed itself, finally giving the federal government the constitutional green light it needed to implement its massive program towards national economic recovery.

* * *

There has been a long-standing debate on whether to nationalize corporate law, but so far the federal government has bowed to tradition and left corporate law to the states. In theory, the disadvantages stemming from the lack of uniformity in corporate law could well be outweighed by the advantages likely to result from state experimentation and innovation. In fact, however, the potential for diversity has, to a significant extent, turned to a race to the bottom, with a large number of truly national—even many multi-national—corporations choosing the tiny state of Delaware as their state of incorporation. Not surprisingly, Delaware corporate law is generally the most favorable law from the standpoint for the interests of corporate management. * * *

* * * [T]he structural brand of federalism that has prevailed throughout the history of the United States has fallen short of the objectives set and proclaimed for it. This is not to say that American federalism has produced no significant benefits * * * Actually, federal-

40. The history of the United States is replete with examples of state discrimination against particular minorities. For example, California enacted laws prohibiting Japanese ownership of land while New Eng-land states adopted discriminatory policies against the Irish. * * *

41. Pursuant to U.S. Con. Art 1 Sec. 8, the U.S. Congress is empowered to regulate commerce between the states. * * *

ism is very deeply entrenched in the United States and so are the flexibility and pragmatism which made possible for it to survive through so many important changes. * * * [T]he future shape of federalism should depend on a cogent apportionment of economic and non-economic values so as to allow for the carving out of a defensible area of state sovereignty even in the face of the pursuit of a truly unified regulation of the nation's economy. In the end, American federalism may be well suited to accommodate both unity and diversity, if only Americans could build a consensus on which unity and what kind of diversity.

A.2. GERMANY: COOPERATIVE FEDERALISM

German federalism is deeply entrenched in the Basic law, and the division of the German Federation into *Länder* is permanently enshrined in the country's constitutional landscape as Art. 79 (3) of the Basic Law prohibits any amendment that would undermine the federal structure of the republic. Germany is currently comprised of sixteen *Länder*, which bear a close and complex relationship to the federal government. One of the predominant features of that relationship is the obligation imposed on both the federal government and the *Länder* to continuously engage in active cooperation. Although cooperative federalism is not an exclusively German preserve—e.g., U.S. federalism is also to a significant extent cooperative, see Daniel Halberstam and Roderick M. Hills, Jr., *State Autonomy in Germany and the United States* 574 Annals 173, 175 (2001)—it is central and predominant in Germany in ways that it is not in many other countries, including the U.S.

German cooperative federalism relies on the principle of comity (*Bundestreue*), "which obligates federal and state governments to consider each other's interests in exercising their authority." Kommers, *op. cit.* at 69. The principle of comity is not found in the text of the Basic Law. It has been elaborated by the German Federal Constitutional Court (GFCC), which has cast federalism as "essentially a relationship of trust between state and national governments. Each government has a duty to keep 'faith' (*Treue*) with the other and respect the rightful prerogatives of the other." *Id*. Consider the role of the principle of comity in the following case.

TELEVISION I CASE
Federal Constitutional Court (Germany).
12 BVerfGE 205 (1961).[b]

[The television controversy grew out of Chancellor Konrad Adenauer's effort to create a federally operated television station. At the time, one major television channel controlled by the states (*Länder*) already operated in the Federal Republic. The Chancellor, who was also the leader of the Christian Democratic Union, was strongly opposed by the states under the control of the Social Democratic party. Finally, and notwithstanding opposition from both Social Democratic and Christian

b. Reproduced from Donald P. Kommers, *The Constitutional Jurisprudence of* *the Federal Republic of Germany* 69–73 (2d ed. 1997).

Democratic states, the Chancellor established a second television station by decree. Several states immediately challenged the validity of the decree before the Court. They relied on Arts. 30 and 70 (1) of the Basic Law, claiming that these provisions conferred no such power on the federation. In response, the federation relied on Arts. 87 (1) and 73 (7), which confer power on the federation to regulate "postal and telecommunication services."]

Judgement of the Second Senate:

D. II. (b) The Basic Law regulates the legislative authority of federation and states on the basis of a principle that favors the jurisdiction of the states. * * * The federation has legislative authority only insofar as the Basic Law confers it. (Article 70 [1]) Thus, as a rule, federal legislative powers can be derived only from an express statement to that effect in the Basic Law. In cases of doubt there is no presumption in favor of the federation's jurisdiction. Rather, the systematic order of the Basic Law demands a strict interpretation of Article 73 [and other provisions which confer power on the federation].

In addition, broadcasting is a cultural matter. To the extent that cultural affairs are subject to governmental regulation at all, the Basic Law has made a fundamental decision (Articles 30, 70 *et seq.*) *that they come within* the jurisdiction of the states * * *

Exceptions occur only when special provisions of the Basic Law provide that the federation has authority. This fundamental decision of the Constitution, a decision in favor of the federal structure of the nation in the interest of an effective division of powers, specifically prohibits the assumption that the federation has jurisdiction over cultural matters. The federation has authority only when there is a clear exception spelled out in the Basic Law. This sort of provision is lacking here.

(c) Article 87 (1) provides that the federal postal service shall be conducted as a matter of direct federal administration. [We] can draw no conclusions as to the extent of the federation's legislative authority from this.

[The states usually administer federal laws "as matters of their own concern" (Article 83). Under Article 87 (1), however, the federal government administers selected subjects, such as federal railroads, and the federal administration in these areas does not define the full extent of the national government's *legislative* authority.]

* * * Moreover, "postal and telecommunication services" in Article 73 (7) and "federal postal administration" in Article 87 (1), refer to the same subject. The scope of "federal postal administration" follows from what is to be understood by "postal and telecommunication services".

4. The public interest demands the regulation of radio communications—something only the federation can do effectively. This is also true of broadcasting. To prevent chaos, the allocation and delimitation of frequency ranges of stations, determination of their locations and transmitting powers * * * control of radio communication, protection from widespread and local disturbances, and implementation of international agreements must be subject to uniform regulations.

Article 73 makes it possible to enact uniform regulations that are indispensable to these and similar matters. But implementation of this objective does not require that, in addition to technical questions of radio communication, federal law [should] also regulate the production of broadcasts * * *

(c) The federation has no authority to regulate broadcasting beyond the technical aspects of transmission * * *

7.   (b) The federation must * * * observe the principle of profederal behavior * * * This principle would be violated if the federation today used its authority to regulate the telecommunication system so as to deprive existing broadcasting companies of the right to dispose of transmitting facilities which they own and operate. The same would be true if the federation took away from these companies their frequency ranges, and in distributing frequencies to be used now or in the future, did not duly consider the companies in light of state regulations concerning producers of programs * * *

E.   II. In the German federal state the unwritten constitutional principle of the reciprocal obligation of the federation and the states to behave in a profederal manner governs all constitutional relationships between the nation as a whole and its members and the constitutional relationships among members * * * From this principle the federal Constitution has developed a number of concrete legal obligations. In considering the constitutionality of the so-called horizontal financial adjustment, this court said: "The federal principle by its nature creates not only rights but also obligations. One of these obligations consists in financially strong states having to give assistance within certain limits to financially weaker states* * * " [citing the *Finance Equalization I Case*, 1 BVerfGE 117, 131 (1952)]. Furthermore, in cases where a law demands that the federation and the states come to an understanding, this constitutional principle can create an increased obligation of cooperation on all parties concerned * * * In the decision which concerned granting Christmas bonuses to public employees, this court held that states must maintain *Bundestreue* [loyalty to the union] and therefore show consideration for the overall financial structure of federation and states * * * This legal restraint, derived from the concept of loyalty to the union, becomes even more evident in the exercise of legislative powers: "If the effects of a law are not limited to the territory of a state, the state legislature must show consideration for the interests of the federation and other states* * * " [citing the *North Rhine–Westphalia Salaries Case*, 4 BVerfGE 115, 140 (1954)]. The constitutional principle of the obligation to act in a profederal manner can further imply the duty of states to observe international treaties concluded by the federation * * * Finally, under the circumstances, loyalty to the union can obligate a state to use its supervisory authority over local governments to intervene against communities that encroach upon an exclusive federal competency * * * In the execution of federal jurisdiction over the field of broadcasting, the principle of profederal behavior is also of fundamental importance * * *

Previous decisions show that additional concrete obligations of the states can be developed from this principle—obligations that surpass constitutional obligations explicitly laid down in the Basic Law * * *

The case at hand offers an occasion to develop further the constitutional principle of the obligation to act profederally in a different direction: The rule of profederal behavior also governs the procedure and style of the negotiations required in constitutional life between the federation and its members as well as between the states. In the Federal Republic of Germany all states have the same constitutional status; they are states entitled to equal treatment when dealing with the federation. Whenever the federation tries to achieve a constitutionally relevant agreement in a matter in which all states are interested and participating, the obligation to act in a profederal manner prohibits the federal government from treating state governments differently because of their party orientation and, in particular, from inviting to politically decisive discussions only representatives from those state governments politically close to the federal government and excluding state governments which are close to opposition parties in the federal parliament * * *

[The Court found that the federal government had acted inappropriately by consulting with *Länder* controlled by the Christian Democrats but not those under the administration of the Social Democrats.]

Daniel Halberstam and Roderick M. Hills, Jr., STATE AUTONOMY IN GERMANY AND THE UNITED STATES

574 Annals 173, 175–178, 180–181 (2001).

* * *

I.   COOPERATIVE FEDERALISM: GERMAN AND AMERICAN SYSTEMS COMPARED

[T]he German and American systems of cooperative federalism * * * differ in important ways. [T]hree salient differences merit discussion.

First, the Grundgesetz (the German Constitution, or Basic Law) provides for the formal representation of state governments in the federal legislative process through the Bundesrat. Each *Land* government sends members of its cabinet to represent the interests of the *Land* in the Bundesrat. As these officials are simultaneously delegates to the Bundesrat and officers of the *Land* government and can be instructed and recalled by the *Land* government, their representation of *Land* interests is more direct than the U.S. senator's representation of state interests even prior to the ratification of the Seventeenth Amendment, when senators were chosen (but not instructed or recallable) by state legislatures. In return for this closer representation of the *Länder* governments in the Bundesrat, however, the German framers of the Grundgesetz who favored federalism had to limit the jurisdiction of the Bundesrat. The Bundesrat does not have the same capacity as the U.S. Senate to stop federal legislation but instead can veto only those laws that affect the administrative duties of the *Länder*.

* * *

The second respect in which the German and U.S. constitutional rules regarding cooperative federalism differ is that, apart from those areas enumerated in Article 87 in the Grundgesetz in which the federation must maintain its own implementing bureaucracy, the Grundgesetz gives the *Länder* a monopoly on the implementation of federal law, either as the agents of the federation or as a matter of their own concern. The federation can take measures to ensure that the *Länder* execute federal laws faithfully, but, when the *Länder* execute such laws as a matter of their own concern, the measures available to the federation are strictly limited by Grundgesetz Article 84. In particular, the federation cannot create its own federal field offices or send commissioners to any but the highest *Länder* authorities without the consent of the Bundesrat.

* * *

A third difference between the U.S. and German systems of federalism is that the *Länder* have much more limited capacity to initiate their own tax and regulatory policies absent federal authorization, because the German doctrine of field preemption is broader than the analogous American doctrine. Article 72(1) of the Grundgesetz provides that *Länder* may exercise concurrent powers "only so long as and to the extent that the federation does not exercise its right to legislate." This provision has been construed to forbid the *Länder* from imposing taxes that are also imposed by the federation. As a result, Article 106 of the Grundgesetz precisely specifies the taxes that each level of government can impose, leaving the *Länder* with the relatively unimportant sources of revenue enumerated in Article 106(2).

* * *

II. THE PRACTICAL EFFECTS OF DIFFERENT CONSTITUTIONAL STRUCTURES

We will suggest that two general consequences plausibly follow from the differences in constitutional structure. We stress that these are tentative hypotheses that can be confirmed only through more careful empirical work. Indeed, it is quite possible that the effects of, for example, the political culture or the political party system overpower any appreciable effects of constitutional structure. To the extent that the constitutional structure has practical effects, however, we speculate that (1) the U.S. system of federalism is likely to provide states with less effective protection from the federal government than the Grundgesetz provides to the *Länder* but (2) the German protections for the *Länder* arguably impose a greater cost than the American system in terms of efficient and flexible administration of national laws.

* * *

[The U.S. Constitution, as buttressed by the *Printz* decision, see Subsection C.2.3.a. below,] prevents Congress from simply taking over the states' bureaucratic structures cost-free for its own policy programs. Instead, Congress either has to undergo the political risk and fiscal

expense of creating its own structures or must pay the state govern-ments a grant acceptable to them in return for the states' services.
* * *

Nevertheless, [this may not] protect state autonomy as effectively as German law does. How can one be sure that the vagaries of intergovern-mental deal making will ensure that the states will be left with enough discretion to implement federal law? Perhaps Congress will bypass states and use federal agencies even when it is inefficient to do so, simply because Congress has a self-interested desire to monopolize patronage or credit-taking. By contrast, German federalism gives the *Länder* the surer protections of a constitutional entitlement to administer federal statutes and a collective rather than individual veto over federal mandates. In short, it seems hard to argue with the conclusion that German law protects state autonomy more reliably than U.S. federalism does.

This extra protection of federalism, however, comes at a price. Our second hypothesis is that, when compared to the U.S. system of coopera-tive federalism, the German system tends to produce a "joint decision trap"—the tendency in German federalism to require consent from multiple actors for political action, resulting in the obstruction of clear and effective policymaking. By giving the *Länder* a collective veto (through the Bundesrat) and a monopoly (through Articles 83–86 of the Grundgesetz) over the implementation of federal law, the German sys-tem locks the two levels of government—*Länder* and federation—into a position in which neither can dispense with the other in executing any policy of significance. This collective veto over federal lawmaking gives the *Länder* far greater capacity to hold federal lawmaking hostage to their demands for policy concessions or simply for more revenue, even when this is not justified by their superior regulatory performance. * * *

* * *

* * * The federation, therefore, must enter into lengthy, complex, and publicly invisible negotiations with the Byzantine networks of ap-pointed and elected officials of the *Länder* to secure passage and faithful implementation of the law.

* * *

A.3. SWITZERLAND: PREDOMINANCE OF THE CANTONS

Thomas Fleiner, SWITZERLAND: CONSTITUTION OF THE FEDERAL STATE AND THE CANTONS, in FEDERALISM AND MULTIETHNIC STATES: THE CASE OF SWITZERLAND

103–107, 109–113, 116–117 (Lidija R. Basta Fleiner
and Thomas Fleiner eds., 2d ed. 2000).

A. FEDERALISM AS BASIS OF THE SWISS FEDERATION

Switzerland is certainly one of the smallest existing federal states.
* * * The size of the population of Switzerland is about 6,3 Million

* * *. Still Switzerland is divided in 26 different cantons each of them being a state with sovereign jurisdiction. * * *

1. *Preserving Cantonal Identity*

Historically Switzerland as a country has emerged from the traditional confederation of the old mediaeval states of Switzerland. Although Switzerland has become technically a federal state, it is still called confederation. * * * Thanks to their independence, the cantons have been able to develop their own historical identity as states with their own cultural and legal traditions. This pluralistic diversity with regard to their independent legal system could be maintained even though the cantons did become part of the Confederation of Switzerland.

* * *

The cantons were only able to preserve this identity because they:

—Had adopted their own Constitution and could shape autonomous democratic institutions and rights of citizens;

—did produce their own court system and did enact their own codes of procedure;

—did decide independently how Church and State should collaborate together or whether Church and State should be separated:

—did grant autonomous jurisdiction to their districts and municipalities according to their own cultural and economical tradition and did give their internal structure an independent feature.

2. *Relationship between the Federal Government and the Cantons*

Those who want to examine the relationship between the federal government and the cantons have to study the historical developments of the Swiss Confederation. Contrary to Austria, Germany, Canada, India or now Belgium, the cantons of Switzerland did not emerge as autonomous decentralized districts out of the central state. On the contrary the Confederation of Switzerland emerged with the sovereign will of its former 25 (with the new Canton Jura now 26) sovereign and independent member states.

The sovereignty of the Confederation has been transferred to the central government by then existing full sovereignty of the cantons. Article 3 of the federal Constitution determines that cantons are sovereign, as far as their sovereignty is not restricted or limited by the federal Constitution. This provision is the formal confirmation for the very truth that the residual power, the residual sovereignty finds its roots in the cantonal autonomy and not in a central organ such as for instance the crown, which has residual jurisdiction in the UK.

* * * The Swiss federal system developed its own concept of federalism in the last century. * * * Th[e] cantons do execute and implement federal laws with cantonal courts and cantonal agencies. * * *

As most ways of collaboration between cantonal and federal agencies are not regulated by law but based on tradition and informal consent, there [are] * * * very few concrete and detailed regulations providing control, collaboration, coordination, execution and sanctions with regard to the cantonal execution of federal orders. Thus conflictual situations are not regulated. * * *

There is also a gap between reality and law if one seeks to determine the factual influence of the cantons in the decision-making process of the federal government. The cantons can influence federal decisions not only through the second chamber (the Swiss Senate) but also through the House of Representatives the so-called National Council. As cantonal territories are the boundaries for constituency for the election of the members of the National Council, the parties responsible for the selection of the candidates are cantonal. Thus a member of the National Council always needs the support of his cantonal party in order to be reelected. Thus the very political power in Switzerland is not to be found in the federal but in the cantonal parties. Therefore Switzerland is, not only legally but also in reality, a politically decentralized country. This may be the most important difference with the federalism of Germany which politically is very centralized by the party system.

* * *

3. *Sovereignty of the Cantons*

According to article 3 of the federal Constitution the cantons are sovereign in as much as their sovereignty is not limited by the federal Constitution. For the federal Constitution the cantons are member States. They have limited but nevertheless independent and external responsibilities like sovereign states.

* * *

The very fact that the state authority is subject to direct democratic control by citizens, is the very reason for a still very decentralized and federal Switzerland. * * * Direct democracy has stopped lots of projects giving more but not absolutely necessary power to the central government.

If the cantonal government violates federal law, it is politically responsible to the citizens of its canton. There does not exist any disciplinary responsibility of cantonal governments with regard to the federal government. Nor has the federal government the possibility to enforce federal law with contempt of court.

4. *Autonomy of the Cantons*

The autonomy of the cantonal governments, that is their rights for self-determination with regard to their internal structure, the organization of the governmental branches (legislature, executive and judiciary) and the contents of the democratic rights of their citizens, belongs to the essentials of the federalism of Switzerland. * * *

Up to 1991 cantons could even decide themselves that women were denied the right to vote. Fortunately, the federal court has now decided that equal protection be applied to voting rights as an obligatory general standard of the federal Constitution for the cantons. * * *

Although the governmental systems of the cantons do not differ very much from one another, they do with regard to the democratic rights of the citizens. Some cantons provide the obligatory referendum for every statutory decision of the parliament while others provide only [for a permissive] referendum, which means that statutory decisions are only submitted to the vote of the citizens if a certain amount of voters require a referendum.

* * *

7. *Direct Democracy, the Twin Sister of Federalism*

Without direct democracy on the three levels of the state: federal, cantonal and municipal, federalism in Switzerland would not have been defended so vigorously by the cantonal citizens. In fact the very reason why federalism in Switzerland is very much alive is direct democracy at the federal, cantonal and municipal levels. With the instrument of direct democracy citizens of cantons and municipalities have great influence on the political activities of their governments. Thus, they are interested to keep as much competence as possible on the cantonal of even municipal level. Every centralizing decision diminishes their power to influence the state politics.

Therefore in several federal referendums, the voters did not accept proposals of governments or parliaments to centralize certain powers because they feared that their possibility to influence politics would diminish. In several instances, the government of the cantons would even be interested to give up certain unpopular powers, which require from them to justify unpopular decisions endangering their reelection. They prefer to confer the responsibility to the central government so that it has to justify unpopular decisions before the citizens.

* * *

A.4. INDIA: MULTIETHNIC FEDERALISM

S.D. Muni, ETHNIC CONFLICT, FEDERALISM, AND DEMOCRACY IN INDIA, in ETHNICITY AND POWER IN THE CONTEMPORARY WORLD

179, 179–180, 187, 188–193 (Kumar Rupesinghe
and Valery A. Tishkov eds., 1996).

India has a highly complex and colorful social mosaic. Yet, although characterized by a vast spread of cultural diversity and heterogeneity, this mosaic is not chaotic. It has a clearly discernible pattern, wherein sociocultural diversity draws its strength and sustenance from India's composite culture and civilizational thrust. This culture has evolved over centuries. * * * [The] * * * composite culture cannot be compared * * * with the melting pot of American society * * * India's socio-cultural mosaic is the true picture of "unity in diversity," * * * where every component, while retaining its specific identity, is a part of a larger whole.

* * * Several cultural markers—language, race, tribe, caste, religion, and region—serve as identity axes for ethnic groups and their mobilization. In most of the ethnic groups, more than one of these cultural markers are pertinent for identification. In other words, India's ethno-communities have multilayered and multidimensional identities that impinge on each other in a non-stratified, dynamic manner. The identity composition of ethno-communities has been further complicated by the imposition of class distinctions, not only between one and another ethno-community, but also within each. Multilayered, non-stratified identity compositions has enabled ethnic groups to assert and reshuffle their cultural markers to advance their perceived objectives.

* * * [T]he ethnic groups do not have territories marked out for them because the cultural markers identifying such groups do not coincide with territorial boundaries. Accordingly, people belonging to specific religions, tribes, castes, races, and languages are found scattered in various territorial regions. * * * [N]ot even the reorganization of states in India on linguistic lines has been able to overcome this aspect.

* * *

Federalism

The foundations of federalism were laid down on the grounds of concern for the unity and integrity of a culturally diverse nation. In view of historical experiences of disruptive and disintegrative sectarian forces and the political context of partition prevailing at the time of independence, the founding fathers of the Indian Constitution wanted to strengthen the Union against possible disintegrative pressures. * * *

With administrative convenience the avowed guiding principle for designing the federation, not much weight was given to the need for reflecting India's cultural design. No specific provisions for religious or cultural minorities were incorporated, except that they were given equal rights. * * *

The Constitution's initial provisions and subsequent amendments provided for self-government under special administrative provisions for Jammu and Kashmir (Schedule IV, article 370) and to the tribal areas of North–East (Nagas, Mizos, Manipuri, Tripura, under articles 371 and 371A–I), but the Constituent Assembly refused to endorse proposals for constituting states on a linguistic basis. * * * [U]nder the force of circumstances[, however,] in 1953, the linguistic basis of reorganizing states was accepted. The Commission Constituted to Reorganize States in the Indian Federation * * * [explained] the criterion of language as the basis for constituting a state [as follows]:

"Linguistic homogeneity provides the only rational basis for reconstituting the state, for it reflects the social and cultural pattern of living obtaining in well-defined regions of the country."

The process of linguistic reorganization of states initiated in 1953 has been carried forward * * * since 1956 and was broadly completed by the end of the 1960s. This was a major development toward incorporating cultural identities into political and administrative units. The federal devolution of power strengthened this expression of cultural diversity.

The devotion of powers between the Union (or the centre) and the states was laid down in separate lists prepared for this purpose. Accordingly, the list of states' "exclusive" powers includes: public order; police; education; local government; roads and transport; agriculture; land and land revenue; forests; fisheries; industry and trade (limited); state Public Service Commissions; and Courts (except the Supreme Court). The states can also make laws along with the centre (provided the two do not clash), on subjects included in a "Concurrent List". These subjects include: criminal laws and their administration; economic and social planning; commercial and industrial monopolies; shipping and navigation on the inland waterways; drugs; ports (limited); courts and civil procedures. The arrangement for distribution of powers between the Union and the states has remained generally stable. One of the controversial aspects of centre-state relations has been the allocation of economic resources by the Union to the states. Such allocation is carried out by the Planning Commission in the area of developmental expenditure and has led to complaint by the states that the resources provided are inadequate. * * * [S]uccessive Finance Commissions have gradually enlarged the scope of devolution of taxes to the states. * * *

* * * [A]n elaborate structure of power devolution has combined with the linguistic basis of federal unity to facilitate the management of cultural diversity in India and help mitigate pulls toward separatism and disintegration. Centre-state relations, whether based on ethnicity or otherwise, have not been peaceful or tension-free, but the competition has tended to focus on securing resources and greater power. States of diverse languages and cultures have often joined together to enhance their bargaining power. In some cases the Indian federal structure even provided for such bargaining through bodies such as the Inter–State and National Development Councils. * * * Some scholars have described the federal system in India as one of "coalition and administration" or one with a "high degree of collaborative partnership." In addition, both at the central and state levels, a consciously followed approach to preserve and promote the cultural specificities of diverse groups has helped such groups identify with the national mainstream. All this has contributed to the secularization of ethnicity and has thus helped strengthen integrative forces.

It is interesting to note that most of the ethnic conflicts are between one given ethnic group and the Union of India, as if there were no ethnic contradictions and incompatibilities between individual groups. As noted earlier, the issues involved in such conflicts are invariably mixed with questions of sharing economic resources and decision-making power.

The functioning of federalism has nevertheless also had undesirable implications for the ethnic scene in India. The linguistic reorganization of the states gave impetus to various groups of specific cultural markers and ethnic identities to seek political expression and legitimacy. This was because ethnic identity was provided a territory under the scheme of reorganization. The importance of ethnic territory in ethnic conflict is very crucial, as can be gathered from recent developments in the Punjab and Kashmir and earlier events in Assam. In the Punjab and Kashmir conflicts, along with the transformation of identities and issues, the territorial base of ethnicity is being perfected by driving out Punjabi-speaking Hindus from the Punjab and Kashmiri-speaking Hindus from Kashmir. The potential for conflict formation along ethnic identity lines has thus been encouraged.

This potential has been further sharpened because linguistic reorganization in a vast and diverse country like India cannot be perfectly precise. On the periphery of the newly formed linguistic states, unassimilated linguistic minorities continued to exist. Then many other linguistic groups continued to remain in the larger Hindi-speaking states without being accommodated in the new political arrangement. The dissatisfactions of some of the unrecognized minority linguistic groups also continue to simmer. Such problems exist with regard to the Konkan region of Maharasthra/Goa, Nepali-speaking groups of Darjeeling, Sikkim, and Assam, and Maithili and Avadhi language groups in Bihar. * * *

In a very significant way, federalism has fueled ethnic conflict through the use of the Union's special provisions over the states. The use of article 356, which provides for imposition of presidential rule in a state in the "event of the failure of constitutional machinery," has been the subject of considerable controversy and debate in this regard. Political use of this provision has been extensive, particularly by the Congress-ruled centre. It can be employed to dismiss the state government of an opposition party or to manipulate political advantages for a ruling party or a particularly favoured political leader. In such manipulative machinations, the centre-appointed governor has played a decisive role, bringing the status and integrity of the governorship into considerable disrepute. The victimized party and leaders have sought to project this abuse of power as an instance of suppression of the political rights of the dominant ethnic group in the given state. * * *

Based on federal experience in India, it may not be out of place to assume that the structure of federalism and its inherent resilience can cope with the pressures of ethnicity and conflicts. It can even help resolve, or at least contain, some of these pressures, if the imperatives of federal devolution of power and obligations of mutual accommodation and adjustments are observed sincerely. * * * Against this, politically motivated distortions and manipulation of federal powers and institutions can worsen ethnic conflicts. Punjab and Kashmir are painful illustrations of this * * *

In an important way, federal relations have been vitiated by the breakdown of the Congress Party's dominance of the centre and the states since the 1960s and the emergence of political incompatibility and competition between the party ruling at the centre and in the various states. As these incompatibilities have grown, demands for redefining and restructuring these relations have been most pronounced, because the forum consisting of a single party in Power everywhere could not be utilized to sort out federal tensions. * * *

A.5. CANADA: ASYMMETRICAL FEDERALISM

Unlike in Germany and the U.S., where federalism is clearly distributive, in Canada, federalism confronts a tension between distributive- and identity-based objectives. From the standpoint of the English-speaking provinces, federalism is essentially regulative and hence distributive, and national identity resides at the federal rather than the provincial level. For French-speaking Quebec, however, collective identity as a distinct national group operates at the provincial level, and federalism is primarily a matter of identity rather than one of regulation or distribution. Moreover, because the Québécois seek to fulfill their national-identity aspirations at a provincial level, they have oscillated between asymmetrical federalism—which would entail Quebec having the same powers of autonomy as the federal unit has for the English-speaking provinces in return for Quebec remaining in the federation—and secession from Canada.

Quebec refused to ratify the 1982 Canadian Constitution. In 1995, Quebec voters rejected secession in a referendum by the slimmest of margins. On the other hand, while Canada's federalism is somewhat asymmetrical, it is nowhere nearly as asymmetrical as Quebec and its supporters would wish. Indeed Canadian asymmetrical federalism, to date, has been much more an aspiration than a reality, notwithstanding several efforts to institutionalize it.

Quebec's position, underlying its support for asymmetrical federalism, was elaborated in the following case.

RE QUEBEC OBJECTION TO A RESOLUTION TO AMEND THE CONSTITUTION

Supreme Court (Canada).
[1982] 2 S.C.R. 793.

[Quebec refused to ratify the 1982 Canadian Constitution—technically this new constitution was the product of amendment rather than of constitution-making from scratch—which was adopted after a unanimous vote of all the other provinces. In this case Quebec argued that it held a veto power over the new constitution, but the Court rejected that argument. The following excerpts reveal the arguments made on Quebec's behalf.]

Judgment

* * *

VI. *WHETHER QUEBEC HAS A CONVENTIONAL POWER OF VETO*

* * *

The reason advanced by the appellant for the existence of a conventional rule of a power of veto for Quebec is the principle of duality, this principle being however understood in a special sense.

The expression of "Canadian duality" is frequently used to refer to the two larger linguistic groups in Canada and to the constitutional protection afforded to the official languages by provisions such as s. 133 of the Constitution Act, 1867 and s. 23 of the Manitoba Act, 1870.

Counsel for the appellant characterized this aspect of the Canadian duality as the "federal" aspect and recognized that the central government had a role to play in this respect within the framework of federal institutions as well as outside Quebec. But he also made it clear that what he meant by the principle of duality embraced much more than linguistic or cultural differences. What was meant by the principle of duality was what counsel called its "Quebec" aspect which he defined more precisely in his factum at pp. 8 and 16:

> [TRANSLATION] In the context of this reference, the word "duality" covers all the circumstances that have contributed to making Quebec a distinct society, since the foundation of Canada and long before, and the range of guarantees that were made to Quebec in 1867, as a province which the Task Force on Canadian Unity has described as "the stronghold of the French–Canadian people" and the "living heart of the French presence in North America". These circumstances and these guarantees extend far beyond matters of language and culture alone: the protection of the British North America Act was extended to all aspects of Quebec society—language, certainly, but also the society's values, its law, religion, education, territory, natural resources, government and the sovereignty of its legislative assembly over everything which was at the time of a "local" nature.

In 1867, the French Canadian minority became a majority within the Quebec Legislature. This is what accounts for the special nature of this province, and it is the reason underlying the convention that the powers of its Legislature cannot be reduced without consent.

One finds another expression of the principle of duality understood in this sense in the preamble of the above quoted Decree No. 3367–81, dated December 9, 1981, the fourth paragraph of which states in concise terms:

> [TRANSLATION] Whereas Quebec forms a distinct society within the Canadian federation;

Another more elaborate expression of the principle of duality understood in the special sense urged by counsel for the appellant is to be found in a resolution passed by the Quebec National Assembly on December 1, 1981, and more particularly in condition no. 1 of the Resolution:

> [TRANSLATION] ... that the National Assembly of Quebec, having in mind the right of the people of Quebec to self-determination and exercising its historical right to be a party to and approve any change in the Constitution of Canada which might affect the rights and powers of Quebec, states that it cannot approve the proposal to patriate the constitution unless it includes the following conditions:

> 1. It shall be recognized that the two founding people of Canada are fundamentally equal, and that within the Canadian federation Quebec forms a society distinct by its language, culture and institutions, one which possesses all the attributes of a distinct national community;

> "2. The constitutional amending formula:

> > a) shall either preserve Quebec's right of veto, or

> > b) Shall be the one approved in the constitutional agreement signed by Quebec on April 16, 1981, affirming the right of Quebec not to have imposed on it any change which would reduce its powers or

rights, and if such a reduction were to take place, to be given reasonable compensation as a matter of right;"

* * *

Peter Hogg, SPECIAL STATUS, IN CONSTITUTIONAL LAW OF CANADA

108–110 (4th ed. 1997).

* * * [T]he provinces are not equal in wealth, status or actual power. Nor is their constitutional situation exactly equal. A number of the provisions of the Constitution apply to only one or only some of the provinces.[16] And the terms upon which each province was admitted usually included unique terms[17] which operate as legally enforceable provisions applicable only to that province.[18]

While the provinces are not perfectly equal, the differences are not so marked as to justify the description "special status" for any province. "Special status" is the term which has been applied to proposals for constitutional change under which one province (most likely, Quebec) would possess larger powers than the other provinces.[19] This could arise under the new amending procedures if Quebec (or any other province) opted out of a constitutional amendment transferring a provincial power to the federal Parliament. * * * [S]pecial status for one or a few provinces would impose severe strains on central institutions, and especially the federal Parliament. If the Parliament had authority to regulate a matter, say, product standards * * * everywhere except in Quebec, the members of parliament and senators from Quebec would presumably be permitted to vote on a bill regulating product standards, and they might have to do so in order to preserve a governmental majority, but the bill when enacted would not apply in Quebec. This problem has never been solved by political scientists, and it means that special status is a viable constitutional arrangement only up to a point. Of course, Quebec already enjoys a de facto special status, as the only province that has opted out of the Canada Pension Plan and the Hospital Insurance Plan (and some other national shared-cost programmes). But these arrangements do not

---

16. For example, Constitution Act, 1867, ss. 93 (denominational schools), 94 (uniformity of laws), 133 (language); Constitution Act, 1982, ss. 6(4) (affirmative action), 16 (2) 17(2), 18(2), 19(2), 20(2), 59 (language).

17. For example, the denominational schools guarantees in s. 20 of the Manitoba Act, 1870, s. 17 of the Alberta Act, s. 17 of the Saskatchewan Act and s. 17 of the Terms of Union of Newfoundland; the language guarantee in s. 23 of the Manitoba Act, 1870; and provisions regarding the natural resources of Manitoba, Alberta and Saskatchewan enacted by the Constitution Act, 1930.

18. *The Queen (Can.)* v. *The Queen (P.E.I.)* [1978] I.F.C. 533 (C.A.) (enforcing

terms of union promising ferry service); *Jack* v. *The Queen* [1980] 1 S.C.R. 294 (interpreting term of union regarding policy towards Indians); *Moosehunter* v. *The Queen* [1981] 1 S.C.R. 282 (enforcing term of natural resources agreement guaranteeing Indian hunting rights); *B.C.* v. *Can.* [1994] 2 S.C.R. 41 (interpreting term of union promising construction of railway).

19. "Special status" under which Quebec would remain within Canada, must be distinguished from "sovereignty-association", under which Quebec would secede from Canada and would retain only an economic association with (the rest of) Canada: * * *

give to Quebec any special *constitutional* powers: the other nine provinces continue to possess the same powers as Quebec over pensions and hospital insurance, and they could if they chose follow an independent course like Quebec.

The Meech Lake Constitutional Accord of 1987 was a failed attempt to reconcile Quebec to the terms of the Constitution Act, 1982, by which the province was legally bound, but to which it had never given its assent. The Accord made provision for (1) the recognition of Quebec as a distinct society, (2) a provincial role in immigration, (3) a provincial role in appointments to the Supreme Court of Canada, (4) a limitation of the federal spending power and (5) a veto for Quebec over some kinds of constitutional amendments. Although these five points were sought by Quebec alone, the Accord was carefully drafted to avoid making special provision for Quebec, and the new provincial powers were confirmed on all provinces, not just Quebec. This even included the veto over constitutional amendments which took the form of a unanimity requirement, conferring a veto on all provinces.

The one point that would not yield to the ingenious avoidance of special provision for Quebec[23] was the recognition of Quebec as a "distinct society". In my opinion, even this provision could not plausibly be regarded as creating a special status for Quebec, in that it was an interpretative provision only. It did not directly confer any new powers on the province, and if its interpretative role did lead to some expansion of Quebec's powers, that expansion was bound to be minor—well within the range of variation in provincial powers that is now to be found within the Constitution of Canada. Nevertheless, there was much public debate about the undesirability of special status for Quebec, and the distinct society clause was the major objection that led to the failure by two provinces to ratify the Accord, which caused the Accord to lapse.[24]

Will Kymlicka, ASYMMETRIC FEDERALISM, in POLITICS IN THE VERNACULAR: MINORITY NATIONALISM AND MULTINATION FEDERALISM

91, 104–105 (2001).

In a federal system which contains both regional-based and nationality based units * * * it seems likely that demands will arise for some form of *asymmetrical federalism*—i.e. for a system in which some federal units have greater self-governing powers than others. Unfortunately, it has proven extraordinarily difficult to negotiate such an asymmetrical model. There seems to be great resistance, particularly on the part of

23. To be strictly accurate, the Accord also guaranteed that three of the judges of the Supreme Court of Canada would come from Quebec. This provision, although singling out Quebec for special treatment, was not controversial, because it constitutionalized a longstanding statutory requirement.

24. The "distinct society" clause was also part of the unsuccessful Charlottetown Accord of 1992 * * * The Accord also repeated the guarantee that three judges of the Supreme Court of Canada would come from Quebec (see previous note). The Accord contained a new guarantee that Quebec's representation in the House of Commons would never fall below 25 per cent. This special provision for Quebec (along with the distinct society clause) seems to have been an important factor in the defeat of the Accord in the western provinces.

majority groups, to accepting the idea that federal units can differ in their rights and powers. As a result, national minorities have found it very difficult to secure the rights and recognition that they seek.

The difficulty in negotiating asymmetry is, in one sense, quite puzzling. If most English-speaking Canadians want a strong federal government, and most Québécois want a strong provincial government, asymmetry would seem to give both groups what they want. It seems perverse to insist that all subunits have the same powers, if it means that English-speaking Canadians have to accept a more decentralized federation than they want, while French–Canadians have to accept a more centralized federation than they want.

Yet most English-speaking Canadians overwhelmingly reject the idea of 'special status' for Quebec. To grant special rights to one province on the grounds that it is nationality-based, they argue, is somehow to denigrate the other provinces, and to create two classes of citizens.[22] Similar sentiments have been expressed in Spain about the demand for asymmetrical status by the Basques and Catalans. Some commentators-such as Charles Taylor-argue that this simply reflects confused moral thinking. Liberal democracies are deeply committed to the principle of the moral equality of persons, and equal concern and respect for their interests. But equality for individual citizens does not require equal powers for federal units. On the contrary, special status for nationality-based units can be seen as promoting this underlying moral equality, since it ensures that the national identity of minorities receives the same concern and respect as the majority nation. Insofar as English-speaking Canadians view the federal government as their 'national' government, respecting their national identity requires upholding a strong Federal government; insofar as Québécois view Quebec as their national government, respecting their national identity requires upholding a strong provincial government. Accommodating these differing identities through asymmetrical federalism does not involve any disrespect or invidious discrimination.[25]

It is difficult to avoid the conclusion that much of the opposition to asymmetry amongst the majority national group is rooted in a latent ethnocentrism—i.e. a refusal to recognize that the minority has a distinct national identity that is worthy of respect. This fits into the long history neglecting or denigrating the desire of national minorities to remain culturally distinct societies, which I discussed earlier.

A.6. BELGIUM: FROM CENTRALIZATION TO ETHNIC FEDERALISM TO CONFEDERATION?

Belgium's 1831 Constitution established the country as a unitary state with a bicameral parliament and a constitutional monarch. Al-

22. * * * [A] poll show[ed] 83 per cent opposition to special status. A certain amount of *de facto* asymmetry in powers has been a long-standing aspect of Canadian federalism, but most English–Canadians have been unwilling to formally recognize or entrench this in the constitution, let alone to extend it.

25. English–Canadians often say to Quebeckers, "Why can't we all be Canadians first, and members of provinces second?" without realizing that this involves asking the Québécois to subordinate their national identity, whereas for English–Canadians it simply involves strengthening their national identity *vis-à-vis* their regional identity.

though Belgium's population was divided among French and Dutch speakers, French was the country's official language.

Although Belgium has long had a Flemish majority, French remained the official language as the French-speaking region was the most prosperous and Flemish elites were fluent in French. See Richard Cullen, *Adaptive Federalism in Belgium*, 13 UNSW L.J. 347, 350 (1990).

This situation changed as Wallonia declined economically, the Flemish region became economically predominant, and the adoption of universal suffrage gave the Flemish majority a stronger political voice. *Id.* at 350–51. Major linguistic reform ensued in 1962–1963, bringing unilingualism to the Dutch-speaking population in Flanders. *Id.* Moreover, as a consequence of the institutionalization of unilingualism, the various linguistic communities became increasingly antagonistic toward one another, threatening the viability of the unitary state and prompting constitutional changes that would set Belgium on a course toward federalism.

Robert Senelle, THE REFORM OF THE BELGIAN STATE, in FEDERALIZING EUROPE: THE COSTS, BENEFITS AND PRECONDITIONS OF FEDERAL POLITICAL SYSTEMS

266, 270–272, 281, 287–288, 293–294, 315–316 (Joachim
Jens Hesse and Vincent Wright eds., 2001).

When the Belgian political classes realized in the early 1970s that the unitary state was a thing of the past, the political parties began the slow process that was to lead, a quarter-century later, to the federalization of the kingdom. That fundamental reform was carried out in four phases, each of which entailed a revision of the Constitution (1970–1980—1988–1993). Belgians gradually accepted the obvious truth that it was only under a federal system that Belgium would be able to survive.
* * *

* * * The present constitutional system changing Belgium into a federal state was brought about as a result of the four revisions of the Constitution between 1970 and 1993. Article 1 of the new Constitution states that Belgium is a federal state.

According to Article 4 of the Constitution Belgium has four linguistic regions: the French-speaking Region, the Dutch-speaking Region, the bilingual Region of Brussels–Capital, and the German-speaking Region. Each commune of the Kingdom is part of one of these linguistic regions.
* * *

According to Article 2 of the Constitution Belgium is made up of three Communities: the French Community, the Flemish Community, and the German-speaking Community. According to Article 3 of the Constitution Belgium is made up of three Regions: the Walloon Region, the Flemish Region, and the Brussels Region. * * *

* * *

Partly because the reform of the Belgian state is moving towards federalization, the monarchy is now of supreme importance. To transform a unitary state that has been highly centralized * * * into a federal state is a difficult and hazardous political venture. All federal structures presuppose what is referred to as 'federal loyalty', or to use the time-honored German expression, *Bundestreue*. The Belgians are now in the position of having to accustom themselves to observe federal loyalty, a notion quite unknown to them as recently as a quarter of a century ago. Were it not for the monarchy as symbol of the cohesion of the kingdom and therefore the visible incarnation of federal loyalty, the Belgian experiment would be doomed to failure.

Even prior to the 1993 Reform, the Constitution had ruled that the Council of Ministers should be composed of an equal number of French- and Dutch-speaking ministers, with the possible exception of the Prime Minister. * * *

    * * *

3. Federal Powers

Until the 1993 Reform the Communities and Regions had only the powers vested in them, the residual powers being held by the national authority, by virtue of a combination of constitutional provisions. Article 35 of the Constitution reads as follows:

> The federal Authority has powers only in matters expressly assigned to it by the Constitution and the laws enacted thereunder.

> The Communities or Regions, in their respective domains, have powers in other matters, subject to the conditions and rules established by law. That law must be adopted by a majority as defined in the last paragraph of Article 4.

'Majority' here means a majority of the votes in each language group of each chamber, on condition that the majority of the members of each group is assembled, and further provided that that total votes given in favor by both language groups represent two-thirds of the votes cast.

In stressing the dynamics of federalism, the revised Constitution provides that from now on residual powers will be vested in the Regions and the Communities, in their respective domains. However, this new system will not come into effect until a list of federal powers has been drawn up. This list must be drafted by a legislator acting under a special majority.

It should be emphasized that the Belgian constitutional system includes exclusive powers held by the federal authority and by the Communities and Regions. Thus, in Belgium there can hardly be said to be concurrent powers such as exist in most federal constitutional systems-for example, Switzerland or the Federal Republic of Germany. Though regrettable, this state of affairs is the consequence of the process through which Belgian federalism has been fashioned: it has always had to contend with a profound mistrust of the central authority on the part of the advocates of federalism. * * *

    * * *

The subdivision of the federated states of Belgium into Communities and Regions is one of the oddest aspects of Belgium's federal system. Community issues fall within the competence of the Flemish Council for the Flemish Community, that of the Council of the French-speaking Community for the French community. Regional issues are handled by the Flemish Council for the Flemish Region, and by the Regional Walloon Council for the Walloon Region. Since 1980 the Constitution has allowed the exercise of the Flemish Region's powers to be devolved to the Flemish Community, and those of the Walloon Region to the French Community. This prerogative was immediately taken up by the Dutch-speaking Community but has never been used by the French-speaking Community. As far as the Dutch-speaking side is concerned, the Community is a privileged collective entity, whereas on the French-speaking side there is a strong tendency to give the Region more prominence.

* * * Regarding the competence of the communities Art. 127 of the Constitution provides as follows:

Art. 127 § 1. The French and Dutch Community Councils, respectively, establish by decree;

1. cultural issues;

2. education, with the exception of:

    a) the determination of the beginning and of the end of mandatory scholarity;

    b) minimum standards for the granting of diplomas;

    c) attribution of pensions

3. inter-Community co-operation, in addition to international co-operation, including the drafting of treaties for those matters described in 1 and 2.

A law adopted by majority vote as described in Article 4, last paragraph, establishes those cultural matters described in 1., types of co-operation described in 3.

§ 2. These decrees have force of law in French-language and in Dutch-language Regions respectively, as well as in those institutions established in the bilingual Region of Brussels–Capital which, on account of their activities, must be considered as belonging exclusively to one Community or the other.

* * *

CO–OPERATION AND SETTLEMENT OF CONFLICTS
BETWEEN THE FEDERAL AUTHORITY, THE
COMMUNITIES, AND THE REGIONS

[P] 1. CO–OPERATION

* * * Powers are allocated exclusively between the federal authority, the Communities, and the Regions. The federated bodies also enjoy extensive autonomy, since their legal provisions (decrees and orders) are not in principle subordinated to those of the federal authority. The Belgian Constitution does not contain the famous principle set out in Article 31 of the Constitution of the Federal Republic of Germany, under

which federal law takes precedence over the law of the *Länder*—hence the importance attached by the Constituent body and the legislature to co-ordination and co-operation between the various authorities. By virtue of the concentration and co-operation procedures the authorities are able to harmonize their policies on similar issues and thus achieve optimum efficiency: it often happens that several authorities may have responsibility for a given issue, each being in charge of one particular aspect of it.

Formal Co-operation Agreements

The co-operation agreement is the classic device used by the federal authority and the federated bodies to harmonize their policies in accordance with the content of the agreement, each respecting the autonomy of the other. Some agreements must be approved by law, decree, or order. Co-operation agreements are compulsory on certain issues, such as transport between adjacent areas, and roads and waterways that extend beyond a single region.

Any disputes that may arise in relation to a co-operation agreement cannot be brought before an ordinary court but must come before special co-operation tribunals having sole jurisdiction over disputes of this type: they are not permanent but are set up whenever a conflict arises. They are composed of a presiding judge and two or more members appointed by the parties to the dispute. * * *

Notes and Questions

1. American pragmatism coupled with broad latitude in judicial interpretation allows for great fluctuation in the boundaries between federal and state powers in the U.S. Furthermore, state interests have a direct impact on the make-up of the federal government. Each state has two senators, and although seats in the House of Representatives are apportioned on a population basis, all House districts are completely within a single state; finally, the President is elected indirectly by winning a majority in the Electoral College, which depends on state majorities rather than on the national majority. Because of this, some have suggested that apportionment of powers among the federal government and the states ought to be left to elected federal officials. See *Garcia v. San Antonio Metropolitan Transit Authority*, 469 U.S. 528 (1985); Jesse H. Choper, *Judicial Review and the National Political Process* (1980). Since U.S. federalism is regulative and distributive, should courts or democratic majorities determine the line between federal and state powers? Would a different answer emerge for an identity-based federal system?

2. Given that the U.S. economy has long been national (if not transnational) and that all human activity taken in the aggregate has a significant economic impact—e.g., crime, health issues, education—arguably, a purely pragmatic approach could eventually lead virtually to exclusive federal control. Thus if pragmatism is equated with efficiency, national regulation would result in greater efficiency than divided and potentially inconsistent regulation. Under such circumstances, federalism may require confining pragmatism within certain categorical bounds. See *United States v. Lopez*, 514 U.S. 549 (1995), in Subsection C.2.2.a. below (5–4 decision relying on

categorical distinction between economic and noneconomic activities); *United States v. Morrison*, 529 U.S. 598 (2000) (Federal Violence Against Women Act unconstitutional on grounds that rape is not an economic act). Assuming this trend continues, the U.S. Supreme Court (USSC) risks reshaping federalism in ways that are contrary to the will of both national and state majorities. Indeed the Violence Against Women Act involved in *Morrison* was not only broadly supported in the U.S. Congress but also by at least 36 of the 50 U.S. states. Should the discrepancy between the judicial approach and that of the political branches at both the federal and state levels raise significant concerns?

3. German federalism requires far greater cooperation between the federation and federated entities than its U.S. counterpart, not only because of judicial imposition of a strong duty of comity, as made plain in the *Television I Case* above, but also because of two structural features. The first is state administration of federal law; the second is the way the interests of the *Länder* figure in Germany's second legislative body, the Bundesrat. As stressed in note 1, above, in the U.S., state interests have an impact on the make-up of the Congress in that all federal legislators depend on an electorate encompassed within a single state, but otherwise the Congress remains independent from the states. In Germany, in contrast, while the first chamber of the federal legislature—the Bundestag—is no more dependent on the *Länder* than the U.S. Congress is on the states, the second chamber—the Bundesrat—depends entirely on the *Länder* in their capacity as federated entities. As Professor Kommers states:

> The Council of State Governments (Bundesrat), the mainstay of German federalism, was designed to safeguard the interests of the *Länder*. Unlike the United States Senate, the Bundesrat represents the *Länder* in their corporate capacities. Thus each *Land* delegation or the person appointed to represent the state, votes as a unit in accordance with instructions of the *Land* government * * * Each state is entitled to at least three voting members, but * * * states with more than two million people are entitled to four votes, those with more than six million receive five votes, and those with more than seven million receive six votes. * * *

> The Basic Law does not place the Bundesrat on an equal footing with the Bundestag. As the popularly elected house, the Bundestag is the nation's highest parliamentary body. By contrast, the Bundesrat enjoys the right to *participate* in the national legislative process. Yet it has a suspensive veto over legislation generally and an absolute veto over all legislation affecting the vital interests of the *Länder*. A suspensive veto can be overridden by an equivalent vote in the Bundestag. If the legislation affects the interests of the *Länder*, the Bundesrat's consent is required. Actions constitutionally requiring the Bundesrat's consent include proposed constitutional amendments, all laws affecting state tax revenues, and all laws and directives impinging on the administration of federal law by a state.

Kommers, *op. cit.* at 96–97.

Professors Halberstam and Hills argue that German federalism is less flexible than that in the U.S. because of the role of the *Länder* in administering federal law. Is this a defect of German federalism? Or does it depend on whether flexibility or cooperation is deemed more desirable? In his dissenting opinion in *Printz v. United States*, 521 U.S. 898 (1997), in Subsection C.2.3.a. below, Justice Breyer states that German federalism allows for greater independence of the states, because of the latter's administration of federal law, than does U.S. federalism, which entrusts the administration of federal law to federal agents. Do you agree?

4. Switzerland, India, Canada, and Belgium all have federal systems that are to a significant extent identity based. Identity-based federalism seems well suited for the majority group in a federated unit. For example, the French-speaking population in Quebec seems better off as a majority in that province than as a minority in Canada. Similarly, the Catholic majority in a given Swiss canton seems better off than it would be as a minority in a predominantly Protestant Switzerland. But what about the minorities within a federated entity? If such a minority belongs to the national majority (e.g., English speakers in Quebec or Protestants in a Catholic Swiss canton), then presumably they would be better off if their country became unitary. But what about minorities within a state who are also minorities on a national scale, such as the Japanese in California or the Irish in New England (see Professor Rosenfeld's article in Subsection A.1. above)? Are not relatively large majorities on a statewide basis that are relatively small on a nationwide basis better off under federal, as opposed to state, protection?

5. Unlike in the U.S. or Germany, the Swiss Constitution does not provide a formal mechanism to resolve conflicts between the federal government and the cantons. Does that make Switzerland more akin to a confederation than a federation? In comparing the relative success in securing state, as opposed to federal, control in areas apparently entrusted to the federated entities, is direct democracy as practiced in the Swiss cantons an effective tool?

6. Asymmetrical federalism, like that envisioned in the failed Lake Meech Accord in Canada, seems inherently problematic. Professor Kymlicka claims, however, that it is puzzling that Canadians are unwilling to embrace it, given that Anglophones identify more with the federation and Francophones with Quebec. Can the distinction between individual and collective equality mentioned by Kymlicka aid in dispelling the impression that unequal treatment of different provinces is unfair? See the discussion on group rights in Chapter 6. Because Canadian federalism allows a province to opt out of certain federal legislation, it seems particularly unfair, as Professor Hogg notes, to allow federal legislators from a province that has opted out to vote for a law that will not bind their electorate. Could this problem be avoided by moving from a federation to a confederation and allowing more cooperation among those federated entities that do not seek added powers?

B. DECENTRALIZATION IN NONFEDERAL STATES

In unitary states, there is no splitting of the atom of sovereignty. In both federations and confederations, sovereignty is apportioned among federated and federal sovereigns. In decentralized unitary states, sovereignty remains national, but some powers may be delegated to regional or local administrators. In a strictly unitary state, all powers would emanate from the center and radiate in various degrees to the periphery. Many nonfederal states with various degrees of decentralization stand somewhere between these two ends of the spectrum, and the lines between federal and nonfederal arrangements are sometimes blurred. Consider the differences concerning decentralization in the following unitary states: France, Spain, Italy, and the United Kingdom.

B.1. FRANCE: CAN DECENTRALIZATION WORK IN THE PARADIGMATIC CASE OF THE INDIVISIBLE REPUBLIC?

France is the paradigmatic example of a unitary state. All legal and political power resides in the central government. Subnational units, such as the regions, *departments*, or local communities, are administrative rather than political in nature. Although a unitary state, contemporary France has moved from full centralization through "deconcentration" and decentralization: As Professor Favoreu explains in Louis Favoreu et al., *Droit constitutionnel* 459 (1998): " 'Deconcentration' consists in the delegation of powers of decision residing in the national ministries to prefects or other agents named by such ministries. These agents remain, nonetheless, under the hierarchical powers of the ministers. Decentralization, on the other hand, involves a transfer of decision-making powers from the central government to other public entities, such as territorial collectivities administered by locally elected officials and subjected to controls under law."

Moreover, as Professor Favoreu further specifies, local collectivities operate under narrow constraints. They are free to administer, but their autonomy is severely limited by the constitutional principle of the indivisibility of the republic. *Id.* at 459–60.

As Professor John Bell emphasizes in *Devolution French Style*, 6 European Public Law 139 (2000):

> France has * * * deep-seated difficulties with devolution * * * Article 1 of the Constitution of the Fifth Republic of 1958 states that 'France is an indivisible ... Republic' and Article 3 forbids any section of the people from arrogating to itself national sovereignty. These provisions have been interpreted in a fairly fundamentalist way by the *Conseil constitutionnel* and by the legislature. In Decision No. 91–290 DC of 9 May 1991, the *Conseil constitutionnel* held that the recognition of a "Corsican people" in a law was unconstitutional. More recently, in Decision No. 99–412 DC of 15 June 1999, it held that France could not sign the European Charter on minority languages insofar as it conferred rights on 'groups' of speakers of minority languages and recognized the right to speak a language other than French in public life (including in court and in administrative and public services). Everyone is a French citizen and has to be treated as such, rather than as belonging to special minorities with particular interests.

In 1982, France introduced a program of decentralization that included a special statute for Corsica, intending to afford it greater fiscal and administrative autonomy. The statute has not been a success. As one observer noted:

Clear-cut autonomy has not been established in Corsica by the legislation of 1982. Local demands have been only partially satisfied and a mixture of disappointment and anger remains. The unitary state and the clan system of political influence have apparently emerged victorious. A little has been conceded here and there. Perhaps true autonomy cannot come from the 1958 Constitution of France because no real negotiations can take place between region and state; all is *octroyé*. The French state may be constitutionally unable to move towards a federal system without major constitutional change, which will allow such negotiations and which would construct a real and effective means of arbitration between two levels of power. The Corsican nationalists and separatists are pointing to the need for a more fundamental revision of the relationship. They do not believe that the central state can abandon its authority; this can only be wrested from it, if necessary by violence.

Peter Savigear, *Autonomy and the Unitary State: The Case of Corsica*, in *Federalism and Nationalism* 96, 110–11 (Murray Forsyth ed., 1989).

In the face of mounting pressure, including violence, the French government prompted the passage of a law granting greater self-government rights to Corsica and authorizing the Corsican Parliament to exercise certain limited powers to adapt national legislation to suit Corsica's needs. In its Decision 2001–454 DC of 17 Jan. 2002, the French Constitutional Council held the law in question unconstitutional for breaching the principle of national unity. The Council emphasized that only France's Parliament was entitled to enact laws. In contrast, the Corsican Parliament could modify regulations issued in Paris to accommodate Corsica's needs only under certain conditions. The invalidated law—the first of its kind—had been unacceptable not only to opposition parties but also to members of the government, prompting the resignation of the Minister of the Interior. See "New Reverse for Jospin, Corsica Bill ruled Unconstitutional", *Agence France Press,* January 17, 2002. The prospects for genuine devolution in France appear dim.

B.2. SPAIN AND ITS AUTONOMOUS REGIONS: HALFWAY BETWEEN THE UNITARY STATE AND FEDERALISM?

Juan José Solozábal, SPAIN: A FEDERATION IN THE MAKING?, in FEDERALIZING EUROPE: THE COSTS, BENEFITS AND PRECONDITIONS OF FEDERAL POLITICAL SYSTEMS

240, 245–250, 253–259 (Joachim Jens Hesse and Vincent Wright eds., 1996).

1. THE SOCIO–POLITICAL FOUNDATION OF THE SPANISH AUTONOMOUS STATE

The Spanish Constitution of 1978 established a model for territorial organization which may be considered to be midway between a unitary state and a federal one. Both politicians and constitutionalists have agreed on the terms 'autonomous state' *(estado autonómico)* or state of autonomous territories' *(estado de las autonomías territoriales)* to describe this model, although nowhere do these labels actually appear in the Constitution.

The socio-political dynamics operating in Spain when the new Constitution was drafted prevented its authors from considering any of the proven models of territorial organization, whether centralized or federal, as an option for Spain.

The Crisis of the Centralized State.

The crisis of the Franco regime also reflected the crisis of the centralized model, of which it was certainly an archetype. The intensification of centralized power during the Franco regime resulted in the centralized model being equated with the abuse of power, despite the examples of the French and British centralized states * * * in which this model is perfectly compatible with democracy.

* * *

2. ORGANIZATIONAL AND LEGAL FEATURES OF THE AUTONOMOUS STATE

* * * In Spain, the autonomous division of the state is not a simple formula for organizing power from the standpoint of technical perfection, in a distribution derived solely or principally from demands for efficiency or even as a means for bringing political decisions closer to the individual citizen. The Autonomous State cannot be considered as an original political variation from the standpoint of its vertical disposition of power nor due to its innovative constitutional design, but rather as a valiant if risky attempt to offer an institutional solution to the problems arising from political factionalism and peripheral nationalisms. This explains the originality of Spain's decentralized state, which does not reside so much in the uniqueness of its organizational features or in the peculiarities of the delimitations of powers which have been established between central entities and the autonomous community but rather in the nationalist tensions which justify its existence and which it seeks to address.

The Spanish Autonomous State is a state which is politically decentralized. Within it coexist, on the one hand, a central or general political organization with jurisdiction in the entire national territory (with a complete level of authorities: a parliament, a government, and a common court system): and, on the other, a level of regional authorities with their corresponding parliaments and governments. In the legal realm, there is a system of norms produced by central organs, and another seventeen territorial legal sub-systems of laws resulting from the normative activity of the corresponding regional organs.

It should be stated that, as in the political arena, the presence of a variety of political centres does not hinder the unity of the state as a common organization corresponding to the existence of a single Spanish people to which the Constitution in Article 1 attributes the sovereignty of the nation. In the legal arena, the central legal system and the territorial legal systems form a general type of super-system of norms which displays a certain degree of homogeneity, a consequence of the pre-eminent role which the Constitution plays in it, as the base for legal order as stipulated in Article 9–2, whose structural, organizational, and value principles apply throughout the system, and within which it plays a role in integrating the central state's legal order.

These are features which the Autonomous State shares with the unitary model, but we should not forget that, as opposed to this type of legal and political system, the entities comprising the Autonomous State (the Autonomous Communities), enjoy true legislative capacity to the extent that, within the political framework outlined in the Constitution, the Parliaments of the Autonomous Communities may pass laws which have the same status and force as those of the state and which are barely distinguishable from them, although they are of doubtful justification from a constitutional standpoint. This is a reference to the fact that the laws of the Autonomous Communities, as opposed to general laws passed in the central parliament, are never subjected to suspension. Thus while in a unitary state decentralization is merely administrative in nature, in the Autonomous State decentralization takes on true political significance, which is reflected in this attribution of legislative power to the Autonomous Communities.

The Second Chamber or Senate

On the other hand, the Autonomous State does not reflect many of the features of a federalist state. It is true that certain characteristics or 'federal instrumentalities' do exist (although they might be considered to be insufficient), which include the presence of a Senate. * * *

The differences between the Spanish autonomous state and a federal state should not be overlooked and are based principally on the fact that in the Spanish system the Autonomous Communities do not possess real constitutional power * * * There is a difference between sovereignty, understood as original and unlimited legal political power which belongs to the central state, and autonomy defined as the derived and limited power of the different regions and nationalities.

* * * [A]s the norm which organizes and grants specific powers to the Autonomous Communities, in accordance with the precepts of the Constitution, the Statute of Autonomy is the basic institutional norm of the Community. It is, thus, 'within the limits of the Constitution', the highest norm of the territorial legal order to which all other laws and regulations are subordinate, and it expresses the values and contains the sources of this order. The position of the Statute within the territorial legal system is clearly rooted in the principle of hierarchy and, in this sense, does not seem to present any major problems.

The Spanish Senate carries out only modest functions as the institution of participation of the Autonomous Communities in the formation of the will of the nation-state. In the first place, the powers of the Spanish Senate are not comparable with those exercised by an authentic lower chamber. Thus, with respect to its legislative function, any amendments or vetoes which the Senate makes to draft laws remitted to it by the Congress may eventually be overridden. And, in the second place, the government of the nation is not politically responsible to the Senate, in the sense that the Senate cannot exercise any extraordinary control over the government. In addition, the Senate lacks practically any authority in matters concerning the Autonomous Communities.

* * *

Variation in Power between the Autonomous Communities

* * *

Perhaps the most outstanding feature of the Spanish Autonomous State is the absence of uniformity in it organizational structure, and above all, in the distribution of powers among its members. The differences between Autonomous Communities having ordinary statutes and those having special ones reside in the manner in which they assumed autonomy and, consequently, in the elaboration of their statutes (the contents of the statutes of the Special Autonomous Communities were agreed upon previously and were subjected to a referendum in their respective territories). Above all, the differences lie in the powers granted in these statutes, which in the case of the ordinary Communities are limited to those outlined in Article 148 of the Constitution while the special Communities exercise their powers in the much wider framework of Article 149.

The authors of the Spanish Constitution wanted to reserve the special status for the so-called historical nationalities within Spain: those territories with specific historical and cultural features, and especially those with their own language (which is the Basque Country, Catalonia, and Galicia), as well as with some previous experience of self-government. Other regions were not excluded from this status, but their access to this degree of self-government was made more difficult. Thus, in addition to these three, Andalusia has also achieved a special statute, and in practice Navarre (which attained autonomy through a procedure based on its special historical status), and the Canary Islands and Valencia enjoy a level of powers similar to these, although not granted through an autonomy statute, but rather by means of an organic law. The eleven remaining regions of Spain have adopted an ordinary status of autonomy.

* * *

4.   REDUCING NATIONALIST TENSIONS

* * *

With respect to the Autonomous State's capacity for consolidation, it is worth pointing out that, in general terms, the current regions' capacity to reduce territorial sectionalism is similar to the federal model's capacity do so. Regarding the capacity of federalism to reduce tensions derived from territorial sectionalism, we should first note, as a word of caution, that the federal model is not the only answer to problems derived from territorial sectionalism, but rather is principally a technique of decentralization and distribution of political power. Without a doubt, the federal system's performance has been more satisfactory in the task which we might term the technical division of power, than as an answer to problems of a nationalist origin, principally because these problems are very difficult to solve without recognizing the nationalist communities' right to self-government. * * *

* * * What is the situation in Spain? Briefly, the country started with an inadequate constitutional framework, especially with regard to the Constitution's inclusion of the participatory part of the federal formula. These inadequacies have not been adequately compensated for on the political plane. This is demonstrated by the absence of mechanisms of co-operation and, above all, of the political will to co-operate. * * *

Notes and Questions

1. Regionalism has a number of distinct meanings. In Italy, it is constitutionally mandated; in Britain (in regard to Scotland), it is based on an Act of Parliament. The constitutional status of the region does not determine its legal status. Compare the following two approaches:

[Italy opted for a regional state in its 1947 Constitution. The Italian concept was based on the assumption] that in a regional state, the powers of the regions (as well as those of the member states in a federal state) are completely guaranteed by the Constitution, while the powers of the local government in a unitary state are based on parliamentary statutes only. Therefore, [Ambrosini, who developed the idea of the regional state for the Constituent Assembly,] tried to guarantee the allocation of functions to the regions in the new Constitution, notwithstanding that those functions were supposed to be an expression of a devolution of power by the state to the new autonomous entities (and not the manifestation of the original sovereignty of the regions). However, he was not able to avoid entrusting to the national legislator the task of implementing the regional reform designed in the Constitution and of transferring, by ordinary legislation to the regions, the state functions which the Constitution assigned them.

* * *

[Implementing regionalism required considerable time.] In 1970, Parliament adopted the necessary legislation delegating the implementation of the reform to the Cabinet, and the ordinary regions were able to start functioning as originally intended. But it was immediately evident that the central government preferred a cautious line in dealing with the problem. Powers were transferred to the regions in a piecemeal fashion, in such a way that the national authority could keep a significant amount of influence on regional matters and, therefore, could control the formation and development of regional policies.

* * * [T]he financial autonomy of the regions was not established and they still depended on financial transfers from the state, which became more and more difficult to implement as the state fiscal crisis grew and public debt increased. * * * Moreover, the Government has been entrusted with the task of coordinating and directing the administrative activities of the regions, and the Constitutional Court decided that this new state function as well as the state substitution for the regions does not conflict with the Constitution.

Sergio Bartole, *Regionalism and Federalism in the Italian Constitutional Experience*, in *Autonomy: Applications and Implications* 173–75 (Markku Suksi ed., 1998).

With respect to the United Kingdom:

[T]he [Royal Commission on the Constitution, known as the] Kilbrandon Commission[,] defined devolution as the delegation of central government power without the relinquishment of sovereignty. This implies that the devolving authority 'reserves the power to revoke or redefine the nature of the delegation at any future date.[21] Devolution can take a number of forms, but only two of these are relevant to the present discussion. Legislative devolution involves the transfer of powers to regional assemblies to determine policy on a selected range of subjects, to enact legislation to give effect to that policy and to provide the administrative machinery for its execution, while reserving the Parliament the ultimate power to legislate for the regions on all matters. Executive devolution is more restricted than this. In this model Parliament and the central government would still be responsible for legislation and major policy issues, while regional assemblies would be responsible for general administration, and would have the task of devising and executing specific policies for their regions within the framework of the central government policy. Of these, legislative devolution is the more decentralizing in effect, and has the potential to lead to quasi-independent regional governments.

Abimbola A. Olowofoyeku, *Devolution: Conceptual and Implementational Problems*, 29 Anglo–American Law Review, 137, 137–38 (2000)

2. As the French Constitutional Council's recent decision regarding Corsica demonstrates, France remains politically centralized, with its national Parliament retaining a monopoly on lawmaking. Do deconcentration and administrative decentralization seem capable of producing any significant devolution of powers? Does it matter whether the purpose for devolution is identity based or distributive? The aspirations of certain regions of France, such as Corsica and Brittany, are identity based. Are these aspirations likely to be frustrated so long as the French Constitution maintains its present emphasis on unity and indivisibility?

Compared with attempts at devolution in France, those in the UK are more significant. Because they have their own Parliament and fairly extended lawmaking powers, Scots enjoy a far greater degree of autonomy than Corsicans. Is such greater autonomy more or less likely to fuel moves toward secession? Note that the Scottish Parliament has legislative powers only in areas expressly delegated by an act of Parliament, and its powers to tax are limited to a power to vary the basic rate of the income tax.

3. [A distinguished Belgian scholar,] Francis Delpérée[24] [has argued that] since 1967 * * * distinguishing the regional state from the federal state is not possible. Federal states are frequently created on the basis of a partial devolution of powers of a state to newly created intermediate entities.

* * * [M]any authors shared the idea that [federated entities] have a traditional sovereignty and, therefore, differ from the regions, which have an autonomy given to them solely by the central state. However, constitutional developments have outgrown this idea. The growing complexity of post-industrial contemporary society, the expansion of the social state and the increasing connection between the internal and

---

21. I. Loveland, *Constitutional Law, A Critical Introduction* (London: Butterworths, 1996) 420–1.

24. F. Delpérée, "Le Belgique, Etat fedéral, *Rev. dr. publ.* (1972), pp. 607–660.

external affairs of the states have favoured, on one hand, the enlargement of the powers of the authorities of the federal states and, on the other, the downgrading of the powers of the [federated] states. Step by step the federal states have started to look like unitary states, while the [federated] states have become dependent on the decisions of the central authorities, even in the fields originally retained by them. The experience of the New Deal in United States of American and the example of the German social state offer a strong justification for examining afresh the old theory of the federal state and of its distinction from the regional state.

Bartole, *op. cit.* at 186.

In discussing Italy, Professor Bartole argues that it is difficult, today, to draw any sharp distinction between federalism and decentralization. Is that not even more true with respect to Spain and the UK? Although none of the countries discussed in this section is federal in any formal sense, from a functional standpoint are they not all, except France, to a significant extent like federal countries?

4. *Asymmetrical regionalism.* "Decentralization and even federalization may also be used to afford a special status to particular areas of a country presenting specific problems: special status regions in Italy, autonomous areas in Portugal." M. Bothe, *Final Report*, in *Federalism and Decentralization* 417 (T. Fleiner–Gerster and S. Hutter eds., 1987). This might prove useful in solving problems of special regions or ethnic minorities being in the majority in certain parts of a country but may leave large territories of the majority population without self-rule. In the context of Scottish devolution the "West Lothian Question" emerged: "How can it be tolerable for Scottish Members of Parliament to continue to vote at Westminster on legislation governing England on matters about which, since they are devolved matters in Scotland, they themselves—let alone their English counterparts—have no say and no responsibility in Scotland?" T. Dalyell, HC Deb, 12 January 1998, col. 83; compare Douglas Hogg MP (col. 77); and see, generally, T. Dalyell, *Devolution: The End of Britain?* 245–48 (1977).

What is the solution to such objections? Should Scottish MPs be denied the vote in the above situation? Is federalism the answer? The drive toward decentralization seems fueled by identity-based concerns in many cases (although, in Italy, the Northern League's drive toward federalization was motivated above all by distributive objectives). Similarly, Belgium's transformation from a unitary to a federal state and the redrawing of India's federal map were also driven by identity-based aspirations. Does this suggest that deconcentration or mere decentralization is more likely to succeed and be accepted as satisfactory in contexts where distributive concerns predominate?

Asymmetrical decentralization may have different implications. In France, where such decentralization has been rather minimal, the Constitutional Council upheld the Corsican Parliament's right to modify regulations issued in Paris. At the other end of the spectrum, both in Spain and in the UK, decentralization and devolution, respectively, have been asymmetrical; while in Italy, regional decentralization has been asymmetrical to the extent that German-and French-speaking regions have obtained certain rights that have not been extended to their Italian-speaking counterparts. Significantly, in the UK, Italy, and France, asymmetrical arrangements resulted from initiatives of their national parliaments. Only in Spain is asymmetrical decentralization directly traceable to the Constitution. Particularly when this is contrasted with the failure of Canada's Lake Meech Accord, does it suggest that asymmetrical arrangements are most likely to occur as the result of political expediency? Consider, in that respect, that the greater devolution of powers to Scotland than to Wales was apparently motivated by the UK Parliament's fear that Scotland might more readily seek independence.

5. Spain's asymmetrical decentralization is traceable to its Constitution, but this seems more the latter's byproduct than a consequence of its explicit design. Faced with the difficult task of having to accommodate both those who insisted on national unity and the demands for greater autonomy by Catalonians and Basques, Spanish constitution-makers chose to produce a constitutional document marked by ambiguity. Accordingly, they divided the country into several autonomous communities, but only a few of those were politically organized to function as such. Therefore, from a formal standpoint, all of Spain is divided into autonomous communities with equivalent powers. From a practical standpoint, however, only Catalonians and Basques had the requisite infrastructure to fully benefit from their newly minted constitutional prerogatives. See Francisco Rubio Llorente, *The Writing of the Constitution of Spain*, in *Constitution Makers on Constitution–Making* 239 (Robert A. Goldwin and Art Kaufman eds., 1988). Contrast the Spanish situation with its Canadian counterpart in the context of Lake Meech.

6. *Federalism and local autonomy.* Both federal and nonfederal governing systems confront the problem of local autonomy in terms of democratic self-rule. Some federal constitutions, such as the German Basic Law, ascribe powers to local units encompassed within a *Land*; while others, such as the U.S. Constitution, do not. Article 28, Paragraph 2, of the German Basic Law declares: "The communes [towns, counties, and municipalities] must be guaranteed the right to regulate, on their own responsibility, all the affairs of the local community within the limits set by law." On the other hand, under the U.S. Constitution federalism is exclusively a matter between the federal government and the states. Moreover, to the extent that any subunit of a state is involved, it is treated as if it were a state. For example, if a law enacted by Boston were deemed in conflict with a valid federal power, it would be treated for federal constitutional purposes exactly the same as an equivalent law enacted by Massachusetts, where Boston is located. Conversely, the federal Constitution has nothing to say about how powers ought to be apportioned between any state and its subdivisions. A state constitution may apportion such powers within the state as it sees fit. In addition, individual rights provisions within the federal Constitution may have an impact on how powers may be constitutionally apportioned between a state and its subdivisions. See *Romer v. Evans*, 517 U.S. 620 (1996), in Chapter 6 (state constitution ban against protection of homosexuals from discrimination in conflict with local municipal laws to the contrary held unconstitutional as violative of federal equal protection rights).

C. THE CONFRONTATION BETWEEN THE FEDERATION AND FEDERATED GOVERNMENTS

Regardless of how powers are apportioned between a federation and federated entities, conflicts seem inevitable. These revolve primarily around the interplay between the two orders of democracy; namely, that of the federation and those of the federated entities, dealt with in Subsection C.1., and around the proper boundaries of apportioned powers—be they exclusive, concurrent, or delegated—and whether they be used to regulate private conduct or federated-entity activities, considered in Subsection C.2.

C.1. FEDERAL SOVEREIGNTY, FEDERAL–ENTITY SOVEREIGNTY AND DEMOCRACY

In a confederation, it is the confederated entities as such that have a voice at the confederal level, leaving no room for conflicts among electorates. In contrast, voters in a federal system vote both at the federated and federal levels. This can create problems. For example, can a majority of voters in the federal entity, who are all voters in the federated entities, impose a policy on a federated entity notwithstanding that a majority of the voters in the latter have cast their votes against it? Conversely, can the votes in one federated entity impose a policy with repercussions throughout the rest of the federation?

The German Basic Law enshrines federalism by making it unamendable, see Art 79 (3), but it allows for changing the number or boundaries of the *Länder*. As Professor Kommers notes:

> Article 29 of the Basic Law provides that "the federal territory, may be reorganized to ensure that the states by their size and capacity are able effectively to fill the functions incumbent upon them." Any proposal for redrawing state boundary lines needs the sanction of federal law and the approval of the majority of the voters in the affected states. Under the terms of Article 29 (3), however, two-thirds of the voters in the particular area affected by such a proposal may, by their approval overcome a majority. vote against it in any one of the affected states "unless in the entire territory of the affected *Land* a majority of two-thirds rejects the modification."

The *Southwest State* case arose out of the decision of the Allied powers to divide the former states of Württemberg and Baden into three southwestern states: Württemberg-Baden, Baden, and Württemberg-Hohenzollern. Germans bridled over this arrangement because it split up two historic states, sundering a relatively integrated political community. Article 118 of the Basic Law sought to cope with this situation. As *a lex specialis*, it modified the general policy of Article 29 by authorizing the southwestern states to reorganize themselves, by mutual agreement. The most likely possibilities were the restoration of the former states of

Baden and Württemberg and the consolidation of the three existing states into a single state. Unable to agree on a plan of reorganization, the states effectively turned the matter over to the federal government. Article 118 empowered the federal government to reorganize these states by law in the absence of a tri-state agreement.

Southwest arose under an earlier version of Article 29. In its original form it required the reorganization of the federal territory as a whole by federal law. A majority of voters in an area affected by a proposed boundary change had to approve the proposal in a referendum. In addition, Article 29 (4) required the Bundestag to reintroduce the law if it should be rejected by the voters; if it was reenacted, a majority of voters would have to approve the measure in a national referendum. Article 118, as noted, circumvented these procedures with respect to the reorganization of the southwestern states.

Kommers, *op. cit.* at 62.

SOUTHWEST STATE CASE

Federal Constitutional Court (Germany).
1 BVerfGE 14 (1951).[c]

[When tri-state negotiations collapsed, in November 1950, the federal government enacted two reorganization statutes. The first extended the terms of the Württemberg-Hohenzollern and Baden legislatures, a measure designed to avoid new state elections in April 1951 because reorganization was likely to be approved. The second specified the procedures by which the proposed referendum would be carried out. The proposal provided for merging the three states into the single state of Baden–Württemberg, subject to the approval of a majority of voters in three of four electoral districts established for purposes of the referendum. The small and cohesive 150–year-old state of Baden challenged the constitutionality of these statutes on the ground that they violated the principles of democracy and federalism: democracy, because the electoral districts were created in such a way as to dilute the votes of persons casting ballots in Baden; and federalism, because the federal government is powerless to tamper with the legislature of an independent state.]

Judgment of the Second Senate:

D.   [First Reorganization Law]

3.   The Basic Law has chosen democracy as the basis for the governmental system (Articles 20, 28): The Federal Republic is a democratic, federal state. The constitutional order in the states must conform to the principles of a democratic state based on the rule of law within the meaning of the Basic Law. The federation guarantees that the constitutional order of the states will conform to this political order.

As prescribed by the Basic Law, democracy requires not only that parliament control the government but also that the right to vote of eligible voters is not removed or impaired by unconstitutional means * * * It is true that the democratic principle does not imply that the

---

c. Reproduced from Donald P. Kommers, *The Constitutional Jurisprudence of*   *the Federal Republic of Germany* 62–66 (2d ed. 1997).

term of a state legislature must not exceed four years or that it cannot be extended for important reasons. But this principle does require that the term of a state legislature, whose length was set by the people in accepting their constitution, can be extended only through procedures prescribed in that constitution, i.e., only with the consent of the people.

If the federation prevents an election scheduled by the state constitution without the consent of the people of the state, then it violates the fundamental right of a citizen in a democratic state, the right to vote, as protected by Article 28 (3) of the Basic Law.

4.   Another fundamental principle of the Basic Law is that of federalism (Articles 20, 18, 30). As members of the federation *Länder* are states with their own sovereign power. This power, even if limited in subject matter, is not derived from the federation but recognized by it. As long as it remains within the framework of Article 28 (1), a state's constitutional order falls within the state's jurisdiction. In particular, it is exclusively incumbent upon the state to determine the rule that governs the formation of the state's constitutional organs and their functions. Th[e] state's competency also includes setting regulations which determine how often and on what occasions citizens may vote as well as when and under what conditions the term of a state legislature expires.

This rule also applies equally to legislation [enacted] pursuant to Article 118. It is true that, in order to effect reorganization, the federal legislature has power to "retrench" the states of Baden, Württemberg-Baden, and Württemberg-Hohenzollern. But it cannot disturb the constitutional structures of these states as long as they exist in their entirety.

One may not argue that, by eliminating the three state legislatures in the process of reorganization, the federation shortens their terms of office and consequently can also extend them for a transitional period.

Elimination of the state legislatures is a necessary consequence of the elimination of these states; thus [this act] does not constitute a curtailment of [the legislatures'] terms of office. By contrast, extension of the legislative terms may occur with respect to existing state legislatures. This extension requires a special legislative act which the federation cannot pass for the aforementioned reasons. A state cannot dispose of its legislative authority. And the federation cannot by virtue of a state's consent obtain legislative authority which the Basic Law does not grant. Therefore, the fact that Württemberg-Hohenzollern consented to the measure taken by the federation is without legal significance.

5.   Article 118 [2] authorizes the federal legislature only to regulate "reorganization" and thus draws constitutional limits. The federal legislature could extend the electoral terms of the state legislatures only if the "matter cannot be effectively regulated by legislation of individual states" [Article 72 (2) of the Basic Law]. This limitation precludes extending the term of state legislatures. Such authority remains primarily a matter for the states.

6.   In view of these legal restraints, reasons neither of practicality, political necessity, nor similar considerations can confer unfettered dis-

cretion on the federal legislature to enact any regulations that seem reasonable and proper under the guise of reorganizing states * * *

7. The Federal Constitutional Court must hold a legal provision null and void if it is inconsistent with the Basic Law: Hence we declare that the First Reorganization Law is null and void.

E. [Second Reorganization Law]

8. (a) It has been asserted that a federation cannot eliminate a member state against its population's will. As a rule, a federal constitution guarantees the existence and territory of member states. But the Basic Law expressly deviates from this rule. Article 79 (3) guarantees as an inviolable principle only that the federation must be divided "into states." The Basic Law does not contain any guarantee for presently existing states and their borders. On the contrary, it provides—as follows from Articles 29 and 118—for changes in territorial conditions of individual states as well as for a reorganization of federal territory which may entail the elimination of one or more existing states. This reorganization may even be effected against the will of the population of the state concerned. The Basic Law thus espouses a "changeable federal state".

(b) It follows from Article 29 (4), however, that an ordinary federal law cannot supersede the will of a member state's population—only a new vote of the federal legislature and a referendum of the entire federal population can do so. Thus only the will of the population of the higher unit suffices, and not merely the will of the population of one or several neighboring states.

(c) Baden claims that, aside from the principle contained in Article 29 (4), other clauses of the Basic Law recognize the democratic principle (Articles 20, 28). Democracy means self-determination of the people. [The Second Reorganization Law] Baden argues[,] deprives the people of Baden of this right because it forces them to become part of a southwest state against their will.

That, in principle, a people must themselves determine their basic order certainly follows from the notion of democracy. The state of Baden, as a member of the federation, is a stare to which necessarily belongs a body politic. This body politic possesses the right of self-determination. It is decisive, however, that Baden as a member state of the federation is not autonomous and independent but is part of a federal order which restricts its sovereign power in various respects. * * * To a certain extent a tension exists between the principles of democracy, and federalism concerning the position of a member state in the federation. There can be a compromise between the two only if both suffer certain restrictions. In the case of reorganization of federal territory consigned to the federation, it is the nature of things that the people's right to self-determination in a state be restricted in the interest of the more comprehensive unit. Within the scope of what is possible in a federal state, the Basic Laws provisions in Article 29 and in Article 118 safeguard the democratic principle by setting forth that the bodies politic, respectively; of the federation and of the area to be reorganized will ultimately decide. * * *

McCULLOCH v. MARYLAND

Supreme Court (United States).
17 U.S. 316 (1819).

[For the facts and first part of this decision, see Subsection A.1. above.]

3. [May] the state of Maryland, without violating the constitution, tax [the Baltimore] branch of the federal Bank? That the power of taxation is one of vital importance; that it is retained by the states; that it is not abridged by the grant of a similar power to the government of the Union; that it is to be concurrently exercised by the two governments—are truths which have never been denied. But such is the paramount character of the constitution, that its capacity to withdraw any subject from the action of even this power, is admitted.

The argument on the part of the state of Maryland, is, not that the states may directly resist a law of congress, but that they may exercise their acknowledged powers upon it, and that the constitution leaves them this right, in the confidence that they will not abuse it.

The people of a state * * * give to their government a right of taxing themselves and their property, and as the exigencies of government cannot be limited, they prescribe no limits to the exercise of this right, resting confidently on the interest of the legislator, and on the influence of the constituent over their representative, to guard them against its abuse. But the means employed by the government of the Union have no such security, nor is the right of a state to tax them sustained by the same theory. Those means are not given by the people of a particular state, not given by the constituents of the legislature, which claim the right to tax them, but by the people of all the states. They are given by all, for the benefit of all—and upon theory, should be subjected to that government only which belongs to all.

The sovereignty of a state extends to everything which exists by its own authority, or is introduced by its permission; but does it extend to those means which are employed by congress to carry into execution powers conferred on that body by the people of the United States? We think it demonstrable, that it does not. Those powers are not given by the people of a single state. They are given by the people of the United States, to a government whose laws, made in pursuance of the constitution, are declared to be supreme. Consequently, the people of a single state cannot confer a sovereignty which will extend over them.

Would the people of any one state trust those of another with a power to control the most insignificant operations of their state government? We know they would not. Why, then, should we suppose, that the people of any one state should be willing to trust those of another with a power to control the operations of a government to which they have confided their most important and most valuable interests? In the legislature of the Union alone, are all represented. The legislature of the Union alone, therefore, can be trusted by the people with the power of controlling measures which concern all, in the confidence that it will not be abused. This, then, is not a case of confidence, and we must consider it is as it really is.

It has also been insisted, that, as the power of taxation in the general and state governments is acknowledged to be concurrent, every argument which would sustain the right of the general government to tax banks chartered by the states, will equally sustain the right of the states to tax banks chartered by the general government. But the two cases are not on the same reason. The people of all the states have created the general government, and have conferred upon it the general power of taxation. The people of all the states, and the states themselves, are represented in congress, and, by their representatives, exercise this power. When they tax the chartered institutions of the states, they tax their constituents; and these taxes must be uniform. But when a state taxes the operations of the government of the United States, it acts upon institutions created, not by their own constituents, but by people over whom they claim no control. It acts upon the measures of a government created by others as well as themselves, for the benefit of others in common with themselves. The difference is that which always exists, and always must exist, between the action of the whole on a part, and the action of a part on the whole—between the law of a government declared to be supreme, and those of a government which, when in opposition to those laws, is not supreme.

The court has bestowed on this subject its most deliberate consideration. The result is a conviction that the states have no power, by taxation or otherwise, to retard, impede, burden, or in any manner control, the operations of the constitutional laws enacted by congress to carry into execution the powers vested in the general government. This is, we think, the unavoidable consequence of that supremacy which the constitution has declared. We are unanimously of opinion, that the law passed by the legislature of Maryland, imposing a tax on the Bank of the United States, is unconstitutional and void.

Notes and Questions

1.   The USSC in *McCulloch* went on to specify that its decision did not preclude Maryland from collecting real estate taxes from the Federal Bank branch in Baltimore or other state taxes from Maryland citizens with deposits in the Federal Bank. Is that consistent with the main thrust of the Court's opinion?

2.   Does the GFCC's distinction between a federally decreed prolongation of a *Land* legislature's term and abolition of the same as part of a reorganization of federated entities make sense? Are not both equally likely to undermine the federated entity's integrity as a limited sovereign? The German Basic Law and the *Southwest State Case* make it clear that what is paramount to German federalism is the maintenance of a federal republic rather than preserving any particular number or identity of *Länder*. In short, German federalism is above all distributive, and consistent with this, the federal electorate can legitimately have the last word concerning the reorganization of federated entities. But what about the treatment of similar issues in the context of identity-based federalism? Should not the electorate

of an identity-based federated entity have a veto power over any attempt by the federation to subdivide it or merge it into a larger unit? For an analysis of the newly formed Swiss canton of Jura, see Lidija R. Basta Fleiner, *Minority and Legitimacy of a Federal State*, in *Federalism and Multiethnic States: The Case of Switzerland* 86–94 (Lidija R. Basta Fleiner and Thomas Fleiner eds., 2000), Cf. the *Quebec Secession Case*, in Chapter 2, for the converse problem of federation acquiescence in a federated entity's projected secession.

C.2. CONFRONTATION AND COOPERATION BETWEEN THE FEDERATION AND THE FEDERATED GOVERNMENTS

C.2.1. DETERMINATION OF STATE CONSTITUTIONAL STRUCTURES BY THE FEDERATION

The U.S. Constitution allows for nearly absolute freedom in the determination of the internal constitutional structures of the constituent states. It forbids eliminating a state without its consent, but, otherwise, the only express constitutional constraint is the Guarantee Clause of Article IV Sect. 4: "The United States shall guarantee to every State in this Union a Republican Form of Government." This provision is nonjusticiable, leaving enforcement up to the U.S. Congress. In other countries, however, the federal government has an acknowledged power in defining the internal constitutional structures of the federated units, as the *Altai Territory Case* below indicates. Further, both the interim and current South African constitutions expressly require that the provinces submit their constitutions to the South African Constitutional Court (SACC) for certification. The South African Constitution specifically authorizes the provinces to adopt their own constitutions. A provincial constitution must be consistent with the national constitution but can provide for "provincial legislative or executive structures and procedures that differ from those provided for by the National Constitution." The Russian Constitutional Court (RCC) considered a similar possibility in relation to the "subjects of the federation," as the federated entities are called in the Russian Constitution.

ALTAI TERRITORY CASE

[CONSTITUTIONALITY OF CERTAIN PROVISIONS OF
THE BASIC LAW OF THE ALTAI TERRITORY].
Constitutional Court (Russia).
Decision 2–P of 18 January 1996.

[The constituent entities (subjects) of the Russian Federation have their own constitutions or charters. These fundamental laws are enacted by the respective legislatures. In many constituent entities, various procommunist groups commanded legislative majorities at the time of the drafting of these basic laws. The procommunists, partly following the Leninist tradition of supremacy of the representative–legislative body and partly to guarantee their powers vis-à-vis the local executive, which was likely to fall under the spell of the President of the Russian Federation, experimented with various arrangements of division of powers. The Court reviewed these basic laws in a series of cases. In order to evaluate their power-sharing mechanism, the Court had to develop certain separation-of-powers criteria. As this case indicates, the prevalent model was the arrangement found in the Russian Federal Constitution. This is partly explained by a specific understanding of federalism, which requires a certain uniformity within the federation.]

* * *

3. The Constitution of the Russian Federation provides that the subjects of the Russian Federation (RF) may constitute their own system of government by means of adopting respective legislative acts. However, such acts must be in conformity with the fundamentals of the constitutional system, the general principles of the organization of the legislative and executive branches of power (Article 77, part 1), and other provisions of the RF Constitution and federal legislative acts bringing them into effect. State power in the RF subjects must be based on the principles of a democratic, federal rule-of-law state with a republican form of government (Article 1, part 1), integrity and a uniform system of state power (Article 5, part 3), as well as governance on the basis of the separation of the legislative, executive, and judicial branches, and the independence of the branches of power (Article 10).

4. The applicant challenges the constitutionality of Articles 44, 45 and 73.11 of the Altai Basic Law, which determines the competence of the Legislative Assembly to lay down the procedure for forming extra-budgetary and currency funds, adopting the terms for such funds, as well as establishing the procedure for expending credits for administrative and social purposes.

The competence of the branches of power in the RF subjects is based on the rule following from Article 77, part 1, of the RF Constitution. In accordance with this rule, the competencies of the branches of power in the RF subjects are determined by the RF subjects themselves, so long as the constitutional basis and the prerogatives of the federal legislature are not affected. In accordance with this rule, the Legislative Assembly, laying down the procedures as to establishing the said funds, and determining the terms and accountability procedures, cannot be qualified as violating the RF Constitution, nor as encroaching onto the administrative functioning of the Administration of the [Altai] Territory. Essentially, this is the case of the legislative branch realizing its budget powers, which in itself does not upset the balance of power between the legislative and executive branches.

Furthermore, the competence of the Legislative Assembly to lay down procedures as to establishing extra-budgetary and currency funds in the Territory conforms to the Federal Law of 15 April 1993 "On the Fundamentals of Budgetary Prerogatives and Competencies to Form and Expend Extra–Budgetary Funds of the Legislative and Executive Branches of the [RF Subjects]" (Article 22).

* * *

5. At issue is also Article 77 of the Altai Basic Law, which provides that the activities of the Legislative Assembly may not be interrupted or ended before time by a decision of any organ of state power of the RF or the Territory. The activities of the Legislative Assembly and its permanent committees and commissions may be ended only by a decision of the Legislative Assembly itself. The competence of the Legislative Assembly may end only following the expiration of its term of service, or in special cases by a decision of the Legislative Assembly.

In the applicant's view the provisions of the said Article take the Altai Legislative Assembly outside the jurisdiction of the RF. However, the Basic Law stipulates that the legal basis for executing state power in the Territory is based on the RF Constitution, federal laws, the Basic Law, and the laws of the Territory, while the organization and execution of state power in the Territory is based on general principles of the organization of state power in the RF. Nothing in Article 77 states otherwise.

At the same time, the RF Constitution does not provide for the right of federal bodies of power to end or interrupt the activities of lawfully elected legislatures of the RF subjects, due to presumption of conformity of those activities to the RF Constitution and federal laws. The settlement of disputes concerning the competencies of the branches of power of the RF and its subjects is provided for in the RF Constitution and federal laws, e.g., through conciliatory procedures and appeals to the competent courts and other legal mechanisms.

Article 77, part 1, of the Altai Basic Law excludes the possibility of dissolution of the Legislative Assembly by the Head of the Territory's Administration. The measure under certain circumstances may serve as one of the checks and balances between the executive and legislative branches. The legislature, in deciding to include or exclude this measure, must be guided by considerations of the balance of these powers.

* * *

6. Pursuant to Article 71, part 4, para. 2, of the Altai Basic Law, the prerogative to sign the laws of the Territory rests with the Chair of the Legislative Assembly.

The RF Constitution places the adoption of laws within the legislature's exclusive competence. At the same time, the Constitution provides for the veto and promulgation of federal laws by the Head of State as a significant element of the legislative procedure, to ensure separation of powers and to ensure against possible mistakes. As a result, any law adopted by the legislature acquires the force of a legal norm of the uniform system of state power. Adoption and promulgation of laws by one and the same body would upset the balance of power in the legislative sphere. The same holds true, also, for the legislative process on the level of the RF subjects; there, too, the promulgation in principle is a prerogative of the Head of the Administration * * *.

Article 73, para. 12, of the Basic Law places within the competencies of the Legislative Assembly the approval of the government plan for the Territory, the structure of the Administration, and amendments thereto.

This provision does not conflict with the RF Constitution, and conforms to the Federal Law of 5 March 1992 "On the Territorial and Regional Council of the People's Deputies and the Territorial and Regional Administration." The Law provides that the government plan for the Territory and the structure of the Territorial Administration are approved by the representative branch (Article 44.7 and Article 48, part 1.a).

* * *

The applicant draws attention to the following provisions: the Head of the Administration is elected by the Legislative Assembly; the Legislative Assembly approves the structure of the Council of the Administration and the key nominations to the Administration; the Legislative Assembly may express non-confidence not only to the Head of the Administration, but [also the Head] must annually report to the Legislative Assembly on the activities of the executive in the [Altai] Territory.

* * *

The RF Constitution does not contain a specific provision as to procedures for electing the heads of the executive branches in the RF subjects. However, the Constitution provides that people exercise their power directly, as well as through the bodies of state power (Article 3, part 2). In conjunction with Article 32 of the RF Constitution, which affirms the right of citizens to elect the bodies of state power, the meaning of this article allows the conclusion that the highest executive authority receives the mandate from the people and is accountable to the people. Since Russian federalism is founded upon the principle of the integrity and uniform system of state power (Article 5, part 3 of the RF Constitution), the branches of power in the RF subjects are formed in accordance with the same principles as those on the federal level. According to the Federal Law of 6 December 1994 "On the Basic Guarantees of the Voting Rights of Citizens of the Russian Federation," the head of the executive branch of the RF is among those officials elected by citizens (Article 2).

Procedures for forming the executive branch in the RF subjects on the basis of the direct election of the heads of the administration are provided for in the majority of the legislatures of the RF subjects. The Altai Basic Law (Article 83, as of 2 October 1995) provides differently: the Head of the Administration is elected by the Legislative Assembly; a citizen of the RF may be elected subject to satisfying the set requirements. Thereby the Legislative Assembly becomes an electoral college of sorts, whose decision substitutes for the electorate's direct choice. Such an election procedure does not conform to the RF Constitution and federal laws in force. The Head of the Administration, who was elected in such a manner, cannot be considered a legitimate representative of the executive branch since neither the legislative nor the executive branch is empowered to determine the representative for each other, including on the federal level.

These requirements, following from the independence of the executive and legislative branches, and ensuring independence in forming the respective bodies of power, are stipulated in Article 95, part 2 of the RF

Constitution. The Article provides that the Council of the Federation is composed of two representatives from each RF subject: one from the legislative branch and one from the executive branch. This separate representation becomes meaningless if both representatives, the Chair of the Legislative Assembly and the Head of the Administration, are elected by one and the same body.

The constitutional principle of the independence of the executive branch of the RF subject is inevitably violated, if the representative organ acquires the right to approve the structure of the Council of the Administration (Article 82, part 1, para. 2, of the Basic Law). Determining the structure of the Administration is a competence of the Head of the Administration, since he bears responsibility for the activities of the executive branch. For the same reason, the Head of the Administration may not be restricted in his right to dismiss officials enumerated in Article 81, part 3, of the Basic Law. Determining the structure of the Administration is a competence of the Head of the Administration, since he bears responsibility for the activities of the executive branch. For the same reason, the Head of the Administration may not be restricted in his right to dismiss officials, enumerated in Article 81, part 3, of the Basic Law, without the consent of the Legislative Assembly.

* * *

The balance of power and stability of the two branches can be sustained only if the competencies of one branch are balanced by adequate competencies of the other. Possible abuses of the right to dismiss the Administration are checked when the Head of the Administration has the right to dissolve the legislature. The legislature must resolve those issues * * * ensuring cooperation and mutual trust between the two branches.

* * *

As provided in Article 87, part 2, of the Altai Basic Law, the duty of the Head of the Administration to present annual reports on the activities of the executive power to the Legislative Assembly does not conform to the principle of separation of powers insofar as accountability of the executive is thereby introduced to the legislature on all matters within the executive's competence, and the right is introduced to the legislature to give orders or make decisions triggering responsibility for officials in the executive branch.

* * *

Separate Opinion of Justice Vitruk.

The Administration of the Altai Territory challenges the constitutionality of certain provisions of Articles 44, 45, 71, 73, 77, 81–85, 87 of the Altai Basic Law, alleging that the Legislative Assembly of the Territory and its Chair are vested with a number of extra competencies in violation of the constitutional principles of separation of powers, the independence of the branches of power, and the system of checks and balances.

When determining the constitutionality of the provisions of the Altai Basic Law (as well as that of any RF subject) it is essential to consider the following legal principles and the requirements thereof.

1. The principle of separation of powers denotes not only independence of each of the branches of power (legislative, executive, and judicial) within the boundaries of their respective competencies, but also their interaction and cooperation, as preconditioned by the integrity and uniform system of state power, the need to guarantee and protect the rights and freedoms of man and citizen, and to protect other fundamentals of the constitutional system.

However, there are diverse models of organization of state power based on separation of powers. The differences are possible as regards the competencies of the bodies of the legislative and executive branches, the mode of coordination, as defined by the mode of governance (there are also diverse models of those), and by the federal system. The RF subjects are independent in determining their organization of branches of power, so long as they respect the fundamentals of the constitutional system, and the general principles of the organization of state power as stipulated in federal laws (Article 77, part 1, of the RF Constitution). Observance of the constitutional norms and principles, established by federal law, does not denote copying the federal arrangement for the legislative and executive branches, nor does it denote uniformity for all the RF subjects.

In the absence of a specific federal law, the RF subjects may constitute their own system of state power.

* * *

The RF subjects are diverse. The differences are not only in their names, but also in their legal nature, and accordingly in their status. There are republics acknowledged as states; there are territories and regions; there are cities of federal importance—Moscow and St. Petersburg (Moscow being the capital of the RF)—and there are autonomous areas (some of which are located within the territories and regions). All of the RF subjects are equal only in their relations with the federal government, as per Article 5, part 4, of the RF Constitution. Leveling the legal status of the RF subjects (not to mention their economic and social spheres) is an objective tendency. In those conditions, unduly expediting the unification of state power in the RF subjects is premature and may play a negative role in realizing the principle of genuine federalism. This is evidenced also by the diverse practice of demarcating the jurisdiction and competencies between the branches of power of the RF subjects.

* * *

2. Both the federal legislature and the legislatures of the RF subjects consider the strategic objectives for the organization of state power, and other nonlegal factors (socio-economic, political, spiritual, traditional national, and other specifics), that is, they are guided by principles of pragmatism, although within constitutional limits. The Constitutional Court, pursuant to the law, may not be guided by pragmatism alone when deciding a case before it. However, it may and ought to

consider the consequences of its decisions. Therefore, the Constitutional Court in its activities ostensibly does not rule out the principle of self-restraint and should not always strive to go ahead of, or substitute for, the legislature.

3.   Some of the challenged provisions of the Altai Basic Law require the adoption of subsequent legal acts (Article 81, part 3, Article 83, etc.). This also complicated the judicial review of the challenged provisions of the Basic Law by the Constitutional Court, since the Constitutional Court is forced to give its interpretation of those provisions—the interpretation that might not be retained when laws are actually adopted. In other words, the Constitutional Court must guess the intent of the Territory's legislature.

Concerning the specific challenged provisions of the Altai Basic Law:

1.   It is the prerogative of the Legislative Assembly of the Altai Territory to determine the competencies and the procedures relating to the formation, basic organization, and activities of the Administration of the Altai Territory and its Head. In our view the requirements of Article 77, part 2, of the RF Constitution on the uniform system of the executive power in the RF apply only as regards the competencies of the said branch that concern the matters within the exclusive jurisdiction of the RF and the matters within the concurrent jurisdiction of the RF and its subjects. However, there is no such uniformity as regards the matters falling within the jurisdiction of the RF subjects. Moreover, the constitutional provision in question does not provide for only one procedure for forming the executive branch in a subject of the RF. There are also diverse modes to elect the Head of the Administration of the Territory. This issue may as well not be a subject of the federal law on the basic principles of organization of the representative and executive branches in the RF subjects. When the Head of the Administration is elected by the Legislative Assembly on the basis of a competitive, secret vote, the principle of popular government is not violated. Nor is the principle of direct elections to state power in the RF subjects, since the Constitutions and Basic Laws of the RF subjects provide for the list of state bodies, formed on the basis of direct election.

* * *

The Legislative Assembly of the Territory may regularly receive information about the activities of the executive branch of the Territory. Therefore, the provision of Article 87, part 2, of the Altai Basic Law as to the annual report of the Head of the Administration of the Territory on the activities of the executive to the Legislative Assembly is quite logical. This does not denote total accountability of the Territory's Administration to the Legislative Assembly, and inter alia evaluation on the basis of the said reports of the Administration's activities by the Legislative Assembly, with consequent ramifications for the Administration.

* * *

Separate Opinion of Justice Rudkin.

* * *

It is no accident that the RF Constitution omits a specific provision as to the procedure for electing the heads of the executive branch in the RF subjects. This omission is based on the specifics of Russian federalism, as well as the decentralization of state power, whose boundaries are defined by the RF Constitution. Article 3 stipulates a general principle of the organization of state power by means of popular participation, directly or through the bodies of state power and local self-government, the people being the sole bearer of sovereignty. In conjunction with Article 32 of the RF Constitution, which affirms the right of citizens to participate in state government directly or through elected representatives, the meaning of Article 3, therefore, allows the conclusion that the executive branch may be elected by the people directly, as well as be formed by the legislature, or by other constitutional means. The RF Constitution allows for various legal solutions to this problem.

S.R. BOMMAI v. UNION OF INDIA

Supreme Court (India).
(1994) 2 S.C.R. 644.

[For the facts of this case, see Chapter 3.]

Ahmadi, J.

* * *

21. It is common knowledge that shortly after we constituted ourselves into a Republic, the Princely States gradually disappeared leading to the unification of India into a single polity with duality of governmental agencies for effective and efficient administration of the country under central direction and, if I may say so, supervision. The duality of governmental organs on the Central and State levels reflect demarcation of functions in a manner as would ensure the sovereignty and integrity of our country. The experience of partition of the country and its aftermath had taught lessons which were too fresh to be forgotten by our Constitution makers. It was perhaps for that reason that our Founding Fathers thought that a strong Centre was essential to ward off separatist tendencies and consolidate the unity and integrity of the country.

22. A Division Bench of the Madras High Court in *M. Karunnanidhi v. Union of India* AIR 1977 Mad 192: (1977) while dealing with the contention that the Constitution is a federal one and that the States are autonomous having definite powers and independent rights to govern, and the Central Government has no right to interfere in the governance of the State, observed as under :

> "[T]here may be a federation of independent States, as it is in the case of United States of America. As the name itself denotes, it is a Union of States, either by treaty or by legislation by the concerned States. In those cases, the federating units gave certain powers to the federal Government and retained some. To apply the meaning to the word 'federation' or 'autonomy' used in the context of the American Constitution, to our Constitution will be totally misleading."

After tracing the history of the governance of the country under the British rule till the framing of our Constitution, the Court proceeded to add as follows:

"The feature of the Indian Constitution is the establishment of a Government for governing the entire country. In doing so, the Constitution prescribes the powers of the Central Government and the powers of the State Governments and the relations between the two. In a sense, if the word 'federation' can be used at all, it is a federation of various States which were designated under the Constitution for the purpose of efficient administration and governance of the country. The powers of the Centre and States are demarcated under the Constitution. It is futile to suggest that the States are independent, sovereign or autonomous units which had joined the federation under certain conditions. No such State ever existed or acceded to the Union."

23.   Under our Constitution the state as such has no inherent sovereign power or autonomous power which cannot be encroached upon by the Centre. The very fact that under our Constitution, Article 3, Parliament may by law form a new State by separation of territory from any State or by uniting two or more States or parts of States or by uniting any territory to a part of any State, etc., militates against the view that the States are sovereign or autonomous bodies having definite independent rights of governance. In fact, as pointed out earlier in certain circumstances the Central Government can issue directions to States and in emergency conditions assume far reaching powers affecting the States as well, and the fact that the President has powers to take over the administration of States demolishes the theory of an independent or autonomous existence of a State. It must also be realized that unlike the Constitution of the United States of America which recognizes dual citizenship [Section 1(1), 14th Amendment], the Constitution of India, Article 5, does not recognize the concept of dual citizenship. Under the American Constitution all persons born or naturalized in the United States, and subject to the jurisdiction thereof, are citizens of the United States and of the State wherein they reside whereas under Article 5 of the Indian Constitution at its commencement, every person domiciled in the territory of India and (a) who was born in the territory of India; or (b) either of whose parents was born in the territory of India; or (c) who has been ordinarily resident in the territory of India for not less than five years immediately preceding such commencement shall be a citizen of India. Article 9 makes it clear that if any person voluntarily acquires the citizenship of any foreign country, he will cease to be a citizen of India. These provisions clearly negative the concept of dual citizenship, a concept expressly recognized under the American Constitution. The concept of citizenship assumes some importance in a federation because in a country which recognizes dual citizenship, the individual would owe allegiance both to the Federal Government as well as the State Government but a country recognizing a single citizenship does not face complications arising from dual citizenship and by necessary implication negatives the concept of State sovereignty.

24.   Thus the significant absence of the expressions like 'federal' or 'federation' in the constitutional vocabulary, Parliament's powers under

Articles 2 and 3 elaborated earlier, the extraordinary powers conferred to meet emergency situations, the residuary powers conferred by Article 48 read with Entry 97 in List 1 of the VIIth Schedule on the Union, the power to amend the Constitution, the power to issue directions to States, the concept of a single citizenship, the set-up of an integrated judiciary, etc., have led constitutional experts to doubt the appropriateness of the appellation 'federal' to the Indian Constitution. Said Prof. KC Whereas in his work Federal Government:

> "What makes one doubt that the Constitution of India is strictly and fully federal, however, are the powers of intervention in the affairs of the States given by the Constitution to the Central Government and Parliament."

Thus in the United States, the sovereign States enjoy their own separate existence which cannot be impaired; indestructible States having constituted an indestructible Union. In India, on the contrary, Parliament can by law form a new State, alter the size of an existing State, alter the name of an existing State, etc., and even curtail the power, both executive and legislative, by amending the Constitution. That is why the Constitution of India is differently described, more appropriately as 'quasi-federal' because it is a mixture of the federal and unitary elements, leaning-more towards the latter but then what is there in a name, what is important to bear in mind is the thrust and implications of the various provisions of the Constitution bearing on the controversy in regard to scope and ambit of the Presidential power under Article 356 and related provisions.

* * *

K. Ramaswamy, J.

* * *

165. The polyglot Indian society of wide geographical dimensions habiting by social milieu, ethnic variety or cultural diversity, linguistic multiplicity, hierarchical caste structure among Hindus, religious pluralism, majority of rural population and minority urban habitus, the social and cultural diversity of the people furnish a manuscript historical material for and the Founding Fathers of the Constitution to lay federal structure as foundation to integrate India as a united Bharat. Federalism implies mutuality and common purpose for the aforesaid process of change with continuity between the Centre and the States which are the structural units operating on balancing wheel of concurrence and promises to resolve problems and promote social, economic and cultural advancement of its people and to create fraternity among the people. Article 1 is a recognition of the history that Union of India's territorial limits are unalterable and the States are creatures of the Constitution and they are territorially alterable constituents with single citizenship of all the people by birth or residence with no right to cessation. Under Articles 2 and 4 the significant feature is that while the territorial integrity of India is fully ensured and maintained, there is a significant absence of the territorial integrity of the constituent States under Article 3. Parliament may by law form a new State by separation of territory from any State or by uniting two or more States or part of States or

uniting any territory to a part of any State or by increasing the area of any State or diminishing the area of any State, or alter the boundary of any State.

166.   In Berubari Union and Exchange of Enclaves Reference under Article 143(1) of the Constitution of India, Gajendragadkar, J. speaking for eight-judge Bench held that: (SCR p. 285)

"Unlike other federations, the Federation embodied in the said Act was not the result of a pact or union between separate and independent communities of States who came together for certain common purposes and surrendered a part of their sovereignty. The constituent units of the federation were deliberately created and it is significant that they, unlike the units of other federations, had no organic roots in the past. Hence, in the Indian Constitution, by contrast with other Federal Constitutions, the emphasis on the preservation of the territorial integrity of the constituent States is absent. The makers of the Constitution were aware of the peculiar conditions under which, and the reasons for which, the States (originally Provinces) were formed and their boundaries were defined, and so they deliberately adopted the provisions in Article 3 with a view to meet the possibility of the redistribution of the said territories after the integration of the Indian States. In fact it is well-known that as a result of the States Reorganization Act, 1956 (Act XXXVII of 1956), in the place 31 (1960) 3 SCR 250: AIR 1960 SC 845 157 of the original 27 States and one Area which were mentioned in Part D in the First Schedule to the Constitution, there are now only 14 States and 6 other Areas which constitute the Union Territory mentioned in the First Schedule. The changes thus made clearly illustrate the working of the peculiar and striking feature of the Indian Constitution." * * *

167.   Union and States Relations under the Constitution (Tagore Law Lectures) by M.C. Setalvad at p. 10 stated that

"one notable departure from the accepted ideas underlying a federation when the power in the Central Government to redraw the boundaries of States or even to destroy them."

168.   The Constitution decentralizes the governance of the States by a four tier administration i.e. Central Government, State Government, Union Territories, Municipalities and Panchayats. See the Constitution for Municipalities and Panchayats: Part IX (Panchayats) and Part IX–A (Municipalities) introduced through the Constitution 73rd Amendment Act, making the peoples' participation in the democratic process from grass-root level a reality. Participation of the people in governance of the State is sine qua non of functional democracy. Their surrender of rights to be governed is to have direct encounter in electoral process to choose their representatives for resolution of common problems and social welfare. Needless interference in self-governance is betrayal of their faith to fulfill self-governance and their democratic aspirations. The constitutional culture and political morality based on healthy conventions are the fruitful soil to nurture and for sustained growth of the federal institutions set down by the Constitution. In the context of the Indian Constitution federalism is not based on any agreement between federating units but one of integrated whole as pleaded with vision by Dr

BR Ambedkar on the floor of the Constituent Assembly at the very inception of the deliberations and the Constituent Assembly unanimously approved the resolution of federal structure. He poignantly projected the pitfalls flowing from the word "federation".

* * *

CERTIFICATION OF THE CONSTITUTION OF THE PROVINCE OF KWAZULU–NATAL

Constitutional Court (South Africa).
1996 (4) SALR 1098 (CC).

[During the process leading to the interim and final constitutions, the political leadership of the South African Province of KwaZulu–Natal made several attempts to carve out specific powers for itself, sometimes verging on secession and civil war. The 1996 provincial Constitution was seen by many as one of such attempts. (The provinces that actually were quick to have their constitutions where controlled by political parties in opposition to the prevalent ANC party.)]

FULL COURT:

In terms of section 160(1) of the Constitution of the Republic of South Africa, Act 200 of 1993 (the Interim Constitution) a provincial legislature is entitled to pass a constitution for its province by a resolution of a majority of at least two-thirds of all its members. Before such a constitution can have the force of law, this Court must certify, under section 160(4) of the Interim Constitution, that none of its provisions is inconsistent with any provision of the Interim Constitution, including the Constitutional Principles set out in Schedule 4. [As to the Constitutional Principles, see *Certification of the Constitution of the Republic of South Africa* in Chapter 1, Subsection E.1.]

[2] On 15 March 1996, the Legislature of the province of KwaZulu–Natal (KZN) unanimously adopted a Constitution (the provincial Constitution) for that province. * * *

[4] At this stage of constitutional history of South Africa, all law-making power throughout the country is derived from the Interim Constitution. The power throughout the country is derived from the Interim Constitution. The power of a provincial legislature to adopt its own Constitution is to be found in section 160 of the Interim Constitution. It is there provided, in subsection (1), that:

"The provincial legislature shall be entitled to pass a constitution for its province by a resolution of a majority of at least two-thirds of all its members."

This power is additional to the legislative competence which is conferred on provincial legislatures by sections 125 and 126 of the Interim Constitution, but is expressly limited in section 160(3):

"A provincial constitution shall not be inconsistent with a provision of this Constitution, including the Constitutional Principles set out in Schedule 4: Provided that a provincial constitution may—

(a) provide for legislative and executive structures and procedures different from those provided for in this Constitution in respect of a province; and

(b) where applicable, provide for the institution, role, authority and status of a traditional monarch in the province, and shall make such provision for the Zulu Monarch in the case of the province of KwaZulu/Natal.''

The reference to "legislative structures and procedures" clearly relates to the structures and procedures which may be necessary or appropriate for the proper functioning of the provincial organs of government.

[5]   On a proper interpretation of section 160, while a provincial constitution may not be inconsistent with any provision of the Interim Constitution, in terms of the proviso to subsection (3), the legislative and executive structures and procedures may differ from those provided for in the Interim Constitution. We would emphasize however, that whatever meaning is ascribed to structures and procedures they do not relate to the fundamental nature and substance of the democratic state created by the Interim Constitution nor to the substance of the legislative or executive powers of the national Parliament or Government or those of the provinces.

[8]   * * * [A] province cannot by means of the bootstraps of its own constitution confer on its legislature greater powers than those granted it by the Interim Constitution. The same principle must apply, *mutatis mutandis,* to all other powers, of whatever nature, asserted by a province in the provisions of its constitution. Certification requires a two step approach in regard to such provisions. The first is an inquiry as to whether the Interim Constitution or a Constitutional Principle deals, expressly or impliedly, with the power in question and how it deals with it. The second is the determination whether the provision in a provincial constitution is inconsistent with such comparable provision or any other relevant provisions in the Interim Constitution or Constitutional Principles.

[9]   It is also useful, at this stage, to comment briefly on the nature of and the interrelationship between the legislative powers of Parliament and the provincial legislatures. In terms of section 37 of the Interim Constitution, Parliament has general plenary power to legislate for the Republic. That plenary power is not confined to specific functional areas.[2] The legislative competence of provincial legislatures is different and is derived from section 126(1), read with Schedule 6 and section 126(2) as described above.[3] It is not, however, an exclusive legislative competence but one which is exercised concurrently with Parliament.[4]

2. *Ex parte Speaker of the National Assembly: In re: Dispute Concerning the Constitutionality of Certain Provisions of the National Education Policy Bill 83 of 1995* 1996 (3) SALR 289 (CC) para 13.

3. Id and para 7 supra.

4. *Premier, KwaZulu–Natal, and Others v. President of the Republic of South Africa and Others* 1996 (1) SALR 769 (CC) para 25; *Ex parte Speaker of the National Assembly: In re: Dispute Concerning the Constitutionality of Certain Provisions of the National Education Policy Bill 83 of 1995* supra n 2 para 13.

Section 126 restricts neither Parliament's plenary legislative competence nor its last mentioned concurrent competence to legislate; it merely provides in subsections (3) and (4) how a conflict or potential conflict that may exist between an Act of Parliament and provincial legislation is to be resolved and which of the conflicting provisions is to prevail.[5] If the conflict is resolved in favor of one of the conflicting laws the other is not invalidated, it is subordinated and to the extent of the conflict rendered inoperative.[6] A law so subordinated is not nullified;

> "it remains in force and has to be implemented to the extent that it is not inconsistent with the law that prevails [and] [i]f the inconsistency falls away the law would then have to be implemented in all respects."[7]

The inconsistency could fall away and the provisions of the subordinated law become fully operative if the prevailing law were to be repealed or appropriately amended. In effect the consequence of subordination is that the subordinated law, or relevant provision thereof, goes into abeyance.[8]

[13]   In our opinion there are fundamental respects in which the provincial Constitution is fatally flawed. Those flaws can appropriately be considered under three heads:

1.   Usurpation of National Powers; * * *

[14]   In a number of provisions, the provincial Constitution purports to usurp powers and functions of Parliament and the national Government. This process begins in Chapter 1 dealing with "Fundamental Principles". The majority of these principles are those that one would expect to find and would be appropriate in a national constitution. Clause 1(1), for example, provides that:

> "The Province of KwaZulu Natal is a self-governing Province within the Republic of South Africa."

That purports to be an operative provision of the provincial Constitution and not a record of a fact or an aspiration. It is clearly beyond the capacity of a provincial legislature to pass constitutional provisions concerning the status of a province within the Republic. After all, the provinces are the recipients and not the source of power. [The Court relied on the *National Education Policy Bill Case*, see below, and concluded that] [t]here is no provision in the Interim Constitution which empowers a province to regulate its own status.

[16]   Clause 1(5) of Chapter 1 purports to arrange the relationship between the province and the national Government. Clause 1(6) purports to confer autonomous powers in respect of local government. Clause 1(8) states that the provincial Constitution sets out the basis of the interaction between the province and the rest of the Republic. The

5. *Ex parte Speaker of the National Assembly: In re: Dispute Concerning the Constitutionality of Certain Provisions of the National Education Policy Bill 83 of 1995* supra n 2 paras 14 and 15 for an explanation of how such conflict is to be resolved.

6. Id. para 16.

7. Id. para 19.

8. Which the Oxford English Dictionary describes as: "A state of suspension, temporary non-existence or inactivity; dormant or latent condition liable to be at any time revived."

provincial Constitution is replete with other examples of this attempted usurpation of power.

Chapter 3 contains a bill of rights. There can in principle be no objection to a province embodying a bill of rights in its constitution. * * * A significant feature of most constitutions adopted since the Second World War is the embodiment of a justiciable bill of rights; it is indeed a significant feature of the Interim Constitution itself. Under these circumstances it would require the clearest indication in the Interim Constitution that no bill of rights, of any nature, could be embodied in a provincial constitution duly passed pursuant to section 160(1). There is no indication of any such proscription. * * *

[18] It is equally clear, however, that it is constitutionally impermissible for any provision to be embodied in a provincial bill of rights which is inconsistent with any provision of the Interim Constitution (which includes any provision in Chapter 3 itself) or the Constitutional Principles. It is inadvisable to attempt to formulate any comprehensive rule for determining exactly what provisions may, in conformity with section 160, be embodied in a provincial bill of rights. Nevertheless some basic principles must be laid down in order to evaluate the attack directed at the bill of rights in the provincial Constitution.

[19] The powers of a provincial legislature to enact a bill of rights are limited in different ways. In the first place the legislature cannot provide for the provincial bill of rights to operate in respect of matters which fall outside its legislative or executive powers. Bills of rights, with the exception of provisions which may not always be regarded as capable of direct enforcement (such as, for example, certain of the types of provisions which have come to be known as "directive principles of state policy") are conventionally enforced by courts of law striking down or invalidating, for example, legislation and administrative action even when such power of review is not expressly granted in the constitution or bill of rights concerned.[11]

[22] In the second place a province would be precluded from incorporating any provision in its bill of rights which is "inconsistent with" any similar provision in Chapter 3 of the Interim Constitution. This is so because section 7(1) of the Interim Constitution expressly provides that Chapter 3 binds all legislative and executive organs of state "at all levels of government". All the provisions in this Chapter must be applied, for example, to all provincial legislation. Any provision in any provincial law, including a provincial constitution, which purported to limit the operation of the national bill of rights in any way would be in conflict with section 7(1) of the Interim Constitution and would not meet the section 160(3) inconsistency qualification.

[23] A provincial bill of rights could (in respect of matters falling within the province's powers) place greater limitations on the province's powers or confer greater rights on individuals than does the Interim Constitution, and it could even confer rights on individuals which do not

11. The best known example is the US Constitution and Bill of Rights; see *Mar-* *bury v. Madison* 5 US 137 (1803).

exist in the Interim Constitution. An important question is whether such provisions would be inconsistent with the provisions of the Interim Constitution.

[24]   * * * For purposes of the present inquiry as to inconsistency we are of the view that a provision in a provincial bill of rights and a corresponding provision in Chapter 3 are inconsistent when they cannot stand at the same time, or cannot stand together, or cannot both be obeyed at the same time. They are not inconsistent when it is possible to obey each without disobeying either. There is no principal or practical reason why such provisions cannot operate together harmoniously in the same field.

[27]   The way is now clear to consider whether any provision in the bill of rights (Chapter 3) of the provincial Constitution is inconsistent with the Interim Constitution or the Constitutional Principles because it purports to usurp powers or functions of Parliament. The contents of a right to a fair trial are, for instance, referred to in some detail in clause 19(3). Similarly, in clause 21, labour relations are dealt with in some detail. In clause 31 one finds detailed provisions for states of emergency and their suspension. These are all examples of areas falling patently outside the domain of competence of provincial legislatures. Another attempt to usurp national power is the provision in Chapter 3 clause 30(3) where, amongst others, it is asserted that the entrenchment of the rights in terms of the provincial Constitution shall not be construed as—

> "denying the existence of any other rights or freedoms recognized or conferred by the Constitution of the Republic of South Africa ... to the extent that they are not inconsistent with this Constitution."

This bears all the hallmarks of a hierarchical inversion. The provincial Constitution is presented as the supreme law recognizing what is or is not valid in the national Constitution. It has no power to do so.

[31]   The bill of rights in the provincial Constitution is deeply flawed in the many respects already mentioned and will have to be thoroughly redrafted should the KZN Legislature still wish to embody a bill of rights in a provincial constitution. We consider that our certification task in relation to the bill of rights goes no further than identifying its seriously flawed provisions.[16] It would be inappropriate for us in this judgment to embark on what would in effect be a definitive commentary on the provincial bill of rights for the guidance and benefit of the KZN Legislature, with the implication that a bill of rights enacted in conformity with such commentary would pass a later certification process as a matter of course. This would be tantamount to us drafting a bill of rights for the province. We consider that in the present circumstances the general principles we have outlined provide sufficient guidance for the provincial Legislature. In these circumstances the fact that we have identified specific offending provisions in the bill of rights is not to be construed as a finding that there are no other.

16. See section 160(4) of the Interim Constitution and compare with section 71(2).

[32]   In clause 1(2) of Chapter 5, exclusive legislative powers are conferred upon the KZN Legislature. In clause 1(4) executive authority is "conferred" upon the province in certain circumstances. It is unnecessary even to consider whether this conflicts with any corresponding powers of the national Legislature or executive in the Interim Constitution for the simple reason that a province has no authority at all to "confer" any legislative or executive authority, of whatsoever nature, on itself. All such power emanates exclusively from the Interim Constitution.

[33]   A related and equally serious attempted usurpation of power is the provision made in Chapter 8 for the establishment of a constitutional court for KZN and in clause 2(7) of Chapter 14 for the functions of such court to be performed by the provincial division of the Supreme Court pending its establishment. Chapter 8 clause 1(3) purports to confer on such constitutional court exclusive power to decide on the constitutional nature of a dispute and clause 1(4) exclusive jurisdiction to decide disputes in constitutional matters between organs and powers "established or recognized in terms of this Constitution" and to "declare a law of the Province unconstitutional". The Interim Constitution nowhere confers any power on a province to establish courts of law, whatever their jurisdiction may be. Chapter 7 of the Interim Constitution establishes and makes comprehensive provision for court structures. It is also made explicitly clear by sections 101(3)(c), (d) and (e) respectively that it is the provincial or local division of the Supreme Court as established by the Interim Constitution which has jurisdiction to inquire into the constitutionality of "any law applicable within its area of jurisdiction, other than an Act of Parliament"; jurisdiction in relation to disputes of a constitutional nature between local governments or between a local government and a provincial government; and jurisdiction in respect of the determination of questions whether any matter falls within its jurisdiction. The KZN Legislature simply does not have the power it purports to exercise in Chapter 8 of the provincial Constitution.

[34]   Clause 2(1) of Chapter 5 proclaims that "[t]his Constitution recognizes" the exclusive legislative and executive authority of the "national Government" over certain matters and clause 2(2) similarly purports to recognize the "competence" of the "national Parliament" in certain respects. These assertions of recognition purport to be the constitutional acts of a sovereign state. They are inconsistent with the Interim Constitution because KZN is not a sovereign state and it simply has no power or authority to grant constitutional "recognition" to what the national Government may or may not do.

Conclusion

[47]   From the foregoing discussion, it is apparent that the provincial Constitution is fatally flawed and cannot be certified under the provisions of section 160(4) of the Interim Constitution.

Notes and Questions

1. The Indian Supreme Court (ISC) justifies the constitutionally mandated ability of the federal executive to interfere in the affairs of the member-states by the ethnic tensions in India. A similar concern is present in South Africa, where Art. 55(2)(b)(ii) grants the right of oversight of any organ of state, including a department of the provincial government. "This must be seen in the context of the scheme of cooperative government under which provinces will implement national legislation unless an Act of Parliament otherwise provides, and where Parliament is under a constitutional duty to intervene and implement such legislation itself if it is necessary to do so." (*Certification of the Constitution of the Republic of South Africa Case,* below, at para. 295.)

2. Though intervention might also be justified by efficiency reasons and against attempts of secession, these can be problematic:

> On paper, Argentine federalism closely resembles that of the U.S. This is not surprising, since about two-thirds of Argentina's Constitution was copied from that of the U.S. Political authority is divided between the national government and twenty-three semi-autonomous provinces. Each province has its own constitution, executive, legislature, and court system. In actual practice, however, this system differs dramatically from the theoretical conception. The national government almost totally dominates the provinces. Constitutional provisions designed to assure provincial autonomy have been easily brushed aside by federal intervention under Article 6, which authorizes the federal government to intervene in the territory of the provinces to guarantee a republican form of government. Article 6 has been used and abused, allowing the federal government carte blanche to assume total control over any province at any time. This provision, which was taken from the U.S. Constitution, has fallen into disuse in the U.S. In Argentina, on the other hand, it is used continually, usually by the Executive. According to one count, by 1962 Argentina had more than 220 federal interventions, more than of which were ordered by the Executive. In the first four years of his government, the current president, Carlos Menem, has used this power to place four of the twenty-three provinces under federal trusteeship. Generally, mere threat of intervention suffices to secure provincial compliance with the wishes of the federal government. Moreover, the provinces lack fiscal autonomy, leaving them dependent upon the federal government for financial assistance. Even at the federal level power is heavily centralized in the presidency, which dominates both the Legislature and the Judiciary.

> Keith S. Rosenn, *Federalism in the Americas in Comparative Perspective,* 26 U. Miami Inter–Am. L. Rev. 1, 44 (1994).

3. Is public/constitutional order (the fear of secession, extreme diversity, and the like) the fundamental reason for strong central control over the constituent states? Consider the case of India:

> The central government retains enormous control over the economy, setting most economic laws and regulations; state governments have little discretion in revenue raising and spending. The framers of the Indian Constitution created a strong center that could, many Indians

believed, direct economic growth, protect minority rights, and defuse the political and economic tensions that might arise in such a heterogeneous nation.

The Indian revenue collection system places states at the mercy of the central government. The central government raises the bulk of its revenue through taxes and distributes that revenue to the states according to the recommendations of several central agencies. States may raise revenue in only a few areas on their own, chiefly sales, liquor excise, and various fees. States therefore have been dependent on the various commissions and ministries.

* * *

Why would provincial leaders agree to such an asymmetric division of economic control in a heterogeneous, federal country? * * * It should be emphasized that the Constituent Assembly distinguished between economic and political decentralization. While political decentralization was seen as inevitable, economic decentralization was never seriously contemplated given the differences in language, ethnicity, and previous forms of government (e.g., between the British colonial provinces and the princely states).

Nehru and the socialist wing sought to implement central economic planning because they believed it would more quickly create a strong industrial base * * *

In addition, many feared that without central control, the disparities between rich and poor states would increase. * * * Central dominance was * * * considered to be a way to avoid destructive interstate disputes and increase equality across disparate regions. These deliberations did result in a system in which the national government makes all the important economic decisions. But it is far from clear that centralization led to greater equality.

[In addition to these central powers,] the central government has unilateral control over federal provisions in several important ways. For example, state boundaries can be redrawn by a simple majority in Parliament. Even more importantly, the Indian Constitution provides that the President of India may dissolve state[s] * * *."

Sunita Parikh and Barry R. Weingast, *A Comparative Theory of Federalism: India*, 83 Va. L. Rev. 1593, 1607–12 (1994).

4. In the *KwaZulu-Natal Certification Case* it was held that "whatever meaning is ascribed to 'structures and procedures' they do not relate to the fundamental nature and substance of the democratic state created by the Interim Constitution nor to the substance of the legislature or executive powers of the national Parliament or Government or those of the provinces." In view of NT 142 and 143, a provincial constitution is not suitable for an independent or confederal state but rather for governance of a province whose powers are derived from the NT. Thus the SACC clearly reaffirmed the devolutionary status of South African federalism. The provinces are the creatures of devolution.

C.2.2.　EXCLUSIVE AND CONCURRENT POWERS

A frequently mentioned point of departure in the allocation of powers between a federation and its constituent units is that the federation should have jurisdiction in matters that pertain to the whole nation while the units have precedence in their own matters. Fiscal federalists and economists argue that the provision of public goods should be assigned to the lowest jurisdiction compatible with producing that good. See Wallace E. Oates, *Fiscal Federalism* 34–5 (1972). As the Interim Constitution of South Africa (Act 200 of 1993) required: "The level at which decisions can be taken most effectively in respect of the quality and rendering of services, shall be the level responsible and accountable for the quality and the rendering of the services, and such level shall accordingly be empowered by the Constitution to do so." (Schedule 4.CP [Constitutional Principles of the Interim Constitution] XXI.1.) But the dividing lines are unclear, and courts have not consistently approached questions relating to the boundaries between federal and federated-entities powers.

C.2.2.a.　DOMESTIC POWERS

UNITED STATES v. LOPEZ

Supreme Court (United States).
514 U.S. 549 (1995).

Chief Justice Rehnquist delivered the opinion of the Court.

In the Gun–Free School Zones Act of 1990, Congress made it a federal offense "for any individual knowingly to possess a firearm at a place that the individual knows, or has reasonable cause to believe, is a school zone." 18 U.S.C. § 922 (q)(1)(A) (1988 ed., Supp. V). The Act neither regulates a commercial activity nor contains a requirement that the possession be connected in any way to interstate commerce. We hold that the Act exceeds the authority of Congress "to regulate Commerce * * * among the several States * * * " U. S. Const. Art. I, § 8, cl. 3.

On March 10, 1992, respondent, who was then a 12th-grade student, arrived at Edison High School in San Antonio, Texas, carrying a concealed .38 caliber handgun and five bullets. Acting upon an anonymous tip, school authorities confronted respondent, who admitted that he was carrying the weapon. He was arrested and charged * * * with violating the Gun–Free School Zones Act of 1990 * * *

[Lopez was tried, convicted, and sentenced to six months in prison. He appealed, claiming that the federal government lacked the power to criminalize mere gun possession in a school zone.]

We start with first principles. The Constitution creates a Federal Government of enumerated powers. As James Madison wrote, "the powers delegated by the proposed Constitution to the federal government are few and defined. Those which are to remain in the State governments are numerous and indefinite." *The Federalist* No. 45, pp. 292–293 (C. Rossiter ed., 1961). This constitutionally mandated division of authority "was adopted by the Framers to ensure protection of our fundamental liberties." *Gregory v. Ashcroft*, 501 U.S. 452, 458 (1991). "Just as the separation and independence of the coordinate branches of the Federal Government serve to prevent the accumulation of excessive power in any one branch, a healthy balance of power between the States and the Federal Government will reduce the risk of tyranny and abuse from either front." *Ibid.*

The commerce power "is the power to regulate; that is, to prescribe the rule by which commerce is to be governed. This power, like all others vested in congress, is complete in itself, may be exercised to its utmost extent, and acknowledges no limitations, other than are prescribed in the constitution.

* * *

In *United States v. Darby*, 312 U.S. 100 (1941), the Court upheld the Fair Labor Standards Act, stating:

"The power of Congress over interstate commerce is not confined to the regulation of commerce among the states. It extends to those activities intrastate which so affect interstate commerce or the exercise of the power of Congress over it as to make regulation of them appropriate means to the attainment of a legitimate end, the exercise of the granted power of Congress to regulate interstate commerce." *Id.*, at 118.

* * *

In *Wickard v. Filburn*, the Court upheld the application of amendments to the Agricultural Adjustment Act of 1938 to the production and consumption of homegrown wheat. 317 U.S. at 128–129. The *Wickard* Court explicitly rejected earlier distinctions between direct and indirect effects on interstate commerce, stating:

"Even if appellee's activity be local and though it may not be regarded as commerce, it may still, whatever its nature, be reached by Congress if it exerts a substantial economic effect on interstate commerce, and this irrespective of whether such effect is what might at some earlier time have been defined as 'direct' or 'indirect.' " *Id.*, at 125.

The *Wickard* Court emphasized that although Filburn's own contribution to the demand for wheat may have been trivial by itself, that was not "enough to remove him from the scope of federal regulation where, as here, his contribution, taken together with that of many others similarly situated, is far from trivial." *Id.*, at 127–128.

[These cases] ushered in an era of Commerce Clause jurisprudence that greatly expanded the previously defined authority of Congress under that Clause. In part, this was a recognition of the great changes that had occurred in the way business was carried on in this country. Enterprises that had once been local or at most regional in nature had become national in scope. But the doctrinal change also reflected a view that earlier Commerce Clause cases artificially had constrained the authority of Congress to regulate interstate commerce.

But even these modern-era precedents which have expanded congressional power under the Commerce Clause confirm that this power is subject to outer limits. In *Jones & Laughlin Steel*, the Court warned that the scope of the interstate commerce power "must be considered in the light of our dual system of government and may not be extended so as to embrace effects upon interstate commerce so indirect and remote that to embrace them, in view of our complex society, would effectually obliterate the distinction between what is national and what is local and create a completely centralized government." 301 U.S. at 37; see also *Darby*, *supra*, at 119–120 (Congress may regulate intrastate activity that has a "substantial effect" on interstate commerce).

* * *

[2A]

Consistent with this structure, we have identified three broad categories of activity that Congress may regulate under its commerce power. First, Congress may regulate the use of the channels of interstate commerce. See, e.g., *Darby*, 312 U.S. at 114; "The authority of Congress to keep the channels of interstate commerce free from immoral and injurious uses has been frequently sustained, and is no longer open to question". Second, Congress is empowered to regulate and protect the instrumentalities of interstate commerce, or persons or things in interstate commerce, even though the threat may come only from intrastate activities, ("For example, the destruction of an aircraft or . . . thefts from interstate shipments"). Finally, Congress' commerce authority includes the power to regulate those activities having a substantial relation to interstate commerce, i.e., those activities that substantially affect interstate commerce.

Within this final category, admittedly, our case law has not been clear whether an activity must "affect" or "substantially affect" interstate commerce in order to be within Congress' power to regulate it under the Commerce Clause * * * We conclude, consistent with the great weight of our case law, that the proper test requires an analysis of whether the regulated activity "substantially affects" interstate commerce.

We now turn to consider the power of Congress, in the light of this framework, to enact [the challenged law]. The first two categories of authority may be quickly disposed of: [this] is not a regulation of the use of the channels of interstate commerce, nor is it an attempt to prohibit the interstate transportation of a commodity through the channels of commerce; nor can [it] be justified as a regulation by which Congress has sought to protect an instrumentality of interstate commerce or a thing in interstate commerce. Thus, if [this law] is to be sustained, it must be under the third category as a regulation of an activity that substantially affects interstate commerce.

[2B]

First, we have upheld a wide variety of congressional Acts regulating intrastate economic activity where we have concluded that the activity substantially affected interstate commerce. Examples include the regulation of intrastate coal mining; intrastate extortionate credit transactions, restaurants utilizing substantial interstate supplies, inns and hotels catering to interstate guests, and production and consumption of home-grown wheat. These examples are by no means exhaustive, but the pattern is clear. Where economic activity substantially affects interstate commerce, legislation regulating that activity will be sustained.

Even *Wickard*, which is perhaps the most far-reaching example of Commerce Clause authority over intrastate activity, involved economic activity in a way that the possession of a gun in a school zone does not. Roscoe Filburn operated a small farm in Ohio, on which, in the year involved, he raised 23 acres of wheat. It was his practice to sow winter wheat in the fall, and after harvesting it in July to sell a portion of the crop, to feed part of it to poultry and livestock on the farm, to use some in making flour for home consumption, and to keep the remainder for seeding future crops. The Secretary of Agriculture assessed a penalty against him under the Agricultural Adjustment Act of 1938 because he harvested about 12 acres more wheat than his allotment under the Act permitted. The Act was designed to regulate the volume of wheat moving in interstate and foreign commerce in order to avoid surpluses and shortages, and concomitant fluctuation in wheat prices, which had previously obtained. The Court said, in an opinion sustaining the application of the Act to Filburn's activity:

> "One of the primary purposes of the Act in question was to increase the market price of wheat and to that end to limit the volume thereof that could affect the market. It can hardly be denied that a factor of such volume and variability as home-consumed wheat would have a substantial influence on price and market conditions. This may arise because being in marketable condition such wheat overhangs the market and, if induced by rising prices, tends to flow into the market and check price increases. But if we assume that it is never marketed, it supplies a need of the man who grew it which would otherwise be reflected by purchases in the open market. Home-grown wheat in this sense competes with wheat in commerce." 317 U.S. at 128.

[3A]

Section 922(q) is a criminal statute that by its terms has nothing to do with "commerce" or any sort of economic enterprise, however broadly one might define those terms. Section 922(q) is not an essential part of a larger regulation of economic activity, in which the regulatory scheme could be undercut unless the intrastate activity were regulated. It cannot, therefore, be sustained under our cases upholding regulations of activities that arise out of or are connected with a commercial transaction, which viewed in the aggregate, substantially affects interstate commerce.

* * *

The Government's essential contention * * * is that * * * possession of a firearm in a local school zone does indeed substantially affect interstate commerce. The Government argues that possession of a firearm in a school zone may result in violent crime and that violent crime can be expected to affect the functioning of the national economy in two ways. First, the costs of violent crime are substantial, and, through the mechanism of insurance, those costs are spread throughout the population. Second, violent crime reduces the willingness of individuals to travel to areas within the country that are perceived to be unsafe. The Government also argues that the presence of guns in schools poses a substantial threat to the educational process by threatening the learning environment. A handicapped educational process, in turn, will result in a less productive citizenry. That, in turn, would have an adverse effect on the Nation's economic well-being.

* * *

We pause to consider the implications of the Government's arguments. The Government admits, under its "costs of crime" reasoning, that Congress could regulate not only all violent crime, but all activities that might lead to violent crime, regardless of how tenuously they relate to interstate commerce. See Tr. of Oral Arg. 8–9. Similarly, under the Government's "national productivity" reasoning, Congress could regulate any activity that it found was related to the economic productivity of individual citizens: family law (including marriage, divorce, and child custody), for example. Under the theories that the Government presents in support of [the challenged law,] it is difficult to perceive any limitation on federal power, even in areas such as criminal law enforcement or education where States historically have been sovereign. Thus, if we were to accept the Government's arguments, we are hard pressed to posit any activity by an individual that Congress is without power to regulate.

* * *

For instance, if Congress can, pursuant to its Commerce Clause power, regulate activities that adversely affect the learning environment, then, *a fortiori*, it also can regulate the educational process directly. Congress could determine that a school's curriculum has a "significant" effect on the extent of classroom learning. As a result, Congress could mandate a federal curriculum for local elementary and secondary schools because what is taught in local schools has a significant "effect on classroom learning," and that, in turn, has a substantial effect on interstate commerce.

* * *

Admittedly, a determination whether an intrastate activity is commercial or noncommercial may in some cases result in legal uncertainty. But, so long as Congress' authority is limited to those powers enumerated in the Constitution, and so long as those enumerated powers are interpreted as having judicially enforceable outer limits, congressional legislation under the Commerce Clause always will engender "legal uncertainty."

* * *

The possession of a gun in a local school zone is in no sense an economic activity that might, through repetition elsewhere, substantially affect any sort of interstate commerce. Respondent was a local student at a local school; there is no indication that he had recently moved in interstate commerce, and there is no requirement that his possession of the firearm have any concrete tie to interstate commerce.

To uphold the Government's contentions here, we would have to pile inference upon inference in a manner that would bid fair to convert congressional authority under the Commerce Clause to a general police power of the sort retained by the States. Admittedly, some of our prior cases have taken long steps down that road, giving great deference to congressional action * * * The broad language in these opinions has suggested the possibility of additional expansion, but we decline here to proceed any further. To do so would require us to conclude that the Constitution's enumeration of powers does not presuppose something not enumerated, and that there never will be a distinction between what is truly national and what is truly local. This we are unwilling to do.

* * *

Justice Breyer, with whom Justice Stevens, Justice Souter, and Justice Ginsburg join, dissenting.

The issue in this case is whether the Commerce Clause authorizes Congress to enact a statute that makes it a crime to possess a gun in, or near, a school. In my view, the statute falls well within the scope of the commerce power as this Court has understood that power over the last half century.

I

In reaching this conclusion, I apply three basic principles of Commerce Clause interpretation. First, the power to "regulate Commerce * * * among the several States," U.S. Const., Art. I, § 8, cl. 3, encompasses the power to regulate local activities insofar as they significantly affect interstate commerce.

Second, in determining whether a local activity will likely have a significant effect upon interstate commerce, a court must consider, not the effect of an individual act (a single instance of gun possession), but rather the cumulative effect of all similar instances [i.e., the effect of all guns possessed in or near schools].

* * *

Third, the Constitution requires us to judge the connection between a regulated activity and interstate commerce, not directly, but at one remove. Courts must give Congress a degree of leeway in determining the existence of a significant factual connection between the regulated activity and interstate commerce—both because the Constitution delegates the commerce power directly to Congress and because the determination requires an empirical judgment of a kind that a legislature is more likely than a court to make with accuracy. The traditional words "rational basis" capture this leeway. Thus, the specific question before us, as the Court recognizes, is not whether the "regulated activity sufficiently affected interstate commerce," but, rather, whether Congress could have had "*a rational basis*" for so concluding.

* * *

II

Applying these principles to the case at hand, we must ask whether Congress could have had a *rational basis* for finding a significant (or substantial) connection between gun-related school violence and interstate commerce. Or, to put the question in the language of the *explicit* finding that Congress made when it amended this law in 1994: Could Congress rationally have found that "violent crime in school zones," through its effect on the "quality of education," significantly (or substantially) affects "interstate" or "foreign commerce"?

* * *

For one thing, reports, hearings, and other readily available literature make clear that the problem of guns in and around schools is widespread and extremely serious. These materials report, for example, that four percent of American high school students (and six percent of inner-city high school students) carry a gun to school at least occasionally, that 12 percent of urban high school students have had guns fired at them, that 20 percent of those students have been threatened with guns, and that, in any 6–month period, several hundred thousand schoolchildren are victims of violent crimes in or near their schools. And, they report that this widespread violence in schools throughout the Nation significantly interferes with the quality of education in those schools. Based on reports such as these, Congress obviously could have thought that guns and learning are mutually exclusive. Congress could therefore have found a substantial educational problem—teachers unable to teach, students unable to learn—and concluded that guns near schools contribute substantially to the size and scope of that problem.

Having found that guns in schools significantly undermine the quality of education in our Nation's classrooms, Congress could also have found, given the effect of education upon interstate and foreign commerce, that gun-related violence in and around schools is a commercial, as well as a human, problem. Education, although far more than a matter of economics, has long been inextricably intertwined with the Nation's economy.

* * *

In recent years the link between secondary education and business has strengthened, becoming both more direct and more important. Scholars on the subject report that technological changes and innovations in management techniques have altered the nature of the workplace so that more jobs now demand greater educational skills.

* * *

Increasing global competition also has made primary and secondary education economically more important. The portion of the American economy attributable to international trade nearly tripled between 1950 and 1980, and more than 70 percent of American-made goods now compete with imports. Yet, lagging worker productivity has contributed to negative trade balances and to real hourly compensation that has fallen below wages in 10 other industrialized nations. At least some significant part of this serious productivity problem is attributable to students who emerge from classrooms without the reading or mathematical skills necessary to compete with their European or Asian counterparts.

* * *

The economic links I have just sketched seem fairly obvious. Why then is it not equally obvious, in light of those links, that a widespread, serious, and substantial physical threat to teaching and learning *also* substantially threatens the commerce to which that teaching and learning is inextricably tied? That is to say, guns in the hands of six percent of inner-city high school students and gun-related violence throughout a city's schools must threaten the trade and commerce that those schools support. The only question, then, is whether the latter threat is (to use the majority's terminology) "substantial." The evidence of (1) the *extent* of the gun-related violence problem, (2) the *extent* of the resulting negative effect on classroom learning, and (3) the *extent* of the consequent negative commercial effects, when taken together, indicate a threat to trade and commerce that is "substantial." At the very least, Congress could rationally have concluded that the links are substantial.

* * *

To hold this statute constitutional is not to "obliterate" the "distinction between what is national and what is local," nor is it to hold that the Commerce Clause permits the Federal Government to "regulate any activity that it found was related to the economic productivity of individual citizens," to regulate "marriage, divorce, and child custody," or to regulate any and all aspects of education. First, this statute is aimed at curbing a particularly acute threat to the educational process— the possession (and use) of life-threatening firearms in, or near, the classroom. The empirical evidence that I have discussed above unmistakably documents the special way in which guns and education are incompatible. This Court has previously recognized the singularly disruptive potential on interstate commerce that acts of violence may have. Second, the immediacy of the connection between education and the national economic well-being is documented by scholars and accepted by society at large in a way and to a degree that may not hold true for other social institutions. It must surely be the rare case, then, that a statute strikes at conduct that (when considered in the abstract) seems so removed from commerce, but which (practically speaking) has so significant an impact upon commerce. * * *

III

The majority's holding * * * creates three serious legal problems. First, the majority's holding runs contrary to modern Supreme Court cases that have upheld congressional actions despite connections to interstate or foreign commerce that are less significant than the effect of school violence.

* * *

The second legal problem the Court creates comes from its apparent belief that it can reconcile its holding with earlier cases by making a critical distinction between "commercial" and noncommercial "transaction[s]." That is to say, the Court believes the Constitution would distinguish between two local activities, each of which has an identical effect upon interstate commerce, if one, but not the other, is "commercial" in nature. As a general matter, this approach fails to heed this Court's earlier warning not to turn "questions of the power of Congress" upon "formula[s]" that would give "controlling force to nomenclature such as 'production' and 'indirect' and foreclose consideration of the actual effects of the activity in question upon interstate commerce." *Wickard, supra,* at 120.

* * *

More importantly, if a distinction between commercial and noncommercial activities is to be made, this is not the case in which to make it * * * [I]f the majority * * * means to distinguish generally among broad categories of activities, differentiating what is educational from what is commercial, then, as a practical matter, the line becomes almost impossible to draw. Schools that teach reading, writing, mathematics, and related basic skills serve *both* social and commercial purposes, and one cannot easily separate the one from the other. American industry itself has been, and is again, involved in teaching. When, and to what extent, does its involvement make education commercial? Does the number of vocational classes that train students directly for jobs make a difference? Does it matter if the school is public or private, nonprofit or profit seeking? Does it matter if a city or State adopts a voucher plan that pays private firms to run a school? Even if one were to ignore these practical questions, why should there be a theoretical distinction between education, when it significantly benefits commerce, and environmental pollution, when it causes economic harm?

* * *

The third legal problem created by the Court's holding is that it threatens legal uncertainty in an area of law that, until this case, seemed reasonably well settled. Congress has enacted many statutes (more than 100 sections of the United States Code), including criminal statutes (at least 25 sections), that use the words "affecting commerce" to define their scope * * * Do these, or similar, statutes regulate noncommercial activities? More importantly [are] the courts * * * to take *Wickard,* 317 U.S. at 127–128, (and later similar cases) as inapplicable, and to judge the effect of a single noncommercial activity on interstate commerce without considering similar instances of the forbidden conduct? However these questions are eventually resolved, the legal uncertainty now created will restrict Congress' ability to enact criminal laws aimed at criminal behavior that, considered problem by problem rather than instance by instance, seriously threatens the economic, as well as social, well-being of Americans.

IV

In sum, to find this legislation within the scope of the Commerce Clause would permit "Congress * * * to act in terms of economic * * * realities * * * Upholding this legislation would do no more than simply recognize that Congress had a "rational basis" for finding a significant connection between guns in or near schools and (through their effect on education) the interstate and foreign commerce they threaten * * * Respectfully, I dissent.

In 1901, the former colonies in Australia became the states of a "new indissoluble Federal Commonwealth" (Preamble to the 1901 Constitution). There was no preexisting statehood. Section 107 [Continuity of Colony Government] stated: "Every power of the Parliament of a Colony which has become or becomes a State, shall, unless it is by this Constitution exclusively vested in the Parliament of the Commonwealth or withdrawn from the Parliament of the State, continue as at the establishment of the Commonwealth, or as at the admission or establishment of the State, as the case may be." The legislative powers of the Commonwealth Parliament are listed in s 51 (40 paragraphs). This is understood, generally, (in most cases) as concurrent powers, i.e., the states have power in the area, too; in case of conflict the Commonwealth law prevails.

The early judicial understanding of federalism was one of balanced or "co-ordinate federalism, in which the Commonwealth and the States were both financially and politically independent within their own spheres of responsibility." Russell L. Matthew, *The Development of Australian Federalism*, in *Federalism in Australia and the Federal Republic of Germany: A Comparative Study* (Russell L. Matthew ed., 1980). The original judicial understanding of reserved state powers was challenged in a series of cases, leading to the *Engineers' Case* below.

AMALGAMATED SOCIETY OF ENGINEERS v. ADELAIDE STEAMSHIP CO. LTD.

High Court (Australia).
(1920) 28 C.L.R. 129.

[A national union of engineers lodged a claim for an award under the (federal) Conciliation and Arbitration Act 1904–1918. Among the concerned employers, there were three governmental employers. The question posed before the High Court was whether "the Commonwealth had the power to determine national arbitration under (XXXV) s 51, which grants the Commonwealth legislative powers with respect to Conciliation and arbitration for the prevention and settlement of industrial disputes extending beyond the limits of any one State." In earlier cases the High Court granted immunity to state agencies and applied a "reserved state powers" doctrine.]

Robert Menzies, for the claimant. * * * [T]he doctrine of the supremacy of Commonwealth powers [applies]. This is so whether the decision rests on sec. V. of the Act and sec. 109 of the Constitution or on the reasoning of Marshall C.J. in *McCulloch v. Maryland*, 17 U.S. 316 (1819). * * * In America the immunity of States has probably arisen by reason of the historic position of the States at the foundation of the

United States, and the subsequent fight for Federation (see In re Income Tax Acts [No. 4], (1904) 29 VLR 748; Wollaston's Case, (1902) 28 VLR 357). In any case, the operation of the American doctrine is limited to the control of the taxation power. The taxing power is, by its nature, indefinite and capable of effecting general control. Some limit to it may, therefore, be necessary. Looking at the power conferred by sec. 51 (XXXV), * * * [t]he power should be construed fully, and without regard to the alleged "reserved" powers of the States. The specific grant of power must be defined before the residue can be defined. The express grant is only to be cut down by express limitations (*R. v. Burah*, (1878) 3 App. Cas. 889, 904). The maxim *Quando lex a liquid concedit concedere videtur et illud sine quo res ipsa valere non potest* can only apply to a grant of power, and has no application to the powers of the States remaining after the Federal powers have been taken out. For the purposes of this case the word "industrial" in pl. XXXV. provides the only limitation. What is industrial if done by a private employer is industrial if done by a State.

* * *

Sir Edward Mitchell K.C. and Latham, for the States of Victoria, South Australia and Tasmania, intervening. * * * [W]hen the validity of a State law is attacked, the first inquiry is where is the power to enact it. If the answer is that the State had it before Federation, then the next question is whether the Commonwealth Constitution has taken the power away. With regard to powers reserved to the States by the Constitution, the States have powers of legislation as exclusive as are the powers granted exclusively to the Commonwealth. As regards the concurrent powers, sec. 109 determines that the Commonwealth legislation overrides that of the States. * * * That doctrine must have been in the minds of the framers of the Constitution; otherwise there was no necessity to enact sec. 51 (XXXII.) in view of sec. 51 (VI.) or sec. 98 in view of sec. 51 (I.). * * * [Mutual immunity is] to be reciprocal, * * * and is necessary for the effective working of the Constitution in accordance with the intention as disclosed by its terms. The relation between the Crown and the States remains the same as between the Crown and the several colonies before Federation, and as to the powers reserved to the States they are free from the control of the Commonwealth and as supreme as before Federation (*Liquidators of the Maritime Bank of Canada v. Receiver–General of New Brunswick*, (1892) A. C. 437, 442). The maxim Quando lex a liquid concedit concedere videtur et illud sine quo res ipsa valere non potest applies to the reservation of powers for the States as well as to the grant of powers to the Commonwealth. * * * The doctrine of non-interference was present in the minds of the Supreme Court of the United States in *McCulloch v. Maryland*, 17 U.S. 316, 435 (1819) and *Veazie Bank v. Fenno*, 75 U.S. 533, 547, 556 (1869), although it was not applied until *Collector v. Day*, 78 U.S. 113, 127 (1870). In *South Carolina v. United States*, 199 U.S. 437 (1905) the reciprocal nature of the doctrine was recognized as being based on necessity, which is the basis upon which it was put by this Court.

The following written judgments were delivered:—

Knox C.J., Isaacs, Rich and Starke JJ [Justice Gavan Duffy dissenting]

[I]n the circumstances [of legal uncertainty], the manifest duty of this Court to turn its earnest attention to the provisions of the Constitution itself. That instrument is the political compact of the whole of the people of Australia, enacted into binding law by the Imperial Parliament, and it is the chief and special duty of this Court faithfully to expound and give effect to it according to its own terms, finding the intention from the words of the compact, and upholding it throughout precisely as framed. * * *

The chief contention on the part of the States is that what has been called the rule of *D'Emden v. Pedder*, (1904) 1 CLR 91, justifies their immunity from Commonwealth control in respect of State trading. The rule referred to is in these terms, *Id* 91, 111: "When a State attempts to give to its legislative or executive authority an operation which, if valid, would fetter, control, or interfere with, the free exercise of the legislative or executive power of the Commonwealth, the attempt, unless expressly authorized by the Constitution, is to that extent invalid and inoperative." So far from that rule supporting the position taken up on behalf of the States, its language, strictly applied, is destructive of it. An authority has been set up by a State which is claimed to be an executive authority and which, if exempt from Commonwealth legislation, does fetter or interfere with free exercise of the legislative power of the Commonwealth under pl. XXXV. of sec. 51, unless that placitum is not as complete as its words in their natural meaning indicate, or, since sec. 107 applies to State concurrent powers equally with its exclusive powers, unless every Commonwealth legislative power, however complete in itself, is subject to the unrestricted operation of every State Act. It is said that the rule above stated must be read as reciprocal, because some of the reasoning in *D'Emden v. Pedder*, (1904) 1 CLR 91, indicates a reciprocal invalidity of Commonwealth law where the State is concerned. It is somewhat difficult to extract such a statement from the judgment * * *. Those who rely on American authorities for limiting pl. XXXV. in the way suggested, would find in the celebrated judgment of Marshall C.J. in *Gibbons v. Ogden*, 22 U.S. 1, (1824), two passages militating strongly against their contention. One is at p. 189 in these words: "We know of no rule for construing the extent of such powers, other than is given by the language of the instrument which confers them, taken in connection with the purposes for which they were conferred." The other is at p. 196, where, speaking of the commerce power, the learned Chief Justice says: "This power, like all others vested in Congress, is complete in itself, may be exercised to its utmost extent, and acknowledges no limitations, other than are prescribed in the Constitution." In *Keller v. The United States*, 213 U.S. 138, 146 (1909), it is said of the State police power: "That power, like all other reserved powers of the States, is subordinate to those in terms conferred by the Constitution upon the nation." Passing to one of the latest American decisions, *Virginia v. West Virginia*, 246 U.S. 565, 596, 603 (1918), the pre-eminence of federal authority within the ambit of the text of the Constitution is maintained with equal clearness and vigor.

But we conceive that American authorities, however illustrious the tribunals may be, are not a secure basis on which to build fundamentally with respect to our own Constitution. While in secondary and subsidiary matters they may, and sometimes do, afford considerable light and assistance, they cannot, for reasons we are about to state, be recognized as standards whereby to measure the respective rights of the Commonwealth and States under the Australian Constitution. For the proper construction of the Australian Constitution it is essential to bear in mind two cardinal features of our political system which are interwoven in its texture and, notwithstanding considerable similarity of structural design, including the depositary of the residual powers, radically distinguish it from the American Constitution. Pervading the instrument, they must be taken into account in determining the meaning of its language. One is the common sovereignty of all parts of the British Empire; the other is the principle of responsible government. The combined effect of these features is that the expression "State" and the expression "Commonwealth" comprehend both the strictly legal conception of the King in right of a designated territory, and the people of that territory considered as a political organism. The indivisibility of the Crown will be presently considered in its bearing on the specific argument in this case. The general influence of the principle of responsible government in the Constitution may be more appropriately referred to now.

In the words of a distinguished lawyer and statesman, Lord Haldane, when a member of the House of Commons, delivered on the motion for leave to introduce the bill for the Act which we are considering: "The difference between the Constitution which this bill proposes to set up and the Constitution of the United States is enormous and fundamental. This bill is permeated through and through with the spirit of the greatest institution which exists in the Empire, and which pertains to every Constitution established within the Empire–I mean the institution of responsible government, a government under which the Executive is directly responsible to—nay, is almost the creature of—the Legislature. This is not so in America, but it is so with all the Constitutions we have granted to our self-governing colonies. On this occasion we establish a Constitution modeled on our own model, pregnant with the same spirit, and permeated with the principle of responsible government. Therefore, what you have here is nothing akin to the Constitution of the United States except in its most superficial features." With these expressions we entirely agree. * * *

The settled rules of construction which we have to apply have been very distinctly enunciated by the highest tribunals of the Empire. To those we must conform ourselves: for, whatever finality the law gives to our decisions on questions like the present, it is as incumbent upon this Court in arriving at its conclusions to adhere to principles so established as it is admittedly incumbent upon the House of Lords or Privy Council in cases arising before those ultimately final tribunals.

What, then, are the settled rules of construction? * * * In *Attorney-General for Ontario v. Attorney–General for Canada*, (1912) A.C. 571, 503, Lord Loreburn L.C., for the Judicial Committee, said: "In the interpretation of a completely self-governing Constitution founded upon a written organic instrument, such as the British North America Act, if the text is explicit the text is conclusive, alike in what it directs and what it forbids. When the text is ambiguous, as, for example, when the words establishing two mutually exclusive jurisdictions are wide enough to bring a particular power within either, recourse must be had to the context and scheme of the Act."

* * *

Before approaching, for this purpose, the consideration of the provisions of the Constitution itself, we should state explicitly that the doctrine of "implied prohibition" against the exercise of a power once ascertained in accordance with ordinary rules of construction, was definitely rejected by the Privy Council in *Webb v. Outrim*, (1906) 4 CLR 356. Though subsequently reaffirmed by three members of this Court, it has as often been rejected by two other members of the Court, and has never been unreservedly accepted and applied. From its nature, it is incapable of consistent application, because "necessity" in the sense employed—a political sense—must vary in relation to various powers and various States, and, indeed, various periods and circumstances. Not only is the judicial branch of the Government inappropriate to determine political necessities, but experience, both in Australia and America, evidenced by discordant decisions, has proved both the elusiveness and the inaccuracy of the doctrine as a legal standard. Its inaccuracy is perhaps the more thoroughly perceived when it is considered what the doctrine of "necessity" in a political sense means. It means the necessity of protection against the aggression of some outside and possibly hostile body. It is based on distrust, lest powers, if once conceded to the least degree, might be abused to the point of destruction. But possible abuse of powers is no reason in British law for limiting the natural force of the language creating them. It may be taken into account by the parties when creating the powers, and they, by omission of suggested powers or by safeguards introduced by them into the compact, may delimit the powers created. But, once the parties have by the terms they employ defined the permitted limits, no Court has any right to narrow those limits by reason of any fear that the powers as actually circumscribed by the language naturally understood may be abused. This has been pointed out by the Privy Council on several occasions, including the case of the Bank of *Toronto v. Lambe*, (1887) 12 App. Cas. 575, 586–587. * * * The non-granting of powers, the expressed qualifications of powers granted, the expressed retention of powers, are all to be taken into account by a Court. But the extravagant use of the granted powers in the actual working of the Constitution is a matter to be guarded against by the constituencies and not by the Courts. When the people of Australia, to use the words of the Constitution itself, "united in a Federal Commonwealth," they took power to control by ordinary constitutional means any attempt on the part of the national Parliament to misuse its powers. If it be conceivable that the representatives of the people of Australia as a whole would ever proceed * * * to use their national powers to injure the people of Australia considered sectionally, it is certainly within the power of the people themselves to resent and reverse what may be done. No protection of this Court in such a case is necessary or proper.

Therefore, the doctrine of political necessity, as means of interpretation, is indefensible on any ground. The one clear line of judicial inquiry as to the meaning of the Constitution must be to read it naturally in the light of the circumstances in which it was made, with knowledge of the combined fabric of the common law, and the statute law which preceded it, and then *lucet ipsa per se.*

   * * *

The grant of legislative power to the Commonwealth is, under the doctrine of *Hodge v. The Queen*, (1883) 9 App. Cas. 117, 132, and within the prescribed limits of area and subject matter, the grant of an "authority as plenary and as ample ... as the Imperial Parliament in the plenitude of its power possessed and could bestow,"). * * * "The nature and principles of legislation" (to employ the words of Lord Selborne in Burah's Case, (1878) 3 App. Cas. 889, 904, the nature of dominion self-government and the decisions just cited entirely preclude, in our opinion, an a priori contention that the grant of legislative power to the Commonwealth Parliament as representing the will of the whole of the people of all the States of Australia should not bind within the geographical area of the Commonwealth and within the limits of the enumerated powers, ascertained by the ordinary process of construction, the States and their agencies as representing separate sections of the territory. * * *

Applying these principles to the present case, the matter stands thus: Sec. 51 (XXXV.) is in terms so general that it extends to all industrial disputes in fact extending beyond the limits of any one State, no exception being expressed as to industrial disputes in which States are concerned: but subject to any special provision to the contrary elsewhere in the Constitution. The respondents suggest only section 107 as containing by implication a provision to the contrary. The answer is that sec. 107 contains nothing which in any way either cuts down the meaning of the expression "industrial disputes" in sec. 51 (XXXV.) or exempts the Crown in right of a State, when party to an industrial dispute in fact, from the operation of Commonwealth legislation under sec. 51 (XXXV.). Sec. 107 continues the previously existing powers of every State Parliament to legislate with respect to (1) State exclusive powers and (2) State powers which are concurrent with Commonwealth powers. But it is a fundamental and fatal error to read sec. 107 as reserving any power from the Commonwealth that falls fairly within the explicit terms of an express grant in sec. 51, as that grant is reasonably construed, unless that reservation is as explicitly stated. The effect of State legislation, though fully within the powers preserved by sec. 107, may in a given case depend on sec. 109. However valid and binding on the people of the State where no relevant Commonwealth legislation exists, the moment it encounters repugnant Commonwealth legislation operating on the same field the State legislation must give way. This is the true foundation of the doctrine stated in *D'Emden v. Pedder*, (1904) 1 CLR 91 in the so-called rule quoted, which is after all only a paraphrase of sec. 109 of the Constitution. The supremacy thus established by express * * * words of the Constitution has been recognized by the Privy Council without express provision in the case of the Canadian

Constitution (see, e.g., *La Compagnie Hydraulique v. Continental Heat and Light Co.*, (1909) A.C. 194, 198). The doctrine of "implied prohibition" finds no place where the ordinary principles of construction are applied so as to discover in the actual terms of the instrument their expressed or necessarily implied meaning. The principle we apply to the Commonwealth we apply also to the States, leaving their respective acts of legislation full operation within their respective areas and subject matters, but, in case of conflict, giving to valid Commonwealth legislation the supremacy expressly declared by the Constitution, measuring that supremacy according to the very words of sec. 109. That section, which says "When a law of a State is inconsistent with a law of the Commonwealth, the latter shall prevail, and the former shall, to the extent of the inconsistency, be invalid," gives supremacy, not to any particular class of Commonwealth Acts but to every Commonwealth Act, over not merely State Acts passed under concurrent powers but all State Acts, though passed under an exclusive power, if any provisions of the two conflict; as they may—if they do not, then *ceadit quaestio*.

We therefore hold that States, and persons natural or artificial representing States, when parties to industrial disputes in fact, are subject to Commonwealth legislation under pl. XXXV. of sec. 51 of the Constitution, if such legislation on its true construction applies to them.

The impact of the *Engineers' Case* on forging a new national identity is recognized in the following case.

VICTORIA v. THE COMMONWEALTH

High Court (Australia).
(1971) 122 C.L.R. 353.

[The issue was whether it is beyond the power of the Parliament of the Commonwealth of Australia to enact the tax imposed by the Pay-roll Tax Act 1941 to be levied on any of the wages referred to in paragraph 4 of the statement of claim paid or payable by the Crown in the right of the State of Victoria or that the Crown in the right of the State of Victoria shall pay the said tax to the Commonwealth in respect of any such wages.]

Windeyer, J.

4. [U]nlike the Supreme Court of the United States, this Court, the Federal Supreme Court as the Constitution calls it, is not the umpire in conflicts arising from the terms of an agreement or treaty. Our task is simply to interpret and apply the provisions of the Constitution as a statute of the Imperial Parliament.

     * * *

5. I have on other occasions adverted to differing legal consequences that flow from the different origins, historically and juristically, of our Constitution from that of the United States. I shall allude to that again here. I do so because to my mind the phrase "dual sovereignty",

which we sometimes hear, is for law a misleading misnomer when applied to the Commonwealth of Australia. There is dual authority but only one sovereignty. The Commonwealth Constitution was enacted at Westminster in 1900 as a product of the assent and agreement of the peoples of the Australian Colonies. It was sought by Australians, not imposed upon them. The Constitution Act itself was carefully worded so as not to be coercive. Section 3 provided that Western Australia should not become part of the new Commonwealth unless Her Majesty was satisfied that the people of that Colony had agreed thereto. As an agreement of peoples, British subjects in British Colonies, and the enactment thereafter by the sovereign legislature of the British Empire of a law to give effect to their wishes, the Australian federation can be described as springing from an agreement or compact. But agreement became merged in law. The word "compact" is still appropriate but strictly only if used in a different sense—not as meaning a pact between independent parties, but as describing a compaction, a putting of separate things firmly together by force of law. The Colonies which in 1901 became States in the new Commonwealth were not before then sovereign bodies in any strict legal sense; and certainly the Constitution did not make them so. They were self-governing colonies which, when the Commonwealth came into existence as a new Dominion of the Crown, lost some of their former powers and gained no new powers. They became components of a federation, the Commonwealth of Australia. It became a nation. Its nationhood was in the course of time to be consolidated in war, by economic and commercial integration, by the unifying influence of federal law, by the decline of dependence upon British naval and military power and by a recognition and acceptance of external interests and obligations. With these developments the position of the Commonwealth, the federal government, has waxed; and that of the States has waned. In law that is a result of the paramount position of the Commonwealth Parliament in matters of concurrent power. And this legal supremacy has been reinforced in fact by financial dominance. That the Commonwealth would, as time went on, enter progressively, directly or indirectly, into fields that had formerly been occupied by the States, was from an early date seen as likely to occur. This was greatly aided after the decision in the *Engineers' Case* (1920) 28 CLR 129, which diverted the flow of constitutional law into new channels. I have never thought it right to regard the discarding of the doctrine of the implied immunity of the States and other results of the *Engineers' Case* (1920) 28 CLR 129 as the correction of antecedent errors or as the uprooting of heresy. To return today to the discarded theories would indeed be an error and the adoption of a heresy. But that is because in 1920 the Constitution was read in a new light, a light reflected from events that had, over twenty years, led to a growing realization that Australians were now one people and Australia one country and that national laws might meet national needs. For lawyers the abandonment of old interpretations of the limits of constitutional powers was readily acceptable. It meant only insistence on rules of statutory interpretation to which they were well accustomed. But reading the instrument in this light does not to my mind mean that the original judges of the High Court were wrong in their understanding of what at the time of federation was believed to be the effect of the Constitution and in reading it accordingly. As I see it the *Engineers' Case* (1), looked at as an event in legal and constitutional history, was a consequence of developments that had occurred outside the law courts as well as a cause of further developments there. That is not surprising for the Constitution is not an ordinary statute: it is a fundamental law. In any country where the spirit of the common law holds sway the enunciation by courts of constitutional principles based on the interpretation of a written constitution may vary and develop in response to changing circumstances. This does not mean that courts have transgressed lawful boundaries: or that they may do so. (at p 367).

6.   The course of constitutional interpretation in Canada has been different from here. There provincial powers have, by decisions of the Privy Council, tended to increase and federal powers to be restricted: see Halsbury's *Laws of England*, 3rd ed., vol. 5, pp. 499, 500; and I add to the cases there mentioned *Attorney-General (Ontario) v. Winner* (1954) AC 541, a judgment that is indirectly illuminating for us. The different courses that the constitutional law of Australia and Canada have taken is not only the result of differing philosophies of a federal system reflected in the predilections of particular individuals. That may have had an influence, as, for Canada, is pointed out in an interesting article: Robinson, "Lord Haldane and the British North America Act", University of Toronto Law Journal, vol. 20, pp. 55–69 (1970). But the different consequences of judicial interpretation flow mainly from radical differences in the terms of the two instruments to be interpreted, our Constitution and the British North America Act. (at p. 397).

7.   Clearly the Constitution assumes the continued existence of the States as constituent elements in a federation. Rhetorical assertions that the Commonwealth Parliament cannot destroy the States can thus stand without question. But that does not justify, as legal propositions, some unqualified and question begging, assertions that were made in the course of the argument in this case—such as that one government does not tax another government, that any Commonwealth taxation law is invalid which unduly as it was said affects State governments.

Greg Taylor, THE COMMERCE CLAUSE— COMMONWEALTH COMPARISONS

24 B.C. Int'l & Comp. L. Rev. 235, 236–244 (2001).

* * *

Modern American constitutional law on the commerce clause began in 1937 with the New Deal and the "switch in time" by the Court, * * *.[5] [This] together with case law of the 1940s—most notably, the celebrated case of Wickard v. Filburn[7]—gave the commerce clause a potential for expansion that seemed unlimited. This expansion was

5. See, e.g., William Lasser, Justice Roberts and the Constitutional Revolution of 1937—Was There a "Switch In Time"?, 78 TEX L. REV. 1347 (2000); * * *

7. 317 U.S. 111 (1942).

confirmed by the civil-rights cases of the 1960s,[8] which opened up vast new possibilities of congressional regulation of commerce in order to achieve non-commercial aims.

The seemingly limitless possibilities, however, now have been limited by the Supreme Court's decisions in *Lopez* [above] and *Morrison* which, over the strong dissents of four Justices, reveal that the reach of the commerce clause is not unbounded and, more broadly, that judicial review of federal statutes to ensure that they fall within Congress's enumerated powers is not dead, as some had thought it might be. * * *

II. CANADA

A. Distribution of Powers

Section 91 (2) of Canada's Constitution Act of 1867 appears to give the Canadian federal Parliament an even broader power than that contained in the U.S. commerce clause, for it confers on the Canadian Parliament "exclusive Legislative Authority" over "The Regulation of Trade and Commerce." The restriction to inter-state and overseas commerce found in the U.S. provision is not present, and the Canadian provision mentions trade as well as commerce. Nevertheless, the Canadian Supreme Court has conceded to the Canadian federal Parliament much narrower powers than has the U.S. Supreme Court to Congress.

To some extent, this difference must be understood as merely a consequence of the different scheme of distribution of powers which operates in Canada. The U.S. Constitution confers enumerated powers on the central government and leaves the residue with the states. The Canadian Constitution, in section 92, confers exclusive enumerated powers on the provinces and leaves the residue with the center. However, "for greater Certainty, but not so as to restrict the Generality of the" conferral of the residue, section 91 sets out a list of powers conferred exclusively on the center. As already mentioned, one of these is "The Regulation of Trade and Commerce." This scheme for the distribution of powers, which was drafted in the 1860s, was meant to establish strong central control in order to avoid the weaknesses thought to have caused the American Civil War. In practice, however, the Canadian scheme has resulted in much stronger provincial autonomy than exists in the United States. The Courts undoubtedly have been motivated by a concern to allow the provinces some degree of independent legislative authority having regard to the differences among them, especially the difference between English Canada and Quebec.

One consequence of this scheme is that recognizing a power as belonging to the center under section 91(2) withdraws it, at least if the logic of the system is followed, [13] from the competence of the provinces, as the power under section 91(2) is exclusive. [14] Therefore, a jurispru-

---

8. Heart of Atlanta Motel v. United States, 379 U.S. 241 (1964); Katzenbach v. McClung, 379 U.S. 294 (1964); Daniel v. Paul, 395 U.S. 298 (1969); see also Perez v. United States, 402 U.S. 146 (1971).

13. The "double aspect theory" sometimes disturbs this tidy scheme. See, e.g., Bell Canada v. Quebec [1988] 1 S.C. R. 749, 7.

14. For a commentary from an Australian perspective, see Huddart Parker Ltd.

dence as generous to the federal government as the American jurisprudence would result in the virtually complete removal of all authority from the provinces. This consequence is avoided by a generous interpretation of sections 92(13) and (16), which confer exclusive power on the provinces in relation to "Property and Civil Rights in the Province"[15] and "Generally all Matters of a merely local or private Nature in the Province" respectively.[16] It is necessary, under the Canadian "pith and substance" approach to determining the nature of statutes,[17] to decide which heading a particular statute in truth falls under.

B.   The Parsons Tests

As early as 1881, the Privy Council (which, sitting in London, was the final Court of appeal for Canadian constitutional issues until 1949) held in Citizens Insurance of Canada v. Parsons[19] that section 91(2) was, despite the absence of an express limitation to this effect, limited to "regulation of trade in matters of inter-provincial concern" as well as international trade. Secondly, it was held that section 91(2) "may ... include general regulation of trade affecting the whole"[20] of Canada. These are the two branches of trade and commerce which the federal Parliament may regulate in Canada. All other forms of trade and commerce come within provincial authority.

Although a trend slightly more generous to the federal government can be detected in more recent cases, which allow control of intra-provincial transactions when the purpose of the legislation can be said to be extra-provincial,[21] the distinctions made in Parsons, in essence, still constitute good law.[22] It is necessary to determine whether a statute's "pith and substance" is a matter of federal or provincial concern. Thus, the Supreme Court of Canada held in the late 1970s that the transformation of primary agricultural products into food, even for extra-provincial trade, was a matter for regulation by the provinces, as such activity did not come within either of the two Parsons branches.[23] However, it may be otherwise if production quotas are, in "pith and substance," an attempt to control inter-provincial or international prices, for those are

Et al. v. Commonwealth (1931) 44 C.L.R. 492, 526.

15. For the origin of this phrase, see PETER W. HOGG, CONSTITUTIONAL LAW OF CANADA 36, 545–46 (4th e., 1997).

16. On the choice between the two subsections, see HOGG, supra note 15, at 530 n.9.

17. See, e.g. Russell v. R (1882) 7 App. Cas. 829, 839; Union Colliery of British Columbia v. Bryden v. Lower Mainland Dairy Products Board [1938] A.C. 708, 720.

19. (1881) 7 App. Cas. 96, 113.

20. Id.

21. Particularly R v. Klassen (1960) 20 D.L. R. 2d 406 (the Supreme Court of

Canada refused leave to appeal in this case; [1959] S.C.R. ix); Caloil v. Attorney–General (Canada) [1971] S.C.R. 543; see also Labatt Breweries v. Attorney–General (Canada) [1980] 1 S.C.R. 914, 942; General Motors of Canada v. City National Leasing [1989] 1 S.C.R. 641, 659. See Neil Finkelstein, Recent Case, 68 CAN. BAR. REV. 361, 367 (1976); Paul C. Weiler, the Supreme Court and the Law of Canadian Federalism, 23 U. Toronto L.J. 307, 331 (1973).

22. As is shown by Dominion Stores v. R [1980] 1 S.C.

23. Re Agricultural Products Marketing Act [1978] 2 S.C.R. 1198, 1293.

matters for the federal government under the first limb of the Parsons test,[24]—a conclusion that would have delighted President Roosevelt.

C. The Canadian New Deal

One result of the Canadian jurisprudence is that the Canadian New Deal fared rather worse in the courts than did the American New Deal after 1937. Thus, the Privy Council struck down—in a series of three decisions handed down on January 28, 1937, just as President Roosevelt was preparing to reveal his "Court-packing" plan—attempts by the federal Parliament to regulate conditions of labor,[25] to provide unemployment insurance,[26] and to control the marketing of natural products generally.[27] However, the reaction was muted, and there was no "Court-packing" plan. This result is partly due to the fact that the composition of the Privy Council was beyond the influence of the Canadian government. * * *

D. The Current Tests

* * * In Canada, there continues to be a distinction between inter-provincial trade and commerce and other sorts of trade and commerce, as well as between trade and commerce and things that are not trade and commerce.

Thus, a storage facility receiving liquefied natural gas in one province from another province is not within the federal Parliament's trade and commerce power even though the gas is sold to customers: by the time the gas has reached the storage facility, it is no longer part of inter-provincial trade but is part of a local network only.[35] * * * The production of pornographic videos for inter-provincial trade is not a matter for the Canadian government, but for the provinces.[37] The first limb of the Parsons test will not be satisfied, in other words, if a statute deals not with matters of inter-provincial or international concern, but merely with isolated, local manifestations of trade that happen to occur in different provinces or countries. And, in principle, trade and commerce does not include production.

The second limb of the Parsons test—general regulation of trade affecting the whole of Canada—is even now, 120 years after Parsons, not fully explored territory,[39] mostly due to the failure of the federal Parliament to exploit the possibilities inherent in it. However, the outlines of Canadian jurisprudence on this score have emerged relatively recently in cases such as MacDonald v. Vapor Canada Ltd.[41] and General Motors of

24. Central Canada Potash v. Saskatchewan [1979] 1 S.C.R. 42. Now section 92A (2) of the Constitution, added in 1982, might permit provincial legislation in the circumstances considered in this case, see HOGG, supra note 15, at 566, but that has nothing to do with the meaning of the trade and commerce power.

25. See Attorney–General (Canada) v. Attorney–General (Ontario) [1937] A.C. 326.

26. See Attorney–General (Canada) v. Attorney–General (Ontario) [1937] A. C. 355.

27. See Attorney–General (British Columbia) v. Attorney–General (Canada) [1937] A.C. 377

35. Re Ontario Energy Bd. (1986) 32 D.L.R. 4th 706.

37. See It's Adult Video Plus v. British Columbia (1991) 81 D.L.R. 4th 436, 445–54.

39. General Motors of Canada, 1 S.C.R. at 657.

41. 2 S.C.R. 134.

Canada Ltd. v. City Nationwide Leasing.[42] Attempts to codify private law, such as tort law, will be looked upon unfavorably by the Court: in MacDonald, a federal statute prohibiting any act or business practice "contrary to honest industrial or commercial usage in Canada" was seen as an attempt to create a general federal action in tort law, which is a matter that comes under the jurisdiction of the provinces.[43] The statute was therefore invalid. On the other hand, general regulatory schemes dealing not with provincial matters referred to in sections 92(13) and (16), but with well-defined public goods relevant to trade generally, such as fair competition, will be upheld, as in General Motors.

* * *

The Supreme Court of Canada, in its unanimous judgment in General Motors, recognized that its job is to balance, as best it can, the competing claims of federal and provincial legislatures, and developed quite an involved method of doing so.[46] The judgment is very closely reasoned, a first-class example of the judicial craft, and repays study by those who would abandon judicial review of commerce clauses because it is allegedly too difficult to draw boundaries in this area. The case concerned a federal anti-trust statute and the associated right to damages for breach. The right to damages was attacked, and it was vulnerable to attack because rights to damages are generally part of tort law, and thus, as in Vapor Canada, generally fall under provincial control.

In General Motors, the Court assessed, first, the extent to which the damages section intruded on provincial powers, second, the validity of the statute as a whole, and third, the extent to which the damages section was connected to the rest of the statute, to the extent that the statute was valid.[47] In the first step, the Court held that the damages section did indeed encroach on provincial powers, but noted that it was a remedial provision and an adjunct to the rest of the statute rather than a freestanding right to damages. The encroachment, therefore, did not mean that the right to damages was invalid if the rest of the statute was valid and the damages section was sufficiently well integrated into its scheme.[48]

The second step was to assess the validity of the statute. In so doing, a list of five criteria, developed in MacDonald and further elaborated in General Motors, was relevant. It must be stressed, however, that this is not a list of mandatory requirements that a statute must meet in order to be valid under the second limb of Parsons, but merely a helpful list of criteria that the Court will take into account. The list of criteria is as follows: (1) the existence of a general regulatory scheme; (2) the oversight of a regulatory agency; (3) a concern with trade as a whole rather than with a particular trade; (4) the constitutional inability of the provinces, jointly or severally, to enact the scheme concerned; and (5)

---

42. 1 S.C.R. 641.

43. See MacDonald 2 S.C.R. at 141–42, 149.

46. See 1 S.C.R. at 659, 666.

47. See id. at 663–72.

48. See id. at 672–74.

the need for national rather than provincial regulation if a scheme is to be effective.[49]

Although some do not understand the need for the first two criteria, the reason is apparent: public regulation indicates that the matter concerned is of general importance and shows that the federal statute does not merely deal with private grievances or tort laws, which are subjects reserved for the provinces. The last three criteria are, of course, indications that the problem is one which goes beyond intra-provincial trade.

The regulatory scheme at issue in General Motors met all five criteria, and the statute as a whole was therefore valid.[52] The only remaining question was whether the damages section was sufficiently related to the statute as a whole. The "correct approach," the Court indicated, was "to ask whether the provision is functionally related to the general objective of the legislation, and to the structure and the content of the scheme," or whether it had been "tacked on."[53] The Court had little difficulty concluding that the award of damages for breach of a valid anti-trust statute was "functionally related" to that statute.[54] The intrusion into provincial jurisdiction identified in the first stage therefore could be justified by the fact that it was associated in a sufficiently close way with a scheme that, as a whole, was valid. The intrusion was different from that involved in the federal statute invalidated in *Vapor Canada* in a number of respects, chiefly its close connection with a general regulatory scheme and its less broad and undefined nature.[55]

C.2.2.b. FOREIGN RELATIONS

MISSOURI v. HOLLAND

Supreme Court (United States).
252 U.S. 416 (1920).

Justice Holmes delivered the opinion of the Court.

[1] This is [an action] brought by the State of Missouri to prevent a game warden of the United States from attempting to enforce the Migratory Bird Treaty Act of July 3, 1918, c. 128, 40 Stat. 755, and the regulations made by the Secretary of Agriculture in pursuance of the same. The ground of the bill is that the statute is an unconstitutional interference with the rights reserved to the States by the Tenth Amendment, and that the acts of the defendant done and threatened under that authority invade the sovereign right of the State and contravene its will manifested in statutes.

On December 8, 1916, a treaty between the United States and Great Britain was proclaimed by the President. It recited that many species of birds in their annual migrations traversed certain parts of the United States and of Canada, that they were of great value as a source of food

---

49. See MacDonald, 2 S.C.R. at 158, 165; General Motors, 1 S.C.R. at 662.

52. See 1 S.C.R. at 677–683.

53. Id. at 683.

54. See id. at 683–93.

55. Id. at 690–92.

and in destroying insects injurious to vegetation, but were in danger of extermination through lack of adequate protection. It therefore provided for specified close seasons and protection in other forms, and agreed that the two powers would take or propose to their law-making bodies the necessary measures for carrying the treaty out. 39 Stat. 1702. The above mentioned Act of July 3, 1918, entitled an act to give effect to the convention, prohibited the killing, capturing or selling any of the migratory birds included in the terms of the treaty * * * [T]he question raised is the general one whether the treaty and statute are void as an interference with the rights reserved to the States.

[2]   To answer this question it is not enough to refer to the Tenth Amendment, reserving the powers not delegated to the United States, because by Article II, § 2, the power to make treaties is delegated expressly, and by Article VI treaties made under the authority of the United States, along with the Constitution and laws of the United States made in pursuance thereof, are declared the supreme law of the land. If the treaty is valid there can be no dispute about the validity of the statute under Article I, § 8, as a necessary and proper means to execute the powers of the Government. The language of the Constitution as to the supremacy of treaties being general, the question before us is narrowed to an inquiry into the ground upon which the present supposed exception is placed.

[3]   It is said that a treaty cannot be valid if it infringes the Constitution, that there are limits, therefore, to the treaty-making power, and that one such limit is that what an act of Congress could not do unaided, in derogation of the powers reserved to the States, a treaty cannot do. An earlier act of Congress that attempted by itself and not in pursuance of a treaty to regulate the killing of migratory birds within the States had been held bad in the District Court. *United States v. Shauver*, 214 Fed. Rep. 154; *United States v. McCullagh*, 221 Fed. Rep. 288. Those decisions were supported by arguments that migratory birds were owned by the States in their sovereign capacity for the benefit of their people, and that under cases like *Geer v. Connecticut*, 161 U.S. 519, this control was one that Congress had no power to displace. The same argument is supposed to apply now with equal force.

Whether the two cases cited were decided rightly or not they cannot be accepted as a test of the treaty power. Acts of Congress are the supreme law of the land only when made in pursuance of the Constitution, while treaties are declared to be so when made under the authority of the United States * * * We do not mean to imply that there are no qualifications to the treaty-making power; but they must be ascertained in a different way. It is obvious that there may be matters of the sharpest exigency for the national well being that an act of Congress could not deal with but that a treaty followed by such an act could, and it is not lightly to be assumed that, in matters requiring national action, "a power which must belong to and somewhere reside in every civilized government" is not to be found * * * The treaty in question does not contravene any prohibitory words to be found in the Constitution. The only question is whether it is forbidden by some invisible radiation from the general terms of the Tenth Amendment. We must consider what this country has become in deciding what that Amendment has reserved. As most of the laws of the United States are carried out within the States and as many of them deal with matters which in the silence of such laws the State might regulate, such general grounds are not enough to support Missouri's claim. Valid treaties of course "are as binding within the territorial limits of the States as they are elsewhere throughout the dominion of the United States." *Baldwin v. Franks,* 120 U.S. 678, 683. No doubt the great body of private relations usually fall within the control of the State, but a treaty may override its power.

Here a national interest of very nearly the first magnitude is involved. It can be protected only by national action in concert with that of another power. The subject matter is only transitorily within the State and has no permanent habitat therein. But for the treaty and the statute there soon might be no birds for any powers to deal with. We see nothing in the Constitution that compels the Government to sit by while a food supply is cut off and the protectors of our forests and our crops are destroyed. It is not sufficient to rely upon the States. The reliance is vain, and were it otherwise, the question is whether the United States is forbidden to act. We are of opinion that the treaty and statute must be upheld.

CONCORDAT CASE
Federal Constitutional Court (Germany).
6 BVerfGE 309 (1957).[d]

[In 1933, Hitler's regime concluded a concordat with the Holy See. The concordat recognized the right of the Catholic Church to freedom of religion and control over Church properties. It also included guarantees of religious education in the public schools and state-supported confessional schools for the children of Catholic parents. In 1954, Lower Saxony, a predominantly Protestant state, provided nondenominational schools for all children. The federal government, at the urging of the Holy See, contested the validity of the state's new policy, claiming that the state had usurped federal authority to conduct foreign relations. The Court sustained the validity of the concordat under the general principles of international law but then proceeded to rule that Art. 23 of the concordat, guaranteeing confessional schools, was not enforceable in states with conflicting school legislation. * * *]

Judgment of the Second Senate: * * *

E.II. We need not here examine the extent of the state's obligation toward the federation to honor treaties internationally binding upon the Federal Republic of Germany. In no case could the states' obligation toward the federation to honor the concordat's educational provisions * * * be derived from the constitutional order created by the Basic Law. Articles 7, 30 and 70 *et seq.* of the Basic Law have made certain fundamental choices that shape the relationship between federation and states * * * These choices reflect no such obligation. In contrast to the

---

d. Reproduced from Donald P. Kommers, *The Constitutional Jurisprudence of* *the Federal Republic of Germany* 80–82 (2d ed. 1997).

Weimar Constitution, these provisions establish the states as the exclusive custodians of cultural leadership. In the area of denominational organization of the school system, only the provisions of Articles 7 and 141 limit this exclusive authority. This allocation is an important element of the federal structure of the Federal Republic of Germany.

1. We must proceed from the view that the states alone are entitled to make law where they possess exclusive legislative authority. In Articles 30 and 70 *et seq.* the Basic Law very clearly expresses this principle. Only obligations arising from federal constitutional law limit the legislative freedom of the states in this area, because the federal legislature cannot pass a law in an area where states have exclusive legislative authority.

We must therefore consider as an important principle of federal constitutional law that states are subject to no limitation upon their legislative authority other than that imposed by the Basic Law. The principle also applies to state legislation pursuant to [preconstitutional] law having continued validity under Articles 123 (1) and (2). * * *

To bind the states constitutionally to the educational provisions of the concordat would flatly contradict their authority to make educational law freely within the limits of the Constitution.

2. With respect to the organization of the school system along denominated lines, the Basic Law made a specific choice that rejected constitutionally binding the states to the educational provisions of the concordat. Based upon the states' freedom of action, Articles 7 and 141 of the Basic Law establish the limits within which the state legislature should be confined in this particular area * * * This choice is not reconcilable with the educational provisions of the concordat * * *.

3. [One] can correctly understand the meaning of Article 7 * * * only by considering the background of the entire situation surrounding the [framing of the] Basic Law for the area of educational law.

From 1933 to 1945 [the Hitler regime] did not enforce the educational provisions of the concordat and in many cases allowed them to violated.

After the collapse of the Reich in 1945, the states helped to accomplish the civil reconstruction of Germany. They reconstructed civil life during a period when the entire German state was not yet capable of action. As a result, the states could alter previous laws of the Reich during this time. Thus the Basic Law also expressly recognized the changes the states had made in earlier laws of the Reich during this period (Article 125 [2]).

In the governmental structure of the states, the issue of education had particular importance and was the subject of lively dispute; the states often deviated from the educational provisions of the concordat * * *.

The Constitution's framers thus had to proceed from the fact that the new educational law of a large part of the territory enacted under the Basic Law contradicted the educational provisions of the concordat. How these events are to be evaluated from the standpoint of international law cannot concern us here. * * * This legal situation * * * made it imperative for the Basic Law to state expressly any intention to constitutionally obligate the states to fulfill the educational provisions of the concordat. In view of the diversified legal situation in education among the states and the Basic Law's own choices in this area (Articles 7 and 141), the Constitution could not have been silent on educational matters if it wished to oblige the states to observe the educational provisions of the concordat. Moreover, the Basic Law could not have been content generally to ordain the constitutional validity of domestic law corresponding to international treaties of the German Reich. This order neither removed contradictory state laws nor bound the state legislature to the continued validity of the law.

In interpreting the Basic Law, one must proceed from the inner harmony of the constitutional structure which gave the German state a new federal and democratic order in place of a totalitarian dictatorship. The supposition that states are obligated vis-à-vis the federation to observe the concordat's educational provisions is irreconcilable with the basic decisions of the constitutional structure, including [the decision to confer] upon the states supremacy over education as policy.

CERTIFICATION OF THE CONSTITUTION OF THE REPUBLIC OF SOUTH AFRICA

Constitutional Court (South Africa).
1996 (4) SALR 744 (CC).[e]

[The 1993, the Interim Constitution of South Africa (Schedule 4) established certain Constitutional Principles that define an ideal model of federalism for a country where the postapartheid Constitution itself had to make "provision for the complex issues involved in bringing together again in one country, areas which had been separated under apartheid, and at the same time establishing a constitutional State based on respect for fundamental human rights, with a decentralised form of government in place of what had previously been authoritarian rule enforced by a strong central government. On the day the Constitution came into force, 14 structures of government 'ceased to exist'." *Executive Council, Western Cape Legislature and Others v. President of the Republic of South Africa and Others* 1995 (4) SALR 877 (CC) at para. 7.

[In regard to the allocation of powers to the national government and the provincial governments Constitutional Principle XXI stated:

"1. The level at which decisions can be taken most effectively in respect of the quality and rendering of services, shall be the level responsible and accountable for the quality and the rendering of the services, and such level shall accordingly be empowered by the Constitution to do so.

2. Where it is necessary for the maintenance of essential national standards, for the establishment of minimum standards required for the rendering of services, the maintenance of economic unity, the maintenance of national security or the prevention of unreasonable action taken by one province which is prejudicial to the interests of another

e. For other excerpts of this case, see Chapter 1, Subsection E.1.

province or the country as a whole, the Constitution shall empower the national government to intervene through legislation or such other steps as may be defined in the Constitution.

3. Where there is necessity for South Africa to speak with one voice, or to act as a single entity—in particular in relation to other states—powers should be allocated to the national government.

4. Where uniformity across the nation is required for a particular function, the legislative power over that function should be allocated predominantly, if not wholly, to the national government.

5. The determination of national economic policies, and the power to promote interprovincial commerce and to protect the common market in respect of the mobility of goods, services, capital and labour, should be allocated to the national government.

6. Provincial governments shall have powers, either exclusively or concurrently with the national government, inter alia–

> a. for the purposes of provincial planning and development and the rendering of services; and

> b. in respect of aspects of government dealing with specific socio-economic and cultural needs and the general well being of the inhabitants of the province.

7. Where mutual co-operation is essential or desirable or where it is required to guarantee equality of opportunity or access to a government service, the powers should be allocated concurrently to the national government and the provincial governments.

8. The Constitution shall specify how powers which are not specifically allocated in the Constitution to the national government or to a provincial government, shall be dealt with as necessary ancillary powers pertaining to the powers and functions allocated either to the national government or provincial governments.''']

Cooperative Government

[287] The constitutional system chosen by the CA is one of cooperative government in which powers in a number of important functional areas are allocated concurrently to the national and the provincial levels of government. This choice, instead of one of a competitive federalism which some political parties may have favoured, was a choice which the CA was entitled to make in terms of the CPs. Having made that choice, it was entitled to make provision in the NT for the way in which cooperative government is to function. It does this in NT 40 and 41.

[288] NT 40 defines the different levels of government as being distinctive, interdependent and interrelated and requires them to conduct their activities within the parameters of NT 40 and 41. According to NT 41(1), all spheres of government and all organs of state within each sphere must adhere to the principles of cooperative government and inter-governmental relations set out in that section.

[289] These principles, which are appropriate to cooperative government, include an express provision that all spheres of government must exercise their powers and functions in a manner that does not

encroach on the geographical, functional or institutional integrity of government in another sphere.[199]

[290] Inter-governmental cooperation is implicit in any system where powers have been allocated concurrently to different levels of government[200] and is consistent with the requirement of CP XX that national unity be recognized and promoted. The mere fact that the NT has made explicit what would otherwise have been implicit cannot in itself be said to constitute a failure to promote or recognize the need for legitimate provincial autonomy.

[291] Although it was argued that cooperation should be a matter for negotiation between each province and the national government, the only provision in NT 41(1) to which serious objection was taken was the requirement that the different spheres of government should avoid legal proceedings against each other. This has to be read with NT 41(4) which provides:

> "An organ of state involved in an intergovernmental dispute must make every reasonable effort to settle the dispute by means of mechanisms and procedures provided for that purpose, and must exhaust all other remedies before it approaches a court to resolve the dispute."

This provision binds all departments of state and administrations in the national, provincial or local spheres of government.[201] Its implications are that disputes should where possible be resolved at a political level rather than through adversarial litigation. It is consistent with the system of cooperative government which has been established and does not oust the jurisdiction of the courts or deprive any organ of government of the powers vested in it under the NT. The contention advanced on behalf of one of the objectors that litigation between organs of state is not competent under the NT is clearly wrong. Specific provision for such litigation is made in NT 167(4)(a). In our view it cannot be said that NT 41 is inconsistent with CP XX. In so holding we are not unmindful of the fact that NT 41(2) and 41(3) make provision for Acts of Parliament to establish the structures and institutions which will promote and facilitate inter-governmental relations, and prescribe the mechanisms and procedures to facilitate the settlement of inter-governmental disputes. The legislation that is required has national implications and it is appropriate that it should be the subject of national legislation. The legislation will have to respect the integrity of provincial governments and, although it does not have to be passed by the NCOP, it will be subject to constitutional control.

[292] The principles of cooperative government and inter-governmental relations set out in NT 41 are not invasive of the autonomy of a province in a system of cooperative government and the objection that they contravene CP XX must be rejected.

---

199. NT 41(1)(g).
200. *Ex parte Speaker of the National Assembly: In re Dispute Concerning the Constitutionality of Certain Provisions of* the National Education Policy Bill 83 of 1995 1996 (3) SALR 289 (CC) at para 34.
201. NT 239(1)(a).

Notes and Questions

1.   Some federal systems were created through the union of preexisting states or state-like entities (Switzerland, the U.S., and Canada).

The federalist traditions of Canada and the U.S., although they differ in various important respects, are quite distinct from those of Latin America. Canada and the U.S. were colonized by Great Britain, which allowed its colonies substantial freedom in governing themselves. In both countries, federalism was perceived as a useful technique for integrating substantially autonomous colonies into a single nation. Latin America, on the other hand, was colonized by Spain and Portugal, whose heavily centralized regimes permitted their colonies little freedom to govern their own affairs. In Latin America, federalism was perceived as a means to decentralize governments that had been heavily concentrated. Both the U.S. and Canada, with the exception of Quebec, were products of colonizations that synthesized Protestantism, Locke's social compact theory, and the natural rights of Englishmen. This North American inheritance of theology and political theory was far more conducive to the structured dispersal of power among many regional centers than Latin America's inheritance of the centralized, hierarchical organization of Roman Catholicism and Bourbon absolutism. It should not be surprising, therefore, that power in all the Latin American federal nations is far more centralized than in Canada or the U.S.

The Argentine Constitution follows the allocative formula of the U.S. Constitution, specifically delegating a long list of powers to the federal government. Article 121 tracks the language of the U.S. Tenth Amendment, reserving to the provinces all powers not delegated to the federal government, as well as all powers expressly reserved in special pacts made at the time of their incorporation into the federal system. Argentina's Constitution, however, departs radically from the U.S. model by expressly granting the federal government broad general powers to promote the economic prosperity of the nation and the conduct of human development, as well as the power to enact civil, commercial, penal, mining, and labor codes. Once the Argentine Congress enacts these codes, the provinces can no longer regulate any matter covered by them. On the other hand, the Argentine provinces do have the power to enact codes of civil and criminal procedure, which generally follow the codes for the federal capital.

Keith S. Rosenn, *Federalism in the Americas in Comparative Perspective*, 26 U. Miami Inter–Am. L. Rev. 1, 4, 13–14 (1994).

Similarly to Latin America, South Africa, or Australia, the constituent entities did not exist as separate states before the constitutional creation of federalism. These countries are part of the common law tradition and, for a while, were subject to the same Commonwealth judicial influence (through appeal to the Privy Council). Do history and culture explain the arrangement of powers between federations and their states? What might be the impact of economic developments on relations between a federation and its states?

Consider the early position in Australia. Even before the *Engineers' Case*, federal spending had increased because of expanded welfare commitments and World War One expenses, forcing the Commonwealth to impose income taxes (originally a preserve of the states). Competition between the federation and states emerged, resulting, in 1927, in a Financial Agreement, by which a Loan Council of the state and Commonwealth treasurers decided on all government-borrowing matters. During the Great Depression, other elements of cooperative federalism emerged.

R. v. Barger (1908) 6 CLR 41 was an 'excise' case that took the simple ideas of *Peterswald v. Bartley* (1904) 1 CLR 497 much further. Section 2 of the Excise Tax Act 1906 (Cth) imposed excise duties at scheduled rates on various agricultural implements. The section went on to provide that the excise did not apply to goods manufactured under conditions where the remuneration of labour was, for example, "declared by resolution of both Houses of Parliament to be fair and 'reasonable' " or was 'in accordance with an industrial award under the Commonwealth Conciliation and Arbitration Act 1904". The issue before the court was whether § 2 was a law with respect to 'taxation' under § 51(ii) of the Constitution * * *

By 3:2, Issacs and Higgins JJ dissenting, the court held that § 2 could not be supported by § 51(ii). The essential majority argument of Griffith CJ, Barton and O'Connor JJ was that 'It is clear that the power to pass such an Act must be vested *either* in the Parliament *or* in the State legislatures' (emphasis added). Because the subject matter lay within the State legislative power, it therefore could not lie within the Commonwealth's taxation power.

Tony Blackshield and George Williams, *Australian Constitutional Law and Theory: Commentary and Materials* 234–35 (2d ed., 1998).

The scheme of the Australian Constitution, like that of the United States of America, is to confer certain definite powers upon the Commonwealth, and to reserve to the States, whose powers before the establishment of the Commonwealth were plenary, all powers not expressly conferred upon the Commonwealth * * *

The grant of the power of taxation is a separate and independent grant. This is the accepted law in the United States. In interpreting the grant it must be considered not only with reference to other separate and independent grants, such as the power to regulate external and interstate trade and commerce, but also with reference to the powers reserved to the States.

It was not contested in argument that regulation of the conditions of labour is a matter relating to the internal affairs of the States, and is therefore reserved to the States and denied to the Commonwealth, except so far as it can be brought within one of the thirty-nine powers enumerated in § 51 * * *

R. v. Barger, (1908) 6 C.L.R. 41, 67, 69.

2. Argentina and Mexico have constitutional provisions directly modeled on the U.S. Supremacy Clause. Brazil has a similar provision. Venezuela achieves the same result by denying to the states the power to do anything that does not conform to the Constitution and requiring that all exercise of public power conform to the Constitution. The Canadian Constitution Act of 1982 explicitly states that the Constitution is the supreme law of the land and that any inconsistent statute is without effect. All these countries have developed complex systems of judicial review. Even though nothing in the constitutions of the U.S. or Canada explicitly authorizes the federal courts to declare statutes unconstitutional, both countries have developed decentral-

ized systems of judicial review in which all levels of the federal and state judiciaries routinely determine the constitutionality of both federal and state legislation. From 1887 to 1994, the Argentine Supreme Court, also without explicit constitutional authorization, developed a decentralized system of judicial review in which all levels of both the federal and state judiciaries routinely determine the constitutionality of both federal and provincial legislation. Argentina's 1994 constitutional reform now explicitly authorizes judicial review. Brazil has a decentralized system of judicial review, but it is based on specific constitutional authorization that originated in the 1891 Constitution, which first adopted federalism. The 1988 Brazilian Constitution contains an extraordinarily elaborate set of procedures for judicial review, including an abstract action of unconstitutionality that must be brought directly before the Supreme Court. The Mexican Constitution confers the power of judicial review only upon the federal courts. The Venezuelan Constitution confers the power of judicial review only upon the Supreme Court, but Article 20 of the Code of Civil Procedure permits all federal courts to declare state acts unconstitutional.

Keith S. Rosenn, *Federalism in the Americas in Comparative Perspective*, 26 U. Miami Inter–Am. L. Rev. 1, 23 (1994).

3. The actual power arrangements between federation and states evade standard constitutional determination on the basis of allocation of legislative powers. The power of the central government is determined to a great extent through its taxing and spending powers. To the extent that a federal government, for economic or political reasons, concentrates revenues, it will be in the position to increase its powers. But see the emerging constitutional—primarily procedural—limits to this trend in Germany below. The federal governments of Canada and the U.S. collect between 40 and 50 percent of total tax revenues. In the largest federal countries of Latin America, this indicator is in the range of 70 to 96 percent. Transfers to provincial and local governments vary. The Mexican federal government, until recently, retained 80 percent of all revenue; while after the 1988 constitutional amendments, the Brazilian federal government retains only roughly 36 percent of the tax revenue. What really matters is the dependence of the constituent states on transfers. Except for Brazil, Latin American federal (member) states depend on federal transfers for roughly 80 to 90 percent of their needs. In the U.S., up to 30 percent of the states' budgets are dependent upon participation in federal programs. These developments bring up issues of federal commandeering and cooperation. See Subsection C.2.3. below. Obviously the more dependent the state is on federal monies the more likely it is that it will follow the same political line as the federation. Diversity (political, religious, or ethnic) at the state level will become risky as the federal government will have no difficulty in frustrating it through withholding of federal transfers. The issue remains thus: To what extent can constitutional doctrines based on states' residual, inherent, or original powers deal with these issues?

4. That the Supreme Court of Canada has construed the national government's power over "trade or commerce" quite narrowly (for example, not to extend to labeling requirements for products in a single industry) may have little bearing on the proper scope of the U.S. Congress's power to regulate "interstate and foreign commerce." This is, in part, because interpretation of the Canadian "trade-and-commerce" power has been influenced by the enumerated powers of the Canadian provinces over property and civil rights, an enumeration absent from the U.S. Constitution. If even similarly

worded "federalism" provisions call for such different interpretations, the prospects for transnational understandings of particular federalism terms seem rather limited. The potential benefits of comparative constitutional study of federalism may be more modest than those in the individual rights context. Consider the following:

> First, federalism provisions of constitutions are often peculiarly the product of political compromise in historically situated moments, generally designed as a practical rather than a principled accommodation of competing interests. Each federal "bargain" is in important respects unique to the parties' situations, in contrast to constitutional provisions asserted to guarantee universal, or natural, or necessary rights of women and men as persons. Similar phrases or provisions concerning federalism may have different historical meanings in a particular polity, tied in different ways to the political compromises that are usually at the foundation of a federal union. Second, not only are federal systems agreed to as a compromise, but the compromise typically constitutes an interrelated "package" of arrangements. No one element of the package can be compared to a similar-seeming element in a different federal system without more broadly considering the comparability of the whole "package" and the role of the particular element within that federal package. With the current United States Supreme Court's doctrinal emphasis on achieving a "balance" between federal and state power to support structural, nontextual rules limiting national power, it would seem both particularly important, and particularly difficult, to consider the entire package in evaluating any particular claim. To compare federalism issues, then, it might be necessary to compare not just decisions on a particular issue but also the entire interrelated structure of a foreign federal system—a task that is even more difficult, especially for judges and lawyers in adjudication.

Vicki C. Jackson, *Narratives of Federalism: Of Continuities and Comparative Constitutional Experience*, 51 Duke L.J. 223, 273 (2001).

5.   There seems to be an important difference between apportionment of powers within a federation in relation to foreign affairs as opposed to domestic affairs. In the international arena, arguably each nation-state should be able to speak and act as an undivided unit, and, accordingly, the federal government ought to have exclusive powers over foreign relations. This view seems consistent with *Missouri v. Holland* but not with the *Concordat Case*. Presumably, what accounts for that difference is that whereas U.S. federalism is more fluid, German federalism grants few exclusive powers to the *Länder*, but when a *Land* is involved, it affords the *Land* great protection. Even granting that resolution of the constitutional issue has no bearing on a country's treaty obligations under international law, does not the German position loom as inherently problematic?

Undoubtedly, the decision in the *Concordat Case* was made easier by the facts that the Treaty involved had been concluded between Hitler and the Vatican and that Hitler had failed to honor it. Furthermore, the exclusive rights of the *Länder* over education originated in the Basic Law, which came into being after the Treaty was made. But what about the future? Should Germany simply avoid international treaties on education? Or could there be other ways around the exclusive rights of the *Länder* in this area?

6.   When dealing with exclusive powers—whether they reside with the federation or the federated entities—the resolution of legal disputes depends primarily on line drawing. Thus in *Missouri v. Holland* the key question was whether protection of migratory birds was a proper subject for an international treaty. In contrast, in cases involving concurrent powers, avoiding imposition of contradictory legal obligations without trampling on either the federation or federated entities often seems much more delicate. Consider, e.g., *Pacific Gas & Elec. Co. v. State Energy Resources Conservation & Development Comm'n*, 461 U.S. 190 (1983), involving federal regulation of nuclear safety and state power to issue permits to construct nuclear plants based on a determination of economic viability. California denied such permits because of a lack of feasible plans for disposal of nuclear waste. This denial was challenged as an improper safety regulation by the state, but the USSC upheld California's decision, stressing that the lack of a safe means of disposing nuclear waste made the proposed plant uneconomical. In reaching its decision, the Court emphasized that even within the realm of concurrent powers, "[S]tate law is preempted to the extent that it actually conflicts with Federal law. Such a conflict arises when compliance with both Federal and state regulations is a physical impossibility, or where state law stands as an obstacle to the accomplishment and execution of the full purposes and objectives of Congress."

Does the USSC's decision satisfy this criterion? Is this because the facts made the proposed nuclear plant both unsafe and uneconomical, thus justifying denial of a permit to build under both federal and state law?

C.2.3. FEDERATION–FEDERATED ENTITIES INTERACTION AT WORK: COMMANDEERING, NEGOTIATION, COOPERATION AND ACCOMMODATION

C.2.3.a. FEDERAL COMMANDEERING OF THE STATE LEGISLATURE OR EXECUTIVE

NEW YORK v. UNITED STATES

Supreme Court (United States).
505 U.S. 144 (1992).

[This case is summarized in the following case and discussed in *Printz v. United States* below.]

DISPUTE CONCERNING THE CONSTITUTIONALITY OF CERTAIN PROVISIONS OF THE NATIONAL EDUCATION POLICY BILL, NO. 83 OF 1995.

Constitutional Court (South Africa),
1996 (3) SALR 289 (CC).

[1]   Chaskalson P: The Speaker of the National Assembly, acting in terms of sections 98(2)(d) and 98(9) of the Constitution, has referred a dispute concerning the constitutionality of certain provisions of the National Education Policy Bill (B83–95) to this Court for its decision. [The Bill charged the Minister of Education in the national government with determining national education policy.] * * *

The constitutional challenge

[6]   [It was argued that although] it would be competent for Parliament to enact legislation establishing consultative structures and enabling the department of national education to procure information from the provincial education departments, * * * [the Bill] would oblige members of provincial executive councils to promote policies that might be inconsistent with provincial policy, require them where necessary to amend their laws to bring them into conformity with national policy, and in effect would empower the Minister to impose the national policies on the provinces. * * *

[9]   The specific provisions of the Bill to which objection was taken in argument were clauses 3(3), 8(6) and (7), and 9 and 10.

[10]   Clause 3(3) of the Bill provides that:

Whenever the Minister wishes a particular national policy to prevail over the whole or a part of any provincial law on education, the Minister shall inform the provincial political heads of education accordingly, and make a specific declaration in the policy instrument to that effect.

This has to be read with clause 8 which deals with the monitoring and evaluation of education. Clause 8(5) requires the Department of Education to report on investigations undertaken by it, and clauses 8(6) and (7) go on to provide:

(6) If a report prepared in terms of subsection (5) indicates that the standards of education provision, delivery and performance in a province do not comply with the Constitution or with the policy determined in terms of section 3(3), the Minister shall inform the provincial political head of education concerned and require the submission within 90 days of a plan to remedy the situation.

(7) A plan required by the Minister in terms of subsection (6) shall be prepared by the provincial education department concerned in consultation with the Department [of Education], and the Minister shall table the plan in Parliament with his or her comments within 21 days of receipt, if Parliament is then in ordinary session, or, if Parliament is not in ordinary session, within 21 days after the commencement of the first ensuing ordinary session of Parliament.

The provincial political head of education is defined as meaning the member of the [provincial] Executive Council responsible for education in a province.

[11]   Clauses 9 and 10 establish a Council of Education Ministers and a committee called the Heads of Education Departments Committee [with the participation of] the provincial political heads of education. The functions of the Council are to share information and views on education, to co-ordinate action on matters of mutual interest to the provinces and the national government, and to promote a national education policy which takes full account of the policies of the government, the principles [of national education policy] * * *

[12]   None of the objectives of the bill is inconsistent with the Constitution. Parliament has the competence to make laws in respect of education, and the determination of policy is clearly necessary for this

purpose. There can be no objection to providing that consultation shall take place prior to the formulation of policy. This serves to restrict rather than to increase the Minister's powers. And if regard is had to our history of disrupted education and to the present constitutional structure which vests concurrent powers to make laws for education in Parliament and the provinces, consultation with educational bodies, including provincial education departments, is essential for the proper exercise of the power to make policy. The publication and implementation of national education policy and the monitoring and evaluation of education are also not open to objection, unless they are done in a way which infringes the powers of the provinces. This was accepted by all counsel in argument, and the constitutional challenge was limited to a contention that the Bill authorized the Minister to implement policy in a way that infringed the powers of the provinces, and to that extent, was inconsistent with the Constitution.

The powers of Parliament and the provincial legislatures

[13]   In terms of section 37 of the Constitution Parliament has the power to make laws for the Republic. It is a general plenary power and is not confined to specific functional areas. The legislative competence of the provincial legislatures is different. It is derived from section 126(1) of the Constitution which empowers them to make laws with regard to all matters set out in schedule 6 to the Constitution. This must be read with Section 126(2) which provides that they can also make laws which are reasonably necessary for or incidental to the exercise of such legislative competence. Education is a schedule 6 functional area in respect of which the provinces have legislative competence. This is not, however, the exclusive domain of the provinces, but one which they exercise concurrently with Parliament. This is made clear by section 126(2A) of the Constitution which provides:

> Parliament shall be competent, subject to subsections (3) and (4), to make laws with regard to matters referred to in subsections (1) and (2).

[14]   Section 126 of the Constitution does not restrict this power; what it does is to provide in subclauses (3) and (4) how a conflict or potential conflict that may exist between an Act of Parliament and provincial legislation is to be resolved.[2]

[15]   Section 126(5) of the Constitution requires that if it is possible to do so an Act of Parliament and a provincial law should be construed as being consistent with each other. If, or to the extent that, this cannot be done, then the provisions of sections 126(3) and (4) determine which of the conflicting provisions is to prevail. The solution provided is as follows. To the extent that the criteria specified in subsections (a) to (e) of section 126(3) are met the provisions of an Act of Parliament that is of general application will prevail; if, or to the extent that, such criteria are not met the provisions of the provincial law will prevail.

* * *

---

2. *Premier of KwaZulu–Natal and Others v. President of the Republic of South Africa* 1996 (4) SALR 1098 (CC) at para 25; *The Executive Council of the Western Cape Legislature and Others v. President of the Republic of South Africa and Others* 1995 (4) SALR 877 (CC) at para 90.

The argument

[21]   In support of the challenge to the constitutionality of the Bill on the grounds that it obliges provinces to adhere to national education policy, Mr. Trengove placed considerable reliance on the majority judgment of the United States Supreme Court in *New York v. United States*.[7] This case was concerned with a 1985 congressional statute which dealt with the disposal of radioactive waste. The statute was enacted after negotiations involving the affected states. At that time there were three regional disposal facilities and in terms of earlier legislation those facilities would have been entitled as from the beginning of 1986 to exclude waste from non-members. The 1985 statute extended the period during which the existing three sites would accept waste from non-members until 1992, and dealt with the obligations of states after the expiry of that deadline. The legislative scheme was as follows. Each state was made responsible for disposing of waste generated within its territory either by itself or in co-operation with other states. States were authorized to enter into compacts for the establishment of regional disposal facilities, and three sets of incentives were offered to states to encourage them to comply with their obligations under the statute. One set consisted of monetary incentives; one set authorized states with disposal sites to gradually increase the cost of access to their sites and ultimately to deny access to waste generated in the states which did not meet federal deadlines. The third set required a state which had not made arrangements for the disposal of waste either to regulate the disposal of the waste in accordance with the instruction of Congress, or, if required to do so by the generator or owner of the waste, to assume ownership, possession and ultimately responsibility for the waste and any damage caused by it. The validity of the legislation making provision for the incentives was disputed on the grounds that it interfered with state rights. The Court was divided. The majority judgment in the *New York* case is based in the main on the importance of the states' powers under the Tenth Amendment. They concluded that:

> while Congress has substantial power under the Constitution to encourage the States to provide for the disposal of the radioactive waste generated within their borders, the Constitution does not confer upon Congress the ability simply to compel the States to do so.[8]

In the result it was held that the first two incentives were within the Constitution, but the third was not. As the provisions relating to the third incentive could be severed from the rest of the statute, the Act containing only the two incentives remained operative and served:

> Congress objective of encouraging the States to attain local or regional self-sufficiency in the disposal of low level radioactive waste.[9]

The minority took a different view, holding that:

> principles of federalism have not insulated States from mandates by the National Government and that the Courts have upheld "congressional statutes that impose clear directives on state officials."[10]

---

7.   505 U.S. 144 (1992).

8.   *Id*. at 149.

9.   *Id*. at 187.

10.   *Id*. at 207, note 3.

Stevens J, concurring in the dissenting judgment, said that:

[t]he notion that Congress does not have the power to issue a simple command to state governments to implement legislation enacted by Congress . . . is incorrect and unsound.[11]

[22] It was pointed out in *Executive Council of the Western Cape Legislature and Others v. President of the Republic of South Africa and Others*[12] that the powers of Parliament depend ultimately upon "the language of the Constitution, construed in the light of [our] own history." Our history is different to the history of the United States of America, and the language of our Constitution differs materially from the language of the United States Constitution. The history and structure of the United States Constitution are discussed in the judgment of O'Connor J in the *New York* case.[13] The Constitution addressed a situation in which several sovereign states were brought together in a federation. The constitutional scheme agreed upon was that each state would surrender part of its sovereignty to the federal government and retain that part which had not been surrendered. This is reflected in the language of the Constitution. Congress has only those powers specifically vested in it by the Constitution. All other power is vested in the states.[14] Congress can make laws which encroach upon state sovereignty through the supremacy clause,[15] commerce clause,[16] the spending power[17] and the power to make all laws which may be necessary and proper for the implementation of its powers,[18] but cannot otherwise interfere with the rights vested in the states under the Tenth Amendment.

[23] Unlike their counterparts in the United States of America, the provinces in South Africa are not sovereign states. They were created by the Constitution and have only those powers that are specifically conferred on them under the Constitution. Their legislative power is confined to schedule 6 matters and even then it is a power that is exercised concurrently with Parliament. Decisions of the courts of the United States dealing with state rights are not a safe guide as to how our courts should address problems that may arise in relation to the rights of provinces under our Constitution. And this is so whether the issue arises under the provisions of section 126 or any other provision of the Constitution.

[24] Although the Bill establishes structures and procedures which are directed to developing a national policy that will be adhered to by all provinces, and contains provisions which are calculated to persuade the provinces to do so, it does not in my view go so far as to require this to be done. In the circumstances the argument that the Bill empowers the Minister to override provincial law or to compel the provinces to amend

---

11. *Id.* at 211.

12. 1995 (4) SALR 877 (CC) at para 61.

13. *Ibid.* at 155–8 and 161–6.

14. U.S. Const. amend. X.

15. U.S. Const. art. VI, cl. 2.

16. U.S. Const. art. I, section 8 cl. 3.

17. U.S. Const. art. I, section 8 cl. 1.

18. U.S. Const. art. I, section 8 cl. 18.

their laws must be rejected. My reasons for rejecting this interpretation of the Bill are as set out below.

The interpretation of the Bill

[25] The provisions that are challenged must be seen in the context of the Bill as a whole which addresses policy issues in a situation in which Parliament exercises concurrent legislative power with the provincial legislatures in respect of schedule 6 matters.

[26] Clause 3(1) of the Bill provides that national education policy is to be determined by the Minister in accordance with the Constitution and the other provisions of the Bill. Clause 3(2) of the Bill requires that in the formulation of national education policy the Minister shall take account of the provisions of section 126 of the Constitution and the relevant provisions of any provincial law relating to education. This is a clear indication that national education policy should not contradict provincial law, save where it would be permissible for Parliament to authorize this through legislation which in terms of section 126 would prevail over provincial law. Clause 6 contemplates that such legislation may be necessary and provides that it may not be introduced into Parliament without prior consultation with the Council of Education Ministers.

[27] The vesting of concurrent lawmaking powers in Parliament and the provincial legislatures is an arrangement which calls for consultation and co-operation between the national executive and the provincial executives. The Commission on Provincial Government[19] and the Financial and Fiscal Commission,[20] which are important constitutional structures, contemplate that there will be consultation between representatives of the provinces and the national government in regard, *inter alia*, to the allocation of funds and the rationalization of statutory enactments. The Bill, which makes provision for such consultation and co-operation in the field of education, is wholly consistent with the constitutional scheme. Indeed, where both Parliament and the provincial legislatures have exercised or wish to exercise schedule 6 competencies such consultation and co-operation would appear to be essential. It is necessary to enable the national government to obtain the information it may require to enable it to take decisions in regard to educational matters falling within the ambit of sections 126(3)(a) to (e) of the Constitution; it is necessary to avoid conflicting legislative provisions and to rationalize the legislation applicable to schedule 6 matters; and it is necessary to enable provincial and national governments to formulate their plans, including budgetary allocations, for the future. The setting up of a parallel national administration in a province to procure the information that the national government needs, and to implement legislation enacted pursuant thereto, would be neither cost-effective nor efficient, and moreover, would be likely to be more intrusive of provincial structures than legislation which calls for cooperation.

[28] One of the purposes of the Bill is to make provision for the development of a national education policy which will accommodate

19. As to which, see sections 163 to 173 of the Constitution.

20. As to which, see sections 198 to 206 of the Constitution.

differences between the national government and the provinces. Thus clause 9(3)(a) refers to a policy that takes full account of the policies of the government and the needs and interests of the provinces, and the respective powers of Parliament and the provincial legislatures. In so far as the Bill makes provision for consultative structures to be established for this purpose, or for the provision of information by provincial education departments to the national education department, it does not in my view offend any of the provisions of the Constitution.

[29]   Clause 3(3) of the Bill requires the Minister to give notice to the relevant provincial political heads of education if he *wishes* national education policy to prevail over provincial law. Such notice does not enable the Minister to require the provinces to act in conformity with national policy; it merely informs them that it is the Minister's *wish* that they should do so, and lays the ground for the necessary consultation that must take place with the Council. There is, no doubt, an implication that the Minister may take action to secure the implementation of national policy if the expressed wish is not met, but that would depend on further steps including if necessary the enactment of legislation as contemplated by clause 6. The response to the Minister's notice, or the consultation called for under clause 6, could lead to the Minister changing tack, or to consensus between the different administrations as to how differences between them should be resolved.

[30]   The provisions of clauses 8(6) and (7) of the Bill also give rise to no obligation on the part of the provinces to adopt national education policy in preference to their own policy, or to amend their legislation to bring it into conformity with national policy. The provincial political head of education can be called upon to prepare a plan to bring standards of education in his or her province into line with what may be required by the Constitution or national policy, if a report has been made under clause 8(5) that such standards are not being met. There is, however, no obligation imposed on the province by the Bill to implement that plan if it chooses not to do so. That obligation could possibly be imposed by other legislation which passes the test of sections 126(3) and (4), but the Bill itself makes no specific provision for that to be done. It contemplates that such legislation may be enacted, but only after consultation has taken place in terms of clause 6.

[31]   Nothing in the Bill imposes an obligation on the provinces to act in conformity with national education policy. That may possibly be achieved by Parliament through the passing of legislation which prevails over provincial law in terms of section 126(3). Whether such laws will or will not be enacted depends on Parliament; and if enacted, whether they will prevail over any provincial laws that are inconsistent with them, is a matter that should only be determined if and when such laws are passed.
* * *

[32]   The opportunity to participate in the Council and Committee and to be heard on adverse reports was not objected to. The objection was to being required to formulate a remedial plan, or to promote national policy. The word "require" which is used in clause 8(6) has a

peremptory connotation, and this is also true of clause 8(7) which provides that the remedial plan:

> shall be prepared by the provincial education department concerned in consultation with the [national] Department.

[33] It was suggested in argument that the cooperation of a provincial political head of education who wishes to ignore a request made for the submission of a remedial plan, could be secured through a mandamus, or through a threat to withhold financial support for the province's education system, or through some other coercive action. It is by no means clear that a political obligation such as that contemplated by clause 8(6) could be made the subject of a mandamus, particularly if the province is not willing to implement the plan;[21] nor is it clear that the offering or withholding of financial incentives (if otherwise lawful) would be open to objection. If the financial incentives or other action taken to persuade the provinces to agree to national policy are not legitimate they can be challenged under the Constitution or under the well established principle that a power given for a specific purpose may not be misused in order to secure an ulterior purpose;[22] if they are legitimate, then they are not open to objection.[23] These are not, however, issues that need trouble us in this case. It can be assumed that provincial administrations will act in accordance with a law which is consistent with the Constitution. If a law requires a provincial administration to act in a particular manner and that requirement is not constitutional, the law cannot be saved from constitutional challenge simply because there may be inadequate forensic mechanisms under the Constitution for its enforcement. It is therefore necessary to confront and answer the question: can an Act of Parliament require a provincial political head of education to cause a plan to be prepared as to how national standards can best be implemented in the province?

[34] Where two legislatures have concurrent powers to make laws in respect of the same functional areas, the only reasonable way in which these powers can be implemented is through cooperation. And this applies as much to policy as to any other matter. It cannot therefore be said to be contrary to the Constitution for Parliament to enact legislation that is premised on the assumption that the necessary cooperation will be offered, and which requires a provincial administration to participate in cooperative structures and to provide information or formulate plans that are reasonably required by the Minister and are relevant to finding the best solution to an impasse that has arisen. * * *

[37] The executive authority vested in the provinces by section 144 of the Constitution is to administer their own laws. Clauses 9 and 10 do not interfere with this authority in any way. What they do is to establish bodies for the purpose of formulating mutual policies, co-ordinating

---

21. *The King v. The Governor of the State of South Australia,* (1907) 4 C.L.R. 1497, 1511; *Reg. v. Employment Secretary, Ex p. E.O.C.* [1993] 1 W.L.R. 872 *(C.A.),* 877 E–F, 895H–896C; 907G–908G.

22. *Van Eck NO and van Rensburg NO v. Etna Stores* 1947(2) SA 984 (A).

23. In the *New York* case it was held that there was no constitutional objection to the use of financial incentives by Congress to secure the co-operation of the states in the implementation of the plan for the disposal of the waste.

action on matters of mutual interest, and exchanging information. There is no compulsion on the provincial political heads of education or the officials of their departments to participate in the affairs of the Council or the Committee. The Bill gives them the right to do so; but if they choose not to, the only sanction is that national education policy and other plans that may be relevant to them, may be formulated without any input from them and without their particular concerns being adequately taken into account. Neither the Council nor the Committee can require a province to change its laws or to implement national policy; nor can they require the provincial political head of education or members of the provincial education department to refrain from implementing provincial laws or policies. The most that they can do is to give advice or make recommendations which may or may not be followed by the provinces.

[38]   There are no provisions of the Bill that oblige the provinces to follow national education policy, or that empower the Minister to require them to adopt national policy or to amend their own legislation. * * *

[40]   * * * The Bill is not a law; it creates no rights and cannot be made the subject of a declaration of rights. All that this Court is empowered to do is to resolve the dispute as to the constitutionality of the Bill. In the circumstances the only order that can properly be made is that the provisions of the National Education Policy Bill submitted to this Court by the Speaker are not inconsistent with the Constitution on any of the grounds advanced on behalf of the petitioners.

PRINTZ v. UNITED STATES

Supreme Court (United States).
521 U.S. 898 (1997).

Justice Scalia delivered the opinion of the Court.

The question presented in these cases is whether certain interim provisions of the Brady Handgun Violence Prevention Act, Pub. L. 103–159, 107 Stat. 1536, commanding state and local law enforcement officers to conduct background checks on prospective handgun purchasers and to perform certain related tasks, violate the Constitution.

The Gun Control Act of 1968 (GCA), 18 U.S.C. § 921 *et seq.,* establishes a detailed federal scheme governing the distribution of firearms. * * *

In 1993, Congress amended the GCA by enacting the Brady Act. The Act requires the Attorney General to establish a national instant background check system by November 30, 1998, Pub. L. 103–159, and immediately puts in place certain interim provisions until that system becomes operative. Under the interim provisions, a firearms dealer who proposes to transfer a handgun must first: (1) receive from the transferee a statement (the Brady Form), containing the name, address and date of birth of the proposed transferee along with a sworn statement that the transferee is not among any of the classes of prohibited purchasers, (2) verify the identity of the transferee by examining an identification document, and (3) provide the "chief law enforcement officer" (CLEO) of the transferee's residence with notice of the contents (and a copy) of the Brady Form. With some exceptions, the dealer must then wait five business days before consummating the sale, unless the CLEO earlier notifies the dealer that he has no reason to believe the transfer would be illegal.

* * *

When a CLEO receives the required notice of a proposed transfer from the firearms dealer, the CLEO must "make a reasonable effort to ascertain within 5 business days whether receipt or possession would be in violation of the law, including research in whatever State and local recordkeeping systems are available and in a national system designated by the Attorney General." The Act does not require the CLEO to take any particular action if he determines that a pending transaction would be unlawful; he may notify the firearms dealer to that effect, but is not required to do so. If, however, the CLEO notifies a gun dealer that a prospective purchaser is ineligible to receive a handgun, he must, upon request, provide the would-be purchaser with a written statement of the reasons for that determination. Moreover, if the CLEO does not discover any basis for objecting to the sale, he must destroy any records in his possession relating to the transfer, including his copy of the Brady Form. Under a separate provision of the GCA, any person who "knowingly violates [the section of the GCA amended by the Brady Act] shall be fined under this title, imprisoned for no more than 1 year, or both."

Petitioners Jay Printz and Richard Mack, the CLEOs for Ravalli County, Montana, and Graham County, Arizona, respectively, filed separate actions challenging the constitutionality of the Brady Act's interim provisions.

* * *

II

* * * [T]he Brady Act purports to direct state law enforcement officers to participate, albeit only temporarily, in the administration of a federally enacted regulatory scheme. Regulated firearms dealers are required to forward Brady Forms not to a federal officer or employee, but to the CLEOs, whose obligation to accept those forms is implicit in the duty imposed upon them to make "reasonable efforts" within five days to determine whether the sales reflected in the forms are lawful.
* * *

The petitioners here object to being pressed into federal service, and contend that congressional action compelling state officers to execute federal laws is unconstitutional. Because there is no constitutional text speaking to this precise question, the answer to the CLEOs' challenge must be sought in historical understanding and practice, in the structure of the Constitution, and in the jurisprudence of this Court. We treat those three sources, in that order, in this and the next two sections of this opinion.

* * *

[E]arly laws establish, at most, that the Constitution was originally understood to permit imposition of an obligation on state *judges* to enforce federal prescriptions, insofar as those prescriptions related to matters appropriate for the judicial power. That assumption was perhaps implicit in one of the provisions of the Constitution, and was explicit in another. In accord with the so-called Madisonian Compromise, Article III, § 1, established only a Supreme Court, and made the creation of lower federal courts optional with the Congress—even though it was obvious that the Supreme Court alone could not hear all federal cases throughout the United States. And the Supremacy Clause, Art. VI, cl. 2, announced that "the Laws of the United States ... shall be the supreme Law of the Land; and the Judges in every State shall be bound thereby." It is understandable why courts should have been viewed distinctively in this regard; unlike legislatures and executives, they applied the law of other sovereigns all the time.

* * *

[Historical review omitted.]

III

The constitutional practice we have examined above tends to negate the existence of the congressional power asserted here, but is not conclusive. We turn next to consideration of the structure of the Constitution, to see if we can discern among its "essential postulates," a principle that controls the present cases.

A

It is incontestable that the Constitution established a system of "dual sovereignty." Although the States surrendered many of their powers to the new Federal Government, they retained "a residuary and inviolable sovereignty," The Federalist No. 39, at 245 (J. Madison). This is reflected throughout the Constitution's text including (to mention only a few examples) the prohibition on any involuntary reduction or combination of a State's territory, Art. IV, § 3; the Judicial Power Clause, Art. III, § 2, and the Privileges and Immunities Clause, Art. IV, § 2, which speak of the "Citizens" of the States; the amendment provision, Article V, which requires the votes of three-fourths of the States to amend the Constitution; and the Guarantee Clause, Art. IV, § 4, which "presupposes the continued existence of the states and ... those means and instrumentalities which are the creation of their sovereign and reserved rights." Residual state sovereignty was also implicit, of course, in the Constitution's conferral upon Congress of not all-governmental powers, but only discrete, enumerated ones, Art. I, § 8, which implication was rendered express by the Tenth Amendment's assertion that "the powers not delegated to the United States by the Constitution, nor prohibited by it to the States, are reserved to the States respectively, or to the people."

The Framers' experience under the Articles of Confederation had persuaded them that using the States as the instruments of federal governance was both ineffectual and provocative of federal-state conflict.

See The Federalist No. 15. Preservation of the States as independent political entities being the price of union, and "the practicality of making laws, with coercive sanctions, for the States as political bodies" having been, in Madison's words, "exploded on all hands," 2 Records of the Federal Convention of 1787, p. 9 (M. Farrand ed. 1911), the Framers rejected the concept of a central government that would act upon and through the States, and instead designed a system in which the state and federal governments would exercise concurrent authority over the people—who were, in Hamilton's words, "the only proper objects of government," The Federalist No. 15, at 109. We have set forth the historical record in more detail elsewhere, see *New York v. United States,* 505 U.S. at 161–166, It suffices to repeat the conclusion: "The Framers explicitly chose a Constitution that confers upon Congress the power to regulate individuals, not States." *Id.,* at 166. The great innovation of this design was that "our citizens would have two political capacities, one state and one federal, each protected from incursion by the other"—"a legal system unprecedented in form and design, establishing two orders of government, each with its own direct relationship, its own privity, its own set of mutual rights and obligations to the people who sustain it and are governed by it." *U.S. Term Limits, Inc. v. Thornton,* 514 U.S. 779, 838 (1995) (Kennedy, J., concurring). The Constitution thus contemplates that a State's government will represent and remain accountable to its own citizens. *See New York, supra,* at 168–169; *United States v. Lopez,* 514 U.S. 549, 576–577 (1995) (Kennedy, J., concurring). Cf. *Edgar v. MITE Corp.,* 457 U.S. 624, 644 (1982) ("the State has no legitimate interest in protecting nonresidents"). As Madison expressed it: "The local or municipal authorities form distinct and independent portions of the supremacy, no more subject, within their respective spheres, to the general authority than the general authority is subject to them, within its own sphere." The Federalist No. 39, at 245.[11]

* * *

11. Justice Breyer's dissent would have us consider the benefits that other countries, and the European Union, believe they have derived from federal systems that are different from ours. We think such comparative analysis inappropriate to the task of interpreting a constitution, though it was of course quite relevant to the task of writing one. The Framers were familiar with many federal systems, from classical antiquity down to their own time; they are discussed in Nos. 18–20 of The Federalist. Some were (for the purpose here under discussion) quite similar to the modern "federal" systems that Justice Breyer favors. Madison's and Hamilton's opinion of such systems could not be clearer. Federalist No. 20, after an extended critique of the system of government established by the Union of Utrecht for the United Netherlands, concludes:

"I make no apology for having dwelt so long on the contemplation of these federal precedents. Experience is the oracle of truth; and where its responses are unequivocal, they ought to be conclusive and sacred. The important truth, which it unequivocally pronounces in the present case, is that a sovereignty over sovereigns, a government over governments, a legislation for communities, as contradistinguished from individuals, as it is a solecism in theory, so in practice it is subversive of the order and ends of civil polity. . . ." *Id.,* at 138.

Antifederalists, on the other hand, pointed specifically to Switzerland—and its then-400 years of success as a "confederate republic"—as proof that the proposed Constitution and its federal structure was unnecessary. See Patrick Henry, Speeches given before the Virginia Ratifying Convention, 4 and 5 June, 1788, reprinted in The Essential Antifederalist 123, 135–136 (W. Allen & G. Lloyd ed. 1985). The fact is that our federalism is not Europe's. It is "the unique contribution of the Framers to political science and political theory." *United States v.*

This separation of the two spheres is one of the Constitution's structural protections of liberty. "Just as the separation and independence of the coordinate branches of the Federal Government serve to prevent the accumulation of excessive power in any one branch, a healthy balance of power between the States and the Federal Government will reduce the risk of tyranny and abuse from either front." To quote Madison once again:

"In the compound republic of America, the power surrendered by the people is first divided between two distinct governments, and then the portion allotted to each subdivided among distinct and separate departments. Hence a double security arises to the rights of the people. The different governments will control each other, at the same time that each will be controlled by itself." The Federalist No. 51, at 323.

See also The Federalist No. 28, at 180–181 (A. Hamilton). The power of the Federal Government would be augmented immeasurably if it were able to impress into its service—and at no cost to itself—the police officers of the 50 States.

B

We have thus far discussed the effect that federal control of state officers would have upon the first element of the "double security" alluded to by Madison: the division of power between State and Federal Governments. It would also have an effect upon the second element: the separation and equilibration of powers between the three branches of the Federal Government itself. The Constitution does not leave to speculation who is to administer the laws enacted by Congress; the President, it says, "shall take Care that the Laws be faithfully executed," Art. II, § 3, personally and through officers whom he appoints * * *. The Brady Act effectively transfers this responsibility to thousands of CLEOs in the 50 States, who are left to implement the program without meaningful Presidential control * * * The insistence of the Framers upon unity in the Federal Executive—to insure both vigor and accountability—is well known. See The Federalist No. 70 (A. Hamilton). That unity would be shattered, and the power of the President would be subject to reduction, if Congress could act as effectively without the President as with him, by simply requiring state officers to execute its laws.

* * *

IV

* * *

Federal commandeering of state governments is such a novel phenomenon that this Court's first experience with it did not occur until the 1970's * * *

* * *

Lopez, 514 U.S. 549, 575 (1995) (Kennedy, J., concurring) (citing Friendly, Federalism: A Forward, 86 Yale L. J. 1019 (1977)).

When we were * * * confronted squarely with a federal statute that unambiguously required the States to enact or administer a federal regulatory program, our decision should have come as no surprise. At issue in *New York v. United States,* 505 U.S. 144 (1992), were the so-called "take title" provisions of the Low–Level Radioactive Waste Policy Amendments Act of 1985, which required States either to enact legislation providing for the disposal of radioactive waste generated within their borders, or to take title to, and possession of the waste—effectively requiring the States either to legislate pursuant to Congress's directions, or to implement an administrative solution. 505 U.S. 144 at 175–176, 112 S. Ct. 2408, 120 L. Ed. 2d 120. We concluded that Congress could constitutionally require the States to do neither. *Id.,* at 176. "The Federal Government," we held, "may not compel the States to enact or administer a federal regulatory program." *Id.,* at 188.

The Government contends that *New York* is distinguishable on the following ground: unlike the "take title" provisions invalidated there, the background-check provision of the Brady Act does not require state legislative or executive officials to make policy, but instead issues a final directive to state CLEOs. It is permissible, the Government asserts, for Congress to command state or local officials to assist in the implementation of federal law so long as "Congress itself devises a clear legislative solution that regulates private conduct" and requires state or local officers to provide only "limited, non-policymaking help in enforcing that law." "The constitutional line is crossed only when Congress compels the States to make law in their sovereign capacities."

The Government's distinction between "making" law and merely "enforcing" it, between "policymaking" and mere "implementation," is [a difficult one to maintain] * * *. Executive action that has utterly no policymaking component is rare, particularly at an executive level as high as a jurisdiction's chief law-enforcement officer. Is it really true that there is no policymaking involved in deciding, for example, what "reasonable efforts" shall be expended to conduct a background check? It may well satisfy the Act for a CLEO to direct that (a) no background checks will be conducted that divert personnel time from pending felony investigations, and (b) no background check will be permitted to consume more than one-half hour of an officer's time. But nothing in the Act *requires* a CLEO to be so parsimonious; diverting at least *some* felony-investigation time, and permitting at least *some* background checks beyond one-half hour would certainly not be *un*reasonable. Is this decision whether to devote maximum "reasonable efforts" or minimum "reasonable efforts" not preeminently a matter of policy? It is quite impossible, in short, to draw the Government's proposed line at "no policymaking," and we would have to fall back upon a line of "not too much policymaking." How much is too much is not likely to be answered precisely; and an imprecise barrier against federal intrusion upon state authority is not likely to be an effective one.

* * *

It is an essential attribute of the States' retained sovereignty that they remain independent and autonomous within their proper sphere of authority. It is no more compatible with this independence and autonomy that their officers be "dragooned" into administering federal law, than it would be compatible with the independence and autonomy of the United States that its officers be impressed into service for the execution of state laws.

* * *

The Government also maintains that requiring state officers to perform discrete, ministerial tasks specified by Congress does not violate the principle of *New York* because it does not diminish the accountability of state or federal officials. This argument fails even on its own terms. By forcing state governments to absorb the financial burden of implementing a federal regulatory program, Members of Congress can take credit for "solving" problems without having to ask their constituents to pay for the solutions with higher federal taxes. And even when the States are not forced to absorb the costs of implementing a federal program, they are still put in the position of taking the blame for its burdensomeness and for its defects. Under the present law, for example, it will be the CLEO and not some federal official who stands between the gun purchaser and immediate possession of his gun. And it will likely be the CLEO, not some federal official, who will be blamed for any error (even one in the designated federal database) that causes a purchaser to be mistakenly rejected.

The dissent makes no attempt to defend the Government's basis for distinguishing *New York*, but instead advances what seems to us an even more implausible theory. The Brady Act, the dissent asserts, is different from the "take title" provisions invalidated in *New York* because the former is addressed to individuals—namely CLEOs—while the latter were directed to the State itself. That is certainly a difference, but it cannot be a constitutionally significant one. While the Brady Act is directed to "individuals," it is directed to them in their official capacities as state officers; it controls their actions, not as private citizens, but as the agents of the States * * *. To say that the Federal Government cannot control the State, but can control all of its officers, is to say nothing of significance. Indeed, it merits the description "empty formalistic reasoning of the highest order." By resorting to this, the dissent not so much distinguishes *New York* as disembowels it.

Finally, the Government puts forward a cluster of arguments that can be grouped under the heading: "The Brady Act serves very important purposes, is most efficiently administered by CLEOs during the interim period, and places a minimal and only temporary burden upon state officers." There is considerable disagreement over the extent of the burden, but we need not pause over that detail. Assuming *all* the mentioned factors were true, they might be relevant if we were evaluating whether the incidental application to the States of a federal law of general applicability excessively interfered with the functioning of state governments. But where, as here, it is the whole *object* of the law to direct the functioning of the state executive, and hence to compromise the structural framework of dual sovereignty, such a "balancing" analysis is inappropriate. It is the very *principle* of separate state sovereignty that such a law offends, and no comparative assessment of the various interests can overcome that fundamental defect.

We * * * conclude categorically: "The Federal Government may not compel the States to enact or administer a federal regulatory program." The mandatory obligation imposed on CLEOs to perform background checks on prospective handgun purchasers plainly runs afoul of that rule.

V

* * *

We held in *New York* that Congress cannot compel the States to enact or enforce a federal regulatory program. Today we hold that Congress cannot circumvent that prohibition by conscripting the State's officers directly. The Federal Government may neither issue directives requiring the States to address particular problems, nor command the States' officers, or those of their political subdivisions, to administer or enforce a federal regulatory program. It matters not whether policymaking is involved, and no case-by-case weighing of the burdens or benefits is necessary; such commands are fundamentally incompatible with our constitutional system of dual sovereignty * * *.

* * *

Justice Breyer, with whom Justice Stevens joins, dissenting.

* * *

* * * [T]he United States is not the only nation that seeks to reconcile the practical need for a central authority with the democratic virtues of more local control. At least some other countries, facing the same basic problem, have found that local control is better maintained through application of a principle that is the direct opposite of the principle the majority derives from the silence of our Constitution. The federal systems of Switzerland, Germany, and the European Union, for example, all provide that constituent states, not federal bureaucracies, will themselves implement many of the laws, rules, regulations, or decrees enacted by the central "federal" body. They do so in part because they believe that such a system interferes less, not more, with the independent authority of the "state," member nation, or other subsidiary government, and helps to safeguard individual liberty as well. See Council of European Communities, European Council in Edinburgh, 11–12 December 1992, Conclusions of the Presidency 20–21 (1993).

Of course, we are interpreting our own Constitution, not those of other nations, and there may be relevant political and structural differences between their systems and our own. *Cf.* The Federalist No. 20, pp. 134–138 (C. Rossiter ed. 1961) (J. Madison and A. Hamilton) (rejecting certain aspects of European federalism). But their experience may nonetheless cast an empirical light on the consequences of different solutions to a common legal problem—in this case the problem of reconciling central authority with the need to preserve the liberty-enhancing autonomy of a smaller constituent governmental entity. *Cf. id.*, No. 42, p. 268 (J. Madison) (looking to experiences of European countries); *id.*, No. 43, pp. 275, 276 (J. Madison) (same). And that experience here offers empirical confirmation of the implied answer to a question Justice Stevens asks: Why, or how, would what the majority sees as a constitutional alternative—the creation of a new federal gun-law bureaucracy, or the expansion of an existing federal bureaucracy—better promote either state sovereignty or individual liberty? See *ante*, at 7–8, 23 (Stevens, J., dissenting).

As comparative experience suggests, there is no need to interpret the Constitution as containing an absolute principle—forbidding the assignment of virtually any federal duty to any state official. Nor is there a need to read the Brady Act as permitting the Federal Government to overwhelm a state civil service. The statute uses the words "reasonable effort," words that easily can encompass the considerations of, say, time or cost, necessary to avoid any such result.

Regardless, as Justice Stevens points out, the Constitution itself is silent on the matter. *Ante*, at 7, 18, 25 (Stevens, J., dissenting). Precedent supports the Government's position here. *Ante*, at 19, 23–25, 26–34 (Stevens, J., dissenting). And the fact that there is not more precedent— that direct federal assignment of duties to state officers is not common— likely reflects, not a widely shared belief that any such assignment is incompatible with basic principles of federalism, but rather a widely shared practice of assigning such duties in other ways. Thus, there is neither need nor reason to find in the Constitution an absolute principle, the inflexibility of which poses a surprising and technical obstacle to the enactment of a law that Congress believed necessary to solve an important national problem.

For these reasons[, among others,] I * * * dissent.

C.2.3.b. COOPERATION, NEGOTIATION AND ACCOMMODATION

CERTIFICATION OF THE CONSTITUTION OF THE REPUBLIC OF SOUTH AFRICA

Constitutional Court (South Africa).
1996 (4) SALR 744 (CC).

[This case is presented in Chapter 1.]

REFERENCE RE CANADA ASSISTANCE PLAN

Supreme Court (Canada).
[1991] 2 S.C.R. 525.

The judgment of the Court was delivered by Sopinka J.

* * *

The Background

The Canada Assistance Plan (the "Plan") was enacted by S.C. 1966–67, c. 45; * * * it authorizes the government of Canada to enter into agreements with the provincial governments to pay them contributions toward their expenditures on social assistance and welfare. * * * The Plan (s. 6(2)) specifies certain prerequisites for eligibility of provincial expenditures, but leaves for the provinces the determination of which programmes will be operated and how much money will be spent. * * * The Plan is silent as to the authority of Parliament to amend the Plan.

The government of Canada entered into agreements with each of the provincial governments in 1967. * * *

In 1990 the federal government decided to cut expenditures in order to reduce the federal budget deficit. The government has created an Expenditure Control Plan. One feature of this plan is to limit the growth of payments made to financially stronger provinces under the Canada Assistance Plan. Such payments are to grow no more than 5 per cent per annum for fiscal 1991 and fiscal 1992. The provinces affected are those which are not entitled to receive equalization payments from the federal government * * *

* * * [t]he government of British Columbia referred the following questions to the British Columbia Court of Appeal:

> (1) Has the Government of Canada any statutory, prerogative or contractual authority to limit its obligation under the Canada Assistance Plan Act [sic] Act without the consent of British Columbia? [A second question concerned the legitimate expectations of the province created by the Plan. In that regard the Court found that the doctrine of legitimate expectations does not apply to a body exercising legislative functions.]
>
> * * *

In the Court of Appeal, this first question was interpreted as asking whether the federal government, in the absence of any new legislation amending the Plan, could unilaterally modify its obligations under the Plan and the agreement. * * * In my opinion, the first question asks the court to determine whether the agreement obliges the government of Canada to pay to British Columbia the contributions that were authorized when the agreement was signed, or rather whether the obligation is to pay those contributions which are authorized from time to time. Adopting the terminology of Lambert J.A. in the Court of Appeal, the former may be called a "static" interpretation and the latter an "ambulatory" one. * * *

First, [Lambert] said that it is unlikely that the parties would have agreed to an arrangement in which Canada could change the arrangement unilaterally while British Columbia could not. There would be a "want of mutuality." It may be noted, though, that by s. 8(1) of the Plan, which is mirrored in cl. 6(2) of the agreement, the agreement is terminated if the provincial welfare and assistance legislation ceases to be in force. The parties, therefore, acknowledged that both were free to terminate the agreement by appropriate legislation.

   * * *

The written argument of the Attorney General of Manitoba was that the legislation "amounts to" regulation of a matter outside federal authority. I disagree. The agreement under the Plan set up an open-ended cost-sharing scheme, which left it to British Columbia to decide which programmes it would establish and fund. The simple withholding of federal money which had previously been granted to fund a matter within provincial jurisdiction does not amount to the regulation of that matter. Still less is this so where, as in this case, the new legislation simply limits the growth of federal contributions. In oral argument, counsel said that the Government Expenditures Restraint Act "impacts upon [a] constitutional interest" outside the jurisdiction of Parliament. That is no doubt true, but it does not make the Act ultra vires. "Impact" with nothing more is clearly not enough to find that a statute encroaches upon the jurisdiction of the other level of government.

Finally, I turn to the second branch of this argument of the Attorney General of Manitoba. This was the argument that the "overriding principle of federalism" requires that Parliament be unable to interfere in areas of provincial jurisdiction. It was said that, in order to protect the autonomy of the provinces, the court should supervise the federal government's exercise of its spending power. But supervision of the spending power is not a separate head of judicial review. If a statute is neither ultra vires nor contrary to the Canadian Charter of Rights and Freedoms, the courts have no jurisdiction to supervise the exercise of legislative power.

[The appeal is allowed.]

Many constitutions provide rules for the distribution of resources within a federal system. However, since constitutions are meant to endure for many generations and provide general rather than detailed prescriptions, conflicts arise when (1) new developments affect a formerly balanced system, (2) certain states within a federation become more resourceful than others, or (3) detailed short-term decisions must be deduced from general norms. Constitutional law is then confronted with the question of whether a system is competitive rather than cooperative and whether constitutions set limits for change. In Germany, the GFCC reacted to such conflict by establishing an obligation for the legislature to act with regard to the endurance of law through time. Citing the German philosopher Husserl as well as the American political philosopher Rawls, the Court defined a constitutional requirement of standard-setting legislation as an intermediate step between the general long-term rules of a constitution and the concrete short-term decisions concerning financial allocations.

REVENUE REALLOCATION CASE
Federal Constitutional Court (Germany).
BVerfG, 2 BvF 2/98, Nov.11, 1999 BVerfGE 101, 158.[f]

[German federalism, in part, consists of a system of tax distribution, or allocation of tax revenues, between the federation and the states. It is

f. Translated by Stephen Kampmeier and Susanne Baer.

governed by a statute (*"Finanzausgleichsgesetz"* [FAG]) that was challenged by the comparatively rich southern states in an abstract procedure to test the constitutionality of federal laws.]

A.   * * *

I.   The Basic Law vests in the federal legislator the power to set and supplement the steady allocation of funds provided for by the Basic Law, applying flexible standards sufficient to meet current needs.

The law governing the allocation of revenue between the federal government and the states (FAG) first determines the portions of the value added tax (VAT) for the federal government and the states (§ 1 FAG), then distributes the states' part of the VAT and commercial taxes to the states (§§ 2, 3 FAG), regulating in this manner the horizontal allocation of revenue among the states (§§ 4–10 FAG), and deciding on grants of federal supplemental payments. * * *

§ 1   para. 1 ss. 3–6 FAG regulates the vertical distribution of VAT between the federal government and the states as a whole. The FAG last provided for a division of 56:44 between the federal government and the states. [To adjust for family support paid for by the states,] the states' portion of the VAT was raised 5.5 %, thus yielding a division of 50.5% for the federal government and 49.5% for the states * * *

2.   75% of the states' portion of the VAT is distributed among the states according to their respective population and 25% is distributed according to another ratio * * *.

[In addition, the system provides for allocations to the municipalities and for reallocations form the rich to the poor states, with a minimum guarantee of financial strength for each state eventually provided for by the federation.]

III.

[Bavaria and other states claimed that the FAG system violated the Basic Law for a number of reasons. The system should adhere to the standard of reasonableness (*"Angemessenheit"*), which was, they claimed, violated in several regards. They argued that:]

4.   § 10 para. 2, 4 of the FAG is in conflict with the standard of reasonable allocation of revenue because it permits skimming financial resources of one resourceful state at a rate of more than half of the average financial resources available.

a) With a certain historical justification, preserving the historical individuality of the various states and the regional plurality of Germany can be understood as an important goal of the federal system. A prerequisite is, of course, a degree of financial autonomy that must be maintained even when arranging for financial adjustments. The intention of the principle of federalism to safeguard better government by decentralized and localized decision-making, as well as the amount of competition between the individual states, guaranteed for by the principle of federalism, presupposes the conservation of the financial base for such limited state competition. A complete leveling off of all differences in financial power, as produced by the balanced budget law as enforced, conflicts with this basic idea.

A significant legitimizing basis for federalism lies in the drive to innovation brought about through political competition of the states amongst themselves and with the federal government. This command for federal competition, which can be inferred from the principle of federalism, also effects the prescribed division of funds to the states under budgetary constitutional law. This is acutely expressed in the basic distribution according to local tax yields. The individual states are thus involved in the collection of taxes generated by businesses in their areas. The distribution law has the function of allocating tax yields to the states in which they were generated.

b) A level of allocation of revenue set too high would result in a conflict with the principle of local tax yields prescribed above and guaranteed by the principle of federal competition in Article 20, paras. 1 and 2 of the Basic Law. * * *

IV.

[Other states and the federal government argued that:]

§ 10   FAG is constitutional. When the scope of the allocation of revenue is determined, the states that owe balance payments are only burdened up to a degree at which their solvency is not critically weakened and no leveling of state finances is induced. [They] assert that the principle of dividing equally between private and public coffers, derived from Article 14 paras. 1 and 2 of the Basic Law, is not applicable to the allocation of revenue to the states. A measure cannot be based on a "proper midpoint" in the tense relationship between autonomy and federal solidarity, because no quantifiable results can be deduced from it. The "proper midpoint" is not a "calculable midpoint". The legislator who balances the budget determines which midpoint is "correct". * * *

C.   * * *

I.

1.   The allocation of revenues in the federal state is determined in principle by the finance constitution (*"Finanzverfassung"*) of the Basic Law. It results in a constitutional system, flexible and adaptable in itself, whose specific steps can however not be exchanged or stepped over at will. The Basic Law forces the legislator to concretize and supplement the constitutional standards. This is specifically true for the standards of vertical allocation of revenues between the federation and the states. * * *

The finance constitution thus contains no immediately binding standards, but requires the legislator to concretize and supplement the system of distributing and allocating financial resources, which the Basic Law only sketches in indefinite terms, by applicable, general, self binding laws according to the economic conditions and the knowledge from economist science. The legislator must—independent of changing compensation needs and particular distributions and reapportionments—establish long-term feasible criteria from which the resulting concrete distributions and reapportionments expressed in numbers can be derived.

* * * This obligation to regulate also becomes visible in Art. 106 para. 4 s. 1 of the Basic Law. This constitutional norm presupposes a legal standard to determine income and spending of the federation and the states, to then determine the percentage of VAT of each respectively. Without such a long-term legal standard it could not be determined whether the relationship between the income and spending of the federation and the states has developed significantly different.

a) The obligation to reallocate VAT revenue can only be met after the legislator has concretized the "basic principles" of Article 106 para. 3 s. 4 Nr.1, 2 of the Basic Law, and after he has specifically defined and made calculable what is meant by "running income" and "necessary spending" that one can deduce allocation measures from it. On the second step, the legislator has been vested with the power to determine below-average income according to Article 107 para. 1 s. 4 of the Basic Law * * *. On the third step, the horizontal reallocation of finances, the legislator is also obliged to define standards * * *:

b) In sum, the legislator thus faces a double burden: He has to concretize constitutional standards and name standards of allocation. Then, he has to deduce the concrete financial conclusions [from it]. * * * The Basic Law gives, in the steadiness of constitutional law, the general principles for legal tax distribution and general financial allocation; the legislator deduces from it long-term * * * standards; in applying such standards binding for himself ("*Maïstäbegesetz*"), the legislator then develops the short-term law of * * * distribution, subject to regular scrutiny.

With the creation of standards, effective and binding for the long-term, the legislator ensures to begin with that the Federal government and the states interpret the constitutionally prescribed initial facts in the same manner, on the basis of the same indicators thus making possible a comparison of the needs for coverage.

c) The constitutional mandate to create a long-term legal standard applied with concrete financial consequences in the near future is based on a sequence of events that ignores, or at the very least complicates, a pure interest-based agreement over the sums. The financial constitution requires in Article 106 paras. 3, 4, as well as in Article 107 para. 2 of the Basic Law, the creation of a legal standard that manages to effect the constitutional mandate of a legal anticipation of the future (compare G. Husserl, Law and Time: Five Legal-philosophical Essays, 1955, p. 27 ff.) in a manner such that the standards for the distribution of taxes and for the allocation of revenue between the parties are already set, before their later effects can be definitively known. By requiring that the law be based on planning (Article 106 para. 3 s. 4 no. 1 Basic Law), the creation of long-term standards is set, which gives the law its usual attributes of the constitutional state: The law, as a formal act, creates the future on a rationally planned basis, requiring a certain durability of the rule, extends its application to an indefinite number of future cases, achieves a certain distance from those effected by it, directs the attention of the ruling organ also to the future obligatory standard, and safeguards the jurisdiction of the legislature for questions of constitutional interpretation. This openness for a general rule reaching into the future can be preserved, if the legislator enacts the standards-law before the financial interests of the federal government and the individual states are made known to him through the introduction of yields and financial requirements which change every year. Therefore this standards-setting law must be enacted through the FAG at a point in time before its concrete application, and then bundled into continuing obligations that protect its standards and indicators from present-day financial factors, conditions of status, and privilege. Even if there is not a "veil of ignorance" (J. Rawls, A Theory of Justice, 1st edition [in German], 1975, pp. 29 *et seq.*, 159 *et seq.*) covering the decisions of the representatives, the antecedent nature of the standards-law can ensure an institutional constitutional orientation that develops a standard without being able to envision the concrete application thereof. The classical effect of time of precedence and reserved powers, comes to play a role anew even in the provisos of federal law.

d) Legislation is the medium used to elucidate and finalize the constitutionally legal financial apportionment system and the system of allocation of revenue. The regulation of financial adjustments cannot be left in the hands of political forces. The Basic Law does not place its circumspect system of checks and balances of tax yields and allocation of revenue at the end of a graduated and inter-related system of regulation then to be placed at the disposition of the effected corporate bodies. To a much greater extent, it obligates the legislator to develop the Basic Law's financial precepts in such a manner so as to perpetuate federal constitutional principles, so that the financial constitution is made explicit in appropriate standards and the consequences of the distribution and the allocations of revenue can be fairly measured and periodically checked according to standards of the day. A merely contractual understanding of facts and the legal consequences of the allocation of revenue is thereby further precluded because each state that were unready or unwilling at the conclusion of the contract could withdraw from its obligation to reallocate revenue. On the other hand, a mere parliamentary majority does not justify the approved allocation of revenue. The legislator must recognize, evaluate, and balance competing interests. But he may not simply rely on the will of the majority to drawn on another's budget to the detriment of a minority, or to thwart claims for allocation of revenue. With that, a legislative act that effectively shifts the accountability for the law governing the allocation of revenue onto the Federal Council encounters constitutional objections.

2. The financial constitution restricts the standards defining law and the FAG on four levels of finance distribution, particularly according to the following maxims: a) At the first level, the level of the tax yields divided between federal government and the states, the variable vertical distribution of the VAT yield between the federal government and the states as a whole according to Article 106 para. 3 s. 4 of the Basic Law, is tied to constitutionally prescribed rules in the context of rolling receipts, the federal government and the states have equal claims at having their

necessary expenditures covered. The scope of necessary expenditures is to be determined in light of multi-year financial planning, in other words, with a rational business sense and with planned continuity in mind. The claims to cover are to adjust in a sense of a "just" balance—which avoids overburdening the taxpayers and which protects the uniformity of living conditions. The legislator is given the task of differentiating the "necessary" expenditures from those simply estimated in the budget, in other words to evaluate the structure of expenditures in terms of necessity and urgency so as to provide a limit to what can be financed in the budgets of the states and federal government. * * * Pursuant to Article 106 para. 3 s. 4 no. 1, s. 2 of the Basic Law, the scope of the essential expenditures relies on a basis of planning that ensures that the federal government and the states base their determination of necessary expenditures and the rolling receipts on the basis of the same indicators. These indicators, which in a rational business sense are monitored over years, can be adjusted against one another repeatedly, preserved in this manner for the budgetary legislators in state and federal government respectively as a lasting basis for their planning and thereby protecting the lasting prescribed criterion of necessity, which ensures that a generous tax expenditure policy would not be refinanced through a distribution of the VAT and that a frugal expense policy would not have the corresponding effect of reducing claims to tax yields. According to Article 106 para. 3 s. 4 no. 2 of the Basic Law, the claim of cover for necessary expenditures does not satisfy actual needs, but rather encourages consensus concerning the coverage needs of state and federal government. This obligation to weigh the respective claims to cover seeks a just reckoning of allocation of revenue that avoids overburdening the taxpayers and protects the uniformity of the living conditions within the federal territory.

b) On the basis of the distribution of tax yields between federal and state government as a whole set by Article 106 of the Basic Law, Article 107 para. 1 of the Basic Law determines at a second level, the horizontal distribution of tax yields amongst the states, the amount that individual states may claim as their own. The standard for this horizontal tax yield distribution is the "local yield", as clarified in the distribution law, that is to say arising from the power to tax in the respective state jurisdiction. In the context of furnishing the states with their own resources, Article 107, para. 1, s. 4, (second half) of the Basic Law empowers the legislator to implement in this primary distribution of taxes an equalizing standard of distribution for individual states. Generally, the VAT is distributed proportionally according to the number of inhabitants, which better expresses the local yield of this end-user tax than any formal coupling of a tax levy on the business owner and which describes an abstract standard of need called the *uniform per capita provision*. An exception to the general rule, up to one quarter of the states' VAT quota can be attributed to states which generate below average tax yields. After the distribution of these supplemental amounts, the financial allotments of the individual states is determined.

c) These results of the primary tax allotment amongst the states are subsequently corrected again at a third level, called the horizontal allocation of revenue * * *. Article 107 para. 2 of the Basic Law requires an auxiliary revision of this tax yield distribution fundamentally envisioned by the Basic Law in as much as the distribution may not fit with the federal model of solidarity in consideration of the autonomy of the states. This allocation of revenue between the states is intended to reduce, but not do away with, the differences in financial power amongst the states. This financial adjustment between states must find a proper medium between independence, self-sufficiency, and preservation of the state individuality on the one hand and the joint liability for the existence and independence of fellow states of the Republic on the other. This financial adjustment between states is not a means to replace the result of the primary tax yield distribution system as set out in Article 107 para. 1 of the Basic Law with a new system, shaped, for example, solely by the thought of financial equality for the states, but which no longer takes into consideration their autonomy and their own accountability. The obligation to allocate revenues equally as set out in Article 107 para. 2 of the Basic Law does not therefore encourage a financial equalization of the states, but rather a corresponding harmonization of their financial powers according to their responsibilities. The balance between state autonomy and federal solidarity would be in acute jeopardy, if the standards of the horizontal financial adjustment or their consequences were to decidedly weaken the power of the more financially powerful states, or were to lead to a leveling out of state finances. The obligation to equalize the states' relative finances in measured terms and without a general leveling off, also forbids as well a change in the ranking of the financial powers of the states in the context of the horizontal financial adjustment. The harmonizing but not equalizing financial adjustment narrows the distance between each of the 16 states, those owing as well as those deserving adjustments, but does not bridge the gap completely or change the financial rankings of the states. Solidarity amongst the states minimizes differences, but does not do away with them.

d) [In addition, the central government may provide financial means, on a temporary basis, to the financially less well-to-do states, if they fail to possess the budgetary means to cover additional obligations to spend.] However, such federal financial adjustments do not serve to lift temporary financial crises, to finance current projects, or to remedy financial deficits that were a direct and foreseeable result of political decisions of a state. Independence and political autonomy bring with them the condition that the states are fundamentally accountable for the budgetary consequences of their autonomous decisions and themselves must find the means to bridge any short-term financial deficits (Federal Constitutional Court, see cite, *supra*).

II.   According to these constitutionally legal precepts, the legislator is obligated to delineate and explain the standards of financial distribution in legislation in accord with Article 106 and Article 107 of the Basic Law. This obligation follows from the regulations of financial provisions of the Basic Law, whose general standards are to be set by law and to be adjusted according to changes in the budgetary conditions and economic perceptions. (C.I.1.). Even experiences in practical application of allocation of revenue between states and between the state and federal government substantiates the fact that the regulations of the Basic Law require legal definition and supplemental information that primarily and definitively establish standards for the law governing the adjustment of revenue between the federal and state authorities. Moreover, there are a few tests of the Federal Constitutional Court that were not yet met by the legislators. According to Article 106 para. 3 s. 4 of the Basic Law, the legislator shall first clarify the standards for the distribution of the VAT and thereafter promulgate his rules for distribution derived there from (see 1 *infra*). For the horizontal allocation of revenue between the states as well, the legislator will have to promulgate a definitive standard, so that the respective claims for payment or obligations to pay can be developed in a definite, planned, and controllable manner according to constitutionally defining and constitutionally supplementing standards (see 2, *infra*). Similarly regulations about supplemental federal adjustments only have enduring power, if they transparently and verifiably satisfy the law's rules. * * *

1. The constitutional obligation of Article 106 para. 3 s. 4 of the Basic Law has not yet been met.

a) At oral proceedings, the federal government and the states reported that the VAT has not yet been—as constitutionally envisioned—distributed on the basis of a multi-year financial plan. Additionally, no legal definitions have been developed to separate "rolling" receipts from other income or to define the "necessary" expenditures from among the estimated expenditures. With this, the constitutional obligation to fine tune the need for cover of the federal government and the state with the goal of achieving a just reckoning of allocation of revenue (Article 106 para. 3 s. 4 no. 2 of the Basic Law) is lacking the necessary legal definition and supplemental information.

b) According to the constitutional mandate, measurable criteria are to be set forth in a standard-setting law that, from the vantage point of federal uniformity, apply to the federal government and the states in equal measure. The legislator, following the precepts of transparency and parity, is obligated to take definite steps that contribute to finding political compromises within well-defined limits set by definite criteria and rules of procedure. Specifically he will have to decide which expenditures—above and beyond those made mandatory for the federal government and the states by the Basic Law—will be declared "essential" in the future so as to be included in the quotas used to cover.

c) Without the legal definition and a comprehensive adoption of the principles prescribed in Article 106 para. 3 s. 4 of the Basic Law in a manner which can clearly be used as a basis for the distribution of the VAT, the constitutional obligation set forth in Article 106 para. 3, s. 4 no. 2 of the Basic Law can neither be satisfied nor verified. [The FAG provided for the repayment of the obligations of the "German Unity Fund," which was established to cover the budget of those states that joined after the dissolution of East Germany (the "new" Eastern states). This system, too, was found to be unconstitutional, except where it was a genuine interim measure.]

D. The constitutional assessment of the FAG has shown that the inalienable ordering function of the financial constitution can only be discerned by means of concrete standards and explications of the requirements of the Basic Law. A conclusive assessment of individual regulations or of the whole system of the FAG is not at this time in the purview of the Federal Constitutional Court. The constitutional expression of standards for the allocation of revenue between the federal and state authorities is a task left to the legislator. This is required by the openness of the constitutional rules of distribution, out of which follow complex reciprocal coordination within a standardized system of allocations of revenue between the federal and state authorities, as well as being required by the considerable uncertainties in the necessary estimation of contemporary and future business and political developments.

The lack of a developed system of standards does not allow for an unlimited term of validity of the law governing the FAG. The partial revision already envisioned by the legislators themselves for the period beginning in 2005 marks a considerable constitutional juncture: until December 31, 2004 the FAG is in force in light of the more detailed conditions expressed above. In as much as the standards defining law has not be put into force by January 1, 2003, the FAG will on this day be unconstitutional and void. By December 31, 2004, the legislature must revise the FAG on the foundations set forth in and through the enactment of the standards defining law. In the event that such a revision has not taken place on January 1, 2005, the FAG will on this day become unconstitutional and void.

Notes and Questions

1. The issue of tax comity also came up in the South African *Constitution Certification Case*:

> [279] NT [New Text (Draft of the Constitution)] ch 13 deals with finance. In the context of provincial autonomy the objection that is taken is as follows. NT 215 prescribes to the provinces how and when they must prepare their budgets and what must be contained in them, and NT 216 empowers Parliament to prescribe measures to ensure both transparency and expenditure control, by requiring all spheres of government to adhere to recognized accounting practices, uniform expenditure classifications and uniform treasury norms and standards. In terms of NT 216(2) the transfer of funds to a province may be stopped if there is a "serious or persistent material breach of" such measures. NT 217, which deals with procurements, requires all organs of state at all levels of government to contract for goods and services "in accordance with a system which is fair, equitable, transparent, competitive and cost-effective", and it authorizes national legislation to prescribe a framework within which "affirmative action" policies may be implemented. NT 218 provides that loan guarantees by any level of government must comply with conditions set out in national legislation, and NT 219 requires national legislation to prescribe a framework for determining the salaries of traditional leaders and members of councils of traditional leaders, and the upper limit of salaries, allowances or benefits of members of provincial legislatures and members of Executive Councils of provinces.

It is contended that these provisions, taken together, encroach upon the legitimate autonomy of the provinces.

[280]   These provisions must be seen in the context of the requirements of the CPs dealing with the allocation to different levels of government of revenue raised nationally. That is dealt with in the CPs as follows:

"XXVI

Each level of government shall have a constitutional right to an equitable share of revenue collected nationally so as to ensure that the provinces and local governments are able to provide basic services and execute the functions allocated to them.

XXVII

A Financial and Fiscal Commission, in which each province shall be represented, shall recommend equitable fiscal and financial allocations to the provincial and local governments from revenue collected nationally, after taking into account the national interest, economic disparities between the provinces as well as the population and developmental needs, administrative responsibilities and other legitimate interests of each of the provinces."

[281]   NT 214(1) requires an Act of Parliament to make provision for the equitable division of revenue, the determination of each province's share of such revenue, and other allocations out of the national government's share of revenue that may be made to provinces or local governments. The Act has to take account of various factors specified in NT 214(2). For the purpose of addressing the issue of legitimate provincial autonomy, what is important is that the scheme of governmental financing contemplated by the CPs is one which involves a distribution of revenue collected nationally between the various levels of government. The provisions of NT 215 and 216 are rationally connected to such a scheme and serve a legitimate purpose. Uniformity in accounting practices and preparation of budgets will facilitate the equitable allocation of revenue between the various levels of government; indeed, without such uniformity the allocation of revenue on an equitable basis might not be possible. In the circumstances the requirements of NT 215 and 216(1) do not encroach upon the legitimate autonomy of the provinces."

[282]   A province cannot carry out its governmental functions without the equitable share of revenue to which it is entitled. If the transfer of funds to the provinces is to be made, or is liable to be stopped, at the discretion of the national government, that would materially impair the legitimate autonomy of the provinces.

[283]   This, however, is not the effect of NT 214 and 215. Each province has a constitutional right to an equitable share of revenue collected nationally, a right that is recognized in NT 214(1). NT 216(2), which empowers the Minister of Finance in the national government to stop the transfer of funds to an organ of state which is guilty of a serious or persistent material breach of the requirements of the measures established to secure uniformity, does not detract from this right. It is an enforcement mechanism designed to secure compliance with the corresponding obligation to adhere to uniform norms in the budgeting and accounting processes. * * *

Do you find that the South African solution satisfies the requirement of the GFCC?

SOUTH DAKOTA v. DOLE

Supreme Court (United States).
483 U.S. 203 (1987).

Chief Justice Rehnquist delivered the opinion of the Court.

Petitioner South Dakota permits persons 19 years of age or older to purchase beer containing up to 3.2% alcohol. In 1984 Congress enacted 23 U. S. C. § 158 (1982 ed., Supp. III), which directs the Secretary of Transportation to withhold a percentage of federal highway funds otherwise allocable from States "in which the purchase or public possession ... of any alcoholic beverage by a person who is less than twenty-one years of age is lawful." The State sued [claiming] that § 158 violates the constitutional limitations on congressional exercise of the spending power and violates the Twenty-first Amendment to the United States Constitution * * *

In this Court, the parties direct most of their efforts to defining the proper scope of the Twenty-first Amendment. Relying on our statement in *California Retail Liquor Dealers Assn. v. Midcal Aluminum, Inc.*, 445 U.S. 97, 110 (1980), that the "Twenty-first Amendment grants the States virtually complete control over whether to permit importation or sale of liquor and how to structure the liquor distribution system," South Dakota asserts that the setting of minimum drinking ages is clearly within the "core powers" reserved to the States under § 2 of the Amendment. Section 158, petitioner claims, usurps that core power. The Secretary in response asserts that the Twenty-first Amendment is simply not implicated by § 158; the plain language of § 2 confirms the States' broad power to impose restrictions on the sale and distribution of alcoholic beverages but does not confer on them any power to *permit* sales that Congress seeks to *prohibit*. That Amendment, under this reasoning, would not prevent Congress from affirmatively enacting a national minimum drinking age more restrictive than that provided by the various state laws; and it would follow *a fortiori* that the indirect inducement involved here is compatible with the Twenty-first Amendment.

* * *

Despite the extended treatment of the question by the parties, however, we need not decide in this case whether that Amendment would prohibit an attempt by Congress to legislate directly a national minimum drinking age. Here, Congress has acted indirectly under its spending power to encourage uniformity in the States' drinking ages. As we explain below, we find this legislative effort within constitutional bounds even if Congress may not regulate drinking ages directly.

The Constitution empowers Congress to "lay and collect Taxes, Duties, Imposts, and Excises, to pay the Debts and provide for the common Defence and general Welfare of the United States." Art. I, § 8, cl. 1. Incident to this power, Congress may attach conditions on the receipt of federal funds, and has repeatedly employed the power "to further broad policy objectives by conditioning receipt of federal moneys upon compliance by the recipient with federal statutory and administrative directives." *Fullilove v. Klutznick*, 448 U.S. 448, 474 (1980) (opinion of Burger, C. J.). The breadth of this power was made clear in *United States v. Butler*, 297 U.S. 1, 66 (1936), where the Court, resolving a longstanding debate over the scope of the Spending Clause, determined that "the power of Congress to authorize expenditure of public moneys for public purposes is not limited by the direct grants of legislative power found in the Constitution." Thus, objectives not thought to be within Article I's "enumerated legislative fields," *id.*, at 65, may nevertheless be attained through the use of the spending power and the conditional grant of federal funds.

The spending power is of course not unlimited, but is instead subject to several general restrictions articulated in our cases. The first of these limitations is derived from the language of the Constitution itself: the exercise of the spending power must be in pursuit of "the general welfare." In considering whether a particular expenditure is intended to serve general public purposes, courts should defer substantially to the judgment of Congress. Second, we have required that if Congress desires to condition the States' receipt of federal funds, it "must do so unambiguously * * *, enabl[ing] the States to exercise their choice knowingly, cognizant of the consequences of their participation." Third, our cases have suggested (without significant elaboration) that conditions on federal grants might be illegitimate if they are unrelated "to the federal interest in particular national projects or programs." *Massachusetts v. United States*, 435 U.S. 444, 461 (1978) (plurality opinion). See also *Ivanhoe Irrigation Dist. v. McCracken, supra,* at 295, ("The Federal Government may establish and impose reasonable conditions relevant to federal interest in the project and to the over-all objectives thereof"). Finally, we have noted that other constitutional provisions may provide an independent bar to the conditional grant of federal funds. *Lawrence County v. Lead–Deadwood School Dist.*, 469 U.S. 256, 269–270 (1985).

South Dakota does not seriously claim that § 158 is inconsistent with any of the first three restrictions mentioned above. We can readily conclude that the provision is designed to serve the general welfare, especially in light of the fact that "the concept of welfare or the opposite is shaped by Congress * * *." Congress found that the differing drinking ages in the States created particular incentives for young persons to combine their desire to drink with their ability to drive, and that this interstate problem required a national solution. The means it chose to address this dangerous situation were reasonably calculated to advance the general welfare. The conditions upon which States receive the funds, moreover, could not be more clearly stated by Congress. And the State itself, rather than challenging the germaneness of the condition to federal purposes, admits that it "has never contended that the congressional action was ... unrelated to a national concern in the absence of the Twenty-first Amendment." Indeed, the condition imposed by Congress is directly related to one of the main purposes for which highway funds are expended—safe interstate travel. This goal of the interstate highway system had been frustrated by varying drinking ages among the States. A Presidential commission appointed to study alcohol-related accidents and fatalities on the Nation's highways concluded that the lack of uniformity in the States' drinking ages created "an incentive to drink and drive" because "young persons commut[e] to border States where the drinking age is lower." Presidential Commission on Drunk Driving, Final Report 11 (1983). By enacting § 158, Congress conditioned the receipt of federal funds in a way reasonably calculated to address this particular impediment to a purpose for which the funds are expended.

The remaining question about the validity of § 158 * * * is whether the Twenty-first Amendment constitutes an "independent constitutional bar" to the conditional grant of federal funds. Petitioner, relying on its view that the Twenty-first Amendment prohibits *direct* regulation of drinking ages by Congress, asserts that "Congress may not use the spending power to regulate that which it is prohibited from regulating directly under the Twenty-first Amendment." But our cases show that this "independent constitutional bar" limitation on the spending power is not of the kind petitioner suggests. *United States v. Butler, supra*, at 66, for example, established that the constitutional limitations on Congress when exercising its spending power are less exacting than those on its authority to regulate directly.

[T]he "independent constitutional bar" limitation on the spending power is not, as petitioner suggests, a prohibition on the indirect achievement of objectives which Congress is not empowered to achieve directly. Instead, we think that the language in our earlier opinions stands for the unexceptionable proposition that the power may not be used to induce the States to engage in activities that would themselves be unconstitutional. Thus, for example, a grant of federal funds conditioned on invidiously discriminatory state action or the infliction of cruel and unusual punishment would be an illegitimate exercise of the Congress' broad spending power. But no such claim can be or is made here. Were South Dakota to succumb to the blandishments offered by Congress and raise its drinking age to 21, the State's action in so doing would not violate the constitutional rights of anyone.

Our decisions have recognized that in some circumstances the financial inducement offered by Congress might be so coercive as to pass the point at which "pressure turns into compulsion." *Steward Machine Co. v. Davis, supra*, at 590. Here, however, Congress has directed only that a State desiring to establish a minimum drinking age lower than 21 lose a relatively small percentage of certain federal highway funds. Petitioner contends that the coercive nature of this program is evident from the degree of success it has achieved. We cannot conclude, however, that a conditional grant of federal money of this sort is unconstitutional simply by reason of its success in achieving the congressional objective.

When we consider, for a moment, that all South Dakota would lose if she adheres to her chosen course as to a suitable minimum drinking age is 5% of the funds otherwise obtainable under specified highway grant programs, the argument as to coercion is shown to be more rhetoric than fact.

* * *

Here Congress has offered relatively mild encouragement to the States to enact higher minimum drinking ages than they would otherwise choose. But the enactment of such laws remains the prerogative of the States not merely in theory but in fact. Even if Congress might lack the power to impose a national minimum drinking age directly, we conclude that encouragement to state action found in § 158 is a valid use of the spending power.

* * *

Justice O'Connor, dissenting.

* * *

My disagreement with the Court is relatively narrow on the spending power issue: it is a disagreement about the application of a principle rather than a disagreement on the principle itself. I agree with the Court that Congress may attach conditions on the receipt of federal funds to further "the federal interest in particular national projects or programs."

* * *

But the Court's application of the requirement that the condition imposed be reasonably related to the purpose for which the funds are expended is cursory and unconvincing. We have repeatedly said that Congress may condition grants under the spending power only in ways reasonably related to the purpose of the federal program.

* * *

[T]he Court asserts the reasonableness of the relationship between the supposed purpose of the expenditure—"safe interstate travel"—and the drinking age condition. The Court reasons that Congress wishes that the roads it builds may be used safely, that drunken drivers threaten highway safety, and that young people are more likely to drive while under the influence of alcohol under existing law than would be the case if there were a uniform national drinking age of 21. It hardly needs saying, however, that if the purpose of § 158 is to deter drunken driving, it is far too over-and under-inclusive. It is over-inclusive because it stops teenagers from drinking even when they are not about to drive on interstate highways. It is under-inclusive because teenagers pose only a small part of the drunken driving problem in this Nation.

* * *

When Congress appropriates money to build a highway, it is entitled to insist that the highway be a safe one. But it is not entitled to insist as a condition of the use of highway funds that the State impose or change regulations in other areas of the State's social and economic life because of an attenuated or tangential relationship to highway use or safety. Indeed, if the rule were otherwise, the Congress could effectively regulate almost any area of a State's social, political, or economic life on the theory that use of the interstate transportation system is somehow enhanced. If, for example, the United States were to condition highway moneys upon moving the state capital, I suppose it might argue that interstate transportation is facilitated by locating local governments in places easily accessible to interstate highways—or, conversely, that highways might become overburdened if they had to carry traffic to and from the state capital. In my mind, such a relationship is hardly more attenuated than the one which the Court finds supports § 158.

    * * *

There is a clear place at which the Court can draw the line between permissible and impermissible conditions on federal grants.

    * * *

Congress has the power to *spend* for the general welfare, it has the power to *legislate* only for delegated purposes * * *

The appropriate inquiry, then, is whether the spending requirement or prohibition is a condition on a grant or whether it is regulation. The difference turns on whether the requirement specifies in some way how the money should be spent, so that Congress' intent in making the grant will be effectuated. Congress has no power under the Spending Clause to impose requirements on a grant that go beyond specifying how the money should be spent. A requirement that is not such a specification is not a condition, but a regulation, which is valid only if it falls within one of Congress' delegated regulatory powers.

    * * *

If the spending power is to be limited only by Congress' notion of the general welfare, the reality, given the vast financial resources of the Federal Government, is that the Spending Clause gives "power to the Congress to tear down the barriers, to invade the states' jurisdiction, and to become a parliament of the whole people, subject to no restrictions save such as are self-imposed." This, of course was not the Framers' plan and it is not the meaning of the Spending Clause.

    * * *

As discussed above, a condition that a State will raise its drinking age to 21 cannot fairly be said to be reasonably related to the expenditure of funds for highway construction. The only possible connection, highway safety, has nothing to do with how the funds Congress has appropriated are expended. Rather than a condition determining how federal highway money shall be expended, it is a regulation determining who shall be able to drink liquor. As such it is not justified by the spending power. Of the other possible sources of congressional authority for regulating the sale of liquor only the commerce power comes to mind. But in my view, the regulation of the age of the purchasers of liquor, just as the regulation of the price at which liquor may be sold, falls squarely within the scope of those powers reserved to the States by the Twenty-first Amendment.

    * * *

Accordingly, Congress simply lacks power under the Commerce Clause to displace state regulation of this kind.

The immense size and power of the Government of the United States ought not obscure its fundamental character. It remains a Government of enumerated powers. Because § 158 cannot be justified as an exercise of any power delegated to the Congress, it is not authorized by the Constitution. The Court errs in holding it to be the law of the land, and I respectfully dissent.

Notes and Questions

1. As noted above, the German Basic Law, in order to avoid excessive central power, limits the creation of any centrally controlled public administration. Most federal regulation is administered by the states. Compare the German central-state executive relations with the South African approach, where there is a national civil service with centralized services to carry out constitutionally or statutorily mandated functions (though the provinces are free to operate their own administrative structures within the national public service). Does the participation or the representation of the provinces (in the National Council of Provinces) in the legislation in matters on the Constitutional Schedule (4) of Functional Areas of Concurrent National and Provincial Legislative Competence provide protection to the provinces?

2. Consider Justice Breyer's dissent in *Printz*, where he finds that Switzerland and the EU rely nearly exclusively on the executive (public administration) of the composite units. Is this arrangement justified by efficiency considerations, by concerns relating to excessive concentration of powers in the federal government, or both?

3. According to Professor Nicholas Haysom, legal advisor to former President Nelson Mandela, the notion of "cooperative government" in South Africa's new Constitution is based on a break with the nineteenth-century approach to federalism, which allocated "areas of responsibility to one particular area of government only." The approach of the South African Constitution is to empower different areas of government to legislate on the same subject within the scope of their own responsibilities. "Responsibility, in turn, is decided relative to appropriate interest, capacity and effective delivery but the apportionment of it is more complex than merely isolating an area of social life and parceling it out to a single sphere of government." Nicholas Haysom, *The Making of the Constitution* 72 (Paul Bell ed., 1997).

Note on Transnational Federalism: The Case of the European Union

The European Union is neither a full-fledged federation nor a typical confederation. Instead it has some aspects of both. Accordingly, it provides an example of federalism at work in a supranational setting. The cases and comments included in Chapter 1, Subsection D.3. illustrate the potential for problems that confront those who seek to expand federalism beyond the bounds of the nation-state. As illustrated by *Van Gend & Loos v. Netherland Inland Revenue Service*, [1963] CMLR 105, (in Chapter 1, Subsection D.3.) although EU legal norms are ultimately derived from treaties concluded among the nation-states that are members of the Union, they can provide individuals in a member-state with rights against their own country, much like federal law can be invoked by citizens against their own federated entity in a federal nation-state.

Invocation of EU legal norms by individuals against their own country is not problematic in cases that, like *Van Gend*, involve prohibitions against member-states. Indeed in that case countries were prohibited from imposing higher duties on imports than those allowed by the EU, and courts could vindicate individual rights against higher national rates by declaring the latter unenforceable against a country's own citizens. But what about EU legal norms purporting to grant individuals positive rights? What if the EU issues a directive requiring national legislation and a country fails to enact such legislation?

This issue arose before the European Court of Justice (ECJ) in the *Francovich Case*, 1991 ECR I–5357, involving an EEC (the predecessor of the EU) directive requiring states to legislate in order to ensure that employees' wages would be paid in the event that their employer went into bankruptcy. Italy failed to enact the requisite implementing legislation, leaving Francovich without the EEC-prescribed wage payments owed her when her employer went bankrupt. In arguing the case before the ECJ, the Court's Advocate General summarized the state of EEC law as follows:

> Although, as Community law now stands, it is in principle for the legal system of each Member State to determine the legal procedure which will enable Community law to be fully effective, that State power is nevertheless limited by the very obligation of the Member States, under Community law, to ensure such effectiveness.
>
> 1. That is true in respect not only of provisions whose purpose is to grant rights to individuals. The lack of direct effect does not mean that the result sought by Community law is not to grant rights to individuals, but merely that these are not sufficiently precise and unconditional to be relied upon and applied as they stand.
>
> 2. In the event of failure to implement a directive or its incorrect implementation, a Member State deprives Community law of the desired effect. It also commits a breach of Article 5 and the third paragraph of Article 189 of the Treaty, which affirm the binding nature of the directive and require the Member State to take all the measures necessary for its implementation.
>
> 3. Where the breach of that obligation is confirmed by a judgement of the Court of Justice delivered pursuant to Articles 169 to 171 of the Treaty, the binding authority of a judicial decision and Article 171 of the Treaty requires the Member State, which cannot raise any obstacle whatsoever, to take all appropriate measures to make good its default and give the desired effect to Community law. In so doing it may also be required to make reparation for the loss and damage which it has caused to individuals as a result of its unlawful conduct. * * *

In a case like *Francovich*, allowing an individual to obtain damages from her country for failure to implement an EU directive seems sufficient to put the individual in the position she would have been in but for the failure of her country to implement the relevant directive. But what about cases where monetary damages are inadequate, such as, e.g., a case involving the loss of a limb because of a country's failure to implement an EU safety directive?

Chapter 5

DIGNITY, PRIVACY AND
PERSONAL AUTONOMY

This chapter addresses three interrelated and overlapping rights that lie at the heart of many attempts to guarantee the protection of human rights. In most liberal constitutional traditions human dignity is considered the core social value and the bedrock of all fundamental rights. It evokes the individual's desire to be treated with respect (and not to be degraded) and to have one's intrinsic worth recognized. Privacy names an effort primarily directed against a threatening public, that is, the state, to establish protected spheres, places, or spaces within which an individual's own desires are privileged and his or her choices about how to act and be acted upon are unfettered. Personal autonomy describes the capacity to determine and decide for one's self, adding a more active dimension to dignity and privacy. Together, these three rights—human dignity, privacy, and personal autonomy—form a starting point for the constitutional recognition of what it means to be human.

A. PROTECTING FUNDAMENTAL RIGHTS

A.1. WHAT IS PROTECTED?

1. *Starting Points.* Some national constitutions, such as the German Basic Law, and many international instruments, such as the Universal Declaration of Human Rights, the International Covenant on Civil and Political Rights (ICCPR), and the International Covenant on Economic, Social and Cultural Rights (ICESCR), expressly provide for the protection of dignity, privacy, and personal autonomy. In a number of constitutions, such as the U.S. Constitution and the 1958 French Constitution, however, no such protections are mentioned. Nonetheless, courts have introduced these concepts and established grounds for their constitutional protection, deriving them from various other constitutional provisions.

The German Basic Law of 1949 enshrines the right to dignity in Art. 1, Sec. 1: "Human dignity is inviolable. To respect and protect it is the duty of all state authority." Similarly, the post-apartheid South African Constitution of 1996 begins as follows: "1. The Republic of South Africa is one sovereign democratic state founded on the following values: (a) Human dignity, the achievement of equality and the advancement of human rights and freedoms." Continuing in Sec. 10, "everyone has inherent dignity and the right to have their dignity respected and protected." Furthermore, many of the post-communist constitutions, written in the 1990s, adopted similar language. The drafters of these modern constitutions were strongly influenced by international human rights documents and the rights provisions of the German Basic Law, which were themselves inspired by the horrors of World War Two.

Although adopted only in 1982, the Canadian Charter of Rights and Freedoms is similar to the U.S. and French constitutions in that it does not explicitly provide for the protection of human dignity. But there have been subsequent efforts to derive this right from the equality clause. Consider the words of Justice Iacobucci in *Law v. Canada (Minister of Employment and Immigration)*, [1999] 1 S.C.R. 497:

51.   * * * It may be said that the purpose of s. 15(1) [the Charter's equality clause] is to prevent the violation of essential human dignity and freedom through the imposition of disadvantage, stereotyping, or political or social prejudice, and to promote a society in which all persons enjoy equal recognition in law as human beings or as members of Canadian society, equally capable and equally deserving of concern, respect and consideration. Legislation which effects differential treatment between individuals or groups will violate this fundamental purpose where those who are subject to differential treatment fall within one or more enumerated or analogous grounds, and where the differential treatment reflects the stereotypical application of presumed group or personal characteristics, or otherwise has the effect of perpetuating or promoting the view that the individual is less capable, or less worthy of recognition or value as a human being or as a member of Canadian society. Alternatively, differential treatment will not likely constitute discrimination within the purpose of s. 15(1) where it does not violate the human dignity or freedom of a person or group in this way, and in particular where the differential treatment also assists in ameliorating the position of the disadvantaged within Canadian society.

53.   * * * Human dignity means that an individual or group feels self-respect and self-worth. It is concerned with physical and psychological integrity and empowerment. Human dignity is harmed by unfair treatment premised on personal traits or circumstances which do not relate to individual needs, capacities, or merits. It is enhanced by laws which are sensitive to the needs, capacities, and merits of different individuals, taking into account the context underlying their differences. Human dignity is harmed when individuals and groups are marginalized, ignored, or devalued, and is enhanced when laws recognize the full place of all individuals and groups within Canadian society. Human dignity within the meaning of the equality guarantee does not relate to the status or position of an individual in society *per se*, but rather concerns the manner in which a person legitimately feels when confronted with a particular law. * * *

54.   * * * The equality guarantee in s. 15(1) of the Charter must be understood and applied in light of the above understanding of its purpose.

In the so-called *Bioethics Decision* (Cons. Const., July 27, 1994, D. 1995, Somm., 299, *note Favoreu*, DC 94–343/344) the French Constitutional Council found that dignity was a principle of constitutional value, in spite of its absence from the constitutional text, and determined that dignity concerns could trump legislation like any other constitutional right:

> [T]he preamble of the 1946 Constitution reaffirmed and proclaimed (declared) the rights, freedoms (liberties) and constitutional principles in the following terms: "On the morrow of the victory of the free peoples over the regimes that attempted to enslave and degrade the human person, the French people proclaims once more that every human being, without distinction of race, religion or belief possesses inalienable and sacred rights" [a translation from *Constitutions that Made History*]; that the dignity of the human being is safeguarded against all forms of subjugation and degrading treatment as a principle of constitutional value.

Does the absence of dignity language in some national constitutions hamper efforts on the part of constitutional courts to protect fundamental rights? Certain conflicts that are argued as dignity cases in Europe are sometimes adjudicated as free speech, privacy, or other constitutional issues in other parts of the world. Dignity issues may thus come to a court in the guise of liberty or personal autonomy. The central comparative questions are thus: Which specific concepts provide a sound basis for the protection of fundamental rights against which kind of injustice, and what is the difference between a reference to one right or another?

2. *Inspirations.* The concept of dignity—and the related concept of the person—has a long and complex history in religious traditions. Christian theology, for example, understands dignity as a value inherently bound to duties and obligations. Muslim and Confucian theology offer their own distinct interpretations of the concept. However, the understanding of dignity that is prevalent in most contemporary liberal democracies is largely inspired by the philosophy of the Enlightenment, particularly that of Immanuel Kant. For Kant, dignity is a function of autonomy and is captured in the definition of the human being as an end in him or herself; dignity requires mutual respect and recognition. In German jurisprudence this philosophy has been promulgated as "object theory," attributed to Günter Dürig (Theodor Maunz and Günter Dürig, *Kommentar zum Grundgesetz*, Art. 1 Abs. 1 Rn. 28, 34) and captured in the following definition: dignity is the right not to be turned into an object for someone else's needs. If a woman has a duty to carry a pregnancy to birth, as the German Federal Constitutional Court (GFCC) ruled in its *Abortion I Case* (see below), is she turned into an object serving another's need? Would a duty to donate blood or body organs to enable another's survival or welfare be constitutional? See further on the German concepts of dignity in the *Mephisto Case*, in Chapter 7, and *Life Imprisonment* below.

Dignity dictates that human beings be treated as persons, as integral and self-determining subjects. Thus, dignity is fundamental to the rights of liberty and equality since there are no such rights if there is no respect for the person who claims them. However, it is open to debate whether dignity is acquired or innate, a debate particularly relevant to the new legal and ethical challenges of biotechnology. For example, philosopher Peter Singer has argued that since such rights are attached to a concept of rational decisionmaking, they cannot be attributed to human beings who cannot decide, like fetuses or the severely mentally disabled. Peter Singer, *Writings on an Ethical Life* 135 (2000). This position has been strongly contested by those concerned about the civil rights of the disabled.

An alternative, though related, concept of the individual subject finds liberty at the heart of all other rights. Much constitutional reasoning, then, focuses on where exactly the fundamental right to liberty finds its limits. This resonates with the abiding philosophical debates of liberalism: compare John Stuart Mill, *On Liberty* (1859), with Patrick Devlin, *Enforcement of Morals* (1965). On this liberal tradition, see the critical assessment by Carole Pateman, *The Sexual Contract* 11 (1988). Regarding the scope of the right to dignity, consider the reasoning of the Canadian Supreme Court in *R. v. Morgentaler*, [1988] 1 S.C.R. 30 (Justice Wilson, concurring):

> 227.   The idea of human dignity finds expression in almost every right and freedom guaranteed in the *Charter*. Individuals are afforded the right to choose their own religion and their own philosophy of life, the right to choose with whom they will associate and how they will express themselves, the right to choose where they will live and what occupation they will pursue.

> 228.   [An] aspect of the respect for human dignity on which the *Charter* is founded is the right to make fundamental personal decisions without interference from the state. This right is a critical component of the right to liberty. Liberty is a phrase capable of a broad range of meaning. In my view, this right, properly construed, grants the individual a degree of autonomy in making decisions of fundamental personal importance.

The language of the Canadian Court perfectly reflects the liberal conception of liberty as freedom from interference. A slightly different conception of dignity and autonomy, which animates constitutional jurisprudence in parts of Europe, could be seen as having its origin in the political tradition of European republicanism, which understands liberty as freedom from dependence. See Maurizio Viroli, *Republicanism* 67 (2002).

3.   *Understandings.* When constitutions protect fundamental rights, the lines demarcating law and moral philosophy, theology, and metaphysics sometimes blur. Consider the reasoning of Chief Justice Solyóm (concurring) from the Hungarian Constitutional Court (HCC) (Decision 23/1990 (X.31.) AB hat.), which declared the death penalty unconstitutional based on the sanctity of life, 1990, 1 E. Eur. Case Rep. Const. L. 177, 194–95 (1994):

> [The] right to human dignity is not merely a declaration of a moral value. The concept that human dignity is a value a priori and beyond law, and is inaccessible by law in its entirety does not preclude this

value from being regarded as the source of rights—as many international conventions and constitutions do by following natural law—or the law from requiring respect of dignity or the transformation of some of its aspects into a true right.

The right to human dignity has two functions. On the one hand, it means that there is an absolute limit which may not be transgressed by the State or by the coercive power of other people—i.e., it is a seed of autonomy and individual self-determination withdrawn from the control of anybody else by virtue of which, according to the classical wording, man may remain an individual and will not be changed into a tool or object. * * *

The other function of dignity is to ensure equality. [This] means that dignity is indivisible and irreducible, * * * [and that it] must ensure * * * [that] bare lives are not to be treated differently in the legal sense. No one is more or less worthy of life. [The] equality of lives is also guaranteed by dignity.

For concepts that emphasize social justice at the heart of dignity, see *Law v. Canada*, below, and the position of the Indian Supreme Court (ISC) in *Ahmedabad* in Chapter 10. Also, consider what the Polish Constitutional Tribunal said in a decision on tax authority powers about the fundamental right of privacy: "[T]he concept of the right to a private life has recently begun to play a more important role in constitutional provisions and judicial decisions of the courts. However, it has already obtained a permanent place in contemporary democratic States. It is composed of principles and rules concerning different aspects of life of the individual and what they have in common is recognizing the individual's right 'to lead his own life, in accordance with his own will and with all external interference limited to the necessary minimum.'" Quoting A. Kopf (1972), in K. 21/96, 24 April 1997, at III.1., 5 E. Eur. Case Rep. Const. L. 81 (1998). In addition, consider the words of Justice Sachs (concurring) of the South African Constitutional Court (SACC) in *S. v. Makwanyane and Another*, 1995 (3) SALR 391 (CC):

> 389. Historically, constitutionalism was a product of the age of enlightenment. It was associated with the overthrow of arbitrary power and the attempt to ensure that Government functioned according to established principles and processes and in the light of enduring values. It came together with the abolition of torture and the opening up of dungeons. It based itself on the twin propositions that all persons had certain inherent rights that came with their humanity, and that no one had a God-given right to rule over others.

> 390. The second great wave of constitutionalism after World War II, was also a reaction to gross abuse of power, institutionalised inhumanity and organised disrespect for life. Human rights were not merely declared to exist: against the background of genocide and crimes against humanity committed in the name of a racial ideology linked to state sovereignty, firm constitutional limits were placed on State power. In particular, the more that life had been cheapened and the human personality disregarded, the greater the entrenchment of the rights to life and dignity.

A core question is whether the rights to dignity, privacy, and autonomy are primarily protected through processes of constitutional review. Or are they rooted in the cultural and political history from which such decisions spring?

4. *A fundamental right to subsistence?* What is the value of a fundamental right if one lacks the economic means to exercise it? Are claims to life-sustaining subsidies better articulated in terms of dignity or, rather, the rights to life and health? Is an obligation of care inherent in fundamental rights? Compare the Japanese Supreme Court decision in *Asahi v. Japan* in Chapter 10. Do you think a principle obligation like "cultured living," which is used in Japan, justifies individual duties? With such positive rights in mind, is the South African decision on affirmative state obligations to protect women from violence in *Carmichele* (see Chapter 10) an exception to the rule of constitutional liberalism or its consequence? The GFCC draws a right to life-sustaining state subsidies—a "minimum livelihood" allowance—from the right to dignity, interpreted in conjunction with the constitutional principle of the welfare state, which results in specific requirements regarding tax laws, e.g., a tax reduction in favor of children (99 BVerfGE 246). (See further in Chapter 10, notes to *DeShaney*). In India, the ISC interprets the constitutional guarantee of life and personal liberty thus: "We think that the right to life includes the right to live with human dignity and all that goes along with it, namely, the bare necessities of life such as adequate nutrition, clothing and shelter over the head and facilities for reading, writing and expressing oneself in diverse forms, freely moving about and mixing and commingling with fellow human beings." (*Francis Coralie Mullin v. Administrator, Union Territory of Delhi*, (1981) 2 S.C.R. 516, (1981) 1 S.C.C. 608, 618–19; A.I.R. 1981 S.C. 746, 753.) Note that the Indian Court includes among the dignity-related necessities the right to free speech and assembly. Does that inspire a positive side of such liberties as well? See also welfare rights issues in Chapter 10. Consider that the ISC held that dignity entails a right to protection from abuse of the health and strength of workers—men, women and children. (*Bandhua Mukti Morcha v. Union of India*, ((1984) 2 S.C.R. 67, A.I.R. 1984 S.C. 802, (1984) 3 S.C.C. 161.) On the basis of dignity considerations, the Indian Court held that, among others, there is a right to ban injurious drugs (*Vincent Panikurlangara v. Union of India*, (1987) 2 S.C.C. 165) and a right to humane conditions in care facilities (*Vikaram Deo Singh Tomar v. State of Bihar*, A.I.R. 1988 S.C. 1782). See further in Chapter 10.

5. *Universality?* Dignity, just as personal autonomy, has been variously called a value, a right, or the locus of the principle of recognition. It has been subject to at least as much interpretation and debate as other fundamental rights in constitutions. Yet all of these rights are often conceived to be universal standards. Are they, then, not subject to the prevailing norms in a given society? Can an assessment of a violation of a fundamental right proceed without reference to these norms? Consider a perspective from Namibia: "Whilst it is extremely instructive and useful to refer to, and analyse, decisions by other Courts, such as the International Court of Human Rights, or the Supreme Court of Zimbab-

we or the United States of America, the one major and basic consideration in arriving at a decision involves an enquiry into the contemporary norms, aspirations, expectations, sensitivities, moral standards, relevant established beliefs, social conditions, experiences and perceptions of the Namibian people." *S. v. Tcoeib*, 1996 (7) BCLR 996 (NmS).

Note that in some Asian courts "dignity" is attributed to institutions, like courts; e.g., *R. v. Lau Tak Mong*, 1994–3 H.K.C. 634. Then, contempt of court may justify infringements of individual rights based on a dignity interest. From the point of view of constitutionalism, can arguments for the protection of institutions be based on notions of dignity or autonomy?

6. *The fundamental right to privacy.* While some constitutions protect dignity expressly, others protect privacy. Sometimes privacy is statutorily protected only. The preamble of the Australian Privacy Charter of 1994 states that: "Privacy is a value which underpins human dignity and other key values such as freedom of association and freedom of speech. * * * Privacy is a basic human right and the reasonable expectation of every person." Yet consider the argument from President Hamilton of the Irish Supreme Court, working with a constitution with no express protection of privacy: "[T]hough not specifically guaranteed by the Constitution, the right to privacy is one of the fundamental personal rights of the citizen which flow from the Christian and democratic nature of the State. It is not an unqualified right. Its exercise may be restricted by the constitutional rights of others, by the requirements of the common good and is subject to the requirements of public order and morality." (*Kennedy v. Ireland*, [1987] I.R. 587, at 592.) The Irish Court derives privacy, in part, from the "Christian nature of the state." What exactly does this mean? Do secular states endorse different notions of privacy? In a state in which the constitution demands a separation of church and state and prohibits discrimination on religious grounds, would such an argument be valid? How important do you think Christian–Judaic values are in constitutions in states like the U.S. or Germany? In Jewish law privacy is the right to be free from being watched (Jeffrey Rosen, *The Unwanted Gaze: The Destruction of Privacy in America* 18–19 (2000)), which informs Israel's Basic Law on Human Dignity and Liberty: "(a) All persons have the right to privacy and to intimacy," particularly on private premises, (b) against searches, (c) and to secrecy."

The Americans Warren and Brandeis, in 1890, called privacy the most important right, the "right to be let alone" (Samuel D. Warren and Louis D. Brandeis, *The Right to Privacy*, 4 Harv. L. Rev. 193 (1890)), which became part of Justice Brandeis's dissent in *Olmstead v. United States*, 277 U.S. 438, 478 (1928). In a dissent in *Munn v. Illinois*, 94 U.S. 113 (1876), endorsed by the majority in *Allgeyer v. Louisiana*, 165 U.S. 578 (1897), then-Justice Field had already explained: "By the term 'liberty,' as used in the provision, something more is meant than mere freedom from physical restraint or the bounds of a prison. It means freedom to go where one may choose, and to act in such manner, not inconsistent with the equal rights of others, as his judgment may dictate for the promotion of his happiness; that is, to pursue such callings and advocations as may be most suitable to develop his capacities, and give them their highest enjoyment."

The Austrian Supreme Court held, in 1990, that privacy entails the right to withdraw the design of one's private life and information about it from the public and the state. (*Sammlung des Verfassungsgerichts* 1991/12689, March 14, 1991.) Also note that a strong minority of judges on the European Court of Human Rights (ECHR), in a case in which gypsies were not allowed to camp on public grounds, argued that privacy is at least affected when a state does not affirmatively ensure its use: "Measures which affect the applicant's stationing of her caravans have therefore a wider impact than on the right to respect for home. They also affect her ability to maintain her identity as a gypsy and to lead her private and family life in accordance with that tradition." (*Chapman v. United Kingdom*, Application no. 27238/95, 2001.) The judges on the Court from the East European countries held, by and large, that the right to privacy was not violated. Does the understanding of the reach of rights depend on political traditions? Which interpretation seems convincing?

7. *Dignity in international law.* Several international legal norms provide for the protection of dignity in express terms. For some scholars "the United Nations Universal Declaration of Human Rights of 1948 is the single most important reference point of cross-cultural discussion of human freedom and dignity in the world today." Mary Ann Glendon, *Knowing the Universal Declaration of Human Rights*, 73 Notre Dame L. Rev. 1153 (1998). The Declaration provides that:

> Whereas recognition of the inherent dignity and of the equal and inalienable rights of all members of the human family is the foundation of freedom, justice and peace in the world * * *

> Art. 1–All human beings are born free and equal in dignity and rights. They are endowed with reason and conscience and should act towards one another in a spirit of brotherhood.

> Art. 22–Everyone, as a member of society, has the right to social security and is entitled to realization, through national effort and international co-operation and in accordance with the organization and resources of each State, of the economic, social and cultural rights indispensable for his dignity and the free development of his personality.

Human dignity is also explicitly protected in the preamble of the UN Charter, in Art. 10 of the International Covenant on Civil and Political Rights, U.N. Doc. A/6316 (1966), 999 U.N.T.S. 171 (entered into force March 23, 1966), in Art. 13 of the International Covenant on Economic, Social and Cultural Rights, U.N. Doc. A/6316 (1966), 993 U.N.T.S. 3 (entered into force Jan. 3, 1976), and in Art. 1 of the (nonbinding yet symbolically forceful) European Union's Charter of Fundamental Rights (2000). In these documents dignity is associated with the protection of human life, physical integrity, the prohibition against torture and inhuman and degrading treatment, personal autonomy as well as with rights related to self-realization. For instance, Art. 5(2) of the American Convention on Human Rights, O.A.S. Treaty Series No. 36, 1144 U.N.T.S. 123 (entered into force July 18, 1978), provides that "no one shall be subjected to torture or to cruel, inhuman, or degrading punishment or treatment. All persons deprived of their liberty shall be treated with respect for the inherent dignity of the human person."

Note that the European Convention for the Protection of Human Rights and Fundamental Freedoms (hereafter, European HR Convention) does not mention dignity per se. Does this mean that the protection of human dignity is beyond its scope? What does the express protection of human dignity add to a scheme of rights protection beyond what would be protected by other provisions mentioned above? Consider the reasoning of the High Court of Singapore in a case concerning corruption that dealt with the question of the admissibility of certain evidence, *Taw Cheng v. Public Prosecutor*, 1998–1 S.L.R. 943 (Karthigesu J.A.):

> 25.   * * *   [I]n determining the scope of a right or liberty, the importance that the court have regard to the Constitution in its entirety cannot be overstressed. This is necessary in order that the court give equal effect to all the provisions of the Constitution, and not to distort or enhance the interpretation of a particular right to the perversion of the others.   * * *

> 26.   [Thus our] decisions illustrated that no right, even a constitutional one, is absolute. In many cases, the scope of a constitutional right is itself limited by the provisions of the Constitution itself.

Does this mean that no right is absolutely fundamental in the sense of being subject to no limitation? What, then, is fundamental about fundamental rights?

A.2.   DEATH PENALTY AND LIFE IMPRISONMENT

This section takes up an issue that has been considered mostly in terms of a constitutional protection of human dignity: punishment, and the death penalty and life imprisonment in particular. Although other considerations are frequently entailed in the constitutional review of criminal sentencing—due process and equality are chief among them— the following cases illustrate the centrality of dignity claims to the determination of the constitutionality of the extreme sentences of death and life imprisonment. These cases raise many of the issues and problems involved in attempting to constitutionalize fundamental questions closely related to morals and beliefs. On criminal justice issues generally, see Chapter 9.

GREGG v. GEORGIA

Supreme Court (United States).
428 U.S. 153 (1976).

[Following the decision in *Furman v. Georgia*, there was a constitutional "moratorium" on the death penalty in the U.S., from 1972 to 1976. By 1976, state legislation changed some of the features of the death penalty that had made it "cruel and unusual punishment." The Supreme Court upheld the constitutionality of the post-Furman Georgia statute, which provides for the death penalty in certain cases.]

Mr. Justice Stewart delivered the opinion of the Court.

The Court, on a number of occasions, has both assumed and asserted the constitutionality of capital punishment. In several cases, that assumption provided a necessary foundation for the decision, as the Court was asked to decide whether a particular method of carrying out a capital sentence would be allowed to stand under the Eighth Amendment. But until *Furman v. Georgia*, 408 U.S. 238 (1972), the Court never confronted squarely the fundamental claim that the punishment of death always, regardless of the enormity of the offense or the procedure followed in imposing the sentence, is cruel and unusual punishment in violation of the Constitution. Although this issue was presented and addressed in *Furman*, it was not resolved by the Court. Four Justices would have held that capital punishment is not unconstitutional per se; two Justices would have reached the opposite conclusion; and three Justices, while agreeing that the statutes then before the Court were invalid as applied, left open the question whether such punishment may ever be imposed. We now hold that the punishment of death does not invariably violate the Constitution. * * *

But our cases also make clear that public perceptions of standards of decency with respect to criminal sanctions are not conclusive. A penalty also must accord with "the dignity of man," which is the "basic concept underlying the Eighth Amendment." *Trop v. Dulles, supra* at 100 (plurality opinion). This means, at least, that the punishment not be "excessive." When a form of punishment in the abstract (in this case, whether capital punishment may ever be imposed as a sanction for murder), rather than in the particular (the propriety of death as a penalty to be applied to a specific defendant for a specific crime), is under consideration, the inquiry into "excessiveness" has two aspects. First, the punishment must not involve the unnecessary and wanton infliction of pain. * * * Second, the punishment must not be grossly out of proportion to the severity of the crime. * * *

Mr. Justice Brennan, dissenting.

The Cruel and Unusual Punishments Clause "must draw its meaning from the evolving standards of decency that mark the progress of a maturing society." [*Trop v. Dulles*, 356 U.S. 86, 101 (1958)] The opinions of Mr. Justice Stewart, Mr. Justice Powell, and Mr. Justice Stevens today hold that "evolving standards of decency" require focus not on the essence of the death penalty itself but primarily upon the procedures employed by the State to single out persons to suffer the penalty of death. Those opinions hold further that, so viewed, the Clause invalidates the mandatory infliction of the death penalty but not its infliction under sentencing procedures that Mr. Justice Stewart, Mr. Justice Powell, and Mr. Justice Stevens conclude adequately safeguard against the risk that the death penalty was imposed in an arbitrary and capricious manner.

In *Furman v. Georgia*, 408 U.S. 238, 257, (1972) (concurring opinion), I read "evolving standards of decency" as requiring focus upon the essence of the death penalty itself and not primarily or solely upon the procedures under which the determination to inflict the penalty upon a particular person was made. I there said: "From the beginning of our Nation, the punishment of death has stirred acute public controversy. Although pragmatic arguments for and against the punishment have been frequently advanced, this longstanding and heated controversy cannot be explained solely as the result of differences over the practical wisdom of a particular government policy. At bottom, the battle has been waged on moral grounds. The country has debated whether a society for which the dignity of the individual is the supreme value can, without a fundamental inconsistency, follow the practice of deliberately putting some of its members to death. In the United States, as in other nations of the western world, 'the struggle about this punishment has been one between ancient and deeply rooted beliefs in retribution, atonement or vengeance on the one hand, and, on the other, beliefs in the personal value and dignity of the common man that were born of the democratic movement of the eighteenth century, as well as beliefs in the scientific approach to an understanding of the motive forces of human conduct, which are the result of the growth of the sciences of behavior during the nineteenth and twentieth centuries.' It is this essentially moral conflict that forms the backdrop for the past changes in and the present operation of our system of imposing death as a punishment for crime." *Id.*, at 296 [quoting T. Sellin, *The Death Penalty, A Report for the Model Penal Code Project of the American Law Institute* 15 (1959)].

That continues to be my view. For the Clause forbidding cruel and unusual punishments under our constitutional system of government embodies in unique degree moral principles restraining the punishments at our civilized society may impose on those persons who transgress its laws. Thus, I too say: "For myself, I do not hesitate to assert the proposition that the only way the law has progressed from the days of the rack, the screw and the wheel is the development of moral concepts, or, as stated by the Supreme Court ... the application of 'evolving standards of decency'...." [*Novak v. Beto*, 453 F.2d 661, 672 (C.A.5 1971) (Justice Tuttle, concurring in part and dissenting in part).]

This Court inescapably has the duty, as the ultimate arbiter of the meaning of our Constitution, to say whether, when individuals condemned to death stand before our Bar, "moral concepts" require us to hold that the law has progressed to the point where we should declare that the punishment of death, like punishments on the rack, the screw, and the wheel, is no longer morally tolerable in our civilized society. My opinion in *Furman v. Georgia* concluded that our civilization and the law had progressed to this point and that therefore the punishment of death, for whatever crime and under all circumstances, is "cruel and unusual" in violation of the Eighth and Fourteenth Amendments of the Constitution. I shall not again canvass the reasons that led to that conclusion. I emphasize only that foremost among the "moral concepts" recognized in our cases and inherent in the Clause is the primary moral principle that the State, even as it punishes, must treat its citizens in a manner consistent with their intrinsic worth as human beings—a punishment must not be so severe as to be degrading to human dignity. A judicial determination whether the punishment of death comports with human dignity is therefore not only permitted but compelled by the Clause. 408 U.S., at 270.

I do not understand that the Court disagrees that "[i]n comparison to all other punishments today ... the deliberate extinguishment of human life by the State is uniquely degrading to human dignity." *Id.*, at 291. For three of my Brethren hold today that mandatory infliction of the death penalty constitutes the penalty cruel and unusual punishment. I perceive no principled basis for this limitation. Death for whatever crime and under all circumstances "is truly an awesome punishment. The calculated killing of a human being by the State involves, by its very nature, a denial of the executed person's humanity.... An executed person has indeed 'lost the right to have rights.' " *Id.*, at 290. Death is not only an unusually severe punishment, unusual in its pain, in its finality, and in its enormity, but it serves no penal purpose more effectively than a less severe punishment; therefore the principle inherent in the Clause that prohibits pointless infliction of excessive punishment when less severe punishment can adequately achieve the same purposes invalidates the punishment. *Id.*, at 279.

The fatal constitutional infirmity in the punishment of death is that it treats "members of the human race as nonhumans, as objects to be toyed with and discarded. (It is) thus inconsistent with the fundamental premise of the Clause that even the vilest criminal remains a human being possessed of common human dignity." *Id.*, at 273. As such it is a penalty that "subjects the individual to a fate forbidden by the principle of civilized treatment guaranteed by the [Clause]" [*Trop v. Dulles*, 356 U.S., at 99 (plurality opinion of Chief Justice Warren)]. I therefore would hold, on that ground alone, that death is today a cruel and unusual punishment prohibited by the Clause. "Justice of this kind is obviously no less shocking than the crime itself, and the new 'official' murder, far from offering redress for the offense committed against society, adds instead a second defilement to the first." (A. Camus, Reflections on the Guillotine 5–6 (Fridtjof–Karla Pub. 1960).

* * * I would set aside the death sentences imposed in those cases as violative of the Eighth and Fourteenth Amendments.

S. v. MAKWANYANE AND ANOTHER

[SOUTH AFRICA DEATH PENALTY CASE]
Constitutional Court (South Africa).
1995 (3) SALR 391 (CC).

[Two men sentenced to death were awaiting execution on death row. No executions had occurred in South Africa since 1989. The new South African government saw the death penalty as a cruel, inhuman, and degrading punishment, and asked the Court to declare it unconstitutional, while the Attorney–General contended that the death penalty was a necessary and acceptable form of punishment. The case addresses the death penalty in terms of the right not to be subjected to "cruel, inhuman or degrading punishment" provided in section 11(2) of the Constitution.]

Chaskalson P.

* * * Capital punishment was the subject of debate before and during the constitution-making process, and it is clear that the failure to deal specifically in the Constitution with this issue was not accidental. * * *

[5] It would no doubt have been better if the framers of the Constitution had stated specifically, either that the death sentence is not a competent penalty, or that it is permissible in circumstances sanctioned by law. This, however, was not done and it has been left to this Court to decide whether the penalty is consistent with the provisions of the Constitution. That is the extent and limit of the Court's power in this case. * * *

[7] * * * It is a transitional constitution but one which itself establishes a new order in South Africa; an order in which human rights and democracy are entrenched * * *

[8] Chapter Three of the Constitution sets out the fundamental rights to which every person is entitled under the Constitution and also contains provisions dealing with the way in which the Chapter is to be interpreted by the Courts. It does not deal specifically with the death penalty, but in *section* 11(2), it prohibits "cruel, inhuman or degrading treatment or punishment." There is no definition of what is to be regarded as "cruel, inhuman or degrading" and we therefore have to give meaning to these words ourselves.

[9] [This Court] gave its approval to an approach which, whilst paying due regard to the language that has been used, is "generous" and "purposive" and gives expression to the underlying values of the Constitution. * * *

[10] * * * I need say no more in this judgment than that *section* 11(2) of the Constitution must not be construed in isolation, but in its context, which includes the history and background to the adoption of the Constitution, other provisions of the Constitution itself and, in particular, the provisions of Chapter Three of which it is part. It must also be construed in a way which secures for "individuals the full measure" of its protection. Rights with which *section* 11(2) is associated in Chapter Three of the Constitution, and which are of particular importance to a decision on the constitutionality of the death penalty are included in *section* 9, "every person shall have the right to life", *section* 10, "every person shall have the right to respect for and protection of his or her dignity", and *section* 8, "every person shall have the right to equality before the law and to equal protection of the law." Punishment must meet the requirements of *sections* 8, 9 and 10; and this is so, whether these sections are treated as giving meaning to *section* 11(2) or as prescribing separate and independent standards with which all punishments must comply * * *

[26] Death is the most extreme form of punishment to which a convicted criminal can be subjected. Its execution is final and irrevocable. It puts an end not only to the right of life itself, but to all other personal rights which had vested in the deceased under Chapter Three of

the Constitution. It leaves nothing except the memory in others of what has been and the property that passes to the deceased's heirs. * * * [T]he death sentence * * * is also an inhuman punishment for it "involves, by its very nature, a denial of the executed person's humanity", and it is degrading because it strips the convicted person of all dignity and treats him or her as an object to be eliminated by the state. The question is not, however, whether the death sentence is a cruel, inhuman or degrading punishment in the ordinary meaning of these words but whether it is a cruel, inhuman or degrading punishment within the meaning of *section* 11(2) of our Constitution. The accused, who rely on *section* 11(2) of the Constitution, carry the initial onus of establishing this proposition. * * *

[33] The death sentence is a form of punishment which has been used throughout history by different societies. It has long been the subject of controversy. As societies became more enlightened, they restricted the offences for which this penalty could be imposed. The movement away from the death penalty gained momentum during the second half of the present century with the growth of the abolitionist movement. In some countries it is now prohibited in all circumstances, in some it is prohibited save in times of war, and in most countries that have retained it as a penalty for crime, its use has been restricted to extreme cases. According to Amnesty International, 1,831 executions were carried out throughout the world in 1993 as a result of sentences of death, of which 1,419 were in China, which means that only 412 executions were carried out in the rest of the world in that year. Today, capital punishment has been abolished as a penalty for murder either specifically or in practice by almost half of the countries of the world including the democracies of Europe and our neighbouring countries, Namibia, Mozambique and Angola. In most of those countries where it is retained, as the Amnesty International statistics show, it is seldom used.

[34] In the course of the arguments addressed to us, we were referred to books and articles on the death sentence, and to judgments dealing with challenges made to capital punishment in the courts of other countries and in international tribunals. The international and foreign authorities are of value because they analyse arguments for and against the death sentence and show how courts of other jurisdictions have dealt with this vexed issue. For that reason alone they require our attention. They may also have to be considered because of their relevance to *section* 35(1) of the Constitution, which states:

> In interpreting the provisions of this Chapter a court of law shall promote the values which underlie an open and democratic society based on freedom and equality and shall, where applicable, have regard to public international law applicable to the protection of the right entrenched in this Chapter, and may have regard to comparable foreign case law.

[35] Customary international law and the ratification and accession to international agreements is dealt with in *section* 231 of the Constitution which sets the requirements for such law to be binding within South Africa. In the context of *section* 35(1), public international law would include non-binding as well as binding law. They may both be

used under the *section* as tools of interpretation. International agreements and customary international law accordingly provide a framework within which Chapter Three can be evaluated and understood, and for that purpose, decisions of tribunals dealing with comparable instruments, such as the United Nations Committee on Human Rights, the Inter–American Commission on Human Rights, the Inter–American Court of Human Rights, the European Commission of Human Rights, and the European Court of Human Rights, and in appropriate cases, reports of specialised agencies such as the International Labour Organisation may provide guidance as to the correct interpretation of particular provisions of Chapter Three.

[36]   Capital punishment is not prohibited by public international law, and this is a factor that has to be taken into account in deciding whether it is cruel, inhuman or degrading punishment within the meaning of *section* 11(2). International human rights agreements differ, however, from our Constitution in that where the right to life is expressed in unqualified terms they either deal specifically with the death sentence, or authorise exceptions to be made to the right to life by law. This has influenced the way international tribunals have dealt with issues relating to capital punishment, and is relevant to a proper understanding of such decisions.

[37]   Comparative "bill of rights" jurisprudence will no doubt be of importance, particularly in the early stages of the transition when there is no developed indigenous jurisprudence in this branch of the law on which to draw. Although we are told by *section* 35(1) that we "may" have regard to foreign case law, it is important to appreciate that this will not necessarily offer a safe guide to the interpretation of Chapter Three of our Constitution. This * * * is implicit in the injunction given to the Courts in *section* 35(1), which in permissible terms allows the Courts to "have regard to" such law. There is no injunction to do more than this.

[38]   When challenges to the death sentence in international or foreign courts and tribunals have failed, the constitution or the international instrument concerned has either directly sanctioned capital punishment or has specifically provided that the right to life is subject to exceptions sanctioned by law. The only case to which we were referred in which there were not such express provisions in the Constitution, was the decision of the Hungarian Constitutional Court. There the challenge succeeded and the death penalty was declared to be unconstitutional.

[39]   Our Constitution expresses the right to life in an unqualified form, and prescribes the criteria that have to be met for the limitation of entrenched rights, including the prohibition of legislation that negates the essential content of an entrenched right. In dealing with comparative law, we must bear in mind that we are required to construe the South African Constitution, and not an international instrument or the constitution of some foreign country, and that this has to be done with due regard to our legal system, our history and circumstances, and the structure and language of our own Constitution. We can derive assis-

tance from public international law and foreign case law, but we are in no way bound to follow it.

[40]   The earliest litigation on the validity of the death sentence seems to have been pursued in the courts of the United States of America. It has been said there that the "Constitution itself poses the first obstacle to [the] argument that capital punishment is per se unconstitutional". From the beginning, the United States Constitution recognised capital punishment as lawful. The Fifth Amendment (adopted in 1791) refers in specific terms to capital punishment and impliedly recognises its validity. The Fourteenth Amendment (adopted in 1868) obliges the states, not to "deprive any person of life, liberty, or property, without due process of law" and it too impliedly recognises the right of the states to make laws for such purposes. The argument that capital punishment is unconstitutional was based on the Eighth Amendment, which prohibits cruel and unusual punishment. Although the Eighth Amendment "has not been regarded as a static concept" and as drawing its meaning "from the evolving standards of decency that mark the progress of a maturing society", the fact that the constitution recognises the lawfulness of capital punishment has proved to be an obstacle in the way of the acceptance of this argument * * *

[41]   * * * [T]he federal constitutionality of the death sentence as a legitimate form of punishment for murder was affirmed by the United States Supreme Court in *Gregg v. Georgia* [428 U.S. 153 (1976)]. Both before and after *Gregg*'s case, decisions upholding and rejecting challenges to death penalty statutes have divided the Supreme Court, and have led at times to sharply-worded judgments. The decisions ultimately turned on the votes of those judges who considered the nature of the discretion given to the sentencing authority to be the crucial factor.

[42]   Statutes providing for mandatory death sentences, or too little discretion in sentencing, have been rejected by the Supreme Court because they do not allow for consideration of factors peculiar to the convicted person facing sentence, which may distinguish his or her case from other cases * * *

[47]   There seems to me to be little difference between the guided discretion required for the death sentence in the United States, and the criteria laid down by the Appellate Division for the imposition of the death sentence. The fact that the Appellate Division, a court of experienced judges, takes the final decision in all cases is, in my view, more likely to result in consistency of sentencing, than will be the case where sentencing is in the hands of jurors who are offered statutory guidance as to how that discretion should be exercised.

[48]   The argument that the imposition of the death sentence under *section* 277 is arbitrary and capricious does not, however, end there. It also focuses on what is alleged to be the arbitrariness inherent in the application of *section* 277 in practice. Of the thousands of persons put on trial for murder, only a very small percentage are sentenced to death by a trial court, and of those, a large number escape the ultimate penalty on appeal. At every stage of the process there is an element of chance. The outcome may be dependent upon factors such as the way the case is

investigated by the police, the way the case is presented by the prosecutor, how effectively the accused is defended, the personality and particular attitude to capital punishment of the trial judge and, if the matter goes on appeal, the particular judges who are selected to hear the case. Race and poverty are also alleged to be factors. * * *

[52] In holding that the imposition and the carrying out of the death penalty in the cases then under consideration constituted cruel and unusual punishment in the United States, Justice Douglas, concurring in *Furman v. Georgia* [408 U.S. 238, 257 (1972)], said that "[a]ny law which is nondiscriminatory on its face may be applied in such a way as to violate the Equal Protection Clause of the Fourteenth Amendment." Discretionary statutes are:

" * * * pregnant with discrimination and discrimination is an ingredient not compatible with the idea of equal protection of the laws that is implicit in the ban on 'cruel and unusual' punishments." * * *

[56] The United States jurisprudence has not resolved the dilemma arising from the fact that the Constitution prohibits cruel and unusual punishments, but also permits, and contemplates that there will be capital punishment. * * * The difficulties that have been experienced in following this path * * * persuade me that we should not follow this route.

The Right to Dignity

[57] Although the United States Constitution does not contain a specific guarantee of human dignity, it has been accepted by the United States Supreme Court that the concept of human dignity is at the core of the prohibition of "cruel and unusual punishment" by the Eighth and Fourteenth Amendments. [*Trop v. Dulles*, 356 U.S. 86. See also *People v. Anderson*, 6 Cal. 3d 628, 100 Cal. Rptr. 152. ("The dignity of man, the individual and the society as a whole, is today demeaned by our continued practice of capital punishment.")] For Brennan, J this was decisive of the question in *Gregg v. Georgia* * * *

[58] Under our constitutional order the right to human dignity is specifically guaranteed. It can only be limited by legislation which passes the stringent test of being "necessary". The weight given to human dignity by Justice Brennan is wholly consistent with the values of our Constitution and the new order established by it. It is also consistent with the approach to extreme punishments followed by courts in other countries.

[59] In Germany, the Federal Constitutional Court has stressed this aspect of punishment.

Respect for human dignity especially requires the prohibition of cruel, inhuman, and degrading punishments. [The state] cannot turn the offender into an object of crime prevention to the detriment of his constitutionally protected right to social worth and respect. [*Life Imprisonment Case* below.]

[60] That capital punishment constitutes a serious impairment of human dignity has also been recognised by judgments of the Canadian Supreme Court. * * * [It held:]

It is the supreme indignity to the individual, the ultimate corporal punishment, the final and complete lobotomy and the absolute and irrevocable castration. [It is] the ultimate desecration of human dignity . . .

[61]   Three other Judges were of the opinion that

(t)here is strong ground for believing, having regard to the limited extent to which the death penalty advances any valid penological objectives and the serious invasion of human dignity it endangers, that the death penalty cannot, except in exceptional circumstances, be justified in this country. * * *

The International Covenant on Civil and Political Rights

[66]   * * * [A]lthough articles 6(2) to (5) of the International Covenant specifically allow the imposition of the death sentence under strict controls "for the most serious crimes" by those countries which have not abolished it, it provides in *article* 6(6) that "[n]othing in this article shall be invoked to delay or to prevent the abolition of capital punishment by any State Party to the present Covenant". The fact that the International Covenant sanctions capital punishment must be seen in this context. It tolerates but does not provide justification for the death penalty.

[67]   * * * [W]hat is clear from the decisions of the Human Rights Committee of the United Nations is that the death penalty is regarded by it as cruel and inhuman punishment within the ordinary meaning of those words, and that it was because of the specific provisions of the International Covenant authorising the imposition of capital punishment by member States in certain circumstances, that the words had to be given a narrow meaning.

The European Convention on Human Rights

[68]   Similar issues were debated by the European Court of Human Rights in *Soering v. United Kingdom* [11 E.H.R.R. 439 (1989)]. This case was also concerned with the extradition to the United States of a fugitive to face murder charges for which capital punishment was a competent sentence. It was argued that this would expose him to inhuman and degrading treatment or punishment in breach of *article* 3 of the European Convention on Human Rights. *Article* 2 of the European Convention protects the right to life but makes an exception in the case of "the execution of a sentence of a court following [the] conviction of a crime for which this penalty is provided by law." The majority of the Court held that *article* 3 could not be construed as prohibiting all capital punishment, since to do so would nullify *article* 2. * * *

[69]   * * * [A]lthough the offence for which extradition was sought had been committed in the United States, the fugitive who was a German national was also liable to be tried for the same offence in Germany. Germany, which has abolished the death sentence, also sought his extradition for the murders. There was accordingly a choice in regard to the country to which the fugitive should be extradited, and that choice should have been exercised in a way which would not lead to a contravention of *article* 3. What weighed with the Court was the fact that the

choice facing the United Kingdom was not a choice between extradition to face a possible death penalty and no punishment, but a choice between extradition to a country which allows the death penalty and one which does not. We are in a comparable position. A holding by us that the death penalty for murder is unconstitutional, does not involve a choice between freedom and death; it involves a choice between death in the very few cases which would otherwise attract that penalty under *section* 277(1)(a), and the severe penalty of life imprisonment.

Capital Punishment in India

[71]   *Section* 302 of the Indian Penal Code authorises the imposition of the death sentence as a penalty for murder. * * *

[75]   The Supreme Court had recognised in a number of cases that the death sentence served as a deterrent, and the Law Commission of India, which had conducted an investigation into capital punishment in 1967, had recommended that capital punishment be retained. * * *

[76]   * * * [T]he court concluded that:

> . . . the question whether or not [the] death penalty serves any penological purpose is a difficult, complex and intractable issue [which] has evoked strong, divergent views. For the purpose of testing the constitutionality of the impugned provisions as to death penalty . . . on the grounds of reasonableness in the light of Articles 19 and 21 of the Constitution, it is not necessary for us to express any categorical opinion, one way or another, as to which of these antithetical views, held by the Abolitionists and the Retentionists, is correct. It is sufficient to say that the very fact that persons of reason, learning and light are rationally and deeply divided in their opinion on this issue, is ground among others, for rejecting the petitioners' argument that retention of death penalty in the impugned provision, is totally devoid of reason and purpose. * * *

[77]   The Court then went on to [specify that] * * * it was clear that the State could deprive a person of his or her life, by "fair, just and reasonable procedure." In the circumstances, and taking into account the indications that capital punishment was considered by the framers of the constitution in 1949 to be a valid penalty, it was asserted that "by no stretch of the imagination can it be said that death penalty * * * either per se or because of its execution by hanging constitutes an unreasonable, cruel or unusual punishment" prohibited by the Constitution.

[78]   The wording of the relevant provisions of our Constitution are different. The question we have to consider is not whether the imposition of the death sentence for murder is "totally devoid of reason and purpose", or whether the death sentence for murder "is devoid of any rational nexus" with the purpose and object of *section* 277(1)(a) of the Criminal Procedure Act. It is whether in the context of our Constitution, the death penalty is cruel, inhuman or degrading, and if it is, whether it can be justified in terms of *section* 33. * * *

[80]   The unqualified right to life vested in every person by *section* 9 of our Constitution is another factor crucially relevant to the question whether the death sentence is cruel, inhuman or degrading punishment within the meaning of *section* 11(2) of our Constitution. * * *

[83]   An individual's right to life has been described as "[t]he most fundamental of all human rights", [Per Lord Bridge in *R. v. Home Secretary*] and was dealt with in that way in the judgments of the Hungarian Constitutional Court declaring capital punishment to be unconstitutional. * * *

[The Attorney General then argues that the public endorses the view that the death penalty is justified. But, referring to U.S. jurisprudence, the Court says:]

[89]   This Court cannot allow itself to be diverted from its duty to act as an independent arbiter of the Constitution by making choices on the basis that they will find favour with the public. * * *

[95]   The carrying out of the death sentence destroys life, which is protected without reservation under *section* 9 of our Constitution, it annihilates human dignity which is protected under *section* 10, elements of arbitrariness are present in its enforcement and it is irremediable. Taking these factors into account, * * * I am satisfied that in the context of our Constitution the death penalty is indeed a cruel, inhuman and degrading punishment.

Is capital punishment for murder justifiable?

[96]   The question that now has to be considered is whether the imposition of such punishment is nonetheless justifiable as a penalty for murder * * *

[98]   *Section* 33(1) of the Constitution provides, in part, that:

The rights entrenched in this Chapter may be limited by law of general application, provided that such limitation–

    (a) shall be permissible only to the extent that it is–

        (i) reasonable; and

        (ii) justifiable in an open and democratic society based on freedom and equality; and

    (b) shall not negate the essential content of the right in question.

[99]   *Section* 33(1)(b) goes on to provide that the limitation of certain rights, including the rights referred to in *section* 10 and *section* 11 "shall, in addition to being reasonable as required in paragraph (a)(i), also be necessary."

The Two–Stage Approach

[100]   Our Constitution deals with the limitation of rights through a general limitations clause. As was pointed out by Kentridge AJ in *Zuma*'s case, this calls for a "two-stage" approach, in which a broad rather than a narrow interpretation is given to the fundamental rights enshrined in Chapter Three, and limitations have to be justified through the application of *section* 33. In this it differs from the Constitution of the United States, which does not contain a limitation clause, as a result of which courts in that country have been obliged to find limits to constitutional rights through a narrow interpretation of the rights themselves. Although the "two-stage" approach may often produce the

same result as the "one-stage" approach, this will not always be the case.

[101]   The practical consequences of this difference in approach are evident in the present case. In *Gregg v. Georgia*, the conclusion reached in the judgment of the plurality was summed up as follows:

> In sum, we cannot say that the judgment of the Georgia legislature that capital punishment may be necessary in some cases is clearly wrong. Considerations of federalism, as well as respect for the ability of a legislature to evaluate, in terms of its particular state the moral consensus concerning the death penalty and its social utility as a sanction, require us to conclude in the absence of more convincing evidence, that the infliction of death as a punishment for murder is not without justification, and is thus not unconstitutionally severe.

[102]   Under our Constitution, the position is different. It is not whether the decision of the State has been shown to be clearly wrong; it is whether the decision of the State is justifiable according to the criteria prescribed by *section* 33. It is not whether the infliction of death as a punishment for murder "is not without justification", it is whether the infliction of death as a punishment for murder has been shown to be both reasonable and necessary, and to be consistent with the other requirements of *section* 33. It is for the legislature, or the party relying on the legislation, to establish this justification, and not for the party challenging it to show that it was not justified. * * *

[104]   The limitation of constitutional rights for a purpose that is reasonable and necessary in a democratic society involves the weighing up of competing values, and ultimately an assessment based on proportionality. * * *

The Essential Content of the Right

[132]   *Section* 33(1)(b) provides that a limitation shall not negate the essential content of the right. There is uncertainty in the literature concerning the meaning of this provision. It seems to have entered constitutional law through the provisions of the German Constitution, and in addition to the South African constitution, appears, though not precisely in the same form, in the constitutions of Namibia, Hungary, and possibly other countries as well. The difficulty of interpretation arises from the uncertainty as to what the "essential content" of a right is, and how it is to be determined. Should this be determined subjectively from the point of view of the individual affected by the invasion of the right, or objectively, from the point of view of the nature of the right and its place in the constitutional order, or possibly in some other way? Professor Currie [David P. Currie, *The Constitution of the Federal Republic of Germany* (1994)] draws attention to the large number of theories which have been propounded by German scholars as to the how the "essence" of a right should be discerned and how the constitutional provision should be applied. The German Federal Constitutional Court has apparently avoided to a large extent having to deal with this issue by subsuming the enquiry into the proportionality test that it applies and the precise scope and meaning of the provision is controversial. [See Dieter Grimm, *Human Rights and Judicial Review in Germany*, in

Human Rights and Judicial Review: A Comparative Perspective 267, 275 (David H. Beatty ed., 1994).]

[133] If the essential content of the right not to be subjected to cruel, inhuman or degrading punishment is to be found in respect for life and dignity, the death sentence for murder, if viewed subjectively from the point of view of the convicted prisoner, clearly negates the essential content of the right. But if it is viewed objectively from the point of view of a constitutional norm that requires life and dignity to be protected, the punishment does not necessarily negate the essential content of the right. It has been argued before this Court that one of the purposes of such punishment is to protect the life and hence the dignity of innocent members of the public, and if it in fact does so, the punishment will not negate the constitutional norm. On this analysis it would, however, have to be shown that the punishment serves its intended purpose. This would involve a consideration of the deterrent and preventative effects of the punishment and whether they add anything to the alternative of life imprisonment. If they do not, they cannot be said to serve a life protecting purpose. If the negation is viewed both objectively and subjectively, the ostensible purpose of the punishment would have to be weighed against the destruction of the individual's life. For the purpose of that analysis the element of retribution would have to be excluded and the "life saving" quality of the punishment would have to be established.

[134] It is, however, not necessary to solve this problem in the present case. At the very least the provision evinces concern that, under the guise of limitation, rights should not be taken away altogether. It was presumably the same concern that influenced Dickson CJC to say in *R. v. Oakes* that rights should be limited "as little as possible", [[1986] 1 S.C.R. 103, citing *R. v. Big M Drug Mart Ltd.*, [1985] 1 S.C.R. 295] and the German Constitutional Court to hold in the *Life Imprisonment* case that all possibility of parole ought not to be excluded.

The Balancing Process

[135] In the balancing process, deterrence, prevention and retribution must be weighed against the alternative punishments available to the state, and the factors which taken together make capital punishment cruel, inhuman and degrading: the destruction of life, the annihilation of dignity, the elements of arbitrariness, inequality and the possibility of error in the enforcement of the penalty.

[136] The Attorney General argued that the right to life and the right to human dignity were not absolute concepts. Like all rights they have their limits. One of those limits is that a person who murders in circumstances where the death penalty is permitted by *section* 277, forfeits his or her right to claim protection of life and dignity. * * *

[137] This argument is fallacious. The rights vested in every person by Chapter Three of the Constitution are subject to limitation under *section* 33. In times of emergency, some may be suspended in accordance with the provisions of *section* 34 of the Constitution. But subject to this, the rights vest in every person, including criminals convicted of vile crimes. Such criminals do not forfeit their rights under the Constitution and are entitled, as all in our country now are, to assert these rights,

including the right to life, the right to dignity and the right not to be subjected to cruel, inhuman or degrading punishment. Whether or not a particular punishment is inconsistent with these rights depends upon an interpretation of the relevant provisions of the Constitution, and not upon a moral judgment that a murderer should not be allowed to claim them. * * *

[141]   The Attorney General argued that all punishment involves an impairment of dignity. Imprisonment, which is the alternative to the death sentence, severely limits a prisoner's fundamental rights and freedoms. There is only the barest freedom of movement or of residence in prison, and other basic rights such as freedom of expression and freedom of assembly are severely curtailed.

[142]   Dignity is inevitably impaired by imprisonment or any other punishment, and the undoubted power of the state to impose punishment as part of the criminal justice system, necessarily involves the power to encroach upon a prisoner's dignity. But a prisoner does not lose all his or her rights on entering prison.

> [Prisoners retain] those absolute natural rights relating to personality, to which every man is entitled. True [their] freedom had been greatly impaired by the legal process of imprisonment but they were entitled to demand respect for what remained. The fact that their liberty had been legally curtailed could afford no excuse for a further legal encroachment upon it. [It was] contended that the [prisoners] once in prison could claim only such rights as the Ordinance and the regulations conferred. But the directly opposite view is surely the correct one. They were entitled to all their personal rights and personal dignity not temporarily taken away by law, or necessarily inconsistent with the circumstances in which they had been placed. [Justice Innes in *Whittaker v. Roos and Bateman*, 1912 AD 92, at 122–23.]

[143]   A prisoner is not stripped naked, bound, gagged and chained to his or her cell. The right of association with other prisoners, the right to exercise, to write and receive letters and the rights of personality referred to by Innes J are of vital importance to prisoners and highly valued by them precisely because they are confined, have only limited contact with the outside world, and are subject to prison discipline. Imprisonment is a severe punishment; but prisoners retain all the rights to which every person is entitled under Chapter Three subject only to limitations imposed by the prison regime that are justifiable under *section* 33. Of these, none are more important than the *section* 11(2) right not to be subjected to "torture of any kind ... nor to cruel, inhuman or degrading treatment or punishment." There is a difference between encroaching upon rights for the purpose of punishment and destroying them altogether. It is that difference with which we are concerned in the present case.

Conclusion

[144]   The rights to life and dignity are the most important of all human rights, and the source of all other personal rights in Chapter Three. By committing ourselves to a society founded on the recognition of human rights we are required to value these two rights above all

others. And this must be demonstrated by the State in everything that it does, including the way it punishes criminals. This is not achieved by objectifying murderers and putting them to death to serve as an example to others in the expectation that they might possibly be deterred thereby.

[145]   In the balancing process the principal factors that have to be weighed are on the one hand the destruction of life and dignity that is a consequence of the implementation of the death sentence, the elements of arbitrariness and the possibility of error in the enforcement of capital punishment, and the existence of a severe alternative punishment (life imprisonment) and, on the other, the claim that the death sentence is a greater deterrent to murder, and will more effectively prevent its commission, than would a sentence of life imprisonment, and that there is a public demand for retributive justice to be imposed on murderers, which only the death sentence can meet.

[146]   Retribution cannot be accorded the same weight under our Constitution as the rights to life and dignity, which are the most important of all the rights in Chapter Three. It has not been shown that the death sentence would be materially more effective to deter or prevent murder than the alternative sentence of life imprisonment would be. Taking these factors into account, as well as the elements of arbitrariness and the possibility of error in enforcing the death penalty, the clear and convincing case that is required to justify the death sentence as a penalty for murder, has not been made out. * * *

Notes and Questions

1.   *Text.* The U.S. Constitution does not include an explicit right to dignity, but the U.S. Supreme Court (USSC) has found this protection in the Eighth and Fourteenth amendments. Does having an explicit textual basis for dignity claims, as in the South African and German constitutions, provide a sounder basis for protecting fundamental rights?

2.   *Civilized standards.* The SACC refers to the USSC in *Trop v. Dulles*, 356 U.S. 86, 100 (1958). The relevant quote reads: "The basic concept underlying the Eighth Amendment is nothing less than the dignity of man. While the State has the power to punish, the Amendment stands to assure that this power be exercised within the limits of civilized standards. Fines, imprisonment and even execution may be imposed depending upon the enormity of the crime, but any technique outside the bounds of these traditional penalties is constitutionally suspect." Here, Chief Justice Warren (in a plurality but not majority opinion) invokes the concept of dignity but also allows for execution as a legitimate punishment, according to a "civilized standard." How is this standard to be defined and by whom? What is its relationship to the conception of dignity that informs other constitutional cultures?

3.   *Reasonable sentencing?* Consider that Section 302 of the Indian Penal Code authorizes the imposition of the death sentence as a penalty for murder. The ISC has relied on a standard of "reasonableness" in its decision to uphold the constitutionality of capital punishment. In *Jagmohan Singh v. State of Uttar Pradesh*, (1973) S.C.C. 20, the Court held that if the entire

procedure for criminal trial under the Criminal Procedure Code for arriving at the sentence of death is valid, then the imposition of a death sentence in accordance with the procedure established by law cannot be said to be unconstitutional. Later, in *Bachan Singh v. State of Punjab*, (1980) 1 S.C.R. 645, (1980) 2 S.C.C. 684, 751: A.I.R. 1980 S.C. 898, the Court sought to limit the use of capital punishment to the "rarest-of-rare" cases, expressing an abiding concern for the dignity of human life.

4. *Changes over time.* Consider the words of Lord Diplock in *Ong Ah Chuan v. Public Prosecutor*, Privy Council, (1981) 1 MLJ 64, [1981] A.C. 648, a case in which the mandatory death sentences for drug trafficking in Singapore was upheld: "[a] primary object of imposing a death sentence for offences that society regards with particular abhorrence is that it should act as a deterrent; particularly where the offence is one that is committed for profit by an offender who is prepared to take a calculated risk. There is nothing unusual in a capital sentence being mandatory. Indeed its efficacy as a deterrent may be to some extent diminished if it is not. At common law all capital sentences were mandatory * * *." Twenty years later, in *Patrick Reyes v. The Queen*, Privy Council Appeal No. 64 of 2001, [2002] U.K.P.C. 11, [2002] 2 WLR 1034, PC, a mandatory death sentence for any shooting murder in Belize was held to be in violation of the constitutional prohibition against inhuman or degrading punishment.

5. *Deterrence and prevention.* The above ruling by Lord Diplock asserts deterrence as one of the primary objectives of capital punishment. The South African ruling in *Makwanyane* (set out above) outlines a balancing process that includes this consideration. In criminal law one basis for sentencing is to prevent future crimes. Arguably, the only way to guarantee with absolute certainty that an individual will never again commit a crime is to put that individual to death. Can the death penalty be thereby justified under standards of constitutional law? Is it possible to balance fundamental rights with competing state interests like deterrence and prevention? Criminology argues that such general measures show no direct effect in combating crime.

6. *International law.* Article 6(2) of the ICCPR, which entered into force in 1976, requires that states impose a sentence of death "only for the most serious crimes," but in 1991 the Second Optional Protocol to the Covenant (G.A. res. 44/128, annex, 44 U.N. GAOR Supp. (No. 49) at 207, U.N. Doc A/44/49 (1989), entered into force July 11, 1991) requires ratifying states to abolish the death penalty. Note that the preamble to the Covenant explicitly recognizes the inherent dignity of the human person as that from which rights are derived. Protocol No. 6 of the European HR Convention, E.T.S. 114 (entered into force March 1, 1985), prohibits the imposition of the death penalty in peacetime but allows for an exception during times of war or imminent threat of war (Art. 2). Does this exception undermine the position that the death penalty violates the fundamental rights of human beings?

R. v. LATIMER

Supreme Court (Canada).
[2001] 1 S.C.R. 3.

[Robert Latimer, a farmer, admitted to killing his 12–year-old daughter, Tracy, who suffered with a severe case of cerebral palsy since birth. He steadfastly maintained that the killing was motivated by love for his daughter, not wanting her to endure any more pain from her illness or the resultant surgeries. The court sentenced Latimer to life in prison with a mandatory minimum of 10 years imprisonment for second-degree murder. He challenged this as a "cruel and inhuman punishment."]

The Court:

2. * * * The test for what amounts to "cruel and unusual punishment" is a demanding one, and the appellant has not succeeded in showing that the sentence in his case is "grossly disproportionate" to the punishment required for the most serious crime known to law, murder.

71. We conclude that Mr. Latimer's conviction must be upheld. * * *

73. * * * [T]hough the state may impose punishment, the effect of that punishment must not be grossly disproportionate to what would have been appropriate.

74. * * * [In] assessing whether a sentence is grossly disproportionate, the court must first consider the gravity of the offence, the personal characteristics of the offender and the particular circumstances of the case in order to determine what range of sentences would have been appropriate to punish, rehabilitate or deter this particular offender or to protect the public from this particular offender. * * *

75. [In addition,] a full contextual understanding of the sentencing provision also requires a consideration of the actual effect of the punishment on the individual, the penological goals and sentencing principles upon which the sentence is fashioned, the existence of valid alternatives to the punishment imposed, and a comparison of punishments imposed for other crimes in the same jurisdiction. However, not all of these matters will be relevant to the analysis and none of these standing alone will be decisive to a determination of gross disproportionality.

76. While the test is one that attributes a great deal of weight to individual circumstances, it should also be stressed that in weighing the s. 12 considerations the court must also consider and defer to the valid legislative objectives underlying the criminal law responsibilities of Parliament * * *

> It will only be on rare and unique occasions that a court will find a sentence so grossly disproportionate that it violates the provisions of s. 12 of the *Charter*. The test for determining whether a sentence is disproportionately long is very properly stringent and demanding. A lesser test would tend to trivialize the *Charter*. * * *

77. * * * It is not for the court to pass on the wisdom of Parliament with respect to the gravity of various offences and the range of penalties which may be imposed upon those found guilty of committing the offences. Parliament has broad discretion in proscribing conduct as criminal and in determining proper punishment.

[The Court then applies such principles to the case and emphasizes that] one cannot escape the conclusion that Mr. Latimer's actions resulted in the most serious of all possible consequences, namely, the death of the victim, Tracy Latimer. [The Court also considers Latimer's planned action and the victim's weakness.]

86.   Finally, this sentence is consistent with a number of valid penological goals and sentencing principles. Although we would agree that in this case the sentencing principles of rehabilitation, specific deterrence and protection are not triggered for consideration, we are mindful of the important role that the mandatory minimum sentence plays in denouncing murder. Denunciation of unlawful conduct is one of the objectives of sentencing recognized in s. 718 of the *Criminal Code*. As noted by the Court in *R. v. M.* (C.A.), [1996] 1 S.C.R. 500, at para. 81:

> The objective of denunciation mandates that a sentence should communicate society's condemnation of that particular offender's conduct. In short, a sentence with a denunciatory element represents a symbolic, collective statement that the offender's conduct should be punished for encroaching on our society's basic code of values as enshrined within our substantive criminal law.

87.   In summary, the minimum mandatory sentence is not grossly disproportionate in this case.

LIFE IMPRISONMENT CASE

Federal Constitutional Court (Germany).
45 BVerfGE 187 (1977).

[A lower court referred a murder case to the Federal Constitutional Court because the judges deemed the murder and the manslaughter statutes, Sections 211 and 212, respectively, of the Criminal Code, incompatible with the human dignity clause of Art. 1 sec. 1 of the Basic Law. They both provide for life imprisonment in extreme cases—such as homicide to satisfy sexual urges, homicide as a result of greed, homicide to cover up another crime, extreme homicides in general, etc. The lower court maintained that life imprisonment can be shown to destroy human beings within about twenty years. Such long prison terms turn people into spiritual and physical wrecks. The permanent exclusion of the criminal from society destroys him psychologically, and, therefore, the legislature violated its duty to respect human dignity. The court concluded that such law violated the right to life and health (Art. 2 sec. 2), to legal protection (Art. 19 sec. 2), and to equal treatment (Art. 3 sec. 1).]

Judgement of the First Senate:

II.   1. * * * [The] Criminal Code is, within the scope of this review and in compliance with the following text and the restricted interpretation * * * which can be derived therefrom, compatible with the Constitution. [Respect] and protection of human dignity are among the constitutional principles of the Constitution. The free human personality and [human] dignity represent the highest legal values within the constitutional order. The state has the duty to respect and to protect the dignity of human beings. This is founded on the conception of man as a spiritual-moral being, that has the potential to determine himself in freedom and develop from within. This freedom, within the meaning of the Constitution, is not the one of an isolated and self-regarding individual, but rather [it is the freedom of an individual] that is related to the community and bound by it. [Therefore, it] can in principle not be unlimited. The individual must allow those limitations of his freedom to act that the legislator deems bearable [and necessary] in particular factual circumstances, in order to nourish and support the communal living with each other; however, the autonomy of the individual must be protected. This means, also, that within the community each individual must be recognized, as a matter of principle, as a member with equal rights and a value of his own. The sentence "the human being must always remain an end in itself" has unlimited validity in all areas of the law; for the dignity of man as person, which can never be taken away from him, consists particularly therein, that he remains recognized as a person who bears responsibility for himself.

In the area of criminal law, in which highest demands to the maintenance of justice are posed, Article 1 sec 1 of the Constitution determines the understanding of the nature of penal sanctions and the relation between guilt and atonement. The fundamental principle *"nulla poena sine culpa"* has the rank of a constitutional norm. Every penal sanction must bear a just relation to the severity of the offense and the guilt of the offender. The command to respect human dignity means in particular that cruel, inhuman and degrading punishments are not permitted. The offender may not be turned into a mere object of [the state's] fight against crime under violation of his constitutionally protected right to social worth and respect. The fundamental prerequisites of individual and social existence of men must be preserved. From Article 1 sec 1 of the Constitution, in conjunction with the principle to maintain a state based on social justice, one can—and this is particularly true in the execution of criminal punishments—derive the duty of the state to allow [everyone at least] that minimum level of existence at which human dignity is conceived. It would be inconsistent with human dignity perceived in this way if the state were to claim the right to forcefully strip a human of his freedom without [the human] having at least the possibility to ever regain freedom.

[In the course of the discussion] one must never loose sight [of this principle]: The dignity of the human being is something indispensable. The recognition of what is necessary to comply with the command to respect human dignity is, however, inseparable from the historical development. The history of criminal law clearly shows that most cruel punishments were always replaced by milder punishments. * * * The judgment on what is necessary for [the maintenance of] human dignity can therefore only rest on present understanding and claim no right to timeless validity.

2.   If these standards are used in assessing nature and effect of life imprisonment, one reaches the conclusion that no violation of Article 1 section 1. of the Constitution is before the court. [The Court then discussed the negative effects of long prison terms, on which experts come to divergent conclusions.]

c) Regarding such facts, constitutional review must exercise restraint. It is true that the Federal Constitutional Court has the duty to protect the basic rights against [infringements] from the legislator. Therefore, the court is in its review not bound by the legal understanding of the legislator. However, if assessments and actual judgments by the legislator are of importance [for constitutional review], then the court may, as a matter of principle, only overrule legislative acts if such assessments are refutable. It seems worrisome, however, that, even in cases where serious interference with basic rights are under review, uncertainties in the evaluation of facts will burden the holder of the basic right. When the Federal Constitutional Court nevertheless denies a violation of the inviolability of the dignity of man as guaranteed by Article 1 sec 1 of the Constitution, [that decision] is based on the following reasons:

aa) Lifetime imprisonment finds its constitutionally necessary complement in a sensible execution of treatment. Penal institutions are obliged, even in the cases of life imprisonment, to promote the rehabilitation of the inmates. * * * These obligations for the execution of the penal sanctions are based on the Constitution, they can be derived from the inviolability of the dignity of man as guaranteed by Article 1 sec 1 of the Constitution. * * *

The court has emphasized several times that the demand to achieve a reintegration into society [of the criminals] is constitutionally consistent with the self-understanding of a community which put human dignity at its center and which is committed to the principle of social justice. The prisoner's interest in the reintegration into society flows from Article 1 of the Constitution in relation with Article 2 sec 1. of the Constitution. The condemned offender must be granted the chance to reenter the community after having atoned for his crime. It is the duty of the state to take all possible measures it can [reasonably] be expected to bear, which are useful and necessary to achieve this goal of the execution of the criminal penalty.

If one assumes that even [the criminal] sentenced to life imprisonment must principally be granted a possibility to regain his freedom, then he must also have a right to be prepared to reenter the society, even if he will only after a long period of atonement for his crime have the possibility to be obliged to handle a life in freedom. * * *

bb) * * * The assessment of the constitutionality of lifetime imprisonment especially with references to Article 1 sec 1 of the Constitution and the principle of the rule of law (*Rechtsstaatsprinzip*) revealed that a humane execution of the lifetime imprisonment can only be assured if the sentenced criminal has a concrete and principally attainable possibility to regain freedom at a later point in time; for the core of human dignity is struck if the convicted criminal has to give up any hope of regaining his freedom no matter how his personality develops. In order to assure this perspective [to regain freedom at some point in the future], which is the prerequisite for rendering lifetime imprisonment bearable according to the [Court's] understanding of human dignity, in a manner which meets constitutional requirements, the [current] legal rules of parole are not sufficient.

Notes and Questions

1. *Standards.* Compare the underlying rationales for criminal sentencing in the German and Canadian cases above. In particular, are the rights at issue in life imprisonment understood differently? Is the Canadian Court's approach to sentencing in *Latimer*, emphasizing the interest of public safety, consistent with the constitutional guarantee of respect for the dignity of the individual understood by German jurisprudence as a prohibition against the "use of a person as a means to an end"? Note that in matters of criminal sentencing, traditional common law is not troubled by dignity concerns:

> When the following conditions are satisfied, a sentence of life imprisonment is in our opinion justified: (1) where the offence or offences are in themselves grave enough to require a very long sentence; (2) where it appears from the nature of the offences or from the defendant's history that he is a person of unstable character likely to commit such offences in the future; and (3) where if the offences are committed the consequences to others may be specially injurious, as in the case of sexual offences or crimes of violence. [These conditions] justify an indeterminate life sentence. The Home Secretary has of course the power to release the appellant on licence when it is thought safe to release him, if that time comes.

> *Reg. v. Hodgson*, 52 Crim. App. R. 113, 114 (1967).

Would the British conditions for a sentence of life imprisonment satisfy the German constitutional standard? Is there a significant difference in the way criminal sentencing is considered in countries where dignity is explicitly recognized as a constitutional right?

2. *Dignity.* The GFCC's strongly Kantian approach to life imprisonment has considerable following around the world. The Namibian Supreme Court has stated:

> In *S v. Tcoeib* [1993 (1) SACR 274] at 300a, MAHOMED CJ had this in mind when he said that if life imprisonment in the Namibian context would mean detention for the rest of the prisoner's natural life it would be unconstitutional because without hope of release the prisoner is reduced to a thing and stripped of all dignity. The acceptance by Parliament of these Conventions as well as the First Optional Protocol to the ICCPR is a continued expression of and confirmation of the high norms and values of the Namibian people as contained in the Constitution and expressed by other institutions. * * * I respectfully agree with what was stated in these cases. To imprison a person would in many respects invade his or her right and also the right to dignity but these inroads are the necessary result of the incarceration and are sanctioned by the Constitution, article 7. That does not mean that a prisoner can be regarded as a person without dignity.

> *Namunjepo and Others v. Commanding Officer, Windhoek Prison,* 2000 (6) BCLR 671 (NmS).

This language suggests that inroads into the right to dignity might be acceptable, provided its core is untouched. At what point is the core of human dignity struck? According to the German ruling cited above, the answer to this question is "if the convicted criminal has to give up any hope of regaining his freedom no matter how his personality develops." This ruling suggests that the right to dignity includes the right to incarceration under conditions in which rehabilitation is promoted. Does this constitute a broader conception of dignity than that which underlies the prohibition against capital punishment?

3. *Equality.* Considerations on the constitutionality of punishment may arise on the basis of equality concerns, whether or not a question of dignity is directly raised. Consider the USSC's decision in *Skinner v. Oklahoma*, 316 U.S. 535 (1942), which upheld the sterilization of habitual criminals on equal protection grounds without reference to any violation of dignity. See also the Israeli Supreme Court's decision in *Public Committee Against Torture in Israel, et al. v. The State of Israel, The General Security Service, et al.* in Chapter 9. In a case before the SACC, *S. v. Niemand*, 2002 (1) SALR 21 (CC), the appellant, deemed an habitual criminal, contested the constitutionality of a section of the Criminal Procedure Act 51 of 1977 (the CPA) which, read in conjunction with a section of the Correctional Services Act 8 of 1959 (the CSA), stipulated that an habitual criminal must serve a minimum of seven years in prison before being considered for parole. Justice Madala wrote:

[6.]   The argument on behalf of Mr. Niemand was that being declared an habitual criminal violates the fundamental right to be sentenced by a court of law. In the case of persons declared habitual criminals, the duration of their sentence is determined by the parole board and the Commissioner of Correctional Services, these being members of the executive branch of government. Such punishment or treatment is also cruel, inhuman or degrading and violates the provisions of section 12(1)(e) of the Constitution and it unfairly discriminates between habitual criminals and dangerous criminals. Furthermore, the appellant contends that his right of access to court [guaranteed expressly in Art. 34 of the Constitution] has been violated in consequence of such declaration. Less restrictive means could have been adopted to protect society from criminals and therefore the challenged provisions should be struck down.

[7.]   The state argued that such a sentence is not literally indeterminate—implicitly its maximum period is fifteen years. The sentence means imprisonment for a minimum of seven and a maximum of fifteen years, so it was argued. Although no such maximum period was prescribed by the legislation, the Department of Correctional Services has a practice in terms of which no habitual criminal is incarcerated for a period exceeding 15 years. It was further submitted that the parole board and the Commissioner are well qualified and best suited to determine parole eligibility. In any event the exercise of their powers and duties is legislatively prescribed and subject to judicial review. However, should the sentence be found to infringe the rights in question, it is justifiable in terms of section 36 of the Constitution, there being no less restrictive means available to serve the purpose for which it is intended.

Id.

Does a policy of an administrative agency to grant parole after a certain number of years meet the legal requirement of a determinate sentence? Or is a court sentence required? Is such broad administrative power consistent with the conceptions of dignity outlined above? What are the implications for the rule of law? Compare with *Morrison v. Olson* and *Hinds v. The Queen* in Chapter 3. Consider also that German constitutional doctrine requires a parliamentary decision on all matters of decisive relevance to fundamental rights (*"Wesentlichkeitstheorie"*), as does much due process doctrine around the world. What would such doctrine require in the South African case?

4. *Balancing other rights*. The GFCC held in the *Lebach Case*, 35 BVerfGE 202 (1973), that a quasi-documentary about a murder could not be broadcast on television, in order to safeguard the dignity of the murderer by preserving the possibility of his reintegration into society after serving his sentence. Is this consideration sufficient to justify limiting the freedom of the media? Are there other considerations or interests—for instance, deterrence or prevention of crime, debatable as they are—that might take priority over dignity concerns? On free speech, see also Chapter 7.

5. *International law*. The Rome Statute, U.N. Doc. A/Conf.183/9 (1998) (entered into force July 1, 2002), governing the International Criminal Court, allows for the imposition of life imprisonment, "when justified by the extreme gravity of the crime and the individual circumstances of the convicted person." (Article 77 (1)(b). The Statute of the International Tribunal for Rwanda excludes the death sentence, penal servitude or a fine and, in Rule 101 (A), provides that "a convicted person may be sentenced to imprisonment for a term up to and including the remainder of his life." Is this compatible with Canadian constitutional requirements? Is it compatible with the constitutional doctrine of Germany, which ratified the statute? Do you think that sentences of life imprisonment are acceptable—from a fundamental rights point of view—if there is a mandatory review process, like that provided for in Art. 110 of the Rome Statute, which obliges the court to "review the sentence to determine whether it should be reduced" after a period of 25 years has been served?

B. SOURCES OF PRIVACY RIGHTS

This section deals with problems often adjudicated under the right of privacy, a somewhat controversial right that has been widely invoked in different forms across constitutional traditions and in a broad array of cases. Across the globe, privacy cases seem to arise around issues closely connected to gender equality as well as to sexuality. Though highly relevant to people's lives, a right to privacy is rarely manifest in constitutional text and is not recognized in the common law. In addition, it has been criticized by some feminists for reinscribing the subordination of women and by judicial conservatives as a product of illegitimate judicial activism. We discuss the landmark ruling on the "right to privacy" in the U.S. and then move to other decisions which enlarge that perspective. The USSC relies on the "penumbras" of several other specific guarantees in order to derive the privacy right, which has no textual basis in the U.S. Constitution.

GRISWOLD v. CONNECTICUT

Supreme Court (United States).
381 U.S. 479 (1965).

[A challenge was brought against a law that prohibited the use or assisting the use of contraceptives. We also discuss this case in Chapter 2, and quote here only from Justice Stewart's majority opinion to highlight the privacy arguments.]

Mr. Justice Douglas delivered the opinion of the Court.

* * * [S]pecific guarantees in the Bill of Rights have penumbras, formed by emanations from those guarantees that help give them life and substance. See *Poe v. Ullman*, 367 U.S. 497, 516–522, (dissenting opinion). Various guarantees create zones of privacy. The right of association contained in the penumbra of the First Amendment is one, as we have seen. The Third Amendment in its prohibition against the quartering of soldiers 'in any house' in time of peace without the consent of the owner is another facet of that privacy. The Fourth Amendment explicitly affirms the 'right of the people to be secure in their persons, houses, papers, and effects, against unreasonable searches and seizures.' The Fifth Amendment in its Self–Incrimination Clause enables the citizen to create a zone of privacy which government may not force him to surrender to his detriment. The Ninth Amendment provides: 'The enumeration in the Constitution, of certain rights, shall not be construed to deny or disparage others retained by the people.'

The Fourth and Fifth Amendments were described as protection against all governmental invasions 'of the sanctity of a man's home and the privacies of life.' * * *

We have had many controversies over these penumbral rights of 'privacy and repose.' These cases bear witness that the right of privacy which presses for recognition here is a legitimate one.

The present case, then, concerns a relationship lying within the zone of privacy created by several fundamental constitutional guarantees. * * * Such a law cannot stand in light of the familiar principle, so often applied by this Court, that a 'governmental purpose to control or prevent activities constitutionally subject to state regulation may not be achieved by means which sweep unnecessarily broadly and thereby invade the area of protected freedoms.'

Mr. Justice Black [joined by Justice Stewart] dissenting.

* * * The Court talks about a constitutional "right of privacy" as though there is some constitutional provision or provisions forbidding any law ever to be passed which might abridge the "privacy" of individuals. But there is not. There are, of course, guarantees in certain specific constitutional provisions which are designed in part to protect privacy at certain times and places with respect to certain activities. * * *

One of the most effective ways of diluting or expanding a constitutionally guaranteed right is to substitute for the crucial word or words of a constitutional guarantee another word or words, more or less flexible and more or less restricted in meaning. This fact is well illustrated by the use of the term "right of privacy" as a comprehensive substitute for * * * "unreasonable searches and seizures." "Privacy" is a broad, abstract and ambiguous concept which can easily be shrunken in meaning but which can also, on the other hand, easily be interpreted as a constitutional ban against many things other than searches and seizures. * * * I like my privacy as well as the next one, but I am nevertheless compelled to admit that government has a right to. invade it unless prohibited by some specific constitutional provision. * * *

Notes and Questions

1. *Does the text matter?* In 1937, the Australian High Court pointed out (in *Victoria Park Racing and Recreation Grounds Co., Ltd. v. Taylor*, 58 C.L.R. 479), that the common law does not recognize a right to privacy. Can courts in common or civil law systems still recognize it, even if it is not part of the constitutional text? The U.S. Constitution, like the Irish and the French, does not contain an explicit privacy provision. The French Constitutional Council, like the Australian High Court, held that such a right does not exist (Cons. const., Jan. 18, 1995, D. 1997, Somm., 121, *note Tremeau*, CC 94–352, 1995). However, the Council does accept a constitutional right to protection of the home (*Finance Law Case for 1984*, Cons. const., Dec. 19, 1983, A.D.J.A. 1984, 97, *note Philip*, CC 83–164, 1983). International covenants were later brought to bear, when France was found to have violated the privacy provision of the European HR Convention in a case on phonetapping (*Kruslin v. France*, 12 E.H.R.R. 547 (1990)). And, more recently, the French Constitutional Council held that the Constitution requires a statutory basis for searches (Cons. const., July 27, 2000, D. 2001(23), Somm., 1838, *note Jacquinot*, CC 2000–433). Note that the Council has not considered the protection of family relations a constitutional issue: "[it] is for the legislature to determine the terms under which the rights of the family can be reconciled with requirements of the public interest." (*Entry and Residence of Foreigners*, Cons. Const., Sept. 3, 1986, 86–216 DC, para 10.) Can the position of the Council be explained as judicial restraint? Should the decision in *Griswold*, in which the USSC accepted a right to privacy, be considered excessive judicial activism? Does any attempt to find protection for fundamental values that have no explicit basis in constitutional text or history amount to judicial activism? How perfect can constitutions be as guides to government? Is there a difference between a young document and an old one?

Consider that the picture looks different if we shift from "privacy" to other constitutional bases for protecting individual rights. One constitutional scholar has commented, in reference to French jurisprudence, that "the development of a general principle of general freedom may provide a more solid foundation for the idea of privacy as a constitutional value." John Bell, *French Constitutional Law* 148 (1992). In the UK, it was held that no right to privacy existed (*Kaye v. Robertson* [1991] F.S.R. 62 (C.A.)), yet interests called "private" are recognized in the courts. In Germany, free development of the person is the right on which fundamental interests can be based, if no more specific provision is applicable (*Elfes Case,* 6 BVerfGE 32 (1957)). Similarly, the Hungarian Constitutional Court (HCC) has provided for minimal protection to "persons with equal dignity," in the absence of infringement of an explicit constitutional right.

The Puerto Rican Supreme Court implied in a holding on rights to divorce that the right to privacy may be enforced between private as well as against public actors. A provision of the Puerto Rican Civil Code that prohibited men and women from obtaining a divorce on "mutual consent" grounds was declared unconstitutional. The Court held that the provision violated the right to privacy of couples who were conscious of the inexorable rupture of a matrimonial bond but who refused to discuss, and perhaps lie about, their intimate relations in order to fall under one of the fault grounds established by the Civil Code. The Court went on to say that the state cannot violate the couple's protected "zone of privacy" in the absence of a compelling state interest and that "the Constitution of the Commonwealth of Puerto Rico embraces the right of all Puerto Ricans to protect their dignity and private life in divorce proceedings by means of mutually expressing their decision of obtaining a divorce." *Figueroa Ferrer v. E.L.A.*, 107 P.R. Dec. 250, 276 (1978). The Court referred to the intent of the framers of the Constitution but also based the decision on the primacy of the principle of human dignity. This is very much in line with the South African decision in *Carmichele* (see Chapter 10).

What are the best possible bases on which courts can protect fundamental interests? In a case dealing with the right to a hearing when dismissed from public service, a Kuala Lumpur, Malaysia, court, in *Lembaga Tatatertib Perkhidmatan Awam, Hospital Besar Pulau Pinang v. Utra Badi a [sol] l K Perumal*, Court of Appeal, Kuala Lumpur (2000) 3 M.L.J. 281, stated, per Judge Sri Ram Gopal: "When a person is deprived of his reputation, it would amount to a deprivation of 'life' within art. 5(1) of the Federal Constitution. The right to reputation is part and parcel of human dignity. * * * The combined effect of arts. 5(1) and 8(1) of the Federal Constitution is to demand fairness both in procedure and in substance whenever a public law decision has an adverse effect on any of the facets of a person's life. Among these facets are a person's livelihood and his reputation." (Overruled by the Federal Court in 2001, 2001 WL 9513366). Note that the Court of Appeal came to this position relying on Indian precedents. Do you think the right to life or personal integrity is a source of a right to dignity or privacy? What does "life" mean in this context? Does this also protect against informational intrusion? Consider that the Australian Court, like other courts throughout the world, in *Johns v. Australian Securities Commission*, (1993) 178 C.L.R. 408, stated that information collected for one purpose may not be used for another purpose. Is that a privacy right? Is it a dignity interest? Also, consider that the GFCC held that a novel that "dishonors the good name and memory of a now-deceased famous actor" may be banned to protect personality rights, given the dignity interest involved (*Mephisto Case,* 30 BVerfGE 173 (1971) in Chapter 7). Recall, also, the Court's ruling in the *Lebach Case,* 35 BVerfGE 202 (1973), mentioned above. On what other rights can such protections be based?

Today, constitutions guarantee the equality of all citizens. However, it is possible that conflicts might arise between competing rights claims. Consider that most constitutions protect the home from arbitrary search and seizure. Is there, then, a territory in which one might not be protected against threats to dignity or autonomy? Alternatively, the Hong Kong Court of First Instance held, in a case dealing with the poor pay of domestic workers: "any right thinking member of our civilised society must regard such a wage an affront to justice and insult to human dignity." *Andayani v. Chan Oi Ling,*

(2001) 1 H.K.C. 252. The Court argued that domestic workers are in especially dependent and vulnerable positions. Does dignity then limit freedom of contract? Or is there a hierarchy of rights in which freedom trumps dignity?

2. *A right to privacy—a constitutional right against private action?* The definitions of privacy do not tell us against whom privacy rights are directed. Are they directed exclusively at the state, or are they meant to restrict private actors as well? Are fundamental privacy rights, especially those that apply in the home, endangered only by state intervention, or also, and possibly more so, by private actors? Consider that the SACC, in *Carmichele v. Ministers of Safety and Security and of Justice and Constitutional Development*, 2001 (1) SALR 489 (CC), held that public authorities have a duty to actively protect a woman in her home from sexual violence by a known offender, by providing sufficient information to decide on refusal of bail. Compare this to *DeShaney* in Chapter 10, Section C. This position has been endorsed by the ECHR in *Osman v. United Kingdom*, 29 E.H.R.R. 245 (1998) at 305, para 115: "the Convention may also imply in certain well-defined circumstances a positive obligation on the authorities to take preventive operational measures to protect an individual whose life is at risk from the criminal acts of another individual." The GFCC, in its first decision on abortion, below, established a duty on the part of the legislature to act in "all areas of the law." "The jurisprudence of the Federal Constitutional Court is consistently to the effect that the basic right norms contain not only defensive subjective rights for the individual but embody at the same time an objective value system which, as a fundamental constitutional value for all areas of the law, acts as a guiding principle and stimulus for the legislature, executive and judiciary." (39 BVerfGE 1, 41).

However, the USSC has been of a different opinion following the "state action" doctrine (see Chapter 10), according to which constitutional rights are understood to be violated only by governmental action. Is this requirement modified in cases in which fundamental interests of a person, like privacy or dignity, are at issue? Consider *Palmore v. Sidoti*, 466 U.S. 429 (1984), in which the Court held as unconstitutional a decision to take a white child away from a white mother after she had married a black man. The Court stated: "[Private] biases may be outside the reach of the law, but the law cannot, directly or indirectly, give them effect." *Id.* at 433. See also *Shelley v. Kraemer*, 334 U.S. 1 (1948), in which private racist agreements are held to violate the equal protection clause of the U.S. Constitution (see Chapter 10).

3. *The "home" and expectations.* Privacy has traditionally been associated with the home. Thus constitutions often explicitly protect the home against search and seizure, which might be understood as the territorial aspect of privacy. How is this territorial dimension to be understood? Do homeless people have a sphere of privacy in which they are protected? Do employees have a sphere of privacy in the workplace? Are places where people stay against their will, like prisons, protected as "home"? The USSC defines privacy as the sphere in which one can justifiably expect to be left alone. In *Hudson v. Palmer*, 468 U.S. 517, 523 (1984), the Court (Chief Justice Burger) stated, in a case brought by a prisoner against searches of his cell, that:

[We] have repeatedly held that prisons are not beyond the reach of the Constitution. No "iron curtain" separates one from the other. *Wolff v. McDonnell*, 418 U.S. 539, 555 (1974). Indeed, we have insisted that prisoners be accorded those rights not fundamentally inconsistent with imprisonment itself or incompatible with the objectives of incarceration. * * * [It] is also clear that imprisonment carries with it the circumscription or loss of many significant rights. [The] curtailment of certain rights is necessary, as a practical matter, to accommodate a myriad of "institutional needs and objectives" of prison facilities. *Wolff v. McDonnell, supra,* at 555, * * * We must determine here * * * if a "justifiable" expectation of privacy is at stake. * * * [We] hold that society is not prepared to recognize as legitimate any subjective expectation of privacy that a prisoner might have in his prison cell and that, accordingly, the [constitutional] proscription against unreasonable searches does not apply within the confines of the prison cell. The recognition of privacy rights for prisoners in their individual cells simply cannot be reconciled with the concept of incarceration and the needs and objectives of penal institutions.

In response to a complaint by a prisoner that his letters to a civil rights organization were intercepted by prison administrators, the GFCC, in *Prison Correspondence I,* 33 BVerfGE 1 (1973), ruled that a prisoner's rights may be curtailed but only based on legislative action rather than merely administrative power. In this case procedure protects fundamental rights: "It would contravene this encompassing restriction of all state power if prison conditions could be set arbitrarily or at free will. A restriction of rights is only conceivable if it is intended and necessary to reach a social end which is legitimate under the value order of the constitution, and which is acted out in the constitutionally required form."

The European Commission, in *Silver v. United Kingdom*, 3 E.H.R.R. 475, 500 (1980), held that protection of fundamental rights includes respect for private correspondence but that "a balance" must be struck "between the legitimate interests of public order and security," on the one hand, and "the rehabilitation of prisoners," on the other. At what point can speech be considered a threat to prison security?

When U.S. courts hold that privacy is protected only against invasions that one can reasonably expect would not occur, who defines "reasonableness"? If there is a systematic practice of police surveillance, can one nonetheless "reasonably expect" to have one's privacy respected? Does protection of certain fundamental rights rely on the social policies that themselves have the potential to violate such rights?

Consider the ambivalence of the protection of privacy in private places like the home. "[S]laves and servants, as well as women and children, have, in all legal traditions (and in some legal systems still), been legally considered property of the head of the household (*pater familias*), rather than persons. To the extent the household was protected, legal rules accepted the domination and abuse in the privacy of the household." Scholar Anita Allen has commented that "[w]omen have had too much privacy, in the form of confinement in their homes and imposed standards of modesty and reserve; but they have had too little privacy in the form of opportunities for replenishing solitude and independent decisionmaking." Anita L. Allen, *Gender and Privacy in Cyberspace*, 52 Stanford L. Rev. 1175, 1179 (2000).

The USSC held that there is a right to consume pornography in private, *Stanley v. Georgia*, 394 U.S. 557 (1969), while others have argued that pornography violates the rights of people, particularly the rights of women and children. See Catharine A. MacKinnon, *Sex Equality* 1532–1626 (2001). The Court stated that "the makers of our Constitution undertook to secure conditions favorable to the pursuit of happiness." Whose happiness counts? Against what other rights should this happiness be balanced? And is pornography about "happiness"? Consider that the SACC, in *Curtis v. The Minister of Safety and Security and others*, 1996 (3) SALR 617 (CC), with reference to the Canadian decision *R. v. Butler*, [1992] 1 S.C.R. 452, argued that pornography should not be viewed from "a public-morality basis that underpins the American approach," but rather judged according to "a standard based explicitly on the harm believed to be engendered by certain kinds of sexually explicit material." The Court, nonetheless, upheld its use in private. Remember that some crimes, particularly those committed against children and women, many of which are sexual in nature, are committed at home. Should this make a difference in considering the inviolability of privacy rights?

4. *"Private parts."* Places that can be considered private, where searches have to be based on law and be justifiable, are clearly not limited to the home and the prison cell. But does the constitutional protection of privacy extend to the body, to one's "private parts"? In the U.S., it was held that, although vaginal searches "give us cause for concern as they implicate and threaten the highest degree of dignity," after balancing all factors, they did not constitute a violation of privacy, since "the search was not unreasonable by its very nature." *Rodriques v. Furtado*, 950 F.2d 805 (1st Cir.1991). Is a right to dignity at stake here as well, or is this a violation of physical integrity? The USSC also held that surgery may constitute a potentially unconstitutional search in *Winston v. Lee*, 470 U.S. 753 (1985). Consider the constitutional requirements necessary to permit such intrusions. If one can consent to surgery, can one consent to a search of one's house or car in a criminal investigation? If a legal system accepts implied consent in medical cases, does it have to accept implied consent to police activities, or is there a difference? How do you know whether someone has "consented" freely to a violation of privacy? Can one voluntarily forfeit one's privacy? Can one consent to the abridgement of a fundamental right?

C. THE RIGHT TO BODILY SELF–DETERMINATION

Cases on dignity, autonomy, and privacy do not deal only with territorial understandings of constitutional protection but also with decisional aspects of personhood. The right to bodily self-determination—the right to dispose of one's body as one chooses—is an integral component of this. The following cases illustrate that the private is not restricted to the literal space of the home but extends to the private body as well. This is supported by a strong philosophical and jurisprudential tradition that understands autonomy in terms of ownership of one's body. Western thinking tends toward the position that human beings have a broad individual right to make decisions on matters with profound consequences for one's body and one's life. Thus we find the right to privacy prominently in the so-called Biomedicine Convention, the

"Convention for the Protection of Human Rights and Dignity of the Human Being with regard to the Application of Biology and Medicine: Convention on Human Rights and Biomedicine" (Oviedo, 4.IV.1997), a European international treaty that seeks to complement the European HR Convention in an effort to protect the dignity and identity of all human beings without discrimination. See H.D.C. Roscam Abbing, *The Convention on Human Rights and Biomedicine: An Appraisal of the Council of Europe Convention*, European Journal of Health Law 377–87 (1998). But where are the limits of this kind of self-determination? Grand theories often ignore that a right to one's body is bound to social status, race, and gender. In addition, the tradition of self-ownership may, for example, conflict with conceptions of life and the body which stem from theoretical frameworks that view life as a given, either by nature or some metaphysical force, as in certain theological traditions. The long-standing and controversial debates about reproductive rights, at the forefront of which is the right to an abortion, raise these issues in complex ways, which is why we discuss them first. More recently, related questions have arisen around whether, given that one cannot take the life of another person, one has a legal right to take one's own life. Since suicide is not prohibited in most jurisdictions, these cases revolve around the issue of assisted suicide.

C.1. ABORTION

ROE v. WADE

Supreme Court (United States).
410 U.S. 113 (1973).

[A pregnant woman and others challenged the constitutionality of a statute making a crime to "procure an abortion" except "by medical advice for the purpose of saving the life of the mother."]

Justice Blackmun delivered the opinion of the Court.

* * * We forthwith acknowledge our awareness of the sensitive and emotional nature of the abortion controversy, of the vigorous opposing views, even among physicians, and of the deep and seemingly absolute convictions that the subject inspires. One's philosophy, one's experiences, one's exposure to the raw edges of human existence, one's religious training, one's attitudes toward life and family and their values, and the moral standards one establishes and seeks to observe, are all likely to influence and to color one's thinking and conclusions about abortion.

In addition, population growth, pollution, poverty, and racial overtones tend to complicate and not to simplify the problem. * * *

The principal thrust of appellant's attack on the Texas statutes is that they improperly invade a right, said to be possessed by the pregnant woman, to choose to terminate her pregnancy. * * *

The Constitution does not explicitly mention any right of privacy. In a line of decisions, however, * * * [the] Court has recognized that a right of personal privacy, * * * does exist under the Constitution. [Based on precedents] only personal rights that can be deemed "fundamental" or "implicit in the concept of ordered liberty," *Palko v. Connecticut*, 302 U.S. 319, 325 (1937), are included in this guarantee of personal privacy. They also make it clear that the right has some extension to activities relating to marriage * * *; procreation * * *; contraception * * *; family relationships * * *; and childrearing and education * * *.

This right of privacy, whether it be founded in the Fourteenth Amendment's concept of personal liberty and restrictions upon state action, as we feel it is, or [in] the Ninth Amendment's reservation of rights to the people, is broad enough to encompass a woman's decision whether or not to terminate her pregnancy. The detriment that the State would impose upon the pregnant woman by denying this choice altogether is apparent. Specific and direct harm medically diagnosable even in early pregnancy may be involved. Maternity, or additional offspring, may force upon the woman a distressful life and future. Psychological harm may be imminent. Mental and physical health may be taxed by child care. There is also the distress, for all concerned, associated with the unwanted child, and there is the problem of bringing a child into a family already unable, psychologically and otherwise, to care for it. In other cases, as in this one, the additional difficulties and continuing stigma of unwed motherhood may be involved. All these are factors the woman and her responsible physician necessarily will consider in consultation.

On the basis of elements such as these, appellant and some amici argue that the woman's right is absolute and that she is entitled to terminate her pregnancy at whatever time, in whatever way, and for whatever reason she alone chooses. With this we do not agree. * * * [The] Court's decisions recognizing a right of privacy also acknowledge that some state regulation in areas protected by that right is appropriate. * * * [A] State may properly assert important interests in safeguarding health, in maintaining medical standards, and in protecting potential life. At some point in pregnancy, these respective interests become sufficiently compelling to sustain regulation of the factors that govern the abortion decision. The privacy right involved, therefore, cannot be said to be absolute. In fact, it is not clear to us that the claim asserted by some *amici* that one has an unlimited right to do with one's body as one pleases bears a close relationship to the right of privacy previously articulated in the Court's decisions. The Court has refused to recognize an unlimited right of this kind in the past [in cases on vaccination and sterilization]. We, therefore, conclude that the right of personal privacy includes the abortion decision, but that this right is not unqualified, and must be considered against important state interests in regulation.

PLANNED PARENTHOOD OF SOUTHEASTERN PENNSYLVANIA v. CASEY

Supreme Court (United States).
505 U.S. 833 (1992).

Justice O'Connor, Justice Kennedy, and Justice Souter delivered the judgment of the Court and the opinion of the Court with respect to Parts I, II, III, V–A, V–C and VI, and an opinion with respect to other Parts.

I

Liberty finds no refuge in a jurisprudence of doubt. Yet 19 years after our holding that the Constitution protects a woman's right to terminate her pregnancy in its early stages, *Roe v. Wade* 410 U.S. 113, that definition of liberty is still questioned. * * *

At issue in these cases are five provisions of the Pennsylvania Abortion Control Act of 1982, as amended in 1988 and 1989.

* * * *Roe*'s essential holding, the holding we reaffirm, has three parts. First is a recognition of the right of the woman to choose to have an abortion before viability and to obtain it without undue interference from the State. Before viability, the State's interests are not strong enough to support a prohibition of abortion or the imposition of a substantial obstacle to the woman's effective right to elect the procedure. Second is a confirmation of the State's power to restrict abortions after fetal viability, if the law contains exceptions for pregnancies which endanger the woman's life or health. And third is the principle that the State has legitimate interests from the outset of the pregnancy in protecting the health of the woman and the life of the fetus that may become a child. These principles do not contradict one another; and we adhere to each.

II

Constitutional protection of the woman's decision to terminate her pregnancy derives from the Due Process Clause of the Fourteenth Amendment. It declares that no State shall "deprive any person of life, liberty, or property, without due process of law." * * *

It is also tempting, for the same reason, to suppose that the Due Process Clause protects only those practices, defined at the most specific level, that were protected against government interference by other rules of law when the Fourteenth Amendment was ratified. See *Michael H. v. Gerald D.*, 491 U.S. 110, 127–128, n. 6 (1989) (opinion of SCALIA, J.). But such a view would be inconsistent with our law. It is a promise of the Constitution that there is a realm of personal liberty which the government may not enter. * * *

Neither the Bill of Rights nor the specific practices of States at the time of the adoption of the Fourteenth Amendment marks the outer limits of the substantive sphere of liberty which the Fourteenth Amendment protects. See U.S. Const., Amdt. 9. As the second Justice Harlan recognized:

"[T]he full scope of the liberty guaranteed by the Due Process Clause cannot be found in or limited by the precise terms of the specific guarantees elsewhere provided in the Constitution. This 'liberty' is not a series of isolated points pricked out in terms of the taking of property; the freedom of speech, press, and religion; the right to keep and bear arms; the freedom from unreasonable searches and seizures; and so on. It is a rational continuum which, broadly speaking, includes a freedom from all substantial arbitrary impositions and purposeless restraints, . . . and which also recognizes, what a reasonable and sensitive judgment must, that certain interests require particularly careful scrutiny of the state needs asserted to justify their abridgment." *Poe v. Ullman, supra,* [367 U.S.,] at 543, (opinion dissenting from dismissal on jurisdictional grounds).

Justice Harlan wrote as follows on an issue the full Court did not reach in *Poe v. Ullman,* but the Court adopted his position four Terms later in *Griswold v. Connecticut, supra.* * * *

Men and women of good conscience can disagree, and we suppose some always shall disagree, about the profound moral and spiritual implications of terminating a pregnancy, even in its earliest stage. Some of us as individuals find abortion offensive to our most basic principles of morality, but that cannot control our decision. Our obligation is to define the liberty of all, not to mandate our own moral code. The underlying constitutional issue is whether the State can resolve these philosophic questions in such a definitive way that a woman lacks all choice in the matter, except perhaps in those rare circumstances in which the pregnancy is itself a danger to her own life or health, or is the result of rape or incest.

* * * Our cases recognize "the right of the individual, married or single, to be free from unwarranted governmental intrusion into matters so fundamentally affecting a person as the decision whether to bear or beget a child." *Eisenstadt v. Baird, supra,* [405 U.S.,] at 453. * * * At the heart of liberty is the right to define one's own concept of existence, of meaning, of the universe, and of the mystery of human life. Beliefs about these matters could not define the attributes of personhood were they formed under compulsion of the State.

These considerations begin our analysis of the woman's interest in terminating her pregnancy but cannot end it, for this reason: though the abortion decision may originate within the zone of conscience and belief, it is more than a philosophic exercise. Abortion is a unique act. It is an act fraught with consequences for others: for the woman who must live with the implications of her decision; for the persons who perform and assist in the procedure; for the spouse, family, and society which must confront the knowledge that these procedures exist, procedures some deem nothing short of an act of violence against innocent human life; and, depending on one's beliefs, for the life or potential life that is aborted. Though abortion is conduct, it does not follow that the State is entitled to proscribe it in all instances. That is because the liberty of the woman is at stake in a sense unique to the human condition and so unique to the law. The mother who carries a child to full term is subject to anxieties, to physical constraints, to pain that only she must bear. That these sacrifices have from the beginning of the human race been endured by woman with a pride that ennobles her in the eyes of others and gives to the infant a bond of love cannot alone be grounds for the State to insist she make the sacrifice. Her suffering is too intimate and personal for the State to insist, without more, upon its own vision of the woman's role, however dominant that vision has been in the course of our history and our culture. The destiny of the woman must be shaped to a large extent on her own conception of her spiritual imperatives and her place in society.

* * * [M]oreover * * * in some critical respects the abortion decision is of the same character as the decision to use contraception, to which *Griswold v. Connecticut*, *Eisenstadt v. Baird*, and *Carey v. Population Services International* afford constitutional protection. * * *

* * * We have seen how time has overtaken some of *Roe*'s factual assumptions: advances in maternal health care allow for abortions safe to the mother later in pregnancy than was true in 1973, * * * and advances in neonatal care have advanced viability to a point somewhat earlier. * * * But these facts go only to the scheme of time limits on the realization of competing interests, and the divergences from the factual premises of 1973 have no bearing on the validity of *Roe*'s central holding, that viability marks the earliest point at which the State's interest in fetal life is constitutionally adequate to justify a legislative ban on nontherapeutic abortions. The soundness or unsoundness of that constitutional judgment in no sense turns on whether viability occurs at approximately 28 weeks, as was usual at the time of *Roe*, at 23 to 24 weeks, as it sometimes does today, or at some moment even slightly earlier in pregnancy, as it may if fetal respiratory capacity can somehow be enhanced in the future. Whenever it may occur, the attainment of viability may continue to serve as the critical fact, just as it has done since *Roe* was decided; which is to say that no change in *Roe*'s factual underpinning has left its central holding obsolete, and none supports an argument for overruling it.

* * * The country's loss of confidence in the Judiciary [resulting from the disregard of precedent in this case] would be underscored by an equally certain and equally reasonable condemnation for another failing in overruling unnecessarily and under pressure. Some cost will be paid by anyone who approves or implements a constitutional decision where it is unpopular, or who refuses to work to undermine the decision or to force its reversal. The price may be criticism or ostracism, or it may be violence. * * * The promise of constancy, once given, binds its maker for as long as the power to stand by the decision survives and the understanding of the issue has not changed so fundamentally as to render the commitment obsolete. * * *

IV

* * * We conclude that the basic decision in *Roe* was based on a constitutional analysis which we cannot now repudiate. The woman's liberty is not so unlimited, however, that from the outset the State

cannot show its concern for the life of the unborn, and at a later point in fetal development the State's interest in life has sufficient force so that the right of the woman to terminate the pregnancy can be restricted.

* * * We conclude the line should be drawn at viability, so that before that time the woman has a right to choose to terminate her pregnancy. * * *

* * * [T]he concept of viability, as we noted in *Roe*, is the time at which there is a realistic possibility of maintaining and nourishing a life outside the womb, so that the independent existence of the second life can in reason and all fairness be the object of state protection that now overrides the rights of the woman. * * * Consistent with other constitutional norms, legislatures may draw lines which appear arbitrary without the necessity of offering a justification. But courts may not. * * *

On the other side of the equation is the interest of the State in the protection of potential life. * * *

* * * [I]t must be remembered that *Roe v. Wade* speaks with clarity in establishing not only the woman's liberty but also the State's "important and legitimate interest in potential life. * * *

Though the woman has a right to choose to terminate or continue her pregnancy before viability, it does not at all follow that the State is prohibited from taking steps to ensure that this choice is thoughtful and informed. Even in the earliest stages of pregnancy, the State may enact rules and regulations designed to encourage her to know that there are philosophic and social arguments of great weight that can be brought to bear in favor of continuing the pregnancy to full term and that there are procedures and institutions to allow adoption of unwanted children as well as a certain degree of state assistance if the mother chooses to raise the child herself. * * *

We reject the trimester framework, which we do not consider to be part of the essential holding of *Roe*. * * * The trimester framework suffers from these basic flaws: in its formulation it misconceives the nature of the pregnant woman's interest; and in practice it undervalues the State's interest in potential life, as recognized in *Roe*.

As our jurisprudence relating to all liberties save perhaps abortion has recognized, not every law which makes a right more difficult to exercise is, ipso facto, an infringement of that right. * * *

* * * Only where state regulation imposes an undue burden on a woman's ability to make this decision does the power of the State reach into the heart of the liberty protected by the Due Process Clause. * * *

* * * Not all burdens on the right to decide whether to terminate a pregnancy will be undue. In our view, the undue burden standard is the appropriate means of reconciling the State's interest with the woman's constitutionally protected liberty. * * *

* * * [W]e answer the question, left open in previous opinions discussing the undue burden formulation, whether a law designed to further the State's interest in fetal life which imposes an undue burden

on the woman's decision before fetal viability could be constitutional. * * * The answer is no.

Some guiding principles should emerge. What is at stake is the woman's right to make the ultimate decision, not a right to be insulated from all others in doing so. Regulations which do no more than create a structural mechanism by which the State, or the parent or guardian of a minor, may express profound respect for the life of the unborn are permitted, if they are not a substantial obstacle to the woman's exercise of the right to choose. See *infra*, at 899–900 (addressing Pennsylvania's parental consent requirement). Unless it has that effect on her right of choice, a state measure designed to persuade her to choose childbirth over abortion will be upheld if reasonably related to that goal. Regulations designed to foster the health of a woman seeking an abortion are valid if they do not constitute an undue burden. * * *

V

B

We next consider the informed consent requirement. 18 Pa. Cons. Stat. § 3205 (1990). Except in a medical emergency, the statute requires that at least 24 hours before performing an abortion a physician inform the woman of the nature of the procedure, the health risks of the abortion and of childbirth, and the "probable gestational age of the unborn child." The physician or a qualified nonphysician must inform the woman of the availability of printed materials published by the State describing the fetus and providing information about medical assistance for childbirth, information about child support from the father, and a list of agencies which provide adoption and other services as alternatives to abortion. An abortion may not be performed unless the woman certifies in writing that she has been informed of the availability of these printed materials and has been provided them if she chooses to view them.

Our prior decisions establish that as with any medical procedure, the State may require a woman to give her written informed consent to an abortion. * * * In this respect, the statute is unexceptional. Petitioners challenge the statute's definition of informed consent because it includes the provision of specific information by the doctor and the mandatory 24–hour waiting period. The conclusions reached by a majority of the Justices in the separate opinions filed today and the undue burden standard adopted in this opinion require us to overrule in part some of the Court's past decisions, decisions driven by the trimester framework's prohibition of all previability regulations designed to further the State's interest in fetal life. * * *

* * * [R]equiring that the woman be informed of the availability of information relating to fetal development and the assistance available should she decide to carry the pregnancy to full term is a reasonable measure to ensure an informed choice, one which might cause the woman to choose childbirth over abortion. This requirement cannot be considered a substantial obstacle to obtaining an abortion, and, it follows, there is no undue burden.

* * * Whether the mandatory 24–hour waiting period is nonetheless invalid because in practice it is a substantial obstacle to a woman's choice to terminate her pregnancy is a closer question. The findings of fact by the District Court indicate that because of the distances many women must travel to reach an abortion provider, the practical effect will often be a delay of much more than a day because the waiting period requires that a woman seeking an abortion make at least two visits to the doctor. The District Court also found that in many instances this will increase the exposure of women seeking abortions * * *

* * * [A]s we have stated, under the undue burden standard a State is permitted to enact persuasive measures which favor childbirth over abortion, even if those measures do not further a health interest. And while the waiting period does limit a physician's discretion, that is not, standing alone, a reason to invalidate it. * * *

We are left with the argument that the various aspects of the informed consent requirement are unconstitutional because they place barriers in the way of abortion on demand. Even the broadest reading of *Roe*, however, has not suggested that there is a constitutional right to abortion on demand. * * * Rather, the right protected by *Roe* is a right to decide to terminate a pregnancy free of undue interference by the State. Because the informed consent requirement facilitates the wise exercise of that right, it cannot be classified as an interference with the right *Roe* protects. The informed consent requirement is not an undue burden on that right.

C

Section 3209 of Pennsylvania's abortion law provides, except in cases of medical emergency, that no physician shall perform an abortion on a married woman without receiving a signed statement from the woman that she has notified her spouse that she is about to undergo an abortion. * * *

* * * In well-functioning marriages, spouses discuss important intimate decisions such as whether to bear a child. But there are millions of women in this country who are the victims of regular physical and psychological abuse at the hands of their husbands. Should these women become pregnant, they may have very good reasons for not wishing to inform their husbands of their decision to obtain an abortion. * * * Many may fear devastating forms of psychological abuse from their husbands, including verbal harassment, threats of future violence, * * *

The spousal notification requirement is thus likely to prevent a significant number of women from obtaining an abortion. It does not merely make abortions a little more difficult or expensive to obtain; for many women, it will impose a substantial obstacle. We must not blind ourselves to the fact that the significant number of women who fear for their safety and the safety of their children are likely to be deterred from procuring an abortion as surely as if the Commonwealth had outlawed abortion in all cases. * * *

Chief Justice Rehnquist, with whom Justice White, Justice Scalia, and Justice Thomas join, concurring in the judgment in part and dissenting in part.

The joint opinion, following its newly minted variation on *stare decisis*, retains the outer shell of *Roe v. Wade*, 410 U.S. 113 (1973), but beats a wholesale retreat from the substance of that case. We believe that Roe was wrongly decided, and that it can and should be overruled consistently with our traditional approach to stare decisis in constitutional cases.

I

* * *

In arguing that this Court should invalidate each of the provisions at issue, petitioners insist that we reaffirm our decision in *Roe v. Wade*, *supra*, in which we held unconstitutional a Texas statute making it a crime to procure an abortion except to save the life of the mother.[a] * * * Although they reject the trimester framework that formed the underpinning of *Roe*, Justices O'CONNOR, KENNEDY, and SOUTER adopt a revised undue burden standard to analyze the challenged regulations. We conclude, however, that such an outcome is an unjustified constitutional compromise, one which leaves the Court in a position to closely scrutinize all types of abortion regulations despite the fact that it lacks the power to do so under the Constitution. * * *

* * * Unlike marriage, procreation, and contraception, abortion "involves the purposeful termination of a potential life." *Harris v. McRae*, 448 U.S. 297, 325 (1980). The abortion decision must therefore "be recognized as sui generis, different in kind from the others that the Court has protected under the rubric of personal or family privacy and autonomy." *Thornburgh v. American College of Obstetricians and Gynecologists*, *supra*, [476 U.S.,] at 792, (WHITE, J., dissenting). One cannot ignore the fact that a woman is not isolated in her pregnancy, and that the decision to abort necessarily involves the destruction of a fetus. See *Michael H. v. Gerald D.*, *supra*, [491 U.S.,] at 124, n. 4, (To look "at the act which is assertedly the subject of a liberty interest in isolation from its effect upon other people [is] like inquiring whether there is a liberty interest in firing a gun where the case at hand happens to involve its discharge into another person's body").

* * * Because the undue burden standard is plucked from nowhere, the question of what is a "substantial obstacle" to abortion will undoubtedly engender a variety of conflicting views. For example, in the very matter before us now, the authors of the joint opinion would uphold Pennsylvania's 24–hour waiting period, concluding that a "particular burden" on some women is not a substantial obstacle. * * * But the

a. Two years after *Roe*, the GFCC, by contrast, struck down a law liberalizing access to abortion on the grounds that life developing within the womb is constitutionally protected. *Judgment of February 25, 1975*, 39 BVerfGE 1 (translated in Robert Jonas and John Gorby, *West German Abortion Decision: A Contrast to* Roe v. Wade, 9 John Marshall J. Prac. & Proc. 605 (1976)). In 1988, the Canadian Supreme Court followed reasoning similar to that of *Roe* in striking down a law that restricted abortion. *R. v. Morgentaler*, 1 S.C.R. 30, 44 D.L.R. 4th 385 (1988).

authors would at the same time strike down Pennsylvania's spousal notice provision, after finding that in a "large fraction" of cases the provision will be a substantial obstacle. * * * And, while the authors conclude that the informed consent provisions do not constitute an "undue burden," * * *

Furthermore, while striking down the spousal *notice* regulation, the joint opinion would uphold a parental *consent* restriction that certainly places very substantial obstacles in the path of a minor's abortion choice. The joint opinion is forthright in admitting that it draws this distinction based on a policy judgment that parents will have the best interests of their children at heart, while the same is not necessarily true of husbands as to their wives. * * * This may or may not be a correct judgment, but it is quintessentially a legislative one. The "undue burden" inquiry does not in any way supply the distinction between parental consent and spousal consent which the joint opinion adopts. Despite the efforts of the joint opinion, the undue burden standard presents nothing more workable than the trimester framework which it discards today. Under the guise of the Constitution, this Court will still impart its own preferences on the States in the form of a complex abortion code.* * *

Justice Scalia, with whom The Chief Justice, Justice White, and Justice Thomas join, concurring in the judgment in part and dissenting in part.

* * * The States may, if they wish, permit abortion on demand, but the Constitution does not require them to do so. The permissibility of abortion, and the limitations upon it, are to be resolved like most important questions in our democracy: by citizens trying to persuade one another and then voting. * * *

That is, quite simply, the issue in these cases: not whether the power of a woman to abort her unborn child is a "liberty" in the absolute sense; or even whether it is a liberty of great importance to many women. Of course it is both. The issue is whether it is a liberty protected by the Constitution of the United States. I am sure it is not. I reach that conclusion not because of anything so exalted as my views concerning the "concept of existence, of meaning, of the universe, and of the mystery of human life." * * * Rather, I reach it for the same reason I reach the conclusion that bigamy is not constitutionally protected—because of two simple facts: (1) the Constitution says absolutely nothing about it, and (2) the longstanding traditions of American society have permitted it to be legally proscribed.[1]

---

1. The Court's suggestion, ante, at 847–848, that adherence to tradition would require us to uphold laws against interracial marriage is entirely wrong. Any tradition in that case was contradicted by a text—an Equal Protection Clause that explicitly establishes racial equality as a constitutional value. See *Loving v. Virginia*, 388 U.S. 1, 9 (1967) ("In the case at bar, . . . we deal with statutes containing racial classifications, and the fact of equal application does not immunize the statute from the very heavy burden of justification which the Fourteenth Amendment has traditionally required of state statutes drawn according to race"); see also *id.*, at 13 (STEWART, J., concurring in judgment). The enterprise launched in *Roe v. Wade*, 410 U.S. 113 (1973), by contrast, sought to establish—in the teeth of a clear, contrary tradition—a value found nowhere in the constitutional text * * *.

R. v. MORGENTALER

Supreme Court (Canada).
[1988] 1 S.C.R. 30.

Dickson, C.J.

The principal issue raised by this appeal is whether the abortion provisions of the *Criminal Code*, R.S.C. 1970, c. C–34, infringe the "right to life, liberty and security of the person and the right not to be deprived thereof except in accordance with the principles of fundamental justice" as formulated in s. 7 of the *Canadian Charter of Rights and Freedoms*. The appellants, Dr. Henry Morgentaler [and others], have raised thirteen distinct grounds of appeal. * * * It is submitted by the appellants that s. 251 of the *Criminal Code* contravenes s. 7 of the *Canadian Charter of Rights and Freedoms* and that s. 251 should be struck down.

* * * [It] remains true that this Court cannot presume to resolve all of the competing claims advanced in vigorous and healthy public debate. Courts and legislators in other democratic societies have reached completely contradictory decisions when asked to weigh the competing values relevant to the abortion question. See, e.g., *Roe v. Wade*, 410 U.S. 113 (1973); *Paton v. United Kingdom* (1980), 3 E.H.R.R. (European Court of Human Rights); *The Abortion Decision of the Federal Constitutional Court—First Senate—of the Federal Republic of Germany*, February 25, 1975, translated and reprinted in (1976), 9 John Marshall J. Prac. and Proc. 605; and the *Abortion Act, 1967*, 1967, c. 87 (U.K.)

But since 1975, and the first *Morgentaler* decision, the Court has been given added responsibilities. * * * Although no doubt it is still fair to say that courts are not the appropriate forum for articulating complex and controversial programmes of public policy, Canadian courts are now charged with the crucial obligation of ensuring that the legislative initiatives pursued by our Parliament and legislatures conform to the democratic values expressed in the *Canadian Charter of Rights and Freedoms*. * * *

III.   * * * The three appellants are all duly qualified medical practitioners who together set up a clinic in Toronto to perform abortions upon women who had not obtained a certificate from a therapeutic abortion committee of an accredited or approved hospital as required by s. 251(4). The doctors had made public statements questioning the wisdom of the abortion laws in Canada and asserting that a woman has an unfettered right to choose whether or not an abortion is appropriate in her individual circumstances.

Indictments were preferred against the appellants charging that they had conspired with each other with intent to procure abortions contrary to ss. 423(1)(d) and 251(1) of the *Criminal Code*. [The three were acquitted, and on appeal, the Supreme Court was confronted with the matter.] Per Dickson C.J. and Lamer J.:

[State] interference with bodily integrity and serious state-imposed psychological stress, at least in the criminal law context, constitutes a breach of security of the person. Section 251 clearly interferes with a woman's physical and bodily integrity. * * * The harm to the psychological integrity of women seeking abortions was also clearly established.

[The Court found that the law on therapeutic abortion committees is vague.]

Section 251 cannot be saved under s. 1 of the *Charter*. The objective of s. 251 as a whole, namely to balance the competing interests identified by Parliament, is sufficiently important to pass the first stage of the s. 1 inquiry. The means chosen to advance its legislative objectives, however, are not reasonable or demonstrably justified in a free and democratic society. None of the three elements for assessing the proportionality of means to ends is met. Firstly, the procedures and administrative structures created by s. 251 are often unfair and arbitrary. Moreover, these procedures impair s. 7 rights [which reads: "Everyone has the right to life, liberty and security of the person and the right not to be deprived thereof except in accordance with the principles of fundamental justice."] far more than is necessary because they hold out an illusory defence to many women who would *prima facie* qualify under the exculpatory provisions of s. 251(4). Finally, the effects of the limitation upon the s. 7 rights of many pregnant women are out of proportion to the objective sought to be achieved and may actually defeat the objective of protecting the life and health of women.

Per Beetz and Estey JJ.:

Before the advent of the *Charter*, Parliament recognized, in adopting s. 251(4) of the *Criminal Code*, that the interest in the life or health of the pregnant woman takes precedence over the interest in prohibiting abortions, including the interest of the state in the protection of the foetus, when "the continuation of the pregnancy of such female person would or would be likely to endanger her life or health". This standard in s. 251(4) became entrenched at least as a minimum when the "right to life, liberty and security of the person" was enshrined in the *Canadian Charter of Rights and Freedoms* at s. 7.

"Security of the person" within the meaning of s. 7 of the *Charter* must include a right of access to medical treatment for a condition representing a danger to life or health without fear of criminal sanction. If an act of Parliament forces a pregnant woman whose life or health is in danger to choose between, on the one hand, the commission of a crime to obtain effective and timely medical treatment and, on the other hand, inadequate treatment or no treatment at all, her right to security of the person has been violated.

According to the evidence, the procedural requirements of s. 251 of the *Criminal Code* significantly delay pregnant women's access to medical treatment resulting in an additional danger to their health, thereby depriving them of their right to security of the person. * * *

The primary objective of s. 251 of the *Criminal Code* is the protection of the foetus. The protection of the life and health of the pregnant woman is an ancillary objective. The primary objective does relate to concerns which are pressing and substantial in a free and democratic society and which, pursuant to s. 1 of the *Charter*, justify reasonable limits to be put on a woman's right. However, the means chosen in s. 251 are not reasonable and demonstrably justified. The rules unnecessary in respect of the primary and ancillary objectives which they are designed to serve, such as the above-mentioned rules contained in s. 251, cannot be said to be rationally connected to these objectives under s. 1 of the *Charter*. Consequently, s. 251 does not constitute a reasonable limit to the security of the person. * * *

Per Wilson J.:

* * * The right to "liberty" contained in s. 7 guarantees to every individual a degree of personal autonomy over important decisions intimately affecting his or her private life. Liberty in a free and democratic society does not require the state to approve such decisions but it does require the state to respect them.

A woman's decision to terminate her pregnancy falls within this class of protected decisions. It is one that will have profound psychological, economic and social consequences for her. It is a decision that deeply reflects the way the woman thinks about herself and her relationship to others and to society at large. It is not just a medical decision; it is a profound social and ethical one as well.

* * * [The] deprivation of the s. 7 right [by s. 251] offends freedom of conscience guaranteed in s. 2(a) of the *Charter*. The decision whether or not to terminate a pregnancy is essentially a moral decision and in a free and democratic society the conscience of the individual must be paramount to that of the state. Indeed, s. 2(a) makes it clear that this freedom belongs to each of us individually. "Freedom of conscience and religion" should be broadly construed to extend to conscientiously-held beliefs, whether grounded in religion or in a secular morality and the terms "conscience" and "religion" should not be treated as tautologous if capable of independent, although related, meaning. The state here is endorsing one conscientiously-held view at the expense of another. It is denying freedom of conscience to some, treating them as means to an end, depriving them of their "essential humanity".

The primary objective of the impugned legislation is the protection of the foetus. This is a perfectly valid legislative objective. It has other ancillary objectives, such as the protection of the life and health of the pregnant woman and the maintenance of proper medical standards.* * *

[The] value to be placed on the foetus as potential life is directly related to the stage of its development during gestation. * * * The precise point in the development of the foetus at which the state's interest in its protection becomes "compelling" should be left to the informed judgment of the legislature which is in a position to receive submissions on the subject from all the relevant disciplines.

Per McIntyre and La Forest JJ. (dissenting):

Save for the provisions of the *Criminal Code* permitting abortion where the life or health of the woman is at risk, no right of abortion can be found in Canadian law, custom or tradition and the *Charter*, including s. 7, does not create such a right. Section 251 of the *Criminal Code* accordingly does not violate s. 7 of the *Charter*.

The power of judicial review of legislation, although given greater scope under the *Charter*, is not unlimited. The courts must confine themselves to such democratic values as are clearly expressed in the *Charter* and refrain from imposing or creating rights with no identifiable base in the *Charter*. The Court is not entitled to define a right in a manner unrelated to the interest that the right in question was meant to protect.

The infringement of a right such as the right to security of the person will occur only when legislation goes beyond interfering with priorities and aspirations and abridges rights included in or protected by the concept. The proposition that women enjoy a constitutional right to have an abortion is devoid of support in either the language, structure or history of the constitutional text, in constitutional tradition, or in the history, traditions or underlying philosophies of our society. * * *

As to the asserted right to be free from state interference with bodily integrity and serious state-imposed psychological stress, an invasion of the s. 7 right of security of the person, there would have to be more than state-imposed stress or strain. A breach of the right would have to be based upon an infringement of some interest which would be of such nature and such importance as to warrant constitutional protection. This would be limited to cases where the state-action complained of, in addition to imposing stress and strain, also infringed another right, freedom or interest which was deserving of protection under the concept of security of the person. Abortion is not such an interest. * * *

[Section] 251 did not infringe the equality rights of women, abridge freedom of religion, or inflict cruel or unusual punishment.

DAIGLE v. TREMBLAY

Supreme Court (Canada).
[1989] 2 S.C.R. 530.

(Present: Dickson CJ and Lamer, Wilson, La Forest, L'Heureux–Dubé, Sopinka, Gonthier, Cory and McLachlin JJ.)

The judgment delivered by the Court.

[The] father requested an injunction in a Quebec court to enjoin his former partner of 5 months cohabitation from getting an abortion. The trial court granted an injunction, it was affirmed on appeal, while the Supreme Court set it aside. The Court held that the prospective father has standing because "if the respondent's allegations of foetal rights were accepted it would seem that he would be an appropriate person to assert such rights. As the potential father of the foetus in question Mr. Tremblay would appear to have as much interest in the foetus and as much right to speak on its behalf as anyone, save the appellant. * * *

[Issue: is the fetus a human being under the Quebec Charter?

Quebec Charter of Human Rights and Freedoms

Section 1—Every human being has a right to life, and to personal security, inviolability and freedom.

Section 2—Every human being whose life is in peril has a right to assistance.]

* * * In our view the Quebec Charter, considered as a whole, does not display any clear intention on the part of its framers to consider the status of a foetus. This is most evident in the fact that the Charter lacks any definition of "human being" or "person". * * * One can ask why the Quebec legislature, if it had intended to accord a foetus the right to life, would have left the protection of this right in such an uncertain state. As this case demonstrates, even if the respondent's arguments are accepted it will only be at the discretionary request of third parties, such as Mr. Tremblay, that a foetus' alleged right to life will be protected under the Quebec Charter. If the legislature had wished to grant foetuses the right to life, then it seems unlikely that it would have left the protection of this right to such happenstance. * * *

[Issue: Is the fetus a human being under s.7 of the Canadian Charter?]

In our view, it is not necessary in the context of the present appeal to address this issue. This is a civil action between two private parties. For the Canadian Charter to be invoked there must be some sort of state action which is being impugned (see *RWDSU v. Dolphin Delivery Ltd.*, [1986] 2 S.C.R. 573; and *Borowski v. Canada (Attorney General)*, [1989] 1 S.C.R. 342). The argument which alleges that the Charter can, on its own, support the injunction at issue fails to impugn any state action. The respondent pointed to no "law" of any sort which he can claim is infringing his rights or anyone else's rights. The issue as to whether s. 7 could be used to ground an affirmative claim to protection by the state was not raised. Neither the respondent nor any of the interveners who referred to the Canadian Charter as a possible basis for the injunction challenged the correctness of Dolphin Delivery or offered any basis upon which it could be distinguished and, accordingly, it provides a full answer to the Charter argument.

As we have indicated, the Court decided in its discretion to continue the hearing of this appeal although it was moot, in order to resolve the important legal issue raised so that the situation of women in the position in which Ms. Daigle found herself could be clarified. * * *

[Issue: Father's rights.]

The argument based upon "father's rights" (more accurately referred to as "potential father's rights") is the third and final basis on which the substantive rights necessary to support the impugned injunction might be founded. This argument would appear to be based on the proposition that the potential father's contribution to the act of conception gives him an equal say in what happens to the foetus. Little emphasis was put on this argument in the appeal. * * *

There does not appear to be any jurisprudential basis for this argument. No court in Quebec or elsewhere has ever accepted the argument that a father's interest in a foetus which he helped create could support a right to veto a woman's decisions in respect of the foetus she is carrying. * * * This lack of a legal basis is fatal to the argument about "father's rights".

ABORTION I CASE

Federal Constitutional Court (Germany).
39 BVerfGE 1 (1975).[b]

[The Criminal Code was challenged by members of the federal Parliament and by the states. It provided that termination of a pregnancy is legal if performed with the consent of the pregnant woman within the first twelve weeks of the pregnancy.]

C. I. 1 [The Constitution] also protects the life developing within the mother's womb as an independent legal interest. * * * (b) "Everyone" within the meaning of [the Constitution] is "every living human being", or, put differently, every human individual possessing life; "everyone" thus also includes the still unborn human being.

2. The duty of the state to protect every human life can therefore be derived directly from [this] Article * * *. [Also], the developing human life is included in the protection of human dignity * * *. Where human life exists it merits human dignity; it is not decisive whether the holder of this human dignity knows of it and is able to maintain it by himself. The potential capabilities lying in human existence from its inception on are sufficient to justify human dignity.

3. * * * Basic rights not only provide subjective defensive rights of the individual against the state, they also embody an objective order of values which binds basic constitutional decisions in all areas of the law and constitute guidelines and impulses for [legislative, administrative and judicial practice]. * * *

II.1. * * * Human life, as need not further be justified, represents the supreme value within the constitutional order; it is the vital basis for human dignity and the prerequisite [for] all other basic rights.

2. The duty of the state to protect developing human life exists in principle also with respect to the mother. Undoubtedly, the natural union of the unborn life with the mother establishes a special relation for which there is no parallel in any other factual situation of life. Pregnancy belongs to the intimate sphere of women which is constitutionally protected * * *. If [one] were to regard the embryo only as a part of the maternal organism, the termination of a pregnancy would fall within the [mother's] sphere of private life decisions into which the legislator may not intrude. Because the [one about to be born] is an independent human being which is protected by the Constitution, the termination of a pregnancy has a social dimension which makes [it] accessible to and in need of state regulation. It is true that a woman's right to develop her personality, which consists of the freedom of action in a comprehensive sense and therefore also includes the woman's right to take responsibility for herself and to make a decision against parent-

b. Reproduced from Robert Jonas and John Gorby, *West German Abortion Decision: A Contrast to* Roe v. Wade, 9 John

Marshall J. Prac. & Proc. 605 (1976). Available at <www.hrcr.org/safrica/life/39bverfge1.html>.

hood and the duties arising therefrom, also deserves the recognition and protection [of the state]. But this right is not given without limitation— the rights of others, the constitutional order, and moral law limit it. * * * No balance is possible which would guarantee both the protection of the life of the nasciturus and the freedom of the pregnant women to terminate her pregnancy, for the termination of a pregnancy always means the destruction of unborn life. In the necessary balancing process both constitutional values must be perceived in relation to human dignity as the center of the constitution's value system. When using [the right to dignity] as a standard, the decision must favor the protection of the fetus' life over the right of self-determination of the women. [Women] may be limited in some potential personal developments by pregnancy, birth, and childrearing [and her right to self-determination may thus be impaired]. The unborn life, however, gets destroyed by the termination of a pregnancy. Pursuant to the principle of the most careful balancing of competing constitutionally protected positions, * * * the protection of the nasciturus's life must be granted priority. This priority principally lasts for the entire duration of the pregnancy. * * *

3.   From [the discussion] above the constitutionally required fundamental position of the legal order with respect to termination of pregnancies may be deduced:

The legal order may not render the women's right to self-determination into its sole guideline for its regulations. The state must principally assume a duty to carry a pregnancy to terms, a termination [of a pregnancy] must therefore principally be seen as a wrong. The legal order must clearly articulate its disapproval of the termination of pregnancies. The wrong impression must be avoided that a termination of a pregnancy is, for instance, an event socially similar to a trip to the doctor to cure an illness or, even worse, a legally irrelevant alternative to contraception. The state may not avoid its responsibility and declare a legal vacuum by not making a value judgment and leaving this judgment to individuals [who make such decisions only on their own behalf].

III.   * * * [H]ow the state is to fulfill its obligation of an effective protection of life are first to be decided upon by the legislator. * * * 1. Especially with respect to the protection of unborn life the guiding concept is the priority of prevention as opposed to repression. It is therefore the state's task to use sociopolitical means as well as public assistance to safeguard the developing life. * * * To reawaken and strengthen the maternal will to protect [the unborn life] in cases where it has been lost shall be the noblest end of the state's endeavor to protect life. * * *

2.   * * * The legislator is principally not obliged to employ the same criminal sanctions for the protection of unborn life that it deems useful and necessary for the protection of born life. * * *

3.   As has been shown, the duty of the state to protect the developing life also exists with respect to the mother. * * * The incisive effects of a pregnancy upon the mental and physical condition of a woman are evident and require no further exposition. * * * In individual cases serious and even life-threatening situations of conflict may emerge.

* * * Respect for the unborn life conflicts with the woman's right not to be forced to sacrifice her own values to an unbearable degree in order to protect the unborn life. In such a situation of conflict, which usually does not permit a clear cut moral judgment and in which the decision to terminate the pregnancy may be one of conscience and worthy of respect, the legislature has the duty to exercise particular restraint. If, in these cases, [the legislator] does not deem the behavior of the pregnant women deserving of punishment and foregoes the imposition of the means of criminal punishment, then the result of the balancing incumbent upon the legislator must be constitutionally accepted. * * *

Dissenting Opinion by Justices Rupp-von Bruenneck and Simon:

The life of every single human being is self-evidently a central value of the legal order. It is indisputable that the constitutional duty to protect such life also encompasses its preliminary state before birth. The disputes in parliament and before the Federal Constitutional Court did not refer to *whether*, but only to the *how* of this protection. The decision in this matter belongs to the legislator. Under no circumstances can a duty of the state be derived from the constitution to subject every termination of a pregnancy, at any stage, to punishment. The legislator was as free to [opt] for the *Fristenlösung* (counseling and deadline solution) as he was [to opt] for the *Indikationslösung* (indication solution) * * *

A. I. The [authority] of the Federal Constitutional Court to annul decisions of the parliamentary legislator requires sparse use in order to avoid a [dislocation] of power among the constitutional organs. The command of judicial self-restraint, which has been labeled the "life-giving elixir" of the judicial office of the Federal Constitutional Court, is binding in particular when a case does not deal with defending against excesses of state power, but rather when it involves directing, by the means of constitutional judicial control, [the work] of the legislator, who is immediately legitimated by the people, in the positive shaping of the social order. * * *

1. The [constitutional review] asked for in this case goes beyond the realm of classic constitutional control. The Basic Rights, which are at the center of our constitution, guarantee the citizen, in the form of *defensive rights* in relation to the state, a sphere in which [the citizen can engage in a free design of his life and where he may assume the sole responsibility for his life]. The classic function of the Federal Constitutional Court here lies in warding off injuries to this personal sphere caused by excessive interventions of state authorities. At the peak of the scale of state interventions lie penal provisions * * *. [The question is whether the state] is *permitted* to punish at all or in the desired extent.

In the present constitutional dispute the reverse [question] is, for the first time, subject to review, [namely,] whether the state must punish * * *. It is, however, self-evident, that to refrain from punishment is the opposite of a state intervention. * * *

2. Because the Basic Rights, [if seen] as defensive rights, are from the outset unsuitable to prevent the legislator from lifting penal provisions, the majority of the senate wants to find the basis for doing so in a

more extensive meaning of the Basic Rights as *objective value decisions.* [According to the majority's interpretation,] the Basic Rights not only are normative as defensive rights of the individual against the state, but simultaneously contain objective value decisions, the realization of which is to be promoted through active measures by the state authorities. * * *

[Seen] as defensive rights Basic Rights have a relatively clear, identifiable content; in their interpretation and application the [judicial branch] has developed practical, generally accepted criteria for the control of state interventions—for example, the principle of proportionality. In contrast, it is a highly complex question how a value decision is to be effectuated by active measurements by the legislator. The value decisions [which by necessity are phrased in broad terms] could be characterized as constitutional mandates, which determine the direction of all acts by the state, [mandates] however which depend upon a translation into binding regulations. Depending on the evaluation of the factual circumstances, on the concrete goals and their ranking, [and] on the suitability of conceivable means and methods, very different solutions are possible. The decision [as to which solution to adopt], which in many cases requires prior compromises and [which] is arrived at in a trial-and-error process, belongs, pursuant to the fundamental rule of the separation of powers and the democratic principle, within the responsibility of the legislator.

The concept of the objective value decision shall not become the vehicle for transferring specifically legislative functions, [such as] the design of the social order, to the Federal Constitutional Court. Otherwise the court would be forced into a role for which it is neither competent not equipped. * * * [The Court] may only counter the legislator when he has completely disregarded a value decision or when the nature and manner in which [such a decision] was effectuated is obviously erroneous. On the contrary, the majority accuses the legislator, despite seeming recognition of his freedom to design [the effectuation of value decisions], of not having realized, in the majority's opinion, a recognized value decision in the best possible manner. If this [way of arguing] became the general yardstick for review, the command of judicial self-restraint would be given up.

II. 1. * * * Of course, the Constitution presupposes that the state, for the protection of an orderly [social life], can also use its power to punish; however, the meaning of Basic Rights does not aim at demanding [the use of the state's power to punish], but to draw boundaries for such use. [Following a similar line of argument], the Supreme Court of the United States even judged it a violation of a Basic Right to punish termination of pregnancies performed by a physician with the consent of the pregnant woman during the first third of the pregnancy [citing *Roe v. Wade*]. [Such an argument] would go too far under German constitutional law. However, according to the freedom-oriented character of our constitution, the legislator needs a constitutional justification for punishing, but not if he refrains from a punitive sanction because, in his opinion, the threat of punishment does not promise success or seems to be an inadequate reaction for other reasons.

The contrary interpretation of the Basic Rights inevitably leads to a no less worrisome extension of constitutional control: Not only [must it be decided] whether a penal provision interferes too far into the legal sphere of the citizen, but also the reverse, whether the state [does not punish enough]. [In doing this,] the Federal Constitutional Court will, contrary to the opinion of the majority, not be able to limit itself to the question of whether the passing of any penal norm is required, but [the court] will also have to clarify which penal sanction for the protection of a particular legal interest is sufficient. In the final consequence the court could even be forced to review whether the application of a penal norm in a single case sufficiently serves the concept of [the] protection [of Basic Rights].

FAMILY PLANNING ACT AMENDMENT

Constitutional Tribunal (Poland).
Decision dated 28 May 1997 (K. 26/96).[c]

[Provisions of the Act of 30 August 1996 on the amendment to the Act on Family–Planning, Human Embryo Protection and Conditions of Legal Pregnancy Termination] specify the legal status of the fetus and the limits of legal protection of the fetus's goods, in particular its health and life. In considering the constitutionality of particular provisions challenged by the mover it therefore seems necessary to establish first, whether and to what extent the fetus's life and health enjoy protection within the scope of constitutional regulations. This will chart the constitutional bases to control most of the appraised provisions of the Act of 30th August, 1996. There are no provisions relating directly to life protection in the constitutional regulations in force in Poland. This is not to say, however, that human life is not a constitutional value. The basic provision from which constitutional life protection should be educed, is Article 1 of the constitutional provisions continued in force, in particular the rule of a democratic state of law. Such a state is realised only as a community of people; so only people can be proper carriers of rights and duties enacted in such a state.

The basic attribute of a human being is his or her life. Thus depriving somebody of life at the same time annihilates a human being as a carrier of rights and duties. If the content of the rule of a state of law is a constellation of basic directives that are educed from the very essence of a democratically legislated law and that guarantee a minimum of its justice, then respecting in a state of law the value, without which any legal personality is impossible, i.e. human life from the moment it develops, must be a primary directive. In a democratic state of law a human being and the goods most precious to him or her are of paramount value. Such a good is life. So in a democratic state of law life, in each and every stage of its development, must be protected by the Constitution. The value of the constitutionally protected legal good of human life—including life evolving in the pre-natal stage—cannot be

c. Reproduced from strib.htm>.
<www.waw.pdi.net/?polfedwo/english/con-

differentiated. This is so, because there are no sufficiently fine and justified criteria for distinguishing the value of human life according its developmental phase. Human life, therefore, becomes a value protected under the Constitution from the moment it develops. This applies also to the pre-natal stage. Moreover, constitutional protection of the pre-natal phase of human life is also confirmed by the Convention on the Rights of the Child * * * Recognising the value of the life of the conceived human being must be the sole reason for proscribing abortion, a reason that in general applies also to the pregnant woman herself (as shall follow from subsequent considerations). * * *

* * * The protection of human life cannot be taken to mean merely a protection of the minimum of biological functions that are indispensable for survival; it should be understood as a guarantee of correct development, as well as attaining and maintaining a normal mental and physical condition proper to a given developmental age (life stage). * * *

4.1 In accordance with Article 1.2 of the Act of 30th August, * * * a new wording [came into force] * * *.

[The new wording] means that the life of the unborn enjoys legal protection only within limits provided in a clear way by an ordinary act. The term "limits of protection" comprises both a rule which prohibits directly the violation of specific goods—in this case the life of the unborn—and measures provided for the execution of abidance by this rule. The reservation that the life of the unborn enjoys protection exclusively within the limits of the act must mean that only a regulation under an ordinary act becomes the source of a potential prohibition of offending the life of the unborn. * * * [B]estowing such an exclusive power to enact a prohibition itself, is incompatible with the duty to protect constitutional values which is incumbent on the legislator. Conditioning the validity of the prohibition of offence against the life of the unborn upon regulations from ordinary acts must result in a lack of any protection of this life, should the legislator fail to introduce such a prohibition or limit its scope. So the present wording of Article 1 of the Act assigns to the ordinary legislator the right to specify if, and to what extent, the life of the unborn enjoys legal protection. * * *

[T]he new provision does not speak of legal protection of the health of the child—including the conceived child—it does not comprise the declaration that the right to life is inherent and it alters the way of specifying the period of time during which the right to life enjoys legal protection. The repeal of the declaration that the right to life is inherent cannot be taken to be a normative change. Whether a given right or freedom is in fact inherent or not, does not depend on the legislator's will; so it is impossible to nullify (abrogate) the quality of inherence by a statutory act. For the legislator does not have the power to grant or cancel the right to life as a constitutional value. The inherent character of the right to life, therefore, cannot be influenced by the legislator stating it explicitly in statutory provisions or not. In the amended Article 1, the legislator employed a different expression to specify the period of time during which human life enjoys legal protection. * * *

4.3 The challenged provision * * * admitted of the possibility of abortion to be performed only by a doctor, if the pregnant woman had difficult life conditions or a difficult personal situation (Article 4a.1) (1) and the pregnancy did not last longer than 12 weeks (Article 4a. 2) (2). As a formal condition for the doctor to perform an abortion, the woman must submit a written consent (Article 4a. 4) (3), a statement relating to the difficult life conditions or a difficult personal situation, and, moreover, a certificate that she has consulted (4) a doctor from the basic health care, other than the doctor who is to perform the pregnancy termination, or another qualified person (Article 4a. 6). (5) * * *

In evaluating the normative significance of the prescription under Article 4a.1.4, it should be concluded that it legalises specific behaviours that are aimed at abortion. In so doing, it admits of behaviours that are, in principle, outlawed. In the context of the remaining provisions of the Act, especially Article 1 in its new wording, but also the new Articles 152a and 152b of the Penal Code, it should be concluded that also on the basis of new regulations relating to the conceived child, its life enjoys legal protection from the moment of conception; and any acts aimed at taking its life, including, in particular, abortion, are generally outlawed. * * *

The essence of the evaluated regulation from Article 4a.1.4 is the legalisation of actions aimed at taking the life of the foetus and undertaken in conditions specified in this regulation. A constitutional evaluation of this legalisation must therefore determine:

a. whether the good, whose violation the legislator legalises, is a constitutional value, b. whether the legalisation of violations of this good is justifiable on the basis of constitutional values, being, in particular, a result of settling a conflict of specific values, rights or freedoms that are guaranteed in the Constitution, and c. whether the legislator kept the constitutional criteria to be followed in an attempt to settle such conflicts and, in particular, whether the legislator complied with the requirement—which the Tribunal has repeatedly deduced from Article 1 of constitutional provisions (from the rule of a state of law)—to maintain balance in the settling of conflicts that arise between constitutionally protected goods, rights and freedoms.

An acknowledgement of the constitutional value of human life—including its pre-natal phase—does not prejudge that, in some exceptional situations, the protection of this value may be limited or even cancelled due to the need to protect or realise other constitutional values, rights or freedoms. When the ordinary legislator decides to forfeit the protection of a specific constitutional value or even legalise behaviours that violate such a value, the decision must be justified by a conflict of constitutional goods, rights or freedoms presented above. The legislator, however, is not qualified to settle such conflicts in an uncontrolled and arbitrary manner. The legislator should, in particular, follow the results of comparing the value of conflicting goods, rights or freedoms. The criteria that specify the scope of a permissible violation should match the nature of the settled conflict. * * *

A comparison with the remaining grounds for abortion enumerated in Article 4a.1 leads to the conclusion that the so called difficult life conditions, and in particular a difficult personal situation, mean neither a threat to the life or health of the pregnant woman (this is regulated in subparagraph 1), nor genetic defects of the foetus (subparagraph 2) nor do they relate to the pregnancy as a result of a prohibited act (subsection 3). Subparagraph 4, therefore, must have been legislated for a situation which is not embraced by the remaining provisions specified under Article 4a.1. As to *difficult life conditions*, they comprise in particular the material situation, which may deteriorate or loose a chance for improvement in relation to more advanced stages of the pregnancy or as a result of bearing the child. And in case of a *difficult personal situation*, the legislator most probably meant a specific mental state related to becoming with child. A state that may result from strained relations with other people (family members as well as the environment) because of the pregnancy or from the necessity to limit specific needs of the woman, including her rights and personal freedoms. Therefore, although the prerequisites specified under Article 4a.1.4 are fairly vague (this element shall be discussed later), they support the conclusion that this regulation probably protects the following values: that the pregnant woman retains a specific material status that could deteriorate or lose a chance for improvement in relation to continuing the pregnancy and bearing the child; or else that the pregnant woman retains the type of relations with others she used to have before her pregnancy and the extent to which she used to realise her specific need, rights and freedoms.

The prerequisites specified under Article 4a.1.4, however, must be interpreted in the light of paragraph 6 of the same provision. This regulation implies that only the woman herself is entitled to determine the circumstances listed in 4a.1.4, by presenting an appropriate statement concerning this issue. In this way, the legislator has prejudiced that the prerequisites specified under Article 4a.1.4 are to be understood in a subjective way. In the light of this provision, therefore, the woman's subjective conviction that her material situation or her personal relations or else the possibility to realise her own needs, rights and freedoms may perhaps be under threat, becomes a legal good. This shows that the prerequisites specified under Article 4a.1.4 do not refer to extreme situations, such as could, at the same time, be taken to contradict the principle of the protection of the dignity of the human person. In addition, it is possible to conclude from the preamble of the Act that a prerequisite for the enacted regulations was, *inter alia*, the recognition of *every individual's right to decide responsibly if to reproduce*. Weighing against each other the value of the conflicting goods specified in this way disqualifies the regulation under Article 4a.1.4. Human life, as stressed by the preamble of the Act itself, is a *fundamental good of the human being*. The right of the pregnant woman to avoid aggravating her material situation follows from the constitutional protection of the freedom to shape ones living conditions freely and from the right of the woman that pertains to this freedom to satisfy the material needs she and her family may have. But this protection cannot lead so far as to involve the violation of the fundamental good of human life; in comparison with this good, living conditions are a secondary issue and may change. * * *

Due to the ambiguity of the prerequisites formulated by the legislator, it is impossible to identify the constitutionally protected values, by virtue of which the legislator decides to legalise the violation of another constitutional value. * * * The very nature of the recognition that human life is a constitutional value implies a necessary limitation on the rights of a pregnant woman. The evolving life not only makes use of the mother's goods in the biological sense; it may also, for purely factual reasons, limit the mother's possibility to enjoy the rights and freedoms that are vested in her. Also in the private sphere, the evolvement of the life of the child is correlated with a set of responsibilities resting in the child's mother, as well as its father, which rise sharply with the moment of birth.

* * * It remains to be considered, whether the regulation under Article 4a.1.4 is justifiable by virtue of the right to responsibly decide about reproduction. Such a right may indeed be deduced from the scope of basic human rights and freedoms, and, within constitutional provisions, from guarantees provided therein for motherhood and the family. The right to parenthood must be interpreted both positively and negatively. It must signify a prohibition of actions that limit the freedom to reproduce, as well as the prohibition of actions that coerce to reproduce. The right to parenthood concerns, in particular, the decision to conceive a child. In reality any interference in this sphere, be it by the authorities, be it by other people, should be regarded as an intolerable violation of a fundamental right of every human being.

The question arises, whether the right to decide to reproduce can be understood in a broader sense, to comprise also the right to decide about bearing a child. In which case, the introduction of a legal prohibition on bearing a child, a prohibition that would be executed by the state, would be impermissible. Similarly, the legislation of any negative legal consequences relating to bearing a child would also be impermissible. Any public or private interests that might justify the introduction of such a regulation should be challenged by the paramount value of the life of the conceived child and by the right of the parents to reproduce. A separate matter is considering the right to bear a child in its negative aspect, i.e. also as a right to terminate the pregnancy. In this case, due to the development of life, the right to decide about reproduction should in fact be reduced to the right not to have a child. One cannot decide about having a child, when this child is already evolving in the pre-natal phase and, in this sense, the parents already *have* it. The right to have a child, therefore, can be interpreted solely in its positive aspect, and not as a right to annihilate a developing human foetus.

* * * The legislator has legalised acts which occasions the death of the foetus only in respect to those acts which are undertaken before the foetus is 12 weeks old. This criterion is entirely arbitrary in the context of the Act as a whole. For the nature of a potential conflict between constitutionally protected interests of the pregnant woman and constitu-

tionally protected life in the pre-natal phase does not change in any way either before or after the 12th week of pregnancy. * * *

Notes and Questions

1. *The question of life?* Abortion is an issue of life and death only if and insofar as a fetus is considered life for purposes of constitutionally guaranteed fundamental rights. Remember that, for example, the philosophical debate about dignity centers on the question of whether it inheres in the capacity for decisionmaking, or whether dignity is a right attributed to every human being per se. In the case of abortion the question whether the fetus constitutes a rights-bearing subject is often of central importance in constitutional reasoning. If you consider the fetus life, does it necessarily follow that the fetus is a constitutional subject? Is protection based on the mere fact of existence or rather on a capacity to make decisions? If the fetus is considered a living human being, and is thus considered to have a right to full autonomy from the mother, conflicts arise. For although we must assume that autonomy, in this case that of the fetus, cannot "trump" a right to life, like the life of a mother who is unable or unwilling to carry a pregnancy to term, we must also assume that once the fetus is considered an autonomous, rights-bearing subject, its right to life cannot be trumped by the mother's autonomy or privacy interest. The question of life is largely side-stepped in the U.S. cases, in favor of a conception of "viability" in *Planned Parenthood*, which might be understood as the biological capacity for autonomous life. The following dissenting opinion of Dr. Marco Gerardo Monroy Cabra of the Inter–American Commission represents a strong position in favor of understanding the moment of conception as the beginning of life:

> Life is the primary right of every individual. It is the fundamental right and the condition for the existence of all other rights. If human existence is not recognized, there is no subject upon which to predicate the other rights. It is a right that antecedes other rights and exists by the mere fact of being, with no need for the state to recognize it as such. It is not up to the state to decide whether that right shall be recognized in one case and not in another, since that would mean discrimination. The life of the unborn child, the infant, the young, the old, the mentally ill, the handicapped, and that of all human beings in general, must be recognized.

> The foregoing means that if conception produces a human life, and this right is the primary and fundamental one, abortion is an attack on the right to life and, therefore, runs counter to * * * the American Declaration of the Rights and Duties of Man [which reads: "Every human being has the right to life, liberty and security of his person."]. [Thus] abortion laws violate Article 1 of the aforementioned Declaration.

> *White and Potter v. United States,* Inter–American Commission Res. No. 23/81, March 6, 1981, Case 2141, Inter–Am C.H.R. OEA /ser.L./V/II.54, doc. 9 rev. 1 (1981).

The dissent in the Inter–American Commission is comparable to that of the Polish Constitutional Tribunal (K. 26/96, 28 May 1997, 6 E. Eur. Case Rep. Const. L. 38 (1994), above). The decision summarizes a trend that emerged, after the collapse of communism, under the influence of the Catholic Church, which the Human Rights Watch *Global Report On Women's Human Rights*[d] described as follows:

> Poland's first post-communist government acted quickly to reduce women's access to abortion. During the communist regime, a woman could receive an abortion in a state hospital if she presented a note from a doctor attesting to her adverse social or medical circumstances. Obtaining such a note was a formality, and abortion generally was available on demand in the first trimester of pregnancy.

> The situation in Poland changed significantly in the spring of 1990, shortly after the fall of communism, when a new official directive required women seeking an abortion in a state facility to obtain approval from a psychologist and two doctors. Moreover, a doctor could refuse to issue the necessary document without reason. Poland's ombudsman, who is supposed to protect the civil and political rights of Polish citizens through legal action, sued in the constitutional tribunal challenging a doctor's arbitrary power to refuse to issue such a document, but the tribunal held that the regulation was constitutional. [Decision of the Constitutional Tribunal of January 15, 1991.]

> * * * Reflecting the changed political climate with respect to abortion, the Polish Medical College promulgated, with the acquiescence of the government, a medical ethics code in 1991 that contradicted the Polish abortion law existing at that time. The code was approved by the Polish Medical College during its national convention held in mid-December 1991. The Medical College, created in 1989, is a private institution to which all Polish doctors must belong in order to practice medicine, and which has the right by law to revoke a license to practice medicine.

> * * * The medical ethics code stated that a woman carrying a damaged or malformed fetus, due to a hereditary disease or other factors, could not terminate her pregnancy. Doctors who violated the code risked being disciplined by the Medical College with a number of sanctions, including the revocation of their medical licenses.

> * * * The ombudsman filed suit in the constitutional tribunal on January 7, 1992, but the case was dismissed on a technicality.

> In 1993, following the adoption of a new abortion law, the ombudsman again challenged the code. The ombudsman claimed that the code conflicted with the new abortion law, because the new law permitted abortions in cases of fetal defects whereas the code allowed no such exception. That March, the constitutional tribunal ruled that the Medical College cannot penalize a physician who performed an abortion in violation of the code if he or she obeyed the new abortion law. [Judgment of March 17, 1993] Responding to this decision, in December 1993, the Medical College amended its ethics code to conform with Polish law. The Medical College removed the explicit references of when an abortion is and is not permitted. * * * "

Consider, in addition, that the Irish Constitution, in Art. 40 Sec 3(3), reads: "The State acknowledges the right to life of the unborn and, with due

---

d. Human Rights Watch, *Global Report on Women's Human Rights*, adapted from *Hidden Victims: Women in Post–Communist Poland, A Human Rights Watch Short* *Report*, vol. 4, no. 3 (March 1992). Available at <www.hrw.org/about/projects/womrep/General–234.htm>.

regard to the equal right to life of the mother, guarantees in its laws to respect, and, as far as practicable, by its laws to defend and vindicate that right."

In the German decisions on abortion, the GFCC stated that there is a right to life which is inviolable but that a fetus is not a "completed person" and is thus not fully protected. The Court held that women carry the burden of giving birth and that abortions may be permitted in some cases, for which public insurance will not bear the cost (*Abortion I Case*, 39 BVerfGE 1, and *Abortion II Case*, 88 BVerfGE 203 (1993). Is this a relative protection of human life? Consider the comment by Donald P. Kommers, *The Constitutional Jurisprudence of the Federal Republic of Germany* 346–47 (2d ed. 1997): "The German distinction between fetal life and persons is noteworthy in comparative perspective because it allowed the Constitutional Court to engage in a balancing process largely absent in the seminal American case of *Roe v. Wade*."

The French *Decision on the Termination of Pregnancy Act*, although taking a position in favor of the right to life, found no constitutional problem with the statutory scheme that permitted abortion after mandatory counseling:

> The statute referred to the Constitutional Council does not allow any departure from the principle of respect for all human beings from the inception of life—a principle referred to in section 1 of the Act—except in case of need and on the terms and subject to the restrictions contained therein; none of the exceptions allowed by the statute is, as matters stand, inconsistent with any of the fundamental principles recognized by the laws of the Republic, nor with the principle set out in the preamble to the Constitution of 27 October 1946 whereby the nation guarantees health care to all children, nor with any of the other principles of constitutional status established by that text.

Cons. const., Jan 15, 1975, D. 1975, Jur., 529, *note Hamon*, DC 74–54.

Commenting on the French system, Mary Ann Glendon argues that "the French statute *names* the underlying problem as one involving human life, not a conflict involving a woman's individual liberty or privacy and a non-person. While showing great concern for the pregnant woman, it tries, [through counseling] to make her aware of her alternatives without either frightening or unduly burdening her." Mary Ann Glendon, *Abortion and Divorce Law in Western Law* 19 (1987). How do we, or how do courts, know what is an undue burden for pregnant women about to decide on the continuation of a pregnancy?

2. *Are courts to decide?* Are courts qualified to decide these questions? Clearly the USSC is reluctant to engage the issue of life. Might the question be better addressed by medical science, theology, or philosophy? How is constitutional jurisprudence to respond? Or might such questions be best left to the legislature? The HCC, in its first decision on abortion, prior to a notable shift toward a prolife position in its second ruling on the issue, tried to take a deferential position:

> The question of the fetus' legal subjecthood is not a legal subject [and] does not advance the resolution of the problem. [In examining the question,] one is not confronted with the usual task of constitutional interpretation. * * *

The decision about the fetus' legal subjecthood is tantamount to the redefinition of the meaning of human rights. But such a determination, which must precede any interpretation of basic rights, cannot be derived from the inner logic of the Constitution and is not to be found therein; it is an external decision * * *. [T]he legislator can decide that only a fully matured fetus is entitled to legal status with its concomitant absolute right to life, or can, alternatively, create a special legal status for the fetus within which one can distinguish on the basis of age, maturity, or even the "domicile"—inside the uterus versus outside in artificial conditions.

Constitutional Court, Hungary 1991. Decision 64/1991 (XII.17.) AB hat., 17 December 1991, 1 E. Eur. Case Rep. Const. L. 3, 15–20 (1994).

This tendency toward restraint in judicial review of the legislature is essentially the argument of Justices McIntyre and La Forest, dissenting, in *Morgentaler* above.

3. *Privacy or self-determination?* The GFCC, in its first decision on the issue, invalidated a law because it gave women too much privacy in deciding about the continuation of a pregnancy. Is abortion not about privacy but about a liberty interest that could be framed as a "reproductive right"? Consider another opinion: "For if the State has the power to infringe the right of procreative autonomy in favor of birth, then, necessarily, it also has the power to require abortion under some circumstances. If one accepts the former, then imposition of the latter is no more remote than a change in prevailing political ideology." *Armstrong v. State of Montana*, 989 P.2d 364, 380 (Mont.1999). See also Elizabeth Westley, *Emergency Contraception: A Global Overview*, 53 J. Amer. Med. Women's Ass'n 215, 216 (Supp. II 1998). Note that the German criminal law on the termination of pregnancy was unsuccessfully challenged in the ECHR on privacy grounds. The ECHR concluded that not every restriction on the termination of an unwanted pregnancy constituted an interference with the right of respect for the private life of the mother. Article 8(1) of the Convention, therefore, could not be interpreted as meaning that pregnancy and its termination were, in principle, solely a matter of the private life of the mother. *Brüggemann and Scheuten v. Federal Republic of Germany*, 3 E.H.R.R. 244, 253–54 (1977).

4. *Mothers and Fathers.* Most abortion decisions do not discuss the rights of the men involved, nor do they address any right attached to paternity. Should a father's right be allowed to limit the decisional freedom of the mother? Why or why not? Is one parent or progenitor of a child more important than the other? And is it important who becomes the primary caregiver after birth? Do you agree with the Court's conclusion in *Casey* that requiring a married woman to notify her husband prior to obtaining an abortion constitutes an "undue burden"? Does balancing accord adequate protection to human life? Is it compatible with a fundamental right to dignity? Should the condition of pregnancy command a privileged right to dignity, autonomy, or privacy? Consider *Daigle*.

5. *Legislative deadlock.* In 1990, following the Canadian Supreme Court's decision in *Morgentaler* (1988), an attempt was made to reinstitute criminal law control over abortion. A bill was introduced in Parliament (Bill C–43) which provided that "every person who induces an abortion on a female person is guilty of an indictable offence and liable to imprisonment for a term not exceeding two years, unless the abortion is induced by or

under the direction of a medical practitioner who is of the opinion, that if the abortion were not induced, the health or life of the female person would be likely to be threatened." The bill was passed by a narrow margin in the House of Commons but failed in the Senate in a rare tie. The old law is still on the books, although it is not enforced. See Peter W. Hogg and Allison A. Bushell, *The Charter Dialogue Between Courts and Legislatures, Or Perhaps the Charter of Rights Isn't Such a Bad Thing After All*, 35 Osgoode Hall L. J. 75, 113 (1997). In a subsequent Supreme Court decision, a local attempt in Nova Scotia to criminalize abortion was struck down on the basis of federalism considerations. The Court held that the Nova Scotia legislation was *ultra vires* as it interfered with the "pith and substance" of federal jurisdiction in criminal law. The law had prohibited abortions (and other medical procedures) outside accredited hospitals and denied medical insurance coverage for abortions performed in violation of the statute.

6. *Equality?* Courts find different rights at issue in abortion, in addition to or instead of privacy or self-determination. Could sex equality provide a basis on which to protect a woman's right to choose to carry a pregnancy to term? Does equality provide a sounder basis than privacy as determined in *Roe*? Does equality matter in access to abortion facilities? Consider the Canadian position in *Morgentaler*. On the other hand the GFCC does not accept equality as an argument. American scholar Frances Olsen located a trend in USSC decisions when she noted that it "has begun to acknowledge that abortion law has something to do with the role and status of women." The Supreme Court 1988 Term, Frances Olsen, Comment, *Unraveling Compromise*, 103 Harv. L. Rev. 105, 117 (1989). See also Ruth Bader Ginsburg, Comment, *Some Thoughts on Autonomy and Equality in Relation to* Roe v. Wade, 63 N.C. L. Rev. 375 (1985); Ruth Bader Ginsburg, *Speaking in a Judicial Voice*, in *The Unpredictable Constitution* 71 (Norman Dorsen ed., 2002); Sylvia Ann Law, *Rethinking Sex and the Constitution*, 132 U. Pa. L. Rev. 955 (1984). The Court, however, does not acknowledge a right to equality as a decisive factor in these cases. Is this legitimate in light of recent developments in sex discrimination jurisprudence? U.S. feminist legal scholar Catharine A. MacKinnon argues forcefully in *Reflections on Sex Equality Under Law*, 100 Yale L.J. 1281, 1295–97 (1991):

> If discrimination based on pregnancy is discrimination based on sex, one can be different in a way that perfectly tracks the gender line and still be entitled to equal treatment. And if female sexuality is regarded as discriminated against rather than different when women are sexually harassed, given that the line of distinction tracks both biology and sex roles, the law of equality has taken a long step beyond the "similarly situated" requirement. Although implicitly undermined in these ways, neither the "similarly situated" test, nor its statutory version, the comparability requirement, has been exposed as the doctrinal guise of dominance. * * * The more perfect the disparity, the more difficult the showing of discrimination, so long as the basis for disparity is not mythic but real. Until this model based on sameness and difference is rejected or cabined, sex equality law may find itself increasingly unable even to advance women into male preserves * * *. Because the "similarly situated" requirement continues to control access to equality claims, the laws of sexual assault and reproductive control—areas as crucial in the social construction of women's inferior status as they are laden with

misogyny—have not been seen as amenable to constitutional sex equality attack.

7. *Dignity*. According to the German case above, "the developing human life is included in the protection of human dignity." The ruling goes on to state in very clear terms that the right to dignity inheres in human beings per se: "where human life exists it merits human dignity; it is not decisive whether the holder of this human dignity knows of it and is able to maintain it by himself. The potential capabilities lying in human existence from its inception on are sufficient to justify human dignity." This ruling clearly suggests that human *potentiality* is sufficient to warrant a dignity concern. How is this to be balanced against a possible dignity interest of the mother? Could being compelled by the state to give birth constitute a violation of dignity rights? The balancing process outlined in the German ruling would always give priority to the fetus, whose loss of life would presumably constitute the greater affront to dignity. Is this consistent with the German distinction between fetal life and personhood? Does dignity provide a sound conceptual framework for considering the issue?

C.2.   THE RIGHT TO END A LIFE

For many, euthanasia is considered a viable alternative to the protracted suffering caused by chronic or fatal illness or to the severe incapacity caused by severe physical trauma. For others, however, life is understood as a gift of God or, at the very least, as something no human can rightly dispose of, rendering the idea of taking one's own life deliberately an anathema. Still others may not oppose suicide on principle but are concerned about the involvement of a third party in willful death, be it a physician or a relative, and especially about the potential for malfeasance or abuse that might arise in cases of mental incompetence. The following cases deal with various aspects of this issue.

CRUZAN v. DIRECTOR, MISSOURI DEPARTMENT OF HEALTH

Supreme Court (United States).
497 U.S. 261 (1990).

Chief Justice Rehnquist delivered the opinion of the Court.

Petitioner Nancy Beth Cruzan was rendered incompetent as a result of severe injuries sustained during an automobile accident. Copetitioners Lester and Joyce Cruzan, Nancy's parents and coguardians, sought a court order directing the withdrawal of their daughter's artificial feeding and hydration equipment after it became apparent that she had virtually no chance of recovering her cognitive faculties. [Nancy was the victim of an automobile accident and lived for years in a persistent vegetative state. She had no chances to regain her cognitive faculties.] The Supreme Court of Missouri held that because there was no clear and convincing evidence of Nancy's desire to have life-sustaining treatment withdrawn under such circumstances, her parents lacked authority to effectuate such a request. * * *

We granted certiorari to consider the question whether Cruzan has a right under the United States Constitution which would require the hospital to withdraw life-sustaining treatment from her under these circumstances.

At common law, * * * the logical corollary of the doctrine of informed consent is that the patient generally possesses the right not to consent, that is, to refuse treatment. Just this Term, * * * we recognized that prisoners possess "a significant liberty interest in avoiding the unwanted administration of antipsychotic drugs under the Due Process Clause of the Fourteenth Amendment." Still other cases support the recognition of a general liberty interest in refusing medical treatment. But determining that a person has a "liberty interest" under the Due Process Clause does not end the inquiry; "whether respondent's constitutional rights have been violated must be determined by balancing his liberty interests against the relevant state interests." *Youngberg v. Romeo*, 457 U.S. 307, 321 (1982).

Petitioners insist that under the general holdings of our cases, the forced administration of life-sustaining medical treatment, and even of artificially delivered food and water essential to life, would implicate a competent person's liberty interest. Although we think the logic of the cases discussed above would embrace such a liberty interest, the dramatic consequences involved in refusal of such treatment would inform the inquiry as to whether the deprivation of that interest is constitutionally permissible. But for purposes of this case, we assume that the United States Constitution would grant a competent person a constitutionally protected right to refuse lifesaving hydration and nutrition.

Petitioners go on to assert that an incompetent person should possess the same right in this respect as is possessed by a competent person. * * * The difficulty with petitioners' claim is that in a sense it begs the question: An incompetent person is not able to make an informed and voluntary choice to exercise a hypothetical right to refuse treatment or any other right. Such a "right" must be exercised for her, if at all, by some sort of surrogate. Here, Missouri has in effect recognized that under certain circumstances a surrogate may act for the patient in electing to have hydration and nutrition withdrawn in such a way as to cause death, but it has established a procedural safeguard to assure that the action of the surrogate conforms as best it may to the wishes expressed by the patient while competent. Missouri requires that evidence of the incompetent's wishes as to the withdrawal of treatment be proved by clear and convincing evidence. The question, then, is whether the United States Constitution forbids the establishment of this procedural requirement by the State. We hold that it does not.

* * * Missouri relies on its interest in the protection and preservation of human life, and there can be no gainsaying this interest. As a general matter, the States—indeed, all civilized nations—demonstrate their commitment to life by treating homicide as a serious crime. Moreover, the majority of States in this country have laws imposing criminal penalties on one who assists another to commit suicide. We do not think a State is required to remain neutral in the face of an informed and voluntary decision by a physically able adult to starve to death.

But in the context presented here, a State has more particular interests at stake. The choice between life and death is a deeply personal decision of obvious and overwhelming finality. We believe Missouri may legitimately seek to safeguard the personal element of this choice through the imposition of heightened evidentiary requirements. * * * A State is entitled to guard against potential abuses in such situations. Similarly, a State is entitled to consider that a judicial proceeding to make a determination regarding an incompetent's wishes may very well not be an adversarial one, with the added guarantee of accurate factfinding that the adversary process brings with it. * * * Finally, we think a State may properly decline to make judgments about the "quality" of life that a particular individual may enjoy, and simply assert an unqualified interest in the preservation of human life to be weighed against the constitutionally protected interests of the individual.

In our view, Missouri has permissibly sought to advance these interests through the adoption of a "clear and convincing" standard of proof to govern such proceedings. "The function of a standard of proof, as that concept is embodied in the Due Process Clause and in the realm of factfinding, is to 'instruct the factfinder concerning the degree of confidence our society thinks he should have in the correctness of factual conclusions for a particular type of adjudication.'" * * *

We think it self-evident that the interests at stake in the instant proceedings are more substantial, both on an individual and societal level, than those involved in a run-of-the-mine civil dispute. * * *

In sum, we conclude that a State may apply a clear and convincing evidence standard in proceedings where a guardian seeks to discontinue nutrition and hydration of a person diagnosed to be in a persistent vegetative state. * * * The Supreme Court of Missouri held that in this case the testimony adduced at trial did not amount to clear and convincing proof of the patient's desire to have hydration and nutrition withdrawn. In so doing, it reversed a decision of the Missouri trial court which had found that the evidence "suggest[ed]" Nancy Cruzan would not have desired to continue such measures, * * * but which had not adopted the standard of "clear and convincing evidence" enunciated by the Supreme Court. The testimony adduced at trial consisted primarily of Nancy Cruzan's statements made to a housemate about a year before her accident that she would not want to live should she face life as a "vegetable," and other observations to the same effect. The observations did not deal in terms with withdrawal of medical treatment or of hydration and nutrition. We cannot say that the Supreme Court of Missouri committed constitutional error in reaching the conclusion that it did. * * *

The judgment of the Supreme Court of Missouri is *affirmed*.

Scalia, J., concurring.

While I agree with the Court's analysis today, and therefore join in its opinion, I would have preferred that we announce, clearly and promptly, that the federal courts have no business in this field; that American law has always accorded the State the power to prevent, by force if necessary, suicide—including suicide by refusing to take appropriate measures necessary to preserve one's life; that the point at which life becomes "worthless," and the point at which the means necessary to preserve it become "extraordinary" or "inappropriate," are neither set forth in the Constitution nor known to the nine Justices of this Court any better than they are known to nine people picked at random from the Kansas City telephone directory; and hence, that even when it *is* demonstrated by clear and convincing evidence that a patient no longer wishes certain measures to be taken to preserve his or her life, it is up to the citizens of Missouri to decide, through their elected representatives, whether that wish will be honored. It is quite impossible (because the Constitution says nothing about the matter) that those citizens will decide upon a line less lawful than the one we would choose; and it is unlikely (because we know no more about "life and death" than they do) that they will decide upon a line less reasonable. * * *

Brennan, J., with whom Marshall, and Blackmun, JJ., join, dissenting.

"Medical technology has effectively created a twilight zone of suspended animation where death commences while life, in some form, continues. Some patients, however, want no part of a life sustained only by medical technology. Instead, they prefer a plan of medical treatment that allows nature to take its course and permits them to die with dignity." [footnote omitted]

* * * Because I believe that Nancy Cruzan has a fundamental right to be free of unwanted artificial nutrition and hydration, which right is not outweighed by any interests of the State, and because I find that the improperly biased procedural obstacles imposed by the Missouri Supreme Court impermissibly burden that right, I respectfully dissent. Nancy Cruzan is entitled to choose to die with dignity. * * *

Yet Missouri and this Court have displaced Nancy's own assessment of the processes associated with dying. * * * That Missouri and this Court may truly be motivated only by concern for incompetent patients makes no matter. As one of our most prominent jurists warned us decades ago: "Experience should teach us to be most on our guard to protect liberty when the government's purposes are beneficent. . . . The greatest dangers to liberty lurk in insidious encroachment by men of zeal, well meaning but without understanding." * * *

I respectfully dissent.

Stevens, J., dissenting.

* * * Choices about death touch the core of liberty. * * * Nancy Cruzan's death, when it comes, cannot be an historic act of heroism; it will inevitably be the consequence of her tragic accident. But Nancy Cruzan's interest in life, no less than that of any other person, includes an interest in how she will be thought of after her death by those whose opinions mattered to her. There can be no doubt that her life made her dear to her family and to others. How she dies will affect how that life is remembered. The trial court's order authorizing Nancy's parents to cease their daughter's treatment would have permitted the family that cares for Nancy to bring to a close her tragedy and her death. Missouri's

objection to that order subordinates Nancy's body, her family, and the lasting significance of her life to the State's own interests. The decision we review thereby interferes with constitutional interests of the highest order * * *

In short, there is no reasonable ground for believing that Nancy Beth Cruzan has any *personal* interest in the perpetuation of what the State has decided is her life. As I have already suggested, it would be possible to hypothesize such an interest on the basis of theological or philosophical conjecture. But even to posit such a basis for the State's action is to condemn it. It is not within the province of secular government to circumscribe the liberties of the people by regulations designed wholly for the purpose of establishing a sectarian definition of life. * * *

My disagreement with the Court is thus unrelated to its endorsement of the clear and convincing standard of proof for cases of this kind. Indeed, I agree that the controlling facts must be established with unmistakable clarity. The critical question, however, is not how to prove the controlling facts but rather what proven facts should be controlling. In my view, the constitutional answer is clear: The best interests of the individual, especially when buttressed by the interests of all related third parties, must prevail over any general state policy that simply ignores those interests.

WASHINGTON v. GLUCKSBERG

Supreme Court (United States).
521 U.S. 702 (1997).

[Physicians who occasionally treat terminally ill patients claimed that Washington law, which provides that "a person is guilty of promoting a suicide attempt when he knowingly causes or aids another person to attempt suicide" [Wash. Rev. Code § 9A.36.060(1) (1994)], is unconstitutional.]

Chief Justice Rehnquist delivered the opinion of the Court.

The question presented in this case is whether Washington's prohibition against "caus[ing]" or "aid[ing]" a suicide offends the Fourteenth Amendment to the United States Constitution. We hold that it does not. * * *

The plaintiffs asserted "the existence of a liberty interest protected by the Fourteenth Amendment which extends to a personal choice by a mentally competent, terminally ill adult to commit physician-assisted suicide." * * * Relying primarily on *Planned Parenthood of Southeastern Pa. v. Casey*, 505 U.S. 833 (1992), and *Cruzan v. Director, Mo. Dept. of Health*, 497 U.S. 261 (1990), the District Court agreed, 850 F.Supp., at 1459–1462, and concluded that Washington's assisted-suicide ban is unconstitutional because it "places an undue burden on the exercise of [that] constitutionally protected liberty interest." * * * The District Court also decided that the Washington statute violated the Equal Protection Clause's requirement that " 'all persons similarly situated ... be treated alike.' " [A panel of the Court of Appeals for the Ninth Circuit reversed. Upon rehearing, an en banc Ninth Circuit reversed and affirmed the district court's judgment.]

We begin, as we do in all due process cases, by examining our Nation's history, legal traditions, and practices. In almost every State—indeed, in almost every western democracy—it is a crime to assist a suicide. The States' assisted-suicide bans are not innovations. Rather, they are longstanding expressions of the States' commitment to the protection and preservation of all human life. * * *

Though deeply rooted, the States' assisted-suicide bans have in recent years been reexamined and, generally, reaffirmed. * * * Public concern and democratic action are therefore sharply focused on how best to protect dignity and independence at the end of life, with the result that there have been many significant changes in state laws and in the attitudes these laws reflect. Many States, for example, now permit "living wills," surrogate health-care decisionmaking, and the withdrawal or refusal of life-sustaining medical treatment. * * * At the same time, however, voters and legislators continue for the most part to reaffirm their States' prohibitions on assisting suicide. * * *

The Due Process Clause guarantees more than fair process, and the "liberty" it protects includes more than the absence of physical restraint. * * * The Clause also provides heightened protection against government interference with certain fundamental rights and liberty interests. * * *

* * * [W]e "ha[ve] always been reluctant to expand the concept of substantive due process because guideposts for responsible decisionmaking in this unchartered area are scarce and open-ended." Collins, 503 U.S., at 125. By extending constitutional protection to an asserted right or liberty interest, we, to a great extent, place the matter outside the arena of public debate and legislative action. We must therefore "exercise the utmost care whenever we are asked to break new ground in this field," * * * lest the liberty protected by the Due Process Clause be subtly transformed into the policy preferences of the Members of this Court * * *.

Our established method of substantive-due-process analysis has two primary features: First, we have regularly observed that the Due Process Clause specially protects those fundamental rights and liberties which are, objectively, "deeply rooted in this Nation's history and tradition." Second, we have required in substantive-due-process cases a "careful description" of the asserted fundamental liberty interest. * * *

The Washington statute at issue in this case prohibits "aid[ing] another person to attempt suicide," and, thus, the question before us is whether the "liberty" specially protected by the Due Process Clause includes a right to commit suicide which itself includes a right to assistance in doing so.

We now inquire whether this asserted right has any place in our Nation's traditions. Here * * * we are confronted with a consistent and almost universal tradition that has long rejected the asserted right, and continues explicitly to reject it today, even for terminally ill, mentally competent adults. * * *

Respondents contend, however, that the liberty interest they assert is consistent with this Court's substantive-due-process line of cases, if not with this Nation's history and practice. Pointing to Casey *and Cruzan,* respondents read our jurisprudence in this area as reflecting a general tradition of "self-sovereignty," and as teaching that the "liberty" protected by the Due Process Clause includes "basic and intimate exercises of personal autonomy". * * * According to respondents, our liberty jurisprudence, and the broad, individualistic principles it reflects, protects the "liberty of competent, terminally ill adults to make end-of-life decisions free of undue government interference."

The question presented in this case, however, is whether the protections of the Due Process Clause include a right to commit suicide with another's assistance. * * * The history of the law's treatment of assisted suicide in this country has been and continues to be one of the rejection of nearly all efforts to permit it. That being the case, our decisions lead us to conclude that the asserted "right" to assistance in committing suicide is not a fundamental liberty interest protected by the Due Process Clause. The Constitution also requires, however, that Washington's assisted-suicide ban be rationally related to legitimate government interests. * * * This requirement is unquestionably met here. * * *

First, Washington has an "unqualified interest in the preservation of human life." *Cruzan,* 497 U.S., at 282. The State's prohibition on assisted suicide, like all homicide laws, both reflects and advances its commitment to this interest. * * * The State also has an interest in protecting the integrity and ethics of the medical profession. * * *

Next, the State has an interest in protecting vulnerable groups—including the poor, the elderly, and disabled persons—from abuse, neglect, and mistakes. * * * If physician-assisted suicide were permitted, many might resort to it to spare their families the substantial financial burden of end-of-life health-care costs.

The State's interest here goes beyond protecting the vulnerable from coercion; it extends to protecting disabled and terminally ill people from prejudice, negative and inaccurate stereotypes, and "societal indifference." * * *

Finally, the State may fear that permitting assisted suicide will start it down the path to voluntary and perhaps even involuntary euthanasia. * * * Thus, it turns out that what is couched as a limited right to "physician-assisted suicide" is likely, in effect, a much broader license, which could prove extremely difficult to police and contain. Washington's ban on assisting suicide prevents such erosion.* * *

RODRIGUEZ v. BRITISH COLUMBIA

Supreme Court (Canada).
[1993] 3 S.C.R. 519.

[Sue Rodriguez, a 42–year-old mother, suffered from amyotrophic lateral sclerosis. Her condition was rapidly deteriorating and she was soon to lose the ability to swallow, speak, walk, and move her body without assistance. Thereafter, she would lose the capacity to breathe without a respirator, to eat without a gastrotomy, and would eventually become confined to a bed. Her life expectancy was between 2 and 14 months. The appellant did not wish to die so long as she still had the capacity to enjoy life but wished that a qualified physician be allowed to set up technological means by which she might, when she was no longer able to enjoy life, end her life by her own hand, at the time of her choosing. S. 241(b) of the Criminal Code, however, prevented the appellant from having assistance to commit suicide when she was no longer able to do so on her own. Rodriguez challenged the constitutionality of the provision on various grounds.]

Justices La Forest, Sopinka, Gonthier, Iacobucci, and Major:

The most substantial issue in this appeal is whether s. 241(b) infringes s. 7 in that it inhibits the appellant in controlling the timing and manner of her death. I conclude that while the section impinges on the security interest of the appellant, any resulting deprivation is not contrary to the principles of fundamental justice. I would come to the same conclusion with respect to any liberty interest which may be involved. Section 7 of the *Charter* provides as follows:

7. Everyone has the right to life, liberty and security of the person and the right not to be deprived thereof except in accordance with the principles of fundamental justice.

The appellant argues that, by prohibiting anyone from assisting her to end her life when her illness has rendered her incapable of terminating her life without such assistance, by threat of criminal sanction, s. 241(b) deprives her of both her liberty and her security of the person. The appellant asserts that her application is based upon (a) the right to live her remaining life with the inherent dignity of a human person, (b) the right to control what happens to her body while she is living, and (c) the right to be free from governmental interference in making fundamental personal decisions concerning the terminal stages of her life. The first two of these asserted rights can be seen to invoke both liberty and security of the person; the latter is more closely associated with only the liberty interest.

(a) Life, Liberty and Security of the Person

The appellant seeks a remedy which would assure her some control over the time and manner of her death. While she supports her claim on the ground that her liberty and security of the person interests are engaged, a consideration of these interests cannot be divorced from the sanctity of life, which is one of the three Charter values protected by s. 7.

None of these values prevail a priori over the others. All must be taken into account in determining the content of the principles of fundamental justice and there is no basis for imposing a greater burden on the propounder of one value as against that imposed on another.
* * *

Sanctity of life, as we will see, has been understood historically as excluding freedom of choice in the self-infliction of death and certainly in the involvement of others in carrying out that choice. At the very least, no new consensus has emerged in society opposing the right of the state to regulate the involvement of others in exercising power over individuals ending their lives.

The appellant suggests that for the terminally ill, the choice is one of time and manner of death rather than death itself since the latter is inevitable. I disagree. Rather it is one of choosing death instead of allowing natural forces to run their course. The time and precise manner of death remain unknown until death actually occurs. There can be no certainty in forecasting the precise circumstances of a death. Death is, for all mortals, inevitable. Even when death appears imminent, seeking to control the manner and timing of one's death constitutes a conscious choice of death over life. It follows that life as a value is engaged even in the case of the terminally ill who seek to choose death over life.

Indeed, it has been abundantly pointed out that such persons are particularly vulnerable as to their life and will to live and great concern has been expressed as to their adequate protection * * *

* * * That there is a right to choose how one's body will be dealt with, even in the context of beneficial medical treatment, has long been recognized by the common law. To impose medical treatment on one who refuses it constitutes battery, and our common law has recognized the right to demand that medical treatment which would extend life be withheld or withdrawn. In my view, these considerations lead to the conclusion that the prohibition in s. 241(b) deprives the appellant of autonomy over her person and causes her physical pain and psychological stress in a manner which impinges on the security of her person. * * *

The appellant asserts that it is a principle of fundamental justice that the human dignity and autonomy of individuals be respected, and that to subject her to needless suffering in this manner is to rob her of her dignity. * * *

That respect for human dignity is one of the underlying principles upon which our society is based is unquestioned. I have difficulty, however, in characterizing this in itself as a principle of fundamental justice within the meaning of s. 7. While respect for human dignity is the genesis for many principles of fundamental justice, not every law that fails to accord such respect runs afoul of these principles. To state that "respect for human dignity and autonomy" is a principle of fundamental justice, then, is essentially to state that the deprivation of the appellant's security of the person is contrary to principles of fundamental justice because it deprives her of security of the person. This interpretation would equate security of the person with a principle of fundamental justice and render the latter redundant. * * *

The principles of fundamental justice are concerned not only with the interest of the person who claims his liberty has been limited, but with the protection of society. Fundamental justice requires that a fair balance be struck * * *. In my view the balance struck in this case conforms to this requirement. * * *

Section 241(b) has as its purpose the protection of the vulnerable who might be induced in moments of weakness to commit suicide. This purpose is grounded in the state interest in protecting life and reflects the policy of the state that human life should not be depreciated by allowing life to be taken. * * *

[Because it also does not violate the constitutional prohibition of cruel and unusual punishment, nor the prohibition of discrimination of the disabled,] section 241(b) [of the Code] is not contrary to the provisions of the *Charter*.

McLachlin, with L'Heureux–Dubé, JJ., dissenting:

* * * In my view, the denial to Sue Rodriguez of a choice available to others cannot be justified. The potential for abuse is amply guarded against by existing provisions in the *Criminal Code*, as supplemented by the condition of judicial authorization, and ultimately, it is hoped, revised legislation. * * *

In my view, the reasoning of the majority in *R. v. Morgentaler*, [1988] 1 S.C.R. 30, is dispositive of the issues on this appeal. In the present case, Parliament has put into force a legislative scheme which does not bar suicide but criminalizes the act of assisting suicide. The effect of this is to deny to some people the choice of ending their lives solely because they are physically unable to do so. This deprives Sue Rodriguez of her security of the person (the right to make decisions concerning her own body, which affect only her own body) in a way that offends the principles of fundamental justice, thereby violating s. 7 of the *Charter*. The violation cannot be saved under s. 1. This is precisely the logic which led the majority of this Court to strike down the abortion provisions of the *Criminal Code* in *Morgentaler*. In that case, Parliament had set up a scheme authorizing therapeutic abortion. The effect of the provisions was in fact to deny or delay therapeutic abortions to some women. This was held to violate s. 7 because it deprived some women of the right to deal with their own bodies as they chose thereby infringing their security of the person, in a manner which did not comport with the principles of fundamental justice. Parliament could not advance an interest capable of justifying this arbitrary legislative scheme, and, accordingly, the law was not saved under s. 1 of the *Charter*. * * *

It is established that s. 7 of the *Charter* protects the right of each person to make decisions concerning his or her body: *Morgentaler, supra*. This flows from the fact that decisions about one's body involve "security of the person" which s. 7 safeguards against state interference which is not in accordance with the principles of fundamental justice. Security of the person has an element of personal autonomy, protecting the dignity and privacy of individuals with respect to decisions concerning their own body. It is part of the persona and dignity of the human being that he or she have the autonomy to decide what is best for his or her body. This is in accordance with the fact, alluded to by McEACHERN C.J.B.C. below, that "s. 7 was enacted for the purpose of ensuring human dignity and individual control, so long as it harms no one else": (1993), 76 B.C.L.R. (2d) 145, at p. 164. * * * It is argued that the denial to Sue Rodriguez of the capacity to treat her body in a way available to the physically able is justified because to permit assisted suicide will open the doors, if not the floodgates, to the killing of disabled persons who may not truly consent to death. The argument is essentially this. There may be no reason on the facts of Sue Rodriguez's case for denying to her the choice to end her life, a choice that those physically able have available to them. Nevertheless, she must be denied that choice because of the danger that other people may wrongfully abuse the power they have over the weak and ill, and may end the lives of these persons against their consent. Thus, Sue Rodriguez is asked to bear the burden of the chance that other people in other situations may act criminally to kill others or improperly sway them to suicide. She is asked to serve as a scapegoat.

* * * [But the] principles of fundamental justice require that each person, considered individually, be treated fairly by the law.

[In sum,] I conclude that the infringement of s. 7 of the *Charter* by s. 241(b) has not been shown to be demonstrably justified under s. 1 of the *Charter*.

Cory, J., dissenting:

* * * I can see no difference between permitting a patient of sound mind to choose death with dignity by refusing treatment and permitting a patient of sound mind who is terminally ill to choose death with dignity by terminating life preserving treatment, even if, because of incapacity, that step has to be physically taken by another on her instructions. Nor can I see any reason for failing to extend that same permission so that a terminally ill patient facing death may put an end to her life through the intermediary of another, as suggested by Sue Rodriguez. The right to choose death is open to patients who are not physically handicapped. There is no reason for denying that choice to those that are. * * * This will ensure that Sue Rodriguez, who has lived her life with such dignity and courage, may choose to end her life with that same courage and dignity. * * *

Notes and Questions

1. *Disability and autonomy.* In many jurisdictions there is no constitutionally protected right to assisted suicide. See *Death, Dying and the Law* (Sheila A. M. McLean ed., 1996). As in the Canadian case of *Latimer*, in which a father killed his disabled daughter and was sentenced for murder, complicated questions around the legal construction of disability and of understandings of autonomy are raised. For example, is there a difference between the cases dealing with mentally incapacitated patients and those of fully capable persons who wish to die? Does constitutional law draw a distinction between assisted suicide and the termination of life-saving treatment? In *Cruzan*, the USSC recognized "the more specific interest in making decisions about how to confront an imminent death" and ruled that the Constitution granted competent persons a "constitutionally protected right to refuse lifesaving hydration and nutrition." Is this compatible with the reasoning in *Glucksberg*? Note that Chief Justice Rehnquist cited the applicability to *Cruzan*:

The right assumed in *Cruzan*, however, was not simply deduced from abstract concepts of personal autonomy. Given the common-law rule that forced medication was a battery, and the long legal tradition protecting the decision to refuse unwanted medical treatment, our assumption was entirely consistent with this Nation's history and constitutional traditions. The decision to commit suicide with the assistance of another may be just as personal and profound as the decision to refuse unwanted medical treatment, but it has never enjoyed similar legal protection. Indeed, the two acts are widely and reasonably regarded as quite distinct. See *Vacco v. Quill* [521 U.S. 793 (1997)]. In *Cruzan* itself, we recognized that most States outlawed assisted suicide—and even more do today—and we certainly gave no intimation that the right to refuse unwanted medical treatment could be somehow transmuted into a right to assistance in committing suicide. 497 U. S., at 280.

Washington v. Glucksberg, 521 U.S. 702, 725 (1997).

2. *Universality?* The decision in *Rodriguez* relies heavily on the assumption that all "Western democracies" share the same opinion as the Canadian legislature. One of the most liberal approaches to euthanasia can be found in The Netherlands. The Dutch legislature enacted a statute that allows for certain forms of assisted suicide. This decision had been previously endorsed by the Dutch High Court: "In the 1973 *Leeuwarden* case, the Dutch high court excluded physicians who assisted patients from criminal sanctions if they carefully and prudently followed the guidelines of the RDMA. The court found the doctrine of 'force majeure,' something that compels the physician to act, persuasive. The *Leeuwarden* decision illustrated the Dutch consensus that physicians should not endeavor to prolong life under all circumstances." Alison C. Hall, *To Die with Dignity: Comparing Physician–Assisted Suicide in the United States, Japan, and the Netherlands*, 74 Wash. U. L.Q. 803, 826 (1996). How does this affect the argument of the Canadian Court? Do you think that a father who, after careful and prudent deliberation, kills his child to spare her suffering should be held to a different standard than doctors? Who should be empowered to formulate such standards? Should they be subject to review under constitutional law, or is this not a matter for jurists? What kind of circumstances would bring a decision to end somebody else's life into the sphere of constitutional protection? What is the relationship between constitutional protection and "force majeure"?

Consider an approach from a "non-Western" democracy, Japan:

* * * [A] physician at the Tokai University School of Medicine Hospital (Tokai Daigaku) administered a lethal dose of potassium chloride to a fifty-eight-year-old, terminally ill cancer patient. Prosecutors sought a three year sentence for Dr. Masahito Tokunaga and accused him of "behavior that betrayed the nation's faith in doctors." The Yokohama District Court sentenced Tokunaga to a two year suspended prison term. The court established a legal framework strictly limiting a physician's actions in assisting patient death. The court emphasized that the patient must express a clear wish to end life before a doctor may assist the request. * * *

Although the 1995 ruling in the *Tokai Daigaku* case established a clear legal standard, the continuing national debate over the case illustrates the troubling aspects of the decision. The court noted the dilemma of the physician when faced with a request to assist in a patient's suicide. Unlike the Dutch, the Japanese guidelines do not specify that the patient should administer the lethal drug with her own hand. Moreover, the guidelines do not require patient evaluation by several physicians and psychiatrists.

The court expressed dissatisfaction with the lack of hospice facilities and other pain elimination techniques that would obviate the necessity of physician assisted death. The decision noted that patients would not wish for death if their pain could be alleviated. The decision does establish the patient's right to have her wishes regarding death fulfilled. Nonetheless, the court limited the absolute right of the patient to choose death to prevent "a general trend to think lightly of human life." Moreover, the court addressed the critics' concern that the patient must have a clear and voluntary declaration of intent.

Id. at 832–34 (1996).

3. *Balancing fundamentals. Rodriguez* is discussed primarily in terms of individual autonomy, while the dissenting opinions each emphasize a different approach. The majority in the Canadian decision balances this autonomy against other constitutional interests. Is such balancing an unprincipled form of legal reasoning? Some argue that there are no rational criteria for assessing the "weight" of rights, while others maintain that it is clearly rational to assess what kind of constitutional interests are at stake for whom under what circumstances and with what effects in a particular situation. Does the general critique leveled against balancing apply to the *Rodriguez* case? Also consider that the question of assisted suicide may include family rights and the rights and obligations of the medical profession. Some cases of assisted suicide raise the question as to whether the law can shift responsibility for life-or-death decisions to the medical (or any other) profession, since doctors may be the ones to have the final say. Annette E. Clark, *Autonomy and Death*, 71 Tulane L. Rev. 45 (1996). Or should the law grant the power of decisionmaking to family members based on the constitutional right of respect for family life? Here, clashes between the right of an individual and the rights of a collective, like the family, arise again. For a discussion of these issues, see Martha A. Field, *Killing "The Handicapped"—Before and After Birth*, 16 Harv. Women's L.J. 79 (1993).

4. *Church doctrine.* The Colombian Constitutional Court ruled six to three in favor of a constitutional right to doctor-assisted euthanasia for the terminally ill, invalidating Art. 326 of the Penal Code, which considered euthanasia to be homicide. Serge F. Kovaleski, *Colombian High Court Legalizes Mercy Killing: Vatican Assails Assisted Suicide Decision*, Houston Chron., Aug. 24, 1997, at 28A, cited in David Crump, Eugene Gressman, and David S. Day, *Cases and Materials on Constitutional Law* 563–64 (3d ed. 1998): "In announcing the decision, the court's president explained, 'The State has the duty to protect life, but this duty is not absolute—it has a limit. There is not just one morality. Every person can determine their own sense of life, whether it is sacred or not.' " A superficial reading of the Court's jurisprudence might lead to an exaggerated sense of the degree to which the Court's opinions, outside the ambit of abortion, conflict with the teachings of the Catholic Church. In fact, much of the Court's jurisprudence is consistent with liberal strains of Catholic social teachings. For instance, a "constitutionalism of poverty," bears striking similarities to liberation theology's "option for the poor." See Martha I. Morgan, *Taking Machismo to Court: The Gender Jurisprudence of the Colombian Constitutional Court*, 30 U. Miami Inter–Am. L. Rev. 253 (1999).

C.3. DRUGS

The use of drugs arguably does bodily harm to the individual user and social harm to others. Some drugs, like alcohol or tobacco, are mostly not treated as such, while in the case of "soft" drugs, like marijuana or hashish, it has been argued that their use should nevertheless be protected by rights to privacy, self-determination, and liberty, as well as by religious freedom in certain contexts. This section reveals that such cases rely on balancing individual interests and social welfare.

HASHISH CASE

Federal Constitutional Court (Germany).
90 BVerfGE 145 (1994).

[German drug law requires permission of any use of drugs including cannabis but not alcohol or tobacco. It criminalizes production, dealing with, importing, exporting, selling, handling, or obtaining such drugs. Various German lower courts asked the Federal Constitutional Court to consider whether these criminal provisions, when applied to marijuana and cannabis, violate the right to self-determination in conjunction with the rights to dignity, physical integrity, and equality. In this case a man was sentenced to a prison term for selling about 6 kilograms of cannabis to various "friends."]

Article 2 sec. 1 of the Constitution protects every form of human activity without consideration of the importance of the activity for a person's development. However, only the inner core of the right to determine the course of one's own life is accorded absolute protection and thus withdrawn from interference by public authority. Dealings with drugs, and in particular the act of voluntarily becoming intoxicated, cannot be reckoned as part of that absolute core because of the numerous direct and indirect consequences for society. Outside the core the general right to freedom of action is only guaranteed within the limits of the second half of the sentence contained in Article 2, para 1 of the Constitution. This means that it is subject to the limits placed on it in accordance with the constitutional order.

R. v. MALMO–LEVINE

British Columbia Court of Appeal (Canada).
2000 B.C.D. Crim. J. 212.

[M.-L., who was convicted of possession of marijuana, challenged the constitutionality of the prohibition on marijuana possession in the Narcotic Control Act (NCA).]

Braidwood, J.

[41] * * * [C]ourts must consider more closely whether the actions in question engage the liberty interest. * * * The issue in these cases can be boiled down to essentially the question: is the activity of "fundamental personal importance?"

[69] * * * Due to the penal provisions of the NCA, the "liberty" interests of the appellants are automatically engaged. * * * It was not

necessary for the Court to discern whether there is a free-standing "right to smoke recreational drugs" or a "right to control one's bodily integrity" contained within the meaning of "liberty" due to the presence of these penal sanctions. * * *

[71]   The next stage involves identifying and defining the relevant principle or principles of fundamental justice [which may justify a limitation of a fundamental right]. * * *

[97]   The appellants have argued that the so-called "harm principle" is the operative principle of fundamental justice in this case.

[98]   The "harm principle" was articulated best by Victorian philosopher and economist John Stuart Mill in his essay *On Liberty*. He wrote:

> The object of this Essay is to assert one very simple principle, as entitled to govern absolutely the dealing of society with the individual in the way of compulsion and control, whether the means used be physical force in the form of legal penalties, or the moral coercion of public opinion. That principle is, that the sole end for which mankind are warranted, individually or collectively, in interfering with the liberty of action of any of their number, is self-protection. That the only purpose for which power can be rightfully exercised over any member of a civilised community, against his will, is to prevent harm to others. His own good, either physical or moral is not a sufficient warrant. * * * Over himself, over his own body and mind, the individual is sovereign. J.S. Mill, *On Liberty*, ed. by Edward Alexander, (Peterborough: Broadview Press, 1999) pp. 51–2.

[99]   In [another case Justice Wilson, in a dissenting opinion,] considered the ideas of Mill in context of the Charter. She stated:

> "I believe that the framers of the Constitution in guaranteeing 'liberty' as a fundamental value in a free and democratic society had in mind the freedom of the individual to develop and realize his potential to the full, to plan his own life to suit his own character, to make his own choices for good or ill, to be non-conformist, idiosyncratic and even eccentric—to be, in to-day's parlance, 'his own person' and accountable as such. * * * Of course, this freedom is not untrammelled. We do not live in splendid isolation. We live in communities with other people. Collectivity necessarily circumscribes individuality and the more complex and sophisticated the collective structures become, the greater the threat to individual liberty in the sense protected by s. 7." * * *

[103]   The relevance of the harm principle was challenged by counsel during argument. It is now necessary to define this principle and determine its implications for the case at bar. * * *

[131]   I note in passing that the "harm principle" is not absolute, and there would be legitimate exceptions to it. * * * A limit to the harm principle would most likely arise in situations involving vulnerable groups. * * *

[133]   However, I only note such limitations to the harm principle in passing as it is not pertinent to the case at bar. Both Mr. Malmo–Levine and Mr. Caine are healthy adults who do not fall in the category of "vulnerable groups."

[134]   I conclude that on the basis of all of these sources—common law, Law Reform Commissions, the federalism cases, Charter litigation—that the "harm principle" is indeed a principle of fundamental justice within the meaning of s. 7. It is a legal principle and it is concise. Moreover, there is a consensus among reasonable people that it is vital to our system of justice. Indeed, I think that it is common sense that you do not go to jail unless there is a potential that your activities will cause harm to others.

[The question for the Court to answer, then, is whether the deprivation of the appellants' liberty, by criminalizing the use of drugs, is in accordance with the principles of fundamental justice.]

[136]   * * * [T]he focus should have remained on freedom from imprisonment or the threat of imprisonment rather than a free-standing "right to possess recreational drugs" or "the freedom over the integrity of one's person." * * * [It] is an error to confuse the underlying activity—in this case, the possession of a recreational drug—with the s. 7 right of freedom from imprisonment. * * *

[141]   I point out that it is well-established law that Parliament has a wide discretion to designate certain activities to be "criminal" and impose criminal sanctions: * * * [T]he Supreme Court of Canada has ruled that the "purpose" of a criminal law must be to suppress an "evil" that has the potential of inflicting harm to others. However, the Court has not specifically quantified this "evil" for the purposes of establishing a threshold standard of "harm." * * *

[142]   The findings of fact made by the trial judge in Caine show that marihuana indeed poses a risk of harm to others and society. * * * [The trial judge stated that there] is a risk that, upon legalization, rates of use will increase * * *.

[143]   * * * Does the NCA Strike the Right Balance Between the Individual and the State?

[145]   * * * The appellants' right to be free from imprisonment should not be equated with the activity that could possibly lead to their imprisonment. The focus should remain on the effects to an individual's life when placed in prison. * * * Men and women may have their lives, public and private, destroyed; families may be broken up; the state may be put to considerable expense; all these consequences are to be taken into account when determining whether a particular kind of conduct is so obnoxious to social values that it is to be included in the catalogue of crimes. If there is any other course open to society when threatened, then that course is to be preferred. The deliberate infliction of punishment or any other state interference with human freedom is to be justified only where manifest evil would result from failure to interfere. * * *

[154]   [In sum,] in balancing the rights of the individual and the interests of the State in this case, this reality should not be ignored. * * *

[156]   * * * Once again, there is no clear winner in this "balancing test." In the end, I am reminded that a degree of judicial deference is owed to Parliament in matters of public policy. * * *

[159]   Therefore, I find that the legal prohibition against the possession of marihuana does not offend the operative principle of fundamental justice in this case.

Prowse J. (dissenting):—

[165]   * * * [I] am satisfied that the appellants have established that s. 3(1) of the Narcotic Control Act ... breaches their right to life, liberty and security of the person in a manner which is inconsistent with a principle of fundamental justice, in this case, the "harm principle". * * * [The] nature and extent of the harmful effects of marijuana as disclosed by the evidence are not sufficiently serious to justify the imposition of criminal law sanctions, including imprisonment.

NEW JERSEY v. T.L.O.

Supreme Court (United States).
469 U.S. 325 (1985).

[A teacher at a high school, upon discovering a then–14–year-old freshman and her companion smoking cigarettes in a school lavatory in violation of a school rule, took them to the principal's office. After questioning and denial of smoking, her purse was searched, where the principal found a pack of cigarettes, marijuana, and a list of people who owed money to respondent. The state brought delinquency charges against the student, who was adjudged a delinquent. On appeal, the student maintained that the search of the purse was an "unreasonable search and seizure" and that the evidence seized should be suppressed. The New Jersey Supreme Court accepted this claim, and the state brought the case to the Court.]

Justice White delivered the opinion of the Court.

[We] have recognized that even a limited search of the person is a substantial invasion of privacy. * * * We have also recognized that searches of closed items of personal luggage are intrusions on protected privacy interests, for "the Fourth Amendment provides protection to the owner of every container that conceals its contents from plain view." * * * A search of a child's person or of a closed purse or other bag carried on her person, no less than a similar search carried out on an adult, is undoubtedly a severe violation of subjective expectations of privacy.

Of course, the Fourth Amendment does not protect subjective expectations of privacy that are unreasonable or otherwise "illegitimate." * * * To receive the protection of the Fourth Amendment, an expectation of privacy must be one that society is "prepared to recognize as legitimate." * * * The State of New Jersey has argued that, because of the pervasive supervision to which children in the schools are necessarily subject, a child has virtually no legitimate expectation of privacy in articles of personal property "unnecessarily" carried into a school. This argument has two factual premises: (1) the fundamental incompatibility of expectations of privacy with the maintenance of a sound educational environment; and (2) the minimal interest of the child in bringing any items of personal property into the school. Both premises are severely flawed.

How, then, should we strike the balance between the schoolchild's legitimate expectations of privacy and the school's equally legitimate need to maintain an environment in which learning can take place? It is evident that the school setting requires some easing of the restrictions to which searches by public authorities are ordinarily subject. The warrant requirement, in particular, is unsuited to the school environment: requiring a teacher to obtain a warrant before searching a child suspected of an infraction of school rules (or of the criminal law) would unduly interfere with the maintenance of the swift and informal disciplinary procedures needed in the schools. Just as we have in other cases dispensed with the warrant requirement when "the burden of obtaining a warrant is likely to frustrate the governmental purpose behind the search," * * * we hold today that school officials need not obtain a warrant before searching a student who is under their authority.

Notes and Questions

1. *A fundamental interest?* To some, drug use is not a sufficiently important issue to raise basic constitutional concerns. Canadian courts, however, have explicitly discussed the question of the fundamental importance of a given activity. In *Buhlers v. British Columbia*, (1999) 65 BCLR 3d 114, in which the applicant's driver's license had been suspended, the Supreme Court of British Columbia, S99–2119 (1999), considered and rejected a "right to drive" as a liberty. While liberty interests may not necessarily be restricted to the physical liberty of the individual and may, in some circumstances, embrace broader liberties that are fundamentally or inherently personal to the individual and go to the root of a person's dignity and independence, this does not extend to the driving of a motor vehicle on a public highway. "It is not a matter that is fundamental or inherently personal to the individual. * * * To hold otherwise would trivialize the liberty sought to be protected by s. 7." In *Cunningham v. Canada*, [1993] 2 S.C.R. 143, the Canadian Supreme Court stated that the "Charter does not protect against insignificant or 'trivial' limitations of rights." In a German case, The Horseback Riding in The Forest Case (80 BVerfGE 137 (1989)), Justice Grimm, who dissented, argued along the same lines. The majority held, however, that even trivial activities are protected by the Constitution. They argued that to base self-determination on a court's judgment is a contradiction in terms. The dissent argued that this position would lead to the intervention of the Court in such minor cases that it would undermine the idea of fundamental rights protection. With whom do you agree? Who defines what is insignificant to whom?

2. *Law or policy?* The Netherlands is known for its commitment to the decriminalization of drugs. Consider the Dutch policy, Fact sheet: Dutch Drugs Policy,[e] Ministry of Justice, The Netherlands:

e. Reproduced from <www.min-just.nl:8080/a_beleid/fact/cfact7.htm#3>.

Regulations on drugs are laid down in the Opium Act. The Act draws a distinction between hard drugs, (e.g. heroin, cocaine and XTC) which pose an unacceptable hazard to health, and soft drugs (e.g. hashish and marihuana), which constitute a far less serious hazard. The possession of drugs is an offence. However, the possession of a small quantity of soft drugs for personal use is a summary, or minor, offence.

Importing and exporting drugs are the most serious offences under the provisions of the Opium Act, although manufacturing, selling and attempting to import drugs are also offences. As is the case in other countries, the cultivation of hemp is prohibited, except for certain agricultural purposes (e.g. to form windbreaks, and for the production of rope). New legislation is currently being drafted to raise the maximum penalty for commercial hemp production from two to four years' imprisonment.

That the use of drugs is not an offence is based on the principle that everything should be done to stop drug users from entering the criminal underworld where they would be out of the reach of the institutions responsible for prevention and care.

Is this position a matter of social policy only, or might constitutional liberty concerns also play a role?

3. *Harm to society?* The German and Canadian drug cases above speak of determining a threshold of harm for establishing that the state's interest in protecting society takes priority over an individual's liberty interest. Is the reasoning in these cases convincing? Are the fundamental rights of the individual adequately protected in the balance?

4. *Drugs for different purposes.* Should we distinguish between the use of substances for different purposes, like killing pain (as in the case of marijuana), recreation (as in the case of alcohol), or competitive advantage (to take exams or work longer hours)? (Compare this to the medical marijuana proposals in U.S. legislatures and *United States v. Oakland Cannabis Buyers' Cooperative*, 532 U.S. 483 (2001), which provide no medical necessity exception to the Controlled Substances Act's prohibitions on manufacturing and distributing marijuana.) Should the purpose affect the legality of use? Should the right to decide what one does to oneself be limited by the interest of a public health insurance system, which would be responsible for the costs of abusive behavior? Can a national public insurance system refuse to cover such costs? Say there is no such system? What about cases in which smokers sue tobacco companies for damages resulting from longtime enjoyment of nicotine: Are they autonomous actors as imagined by constitutional law? See Thaddeus Mason Pope, *Balancing Public Health Against Individual Liberty: The Ethics of Smoking Regulations*, 61 U. Pitt. L. Rev. 419 (2000). Consider that the French Constitutional Council decided that tobacco advertising may be restricted based on the constitutional right to health, which the state has an obligation to protect. Cons. Const, Jan. 8, 1991, AJDA 1991, 382 *note Wachsmann*, CC 90–283.

5. *A crime?* Is criminal law the best means to combat drug abuse? For the USSC position, see *Employment Division, Dep't of Human Resources of Oregon v. Smith*, 494 U.S. 872 (1990), in Chapter 8. Can a general prohibition be considered constitutional if rules of criminal procedure allow a state prosecutor to stop proceedings in less severe cases? Consider the dissent by Justice Sommer in the German *Hashish Case*, above, at 212:

I cannot fully agree with the majority's decision. Criminalizing the possession, import, and buying of cannabis in small amounts for one's personal use violates [the right to self determination in conjunction with the right to dignity and physical integrity]. Already the threat of punishment—along with imposing and implementing it—carries a special weight as an interference with fundamental rights. The criminal provisions in question [do] not stand the test of proportionality. * * *

Criminal law shall protect the basics of a common social order. It is used as the 'ultima ratio' of such protection, if a specific activity is, beyond its illegality, specifically detrimental to society and unbearable in the ordered living together of the people, its prevention is particularly urgent. Criminal law which accords to the rule of law and governed by the liberal order of the Constitution is thus necessarily fragmented (Adolf Arndt 1968).

Criminal norms address, through the immanent social-ethical judgment of unworthiness on a specific activity, the citizen in personhood, in his honour, and thus have close ties to human dignity. * * * Then, the principle of proportionality has even more meaning as the standard of constitutionality of a criminal provision. [Since it is not anymore evident that the use of cannabis is a severely dangerous act, the provisions in question are overbroad and thus unconstitutional. The argument that a public prosecutor may in certain cases decide to acquit a defendant does not compensate this violation of fundamental rights. Not procedural, but] material penal law has to define what is criminal behavior and what is not.

6. *Obligations?* The use or nonuse of drugs may not only be claimed as a right but also be imposed as an obligation. Generally, constitutional standards change when a person affects the well being of another person by taking drugs. This is what some have argued is the case with pregnant or breast-feeding women. In the U.S., women have been prosecuted for damaging a fetus via drug abuse or simply taking the wrong medicine during pregnancy. See Nancy Kubasek, *The Case Against Prosecutions for Prenatal Drug Abuse*, 8 Tex. J. Women & L. 167 (1999). Note also that the GFCC held that women have an obligation, derived from the right to life, to carry a pregnancy to term. Does this include an obligation to live healthily during pregnancy? Or does this turn a mother into an object for the child's needs and thereby violate her right to dignity? Do fathers have obligations? The issue of obligation also arises in cases that challenge the constitutionality of laws mandating the use of automobile safety belts or the wearing of helmets while riding a motorcycle. Can one be understood to have a legal obligation to act in accordance with one's own well-being? Does this violate a right to self-determination? See *People v. Kohrig*, 498 N.E.2d 1158, 1164–66 (Ill. 1986); Jonathan M. Purver, Annotation, *Validity of Traffic Regulations Requiring Motorcyclists to Wear Protective Headgear*, 32 A.L.R. 3d 1270, § 4 (1970 and Supp. 1998).

7. *Who defines dignity?* The foregoing drug cases illustrate conflicts between an individual and the state. In other cases there are conflicts of a more complex kind. With regard to the work of predominantly female prostitutes in peep shows, employers argue a right to free enterprise and freedom of contract when they are charged with exploiting women. But some women in the sex industry argue a right to self-determination and dignity as well as freedom of contract. In addition, they claim the right of protection

against violence. The almost exclusively male customers argue a right to self-determination as a right to "pleasure." How is it determined whose rights have been violated and at whose expense? Who defines what dignity means to whom? Is dignity violated when people watch others while remaining invisible themselves? Does it make a difference whether those who are watched are naked or dressed? Does it matter that it is usually men watching women?

D. THE RIGHT TO ONE'S OWN IDENTITY

The right to self-determination includes the right to choose how to present oneself to others. It would seem to be an obvious intrusion if the state were to require the wearing of certain clothes or mandate a specific haircut, but it may be a different case in a state-employment setting, as in the military. Beyond that, there are even more-complex cases of informational and representational self-determination.

D.1. SEX, GENDER AND BODY

SHEFFIELD AND HORSHAM v. UNITED KINGDOM

European Court of Human Rights.
27 E.H.R.R. 163 (1998).

[The applicants had been registered at birth as being male and were male-to-female postoperative transsexuals. They had changed their names, which was recorded on their passports and driving licenses, while their birth certificates and social security, national insurance, employment, and police records continued to record their preoperative genders and names. Disclosure of preoperative history caused the applicants' embarrassment and prejudice, and one applicant was precluded from contracting a valid marriage with her male partner.]

40. * * * The applicants complained that the failure of the respondent State to recognise in law that they were of the female sex constituted an interference with their rights to respect for their private lives.

51. The court observes that it is common ground that the applicants' complaints fall to be considered from the standpoint of whether or not the respondent state has failed to comply with a positive obligation to ensure respect for their rights to respect for their private lives. It has not been contended that the failure of the authorities to afford them recognition for legal purposes, in particular by altering the register of births to reflect their new gender status or issuing them with birth certificates whose contents and nature differ from the entries made at the time of their birth, constitutes an "interference."

Accordingly, * * * the issue raised [is] not that the respondent State should abstain from acting to their detriment but that it has failed to take positive steps to modify a system which they claim operates to their prejudice. The Court will therefore proceed on that basis.

52. The court reiterates that the notion of "respect" is not clear-cut, especially as far as the positive obligations inherent in that concept

are concerned: having regard to the diversity of the practices followed and the situations obtaining in the Contracting States, the notion's requirements will vary considerably from case to case. In determining whether or not a positive obligation exists, regard must be had to the fair balance that has to be struck between the general interest of the community and the interests of the individual, the search for which balance is inherent in the whole of the Convention.

53. [In other cases] the Court concluded that the same respondent State was under no positive obligation to modify its system of birth registration in order to allow those applicants the right to have the register of birth updated or annotated to record their new sexual identities or to provide them with a copy birth certificate or a short-form certificate excluding any reference to sex at all or sex at the time of births.

* * * The essence of their complaints concerns the continuing insistence by the authorities on the determination of gender according to biological criteria alone and the immutability of the gender information once it is entered on the register of birth.

56. * * * [The] non-acceptance by the authorities of the respondent State for the time being of the sex of the brain as a crucial determinant of gender cannot be criticised as being unreasonable. The Court would add that * * * it still remains established that gender reassignment surgery does not result in the acquisition of all the biological characteristics of the other sex. * * *

58. The Court * * * conclude[s] that on the basis of scientific and legal developments alone the respondent State can no longer rely on a margin of appreciation to defend its continuing refusal to recognise in law a transsexual's post-operative gender. For the Court, it continues to be the case that transsexualism raises complex scientific, legal, moral and social issues, in respect of which there is no generally shared approach among the Contracting States.

59. Nor is the Court persuaded that the applicants' case histories demonstrate that the failure of the authorities to recognise their new gender gives rise to detriment of sufficient seriousness as to override the respondent State's margin of appreciation in this area. * * * It cannot be denied that the incidents alluded to by Miss Sheffield were a source of embarrassment and distress to her and that Miss Horsham, if she were to return to the United Kingdom, would equally run the risk of having on occasions to identify herself in her pre-operative gender. At the same time, it must be acknowledged that an individual may with justification be required on occasions to provide proof of gender as well as medical history. This is certainly the case of life assurance contracts which are *uberrimae fidei*. It may possibly be true of motor insurance where the insuror may need to have regard to the sex of the driver in order to make an actuarial assessment of the risk. Furthermore, it would appear appropriate for a court to run a check on whether a person has a criminal record, either under his or her present name or former name, before accepting that person as a surety for a defendant in criminal proceedings. However, quite apart from these considerations the situa-

tions in which the applicants may be required to disclose their pre-operative gender do not occur with a degree of frequency which could be said to impinge to a disproportionate extent on their rights to respect for their private lives. The Court observes also that the respondent State has endeavoured to some extent to minimise intrusive inquiries as to their gender status by allowing transsexuals to be issued with driving licences, passports and other types of official documents in their new name and gender, and that the use of birth certificates as a means of identification is officially discouraged.

60.   * * * [T]he Court reiterates that this area needs to be kept under review by Contracting States.

61.   For the above reasons, the Court considers that the applicants have not established that the respondent State has a positive obligation under * * * the Convention to recognise in law their post-operative gender. Accordingly, there is no breach of that provision in the instant case.

[The Court also denied a violation of the right to form a family, which, in the European Convention, explicitly refers to "Men and women of marriageable age."]

Bernhardt, Thor Vilhjalmsson, Spielmann, Palm, Wildhaber, Makarczyk and Voicu, JJ., partly dissenting:

Once again the Court is confronted with the difficult and profoundly human problems associated with transsexualism. * * * The essence of their complaint is that in certain situations—for example, in taking out motor, house or life insurance, entering into other types of contracts, standing as surety in court proceedings—they are obliged to produce a birth certificate indicating their sex as recorded at birth which is in plain contradiction with their new post-operative appearance after gender reassignment surgery. Such situations, they contend, cause intense humiliation, distress and embarrassment. * * *

We are of the conviction that in the almost 12 years since [the other case] was decided important developments have occurred in this area. [But] U.K. law has remained at a standstill. No review of the legal situation of transsexuals has taken place.

In our opinion the fair balance that is inherent in the Convention tilts decisively in favour of protecting the transsexuals' right to privacy.

* * * [The] problems of such transsexuals are being dealt with in a respectful and dignified manner by a large number of Convention countries. We do not believe that the Court need wait until every Contracting Party has amended its law in this direction before deciding that [the Convention] gives rise to a positive obligation to introduce reform. Bearing in mind that the Convention must be interpreted in the light of modern day conditions, enough has been achieved today in Europe to sustain this argument.

We accept, as the Court observes * * *, that transsexualism raises complex scientific, legal, moral and social issues, in respect of which there is no generally shared approach among the Contracting States. However, what this means is that the legal recognition of a change of sex—or its repercussions in areas of law such as marriage, affiliation, privacy, adoption etc—takes diverse forms in the different countries. But how can we expect uniformity in such a complex area where legal change will necessarily take place against the background of the States' traditions and culture? However, the essential point is that in these countries, unlike in the United Kingdom, change has taken place—whatever its precise form is—in an attempt to alleviate the distress and suffering of the post-operative transsexual and that there exists in Europe a general trend which seeks in differing ways to confer recognition on the altered sexual identity. * * *

We are convinced, therefore, * * * that the States' margin of appreciation in this area can no longer serve as a defence in respect of policies which lead inevitably to embarrassing and hurtful intrusions into the private lives of such persons. * * * [and that] solutions can be found which respect the dignity and sense of privacy of post-operative transsexuals.

Van Dijk, J., partly dissenting:

* * * [I] would not characterize the issue of the legal status of post-operative transsexuals as one of minorities, but rather as one of privacy: everyone's right to live one's life as one chooses without interference, and everyone's right to act and be treated according to the identity that corresponds best to one's innermost feelings, provided by doing so one does not interfere with public interests or the interests of others. Even if there were only one post-operative transsexual in the United Kingdom claiming legal recognition of the reassignment of his or her sex, that would not make the claim any weaker. * * *

[And with] respect to [the right to marriage] I can be quite brief. * * * [The] applicants have to be considered as persons of the new sex for legal purposes, including for [this right]. * * * Only in that way is their choice of a new sexual identity socially respected and legally recognised.

TRANSSEXUALS CASE

Federal Constitutional Court (Germany).
49 BVerfGE 286 (1978).[f]

[The complainant had undergone surgery and changed sex from male to female. Lower courts were divided on the question whether to change the birth certificate.]

B.   1. According to the medical opinion before the court, the complainant is psychologically a woman. * * * Yet the complainant is treated as a man in the eyes of the law. The possibility of living a normal, healthy, and socially adjusted life as a woman is thus denied to this person. * * *

2.   (a) [The Constitution] protects the dignity of a person as he understands himself in his individuality and self-awareness. This is

f. Reproduced from Donald P. Kommers, *The Constitutional Jurisprudence of* *the Federal Republic of Germany* 330–332 (2d ed. 1997).

connected with the idea that each person is responsible for himself and controls his own destiny. [The Constitution also] guarantees the free development of a person's abilities and strengths. Human dignity and the constitutional right to free development of personality demand, therefore, that one's civil status be governed by the sex with which he is psychologically and physically identified. Our law and society are based on the principle that each person is either "masculine" or "feminine," and that this identification is independent of any possible genitalic anomalies. It is doubtful, however, that the theory of gender immutability, determined by sexual characteristics apparent at birth, can be maintained with the absolute certitude reflected in [the lower court decision, which denied the change of the birth certificate]. Various forms of biological intersexuality are known to modern medicine. * * *

(b) The right to free development of personality is protected only within the limits of the moral law. In the present case the moral law has not been infringed. Whether an operation, not therapeutically necessary, to change a person's sex should be regarded as immoral is not the issue here. * * * [Because medical opinion deemed it necessary,] the sexual change secured by the complainant cannot be considered immoral. * * *

Suffice it to say that the ability of a man to conceive a child or of a woman to bear a child is not a prerequisite for marriage. * * * The marriage partners form this community on the basis of their own ideas and expectations. It may be that many people reject the idea of a marriage between a male transsexual and a man as something deserving of moral condemnation. Such irrational fears, however, may not stand in the way of marriage. * * * [T]ranssexuals do not seek homosexual relationships. Rather, they desire normal relations * * *.

Notes and Questions

1. *Sex and gender.* "Sex" has been defined as a biological phenomenon, on which distinctions may be based in rare cases, while sex discrimination is now commonly understood to be legally relevant as an aspect of gender—the socially constructed form of sexuality or, for some, of culturally embedded experience. A fundamental challenge to personal privacy, dignity, and capacity for self-determination arises when gender identity is disrespected by the state. Why does the issue of gender identity seem to come up only in cases brought by transsexuals? Is nobody else's gender identity ever violated? Consider that some people experience harassment when they appear to be of the "wrong" gender.

2. *European attitudes.* The ECHR has decided several cases on transsexuality. In *Rees v. United Kingdom*, 9 E.H.R.R. 56 (1986), it held that Rees, a postoperative transsexual, had no right to have the birth register modified to reflect his postoperative identity. The Court, however, was "conscious of the seriousness of the problems affecting these persons and the distress they suffer" (para. 47). Recalling that the Convention must be interpreted and applied in light of current circumstances, the ruling stated that "the need for appropriate legal measures should therefore be kept under review having regard particularly to scientific and societal developments." *Id.* In *Cossey v. United Kingdom*, 13 E.H.R.R. 622 (1990), [the

Court was faced with essentially the same question and, by a narrow vote, reaffirmed *Rees*. It noted that there was still little common ground between the contracting states in this area and that the states enjoyed a wide margin of discretion. Again, it stressed the importance of continuing review of the relevant legal measures. In *B. v. France*, 16 E.H.R.R. 1 (1992), the Court held that more far-reaching disabilities, to which the postoperative transsexual was subject under French law, violate the privacy rights of that person.

The European Court of Justice (ECJ) has ruled differently. In Case C–13/94, *P. v. S.*, 1996 E.C.R. I–2143, [1996] 2 C.M.L.R. 247, involving the dismissal of a transsexual from work, it held that unfair treatment arising from gender reassignment constituted discrimination on grounds of sex and the principle of equal treatment for men and women. The ECJ rejected the argument of the UK government that the employer would also have dismissed a male-to-female transsexual, as he had a female-to-male transsexual, by saying:

> Where a person is dismissed on the ground that he or she intends to undergo, or has undergone, gender reassignment, he or she is treated unfavourably by comparison with persons of the sex to which he or she was deemed to belong before undergoing gender reassignment.

> To tolerate such discrimination would be tantamount, as regards such a person, to a failure to respect the dignity and freedom to which he or she is entitled, and which the court has a duty to safeguard. * * *

3. *Law and (ab)normalities.* In a concurrence to *Sheffield and Horsham*, 27 E.H.R.R. 163 (1998), three judges (De Meyer, Valticos, and Morenilla, concurring) stated: "Situations which depart from the normal and natural order of things must not give rise to aberrations in the field of fundamental rights. In that field arguments derived from scientific, legal or societal developments, the variety of practices and conditions or the lack of a consensus or a common approach, are not necessarily relevant. Arguments based on the margin of appreciation that states are said to have are not relevant at all. Common sense must be sufficient."

In the German *Transsexuals Case*, the GFCC rejected "irrational fears" but invoked them one sentence later with a reference to "normal relations." Is common sense an adequate basis? If the function of fundamental rights is to protect individuals from majoritarian intrusion, can this argument be accepted? The judges added that, "like any other human being, a transsexual must come to terms with his past." Might that be more difficult for some than for others? What about a person convicted of a criminal offence who, after having completed a jail sentence, faces social exclusion upon release? But also consider a decision from the Singapore High Court, *Lim Ying v. Hiok Kian Ming Eric*, (1992) 1 S.L.R. 184: "If the 'assignment' to the female sex is made after the operation, then the operation has changed the sex. From this it would follow that if a 50–year-old male transsexual, married and the father of children, underwent the operation, he would then have to be regarded in law as a female and capable of 'marrying' a man. The results would be nothing if not bizarre." What exactly is "bizarre" about this? Is this acceptable language for constitutional review? Is there a constitutional right to live in ways that others consider "bizarre"?

4. *Who defines dignity?* Who is charged with establishing the limits of self-determination? Consider an attempt by nongovernmental organizations, in the International Bill of Gender Rights (adopted on June 17, 1995), Fifth

Int'l Conf. on Transgender Law & Emp. Pol'y 41–43,[g] to define what the right to privacy and identity may mean from the perspective of transsexuals and transgender people:

> All human beings carry within themselves an ever-unfolding idea of who they are and what they are capable of achieving. The individual's sense of self is not determined by chromosomal sex, genitalia, assigned birth sex, or initial gender role. Thus, the individual's identity and capabilities cannot be circumscribed by what society deems to be masculine or feminine behavior. It is fundamental that individuals have the right to define, and to redefine as their lives unfold, their own gender identities, without regard to chromosomal sex, genitalia, assigned birth sex, or initial gender role.

> Therefore, all human beings have the right to define their own gender identity regardless of chromosomal sex, genitalia, assigned birth sex, or initial gender role, and further, no individual shall be denied Human or Civil Rights by virtue of a self-defined gender identity which is not in accord with chromosomal sex, genitalia, assigned birth sex, or initial gender role.

> The Right to Free Expression of Gender Identity

> * * *

> The Right to Secure and Retain Employment and to Receive Just Compensation

> * * *

> The Right of Access to Gendered Space and Participation in Gendered Activity

> * * *

> The Right to Control and Change One's Own Body

> * * *

> The Right to Competent Medical and Professional Care

> * * *

> The Right to Freedom from Psychiatric Diagnosis and Treatment

> * * *

> The Right to Sexual Expression

> * * *

> The Right to Form Committed, Loving Relationships and Enter into Marital Contracts

> * * *

> The Right to Conceive, Bear, or Adopt Children; the Right to Nurture and Have Custody of Children and to Exercise Parental Capacity.

> * * *

5. *Physical appearance.* Identity is often linked to physical appearance. A right to identity—based on dignity, privacy or self-determination—is often invoked to defend one's right to choose how to appear in the world. In some workplace settings, a certain length of hair is argued to be a safety require-

g. Reproduced from <www.pfc.org.uk/ gendrpol/gdrights.htm>.

ment. Does long hair hinder soldiers or police personnel from maximally performing their duties? Can helmets or other protective gear be produced to allow people to keep their hair long? Does it matter that longer hair tends to be gender specific? In 1999, the highest German administrative court held (BVerwG, 1 WB 24/99) that "it is not constitutionally objectionable that female soldiers are allowed to carry their hair longer than male soldiers." The judges argued that since male soldiers potentially saw combat and, at the time, women were not allowed to serve in combat units, practical considerations required a different standard. However, in 2000, the ECJ (Case C–285/98, *Kreil v. Germany*, [2000] E.C.R. I–69, [2002] 1 C.M.L.R. 36) required that women be allowed to serve in combat units. Will they now be required to cut their hair? Does this violate their right to self-determination? Can the right to self-determination be circumscribed according to the requirements of employment? Also consider the case of the Spanish Constitutional Tribunal, TC, Oct. 30, 1987 (R.T.C. No. IV, p. 231), in which an experienced senior waiter was dismissed after disregarding his employer's objection to his beard. The company argued that there was a long-standing custom in the regional hotel industry against waiters having "capillary additions," while the waiter claimed his physical appearance was protected by the constitutional right to privacy. The Court disagreed and defined privacy to exclude a person's physical appearance, holding that the restriction on beards lacked "constitutional relevance" and was a question of ordinary legality. Do you agree? Remember the German case, above, on riding horses. Again, who decides what is fundamental, and thus of constitutional relevance, and for whom?

D.2. INFORMATIONAL SELF–DETERMINATION AND THE RIGHT TO ANONYMITY

Identity rests not only on physical appearance but also on personal history and information about one's self, thus on personal data. Consider the following analysis by Gebhard Rehm, *Just Judicial Activism? Privacy and Informational Self–Determination in U.S. and German Constitutional Law*, 32 UWLA L. Rev. 275, 275–79 (2001):

> * * * Technical progress in general, computerized data banks permitting the combination of personal data such as credit card payments in seconds in particular, and the booming expansion of the Internet, which allows not only executing, but also recording formerly largely anonymous transactions like shopping, to name but a few factors, have increasingly spawned the fear of perfect categorization of individuals in personal profiles and of complete surveillance. In the age of automatic data processing, huge amounts of personal information are available and accessible to almost everyone interested. * * * In some respects, the situation has become frighteningly similar to George Orwell's "1984" vision of a totalitarian state keeping its citizens under complete surveillance. That an *Orwellian* society, consisting of degrading human beings to mere objects of state action, is inconsistent with the Kantian idea of man as a rational being, that underlies a democratic society based on the rule of law, hardly needs explanation. But every single move towards a society with more rather than less surveillance also gnaws at Kant's ideal because it leads to more heteronomous decisionmaking. The more

others know about individuals, particularly those who wield a certain power over them such as government or employers, the more the individuals will feel urged to subordinate their own judgment to that of others.

Unlimited collection and availability of data not only conflicts with the philosophical values that are at the core of democratic societies, but also has negative legal implications. It violates the spirit of liberties that human beings enjoy in a democratic and liberal society. Surveillance of one's behavior, even the fear of being controlled, tends to have a chilling effect on the enjoyment of freedom. * * *

On the other hand, a right to protect one's data against public knowledge cannot be absolute. The discharge of governmental functions requires a solid basis of information. * * *

This conflict of countervailing interests regarding privacy did not go unnoticed by neither the German Federal Constitutional Court nor the U.S. Supreme Court. Both courts have tried to cope with this challenge by recognizing a constitutional right of each individual to control the flux of certain personal information. The Federal Constitutional Court has called this right, somewhat clumsily, the "right to informational self-determination," [*Census Case*, 65 BVerfGE 1 (1983)] the U.S. Supreme Court subsumes this right under the right to privacy. The constitutional right to privacy encompasses, however, the protection of basically two interests: firstly, the individual interest in avoiding the disclosure of personal matters (the "informational aspect"), and secondly, the interest in the independence in making certain kinds of important decisions (the "decisionmaking aspect") [*Whalen v. Roe*, 429 U.S. 589, 599–601 (1977)].

* * * [T]he differences in structure, scope and level of protection between the right to informational self-determination and the right to privacy are by no means negligible. The German Federal Constitutional Court has derived a comprehensive right to privacy from the right to personhood which is guaranteed in Art. 1, 2 GG. The U.S. Supreme Court, in contrast, has refused to recognize an all-embracing right to privacy as a matter of federal constitutional law that in principle protects against disclosure of any data.

LUSTRATION CASE

Constitutional Court (Hungary).
Decision 60/1994 (XII.22.) AB hat.[h]

[In 1994, the Hungarian Parliament approved an Act mandating background checks on individuals holding certain key offices.]

1.   * * * The Court declares that data and records on individuals in positions of public authority and those who participate in political life—including those responsible for developing public opinion—that reveal that these persons at one time carried out activities contrary to the principles of a constitutional state, or belonged to State organs that at one time pursued activities contrary to the same, count as information of public interest * * *.

h. Reproduced from 2 E. Eur. Case Rep.
Const. L. 159 (1995).

2. The Constitutional Court declares that [certain sections of the Act] concerning background checks on individuals who hold certain key offices * * * is unconstitutional. [It] declares that * * * the Act fails to establish consistent criterion to distinguish between public and personal data, and this leads to an unconstitutional distinction between those who are subject to background checks and those who are not, even though they otherwise fall under the same criteria. With respect to the groups of individuals referred to explicitly, the Act draws such a distinction between checks conducted on persons in the print media as opposed to those in the electronic media. To eliminate this discrimination, the legislature must establish a consistent standard within the constitutional framework * * * based on its own judgment. * * *

5. a)[In addition, the Court] declares that Parliament created an unconstitutional situation by failing to guarantee the practice of the right to informational self-determination, especially the right of individuals at issue on whom the organizations or individuals defined in * * * the Act collected information, or who appeared in reports they compiled to review their own records to delete these records. * * *

c) Parliament created an unconstitutional situation * * * in failing to oblige all authorities who keep public records, including the minister-without-portfolio for the secret services, to guarantee the conditions for the review of the records of those under scrutiny. The Constitutional Court calls upon Parliament to meet its legislative obligation * * *

REASONING

III

* * * 'Lustration laws' such as the Act at issue in this decision are typical products of the change of system underway in the former socialist countries of East–Central Europe. The lustration, or background checks, generally served two different purposes, and accordingly, the laws come in two types. The majority of lustration laws lay down rules on incompatibility. Those who held certain State or party positions in the former socialist system, and further, those who belonged to the ranks of the political police or were to be found among its secret informers, may not occupy certain positions as the change of system unfolds. Particular laws extend to employees of institutions of culture, (higher) education, and academia, public service radio and television, and also to lawyers (see the Czech and Slovak lustration or purification law of 1991, and the * * * 1990 treaty uniting * * * Germany * * *, [and the] laws * * * in Bulgaria [and] Albania). Constitutional Court decisions were rendered on each of these acts in the respective countries. * * * [T]he constitutional complaints concerned violations of the right to freely choose employment and occupation, and of international agreements which guaranteed social welfare rights.

A consummate example of the other type of lustration law is Germany's 'Stasi Act.' In this case, the primary aim was nothing other than bringing completely to the light of day the activities of the former State security organs and secret agents. Calls for the public naming of former agents were to be heard in other countries as well, but did not come to pass. * * *

The 'lustration' or background check thus came in two types, according to purpose. One aimed to guarantee personnel replacements in certain key positions, and at the same time keep the nations transition as defined in the Constitution from being endangered by those who in the past stood actively and in their professional capacity against the principles of a constitutional state. The other aimed toward a genuine public disclosure of the nature of the previous regime, to guarantee a measure of redress, and simultaneously to symbolise the irreversibility of the changes, through revealing the activities of the secret services.

* * * [T]he Act at issue * * * was created with the same purpose. * * * [But] it can not be said * * * that it aims primarily to avert a suspension of or risk to the transition. Nor was the identity of the one-time agents publicly disclosed; indeed, the post-socialist era legislative process only broadened the veil of secrecy. * * * Even the content of the Act differed from that in other countries; it neither declares incompatibility between personnel in past and present offices, nor proposes to unveil the whole previous system of political informing, least of all with respect to those who had been under observation. The Act in fact promotes the transparency of those in prominent political and other public roles, and thus of the life of the nation in general. In it, there is a confluence of the moral obligation that remained in the wake of the transition: the unveiling of deceit, publicity rather than punishment and the value system normal to a constitutional state.

The Act must therefore be examined in view of present-day, normal legal conditions characteristic of a constitutional state. Owing to the passage of time, the legal peculiarities of the transition period can today hardly be validated within the framework of obligations presumed by a constitutional state. It must also be taken into account, however, that the change of system, from a political perspective, in fact marked a revolutionary change in that prior to the Constitution, Hungary was by definition not a constitutional state. * * * The Constitutional Court also clarified that the legislature is accorded different measures of constitutional manoeuverability to consider a historical situation * * *.

The Act must therefore be examined in view of the fact that in a constitutional state, the fundamental right to the freedom of information presumes that the functioning of the State is transparent to its citizens. For this reason, the scope of private life of individuals who hold positions of public authority or who partake in political life—with respect to aspects in connection with these public activities—is restricted. Entirely independent of the original goals of the lustration laws, "public" information on individuals in certain positions of public authority today necessarily includes information revealing previous activity expressly contradictory to the principles of a constitutional state, or individuals' memberships in an organization which pursued such activity. In defining the range of such activity, the Constitutional Court must consider the transition as a historical fact. The constitutional issue at the crux of the matter involves striking a balanced circumscription of the circle of individuals at issue and the information of public interest on them.

Nor can it be overlooked that the very system of records at issue, maintained to the present day, is itself unconstitutional, and that these records both those of the agents who supplied the information, and those of the individuals who are the subjects of the files must therefore be brought into harmony with the Constitution. Continued secrecy, constitutionally speaking, is an insufficient solution. * * *

IV

* * *

[Yet] it does not follow from the declassification of the secret records at issue in the Act that the information therein must necessarily be made available to all, or rather, that the information automatically becomes of public interest. * * * It is actually the office held by the individual under scrutiny which determines whether the information is of public interest. * * *

The shedding of light on the past, and with it an objective evaluation of the importance of the change of regime, presumes the public disclosure of the activities of the former secret services. With regard to such records, even laws which otherwise protect the security of information, personal and otherwise, regularly make exceptions to the rule, given suitable guarantees and in order to serve the interest of public knowledge. * * * Just as violations of the right to (informational) self-determination require clarification of just who may gain access to secret service files which concern them, so that they may understand the true extent to which the past regime influenced their personal fate, and in this way, at least, temper the transgression against their human dignity, so too the nagging issue of the past in the larger sense, as it concerns the nation as a whole, can be resolved only if the secrecy of former secret service records is not further maintained.

[But an] unconditional secrecy of the data in the records * * * is unconstitutional * * *

The fundamental right to the protection of personal records and to access information of public interest are properly interpreted in light of each other. * * * This is natural, for informational self-determination and the freedom of information are two complimentary preconditions for individual autonomy. * * *

* * * The legislature is thus not entirely free either to decide whether to destroy secret service records, although as earlier noted they engendered an unconstitutional situation from their very incipience; or to continue handling them as secret; or to disclose their contents and if disclosure is allowed, to decide who shall have access to the records. * * * Drawing the line * * ** offers the legislature fairly broad room to manoeuvre. * * * This political decision about the precise determination of the range of information subject to the probe and the range of information to be deemed personal cannot be based upon the Constitu-

tion, but instead on the constitutional certainty that the records neither can be kept secret, nor be brought entirely to light. * * *

TAX DATA CASE

Constitutional Tribunal (Poland).
Decision dated 24 April 1997 (K. 21/96).

[A statute allowed tax authorities to obtain information on financial matters from banks that, before the law was passed, was disclosed only when requested by a court or a prosecutor. In addition, banks were allowed to exchange information on customers. The statute said that a legitimate interest in tax equity justified fiscal and bank secrecy. The statute also authorized the Minister of Finance and the President of the Supreme Chamber of Control to publish information about the amount of taxes paid or tax arrears of individual taxpayers engaged in commercial activity.]

Generally, it is accepted that privacy refers to the protection of information concerning a given person, guaranteeing, inter alia, a state of independence where the individual may decide upon the scope and extent on his life disclosed and communicated to third persons.

[This] is a necessary element of a democratic State.

[The] right to private life also includes the protection of confidentiality of data related to the financial situation of citizens and therefore relates also to bank accounts (and similar) * * * and transactions connected with them. This especially applies to those situations where a citizen is acting as a private person and not as a business entity.

[Thus] regulation[s] permitting public disclosure of information on the amount of taxes or the outstanding liabilities may be recognized as a repressive regulation. Publication of information, even on real facts, may cause adverse consequences to interested parties, both for their business and their reputation, i.e. personal dignity. Therefore introducing the possibility of undertaking such actions towards the citizen must comply both with substantive (principle of definition) and procedural (court protection) requirements. Failure to meet these requirements must mean non-constitutionality of the regulation in question.

JOHNS v. AUSTRALIAN SECURITIES COMMISSION

Supreme Court (Australia).
178 C.L.R. 408 (1993).

[Johns was questioned in a special proceeding by a Commissioner, as to which] Section 22 of the Act directs that an examination under s.19 "shall take place in private", the inspector being given discretion as to who may be present in addition to the inspector, the examinee's lawyer and any staff member approved by the A.S.C. ((5) ss.22(2), 23). The Act thus maintains the traditional privacy of examinations into the affairs of a company. Privacy has been observed in conducting such examinations out of consideration for the commercial reputation of the company and the protection of witnesses.

[The statute] provides for the making of a record of statements made at an examination—the transcripts in this case—and * * * [for] the distribution of such transcripts. Although [it] insist[s] on privacy in the conduct of an examination, [it] contains no express restriction on the giving of copies of transcripts. * * *

A statute which confers a power to obtain information for a purpose defines, expressly or impliedly, the purpose for which the information when obtained can be used or disclosed. The statute imposes on the person who obtains information in exercise of the power a duty not to disclose the information obtained except for that purpose. If it were otherwise, the definition of the particular purpose would impose no limit on the use or disclosure of the information. The person obtaining information in exercise of such a statutory power must therefore treat the information obtained as confidential whether or not the information is otherwise of a confidential nature. Where and so far as a duty of non-disclosure or non-use is imposed by the statute, the duty is closely analogous to a duty imposed by equity on a person who receives information of a confidential nature in circumstances importing a duty of confidence.

* * * The purposes for which information may legitimately be used or disclosed are one thing; the means by which information is used or disclosed are another. * * *

Prima facie, it is the privilege of any person who possesses information to keep the information confidential. That person may wish not to disclose it at all or may wish to disseminate it or to authorize its dissemination only for a limited purpose or to a limited class of persons. * * *

M.S. v. SWEDEN

European Court of Human Rights.
28 E.H.R.R. 313 (1997).

[Ms. M.S. was diagnosed as a child as having spondylolisthesis, a condition affecting the spine that can cause chronic back pain. In her adult life, she slipped and fell at work, injuring her back. She then went to a hospital several times and was unable to return to work for a long period of time. When she made a claim for compensation to the Social Insurance Office, her lawyer requested a copy of the file that had been compiled by the Office for the purposes of her claim. From the file she learned that the Office had asked the clinic for data and had received medical records. The Office rejected her claim on the basis of information therein.]

32. The Court observes that under the relevant Swedish law, the applicant's medical records at the clinic were governed by confidentiality * * *. Communication of such data by the clinic to the Office would be permissible under the Insurance Act only if the latter authority had made a request and only to the extent that the information was deemed to be material to the application of the Insurance Act * * *. This assessment was left exclusively to the competent authorities, the applicant having no right to be consulted or informed beforehand * * *

It thus appears that the disclosure depended not only on the fact that the applicant had submitted her compensation claim to the Office but also on a number of factors beyond her control. It cannot therefore be inferred from her request that she had waived in an unequivocal manner her right under Article 8 § 1 of the Convention to respect for private life with regard to the medical records at the clinic. * * *

37. However, * * * [t]he Court is satisfied that the interference had a legal basis and was foreseeable; in other words, that it was "in accordance with the law".

38. * * * The communication of the data was potentially decisive for the allocation of public funds to deserving claimants. It could thus be regarded as having pursued the aim of protecting the economic well-being of the country. Indeed this was not disputed before the Court. * * *

41. The Court reiterates that the protection of personal data, particularly medical data, is of fundamental importance to a person's enjoyment of his or her right to respect for private and family life as guaranteed by Article 8 of the Convention. * * *

Bearing in mind the above considerations and the margin of appreciation enjoyed by the State in this area, the Court will examine whether, in the light of the case as a whole, the reasons adduced to justify the interference were relevant and sufficient and whether the measure was proportionate to the legitimate aim pursued * * *.

42. * * * In the absence of objective information from an independent source, it would have been difficult for the Office to determine whether the claim was well-founded.

43. In addition, under the relevant law it is a condition for imparting the data concerned that the Office has made a request and that the information be of importance for the application of the Insurance Act * * *. The Office, as the receiver of the information, was under a similar duty to treat the data as confidential.

In the circumstances, the contested measure was therefore subject to important limitations and was accompanied by effective and adequate safeguards against abuse * * *

44. Having regard to the foregoing, the Court considers that there were relevant and sufficient reasons for the communication of the applicant's medical records by the clinic to the Office and that the measure was not disproportionate to the legitimate aim pursued. Accordingly, it concludes that there has been no violation of the applicant's right to respect for her private life, as guaranteed by Article 8 of the Convention.

GASKIN v. UNITED KINGDOM

European Court of Human Rights.
12 E.H.R.R. 36 (1989).

[Gaskin claimed access to files about his childhood, which were part of files of childcare facilities.]

38. As the Court held in [before] * * *, "although the essential object * * * is to protect the individual against arbitrary interference by the public authorities, there may in addition be positive obligations inherent in an effective 'respect' for family life."

39. The Commission considered that "respect for private life requires that everyone should be able to establish details of their identity as individual human beings and that in principle they should not be obstructed by the authorities from obtaining such very basic information without specific justification." * * * [It] noted that * * * the information compiled and maintained by the local authority related to the applicant's basic identity, and indeed provided the only coherent record of his early childhood and formative years, it found the refusal to allow him access to the file to be an interference with his right to respect for his private life falling to be justified * * *.

40. The Government contended that * * * the present case involved essentially the positive obligations of the State * * *, [that is] a failure by the State to secure through its legal or administrative system the right to respect for private and family life. * * * [It argued there that this] entailed a wide margin of appreciation for the State. The question [is thus] whether * * * a fair balance was struck between the * * * public interest * * * in the efficient functioning of the child care system * * *, and the applicant's interest in having access to a coherent record of his personal history * * *.

42. * * * [The] Court, in determining whether or not such a positive obligation exists, will have regard to the "fair balance that has to be struck between the general interest of the community and the interests of the individual * * *."

43. * * * [It] considers that the confidentiality of the contents of the file contributed to the effective operation of the child care system and, to that extent, served a legitimate aim, by protecting not only the rights of contributors but also of the children in need of care. * * *

49. In the Court's opinion, persons in the situation of the applicant have a vital interest, protected by the Convention, in receiving the information necessary to know and to understand their childhood and early development. On the other hand, it must be borne in mind that confidentiality of public records is of importance for receiving objective and reliable information, and that such confidentiality can also be necessary for the protection of third persons. Under the latter aspect, a system like the British one, which makes access to records dependent on the consent of the contributor, can in principle be considered to be compatible with the obligations under [the Convention], taking into account the State's margin of appreciation. * * * [U]nder such a system the interests of the individual seeking access to records relating to his private and family life must be secured when a contributor to the records either is not available or improperly refuses consent. Such a system is only in conformity with the principle of proportionality if it provides that an independent authority finally decides whether access has to be granted in cases where a contributor fails to answer or withholds

consent. No such procedure was available to the applicant in the present case.

Accordingly, the procedures followed failed to secure respect for Mr Gaskin's private and family life * * *. There has therefore been a breach of that provision.

Notes and Questions

1. *"Habeas data"*. The right to anonymity has been conceived as the informational aspect of the right to privacy, translating into a right to control the use of personal data. It has been accepted in many jurisdictions, e.g., in Puerto Rico *(Lopez Vives v. Policía de P.R.*, 118 P.R. Dec. 219 (1987)). The constitutional limits on access to personal data have already been considered above with regard to the integrity of the home as the territorial dimension of the right to be let alone. Now, we are dealing with the far vaster purview of the circulation of information. As noted in the following excerpt, the GFCC considered the problem of modern data collection in 1969 and in 1983 in regard to governmental census.

The Court held [in the *Census Case*, 65 BVerfGE 1 (1983)] that, based on the right to personhood, every individual has, in principle, a right to control the flux of all information relating to her. It abandoned the distinction between different personality spheres for the purpose of delineating the scope of the right. Though subject to a balancing test, the right to privacy therefore, in principle, protects against disclosure of data relating to individuals in any respect. The Court reasoned that the present and prospective conditions of automatic data processing permit a wide variety of abuses against which the individual has to be protected by being able to control the disclosure of data. Technical means of storing highly personalized information about individuals are practically unlimited and these data can be retrieved in a matter of seconds with the aid of automatic data processing, irrespective of distance. Information can be joined to other data collections, particularly when constructing integrated information systems to produce a partial or virtually complete personal profile, with the individual concerned having only insufficient means of controlling either its veracity or use. In view of the conditions of modern automatic data processing, there are no more inconsequential data. The question is not whether the data concern intimate actions, but how they can be joined to other data. What matters are the possible uses and abuses. The right to informational self-determination therefore protects the individual against unlimited investigation, storage, use and transmission of personal data. As an aspect of the general right to personhood, it encompasses the right of the individual to decide for himself, on the basis of the idea of self-determination, when and within what limits facts about his personal life shall be disclosed. This right would be infringed if the automatic processing of data could result in the reconstruction or release of the personality profiles of particular individuals.

Gebhard Rehm, *Just Judicial Activism? Privacy and Informational Self–Determination in U.S. and German Constitutional Law*, 32 U.West.L.A. L. Rev. 275, 312–13 (2001).

The GFCC emphasized the importance of knowledge as part of informational self-determination: "It would be incompatible with the right to informational self-determination if a legal order would permit a societal structure where the citizen could not be sure who knows something about him, what they know about him, when this information can be released, and what occasions the release of this data." *Census Case*, 65 BVerfGE 1 (1983).

Does this principle extend to the police taking surveillance videotapes in public places? Do constitutional standards differ if a state is in a period of transition or emergency? Is a limitation on a right to personal data compatible with the fundamental character of dignity and self-determination? If so, under what circumstances? Consider the Hungarian decision on lustration laws: Should the legislature be able to draw the line, or is this an issue of constitutional law? The HCC demanded safeguards against unlimited data transfer, based on an argument similar to the GFCC in the *Microcensus Case* (27 BVerfGE 1 (1969)). However, in practice, the technology is deliberately designed not to allow for such control. Should the law have something to say about the design of technology? Does the nature or structure of technology itself ever constrain the law? Is this a freedom of speech issue, or can freedom of speech be limited by considerations of privacy and dignity? On one aspect of this, consider Lawrence E. Rothstein, *Privacy or Dignity?: Electronic Monitoring in the Workplace*, 19 N.Y.L. Sch. J. Int'l & Comp. L. 379, 382 (2000):

> [In the U.S., privacy] highlights a "possessive individualism." Privacy implies notions of property, individualism, ownership and expectations with regard to the exclusion of outsiders without specific legal rights to the work premises. * * * Privacy is associated with one's home, with intimate relations, and with premises under a person's control. * * * This possessive, territorial view of privacy finds clear expression in the workplace.

> When a worker sells her capacity to labor, she alienates certain aspects of the person and puts them under the control of the employer. Thus in the U.S., workers in the workplace, except occasionally in restrooms and employee locker rooms, are not generally protected from surveillance on the grounds that the premises and equipment are possessions of the employer and the employee can have no legitimate expectation of intimacy or of protection from employer intrusion. * * *

> Where Anglo–American jurisdictions emphasize the concept of privacy in their legal protection of workers from monitoring and surveillance, continental European countries manifest a concept of human dignity more related to notions of community and citizenship than property. French, Italian, German and Spanish do not even have a direct equivalent of the English word "privacy." The concept of human dignity is a social one that promotes a humane and civilized life. The protection of human dignity allows a broader scope of action against treating people in intrusive ways. * * * At work, human dignity is denied by treating the employee as a mere factor of production with fixed capacities and vulnerabilities determining her behavior and ignoring both the worker's individuality in the face of statistical probabilities and the human potential to overcome or compensate for physical obstacles. The worker's dignity is denied when she is treated as a mechanism transparent to

the view of others at a distance and therefore manipulable or disposable without the ability to confront the observer.

[Rothstein then describes French and Italian labor laws and concludes:] In France and Italy, unlike the U.S., there is legal recognition that private power is as much an attack on dignity and liberty as is public power.

What are the differences entailed in protecting workplace rights through conceptions of dignity versus those of privacy? Does one provide a stronger basis than the other? Do these differences lead to a substantially different jurisprudence of fundamental rights? Are there any implications for the U.S. "state action" doctrine?

2. *Doctrine.* What is the doctrinal basis for a right of habeas data or informational self-determination? Is this fundamentally a dignity interest, like the right to respect for one's individuality and the right not to be turned into an object of someone else's interest? Or is this about self-determination, such as the right to decide how one is viewed by others? The GFCC combines the right to dignity with the right to self-determination to create a right of "informational self-determination." Why? Compare Spiros Simitis, *Reviewing Privacy in an Information Society*, 135 U. Pa. L. Rev. 707 (1987); David H. Flaherty, *Protecting Privacy in Surveillance Societies: The Federal Republic of Germany, Sweden, France, Canada, and the United States* (1989). American legal scholar Lawrence Lessig, *The Architecture of Privacy*, Taiwan Net '98 Conference,[i] calls for moving "beyond a debate about privacy that is not really the appropriate debate in cyberspace." *Id.* at 23. Do you agree that privacy is not the correct approach? By what reasoning could privacy be considered an inappropriate constitutional response to issues of data transfer? According to Lessig, the issue is better framed as local control of data. What is the constitutional status of this concept? See also Anita L. Allen, *Privacy-as-Data Control: Conceptual, Practical, and Moral Limits of the Paradigm*, 32 Conn. L. Rev. 861 (2000).

3. *Anonymity.* If there is a right to decide about personal data, it may include the right to use, or to withhold the use of, your name. Consider the argument of the District Court of Georgia, United States 1997, in *A.C.L.U. v. Miller*, 977 F.Supp. 1228 (N.D.Ga.1997), in which plaintiffs challenged the constitutionality of an act that made it a crime for any person to knowingly transmit false or unauthorized personal data through a computer network. They argued that the act had large implications for Internet users, many of whom "falsely identify" themselves on a regular basis to communicate about sensitive topics. The court concluded that the statute curtailed protected speech in order to avoid social ostracism, to prevent discrimination and harassment, and to protect privacy, and was not drafted with the precision required for laws regulating speech. Even if the statute could be used constitutionally under certain circumstances—i.e., to prosecute persons who intentionally "falsely identify" themselves in order to deceive or defraud the public, or to persons whose commercial use of trade names and logos creates a substantial likelihood of confusion or the dilution of a famous mark—the statute is nevertheless overbroad because it operates unconstitutionally for a substantial category of the speakers it covers. The USSC, in *McIntyre v. Ohio Elections Comm'n*, 514 U.S. 334 (1995), decided that a prohibition against the distribution of anonymous leaflets was not constitutionally valid. Is there

i. Available at <http://lessig.org/content/articles/>.

thus a difference between the distribution of information on the Internet and on the street? Whose privacy interests are at stake, the speakers or the people being spoken about?

4. *Data in courts.* Is the German case about privacy, dignity, and self-determination, or is it about equality and discrimination? How would you assess the right of an injured party to name an offender against the offender's right to remain anonymous? Is there a difference between a private individual making an accusation in public, as happened in this case, and a public figure making a private individual's name public? Is it, for example, compatible with fundamental constitutional rights to allow courts to publish the names of defendants? Is it legitimate to do so before and/or after a verdict has been reached? Consider that German courts do not release names of people involved in cases when they publish decisions, while Northern American courts do. Also consider that the British House of Lords held, in *R. v. P. and Others,* [2001] 2 All ER 58, that information gained from wiretapping is admissible into evidence, and hence into the public record, if there are procedural safeguards against abuse. What if court hearings disclose personal data of people with only incidental or tangential involvement in cases? Particular consideration has been given to withholding data on children from public disclosure, but even this consideration has to be made compatible with the right to a public hearing in court. In a case before the ECHR, *B. and P. v. United Kingdom,* 34 E.H.R.R. 19 (2002), in which two fathers fought for child custody, the judge closed the hearing to the public, which the fathers claimed violated their right to a fair trial. The Court said:

> However, requirement to hold a public hearing is subject to exceptions. This is apparent from the text of art 6(1) itself, which contains the provision that "the press and public may be excluded from all or part of the trial * * * where the interests of juveniles or the private life of the parties so require, or to the extent strictly necessary in the opinion of the court in special circumstances where publicity would prejudice the interests of justice." [In the present case the] applicants [had sought to hold in public proceedings that] concerned the residence of each man's son following the parents' divorce or separation. The Court considers that such proceedings are prime examples of cases where the exclusion of the press and public may be justified in order to protect the privacy of the child and parties and to avoid prejudicing the interests of justice. To enable the deciding judge to gain as full and accurate a picture as possible of the advantages and disadvantages of the various residence and contact options open to the child, it is essential that the parents and other witnesses felt able to express themselves candidly on highly personal issues without fear of public curiosity or comment.

Should there be a right to access data about other people? Under what circumstances? Consider that in Argentina the Supreme Court ruled that an individual had a right to know where his brother was taken by the secret police, *Urteaga v. Estado Mayor Conjunto de las Fuerzas Armadas,* Argentina Supreme Court, [1999–I] J.A. 22. Is this a reaction to a specific historical situation only? Should such a right apply to relatives in all circumstances or to the public in general? Can you imagine a conflict of rights when prisoners fear stigmatization if information about them becomes public?

5. *Public and private.* A large percentage of data is processed by private rather than by public actors. Should constitutional rights bear on the actions of both? In the U.S., protection from intrusion by private actors is not guaranteed by the Constitution. For example, in *Intel Corp. v. Hamidi*, 114 Cal.Rptr.2d 244 (Cal.Ct.App.2001), a court decided that limitations of communication on a corporation's e-mail system are not subject to constitutional free speech protection since such a system is a private, and not public, forum. Even connection to the Internet does not render it a public space. Do you agree? Or does the Internet transform the categories of "public" and "private"? Is there a difference if data are used for a private purpose as compared with a public one? The USSC, in *Chandler v. Miller*, 520 U.S. 305 (1997), decided that drug testing as a means to obtain medical data on a person is not constitutionally valid if it is designed as an entry requirement for public office. What is the constitutional interest of the public employer, which has to be balanced against the personal interest of medical-data protection? Also consider that there are rights of access to public files but not to most private data. For example, the ISC understands access to government information as an issue of freedom of speech, *S.P. Gupta and Others v. President of India*, A.I.R. 1982 S.C. 149, 234. However, the information governments keep may well relate to the private lives of individuals and thus touch upon privacy interests. Consider the Israeli decision *Shalit et al. v. Peres et al.*, 44 (3) P.D. 353 (1990). The USSC has held that there is a common law right "to inspect and copy public records and documents, including judicial records and documents." *Nixon v. Warner Communications, Inc.*, 435 U.S. 589, 597 (1978). However, the right of access is not absolute. "[E]very court has supervisory power over its own records and files, and access has been denied where court files might have become a vehicle for improper purposes." 435 U.S. at 598. The hindering of business activity may even be a consideration for limiting access. See the ECHR in *Rotaru v. Romania* (Application no. 28341/95), 4 May 2000; *Niemietz v. Germany*, 16 E.H.R.R. 97 (1992); and *Halford v. United Kingdom*, 24 E.H.R.R. 523 (1997).

The USSC, in *United States Department of Justice v. Reporters Committee for Freedom of the Press*, 489 U.S. 749 (1989), on the question of access to a criminal's "rap sheet," drew a distinction between access in the interest of targeting a private person (i.e., by reporting in the mass media) and access in the interest of monitoring the government (i.e., civil rights activities). The ECHR, for example, in *Guerra v. Italy*, 26 E.H.R.R. 357 (1998), held that citizens may have a right to public data if their health is endangered. See Chapter 10. There is also a long Swedish tradition (since 1766, when Sweden adopted a freedom of information act), which is slowly informing EU law, that allows for broad access to public files. For example, in 1999, the Czech Republic passed the Free Access to Information Law (Act no 106/1999), under which all citizens have the right to be provided with information by state and local administrative bodies, with exceptions for classified information, business secrets, and personal data.

6. *Type of data.* Regarding data protection, one may want to look at the nature of the data in question. Compare *M.S.* and *Gaskin*: Is there a decisive difference? In the U.S., a young woman brought several rolls of film from a vacation to a supermarket to be developed. On one of the rolls of film was a picture, taken by her sister, of her and a friend naked in the shower. When she received the developed photographs, a written notice stated that one or

more of the photographs had not been printed because of their "nature." The woman subsequently learned that an employee had printed the photo and that the picture was circulating in the community. The Minnesota Supreme Court, in *Lake v. Wal–Mart*, 582 N.W.2d 231 (Minn.1998), held: "One's naked body is a very private part of one's person and generally known to others only by choice. This is a type of privacy interest worthy of protection. Therefore, without consideration of the merits of Lake and Weber's claims, we recognize the torts of intrusion upon seclusion, appropriation, and publication of private facts." Is this reasoning sound? Can you imagine "a type of privacy interest" not worthy of protection? How about a student's class notes distributed to a general public: Do they deserve privacy protection? Would pictures of people who are fully or partially clothed make a difference? What about medical data? In *Yesimhovitz v. Baruch and Bros.*, 447/72, 27 (2) P.D. 253 (1973), the Supreme Court of Israel held that disclosure of medical records for tax purposes does not violate the Constitution and that there is no duty of confidentiality for doctors when a patient discloses an illegal act. Consider the comment by Steven Silverstein, *Medical Confidentiality in Israeli Law*, 30 J. Marshall L. Rev. 747, 755 (1997)]:

> Notably, the differences between Israel and the United States regarding the disclosure of medical information relating to possible violent acts do not necessarily reflect a greater respect for medical secrecy in the United States. Rather, Israel's more expansive exceptions can be attributed to cultural and societal differences between the two countries, which are unrelated to the doctor-patient relationship. Indeed, it is difficult to compare a society of five million people with a compulsory army and large portions of civilians carrying weapons, with a society with almost 300 million people with a voluntary army and more unlicensed guns than licensed guns.

Consider that data on bank accounts has for a long time been considered very private and thus protected. Is it compatible with constitutional protections of privacy to release such information to the public or to police investigators to prevent, for example, money laundering or the financing of international terrorism? Compare Anita Ramasastry, *Secrets and Lies? Swiss Banks and International Human Rights*, 31 Vand. J. Transnat'l L. 325, 341–342 (1998). On January 20, 1995, in Belize, the Supreme Court held (*SEC v. Swiss Trade*, [1995] (Belize) (No. 85)) that data kept by private companies is protected not only under rules of confidentiality but also to protect businesses from foreign investigators (in this case, from U.S. officials). Can constitutions protect against transnational searches?

E. INTIMACY

Self-determination, privacy and dignity, as well as the right to respect for who you are and aspire to be, may provide the constitutional standards on which to consider intimate relationships and sexuality, including transsexuality and sexual orientation. As in other parts of this chapter, such cases often raise other constitutional questions, for example, equality or freedom of association. The main focus here is on whether a right to intimacy can be considered constitutionally protected.

E.1. FAMILIES

ELSHOLZ v. GERMANY

European Court of Human Rights.
34 E.H.R.R. 58 (2002).

[Elsholz alleged that the refusal to grant him access to his son, a child born out of wedlock, amounted to a breach of his right to family life.]

43. * * * The Court recalls that the notion of family under this provision is not confined to marriage-based relationships and may encompass other *de facto* "family" ties where the parties are living together out of wedlock. A child born out of such a relationship is *ipso jure* part of that "family" unit from the moment and by the very fact of his birth. Thus there exists between the child and his parents a bond amounting to family life * * *. * * * The Court further recalls that the mutual enjoyment by parent and child of each other's company constitutes a fundamental element of family life, even if the relationship between the parents has broken down, and domestic measures hindering such enjoyment amount to an interference with the right protected * * *.

44. The Court notes that the applicant lived with his son from his birth * * * for about one and a half years. He continued to see his son frequently until July 1991. The subsequent decisions refusing the applicant access to his son therefore interfered with the exercise of his right to respect for his family life * * *

45. The interference * * * constitutes a violation * * * unless it is "in accordance with the law", pursues an aim or aims that are legitimate * * * and can be regarded as "necessary in a democratic society". * * *

46. It was undisputed before the Court that the relevant decisions had a basis in national law, * * *.

47. In the Court's view the court decisions of which the applicant complained were clearly aimed at protecting the "health or morals" and the "rights and freedoms" of the child. Accordingly they pursued legitimate aims * * *

48. In determining whether the impugned measure was "necessary in a democratic society", the Court will consider whether, in the light of the case as a whole, the reasons adduced to justify this measure were relevant and sufficient for the purposes of * * * the Convention. Undoubtedly, consideration of what lies in the best interest of the child is of crucial importance in every case of this kind. Moreover, it must be borne in mind that the national authorities have the benefit of direct contact with all the persons concerned. It follows from these considerations that the Court's task is not to substitute itself for the domestic authorities in the exercise of their responsibilities regarding custody and access issues, but rather to review, in the light of the Convention, the decisions taken by those authorities in the exercise of their power of appreciation * * *.

49. The margin of appreciation to be accorded to the competent national authorities will vary in accordance with the nature of the issues

and the importance of the interests at stake. Thus, the Court recognises that the authorities enjoy a wide margin of appreciation, in particular when assessing the necessity of taking a child into care. However, a stricter scrutiny is called for in respect of any further limitations, such as restrictions placed by those authorities on parental rights of access, and of any legal safeguards designed to secure an effective protection of the right of parents and children to respect for their family life. Such further limitations entail the danger that the family relations between the parents and a young child would be effectively curtailed * * *.

50. The Court further recalls that a fair balance must be struck between the interests of the child and those of the parent * * * and that in doing so particular importance must be attached to the best interests of the child which, depending on their nature and seriousness, may override those of the parent. In particular, the parent cannot be entitled * * * to have such measures taken as would harm the child's health and development.

51. In the present case the Court notes that the competent national courts * * * took into account the strained relations between the parents, considering that it did not matter who was responsible for the tensions, and found that any further contact would negatively affect the child.

52. The Court does not doubt that these reasons were relevant. However, it must be determined whether * * * the applicant has been involved in the decision-making process * * * to a degree sufficient to provide him with the requisite protection of his interests * * *. It recalls that in the present case the District Court considered it unnecessary to obtain an expert opinion on the ground that the facts had been clearly and completely established * * *. In this connection, the District Court referred to the strained relations between the parents and in particular to the mother's objections to the applicant which she imparted to the child. The Court considers that the reasons given by the District Court are insufficient to explain why, in the particular circumstances of the case, expert advice was not considered necessary, as recommended by the Erkrath Youth Office. Moreover, taking into account the importance of the subject-matter, namely, the relations between a father and his child, the Regional Court should not have been satisfied, in the circumstances, by relying on the file and the written appeal submissions without having at its disposal psychological expert evidence in order to evaluate the child's statements. * * *

53. The combination of the refusal to order an independent psychological report and the absence of a hearing before the Regional Court reveals, in the Court's opinion, an insufficient involvement of the applicant in the decision-making process. The Court thus concludes that the national authorities overstepped their margin of appreciation, thereby violating the applicant's rights * * *.

Partly dissenting opinion by J Baka, joined by Judges Palm, Hedigan and Levits

[I agree that] the relevant decisions of the national courts were in accordance with the law and that they served a legitimate aim, namely protecting the interests of the child * * *. I however disagree with the majority's opinion that "the refusal to order an independent psychological report and the absence of a hearing before the Regional Court" amounts to "an insufficient involvement of the applicant in the decision-making process, consequently the national authorities overstepped their margin of appreciation" * * *.

The Court has constantly emphasised that the national authorities are better placed to evaluate the evidence adduced before them * * *. It has also pointed out that "as a general rule, it is for the national courts to assess the evidence before them as well as the relevance of the evidence which defendants seek to adduce." * * *

The margin of appreciation left for the national courts is even broader in cases like the present one which concerns primarily the interests of the child's well-being. * * * After the oral hearings and the two lengthy interviews with the child only this court had the benefit of direct contact with the members of the family and was able to clarify fully the strained relationship between the parents and to decide according to the best interests of the child. After this careful examination only this court was in a position to say that it was clearly unnecessary in the particular circumstances of the case to accept the recommendation of the Erkrath Youth Office to obtain psychological expert opinion on the question of access rights. The opposite decision would have been not only unjustified but it could also have caused additional unnecessary stress to the child. * * *

MOORE v. EAST CLEVELAND

Supreme Court (United States).
431 U.S. 494 (1977).

[A housing ordinance limited occupancy of a dwelling unit to members of a single family, and defined "family" not to include grandparents living with a child and grandchildren. A grandmother was convicted of a criminal violation of the ordinance and complained to the Court.]

Mr. Justice Powell announced the judgment of the Court, and delivered the opinion in which Mr. Justice Brennan, Mr. Justice Marshall, and Mr. Justice Blackmun joined.

* * * East Cleveland * * * has chosen to regulate the occupancy of its housing by slicing deeply into the family itself. This is no mere incidental result of the ordinance. On its face it selects certain categories of relatives who may live together and declares that others may not. In particular, it makes a crime of a grandmother's choice to live with her grandson in circumstances like those presented here.

When a city undertakes such intrusive regulation of the family, * * * the usual judicial deference to the legislature is inappropriate.

"This Court has long recognized that freedom of personal choice in matters of marriage and family life is * * * protected * * *." * * * A host of cases * * * have consistently acknowledged a "private realm of family life which the state cannot enter." * * * Of course, the family is not beyond regulation. * * * But when the government intrudes on choices concerning family living arrangements, this Court must examine carefully the importance of the governmental interests advanced and the extent to which they are served by the challenged regulation.

When thus examined, this ordinance cannot survive. The city seeks to justify it as a means of preventing overcrowding, minimizing traffic and parking congestion, and avoiding an undue financial burden on East Cleveland's school system. Although these are legitimate goals, the ordinance before us serves them marginally, at best. For example, the ordinance permits any family consisting only of husband, wife, and unmarried children to live together, even if the family contains a half dozen licensed drivers, each with his or her own car. At the same time, it forbids an adult brother and sister to share a household, even if both faithfully use public transportation. The ordinance would permit a grandmother to live with a single dependent son and children, even if his school-age children number a dozen, yet it forces Mrs. Moore to find another dwelling for her grandson John, simply because of the presence of his uncle and cousin in the same household. We need not labor the point. * * *

Our decisions establish that the Constitution protects the sanctity of the family precisely because the institution of the family is deeply rooted in this Nation's history and tradition. It is through the family that we inculcate and pass down many of our most cherished values, moral and cultural.

Ours is by no means a tradition limited to respect for the bonds uniting the members of the nuclear family. The tradition of uncles, aunts, cousins, and especially grandparents sharing a household along with parents and children has roots equally venerable and equally deserving of constitutional recognition. Over the years, millions of our citizens have grown up in just such an environment, and most, surely, have profited from it. Even if conditions of modern society have brought about a decline in extended family households, they have not erased the accumulated wisdom of civilization, gained over the centuries and honored throughout our history, that supports a larger conception of the family. Out of choice, necessity, or a sense of family responsibility, it has been common for close relatives to draw together and participate in the duties and the satisfactions of a common home. Decisions concerning childrearing, which [we] have recognized as entitled to constitutional protection, long have been shared with grandparents or other relatives who occupy the same household—indeed who may take on major responsibility for the rearing of the children. Especially in times of adversity, such as the death of a spouse or economic need, the broader family has tended to come together for mutual sustenance and to maintain or rebuild a secure home life. This is apparently what happened here.

Whether or not such a household is established because of personal tragedy, the choice of relatives in this degree of kinship to live together may not lightly be denied by the State. *Pierce* struck down an Oregon law requiring all children to attend the State's public schools, holding that the Constitution "excludes any general power of the State to standardize its children by forcing them to accept instruction from public teachers only." 268 U.S. at 535. By the same token, the Constitution prevents East Cleveland from standardizing its children—and its adults—by forcing all to live in certain narrowly defined family patterns.

SEX EDUCATION CASE

Federal Constitutional Court (Germany).
47 BVerfGE 46 (1977).[j]

[In 1970, a German state issued guidelines on education in public schools, which included among others the teaching of sexual development, procreation, and responsibilities of parenthood. Parents complained to the Court for violation of their right as parents as guaranteed in the Constitution.]

C. I. 2.(a) [Article 6 section 2 of the Constitution] designates the care and upbringing of children as "the natural right of, and a duty primarily incumbent on, the parents." The national community's task is "to watch over their endeavours with respect." * * * The parental freedom to choose ways in which to meet their responsibility is constitutionally protected against encroachments by the state, providing that such encroachments are not within the ambit of the state's mandate as guardian of the national community * * *.

(b) [O]ne must ask whether the state is ever permitted to get involved in sex education in school and if so, to what extent it may do so. * * * The Federal Constitutional Court has pointed out, the state supervision * * * incorporates the authority to plan and organize the educational system with the objective of affording all young citizens educational opportunities geared to contemporary life in [this] society and commensurate with their abilities. * * * That is why the state may pursue its own educational goals independent of the parents. The general mandate of the school * * * is not classified as inferior but, rather, as equal to the parents' right. [It is not] restricted merely to the act of imparting knowledge. Rather, [it] also includes [the premise] that every single child must be brought up to be a responsible member of society. * * * For this reason the state must be allowed to treat sex education as an important element of the general education of a young person. * * *

3. (b) [However], [t]here must be a balancing process between the implementation of sex education in school and sex education at home * * *. Thus [it] must be planned and implemented with the greatest possible cooperation between parents and school. [There is no] parental right of collaboration in the structure and format of sex education [because the constitution guarantees only individual rights to each parent. But to] be sure, parents are entitled to demand necessary restraint and tolerance in sex education [also regarding religious freedom, freedom from discrimination and the principle of neutrality of the civil service.] * * *

j. Reproduced from Donald P. Kommers, *The Constitutional Jurisprudence of*   *the Federal Republic of Germany* 500–503 (2d ed. 1997).

Notes and Questions

1. *What constitutes a family?* Do interests of privacy and self-determination provide a sound basis for the protection of rights of the family and the relationship between adult caregivers and children? Many constitutions as well as human rights documents extend explicit protections to family life. Who is protected under them? If privacy is a right that relates to self-determination, then who is to be charged with making collective determinations for a unit that consists of more than a single individual? Consider that most national constitutional courts, like the ECHR, define a family minimally as an adult and a child, but that most jurisdictions shy away from granting parental rights if the adult is a homosexual. In Great Britain, the House of Lords held in 1977, in *Re D.*, [1977] 1 All ER 145, [1977] A.C. 602 (HL), that a gay father had no right to custody, while another court held in 1991, in *B. v. B.*, [1991] Fam. 174, [1991] 1 F.L.R. 402, that a lesbian mother could have custody of a son if she intended to raise him as a heterosexual and she ensured that he exhibited "unequivocal boyish appearance and conduct." Is that consistent with fundamental rights? Are these rights about protecting the parents, the children, or someone else's ideas? If the interests of parents and children are in conflict, how are they to be balanced? Is it a valid constitutional argument to require heterosexuality of either parent, despite the fact that there is no proven connection between the sexual orientation of parents and their children? Should parental sexual orientation be a factor in determining family rights?

2. *Does self-determination extend to others?* When parental rights conflict with public requirements, like going to school, with children's needs, or with a public sentiment regarding minorities, how are they to be balanced? What kind of constitutional interest can be balanced against the right of parents to educate their children as they see fit? Is the parents' right a family right, a privacy right, or a right to collective self-determination? The GFCC held that the social interest in raising responsible citizens justifies certain infringements on parental and family rights, while the *Pierce Case*, referred to by the USSC, rejected the state's attempt to "standardize." Is there a constitutional obligation to educate children? Is there a constitutional obligation to protect them? Where is the limit to state intervention in the family in cases of, for example, neglect or abuse? Is it constitutional to intervene on grounds of protecting morals or is actual harm required? Since traditional gender roles, of women as caregivers and men as income providers, are subject to change, many cases have been brought by fathers claiming equal rights as parents. In *Nguyen v. INS*, 533 U.S. 53 (2001), the USSC found constitutional a law that required fathers to demonstrate paternity in order to confer nationality on their children, for the purpose of gaining citizenship rights, while mothers conferred such rights automatically in the act of giving birth. Such holdings are usually justified by reference to the biological fact of birth, whereas medical tests are necessary to definitively establish paternity. Do guarantees of self-determination provide for a right to have or refuse such tests? Can a father compel a child—or a child, a father—to undergo medical procedures for the purpose of establishing paternity?

E.2. INTIMATE PARTNERS

A further dimension of a right to privacy and personal autonomy is the right to have intimate relations with whomever you choose, regardless of creed, national origin, skin color, or—to name the two most recent criteria for constitutional challenges—biological sex or sexual orientation.

LOVING v. VIRGINIA

Supreme Court (United States).
388 U.S. 1 (1967).

[The state of Virginia, like 15 other U.S. states at the time, had antimiscegenation statutes that aimed at prohibiting and punishing interracial marriages. The Lovings, a "white" and a "colored" person, were convicted and sentenced for violating these laws. (Excerpts of this case are also presented in Chapter 6.)]

Chief Justice Warren delivered the opinion of the Court.

This case presents a constitutional question never addressed by this Court: whether a statutory scheme adopted by the State of Virginia to prevent marriages between persons solely on the basis of racial classifications violates the Equal Protection and Due Process Clauses of the Fourteenth Amendment. For reasons which seem to us to reflect the central meaning of those constitutional commands, we conclude that these statutes cannot stand consistently with the Fourteenth Amendment. * * *

While the state court is no doubt correct in asserting that marriage is a social relation subject to the State's police power, * * * the State does not contend in its argument before this Court that its powers to regulate marriage are unlimited notwithstanding the commands of the Fourteenth Amendment. * * * [The state also argues that] this Court should defer to the wisdom of the state legislature in adopting its policy of discouraging interracial marriages. * * *

Justice Stewart, joined by Justice Douglas (concurring).

[Next to violating the right to equality because they sustain "White Supremacy," these] statutes also deprive the Lovings of liberty without due process of law in violation of the Due Process Clause of the Fourteenth Amendment. The freedom to marry has long been recognized as one of the vital personal rights essential to the orderly pursuit of happiness by free men. Marriage is one of the "basic civil rights of man," fundamental to our very existence and survival. * * * To deny this fundamental freedom on so unsupportable a basis as the racial classifications embodied in these statutes, classifications so directly subversive of the principle of equality at the heart of the Fourteenth Amendment, is surely to deprive all the State's citizens of liberty without due process of law. The Fourteenth Amendment requires that the freedom of choice to marry not be restricted by invidious racial discriminations. Under our Constitution, the freedom to marry, or not marry, a person of another race resides with the individual and cannot be infringed by the State.

ZABLOCKI v. REDHAIL

Supreme Court (United States).
434 U.S. 374 (1978).

Mr. Justice Marshall delivered the opinion of the Court.

At issue in this case is the constitutionality of a Wisconsin statute * * * which provides that members of a certain class of Wisconsin residents may not marry, within the State or elsewhere, without first obtaining a court order granting permission to marry. The class is defined by the statute to include any "Wisconsin resident having minor issue not in his custody and which he is under obligation to support by any court order or judgment." The statute specifies that court permission cannot be granted unless the marriage applicant submits proof of compliance with the support obligation and, in addition, demonstrates that the children covered by the support order "are not then and are not likely thereafter to become public charges." * * *

After being denied a marriage license because of his failure to comply with [this law], appellee brought this class action * * * challenging the statute as violative * * * of the Equal Protection and Due Process Clauses of the Fourteenth Amendment [of the Constitution]. * * *

[*Loving* established the constitutional protection of the right to marry.] Although *Loving* arose in the context of racial discrimination, prior and subsequent decisions of this Court confirm that the right to marry is of fundamental importance for all individuals. Long ago, * * * the Court characterized marriage as "the most important relation in life," * * * and as "the foundation of the family and of society, without which there would be neither civilization nor progress." * * * [The] Court recognized that the right "to marry, establish a home and bring up children" is a central part of the liberty * * * and * * * marriage was described as "fundamental to the very existence and survival of the race" * * *. More recent decisions have established that the right to marry is part of the fundamental "right of privacy" * * *.

"We deal with a right of privacy older than the Bill of Rights—older than our political parties, older than our school system. Marriage is a coming together for better or for worse, hopefully enduring, and intimate to the degree of being sacred. It is an association that promotes a way of life, not causes; a harmony in living, not political faiths; a bilateral loyalty, not commercial or social projects. Yet it is an association for as noble a purpose as any involved in our prior decisions." * * *

It is not surprising that the decision to marry has been placed on the same level of importance as decisions relating to procreation, childbirth, child rearing, and family relationships. As the facts of this case illustrate, it would make little sense to recognize a right of privacy with respect to other matters of family life and not with respect to the decision to enter the relationship that is the foundation of the family in our society. The woman whom appellee desired to marry had a fundamental right to seek an abortion of their expected child, * * * or to bring the child into life to suffer the myriad social, if not economic, disabilities that the status of illegitimacy brings. * * * Surely, a decision to marry and raise the child in a traditional family setting must receive equivalent protection. And, if appellee's right to procreate means anything at all, it must imply some right to enter the only relationship in which the State of Wisconsin allows sexual relations legally to take place.

By reaffirming the fundamental character of the right to marry, we do not mean to suggest that every state regulation which relates in any way to the incidents of or prerequisites for marriage must be subjected to rigorous scrutiny. To the contrary, reasonable regulations that do not significantly interfere with decisions to enter into the marital relationship may legitimately be imposed. * * * The statutory classification at issue here, however, clearly does interfere directly and substantially with the right to marry. * * *

Rehnquist, J., dissenting:

I [reject] the Court's conclusion that marriage is the sort of "fundamental right" which must invariably trigger the strictest judicial scrutiny. * * * I would view this legislative judgment in the light of the traditional presumption of validity. I think that under the Equal Protection Clause the statute need pass only the "rational basis test," * * * and that under the Due Process Clause it need only be shown that it bears a rational relation to a constitutionally permissible objective. * * * The statute so viewed is a permissible exercise of the State's power to regulate family life and to assure the support of minor children, despite its possible imprecision in the extreme cases envisioned in the concurring opinions. * * *

[Here,] the Wisconsin Legislature has "adopted this rule in the course of constructing a complex social welfare system that necessarily deals with the intimacies of family life." * * * Because of the limited amount of funds available for the support of needy children, the State has an exceptionally strong interest in securing as much support as their parents are able to pay. * * * In the case of some applicants, this statute makes the proposed marriage legally impossible for financial reasons; in a similar number of extreme cases, the Social Security Act makes the proposed marriage practically impossible for the same reasons. I cannot conclude that such a difference justifies the application of a heightened standard of review to the statute in question here. In short, I conclude that the statute, despite its imperfections, is sufficiently rational to satisfy the demands of the Fourteenth Amendment.

ONTARIO v. M & H.

Supreme Court (Canada).
[1999] 2 S.C.R. 3.

[Two women, who had been living together, separated. One of them claimed the financial support that is usually given to spouses under Canadian family law.]

Cory and Iacobucci JJ (Lamer C.J.C., L'Heureux–Dubé, McLachlin and Binnie JJ, concurring)

3. The crux of the issue is that this differential treatment discriminates in a substantive sense by violating the human dignity of individuals in same-sex relationships. * * * [The] inquiry into substantive discrimination is to be undertaken in a purposive and contextual manner. * * * First, individuals in same-sex relationships face significant pre-existing disadvantage and vulnerability, which is exacerbated by the impugned legislation. Second, the legislation at issue fails to take into account the claimant's actual situation. Third, there is no compelling argument that the ameliorative purpose of the legislation does anything to lessen the charge of discrimination in this case. Fourth, the nature of the interest affected is fundamental, namely the ability to meet basic financial needs following the breakdown of a relationship characterized by intimacy and economic dependence. The exclusion of same-sex partners from the benefits of the spousal support scheme implies that they are judged to be incapable of forming intimate relationships of economic interdependence, without regard to their actual circumstances. Taking these factors into account, it is clear that the human dignity of individuals in same-sex relationships is violated by the definition of "spouse" in [family law].

4. This infringement is not justified * * * because there is no rational connection between the objectives of the spousal support provisions and the means chosen to further this objective. * * *

Gonthier J. (dissenting)

* * * [I] believe that the impugned section is constitutionally sound.

Plainly, this appeal raises elemental social and legal issues. Indeed, it is no exaggeration to observe that it represents something of a watershed. * * * [The] majority contends * * * that it need not consider whether a constitutionally mandated expansion of the definition of "spouse" would open the door to a raft of other claims, because such a concern is "entirely speculative". I cannot agree. The majority's decision makes further claims not only foreseeable, but very likely.

Notes and Questions

1. *What is marriage?* With the sole exception of the dissent in *Zablocki*, all of the foregoing rulings argue that marriage is among the fundamental rights recognized by constitutional law. What are the bases for this position? In the Canadian case it is extended to same-sex partners, while in other jurisdictions this has been rejected as a violation of the very notion of "marriage." This is also an issue for cases in which people have changed their sex/gender. Consider the decision by the Family Court in Otahuhu, New Zealand, 1991, in *M. v. M.*, [1991] NZFLR 337, on the validity of a marriage:

[U]ltimately the question has to be answered whether * * * Mrs M, was a woman on 9 September 1977, or whether she was a man, or whether she occupied some kind of sexual twilight zone. She was born male, and her chromosomal structure has not changed. Is that the end of it? * * *

[It] is possible to conclude as a matter of evidence that the genetic starting point, the immutable biological factors, will not be determinative. Why should they be? Accepting that it cannot be a question to be decided merely upon sympathetic or compassionate grounds, nevertheless a consideration of the evidence may lead to the finding that the cumulative effect of the changes that have occurred is to have brought about a change of sex in a real sense, albeit that the chromosome structure is perforce unchanged and the sexual organs are the work of man and not any deity. * * *

The applicant's core identity * * * is that of a woman; her body has been brought into harmony with her psychological sex. * * *

[Thus] [t]here will be a declaration that the marriage was and remains a valid one.

An American commentator argued that any rejection of claims to reclassify the sex of transsexuals would seem inconsistent with the values of privacy as well as dignity. In addition, transsexuals would be forced to suffer while society would lose nothing if it grants the right to lead a normal life. See Corbett, Anonymous Note, *Transsexuals in Limbo: The Search for a Legal Definition of Sex*, 31 Md. L. Rev. 235, 253–54 (1971). Some people, however, consider lifestyles fundamentally different from their own to be problematic. For them, there is "a loss" to their sense of propriety and to civic morality. Should constitutions protect such interests?

In the Canadian case above, what is basis of the institution of marriage: love, emotion, commitment, solidarity, social order, hierarchy, paternal linkage and inheritance, money, and morality (and whose morality?)? In the U.S., the Defense of Marriage Act of 1996, H.R. 3396, 104th Cong. § 7 (1996), 110 Stat. 2419 (1996), defined marriage as a legal union between one man and one woman, after a Hawaiian court, in *Baehr v. Lewin*, 852 P.2d 44 (Haw.1993), intimated that under the state's constitution, the same constitutional protection might be owed to homosexual partnerships and married couples. Does the law violate the dignity of same-sex partners who are seeking the protection of a legal union? Does it change the character of marriage rights not to extend them to same-sex couples? What is the constitutional basis for this exclusion? Note that the Canadian province of Quebec extends partnership rights to both hetero and homosexual adults, without privilege on either side.

2. *Who decides?* In 1999, the GFCC rejected the claim of a constitutional right of homosexuals to marry, holding that such a fundamental change in the notion of marriage, a term present in the constitutional text, would need to be made by the legislature rather than by a court. The Canadian Supreme Court, in *Ontario v. M & H.*, [1999] 2 S.C.R. 3 (Justice Bastarache), argued as follows:

285. * * * The scope of the legal issues raised and the implications of our decision may in fact be greater than expected when the action was first initiated. This explains why we have heard forceful presentations by interveners, and why emotions run high. It is easy to understand, in this context, why the Court has been invited by some parties to take sides; but this is not the role of a court. A court's role is to give a generous and liberal interpretation to s. 15(1) of the *Canadian Charter of Rights and Freedoms*, and to apply s. 1 of the *Charter* in a fair and reasonable way in order to determine, in legal terms, whether the legislature has breached its obligations under the *Charter*.

Does the presence of the concept of marriage in the constitutional text make a difference here? Does this ruling constitute an abdication of the responsibility to protect fundamental rights, or is it merely an example of sound judicial restraint?

E.3.   SEXUALITY AND PROCREATION

Sexual activity is a central component of the intimate sphere. It can be understood as one decisional aspect of the right to privacy and also in terms of an emanation of the right to autonomy. The following cases deal primarily with the constitutional considerations reacting to behavior that is deemed a deviation from what is considered "normal." In each case the criminalization of such intimate behavior is challenged.

GRISWOLD v. CONNECTICUT

Supreme Court (United States).
381 U.S. 479 (1965).

[Doctors and nondoctors were criminalized for giving and providing information about contraceptives. This case (also about autonomy) is discussed above in Section B and in Chapter 2.]

TOONEN v. AUSTRALIA

Human Rights Committee (United Nations).
UN Doc CCPR/C/50/D/488/1992 (1994).

* * * The author [of the complaint] is an activist for the promotion of the rights of homosexuals in Tasmania, one of Australia's six constitutive states. He challenges [provisions of the] Criminal Code * * * which criminalize various forms of sexual contacts between men, including all forms of sexual contacts between consenting adult homosexual men in private.

[He] observes that the * * * [provisions] empower Tasmanian police officers to investigate intimate aspects of his private life and to detain him, if they have reason to believe that he is involved in [such] sexual activities. * * * Mr. Toonen further argues that the criminalization of homosexuality in private has not permitted him to expose openly his sexuality and to publicize his views on reform of the relevant laws on sexual matters, as he felt that this would have been extremely prejudicial to his employment. [He] contends that [the criminal laws] have created the conditions for discrimination in employment, constant stigmatization, vilification, threats of physical violence and the violation of basic democratic rights. * * *

The Committee is called upon to determine whether Mr. Toonen has been the victim of an unlawful or arbitrary interference with his privacy [and discusses whether he has been discriminated against in his right to equal protection of the law, which is not documented here].

[It] is undisputed that adult consensual sexual activity in private is covered by the concept of "privacy", and that Mr. Toonen is * * * affected by the * * * existence of the Tasmanian laws [that] "interfere" with [his] privacy, even if these provisions have not been enforced for a decade. * * *

[Any] interference with privacy must be proportional to the end sought and be necessary in the circumstances of any given case.

[The] authorities submit that the challenged laws are justified on public health and moral grounds, as they are intended in part to prevent the spread of HIV/AIDS in Tasmania, and because * * * moral issues must be deemed a matter for domestic decision.

As far as the public health argument * * * is concerned, the Committee notes that the criminalization of homosexual practices cannot be considered a reasonable means or proportionate measure to achieve the aim of preventing the spread of AIDS/HIV. * * * Criminalization of homosexual activity [drives people underground and thus runs] counter to the implementation of effective education programmes in respect of the HIV/AIDS prevention. [Also,] no link has been shown between the continued criminalization of homosexual activity and the effective control of the spread of the HIV/AIDS virus.

The Committee cannot accept either that * * * moral issues are exclusively a matter of domestic concern, as this would open the door to withdrawing from the Committee's scrutiny a potentially large number of statutes interfering with privacy.

ADT v. UNITED KINGDOM

European Court of Human Rights.
31 E.H.R.R. 33 (2000).

[Police conducted a search under warrant of the applicant's home, seizing various items, including photographs and a list of video tapes. The tapes contained footage of the applicant and up to four other adult men engaging in sexual acts in the applicant's home. He was prosecuted and convicted under the Sexual Offences Act.]

20.   The applicant complained that his conviction for gross indecency constituted a violation of his right to respect for his private life * * *

21.   By reference to *Laskey v. UK*, (1997) 24 EHRR 39 at 56–57 (para 36), the government contend that there was no interference with the applicant's right to respect for his private life as the sexual activity in the present case fell outside the scope of 'private life' within the meaning of art 8(1) of the convention. They point, first, to the number of individuals present and, secondly, to the fact that the sexual activities were recorded on video tape. * * *

23.   The court recalls that the mere existence of legislation prohibiting male homosexual conduct in private may continuously and directly affect a person's private life * * *

25.   As to the government's comments in connection with the scope of 'private life' * * * [the] applicant's conviction related not to any offence involving the making or distribution of the tapes, but solely to the acts themselves. * * *

26.   The court thus considers that the applicant has been the victim of an interference with his right to respect for his private life * * *

29. An interference with the exercise of [a right to privacy] will not be [justified] unless it is 'in accordance with the law', has an aim or aims that is or are legitimate under that paragraph and is 'necessary in a democratic society' for the aforesaid aim or aims * * *

31. The cardinal issue in the case is whether existence of the legislation in question, and its application in the prosecution and conviction of the applicant, were 'necessary in a democratic society' for these aims.

32. The court recalls that in *Dudgeon v. UK*, (1981) 4 EHRR 149 at 167 (para 60), in which the court was considering the existence of legislation, the Court found no 'pressing social need' for the criminalisation of homosexual acts between two consenting male adults over the age of 21 years, and that such justifications as there were for retaining the law were outweighed by the:

'. . . detrimental effects which the very existence of the legislative provisions in question can have on the life of a person of homosexual orientation like the applicant. Although members of the public who regard homosexuality as immoral may be shocked, offended or disturbed by the commission by others of private homosexual acts, this cannot on its own warrant the application of penal sanctions when it is consenting adults alone who are involved.'

* * *

34. There are differences between those decided cases and the present application. The principal point of distinction is that in the present case the sexual activities involved more than two men, and that the applicant was convicted for gross indecency as more than two men had been present. * * *

36. It is not the court's role to determine whether legislation complies with the convention in the abstract. The court will therefore consider the compatibility of the legislation in the present case with the convention in the light of the circumstances of the case, that is, that the applicant wished to be able to engage, in private, in non-violent sexual activities with up to four other men.

37. The court can agree with the government that, at some point, sexual activities can be carried out in such a manner that state interference may be justified, either as not amounting to an interference with the right to respect for private life, or as being justified for the protection, for example, of health or morals. The facts of the present case, however, do not indicate any such circumstances.

BOWERS v. HARDWICK

Supreme Court (United States)
478 U.S. 186 (1986)

[Hardwick was charged with violating the Georgia statute criminalizing sodomy by committing that act with another adult male in the bedroom of his home. He challenged the constitutionality of the statute.]

Justice White delivered the opinion of the Court.

* * * This case does not require a judgment on whether laws against sodomy between consenting adults in general, or between homosexuals in particular, are wise or desirable. It raises no question about the right or propriety of state legislative decisions to repeal their laws that criminalize homosexual sodomy, or of state court decisions invalidating those laws on state constitutional grounds. The issue presented is whether the Federal Constitution confers a fundamental right upon homosexuals to engage in sodomy, and hence invalidates the laws of the many States that still make such conduct illegal and have done so for a very long time. The case also calls for some judgment about the limits of the Court's role in carrying out its constitutional mandate.

We [disagree with the opinion] that the Court's prior cases have construed the Constitution to confer a right of privacy that extends to homosexual sodomy * * *. [We dealt] with childrearing and education * * *; with family relationships * * *; with procreation * * *; with marriage * * *; with contraception * * *; with abortion, [thus with] a fundamental individual right to decide whether or not to beget or bear a child. [But] we think it evident that none of the rights announced in those cases bears any resemblance to the claimed constitutional right of homosexuals to engage in acts of sodomy that is asserted in this case. No connection between family, marriage, or procreation on the one hand and homosexual activity on the other has been demonstrated. * * * [To] announce, as the Court of Appeals did, a fundamental right to engage in homosexual sodomy * * * we are quite unwilling to do. * * *

Blackmun, Brennan, Marshall, Stevens, JJ., dissenting:

This case is no more about "a fundamental right to engage in homosexual sodomy," as the Court purports to declare, * * * than [the case on watching pornography or placing phone calls] was about a fundamental right to watch obscene movies * * *. Rather, this case is about "the most comprehensive of rights and the right most valued by civilized men," namely, "the right to be let alone." * * *

The statute at issue * * * denies individuals the right to decide for themselves whether to engage in particular forms of private, consensual sexual activity. [The] fact that the moral judgments expressed by [such] statutes * * * may be "natural and familiar ... ought not to conclude our judgment upon the question whether statutes embodying them conflict with the Constitution of the United States." * * * I believe that "[i]t is revolting to have no better reason for a rule of law than that so it was laid down in the time of Henry IV. It is still more revolting if the grounds upon which it was laid down have vanished long since, and the rule simply persists from blind imitation of the past." (Holmes, *The Path of the Law*, 10 Harv. L. Rev. 467, 469 (1897)) I believe we must analyze respondent Hardwick's claim in the light of the values that underlie the constitutional right to privacy. If that right means anything, it means that, before Georgia can prosecute its citizens for making choices about the most intimate aspects of their lives, it must do more than assert that the choice they have made is an "abominable crime not fit to be named among Christians." * * *

* * * No matter how uncomfortable a certain group may make the majority of this Court, we have held that "[m]ere public intolerance or animosity cannot constitutionally justify the deprivation of a person's physical liberty." * * *

NATIONAL COALITION FOR GAY AND LESBIAN EQUALITY v. MINISTER OF JUSTICE AND OTHERS

Constitutional Court (South Africa).
1999 (1) SALR 6 (CC).

Sachs J.

28. * * * In my view, * * * the common-law crime of sodomy * * * constitutes an infringement of the right to dignity which * * * is a cornerstone of our Constitution. Its importance is further emphasised by the role accorded to it in section 36 of the Constitution which provides that:

> "The rights in the Bill of Rights may be limited only in terms of law of general application to the extent that the limitation is reasonable and justifiable in an open and democratic society based on human dignity, equality and freedom...."

Dignity is a difficult concept to capture in precise terms. At its least, it is clear that the constitutional protection of dignity requires us to acknowledge the value and worth of all individuals as members of our society. The common-law prohibition on sodomy criminalises all sexual intercourse per anum between men: regardless of the relationship of the couple who engage therein, of the age of such couple, of the place where it occurs, or indeed of any other circumstances whatsoever. In so doing, it punishes a form of sexual conduct which is identified by our broader society with homosexuals. Its symbolic effect is to state that in the eyes of our legal system all gay men are criminals. The stigma thus attached to a significant proportion of our population is manifest. But the harm imposed by the criminal law is far more than symbolic. As a result of the criminal offence, gay men are at risk of arrest, prosecution and conviction of the offence of sodomy simply because they seek to engage in sexual conduct which is part of their experience of being human. Just as apartheid legislation rendered the lives of couples of different racial groups perpetually at risk, the sodomy offence builds insecurity and vulnerability into the daily lives of gay men. There can be no doubt that the existence of a law which punishes a form of sexual expression for gay men degrades and devalues gay men in our broader society. As such it is a palpable invasion of their dignity and a breach of section 10 of the Constitution.

EGAN v. CANADA

Supreme Court (Canada).
[1995] 2 S.C.R. 513.

[The Court decided that sexual orientation is protected as an equality right. We discuss this case in Chapter 6.]

Notes and Questions

1. *Procreation and its costs.* In *Carey v. Population Services Int'l*, 431 U.S. 678 (1977), the USSC held unconstitutional a prohibition against marketing and selling contraceptives to minors. On the other hand it upheld the exclusion of contraception from medical insurance coverage in *Harris v. McRae*, 448 U.S. 297 (1980). What is the value of a right that cannot be exercised due to a lack of means? Can a constitutional right be conditional on market access? Is this the effective outcome of the *Harris* decision? Remember that the GFCC, in the *Abortion I Case* above, argued that duties of the state to protect life may arise. Is this argument applicable here?

2. *Privacy.* Courts have rarely been called upon to decide whether heterosexual activity is constitutionally protected but have often been asked to do so with regard to homosexual activity. Many arguments are based on equality, but some focus on dignity or privacy as well. Note that scholars have argued that "the individualistic concept of privacy * * * is an imprisoning strategy." Jed Rubenfeld, *The Right of Privacy*, 102 Harv. L. Rev. 737, 777 (1989). How so? What are its limitations? What is homosexuality about: conduct, commitment, identity, lifestyle, the public, or the private? Is the right to intimate relationships based on respect for dignity, a sphere of privacy, or individual or collective self-determination? Consider the decision by the ECHR in *Laskey, Jaggard and Brown v. United Kingdom*, 24 E.H.R.R. 39 (1997):

> 36.   The Court observes that not every sexual activity carried out behind closed doors necessarily falls within the scope of [the right to private life]. In the present case, the applicants were involved in consensual sado-masochistic activities for purposes of sexual gratification. There can be no doubt that sexual orientation and activity concern an intimate aspect of private life. * * *

> 45.   The applicants have contended that, in the circumstances of the case, the behaviour in question formed part of private morality which is not the State's business to regulate. In their submission the matters for which they were prosecuted and convicted concerned only private sexual behaviour.

> The Court is not persuaded by this submission. It is evident from the facts established by the national courts that the applicants' sado-masochistic activities involved a significant degree of injury or wounding which could not be characterised as trifling or transient. This, in itself, suffices to distinguish the present case from those applications which have previously been examined by the Court concerning consensual homosexual behaviour in private between adults where no such feature was present.

> 50.   In sum, the Court finds that the national authorities were entitled to consider that the prosecution and conviction of the applicants were necessary in a democratic society for the protection of health * * *.

Do you think the "harm principle" is the appropriate limit to privacy? Is consent significant in this determination? Remember *Carmichele* above and the philosophy of J. S. Mill. Are morals, traditions, or beliefs constitutionally justifiable limits as well? In *Dudgeon v. United Kingdom*, 4 E.H.R.R. 149, 167 (1981), the ECHR held that there is no "pressing social need" to interfere with privacy regarding sexual practices. In *Modinos v. Cyprus*, 16 E.H.R.R. 485 (1993), the Court ruled that even a statute that could not be enforced violates the right to privacy because of the chilling effect it has on private activity. If you take the U.S. decision into account, which arguments are most convincing? Also consider that in *Stanley v. Georgia*, 394 U.S. 557 (1969), the USSC held that the Constitution protects the private use of pornography, which some believe causes harm to others. The Court said that "if the First Amendment means anything, it means that a State has no business telling a man, sitting alone in his house, what books he may read or what films he may watch." But in *Hardwick*, the Court states that a similarly situated man has no unfettered right to have sex. Is this reasoning convincing, or consistent?

3. *Difference.* Consider that, historically, women were not thought to have sexual desires but were instead considered to be passive instruments for the satisfaction of the desire of men. Lesbian sexuality was thus unthinkable and until very recently has rarely been an issue before the courts. The GFCC (*Homosexuality Case*, 6 BVerfGE 389) stated in 1957:

> In the area of homosexuality, biological differences justify a different treatment of the sexes as well. * * * [The] prohibition to differentiate between men and women does only apply if the social activity to be regulated is essentially comparable, that is, when the activity, without regard to the sex of those affected, contains further essential elements which are comparable on their own. [Comparability] is only missing when the biological difference between the sexes shapes the social activity in question to a degree which completely renders irrelevant other potentially comparable elements. [These reasons] exclude the applicability of [sex equality rights] in the area of criminal law of sexual offences, to which the sex drive of the human being is the constitutive element. [Here,] the criminal offence [of male homosexual conduct] is fundamentally defined by the fact that a man appears as a male gendered being, and a woman as a female gendered being, and that typical and specific dangers arise from the biological specificity of both sexes. * * * This enables lesbian women to abstain from sexuality longer while the homosexual man has a tendency to fall to an uninhibited sexual desire. [Thus] lesbian love and male homosexuality are in the legal sense incomparable facts.

What do we know about sex/gender differences today that might force a reconsideration of this argument? If dignity guarantees a right to respect for individuality—that is, difference—and privacy can be seen to guarantee a right to live according to one's choices—as long as one does not interfere with another's right to the same—can it be constitutionally valid to allow sexual and gender differences to matter in the protection of fundamental rights? Or does the very notion of fundamental rights entail the guarantee that such differences be irrelevant? Consider also the impact of racist stereotypes on notions of sexuality and gender.

4. *Sexualities and tolerance.* Many cases arise out of a need for protection from discrimination on the part of homosexuals in traditionally masculine institutions, like the military. In *Smith and Grady v. United Kingdom*, 29 E.H.R.R. 493 (1999), the ECHR decided that:

> 71. [I]nvestigations by the military police into the applicants' homosexuality, which included detailed interviews with each of them and with

third parties on matters relating to their sexual orientation and practices, together with the preparation of a final report for the armed
forces' authorities on the investigations, constituted a direct interference with the applicants' right to respect for their private lives. Their
consequent administrative discharge on the sole ground of their sexual
orientation also constituted an interference with that right * * *.

Such an interference is justified only if it can be considered "necessary in a
democratic society." But since the hallmarks of a "democratic society"
include, according to the Court, "pluralism, tolerance and broadmindedness," it did not find such a necessity. The ECHR also cited a report on the
issue:

> The HPAT observed that there were a wide variety of official positions
> and legal arrangements evolving from local legal and political circum-
> stances and ranging from a formal prohibition of all homosexual activity
> (the United States), to administrative arrangements falling short of real
> equality (France and Germany), to a deliberate policy to create an
> armed force friendly to homosexuals (the Netherlands).

Is self-determination more or less protected in the military than in a
civilian institution? The USSC, in *Boy Scouts v. Dale*, 528 U.S. 1109 (2000),
held that gay men can be expelled from the Boy Scouts because of their
sexual orientation. Justice Kirby, of the Australian High Court, evaluated
that holding from a comparative perspective (Michael Kirby, *Law and
Sexuality: The Contrasting Case of Australia*, 12 Stan. L. & Pol'y Rev. 103,
107 (2001)):

> The narrow decision of the United States Supreme Court [attracted]
> only modest notice in Australia. The chief reasons for this probably lie
> in the fact that the Boys Scouts movement in Australia has no equiva-
> lent policy excluding scouts on the grounds of their sexuality. The
> notion that a Queen's Scout (the equivalent to an Eagle Scout—the
> status Mr. Dale had attained) would be expelled from the movement as
> not "morally straight" or "clean" because of his sexuality is unthink-
> able. The leadership of scouting in Australia would share the opinion of
> the spokesman for Scouts Canada, commenting on the Dale decision:
> "It's our perspective that sexual orientation has no bearing on the
> ability of a person to participate in or deliver our programmes."

> A second reason for the lack of attention to the Dale decision lies in the
> view commonly held in Australia and in other countries which do not
> share the First Amendment jurisprudence of the United States, that
> core expressive values, including the ability to associate to express
> discriminatory messages, are not beyond remedial law designed to
> protect vulnerable minorities from the damage that expression can
> sometimes do. Such minorities have long suffered from extreme types of
> expression. Those affected include persons identified by race, skin col-
> our, sex, and sexuality. Lawyers in the United States have to be told
> that, by world standards, including those expressed in international
> human rights law where other values are acknowledged, First Amend-
> ment jurisprudence is often regarded as somewhat extreme.[k]

Is there a meaningful difference between the infringement of a fundamental
right by a private or state actor? What is this distinction ultimately about—
equality, freedom of contract, dignity, privacy, or self-determination?

---

k. For an opposing view, see Richard
Posner, *Against Constitutional Theory,* 73
N.Y.U.L.Rev. 1 (1998), reprinted in The
Unpredictable Constitution (Norman Dor-
sen ed., 2002) at 217.

Chapter 6

EQUALITY, MINORITY AND GROUP RIGHTS

Equality rights in contemporary constitutional democracies are grounded in the widely held belief that all persons are inherently equal, a belief that is paramount both in the American Declaration of Independence's proclamation "All men are created equal" and in the French Revolution's call for "Liberty, Equality and Fraternity." This notion of equality stands in sharp contrast to feudal society's conception of persons as inherently unequal, depending on their birth or vocation, and a hierarchy in which members of the aristocracy and clergy were treated as superior to commoners and thus entitled to privileges and prerogatives denied commoners.

Equality rights are potentially the most broadly encompassing among fundamental rights. This is because all laws classify—e.g., a law that prohibits those under 18 years of age from driving automobiles divides the population into two classes: those over and under 18—and because everyone, conceivably, can claim that a particular classification casts him or her as an unequal. Either a person treated differently may claim an entitlement to being treated the same, or a person treated the same as others may claim that he or she is entitled to different treatment as an equal—e.g., where a state provides the same medical benefit to all, a very sick person may claim that the policy violates her right to equality because her medical needs cannot be satisfied in the same way that her healthy fellow citizens' needs are.

Equality rights may be conceived of or protected very differently, depending on whether they are imagined narrowly or broadly, used to protect individuals or groups, or construed as outlawing certain types of discrimination rather than as mandating an equal apportionment of benefits and burdens throughout the polity. These issues are explored in this chapter. Section A. addresses general issues, such as the contrast between formal and substantive equality and the scope of constitutional equality. In addition, we ask these questions: Who is to be deemed equal to whom? And, in respect to what are equals to be deemed equal? Section B. focuses on the widely held conception of constitutional equality as a device to attack particular inequalities through deployment of the anti-discrimination principle. Section C. examines the special issues raised by equality rights in certain special contexts, such as voting, education, and access to justice, in which denials of equality would threaten not only individuals or groups but also the integrity of the prevailing constitutional order. Section D. centers on the controversies raised by affirmative action and the tensions it produces between individual equality and group-based equality. Finally, Section E. deals with the special issues introduced by group-equality claims advanced by certain racial, national, ethnic, and linguistic minorities.

A. FORMAL VS. SUBSTANTIVE EQUALITY: THE SCOPE OF CONSTITUTIONAL EQUALITY AND THE SUBJECT AND DOMAIN OF EQUALITY

Debate about constitutional equality often reflects confusion or misunderstanding concerning key concepts and the relationship among them. For example, whereas there is broad-based consensus on formal equality—all equals should be treated equally—this does not extend to substantive equality—who is equal to whom and in what respects. The following excerpts discuss several of the key concepts.

Michel Rosenfeld, TOWARDS A RECONSTRUCTION OF CONSTITUTIONAL EQUALITY, in WESTERN RIGHTS? POST–COMMUNIST APPLICATION

161–166, 170–175.
(András Sajó ed., 1996).

1. Centrality and Elusiveness of Constitutional Equality

Constitutional equality is central yet elusive. It is central as * * * potentially the most pervasive of constitutional rights. Consistent with the requirement of formal equality—those who are similarly situated ought to be similarly treated—any law can be attacked on constitutional equality grounds—either for failing to treat *all* those similarly situated similarly, or for treating similarly *some* who are not similarly situated. Furthermore, equality concerns also permeate other fundamental constitutional rights such as freedom of expression rights,[3] free exercise of religion rights,[4] and abortion rights.[5] [See also Section C. below.]

Notwithstanding its virtual omnipresence, constitutional equality is singularly elusive. It is difficult to pin down owing to disputes regarding its relevant *subject*—who is to be equal to whom—and proper *domain*— what things are to be allocated equally. For example, is the proper

3. See, *e.g.*, K.L. Karst, "Equality as a Central Principle in the First Amendment," 43 *University of Chicago Law Review* 20 (1975).

4. See C.L. Eisgruber and L.G. Sager, "The Vulnerability of Conscience: The Constitutional Basis for Protecting Religious Conduct", 61 *University of Chicago Law Review* 1245 (1994).

5. See Ruth Bader Ginsburg, "Some Thoughts on Autonomy and Equality in Relation to *Roe v. Wade*," 63 *North Carolina Law Review* 375 (1985); *see also* K.L. Karst, "Foreword: Equal Citizenship Under the Fourteenth Amendment," 91 *Harvard Law Review* 1, 57–59 (1977).

subject of constitutional equality the individual or the group? Should it be limited to citizens or include aliens? On the other hand, should the proper domain of constitutional equality be limited to formal rights? Or should it extend to all the products of social cooperation? Or to some but not all of those? Beyond that, and perhaps even more important it is hard to get a handle on constitutional equality due to great difficulties in successfully integrating different levels of abstraction,[7] and in successfully circumscribing the appropriate frame of reference.[8] Indeed, frustrations stemming from attempts to pin down equality may become so great as to promote the belief that equality is ultimately an empty concept.[9]
* * *

Ideally, constitutional equality should account for all *relevant* identities and differences. But in any pluralist society with conflicting conceptions of the good, no consensus on the relevance of all-imaginable identities and differences is conceivable. * * * [Accordingly,] [w]hat ordinarily come under the rubric of constitutional equality * * * are certain proscriptions against inequality, or more precisely against *some inequalities*. [See Section B. below.] * * *

Viewing constitutional equality in terms of proscriptions against certain inequalities conforms with current constitutional practice in the United States and in other major constitutional democracies.[11] * * *

2. The Framework for Reconstruction: Setting Normative Ideals Against the Dialectics of Equality

The struggle for equality, against which constitutional equality must be set, is historically grounded in the rejection of the privileges of birth and status characteristic of hierarchical feudal societies. This struggle, moreover, unfolds in a dialectical process comprising three different

---

7. For example, while there is a wide-ranging consensus in the United States concerning constitutional equality at the highest levels of abstraction, see M. Rosenfeld, "*Metro Broadcasting, Inc. v. FCC*: Affirmative Action at the Crossroads of Constitutional Liberty and Equality," 38 *UCLA Law Review* 583, 588 (1991) (equal protection requires upholding the equal worth, dignity and respect of every individual, regardless of race or ethnic origin), bitter contentiousness often mars consideration of constitutional equality at lower levels of abstraction as vividly illustrated by the Supreme Court's closely divided affirmative action jurisprudence. * * * [See Section D. below.]

8. The "frame of reference" of an equality claim includes, among other things, the historical time slice against which must be set a baseline making it possible to measure equalities and inequalities, and the *locus* in the sociopolitical space in relation to which one must carry out the comparisons inevitably called for by every equality claim. For a good example of a profound disagreement on constitutional equality based in signifi-

cant part on vastly divergent views concerning the appropriate frame of reference, compare Justice O'Connor's majority opinion with Justice Marshall's dissent in *City of Richmond v. J.A. Croson Co.*, 488 U.S. 469 (1989). For an extensive analysis of these two contrasting opinions, see M. Rosenfeld, "Decoding *Richmond:* Affirmative Action and the Elusive Meaning of Constitutional Equality," 87 *Michigan Law Review* 1729 (1989).

9. See P. Westen, "The Empty Idea of Equality," 95 *Harvard Law Review* 537 (1982).

11. In the United States, this is achieved through the use of stricter scrutiny in the cases of certain inequalities such as those based on race, see, e.g., Korematsu v. United States, 323 U.S. 214 (1944) or on sex, see e.g., Craig v. Boren, 429 U.S. 190 (1976). For France, see J. Bell, *French Constitutional Law*, Oxford (1992). For Germany, see T. Würtenberger, "Equality" in *The Constitution of the Federal Republic of Germany*, U. Karpen ed., Baden–Baden (1988) 67–90.

stages marking a logical progression[14] from inequality to the ideal of constitutional equality. [The base line of this process is that all human beings are inherently equal. From there,] [i]n the first stage of this dialectic, difference is correlated to inequality—that is, those who are characterized as different are legitimately treated [better or worse, as the case may be]. In the second stage, identity is correlated to equality— that is, everyone will be entitled to be treated the same so long as he or she meets certain criteria adopted as criteria of identity. Finally, in the third stage, difference is correlated to equality—that is, everyone will be treated in proportion to his or her needs and aspirations.

To briefly illustrate this three-stage dialectic, let us consider the relationship between men and women. In stage one, differences—whether real or constructed—between men and women provide grounds for treating women as inferiors. In stage two, women make claims to equality by stressing identities between the sexes and downplaying differences. Also, because these claims are raised in a setting dominated by men, the identity that women must embrace in their quest for equality is a male-oriented identity. For example, for professional women to achieve equality at the workplace, they would have to adapt to an environment designed for males, and sacrifice childbearing and childrearing in order to have the same chances for promotion as men have. In contrast, in stage three, women would pursue equality in a way that accounts for differences between the sexes without disadvantaging women. For instance, women would demand the same career prospects as men, but with special allowances for childbearing and childrearing. By the same token, in stage three a woman's right to an abortion would be encompassed within her right to equality as it would give her a right over her body that would be the equivalent to that which a man has over his.[16]

The transition between stage one and stage two requires a shift in focus from differences to identities. That shift, in turn necessitates a movement towards greater abstraction. For example, for a woman to buttress the claim that she is, for relevant purposes, identical to men, she will have to construct a more abstract identity between human beings by downplaying those differences that give shape to gender identity. Accordingly, to achieve second-stage equality as identity, a woman would have to repress feminine tendencies which would stand as obstacles to access to the world of men.

In the third stage, the pursuit of equality as difference involves not so much a return to concrete differences, as reconciliation between the latter and abstract (second-stage) identities through a proper integration of different levels of abstraction. Thus, for example, third-stage reasoning would go somewhat as follows: men and women are equal as human beings, but to some extent have different needs and aspirations. Accord-

---

14. This *logical* progression need not correspond to a historical one as the dialectic in question operates at the level of [normative aspiration].

16. See Ginsburg, "Some Thoughts on Autonomy and Equality in Relation to *Roe*

v. Wade," *supra* note 5; see also K.L. Karst, "Foreword: Equal Citizenship Under the Fourteenth Amendment," 91 *Harvard Law Review* 1, 57–59 (1977).

ingly, to reconcile abstract equality and concrete differences, men and women ought to be equally treated in proportion to their different needs and aspirations. * * * [T]hird-stage equality as difference is an ideal which must be approximated but can never be reached. In addition, the transition between second-stage and third-stage equality is fraught with danger, for by refocusing on differences one runs the risk of provoking a regression to a first-stage correlation of difference and inequality. Because of this, the pursuit of greater constitutional equality must be mindful of the danger of regression and devise safeguards designed to avoid it.

* * *

* * * [A]lthough there is wide ranging diversity among different constitutional norms and practices, there seem to be certain constant features that span across most, if not all, of the vast expanse delimited by contemporary constitutional norms and practices. Thus, equality in the context of contemporary constitutions implies that all persons who are members of the same constitutional polity: 1) shall be guaranteed the *same* constitutional rights; and 2) shall be equal *before* and *under* the law, or in a somewhat different formulations, shall be entitled to the *equal protection* of the law. To be sure, these broadly articulated norms are susceptible to being construed in many different ways. Nevertheless, they impose some measure of constraint on how relevant variables may be used to delimit constitutional equality in a given set of circumstances. Furthermore, all claims to constitutional equality and all constitutional measures adopted to meet such claims are likely to be ultimately reducible to one of the three following principles: 1) the equal treatment principle; 2) the equal consideration principle; and 3) the equal result principle. Also, pursuit of the equal treatment principle corresponds to the achievement of *marginal* equality; pursuit of the equal result principle to the achievement of *global* equality;[26] and pursuit of the equal consideration principle * * * to the achievement of equality of opportunity. However, to determine which of these principles ought to predominate in given circumstances, and what its specific content ought to be like, it is first necessary to obtain a better grasp of the variables that play such an important role in shaping the struggle for constitutional equality.

3. The Interplay Between Identity and Difference Inclusion and Exclusion

Laws classify and delimit different classes which, in most cases, are slated for dissimilar treatment[, depending on class membership]. For example, a law that prohibits those under eighteen years of age from driving automobiles divides persons into two distinct classes, and prescribes dissimilar treatment depending on class membership. Such a law makes differences based on age legally relevant, and other differences legally irrelevant. * * *

---

26. "Marginal equality is defined with respect to (often small) *changes* from the status quo, with the changes being equal in magnitude for all. Global equality is defined with respect to holdings above zero, with their amounts or end states being equal." D. Rae, et al., *Equalities,* Cambridge (1981) 51.

Inasmuch as a legally relevant identity is arrived at through disregarding certain differences, such identity is *constructed* rather than given. Furthermore, where such identity is set against a deeply entrenched attachment to certain differences, its construction is likely to be difficult and belabored. In contrast to identity, difference may appear to be given rather than constructed, but legally relevant difference is as constructed as is identity. Thus for example, although there are biological differences between the sexes, gender-based legally relevant differences are nonetheless constructed. In some cases such construction may be more obvious than in others. In *Bradwell v. State*,[29] the United States Supreme Court upheld a state ban against women practicing law on the ground that a woman's proper role was that of wife and mother. Such a role, made legally relevant for purposes of determining eligibility to practice law, is unmistakably a social construct. In other cases, however, the construct may be more concealed. In *Michael M. v. Superior Court of Sonoma Country*,[30] the Supreme Court upheld the statutory rape conviction of a male under eighteen years old even though the law made it a crime to have consensual sex with a female under eighteen but not with a male under eighteen. In support of its decision, the Supreme Court stressed that females but not males risk pregnancy as a consequence of sexual intercourse. Whereas the latter difference is not a mere social construct, making it legally relevant for purposes of defining statutory rape inevitably involves a social construct. One may seek to hide this social construct behind the natural difference with which it has been associated. But the fact remains that without some such construct, the natural difference standing alone does not provide sufficient backing for the legally grounded difference. Indeed the mere fact that consensual sex among heterosexuals can result in the female getting pregnant does not, of itself, afford a rationale for punishing the male but not the female.

* * *

Not only are the possibilities of constructing identities and differences seemingly infinite, but preferences for certain identities or differences are bound to vary as a function of diverging conceptions of the good. Thus, for instance, constructed identities and differences around gender will fluctuate greatly according to whether their proponents adhere to certain traditionalist outlooks or to egalitarian precepts. Traditionalists will thus tend to construct gender-based differences to the detriment of identities, with an eye to legitimating a gender hierarchy. Egalitarians, on the other hand, will tend to construct identities and other kinds of differences more geared towards parity among the sexes than toward subordination.

* * *

At first, it may seem that identity is always linked to inclusion and difference to exclusion. Thus, gender, ethnic and racial identity are often promoted as markers for inclusion whereas gender, ethnic and racial differences have all too frequently been used as markers for exclusion and oppression. Moreover, to the extent that difference goes hand in

---

29. 83 U.S. 130 (1873).   **30.** 450 U.S. 464 (1981).

hand with exclusion, constitutional equality could be easily satisfied through prohibition of the use of certain differences as the basis for legal classifications. Accordingly, a color-blind,[34] gender-blind,[35] etc., constitution would afford the best possible protection against the implantation of the inequalities posing the greatest threats to the achievement of constitutional equality.

Upon closer consideration, however, neither is identity strictly correlated to inclusion, nor difference to exclusion. For example, in a society comprising a linguistic majority and a linguistic minority, constructing an identity that transcends language differences, and prescribing public education exclusively in the majority language may well exacerbate the linguistic minority's sense of exclusion rather than foster national integration. On the other hand, taking into account religious differences for purposes of facilitating compliance with a person's chosen religion may well promote inclusion of diverse religious traditions within the polity.

The *same* difference, moreover, may, depending on the circumstances, form the basis for inclusion or exclusion. Thus religious differences, which can be stressed to achieve inclusion, can also easily be used for purposes of exclusion, as when they are relied upon to discriminate in employment.[36] Accordingly, so far as constitutional equality requires pursuing inclusion, it ought to, at times take certain differences into account, and at other times, disregard them. In general, a sphere of activity with respect to which a particular difference ought to be disregarded constitutes a "sphere of assimilation."[37] In contrast, a sphere of activity in relation to which a particular differences ought to count amounts to a "sphere of differentiation."[38]

Consider the following cases with respect to the nexus between the principle of formal equality—all equals should be treated equally—and different conceptions of substantive equality, i.e., who is equal to whom and in what respect they ought to be deemed equal.

TRIMBLE v. GORDON

Supreme Court (United States).
430 U.S. 762 (1977).

[In a 5–4 decision, the Court held unconstitutional an Illinois law providing that illegitimate children could not inherit from their father if

34. Cf. *Plessy v. Ferguson*, 163 U.S. 559 ("Our constitution is color-blind") (Harlan, J. dissenting).

35. Cf. Art. 3 (2) of the German Constitution, which provides: "Men and women have equal rights." Pursuant to an October 27, 1994 amendment, the following was added: "The state fosters the actual achievement of equal entitlement between men and women and strives to eliminate existing disadvantages."

36. Such discrimination can be achieved either by using religious difference directly as a basis for legal classification, such as in a law that prohibits hiring

members of certain religions, or by formally ignoring religious differences, but imposing a facially neutral criterion that is substantively discriminatory, such as a law that allows employers not to hire any employee who refuses to work on any day other than Sunday, and thus for all practical purposes discriminates against Sabbatarians.

37. See M. Rosenfeld, *Affirmative Action and Justice: A Philosophical and Constitutional Inquiry* 224 (1991).

38. *Id.*

he died without a will, given that legitimate children, under Illinois law, did inherit from their father if he died without a will. The following excerpts are from the dissenting opinion of then—Justice Rehnquist.]

Mr. Justice Rehnquist, dissenting.

The Fourteenth Amendment's prohibition against "any State * * * deny[ing] to any person * * * the equal protection of the laws" is undoubtedly one of the majestic generalities of the Constitution. * * *

Unfortunately, more than a century of decisions under this Clause of the Fourteenth Amendment have a syndrome wherein this Court seems to regard the Equal Protection Clause as a cat-o'-nine-tails to be kept in the judicial closet as a threat to legislatures which may, in the view of the judiciary, get out of hand and pass "arbitrary," "illogical," or "unreasonable" laws. Except in the area of the law in which the Framers obviously meant it to apply—classifications based on race or on national origin, the first cousin of race—the Court's decisions can fairly be described as an endless tinkering with legislative judgments, a series of conclusions unsupported by any central guiding principle.

* * *

The Equal Protection Clause is itself a classic paradox, and makes sense only in the context of a recently fought Civil War. It creates a requirement of equal treatment to be applied to the process of legislation—legislation whose very purpose is to draw lines in such a way that different people are treated differently. The problem presented is one of sorting the legislative distinctions which are acceptable from those which involve invidiously unequal treatment.

All constitutional provisions for protection of individuals involve difficult questions of line drawing. But most others have implicit within them an understandable value judgment that certain types of conduct have a favored place and are to be protected to a greater or lesser degree. * * *

In the case of equality and equal protection, the constitutional principle—the thing to be protected to a greater or lesser degree—is not even identifiable from within the four corners of the Constitution. For equal protection does not mean that all persons must be treated alike. Rather, its general principle is that persons similarly situated should be treated similarly. But that statement of the rule does little to determine whether or not a question of equality is even involved in a given case. For the crux of the problem is *whether persons are similarly situated* for purposes of the state action in issue. Nothing in the words of the Fourteenth Amendment specifically addresses this question in any way.

The essential problem of the Equal Protection Clause is therefore the one of determining where the courts are to look for guidance in defining "equal" as that word is used in the Fourteenth Amendment.

Since the Amendment grew out of the Civil War and the freeing of the slaves, the core prohibition was early held to be aimed at the protection of blacks. If race was an invalid sorting tool where blacks were concerned, it followed logically that it should not be valid where other races were concerned either. A logical, though not inexorable, next step, was the extension of the protection to prohibit classifications resting on national origin.

The presumptive invalidity of all of these classifications has made decisions involving them, for the most part, relatively easy. But when the Court has been required to adjudicate equal protection claims not based on race or national origin, it has faced a much more difficult task. In cases involving alienage, for example, it has concluded that such classifications are "suspect" because, though not necessarily involving race or national origin, they are enough like the latter to warrant similar treatment. *In re Griffiths,* 413 U.S. 717 (1973). While there may be individual disagreement as to how such classes are to be singled out and as to whether specific classes are sufficiently close to the core area of race and national origin to warrant such treatment, one cannot say that the inquiry is not germane to the meaning of the Clause.

Illegitimacy, which is involved in this case, has never been held by the Court to be a "suspect classification." Nonetheless, in several opinions of the Court, statements are found which suggest that although illegitimates are not members of a "suspect class," laws which treat them differently from those born in wedlock will receive a more far-reaching scrutiny under the Equal Protection Clause than will other laws regulating economic and social conditions. The Court's opinion today contains language to that effect. * * * [T]his language is a source * * * of confusion, since the unanswered question remains as to the precise sort of scrutiny to which classifications based on illegitimacy will be subject.

    * * *

Every law enacted, unless it applies to all persons at all times and in all places, inevitably imposes sanctions upon some and declines to impose the same sanctions on others. But these inevitable concomitants of legislation have little or nothing to do with the Equal Protection Clause of the Fourteenth Amendment, unless they employ means of sorting people which the draftsmen of the Amendment sought to prohibit. * * *

Here the Illinois Legislature was dealing with a problem of interstate succession of illegitimates from their fathers, which, as the Court concedes, frequently presents difficult problems of proof. * * * [Accordingly, t]he circumstances which justify the distinction between illegitimates and legitimates contained in § 12 are apparent with no great exercise of imagination * * *

UNIVERSITY PROFESSORS CASE

Constitutional Council (France).
83–165 DC of 20 January 1984.[a]

In the aftermath of May 1968 higher education was reformed, and the universities were broken up into smaller units. Instead of large

---

   a. As summarized in John Bell, *French Constitutional Law* 155–56, 208 (1992).

faculties, the new universities are made up of a series of 'units of study and research,' run by the tenured professors. Teaching is done by both tenured professors and non-tenured *matres-assistants* and *assistants*. The universities are governed by elected councils and committees, composed initially of academic staff and students. As part of their plans to 'democratize' the public sector, the provisions on representation in the universities were extended by the Socialists to include all categories of university employees and students. The role of the academic staff was reduced, and there were many who considered that such changes would endanger academic freedom, since decisions would be taken to comply with pressures from politically motivated staff or students, rather than on academic grounds.

Under the new *loi* on universities, professors, non-tenured teachers and researchers, and personnel from libraries and museums were to form one electoral body to choose representatives for the governing council of the university. Given the structure of the universities, the teachers and researchers would outnumber the professors, and it was claimed, this would leave the appointment of the representatives of the latter group in the hands of the former, contrary to the principle of equality in elections. The Conseil struck down the provision * * * on this ground, [and on academic freedom grounds] * * * [B]ecause professors were outnumbered by the other groups, 'the independence of the professors was threatened' in a number of respects. Professors required freedom in their tasks of preparing programmes, attending to students, co-ordinating teaching teams, and in their necessary involvement in decisions on promotions of teachers and researchers. This freedom would be impaired by belonging to the same electoral group as the teachers and researchers, presumably because they would feel beholden to their potential electors. In any case, the professors would not be able to choose their members on the basis of their own assessment of their colleagues, and they could not be sure of an unbiased representation, since the delegates would be chosen by the majority group, the teachers and researchers. * * *

Equality of treatment requires not merely the prohibition of irrelevant discrimination, but also a respect for relevant differences, [and accordingly] university professors had to be given distinct representation in the government of the university. * * *

Thomas Würtenberger, EQUALITY, IN THE CONSTITUTION OF THE FEDERAL REPUBLIC OF GERMANY

67, 72–73 (Ulrich Karpen ed., 1988).

* * *

Equality through legislation does not require that everyone should be treated equally without any differences in every aspect. The legislator has neither a duty to create equality of status nor to realize factual equality between men:[19] The allocation of equal status would require a distributive state (*Zuteilungsstaat*) destroying freedom. Thus the legislator must differentiate when distributing burdens, services and privileges. In this differentiation the legislator must be careful that equal facts and circumstances should be treated equally, and unequal facts and circumstances should not be treated equally. In any event there are never facts and circumstances which are equal in every element i.e. identical. Facts and circumstances can only be evaluated as equal or unequal with regard to individual specially characteristic elements. Therefore it is the task of the legislator, in the framework of the policy for which he is responsible, to choose out the elements he wants to form the basis of unequal or equal treatment. The legislator has a far-reaching latitude in the evaluation of facts and circumstances as equal or unequal. The parliamentary majority of the day decides, according to its political aims, to what extent and in what way equality through the law should be realized. In spite of this latitude, the legislator is in any case obliged to consider significant existing inequalities. Within the framework of demo-cratically legitimated policy, laws have to provide proper, reasonable and just solutions to problems.

The important point of reference in the application of the general principle of equality is the idea of justice. Whatever justice requires as equal or unequal treatment in a particular case, depends on the prevail-ing moral and cultural order, and is also developed, in terms of legal psychology, from the generally prevailing ideas of justice.[23] The generally prevalent moral and cultural values as well as the ideas of justice find on the one hand their point of reference in the basic values of the constitu-tion, but on the other hand can also change from time to time. The interpretation of the principle of equality depends not only on social and cultural changes, rather also on changes of legal consciousness.

Susanne Baer, CONSTITUTIONAL EQUALITY: THE JURISPRUDENCE OF THE GERMAN CONSTITUTIONAL COURT

5 Colum. J. Eur. L. 249, 251–256, 258–260, 279 (1999).

II. DOCTRINE

A. The Range of Equality Guarantees

* * * [T]he general right to equality guaranteed in art. 3, para. 1 of the Grundgesetz, * * * provides that "all persons shall be equal before the law." Under this provision, equality is limited to general equality, since more specific constitutional provisions such as art. 3, paras. 2 and

---

19. *Maunz/Zippelius*, Deutsches Staats-recht, 26th ed. (1985), § 25 I; *R. Alexy*, Theorie der Grundrechte (1985), pp. 359 f.

23. *Maunz/Zippelius* (n. 19), § 25 I; BVerfGE 9, 338 (349); 13, 225 (228); 42, 64 (72).

3, or art. 33, para. 2 cover equality based on gender, ethnicity, heritage, language, religion or belief, or equality in the public service. Other sources from which German lawyers may draw a general right to equality include art. 14 of the European Convention of Human Rights and Freedoms and the fundamental European law principle of equality developed by the European Court of Justice. In addition, Germany has ratified several international treaties which guarantee equality and, notably, also explicitly guarantee equality with respect to personal and property assets (*Vermögen*), * * *.[13] Finally, there is an equality guarantee in each of the constitutions of the states of the Federal Republic of Germany.[14] In practice, however, the Grundgesetz dominates German equality doctrine.

B. Applicability of Equality Analysis

Which doctrinal analysis is to be applied * * * depends upon the manner in which * * * cases are re-constructed for purposes of constitutional law. Questions of general equality only arise if a set of facts is reconstructed to show certain characteristics. In this reconstruction, narratives are formed out of complex sets of information; a case is never already a case when it enters the realm of law. In particular, this occurs if a social discrepancy is recognized to arise between legally comparable groups or situations. Only then will the German constitutional right to general equality derived from art. 3, para. 1 of the Grundgesetz be applicable.

* * *

2. The Search for the Tertium Comparationis

When we construct a case so as to raise the issue of equality, we have to decide what exactly we wish to compare. At this stage of the analysis, the question is whether a case is about a comparison between groups of persons, between individuals, or between situations. The answer to this question is called the tertium comparationis, the third aspect, which is basis for a comparison between two sets of facts or their common denominator.

* * *

In German constitutional law, it is often said that dignity is the tertium comparationis. After all, the right to dignity in art. 1 of the Grundgesetz is seen as the first and most basic constitutional right which requires courts to compare individuals as individuals to individuals. If we accept this as the basis of equality doctrine, we can raise an equality claim against every law because it is intrinsic to the very nature of laws to differentiate between and not discriminate against individuals. As a result, the legislature, the administration and the courts would be forced to demonstrate that their value judgements and distributive decisions are well founded, in harmony with constitutional requirements

---

13. The concept of *Vermögen* includes personal property as well as all assets to which a person has a claim. As a word, the term even includes the personal abilities of an individual. * * *

14. An unusual version of equality law can be found in Art. 7, § 2 of the constitution of the state of Brandenburg, which literally provides that "each person owes every other person respect for his or her dignity." See BbVerf Art. 7(2) * * *

and free from unjustifiable differences. While this does not sound like a bad idea, such a broad equality concept runs the danger of weakening itself. The more general the concept of equality, the less force and specificity it will have. The early decisions of the Federal Constitutional Court, in which the Court applied a general idea of justice drawn from philosophy rather than law instead of a more specific equality doctrine, prove the point. * * *

In sum, the Grundgesetz does not give us much guidance in our search for the tertium comparationis.[29] Even the enumeration of prohibited grounds for discrimination, such as gender and race, does not tell us whether a certain social inequality is based on, relevant to, or constitutive of, sexual or racial difference. The standards for choosing the tertium comparationis are not to be found in doctrine, but are left to epistemology.

* * *

C. Justifications for Inequality: from Arbitrariness to Proportionality

* * * In Germany, the right to equality is violated when the state makes an unjustified distinction between people or situations. As previously noted, the crux of the matter lies in the manner in which distinction is constructed and on what justifications are deemed to be permissible.

1. A Glimpse of History: Formal vs. Material Equality

Prior to 1945, some German positivists, most conservatives and, later the fascists understood equality to be a symmetrical right which prohibited distinctions between what is similar. They favored the formal version of the Aristotelian approach to equality. However, some liberal scholars of the Weimar Republic were of the opinion that equality is not a right against formal distinctions alone. Their material interpretation of equality did not merely prohibit any distinction but only the relevant ones: according to them, inequality occurs when something is treated unequally while being "substantially the same"[44] or when something is treated equally which is "substantially unalike." They argued that, since "substantially" implies an assessment of the issues, the criteria of substance and relevance imply that some notion of justice is an intrinsic part of equality. After 1945, this second interpretation found a strong adherent in the Federal Constitutional Court and in the Grundgesetz itself.

In German constitutional law today, art. 3, para. 1 of the Grundgesetz is neither deemed to secure a purely formal equality, nor is this specific provision considered necessary to secure such equality. First, since art. 3, para. 1 states that all state power is bound by law, formal

29. Another more subtle problem involves comparability. The problem is that the tertium comparationis is usually a dominant standard which does not allow for pluralism or, in the words of contemporary theory, differences. To pose the question a bit differently: Why must blue-collar employees be similarly situated to white-collar employees in order to claim equality? Why must female athletes be similar to male athletes to have a gender equality right to their own sport?

44. See, e.g., BVerfGE 49, 148 (165).

equality (*Rechtsanwendungsgleichheit*) is already a part of the constitution. This interpretation is based upon an understanding of the Grundgesetz which holds that to be bound by law means that there is equal application of law since the very nature of law demands universal application. Second, the fundamental rights guaranteed by the Grundgesetz do not distinguish between groups but instead treat all the same. Thus, if art. 3, para. 1 is not to be found superfluous, it must have more than a merely formal meaning.

The search for the material meaning of equality developed out of a specific factual context. Generally, it followed society's path towards greater diversification and pluralism which is a legal path towards an increase in equality challenges. Doctrinally speaking, the jurisprudence developed in a primarily area-specific manner. For example, several post–1945 and post–1989 cases dealt with problems unprecedented in the limited national history of the Federal Republic. After 1945, the Court was confronted with the problems posed by the post-war influx of refugees; in the wake of 1989, the Court was presented with issues relating to the thousands of new and indigent citizens from the former German Democratic Republic.[49] The Court's solution was to create a doctrine of area-specific tests applicable to specific fields of regulation such as those responding to the exceptional situation after a change of regime. In the area of tax law, the Court now uses a doctrine of vertical and horizontal tax justice which requires equal factual and legal treatment based on the social difference in economic capability of the individual. For purposes of welfare legislation, which is now increasingly difficult to finance and manage, the Court developed a doctrine of permissible justifications based on generalizations and administrative efficiency and applies a lower standard of review * * *.[50] In addition, it has established the welfare clause in art. 20 of the Grundgesetz to be a dynamic force behind the right to equality.[51]

       * * *

To conclude, the area of equality doctrine is particularly interesting since three fundamental questions of jurisprudence converge. First, is this doctrine able to capture the complexity of social life, to translate it into cases and to adequately resolve them? This question is particularly obvious in the discussion of who or what should be compared and is comparable enough to be treated as an equality case. Second, how much power should be vested in courts rather than in legislatures or civil society? This issue is seen in the structural discussion of functions of judicial review. * * * Finally, does and should law preserve or change the status quo? This question is found in the area of equality of people with little economic power, of groups of non-dominant ethnicity and of

---

49. See, e.g., BVerfGE 71, 66 (76); BVerfGE 53, 164 (177). Referring to periods of economic recession in his dissent, Justice Katzenstein argues that constitutional standards should not carry equal weight at all times. See BVerfGE 62, 256 (289, 294).

50. In such areas, the state has to deal with numerous similar problems. There-

fore, I wonder whether area-specific criteria are necessary or whether the mass-problems and generalizations criteria are sufficient.

51. See, e.g., BVerfGE 74, 9 (24) (unemployment benefits for students).

women. The jurisprudence of the Federal Constitutional Court is moving towards a more sensitive recognition of these issues by adopting area-specific doctrines and the proportionality test. Whether this doctrinal development will serve to further reduce social inequalities remains to be seen.

A.1.   THE SUBJECT OF EQUALITY: WHO IS EQUAL TO WHOM?

Michel Rosenfeld, AFFIRMATIVE ACTION AND JUSTICE: A PHILOSOPHICAL AND CONSTITUTIONAL INQUIRY

15–16 (1991).

The subject of equality is determined by the response to the question of "who is to be equal to whom". There are two different possible answers to this question. The first is that each individual member of a relevant class is the equal of every other individual member of that class. This means that the individual is the subject of equality and that * * * "individual regarding equality" is involved. An example of an individual-regarding equality is provided by the "one-person-one-vote" principle, which defines a class comprised of all those who are citizens and which grants each individual member of that class the same right to vote as any other member of that class.

The second possible subject of equality is the group. Once the class of all those who are to be treated equally has been defined, then in contrast to cases of individual-regarding equality, equality is not between individuals but between subclasses. To illustrate, let us assume there is a class of one hundred persons divided into two subclasses, S1 and S2, of fifty persons each. Let us assume further that there are two hundred equal lots of good G available for distribution to the class. Group-regarding equality would be satisfied if S1 and S2 each received one hundred G's. Moreover, group-regarding equality but not individual-regarding equality would remain satisfied no matter what the particular distribution of G's made by each subclass among its own members. Thus, group-regarding equality is as compatible with equal distribution within each subclass as with equal distribution in one subclass but not the other (e.g., two G's for each member of S1, and one G for half of the members of S2 and three G's for the other half of the members of S2) and with unequal distribution within both subclasses.

As demonstrated by the following example, group-regarding equality may well produce inequalities between individual members of different groups. This would be the case if group S3 has fifty members, group S4 one hundred members, each group receives one hundred lots of G, and each group adheres to a rule of equal distribution among its members. Under those circumstances each individual member of S3 would receive two G's whereas each individual member of S4 would receive only one G. Moreover, individual-regarding equality produces group-regarding inequality whenever the relevant groups are of different sizes. Thus, if every individual is to receive one G, and if group S5 is comprised of one hundred individuals but group S6 of only fifty, S5 will receive twice as many G's as does S6.

In the United States, equal protection rights are accorded to the individual and not groups—see *Shelley v. Kraemer*, 334 U.S. 1 (1948), excerpted in Chapter 10—and are thus individual regarding. In *Regents of the University of California v. Bakke*, 438 U.S. 265, 299, 309–310 (1978), see Section D. below, an affirmative action case involving race-based preferences in medical school admissions, Justice Powell concluded that it was unconstitutional to disadvantage a white person on account of his race in order to address group-related grievances unless this was necessary to accomplish a compelling state interest. For further discussion of the clash between individual-and group-regarding equality in the context of affirmative action, see Section D. below.

MAHE v. ALBERTA

Supreme Court (Canada).
[1990] 1 S.C.R. 342.

[Group equality and linguistic rights. This case is presented in Section E. below.]

A.2. THE DOMAIN OF EQUALITY: IN RESPECT TO WHAT ARE EQUALS TO BE EQUAL?

Michel Rosenfeld, AFFIRMATIVE ACTION AND JUSTICE: A PHILOSOPHICAL AND CONSTITUTIONAL INQUIRY

16 (1991).

If we assume agreement on a particular subject of equality, the next logical task seems to require the determination of what Rae terms the "domain of equality." According to Rae's definition, domain of equality refers to the "classes of things that are to be allocated equally." Moreover, a domain of equality may be broad or narrow. Taking any two domains of equality, Domain I and Domain II, Rae stipulates that "Domain I is broad in relation to II if, first everything in II is also in I, and, second, some of the things in I are not in II." Thus, for instance, if Domain I were to consist of 100 tons of gold and one peanut and Domain II of 100 tons of gold, Domain I would be broad in relation to Domain II. [Douglas Rae et al., *Equalities* 45–46 (1981).]

Rae argues that the distinction between broad and narrow domains of equality highlights a persistent difficulty confronted by all proponents of equality since Locke. As Rae indicates, Locke advocates equal individual rights before the state but finally rejects any right to equal allocation of all goods susceptible of being divided into equal lots for purposes of allocation to the relevant individual-regarding subject-class (ibid., 47).

Once one advocates the equal allocation of *certain* classes of things, however, the question arises: Why only those classes of things and not other classes of things? Why not *all* classes of things? Moreover, since, according to Rae, almost no political thinkers have seriously endorsed "equal everything in the world for everyone in the world" (ibid., 48, 166), these difficult questions arise for a broad spectrum of political thinkers extending from Nozick to Marx.

In theory the domain of constitutional equality could fall anywhere within the spectrum spanning from purely formal rights to equalization of all the benefits and burdens created through, or affected by, social interaction. Equality rights in contemporary constitutions fall between these two extremes and can be distinguished, according to whether they encompass a broader or narrower domain of equality. Constitutions that provide for greater social, economic, and welfare rights (see generally Chapter 10, especially Section C.) encompass a broader domain of equality and mandate a higher degree of state intervention. For example, some constitutions, such as the Italian or the Hungarian one, recognize some equal right to free healthcare (see Chapter 10, Section C.), thus imposing positive obligations on the state to deliver or underwrite medications or health treatments. In contrast, a constitution that guarantees only an equal right of access to nongovernmental healthcare—cf. the interpretation of the U.S. Constitution as guaranteeing a right to an abortion but not to a state-paid abortion for indigent women, see *Harris v. McRae*, 448 U.S. 297 (1980) (upholding ban on government funding of medically necessary abortions)—would only bar the state from interfering with, or limiting, access to such nongovernmental healthcare. Extensive positive rights raise problems of scope and implementation that most negative rights do not. For example, a universal right to free healthcare raises problems concerning state budgeting, resource allocation, and implementation that repeal of a racially discriminatory law relating to access to private housing or employment does not. Cf. the Hungarian and Polish constitutional courts' interpretation of rights to free healthcare arising under their respective constitutions as nonindividual rights. This important issue is discussed further in Chapter 10, Section C. In what follows, we focus on the domain of constitutional equality rather than on the implications concerning the contour or scope of corresponding rights.

PLESSY v. FERGUSON

Supreme Court (United States).
163 U.S. 537 (1896).

[A challenge under the Equal Protection Clause was brought against enforcement of a Louisiana law requiring "separate but equal" accommodations for "white" and "colored" railroad passengers. Plessy, who claimed he had only one-eighth African blood, was arrested for sitting in a "whites-only" railroad car. A divided Supreme Court upheld the law as constitutional.]

Mr. Justice Brown delivered the opinion of the Court.

* * *

2. By the Fourteenth Amendment, all persons born or naturalized in the United States, and subject to the jurisdiction thereof, are made citizens of the United States and of the State wherein they reside; and the States are forbidden from making or enforcing any law which shall deny to any person within their jurisdiction the equal protection of the laws.

* * *

The object of the amendment was undoubtedly to enforce the absolute equality of the two races before the law, but in the nature of things it could not have been intended to abolish distinctions based upon color, or to enforce social, as distinguished from political equality, or a commingling of the two races upon terms unsatisfactory to either. Laws permitting, and even requiring, their separation in places where they are liable to be brought into contact do not necessarily imply the inferiority of either race to the other, and have been generally, if not universally, recognized as within the competency of the state legislatures in the exercise of their police power. The most common instance of this is connected with the establishment of separate schools for white and colored children, which has been held to be a valid exercise of the legislative power even by courts of States where the political rights of the colored race have been longest and most earnestly enforced.

* * *

Laws forbidding the intermarriage of the two races may be said in a technical sense to interfere with the freedom of contract, and yet have been universally recognized as within the police power of the State.

The distinction between laws interfering with the political equality of the negro and those requiring the separation of the two races in schools, theatres and railway carriages has been frequently drawn by this court.

* * * [I]t is also suggested * * * that the same argument that will justify the state legislature in requiring railways to provide separate accommodations for the two races will also authorize them to require separate cars to be provided for people whose hair is of a certain color, or who are aliens, or who belong to certain nationalities, or to enact laws requiring colored people to walk upon one side of the street, and white people upon the other, or requiring white men's houses to be painted white, and colored men's black, or their vehicles or business signs to be of different colors, upon the theory that one side of the street is as good as the other, or that a house or vehicle of one color is as good as one of another color. The reply to all this is that every exercise of the police power must be reasonable, and extend only to such laws as are enacted in good faith for the promotion for the public good, and not for the annoyance or oppression of a particular class.

* * *

So far, then, as a conflict with the Fourteenth Amendment is concerned, the case reduces itself to the question whether the statute of Louisiana is a reasonable regulation, and with respect to this there must necessarily be a large discretion on the part of the legislature. In determining the question of reasonableness it is at liberty to act with reference to the established usages, customs and traditions of the people, and with a view to the promotion of their comfort, and the preservation of the public peace and good order. Gauged by this standard, we cannot say that a law which authorizes or even requires the separation of the two races in public conveyances is unreasonable, or more obnoxious to the Fourteenth Amendment than the acts of Congress requiring separate schools for colored children in the District of Columbia, the constitutionality of which does not seem to have been questioned, or the corresponding acts of state legislatures.

We consider the underlying fallacy of the plaintiff's argument to consist in the assumption that the enforced separation of the two races stamps the colored race with a badge of inferiority. If this be so, it is not by reason of anything found in the act, but solely because the colored race chooses to put that construction upon it. The argument necessarily assumes that if, as has been more than once the case, and is not unlikely to be so again, the colored race should become the dominant power in the state legislature, and should enact a law in precisely similar terms, it would thereby relegate the white race to an inferior position. We imagine that the white race, at least, would not acquiesce in this assumption. The argument also assumes that social prejudices may be overcome by legislation, and that equal rights cannot be secured to the Negro except by an enforced commingling of the two races. We cannot accept this proposition. If the two races are to meet upon terms of social equality, it must be the result of natural affinities, a mutual appreciation of each other's merits and a voluntary consent of individuals.

* * *

Mr. Justice Harlan dissenting.

* * *

It is one thing for railroad carriers to furnish, or to be required by law to furnish, equal accommodations for all whom they are under a legal duty to carry. It is quite another thing for government to forbid citizens of the white and black races from travelling in the same public conveyance, and to punish officers of railroad companies for permitting persons of the two races to occupy the same passenger coach. If a State can prescribe, as a rule of civil conduct, that whites and blacks shall not travel as passengers in the same railroad coach, why may it not so regulate the use of the streets of its cities and towns as to compel white citizens to keep on one side of a street and black citizens to keep on the other? Why may it not, upon like grounds, punish whites and blacks who ride together in street cars or in open vehicles on a public road of street? Why may it not require sheriffs to assign whites to one side of a courtroom and blacks to the other? And why may it not also prohibit the commingling of the two races in the galleries of legislative halls or in public assemblages convened for the considerations of the political questions of the day? Further, if this statute of Louisiana is consistent with the personal liberty of citizens, why may not the State require the separation in railroad coaches of native and naturalized citizens of the United States, or of Protestants and Roman Catholics?

* * *

The white race deems itself to be the dominant race in this country. And so it is, in prestige, in achievements, in education, in wealth and in power. So, I doubt not, it will continue to be for all time, if it remains true to its great heritage and holds fast to the principles of constitutional liberty. But in view of the Constitution, in the eye of the law, there is in this country no superior, dominant, ruling class of citizens. There is no caste here. Our Constitution is color-blind, and neither knows nor tolerates classes among citizens. In respect of civil rights, all citizens are equal before the law. The humblest is the peer of the most powerful. The law regards man as man, and takes no account of his surroundings or of his color when his civil rights as guaranteed by the supreme law of the land are involved. It is, therefore, to be regretted that this high tribunal, the final expositor of the fundamental law of the land, has reached the conclusion that it is competent for a State to regulate the enjoyment by citizens of their civil rights solely upon the basis of race. * * *

BROWN v. BOARD OF EDUCATION

Supreme Court (United States).
347 U.S. 483 (1954).

Mr. Chief Justice Warren delivered the opinion of the Court.

These cases come to us from the States of Kansas, South Carolina, Virginia, and Delaware.

* * *

In each of the cases, minors of the Negro race, through their legal representatives, seek the aid of the courts in obtaining admission to the public schools of their community on a nonsegregated basis. In each instance they had been denied admission to schools attended by white children under laws requiring or permitting segregation according to race. This segregation was alleged to deprive the plaintiffs of the equal protection of the laws under the Fourteenth Amendment. [A] three-judge federal district court denied relief to the plaintiffs on the so-called "separate but equal" doctrine announced by this court in *Plessy v. Ferguson*, 163 U.S. 537 [1896].

* * *

The plaintiffs contend that segregated public schools are not "equal" and cannot be made "equal," and that hence they are deprived of the equal protection of the laws. * * *

In the first cases in this Court construing the Fourteenth Amendment, decided shortly after its adoption, the Court interpreted it as proscribing all state-imposed discriminations against the Negro race. The doctrine of "separate but equal" did not make its appearance in this Court until 1896 in the case of *Plessy v. Ferguson*, *supra*, involving not education but transportation. American courts have since labored with the doctrine for over half a century.

* * * [T]here are findings below that the Negro and white schools involved have been equalized, or are being equalized, with respect to buildings, curricula, qualifications and salaries of teachers, and other "tangible" factors. Our decision, therefore, cannot turn on merely a comparison of these tangible factors in the Negro and white schools involved in each of the cases. We must look instead to the effect of segregation itself on public education.

In approaching this problem, we cannot turn the clock back to 1868 when the Amendment was adopted, or even to 1896 when *Plessy v. Ferguson* was written. We must consider public education in the light of its full development and its present place in American life throughout the Nation. Only in this way can it be determined if segregation in public schools deprives these plaintiffs of the equal protection of the laws.

Today, education is perhaps the most important function of state and local governments. Compulsory school attendance laws and the great expenditures for education both demonstrate our recognition of the importance of education to our democratic society. It is required in the performance of our most basic public responsibilities, even service in the armed forces. It is the very foundation of good citizenship. Today it is a principal instrument in awakening the child to cultural values, in preparing him for later professional training, and in helping him to adjust normally to his environment. In these days, it is doubtful that any child may reasonably be expected to succeed in life if he is denied the opportunity of an education. Such an opportunity, where the state has undertaken to provide it, is a right which must be made available to all on equal terms.

We come then to the question presented: Does segregation of children in public schools solely on the basis of race, even though the physical facilities and other "tangible" factors may be equal, deprive the children of the minority group of equal educational opportunities? We believe that it does.

To separate [children] from others of similar age and qualifications solely because of their race generates a feeling of inferiority as to their status in the community that may affect their hearts and minds in a way unlikely ever to be undone. The effect of this separation on their educational opportunities was well stated by a finding in the Kansas case by a court which nevertheless felt compelled to rule against the Negro plaintiffs:

> "Segregation of white and colored children in public schools has a detrimental effect upon the colored children. The impact is greater when it has the sanction of the law; for the policy of separating the races is usually interpreted as denoting the inferiority of the Negro group. A sense of inferiority affects motivation of a child to learn. Segregation with the sanction of law, therefore, has a tendency to [retard] the educational and mental development of Negro children and to deprive them of some of the benefits they would receive in a racial[ly] integrated school system."

Whatever may have been the extent of psychological knowledge at the time of *Plessy v. Ferguson* contrary to this finding is rejected.

We conclude that in the field of public education the doctrine of "separate but equal" has no place. Separate educational facilities are inherently unequal. Therefore, we hold that the plaintiffs and others similarly situated for whom the actions have been brought are, by reason of the segregation complained of, deprived of the equal protection of the laws guaranteed by the Fourteenth Amendment. * * *

In both *Plessy* and *Brown*, the Court construes the Equal Protection Clause as requiring equality between blacks and whites, or, in the theoretical terms discussed above, that all black and white individuals are subjects of constitutional equality. In *Plessy*, however, the Court circumscribes the domain of constitutional racial equality to the realm of civil and political rights, not extending it to social relations. On the other hand, by branding state-enforced racial segregation in public schools as unconstitutional, *Brown* enlarges the domain of constitutional equality beyond mere civil (i.e., property and contract) and political rights (i.e., freedom of speech and assembly, voting, and eligibility to run for political office). Accordingly, racial equality is not only a matter of properly defining the subject class but also one of framing an appropriate domain of benefits and burdens.

Constitutional rights that define the domain of equality do not necessarily have to be cast as equality rights. For example, Art. 21 of the Constitution of India has been interpreted as specifying that the right to life requires that everyone have decent shelter and imposes on the state the duty to build such shelter if necessary. Although often characterized as a right to decent shelter, this right is the equivalent of an equality right guaranteeing decent shelter to all subjects of constitutional equality and enjoining the state to provide shelter to those who cannot obtain it otherwise. This right is considered in the following case.

AHMEDABAD MUNICIPAL CORPORATION v. NAWAB KHAN GULAB KHAN & ORS

Supreme Court (India).
(1995) 1 S.C.C. 520.

[This case is presented in Chapter 10, Section C.]

NUMERUS CLAUSUS I CASE

Federal Constitutional Court (Germany).
33 BVerfGE 303 (1972).

[Based on the German Basic Law's commitment to a "social welfare state" (*Sozialstaat*), the Federal Constitutional Court recognized a qualified equal right to free university education extended to all secondary school graduates. The Court's opinion is presented in Chapter 10, Section C.]

DANDRIDGE v. WILLIAMS

Supreme Court (United States).
397 U.S. 471 (1970).

Mr. Justice Stewart delivered the opinion of the Court.

This case involves the validity of a method used by Maryland, in the administration of an aspect of its public welfare program, to reconcile the demands of its needy citizens with the finite resources available to meet those demands. Like every other State in the Union, Maryland participates in the Federal Aid to Families With Dependent Children (AFDC) program, 42 U.S.C. § 601 *et seq.* (1964 ed. and Supp. IV), which originated with the Social Security Act of 1935. Under this jointly financed program, a State computes the so-called "standard of need". Other States provide that each family unit shall receive a percentage of the determined need. Still others provide grants to most families in full accord with the ascertained standard of need, but impose an upper limit on the total amount of money any one family unit may receive. Maryland, through administrative adoption of a "maximum grant regulation," has followed this last course. This suit was brought by several AFDC recipients to enjoin the application of the Maryland maximum grant regulation on the ground that it is in conflict * * * with the Equal Protection Clause of the Fourteenth Amendment. * * *

The [welfare recipients involved here] have large families, so that their standards of need as computed by the State substantially exceed the maximum grants that they actually receive under the regulation. The[y claim] that the maximum grant limitation operates to discriminate against them merely because of the size of their families, in violation of the Equal Protection Clause of the Fourteenth Amendment. [See further excerpts and discussion in Chapter 10.]

* * *

II

* * * [A] State * * * may not * * * impose a regime of invidious discrimination in violation of the Equal Protection Clause of the Fourteenth Amendment. Maryland says that its maximum grant regulation is wholly free of any invidiously discriminatory purpose or effect, and that the regulation is rationally supportable on at least four entirely valid grounds. The regulation can be clearly justified, Maryland argues, in terms of legitimate state interests in encouraging gainful employment, in maintaining an equitable balance in economic status as between welfare families and those supported by a wage-earner, in providing incentives for family planning, and in allocating available public funds in such a way as fully to meet the needs of the largest possible number of families * * *.

* * *

In the area of economics and social welfare, a State does not violate the Equal Protection Clause merely because the classifications made by its laws are imperfect. If the classification has some "reasonable basis," it does not offend the Constitution simply because the classification "is not made with mathematical nicety or because in practice it results in some inequality." *Lindsley v. Natural Carbonic Gas Co.*, 220 U.S. 61, 78 [1911].

To be sure, the cases * * * enunciating this fundamental standard under the Equal Protection Clause, have in the main involved state regulation of business or industry. The administration of public welfare assistance, by contrast, involved the most basic economic needs of impoverished human beings. We recognize the dramatically real factual difference between the [former] cases and this one, but we can find no basis for applying a different constitutional standard. It is a standard that has consistently been applied to state legislation restricting the availability of employment opportunities. And it is a standard that is true to the principle that the Fourteenth Amendment gives the federal courts no power to impose upon the States their views of what constitutes wise economic policy.

Under this long-established meaning of the Equal Protection Clause, it is clear that the Maryland maximum grant regulation is constitutionally valid. We need not explore all the reasons that the State advances in justification of the regulation. It is enough that a solid foundation of the regulation can be found in the State's legitimate interest in encouraging employment and in avoiding discrimination between welfare families and the families of the working poor. By combining a limit on the recipient's grant with permission to retain money earned, without reduction in the amount of the grant, Maryland provides an incentive to seek gainful employment. And by keying the maximum family AFDC grants to the minimum wage a steadily employed head of a household receives, the State maintains some semblance of an equitable balance between families on welfare and those supported by an employed breadwinner.

It is true that in some AFDC families there may be no person who is employable. It is also true that with respect to AFDC families whose determined standard of need is below the regulatory maximum, who therefore receive grants equal to the determined standard, the employment incentive is absent. But the Equal Protection Clause does not require that a State must choose between attacking every aspect of a problem or not attacking the problem at all. It is enough that the State's action be rationally based and free from invidious discrimination. The regulation before us meets that test.

* * *

Mr. Justice Marshall, whom Mr. Justice Brennan joins, dissenting.

I

* * *

The Court recognizes, as it must, that this case involves "the most basic economic needs of impoverished human beings," and that there is therefore a "dramatically real factual difference" between the instant case and those decisions upon which the Court relies. The acknowledgment that these dramatic differences exist is a candid recognition that the Court's decision today is wholly without precedent. I cannot subscribe to the Court's sweeping refusal to accord the Equal Protection Clause any role in this entire area of the law, and I therefore dissent from * * * the Court's decision.

* * *

II

The Maryland AFDC program in its basic structure operates uniformly with regard to all needy children by taking into account the basic subsistence needs of all eligible individuals in the formulation of the standards of need for families of various sizes. However, superimposed upon this uniform system is the maximum grant regulation, the operative effect of which is to create two classes of needy children and two classes of eligible families: those small families and their members who receive payments to cover their subsistence needs and those large families who do not.

This classification process effected by the maximum grant regulation produces a basic denial of equal treatment. Persons who are concededly similarly situated (dependent children and their families), are not afforded equal, or even approximately equal, treatment under the maximum grant regulation. Subsistence benefits are paid with respect to some needy dependent children; nothing is paid with respect to others. Some needy families receive full assistance as calculated by the State: the assistance paid to other families is grossly below their similarly calculated needs.

Yet as a general principle, individuals should not be afforded different treatment by the State unless there is a relevant distinction between them, and "a statutory discrimination must be based on differences that are reasonably related to the purposes of the Act in which it is found." *Morey v. Doud*, 354 U.S. 457, 465 (1957). Consequently, the State may not, in the provision of important services or the distribution of governmental payments, supply benefits to some individuals while denying them to others who are similarly situated.

In the instant case, the only distinction between those children with respect to whom assistance is granted and those children who are denied such assistance is the size of the family into which the child permits himself to be born. The class of individuals with respect to whom payments are actually made (the first four or five eligible dependent children in a family), is grossly underinclusive in terms of the class that the AFDC program was designed to assist, namely, *all* needy dependent children. Such underinclusiveness manifests "a prima facie violation of the equal protection requirement of reasonable classification," compelling the State to come forward with a persuasive justification for the classification.

The Court never undertakes to inquire for such a justification; rather it avoids the task by focusing upon the abstract dichotomy between two different approaches to equal protection problems that have been utilized by this Court.

Under the so-called "traditional test", a classification is said to be permissible under the Equal Protection Clause unless it is "without any reasonable basis." *Lindsley v. Natural Carbonic Gas Co.*, 220 U.S. 61, 78 (1911). On the other hand, if the classification affects a "fundamental right", then the state interest in perpetuating the classification must be "compelling" in order to be sustained. See, e.g., *Shapiro v. Thompson*, [394 U.S. 618 (1969)]; *Harper v. Board of Elections*, 383 U.S. 663 (1966); *McLaughlin v. Florida*, 379 U.S. 184 (1964).

This case simply defies easy characterization in terms of one or the other of these "tests." The cases relied on by the Court, in which a "mere rationality" test was actually used, e.g., *Williamson v. Lee Optical Co.*, 348 U.S. 483 (1955) [see Chapter 10], are most accurately described as involving the application of equal protection reasoning to the regulation of business interests. The extremes to which the Court has gone in dreaming up rational bases for state regulation in that area may in many instances be ascribed to a healthy revulsion from the Court's earlier excesses in using the Constitution to protect interests that have more than enough power to protect themselves in the legislative halls. This case, involving the literally vital interests of a powerless minority—poor families without breadwinners—is far removed from the area of business regulation, as the Court conceded. Why then is the standard used in those cases imposed here? We are told no more than that this case falls in "the area of economics and social welfare," with the implication that from there the answer is obvious.

* * *

In the final analysis, Maryland has set up an AFDC program structured to calculate and pay the minimum standard of need to dependent children. Having set up that program, however, the State denies some of those needy children the minimum subsistence standard of living, and it does so on the wholly arbitrary basis that they happen to be members of large families. * * *

Appellees are not a gas company or an optical dispenser; they are needy dependent children and families who are discriminated against by the State. The basis of that discrimination—the classification of individuals into large and small families—is too arbitrary and too unconnected to the asserted rationale, the impact on those discriminated against—the denial of even a subsistence existence—too great, and the supposed interests served too contrived and attenuated to meet the requirements of the Constitution. In my view Maryland's maximum grant regulation is invalid under the Equal Protection Clause of the Fourteenth Amendment.

CUMULATION OF PENSIONS AND SALARIES

Constitutional Council (France).
85–200 DC of 16 January 1986.[b]

* * * The *loi* proposed an increase of 40 per cent (from 10 per cent to 50) in the solidarity payment due from retired persons who, while in

b. As summarized by John Bell, *French* Constitutional Law *212 (1992).*

receipt of a pension, take up paid employment. This was to be paid by both employer and employee if the employee's combined income from his pension and salary was more than 2 1/2 times the national minimum wage (the *salaire minimum interprofessionnel de croissance* (SMIC)). In an argument raised of its own initiative, the Conseil recalled that article 13 [of the 1789 Declaration] required the contribution to the common good to be according to the resources of individuals, and this did not prevent the legislature from imposing on one social group the burden of helping one or more other social groups, in this case the unemployed. All the same, the level of payment here amounted to 'a clear breach of the principle of the equality before public burdens of all citizens', and so the 50 per cent figure was declared unconstitutional. The burden of relieving social problems should not fall disproportionately on one section of society, even though there may be an obligation on that section to contribute to the cost.

Notes and Questions

1.   Because the formal principle of equality—all equals should be treated equally (and as a corollary, all unequals treated unequally)—is silent on who is equal to whom or in what respect are two subjects supposed to be equal to one another, equality is arguably an empty concept. See Peter Westen, *The Empty Idea of Equality*, 95 Harv. L. Rev. 537 (1982). Thus, for example, formal equality is compatible both with the proposition that men are equal to women and with the contrary proposition that men and women are unequal. Furthermore, formal equality is equally compatible with the notion that equality should be measured in terms of need, merit, or wealth. Accordingly, formal equality is of no help in deciding whether medical treatment should be provided on the basis of need or wealth—i.e., equally available only to those who can afford it. Under this line of analysis the concept of equality is superfluous and purely parasitic on other normative concepts. For example, if one is convinced that medical treatment should be allocated according to need or that human dignity requires that everyone should have decent shelter, it is not equality but moral convictions about helping the needy or protecting human dignity that are decisive. Is this analysis convincing? Or is it more persuasive to assert that whereas formal equality taken by itself may be completely indeterminate, the conclusion "to each according to need" or "to each treatment compatible with equal dignity" cannot be defended without embracing certain conceptions of substantive equality. Why, for instance, should everyone be treated with the same dignity if one is convinced of the moral validity of a caste system, in which those at the top are regarded as righteous and virtuous and those at the bottom as abject and barely human?

2.   The French *University Professors Case* indicates that constitutional equality cannot always be satisfied through equal treatment. By requiring that university professors be granted a separate vote from faculty assistants and staff, the Constitutional Council established that certain relevant differences warrant different treatment. Underlying this decision is the principle that university professors have a special responsibility to set academic policy and that responsibility would be diluted or frustrated if they had to vote together with assistants and staff. Is this a genuine equality concern? Or is the real driving force here academic freedom, thus making this an example

of liberty trumping equality? Compare *Hunt v. Washington State Apple Advertising Comm'n*, 432 U.S. 333 (1977), holding that subjecting superior apples from out of state to a grading system that lumped them together with inferior local apples amounts to impermissible discrimination against the products of another state. Is *Hunt* in substance more of an equality case than *University Professors* because it can be explained in terms of equality based on proportionality whereas *University Professors* cannot? Or is the latter case also about proportionality (relating to expertise concerning the curriculum) from the standpoint of setting the academic agenda even if not from the more general standpoint of university self-governance?

3. The *Mahe* case deals with equality among linguistic groups. Some instances of group equality, such as local autonomy for all different ethnic groups within a country, cannot be recast in terms of individual-regarding equality. Is that also true of the linguistic rights at stake in *Mahe*? Cannot these linguistic rights be recast as the right of each individual to receive public schooling in his or her ancestral native language? Or does the fact that this linguistic right is linked to the linguistic self-identity of Francophones and Anglophones make it exclusively group-regarding? What about the proviso that availability of education in one's language depends on the existence of a sufficient number of others in the same position within the same school district? Does that make the right involved a collective one?

4. *Plessy* and *Brown* suggest that whereas questions relating to the subject of equality and those pertaining to its domain may be clearly distinct from a theoretical standpoint, they cannot be neatly untangled from the standpoint of substantive equality. If one deems that there can be no meaningful equality between the races unless social barriers as well as political ones are removed, then, in essence, *Plessy* does not treat blacks and whites as equal subjects. Can the same be said about basic welfare rights? That is, are those with no means to satisfy their minimum-subsistence or shelter needs not the equals of those who can provide for their own basic needs? Can the subject of equality ever remain stable notwithstanding fluctuations in the relevant domain of equality? Consider, for example, abolishing state-sponsored childcare for working mothers. Does it necessarily follow from this that women can no longer be the equals of men at the workplace? Does it matter whether equality between the sexes is considered, for all relevant purposes, a second-or third-stage equality?

B. FRAMING CONSTITUTIONAL EQUALITY IN TERMS OF ATTACKS ON PARTICULAR IN-EQUALITIES: THE ANTIDISCRIMINATION APPROACH

Many constitutional equality provisions are stated in very general terms. For example, Art. 2 of the 1958 French Constitution and Art. 3 (1) of the German Basic Law guarantee "equality before the law," and the Fourteenth Amendment of the U.S. Constitution guarantees the "equal protection of the laws." Notwithstanding provisions such as these, constitutional equality provisions are not customarily construed as requiring the state to pursue full equality for all recognized subjects of equality. As we shall see, constitutional equality is generally construed as affording protection against particular inequalities, either through a partial determination of a constitutionally recognized domain of equality—e.g., subsistence, shelter, free education (see Chapter 10, Section C.)—or through a ban on certain kinds of discrimination. For example, although the U.S. Equal Protection Clause does not address race explicitly, the U.S. Supreme Court (USSC) has interpreted it as prohibiting invidious racial discrimination. For its part, Art. 3 (3) of the German Basic Law provides that "No person shall be favored or disfavored because of sex, parentage, race, language, homeland and origin, or religious or political opinion * * *." Furthermore, Section 15(1) of the 1982 Canadian Charter of Rights and Freedoms combines a general approach to equality with a ban against certain kinds of discrimination. It provides: "Every individual is equal before and under the law and has the right to the equal protection and equal benefit of the law without discrimination and in particular, without discrimination based on race, national or ethnic origin, colour, religion, sex, age or mental or physical disability." Finally, though general in terms, the 1958 French Constitution incorporates the Preamble of the 1946 Constitution, which bans discrimination on grounds of, among others, race, religion, or sex.

To the extent that constitutional equality provisions operate as banning or disfavoring particular types of discrimination, they espouse an antidiscrimination approach. In broad terms such an approach tends to create two kinds of problems. Where the prohibited or disfavored grounds of discrimination are not spelled out in the constitutional text, as in the U.S., determinations must be made concerning which types of discrimination are forbidden and which are not. For example, is discrimination on the basis of illegitimacy permissible? See *Trimble v. Gordon* above (Court majority holding it impermissible; the dissent deeming it permissible). On the other hand even in constitutions where the impermissible grounds of discrimination are spelled out, not all legal distinctions on the relevant grounds need be considered unconstitutional. For example, Section 15 (1) of the Canadian Constitution prohibits discrimination on the basis of age; yet no one would seriously argue that a law prohibiting those younger than 16 from driving automobiles should be deemed unconstitutional. In short, the antidiscrimination approach does not mandate that all laws grant equal treatment to all classes affected by the relevant legislation. The question under the antidiscrimination approach is this: When is equal treatment mandatory, and when is it not?

B.1. ANTIDISCRIMINATION IN GENERAL: LEGAL CLASSIFICATIONS, RATIONALITY AND PROPORTIONALITY

To aid us in determining what makes prohibiting young children from driving automobiles acceptable while making exclusion of those over 40 from most employment unacceptable, we can turn to the concepts of rationality and proportionality. It is obviously rational to keep young children from driving on public roads, and given the great danger that such driving would present, imposing a complete ban certainly does not seem a disproportionate measure. Conversely, it would be irrational to assume that those over 40 are not overall roughly as capable as younger people to perform satisfactorily in a vast number of jobs, and it would be plainly disproportionate to impose a total ban on employment to weed out those who are not as able as younger workers to perform their jobs adequately. While these examples may seem obvious, consider the issues raised in the following cases.

RAILWAY EXPRESS AGENCY, INC. v. NEW YORK

Supreme Court (United States).
336 U.S. 106 (1949).

Mr. Justice Douglas delivered the opinion of the Court.

Section 124 of the Traffic Regulations of the City of New York * * * provides:

"No person shall operate, or cause to be operated, in or upon any street an advertising vehicle; provided that nothing herein contained shall prevent the putting of business notices upon business delivery vehicles, so long as such vehicles are engaged in the usual business or regular work of the owner and not used merely or mainly for advertising"

Appellant is engaged in a nation-wide express business. It operates about 1, 900 trucks in New York City and sells the space on the exterior sides of these trucks for advertising. That advertising is for the most part unconnected with its own business. It was convicted in the magistrate's court and fined. * * *

[The New York courts] concluded that advertising on vehicles using the streets of New York City constitutes a distraction to vehicle drivers and to pedestrians alike and therefore affects the safety of the public in the use of the streets. We do not sit to weigh evidence in order to determine whether the regulation is sound or appropriate; nor is it our function to pass judgment on its wisdom.

The question of equal protection of the laws is pressed more strenuously on us. It is pointed out that regulation draws the line between advertisements of products sold by the owner of the truck and general advertisements. It is argued that unequal treatment on the basis of such a distinction is not justified by the aim and purpose of the regulation. It is said, for example, that one of appellant's trucks carrying the advertisement of a commercial house would not cause any greater distraction of pedestrians and vehicle drivers than if the commercial house carried the same advertisement on its own truck. Yet the regulation allows the latter to do what the former is forbidden from doing. It is therefore contended that the classification which the regulation makes has no relation to the traffic problem since a violation turns not on what kind of advertisements are carried on trucks but on whose trucks they are carried.

That, however, is a superficial way of analyzing the problem, even if we assume that it is premised on the correct construction of the regulation. The local authorities may well have concluded that those who advertise their own wares on their trucks do not present the same traffic problem in view of the nature or extent of the advertising which they use. It would take a degree of omniscience which we lack to say that such is not the case. If that judgment is correct, the advertising displays that are exempt have less incidence on traffic than those of appellants.

We cannot say that the judgment is not an allowable one. Yet if it is, the classification has relation to the purpose for which it is made and does not contain the kind of discrimination against which the Equal Protection Clause affords protection. It is by such practical considerations based on experience rather than by theoretical inconsistencies that the question of equal protection is to be answered. And the fact that New York City sees fit to eliminate from traffic this kind of distraction but does not touch what may be even greater ones in a different category, such as the vivid displays on Times Square, is immaterial. It is no requirement of equal protection that all evils of the same genus be eradicated or none at all.

RE AMENDMENTS OF THE CODE OF SOCIAL SECURITY AND HEALTH

Constitutional Council (France).
89–269 DC of 22 January 1990.

[Parliamentary amendments sought to make changes in the Code of Social Security and Health. The Council addressed the constitutionality of Art. 17 governing payments to physicians. Specifically, objection was made concerning differences between the reimbursements made to specialists and those made to general practitioners.]

* * *

23. Considering that, by virtue of the eleventh paragraph of the Preamble to the Constitution of 4 October 1958, the nation guarantees to all, especially to the child, the mother, and aged workers, the protection of health, material security, rest, and leisure;

24. Considering that it incumbent upon the legislature as well as on the regulatory authority, within their respective competencies and respecting the principles laid down by paragraph 11 of the Preamble, to determine their concrete modes of application; that, in particular, their role is to determine the appropriate rules designed to realize the objective defined by the Preamble; that, in this respect, recourse to an agreement to govern the relationships between the primary funds for sickness insurance and doctors aims to reduce the portion of medical fees that remains to be paid by persons covered by social insurance, and, in consequence, to permit the effective application of the principle laid down by the cited provisions of the Preamble; that the possibility of arranging, by special agreements, the relationships between the primary funds for sickness insurance and, respectively, general practitioners and specialists has, as its purpose, making the conclusion of such agreements easier, that, in this situation, it could not be objected against article 17 of the *loi* that it disregards the provisions of the eleventh paragraph of the Preamble of the 1946 Constitution * * *.

John Bell, THE PRINCIPLE OF EQUALITY, in FRENCH CONSTITUTIONAL LAW

223 (1992).

* * * [I]t cannot be said that discrimination in a *loi* is, in itself, suspect. Provided that Parliament offers a justification related to the policy of the *loi*, the Conseil will nearly always defer to its assessment. Thus, in the *Credit Corporations* decision[65] the Conseil upheld an authorization for some, though not all, credit corporations to compete with banks in the provision of services, since those authorized, such as the Bank of France and the Posts and Telecommunications, offered stronger guarantees of security for investors. The reasons justified a difference of treatment within the activity of credit provision. By contrast, separate but similar professions could be subjected to the same insurance scheme if Parliament thought it appropriate.[66] It is not so much inequality that is the concern of the Conseil, as the rationality of the relationship between the measures proposed and the purpose of the *loi* or of the constitutionally protected values that they are designed to secure. As long as Parliament can justify the measures in terms of these objectives, and does not appear to have acted disproportionately, then the solution adopted will be accepted by the Conseil whether it involves equal treatment or not. Only where there is no rational relationship between the discrimination and the purpose of the *loi,* will a provision be invalid. For example, where different appointment procedures were used to engage doctors as heads of service and heads of department, the Conseil found no public interest reason to justify this discrimination, especially when the doctors were performing tasks in the same public service.[67]

Susanne Baer, THREE CURRENT APPROACHES TO JUSTIFYING INEQUALITY: STRICT FORMALISM, ARBITRARINESS AND PROPORTIONALITY, in CONSTITUTIONAL EQUALITY: THE JURISPRUDENCE OF THE GERMAN CONSTITUTIONAL COURT

5 Colum. J. Eur. L. 249, 260–267 (1999).

For a long time, excluding this application of standards of review specific to certain areas, the constitutional doctrine of justifications for inequality consisted of arbitrariness (or, in U.S. terms, rational basis review) alone. This older approach is still present in today's jurisprudence, but it is increasingly superceded, or at least supplemented, by a more specific formula, which is generally interpreted as a proportionality approach. Seen as a whole, the Federal Constitutional Court has tended to replace the rigid area-based approach to equality cases with a flexible variety of tests. As seen in *Romer*, [see below] the rigidity of group-based doctrine reaches its limits sooner or later. Thus, the German develop-

---

65. CC decision no. 83–167 DC of 19 Jan. 1984, *Rec.* 23.

66. CC decision no. 82–182 DC of 18 Jan. 1985 * * *

67. CC decision of 29 July 1991, *Hospital Reforms, Le Monde,* 31 July 1991 * * *

ment of a doctrine of flexibility may be an inspiration to doctrine overseas.

a. Strict formalism

The doctrinal test of strict formalism is used in cases in which fundamental liberty rights are affected. It requires the administration of such liberties to be strictly equal and blind to social differences. Three prominent cases applying this doctrine involve, respectively, the equality of candidates in test situations, the equality of political parties and the equality in matters of elections and voting. The application of strict formalism to cases involving traditional forms of political participation may come as no surprise. Strict formalism in cases involving test situations, however, can only be explained by bearing some additional factors in mind: first, tests and elections share the characteristics of competitive situations; second, the constitutional right of freedom of employment, guaranteed by art. 12 of the Grundgesetz, results in a specific kind of scrutiny; and third, test situations offer the chance to doctrinally grasp the concept of equality of opportunity which is particularly appealing to those who believe that factual equality cannot and should not be attained by means of law. The strictly formal test employed by the Constitutional Court reduces the right to equality to a right of equality of opportunity rather than a right of equality of results.

b. Arbitrariness

Yet another test used by the Court is the arbitrariness test. It is applied in cases of appellate review of lower court judgments or of review of legislation involving the regulation of so-called "mass phenomena," entailing the large-scale administration of similar fact patterns (*Massenverwaltung*). In such cases, permissible justifications of unequal treatment include administrative convenience, administrative efficiency, generalization for practical reasons and complexity of the matter. The last justification forces the Court to grant the legislature time to test the law and may be seen as a German version of the U.S. Supreme Court's "one step at a time" approach to difficult issues.

c. Proportionality

In 1980, the Constitutional Court, particularly the First Senate, introduced and developed the highest level of scrutiny to date. Despite its history, it is called the "new" formula of equality. Simply put, it states: if unequal treatment of various groups of those addressed by a law shall be upheld under art. 3, para. 1 of the Grundgesetz, "there must be differences of such type and weight between them that they can justify unequal treatment. Unequal treatment and justification must be adequately related to each other."[60] The Court thereby requires an adequate justification of unequal treatment rather than simply—and broadly—prohibiting evident arbitrariness. However, it is not clear whether treatment is based on legislative design or motive or whether the Court will move further in the direction of a search for actual disadvantage.

---

60. *See* BVerfGE 82, 126 (146); BVerfGE 55, 72 (88).

Almost all interpreters see the quoted phrase as a code for proportionality. * * * [Some] defend the specificity of the equality analysis, upholding the standard of comparability and rejecting the implicit analogization of the equality doctrine to the proportionality doctrine of liberty tests. In sum, all tests are neither exclusive nor independent of each other. The German Constitutional Court uses a flexible system of sliding tests which resembles Justice Marshall's sliding scale[63] and which I will presently introduce.

3. Criteria to Determine which Test to Use

The question is when to apply each test. In today's jurisprudence, one central criterion used to assess the strictness of scrutiny or to choose the adequate test is the detrimental effect of the law in question. Sometimes it is really called disadvantage, although often, it is hidden behind weaker terms. In the area of gender equality, the Constitutional Court and the second sentence of art. 3, para. 2 of the amended Grundgesetz now explicitly state that de facto inequality is decisive. However, in the jurisprudence of art. 3, para. 1, detrimental effects are often only measured in legal terms rather than in social or empirical ones, and so they are based on reasons given, goals pursued, or distinctions made by the state instead of on disparate impact.

According to the Court, the intensity of scrutiny increases the more closely the distinctions are based on the persons or groups named in art. 3, para. 3. The Court started with a stricter focus on social effects, so that distinctions between groups of persons and between situations, which have an unequal effect on groups of persons are subject to stricter scrutiny. However, the Court took a step back when it stated that strict scrutiny would only apply if a law was based on personal characteristics which are considered immutable, rather than on situations which persons choose. Thus, if a law is related to behavior which may be avoided and which thus may represent a mutable characteristic, the standard of review will be less strict. However, the Court still focuses on disparate effects when it states that the intensity of scrutiny also increases the more a distinction amounts to discrimination against a minority.

Furthermore, in Germany, the standard of scrutiny escalates the more a basic right to liberty is affected. This is sometimes seen as a part of the area-specific doctrine. For example, strict scrutiny—in this case, a rigid version of formal equality—applies in election and voting matters, [see Subsection C.1. below] in cases in which people are required to be part of a collective system, and, although hesitantly, in cases regarding the survival and protection of parents who raise children and of heterosexual monogamous families. * * *

4. Proportionality in Detail

The German Constitutional Court has applied many versions of the proportionality test between the lowest and the highest level of scrutiny. The proportionality test analysis itself may be divided into three steps which respectively ask: (1) whether the rule adheres to a legitimate goal; (2) whether is it an appropriate and necessary means of attaining that

---

63. *See* Dandridge v. Williams, 397 U.S. 474 (1970). * * *

goal; and (3) whether the detrimental, unequal or even disadvantageous effects are adequately related or proportionate, in a narrow sense, to the value of the goal pursued. We will find criteria which modify each step of the test in relation to the law in question.

It is interesting to note that the proportionality test has its origins in the law which governs direct state intervention and that it only entered constitutional doctrine in the 1950's, propelled by the liberal impetus to restrain administrative forces from infringing upon individual rights. The use of proportionality in constitutional law was a response to the doctrinal need for more specific standards regarding the open wording of liberty rights such as those found in art. 12. Thus, the implementation of the proportionality test into equality doctrine may signify a step towards a liberty-type test in equality rights cases.

a.   The legitimate goal of the law

The first step of the proportionality test is the requirement that a law, or a distinction, have a legitimate goal. This can be seen as a de minimis requirement of rationality, or, more specifically, of a rational assessment of all relevant aspects of the law (*Wertungsrationalitat*).

* * *

One threshold question is whether we assess the legitimacy of the goal in a subjective or in an objective manner. Should we rely on the reasoning explicitly stated by the legislature, on the general public consensus, on the consensus of only those persons affected or on anything the justices can think of? In German constitutional law, the standard is objective and is thus based neither on legislative intent nor on social consensus.

* * *

b.   The necessity of the law

The second step of the proportionality test asks whether unequal treatment is necessary or appropriate. In German equality doctrine, this part of the test is seen as particularly dangerous with respect to the separation of powers because it requires the Court to assess the relative value of the implicated interests and rights and to decide whether the legislature has chosen the mildest remedy available. Therefore, some academics call upon the Court to restrict its discretion in the execution of the second step of the proportionality test. The Court itself applies both a weak and a strong version of the test.

The weak version is applied in cases in which the purpose of the law is to grant state benefits. For instance, such a low standard of scrutiny is applied to regulations in the area of education, specifically as regards the schooling system and the opening of universities. Likewise, in adherence to the area-specific doctrine, the Court sets a low standard of review in cases pertaining to welfare law, particularly state subsidies. Distinguishing "donative" from "intrusive" state activity, the Court requires that the state distribute resources equally in cases of donative state activity, yet grants it the discretion to determine where and how to spend those resources. Derivative claims to benefits, which are really doctrinally based on the art. 20, para. 1 welfare state provision rather than on art.

3, para. 1, are the extreme exception and have been successful only in cases involving the access to higher education and to private school.

The level of scrutiny increases where the state withdraws a benefit from particular groups of people in times of economic recession. This higher level of scrutiny can be interpreted as a result of the transformation of a benefit into an intrusion, but it can also be based on the requirement of consistency as an expression of equality of laws pursuant to the doctrine of *Systemgerechtigkeit*. A stricter version of the necessity test is also applied in cases where a law intrudes directly. Again, the obvious problem is that the level of scrutiny depends on the initial construction of the case, since state intervention usually burdens some while benefiting others: if the focus is on the benefit granted, the standard is weak; if it is on the burden imposed, the standard rises. Additionally, the distinction between benefit and intrusion has not gone unchallenged. For example, the Court granted greater legislative freedom in the area of economic legislation where it is particularly difficult to distinguish between a benefit and an intervention. In cases involving economic legislation, a focus on detriments rather than on distinctions might also prove to be a helpful alternative.

c.   Proportionality in the narrower sense

The third step of the proportionality test involves scrutinizing proportionality in the narrower sense. To some, this is the most problematic part of the test. Briefly stated, it requires the Court to balance all aspects, interests and rights implicated in a case. For example, the Court may weigh the burden a law imposes on a citizen against the long-term benefit such citizen derives from the law. As stated by the constitutional scholar Bernhard Schlink, the Court applies a necessarily decisionistic interpersonal benefit comparison.[98] To some, this may simply be politics. What might be most important is that this step of the equality test serves as a safety net regarding all aspects which have not yet surfaced in earlier parts of the test. * * *

B.2.   TARGETING PARTICULAR INEQUALITIES

ANDREWS v. LAW SOCIETY OF BRITISH COLUMBIA

Supreme Court (Canada).
[1989] 1 S.C.R. 143.

[The Court held that barring noncitizens residing in Canada from practicing law was unconstitutional. The dissenting opinion of Justice McIntyre, which states the facts of the case, is followed by the concurring opinion of Justice La Forest.]

McIntyre J. (dissenting) (Lamer J. concurring)

This appeal raises only one question. Does the citizenship requirement for entry into the legal profession contained in s. 42 of the

---

98. Schlink, quoted in Osterloh [Art. 3   [(Michael Sachs, ed. 1996)].
GG, in Gundgesetz, Komentar], at n. 22

Barristers and Solicitors Act, R.S.B.C. 1979, c. 26 (the "Act"), contravene s. 15 (1) of the Canadian Charter of Rights and Freedoms? Section 42 provides:

42. The benchers may call to the Bar of the Province and admit as solicitor of the Supreme Court

(a) Canadian citizen * * * and s. 15 of the Charter states:

15. (1) Every individual is equal before and under the law and has the right to the equal protection and equal benefit of the law without discrimination and, in particular without discrimination based on race, national or ethnic origin, colour, religion, sex, age or mental or physical disability.

(2) Subsection (1) does not preclude any law, program or activity that has as its object the amelioration of conditions of disadvantaged individuals or groups including those that are disadvantaged because of race, national or ethnic origin, colour, religion, sex, age or mental or physical disability.

The respondent Andrews was a British subject permanently resident in Canada at the time these proceedings were commenced. He had taken law degrees at Oxford and had fulfilled all the requirements for admission to the practice of law in British Columbia, except that of Canadian citizenship. * * * [T]he Chief Justice stated the constitutional questions [in this case] in the following terms:

Does the Canadian citizenship requirement to be a lawyer in the Province of British Columbia as set out in s. 42 of the Barristers and Solicitors Act, R.S.B.C. 1979, c. 26 infringe or deny the rights guaranteed by s. 15 (1) of the Canadian Charter of Rights and Freedoms?

If the Canadian citizenship requirement to be a lawyer in the Province of British Columbia as set out in s. 42 of the Barristers and Solicitors Act, R.S.B.C. 1979, c. 26 infringes or denies the rights guaranteed by s. 15 (1) of the Canadian Charter of Rights and Freedoms, is it justified by s. 1 of the Canadian Charter of Rights and Freedoms? * * *

The concept of equality

Section 15(1) of the Charter provides for every individual a guarantee of equality before and under the law, as well as the equal protection and equal benefit of the law without discrimination. This is not a general guarantee of equality; it does not provide for equality between individuals or groups within society in a general or abstract sense, nor does it impose on individuals or groups an obligation to accord equal treatment to others. It is concerned with the application of the law. * * *

The concept of equality has long been a feature of Western thought. As embodied in s. 151(1) of the Charter, it is an elusive concept and, more than any of the other rights and freedoms guaranteed in the Charter, it lacks precise definition. * * *

It was a wise man who said that there is no greater inequality than the equal treatment of unequals. The same thought has been expressed in this court in the context of s. 2(b) of the Charter in *R. v. Big M Drug Mart Ltd.*, [1985] 1 S.C.R. 295, where DICKSON J. said at p. 347:

The equality necessary to support religious freedom does not require identical treatment of all religions. In fact, the interests of true equality may well require differentiation in treatment. In simple terms, then, it may be said that a law which treats all identically and which provides equality before and under the law—and in human affairs an approach is all that can be expected—the main consideration must be the impact of the law on the individual or the group concerned. Recognizing that there will always be an infinite variety of personal characteristics, capacities, entitlements and merits among those subject to a law, there must be accorded, as nearly as may be possible, an equality of benefit and protection and no more of the restrictions, penalties or burdens imposed upon one than another. In other words, the admittedly unattainable ideal should be that a law expressed to bind all should not because of irrelevant personal differences have a more burdensome or less beneficial impact on one than another.

McLachlin J.A. in the Court of Appeal expressed the view, at p. 605, that:

* * * the essential meaning of the constitutional requirement of equal protection and equal benefit is that persons who are "similarly situated be similarly treated" and conversely, that persons who are "differently situated be differently treated:" * * * The similarly situated test is a restatement of the Aristotelian principle of formal equality— that "things that are alike should be treated alike, while things that are unalike should be treated unalike in proportion to their unlikeness": Ethica Nichomacea (1925), trans. W. Ross, Book VC, at p. 1131a–6.

The test as stated, however, is seriously deficient in that it excludes any consideration of the nature of the law. If it were to be applied literally, it could be used to justify the Nuremberg laws of Adolf Hitler. Similar treatment was contemplated for all Jews. The similarly situated test would have justified the formalistic separate but equal doctrine of *Plessy v. Ferguson*, 163 U.S. 537, 41 L.Ed. 256 (1896) * * *.

* * *

* * * Section 15 spells out four basic rights: (1) the right to equality before the law; (2) the right to equality under the law; (3) the right to equal protection of the law; and (4) the right to equal benefit of the law. * * *

It is clear that the purpose of s. 15 is to ensure equality in the formulation and application of the law. The promotion of equality entails the promotion of a society in which all are secure in the knowledge that they are recognized at law as human beings equally deserving of concern, respect and consideration. It has a large remedial component. * * *

Discrimination

The right to equality before and under the law, and the rights to the equal protection and benefit of the law contained in s. 15, are granted with the direction contained in s. 15 itself that they be without discrimination. Discrimination is unacceptable in a democratic society because it epitomizes the worst effects of the denial of equality, and discrimination reinforced by law is particularly repugnant. The worst oppression will result from discriminatory measures having the force of law. It is against this evil that s. 15 provides a guarantee.

* * *

Discrimination * * * means practices or attitudes that have, whether by design or impact, the effect of limiting an individual's or a group's right to the opportunities generally available because of attributed rather than actual characteristics * * *

[D]iscrimination may be described as a distinction, whether intentional or not but based on grounds relating to personal characteristics of the individual or group, which has the effect of imposing burdens, obligations or disadvantages on such individual or group not imposed upon others, or which withholds or limits access to opportunities, benefits and advantages available to other members of society. Distinctions based on personal characteristics attributed to an individual solely on the basis of association with a group will rarely escape the charge of discrimination, while those based on an individual's merits and capacities will rarely be so classed.

The court in the case at bar must address the issue of discrimination as the term is used in s. 15(1) of the Charter. * * * [D]iscrimination in s. 15(1) is limited to discrimination caused by the application or operation of law, whereas the Human Rights Acts apply also to private activities. Furthermore, and this is a distinction of more importance, all the Human Rights Acts passed in Canada specifically designate a certain limited number of grounds upon which discrimination is forbidden. Section 15(1) of the Charter is not so limited. The enumerated grounds in s. 15(1) are not exclusive and the limits, if any, on grounds for discrimination which may be established in future cases await definition. The enumerated grounds do, however, reflect the most common and probably the most socially destructive and historically practised bases of discrimination and must, in the words of s. 15(1), receive particular attention. Both the enumerated grounds themselves and other possible grounds of discrimination recognized under s. 15(1) must be interpreted in a broad and generous manner, reflecting the fact that they are constitutional provisions not easily repealed or amended but intended to provide a "continuing framework for the legitimate exercise of governmental power" and, at the same time, for "the unremitting protection" of equality rights: see *Hunter v. Southam Inc.*, [1984] 2 S.C.R. 145 at 155.

* * *

Relationship between s. 15(1) and s. 1 of the Charter

* * *

[W]hen confronted with a problem under the Charter, the first question which must be answered will be whether or not an infringement of a guaranteed right has occurred. Any justification of an infringement which is found to have occurred must be made, if at all, under the broad provisions of s. 1. * * *

Approaches to s. 15(1)

Three main approaches have been adopted in determining the role of s. 15(1), the meaning of discrimination set out in that section, and the relationship of s. 15(1) and s. 1. The first one, which was advanced by Professor Peter Hogg in Constitutional Law of Canada, 2nd ed. (1985), would treat every distinction drawn by law as discrimination under s. 15(1). There would then follow a consideration of the distinction under the provisions of s. 1 of the Charter. He said at pp. 800–801:

> I conclude that s. 15 should be interpreted as providing for the universal application of every law. When a law draws a distinction between individuals, on any ground, that distinction is sufficient to constitute a breach of s. 15, and to move the constitutional issue to s. 1. The test of validity is that stipulated by s. 1, namely, whether the law comes within the phrase "such reasonable limits prescribed by laws can be demonstrably justified in a free and democratic society". He reached this conclusion on the basis that, where the Charter right is expressed in unqualified terms, s. 1 supplies the standard of justification for any abridgment of the right. He argued that the word "discrimination" in s. 15(1) could be read as introducing a qualification in the section itself, but he preferred to read the word in a neutral sense because this reading would immediately send the matter to s. 1, which was included in the Charter for this purpose.

The second approach put forward by McLachlin J.A. in the Court of Appeal involved a consideration of the reasonableness and fairness of the impugned legislation under s. 15(1). She stated:

> * * * The ultimate question is whether a fair-minded person, weighing the purposes of legislation against its effects on the individuals adversely affected, and giving due weight to the right of the Legislature to pass laws for the good of all, would conclude that the legislative means adopted are unreasonable or unfair. She assigned a very minor role to s. 1 which would, it appears, be limited to allowing in times of emergency, war or other crises the passage of discriminatory legislation which would normally be impermissible.

A third approach, sometimes described as an "enumerated or analogous grounds" approach, adopts the concept that discrimination is generally expressed by the enumerated grounds. Section 15(1) is designed to prevent discrimination based on these and analogous grounds. The approach is similar to that found in human rights and civil rights statutes which have been enacted throughout Canada in recent times. The following excerpts from the judgment of Hugessen J.A. in *Smith, Kline & French Laboratories v. Can. (A.G.), supra,* for Canada, [1987] 2 F.C. [359], 367–69, illustrate this approach:

> The rights which it [s. 15] guarantees are not based on any concept of strict, numerical equality amongst all human beings. If they were, virtually all legislation, whose function it is, after all, to define, distinguish and make categories, would be in prima facie breach of section 15 and would require justification under section 1. This would be to turn the exception into the rule. Since the courts would be obliged to look for and find section 1 justification for most legislation, the alternative being anarchy, there is a real risk of paradox: the broader the reach given to

section 15 the more likely it is that it will be deprived of any real content.

The answer, in my view, is that the text of the section itself contains its own limitations. It only proscribes discrimination amongst the members of categories which are themselves similar. Thus the issue, for each case, will be to know which categories are permissible in determining similarity of situation and which are not. It is only in those cases where the categories themselves are not permissible, where equals are not treated equally, that there will be a breach of equality rights * * *

As far as the text of section 15 itself is concerned, one may look to whether or not there is "discrimination", in the pejorative sense of that word, and as to whether the categories are based upon the grounds enumerated or grounds analogous to them. The inquiry, in effect, concentrates upon the personal characteristics of those who claim to have been unequally treated. Questions of stereotyping, of historical disadvantagement, in a word, of prejudice, are the focus and there may even be a recognition that for some people equality has a different meaning than for others. The analysis of discrimination in this approach must take place within the context of the enumerated grounds and those analogous to them. The words "without discrimination" require more than a mere finding of distinction between the treatment of groups or individuals. Those words are a form of qualifier built into s. 15 itself and limit those distinctions which are forbidden by the section to those which involve prejudice or disadvantage.

I would accept the criticisms of the first approach made by McLachlin J.A. in the Court of Appeal. She noted that the labelling of every legislative distinction as an infringement of s. 15(1) trivializes the fundamental rights guaranteed by the Charter and, secondly, that to interpret "without discrimination" as "without distinction" deprives the notion of discrimination of content. * * *

I would reject, as well, the approach adopted by McLachlin J.A. She seeks to define discrimination under s. 15(1) as an unjustifiable or unreasonable distinction. In so doing, she avoids the mere distinction test but also makes a radical departure from the analytical approach to the Charter which has been approved by this court. In the result, the determination would be made under s. 15(1) and virtually no role would be left for s. 1.

The third or "enumerated and analogous grounds" approach most closely accords with the purposes of s. 15 and the definition of discrimination outlined above and leaves questions of justifications to s. 1. However, in assessing whether a complainant's rights have been infringed under s. 15(1), it is not enough to focus only on the alleged grounds of discrimination and decide whether or not it is an enumerated or analogous ground. The effect of the impugned distinction or classification on the complainant must be considered. Once it is accepted that not all distinctions and differentiations created by law are discriminatory, then a role must be assigned to s. 15(1) which goes beyond the mere recognition of a legal distinction. A complainant under s. 15(1) must show not only that he or she is not receiving equal treatment before and under the law or that the law has a differential impact on him or her in the protection or benefit accorded by law but, in addition, must show that the legislative impact of the law is discriminatory.

Where discrimination is found, a breach of s. 15(1) has occurred— and where 15(2) is not applicable—any justification, any consideration of the reasonableness of the enactment, indeed, any consideration of factors which could justify the discrimination and support the constitutionality of the impugned enactment would take place under s. 1. This approach would conform with the directions of this court in earlier decisions concerning the application of s. 1 and at the same time would allow for the screening out of the obviously trivial and vexatious claim. In this, it would provide a workable approach to the problem.

It would seem to me apparent that a legislative distinction has been made by s 42 of the Barristers and Solicitors Act between citizens and non-citizens with respect to the practice of law. The distinction would deny admission to the practice of law to non-citizens who in all other respects are qualified. Have the respondents because of s. 42 of the Act been denied equality before and under the law or the equal protection of the law? In practical terms it should be noted that the citizenship requirement affects only those non-citizens who are permanent residents. The permanent resident must wait for a minimum of three years from the date of establishing permanent residence status before citizenship may be acquired. The distinction therefore imposes a burden in the form of some delay on permanent residents who have acquired all or some of their legal training abroad and is, therefore, discriminatory.

The rights guaranteed in s. 15(1) apply to all persons whether citizens or not. A rule which bars an entire class of persons from certain forms of employment, solely on the grounds of a lack of citizenship status and without consideration of educational and professional qualifications or the other attributes or merits of individuals in the group, would, in my view, infringe s. 15 equality rights. Non-citizens, lawfully permanent residents of Canada, are—in the words of the United States Supreme Court in *U.S. v. Carolene Prod. Co.*, 304 U.S. 144 at 152–53, n. 4 (1938) * * *—a good example of a "discrete and insular minority" who come within the protection of s. 15.

Section 1

Having accepted the proposition that s. 42 has infringed the right to equality guaranteed in s. 15, it remains to consider whether, under the provisions of s. 1 of the Charter, the citizenship requirement which is clearly prescribed by law is a reasonable limit which can be "demonstrably justified in a free and democratic society".

The onus of justifying the infringement of a guaranteed Charter right must, of course, rest upon the parties seeking to uphold the limitation, in this case, the Attorney General of British Columbia and the Law Society of British Columbia. As is evident from the decisions of this court, there are two steps involved in the s. 1 inquiry. First, the importance of the objective underlying the impugned law must be assessed. In *Oakes*, [see Chapter 2] it was held that to override a Charter-guaranteed right the objective must relate to concerns which are "pressing and substantial" in a free and democratic society. However, given the broad ambit of legislation which must be enacted to cover various aspects of the civil law dealing largely with administrative and regulatory matters and the necessity for the legislature to make many distinctions between individuals and groups for such purposes, the standard of "pressing and substantial" may be too stringent for application in all cases. To hold otherwise would frequently deny the community-at-large the benefits associated with sound social and economic legislation. In my opinion, in approaching a case such as the one before us, the first question the court should ask must relate to the nature and the purpose of the enactment, with a view to deciding whether the limitation represents a legitimate exercise of the legislative power for the attainment of a desirable social objective which would warrant overriding constitutionally protected rights. The second step in a s. 1 inquiry involves a proportionality test whereby the court must attempt to balance a number of factors. The court must examine the nature of the right, the extent of its infringement and the degree to which the limitation furthers the attainment of the desirable goal embodied in the legislation. Also involved in the inquiry will be the importance of the right to the individual or group concerned, and the broader social impact of both the impugned law and its alternatives. * * *

The s. 15(1) guarantee is the broadest of all guarantees. It applies to and supports all other rights guaranteed by the Charter. However, it must be recognized that Parliament and the legislatures have a right and a duty to make laws for the whole community: in this process, they must make innumerable legislative distinctions and categorizations in the pursuit of the role of the government. When making distinctions between groups and individuals to achieve desirable social goals, it will rarely be possible to say of any legislative distinction that it is clearly the right legislative choice or that it is clearly a wrong one. As stated by the Chief Justice in *R. v. Edwards Books & Art Ltd.*, [[1986] 2 S.C.R. 713,] 781–82:

A "reasonable limit" is one which, having regard to the principles enunciated in *Oakes*, it was reasonable for the legislature to impose. The courts are not called upon to substitute judicial opinions for legislative ones as to the place at which to draw a precise line. In dealing with the many problems that arise, legislatures must not be held to the standard of perfection, for in such matters perfection is unattainable. I would repeat the words of my colleague, La Forest J., in *R. v. Edwards Books & Art Ltd.*, at p. 795:

By the foregoing, I do not mean to suggest that this Court should as a general rule, defer to legislative judgments when those judgments trench upon rights considered fundamental in a free and democratic society. Quite the contrary, I would have thought the Charter established the opposite regime. On the other hand, having accepted the importance of the legislative objective, one must in the present context recognize that if the legislative goal is to be achieved, it will inevitably be achieved to the detriment of some. Moreover, attempts to protect the rights of one group will also inevitably impose burdens on the rights of other groups. There is no perfect scenario in which the rights of all can be equally protected.

In seeking to achieve a goal that is demonstrably justified in a free and democratic society, therefore, a legislature must be given reasonable room to manoeuvre to meet these conflicting pressures.

Disposition

I now turn to the case at bar. * * *

* * *

There is no difficulty in determining that in general terms the Barristers and Solicitors Act of British Columbia is a statute enacted for a valid and desirable social purpose, the creation and regulation of the legal profession and the practice of law. The narrower question, however, whether the requirement that only citizens be admitted to the practice of law in British Columbia serves a desirable social purpose of sufficient importance to warrant overriding the equality guarantee. * * *

The lawyer has, as well, what may be termed a public function. * * * To discharge these duties, familiarity is required with Canadian history, constitutional law, regional differences and concerns within the country and, in fact, with the whole Canadian governmental and political process. It is entirely reasonable, then, that legislators consider and adopt measures designed to maintain within the legal profession a body of qualified professionals with a commitment to the country and to the fulfillment of the important tasks which fall to it.

* * *

Public policy, of which the citizenship requirement in the Barristers and Solicitors Act is an element, is for the legislature to establish. The role of the Charter, as applied by the courts, is to ensure that in applying public policy the legislature does not adopt measures which are not sustainable under the Charter. It is not, however, for the courts to legislate or to substitute their views on public policy for those of the legislature. * * *

The essence of s. 1 is found in the expression "reasonable" and it is for the court to decide if s. 42 of the Barristers and Solicitors Act of British Columbia is a reasonable limit. * * * In my view, the citizenship requirement is reasonable and sustainable under s. 1. It is chosen for the achievement of a desirable social goal: one aspect of the due regulation and qualification of the legal profession. This is an objective of importance and the measure is not disproportionate to the object to be attained. The maximum delay imposed upon the non-citizen from the date of acquisition of permanent resident status is three years. * * *

La Forest J.

* * *

* * * The characteristic of citizenship is one typically not within the control of the individual and, in this sense, is immutable. Citizenship is, at least temporarily, a characteristic of personhood not alterable by conscious action and in some cases not alterable except on the basis of unacceptable costs.

Moreover, non-citizens are an example without parallel of a group of persons who are relatively powerless politically, and whose interests are likely to be compromised by legislative decisions. History reveals that Canada did not for many years resist the temptation of enacting legislation the animating rationale of which was to limit the number of persons entering into certain employment. Discrimination on the basis of nationality has from early times been an inseparable companion of discrimination on the basis of race and national or ethnic origin, which are listed in s. 15.

   * * *

There is no question that citizenship may, in some circumstances, be properly used as a defining characteristic for certain types of legitimate governmental objectives. * * * Nonetheless, it is, in general, irrelevant to the legitimate work of government in all but a limited number of areas. By and large, the use in legislation of citizenship as a basis for distinguishing between persons, here for the purpose of conditioning access to the practice of a profession, harbours the potential for undermining the essential or underlying values of a free and democratic society that are embodied in s. 15. * * *

While it cannot be said that citizenship is a characteristic which "bears no relation to ability to perform or contribute to society" (*Frontiero v. Richardson*, 411 U.S. 677 at 686 (1973)), it certainly typically bears an attenuated sense of relevance to these. That is not to say that no legislative conditioning of benefits (for example) on the basis of citizenship is acceptable in the free and democratic society that is Canada, merely that legislation purporting to do so ought to be measured against the touchstone of our Constitution. It requires justification.

   * * *

Citizenship does not ensure familiarity with Canadian institutions and customs. Only citizens who are not natural-born Canadians are required to have resided in Canada for a period of time. Natural-born Canadians may reside in whatever country they wish and still retain their citizenship. In short, citizenship offers no assurance that a person is conscious of the fundamental traditions and rights of our society. The requirement of citizenship is not an effective means of ensuring that the persons admitted to the bar are familiar with this country's institutions and customs. * * *

   * * *

I would conclude that although the governmental objectives, as stated, may be defensible, it is simply misplaced vis-à-vis the legal professional as a whole. However, even accepting the legitimacy and importance of the legislative objectives, the legislation exacts too high a price on persons wishing to practise law in that it may deprive them, albeit perhaps temporarily, of the "right" to pursue their calling.

   * * *

[Accordingly, exclusion of noncitizens from the practice of law is not justified by s. 1.]

KOREMATSU v. UNITED STATES

Supreme Court (United States).
323 U.S. 214 (1944).

Mr. Justice Black delivered the opinion of the Court.

The petitioner, an American citizen of Japanese descent, was convicted in a federal district court for remaining in San Leandro, California, a "Military Area" contrary to Civilian Exclusion Order No. 34 of the Commanding General of the Western Command, U.S. Army, which directed that after May 9, 1942, all persons of Japanese ancestry should be excluded from that area. No question was raised as to petitioner's loyalty to the United States. * * *

I

It should be noted, to begin with, that all-legal restrictions which curtail the civil rights of a single racial group are immediately suspect. That is not to say that all such restrictions are unconstitutional. It is to say that courts must subject them to the most rigid scrutiny. Pressing public necessity may sometimes justify the existence of such restrictions; racial antagonism never can.

* * *

VII

* * *

It is said that we are dealing here with the case of imprisonment of a citizen in a concentration camp solely because of his ancestry, without evidence or inquiry concerning his loyalty and good disposition towards the United States. Our task would be simple, our duty clear, were this a case involving the imprisonment of a loyal citizen in a concentration camp because of racial prejudice. Regardless of the true nature of the assembly and relocation centers—and we deem it unjustifiable to call them concentration camps with all the ugly connotations that term implies—we are dealing specifically with nothing but an exclusion order. To cast this case into outlines of racial prejudice, without reference to the real military dangers which were presented, merely confuses the issue. Korematsu was not excluded from the Military Area because of hostility to him or his race. He *was* excluded because we are at war with the Japanese empire, because the properly constituted military authorities feared an invasion of our West Coast temporarily, and finally, because Congress, reposing its confidence in this time of war in our military leaders—as inevitably it must—determined that they should have the power to do just this. There was evidence of disloyalty on the part of some, the military authorities considered that the need for action was great, and time was short. We cannot—by availing ourselves of the calm perspective of hindsight—now say that at that time these actions were unjustified.

Mr. Justice Murphy, dissenting.

This exclusion of "all persons of Japanese ancestry, both alien and non-alien," from the Pacific Coast area on a plea of military necessity in the absence of martial law ought not to be approved. Such exclusion goes over "the very brink of constitutional power" and falls into the ugly abyss of racism.

In dealing with matters relating to the prosecution and progress of a war, we must accord great respect and consideration to the judgments of the military authorities who are on the scene and who have full knowledge of the military facts. The scope of their discretion must, as a matter of necessity and common sense, be wide. And their judgments ought not to be overruled lightly by those whose training and duties ill-equip them to deal intelligently with matters so vital to the physical security of the nation.

At the same time, however, it is essential that there be definite limits to military discretion, especially where martial law has not been declared. Individuals must not be left impoverished of their constitutional rights on a plea of military necessity that has neither substance nor support. Thus, like other claims conflicting with the asserted constitutional rights of the individual, the military claim must subject itself to the judicial process of having its reasonableness determined and its conflicts with other interests reconciled. "What are the allowable limits of military discretion, and whether or not they have been overstepped in a particular case, are judicial questions." *Sterling v. Constantin,* 287 U.S. 378, 401 [1932].

The judicial test of whether the Government, on a plea of military necessity, can validly deprive an individual of any of his constitutional rights is whether the deprivation is reasonably related to a public danger that is so "immediate, imminent, and impending" as not to admit of delay and not to permit the intervention of ordinary constitutional processes to alleviate the danger. Civilian Exclusion Order No. 34, banishing from a prescribed area of the Pacific Coast "all persons of Japanese ancestry, both alien and non-alien," clearly does not meet that test. Being an obvious racial discrimination, the order deprives all those within its scope of the equal protection of the laws * * * Yet no reasonable relation to an "immediate, imminent, and impending" public danger is evident to support this racial restriction which is one of the most sweeping and complete deprivations of constitutional rights in the history of this nation in the absence of martial law.

* * *

The military necessity which is essential to the validity of the evacuation order * * * resolves itself into a few intimations that certain individuals actively aided the enemy, from which it is inferred that the entire group of Japanese Americans could not be trusted to be or remain loyal to the United States. No one denies, of course, that there were some disloyal persons of Japanese descent on the Pacific Coast who did all in their power to aid their ancestral land. Similar disloyal activities have been engaged in by many persons of German, Italian and even more pioneer stock in our country. But to infer that examples of individual disloyalty prove group disloyalty and justify discriminatory action against the entire group is to deny that under our system of law individual guilt is the sole basis for deprivation of rights. Moreover, this inference, which is at the very heart of the evacuation orders, has been used in support of the abhorrent and despicable treatment of minority groups by the dictatorial tyrannies which this nation is now pledged to destroy. * * *

No adequate reason is given for the failure to treat these Japanese Americans on an individual basis by holding investigations and hearings to separate the loyal from the disloyal, as was done in the case of persons of German and Italian ancestry. See House Report No. 2124 (77th Cong., 2d Sess.) 247–52. It is asserted merely that the loyalties of this group "were unknown and time was of the essence" yet nearly four months elapsed after Pearl Harbor before the first exclusion order was issued; nearly eight months went by until the last order was issued; and the last of these "subversive" persons was not actually removed until almost eleven months had elapsed. Leisure and deliberation seem to have been more of the essence than speed. * * *

       * * *

I dissent, therefore, from this legalization of racism. Racial discrimination in any form and in any degree has no justifiable part whatever in our democratic way of life. It is unattractive in any setting but it is utterly revolting among a free people who have embraced the principles set forth in the Constitution of the United States. All residents of this nation are kin in some way by blood or culture to a foreign land. Yet they are primarily and necessarily a part of the new and distinct civilization of the United States. They must accordingly be treated at all times as the heirs of the American experiment and as entitled to *all the rights and freedoms* guaranteed by the Constitution.

Notes and Questions

1. The antidiscrimination approach seems to rest on a paradox. Since the very purpose of the vast majority of laws—provided the term is properly understood—is to discriminate, the antidiscrimination approach appears prone to undermining what the process of legislation is designed to achieve. To be sure, we are dealing here with two senses of "discriminate." In the first sense "discriminate" means to distinguish in a useful and knowledgeable way, as connoted by the expression "X has a discriminating eye." In the second sense "discriminate" is understood pejoratively, as unjustifiably excluding others or as "invidiously" discriminating against a person or group. Ideally, then, the legislature will enact laws that discriminate in the first sense and the constitutional judge will ascertain that such laws do not discriminate in the second sense. The problem is that there is often no agreement on whether a law is discriminating in the first or second sense. For example, if the exclusions in *Korematsu* could be justified as the only means of discriminating between law-abiding citizens and traitors in time of war, then the case would involve discrimination in the first sense. But if the classification in that case was motivated by animus against those of Japanese ancestry, then it ought to have been struck down as invidiously discriminatory. Does this make the antidiscrimination approach practically unworkable?

Or is *Korematsu* merely an unusually hard case because of the overlap between security concerns in time of war and racial or ethnic bias?

2. As applied in general, the antidiscrimination approach largely amounts to a requirement of proportionality and is hence subject to the latter's virtues and vices. See the discussion in Chapter 2, Subsection C.2.3.b. Furthermore, to the extent that proportionately can be equated to rationality—i.e., to there being a rational nexus between legislative means and ends—the antidiscrimination approach results in a confluence between due process and equality rights. See, e.g., *Williamson v. Lee Optical Co.,* 348 U.S. 483 (1955) (same rationality test used under due process and under equal protection rights). Does the antidiscrimination approach, when applied so generally, merely amount to a prohibition against irrational laws having little to do with equality? Is the distinction between a van owner's advertisement and that of another business upheld in *Railway Express,* which seems both seriously underinclusive (i.e., it prohibits only a small fraction of the distractions that threaten the safety of drivers and pedestrians on New York streets) and overinclusive (i.e., not all signs on rented space on vans are likely to be distracting or at least not nearly as distracting as permissible signs), have anything to do with equality? Is it even rational? What about the Court's conclusion that equal protection allows legislatures to tackle problems one step at a time? Does that undermine the possibly of being bound by any cogent notion of equality? Does the French Constitutional Council's decision in the *Amendments of the Code of Social Security and Health* fare any better from the standpoint of equality than *Railway Express*? Or does it reduce equality to mere rationality or to any coherent notion of efficiency?

3. Equality concerns could be largely satisfied if laws were not under- or overinclusive. For example, in the context of *Korematsu,* if a law that targeted actual traitors and no one else could have been crafted, then the law would have clearly satisfied equal protection. The problem is that in the overwhelming majority of cases no such laws can be crafted. Accordingly, even laws that clearly comport with constitutional equality requirements are typically both under-and overinclusive. The question, then, is how under-or overinclusive must a law be before it ought to be adjudged unconstitutional? Returning to *Korematsu,* if as the dissent indicates interning Japanese Americans is no more likely to protect against traitors than having no law, the law in question would be irrational and hence unconstitutional under the most general conception of the antidiscrimination approach. If, on the other hand, as the majority believes, it is the only way to get needed protection against traitors, though it will inevitably harm innocent people and fail to reach all traitors, the law can pass constitutional muster although it risks exacerbating racial inequality.

4. Although the legal standard articulated in *Korematsu* has been prevalent ever since, the case itself has been steeped in infamy. In 1984, Korematsu's conviction was vacated by a lower federal court, 584 F.Supp. 1406 (N.D.Cal.1984), on the grounds of government misconduct in the submission of false information to the Supreme Court. In 1988, the U.S. Congress enacted a law apologizing for the internment of Japanese Americans during World War Two and providing for reparations.

5. As opposed to cases generally applying the antidiscrimination approach, cases such as *Andrews* and *Korematsu,* which involve particular

targeted inequalities, require more than a rational nexus between the challenged legal classification and the purpose of the challenged law. In both cases the classifications, respectively on nationality and on race or ethnic origin, were not deemed absolutely impermissible. Does the fact that there were dissenting opinions in both cases suggest that cases involving targeted inequalities are no more easy to resolve under the antidiscrimination approach than those falling in the general category? Or is *Korematsu* special because of government misrepresentation of the facts or wartime exigencies? And *Andrews* because the practice of law is borderline between a public function, such as being a police officer or municipal government officer— functions in relation to which discrimination on the basis of nationality has been upheld—and a purely private calling, such as being an architect or factory worker—occupations in relation to which restrictions based on nationality have routinely been struck down as unconstitutional?

B.3. UNTANGLING PERMISSIBLE FROM IMPERMISSIBLE INEQUALITIES UNDER THE ANTIDISCRIMINATION APPROACH

Even if there were a consensus concerning which inequalities are forbidden or highly disfavored under a constitution and which are permissible, in certain cases it may be difficult to determine whether a permissible or an impermissible inequality is at stake, though such determination is crucial to the disposition of a case under the antidiscrimination approach. Consider the following two cases, which arguably involve impermissible inequalities based on sex.

PERSONNEL ADMINISTRATOR OF MASSACHUSETTS v. FEENEY

Supreme Court (United States).
442 U.S. 256 (1979).

Mr. Justice Stewart delivered the opinion of the Court.

I

This case presents a challenge to the constitutionality of the Massachusetts veterans' preference statute, Mass. Gen. Laws Ann., ch. 31, § 23, [which provides that] all veterans who qualify for state civil service positions must be considered for appointment ahead of any qualifying nonveterans. The preference operates overwhelmingly to the advantage of males.

The appellee Helen B. Feeney is not a veteran. She brought this action * * * alleging that the absolute-preference formula established in ch. 31, § 23, inevitably operates to exclude women from consideration for the best Massachusetts civil service jobs and thus unconstitutionally denies them the equal protection of the laws. * * *

The Federal Government and virtually all of the States grant some sort of hiring preference to veterans. The Massachusetts preference, which is loosely termed an "absolute lifetime" preference, is among the most generous. It applies to all positions in the State's classified civil service, which constitute approximately 60% of the public jobs in the State. It is available to "any person, male or female, including a nurse," who was honorably discharged from the United States Armed Forces after at least 90 days of active service, at least one day of which was during "wartime." Persons who are deemed veterans and who are otherwise qualified for a particular civil service job may exercise the preference at any time and as many times as they wish.

* * *

The veterans' hiring preference in Massachusetts, as in other jurisdictions, has traditionally been justified as a measure designed to reward veterans for the sacrifice of military service, to ease the transition from military to civilian life, to encourage patriotic service, and to attract loyal and well-disciplined people to civil service occupations. * * *

The first Massachusetts veterans' preference statute defined the term "veterans" in gender-neutral language. See 1896 Mass. Acts, ch. 517 § 1 ("a person" who served in the United States Army or Navy), and subsequent amendments have followed this pattern, * * * Women who have served in official United States military units during wartime, then have always been entitled to the benefit of the preference.

* * *

Notwithstanding the apparent attempts by Massachusetts to include as many military women as possible within the scope of the preference, the statute today benefits an overwhelmingly male class. This is attributable in some measure to the variety of federal statutes, regulations, and policies that have restricted the number of women who could enlist in the United States Armed Forces, and largely to the simple fact that women have never been subjected to a military draft.

When this litigation was commenced, then, over 98% of the veterans in Massachusetts were male; only 1.8% were female. And over one-quarter of the Massachusetts population were veterans. During the decade between 1963 and 1973 when the appellee was actively participating in the State's merit selection system, 47, 005 new permanent appointments were made in the classified official service. Forty-three percent of those hired were women, and 57% were men. Of the women appointed, 1.8% were veterans, while 54% of the men had veteran status.

At the outset of this litigation appellants conceded that for "many of the permanent positions for which males and females have competed" the veterans' preference has "resulted in a substantially greater proportion of female eligibles than male eligibles" not being certified for consideration. The impact of the veterans' preference law upon the public employment opportunities of women has thus been severe. This impact lies at the heart of the appellee's federal constitutional claim.

II

The sole question for decision on this appeal is whether Massachusetts, in granting an absolute lifetime preference to veterans, has discriminated against women in violation of the Equal Protection Clause of the Fourteenth Amendment.

The equal protection guarantee of the Fourteenth Amendment does not take from the States all power of classification. Most laws classify, and many affect certain groups unevenly, even though the law itself treats them no differently from all other members of the class described by the law. When the basic classification is rationally based, uneven effects upon particular groups within a class are ordinarily of no constitutional concern. The calculus of effects, the manner in which a particular law reverberates in a society, is a legislative and not a judicial responsibility. In assessing an equal protection challenge, a court is called upon only to measure the basic validity of the legislative classification. *Railway Express Agency v. New York,* 336 U.S. 106. When some other independent right is not at stake, see, e.g., *Shapiro v. Thompson,* 394 U.S. 618 [(1969)], and when there is no "reason to infer antipathy," *Vance v. Bradley,* 440 U.S. 93, 97 [(1979)], it is presumed that "even improvident decisions will eventually be rectified by the democratic process * * *." *Ibid.*

Certain classifications, however, in themselves supply a reason to infer antipathy. Race is the paradigm. A racial classification, regardless of purported motivation, is presumptively invalid and can be upheld only upon an extraordinary justification. This rule applies as well to a classification that is ostensibly neutral but is an obvious pretext for racial discrimination. But * * * even if a neutral law has a disproportionately adverse effect upon a racial minority, it is unconstitutional under the Equal Protection Clause only if that impact can be traced to a discriminatory purpose.

Classifications based upon gender, not unlike those based upon race, have traditionally been the touchstone for pervasive and often subtle discrimination. This Court's recent cases teach that such classifications must bear a close and substantial relationship to important governmental objectives, *Craig v. Boren,* 429 U.S. 190, 197 [(1976)], and are in many settings unconstitutional. Although public employment is not a constitutional right, and the States have wide discretion in framing employee qualifications, * * * any state law overtly or covertly designed to prefer males over females in public employment would require an exceedingly persuasive justification to withstand a constitutional challenge under the Equal Protection Clause of the Fourteenth Amendment.

    * * *

When a statute gender-neutral on its face is challenged on the ground that its effects upon women are disproportionately adverse, a twofold inquiry is * * * appropriate. The first question is whether the statutory classification is indeed neutral in the sense that it is not gender based. If the classification itself, covert or overt, is not based upon gender, the second question is whether the adverse effect reflects invidious gender-based discrimination. In this second inquiry, impact provides an "important starting point," but purposeful discrimination is "the condition that offends the Constitution." *Swann v. Charlotte–Mecklenburg Board of Education*, 402 U.S. 1, 16 [(1971)].

It is against this background of precedent that we consider the merits of the case before us.

II

A

The question whether ch. 31, § 23, establishes a classification that is overtly or covertly based upon gender must first be considered. The appellee has conceded that ch. 31, § 23, serves legitimate and worthy purposes; second, that the absolute preference was not established for the purpose of discriminating against women. * * *

If the impact of this statute could not be plausibly explained on a neutral ground, impact itself would signal that the real classification made by the law was in fact not neutral. But there can be but one answer to the question whether this veteran preference excludes significant numbers of women from preferred state jobs because they are women or because they are nonveterans. Apart from the facts that the definition of "veterans" in the statute has always been neutral as to gender and that Massachusetts has consistently defined veteran status in a way that has been inclusive of women who have served in the military, this is not a law that can plausibly be explained only as a gender-based classification. Indeed, it is not a law that can rationally be explained on that ground. Veteran status is not uniquely male. Although few women benefit from the preference, the nonveteran class is not substantially all female. To the contrary, significant numbers of nonveterans are men, and nonveterans—male as well as female—are placed at a disadvantage. Too many men are affected by ch. 31, § 23, to permit the inference that the statute is but a pretext for preferring men over women.

Moreover, as the District Court implicitly found, the purposes of the statute proved the surest explanation for its impact. Just as there are cases in which impact alone can unmask an invidious classification, cf. *Yick Wo v. Hopkins,* 118 U.S. 356 [(1886)], there are others, in which—notwithstanding impact—the legitimate noninvidious purposes of a law cannot be missed. This is one. The distinction made by ch. 31, § 23, is, as it seems to be, quite simply between veterans nonveterans, not between men and women.

The dispositive question, then, is whether the appellee has shown that a gender-based discriminatory purpose has, at least in some measure, shaped the Massachusetts veterans' preference legislation. As did the District Court, she points to two basic factors which in her view distinguish ch. 31, § 23, from * * * neutral rules. * * *

The first is the nature of the preference, which is said to be demonstrably gender biased in the sense that it favors a status reserved under federal military policy primarily to men. The second concerns the impact of the absolute lifetime preference upon the employment opportunities of women, an impact claimed to be too inevitable to have been unintended. The appellee contends that these factors, coupled with the fact that the preference itself has little if any relevance to actual job performance, more than suffice to prove the discriminatory intent required to establish a constitutional violation.

II

The contention that this veterans' preference is "inherently nonneutral" or "gender-biased" presumes that the State, by favoring veterans, intentionally incorporated into its public employment policies the panoply of sex-based and assertedly discriminatory federal laws that have prevented all but a handful of women from becoming veterans. There are two serious difficulties with this argument. First, it is wholly at odds with the District Court's central finding that Massachusetts has not offered a preference to veterans for the purpose of discriminating against women. Second, it cannot be reconciled with the assumption made by both the appellee and the District Court that a more limited hiring preference for veterans could be sustained. Taken together, these difficulties are fatal.

To the extent that the status of veteran is one that few women have been enabled to achieve, every hiring preference for veterans, however modest or extreme, is inherently gender-biased. If Massachusetts by offering such a preference can be said intentionally to have incorporated into its state employment policies the historical gender-based federal military personnel practices, the degree of the preference would or should make no constitutional difference. Invidious discrimination does not become less so because the discrimination accomplished is of a lesser magnitude. Discriminatory intent is simply not amenable to calibration. It either is a factor that has influenced the legislative choice or it is not. The District Court's conclusion that the absolute veterans' preference was not originally enacted or subsequently reaffirmed for the purpose of giving an advantage to males as such as necessarily compels the conclusion that the State intended nothing more than to prefer "veterans." Given this finding, simple logic suggests that an intent to exclude women from significant public jobs was not at work in this law. To reason that it was, by describing the preference as "inherently nonneutral" or "gender-biased," is merely to restate the fact of impact, not to answer the question of intent.

To be sure, this case is unusual in that it involves a law that by design is not neutral. The law overtly prefers veterans as such. * * * [I]t does not purport to define a job-related characteristic. To the contrary, it confers upon a specifically described group—perceived to be particularly deserving—a competitive headstart. But the District Court found, and the appellee has not disputed, that this legislative choice was legitimate. The basic distinction between veterans and nonveterans, having been found not gender-based, and the goals of the preference having been found worthy, ch. 31 must be analyzed as is any other neutral law that casts a greater burden upon women as a group than upon men as a group. The enlistment policies of the Armed Services may well have discriminated on the basis of sex. But the history of discrimination against women in the military is not on trial in this case.

Mr. Justice Marshall, with whom Mr. Justice Brennan joins, dissenting.

Although acknowledging that in some circumstances, discriminatory intent may be inferred from the inevitable or foreseeable impact of a statute, the Court concludes that no such intent has been established here. I cannot agree. In my judgment, Massachusetts' choice of an absolute veterans' preference system evinces purposeful gender based discrimination. And because the statutory scheme bears no substantial relationship to a legitimate governmental objective, it cannot withstand scrutiny under the Equal Protection Clause.

I

* * * [Th]e critical constitutional inquiry is not whether an illicit consideration was the primary or but-for cause of a decision, but rather whether it had an appreciable role in shaping a given legislative enactment.

In the instant case, the impact of the Massachusetts statute on women is undisputed. * * *

Appellants here advance three interests in support of the absolute-preference system:

(1) assisting veterans in their readjustment to civilian life; (2) encouraging military enlistment; and (3) rewarding veterans. Although each of these goals is unquestionably legitimate, the "mere recitation of a benign, compensatory purpose" cannot of itself insulate legislative classifications from constitutional scrutiny. *Weinberger v. Wiesenfeld*, [420 U.S. 636,] 648 [(1975)]. And in this case, the Commonwealth has failed to establish a sufficient relationship between its objectives and the means chosen to effectuate them.

With respect to the first interest, facilitating veterans' transition to civilian status, the statute is plainly overinclusive. By conferring a permanent preference, the legislation allows veterans to invoke their advantage repeatedly, without regard to their date of discharge. As the record demonstrates, a substantial majority of those currently enjoying the benefits of the system are not recently discharged veterans in need of readjustment assistance.

Nor is the Commonwealth's second asserted interest, encouraging military service, and a plausible justification for this legislative scheme. In its original and subsequent reenactments, the statute extended benefits retroactively to veterans who had served during a prior specified period. If the Commonwealth's "actual purpose" is to induce enlistment, this legislative design is hardly well suited to that end.

Finally, the Commonwealth's third interest, rewarding veterans, does not "adequately justify the salient features" of this preference system. Where a particular statutory scheme visits substantial hardship on a class long subject to discrimination, the legislation cannot be sustained unless "carefully tuned to alternative considerations." * * * Unlike [other] benefits, the costs of which are distributed across the taxpaying public generally, the Massachusetts statute exacts a substantial price from a discrete group of individuals who have long been subject to employment discrimination and who, "because of circumstances totally beyond their control, have [had] little if any chance of becoming members of the preferred class."

In its present unqualified form, the veterans' preference statute precluded all but a small fraction of Massachusetts's women from obtaining any civil service position also of interest to men. Given the range of alternatives available, this degree of preference is not constitutionally permissible.

SUPPRESSION OF RAPE DECISION

Constitutional Council (France).
80–125 DC of 19 Dec. 1980.

[The French Penal Code made indecent acts with a minor under 15 years of age punishable, but made indecent or unnatural acts with a minor under 18 punishable if those involved were of the same sex. This was challenged as contrary to the principle of equality.]

DECISION

* * * It is alleged that the challenged provisions violate the principle of equality before the law both "among delinquents" and "among victims."

Given that Article 34 of the Constitution provides that "The law (*loi*) sets the rules concerning the definition of crimes and delicts as well as regarding the determination of their corresponding punishments;"

Given that the principle of equality as it relates to criminal law under Article 6 of 1789 Declaration of the Rights of Man and of the Citizen incorporated by reference in the Preamble of 1958 Constitution does not preclude criminal law from differentiating between acts which are of a different nature;

Considering that the law concerning the suppression of rape and against certain attempts against prevailing mores can distinguish in the context of the protection of minors, without infringing upon the principle of equality, between acts between persons of the same sex and those between persons of different sexes;

Considering that the law provides an identical sanction for the violator whether the latter be male or female, and that it provides the same protection to victims regardless of their sex, the law does not violate the principle of equality [as it applies to equality between the sexes].

[Accordingly, the challenged law is consistent with the Constitution.]

B.4. DISCRIMINATION BASED ON RACE, ETHNICITY OR RELIGION

LOVING v. VIRGINIA

Supreme Court (United States).
388 U.S. 1 (1967).

[Excerpts of this case are also presented in Chapter 5.]

Mr. Chief Justice Warren delivered the opinion of the Court.

This case presents a constitutional question never addressed by this Court: whether a statutory scheme adopted by the State of Virginia to prevent marriages between persons solely on the basis of racial classifications violates the Equal Protection * * * Clause[ ] of the Fourteenth Amendment. For reasons which seem to us to reflect the central meaning of [that] constitutional command[ ], we conclude that these statutes cannot stand consistently with the Fourteenth Amendment.

In June 1958, two residents of Virginia, Mildred Jeter, a Negro woman, and Richard Loving, a white man, were married in the District of Columbia pursuant to its laws. Shortly after their marriage, the Lovings returned to Virginia and established their marital abode in Caroline County. At the October Term, 1958, of the Circuit Court of Caroline County, a grand jury issued an indictment charging the Lovings with violating Virginia's ban on interracial marriages. On January 6, 1959, the Lovings pleaded guilty to the charge and were sentenced to one year in jail; however, the trial judge suspended the sentence for a period of 25 years on the condition that the Lovings leave the State and not return to Virginia together for 25 years. He stated in an opinion that:

> "Almighty God created the races white, black, yellow, malay and red, and he placed them on separate continents. And but for the interference with his arrangement there would be no cause for such marriages. The fact that he separated the races shows that he did not intend for the races to mix."

* * *

The two statutes under which appellants were convicted and sentenced are part of a comprehensive statutory scheme aimed at prohibiting and punishing interracial marriages. * * *

Virginia is now one of 16 States which prohibit and punish marriages on the basis of racial classifications. Penalties for miscegenation arose as an incident to slavery and have been common in Virginia since the colonial period. The present statutory scheme dates from the adoption of the Racial Integrity Act of 1924, passed during the period of extreme nativism which followed the end of the First World War. The central features of this Act, and current Virginia law, are the absolute prohibition of a "white person" marrying other than another "white person," a prohibition against issuing marriage licenses until the issuing official is satisfied that the applicants' statements as to their race are correct, certificates of "racial composition" to be kept by both local and state registrars, and the carrying forward of earlier prohibitions against racial intermarriage.

* * *

[T]he State argues that the meaning of the Equal Protection Clause, as illuminated by the statements of the Framers, is only that state penal laws containing an interracial element as part of the definition of the offense must apply equally to whites and Negroes in the sense that members of each race are punished to the same degree. Thus, the State contends that, because its miscegenation statutes punish equally both the white and the Negro participants in an interracial marriage, these statutes, despite their reliance on racial classifications, do not constitute an invidious discrimination based upon race. The second argument advanced by the State assumes the validity of its equal application theory. The argument is that, if the Equal Protection Clause does not outlaw miscegenation statutes because of their reliance on racial classifications, the question of constitutionality would thus become whether there was any rational basis for a State to treat interracial marriages differently from other marriages. On this question, the State argues, the scientific evidence is substantially in doubt and, consequently, this Court should defer to the wisdom of the state legislature in adopting its policy of discouraging interracial marriages.

Because we reject the notion that the mere "equal application" of a statute containing racial classifications is enough to remove the classifications from the Fourteenth Amendment's proscription of all invidious racial discriminations, we do not accept the State's contention that these statutes should be upheld if there is any possible basis for concluding that they serve a rational purpose. The mere fact of equal application does not mean that our analysis of these statutes should follow the approach we have taken in cases involving no racial discrimination where the Equal Protection Clause has been arrayed against a statute discriminating between the kinds of advertising which may be displayed on trucks in New York City, *Railway Express Agency, Inc. v. New York*, 336 U.S. 106 (1949) * * *. In * * * cases, involving distinctions not drawn according to race, the Court has merely asked whether there is any rational foundation for the discriminations, and has deferred to the wisdom of the state legislatures. In the case at bar, however, we deal with statutes containing racial classifications, and the fact of equal application does not immunize the statute from the very heavy burden of justification which the Fourteenth Amendment has traditionally required of state statutes drawn according to race.

* * *

There can be no question but that Virginia's miscegenation statutes rest solely upon distinctions drawn according to race. The statutes proscribe generally accepted conduct if engaged in by members of different races. Over the years, this Court has consistently repudiated "distinctions between citizens solely because of their ancestry" as being "odious to a free people whose institutions are founded upon the doctrine of equality." *Hirabayashi v. United States*, 320 U.S. 81, 100 (1943). At the very least, the Equal Protection Clause demands that racial classifications, especially suspect in criminal statutes, be subjected to the "most rigid scrutiny," *Korematsu v. United States*, 323 U.S. 214, 216 (1944), and, if they are ever to be upheld, they must be shown to be necessary to the accomplishment of some permissible state objective, independent of the racial discrimination which it was the object of the Fourteenth Amendment to eliminate. * * *

There is patently no legitimate overriding purpose independent of invidious racial discrimination which justifies this classification. The fact that Virginia prohibits only interracial marriages involving white persons demonstrates that the racial classifications must stand on their own justification, as measures designed to maintain White Supremacy. We have consistently denied the constitutionality of measures which restrict the rights of citizens on account of race. There can be no doubt that restricting the freedom to marry solely because of racial classifications violates the central meaning of the Equal Protection Clause.

* * *

THLIMMENOS v. GREECE

European Court of Human Rights.
31 E.H.R.R. 15 (2001).

[Thlimmenos, a Jehovah's Witness, was convicted by a Greek military tribunal for insubordination, for refusing to wear a military uniform at a time of general mobilization into the Greek armed forces. Because the refusal was on religious grounds, the tribunal found extenuating circumstances but nonetheless imposed a prison term as punishment. Several years after he completed his prison term, Thlimmenos took the state examination to become a chartered accountant. Although he passed his examination with great distinction, he was refused certification because of his past felony conviction.]

* * *

III. *Alleged violation of Article 14 of the Convention taken in conjunction with Article 9.*

33.   The Court notes that the applicant did not complain about his initial conviction for insubordination. The application complained that the law excluding persons convicted of a felony from appointment to a chartered accountant's post did not distinguish between persons convicted as a result of their religious beliefs and persons convicted on other grounds. The applicant invoked Article 14 of the Convention taken in conjunction with Article 9, which provide:

Article 14

The enjoyment of the rights and freedoms set forth in [the] Convention shall be secured without discrimination on any ground such as sex, race, colour, language, religion, political or other opinion, national or social origin, association with a national minority, property, birth or other status.

Article 9

1.   Everyone has the right to freedom of thought, conscience and religion; this right includes freedom to change his religion or belief and freedom, either alone or in community with others and in public or private, to manifest his religion or belief, in worship, teaching, practice and observance.

2.   Freedom to manifest one's religion or beliefs shall be subject only to such limitations as are prescribed by law and are necessary in a democratic society in the interests of public safety, for the protection of public order, health or morals, or for the protection of the rights and freedoms of others.

* * *

B. *The Court's assessment*

* * *

40. The Court recalls that Article 14 has no independent existence, since it has effect solely in relation to the rights and freedoms safeguarded by the other substantive provisions of the Convention and its Protocols. However, the application of Article 14 does not presuppose a breach of one or more of such provisions and to this extent it is autonomous. For Article 14 to become applicable it suffices that the facts of a case fall within the ambit of another substantive provision of the Convention or its Protocols.

* * *

42. [T]he applicant does not complain of the distinction that the rules governing access to the profession make between convicted persons and others. His complaint rather concerns the fact that in the application of the relevant law no distinction is made between persons convicted of offences committed exclusively because of their religious beliefs and persons convicted of other offences. * * * In essence, the applicant's argument amounts to saying that he is discriminated against in the exercise of his freedom of religion, as guaranteed by Article 9, in that he was treated like any other person convicted of a felony although his own conviction resulted from the very exercise of this freedom. Seen in this perspective, the Court accepts that the "set of facts" complained of by the applicant—his being treated as a person convicted of a felony for the purposes of an appointment to a chartered accountant's post despite the fact that the offence for which he had been convicted was prompted by his religious beliefs—"falls within the ambit of a Convention provision", namely Article 9.

43. In order to reach this conclusion, the Court, as opposed to the Commission, does not find it necessary to examine whether the applicant's initial conviction and the authorities' subsequent refusal to appoint him amounted to interference with his rights under Article 9(1). In particular, the Court does not have to address, in the present case, the question whether, notwithstanding the wording of Article 4(3)(b), the imposition of such sanctions on conscientious objectors to compulsory military service may in itself infringe the right to freedom of thought, conscience and religion guaranteed by Article 9(1).

44. The Court has so far considered that the right under Article 14 not to be discriminated against in the enjoyment of the rights guaranteed under the Convention is violated when States treat differently persons in analogous situations without providing an objective and reasonable justification. However, the Court considers that this is not the only facet of the prohibition of discrimination in Article 14. The right not to be discriminated against in the enjoyment of the rights guaranteed under the Convention is also violated when States without an objective and reasonable justification fail to treat differently persons whose situations are significantly different.

45.   It follows that Article 14 is of relevance to the applicant's complaint and applies in the circumstances of this case in conjunction with Article 9 thereof.

46.   The next question to be addressed is whether Article 14 has been complied with. According to its case law, the Court will have to examine whether the failure to treat the applicant differently from other persons convicted of a felony pursued a legitimate aim. If it did the Court will have to examine whether there was a reasonable relationship of proportionality between the means employed and the aim sought to be realised.

47.   The Court considers that, as a matter of principle, States have a legitimate interest to exclude some offenders from the profession of chartered accountant. However, the Court also considers that, unlike other convictions for serious criminal offences, a conviction for refusing on religious or philosophical grounds to wear the military uniform cannot imply any dishonesty or moral turpitude likely to undermine the offender's ability to exercise this profession. Excluding the applicant on the ground that he was an unfit person was not, therefore, justified. The Court takes note of the Government's argument that persons who refuse to serve their country must be appropriately punished. However, it also notes that the applicant did serve a prison sentence for his refusal to wear the military uniform. In these circumstances, the Court considers that imposing a further sanction on the applicant was disproportionate. It follows that the applicant's exclusion from the profession of chartered accountants did not pursue a legitimate aim. As a result, the Court finds that there existed no objective and reasonable justification for not treating the applicant differently from other persons convicted of a felony.

48.   It is true that the authorities had no option under the law but to refuse to appoint the applicant a chartered accountant. However, contrary to what the Government's representative appeared to argue at the hearing, this cannot absolve the respondent State from responsibility under the Convention. The Court has never excluded that legislation may be found to be in direct breach of the Convention. In the present case the Court considers that it was the State having enacted the relevant legislation which violated the applicant's right not to be discriminated against in the enjoyment of his right under Article 9. That State did so by failing to introduce appropriate exceptions to the rule barring persons convicted of a felony from the profession of chartered accountants.

49.   The Court concludes, therefore, that there has been a violation of Article 14 of the Convention taken in conjunction with Article 9.

B.5.   DISCRIMINATION BASED ON SEX OR GENDER

Whereas equality among members of different races or ethnic groups calls for equal treatment in almost all cases, equality between men and women requires a much more varied approach. Indeed, while race or ethnicity should be deemed irrelevant from the standpoint of apportioning benefits and burdens among individuals apart from affirmative action issues, see Section D. below, differences based on gender or sex appear irrelevant in some circumstances but not in others.

In some instances it is obvious that equality between the sexes calls for equal treatment. Thus equally qualified men and women ought to enjoy equal treatment in employment. In certain other instances, however, equality between the sexes may require different treatment. For example, as mentioned above, if men and women are equally to have control over their own bodies, then arguably depriving women of the option of having an abortion would result in the state denying to women, but not men, full control over their own bodies. Differences between the sexes, therefore, may justify or even require different treatment. But which differences? Historically, men and women have been distinguished from each other on the basis of various differences: (1) physical, (2) psychological, and (3) social (i.e., differences relating to ascription of roles within society). This raises at least two different gender-based questions that must be answered before determining whether constitutional equality ought to mandate equal treatment or allow (or mandate) different treatment. First, is the claimed difference real or stereotypical? And, second, even if the difference is real, is it nonetheless irrelevant for purposes of the case at hand? Cf. *Michael M. v. Superior Court*, 450 U.S. 464 (1981), which upheld making it a crime for a male to have consensual sex with a female under 18 years of age, in a case involving both a male and female under 18. The Court reasoned that since females could become pregnant, they had an incentive that males lacked not to engage in sex, hence justifying limiting criminal sanctions to males in order to equalize deterrence between the sexes. For the dissenting justices, however, the true reason for unequal treatment was not a physical difference but a social stereotype about female chastity and a (social) psychological stereotype about a young female's putative lack of capacity truly to consent to sexual intercourse.

NOCTURNAL EMPLOYMENT CASE
Federal Constitutional Court (Germany).
85 BVerfGE 191 (1992).[c]

[A supervisor in a cake factory was fined for employing women to wrap cakes at night, in violation of a statute basically forbidding the employment of women as blue-collar workers (*Arbeiterinnen*) during the night. After exhausting her ordinary judicial remedies, the supervisor filed a constitutional complaint, arguing that the law offended the equality provisions of Art. 3 (1) and (2) of the Basic Law.]

A.   The constitutional complaint is justified * * * The prohibition of nocturnal employment of women is incompatible with Article 3 (1) and (3). The imposition of a fine on the basis of this unconstitutional law violates the complainant's general freedom of action under Article 2 (1) of the Basic Law.

c. Reproduced from Donald P. Kommers, *The Constitutional Jurisprudence of*   *the Federal Republic of Germany* 291–93 (2d ed. 1997).

I. The ban on night work for women * * * offends Article 3 (3).

1. Under this provision no one may be disadvantaged or favored on the basis of sex. This paragraph reinforces the general equality provision of Article 3 (1) by imposing more stringent limitations on legislative judgment. Like the other characteristics listed in paragraph 3, sex basically may not be employed as a basis for unequal treatment. This is true even if the law in question is intended not to establish the forbidden inequality for its own sake but to pursue some independent goal.

With respect to the question whether a law unjustifiably discriminates against women, Article 3 (2) imposes no additional restrictions. What Article 3 (2) adds to the discrimination ban of Article 3 (3) is an affirmative command of equal opportunity [*Gleichberechtigungsgebot*] that extends to the real social world [*die gesellschaftliche Wirklichkeit*]. The provision that "men and women shall have equal rights" is designed not only to do away with legal norms that base advantages or disadvantages on sex but also to bring about equal opportunity for men and women in the future. Its aim is the equalization of living conditions. Thus women must have the same earning opportunities as men * * * Traditional role conceptions that lead to increased burdens or disadvantages for women may not be entrenched by state action * * * De facto disadvantages typically suffered by women may be made up for by rules that favor women * * *

The present case is concerned not with the equalization of conditions but with the removal of an inequality imposed by law. [The statute] treats women laborers unequally because of their sex. It is true that the rule is addressed to employers. But the consequences of the rule are felt immediately by female workers. Unlike men, they are deprived of the opportunity to work at night. This is an inequality imposed by law on the basis of sex.

2. Not every inequality based on sex offends Article 3 (3). Gender distinctions may be permissible to the extent that they are indispensably necessary [*zwingend erforderlich*] to the solution of problems that by their nature can arise only for women or only for men. But this is not such a case.

(a) The prohibition of nocturnal employment was originally based upon the assumption that women laborers were constitutionally more susceptible to harm from night work than men. Studies in occupational medicine provide no firm basis for this assumption. Working at night is fundamentally harmful to everyone * * *

(b) Insofar as investigations show that women are more seriously harmed by night work, this conclusion is generally traced to the fact that they are also burdened with housework and child rearing * * * Women who carry out these duties in addition to night work outside the home * * * obviously suffer the adverse consequences of nocturnal employment to an enhanced degree * * *

But the present ban on night work for all female laborers cannot be supported on this ground, for the additional burden of housework and child rearing is not a sufficiently gender specific characteristic. For the woman to mind the house and the children does correspond with the traditional division of responsibility between husband and wife, and it cannot be denied that she often fills this role even when she is as busy as her male partner with outside work. But this double burden falls with full weight only upon those women with children requiring care who are single or whose male partners leave childcare and housework to them despite their nightly jobs. It falls equally upon single men who bring up children * * * The undeniable need for protection of night laborers, male and female, who have children to bring up and a household to manage can better be met by rules that focus directly on these circumstances.

3. In support of the prohibition of night work it is also argued that women are subject to particular dangers on their way to and from their place of nocturnal employment. In many cases that is no doubt true, but it does not justify forbidding all women laborers to work at night. The state may not escape its responsibility to protect women from being attacked in the public streets by restricting their occupational freedom in order to keep them from leaving their houses at night * * * Furthermore, this argument is not so generally applicable to women laborers as a group as to justify disadvantaging all of them. Particular risks might be avoided, for example, by providing a company bus to take employees to work.

4. The infringement of the discrimination ban of Article 3 (3) is not justified by the equal opportunity command of Article 3 (2). The prohibition of night work * * * does not promote the goals of this provision. It is true that it protects a number of women * * * from nocturnal employment that is hazardous to their health. But this protection is coupled with significant disadvantages: Women are thereby prejudiced in their search for jobs. They may not accept work that must be done even in part at night. In some sectors this has led to a clear reduction in the training and employment of women. In addition, women laborers are not free to dispose as they choose of their own working time. One result of all this may be that women will continue to be more burdened than men by child rearing and housework in addition to work outside the home, and that the traditional division of labor between the sexes may be further entrenched. To this extent the prohibition of night work impedes the elimination of the social disadvantages suffered by women.

CRAIG v. BOREN

Supreme Court (United States).
429 U.S. 190 (1976).

Mr. Justice Brennan delivered the opinion of the Court.

The interaction of two sections of an Oklahoma statute, Okla. Stat., Tit. 37, §§ 241 and 245 (1958 and Supp. 1976), prohibits the sale of "nonintoxicating" 3.2% beer to males under the age of 21 and to females under the age of 18. The question to be decided is whether such a gender-based differential constitutes a denial to males 18–20 years of age of the equal protection of the laws in violation of the Fourteenth Amendment.

* * *

II

A

Before 1972, Oklahoma defined the commencement of civil majority at age 18 for females and age 21 for males. In contrast, females were held criminally responsible as adults at age 18 and males at age 16. After the Court of Appeals for the Tenth Circuit held in 1972, on the authority of *Reed v. Reed*, 404 U.S. 71 (1971), that the age distinction was unconstitutional for purposes of establishing criminal responsibility as adults, *Lamb v. Brown*, 456 F. 2d 18 [1972], the Oklahoma Legislature fixed age 18 as applicable to both males and females. Okla. Stat., In 1972, 18 also was established as the age of majority for males and females in civil matters, except that §§ 241 and 245 of the 3.2% beer statute were simultaneously codified to create an exception to the gender-free rule.

Analysis may appropriately begin with the reminder that *Reed* emphasized that statutory classifications that distinguish between males and females are "subject to scrutiny under the Equal Protection Clause." 404 U.S., at 75. To withstand constitutional challenge, previous cases establish that classifications by gender must serve important governmental objectives and must be substantially related to achievement of those objectives. * * * Decisions following *Reed* * * * have rejected administrative ease and convenience as sufficiently important objectives to justify gender-based classifications. See, e.g., *Stanley v. Illinois*, 405 U.S. 645, 656 (1972); *Frontiero v. Richardson*, 411 U.S. 677, 690 (1973); cf. *Schlesinger v. Ballard*, 419 U.S. 498, 506–507 (1975). And only two Terms ago, *Stanton v. Stanton*, 421 U.S. 7 (1975), * * * held that *Reed* required invalidation of a Utah differential age-of-majority statute, notwithstanding the statute's coincidence with and furtherance of the State's purpose of fostering "old notions" of role typing and preparing boys for their expected performance in the economic and political worlds. 421 U.S., at 14–15.[6]

Reed v. Reed has also provided the underpinning for decisions that have invalidated statutes employing gender as an inaccurate proxy for other, more germane bases of classification. Hence, "archaic and over-broad" generalizations, *Schlesinger v. Ballard*, *supra*, at 508, concerning the financial position of servicewomen, *Frontiero v. Richardson*, *supra*, at 689 n. 23, and working women, *Weinberger v. Wiesenfeld*, 420 U.S. 636, 643 (1975), could not justify use of a gender line in determining eligibility for certain governmental entitlements. Similarly, increasingly outdated misconceptions concerning the role of females in the home rather than in the "marketplace and world of ideas" were rejected as loose-fitting characterizations incapable of supporting state statutory schemes that were premised upon their accuracy. *Stanton v. Stanton*,

---

6. *Kahn v. Shevin*, 416 U.S. 351 (1974) and *Schlesinger v. Ballard*, 419 U.S. 498 (1975), upholding the use of gender-based classifications, rested upon the Court's perception of the laudatory purposes of those laws as remedying disadvantageous conditions suffered by women in economic and military life. See 416 U.S., at 353–354; 419 U.S. at 508. Needless to say, in this case Oklahoma does not suggest that the age-sex differential was enacted to ensure the availability of 3.2% beer for women as compensation for previous deprivations.

supra; *Taylor v. Louisiana*, 419 U.S. 522, 535 n. 17 (1975). In light of the weak congruence between gender and the characteristic or trait that gender purported to represent, it was necessary that the legislatures choose either to realign their substantive laws in a gender-neutral fashion, or to adopt procedures for identifying those instances where the sex-centered generalization actually comported with fact. See, e.g., *Stanley v. Illinois, supra*, at 658; cf. *Cleveland Board of Education v. LaFleur*, 414 U.S. 632, 650 (1974).

* * * We turn then to the question whether, under Reed, the difference between males and females with respect to the purchase of 3.2% beer warrants the differential in age drawn by the Oklahoma statute. We conclude that it does not.

     * * *

C

We accept for purposes of discussion the District Court's identification of the objective underlying §§ 241 and 245 as the enhancement of traffic safety. Clearly, the protection of public health and safety represents an important function of state and local governments. However, appellees' statistics in our view cannot support the conclusion that the gender-based distinction closely serves to achieve that objective and therefore the distinction cannot under *Reed* withstand equal protection challenge.

The appellees introduced a variety of statistical surveys. First, an analysis of arrest statistics for 1973 demonstrated that 18–20–year-old male arrests for "driving under the influence" and "drunkenness" substantially exceeded female arrests for that same age period. Similarly, youths aged 17–21 were found to be overrepresented among those killed or injured in traffic accidents, with males again numerically exceeding females in this regard. Third, a random roadside survey in Oklahoma City revealed that young males were more inclined to drive and drink beer than were their female counterparts. * * * Conceding that "the case is not free from doubt," 399 F. Supp., at 1314, the District Court nonetheless concluded that this statistical showing substantiated "a rational basis for the legislative judgment underlying the challenged classification." *Id*. at 1307.

Even were this statistical evidence accepted as accurate, it nevertheless offers only a weak answer to the equal protection question presented here. The most focused and relevant of the statistical surveys, arrests of 18–20–year-olds for alcohol-related driving offenses, exemplifies the ultimate unpersuasiveness of this evidentiary record. Viewed in terms of the correlation between sex and the actual activity that Oklahoma seeks to regulate—driving while under the influence of alcohol—the statistics broadly establish that .18% of females and 2% of males in that age group were arrested for that offense. While such a disparity is not trivial in a statistical sense, it hardly can form the basis for employment of a gender line as a classifying device. Certainly if maleness is to serve as a proxy for drinking and driving, a correlation of 2% must be considered an unduly tenuous "fit."[12] Indeed, prior cases have consistently rejected the use of sex as a decisionmaking factor even though the statutes in question certainly rested on far more predictive empirical relationships than this.[13]

Moreover, the statistics exhibit a variety of other shortcomings that seriously impugn their value to equal protection analysis. Setting aside the obvious methodological problems,[14] the surveys do not adequately justify the salient features of Oklahoma's gender-based traffic-safety law. None purports to measure the use and dangerousness of 3.2% beer as opposed to alcohol generally, a detail that is of particular importance since, in light of its low alcohol level, Oklahoma apparently considers the 3.2% beverage to be "nonintoxicating." Moreover, many of the studies, while graphically documenting the unfortunate increase in driving while under the influence of alcohol, make no effort to relate their findings to age-sex differentials as involved here. Indeed, the only survey that explicitly centered its attention upon young drivers and their use of beer—albeit apparently not of the diluted 3.2% variety—reached results that hardly can be viewed as impressive in justifying either a gender or age classification.

There is no reason to belabor this line of analysis. It is unrealistic to expect either members of the judiciary or state officials to be well versed in the rigors of experimental or statistical technique. But this merely illustrates that proving broad sociological propositions by statistics is a dubious business, and one that inevitably is in tension with the normative philosophy that underlies the Equal Protection Clause. Suffice to say that the showing offered by the appellees does not satisfy us that sex represents a legitimate, accurate proxy for the regulation of drinking and driving. In fact, when it is further recognized that Oklahoma's statute prohibits only the selling of 3.2% beer to young males and not their drinking the beverage once acquired (even after purchase by their 18–20–year-old female companions), the relationship between gender and traffic safety becomes far too tenuous to satisfy *Reed's* requirement that the gender-based difference be substantially related to achievement of the statutory objective. * * *

12. Obviously, arrest statistics do not embrace all individuals who drink and drive. But for purposes of analysis, this "underinclusiveness" must be discounted somewhat by the shortcomings inherent in this statistical sample, see n. 14, *infra.* In any event, we decide this case in light of the evidence offered by Oklahoma and know of no way of extrapolating these arrest statistics to take into account the driving and drinking population at large, including those who avoided arrest.

13. For example, we can conjecture that in *Reed,* Idaho's apparent premise that women lacked experience in formal business matters (particularly compared to men) would have proved to be accurate in substantially more than 2% of all cases. And in both *Frontiero* and *Wiesenfeld,* we expressly found appellees' empirical defense

of mandatory dependency tests for men but not women to be unsatisfactory, even though we recognized that husbands are still far less likely to be dependent on their wives than vice versa. See, e.g., 411 U.S., at 688–690.

14. The very social stereotypes that find reflection in age-differential laws, see *Stanton v. Stanton,* 421 U.S. 7, 14–15 (1975), are likely substantially to distort the accuracy of these comparative statistics. Hence "reckless" young men who drink and drive are transformed into arrest statistics, whereas their female counterparts are chivalrously escorted home. See, e.g., W. Reckless & B. Kay, The Female Offender 4, 7, 13, 16–17 (Report to Presidential Commission on Law Enforcement and Administration of Justice, (1967). * * *

Mr. Justice Rehnquist, dissenting.

The Court's disposition of this case is objectionable on two grounds. First is its conclusion that men challenging a gender-based statute which treats them less favorably than women may invoke a more stringent standard of judicial review than pertains to most other types of classifications. Second is the Court's enunciation of this standard, without citation to any source, as being that "classifications by gender must serve important governmental objectives and must be substantially related to achievement of those objectives." * * * I think the Oklahoma statute challenged here need pass only the "rational basis" equal protection analysis expounded in cases such as *McGowan v. Maryland*, 366 U.S. 420 (1961), and *Williamson v. Lee Optical Co.*, 348 U.S. 483 (1955), and I believe that it is constitutional under that analysis.

In *Frontiero v. Richardson*, [411 U.S. 677 (1973)] the opinion for the plurality sets forth the reasons of four Justices for concluding that sex should be regarded as a suspect classification for purposes of equal protection analysis. These reasons center on our Nation's "long and unfortunate history of sex discrimination," 411 U.S., at 684, which has been reflected in a whole range of restrictions on the legal rights of women, not the least of which have concerned the ownership of property and participation in the electoral process. Noting that the pervasive and persistent nature of the discrimination experienced by women is in part the result of their ready identifiability, the plurality rested its invocation of strict scrutiny largely upon the fact that "statutory distinctions between the sexes often have the effect of invidiously relegating the entire class of females to inferior legal status without regard to the actual capabilities of its individual members." *Id.*, at 686–687.

Subsequent to *Frontiero*, the Court has declined to hold that sex is a suspect class, *Stanton v. Stanton*, *supra*, at 13, and no such holding is imported by the Court's resolution of this case. However, the Court's application here of an elevated or "intermediate" level scrutiny, like that invoked in cases dealing with discrimination against females, raises the question of why the statute here should be treated any differently from countless legislative classifications unrelated to sex which have been upheld under a minimum rationality standard. * * *

Most obviously unavailable to support any kind of special scrutiny in this case, is a history or pattern of past discrimination, such as was relied on by the plurality in *Frontiero* to support its invocation of strict scrutiny. There is no suggestion in the Court's opinion that males in this age group are in any way peculiarly disadvantaged, subject to systematic discriminatory treatment, or otherwise in need of special solicitude from the courts.

The Court does not discuss the nature of the right involved, and there is no reason to believe that it sees the purchase of 3.2% beer as implicating any important interest, let alone one that is "fundamental" in the constitutional sense of invoking strict scrutiny. Indeed, the Court's accurate observation that the statute affects the selling but not the drinking of 3.2% beer, further emphasizes the limited effect that it has on even those persons in the age group involved. There is, in sum, nothing about the statutory classification involved here to suggest that it affects an interest, or works against a group, which can claim under the Equal Protection Clause that it is entitled to special judicial protection.

It is true that a number of our opinions contain broadly phrased dicta implying that the same test should be applied to all classifications based on sex, whether affecting females or males. *E.g., Frontiero v. Richardson, supra*, at 688; *Reed v. Reed*, 404 U.S. 71, 76 (1971). However, before today, no decision of this Court has applied an elevated level of scrutiny to invalidate a statutory discrimination harmful to males, except where the statute impaired an important personal interest protected by the Constitution.[1] There being no such interest here, and there being no plausible argument that this is a discrimination against females,[2] the Court's reliance on our previous sex-discrimination cases is ill-founded. It treats gender classification as a talisman which—without regard to the rights involved or the persons affected—calls into effect a heavier burden of judicial review.

The Court's conclusion that a law which treats males less favorably than females "must serve important governmental objectives and must be substantially related to achievement of those objectives" apparently comes out of thin air. The Equal Protection Clause contains no such language, and none of our previous cases adopt that standard. I would think we have had enough difficulty with the two standards of review which our cases have recognized—the norm of "rational basis," and the "compelling state interest" required where a "suspect classification" is involved—so as to counsel weightily against the insertion of still another "standard" between those two. How is this Court to divine what objectives are important? How is it to determine whether a particular law is "substantially" related to the achievement of such objective, rather than related in some other way to its achievement? Both of the phrases used are so diaphanous and elastic as to invite subjective judicial preferences or prejudices relating to particular types of legislation, masquerading as judgments whether such legislation is directed at "important" objectives or, whether the relationship to those objectives is "substantial" enough.

I would have thought that if this Court were to leave anything to decision by the popularly elected branches of the Government, where no constitutional claim other than that of equal protection is invoked, it would be the decision as to what governmental objectives to be achieved by law are "important," and which are not. As for the second part of the

1. In *Stanley v. Illinois*, 405 U.S. 645 (1972), the Court struck down a statute allowing separation of illegitimate children from a surviving father but not a surviving mother, without any showing of parental unfitness. The Court stated that "the interest of a parent in the companionship, care, custody, and management of his or her children 'come[s] to this Court with a momentum for respect lacking when appeal is made to liberties which derive merely from shifting economic arrangements.' " * * *

2. I am not unaware of the argument from time to time advanced, that all dis-criminations between the sexes ultimately redound to the detriment of females, because they tend to reinforce "old notions" restricting the roles and opportunities of women. As a general proposition applying equally to all sex categorizations, I believe that this argument was implicitly found to carry little weight in our decisions upholding gender based differences. See *Schlesinger v. Ballard*, 419 U.S. 498 (1975); * * * [Accordingly,] it can be dismissed as an insubstantial consideration.

Court's new test, the Judicial Branch is probably in no worse position than the Legislative or Executive Branches to determine if there is any rational relationship between a classification and the purpose which it might be thought to serve. But the introduction of the adverb "substantially" requires courts to make subjective judgments as to operational effects, for which neither their expertise nor their access to data fits them. And even if we manage to avoid both confusion and the mirroring of our own preferences in the development of this new doctrine, the thousands of judges in other courts who must interpret the Equal Protection Clause may not be so fortunate.

II

The applicable rational-basis test is one which "permits the States a wide scope of discretion in enacting laws which affect some groups of citizens differently than others. The constitutional safeguard is offended only if the classification rests on grounds wholly irrelevant to the achievement of the State's objective. State legislatures are presumed to have acted within their constitutional power despite the fact that, in practice, their laws result in some inequality. A statutory discrimination will not be set aside if any state of facts reasonably may be conceived to justify it." *McGowan v. Maryland*, 366 U.S., at 425–426 [citations omitted].

Our decisions indicate that application of the Equal Protection Clause in a context not justifying an elevated level of scrutiny does not demand "mathematical nicety" or the elimination of all inequality. Those cases recognize that the practical problems of government may require rough accommodations of interests, and hold that such accommodations should be respected unless no reasonable basis can be found to support them. *Dandridge v. Williams*, 397 U.S. [471 (1970)], 485. Whether the same ends might have been better or more precisely served by a different approach is no part of the judicial inquiry under the traditional minimum rationality approach. *Richardson v. Belcher*, 404 U.S. [78,] 84 [(1971)].

* * *

One survey of arrest statistics assembled in 1973 indicated that males in the 18–20 age group were arrested for "driving under the influence" almost 18 times as often as their female counterparts, and for "drunkenness" in a ratio of almost 10 to 1. Accepting, as the Court does, appellants' comparison of the total figures with 1973 Oklahoma census data, this survey indicates a 2% arrest rate among males in the age group, as compared to a .18% rate among females.

* * *

The Court's criticism of the statistics relied on by the District Court conveys the impression that a legislature in enacting a new law is to be subjected to the judicial equivalent of a doctoral examination in statistics. Legislatures are not held to any rules of evidence such as those which may govern courts or other administrative bodies, and are entitled to draw factual conclusions on the basis of the determination of probable cause which an arrest by a police officer normally represents. In this situation, they could reasonably infer that the incidence of drunk driving is a good deal higher than the incidence of arrest.

* * *

The rationality of a statutory classification for equal protection purposes does not depend upon the statistical "fit" between the class and the trait sought to be singled out. It turns on whether there may be a sufficiently higher incidence of the trait within the included class than in the excluded class to justify different treatment. Therefore the present equal protection challenge to this gender-based discrimination poses only the question whether the incidence of drunk driving among young men is sufficiently greater than among young women to justify differential treatment. Notwithstanding the Court's critique of the statistical evidence, that evidence suggests clear differences between the drinking and driving habits of young men and women. Those differences are grounds enough for the State reasonably to conclude that young males pose by far the greater drunk-driving hazard, both in terms of sheer numbers and in terms of hazard on a per-driver basis. The gender-based difference in treatment in this case is therefore not irrational.

* * *

PRESIDENT OF THE REPUBLIC OF
SOUTH AFRICA v. HUGO

Constitutional Court (South Africa).
1997 (4) SA 1 (CC).

Goldstone J:

* * *

[30]   In the present case we are asked to decide whether rights of male prisoners have been violated by the manner in which the President exercised his power to pardon or reprieve prisoners in the impugned part of the Presidential Act. Here the President did not exercise his power of pardon or reprieve in a single case. He exercised it "wholesale" as it were—in general terms. * * *

[31]   Where the power of pardon or reprieve is used in general terms and there is an "amnesty" accorded to a category or categories of prisoners, discrimination is inherent. The line has to be drawn somewhere, and there will always be people on one side of the line who do not benefit and whose positions are not significantly different to those of persons on the other side of the line who do benefit. * * *

[32]   The respondent [a prisoner serving fifteen years, with children, whose wife had died] argued that the Presidential Act was in conflict with section 8 of the interim Constitution in that by releasing all mothers whose children were under the age of twelve, it discriminated against fathers of children of a similar age. Section 8 of the interim Constitution provides as follows:

"(1) Every person shall have the right to equality before the law and to equal protection of the law.

(2) No person shall be unfairly discriminated against, directly or indirectly, and, without derogating from the generality of this provision, on one or more of the following grounds in particular: race, gender, sex, ethnic or social origin, colour, sexual orientation, age, disability, religion, conscience, belief, culture or language.

(3) (a) This section shall not preclude measures designed to achieve the adequate protection and advancement of persons or groups or categories of persons disadvantaged by unfair discrimination, in order to enable their full and equal enjoyment of all rights and freedoms.

(b) * * *

(4) *Prima facie* proof of discrimination on any of the grounds specified in subsection (2) shall be presumed to be sufficient proof of unfair discrimination as contemplated in that subsection, until the contrary is established."

[33]   The respondent argues that in releasing mothers of small children but not fathers, the President discriminated on the grounds of sex. The advantage that was afforded mothers was not afforded to fathers of small children and that failure is sufficient to establish discrimination within the context of section 8(2) of the interim Constitution. * * *

[34]   In his affidavit, the President stated that in regard to the special remission of all mothers of minor children, he

"was motivated predominantly by a concern for children who had been deprived of the nurturing and care which their mothers would ordinarily have provided. Having spent many years in prison myself, I am well aware of the hardship which flows from incarceration. I am also well aware that imprisonment inevitably has harsh consequences for the family of the prisoner."

* * *

[37]   The reason given by the President for the special remission of sentence of mothers with small children is that it will serve the interests of children. To support this, he relies upon the evidence of Ms. Starke that mothers are, generally speaking, primarily responsible for the care of small children in our society. * * *

[38]   * * * The generalisation upon which the President relied is * * * a fact which is one of the root causes of women's inequality in our society. That parenting may have emotional and personal rewards for women should not blind us to the tremendous burden it imposes at the same time. It is unlikely that we will achieve a more egalitarian society until responsibilities for child rearing are more equally shared.

[39]   The fact, therefore, that the generalisation upon which the appellants rely is true, does not answer the question of whether the discrimination concerned is fair. Indeed, it will often be unfair for discrimination to be based on that particular generalisation. Women's responsibilities in the home for housekeeping and child rearing have historically been given as reasons for excluding them from other spheres of life. * * *

[41]   The prohibition on unfair discrimination in the interim Constitution seeks not only to avoid discrimination against people who are members of disadvantaged groups. It seeks more than that. At the heart of the prohibition of unfair discrimination lies a recognition that the purpose of our new constitutional and democratic order is the establishment of a society in which all human beings will be accorded equal dignity and respect regardless of their membership of particular groups. The achievement of such a society in the context of our deeply inegalitarian past will not be easy, but that the goal of the Constitution should not be forgotten or overlooked. * * *

It is not enough for the appellants to say that the impact of the discrimination in the case under consideration affected members of a group that were not historically disadvantaged. They must still show in the context of this particular case that the impact of the discrimination on the people who were discriminated against was not unfair. In section 8(3), the interim Constitution contains an express recognition that there is a need for measures to seek to alleviate the disadvantage which is the product of past discrimination. We need, therefore, to develop a concept of unfair discrimination which recognises that although a society which affords each human being equal treatment on the basis of equal worth and freedom is our goal, we cannot achieve that goal by insisting upon identical treatment in all circumstances before that goal is achieved. Each case, therefore, will require a careful and thorough understanding of the impact of the discriminatory action upon the particular people concerned to determine whether its overall impact is one which furthers the constitutional goal of equality or not. A classification which is unfair in one context may not necessarily be unfair in a different context.

[42]   According to the affidavits filed, the President intended by the special remission of the prison sentences of mothers to further the best interests of children. There is no doubt of his good faith. However, the fact that the President, in good faith, did not intend to discriminate unfairly and had in mind the benefit of children is not sufficient, to establish that the impact of the discrimination upon fathers was not unfair.

[43]   To determine whether that impact was unfair it is necessary to look not only at the group who has been disadvantaged but at the nature of the power in terms of which the discrimination was effected and, also at the nature of the interests which have been affected by the discrimination.

[44]   The power to pardon duly convicted prisoners in terms of which the President acted is conferred upon him by the interim Constitution. The power of pardon is one which is recognised in many democratic countries. * * *

The pardoning power in the interim Constitution * * *. It is not a private act of grace in the sense that the pardoning power in a monarchy may be. It is a recognition in the interim Constitution that a power should be granted to the President to determine when, in his view, the public welfare will be better served by granting a remission of sentence or some other form of pardon.

* * * [The pardoning power] * * * provide[s] an opportunity to the President to consider carefully the implications of the remission he proposed. In particular, he took into account the interests of the public and the administration of justice. * * *

[46] Male prisoners outnumber female prisoners almost fiftyfold. A release of all fathers would have meant that a very large number of men prisoners would have gained their release. As many fathers play only a secondary role in child rearing, the release of male prisoners would not have contributed as significantly to the achievement of the President's purpose as the release of mothers. In addition, the release of a large number of male prisoners in the current circumstances where crime has reached alarming levels would almost certainly have led to considerable public outcry. In the circumstances it must be accepted that it would have been very difficult, if not impossible, for the President to have released fathers on the same basis as mothers. Were he obliged to release fathers on the same terms as mothers, the result may have been that no parents would have been released at all.

[47] In this case, two groups of people have been affected by the Presidential Act: mothers of young children have been afforded an advantage: an early release from prison; and fathers have been denied that advantage. The President released three groups of prisoners as an act of mercy. The three groups—disabled prisoners, young people and mothers of young children—are all groups who are particularly vulnerable in our society, and in the case particularly of the disabled and mothers of young children, groups who have been the victims of discrimination in the past. The release of mothers will in many cases have been of real benefit to children which was the primary purpose of their release. The impact of the remission on those prisoners was to give them an advantage. As mentioned, the occasion the President chose for this act of mercy was 10 May 1994, the date of his inauguration as the first democratically elected President of this country. It is true that fathers of young children in prison were not afforded early release from prison. But although that does, without doubt, constitute a disadvantage, it did not restrict or limit their rights or obligations as fathers in any permanent manner. It cannot be said, for example, that the effect of the discrimination was to deny or limit their freedom, for their freedom was curtailed as a result of their conviction, not as a result of the Presidential Act. That Act merely deprived them of an early release to which they had no legal entitlement. * * *

* * *

Chaskalson P, Mahomed DP, Ackermann, Langa, Madala, and Sachs JJ concur in the judgement of Goldstone J.

Kriegler J:

* * *

[64] My dissent is narrowly based * * * In my view the pardon, although issued in good faith, for ostensibly rational reasons and manifestly to the advantage of some members of a traditionally disadvantaged class, is (i) inconsistent with the prohibition against gender or sex

discrimination contained in s 8(2); (ii) has not been shown to be fair; and (iii) is therefore invalid.

* * *

[74] The importance of equality in the constitutional scheme bears repetition. The South African Constitution is primarily and emphatically an egalitarian constitution. The supreme laws of comparable constitutional states may underscore other principles and rights. But in the light of our own particular history, and our vision for the future, a constitution was written with equality at its centre. Equality is our Constitution's focus and organising principle. The importance of equality rights in the Constitution, and the role of the right to equality in our emerging democracy, must both be understood in order to analyse properly whether a violation of the right has occurred.

[75] * * * Although the Constitution does not establish levels of scrutiny in the manner of the American Constitution, it is nevertheless worth noting that race and sex/gender are given special mention in the Preamble[6] and head the list of s 8(2) categories. The drafters of the Constitution could hardly have established a presumption of unfairness in s 8(4) only to have the burden of rebuttal under the section discharged with relative ease.

[76] Therefore, in terms of s 8(4), read both textually and contextually, unless and "until the contrary is established", a distinction drawn on the basis of gender or sex, such as the one here, must be found to be unfair. If no rebuttal is apparent, that is the end of the matter— the presumption of unfairness, which entails unconstitutionality under s 8(2), stands. Where some rebuttal is proffered, one must examine it to see whether it indeed "establishes" (i.e., proves) the fairness of the distinction.

[77] What kinds of facts are likely to discharge the burden of rebuttal imposed on the President by s 8(4)? I would make three observations here. First, the fact that discrimination is unintended or in good faith does not render it fair. Once the subject action or legislation is found to create adverse effects on a discriminatory basis, there is no further requirement, e.g., of bad faith or malice. My second observation is that the "rebutting" factors can seldom, if ever, in themselves be discriminatory or otherwise objectionable. True as it may be that our society currently exhibits deeply entrenched patterns of inequality, these cannot justify a perpetuation of inequality. A statute or conduct that presupposes these patterns is unlikely to be vindicated by relying on them. One that not only presupposes them but also is likely to promote their continuation is even less likely to pass muster. Third, factors that would or could justify interference with the right to equality in a section 33(1) analysis, are to be distinguished from those relevant to the enquiry

---

6. The first paragraph of the Preamble expresses the need to

* * * create a new order in which all South Africans will be entitled to a common South African citizenship in a sovereign and democratic constitutional state in which there is *equality between men and women and people of all races* so that all citizens shall be able to enjoy and exercise their fundamental rights and freedoms * * * (emphasis added).

under section 8(4). The one is concerned with justification, possibly notwithstanding unfairness; the other is concerned with fairness and with nothing else. I turn from these general comments to the case at hand.

[78]   In my respectful view, the majority errs on all three counts. * * *

[80]   * * * What I cannot endorse, is the majority's conclusion that although the discrimination inherent in the Act was based on that very stereotyping,[8] it is nevertheless vindicated. In my view the notion relied upon by the President, namely that women are to be regarded as the primary care givers of young children, is a root cause of women's inequality in our society. It is both a result and a cause of prejudice; a societal attitude which relegates women to a subservient, occupationally inferior yet unceasingly onerous role. It is a relic and a feature of the patriarchy which the Constitution so vehemently condemns. * * * One of the ways in which one accords equal dignity and respect to persons is by seeking to protect the basic choices they make about their own identities. Reliance on the generalisation that women are the primary care givers is harmful in its tendency to cramp and stunt the efforts of both men and women to form their identities freely.

[81]   Is it relevant that an inherently objectionable generalisation has been used in this case for the benefit of a particular group of women prisoners? * * * My first response is a narrow one. It is merely to say that the President has nowhere mentioned that it was his purpose to benefit women generally or the released mothers in particular. There is no suggestion of compensation for wrongs of the past or an attempt to make good for past discrimination against *women*. On the contrary, the whole thrust of the President's affidavit, and the raison d'être for the main supporting affidavit, is the interest of *children*. * * *

[I]

[82]   * * * In very narrow circumstances a generalisation—although reflecting a discriminatory reality—could be vindicated if its ultimate implications were equalising. But I would suggest that at least two criteria would have to be satisfied for this to be the case. First, there would have to be a strong indication that the advantages flowing from the perpetuation of a stereotype compensate for obvious and profoundly troubling disadvantages. Second, the context would have to be one in which discriminatory benefits were apposite.

[83]   I illustrate what I mean by examining how these criteria are to be applied in the instant case. In terms of the first criterion, the benefits in this case are to a small group of women—the 440 released

---

8. The word "stereotype" appears to have its ordinary meaning in the judgements of the United States Supreme Court. One possible definition, in *Mississippi University for Women v. Hogan* 458 US 718, 725 (1982), is "fixed notions concerning the roles and abilities of males and females". The Canadian Supreme Court is slightly clearer on the meaning of "stereotype". The enumerated and analogous grounds set out in the Charter's s 15(1) serve as indicators of discrimination because "distinctions made on these grounds are typically stereotypical, being based on presumed rather than actual characteristics." *Miron v. Trudel* (1995) 29 CRR (2d) 189 at 200.

from prison—and the detriment is to all South African women who must continue to labour under the social view that their place is in the home. In addition, men must continue to accept that they can have only a secondary/surrogate role in the care of their children. The limited benefit in this case cannot justify the reinforcement of a view that is a root cause of women's inequality in our society. * * *

[84]   The second criterion, it will be recalled, requires some connection between the discriminatory action and the advantage to the previously disadvantaged. On that basis the limited and parochial benefits flowing from the Act are dubious. From the fact that women have suffered discrimination *generally*, it cannot be argued that they deserve compensatory benefits in *any* context. I suggest that the relevant context in this case is a penal one, for the effect of the Presidential Act is felt by prisoners. It has not been suggested that women have suffered systematic discrimination in a penal context. The point here is that there is an advantage unrelated to any compensable past disadvantage. * * *

B.6. DISCRIMINATION BASED ON SEXUAL ORIENTATION

EGAN v. CANADA

Supreme Court (Canada).
[1995] 2 S.C.R. 513.

[The Old Age Security Act provides pension benefits that in certain cases include a spouse's allowance.]

* * *

JUDGMENT:

The reasons of Lamer C.J. and La Forest, Gonthier and Major JJ. were delivered by

1.   La Forest J.—This appeal concerns the constitutionality of ss. 2 and 19 (1) of the Old Age Security Act, R.S.C., 1985, c. 0–9, which accord to spouses of pensioners under the Act whose income falls below a stipulated amount, an allowance when they reach the age of 60, payable until they themselves become pensioners at age 65. The appellants maintain these provisions violate s. 15 of the Canadian Charter of Rights and Freedoms as discriminating against persons living in a homosexual relationship because the effect of the definition of "spouse" in s. 2 is to restrict the allowances to spouses in a heterosexual union, i.e. those who are legally married or who live in a common law relationship.

* * *

5.   The appellants' claim before this Court is that the Act contravenes s. 15 of the Charter in that it discriminates on the basis of sexual orientation. To establish that claim, it must first be determined that s. 15's protection of equality without discrimination extends to sexual orientation as a ground analogous to those specifically mentioned in the section. This poses no great hurdle for the appellants; the respondent Attorney General of Canada conceded this point. While I ordinarily have

reservations about concessions of constitutional issues, I have no difficulty accepting the appellants' contention that whether or not sexual orientation is based on biological or physiological factors, which may be a matter of some controversy, it is a deeply personal characteristic that is either unchangeable or changeable only at unacceptable personal costs, and so falls within the ambit of s. 15 protection as being analogous to the enumerated grounds. * * *

7. The nature of discrimination within the meaning of s. 15(1) of the Charter was first discussed by this Court in the seminal case of Andrews v. Law Society of British Columbia, [1989] 1 S.C.R. 143. In the principal reasons in that case, McIntyre J., at p. 175, underlined the importance in a constitutional document, which is not easily modified, of achieving a workable balance that permits government to perform effectively its function of making ongoing choices in the interests of society and the work of the courts in ensuring protection for the equality rights described in s. 15. * * *

8. What then is discrimination? * * * [T]he relevant question * * * is * * * whether the impugned provision amounts to discrimination * * *

9. As Gonthier J. has noted in *Miron v. Trudel*, this involves a three-step analysis, which he puts this way:

"The first step looks to whether the law has drawn a distinction between the claimant and others. The second step then questions whether the distinction results in disadvantage, and examines whether the impugned law imposes a burden, obligation or disadvantage on a group of persons to which the claimant belongs which is not imposed on others, or does not provide them with a benefit which it grants others * * *

The third step assesses whether the distinction is based on an irrelevant personal characteristic which is either enumerated in s. 15(1) or one analogous thereto."

10. There is no question that the first step is satisfied in this case. Parliament has clearly made a distinction between the claimant and others. * * *

13. I turn then to the third step of the analysis described by Gonthier J. Since it has already been accepted that "sexual orientation" is an analogous ground under s. 15(1), all that remains to be considered under this step is whether the distinction made by Parliament is relevant, what Gonthier J. describes in *Miron v. Trudel*, at p. 436, as the second aspect of this third step. He there notes that in assessing relevancy for this purpose one must look at "the nature of the personal characteristic and its relevancy to the functional values underlying the law". At this stage, he adds, one must necessarily undertake a form of comparative analysis to determine whether particular facts give rise to inequality * * *.

17. * * * [The Old Age Security Act's] objective is clear and singular in purpose. It is to ensure that when a couple is in a situation where one of the spouses has been forced to retire, and that couple has

to live on the pension of a single person, that there should be a special provision, when the breadwinner has been forced to retire at or after 65, to make sure that particular couple will be able to rely upon an income which would be equivalent to both members of the couple being retired * * *

19.   The singling out of legally married and common law couples as the recipients of benefits necessarily excludes all sorts of other couples living together such as brothers and sisters or other relatives, regardless of sex, and others who are not related, whatever reasons these other couples may have for doing so and whatever their sexual orientation. * * *

20.   What reason or purpose, then, can be assigned to the distinction made by Parliament? It seems to me that it is both obvious and deeply rooted in our fundamental values and traditions, values and traditions that could not have been lost on the framers of the Charter. Simply stated, what Parliament clearly had in mind was to accord support to married couples who were aged and elderly, and this for the advancement of public policy central to society. Moreover, in recognition of changing social realities, s. 2 was amended so that whenever the term "spouse" was used in the Act it was to be construed to extend beyond legal married couples to couples in a common law marriage.

21.   [M]arriage has from time immemorial been firmly grounded in our legal tradition, one that is itself a reflection of long-standing philosophical and religious traditions. But its ultimate raison d'être transcends all of these and is firmly anchored in the biological and social realities that heterosexual couples have the unique ability to procreate, that most children are the product of these relationships, and that they are generally cared for and nurtured by those who live in that relationship. In this sense, marriage is by nature heterosexual. It would be possible to legally define marriage to include homosexual couples, but this would not change the biological and social realities that underlie the traditional marriage.

* * *

25.   Viewed in the larger context, then, there is nothing arbitrary about the distinction supportive of heterosexual family units. And for the reasons set forth by Gonthier J. in *Miron*, I am not troubled by the fact that not all these heterosexual couples in fact have children. It is the social unit that uniquely has the capacity to procreate children and generally cares for their upbringing, and as such warrants support by Parliament to meet its needs. This is the only unit in society that expends resources to care for children on a routine and sustained basis. * * *

26.   Neither in its purpose or effect does the legislation constitute an infringement of the fundamental values sought to be protected by the Charter. None of the couples excluded from benefits under the Act are capable of meeting the fundamental social objectives thereby sought to be promoted by Parliament. * * *

27. Homosexual couples are not, therefore, discriminated against; they are simply included with these other couples.

* * *

29. Had I concluded that the impugned legislation infringed s. 15 of the Charter, I would still uphold it under s. 1 of the Charter * * *

The following are the reasons delivered by

113. Cory and Iacobucci JJ. (dissenting) * * * In these joint reasons CORY J. has dealt with the issues pertaining to the breach of s. 15(1) of the Charter while Iacobucci J. has considered the applicability of s. 1 of the Charter and the appropriate remedy.

Cory J.

* * *

Adverse Effect Discrimination or Direct Discrimination

137. The respondent contends that the majority of the Court of Appeal was correct when it found that this was a case of adverse effect discrimination. I cannot agree with that argument.

138. Direct discrimination involves a law, rule or practice which on its face discriminates on a prohibited ground. Adverse effect discrimination occurs when a law, rule or practice is facially neutral but has a disproportionate impact on a group because of a particular characteristic of that group. The distinction between direct discrimination and adverse effect discrimination was set out in *Ontario Human Rights Commission v. Simpsons–Sears Ltd.*, [1985] 2 S.C.R. 536, at p. 551, in these words:

"A distinction must be made between what I would describe as direct discrimination and the concept already referred to as adverse effect discrimination in connection with employment. Direct discrimination occurs in this connection where an employer adopts a practice or rule which on its face discriminates on a prohibited ground. For example, "No Catholics or no women or no blacks employed here." * * * It [adverse effect discrimination] arises where an employer for genuine business reasons adopts a rule or standard which is on its face neutral, and which will apply equally to all employees, but which has a discriminatory effect upon a prohibited ground on one employee or group of employees in that it imposes, because of some special characteristic of the employee or group, obligations, penalties, or restrictive conditions not imposed on other members of the work force."

Although that case dealt with the Ontario Human Rights Code, the same definition has been adopted in s. 15(1) cases: see Andrews, *supra*, at p. 165.

139. The law challenged in this case is, quite simply, not facially neutral. Section 2 of the Act defines "spouse" as being "a person of the opposite sex." It thereby draws a clear distinction between opposite-sex couples and same-sex couples. * * *

The Application of Section 15(1) to the Situation Presented in this Case

1.   Denial of Equal Benefit of the Law

* * *

(a) Whom Does the Act Seek to Benefit?

141.   Looking at the plain wording of the Act, as opposed to any proposed objective of the legislation, it is clear that, in circumstances where the combined income of the pensioner and the opposite-sex spouse falls below a certain level, the Act confers a spousal benefit upon the opposite-sex spouse who is between the ages of 60 and 64. It is not necessary that the spouses be married. The only two requirements for eligibility are that the spouses have lived together for one year and that their combined income falls below the fixed level.

142.   The respondent seems to contend that the Act was not one of general application. It is argued that the appellants were not denied equal benefit of the law because the legislation was only intended to confer a benefit upon either heterosexual couples who have raised children or upon dependent female spouses. These submissions cannot be accepted.

143.   The Act makes no reference to children.

* * *

(b) Does the Distinction Constitute a Denial of Equal Benefit of the Law?

* * *

151.   * * * [I]t seems clear that the denial of the spousal allowance to homosexual couples constitutes a clear denial of equal benefit of the law. The spousal allowance confers an economic benefit which, as a result of the statute's definition of spouse, is denied to homosexual common law couples. Thus, they have been denied equal benefit of the law.

* * *

161.   The law confers a significant benefit by providing state recognition of the legitimacy of a particular status. The denial of that recognition may have a serious detrimental effect upon the sense of self-worth and dignity of members of a group because it stigmatizes them even though no economic loss is occasioned. This principle has been recognized in the cases of the U.S. Supreme Court dealing with the segregation of races. * * * The choice of a spouse is a matter of great importance to the individuals involved. A very real benefit which is derived from the payment of the spousal allowance is the recognition by the state of the societal benefits which flow from supporting a couple who, for at least a year, have established a stable relationship which involves cohabitation, commitment, intimacy and economic interdependence. This benefit of the law is very significant. Its importance can be seen by considering what the result might be if, for example, the benefit were to be denied to couples because the individuals were of different races or different religions. The public outcry would, I think, be immediate and well merited. Such legislation would clearly infringe s. 15(1) because its provisions would indicate that the excluded groups were

inferior and less deserving of benefits. Similarly, an Act which denies equal benefits to homosexual couples who live in a loving and stable common law relationship as a result of their sexual orientation would appear to equally infringe s. 15(1) of the Charter.

* * *

2.   Does the Distinction Result in Discrimination?

(a) Distinction on the Basis of a Personal Characteristic

164.   The first question to be resolved, * * * is whether the distinction set out in s. 2 of the Old Age Security Act is one "based on" personal characteristics. It is my view that the distinction in the Act is indeed based on a personal characteristic, specifically, sexual orientation.

165.   The respondent argues that the distinction was not drawn in reliance upon a personal characteristic but rather on the basis of "spousal" as opposed to "non-spousal" status. The respondent submits that homosexual common law couples are non-spousal couples just as are siblings, parent-child relationships, roommates or any other non-spousal household excluded from the Act. * * * With respect, I cannot accept that position. To say that the distinction is between "spouses" and "non-spouses" is to avoid the very issue which is presented by the legislation in this case, namely the definition of a "spouse".

* * *

167.   * * * [T]he question is whether the difference in treatment is closely related to a personal characteristic of a group to which the claimant belongs. On this issue, I think the reasoning of Linden J.A. was appropriate and bears repetition. He stated (at p. 431):

> "While a distinction must be based on grounds relating to personal characteristics of the individual or group in order to be discriminatory, the words "based on" do not mean that the distinction must be designed with reference to those grounds. Rather, the relevant consideration is whether the distinction affects the individual or group in a manner related to their personal characteristics * * * "

* * *

(b) Is Sexual Orientation an Analogous Ground?

171.   The reasons in *Andrews*, *supra*, and *Turpin*, *supra*, indicate that in order to determine whether the basis of distinction is analogous to the enumerated grounds, it is first necessary to identify the group which is affected. It is true that in some cases it may be useful to determine whether or not the affected group forms a "discrete and insular minority" which is lacking in political power and, thus, vulnerable to having its interests overlooked or its rights to equal concern and respect violated. Yet, that search is not really an end in itself. While historical disadvantage or a group's position as a discrete and insular minority may serve as indicators of an analogous ground, they are not prerequisites for finding an analogous ground. They may simply be of assistance in determining whether the interest advanced by a claimant is the sort of interest that s. 15(1) was designed to protect. The fundamental consideration underlying the analogous grounds analysis is whether

the basis of distinction may serve to deny the essential human dignity of the Charter claimant. Since one of the aims of s. 15(1) is to prevent discrimination against groups which suffer from a social or political disadvantage it follows that it may be helpful to see if there is any indication that the group in question has suffered discrimination arising from stereotyping, historical disadvantage or vulnerability to political and social prejudice.

173.   The historic disadvantage suffered by homosexual persons has been widely recognized and documented. * * *

* * *

(c) Is There Discrimination?

179.   In my opinion, the distinction drawn by s. 2 of the Old Age Security Act on the basis of sexual orientation does constitute discrimination. * * *

[T]he existence of discrimination is determined by assessing the prejudicial effect of the distinction against s. 15(1)'s fundamental purpose of preventing the infringement of essential human dignity. The legislature's reliance upon stereotypical reasoning may very well be an extremely significant factor in determining whether discrimination exists. However, in light of the facts presented in this appeal, it is not necessary to elaborate upon other considerations which may also give rise to discrimination. Ultimately, it must be remembered that the question as to whether or not there is discrimination should be addressed from the perspective of the person claiming a Charter violation.

180.   In the present appeal, looking at the Act from the perspective of the appellants, it can be seen that the legislation denies homosexual couples equal benefit of the law. The Act does this not on the basis of merit or need, but solely on the basis of sexual orientation. * * * The effect of the impugned provision is clearly contrary to s. 15's aim of protecting human dignity, and therefore the distinction amounts to discrimination on the basis of sexual orientation.

* * *

Iacobucci J. [Justice Iacobucci applied the *Oakes* test. See Chapter 2.]

* * *

(ii) Is This Goal Pressing and Substantial?

189.   The appellants concede that the alleviation of poverty in elderly households is a goal of pressing and substantial importance. I agree. Moreover, as noted by Lamer C.J. in *Schachter v. Canada*, [[1992] 2 S.C.R. 679,] 721, "it will be a rare occasion when a benefit conferring scheme is found to have an unconstitutional purpose". The legislation thus satisfies the first component of the *Oakes* test.

(b) The Second Element of *Oakes*: Proportionality Analysis

190.   I conclude that the underinclusiveness of the Act is not a reasonable limit. Although the purpose of the legislation is laudable, it has been implemented in a discriminatory manner in that an equally

deserving group meeting the criteria established by the law is denied benefits based on an irrelevant personal characteristic.

(i) The Legislation Is Not Rationally Connected to Its Objective

191. If the goal of the legislation is the alleviation of poverty among cohabiting elderly "spouses", then how can this be but incompletely attained by denying otherwise eligible households the spousal allowance merely because of discrimination based on sexual orientation? The exclusion of same-sex partners is simply not rationally connected to the goal of alleviating poverty among elderly couples. * * *

ROMER v. EVANS

Supreme Court (United States).
517 U.S. 620 (1996).

Mr. Justice Kennedy delivered the opinion of the Court.

I

The enactment challenged in this case is an amendment ["Amendment 2"] to the Constitution of the State of Colorado, adopted in a 1992 statewide referendum. * * * The impetus for the amendment and the contentious campaign that preceded its adoption came in large part from ordinances that had been passed in various Colorado municipalities. For example, the cities of Aspen and Boulder and the city and County of Denver each had enacted ordinances which banned discrimination in many transactions and activities, including housing, employment, education, public accommodations, and health and welfare services. What gave rise to the statewide controversy was the protection the ordinances afforded to persons discriminated against by reason of their sexual orientation. See Boulder Rev. Code § 12–1–1 (defining "sexual orientation" as "the choice of sexual partners, i.e., bisexual, homosexual or heterosexual"); Denver Rev. Municipal Code, Art. IV, § 28–92 (defining "sexual orientation" as "the status of an individual as to his or her heterosexuality, homosexuality or bisexuality"). Amendment 2 repeals these ordinances to the extent they prohibit discrimination on the basis of "homosexual, lesbian or bisexual orientation, conduct, practices or relationships."

Yet Amendment 2, in explicit terms, does more than repeal or rescind these provisions. It prohibits all legislative, executive or judicial action at any level of state or local government designed to protect the named class, a class we shall refer to as homosexual persons or gays and lesbians. The amendment reads:

> "No Protected Status Based on Homosexual, Lesbian or Bisexual Orientation. Neither the State of Colorado, through any of its branches or departments, nor any of its agencies, political subdivisions, municipalities or school districts, shall enact, adopt or enforce any statute, regulation, ordinance or policy whereby homosexual, lesbian or bisexual orientation, conduct, practices or relationships shall constitute or otherwise be the basis of or entitle any person or class of persons to have or claim

any minority status, quota preferences, protected status or claim of discrimination." * * *

Soon after Amendment 2 was adopted, this litigation [was commenced] to declare its invalidity and enjoin its enforcement * * *

II

The State's principal argument in defense of Amendment 2 is that it puts gays and lesbians in the same position as all other persons. So, the State says, the measure does no more than deny homosexuals special rights. This reading of the amendment's language is implausible. We rely not upon our own interpretation of the amendment but upon the authoritative construction of Colorado's Supreme Court. The state court, deeming it unnecessary to determine the full extent of the amendment's reach, found it invalid even on a modest reading of its implications. The critical discussion of the amendment * * * is as follows:

"The immediate objective of Amendment 2 is, at a minimum, to repeal existing statutes, regulations, ordinances, and policies of state and local entities that barred discrimination based on sexual orientation."

"The 'ultimate effect' of Amendment 2 is to prohibit any governmental entity from adopting similar, or more protective statutes, regulations, ordinances, or policies in the future unless the state constitution is first amended to permit such measures." [*Evans I.*] 854 P.2d [1270,] 1284–1285 [(1993)].

Sweeping and comprehensive is the change in legal status effected by this law. So much is evident from the ordinances the Colorado Supreme Court declared would be void by operation of Amendment 2. Homosexuals, by state decree, are put in a solitary class with respect to transactions and relations in both the private and governmental spheres. The amendment withdraws from homosexuals, but no others, specific legal protection from the injuries caused by discrimination, and it forbids reinstatement of these laws and policies.

The change Amendment 2 works in the legal status of gays and lesbians in the private sphere is far reaching, both on its own terms and when considered in light of the structure and operation of modern antidiscrimination laws. That structure is well illustrated by contemporary statutes and ordinances prohibiting discrimination by providers of public accommodations. "At common law, innkeepers, smiths, and others who 'made profession of a public employment,' were prohibited from refusing, without good reason, to serve a customer." *Hurley v. Irish–American Gay, Lesbian and Bisexual Group of Boston, Inc.*, 515 U.S. 557, 571 (1995). The duty was a general one and did not specify protection for particular groups. The common-law rules, however, proved insufficient in many instances, and it was settled early that the Fourteenth Amendment did not give Congress a general power to prohibit discrimination in public accommodations, *Civil Rights Cases*, 109 U.S. 3, 25, 27 (1883). In consequence, most States have chosen to counter discrimination by enacting detailed statutory schemes.

* * *

Amendment 2 bars homosexuals from securing protection against the injuries that these public-accommodations laws address. That in itself is a severe consequence, but there is more. Amendment 2, in addition, nullifies specific legal protections for this targeted class in all transactions in housing, sale of real estate, insurance, health and welfare services, private education, and employment.

Not confined to the private sphere, Amendment 2 also operates to repeal and forbid all laws or policies providing specific protection for gays or lesbians from discrimination by every level of Colorado government. * * *

Amendment 2's reach may not be limited to specific laws passed for the benefit of gays and lesbians. It is a fair, if not necessary, inference from the broad language of the amendment that it deprives gays and lesbians even of the protection of general laws and policies that prohibit arbitrary discrimination in governmental and private settings. * * *

* * * [W]e cannot accept the view that Amendment 2's prohibition on specific legal protections does no more than deprive homosexuals of special rights. To the contrary, the amendment imposes a special disability upon those persons alone. Homosexuals are forbidden the safeguards that others enjoy or may seek without constraint. * * *We find nothing special in the protections Amendment 2 withholds. These are protections taken for granted by most people either because they already have them or do not need them; these are protections against exclusion from an almost limitless number of transactions and endeavors that constitute ordinary civic life in a free society.

III

The Fourteenth Amendment's promise that no person shall be denied the equal protection of the laws must coexist with the practical necessity that most legislation classifies for one purpose or another, with resulting disadvantage to various groups or persons. We have attempted to reconcile the principle with the reality by stating that, if a law neither burdens a fundamental right nor targets a suspect class, we will uphold the legislative classification so long as it bears a rational relation to some legitimate end.

Amendment 2 fails, indeed defies, even this conventional inquiry. First, the amendment has the peculiar property of imposing a broad and undifferentiated disability on a single named group, an exceptional and, as we shall explain, invalid form of legislation. Second, its sheer breadth is so discontinuous with the reasons offered for it that the amendment seems inexplicable by anything but animus toward the class it affects; it lacks a rational relationship to legitimate state interests.

Taking the first point, even in the ordinary equal protection case calling for the most deferential of standards, we insist on knowing the relation between the classification adopted and the object to be attained. * * * By requiring that the classification bear a rational relationship to an independent and legitimate legislative end, we ensure that classifications are not drawn for the purpose of disadvantaging the group burdened by the law. * * *

Amendment 2 confounds this normal process of judicial review. It is at once too narrow and too broad. It identifies persons by a single trait and then denies them protection across the board. The resulting disqualification of a class of persons from the right to seek specific protection from the law is unprecedented in our jurisprudence. * * *

It is not within our constitutional tradition to enact laws of this sort. Central both to the idea of the rule of law and to our own Constitution's guarantee of equal protection is the principle that government and each of its parts remain open on impartial terms to all who seek its assistance. "Equal protection of the laws is not achieved through indiscriminate imposition of inequalities." *Sweatt v. Painter*, 339 U.S. 629, 635 (1950). Respect for this principle explains why laws singling out a certain class of citizens for disfavored legal status or general hardships are rare. A law declaring that in general it shall be more difficult for one group of citizens than for all others to seek aid from the government is itself a denial of equal protection of the laws in the most literal sense. "The guaranty of 'equal protection of the laws' is a pledge of the protection of equal laws": *Skinner v. Oklahoma ex rel. Williamson*, 316 U.S. 535, 541 (1942)

* * *

* * * Amendment 2, * * * in making a general announcement that gays and lesbians shall not have any particular protections from the law, inflicts on them immediate, continuing, and real injuries that outrun and belie any legitimate justifications that may be claimed for it. We conclude that, in addition to the far-reaching deficiencies of Amendment 2 that we have noted, the principles it offends, in another sense, are conventional and venerable; a law must bear a rational relationship to a legitimate governmental purpose, *Kadrmas v. Dickinson Public Schools*, 487 U.S. 450, 462, (1988), and Amendment 2 does not.

The primary rationale the State offers for Amendment 2 is respect for other citizens' freedom of association, and in particular the liberties of landlords or employers who have personal or religious objections to homosexuality. Colorado also cites its interest in conserving resources to fight discrimination against other groups. The breadth of the Amendment is so far removed from these particular justifications that we find it impossible to credit them. * * *

* * * A State cannot so deem a class of persons a stranger to its laws. Amendment 2 violates the Equal Protection Clause.

Mr. Justice Scalia, with whom the Chief Justice and Mr. Justice Thomas join, dissenting.

The Court has mistaken a Kulturkampf for a fit of spite. The constitutional amendment before us here is not the manifestation of a " 'bare * * * desire to harm' " homosexuals, but is rather a modest attempt by seemingly tolerant Coloradans to preserve traditional sexual mores against the efforts of a politically powerful minority to revise those mores through use of the laws. * * *

In holding that homosexuality cannot be singled out for disfavorable treatment, the Court contradicts a decision, unchallenged here, pronounced only 10 years ago, see *Bowers v. Hardwick*, 478 U.S. 186 (1986), and places the prestige of this institution behind the proposition that opposition to homosexuality is as reprehensible as racial or religious bias. Whether it is or not is *precisely* the cultural debate that gave rise to the Colorado constitutional amendment (and to the preferential laws against which the amendment was directed). Since the Constitution of the United States says nothing about this subject, it is left to be resolved by normal democratic means, including the democratic adoption of provisions in state constitutions. This Court has no business imposing upon all Americans the resolution favored by the elite class from which the Members of this institution are selected, pronouncing that "animosity" toward homosexuality, is evil. I vigorously dissent.

I

* * *

The amendment prohibits *special treatment* of homosexuals, and nothing more. It would not affect, for example, a requirement of state law that pensions be paid to all retiring state employees with a certain length of service; homosexual employees, as well as others, would be entitled to that benefit. But it would prevent the State or any municipality from making death-benefit payments to the "life partner" of a homosexual when it does not make such payments to the long-time roommate of a nonhomosexual employee. * * *

Despite all of its hand wringing about the potential effect of Amendment 2 on general antidiscrimination laws, the Court's opinion ultimately does not dispute all this, but assumes it to be true. The only denial of equal treatment it contends homosexuals have suffered is this: They may not obtain *preferential* treatment without amending the state constitution. That is to say, the principle underlying the Court's opinion is that one who is accorded equal treatment under the laws, but cannot as readily as others obtain *preferential* treatment under the laws, has been denied equal protection of the laws. If merely stating this alleged "equal protection" violation does not suffice to refute it, our constitutional jurisprudence has achieved terminal silliness.

* * *

II

I turn next to whether there was a legitimate rational basis for the substance of the constitutional amendment—for the prohibition of special protection for homosexuals. It is unsurprising that the Court avoids discussion of this question, since the answer is so obviously yes. The case most relevant to the issue before us today is not even mentioned in the Court's opinion * * *. * * * Respondents (who, unlike the Court, cannot afford the luxury of ignoring inconvenient precedent) counter *Bowers* with the argument that a greater-includes-the-lesser rationale cannot justify Amendment 2's application to individuals who do not engage in homosexual acts, but are merely of homosexual "orientation." * * *

The Court evidently agrees that "rational basis"—the normal test for compliance with the Equal Protection Clause—is the governing standard. The trial court rejected respondents' argument that homosexuals constitute a "suspect" or "quasi-suspect" class, and respondents elected not to appeal that ruling to the Supreme Court of Colorado. See 882 P.2d 1335, 1341, n. 3 (1994). And the Court implicitly rejects the Supreme Court of Colorado's holding, *Evans v. Romer*, 854 P.2d 1270, 1282 (1993), that Amendment 2 infringes upon a "fundamental right" of "independently identifiable class[es]" to "participate equally in the political process."

But assuming that, in Amendment 2, a person of homosexual "orientation" is someone who does not engage in homosexual conduct but merely has a tendency or desire to do so, *Bowers* still suffices to establish a rational basis for the provision. If it is rational to criminalize the conduct, surely it is rational to deny special favor and protection to those with a self-avowed tendency or desire to engage in the conduct. Indeed, where criminal sanctions are not involved, homosexual "orientation" is an acceptable stand-in for homosexual conduct. A State "does not violate the Equal Protection Clause merely because the classifications made by its laws are imperfect," *Dandridge v. Williams*, 397 U.S. 471, 485 (1970).

* * *

III

* * *

[T]hough Coloradans are, as I say, *entitled* to be hostile toward homosexual conduct, the fact is that the degree of hostility reflected by Amendment 2 is the smallest conceivable. The Court's portrayal of Coloradans as a society fallen victim to pointless, hate-filled "gay-bashing" is so false as to be comical. Colorado not only is one of the 25 States that have repealed their antisodomy laws, but was among the first to do so. See 1971 Colo. Sess. Laws, ch. 121, § 1. But the society that eliminates criminal punishment for homosexual acts does not necessarily abandon the view that homosexuality is morally wrong and socially harmful; often, abolition simply reflects the view that enforcement of such criminal laws involves unseemly intrusion into the intimate lives of citizens. * * *

By the time Coloradans were asked to vote on Amendment 2, * * * [t]hree Colorado cities—Aspen, Boulder, and Denver—had enacted ordinances that listed "sexual orientation" as an impermissible ground for discrimination, equating the moral disapproval of homosexual conduct with racial and religious bigotry. * * * I do not mean to be critical of these legislative successes; homosexuals are as entitled to use the legal system for reinforcement of their moral sentiments as is the rest of society. But they are subject to being countered by lawful, democratic counter-measures as well.

That is where Amendment 2 came in. It sought to counter both the geographic concentration and the disproportionate political power of homosexuals by (1) resolving the controversy at the statewide level, and (2) making the election a single-issue contest for both sides. It put directly, to all the citizens of the State, the question: Should homosexuality be given special protection? They answered no. The Court today asserts that this most democratic of procedures is unconstitutional. Lacking any cases to establish that facially absurd proposition, it simply asserts that it *must* be unconstitutional, because it has never happened before.

* * *

IV

* * *

When the Court takes sides in the culture wars, it tends to be with the knights rather than the villeins—and more specifically with the Templars, reflecting the views and values of the lawyer class from which the Court's Members are drawn. * * * This * * * view of what "prejudices" must be stamped out may be contrasted with the more plebeian attitudes that apparently still prevail in the United States Congress, which has been unresponsive to repeated attempts to extend to homosexuals the protections of federal civil rights laws.

* * * Today's opinion has no foundation in American constitutional law, and barely pretends to. The people of Colorado have adopted an entirely reasonable provision which does not even disfavor homosexuals in any substantive sense, but merely denies them preferential treatment. Amendment 2 is designed to prevent piecemeal deterioration of the sexual morality favored by a majority of Coloradans, and is not only an appropriate means to that legitimate end, but a means that Americans have employed before. Striking it down is an act, not of judicial judgment, but of political will. I dissent.

Notes and Questions

1. *Feeney* and *Suppression of Rape* suggest that framing the relevant inequality connected to a particular law can be crucial in determining its constitutionality. Had *Feeney* and *Suppression of Rape* been interpreted as involving gender-based discrimination, both laws probably would have been struck down as unconstitutional. Did both courts strain to find that the laws did not involve gender-based discrimination? Would it have been equally logical to have decided that the laws involved imposed gender-based discrimination? Notice that this problem would be unlikely to arise if substantive equality rather than antidiscrimination were the proper constitutional standard. For example, if equal protection required equality of opportunity regarding public employment, then the preference for veterans upheld in *Feeney* would clearly be unconstitutional. Similarly, if homosexual sex were deemed either on a par with heterosexual sex or as a deviant type of behavior akin to incest, then the law challenged in *Suppression of Rape* would be either clearly constitutional or clearly unconstitutional.

2. Prohibition of discrimination on the basis of race, ethnic origin, or religion would seem relatively straightforward. Yet close consideration of *Loving* and *Thlimmenos* reveals that such cases can also raise difficult issues. On one level *Loving* is an easy case because the laws involved serve a racist purpose rather than racist means toward a legitimate state purpose. On closer look, however, is not *Loving* better viewed as a freedom of

association case rather than an equality case? Are not all races treated the same much as both sexes were treated the same in *Suppression of Rape*? Is not the real issue that government should not interfere with the choice of one's marital partner based on any grounds other than public health or public morality? On further thought, does *Loving* involve discrimination as between intraracial and interracial couples? Is that tantamount to discrimination based on race?

On the other hand, does not *Thlimmenos* raise the same issue as *Feeney*? In other words, is Thlimmenos discriminated against because of his conviction as a felon or because of his Jehovah's Witness creed? Would it make a difference if instead of having been convicted for pacifism he had been convicted of having consumed an illegal drug as part of a religious worship service? Cf. *Employment Division, Dept. of Human Resources v. Smith*, 494 U.S. 872 (1990) (ingestion of peyote is a crime and the constitution does not provide for exceptions from generally applicable criminal laws on freedom of religion grounds). (See Chapter 8, Subsection A.3.)

3.   The three cases involving gender-based discrimination seem consistent to the extent that they each start from a constitutional presumption against gender-based classifications. Beyond that, the cases differ in that *Nocturnal Employment* clearly involves a law that disadvantages women workers, whereas *Craig* and *Hugo*, at least in the first instance, disadvantage men. Should that make a difference?

Compare *Nocturnal Employment* with *Muller v. Oregon*, 208 U.S. 412 (1908), which held that limiting the number of hours that women can work in factories is constitutional though a similar limitation on men would be unconstitutional. The Court emphasized that women are weaker and must have time left to care for children at home. *Muller*, which is no longer valid after *Craig*, relied on physical and social differences between the sexes. So did the law struck down in *Nocturnal Employment*.

Were the physical differences involved genuine or stereotypical? On the assumption that the social differences were real—i.e., that they truly reflected how society prescribed different social roles for men and women—should courts adjudicating sex-equality cases ignore such differences or take them into account? In the context of *Muller*, poor women had to work and care for their children. By the same token, the women in question were barred by law from earning as much as men with the same skills. In light of this, was the Court's opinion justified? Is this a situation that can be remedied only by a legislature? Is that what the Court in *Nocturnal Employment* intimates? *Nocturnal Employment,* decided 80 years later than *Muller,* confronts some of the same issues but resolves them differently. Is that because the German Federal Constitutional Court (GFCC) is willing to confront stereotypes? Or because society has significantly evolved since the early twentieth century? Or both?

Should real physical differences in some cases be required to be taken into account to satisfy constitutional equality between the sexes? Consider *Geduldig v. Aiello*, 417 U.S. 484 (1974), where the Court held that exclusion of "disability that accompanies normal pregnancy and childbirth" from California's disability insurance system was constitutional. The Court's majority concluded that such exclusion did not amount to discrimination based on sex since not all women experience pregnancy. The dissent found that California had imposed a sex-based classification and concluded that it was unconstitutional as disabilities affecting only men, such as those related to prostate conditions or voluntary circumcision, were covered. After the Court's decision, the U.S. Congress enacted a federal law requiring inclusion of pregnancy and childbirth in plans such as California's. From the standpoint of an antidiscrimination standard prohibiting sex-based discrimination, should the California disability insurance system have been unconstitutional?

4. Both *Craig* and *Hugo* involved gender-based classifications that appear to disadvantage men. In *Craig* the relevant classification was held unconstitutional, whereas in *Hugo* it was upheld. Given traditional discrimination and injustices against women, should laws that disfavor men be treated more leniently? Was the Court in *Craig* worried about men or about reinforcing gender-based stereotypes generally detrimental to women, notwithstanding the latter's occasionally more favorable treatment? What about *Hugo*? How much does upholding different treatment of fathers and mothers reflect actual social differences? What about the danger of reinforcing stereotypes? How does the fact that the prison population is disproportionately male figure in the decision?

5. The U.S. equal protection jurisprudence differentiates between discrimination based on race or ethnic origin, which is subjected to "strict scrutiny," see *Korematsu* above, and discrimination based on gender, which must meet "intermediate scrutiny," see *Craig* above. One explanation is that some believe blacks historically have suffered greater injustices in the U.S. than women, thus necessitating greater judicial vigilance against legal classifications that disadvantage blacks and other minorities. Another explanation is that greater legislative flexibility is required in the context of gender-related classifications, as certain differences in the treatment of males and females ought to be maintained or pursued. Consider, in this connection, the different attitudes toward single-race schools outlawed in *Brown*, above, and single-sex schools, recognized as legitimate. See *United States v. Virginia,* 518 U.S. 515 (1996) (noting that it is the mission of some single-sex schools "to dissipate rather than perpetuate, traditional gender classifications"). In this case the Court, in a majority opinion by Justice Ruth Bader Ginsburg, who had championed women's equality as a civil rights lawyer before joining the Bench, held an exclusively male state military academy to have unconstitutionally denied admission to qualified women who had been willing to adhere to the rigorous regimen imposed on male students. In the course of her opinion Justice Ginsburg noted: "Physical differences between men and women are * * * enduring: The two sexes are not fungible * * * . Inherent differences between men and women, we have come to appreciate, remain cause for celebration, but not for denigration for members of either sex or for artificial constraints on an individual's opportunity."

Unlike in other contexts for single-sex schools, there was no comparable opportunity for women who wished to go to a military academy in Virginia. Justice Ginsburg concluded that Virginia had failed to prove it had "an exceedingly persuasive justification" for its single-sex military academy. While Justice Ginsburg used the above formulation in the context of applying "intermediate scrutiny," the dissent accused her of having in effect smuggled in "strict scrutiny" to decide gender-discrimination cases. Be that as it may, are single-sex schools more difficult to justify under strict scrutiny than intermediate scrutiny?

6. Notice the contrast between the respective approaches of the U.S. and Canadian supreme courts when it comes to constitutional equality in general and discrimination of homosexuals in particular. The U.S. approach appears to rely exclusively on the antidiscrimination principle, whereas the Canadian seems more nuanced as it blends antidiscrimination with contextual and substantive considerations. The Canadian Court further refined the approach it used in *Egan* in *Law v. Canada (Minister of Employment and Immigration)*, [1999] 1 S.C.R. 497:

> [These are] * * * the main guidelines for analysis under s. 15(1) to be derived from the jurisprudence of this Court, * * *. [T]hese guidelines should not be seen as a strict test, but rather should be understood as points of reference for a court that is called upon to decide whether a claimant's right to equality without discrimination under the Charter has been infringed. * * *
>
> General Approach
>
> (1) It is inappropriate to attempt to confine analysis under s. 15(1) of the Charter to a fixed and limited formula. A purposive and contextual approach to discrimination analysis is to be preferred, in order to permit the realization of the strong remedial purpose of the equality guarantee, and to avoid the pitfalls of a formalistic or mechanical approach.
>
> (2) The approach adopted and regularly applied by this Court to the interpretation of s. 15(1) focuses upon three central issues:
>
>> (A) whether a law imposes differential treatment between the claimant and others, in purpose or effect;
>>
>> (B) whether one or more enumerated or analogous grounds of discrimination are the basis for the differential treatment; and
>>
>> (C) whether the law in question has a purpose or effect that is discriminatory within the meaning of the equality guarantee.
>
> The first issue is concerned with the question of whether the law causes differential treatment. The second and third issues are concerned with whether the differential treatment constitutes discrimination in the substantive sense intended by s. 15(1).
>
> (3) Accordingly, a court that is called upon to determine a discrimination claim under s. 15(1) should make the following three broad inquiries:
>
>> A. Does the impugned law (a) draw a formal distinction between the claimant and others on the basis of one or more personal characteristics, or (b) fail to take into account the claimant's already disadvantaged position within Canadian society resulting in substantively differential treatment between the claimant and others on the basis of one or more personal characteristics?
>>
>> B. Is the claimant subject to differential treatment based on one or more enumerated and analogous grounds?
>>
>> and
>>
>> C. Does the differential treatment discriminate, by imposing a burden upon or withholding a benefit from the claimant in a manner which reflects the stereotypical application of presumed group or personal characteristics, or which otherwise has the effect

of perpetuating or promoting the view that the individual is less capable or worthy of recognition or value as a human being or as a member of Canadian society, equally deserving of concern, respect, and consideration?

Purpose

(4) In general terms, the purpose of s. 15(1) is to prevent the violation of essential human dignity and freedom through the imposition of disadvantage, stereotyping, or political or social prejudice, and to promote a society in which all persons enjoy equal recognition at law as human beings or as members of Canadian society, equally capable and equally deserving of concern, respect and consideration.

(5) The existence of a conflict between the purpose or effect of an impugned law and the purpose of s. 15(1) is essential in order to found a discrimination claim. The determination of whether such a conflict exists is to be made through an analysis of the full context surrounding the claim and the claimant.

Comparative Approach

(6) The equality guarantee is a comparative concept, which ultimately requires a court to establish one or more relevant comparators. The claimant generally chooses the person, group, with whom he or she wishes to be compared for the purpose of the discrimination inquiry. However, where the claimant's characterization of the comparison is insufficient, a court may, within the scope of the ground or grounds pleaded, refine the comparison presented by the claimant where warranted. Locating the relevant comparison group requires an examination of the subject matter of the legislation and its effects, as well as a full appreciation of context.

Context

(7) The contextual factors which determine whether legislation has the effect of demeaning a claimant's dignity must be construed and examined from the perspective of the claimant. The focus of the inquiry is both subjective and objective. The relevant point of view is that of the reasonable person, in circumstances similar to those of the claimant, who takes into account the contextual factors relevant to the claim.

(8) There is a variety of factors which may be referred to by a s. 15(1) claimant in order to demonstrate that legislation demeans his or her dignity. The list of factors is not closed. Guidance as to these factors may be found in the jurisprudence of this Court, and by analogy to recognized factors.

(9) Some important contextual factors influencing the determination of whether s. 15(1) had been infringed are, among others:

(10) Although the s. 15(1) claimant bears the onus of establishing an infringement of his or her equality rights in a purposive sense through reference to one or more contextual factors, it is not necessarily the case that the claimant must adduce evidence in order to show a violation of human dignity or freedom. Frequently, where differential treatment is based on one or more enumerated or analogous grounds, this will be

sufficient to found an infringement of s. 15(1) in the sense that it will be evident on the basis of judicial notice and logical reasoning that the distinction is discriminatory within the meaning of the provision.

7. Turning to discrimination on the basis of sexual orientation, the Canadian Court in *Egan* characterizes it as an "analogous" ground to those explicitly enumerated in s. 15(1), whereas the U.S. Court, in *Romer*, does not single it out as an inequality to be combated through use of the antidiscrimination principle since it subjects it to "minimum scrutiny." Paradoxically, the *Egan* majority upholds the exclusion of homosexual couples from certain pension benefits available to married couples and unmarried heterosexual couples living together. The *Romer* majority, on the other hand, holds that the discrimination against homosexuals imposed by the Colorado constitutional amendments violates equal protection. What accounts for these results? That the challenged Canadian law merely failed to extend a benefit available to some but not all heterosexuals (e.g., heterosexual siblings living together were also excluded)? And that the challenged Colorado amendment imposed a systematic disadvantage on homosexuals but not on anyone else? Or that the Canadian criterion for constitutional equality is diluted through application of Section 1? Is the *Romer* majority's conclusion that the Colorado amendment failed to meet the minimum scrutiny standard genuinely credible? Recall that Colorado sought to justify its amendment as a means to protect the freedom of those who had religious objections to interacting with homosexuals and to save the state's resources to better fight other kinds of discrimination. Are these objectives illegitimate? And are not the means employed more likely than not to advance the state's objectives? Compare *Railway Express* above. Is not the *Romer* majority in fact employing higher scrutiny, thus in effect making discrimination on the basis of sexual orientation presumptively unacceptable under the antidiscrimination principle?

C. EQUALITY IN SPECIAL CONTEXTS AND IN CONNECTION WITH OTHER CONSTITUTIONAL RIGHTS

There are certain contexts in which the achievement of equality seems particularly important because the absence of equality would not only cause individual or collective injustices but also threaten some fundamental rights or the very legitimacy of constitutional government as a whole. For example, without equal access to the ballot box, democracy itself becomes compromised; without equal education, equality of opportunity is threatened; and without equal access to the courts, the system of justice is undermined. On the other hand, in some cases where constitutional rights other than equality are at stake, equality concerns may still play an important or even determinative role.

C.1. ELECTIONS

The right to vote in a democracy may be of little value unless every eligible voter has an equal vote. But what does that entail?

HARPER v. VIRGINIA BOARD OF ELECTIONS

Supreme Court (United States).
383 U.S. 663 (1966).

[This case is presented in Chapter 11.]

REYNOLDS v. SIMS

Supreme Court (United States).
377 U.S. 533 (1964).

[See the excerpt in Chapter 11, Subsection C.]

APPORTIONMENT II CASE

Federal Constitutional Court (Germany).
16 BVerfGE 130 (1963).

[This case is presented in Chapter 11.]

ELECTIONS IN NEW CALEDONIA

Constitutional Council (France).
85–196 DC of 8 August 1985.[d]

Background: As part of the attempt to resolve the political situation in the colony of New Caledonia, it was proposed to institute a new electoral system and a new Congress with greater powers. The electoral system was to meet the aspirations of the native population (now a minority) by weighting representation in favour of their region. A challenge was made to these provisions by the right-wing parties, who drew their support from the settler community.

DECISION

On the principle of equality

12.   Considering that the deputies making of the references claim that articles 3 to 5 of the *loi* are contrary to the principle of equality, as, according to them, they tend 'to confer the majority within the Congress to an ethnic group that is not majoritarian in number in the population of the territory'; that they consider, in fact, that 'by the over-representation of some regions and the reduced representation of another', the criticized provisions disregard both the principles of equality in voting and of equality before the law without distinction as to origin, race, or religion, declared respectively by the third paragraph of article 3 and by the first paragraph of article 2 of the Constitution * * *

14.   Considering that, by the terms of article 2 § 1, cited above, of the Constitution, the Republic 'ensures equality before the law to all citizens, without distinction as to origin, race, or religion'; that, according to article 3 § 3, suffrage 'shall always be universal, equal, secret'; that article 6 of the Declaration of the Rights of Man and of the Citizen of 1789 provides that the law 'most be the same for all, whether it

d.   Reproduced from John Bell, *French Constitutional Law* 350–52 (1992).

protects or punishes. All citizens, being equal in its eyes, are equally eligible for all public dignities, positions, and employment according to their abilities, and without distinction other than that of their virtues and talents';

15. Considering that these provisions do not prevent the legislature, in accordance with article 74 of the Constitution, from being able to create and delimit regions within the framework of: the specific organization of an overseas territory, taking account of all relevant matters, especially the geographical division of populations; that, in doing that, article 3 of the *loi* does not breach article 2 of the Constitution;

16. But considering that, in order to be representative of the territory and its inhabitants in accordance with article 3 of the Constitution, the Congress, whose role as the deliberating organ of an overseas territory is not limited to the mere administration of the territory, must be elected on an essentially demographic basis, that, even if it does not follow that representation must be necessarily proportional to the population of each region, nor that other requirements of the public interest cannot be taken into account, these considerations can only be brought in, however, to a limited extent, which, in this case, is manifestly exceeded * * *

17. Considering that, thus the statement of the number [of seats for each region] appearing in paragraph 2 of article 4 of the *loi* must be declared to be inconsistent with the Constitution; that, in consequence, paragraph 2, inseparable from the statement of these numbers, must be declared incompatible as a whole with the Constitution * * *

BUSH v. GORE

Supreme Court (United States).
531 U.S. 98 (2000).

PER CURIAM.

I

On November 8, 2000, the day following the Presidential election, the Florida Division of Elections reported that petitioner Bush had received 2,909,135 votes, and respondent Gore had received 2,907,351 votes, a margin of 1,784 for Governor Bush. Because Governor Bush's margin of victory was less than "one-half of a percent * * * of the votes cast," an automatic machine recount was conducted under § 102.141(4) of the election code, the results of which showed Governor Bush still winning the race but by a diminished margin. Vice President Gore then sought manual recounts in Volusia, Palm Beach, Broward, and Miami–Dade Counties, pursuant to Florida's election protest provisions. A dispute arose concerning the deadline for local county canvassing boards to submit their returns to the Secretary of State (Secretary). The Secretary declined to waive the November 14 deadline imposed by statute. The Florida Supreme Court, however, set the deadline at November 26. We granted certiorari and vacated the Florida Supreme Court's decision, finding considerable uncertainty as to the grounds on which it was based. On December 11, the Florida Supreme Court issued a decision on remand reinstating that date.

On November 26, the Florida Elections Canvassing Commission certified the results of the election and declared Governor Bush the winner of Florida's 25 electoral votes. On November 27, Vice President Gore, pursuant to Florida's contest provisions, filed a complaint in Leon County Circuit Court contesting the certification. Fla. Stat. Ann. § 102.168 (Supp.2001). He sought relief pursuant to 102.168(3)(c), which provides that "[r]eceipt of a number of illegal votes or rejection of a number of legal votes sufficient to change or place in doubt the result of the election" shall be grounds for a contest. The Circuit Court denied relief, stating that Vice President Gore failed to meet his burden of proof. He appealed to the First District Court of Appeal, which certified the matter to the Florida Supreme Court.

Accepting jurisdiction, the Florida Supreme Court affirmed in part and reversed in part. See *Gore v. Harris,* 772 So.2d 1243 (2000). The court held that the Circuit Court had been correct to reject Vice President Gore's challenge to the results certified in Nassau County and his challenge to the Palm Beach County Canvassing Board's determination that 3,300 ballots cast in that county were not, in the statutory phrase, "legal votes."

The Supreme Court held that Vice President Gore had satisfied his burden of proof with respect to his challenge to Miami–Dade County's failure to tabulate, by manual count, 9,000 ballots on which the machines had failed to detect a vote for President ("undervotes"). *Id.,* at 1256. Noting the closeness of the election, the court explained that "[o]n this record, there can be no question that there are legal votes within the 9,000 uncounted votes sufficient to place the results of this election in doubt." *Id.,* at 1261. A "legal vote," as determined by the Supreme Court, is "one in which there is a 'clear indication of the intent of the voter.' " *Id.,* at 1257. The court therefore ordered a hand recount of the 9,000 ballots in Miami–Dade County. Observing that the contest provisions vest broad discretion in the circuit judge to "provide any relief appropriate under such circumstances," *§ 102, 168 (8),* the Supreme Court further held that the Circuit Court could order "the Supervisor of Elections and the Canvassing Boards, as well as the necessary public officials, in all counties that have not conducted a manual recount or tabulation of the undervotes * * *to do so forthwith, said tabulation to take place in the individual counties where the ballots are located." *Id.,* at 1262.

The Supreme Court also determined that both Palm Beach County and Miami–Dade County, in their earlier manual recounts, had identified a net gain of 215 and 168 legal votes for Vice President Gore. *Id.,* at 1260. Rejecting the Circuit Court's conclusion that Palm Beach County lacked the authority to include the 215 net votes submitted past the November 26 deadline, the Supreme Court explained that the deadline was not intended to exclude votes identified after that date through ongoing manual recounts. As to Miami–Dade County, the court concluded that although the 168 votes identified were the result of a partial recount, they were "legal votes [that] could change the outcome of the election." *Ibid.* The Supreme Court therefore directed the Circuit Court to include those totals in the certified results, subject to resolution of the actual vote total from the Miami–Dade partial recount. The petition presents the following question[ ]: * * * whether the use of standardless manual recounts violates the Equal Protection and Due Process Clauses. * * * [W]e find a violation of the Equal Protection Clause.

II

A

The closeness of this election, and the multitude of legal challenges which have followed in its wake, have brought into sharp focus a common, if heretofore unnoticed, phenomenon. Nationwide statistics reveal that an estimated 2% of ballots cast do not register a vote for President for whatever reason, including deliberately choosing no candidate at all or some voter error, such as voting for two candidates or insufficiently marking a ballot. In certifying election results, the votes eligible for inclusion in the certification are the votes meeting the properly established legal requirements.

This case has shown that punchcard balloting machines can produce an unfortunate number of ballots which are not punched in a clean, complete way by the voter. After the current counting, it is likely legislative bodies nationwide will examine ways to improve the mechanisms and machinery for voting.

B

* * *

The right to vote is protected in more than the initial allocation of the franchise. Equal protection applies as well to the manner of its exercise. Having once granted the right to vote on equal terms, the State may not, by later arbitrary and disparate treatment, value one person's vote over that of another. See, e.g., *Harper v. Virginia Bd. of Elections,* 383 U.S. 663, 665 (1966) ("[O]nce the franchise is granted to the electorate, lines may not be drawn which are inconsistent with the Equal Protection Clause of the Fourteenth Amendment"). It must be remembered that "the right of suffrage can be denied by a debasement or dilution of the weight of a citizen's vote just as effectively as by wholly prohibiting the free exercise of the franchise." *Reynolds v. Sims,* 377 U.S. 533, 555 (1964). There is no difference between the two sides of the present controversy on these basic propositions. Respondents say that the very purpose of vindicating the right to vote justifies the recount procedures now at issue. The question before us, however, is whether the recount procedures the Florida Supreme Court has adopted are consistent with its obligation to avoid arbitrary and disparate treatment of the members of its electorate.

Much of the controversy seems to revolve around ballot cards designed to be perforated by a stylus but which, either through error or deliberate omission, have not been perforated with sufficient precision for a machine to register the perforations. In some cases a piece of the card—a chad—is hanging, say, by two corners. In other cases there is no separation at all, just an indentation.

The Florida Supreme Court has ordered that the intent of the voter be discerned from such ballots. For purposes of resolving the equal protection challenge, it is not necessary to decide whether the Florida Supreme Court had the authority under the legislative scheme for resolving election disputes to define what a legal vote is and to mandate a manual recount implementing that definition. The recount mechanisms implemented in response to the decisions of the Florida Supreme Court do not satisfy the minimum requirement for nonarbitrary treatment of voters necessary to secure the fundamental right. Florida's basic command for the count of legally cast votes is to consider the "intent of the voter." This is unobjectionable as an abstract proposition and a starting principle. The problem inheres in the absence of specific standards to ensure its equal application. The formulation of uniform rules to determine intent based on these recurring circumstances is practicable and, we conclude, necessary.

The law does not refrain from searching for the intent of the actor in a multitude of circumstances; and in some cases the general command to ascertain intent is not susceptible to much further refinement. In this instance, however, the question is not whether to believe a witness but how to interpret the marks or holes or scratches on an inanimate object, a piece of cardboard or paper which, it is said, might not have registered as a vote during the machine count. The factfinder confronts a thing, not a person. The search for intent can be confined by specific rules designed to ensure uniform treatment. * * *

A monitor in Miami–Dade County testified at trial that he observed that three members of the county canvassing board applied different standards in defining a legal vote. And testimony at trial also revealed that at least one county changed its evaluative standards during the counting process. Palm Beach County, for example, began the process with a 1990 guideline which precluded counting completely attached chads, switched to a rule that considered a vote to be legal if any light could be seen through a chad, changed back to the 1990 rule, and then abandoned any pretense of a *per se* rule, only to have a court order that the county consider dimpled chads legal. This is not a process with sufficient guarantees of equal treatment.

An early case in our one-person, one-vote jurisprudence arose when a State accorded arbitrary and disparate treatment to voters in its different counties. The Court found a constitutional violation. We relied on these principles in the context of the Presidential selection process where we invalidated a county-based procedure that diluted the influence of citizens in larger counties in the nominating process. There we observed that "[t]he idea that one group can be granted greater voting strength than another is hostile to the one man, one vote basis of our representative government."

The State Supreme Court ratified this uneven treatment. It mandated that the recount totals from two counties, Miami–Dade and Palm Beach, be included in the certified total. The court also appeared to hold *sub silentio* that the recount totals from Broward County, which were not completed until after the original November 14 certification by the Secretary, were to be considered part of the new certified vote totals even though the county certification was not contested by Vice President Gore. Yet each of the counties used varying standards to determine what was a legal vote. Broward County used a more forgiving standard than Palm Beach County, and uncovered almost three times as many new votes, a result markedly disproportionate to the difference in population between the counties.

In addition, the recounts in these three counties were not limited to so-called undervotes but extended to all of the ballots. The distinction has real consequences. A manual recount of all ballots identifies not only those ballots which show no vote but also those which contain more than one, the so-called overvotes. Neither category will be counted by the machine. This is not a trivial concern. At oral argument, respondents estimated there are as many as 110,000 overvotes statewide. As a result, the citizen whose ballot was not read by a machine because he failed to vote for a candidate in a way readable by a machine may still have his vote counted in a manual recount; on the other hand, the citizen who marks two candidates in a way discernible by the machine will not have the same opportunity to have his vote count, even if a manual examination of the ballot would reveal the requisite indicia of intent. Furthermore, the citizen who marks two candidates, only one of which is discernible by the machine, will have his vote counted even though it should have been read as an invalid ballot. The State Supreme Court's inclusion of vote counts based on these variant standards exemplifies concerns with the remedial processes that were under way.

The question before the Court is not whether local entities, in the exercise of their expertise, may develop different systems for implementing elections. Instead, we are presented with a situation where a state court with the power to assure uniformity has ordered a statewide recount with minimal procedural safeguards. When a court orders a statewide remedy, there must be at least some assurance that the rudimentary requirements of equal treatment and fundamental fairness are satisfied.

Given the Court's assessment that the recount process underway was probably being conducted in an unconstitutional manner, the Court stayed the order directing the recount so it could hear this case and render an expedited decision. The contest provision, as it was mandated by the State Supreme Court, is not well calculated to sustain the confidence that all citizens must have in the outcome of elections. The State has not shown that its procedures include the necessary safeguards. The problem, for instance, of the estimated 110,000 overvotes has not been addressed. * * *

Upon due consideration of the difficulties identified to this point, it is obvious that the recount cannot be conducted in compliance with the requirements of equal protection * * * without substantial additional work. It would require not only the adoption (after opportunity for argument) of adequate statewide standards for determining what is a legal vote, and practicable procedures to implement them, but also orderly judicial review of any disputed matters that might arise. In addition, the Secretary has advised that the recount of only a portion of the ballots requires that the vote tabulation equipment be used to screen out undervotes, a function for which the machines were not designed. If a recount of overvotes were also required, perhaps even a second screening would be necessary. Use of the equipment for this purpose, and any new software developed for it, would have to be evaluated for accuracy by the Secretary, as required by Fla. Stat. Ann. § 101.015 (Supp. 2001).

The Supreme Court of Florida has said that the legislature intended the State's electors to "participat[e] fully in the federal electoral process," as provided in 3 U.S.C. § 5. That statute, in turn, requires that any controversy or contest that is designed to lead to a conclusive selection of electors be completed by December 12. That date is upon us, and there is no recount procedure in place under the State Supreme Court's order that comports with minimal constitutional standards. Because it is evident that any recount seeking to meet the December 12 date will be unconstitutional for the reasons we have discussed, we reverse the judgment of the Supreme Court of Florida ordering a recount to proceed.

Seven Justices of the Court agree that there are constitutional problems with the recount ordered by the Florida Supreme Court that demand a remedy. See *post,* at 545 (Souter, J., dissenting); *post,* at 551, 557–558 (Breyer, J., dissenting). The only disagreement is as to the remedy. Because the Florida Supreme Court has said that the Florida Legislature intended to obtain the safe-harbor benefits of *3 U.S.C. § 5, Justice Breyer's proposed remedy—remanding to the Florida Supreme Court for its ordering of a constitutionally proper contest until December 18—contemplates action in violation of the Florida Election Code, and hence could not be part of an "appropriate" order authorized by* Fla. Stat. Ann. § 102.168(8) (Supp. 2001).

Justice Stevens with whom Justice Ginsburg and Justice Breyer join, dissenting.

      * * *

Admittedly, the use of differing substandards for determining voter intent in different counties employing similar voting systems may raise serious concerns. Those concerns are alleviated—if not eliminated—by the fact that a single impartial magistrate will ultimately adjudicate all objections arising from the recount process. Of course, as a general matter, "[t]he interpretation of constitutional principles must not be too literal. We must remember that the machinery of government would not work if it were not allowed a little play in its joints." *Bain Peanut Co. of Tex. v. Pinson,* 282 U.S. 499, 501 (1931) (Holmes, J.). If it were otherwise, Florida's decision to leave to each county the determination of what balloting system to employ—despite enormous differences in accuracy[4]—might run afoul of equal protection. So, too, might the similar

---

4. The percentage of nonvotes in this election in counties using a punchcard sys-   tem was 3.92% in contrast, the rate of error under the more modern optical-scan sys-

decisions of the vast majority of state legislatures to delegate to local authorities certain decisions with respect to voting systems and ballot design.

Even assuming that aspects of the remedial scheme might ultimately be found to violate the Equal Protection Clause, I could not subscribe to the majority's disposition of the case. As the majority explicitly holds, once a state legislature determines to select electors through a popular vote, the right to have one's vote counted is of constitutional stature. As the majority further acknowledges, Florida law holds that all ballots that reveal the intent of the voter constitute valid votes. Recognizing these principles, the majority nonetheless orders the termination of the contest proceeding before all such votes have been tabulated. Under their own reasoning, the appropriate course of action would be to remand to allow more specific procedures for implementing the legislature's uniform general standard to be established.

In the interest of finality, however, the majority effectively orders the disenfranchisement of an unknown number of voters whose ballots reveal their intent—and are therefore legal votes under state law—but were for some reason rejected by ballot-counting machines. It does so on the basis of the deadlines set forth in Title 3 of the United States Code. But, * * * those provisions merely provide rules of decision for Congress to follow when selecting among conflicting slates of electors. They do not prohibit a State from counting what the majority concedes to be legal votes until a bona fide winner is determined. Indeed, in 1960, Hawaii appointed two slates of electors and Congress chose to count the one appointed on January 4, 1961, well after the Title 3 deadlines. See Josephson & Ross, *Repairing the Electoral College, 22 J. Legis. 145, 166, n. 154 (1996).*[5] Thus, nothing prevents the majority, even if it properly found an equal protection violation, from ordering relief appropriate to remedy that violation without depriving Florida voters of their right to have their votes counted. As the majority notes, "[a] desire for speed is not a general excuse for ignoring equal protection guarantees." *Ante,* at 532.

C.2. EDUCATION

The right to an equal education may be considered fundamental in its own right or as an indispensable means toward securing other key constitutional interests, such as, for example, the need for an educated electorate in a well-functioning democracy. Education is important to the

---

tems was only 1.43% *Siegel v. Lepore,* 234 F. 3d 1163, 1202, 1213 (charts C and F) (C.A. 11, Dec. 6, 2000). Put in other terms, for every 10,000 votes cast, punchcard systems result in 250 more nonvotes than optical-scan systems. A total of 3,718,305 votes were cast under punchcard systems, and 2,353,811 votes were cast under optical-scan systems. *Ibid.*

5. Republican electors were certified by the Acting Governor on November 28, 1960.

A recount was ordered to begin on December 13, 1960. Both Democratic and Republican electors met on the appointed day to cast their votes. On January 4, 1961, the newly elected Governor certified the Democratic electors. The certification was received by Congress on January 6, the day the electoral votes were counted. Josephson & Ross, 22 J. Legis, at 166, n. 154.

development and advancement of every person, so providing it for some but not for others would belie treating the latter with equal concern and respect. Beyond that, equality in education seems indispensable in order to extend equality of opportunity to all members of society.

NUMERUS CLAUSUS I CASE

Federal Constitutional Court (Germany).
33 BVerfGE 303 (1972).

[This case is presented in Chapter 10.]

———————

In *Parity Between Private and Public Education*, 93–329 DC of 13 January 1994, the French Constitutional Council held unconstitutional a law that would have allowed local government officials to subsidize private schools—including religious schools—in a way that would deprive public schools of funds needed to provide a free and secular (*laïque*) education for all. The Council emphasized that "although state subsidies to private schools, including religious ones, is permissible, the principle of equality requires that subsidies be proportionate. To the extent that public schools bear a greater burden than private schools in securing a free and equal secular education for all, they are entitled to higher state subsidies. Accordingly, constitutional equality requires that government subsidies be proportionate to the respective missions of these two types of schools." And since religious schools contribute less to achievement of a secular education, they should not be entitled to the same level of funding as public schools.

San Antonio Independent School District v. Rodriguez, 411 U.S. 1 (1973), involved an equal protection challenge to Texas's free public school education financed through neighborhood-based property taxes. Consistent with this, rich neighborhoods spent more per pupil than poor neighborhoods. In San Antonio's rich Alamo District, the per pupil expenditure amounted to more than 60 percent of that in the much less affluent Edgewood District. The parents of children who attended the Edgewood public schools challenged the constitutionality of San Antonio's school financing system. In a 5–4 decision the Court held that there had been no violation of equal protection. In reaching its conclusion, the majority decided that education was not a fundamental right and that the city's method for financing public education was a reasonable means to the legitimate state purpose of fostering local (neighborhood) control of public schools. The Court's majority also refused to accept the plaintiff's argument that the San Antonio financing system amounted to discrimination against the poor. In so doing, the majority reasoned that if there was discrimination it was not against poor individuals but against poor neighborhoods Thus a wealthy individual residing at the edge of a poor neighborhood would be entitled to less per-pupil expenditures than a poor child residing within the boundaries of a rich neighborhood. The majority also emphasized that at most the case involved a relative disadvantage—as opposed to an absolute deprivation—on account of poverty. Finally, the majority stressed that a lesser-per-pupil expenditure did not necessarily result in an inferior education. In contrast, the dissenting justices concluded that education was a fundamental right, particularly because it was a prerequisite to significant participation in the political process. According to them, deprivation of equal educational opportunities should be subjected to strict scrutiny. Under that standard, the San Antonio system was unconstitutional as there clearly were reasonable alternative means of financing public education that would not be discriminatory—e.g., statewide financing based on equal per-pupil expenditures.

C.3. ACCESS TO JUSTICE

Justice cannot be achieved unless equal access to the judicial process is guaranteed. This means both that there can be no *equality* without equal access to justice and no *justice* without an equal opportunity to be heard by the courts. See Chapter 9. Accordingly, equal access to justice ranks as a fundamental interest, as courts recognize.

Griffin v. Illinois, 351 U.S. 12 (1956), dealt with a challenge to a requirement in Illinois that a convicted criminal defendant provide a trial transcript to the appellate court before his or her conviction could be reviewed. Griffin, who lacked the means to pay for a transcript of his trial, charged that the state's refusal to pay for his transcript amounted to a denial of his equal protection rights. The Court's majority held that Griffin's constitutional rights had been violated, and a plurality of the justices stated that equal protection calls:

> for procedures in criminal trials which allow no invidious discriminations. [In] criminal trials a state can no more discriminate on account of poverty than on account of religion, race or color. Plainly the ability to pay costs in advance bears no rational relationship to a defendant's guilt or innocence and could not be used as an excuse to deprive a defendant of a fair trial. [There] is no meaningful distinction between a rule which would deny the poor the right to defend themselves in a trial court and one which effectively denies the poor an adequate appellate review accorded to all who have money enough to pay the costs in advance.

In his dissent, Justice Harlan emphasized that: "All that Illinois has done is to fail to alleviate the consequences of differences in economic circumstances that exist wholly apart from any state action. The Court thus holds that, at least in this area of criminal appeals, [equal protection] imposes on the states an affirmative duty to lift the handicaps flowing from differences in economic circumstances. That holding produces the anomalous result that a constitutional admonition to the states to treat all persons equally means in this instance that Illinois must give to some what it requires others to pay for."

In a subsequent case, *Douglas v. California*, 372 U.S. 353, 362 (1963), holding that the state must appoint free counsel for an indigent who appeals a criminal conviction, Justice Harlan wrote the following in his dissent: "[The Court's decision] read[s] into the Constitution a philosophy of leveling that [is] foreign to many of our basic concepts of the proper relations between government and society. The state may have a moral obligation to eliminate the evils of poverty, but it is not required by [equal protection] to give to some whatever others can afford."

In Germany, similar concerns are addressed as follows:

the equality of weapons, *("Waffengleichheit")* is an important component of the equality principle in labour law as well as in procedural law. The aim of the procedural equality of weapons is to divide the risk of litigation equally among the parties. Equal procedural positions are intended to enable the parties to fight with equal weapons for a proper and correct decision.[112] Equality of weapons demands, for example, in criminal procedure court-assigned defense if, in serious cases, the accused cannot afford the costs of a privately appointed defense counsel,[113] or that the parties have the equal right to be heard (Art. 103 para. 1 GG) and the equal right to plead attacks and defences.

Würtenberger, *op. cit.* at 90.

C.4. EQUALITY AND OTHER CONSTITUTIONAL RIGHTS

Equality can figure implicitly or explicitly in the definition or delimitation of other constitutional rights. For example, the notion of "equality of weapons" in judicial proceedings, mentioned above, seems just as important to "due process" rights as it does to equality rights. The context of judicial proceedings may seem *sui generis*—inasmuch as depriving one party to a litigation the tools possessed by that party's adversary would seem to lead inevitably to a deprivation of justice. Equality, however, has figured in the shaping of other rights that might stand on their own, such as freedom of speech, freedom of religion and privacy, or intimate association rights. Consider the following cases.

R.A.V. v. City of St. Paul, Minnesota, 505 U.S. 377 (1992), included in Chapter 7, held a municipal hate-speech provision unconstitutional. In his opinion for the Court, Justice Scalia found the provision in question, which outlawed expression insulting and offensive against traditionally discriminated groups, to be unconstitutional because it amounted to viewpoint discrimination inasmuch as it outlawed a type of expression depending on the target group involved. The provision outlawed highly offensive expression, demeaning on the basis of "race, color, creed, religion or gender," but not similar expression directed against homosexuals.

In *Estate of Thornton v. Caldor, Inc.*, 472 U.S. 703 (1985), the USSC struck down a Connecticut law that provided that "No person who states that a particular day of the week is observed as his Sabbath may be required to work on such a day. An employee's refusal to work on his Sabbath shall not constitute grounds for his dismissal." The central issue raised by this law was whether it favored particular religions in

112. BVerfGE 52, 131 ff. (156); 54, 117 (124 f.).

113. BVerfGE 39, 238 (243); 46, 202 (210 f.); 63, 380 (390 f.).

contravention to the Establishment Clause (see Chapter 8) or whether it amounted to an antidiscrimination provision resulting in an equal treatment of all religions. The Court concluded that the mandatory absolute deference to the Sabbath observer amounted to a constitutional violation because the disputed law clearly advanced a "particular religious practice."

In *Suppression of Rape*, above, and in *Bowers v. Hardwick*, 478 U.S. 186 (1986), included in Chapter 5, equality issues lurked in the context of privacy rights and the corruption of morals. In the *Suppression of Rape* different penalties, depending on whether homosexual or heterosexual sex with a minor was involved, were justified on the ground that same-sex relationships are inherently different from opposite-sex ones. But what if such differences were deemed constitutionally irrelevant? In *Bowers* the Court dealt with an antisodomy law equally applicable to homosexuals and heterosexuals, to married and to unmarried couples. The Court's majority upheld the criminalization of homosexual sodomy without discussing whether such criminalization would be unconstitutional if extended to heterosexuals or at least to married couples. The Court's conclusion was that homosexual sodomy between consenting adults in their homes was not protected by constitutional privacy rights. To the dissent, however, the question was whether adult individuals are constitutionally entitled to choose willing partners for intimate associations, including sexual relations. Since the Court's precedents established that constitutional privacy protected such relations in marriage and between unmarried heterosexual partners, the dissenters concluded there was no valid nonreligious reason not to extend the same right to homosexuals.

Notes and Questions

1. The right to vote is of little value in a democracy unless it is a right to an equal vote; but what about apportioning issues or group-related concerns, such as those that are prompted by the law struck down as unconstitutional in the *Elections in New Caledonia Case*? Furthermore, do the equal protection concerns in *Bush v. Gore* make sense, given that Florida voters in counties with punch-card machines were several times more likely not to have their votes counted than their counterparts in counties with optical-scan machines? Is it possible to frame cogent equality issues in the face of all the apparent inequalities that affected the Florida election for president in 2000? For a collection of opposing views on this subject, see *The Longest Night: Polemics and Perspectives on Election 2000* (Arthur J. Jacobson and Michel Rosenfeld eds., 2002).

2. Can special concern for equality in voting and access to justice and education be viewed as an extension of the same concerns that lend support to the antidiscrimination approach? In other words, are inequalities relating to essential benefits, such as the vote and access to justice or to an education, analogous to inequalities relating to immutable or difficult-to-eradicate traits, such as sex, race, or religion? Or, are these inequalities better dealt with in terms of a substantive standard, such as equality of opportunity?

3. Equality rights, as emphasized by the Canadian Supreme Court in *Law v. Canada,* above, are fundamentally *comparative in nature.* For example, if, in the context of *Hugo,* President Mandela had not decided to grant an amnesty to prisoners who were mothers of small children, Hugo would have had no equality claim whatsoever. In contrast, freedom of speech, religion, and privacy are not inherently comparative. If the state arrests a citizen for criticizing government policy, for example, it is not a valid defense to a free speech claim to point out that all other citizens who have been similarly critical have also been arrested. In this light, what genuine role does equality play, if any, in *R.A.V., Calder,* or *Bowers*? With respect to *R.A.V.,* how relevant is the fact that the city ordinance involved prohibited race-based and gender-based hate speech but not homophobic hate speech for purposes of determining whether such prohibition is constitutional? Are the comparative focuses of the Court in *Caldor* and of the dissent in *Bowers* more persuasive inasmuch as they are invoked to indicate the contours of rights undisputedly recognized in a majority of cases (i.e., members of mainstream religions and heterosexuals engaging in intimate relations, respectively)?

D. AFFIRMATIVE ACTION AND THE INTERPLAY BETWEEN INDIVIDUAL AND GROUP EQUALITY: BEYOND ANTIDISCRIMINATION?

Affirmative action, at least to the extent that it involves preferential treatment of members of particular groups, is controversial as it appears to straddle the boundary between individual-regarding and group-regarding equality. Where the group is considered the proper subject of equality, affirmative action can be easily justified. For example, if public employment is to be equally apportioned among members of two different ethnic groups, then overrepresentation of one of these would justify favoring members of the other until the desired balance is achieved. But where the individual is the subject of equality, preferences for some on account of group affiliation seem hard to justify. Nevertheless, proponents of affirmative action argue that temporary unequal treatment (marginal inequality) is sometimes the only viable way to achieve equality (global equality) among presently unequally situated individuals.

REGENTS OF UNIV. OF CALIFORNIA v. BAKKE

Supreme Court (United States).
438 U.S. 265 (1978),

[The University of California at Davis Medical School adopted a dual-admissions program. Every year the Medical School admitted 100 entering students, 84 of whom were admitted based exclusively on the results of an entrance examination and grade average. The remaining 16 places were reserved for minority applicants. Alan Bakke, a white applicant who was denied admission to the Medical School, had entry exam results and a grade average below those of the 84 accepted to the Medical School through the regular admissions program but higher than the 16 admitted through the preferential admissions program. Bakke sued, claiming that the latter's dual-admissions policy violated his equal protection rights. The Court held in a 5–4 decision that Bakke was entitled to admission at the Medical School. Four justices took the position that Davis's dual-admissions program violated a federal statute; hence it was unnecessary to reach the constitutional issue. Four other justices held that Davis's preferential admissions was constitutional. Only Justice Powell concluded that the preferential admissions program violated equal protection.]

Mr. Justice Powell announced the judgment of the Court.

* * *

Bakke * * * alleged that the Medical School's special admissions program operated to exclude him from the school on the basis of his race, in violation of his rights under the Equal Protection Clause of the Fourteenth Amendment * * * The University cross-complained for a declaration that its special admissions program was lawful. The trial court found that the special program operated as a racial quota, because minority applicants in the special program were rated only against one another, and 16 places in the class of 100 were reserved for them. * * *

III

A

* * *

The special admissions program is undeniably a classification based on race and ethnic background.

* * *

Petitioner argues that the court below erred in applying strict scrutiny to the special admissions program because white males, such as respondent, are not a "discrete and insular minority" requiring extraordinary protection from the majoritarian political process. This rationale, however, has never been invoked in our decisions as a prerequisite to subjecting racial or ethnic distinctions to strict scrutiny. Nor has this Court held that discreteness and insularity constitute necessary preconditions to a holding that a particular classification is invidious. * * *

Over the past 30 years, this Court has embarked upon the crucial mission of interpreting the Equal Protection Clause with the view of assuring to all persons "the protection of equal laws," in a Nation confronting a legacy of slavery and racial discrimination. * * *

Petitioner urges us to adopt for the first time a more restrictive view of the Equal Protection Clause and hold that discrimination against members of the white "majority" cannot be suspect if its purpose can be characterized as "benign." The clock of our liberties, however, cannot be turned back to 1868.

* * * The concepts of "majority" and "minority" necessarily reflect temporary arrangements and political judgments. As observed above, the white "majority" itself is composed of various minority groups, most of which can lay claim to a history of prior discrimination at the hands of the State and private individuals. Not all of these groups can receive preferential treatment and corresponding judicial tolerance of distinctions drawn in terms of race and nationality, for then the only "majority" left would be a new minority of white Anglo–Saxon Protestants. There is no principled basis for deciding which groups would merit "heightened judicial solicitude" and which would not. Courts would be asked to evaluate the extent of the prejudice and consequent harm suffered by various minority groups. Those whose societal injury is thought to exceed some arbitrary level of tolerability then would be entitled to preferential classifications at the expense of individuals belonging to other groups. Those classifications would be free from exacting judicial scrutiny. As these preferences began to have their desired effect, and the consequences of past discrimination were undone, new judicial rankings would be necessary. The kind of variable sociological and political analysis necessary to produce such rankings simply does not lie within the judicial competence—even if they otherwise were politically feasible and socially desirable.

Moreover, there are serious problems of justice connected with the idea of preference itself. First, it may not always be clear that a so-called preference is in fact benign. Courts may be asked to validate burdens imposed upon individual members of a particular group in order to advance the group's general interest. Nothing in the Constitution supports the notion that individuals may be asked to suffer otherwise impermissible burdens in order to enhance the societal standing of their ethnic groups. Second, preferential programs may only reinforce common stereotypes holding that certain groups are unable to achieve success without special protection based on a factor having no relationship to individual worth. Third, there is a measure of inequity in forcing innocent persons in respondent's position to bear the burdens of redressing grievances not of their making.

By hitching the meaning of the Equal Protection Clause to these transitory considerations, we would be holding, as a constitutional principle, that judicial scrutiny of classifications touching on racial and ethnic background may vary with the ebb and flow of political forces. Disparate constitutional tolerance of such classifications well may serve to exacerbate racial and ethnic antagonisms rather than alleviate them. Also, the mutability of a constitutional principle, based upon shifting political and social judgments, undermines the chances for consistent application of the Constitution from one generation to the next, a critical feature of its coherent interpretation. * * *

If it is the individual who is entitled to judicial protection against classifications based upon his racial or ethnic background because such distinctions impinge upon personal rights, rather than the individual only because of his membership in a particular group, then constitutional standards may be applied consistently. * * *

IV

We have held that in "order to justify the use of a suspect classification, a State must show that its purpose or interest is both constitutionally permissible and substantial, and that its use of the classification is 'necessary * * * to the accomplishment' of its purpose or the safeguarding of its interest." *Loving v. Virginia*, 388 U.S. [1,] 11 [(1967)]. The special admissions program purports to serve the purposes of: (i) "reducing the historic deficit of traditionally disfavored minorities in medical schools and in the medical profession," (ii) countering the effects of societal discrimination;[43]

B

* * *

We have never approved a classification that aids persons perceived as members of relatively victimized groups at the expense of other innocent individuals in the absence of judicial, legislative, or administrative findings of constitutional or statutory violations. After such findings have been made, the governmental interest in preferring members of the injured groups at the expense of others is substantial, since the legal rights of the victims must be vindicated. In such a case, the extent of the injury and the consequent remedy will have been judicially, legislatively, or administratively defined. Also, the remedial action usually remains subject to continuing oversight to assure that it will work the least harm possible to other innocent persons competing for the benefit. Without such findings of that the government has any greater interest in helping one individual than in refraining from harming another. Thus, the government has any greater interest in helping one individual than in refraining from harming another. Thus, the government has no compelling justification for inflicting such harm.

Petitioner does not purport to have made, and is in no position to make, such findings. Its broad mission is education, not the formulation of any legislative policy or the adjudication of particular claims of illegality. * * * [I]solated segments of our vast governments structures are not competent to make those decisions, at least in the absence of legislative mandates and legislatively determined criteria.

Hence, the purpose of helping certain groups whom the faculty of the Davis Medical School perceived as victims of "societal discrimination" does not justify a classification that imposes disadvantages upon

---

43. A number of distinct subgoals have been advanced as falling under the rubric of "compensation for past discrimination." For example, it is said that preferences for Negro applicants may compensate for harm done them personally, or serve to place them at economic levels they might have attained but for discrimination against their forebears. Greenawalt, [*Judicial Scrutiny of "Benign" Racial Preference in Law School Admissions*, 75 Colum. L. Rev. 559 (1975)], at 5581–586. Another view of the "compensation" goal is that is serves as a form of reparation by the "majority" to a victimized group as a whole. B. Bittker, The Case for Black Reparations (1973). That justification for racial or ethnic preference has been subjected to much criticism. *E.g.,* Greenawalt, *supra* * * *, at 581; Posner, [*The DeFunis Case and the Constitutionality of Preferential Treatment of Racial Minorities*, 1974 Sup. Ct. Rev. 1], at 16–17, and n. 33. Finally, it has been argued that ethnic preferences "compensate" the group by providing examples of success whom other members of the group will emulate, thereby advancing the group's interest and society's interest in encouraging new generations to overcome the barriers and frustrations of the past. Redish, [*Preferential Law School Admissions and the Equal Protection Clause: An Analysis of the Competing Arguments*, 22 UCLA L. Rev. 343 (1974)], at 391. For purposes of analysis these subgoals need not be considered separately. * * *

persons like respondent, who bear no responsibility for whatever harm the beneficiaries of the special admissions program are thought to have suffered. To hold otherwise would be to convert a remedy heretofore reserved for violations of legal rights into a privilege that all institutions throughout the Nation could grant at their pleasure to whatever groups are perceived as victims of societal discrimination. That is a step we have never approved.

Petitioner identifies, as another purpose of its program, improving the delivery of health-care services to communities currently under-served. It may be assumed that in some situations a State's interest in facilitating the health care of its citizens is sufficiently compelling to support the use of a suspect classification. But there is virtually no evidence in the record indicating that petitioner's special admissions program is either needed or geared to promote that goal. * * *

The fourth goal asserted by petitioner is the attainment of a diverse student body. This clearly is a constitutionally permissible goal for an institution of higher education. Academic freedom, though not a specifi-cally enumerated constitutional right, long has been viewed as a special concern of the First Amendment. The freedom of a university to make its own judgments as to education includes the selection of its student body. * * *

The atmosphere of "speculation, experiment and creation"—so es-sential to the quality of higher education—is widely believed to be promoted by a diverse student body. As the Court noted in *Keyishian* [*v. Boards of Regents*, 385 U.S. 589, 603 (1967)], it is not too much to say that the "nation's future depends upon leaders trained through wide exposure" to the ideas and mores of students as diverse as this Nation of many peoples.

Thus in arguing that its universities must be accorded the right to select those students who will contribute the most to the "robust exchange of ideas," petitioner invokes a countervailing constitutional interest, that of the First Amendment. In this light, petitioner must be viewed as seeking to achieve a goal that is of paramount importance in the fulfillment of its mission. * * *

Ethnic diversity, however, is only one element in a range of factors a university properly may consider in attaining the goal of a heterogeneous student body. Although a university must have a wide discretion in making the sensitive judgments as to who should be admitted, constitu-tional limitations protecting individual rights may not be disregarded. Respondents urges—and the courts below have held—that petitioner's dual admissions program is a racial classification that impermissibly infringes his rights under the Fourteenth Amendment. As the interest of diversity is compelling in the context of a university's admissions pro-gram, the question remains whether the program's racial classification is necessary to promote this interest.

V

A

It may be assumed that the reservation of a specified number of seats in each class for individuals from the preferred ethnic groups would contribute to the attainment of considerable ethnic diversity in the student body. But petitioner's argument that this is the only effective means of serving the interest of diversity is seriously flawed. In a most fundamental sense the argument misconceives the nature of the state interest that would justify consideration of race or ethnic groups, with the remaining percentage an undifferentiated aggregation of students. The diversity that furthers a compelling state interest encompasses a far broader array of qualifications and characteristics of which racial or ethnic origin is but a single though important element. Petitioner's special admissions program, focused *solely* on ethnic diversity, would hinder rather than further attainment of genuine diversity.

Nor would the state interest in genuine diversity be served by expanding petitioner's two-track system into a multitrack program with a prescribed number of seats set aside for each identifiable category of applicants. Indeed, it is inconceivable that a university would thus pursue the logic of petitioner's two-track program to the illogical end of insulating each category of applicants with certain desired qualifications from competition with all other applicants.

The experience of other university admissions programs, which take race into account in achieving the educational diversity valued by the First Amendment, demonstrates that the assignment of a fixed number of places to a minority group is not a necessary means toward that end. An illuminating example is found in the Harvard College program:

> "In recent years Harvard College has expanded the concept of diversity to include students from disadvantaged economic, racial and ethnic groups. Harvard College now recruits not only Californians or Louisianians but also blacks and Chicanos and other minority students * * *
>
> In practice, this new definition of diversity has meant that race has been a factor in some admission decisions. When the Committee on Admissions reviews the large middle group of applicants who are 'admissible' and deemed capable of doing good work in their courses, the race of an applicant may tip the balance in his favor just as geographic origin or a life spent on a farm may tip the balance in other candidates' cases. A farm boy from Idaho can bring something to Harvard College that a Bostonian cannot offer. Similarly, a black student can usually bring something that a white person cannot offer * * * "

In such an admissions program, race or ethnic background may be deemed a "plus" in a particular applicants file, yet it does not insulate the individual from comparison with all other candidates for the available seats. The file of a particular black applicant may be examined for his potential contribution to diversity without the factor of race being decisive when compared, for example, with that of an applicant identified as an Italian–American if the latter is thought to exhibit qualities more likely to promote beneficial educational pluralism. Such qualities could include exceptional personal talents, unique work or service experience, leadership potential, maturity, demonstrated compassion, a history of overcoming disadvantage, ability to communicate with the poor, or other qualifications deemed important. In short, an admissions program operated in this way is flexible enough to consider all pertinent elements of diversity in light of the particular qualifications of each applicant, and to place them on the same footing for consideration, although not necessarily according them the same weight. Indeed, the weight attributed to a particular quality may vary from year to year depending upon the "mix" both of the student body and the applicants for the incoming class.

* * *

The fatal flaw in petitioner's preferential program is its disregard of individual rights as guaranteed by the Fourteenth Amendment. Such rights are not absolute. But when a State's distribution of benefits or imposition of burdens hinges on ancestry or the color of a person's skin, that individual is entitled to a demonstration that the challenged classification is necessary to promote a substantial state interest. Petitioner has failed to carry this burden. * * *

Opinion of Mr. Justice Brennan, Mr. Justice White, Mr. Justice Marshall, and Mr. Justice Blackmun, concurring in the judgment in part and dissenting in part.

The Court today * * * affirms the constitutional power of [the government] to act affirmatively to achieve equal opportunity for all. The difficulty of the issue presented—whether government may use race-conscious programs to redress the continuing effects of past discrimination—and the mature consideration which each of our Brethren has brought to it have resulted in many opinions, no single one speaking for the Court. But this should not and must not mask the central meaning of today's opinions: Government may take race into account when it acts not to demean or insult any racial group, but to remedy disadvantages cast on minorities by past governments or administrative bodies with competence to act in this area.

I

Our Nation was founded on the principle that "all Men are created equal". Yet candor requires acknowledgement that the Framers of our Constitution, to forge the 13 Colonies into one Nation, openly compromised this principle of equality with its antithesis: slavery. The consequences of this compromise are well known and have aptly been called our "American Dilemma." Still, it is well to recount how recent the time has been, if it has yet come, when the promise of our principles has flowered into the actuality of equal opportunity for all regardless of race or color.

The Fourteenth Amendment, the embodiment in the Constitution of our abiding belief in human equality, has been the law of our land for only slightly more than half of its 200 years. And for half of that half, the Equal Protection Clause of the Amendment was largely moribund * * *. Worse than desuetude, the Clause was early turned against those whom it was intended to set free, condemning them to a "separate but equal" status before the law, a status always separate but seldom equal. Not until 1954—only 24 years ago—was this odious doctrine interred by our decision in *Brown v. Board of Education*, 347 U.S. 483 [(1954)] (*Brown I*), and its progeny, which proclaimed that separate schools and public facilities of all sorts were inherently unequal and forbidden under our Constitution. * * *

Against this background, claims that law must be "colorblind" or that the datum of race is no longer relevant to public policy must be seen as aspiration rather than as description of reality. This is not to denigrate aspiration; for reality rebukes us that race has too often been used by those who stigmatize and oppress minorities. Yet we cannot—and, as we shall demonstrate, need not under our Constitution—let color blindness become myopia which masks the reality that many "created equal" have been treated within our lifetimes as inferior both by the law and by their fellow citizens.

* * *

III

A

* * *

We conclude, * * * that racial classifications are not *per se* invalid under the Fourteenth Amendment. Accordingly, we turn to the problem of articulating what our role should be reviewing state action that expressly classifies by race.

* * *

Unquestionably we have held that a government practice or statute which restricts "fundamental rights" or which contains "suspect classifications" is to be subjected to "strict scrutiny" and can be justified only if it furthers a compelling government purpose and, even then only if no less restrictive alternative is available. But no fundamental right is involved here. Nor do whites as a class have any of the "traditional indicia of suspectness: the class is not saddled with such disabilities, or subjected to such a history of purposeful unequal treatment, or relegated to such a position of political powerlessness as to command extraordinary protection from the majoritarian political process."

Moreover, if the University's representations are credited, this is not a case where racial classifications are "irrelevant and therefore prohibited." Nor has anyone suggested that the University's purposes contravene the cardinal principle that racial classifications that stigmatize—because they are drawn on the presumption that one race is inferior to another or because they put the weight of government behind racial hatred and separatism—are invalid without more.

On the other hand, the fact that this case does not fit neatly into our analytic framework for race cases does not mean that it should be analyzed by applying the very loose rational-basis standard of review that is the very least that is always applied in equal protection cases. "[The] mere recitation of a benign, compensatory purpose is not an automatic shield which protects against any inquiry into the actual purposes underlying a statutory scheme." *Califano v. Webster*, 430 U.S. 313, 317 (1977). Instead, a number of considerations—developed in gender-discrimination cases but which carry even more force when applied to racial classifications—lead us to conclude that racial classifications designed to further remedial purposes "must serve important governmental objectives and must be substantially related to achievement of those objectives." *Califano v. Webster, supra,* at 317, quoting *Craig v. Boren,* 429 U.S. 190, 197 (1976).

First, race, like, "gender-based classifications too often [has] been inexcusably utilized to stereotype and stigmatize politically powerless segments of society." While a carefully tailored statute designed to remedy past discrimination could avoid these vices, we nonetheless have recognized that the line between honest and thoughtful appraisal of the effects of past discrimination and paternalistic stereotyping is not so clear and that a statute based on the latter is patently capable of stigmatizing all women with a badge of inferiority. State programs designed ostensibly to ameliorate the effects of past racial discrimination obviously create the same hazard of stigma, since they may promote racial separatism and reinforce the views of those who believe that members of racial minorities are inherently incapable of succeeding on their own.

Second, race, like gender and illegitimacy is an immutable characteristic which its possessors are powerless to escape or set aside. While a classification is not *per se* invalid because it divides classes on the basis of immutable characteristics, it is nevertheless true that such divisions are contrary to our deep belief that "legal burdens should bear some relationship to individual responsibility or wrongdoing," and that the advancement sanctioned, sponsored, or approved by the State should ideally be based on individual merit or achievement, or at the least on factors, within the control of an individual.

    * * *

IV

Davis' articulated purpose of remedying the effects of past societal discrimination is, under our cases, sufficiently important to justify the use of race-conscious admissions programs where there is a sound basis for concluding that minority underrepresentation is substantial and chronic, and that the handicap of past discrimination is impeding access of minorities to the Medical School.

A

Finally, the conclusion that state educational institutions may constitutionally adopt admissions programs designed to avoid exclusion of historically disadvantaged minorities, even when such programs explicitly take race into account, finds direct support in our cases construing congressional legislation designed to overcome the present effects of past discrimination.

* * * [T]he presence or absence of past discrimination by universities or employers is largely irrelevant to resolving respondent's constitutional claims. The claims of those burdened by the race-conscious actions of a university or employer who has never been adjudged in violation of an antidiscrimination law are not any more or less entitled to deference than the claims of the burdened nonminority workers in *Franks v. Bowman Transportation Co.,* [424 U.S. 747 (1976)], for in each case the employees are innocent of past discrimination. And, although it might be argued that, where an employer has violated an antidiscrimination law, the expectations of nonminority workers are themselves products of discrimination and hence "tainted," and therefore more easily upset, the same argument can be made with respect to respondent. If it was reasonable to conclude—as we hold that it was—that the failure of minorities to qualify for admission at Davis under regular procedures was due principally to the effects of past discrimination, then there is a reasonable likelihood that, but for pervasive racial discrimination, respondent would have failed to qualify for admission even in the absence of Davis' special admissions program.

* * *

C

The second prong of our test—whether the Davis program stigmatizes any discrete group or individual and whether race is reasonably used in light of the program's objectives—is clearly satisfied by the Davis program.

It is not even claimed that Davis' program in any way operates to stigmatize or single out any discrete and insular, or even any identifiable, nonminority group. Nor will harm comparable to that imposed upon racial minorities by exclusion or separation on grounds of race be the likely result of the program. It does not, for example, establish an exclusive preserve for minority students apart from and exclusive of whites. Rather, its purpose is to overcome the effects of segregation by bringing the races together. True, whites are excluded from participation in the special admissions program, but this fact only operates to reduce the number of whites to be admitted in the regular admissions program in order to permit admission of a reasonable percentage—less than their proportion of the California population—of otherwise underrepresented qualified minority applicants.

Nor was Bakke in any sense stamped as inferior by the Medical School's rejection of him. * * *

Finally, Davis' special admissions program cannot be said to violate the Constitution simply because it has set aside a predetermined number of places for qualified minority applicants rather than using minority status as a positive factor to be considered in evaluating the applications of disadvantaged minority applicants. For purposes of constitutional adjudication, there is no difference between the two approaches. In any admissions program which accords special consideration to disadvantaged racial minorities, a determination of the degree of preference to be given is unavoidable, and any given preference that results in the exclusion of a white candidate is not more or less constitutionally acceptable than a program such as that at Davis.

* * *

STATE OF UTTAR PRADESH v. PRADIP TANDON

Supreme Court (India).
(1975) 1 S.C.C. 267.

[The state reserved a number of places in its medical school for candidates from rural areas, hill areas, and the Uttrakhand area. Out of a total 782 places, 117 were reserved for candidates from the rural area and 25 each for candidates from the other two areas. The reservation of places was challenged as unconstitutional by other applicants to the state medical school.]

The Judgment of the Court was delivered by Ray, C.J.

The principal question for consideration in these appeals * * * is whether the instructions framed by the State in making reservations in favour of candidates from rural areas, hill areas and Uttrakhand are constitutionally valid. These reservations were made by the State Government for admission of students to medical colleges in the State of Uttar Pradesh.

* * *

5. The affidavit evidence on behalf of the State was this. The Government in the years 1952 and 1953 made reservations for Kisan hill area candidates. The Government reviewed the position from time to time. The reservations are considered necessary to attract graduates from those areas which are otherwise handicapped in the matter of education. It is necessary to feed the dispensaries with medical men in adequate number to serve the people inhabiting those areas. The rural, hill and Uttrakhand areas lack educational facilities. People living there are illiterate or have a very modest education. Their economic condition is unsatisfactory. The level of income is low. There is acute poverty. There is lack and in some cases total absence of communication and transportation. Historically these areas have been neglected. People living in those areas are socially backward. The percentage of education among them is low. Candidates from those areas on account of various difficulties and handicaps cannot generally compete on parallel or equal footing with other candidates. The State maintains and financially supports the medical colleges. The State can, therefore, claim to lay down the criterion for admission to those colleges. The State classified these rural, hill and Uttrakhand areas as socially and educationally backward areas.

* * *

11. The Attorney General laid considerable stress on the feature that rural India is socially and educationally backward by reason of poverty. He said that the Court should take judicial notice of the extreme poverty in these areas. The rural people were said to have common traits of agriculture and they were all conditioned by economic poverty. Articles 41 and 46 were put in the forefront that the right to education was one of the provisions in the Directive Principles of State Policy. The State is to promote with special care the educational and economic interests of the weaker sections of the people.

12. Article 15(1) states that the State shall not discriminate against any citizen on grounds only of religion, race, caste, sex, place of birth or any of them. The Attorney General submitted that the reservation was not grounds only of place of birth or caste. Article 29(2) states that no citizen shall be denied admission into any educational institution maintained by the State or receiving aid out of State funds on grounds only of religion, race, caste, language or any of them. It is said by the Attorney General that * * * place of birth is not mentioned in Article 29(2). The Attorney General submitted that the reservations in the present case were not on ground of place of birth but on ground of residence, and, therefore, the reservations would not fall within the mischief of either Article 15(1) or Article 29(2).

13. Article 15(4) was added by the Constitution First Amendment Act, 1951. The object of the amendment was to bring Articles 15 and 29 in line with Article 16(4). Article 16(4) states that nothing in that Article shall prevent the State from making any provision for the reservation of appointments or posts in favour of any backward class of citizens which in the opinion of the State is not adequately represented in the services under the State. In the *State of Madras v. Smt. Champakam Dorairajan*[3] the reservation for seats for non-Brahmins, backward Hindus, Brahmins, Harijans, Anglo–Indians and Indian Christians and Muslims was held to offend Articles 15(1) and 29(2). This Court pointed out that the omission of a clause like Article 16(4) from Article 29 indicated the intention of the Constitution makers not to introduce communal consideration in matters of admission to educational institutions.

14. Article 15(4) speaks of socially and educationally backward classes of citizens. The State described the rural, hill, and Uttrakhand areas as socially and educationally backward areas. The Constitution does not enable the State to bring socially and educationally backward areas within the protection of Article 15(4). The Attorney General however submitted that the affidavit evidence established the rural, hill, and Uttrakhand areas to have socially and educationally backward classes of citizens. The backwardness contemplated under Article 15(4) is both social and educational. Article 15(4) speaks of backwardness of classes of citizens. The accent is on classes of citizens. Article 15(4) also speaks of Scheduled Castes and Scheduled Tribes. Therefore, socially and educationally backward classes of citizens in Article 15(4) could not be equated with castes. * * *

15. Broadly stated, neither caste nor race nor religion can be made the basis of classification for the purposes of determining social and educational backwardness within the meaning of Article 15(4). When Article 15(1) forbids discrimination on grounds only of religion, race, caste, caste cannot be made one of the criteria for determining social and educational backwardness. If caste or religion is recognised as a criterion of social and educational backwardness Article 15(4) will stultify Article 15(1). It is true that Article 15(1) forbids discrimination only on the ground of religion, race, caste, but when a classification takes recourse to caste as one of the criteria in determining socially and educationally

3. 1951 SCR 525: AIR 1951 SC 226: 1951 SCJ 313.

backward classes the expression "classes" in that case violates the rule of *expression unius est exclusio alterius*. The socially and educationally backward classes of citizens are groups other than groups based on caste.

16. * * * It is difficult to define the expression "socially and educationally backward classes of citizens". The traditional unchanging occupations of citizens may contribute to social and educational backwardness. The place of habitation and its environment is also a determining factor in judging the social and educational backwardness.

* * *

20. Educational backwardness is ascertained with reference to these factors. Where people have traditional apathy for education on account of social and environmental conditions or occupational handicaps, it is an illustration of educational backwardness. The hill and Uttrakhand areas are inaccessible. There is lack of educational institutions and educational aids. People in the hill and Uttrakhand areas illustrate the educationally backward classes of citizens because lack of educational facilities keep them stagnant and they have neither meaning and values nor awareness for education.

* * *

22. In *Triloki Nath v. State of J. & K.* [(1969) 1 S.C.R. 103: AIR 1969 SC 1] this Court said that the members of an entire caste or community may, in the social, economic and educational scale of values at a given time, be backward and may, on that account be treated as a backward class, but that is not because they are members of a caste or community, but because they form a class.

23. In *Balaji's case* this Court said that social backwardness is in the ultimate analysis the result of poverty to a large extent and that the problem of backward classes is in substance the problem of rural India. Extracting these observations the Attorney General contended that poverty is not only relevant but is one of the elements in determining social backwardness. We are unable to accept the test of poverty as the determining factor of social backwardness.

* * *

25. Some people in the rural areas may be educationally backward, some may be socially backward, there may be few who are both socially and educationally backward, but it cannot be said that all citizens residing in rural areas are socially and educationally backward.

26. Eighty per cent of the population in the State of Uttar Pradesh in rural areas cannot be said to be a homogeneous class by itself. They are not of the same kind. Their occupation is different. Their standards are different. Their lives are different. Population cannot be a class by itself. Rural element does not make it a class. To suggest that the rural areas are socially and educationally backward is to have reservation for the majority of the State.

27. On behalf of the State it is said that it is necessary to have reservation of seats for the people from rural areas in order to attract people from those areas who are otherwise handicapped in the matter of

education, so that they can serve the people in the rural areas on completion of their medical education. In order to attract medical men for service in rural areas arrangements are to be made to attract them. The special need for medical men in rural areas will not make the people in the rural areas socially and educationally backward classes of citizens.

28.   It was said that the number of marks obtained by candidates from rural areas showed that they were much lower than the marks obtained by general candidates and this would indicate educational backwardness. That is neither a valid nor a justifiable ground for determining social and educational backwardness. Educational institutions should attract the best talents. It has been held by this Court in *Balaji's case (supra)* that 50 per cent of the seats in educational institutions should be left open to general competition. In the present case, it appears that 85 candidates from rural areas were selected in the general seats. One candidate from Uttrakhand area, 7 candidates from hill areas and one Scheduled Caste candidate also competed for the general seats. The candidates from hill areas, Uttrakhand division and Scheduled Castes are exceptions and their performance will not detract from the reservations for Scheduled Caste, hill and Uttrakhand areas. The performance of 85 candidates from rural areas speaks eloquently for the high standards of education in rural areas.

29.   The reservation for rural areas cannot be sustained on the ground that the rural areas represent socially and educationally backward classes of citizens. This reservation appears to be made for the majority population of the State. Eighty per cent of the population of the State cannot be a homogeneous class. Poverty in rural areas cannot be the basis of classification to support reservation for rural areas. Poverty is found in all parts of India. In the instructions for reservation of seats from rural areas must submit a certificate of the District Magistrate of the District to which he belonged that he was born in a rural area and had a permanent home there, and is residing there or that he was born in India and his parents and guardians are still living there and earn their livelihood there. The incident of birth in rural areas is made the basic qualification. No reservation can be made on the basis of place of birth, as this would offend Article 15.

30.   The onus of proof is on the State to establish that the reservations are for socially and educationally backward classes of citizens.
        * * *

37.   In the present case, the reservation for the rural area cannot be upheld because there is no classification based on residence between students coming from within the State and others coming from without. The object of providing medical education to students in Uttar Pradesh is to secure the best possible students for admission to these colleges. It is in this context that district-wise allocation was held by this Court in *Rajendran v. State of Madras*[11] to violate Article 14. The university wide distribution of seats which was found to be valid in *Chanchala's case*

11. (1968) 2 SCR 786: AIR 1968 SC
1012: (1968) 2 SCJ 801.

[*D.N. Chanchala v. State of Mysore*, 1971 Supp. S.C.R. 608: (1971) 2 S.C.C. 293] does not have any application in the present case.

38.   The submission of the Attorney General that rural population would be source for drawing students cannot be upheld. An illustration of different sources of categories of students is *Chitra Ghosh v. Union of India*[12]. There the categories of students were classified as residents of Delhi; sons/daughters of Central Government servants posted in Delhi; candidates whose father is dead and is wholly dependent on brother/sister who is a Central Government servant posted in Delhi; sons/daughters of residents of Union Territories including displaced persons registered therein; sons/daughters of Central Government servants posted in Indian Missions abroad; cultural scholars; Colombo Plan Scholars; Thailand Scholars and Jammu & Kashmir State Scholars. Rural areas in Uttar Pradesh cannot be said to be a source for reservation of the type in *Chitra Ghosh's case*.

39.   The Attorney General relied on *Beryl F. Carroll v. Greenwich Insurance Co. of New York*[13]; *Weaver v. Palmer Brothers Co.*[14] and *West Coast Hotel Co. v. Ernest Parrish*[15] in support of the proposition that if an evil is especially experienced in a particular branch of business, the Constitution embodies no prohibition of laws confined to the evil or doctrinaire requirement that they should be couched in all embracing terms. It was said that if the law was intended to remove the evil where it was most felt it was not to be overthrown because there were other instances to which it might have been applied. This rule really means that there is no doctrinaire requirement that the legislation should be couched in all embracing terms. A case of under classification would be an instance of this rule. The present case of classification of rural areas is not one of under classification. This is a case of discrimination in favour of the majority of rural population to the prejudice of students drawn from the general category. This classification is unconstitutional.

* * *

42.   For these reasons we hold that the reservation in favour of candidates from rural areas is unconstitutional. The reservations for the hill and Uttrakhand areas are severable and these are valid.

HELLMUT MARSCHALL v. LAND NORDHEIN–WESTFALEN

European Court of Justice.
[1998]1 C.M.L.R. 547 (1997).

[Marschall, a male teacher, applied for a promotion that was eventually awarded to an equally qualified female teacher. This was done pursuant to the Civil Servant Act of the German *Land* of Nordhein–Westfalen, which provided that, where women were underrepresented in the workforce, a woman candidate ought to be awarded a position over an equally qualified man.]

12.   (1970) 1 SCR 413: (1969) 2 SCC 228.

13.   50 L Ed 246.

14.   70 L Ed 654.

15.   81 L Ed 703.

JUDGMENT

[1]   * * * [T]he Verwaltungsgericht (Administrative Court) Gelsen-kirchen referred to th[is] Court for a preliminary ruling under Article 177 E.C. a question on the interpretation of Article 2(1) and (4) of Council Directive 76/207 on the implementation of the principle of equal treatment for men and women as regards access to employment, voca-tional training and promotion, and working conditions hereinafter "the Directive".

[2]   That question has been raised in proceedings between Helmut Marschall and Land NordrheinWestfalen (Land of North Rhine–West-phalia, hereinafter "the Land") concerning his application for a higher-grade post at the Gesamtschule (comprehensive school) Schwerte in Germany.

[3]   The * * * (Law on Civil Servants of the Land) * * * provides:

"Where, in the sector of the authority responsible for promotion, there are fewer women than men in the particular higher grade post in the career bracket, women are to be given priority for promotion in the event of equal suitability, competence and professional performance, unless reasons specific to an individual [male] candidate tilt the balance in his favour."

[4]   According to the observations of the Land, the rule of priority laid down by that provision introduced an additional promotion criteri-on, that of being a female, in order to counteract applying for the same post: where qualifications are equal, employers tend to promote men rather than women because they apply traditional promotion criteria which in practice put women at a disadvantage, such as age, seniority and the fact that a male candidate is a head of household and sole breadwinner for the household.

[5]   In providing that priority is to be given to the promotion of women "unless reasons specific to an individual [male] candidate tilt the balance in his favour", the legislature deliberately chose, according to the Land, a legally imprecise expression in order to ensure sufficient flexibility and, in particular, to allow the administration latitude to take into account any reasons which may be specific to individual candidates. Consequently, notwithstanding the rule of priority, the administration can always give preference to a male candidate on the basis of promotion criteria, traditional or otherwise.

[6]   According to the order for reference, Mr. Marschall works as a tenured teacher for the Land, his salary being that attaching to the basic grade in career bracket A12.

                       * * *

[10]   The Verwaltungsgericht, finding that Mr. Marschall and the woman candidate selected were equally qualified for the post, decided that the outcome of the proceedings depended on the compatibility of the provision in question with Article 2(1) and (4) of the Directive.

[11]   Relying on the judgment of this Court in Case C–450/93, *Kalanke v. Freie Hansestadt Bremen* [[1996] 1 C.M.L.R. 175 (1995)], the Verwaltungsgericht considers that the priority which the provision in

question accords in principle to women seems to constitute discrimination within the meaning of Article 2(1) of the Directive and that such discrimination is not eliminated by the possibility of giving preference, exceptionally, to male candidates.

[12]   That court also doubts whether the provision in question is covered by the exception provided for in Article 2(4) of the Directive allows only measures for promoting equality of opportunity.

[13]   The Verwaltungsgericht therefore decided to stay proceedings and to refer the following question to the Court for a preliminary ruling:

Does Article 2(1) and (4) of Council Directive 76/207 on the implementation of the principle of equal treatment for men and women as regards access to employment, vocational training and promotion, and working conditions, preclude a rule of national law which provides that, sectors of the public service in which fewer women than men are employed in the relevant higher grade post in a career bracket, women must be given priority where male and female candidates for promotion are equally qualified (in terms of suitability, competence and professional performance), unless reasons specific to an individual male candidate tilt the balance in his favour.

[14]   The *Land*, the Spanish, Austrian, Finnish, Swedish and Norwegian Governments and the Commission consider that a national rule such as the provision in question constitutes a measure for promoting equality of opportunity between men and women which falls within the scope of Article 2(4) of the Directive.

[15]   The *Land* observes in this regard that the priority accorded to female candidates is intended to counteract traditional promotion criteria without, however, replacing them. The Austrian Government considers that a national rule such as that in question is designed to correct discriminatory procedures in the selection of staff.

[16]   The Finnish, Swedish and Norwegian Governments add that the national rule in question promotes access by women to posts of responsibility and thus helps to restore balance to labour markets which, in their present state, are still broadly partitioned on the basis of gender in that they concentrate female labour in lower positions in the occupational hierarchy. According to the Finnish Government, past experience shows in particular that action limited to providing occupational training and guidance for women or to influencing the sharing of occupational and family responsibilities is not sufficient to put an end to this partitioning of labour markets.

[17]   Finally, the *Land* and all those governments take the view that the provision in question does not guarantee absolute and unconditional priority for women and that it is therefore within the limits outlined by the Court in Kalanke.

[18]   The French and the United Kingdom Governments, on the other hand, consider that the provision in question is not covered by the derogation provided for in Article 2(4) of the Directive.

[19]   Those two governments submit that in providing for priority to be accorded to female candidates the provision goes further than

promoting equality of opportunity and aims to bring about equality of representation between men and women, so that the Court's reasoning in Kalanke applies.

[20]   Nor, in their view, does the presence of a saving clause make the provision in question any less discriminatory. That clause applies only exceptionally and therefore has no impact in a "normal" case where there are no reasons specific to the male candidate which are such as to outweigh the general requirement to appoint the female candidate. Since, moreover, it is formulated in terms that are both general and imprecise the clause is contrary to the principle of legal certainty.

[21]   The Court observes that the purpose of the Directive, as is clear from Article 1(1), is to put into effect in the Member States the principle of equal treatment for men and women as regards, *inter alia,* access to employment, including promotion. Article 2(1) states that the principle of equal treatment

[22]   According to Article 2(4), the Directive is to "be without prejudice to measures to promote equal opportunity for men and women, in particular by removing existing inequalities which affect women's opportunities in the areas referred to in Article 1(1)".

[23]   In paragraph [16] of its judgment in *Kalanke*, the Court held that a national rule which provides that, where equally qualified men and women are candidates for the same promotion in fields where there are fewer women than men at the level of the relevant post, women are automatically to be given priority, involves discrimination of grounds of sex.

[24]   However, unlike the provisions in question in *Kalanke*, the provision in question in this case contains a clause to the effect that women are not to be given priority in promotion if reasons specific to an individual male candidate tilt the balance in his favour.

[25]   It is therefore necessary to consider whether a national rule containing such a clause is designed to promote equality of opportunity between men and women within the meaning of Article 2(4) of the Directive.

[26]   Article 2(4) is specifically and exclusively designed to authorise measures which, although discriminatory in appearance, are in fact intended to eliminate or reduce actual instances of inequality which may exist in the reality of social life.

[27]   It thus authorises national measures relating to access to employment, including promotion, which give a specific advantage to women with a view to improving their ability to compete on the labour market and to pursue a career on an equal footing with men.

[28]   As the Council stated in the third recital in the preamble to Recommendation 84/635 of 13 December 1984 on the promotion of positive action for women, "existing legal provisions on equal treatment, which are designed to afford rights to individuals, are inadequate for the elimination of all existing inequalities unless parallel action is taken by governments, both sides of industry and other bodies concerned, to

counteract the prejudicial effects on women in employment which arise from social attitudes, behaviour and structures.''

[29]   As the *Land* and several governments have pointed out, it appears that even where male and female candidates are equally qualified, male candidates tend to be promoted in preference to female candidates particularly because of prejudices and stereotypes concerning the role and capacities of women in working life and the fear, for example, that women will interrupt their careers more frequently, that owing to household and family duties they will be less flexible in their working hours, or that they will be absent from work more frequently because of pregnancy, childbirth and breastfeeding.

[30]   For these reasons, the mere fact that a male candidate and a female candidate are equally qualified does not mean that they have the same chances.

[31]   It follows that a national rule in terms of which, subject to the application of the saving clause, female candidates for promotion who are equally as qualified as the male candidates are to be treated preferentially in sectors where they are under-represented may fall within the scope of Article 2(4) if such a rule may counteract the prejudicial effects on female candidates of the attitudes and behaviour described above and thus reduce actual instances of inequality which may exist in the real world.

[32]   However, since Article 2(4) constitutes a derogation from an individual right laid down by the Directive, such a national measure specifically favouring female candidates cannot guarantee absolute and unconditional priority for women in the vent of a promotion without going beyond the limits of the exception laid down in that provision.

[33]   Unlike the rules at issue in *Kalanke*, a national rule which, as in the case in point in the main proceedings, contains a saving clause does not exceed those limits if, in each individual case, it provides for male candidates who are equally as qualified as the female candidates a guarantee that the candidatures will be the subject of an objective assessment which will take account of all criteria specific to the individual candidates and will override the priority accorded to female candidates where one or more of those criteria tilts the balance in favour of the male candidate. In this respect, however, it should be remembered that those criteria must not be such as to discriminate against female candidates.

[34]   It is for the national court to determine whether those conditions are fulfilled on the basis of an examination of the scope of the provision in question as it has been applied by the *Land*.

[35]   The answer to be given to the national court must therefore be that a national rule which, in a case where there are fewer women than men at the level of the relevant post in a sector of the public service, and both female and male candidates for the post are equally qualified in terms of their suitability, competence and professional performance, requires that priority be given to the promotion of female candidates unless reasons specific to an individual male candidate tilt the

balance in his favour is not precluded by Article 2(1) and (4) of the Directive, provided that:

>—in each individual case the rule provides for male candidates who are equally as qualified as the female candidates a guarantee that the candidatures will be the subject of an objective assessment which will take account of all criteria specific to the individual candidates and will override the priority accorded to female candidates where one or more of those criteria tilts the balance in favour of the male candidate, and

>—such criteria are not such as to discriminate against the female candidates.

FEMININE QUOTAS CASE

Constitutional Council (France).
82–146 DC of 18 November 1982.[e]

Background: A parliamentary amendment by Socialist deputies was inserted into a *loi* amending the Electoral Code for local elections. The provision in question sought to require that the lists of candidates drawn up by the parties, from which the electors would choose, should contain a maximum of 75 per cent of persons of the same sex. In other words, women would be guaranteed a minimum of 25 per cent of the places on the list of candidates. The Government is understood to have indicated to the Conseil that it did not attach much importance to the provision, and the Conseil, seized of the *loi* on other grounds, declared the provision *unconstitutional*.

DECISION:

* * *

4.   Considering that, by virtue of article 4 of the *loi* submitted to the Conseil, municipal councilors of towns of 3,500 inhabitants or more are elected by voting from a list; that voters can alter neither the content nor the order of presentation on the lists, and, by virtue of article L260 *bis*: 'the lists of candidates cannot include more than 75 per cent of persons of the same *sex*';

5.   Considering that, according to article 3 of the Constitution:

"National sovereignty belongs to the people, which shall exercise it by its representatives and by means of referendum.

No section of the people, nor any individual, may arrogate its exercise to itself.

Suffrage may be direct or indirect, under the conditions provided by the Constitution. It shall always be universal, equal, and secret.

Within the terms settled by *loi*, all adult French nationals of both sexes, enjoying their civil and political rights, are voters."

and according to article 6 of the Declaration of Rights and Man and of the Citizen:

"All citizens, being equal [in the eyes of the law], are equally eligible for all public dignities, positions, and employment according to their abili-

e. Reproduced from John Bell, *French Constitutional Law* 349–50 (1992).

ties, and without distinction other than that of their virtues and talents'';

6.   Considering that it follows from a comparison of these texts that the status of citizen itself gives rise to the right to vote and to be eligible on identical terms to all who are not excluded by reason of age, incapacity, or nationality, or for any reason designed to protect the freedom of the voter or the independence of the person elected; that these principles of constitutional value oppose any division of voters or eligible candidates into categories; that this applies for all political elections, especially for the election of municipal councillors;

7.   Considering that it follows from what has been said that the rule that, in establishing the lists to be submitted to voters, includes a distinction between candidates by reason of their sex is contrary to the constitutional principles mentioned above; that, thus, article L260 *bis* of the Electoral Code, as provided under article 4 of the *loi* submitted for scrutiny by the Conseil constitutional, must be declared contrary to the Constitution * * *

Notes and Questions

1.   Increasing the number of women representatives in Parliament again became an important political issue in the 1990s. In 1999, the French Constitution was amended to allow for "parity" between men and women who aspired to hold public office. A clause providing that "laws shall favor equal access by men and women to elective offices and positions" was added to Art. 3. Furthermore, the following clause was added to Art. 4: [political parties] "shall contribute to the implementation of the principle set out in the last clause of Article 3 as provided by law." Subsequent to these amendments, French electoral law required that the lists of political parties for certain elections be made up of an equal number of men and women and that the order within such lists alternate between male and female candidates. For other types of elections, the new law requires overall parity, amounting to an approximate 50–50 quota. Political parties who fail to abide by these guidelines are liable to forfeit part of their state financing. These laws were challenged as imposing quotas that were constitutionally impermissible even in the context of the new amendments. The Constitutional Council, in 2000–429 DC of 30 May 2000, largely upheld the constitutionality of the laws, with certain minor exceptions not relevant here.

The Italian Constitutional Court (ICC) struck down a law requiring that a political party's electoral list contain no more than two thirds of its candidates of the same sex. ICC–422 of 6 September 1995. Belgium also adopted a law similar to the Italian one, but its constitutionally has yet to be considered by its constitutional tribunal, the Cour d'Arbitrage.

2.   In 1994, Germany amended Art. 3 of its Basic Law to permit for affirmative action in favor of women—a policy that was felt necessary to remedy some of the inequities suffered by East German women as a consequence of the implantation of capitalism in the former regions after reunification. Article 3(2) now reads: "Men and women are equal. The state supports the effective realization of equality of women and men and works towards abolishing present disadvantages."

Regarding the current status of affirmative action in Germany, consider the following:

A.   General Methodology of German Positive Action Law

* * * [The Basic Law's] equality provisions were amended in 1994 to strengthen the positive action position of the now unified Germany. The amendment mandated the nation to work affirmatively to remove the existing disadvantages that women suffer in employment.

The practical effect of positive action law takes place through state specific statutes. Most statutes impose either quotas or binding goals on hiring and promotional processes. A "soft" quota requires preferential hiring for women with equal or "equivalent" qualifications. A "hard" quota requires preferences for less qualified women who meet formal requirements, often taking into account non-traditional skills when evaluating the quality of candidates. A binding goal is a strong preference for women with the "necessary" qualifications. The functional difference between quotas and goals is that there is no legal obligation to hire women over men in a state that only uses goals rather than quotas.

B.   Limited Scope of German Positive Action Law

German positive action law affects only the public sector. * * * Currently, the only form of positive action applied to the private sector is the use of incentives—subsidies—to private employers who voluntarily put in place positive action plans. Only three of the sixteen German states provide such incentives.

* * * Since the federal government has not yet legislated any effective positive action obligations for private employers, only public actors are bound to follow positive action statutes imposed by the states. The immediate resulting effect on East German women after reunification was devastating. While under the Socialist regime women were duty bound by the state to work full-time these women are now confronted with an inability to participate successfully in the labor market. * * *

C.   An Exception to German Positive Action Law

* * * [A]t least one exception to German positive action law still exists * * * based on the realization of "natural" or biological gender differences that are absolutely necessary conditions to employment. Biological differences include, among others, motherhood and physical strength. For example, valid provisions under German law exist that discriminate against women on the basis that the job requires the ability to carry heavy loads. While these differences in law must be absolutely necessary to fit the biological abilities of one gender to be constitutional, these restrictions based on sex seem short-sighted in that they are determined by the sex of a person rather than by his or her actual ability. The experience of women in East Germany demonstrates this shortsightedness, as many women in pre-unification East Germany were required to perform jobs that required physical strength and were traditionally dominated by men, such as blue-collar jobs. By assuming a general lack of capacity because of gender and not recognizing the individual abilities of women, German positive action law fails to support the gains made in women's employment in East Germany.

Given the rates of female unemployment in post-reunification Germany, it is obvious that German positive action law failed to provide East German women with employment protection during the economic transition of the two nations. * * * Despite its shortcomings, however, German positive action law has been increasingly effective in promoting the employment of women."

You Can't Go Home Again: A Reluctant Return to Traditional Gender Roles in Post–Reunification Germany (Book Review), Cynthia M. Guizzetti, 21 B.C. Third World L.J. 145 (2001).

What does Germany's recent experience with affirmative action for women suggest? That absent robust intervention market forces tend to strongly disadvantage women? Are such disadvantages due to prejudice? Or to pervasive social mores extending beyond the workplace?

3. The situation in India, which has resorted to affirmative action much before other constitutional democracies, is significantly different than that of other countries that have used affirmative action. Although India has used affirmative action to ameliorate the fate of women, its primary focus has been on castes.

India boldly announced a commitment to affirmative action in its 1950 Constitution, which reserves seats for members of India's lowest social castes in both the House of the People and the state legislative assemblies.[96] The constitution also permits the government to "reserv[e]" public "appointments or posts" for members of "any backward class of citizens which, in the opinion of the State, is not adequately represented in the services under the State."[97] This permission expressly qualifies a clause otherwise prohibiting discrimination in government employment.[98]

---

96. See India Const. Art. 330: id. art. 332. The constitution reserves these seats for members of "Scheduled Castes" and Scheduled Tribes." The "Scheduled Castes" are India's untouchables, citizens at the bottom of the traditional Hindu Class system. See Marc Galanter, Competing Equalities: Law and the Backward Classes in India 122 (1984). The "Scheduled Tribes" are "groups distinguished by tribal characteristics' and by their spatial and cultural isolation from the bulk of the population." Id. at 147. Members of scheduled castes make up about 15.8 percent of India's population, while the scheduled tribes constitute about 7.8 percent. See E.J. Prior, Constitutional Fairness or Fraud on the Constitution? Compensatory Discrimination in India, *28 Case W. Res. J. Int'L. 63, 67 nn. 18–19 (1996).*

97. India Const. Art. 16(4). A 1995 amendment added a similar proviso for promotions within the public service, although the latter protection applies only to members of "the Scheduled Castes and the Scheduled Tribes." Id. art. 16(4A).

The category "backward classes" in Article 16(4), as well as in the articles mentioned below, includes the scheduled castes, the scheduled tribes, and other castes suffering from disadvantage. As decisions of the Indian Supreme Court show, the proper definition of "backward classes" under these constitutional provisions is not self-evident. See, e.g., *Balaji v. State of Mysore*, A.I.R. 1963 S.C. 649 (caste may constitute one criterion for determining backwardness, but the state must look to other factors as well); *Chitralekha v. State of Mysore*, A.I.R. 1964 S.C. 1823 (consideration of caste in determining backwardness is permissible but not mandatory); *P. Rajendran v. State of Madras*, A.I.R. 1968 S.C. 1012 (state may determine that entire caste is backward and then use caste to designate backwardness); *Vasanth Kumar v. State of Karnataka*, A.I.R. 1985 S.C. 1495 (affirming use of caste as unit for identifying backward classes); *Indra Sawhney v. Union of India*, A.I.R. 1993 S.C. 477 (stating standards to determine backwardness).

98. See India Const. Art. 16(2); see also id. art. 16(1) (guaranteeing "equality of opportunity for all citizens in matters relating to employment or appointment to any office under the State").

Furthermore, India's constitution imposes a duty on the state to "promote with special care the educational and economic interests of the weaker sections of the people, and in particular, of the [most disadvantaged castes]."[99] Although this language appears in a portion of the constitution that is not judicially enforceable, it enunciates a positive governmental responsibility to assist disadvantaged classes. India's constitution thus unambiguously authorizes affirmative action and affirmatively encourages it.

Indeed, a desire to ensure the legitimacy of affirmative action prompted the first amendment to India's Constitution in 1951. In April that year, the Supreme Court of India struck down a "reservation" or quota for students from disadvantaged classes at a state-run medical school, noting that the constitution allowed such reservations only in allocating legislative seats or government employment.[100] Within two months, India altered its constitution to permit affirmative action in education and other contexts. Article 15(4) now expressly provides that "[n]othing in [the constitution's anti-discrimination articles] shall prevent the State from making any special provision for the advancement of any socially and educationally backward classes of citizens."[101]

Some of India's states have maintained affirmative action or "reservation" programs at least since the nation's independence.[102] These programs reserve public university seats or government positions for members of India's disadvantaged castes. In a series of decisions dating back to 1963, India's Supreme Court has upheld the court constitutionality of these programs, although the court has imposed some constraints on their administration. Notably, the court placed a fifty percent ceiling on the number of positions that can be reserved for disadvantaged citizens.[104] A limit so high may appear startling to observers from legal systems more skeptical of affirmative action.

Since 1970, India's affirmative action programs have expanded in both geographic scope (more states have adopted programs) and magnitude (more classes have been catalogued as disadvantaged). The central government was slower than some states to support preferences.[105] In 1990, however, Prime Minister V.P. Singh announced that he would carry out the expansive recommendations of the ten-year old Mandal

---

99. Id. art. 46. The final portion of the article directs special attention to the "Scheduled Castes and the Scheduled Tribes," but the initial clause appears to include other "weaker sections of the people" as well. Id.

100. See *State of Madras v. Champakam Dorairajan*, A.I.R. 1951 S.C. 226.

101. India Const. Art. 15(4). Paralleling other constitutional references to the most disadvantaged castes, the provision adds: "or the Scheduled Castes and the Scheduled Tribes." Id.

102. Some of the programs continue systems imposed under British rule, which heightens the controversy surrounding them. See Prior, supra note 96, at 72–73.

104. See *Balaji v. State of Mysore*, A.I.R. 1963 S.C. 649: see also *Devadasan v. Union of India*, A.I.R. 1964 S.C. 179 (limit-ing carry forward of unfilled reserved positions); *Indra Sawhney v. Union of India*, A.I.R. 1993 S.C. 477 (affirming fifty percent rule). * * *

105. The central government appointed its first Backward Classes Commission in 1953 and received that Commission's report two years later. Parliament, however, rejected the report and the Commission's recommendations were never implemented. See Prior, supra, note 96, at 80–81. The government did not appoint a second commission until 1978, when the commission led by B.P. Mandal began work. The Mandal Commission submitted its report and recommendations at the end of 1980. For a decade, nothing was done to implement them. See *id.* at 69, 81–86.

Commission Report.[106] Three years later, India's Supreme Court upheld the constitutionality of most of those recommendations and the central government began to implement them.[107]

Affirmative action (sometimes called "compensatory discrimination") has provoked its share of controversy, including violent resistance, in India. A 1968 survey showed that high caste and highly educated citizens strongly opposed reservations in government employment. In 1990, when Prime Minister Singh first announced implementation of the Mandal Commission Report, riots erupted across India, and the protests contributed to the fall of Singh's government. More isolated episodes of violence occurred after India's Supreme Court, in 1993, upheld the constitutionality of the Commission's approach. The judicial ruling, however, may have tempered opposition to some degree.

Few citizens of India deny either a long history of overt discrimination against disfavored castes or the persistence of deep-seated bias against those groups. Perhaps that public recognition explains, in part, why "reservations" beyond any set-asides tolerable in the United States have survived in India. A 1964 opinion of the Mysore High Court stated the case this way:

> "[T]here can be neither stability nor real progress if predominant sections of an awakened Nation live in primitive conditions, confined to unremunerative occupations and having no share in the good things of life, while power and wealth [are] confined in the hands of only a few * * * [The] Nation's interest will be best served—taking a long range view—of the backward classes are helped to march forward and take their place in a line with the advanced sections of the people."[112]

Ruth Bader Ginsburg and Deborah Jones Merrit, *Affirmative Action: An International Human Rights Dialogue*, 21 Cardozo L. Rev. 253, 273–77 (1999).

Are there fundamental differences between affirmative action programs based on caste as opposed to race or sex? What about affirmative action based on poverty?

4. In the U.S., gender-based affirmative action has been treated differently than race-based affirmative action. As there was no majority in *Bakke* that could agree on the proper standard of review for race-based affirmative action, the matter was left open. The Court finally agreed that race-based affirmative action had to be subjected to strict scrutiny. See *Richmond v. J.A. Croson Co.*, 488 U.S. 469 (1989). For an analysis of the cases decided between 1978 and 1989, see Michel Rosenfeld, *Affirmative Action and Justice: A Philosophical and Constitutional Inquiry* 163–215 (1991). In contrast, gender-based affirmative action is presumably subject to intermediate scrutiny. Cf. *Johnson v. Transportation Agency*, 480 U.S. 616 (1987) (Court upheld on statutory grounds, mirroring an intermediary scrutiny standard, a preferential promotion of a woman over a slightly better qualified man in a line of work (road maintenance) with few women). Is this

---

106. See *id.* at 63–69.

107. See Indra Sawhney, A.I.R. 1993 S.C. at 477; Prior, *supra* note 96, at 70, 90–94.

112. *D.G. Viswanath v. Government of Mysore*, 1964 A.I.R. 51 (Mys.) 132, 136.

difference, which makes it easier for gender-based preferences to survive constitutional challenges, justified? Note that the result in *Johnson* would have been struck down by the European Court of Justice using the standard upheld in *Marschall* above. Which of the two standards seems preferable? Should it make a difference whether a job traditionally unavailable to women is involved?

E. PROTECTING IDENTITY: RACIAL, NATIONAL, ETHNIC AND LIN- GUISTIC MINORITIES

"Constitutionalism is the end product of social, economic, cultural, and political progress; it can become a tradition only if it forms part of the shared history of a people." H.W.O. Okoth–Ogendo, *Constitutions without Constitutionalism: Reflections on an African Political Paradox*, in *Constitutionalism and Democracy: Transitions in the Contemporary World* 65, 80 (Douglas Greenberg et al. eds., 1993). What if that history is not shared, or if the shared history is a history of nations, ethnicities, or religious groups that oppress each other? What if immigrants represent a tradition that is alien to that of the prevailing majority? Do minority groups or their members have the right to protection of their identity? Which minorities have this right? National, ethnic, linguistic, racial, or religious? Is a history of consistent discrimination by the majority against "social outcasts" sufficient to justify creating a protected-minority status? Note that a group that is called "ethnic" in one country might be called a "national" minority in another; the two terms are not clearly distinct. Religion may also serve as a crosscutting dividing line. Which elements of personal identity are to be protected? Language, customs and traditions, political self-determination? Moreover, are group-identity rights, e.g., local self-government for geographically concentrated ethnic minorities, consistent with equality among all citizens?

Professor Karst has characterized the issues: "When can government properly treat membership in a racial or ethnic group as legally relevant? Do the members of a cultural minority have a constitutional stake in the preservation of their language and culture? When does governmental support for religion amount to impermissible official sponsorship? Should questions like these be left to cultural politics, or resolved as questions of constitutional law?" Kenneth L. Karst, *Paths to Belonging: The Constitution and Cultural Identity*, 64 N.C. L. Rev. 303, 305 (1986). Who are the subjects of these rights, individual members of the group or the group as such (though not necessarily represented by its democratically determined or traditional leaders)?

The section addresses these questions, including language rights and the extent to which minorities are entitled to their own autonomous institutions (e.g., in education). Subsection E.1. deals with majority efforts to protect the majority's identity. Subsection E.2. considers the arrangements necessary to protect the identity of minority groups in an educational setting. Subsection E.3. addresses special problems of aboriginal identity and self-rule. The cases deal with the right of an aboriginal group to determine the legal status of its members, where this right conflicts with general rules of the state.

E.1.   PROTECTING MAJORITY IDENTITY

FORD v. QUEBEC (ATTORNEY GENERAL)

Supreme Court (Canada).
[1988] 2 S.C.R. 712.

[This case involved a challenge to those provisions of the Quebec Charter of the French Language, RSQ, c. C–11 (as amended) that required French only on public signs and posters and in commercial advertising. The appellants challenged these provisions successfully under both the Canadian Charter of Rights and Freedoms and the Quebec Charter of Human Rights and Freedoms, RSQ, c. C–12, ss. 3 and 52.]

The Court (Dickson C.J. and Beetz, Estey, McIntyre, Lamer, Wilson and Le Dain JJ.)

Appeal dismissed.

VII.   Whether the Freedom of Expression Guaranteed by s. 2(b) of the Canadian Charter of Rights and Freedoms and by s. 3 of the Quebec Charter of Human Rights and Freedoms includes the freedom to express oneself in the language of one's choice.

In so far as this issue is concerned, the words "freedom of expression" in s. 2(b) of the Canadian Charter and s. 3 of the Quebec Charter should be given the same meaning. As indicated above, both the Superior Court and the Court of Appeal held that freedom of expression includes the freedom to express oneself in the language of one's choice. * * *

The conclusion of the Superior Court and the Court of Appeal on this issue is correct. Language is so intimately related to the form and content of expression that there cannot be true freedom of expression by means of language if one is prohibited from using the language of one's choice. Language is not merely a means or medium of expression; it colours the content and meaning of expression. It is, as the preamble of the Charter of the French Language itself indicates, a means by which a people may express its cultural identity. It is also the means by which the individual expresses his or her personal identity and sense of individuality. That the concept of "expression" in s. 2(b) of the Canadian Charter and s. 3 of the Quebec Charter goes beyond mere content is indicated by the specific protection accorded to "freedom of thought, belief [and] opinion" in s. 2 and to "freedom of conscience" and "freedom of opinion" in s. 3. That suggests that "freedom of expression" is intended to extend to more than the content of expression in its narrow sense.

The Attorney General of Quebec made several submissions against the conclusion reached by the Superior Court and the Court of Appeal on this issue, the most important of which may be summarized as follows: (a) in determining the meaning of freedom of expression the Court should apply the distinction between the message and the medium which must have been known to the framers of the Canadian and Quebec

Charters; (b) the express provision for the guarantee of language rights in ss. 16 to 23 of the Canadian Charter indicates that it was not intended that a language freedom should result incidentally from the guarantee of freedom of expression in s. 2(b); (c) the recognition of a freedom to express oneself in the language of one's choice under s. 2(b) of the Canadian Charter and s. 3 of the Quebec Charter would undermine the special and limited constitutional position of the specific guarantees of language rights in s. 133 of the Constitution Act, 1867 and ss. 16 to 23 of the Canadian Charter that was emphasized by the Court in *MacDonald v. City of Montreal*, [1986] 1 S.C.R. 460, and *Société des Acadiens du Nouveau–Brunswick Inc. v. Association of Parents for Fairness in Education*, [1986] 1 S.C.R. 549; and (d) the recognition that freedom of expression includes the freedom to express oneself in the language of one's choice would be contrary to the views expressed on this issue by the European Commission of Human Rights and the European Court of Human Rights.

The distinction between the message and the medium was applied by DUGAS J. of the Superior Court in *Devine v. Procureur general du Quebec*, [[1982] C.S. 355], in holding that freedom of expression does not include freedom to express oneself in the language of one's choice. It has already been indicated why that distinction is inappropriate as applied to language as a means of expression because of the intimate relationship between language and meaning. As one of the authorities on language quoted by the appellant Singer in the Devine appeal, J. Fishman, The Sociology of Language (1972), at p. 4, puts it: " * * * language is not merely a means of interpersonal communication and influence. It is not merely a carrier of content, whether latent or manifest. Language itself is content, a reference for loyalties and animosities, an indicator of social statuses and personal relationships, a marker of situations and topics as well as of the societal goals and the large-scale value-laden arenas of interaction that typify every speech community." As has been noted this quality or characteristic of language is acknowledged by the Charter of the French Language itself where, in the first paragraph of its preamble, it states: "Whereas the French language, the distinctive language of a people that is in the majority French-speaking, is the instrument by which that people has articulated its identity."

The second and third of the submissions of the Attorney General of Quebec which have been summarized above, with reference to the implications for this issue of the express or specific guarantees of language rights in s. 133 of the Constitution Act, 1867, and ss. 16 to 23 of the Canadian Charter of Rights and Freedoms, are closely related and may be addressed together. These special guarantees of language rights do not, by implication, preclude a construction of freedom of expression that includes the freedom to express oneself in the language of one's choice. A general freedom to express oneself in the language of one's choice and the special guarantees of language rights in certain areas of governmental activity or jurisdiction—the legislature and administration, the courts and education—are quite different things. The latter have, as this Court has indicated in *MacDonald*, *supra*, and *Société des Acadiens*, *supra*, their own special historical, political and constitutional basis. The central unifying feature of all of the language rights given explicit recognition in the Constitution of Canada is that they pertain to governmental institutions and for the most part they oblige the government to provide for, or at least tolerate, the use of both official languages. In this sense they are more akin to rights, properly understood, than freedoms. They grant entitlement to a specific benefit from the government or in relation to one's dealing with the government. Correspondingly, the government is obliged to provide certain services or benefits in both languages or at least permit use of either language by persons conducting certain affairs with the government. They do not ensure, as does a guaranteed freedom, that within a given broad range of private conduct, an individual will be free to choose his or her own course of activity. The language rights in the Constitution impose obligations on government and governmental institutions that are in the words of Beetz J. in *MacDonald*, a "precise scheme", providing specific opportunities to use English or French, or to receive services in English or French, in concrete, readily ascertainable and limited circumstances. In contrast, what the respondents seek in this case is a freedom as that term was explained by Dickson J. (as he then was) in *R. v. Big M Drug Mart Ltd.*, [1985] 1 S.C.R. 295, at p. 336: "Freedom can primarily be characterized by the absence of coercion or constraint. If a person is compelled by the state or the will of another to a course of action or inaction which he would not otherwise have chosen, he is not acting of his own volition and he cannot be said to be truly free. One of the major purposes of the Charter is to protect, within reason, from compulsion or restraint." The respondents seek to be free of the state imposed requirement that their commercial signs and advertising be in French only, and seek the freedom, in the entirely private or non-governmental realm of commercial activity, to display signs and advertising in the language of their choice as well as that of French. Manifestly the respondents are not seeking to use the language of their choice in any form of direct relations with any branch of government and are not seeking to oblige government to provide them any services or other benefits in the language of their choice. In this sense the respondents are asserting a freedom, the freedom to express oneself in the language of one's choice in an area of non-governmental activity, as opposed to a language right of the kind guaranteed in the Constitution. The recognition that freedom of expression includes the freedom to express oneself in the language of one's choice does not undermine or run counter to the special guarantees of official language rights in areas of governmental jurisdiction or responsibility. The legal structure, function and obligations of government institutions with respect to the English and French languages are in no way affected by the recognition that freedom of expression includes the freedom to express oneself in the language of one's choice in areas outside of those for which the special guarantees of language have been provided.

The decisions of the European Commission of Human Rights and the European Court of Human Rights on which the Attorney General of Quebec relied are all distinguishable on the same basis, apart from the fact that, as Bisson J.A. observed in the Court of Appeal, they arose in an entirely different constitutional context. They all involved claims to language rights in relations with government that would have imposed some obligation on government. * * *

Whether the s. 1 and s. 9.1 Materials Justify the Prohibition of the Use of Any Language Other than French

The section 1 [of the Canadian Charter] and s. 9.1 [of the Quebec Charter] materials consist of some fourteen items ranging in nature from the general theory of language policy and planning to statistical analysis of the position of the French language in Quebec and Canada. The material deals with two matters of particular relevance to the issue in the appeal: (a) the vulnerable position of the French language in Quebec and Canada, which is the reason for the language policy reflected in the Charter of the French Language; and (b) the importance attached by language planning theory to the role of language in the public domain, including the communication or expression by language contemplated by the challenged provisions of the Charter of the French Language. As to the first, the material amply establishes the importance of the legislative purpose reflected in the Charter of the French Language and that it is a response to a substantial and pressing need. Indeed, this was conceded by the respondents both in the Court of Appeal and in this Court. The vulnerable position of the French language in Quebec and Canada was described in a series of reports by commissions of inquiry beginning with the Report of the Royal Commission on Bilingualism and Biculturalism in 1969 and continuing with the Parent Commission and the Gendron Commission. It is reflected in statistics referred to in these reports and in later studies forming part of the materials, with due adjustment made in the light of the submissions of the appellant Singer in Devine with respect to some of the later statistical material. The causal factors for the threatened position of the French language that have generally been identified are: (a) the declining birth rate of Quebec francophones resulting in a decline in the Quebec francophone proportion of the Canadian population as a whole; (b) the decline of the francophone population outside Quebec as a result of assimilation; (c) the greater rate of assimilation of immigrants to Quebec by the anglophone community of Quebec; and (d) the continuing dominance of English at the higher levels of the economic sector. These factors have favoured the use of the English language despite the predominance in Quebec of a francophone population. Thus, in the period prior to the enactment of the legislation at issue, the "visage linguistique" of Quebec often gave the impression that English had become as significant as French. This "visage linguistique" reinforced the concern among francophones that English was gaining in importance, that the French language was threatened and that it would ultimately disappear. It strongly suggested to young and ambitious francophones that the language of success was almost exclusively English. It confirmed to anglophones that there was no great need to learn the majority language. And it suggested to immigrants that the prudent course lay in joining the anglophone community. The aim of such provisions as ss. 58 and 69 of the Charter of the French Language was, in the words of its preamble, "to see the quality and influence of the French language assured". The threat to the

French language demonstrated to the government that it should, in particular, take steps to assure that the "visage linguistique" of Quebec would reflect the predominance of the French language.

The section 1 and s. 9.1 materials establish that the aim of the language policy underlying the Charter of the French Language was a serious and legitimate one. They indicate the concern about the survival of the French language and the perceived need for an adequate legislative response to the problem. Moreover, they indicate a rational connection between protecting the French language and assuring that the reality of Quebec society is communicated through the "visage linguistique". The section 1 and s. 9.1 materials do not, however, demonstrate that the requirement of the use of French only is either necessary for the achievement of the legislative objective or proportionate to it. That specific question is simply not addressed by the materials. Indeed, in his factum and oral argument the Attorney General of Quebec did not attempt to justify the requirement of the exclusive use of French. He concentrated on the reasons for the adoption of the Charter of the French Language and the earlier language legislation, which, as was noted above, were conceded by the respondents. The Attorney General of Quebec relied on what he referred to as the general democratic legitimacy of Quebec language policy without referring explicitly to the requirement of the exclusive use of French. In so far as proportionality is concerned, the Attorney General of Quebec referred to the American jurisprudence with respect to commercial speech, presumably as indicating the judicial deference that should be paid to the legislative choice of means to serve an admittedly legitimate legislative purpose, at least in the area of commercial expression. He did, however, refer in justification of the requirement of the exclusive use of French to the attenuation of this requirement reflected in ss. 59 to 62 of the Charter of the French Language and the regulations. He submitted that these exceptions to the requirement of the exclusive use of French indicate the concern for carefully designed measures and for interfering as little as possible with commercial expression. The qualifications of the requirement of the exclusive use of French in other provisions of the Charter of the French Language and the regulations do not make ss. 58 and 69 any less prohibitions of the use of any language other than French as applied to the respondents. The issue is whether any such prohibition is justified. In the opinion of this Court it has not been demonstrated that the prohibition of the use of any language other than French in ss. 58 and 69 of the Charter of the French Language is necessary to the defence and enhancement of the status of the French language in Quebec or that it is proportionate to that legislative purpose. Since the evidence put to us by the government showed that the predominance of the French language was not reflected in the "visage linguistique" of Quebec, the governmental response could well have been tailored to meet that specific problem and to impair freedom of expression minimally. Thus, whereas requiring the predominant display of the French language, even its marked predominance, would be proportional to the goal of promoting and maintaining a French "visage linguistique" in Quebec and therefore justified under the Quebec Charter and the Canadian Charter, requiring the exclusive use of French has not been so justified. French could be required in addition to any other language or it could be required to have greater visibility than that accorded to other languages. Such measures would ensure that the "visage linguistique" reflected the demography of Quebec: the predominant language is French. This reality should be communicated to all citizens and non-citizens alike, irrespective of their mother tongue. But exclusivity for the French language has not survived the scrutiny of a proportionality test and does not reflect the reality of Quebec society. Accordingly, we are of the view that the limit imposed on freedom of expression by s. 58 of the Charter of the French Language respecting the exclusive use of French on public signs and posters and in commercial advertising is not justified under s. 9.1 of the Quebec Charter. In like measure, the limit imposed on freedom of expression by s. 69 of the Charter of the French Language respecting the exclusive use of the French version of a firm name is not justified under either s. 9.1 of the Quebec Charter or s. 1 of the Canadian Charter.

Appeal dismissed.

MENTZEN CASE

Constitutional Court (Latvia).
Case No. 2001–04–0103.[f]

[The Latvian Language Law provides that "personal names shall be reproduced in accordance with the traditions of the Latvian language and shall be spelled in accordance with the norms of literary language currently in force." According to the Regulations on Spelling and Identification of Names and Surnames of the Cabinet of Ministers (No. 295), "names and surnames of foreign origin shall be reproduced in Latvian (i.e., are spelled using Latvian letters and sounds) as near as possible to their pronunciation and in accordance with the law on reproduction of foreign proper nouns." The original spelling of the name shall be included on a different page in the passport, among "special notes." Juta Mentzen—the holder of a German family name—challenged these provisions on privacy grounds (Art. 96 of the Latvian Constitution), after her name was transcribed as "Mencena" in her passport, and as a consequence, she faced difficulties in dealing with German authorities.]

3.2.   * * * Personal name is one of the elements of language and determining in compliance with what regulations it shall be used, influences the whole language system. * * * [W]hen evaluating if the limitation on private life has a legitimate objective, the role of the Latvian language in Latvia has to be taken into consideration.

* * *

The Constitutional Court agrees * * * that a person's surname is used not only by the holder but by society as well; therefore the spelling of a surname can be regulated for the convenience of the society and other people.

Taking into account historical features and the fact that the number of Latvians in the state territory has decreased during the 20th century;

f. Available   at   www.satv.tie-sa.gov.lv./Eng/Spriedumi/04–0103(01).htm.

that in the biggest cities, including Riga, Latvians are a minority; and, that the Latvian language only recently has regained its status as the state language; the necessity of protecting the state language and strengthening its usage is closely connected to the democratic system of the state of Latvia.

* * * [I]n the era of globalization Latvia is the only place in the world where the existence and development of the Latvian language and together with it the existence of the Latvian nation may be guaranteed. Limitation of the usage of the Latvian language as the state language in the state territory shall be regarded as a threat to the democratic system. * * *

Thus—the privacy rights of the applicant can be limited to protect the right of other inhabitants of Latvia to use the Latvian language freely in the entire territory, and to protect the democratic state system.

4.1.   Inviolability of a person's private life is one of the fundamental values of a democratic society. However, there are limits even to this fundamental right.

* * *

The discomfort the applicant has experienced because of the spelling of her surname in the passport cannot be regarded as a sufficient reason not to apply the Regulations issued in connection with Language Law.

The Constitutional Court holds that the threat to the functioning of the Latvian language as a unified system posed by the spelling of foreign personal names in the documents only in their original form is much greater than the discomfort a person may experience as a consequence of a Latvian spelling of his or her surname in the passport.

Under the above circumstances the functioning of the Latvian language as a unified system is a social necessity in Latvia and not a capricious exercise of state power.

[Accordingly, the Court upheld the provisions of the law requiring the Latvian transliteration of foreign names. The Court found, however, that including the original spelling of the name only in the "special notes" section was disproportionate and hence unconstitutional.]

Notes and Questions

1.   In Quebec, the precarious situation of French speakers in a predominantly English-speaking Canada may explain the concern regarding the use of language in public space. However, remember that

[i]n all times and places, cultural differences have bred suspicion and fear. In times of trouble, those fears tend to focus on particular groups of cultural outsiders as a source of danger. It becomes convenient to make scapegoats of 'them'—the people who look different from 'us' or whose language or behavior is foreign to our own. Cultural majorities have sought to force outsiders to conform to the prevailing cultural norms; alternatively, they have sought to dominate and suppress the outsiders, separating them from the public life of the community. * * * If my group identity tells me where I belong—and *that* I belong—it also

tells me that you, who do not wear the same identifying labels, do not belong. We can trust the members of our own cultural group because we know the meanings of their behavior and know what to expect of them. Conversely, distrust of the members of a different cultural group flows from fear, not just of the unknown but the fear that outsiders threaten our own acculturated views of the natural order of society.

Karst, *op. cit.* at 309.

2. *The aftermath of* Ford. Following the decision of the Canadian Supreme Court, Quebec amended its legislation on commercial signs. Anglo–Saxon citizens living in Quebec challenged the amended legislation before the UN Human Rights Committee, arguing that it violated Art. 29 of the International Covenant on Civil and Political Rights, protecting minority rights, and Art. 19 of the Covenant, protecting freedom of speech. In *Ballantyne, Davidson, McIntyre v. Canada*, Communications Nos. 359/1989 and 385/1989, U.N. Doc. CCPR/C/47/D/359/1989 and 385/1989/Rev.1 (1993), the UN Human Rights Committee found:

> 11.2   * * * [T]he minorities referred to in article 27 are minorities within such a State, and not minorities within any province. A group may constitute a majority in a province but still be a minority in a State and thus be entitled to the benefits of article 27. English speaking citizens of Canada cannot be considered a linguistic minority. The authors therefore have no claim under article 27 of the Covenant.

> 11.3   * * * In the Committee's opinion, the commercial element in an expression taking the form of outdoor advertising cannot have the effect of removing this expression from the scope of protected freedom. The Committee does not agree either that any of the above forms of expression can be subjected to varying degrees of limitation, with the result that some forms of expression may suffer broader restrictions than others.

> 11.4   * * * While the restrictions on outdoor advertising are indeed provided for by law, the issue to be addressed is whether they are necessary for the respect of the rights of others. The rights of others could only be the rights of the francophone minority within Canada under article 27. This is the right to use their own language, which is not jeopardized by the freedom of others to advertise in other than the French language. * * * The Committee believes that it is not necessary, in order to protect the vulnerable position in Canada of the francophone group, to prohibit commercial advertising in English. This protection may be achieved in other ways that do not preclude the freedom of expression, in a language of their choice, of those engaged in such fields as trade. * * *

In 1993, the Quebec law was amended again to allow for English to appear on commercial signs, provided that French remained predominant. Charter of the French Language, R.S.Q. 1985, c. C–11, s.48, as amended by S.Q. 1993, c.40.

3. *Protection of the official language.* The Quebec Charter is not unique in its attempt to protect and promote an official language via legislative means. In 1994, France enacted Law No. 94–665 of 4 August 1994 relative to the use of the French language:

Art. 2

The use of French shall be mandatory for the designation, offer, presentation, instructions for use, and description of the scope and conditions of a warranty of goods, products and services, as well as bills and receipts.

The same provisions apply to any written, spoken, radio and television advertisement. * * *

Art. 3

Any inscription or announcement posted or made on a public highway, in a place open to the public or in a public transport system and designed to inform the public must be expressed in French. * * *

Art. 5

Whatever the substance and form, contracts signed by a public corporate body or a private person on a public service assignment must be drafted in French. Such contracts may neither contain expressions nor terms in a foreign language where a French term or expression with the same meaning exists and is approved under the conditions provided for by the rules relative to the enhancement of the French language * * *

The contracts referred to herein, which are entered into with one or more foreign contracting parties may include, in addition to the French version, one or more versions in a foreign language that shall equally be taken as authentic. * * *

Art. 6

Any participant in an event, seminar or convention organised in France by natural persons or corporate bodies of French nationality has the right to express himself in French. Documents distributed to participants before and during the meeting for the presentation of the programme must be drafted in French and may include translations in one or more foreign languages.

Violators of the law are subject to fines as prescribed in Decree No. 95–240 of 3 March 1995, set down for the application of the law of 4 August 1994 relative to the use of the French language. The Constitutional Council upheld these provisions (94–345 DC of 29 July 1994) against challenges based on freedom of speech, freedom of enterprise, and equality. Summary in English, in BCCL, 1994–2 at 122. Does the French law meet the standards established by the UN Human Rights Committee in *Ballantyne*?

4. Language proficiency and political participation. Language-proficiency requirements were widespread in the former Soviet republics as criteria for obtaining citizenship in the newly independent states. A large segment of the population in these states was ethnically Russian and did not speak the official languages of the new states. Legislation mandating language proficiency in a new republic's traditional language was often upheld by constitutional courts but was later softened or abandoned in response to international pressure, as, for example, in Estonia. Language-proficiency requirements were a means of large-scale exclusion from the political community.

Language-proficiency requirements may also be imposed more subtly to undermine the political impact of the targeted ethnic group. Language-proficiency requirements imposed on candidates running for a public office might look *prima facie* justifiable. A good command of the official language, for example, might be a prerequisite for participating in public discourse and administering public affairs. The promotion of the official language might also be based on more-symbolic considerations related to preserving national identity and sovereignty. Thus, "[although] France has shown unusual intolerance of ethnic distinctiveness, even for a Western European country, * * * cultural and linguistic diversity was an unproblematic fact of life in France until the 1790s, when in the aftermath of the French Revolution a need for a unifying national identity, expressed in part by a single national language, was rather suddenly perceived." Adeno Addis, *Cultural Integrity and Political Unity: The Politics of Language in Multilingual States*, 33 Ariz. St. L.J. 719, 731 n.31 (2001).

According to Art. 43(3) of the Kyrgyz Constitution, the president "must be a citizen of Kyrgyzstan, no younger than 35 years of age, and no older than 65 years of age, who has command of the state language, and who has resided in the Republic for no less than 15 years before the nomination of his/her candidacy to the President's Office." Article 5(1) of the Constitution provides that Kyrgyz is the official language. In the 2000 presidential race, only six of 20 candidates passed a language test, conducted by seven academic experts appointed by the Central Election Commission, while one candidate refused to take the exam.[g] A large percentage of the population of Kyrgyzstan—a former Soviet republic—is of Russian ethnicity; the Russian and the Kyrgyz languages differ substantially. Does the wording of Art. 43(3)[h] call for a language test? (The test requirement itself is prescribed in Art. 61 of the Electoral Code.) Article 5(2) of the Kyrgyz Constitution provides that the "Kyrgyz Republic guarantees the preservation, equal and free development and functioning of the Russian language and all the other languages, used by the population of the Republic," while pursuant to Art. 5(3), "[i]nfringement upon citizens' rights and freedoms based upon lack of knowledge or command of the state language is not allowed."

Recently the European Court of Human Rights (ECHR) reviewed a language-proficiency requirement that was imposed on candidates for parliamentary seats in Latvia. Under Latvian law, citizens who were educated in languages other than Latvian and intend to register as candidates must present a certificate of language proficiency. Podkolzina, a member of the Russian-speaking minority and a candidate of the prominority coalition "For Human Rights in United Latvia," was removed from the list of candidates for the 1998 general elections, after the State Language Center refused to accept her old Latvian language-proficiency certificate. When visited by an examiner and witnesses at her workplace, she refused to take a new written language test. She challenged the Latvian legislation, *inter alia*, under Art. 3 of Protocol No. 1 of the European Convention for the Protection of Human Rights and Fundamental Freedoms (hereafter, European HR Convention) (right to stand as a candidate in elections). In *Podkolzina v. Latvia*, Case no. 46726/99, Judgement of April 9, 2002, the ECHR found that while it was legitimate for Latvia to determine the working language of its national parliament, the rules on language proficiency did not establish objective guarantees. The Court also found that the test performed in *Podkolzina* violated procedural fairness and legal certainty.

g. See *www.eurasianet.org/departments/insight/articles/eav092600.shtml.*

h. Available in English at www.kyrgyzstan.org/Law/constitution.htm.

Is the statutory promotion of an official language more justifiable if the protected language is spoken by relatively few people (one to two million) in a nation-state that was once subject to suppression of its language and that has a sizeable linguistic (ethnic) minority?

5. *Identity as an obstacle to political participation.* Proxies based on identity or ethnic origin might become effective tools for banning certain groups from the political arena. The most extreme form of such restrictions is the official denial of the presence or existence of ethnic minorities in a country, such as the Kurds in Turkey. Similarly, "[w]hen it signed the European Charter of Regional and Minority Languages, France made a declaration that it has no linguistic minorities in its territory. Even though there are regional languages within its borders (not to mention linguistic minorities from France's former colonies), France denied that languages other than French exist and are spoken. It is ironical that while it suppresses minority languages within its borders, France is often at the forefront promoting French as a minority language in other countries such as Canada and Belgium." Addis, *op. cit.* at 730–731. Exclusionary measures may take less drastic forms and still result in the effective disenfranchisement of a segment of the population. Consider the following examples.

In 1990, in the wake of democratic transition in Bulgaria, a political party formed by ethnic Turks was registered as the Movement for Rights and Freedoms (MRF). In the first democratic elections the MRF won a sufficient percentage of the vote to enter Parliament, forming a short-lived coalition with the winning party. Article 11.4 of the Bulgarian Constitution, enacted by a parliamentary majority after the elections, provides that "(t)here shall be no political parties on ethnic, racial, or religious lines, nor parties which seek the violent usurpation of state power."[i] The provision was intended to curtail the effective political participation of various ethnic minorities in Bulgaria, primarily the Turks, Roma (Gypsies), and Macedonians. Many MRF representatives refused to support the adoption of the clause. Is Art. 11.4 compatible with freedom of association? Note that in addition to ethnic differences, ethnic Turks and Macedonians are overwhelmingly Muslim, in a country where the Constitution (Art. 13.3) declares that "Eastern Orthodox Christianity is considered the traditional religion in the Republic of Bulgaria." Following the adoption of the clause, the party that lost the elections—the former communist party—challenged the reregistration of the MRF on the basis of Art. 11.4 of the Constitution.

A split Constitutional Court upheld the registration of the MRF. In its decision the Court interpreted Art. 11.4 of the Bulgarian Constitution narrowly, emphasizing the importance of the historic context in which the MRF was formed. It ruled that the provision should be read in conjunction with other constitutional provisions so that Art. 11.4 prohibits only political parties that are formed on an ethnic basis with the intention to violently usurp state power. The decision of the Court was celebrated as a landmark of constitutionalism and the rule of law in Bulgaria. Without the MRF, the government would have lost its majority.

In 2000, the Constitutional Court found that a political party called "United Macedonian Organization Ilinden–Party for Economic Development

i. See Rumyana Kolarova, *Tacit Agreements in the Bulgarian Transition to Democracy: Minority Rights and Constitution-* *alism*, U. Chi. L. Sch. Roundtable 23, 41 n.71 (1993).

and Integration of the Population'' was unconstitutional under Art. 11.4. (Decision No. 1 of February 29, 2000.) While the party was registered as all-Bulgarian, its members were Macedonians, and the Constitutional Court found that the party of ethnic Macedonians constituted a threat to the territorial integrity of the Bulgarian state. In reaching its decision, the Court examined not only the party's official founding documents but also the activities and statements of party officials.[j] The Macedonian minority is not recognized officially in Bulgaria. Compare with the restrictions on religion/ethnicity-based party formation in India. See Chapter 11.

Although ethnic politics was not always welcome in the U.S., the current position markedly differs from the Bulgarian approach:

> Facing either hostility or indifference, the members of a cultural minority may conclude that they will fare better if they act as a group, particularly when their aims can be satisfied only by participation in the larger community. The pursuit of political goals by people identified by race, ethnicity, or religion has been a fixture of American politics since the colonial era and must be seen as a permanent feature of the politics of a multicultural society. Often, when an issue becomes prominent in cultural politics, it takes on an importance that transcends any immediate effects of the issue's resolution on people's day-to-day lives. The obvious explanation is that the issue has become a symbol of cultural identity and ultimately of individual worth. With the stakes so high, it is no wonder feelings are intense.

Karst, *op. cit.* at 328.

E.2. LANGUAGE RIGHTS OF MINORITIES

MAHE v. ALBERTA

Supreme Court (Canada).
[1990] 1 S.C.R. 342.

Dickson C.J. and Wilson, La Forest, L'Heureux–Dubé, Sopinka, Gonthier and Cory JJ.

* * * Section 23 [of the Canadian Charter of Rights and Freedoms] is one component in Canada's constitutional protection of the official languages.[k] The section is especially important in this regard, however,

---

j. Unofficial English summary at www.infotel.bg/juen/resh/rks-eng.htm.

k. Section 23, Minority Language Educational Rights—

(1) Citizens of Canada

   a) whose first language learned and still understood is that of the English or French linguistic minority population of the province in which they reside, or

   b) who have received their primary school instruction in Canada in English or French and reside in a province where the language in which they received that instruction is the language of the English or French linguistic minority population of the province, have

the right to have their children receive primary and secondary school instruction in that language in that province.

(2) Citizens of Canada of whom any child has received or is receiving primary or secondary school instruction in English or French in Canada, have the right to have all their children receive primary and secondary school instruction in the same language. Application where numbers warrant

(3) The right of citizens of Canada under subsections (1) and (2) to have their children receive primary and secondary school instruction in the language of the English or French linguistic minority population of a province

because of the vital role of education in preserving and encouraging linguistic and cultural vitality. It thus represents a linchpin in this nation's commitment to the values of bilingualism and biculturalism.

The appellants claim that their rights under s. 23 are not satisfied by the existing educational system in Edmonton nor by the legislation under which it operates, resulting in an erosion of their cultural heritage, contrary to the spirit and intent of the Charter. In particular, the appellants argue that s. 23 guarantees the right, in Edmonton, to the "management and control" of a minority-language school—that is, to a Francophone school run by a Francophone school board. Our task then is to determine the meaning of s. 23 of the Charter. * * *

The appellants * * * are parents whose first language learned and still understood is French. * * * [Appellants] have school age children, and thus qualify under s. 23(1) of the Charter as persons who, subject to certain limitations, "have the right to have their children receive primary and secondary school instruction" in the language of the linguistic minority population of the province—in this case, the French language. They may therefore conveniently be called "s. 23 parents", and their children "s. 23 students". * * *

The primary issue raised by this appeal is the degree, if any, of "management and control" of a French language school which should be accorded to s. 23 parents in Edmonton. (The phrase "management and control", it should be noted, is not a term of art: it appears to have been introduced in earlier s. 23 cases and has now gained such currency that it was utilized by all the groups in this appeal.) The appellants appear to accept that, with a few exceptions, the government has provided whatever other services or rights might be mandated in Edmonton under s. 23: their fundamental complaint is that they do not have the exclusive management and control of the existing Francophone schools. * * *

There are two general questions which must be answered in order to decide this appeal: (1) do the rights which s. 23 mandates, depending upon the numbers of students, include a right to management and control; and (2) if so, is the number of students in Edmonton sufficient to invoke this right? I will begin with the first question.

(1) The purpose of s. 23

The general purpose of s. 23 is clear: it is to preserve and promote the two official languages of Canada, and their respective cultures, by ensuring that each language flourishes, as far as possible, in provinces where it is not spoken by the majority of the population. The section aims at achieving this goal by granting minority language educational rights to minority language parents throughout Canada.

My reference to cultures is significant: it is based on the fact that any broad guarantee of language rights, especially in the context of

a) applies wherever in the province the number of children of citizens who have such a right is sufficient to warrant the provision to them out of public funds of minority language instruction; and

b) includes, where the number of those children so warrants, the right to have them receive that instruction in minority language educational facilities provided out of public funds.

education, cannot be separated from a concern for the culture associated with the language. Language is more than a mere means of communication, it is part and parcel of the identity and culture of the people speaking it. It is the means by which individuals understand themselves and the world around them. The cultural importance of language was recognized by this Court in *Ford v. Quebec (Attorney General)*, [1988] 2 S.C.R. 712, at 748–49. * * *

In addition, it is worth noting that minority schools themselves provide community centres where the promotion and preservation of minority language culture can occur; they provide needed locations where the minority community can meet and facilities which they can use to express their culture.

A further important aspect of the purpose of s. 23 is the role of the section as a remedial provision. It was designed to remedy an existing problem in Canada, and hence to alter the status quo. * * *

In my view the appellants are fully justified in submitting that "history reveals that s. 23 was designed to correct, on a national scale, the progressive erosion of minority official language groups and to give effect to the concept of the 'equal partnership' of the two official language groups in the context of education."

The remedial aspect of s. 23 was indirectly questioned by the respondent and several of the interveners in an argument which they put forward for a "narrow construction" of s. 23.

[Reference to Justice Beetz's comments on the political nature of language rights and the restrictive role of the courts in their interpretation is omitted.]

I do not believe that these words support the proposition that s. 23 should be given a particularly narrow construction, or that its remedial purpose should be ignored. Beetz J. makes it clear in this quotation that language rights are not cast in stone nor immune from judicial interpretation. * * * Beetz J.'s warning that courts should be careful in interpreting language rights is a sound one. Section 23 provides a perfect example of why such caution is advisable. The provision provides for a novel form of legal right, quite different from the type of legal rights which courts have traditionally dealt with. Both its genesis and its form are evidence of the unusual nature of s. 23. Section 23 confers upon a group a right which places positive obligations on government to alter or develop major institutional structures. * * *

(2) The Context of s. 23(3)(b): An Overview of s. 23

The proper way of interpreting s. 23, in my opinion, is to view the section as providing a general right to minority language instruction. Paragraphs (a) and (b) of subs. (3) qualify this general right: para. (a) adds that the right to instruction is only guaranteed where the "number of children" warrants, while para. (b) further qualifies the general right to instruction by adding that where numbers warrant it includes a right to "minority language educational facilities". In my view, subs. (3)(b) is included in order to indicate the upper range of possible institutional requirements which may be mandated by s. 23 (the government may, of course, provide more than the minimum required by s. 23).

Another way of expressing the above interpretation of s. 23 is to say that s. 23 should be viewed as encompassing a "sliding scale" of requirement, with subs. (3)(b) indicating the upper level of this range and the term "instruction" in subs. (3)(a) indicating the lower level. The idea of a sliding scale is simply that s. 23 guarantees whatever type and level of rights and services is appropriate in order to provide minority language instruction for the particular number of students involved.

The sliding scale approach can be contrasted with that which views s. 23 as only encompassing two rights—one with respect to instruction and one with respect to facilities—each providing a certain level of services appropriate for one of two numerical thresholds. On this interpretation of s. 23, which could be called the "separate rights" approach, a specified number of s. 23 students would trigger a particular level of instruction, while a greater, specified number of students would require, in addition, a particular level of minority language educational facilities. Where the number of students fell between the two threshold numbers, only the lower level of instruction would be required.

* * * The sliding scale approach ensures that the minority group receives the full amount of protection that its numbers warrant. * * * If, for instance, the appellants succeeded in persuading this Court that s. 23 mandates a completely separate school board—as opposed to some sort of representation on an existing board—then other groups of s. 23 parents with slightly fewer numbers might find themselves without a right to any degree of management and control—even though their numbers might justify granting them some degree of management and control.

The only way to avoid the weaknesses of the separate rights approach would be to lower the numbers requirement—with the result that it would be impractical to require governments to provide more than the minimum level of minority language educational services. In my view, it is more sensible, and consistent with the purpose of s. 23, to interpret s. 23 as requiring whatever minority language educational protection the number of students in any particular case warrants. Section 23 simply mandates that governments do whatever is practical in the situation to preserve and promote minority language education.

There are outer limits to the sliding scale of s. 23. In general, s. 23 may not require that anything be done in situations where there are a small number of minority language students. There is little that governments can be required to do, for instance, in the case of a solitary, isolated minority language student. Section 23 requires, at a minimum, that "instruction" take place in the minority language: if there are too few students to justify a programme which qualifies as "minority language instruction", then s. 23 will not require any programmes be put in place.

     * * *

In my view, the words of s. 23(3)(b) are consistent with and supportive of the conclusion that s. 23 mandates, where the numbers warrant, a measure of management and control. * * * If the term "minority language educational facilities" is not viewed as encompassing a degree of management and control, then there would not appear to be any purpose in including it in s. 23.

* * *

The foregoing textual analysis of s. 23(3)(b) is strongly supported by a consideration of the overall purpose of s. 23. * * * Such management and control is vital to ensure that their language and culture flourish. It is necessary because a variety of management issues in education, e.g., curricula, hiring, expenditures, can affect linguistic and cultural concerns. * * *

Furthermore, as the historical context in which s. 23 was enacted suggests, minority language groups cannot always rely upon the majority to take account of all of their linguistic and cultural concerns. Such neglect is not necessarily intentional: the majority cannot be expected to understand and appreciate all of the diverse ways in which educational practices may influence the language and culture of the minority. * * *

The appellants argue for a completely independent Francophone school board. Much is to be said in support of this position and indeed it may be said to reflect the ideal.

* * *

Historically, separate or denominational boards have been the principal bulwarks of minority language education in the absence of any provision for minority representation and authority within public or common school boards. Such independent boards constitute, for the minority, institutions which it can consider its own with all this entails in terms of opportunity of working in its own language and of sharing a common culture, interests and understanding and being afforded the fullest measure of representation and control. * * *

[W]here the number of students enrolled in minority schools is relatively small, the ability of an independent board to fulfill this purpose may be reduced and other approaches may be appropriate whereby the minority is able to identify with the school but has the benefit of participating in a larger organization through representation and a certain exclusive authority within the majority school board. Under these circumstances, such an arrangement avoids the isolation of an independent school district from the physical resources which the majority school district enjoys and facilitates the sharing of resources with the majority board, something which can be crucial for smaller minority schools.

* * *

What is essential, however, to satisfy that purpose is that the minority language group have control over those aspects of education which pertain to or have an effect upon their language and culture. This degree of control can be achieved to a substantial extent by guaranteeing representation of the minority on a shared school board and by giving these representatives exclusive control over all of the aspects of minority education which pertain to linguistic and cultural concerns.

To give but one example, the right to tax (which would accompany the creation of an independent school district), is not, in my view, essential to satisfy the concerns of s. 23 with linguistic and cultural security.

* * *

At this stage of early development of s. 23 jurisprudence, the appropriate response for the courts is to describe in general terms the requirements mandated. It is up to the public authorities to satisfy these general requirements. Where there are alternative ways of satisfying the requirements, the public authorities may choose the means of fulfilling their duties. In some instances this approach may result in further litigation to determine whether the general requirements mandated by the court have been implemented. I see no way to avoid this result, as the alternative of a uniform detailed order runs the real risk of imposing impractical solutions. Section 23 is a new type of legal right in Canada and thus requires new responses from the courts.

* * *

In my view, the measure of management and control required by s. 23 of the Charter may, depending on the numbers of students to be served, warrant an independent school board. Where numbers do not warrant granting this maximum level of management and control, however, they may nonetheless be sufficient to require linguistic minority representation on an existing school board. In this latter case:

(1) The representation of the linguistic minority on local boards or other public authorities which administer minority language instruction or facilities should be guaranteed;

(2) The number of minority language representatives on the board should be, at a minimum, proportional to the number of minority language students in the school district, i.e., the number of minority language students for whom the board is responsible;

(3) The minority language representatives should have exclusive authority to make decisions relating to the minority language instruction and facilities, including:

(a) expenditures of funds provided for such instruction and facilities;

(b) appointment and direction of those responsible for the administration of such instruction and facilities;

(c) establishment of programs of instruction;

(d) recruitment and assignment of teachers and other personnel; and

(e) making of agreements for education and services for minority language pupils.

* * *

I think it should be self-evident that in situations where the above degree of management and control is warranted the quality of education provided to the minority should in principle be on a basis of equality with the majority. This proposition follows directly from the purpose of s. 23.

However, the specific form of educational system provided to the minority need not be identical to that provided to the majority. * * *

[P]rovincial and local authorities may, of course, give minority groups a greater degree of management and control than that described above. * * *

Appeal allowed.

BELGIAN LINGUISTIC CASE

[CASE "RELATING TO CERTAIN ASPECTS OF THE LAWS ON
THE USE OF LANGUAGES IN EDUCATION IN BELGIUM" v. BELGIUM].
European Court of Human Rights.
1 E.H.R.R. 252 (1968).

[French-speaking parents challenged the Belgian legislation on education, which divided the country into regions in order to determine the language of instruction at schools. The challenge was brought under Art. 2 of Protocol No. 1 to the European HR Convention, with reference to the "right of parents to ensure such education and teaching in conformity with their own religious and philosophical convictions." Additional claims were brought, *inter alia*, under Art. 8 (privacy), and Art. 14 (equal protection) of the European HR Convention.]

The Court:

* * *

4. The first sentence of Article 2 of the Protocol * * * guarantees, in the first place, a right of access to educational institutions existing at a given time, but such access constitutes only a part of the right to education. For the "right to education" to be effective, it is further necessary that, inter alia, the individual who is the beneficiary should have the possibility of drawing profit from the education received, that is to say, the right to obtain, in conformity with the rules in force in each State, and in one form or another, official recognition of the studies which he has completed. * * *

5. The right to education guaranteed by the first sentence of Article 2 of the Protocol (P1–2) by its very nature calls for regulation by the State, regulation which may vary in time and place according to the needs and resources of the community and of individuals. It goes without saying that such regulation must never injure the substance of the right to education nor conflict with other rights enshrined in the Convention.

* * * The Convention * * * implies a just balance between the protection of the general interest of the Community and the respect due to fundamental human rights while attaching particular importance to the latter.

6. The second sentence of Article 2 of the Protocol does not guarantee a right to education; this is clearly shown by its wording:

"* * * In the exercise of any functions which it assumes in relation to education and to teaching, the State shall respect the right of parents to ensure such education and teaching in conformity with their own religious and philosophical convictions."

This provision does not require of States that they should, in the sphere of education or teaching, respect parents' linguistic preferences, but only their religious and philosophical convictions. To interpret the terms "religious" and "philosophical" as covering linguistic preferences would amount to a distortion of their ordinary and usual meaning and to read into the Convention something which is not there. * * * The second sentence of Article 2 is therefore irrelevant to the problems raised in the present case.

7. According to the express terms of Article 8 (1) of the Convention, "everyone has the right to respect for his private and family life, his home and his correspondence".

This provision by itself in no way guarantees either a right to education or a personal right of parents relating to the education of their children: its object is essentially that of protecting the individual against arbitrary interference by the public authorities in his private family life.

However, it is not to be excluded that measures taken in the field of education may affect the right to respect for private and family life or derogate from it; this would be the case, for instance, if their aim or result were to disturb private or family life in an unjustifiable manner, inter alia by separating children from their parents in an arbitrary way.

As the Court has already emphasised, the Convention must be read as a whole. Consequently a matter specifically dealt with by one of its provisions may also, in some of its aspects, be regulated by other provisions of the Convention.

The Court will therefore examine the facts of the case in the light of the first sentence of Article 2 of the Protocol as well as of Article 8 of the Convention.

8. According to Article 14 of the Convention, the enjoyment of the rights and freedoms set forth therein shall be secured without discrimination ("*sans distinction aucune*") on the ground, inter alia, of language; and by the terms of Article 5 of the Protocol, this same guarantee applies equally to the rights and freedoms set forth in this instrument. It follows that both Article 2 of the Protocol and Article 8 of the Convention must be interpreted and applied by the Court not only in isolation but also having regard to the guarantee laid down in Article 14.

9. While it is true that this guarantee has no independent existence in the sense that under the terms of Article 14 it relates solely to "rights and freedoms set forth in the Convention", a measure which in itself is in conformity with the requirements of the Article enshrining the right or freedom in question may however infringe this Article when read in conjunction with Article 14 for the reason that it is of a discriminatory nature.

Thus, persons subject to the jurisdiction of a Contracting State cannot draw from Article 2 of the Protocol the right to obtain from the public authorities the creation of a particular kind of educational establishment; nevertheless, a State which had set up such an establishment could not, in laying down entrance requirements, take discriminatory measures within the meaning of Article 14. * * *

10. * * * Article 14 does not forbid every difference in treatment in the exercise of the rights and freedoms recognised. * * *

It is important, then, to look for the criteria which enable a determination to be made as to whether or not a given difference in treatment, concerning of course the exercise of one of the rights and freedoms set forth, contravenes Article 14. On this question the Court, following the principles which may be extracted from the legal practice of a large number of democratic States, holds that the principle of equality of treatment is violated if the distinction has no objective and reasonable justification. The existence of such a justification must be assessed in relation to the aim and effects of the measure under consideration, regard being had to the principles which normally prevail in democratic societies. A difference of treatment in the exercise of a right laid down in the Convention must not only pursue a legitimate aim: Article 14 is likewise violated when it is clearly established that there is no reasonable relationship of proportionality between the means employed and the aim sought to be realised.

* * * The national authorities remain free to choose the measures which they consider appropriate in those matters which are governed by the Convention. Review by the Court concerns only the conformity of these measures with the requirements of the Convention.

11. In the present case the Court notes that Article 14, even when read in conjunction with Article 2 of the Protocol, does not have the effect of guaranteeing to a child or to his parent the right to obtain instruction in a language of his choice. The object of these two Articles, read in conjunction, is more limited: it is to ensure that the right to education shall be secured by each Contracting Party to everyone within its jurisdiction without discrimination on the ground, for instance, of language. * * * Furthermore, to interpret the two provisions as conferring on everyone within the jurisdiction of a State a right to obtain education in the language of his own choice would lead to absurd results, for it would be open to anyone to claim any language of instruction in any of the territories of the Contracting Parties.

MEYER v. STATE OF NEBRASKA

Supreme Court (United States).
262 U.S. 390 (1923).

[Act Neb. April 9, 1919, Laws 1919, c. 249, prohibited the teaching of any subject in any language other than the English language or the teaching of languages other than the English language to pupils who had not passed the eighth grade. Plaintiff was convicted for teaching German to a 10–year-old child.[1]]

Mr. Justice McReynolds delivered the opinion of the Court.

---

1. The reason given by Meyer was that he intended to help children to participate in Lutheran services, which were taught in German. It is possible to construe the issue as one of free exercise of religion. The law in *Meyer* must be understood in the context of the strong anti-German sentiment prevailing in the U.S. after World War One.

The Supreme Court of [Nebraska] affirmed the judgment of conviction.

* * *

While this court has not attempted to define with exactness the liberty thus guaranteed, the term has received much consideration and some of the included things have been definitely stated. Without doubt, it denotes not merely freedom from bodily restraint but also the right of the individual to contract, to engage in any of the common occupations of life, to acquire useful knowledge, to marry, establish a home and bring up children, to worship God according to the dictates of his own conscience, and generally to enjoy those privileges long recognized at common law as essential to the orderly pursuit of happiness by free men.
* * *

Corresponding to the right of control, it is the natural duty of the parent to give his children education suitable to their station in life; and nearly all the states, including Nebraska, enforce this obligation by compulsory laws.

Practically, education of the young is only possible in schools conducted by especially qualified persons who devote themselves thereto. The calling always has been regarded as useful and honorable, essential, indeed, to the public welfare. Mere knowledge of the German language cannot reasonably be regarded as harmful. Heretofore it has been commonly looked upon as helpful and desirable. Plaintiff in error taught this language in school as part of his occupation. His right thus to teach and the right of parents to engage him so to instruct their children, we think, are within the liberty of the [Fourteenth] amendment.

* * *

It is said the purpose of the legislation was to promote civic development by inhibiting training and education of the immature in foreign tongues and ideals before they could learn English and acquire American ideals, and 'that the English language should be and become the mother tongue of all children reared in this state.'[m] It is also affirmed that the foreign born population is very large, that certain communities commonly use foreign words, follow foreign leaders, move in a foreign atmosphere, and that the children are thereby hindered from becoming citizens of the most useful type and the public safety is imperiled.

* * *

The desire of the Legislature to foster a homogeneous people with American ideals prepared readily to understand current discussions of civic matters is easy to appreciate. Unfortunate experiences during the late war and aversion toward every character of truculent adversaries were certainly enough to quicken that aspiration. But the means adopted, we think, exceed the limitations upon the power of the state and conflict with rights assured to plaintiff in error. The interference is

m. This was understood by the Nebraska Supreme Court as a legitimate use of the state's police power, which is not subject to judicial review.

plain enough and no adequate reason therefore in time of peace and domestic tranquility has been shown.

* * *

Reversed.

Mr. Justice Holmes and Mr. Justice Sutherland, dissent.

LAU v. NICHOLS

Supreme Court (United States).
414 U.S. 563 (1974).

[In a class action suit against the officials of the of the San Francisco Unified School District, non-English-speaking Chinese students challenged their unequal educational opportunities. In the integrated school system of California, only half of the Chinese students speaking no or very little English received special English instruction. The lower courts did not find a violation of equal protection under the Fourteenth Amendment or s. 601 of the Civil Rights Act.]

Mr. Justice Douglas delivered the opinion of the Court.

* * *

[S]71 of the California Education Code states that 'English shall be the basic language of instruction in all schools.' That section permits a school district to determine 'when and under what circumstances instruction may be given bilingually.' That section also states as 'the policy of the state' to insure 'the mastery of English by all pupils in the schools.' And bilingual instruction is authorized 'to the extent that it does not interfere with the systematic, sequential, and regular instruction of all pupils in the English language.' Moreover, s 8573 of the Education Code provides that no pupil shall receive a diploma of graduation from grade 12 who has not met the standards of proficiency in 'English,' as well as other prescribed subjects. Moreover, by s 12101 of the Education Code (Supp. 1973) children between the ages of six and 16 years are (with exceptions not material here) 'subject to compulsory full-time education.'

Under these state-imposed standards there is no equality of treatment merely by providing students with the same facilities, textbooks, teachers, and curriculum; for students who do not understand English are effectively foreclosed from any meaningful education.

Basic English skills are at the very core of what these public schools teach. Imposition of a requirement that, before a child can effectively participate in the educational program, he must already have acquired those basic skills is to make a mockery of public education. We know that those who do not understand English are certain to find their classroom experiences wholly incomprehensible and in no way meaningful.

[2]   We do not reach the Equal Protection Clause argument which has been advanced but rely solely on s 601 of the Civil Rights Act of 1964, to reverse the Court of Appeals.

That section bans discrimination based 'on the ground of race, color, or national origin,' in 'any program or activity receiving Federal financial assistance.' The school district involved in this litigation receives large amounts of federal financial assistance. The Department of Health, Education, and Welfare (HEW), which has authority to promulgate regulations prohibiting discrimination in federally assisted school systems, in 1968 issued one guideline that '(s)chool systems are responsible for assuring that students of a particular race, color, or national origin are not denied the opportunity to obtain the education generally obtained by other students in the system.' 33 Fed.Reg. 4955. In 1970 HEW made the guidelines more specific, requiring school districts that were federally funded 'to rectify the language deficiency in order to open' the instruction to students who had 'linguistic deficiencies,' 35 Fed.Reg. 11595.

By s 602 of the Act HEW is authorized to issue rules, regulations, and orders to make sure that recipients of federal aid under its jurisdiction conduct any federally financed projects consistently with s 601. HEW's regulations, specify that the recipients may not

'(ii) Provide any service, financial aid, or other benefit to an individual which is different, or is provided in a different manner, from that provided to others under the program;

(iv) Restrict an individual in any way in the enjoyment of any advantage or privilege enjoyed by others receiving any service, financial aid, or other benefit under the program.

Discrimination among students on account of race or national origin that is prohibited includes 'discrimination * * * in the availability or use of any academic * * * or other facilities of the grantee or other recipient.' *Id.*, s 80.5(b).

Discrimination is barred which has that effect even though no purposeful design is present: a recipient 'may not * * * utilize criteria or methods of administration which have the effect of subjecting individuals to discrimination' or have 'the effect of defeating or substantially impairing accomplishment of the objectives of the program as respect individuals of a particular race, color, or national origin.' *Id.*, s 80.3(b)(2).

It seems obvious that the Chinese-speaking minority receive fewer benefits than the English-speaking majority from respondents' school system which denies them a meaningful opportunity to participate in the educational program—all earmarks of the discrimination banned by the regulations. In 1970 HEW issued clarifying guidelines, which include the following:

'Where inability to speak and understand the English language excludes national origin-minority group children from effective participation in the educational program offered by a school district, the district must take affirmative steps to rectify the language deficiency in order to open its instructional program to these students.'

'Any ability grouping or tracking system employed by the school system to deal with the special language skill needs of national origin-minority group children must be designed to meet such language skill needs as soon as possible and must not operate as an educational deadend or permanent track.'

Respondent school district contractually agreed to 'comply with title VI of the Civil Rights Act of 1964 * * * and all requirements imposed by or pursuant to the Regulation' of HEW (45 CFR pt. 80) which are 'issued pursuant to that title . . .' and also immediately to 'take any measures necessary to effectuate this agreement.' The Federal Government has power to fix the terms on which its money allotments to the States shall be disbursed. * * *

Reversed and remanded.

Mr. Justice White concurs in the result.

Mr. Justice Stewart, with whom The Chief Justice and Mr. Justice Blackmun join, concurring in the result (omitted).

Mr. Justice Blackmun, with whom The Chief Justice joins, concurring in the result.

I join Mr. Justice Stewart's opinion and thus I, too, concur in the result. Against the possibility that the Court's judgment may be interpreted too broadly, I stress the fact that the children with whom we are concerned here number about 1,800. This is a very substantial group that is being deprived of any meaningful schooling because the children cannot understand the language of the classroom. We may only guess as to why they have had no exposure to English in their preschool years. Earlier generations of American ethnic groups have overcome the language barrier by earnest parental endeavor or by the hard fact of being pushed out of the family or community nest and into the realities of broader experience.

I merely wish to make plain that when, in another case, we are concerned with a very few youngsters, or with just a single child who speaks only German or Polish or Spanish or any language other than English, I would not regard today's decision, or the separate concurrence, as conclusive upon the issue whether the statute and the guidelines require the funded school district to provide special instruction. For me, numbers are at the heart of this case and my concurrence is to be understood accordingly.

AHMEDABAD ST. XAVIER'S COLLEGE SOCIETY v. STATE OF GUJARAT

Supreme Court (India).
(1974)1 S.C.C. 717.[n]

[The petitioner, an educational institution that sought to provide higher education to Christian students, challenged certain provisions of the Gujarat University (Amendment) Act, 1972 that enabled the university to regulate certain matters, as being violative of the petitioner's

n. The issue is currently being reviewed by a 11–judge Constitution Bench of the Supreme Court (hearings began on April 2, 2002) and may well result in the entire law on the subject being rewritten as the purpose of constituting a Bench of this strength is to ensure that the present Bench is not constrained by the binding precedents of earlier Constitution Benches.

right to administer educational institutions guaranteed by Arts. 29 and 30.[o] Institutions that are maintained wholly by state funds are prohibited from providing religious instruction; furthermore, institutions that receive state funds are prohibited from compelling persons to attend any religious worship.[p]]

[The case resulted in a 7–2 decision, with the majority striking down the impugned provisions as being violative of the petitioner organization's right to administration.]

Ray, C.J. (on *behalf of himself and Palekar*, J.)

5.   Articles 29 and 30 confer four distinct rights. First is the right of any section of the resident citizens to conserve its own language, script or culture as mentioned in Article 29(1). Second is the right of all religious and linguistic minorities to establish and administer educational institutions of their choice as mentioned in Article 30(1). Third is the right of an educational institution not to be discriminated against in the matter of State aid on the ground that it is under the management of a religious or linguistic minority as mentioned in Article 30(2). Fourth is the right of the citizen not to be denied admission into any State maintained or State aided educational institution on the ground of religion, caste, race or language, as mentioned in Article 29(2).

6.   It will be wrong to read Article 30(1) as restricting the right of minorities to establish and administer educational institutions of their choice only to cases where such institutions are concerned with language, script or culture of the minorities. The reasons are these. * * * [T]he conservation of language, script or culture under Article 29(1) may be by means wholly unconnected with educational institutions and similarly establishment and administration of educational institutions by a minority under Article 30(1) may be unconnected with any motive to conserve language, script or culture. A minority may administer an institution for religious education which is wholly unconnected with any question of conserving a language, script or culture.

o. The text of the two provisions is as follows:

29. Protection of interests of minorities.–

(1) Any section of the citizens residing in the territory of India or any part thereof having a distinct language, script or culture of its own shall have the right to conserve the same.

(2) No citizen shall be denied admission into any educational institution maintained by the State or receiving aid out of State funds on grounds only of religion, race, caste, language or any of them.

30. Right of minorities to establish and administer educational institutions.–

(1) All minorities, whether based on religion or language, shall have the right to establish and administer educational institutions of their choice.

(1A) In making any law providing for the compulsory acquisition of any property of any educational institution established and administered by a minority, referred to in clause (1), the State shall ensure that the amount fixed by or determined under such law for the acquisition of such property is such as would not restrict or abrogate the right guaranteed under that clause.

(2) The State shall not, in granting aid to educational institutions, discriminate against any educational institution on the ground that it is under the management of a minority, whether based on religion or language.

p. Article 28 of the Constitution of India.

7. If the scope of Article 30(1) is to establish and administer educational institutions to conserve language, script or culture of minorities, it will render Article 30 redundant. If rights under Articles 29(1) and 30(1) are the same then the consequence will be that any section of citizens not necessarily linguistic or religious minorities will have the right to establish and administer educational institutions of their choice. The scope of Article 30 rests on linguistic or religious minorities and no other section of citizens of India has such a right.

8. The right to establish and administer educational institutions of their choice has been conferred on religious and linguistic minorities so that the majority who can always have their rights by having proper legislation do not pass a legislation prohibiting minorities to establish and administer educational institutions of their choice. If the scope of Article 30(1) is made an extension of the right under Article 29(1) as the right to establish and administer educational institutions for giving religious instruction or for imparting education in their religious teachings or tenets, the fundamental right of minorities to establish and administer educational institutions of their choice will be taken away.

9. * * * The whole object of conferring the right on minorities under Article 30 is to ensure that there will be equality between the majority and the minority. If the minorities do not have such special protection they will be denied equality.

       * * *

12. The real reason embodied in Article 30(1) of the Constitution is the conscience of the nation that the minorities, religious as well as linguistic, are not prohibited from establishing and administering educational institutions of their choice for the purpose of giving their children the best general education to make them complete men and women of the country. The minorities are given this protection under Article 30 in order to preserve and strengthen the integrity and unity of the country. The sphere of general secular education is intended to develop the commonness of boys and girls of our country. This is in the true spirit of liberty, equality and fraternity through the medium of education. If religious or linguistic minorities are not given protection under Article 30 to establish and administer educational institutions of their choice, they will feel isolated and separate. General secular education will open doors of perception and act as the natural light of mind for our countrymen to live in the whole.

[One of the issues concerned the "affiliation" of minority educational institutions with state-funded universities, i.e., to what extent should the all-university regulations apply to minority institutions in regard to "establishment" (syllabi, qualifications of teachers) and terms and conditions of management?]

17. When a minority institution applies to a University to be affiliated, it expresses its choice to participate in the system of general education and courses of instruction prescribed by that University. Affiliation is regulating courses of instruction in institutions for the purpose of co-ordinating and harmonizing the standards of education. With regard to affiliation to a University, the minority and non-minority

institutions must agree in the pattern and standards of education. Regulatory measures of affiliation enable the minority institutions to share the same courses of instruction and the same degrees with the non-minority institutions.

* * *

19.   The entire controversy centres round the extent of the right of the religious and linguistic minorities to administer their educational institutions. The right to administer is said to consist of four principal matters. First is the right to choose its managing or governing body. It is said that the founders of the minority institution have faith and confidence in their own committee or body consisting of persons elected by them. Second is the right to choose its teachers. It is said that minority institutions want teachers to have compatibility with the ideals, aims and aspirations of the institution. Third is the right not to be compelled to refuse admission to students. In other words, the minority institutions want to have the right to admit students of their choice subject to reasonable regulations about academic qualifications. Fourth is the right to use its properties and assets for the benefit of its own institution.

20.   The right conferred on the religious and linguistic minorities to administer educational institutions of their choice is not an absolute right. This right is not free from regulation. Just as regulatory measures are necessary for maintaining the educational character, and content of minority institutions similarly regulatory measures are necessary for ensuring orderly, efficient and sound administration. * * *

21.   On behalf of the petitioners, it. is said that the right to administer means autonomy in administration.

* * *

30.   * * * [T]he appointment of teachers is an important part in educational institutions. The qualifications and the character of the teachers are really important. The minority institutions have the right to administer institutions. This right implies the obligation and duty of the minority institutions to render the very best to the students. In the right of administration, checks and balances in the shape of regulatory measures are required to ensure the appointment of good teachers and their conditions of service. The right to administer is to be tempered with regulatory measures to facilitate smooth administration. The best administration will reveal no trace or colour of minority. A minority institution should shine in exemplary eclectism in the administration of the institution. The best compliment that can be paid to a minority institution is that it does not rest on or proclaim its minority character.

* * *

32.   Education should be a great cohesive force in developing integrity of the nation. Education develops the ethos of the nation. Regulations are, therefore, necessary to see that there are no divisive or disintegrating forces in administration.

* * *

41. Autonomy in administration means right to administer effectively and to manage and conduct the affairs of the institutions. * * * In *State of Kerala v. Very Rev. Mother Provincial, etc.* [(1971) 1 S.C.R. 734: (1970) 2 S.C.C. 417] * * * this Court said that if the administration goes to a body in the selection of whom the founders have no say, the administration would be displaced. This Court also said that situations might be conceived when they might have a preponderating voice. That would also effect the autonomy in administration. The provisions contained in Section 33A(*l*)(*a*) of the Act have the effect of displacing the management and entrusting it to a different agency. The autonomy in administration is lost. * * * These provisions in Section 33A(*l*)(*o*) cannot therefore apply to minority institutions.

* * *

45. For these reasons the provisions contained in Sections 40, 41, 33A(*l*)(*a*), 33A(*l*)(f), 51A and 52A cannot be applied to minority institutions. These provisions violate the fundamental rights of the minority institutions.

46. The ultimate goal of a minority institution too imparting general secular education is advancement of learning. This Court has consistently held that it is not only permissible but also desirable to regulate everything in educational and academic matters for achieving excellence and uniformity in standards of education.

47. In the field of administration it is not reasonable to claim that minority institutions will have complete autonomy. Checks on the administration may be necessary in order to ensure that the administration is efficient and sound and will serve the academic needs of the institution. The right of a minority to administer its educational institution involves, as part of it, a correlative duty of good administration.

* * *

Khanna, J (concurring):

* * *

75. * * * Demand had also been made before the partition by sections of people belonging to the minorities for reservation of seats and separate electorates. In order to bring about integration and fusion of the different sections of the population, the framers of the Constitution did away with separate electorates and introduced the system of joint electorates, so that every candidate in an election should have to look for support of all sections of the citizens. Special safeguards were guaranteed for the minorities and they were made a part of the fundamental rights with a view to instill a sense of confidence and security in the minorities. Those provisions were a kind of a Charter of rights for the minorities so that none might have the feeling that any section of the population consisted of first-class citizens and the others of second-class citizens. The result was that minorities gave up their claims for reservation of seats.

* * *

It is in the context of that background that we should view the provisions of the Constitution contained in Articles 25 to 30. The object of Articles 25 to 30 was to preserve the rights of religious and linguistic minorities, to place them on a secure pedestal and withdraw them from the vicissitudes of political controversy. These provisions enshrined a befitting pledge to the minorities in the Constitution of the country whose greatest son had laid down his life for the protection of the minorities. As long as the Constitution stands as it is today, no tampering with those rights can be countenanced. Any attempt to do so would be not only an act of breach of faith, it would be constitutionally impermissible and liable to be struck down by the courts. * * *

76. As in the case of religion so in the case of language, the importance of the matter and the sensitivity of the people on this issue was taken note of by the Constitution-makers. Language has a close relationship with culture. According to the *Royal Commission* on *Bilingualism and Biculturalism* (1965), the vitality of the language is an essential condition for the preservation of a culture and an attempt to provide for cultural equality is primarily an attempt to make provisions for linguistic equality (quoted on page 590 of *Canadian Constitutional Law in a Modern Perspective* by J. Noel Lyon and Ronald G. Atkey).

77. The idea of giving some special rights to the minorities is not to have a kind of a privileged or pampered section of the population but to give to the minorities a sense of security and a feeling of confidence. The great leaders of India since time immemorial had preached the doctrine of tolerance and catholicity of outlook. Those noble ideas were enshrined in the Constitution. Special rights for minorities were designed not to create inequality. Their real effect was to bring about equality by ensuring the preservation of the minority institutions and by guaranteeing to the minorities autonomy in the matter of the administration of those institutions. The differential treatment for the minorities by giving them special rights is intended to bring about an equilibrium, so that the ideal of equality may not be reduced to a mere abstract idea but should become a living reality and result in true, genuine equality, an equality not merely in theory but also in fact. The majority in a system of adult franchise hardly needs any protection. It can look after itself and protect its interests. Any measure wanted by the majority can without much difficulty be brought on the statute book because the majority can get that done by giving such a mandate to the elected representatives. It is only the minorities who need protection, and Article 30, besides some other articles, is intended to afford and guarantee that protection.

        * * *

89. A liberal, generous and sympathetic approach is reflected in the Constitution in the matter of the preservation of the right of minorities so far as their educational institutions are concerned. * * * The minorities are as much children of the soil as the majority and the approach has been to ensure that nothing should be done as might deprive the minorities of a sense of belonging, of a feeling of security, of a consciousness of equality and of the awareness that the conservation of their religion, culture, language and script as also the protection of their

educational institutions is a fundamental right enshrined in the Constitution. The same generous, liberal and sympathetic approach should weigh with the courts in construing Articles 29 and 30 as marked the deliberations of the Constitution-makers in drafting those articles and making them part of the fundamental rights. The safeguarding of the interest of the minorities amongst sections of population is as important as the protection of the interest amongst individuals of persons who are below the age of majority or are otherwise suffering from some kind of infirmity. The Constitution and the laws made by civilized nations, therefore, generally contain provisions for the protection of those interests. It can, indeed, be said to be an index of the level of civilization and catholicity of a nation as to how far their minorities feel secure and are not subject to any discrimination or suppression.

90. * * * The right of the minorities to administer educational institutions does not, however, prevent the making of reasonable regulations in respect of those institutions. The regulations have necessarily to be made in the interest of the institution as a minority educational institution. They have to be so designed as to make it an effective vehicle for imparting education. * * * Regulations made in the true interests of efficiency of instruction, discipline, health, sanitation, morality, public order and the like may undoubtedly be imposed. Such regulations are not restrictions on the substance of the right which is guaranteed: they secure the proper functioning of the institution, in matters educational * * *

ST. STEPHEN'S COLLEGE v. UNIVERSITY OF DELHI

Supreme Court (India).
(1992) 1 S.C.C. 558.

The Judgments of the Court were delivered by

Jagannatha Shetty, J. (*for Kania, J., himself, Fatima Beevi and Yogeswar Dayal, JJ* [Justice Kasliwal, dissenting].)—

Introduction

1. St. Stephen's College at Delhi and Allahabad Agricultural Institute at Naini are two of our premier and renowned institutions. The former has been affiliated to the Delhi University and the latter to the U.P. University. Both are aided educational institutions and getting grant from the State funds. They have their own admission programme which they follow every academic year. The admission programme provides for giving preference in favour of Christian students.

* * *

Question of Law

17. [The issues included, among others, whether]

* * * the College shall admit students on the basis of merit of the percentage of marks secured by the students in the qualifying examinations?

Whether St. Stephen's College and the Allahabad Agricultural Institute are entitled to accord preference to or reserve seats for students of their own community * * *?

* * *

60.   The right to select students for admission is a part of administration. It is indeed an important facet of administration. This power also could be regulated but the regulation must be reasonable just like any other regulation. It should be conducive to the welfare of the minority institution or for the betterment of those who resort to it * * *.

* * *

82.   The core of the argument of counsel for the University and Students Union is that the minority institutions getting government aid are bound by the mandate of Article 29(2) and they cannot prefer their own candidates * * *.

* * *

84.   The access to academic institutions maintained or aided by the State funds is the special concern of Article 29(2). It recognises the right of an individual not to be discriminated under the aegis of religion, race, caste, language or any of them. This is one of the basic principles of a secular State. * * *

85.   The fact that Article 29(2) applies to minorities as well as non-minorities does not mean that it was intended to nullify the special right guaranteed to minorities in Article 30(1). Article 29(2) deals with non-discrimination and it is available only to individuals. The general equality by non-discrimination is not the only goal of minorities. The minority rights under the majority rule implies more than non-discrimination and indeed, it begins with non-discrimination. Protection of interests and institutions and advancement of opportunity are just as important. Differential treatment that distinguishes them from the majority is a must to preserve their basic characteristics. To be blunt, black men do not wish to be white. Jews do not wish to be Protestants. Serbs do not want to be Croats. French Canadians do not want to lose their French heritage. There are many other instances, including the Corsicans in France, the Irish Catholics in Ulster, the French Canadians in Quebec, the Albanians in Kosovo, Yugoslavia, the Tamils in Sri Lanka, the Islamic separatists in the Phillipines, and the Animist and Christian minorities in southern Sudan. The problem in India is not quite different. India is a multicultural and multi-religious society. It is an extraordinary pluralistic and complex society with different religious minorities. Besides there are linguistic aspirations and caste considerations. There may be individuals in the minority group who want to assimilate into the majority, but the group itself has a collective interest for non-assimilation. It is interested in its preservation and promotion as a community. This appears to be the chief reason for which Article 30(1) was incorporated as a fundamental right. Article 27 of the International Covenant on Civil and Political Rights (1966) also lays a foundation in this regard. It states:

"In those States in which ethnic, religious or linguistic minorities exist, persons belonging to such minorities shall not be denied the right, in community with the other members of their group, to enjoy their own culture, to profess and practise their own religion, or to use their own language."

86. Yet another submission which counsel argued is that in a secular democracy the government fund cannot be utilised to promote the interests of any particular community and Article 29(2) interdicts only when the minority institution seeks and gets State financial aid and the minority institution is not entitled to State aid as of right.

87. It is quite true that there is no entitlement to State grant for minority educational institutions. * * * But under Article 30(2), the State is under an obligation to maintain equality of treatment in granting aid to educational institutions. Minority institutions are not to be treated differently while giving financial assistance. They are entitled to get the financial assistance much the same way as the institutions of the majority communities.

88. Second, the receipt of State aid does not impair the rights in Article 30(1). The State can lay down reasonable conditions for obtaining grant-in-aid and for its proper utilisation. The State has no power to compel minority institutions to give up their rights under Article 30(1). * * * In the latter case, this Court observed (at SCR pp. 856–57) that the regulation which may lawfully be imposed as a condition of receiving grant must be directed in making the institution an effective minority educational institution. The regulation cannot change the character of the minority institution. Such regulations must satisfy a dual test; the test of reasonableness, and the test that it is regulative of the educational character of the institution. It must be conducive to making the institution an effective vehicle of education for the minority community or other persons who resort to it. It is thus evident that the rights under Article 30(1) remain unaffected even after securing financial assistance from the government.

89. The educational institutions are not business houses. They do not generate wealth. They cannot survive without public funds or private aid. It is said that there is also restraint on collection of students fees. With the restraint on collection of fees, the minorities cannot be saddled with the burden of maintaining educational institutions without grant-in-aid. They do not have economic advantage over others. It is not possible to have educational institutions without State aid. This was also the view expressed by Das, C.J., in *Kerala Education Bill case*[11]. The minorities cannot therefore, be asked to maintain educational institutions on their own.

        * * *

102. In the light of all these principles and factors, and in view of the importance which the Constitution attaches to protective measures to minorities under Article 30(1), the minority aided educational institutions are entitled to prefer their community candidates to maintain the

---

11. 1959 SCR 995: AIR 1958 SC 956.

minority character of the institutions subject of course to conformity with the University standard. The State may regulate the intake in this category with due regard to the need of the community in the area which the institution is intended to serve. But in no case such intake shall exceed 50 per cent of the annual admission. The minority institutions shall make available at least 50 per cent of the annual admission to members of communities other than the minority community. The admission of other community candidates shall be done purely on the basis of merit.

Notes and Questions

1. While holding that the right of citizens to obtain higher education was constrained by the availability of the state's resources, the Indian Supreme Court (ISC) evolved a scheme to govern admissions into private colleges for medicine and engineering. As the scheme's implementation unfolded, the issue of its applicability to minority educational institutions arose. In one such case a 7–judge bench of the Supreme Court raised questions that are relevant for most programs that aim to promote ethnic identity:

> (2) What are the indicia for treating an educational institution as a minority educational institution? Would an institution be regarded as a minority educational institution only because it was established by a person(s) belonging to a religious or linguistic minority or it is being administered by a person(s) belonging to a religious or linguistic minority?

> (3) Whether the minority's 'right to establish and administer educational institutions of their choice' will include the procedure and method of admission and selection of a student?

2. Minority protection might be concerned with the weakness of a group, but it may also serve the recognition of ethnic/national differences. Which consideration underlies the provisions of the Indian Constitution? In *St. Stephen's College* Justice Jagannatha Shetty held that (para. 28) "Article 30(1) is a protective measure only for the benefit of religious and linguistic minorities and it is essential to make it absolutely clear that no ill-fit or camouflaged institution should get away with the constitutional protection." Do all the justices in *Xavier* interpret this in the same way? Do rights to special education or language use differ whether they apply to a majority or a minority? Is the reasoning of the affirmative action cases above helpful for purposes of answering the last question?

3. Many mainstream liberal democracies have approved assimilation and integration into the majority. See Will Kymlicka, *Multicultural Citizenship: A Liberal Theory of Minority Rights* 14 (1995) (contrasting the U.S. as a "melting pot" with Canada as a multicultural "mosaic"). Assimilation, however, requires change, which individuals and groups may feel will result in serious loss for them. Is assimilation culturally destructive? Does it make a difference if assimilation is required for foreigners who have voluntarily immigrated as opposed to an indigenous population? See E.3. below.

4. Note that *Lau* is a late development in the history of recognizing the special concerns of ethnic minorities. Joyce Kuo discusses the changed

position of the San Francisco School Board on Chinese–Americans in public schools:

> Initially excluding Chinese Americans from attending public schools, the School Board fluctuated several times in its attitude towards these students—first excluding them, then admitting them into a separate school, then excluding them again—until the School Board settled on a segregated system. At the same time, the Chinese American community was divided in how to react to the exclusion and segregation policies, with one group opting to find alternative educational resources and the other group struggling to change the system. * * * [T]his latter group attempt[ed] to appeal to the United States Constitution in order to reverse the discriminatory policies of the state legislatures and school boards. Their lack of success in these cases effectively closed off the option of using the legal system to redress their wrongs. * * * Whereas Japanese Americans were able to successfully overcome the segregation barrier by employing their political power, Chinese Americans were unable to garner similar support and influence to assist them. * * * [However], the Chinese Americans in San Francisco were able to break down the policy of segregation gradually by pursuing case-by-case exceptions, by establishing their interest in public school education through their sheer numbers, and by finally gaining enough leverage to persuade the School Board to open up the public school system.

Joyce Kuo, *Excluded, Segregated and Forgotten: A Historical View of the Discrimination of Chinese Americans in Public Schools,* 5 Asian L.J. 181, 183–184 (1998).

"*Lau* drove a vast expansion of bilingual education programs in the public schools for the bewildering array of language groups that the post–1965 immigration brought to America." Peter H. Schuck, *The Perceived Values of Diversity, Then and Now*, 22 Cardozo L. Rev. 1915, 1935 (2001). For a discussion of the changing attitude toward foreign languages in the U.S., see Michel Rosenfeld, *Bilingualism, National Identity and Diversity in the United States,* 34 Revista de Llengua I Dret 129 (2000) (the U.S. has always been multilingual, and the federal Constitution does not impose any official language; state movements toward "English only" have waxed and waned with the flows of new immigration waves).

5. The choice of the "official" or primary language is itself one measure of assimilation. In the U.S., "[t]here is still a lively debate over the effects of language on an individual's definition of reality, but no one can doubt that language is one of the 'symbol spheres' that define social groups and provide justification for social structures. A distinctive language sets a cultural group off from others, with one consistent unhappy consequence throughout American history: discrimination against members of the cultural minority. Language differences provide both a way to rationalize subordination and a ready means for accomplishing it." Karst, *op. cit.* at 351–352.

6. Compare the educational structures that emerge following the dictates of minority-identity requirements in *Mahe* and *St. Stephen's College.* Are these differences due to differences in the level of education?

E.3.   ABORIGINAL GROUP RIGHTS

SANDRA LOVELACE v. CANADA

Human Rights Committee (United Nations).
Communication No. R.6/24 (29 December 1977).
U.N. Doc. Supp. No. 40 (A/36/40) at 166 (1981).

[Sandra Lovelace] is a 32–year-old woman, living in Canada. She was born and registered as "Maliseet Indian" but has lost her rights and status as an Indian in accordance with section 12 (1) (b) of the Indian Act, after having married a non-Indian on 23 May 1970. Pointing out that an Indian man who marries a non-Indian woman does not lose his Indian status, she claims that the Act is discriminatory on the grounds of sex and contrary to articles 2 (1), 3, 23 (1) and (4), 26 and 27 of the Covenant.

* * *

The State party * * * referred to an earlier public declaration to the effect that it intended to put a reform bill before the Canadian Parliament. It none the less stressed the necessity of the Indian Act as an instrument designed to protect the Indian minority in accordance with article 27 of the Covenant. A definition of the Indian was inevitable in view of the special privileges granted to the Indian communities, in particular their right to occupy reserve lands. Traditionally, patrilineal family relationships were taken into account for determining legal claims. Since, additionally, in the farming societies of the nineteenth century, reserve land was felt to be more threatened by non-Indian men than by non-Indian women, legal enactments as from 1869 provided that an Indian woman who married a non-Indian man would lose her status as an Indian. These reasons were still valid. * * *

[Sandra Lovelace] in her submission * * * disputes the contention that legal relationships within Indian families were traditionally patrilineal in nature.

* * *

The Human Rights Committee recognized that the relevant provision of the Indian Act, although not legally restricting the right to marry as laid down in article 23 (2) of the Covenant, entails serious disadvantages on the part of the Indian woman who wants to marry a non-Indian man and may in fact cause her to live with her fiancé in an unmarried relationship. There is thus a question as to whether the obligation of the State party under article 23 of the Covenant with regard to the protection of the family is complied with. Moreover, since only Indian women and not Indian men are subject to these disadvantages under the Act, the question arises whether Canada complies with its commitment under articles 2 and 3 to secure the rights under the Covenant without discrimination as to sex. On the other hand, article 27 of the Covenant requires States parties to accord protection to ethnic and linguistic minorities and the Committee must give due weight to this obligation.
* * *

In regard to the present communication, however, the Human Rights Committee must also take into account that the Covenant has entered into force in respect of Canada on 19 August 1976, several years after the marriage of Mrs. Lovelace. She consequently lost her status as an Indian at a time when Canada was not bound by the Covenant. The Human Rights Committee has held that it is empowered to consider a communication when the measures complained of, although they occurred before the entry into force of the Covenant, continued to have effects which themselves constitute a violation of the Covenant after that date. It is therefore relevant for the Committee to know whether the marriage of Mrs. Lovelace in 1970 has had any such effects.

* * *

The Committee first observes that from 19 August 1976 Canada had undertaken under article 2 (1) and (2) of the Covenant to respect and ensure to all individuals within its territory and subject to its jurisdiction, the rights recognized in the Covenant without distinction of any kind such as sex, and to adopt the necessary measures to give effect to these rights. Further, under article 3, Canada undertook to ensure the equal right of men and women to the enjoyment of these rights. These undertakings apply also to the position of Sandra Lovelace. The Committee considers, however, that it is not necessary for the purposes of her communication to decide their extent in all respects. The full scope of the obligation of Canada to remove the effects or inequalities caused by the application of existing laws to past events, in particular as regards such matters as civil or personal status, does not have to be examined in the present case, for the reasons set out below.

The Committee considers that the essence of the present complaint concerns the continuing effect of the Indian Act, in denying Sandra Lovelace legal status as an Indian, in particular because she cannot for this reason claim a legal right to reside where she wishes to, on the Tobique Reserve. This fact persists after the entry into force of the Covenant, and its effects have to be examined, without regard to their original cause. Among the effects referred to on behalf of the author the greater number, relate to the Indian Act and other Canadian rules in fields which do not necessarily adversely affect the enjoyment of rights protected by the Covenant. In this respect the significant matter is her last claim, that "the major loss to a person ceasing to be an Indian is the loss of the cultural benefits of living in an Indian community, the emotional ties to home, family, friends and neighbours, and the loss of identity".

Although a number of provisions of the Covenant have been invoked by Sandra Lovelace, the Committee considers that the one which is most directly applicable to this complaint is article 27, which reads as follows:

"In those States in which ethnic, religious or linguistic minorities exist, persons belonging to such minorities shall not be denied the right, in community with the other members of their group, to enjoy their own culture, to profess and practise their own religion, or to use their own language."

It has to be considered whether Sandra Lovelace, because she is denied the legal right to reside on the Tobique Reserve, has by that fact been denied the right guaranteed by article 27 to persons belonging to minorities, to enjoy their own culture and to use their own language in community with other members of their group.

The rights under article 27 of the Covenant have to be secured to "persons belonging" to the minority. At present Sandra Lovelace does not qualify as an Indian under Canadian legislation. However, the Indian Act deals primarily with a number of privileges which, as stated above, do not as such come within the scope of the Covenant. Protection under the Indian Act and protection under article 27 of the Covenant therefore have to be distinguished. Persons who are born and brought up on a reserve who have kept ties with their community and wish to maintain these ties must normally be considered as belonging to that minority within the meaning of the Covenant. Since Sandra Lovelace is ethnically a Maliseet Indian and has only been absent from her home reserve for a few years during the existence of her marriage, she is, in the opinion of the Committee, entitled to be regarded as "belonging" to this minority and to claim the benefits of article 27 of the Covenant. The question whether these benefits have been denied to her, depends on how far they extend.

The right to live on a reserve is not as such guaranteed by article 27 of the Covenant. Moreover, the Indian Act does not interfere directly with the functions which are expressly mentioned in that article. However, in the opinion of the Committee the right of Sandra Lovelace to access to her native culture and language "in community with the other members" of her group, has in fact been, and continues to be interfered with, because there is no place outside the Tobique Reserve where such a community exists. On the other hand, not every interference can be regarded as a denial of rights within the meaning of article 27. Restrictions on the right to residence, by way of national legislation, cannot be ruled out under article 27 of the Covenant.

In this respect, the Committee is of the view that statutory restrictions affecting the right to residence on a reserve of a person belonging to the minority concerned, must have both a reasonable and objective justification and be consistent with the other provisions of the Covenant, read as a whole.

* * *

Whatever may be the merits of the Indian Act in other respects, it does not seem to the Committee that to deny Sandra Lovelace the right to reside on the reserve is reasonable, or necessary to preserve the identity of the tribe. The Committee therefore concludes that to prevent her recognition as belonging to the band is an unjustifiable denial of her rights under article 27 of the Covenant, read in the context of the other provisions referred to.

In view of this finding, the Committee does not consider it necessary to examine whether the same facts also show separate breaches of the other rights invoked. * * * The rights to choose one's residence (article 12), and the rights aimed at protecting family life and children (articles

17, 23 and 24) are only indirectly at stake in the present case. * * * The Committee's finding of a lack of a reasonable justification for the interference with Sandra Lovelace's rights under article 27 of the Covenant also makes it unnecessary, as suggested above (paragraph 12), to examine the general provisions against discrimination (articles 2, 3 and 26) in the context of the present case, and in particular to determine their bearing upon inequalities predating the coming into force of the Covenant for Canada.

R. v. VAN DER PEET

Supreme Court (Canada).
[1996] 2 S.C.R. 507.

[Members of the Sto:lo First Nation of British Columbia challenged fisheries regulations prohibiting the sale or barter of fish caught under their licenses. While the Sto:lo did not contest the facts, they argued that their aboriginal fishing rights included the right to harvest fish for profit. The challenge was based on section 35(1) of the Canadian Constitution Act, providing that the "existing aboriginal and treaty rights of the aboriginal peoples of Canada are hereby recognized and affirmed."]

The judgment of Lamer C.J. and La Forest, Sopinka, Gonthier, Cory, Iacobucci and Major JJ. was delivered by

The Chief Justice

3. In order to define the scope of aboriginal rights, it will be necessary first to articulate the purposes which underpin s. 35(1), specifically the reasons underlying its recognition and affirmation of the unique constitutional status of aboriginal peoples in Canada. Until it is understood why aboriginal rights exist, and are constitutionally protected, no definition of those rights is possible. * * *

19. Aboriginal rights cannot, however, be defined on the basis of the philosophical precepts of the liberal enlightenment. Although equal in importance and significance to the rights enshrined in the *Charter*, aboriginal rights must be viewed differently from *Charter* rights because they are rights held only by aboriginal members of Canadian society. They arise from the fact that aboriginal people are aboriginal. * * *

20. The task of this Court is to define aboriginal rights in a manner which recognizes that aboriginal rights are rights but which does so without losing sight of the fact that they are rights held by aboriginal people because they are aboriginal. The Court must neither lose sight of the generalized constitutional status of what s. 35(1) protects, nor can it ignore the necessary specificity which comes from granting special constitutional protection to one part of Canadian society. The Court must define the scope of s. 35(1) in a way which captures both the aboriginal and the rights in aboriginal rights.

21. The way to accomplish this task is, as was noted at the outset, through a purposive approach to s. 35(1). It is through identifying the interests that s. 35(1) was intended to protect that the dual nature of aboriginal rights will be comprehended. * * * A purposive approach to s. 35(1), because ensuring that the provision is not viewed as static and

only relevant to current circumstances, will ensure that the recognition and affirmation it offers are consistent with the fact that what it is recognizing and affirming are "rights". Further, because it requires the court to analyze a given constitutional provision "in the light of the interests it was meant to protect" (*Big M Drug Mart Ltd.*, [[1985] 1 S.C.R. 295,] 344), a purposive approach to s. 35(1) will ensure that that which is found to fall within the provision is related to the provision's intended focus: aboriginal people and their rights in relation to Canadian society as a whole. * * *

General Principles Applicable to Legal Disputes Between Aboriginal Peoples and the Crown

* * *

24. [The] interpretive principle, articulated first in the context of treaty rights * * * arises from the nature of the relationship between the Crown and aboriginal peoples. The Crown has a fiduciary obligation to aboriginal peoples with the result that in dealings between the government and aboriginals the honour of the Crown is at stake. * * *

25. The fiduciary relationship of the Crown and aboriginal peoples also means that where there is any doubt or ambiguity with regards to what falls within the scope and definition of s. 35(1), such doubt or ambiguity must be resolved in favour of aboriginal peoples. * * * This interpretive principle applies equally to s. 35(1) of the *Constitution Act, 1982* and should, again, inform the Court's purposive analysis of that provision.

Purposive Analysis of Section 35(1)

* * *

28. In identifying the basis for the recognition and affirmation of aboriginal rights it must be remembered that s. 35(1) did not create the legal doctrine of aboriginal rights; aboriginal rights existed and were recognized under the common law: *Calder v. Attorney–General of British Columbia*, [1973] S.C.R. 313. At common law aboriginal rights did not, of course, have constitutional status, with the result that Parliament could, at any time, extinguish or regulate those rights: * * *; it is this which distinguishes the aboriginal rights recognized and affirmed in s. 35(1) from the aboriginal rights protected by the common law. Subsequent to s. 35(1) aboriginal rights cannot be extinguished and can only be regulated or infringed consistent with the justificatory test laid out by this Court in *Sparrow*, [[1990] S.C.R. 1075].

29. The fact that aboriginal rights pre-date the enactment of s. 35(1) could lead to the suggestion that the purposive analysis of s. 35(1) should be limited to an analysis of why a pre-existing legal doctrine was elevated to constitutional status. This suggestion must be resisted. The pre-existence of aboriginal rights is relevant to the analysis of s. 35(1) because it indicates that aboriginal rights have a stature and existence prior to the constitutionalization of those rights and sheds light on the reasons for protecting those rights; however, the interests protected by s. 35(1) must be identified through an explanation of the basis for the legal

doctrine of aboriginal rights, not through an explanation of why that legal doctrine now has constitutional status.

30. In my view, the doctrine of aboriginal rights exists, and is recognized and affirmed by s. 35(1), because of one simple fact: when Europeans arrived in North America, aboriginal peoples were already here, living in communities on the land, and participating in distinctive cultures, as they had done for centuries. It is this fact, and this fact above all others, which separates aboriginal peoples from all other minority groups in Canadian society and which mandates their special legal, and now constitutional, status.

31. More specifically, what s. 35(1) does is provide the constitutional framework through which the fact that aboriginals lived on the land in distinctive societies, with their own practices, traditions and cultures, is acknowledged and reconciled with the sovereignty of the Crown. The substantive rights which fall within the provision must be defined in light of this purpose; the aboriginal rights recognized and affirmed by s. 35(1) must be directed towards the reconciliation of the pre-existence of aboriginal societies with the sovereignty of the Crown. * * *

33. This approach to s. 35(1) is also supported by the prior jurisprudence of this Court. [Analysis of Canadian jurisprudence omitted.]

35. The view of aboriginal rights as based in the prior occupation of North America by distinctive aboriginal societies, finds support in the early American decisions of Marshall C.J. * * * [T]he fact that aboriginal law in the United States is significantly different from Canadian aboriginal law means that the relevance of these cases arises from their articulation of general principles, rather than their specific legal holdings.

36. In *Johnson v. M'Intosh*, 21 U.S. (8 Wheat.) 543 (1823), the first of the Marshall decisions on aboriginal title, the Supreme Court held that Indian land could only be alienated by the U.S. government, not by the Indians themselves. In the course of his decision (written for the court), Marshall C.J. outlined the history of the exploration of North America by the countries of Europe and the relationship between this exploration and aboriginal title. In his view, aboriginal title is the right of aboriginal people to land arising from the intersection of their pre-existing occupation of the land with the assertion of sovereignty over that land by various European nations. The substance and nature of aboriginal rights to land are determined by this intersection (at pp 572–74):

On the discovery of this immense continent, the great nations of Europe were eager to appropriate to themselves so much of it as they could respectively acquire. Its vast extent offered an ample field to the ambition and enterprise of all; and the character and religion of its inhabitants afforded an apology for considering them as a people over whom the superior genius of Europe might claim an ascendency. The potentates of the old world found no difficulty in convincing themselves that they made ample compensation to the inhabitants of the new, by bestowing on them civilization and Christianity, in exchange for unlimited independence. But, as they were all in pursuit of nearly the same object, it was necessary, in order to avoid conflicting settlements, and consequent war with each other, to establish a principle, which all should acknowledge as the law by which the right of acquisition, which they all asserted, should be regulated as between themselves. This principle was, that discovery gave title to the government by whose subjects, or by whose authority, it was made, against all other European governments, which title might be consummated by possession.

The exclusion of all other Europeans, necessarily gave to the nation making the discovery the sole right of acquiring the soil from the natives, and establishing settlements upon it. It was a right with which no Europeans could interfere. It was a right which all asserted for themselves, and to the assertion of which, by others, all assented.

Those relations which were to exist between the discoverer and the natives, were to be regulated by themselves. The rights thus acquired being exclusive, no other power could interpose between them.

In the establishment of these relations, the rights of the original inhabitants were, in no instance, entirely disregarded; but were necessarily, to a considerable extent, impaired. They were admitted to be the rightful occupants of the soil, with a legal as well as just claim to retain possession of it, and to use it according to their own discretion; but their rights to complete sovereignty, as independent nations, were necessarily diminished, and their power to dispose of the soil at their own will, to whomsoever they pleased, was denied by the original fundamental principle, that discovery gave exclusive title to those who made it.

While the different nations of Europe respected the right of the natives, as occupants, they asserted the ultimate dominion to be in themselves; and claimed and exercised, as a consequence of this ultimate dominion, a power to grant the soil, while yet in possession of the natives. These grants have been understood by all, to convey a title to the grantees, subject only to the Indian right of occupancy.

It is, similarly, the reconciliation of pre-existing aboriginal claims to the territory that now constitutes Canada, with the assertion of British sovereignty over that territory, to which the recognition and affirmation of aboriginal rights in s. 35(1) is directed.

37. In *Worcester v. Georgia*, 31 U.S. (6 Pet.) 515 (1832) the U.S. Supreme Court invalidated the conviction under a Georgia statute of a non-Cherokee man for the offence of living on the territory of the Cherokee Nation. The court held that the law under which he was convicted was *ultra vires* the State of Georgia. In so doing the court considered the nature and basis of the Cherokee claims to the land and to governance over that land. Again, it based its judgment on its analysis of the origins of those claims which, it held, lay in the relationship between the pre-existing rights of the "ancient possessors" of North America and the assertion of sovereignty by European nations (at pp. 542–43 and 559):

"* * * power, war, conquest, give rights, which, after possession, are conceded by the world; and which can never be controverted by those on whom they descend. We proceed, then, to the actual state of things, having glanced at their origin; because holding it in our recollection might shed some light on existing pretensions * * *.

The Indian nations had always been considered as distinct, independent political communities, retaining their original natural rights, as the undisputed possessors of the soil, from time immemorial, with the single exception of that imposed by irresistible power, which excluded them from intercourse with any other European potentate than the first discoverer of the coast of the particular region claimed." [Emphasis added.]

Marshall C.J.'s essential insight that the claims of the Cherokee must be analyzed in light of their pre-existing occupation and use of the land—their "undisputed" possession of the soil "from time immemorial"—is as relevant for the identification of the interests s. 35(1) was intended to protect as it was for the adjudication of Worcester's claim.

38. The High Court of Australia has also considered the question of the basis and nature of aboriginal rights. Like that of the United States, Australia's aboriginal law differs in significant respects from that of Canada. In particular, in Australia the courts have not as yet determined whether aboriginal fishing rights exist, although such rights are recognized by statute: *Halsbury's Laws of Australia* (1991), vol. 1, paras. 5–2250, 5–2255, 5–2260 and 5–2265. Despite these relevant differences, the analysis of the basis of aboriginal title in the landmark decision of the High Court in *Mabo v. Queensland [No. 2]* (1992), 175 C.L.R. 1, is persuasive in the Canadian context.

39. The *Mabo* judgment resolved the dispute between the Meriam people and the Crown regarding who had title to the Murray Islands. The islands had been annexed to Queensland in 1879 but were reserved for the native inhabitants (the Meriam) in 1882. The Crown argued that this annexation was sufficient to vest absolute ownership of the lands in the Crown. The High Court disagreed, holding that while the annexation did vest radical title in the Crown, it was insufficient to eliminate a claim for native title; the court held at pp. 50–51 that native title can exist as a burden on the radical title of the Crown: "there is no reason why land within the Crown's territory should not continue to be subject to native title. It is only the fallacy of equating sovereignty and beneficial ownership of land that gives rise to the notion that native title is extinguished by the acquisition of sovereignty".

40. From this premise, Brennan J., writing for a majority of the Court, went on at p. 58 to consider the nature and basis of aboriginal title:

Native title has its origin in and is given its content by the traditional laws acknowledged by and the traditional customs observed by the indigenous inhabitants of a territory. The nature and incidents of native title must be ascertained as a matter of fact by reference to those laws and customs. The ascertainment may present a problem of considerable difficulty, as Moynihan J. perceived in the present case. It is a problem that did not arise in the case of a settled colony so long as the fictions were maintained that customary rights could not be reconciled "with the institutions or the legal ideas of civilized society", *In re Southern Rhodesia*, [1919] A.C., at p. 233, that there was no law before the arrival of the British colonists in a settled colony and that there was no sovereign law-maker in the territory of a settled colony before sovereignty was acquired by the Crown. These fictions denied the possibility of a native title recognized by our laws. But once it is acknowledged that an inhabited territory which became a settled colony was no more a legal desert than it was "desert uninhabited" in fact, it is necessary to ascertain by evidence the nature and incidents of native title.

This position is the same as that being adopted here. "Traditional laws" and "traditional customs" are those things passed down, and arising, from the pre-existing culture and customs of aboriginal peoples. The very meaning of the word "tradition"—that which is "handed down [from ancestors] to posterity", *The Concise Oxford Dictionary* (9th ed. 1995),—implies these origins for the customs and laws that the Australian High Court in *Mabo* is asserting to be relevant for the determination of the existence of aboriginal title. To base aboriginal title in traditional laws and customs, as was done in *Mabo*, is, therefore, to base that title in the pre-existing societies of aboriginal peoples. This is the same basis as that asserted here for aboriginal rights. * * *

43. The Canadian, American and Australian jurisprudence thus supports the basic proposition put forward at the beginning of this section: the aboriginal rights recognized and affirmed by s. 35(1) are best understood as, first, the means by which the Constitution recognizes the fact that prior to the arrival of Europeans in North America the land was already occupied by distinctive aboriginal societies, and as, second, the means by which that prior occupation is reconciled with the assertion of Crown sovereignty over Canadian territory.

[Dissenting opinions of Justices L'Heureux–Dubé and McLachlin omitted.]

Notes and Questions

1. One of the most common issues in aboriginal rights-related constitutional litigation concerns land claims. This is because the aboriginal community's control over land is decisive for the preservation of traditional identity. New Zealand is one of the few countries that attempts to provide some recognition of original titles:

The 1840 Treaty of Waitangi, between the British Crown and the indigenous Maori chiefs of New Zealand, remains a source of controversy. * * * In the Treaty, the Maori chiefs ceded their sovereignty over New Zealand to the British and gave the Crown the exclusive right to purchase Maori land in return for British subjecthood and a guarantee from the Crown to respect Maori ownership of tribal lands, fisheries, and other resources. The Treaty is the cornerstone of New Zealand law, since the state derives its authority over the Maori from the sovereignty of the Crown, which flows from the consent ceded by the Treaty. * * *

Although the text of the Treaty is written in both English and Maori, there is a basic discrepancy concerning a key term of the compact. In the Treaty, the English word "sovereignty" was translated into the word kawanatanga, which in Maori means "governorship." Thus, the Maori believed that they did not cede actual sovereignty; rather, they understood the Treaty to give the British governorship of the islands. Many claims that the Maori have lodged against the Crown stem from this problem of interpretation of whether the Maori ceded their lands or merely the governorship of their lands. * * *

[The Maori tribes may use several land-reclaim tribunals.] In addition to the results from the Tribunal, the Maori have also reclaimed land through settlements and outright purchase. * * *

Carter D. Frantz, *Getting Back What was Theirs? The Reparation Mechanism for the Land Rights Claims of the Maori and the Navajo,* 16 Dickinson J. Int'l L. 489, 491–492, 503 (1998).

2. "On what conceptual foundations do legal claims made by indigenous peoples rest? Uncertainty on this issue has encouraged the flowering of multiple approaches, but it also has done much to heighten national dissensus on questions involving indigenous peoples, and it has been a serious obstacle to negotiation in the United Nations * * * of proposed Declarations on the Rights of Indigenous Peoples." Benedict Kingsbury, *Reconciling Five Competing Conceptual Structures of Indigenous People's Claims in International and Comparative Law,* 34 N.Y.U. J. Int'l L. & Pol. 189 (2001). Professor Kingsbury identifies five grounds for the recognition of indigenous people's rights:

(1) human rights and non-discrimination claims;

(2) minority claims;

(3) self-determination claims;

(4) historic sovereignty claims; and

(5) claims as indigenous peoples, including claims based on treaties or other agreements between indigenous peoples and states.

Id. at 190.

Are these points relevant in *Lovelace, R. v. Van der Peet,* or the *Maori* context?

3. Compare *Santa Clara Pueblo v. Martinez,* 436 U.S. 49 (1978), to *Lovelace. Martinez* involved a challenge based on sex discrimination by a woman member of the Pueblo to a Pueblo ordinance denying membership and inheritance rights to children of women who married outside of the tribe. Children of men who married outside the tribe were not thus disqualified. The woman involved, a full-blooded Pueblo, invoked the Indian Civil Rights Act—a federal law providing members of native tribes living on reservations with fundamental rights, including equal protection rights. The Pueblo maintained that U.S. federal courts lacked jurisdiction because of tribal sovereignty rights extending over intratribal controversies. The federal trial court rejected this argument, but it upheld the challenged ordinance on the ground that the traditional values of patriarchy were of vital importance to the identity and traditions of the tribe. The court of appeals reversed, holding that the woman's equality rights under federal law were superior to the challenged tribal ordinance and had been violated. The Supreme Court reversed the court of appeals on the ground that federal courts lacked jurisdiction to resolve the dispute, leaving it to Pueblo tribal courts to resolve the controversy. Assuming that the disputed ordinance was vital to the identity and cohesion of the Pueblo, *Martinez* presents a paradigmatic

clash between an individual (i.e., a dissenting member's) right and a group right. Is there any way in which these conflicting rights might be reconciled?

4.   Convention No. 169, concerning Indigenous and Tribal Peoples in Independent Countries, adopted on 27 June 1989 by the General Conference of the International Labor Organization at its seventy-sixth session, entry into force on 5 September 1991:

Article 27

1.   Education programmes and services for the peoples concerned shall be developed and implemented in co-operation with them to address their special needs, and shall incorporate their histories, their knowledge and technologies, their value systems and their further social, economic and cultural aspirations. They shall participate in the formulation, implementation and evaluation of plans and programmes for national and regional development which may affect them directly.

2.   The competent authority shall ensure the training of members of these peoples and their involvement in the formulation and implementation of education programmes, with a view to the progressive transfer of responsibility for the conduct of these programmes to these peoples as appropriate.

3.   In addition, governments shall recognise the right of these peoples to establish their own educational institutions and facilities, provided that such institutions meet minimum standards established by the competent authority in consultation with these peoples. Appropriate resources shall be provided for this purpose.

Article 28

1.   Children belonging to the peoples concerned shall, wherever practicable, be taught to read and write in their own indigenous language or in the language most commonly used by the group to which they belong. When this is not practicable, the competent authorities shall undertake consultations with these peoples with a view to the adoption of measures to achieve this objective.

2.   Adequate measures shall be taken to ensure that these peoples have the opportunity to attain fluency in the national language or in one of the official languages of the country.

In certain regards the educational rights of aboriginal children would go beyond those of ethnic/national minorities in Canada or India were the Convention to enter into force (currently a very unlikely possibility). Why does the identity of aboriginal peoples require such a far-reaching departure from the prevailing state system? Note that the Convention provides for rights to be granted to indigenous people regarding the territories in which they live, or used to live, and to natural resources in these territories.

Chapter 7

FREEDOM OF EXPRESSION

In the struggle for freedom against secular and religious oppression, freedom of speech was perceived as crucial in exposing abuses of power and aiding in the search for scientific truth. The constitutional democracies that were born in revolutions abolished censorship. Censorship means preliminary authorization for publication by special church or governmental authorities. Revolutionary constitutions (Virginia, 1776; French Declaration, 1789) declared free speech and expression among the most sacred rights of mankind.[a] In the twentieth century, traditional freedoms of speech and the press were extended to other forms of communication, including modern forms, like broadcasting.[b] Many constitutions, e.g., the German Basic Law, and constitutional practices include or imply in the context of freedom of communication a right to be informed (access to information). This extension perceives speech rights as reaching beyond the right of the speaker and including the right of all citizens to be informed. Freedom in the communicative sphere results from institutional freedoms; the press, publishers, broadcasters, and the Internet are the institutions in which public communication and freedom of speech thrive if guarantees prevail to ensure that they operate freely and independently.

To be sure, formidable differences persist among constitutional free speech systems that are related, among others, to the level of respect for authority required by government, respect for other rights, and people's sensitivities. The differences result in sharp conflicts in a world where communication is increasingly transnational. An international newspaper that publishes an article critical of a government may become the defendant of a libel suit in a country whose laws protect the reputation

---

a. Although most democracies expressly condemn censorship, a number of legal mechanisms exist that are the equivalents of censorship or that may have censorial impact. The most common grounds for prior restraint are public security, the prevention of crime or other illegalities, and the protection of state secrets. Crime prevention involves confiscation of publications and even the means of communication. These interventions, even if they serve legitimate interests, raise a preliminary doubt regarding their constitutional status, given the prohibition of censorship.

b. "[T]he fundamental right to freedom of speech and expression includes the right to communicate effectively and to as large a population [sic] not only in this country but also abroad, as is feasible." *Secretary, Ministry of Info. & Broad. v. Cricket Ass'n of Bengal*, A.I.R. [1995] SC 1236: 2 S.C.C. 161, 250.

of government officials. After having lost the suit for utterances fully protected in the newspaper's country of registration, the plaintiff may seek enforcement in the country of registration, where the judge will face the problem of executing an order that is unconstitutional in his own legal regime. In most cases, notwithstanding considerations of comity, the judge will refuse to enforce the foreign judgment. But if the newspaper wants to remain in circulation in the other country, it must think twice about what it will publish in the future. And in the case of the Internet, the service provider in country A may change the access rules there because of legal actions in country B, where the content that was made accessible by the service provider is found impermissible. See the French Yahoo decisions: *Association "Union des Etudiants Juifs de France" (UEJF), la "Ligue contre le Racisme et l'Antisémitisme" (LI-CRA) v. Yahoo! Inc. (USA), Yahoo! France*, (French Union of Jewish Students and League Against Racism and Anti-Semitism v. Yahoo!) Tribunal de Grande Instance de Paris, 22 May 2000 and 20 November 2000. (Not enforced in the U.S.; *Yahoo!, Inc. v. La Ligue Contre Le Racisme et L'Antisemitisme*, 169 F.Supp.2d 1181 (N.D.Cal.2001).)

This chapter discusses three classic problems of freedom of expression. (Owing to space limitations, not all important matters are considered. The authors particularly regret the omission of pornography issues, which can be treated as obscenity or discrimination, depending on perspective, and "time, place, and manner restrictions.") Section A. looks at the general nature of protected speech. Section B. recognizes and builds on the recognition that the most common conflict between the speech interest and other genuine constitutional values in liberal democracies is in the context of defamatory speech. Depending on the value attributed to the uninhibited functioning of the press, personal dignity is more or less protected. The decisive test of a democracy's robustness is its protection of speech in matters of government criticism, including the reputation of political leaders.

The protection of defamatory and insulting statements gives rise to a particularly controversial question addressed in Section C.: To what extent ought racist statements that humiliate whole groups of people and advocate racial discrimination be included in the class of protected speech? One should consider the past and future social and political consequences of such expressions, but the current differences—primarily between the U.S. and the rest of the world—follow from the general theory of speech and from the use of speech and silence in political discourse.

Only the most crucial (or controversial) and fundamental constitutional issues are considered in the cases presented here. Several other areas of freedom of expression result in conflict and litigation. Hidden forms of prior restraint (seizure, right to reply, state secrets, etc.) continue to exercise a chilling effect on the press. The regulation of obscenity, restrictions on broadcasting, its time, place, and manner (including speech in the classroom and to captive audiences), conflicts of speech and privacy, press privileges, restrictions in the interest of the administration of justice, academic and artistic freedoms, and borderline conflicts, like speech offending religion and restrictions on speech in the civil service, are some of the standard testing grounds for free speech. Electoral speech and campaign regulations are debated in all democracies; a few related issues are discussed below, in Chapter 11, in the context of political rights.

A.   THE SCOPE OF PROTECTION

Defining "protected speech" is more difficult than it seems. Moreover, speech is best understood in light of the reasons that justify its protection. The fundamental justifications are presented in Subsection A.1. Certain utterances are simply declared unprotected because of the alleged or potential harm they may cause. Subversion is prohibited as criminal conduct: But where does subversive agitation begin? (See Subsection A.2.) There are differences among legal cultures regarding the value of speech. Are all forms of speech equal? In some jurisdictions this depends on the content or social function of the speech and the constitutional reasons for speech protection. (See Subsection A.3.) In many cases and approaches most communication is protected in principle, but other interests might prevail against the free speech interest. (See Subsection A.4.)

A.1.   WHY PROTECT SPEECH?

Free speech theories may seem like abstract theories of political philosophy. The following excerpts, however, are from judicial decisions that proved to be watershed moments in shaping new approaches to the protection of speech. Moreover, these ideas serve to check specific legislative and judicial decisions affecting speech. All play some role in every liberal democracy, although the scope and level of protection vary. For example, theories related to democratic government may protect only some forms of speech.

According to the agnostic approach of John Stuart Mill, absolute truth does not exist. In *Abrams* Justice Holmes took the position that "truth" would be the view that prevails in the marketplace of ideas. The "marketplace-of-ideas" argument is based on an assumption about getting closer to truth. A government may seek to suppress opinions "because their expression is thought to impair the authority of a lawful and effective government, interfere with the administration of justice * * * cause offence, invade someone's privacy, or cause a decrease in public order. When these are the motives for suppression, the possibility of losing some truth is relevant but hardly dispositive." Frederick Schauer, *Free Speech: A Philosophical Inquiry* 23 (1982). The advantage of the marketplace-of-ideas approach is that even "false" statements are protected as a valuable part of the learning and communication process. The possibility of government intervention must be countered by other considerations, e.g., by establishing presumptions against the legitimacy of government interference. See the clear and present danger test and balancing in subsections A.2. and A.3. below.

Most theories discuss free speech from the speaker's perspective, although justification might also reside in the interests of the community of recipients. In general the audience's perspective is disregarded: free speech seems to be about the speaker. But this tends to reinforce social hierarchies, and it ignores the powerful effect of speech. Moreover, it skirts this question: About whom or what is the speaker speaking? Audience sensitivities may be legitimate concerns, but they come, certainly, at the expense of free speech. Note that contemporary positions (e.g., *Curtis*, see below) emphasize that speech rights serve the interest of receiving information.

LANGE v. ATKINSON

Court of Appeal, Wellington (New Zealand).
3 NZLR 424, 460 (1998).

Blanchard J:

A judgment is not the occasion for a history of the right to freedom of expression. But, as a legal concept, freedom can be better understood and its scope better assessed if it is put into its wider political and social context and history. Two general references will suffice. The first is the famous statement about freedom of expression made by John Milton in *Areopagitica* (1644). Writing in the midst of the English civil war and in opposition to the licensing of printing, a new technology which had begun to have major impact on political discussion, he asked at pp. 18 and 51–52:

> (What) wisdome can there be to choose, what continence to forbeare, without the knowledge of evill? * * * I cannot praise a fugitive and cloister'd vertue, unexercis'd and unbreath'd, that never sallies out and sees her adversary, but slinks out of the race, where that immortall, garland is to be run for not without dust and heat * * *

> And though all the windes of doctrin were let loose to play upon the earth, so Truth be in the field, we do injuriously by licencing and prohibiting to misdoubt her strength. Let her and Falsehood grapple; who ever knew Truth put to the wors in a free and open encounter?

While it is true that his declaration of the freedom of expression was not absolute (for he excluded "popery and open superstition") the statement remains very broad. It is also functional. According to Milton, knowledge and understanding should be enhanced by the uninhibited exercise of the freedom. That functional element with its resulting benefits is also to be found two centuries later in John Stuart Mill's essay, *On Liberty* (1859):

> If all mankind minus one, were of one opinion, and only one person were of the contrary opinion, mankind would be no more justified in silencing that one person, than he, if he had the power, would be justified in silencing mankind. Were an opinion a personal possession of no value except to the owner; if to be obstructed in the enjoyment of it were simply a private injury, it would make some difference whether the injury was inflicted only on a few persons or on many. But the peculiar evil of silencing the expression of an opinion is, that it is robbing the human race; posterity as well as the existing generation; those who dissent from the opinion, still more than those who hold it. If the opinion is right, they are deprived of the opportunity of exchanging

error for truth: if wrong, they lose, what is almost as great a benefit, the clearer perception and livelier impression of truth, produced by its collision with error.

Alexander Meiklejohn, *Political Freedom* [1960] at p. 27:

When men govern themselves, it is they—and no one else—who must pass judgment upon unwisdom and unfairness and danger. And that means that unwise ideas must have a hearing as well as wise ones, unfair as well as fair, dangerous as well as safe, un-American as well as American.

If then, on any occasion in the United States it is allowable, in that situation, to say that the Constitution is a good document it is equally allowable, in that situation, to say that the Constitution is a bad document. If a public building may be used in which to say, in time of war, that the war is justified, then the same building may be used in which to say that it is not justified. If it be publicly argued that conscription for armed service is moral and necessary, it may likewise be publicly argued that it is immoral and unnecessary. If it may be said that American political institutions are superior to those of England or Russia or Germany, it may with equal freedom, be said that those of England or Russia or Germany are superiors to ours. These conflicting views may be expressed, must be expressed, not because they are valid, but because they are relevant. * * * To be afraid of ideas, any idea, is to be unfit for self government.

WHITNEY v. CALIFORNIA

Supreme Court (United States).
274 U.S. 357 (1927).[c]

Mr. Justice Brandeis, concurring * * *

[W]e must bear in mind why a state is, ordinarily, denied the power to prohibit dissemination of social, economic and political doctrine which a vast majority of its citizens believes to be false and fraught with evil consequence.

Those who won our independence believed that the final end of the state was to make men free to develop their faculties, and that in its government the deliberative forces should prevail over the arbitrary. They valued liberty both as an end and as a means. They believed liberty

c. Fearing anarchism and Bolshevism, a number of states enacted sedition laws after World War One. The California Criminal Syndicalism Act criminalized the advocating of unlawful acts of force as a means of accomplishing or effecting any political change. Membership in groups advocating criminal syndicalism was also a crime. Anita Whitney was convicted for knowingly becoming a member of such a group; although she argued that when she attended the convention to organize the Communist Labor Party of California, the character of the organization could not have been foreseen and that she protested violent opinions. The California Act, as applied, was upheld as a reasonable exercise of police power. Note that these formulations are used in various antisubversion and antiterrorism statutes, which exist in many liberal and illiberal democracies, without being constitutionally challenged, partly because they are narrowly interpreted, if applied at all.

Justice Brandeis agreed with the judgment on the ground that Whitney did not adequately raise the constitutional question of free speech in the lower courts, but he added an extensive opinion discussing the merits of the case.

to the secret of happiness and courage to be the secret of liberty. They believed that freedom to think as you will and to speak as you think are means indispensable to the discovery and spread of political truth; that without free speech and assembly discussion would be futile; that with them, discussion affords ordinarily adequate protection against the dissemination of noxious doctrine; that the greatest menace to freedom is an inert people; that public discussion is a political duty; and that this should be a fundamental principle of the American government. They recognized the risks to which all human institutions are subject. But they knew that order cannot be secured merely through fear of punishment for its infraction; that it is hazardous to discourage thought, hope and imagination; that fear breeds repression; that repression breeds hate; that hate menaces stable government; that the path of safety lies in the opportunity to discuss freely supposed grievances and proposed remedies; and that the fitting remedy for evil counsels is good ones. Believing in the power of reason as applied through public discussion, they eschewed silence coerced by law—the argument of force in its worst form. Recognizing the occasional tyrannies of governing majorities, they amended the Constitution so that free speech and assembly should be guaranteed.

Fear of serious injury cannot alone justify suppression of free speech and assembly. * * * [E]ven advocacy of violation, however reprehensible morally, is not a justification for denying free speech where the advocacy falls short of incitement and there is nothing to indicate that the advocacy would be immediately acted on. The wide difference between advocacy and incitement, between preparation and attempt, between assembling and conspiracy, must be borne in mind. In order to support a finding of clear and present danger it must be shown either that immediate serious violence was to be expected or was advocated, or that the past conduct furnished reason to believe that such advocacy was then contemplated.

* * * If there be time to expose through discussion the falsehood and fallacies, to avert the evil by the processes of education, the remedy to be applied is more speech, not enforced silence. Only an emergency can justify repression.

IRWIN TOY LTD. v. ATTORNEY GENERAL OF QUEBEC

Supreme Court (Canada).
[1989] 1 S.C.R. 927.

Dickson C.J.C., Lamer and Wilson JJ.:

* * * We have already discussed the nature of the principles and values underlying the vigilant protection of free expression in a society such as ours. They * * * can be summarized as follows: (1) seeking and attaining the truth is an inherently good activity; (2) participation in social and political decision-making is to be fostered and encouraged; and (3) the diversity in forms of individual self-fulfillment and human flourishing ought to be cultivated in an essentially tolerant, indeed

welcoming, environment not only for the sake of those who convey a meaning, but also for the sake of those to whom it is conveyed. In showing that the effect of the government's action was to restrict her free expression, a plaintiff must demonstrate that her activity promotes at least one of these principles. It is not enough that shouting, for example, has an expressive element. If the plaintiff challenges the effect of government action to control noise, presuming that action to have a purpose neutral as to expression, she must show that her aim was to convey a meaning reflective of the principles underlying freedom of expression. The precise and complete articulation of what kinds of activity promote these principles is, of course, a matter for judicial appreciation to be developed on a case-by-case basis. But the plaintiff must at least identify the meaning being conveyed and how it relates to the pursuit of truth, participation in the community, or individual self-fulfillment and human flourishing.

CURTIS v. THE MINISTER OF SAFETY AND SECURITY AND OTHERS

Constitutional Court (South Africa).
1996 (3) SALR 617 (CC).

Mokgoro J:

[The charges were based on the possession of videocassettes containing sexually explicit matter. Section 2(1) of the Indecent or Obscene Photographic Matter Act, Act 37 of 1967, a typical example of the oppressive legislation in apartheid South Africa, provides as follows: "Any person who has in his possession any indecent or obscene photographic matter shall be guilty of an offence and liable on conviction to a fine not exceeding one thousand rand or imprisonment for a period not exceeding one year or to both such fine and such imprisonment." The provision was held unconstitutional under the Interim Constitution, providing Justice Mokgoro the opportunity to emphasize in the postpaternalistic situation the self-determination aspect of speech, which serves as the justification for access to information.]

[25] [M]y freedom of expression is impoverished indeed if it does not embrace also my right to receive, hold and consume expressions transmitted by others. Firstly, my right to express myself is severely impaired if others' rights to hear my speech are not protected. And secondly, my own right to freedom of expression includes as a necessary corollary the right to be exposed to inputs from others that will inform, condition and ultimately shape my own expression. Thus, a law which deprives willing persons of the right to be exposed to the expression of others gravely offends constitutionally protected freedoms both of the speaker and of the would-be recipients.

[26] * * * [Of] more relevance here than [the] "marketplace" conception of the role of free speech is the consideration that freedom of speech is a *sine qua non* for every person's right to realise her or his full potential as a human being, free of the imposition of heteronomous power. Viewed in that light, the right to receive others' expressions has more than merely instrumental utility, as a predicate for the addressee's

meaningful exercise of her or his own rights of free expression. It is also foundational to each individual's empowerment to autonomous self-development.

AUSTRALIAN CAPITAL TELEVISION v. THE COMMONWEALTH OF AUSTRALIA

High Court (Australia).
(1992) 177 C.L.R. 106.

[This case is presented in Chapter 2.]

A.2.　SUBVERSION OF THE POLITICAL ORDER: CLEAR AND PRESENT DANGER

In Colonial America, the British prosecuted critiques of the British administration. Courts were accustomed to punishing publishers and authors of pamphlets for "seditious" expression. (Popularly elected assemblies acted similarly against their critics.) Understandably, those who used the press as a weapon in their struggles had every desire to safeguard freedom of speech and the press. It is still debated what the intentions behind the First Amendment were in prohibiting only prior restraint while allowing, at the same time, for all of the common law restrictions. The language of the First Amendment[d] seems to impose an absolute ban on legislative restrictions of expression at a time when the French Declaration of 1789 (Art. 11) expressly allowed them: "The unrestrained communication of thoughts or opinions being one of the most precious rights of man, every citizen may speak, write and publish freely, provided his avowal of them *does not disturb public order as established by law*" (italics added).

Most constitutions and international human rights conventions, including the European Convention for the Protection of Human Rights and Fundamental Freedoms (hereafter, European HR Convention), follow the tradition of the French Declaration and expressly recognize the possibility of restriction by legislation based on specific grounds.

The free speech (First Amendment) position in the contemporary U.S. is often described as an absolutist one, which provides protection to speech to the detriment of other constitutional values and the disregard of social concerns. Notwithstanding fundamental differences between the U.S. and other democracies, this perception is misleading. The text of the U.S. Constitution only purports to protect freedom of speech and the various justifications given to speech. It is the position of the U.S. Supreme Court (USSC) that not all speech (communication) deserves a high level of constitutional protection. Public order must be protected,

---

d. Likewise, the 1948 Universal Declaration of Human Rights (1948) (Art. 19) is silent on speech restrictions: "Everyone has the right to freedom of opinion and expression; this right includes freedom to hold opinions without interference and to seek, receive and impart information and ideas through any media and regardless of frontiers."

even if its disturbance originates in speech. In an early formulation, in *Chaplinsky v. New Hampshire*, 315 U.S. 568 (1942),[e] the USSC said:

> There are certain well-defined and narrowly limited classes of speech, the prevention and punishment of which have never been thought to raise any Constitutional problem. These include the lewd and the obscene, the profane, the libelous, and the insulting or 'fighting words'—those which by their very utterance inflict injury or tend to incite an immediate breach of the peace. [S]uch utterances are no essential part of any exposition of ideas.

"Fighting words" are outside the protection granted to "speech," but otherwise insulting words or communicative conduct do not amount to fighting words if "clearly not 'directed to the person of the hearer.' " *Cohen v. California*, 403 U.S. 15, 20 (1971).[f]

Justice Black, who strongly objected to balancing speech against other interests, argued in *Konigsberg v. State Bar*, 366 U.S. 36, 81 (1961), that "the men who drafted our Bill of Rights did all the 'balancing' that was to be done in this field." But even Black admitted that speech was not protected when it is an integral part of criminal conduct. In the U.S., the potential for abuse of the sedition law was palpably clear in less than ten years after the First Amendment was ratified. The Sedition Act of 1798 was enacted against the Republican opponents of the Adams administration.[g]

What about advocacy of illegality and, in particular, government or group criticism that might lead to disorder or crime? "Intent to commit a crime is not itself criminal," wrote Oliver Wendell Holmes in *The Common Law* 65 (1881). The American approach moved increasingly to a categorical protection of speech, concluding that not all expressions or utterances amount to speech within the safekeeping of the First Amendment. Political speech is granted maximum protection, and only in very rare, specific circumstances is its full protection not granted; for example, if it results in the clear and present danger of serious crime.

In this subsection we discuss landmark cases that indicate how once-nonproblematic subversive and seditious expression became constitution-

---

e. Chaplinsky was a proselytizing Jehovah's Witness. The city marshal warned him to "go slow." Chaplinsky continued with his denunciations of organized religion, and the marshal led him to the police station. Chaplinsky called the marshal "a God damned racketeer" and "a damned Fascist." He was convicted for violating a state statute forbidding anyone to address "any offensive, derisive or annoying word to any other person who is lawfully in any [public place] or call[ing] him by any offensive or derisive name." This has been superseded for almost all issues.

f. During the Vietnam War and while a military draft was in force, Cohen entered a California courthouse with a jacket bearing the clearly visible words "Fuck the Draft."

Cohen's conviction for disturbing the peace by "offensive conduct" was reversed in the Supreme Court.

g. The Act prohibited the publication of false, scandalous, and malicious writing or writings against the government of the United States, or either house of the Congress of the United States, or the President of the United States, with intent to defame [them]; or to bring them [into] contempt or disrepute; or to excite against them [the] hatred of the good people of the United States, or to stir up sedition within the United States, or to excite any unlawful combinations therein, for opposing or resisting any law of the United States, or any [lawful] act of the President of the United States.

ally unsettled. As Justice Brandeis's position in *Whitney* exemplifies, fear of subversion might paralyze speech and therefore democracy: what a government deems subversive might be simply legitimate criticism. In the U.S., more than 30 years of indiscriminate use of the Espionage Act (that was originally directed against the opponents of World War One) passed before it was accepted that agitation might be punished only if it presented a clear and present danger of crime (*Dennis*). Communists, discussing the beauties of armed revolution, were thought to present such a danger during the Cold War. "The Supreme Court has been measured in its protection of subversive advocacy. Communists were allowed to engage in the general advocacy of revolution, but the Court drew the line when advocacy turned into incitement." Owen M. Fiss, *Liberalism Divided: Freedom of Speech and the Many Uses of State Power* 115 (1996). Another decade or two would pass before this test was vigorously applied (*Yates*; *Brandenburg*). The stricter test prevailed in a changed social and political climate, where the underlying assumption might have been that the democracy was now strong enough to resist subversive agitation.

In other countries, the crime of subversive agitation has been less subject to constitutional scrutiny, and

> the conservative view of the state is still reflected in the criminal law. The Irish Constitution specifically preserves the offence of seditious libel, perhaps paradoxically in the very article in which the state guarantees the citizens' rights to express freely their convictions and opinions. [In Australia, the constitutional provision "to make laws with respect to matters incidental to the execution of any power vested" in the Commonwealth] validates the enactment of statutes proscribing incitements to disaffection. * * * In the leading Canadian case, *Boucher v. R.*, the Supreme Court held that there must be an intent to disturb the government by force, * * * The result of all these qualifications, and the changing attitude to the range of permissible restrictions on the expression of political opinion, is that prosecutions for sedition have become virtually unknown [in most western democracies].

Eric Barendt, *Freedom of Speech* 154–55 (1987).

Judicial approaches to speech based on balancing do not presuppose the primacy of speech interests, and constitutional texts allow for the nonprotection of speech under specific circumstances: as free speech can be expressly restricted and, at least at the level of the constitutional text, it is not a supreme constitutional value, the main constitutional task in most countries is to find a proper balance among competing rights and constitutional interests. A similar balancing of political speech and other constitutional interests was still popular in the U.S. in the 1950s. See Justice Frankfurter, concurring in *Dennis* (below). As the *Ceylan* decision below indicates, the protection to speech is granted in a balancing procedure where its classification as legitimate criticism of government is crucial.

ABRAMS ET AL. v. UNITED STATES

Supreme Court (United States).
250 U.S. 616 (1919).

[Criticism of government, bordering on advocacy of subversion, became increasingly a matter of First Amendment concern, beginning with the cases that arose under the Espionage Act, during World War One, thanks to the dissents and concurring opinions of Justices Holmes and Brandeis (*Schenk*; *Abrams*).

[Abrams was charged for violating the Espionage Act of 1917. During World War One, he distributed leaflets encouraging ammunition-factory workers to express solidarity with revolutionary Russia, among others, by striking.]

Mr. Justice Clark delivered the opinion of the Court.

* * *

This is not an attempt to bring about a change of administration by candid discussion, for no matter what may have incited the outbreak on the part of the defendant anarchists, the manifest purpose of such a publication was to create an attempt to defeat the war plans of the government of the United States, by bringing upon the country the paralysis of a general strike, thereby arresting the production of all munitions and other things essential to the conduct of the war.

* * *

Mr. Justice Holmes, dissenting.

* * *

I do not doubt for a moment that by the same reasoning that would justify punishing persuasion to murder, the United States constitutionally may punish speech that produces or is intended to produce a clear and imminent danger that it will bring about forthwith certain substantive evils that the United States constitutionally may seek to prevent. The power undoubtedly is greater in time of war than in time of peace because war opens dangers that do not exist at other times. But as against dangers peculiar to war, as against others, the principle of the right to free speech is always the same. It is only the present danger of immediate evil or an intent to bring it about that warrants Congress in setting a limit to the expression of opinion where private rights are not concerned. Congress certainly cannot forbid all effort to change the mind of the country. Now nobody can suppose that the surreptitious publishing of a silly leaflet by an unknown man, without more, would present any immediate danger that its opinions would hinder the success of the government arms or have any appreciable tendency to do so.

* * *

Persecution for the expression of opinions seems to me perfectly logical. If you have no doubt of your premises or your power and want a certain result with all your heart you naturally express your wishes in law and sweep away all opposition. To allow opposition by speech seems to indicate that you think the speech impotent, as when a man says that he has squared the circle, or that you do not care wholeheartedly for the result, or that you doubt either your power or your premises. But when men have realized that time has upset many fighting faiths, they may come to believe even more than they believe the very foundations of their own conduct that the ultimate good desired is better reached by free trade in ideas—that the best test of truth is the power of the thought to get itself accepted in the competition of the market, and that truth is the only ground upon which their wishes safely can be carried out. That at any rate is the theory of our Constitution. It is an experiment, as all life is an experiment. Every year if not every day we have to wager our salvation upon some prophecy based upon imperfect knowledge. While that experiment is part of our system I think that we should be eternally vigilant against attempts to check the expression of opinions that we loathe and believe to be fraught with death, unless they so imminently threaten immediate interference with the lawful and pressing purposes of the law that an immediate check is required to save the country. I wholly disagree with the argument of the Government that the First Amendment left the common law as to seditious libel in force. History seems to me against the notion. I had conceived that the United States through many years had shown its repentance for the Sedition Act of 1798 by repaying fines that it imposed. Only the emergency that makes it immediately dangerous to leave the correction of evil counsels to time making any exception to the sweeping command, "Congress shall make no law abridging the freedom of speech."

Notes and Questions

1. Justice Holmes's reluctance to acknowledge antigovernmental agitation as genuinely dangerous was partly related to his long held understanding of criminal attempt. It is in this context that he developed the idea that only preliminary acts near the criminal result should be considered attempts: lighting a match near a haystack to start a fire versus buying a box of matches for the same purpose. It was in the context of strong antigovernment agitation at times of political instability (during and after World War One, and later, in the tenser periods of the Cold War) that the boundaries between speech and sedition converged to test liberal democracy and that the boundaries of protected speech were drawn following the concerns of Holmes and Brandeis. The danger to truth and free democratic government represented by this type of criminalization of speech was the foremost concern of Holmes's dissent.

2. The standard argument against Holmes's approach was summarized by a leading comparativist of his day. (The argument is often repeated both by judges of authoritarian regimes and by adherents to militant democracy, who claim that preventive measures are needed to protect democracy.) John Henry Wigmore, Abrams v. U.S.: *Freedom of Speech and Freedom of Thuggery in War–Time and Peace–Time*, 14 Ill. L. Rev. 539, 549–51 (1920):

> None know better than judges that what is lawful for one is lawful for a thousand others. If these five men could, without the law's restraint, urge munition workers to a general strike and armed violences then others could lawfully do so; and a thousand disaffected undesirables,

aliens and natives alike, were ready and waiting to do so. [At a time] when the fate of the civilized world hung in the balance, how could the Minority Opinion interpret law and conduct in such a way as to let loose men who were doing their hardest to paralyze the supreme war efforts of our country? * * * This apotheosis of Truth, however, shows a blindness to the deadly fact that meantime the "power of the thought" of these circulars might "get itself accepted in the competition of the market," by munitions workers, so as to lose the war; * * * This [dissenting opinion, if it had commanded a majority,] would have ended by our letting soldiers die helpless in France, through our anxiety to protect the distribution of a leaflet whose sole purpose was to cut off the soldiers' munitions and supplies. How would this have advanced the cause of Truth?

3. The top leaders of the Communist Party of the United States of America were tried under a federal version of the anarchy acts (the Smith Act of 1940) at the height of McCarthyism. The jury found that they "intended to initiate a violent revolution whenever the propitious occasion appeared." In *Dennis et al. v. United States,* 341 U.S. 494 (1951), the USSC found that "a conviction relying upon speech or press as evidence of violation may be sustained only when the speech or publication created a 'clear and present danger' of attempting or accomplishing the prohibited crime." Applying the test, the Court upheld the conviction. Justice Black dissented:

> The charge was that they agreed to assemble and to talk and publish certain ideas at a later date. * * * The other opinions in this case show that the only way to affirm these convictions is to repudiate directly or indirectly the established "clear and present danger" rule. This the Court does in a way which greatly restricts the protections afforded by the First Amendment. The opinions for affirmance indicate that the chief reason for jettisoning the rule is the expressed fear that advocacy of Communist doctrine endangers the safety of the Republic. Undoubtedly, a governmental policy of unfettered communication of ideas does entail dangers. To the Founders of this Nation, however, the benefits derived from free expression were worth the risk. * * * Public opinion being what it now is, few will protest the conviction of these Communist petitioners. There is hope, however, that in calmer times, when present pressures, passions and fears subside, this or some later Court will restore the First Amendment liberties to the high preferred place where they belong in a free society.

Id. at 579.[h]

In a different political climate the convictions of several "second-string" Communist Party officials were reversed, by reason that the Smith Act did not intend to punish advocacy of an abstract doctrine only advocacy of action. *Yates v. United States*, 354 U.S. 298 (1957).

The clear and present danger test was gradually restated so that probability of harm was no longer the central criterion, and even

h. Justice Douglas also dissented. "So far as the present record is concerned, what petitioners did was to organize people to teach and themselves teach the Marxist–Leninist doctrine."

incitement was protected if the likelihood of dangerous consequences was low. This position was expressed in its fullest form in *Brandenburg*.

BRANDENBURG v. OHIO

Supreme Court (United States).
395 U.S. 444 (1969).

PER CURIAM:

* * * The appellant, a leader of a Ku Klux Klan group, was convicted under the Ohio Criminal Syndicalism statute for "advocat(ing) the duty, necessity, or propriety of crime, sabotage, violence, or unlawful methods of terrorism as a means of accomplishing industrial or political reform" and for "voluntarily assembl(ing) with any society, group, or assemblage of persons formed to teach or advocate the doctrines of criminal syndicalism."

* * * The record shows that a man, identified at trial as the appellant, telephoned an announcer-reporter on the staff of a Cincinnati television station and invited him to come to a Ku Klux Klan "rally" to be held at a farm. [One] film showed 12 hooded figures, some of whom carried firearms. [Another] scene on the same film showed the appellant, in Klan regalia, making a speech. The speech, in full, was as follows:

> [The] Klan has more members in the State of Ohio than does any other organization. We're not a revengent organization, but if our President, our Congress, our Supreme Court, continues to suppress the white, Caucasian race, it's possible that there might have to be some revengeance taken. We are marching on Congress July the Fourth, four hundred thousand strong. From there we are dividing into two groups, one group to march on St. Augustine, Florida, the other group to march into Mississippi. Thank you. * * *

* * * [Statutes, like the Ohio "antianarchism" one, were upheld in the first half of the twentieth century, e.g., in *Whitney*.] More recent precedents like *Dennis* have fashioned the principle that the constitutional guarantees of free speech and free press do not permit a State to forbid or proscribe advocacy of the use of force or of law violation except where such advocacy is directed to inciting or producing imminent lawless action and is likely to incite or produce such action. * * * As we said in *Noto v. United States,* 367 U.S. 290, 297–298 (1961), "the mere abstract teaching [of] the moral propriety or even moral necessity for a resort to force and violence, is not the same as preparing a group for violent action and steeling it to such action."

* * * Accordingly, we are here confronted with a statute which, by its own words and as applied, purports to punish mere advocacy and to forbid, on pain of criminal punishment, assembly with others merely to advocate the described type of action.[4] Such a statute falls within the condemnation of the First and Fourteenth Amendments. [*Whitney* was overruled, and Brandenburg's sentence reversed.]

---

4. Statutes affecting the right of assembly, like those touching on freedom of speech, must observe the established distinctions between mere advocacy and incitement to imminent lawless action. * * *

CEYLAN v. TURKEY

European Court of Human Rights.
30 E.H.R.R. 73 (2000).

THE FACTS

I.   The circumstances of the case

* * *

8.   The applicant, who was at the time the president of the petroleum workers' union wrote an article entitled "The time has come for the workers to speak out—tomorrow it will be too late" in a weekly newspaper published in Istanbul. The article [denouncing the "terrorist" anti-Kurd policies of the government concluded] not only the Kurdish people but the whole of our proletariat must stand up against these laws and the "state terrorism" currently being practiced. Despite all the hurdles erected by the law, we must unite in action with the democratic mass organizations, political parties and every individual or body with which it is possible to work; we must oppose the bloody massacres and state terrorism, using all our powers of organization and coordination. * * *

B.   The proceedings against the applicant

* * *

11.   * * * [T]he National Security Court found the applicant guilty of an offence under Article 312 § 2 and § 3 of the Turkish Criminal Code and sentenced him to one year and eight months' imprisonment, plus a fine of 100,000 Turkish liras. It reached the conclusion that the applicant had incited the population to hatred and hostility by making distinctions based on ethnic or regional origin or social class. * * *

II.   RELEVANT DOMESTIC LAW AND PRACTICE

A.   Criminal Law

15.   Article 312 of the Criminal Code provides:

Non-public incitement to commit an offence: A person who expressly praises or condones an act punishable by law as an offence or incites the population to break the law shall, on conviction, be liable to between six months' and two years' imprisonment and a heavy fine of from six thousand to thirty thousand Turkish liras.

A person who incites the people to hatred or hostility on the basis of a distinction between social classes, races, religions, denominations or regions, shall, on conviction, be liable to between one and three years' imprisonment and a fine of from nine thousand to thirty-six thousand liras. If this incitement endangers public safety, the sentence shall be increased by one third to one half.

The penalties to be imposed on those who have committed the offences defined in the previous paragraph shall be doubled when they have done so by the means listed in Article 311 § 2.

16.   Article 311 § 2 of the Criminal Code provides:

"Public incitement to commit an offence: Where incitement to commit an offence is done by means of mass communication, of whatever type—whether by tape recordings, gramophone records, newspapers, press publications or other published material—by the circulation or distribution of printed papers or by the placing of placards or posters in public places, the terms of imprisonment to which convicted persons are liable shall be doubled. * * * "

2. Legitimate aim

* * *

27. The Government maintained that the aim of the interference in question had been not only to maintain "national security" and "prevent disorder" (as the Commission had found), but also to preserve "territorial integrity."

28. * * * Having regard to the sensitivity of the security situation in south-east Turkey (see *Zana v. Turkey* judgment of November 25, 1997, § 10), and to the need for the authorities to be alert to acts capable of fuelling additional violence, the Court accepts that the applicant's conviction can be said to have been in furtherance of the aims cited by the Government. This is certainly true where, as in south-east Turkey at the time of the circumstances of this case, there was a separatist movement having recourse to methods relying on the use of violence.

3. "Necessary in a democratic society"

* * *

30. The Government submitted that offences similar to that set out in Article 312 of the Turkish Criminal Code were to be found in the legislation of other member States of the Council of Europe, citing, by way of example, Article 130 of the German Criminal Code. They argued that such provisions helped to preserve those States as democracies. Lastly, they submitted that it was not for the Strasbourg institutions to substitute their view for that of the Turkish courts as to whether there had been a "danger" capable of justifying the application of Article 312.

* * *

(b) The Court's assessment

* * *

32. The Court reiterates the fundamental principles underlying its judgments relating to Article 10

(i) Freedom of expression constitutes one of the essential foundations of a democratic society and one of the basic conditions for its progress and for each individual's self-fulfillment. Subject to paragraph 2 of Article 10, it is applicable not only to "information" or "ideas" that are favorably received or regarded as inoffensive or as a matter of indifference, but also to those that offend, shock or disturb. Such are the demands of that pluralism, tolerance and broadmindedness without which there is no "democratic society." As set forth in Article 10, this freedom is subject to exceptions, which must, however, be construed strictly, and the need for any restrictions must be established convincingly.

* * *

(iii) [Although states have a margin of appreciation, the Court has the power to supervise even national courts' decisions.] In exercising its supervisory jurisdiction, the Court must look at the interference in the light of the case as a whole, including the content of the impugned statements and the context in which they were made. In particular, it must determine whether the interference in issue was "proportionate to the legitimate aims pursued" and whether the reasons adduced by the national authorities to justify it are "relevant and sufficient". In doing so, the Court has to satisfy itself that the national authorities applied standards which were in conformity with the principles embodied in Article 10 and, moreover, that they based themselves on an acceptable assessment of the relevant facts.

33. * * * The [article's] style is virulent and the criticism of the Turkish authorities' actions in the relevant part of the country acerbic. * * *

34. The Court recalls, however, that there is little scope under Article 10 § 2 of the Convention for restrictions on political speech or on debate on matters of public interest (see the *Wingrove v. the United Kingdom* judgment of 25 November 1996. § 58). Furthermore, the limits of permissible criticism are wider with regard to the government than in relation to a private citizen or even a politician. In a democratic system the actions or omissions of the government must be subject to the close scrutiny not only of the legislative and judicial authorities but also of public opinion. Moreover, the dominant position which the government occupies makes it necessary for it to display restraint in resorting to criminal proceedings, particularly where other means are available for replying to the unjustified attacks and criticisms of its adversaries. Nevertheless, it certainly remains open to the competent State authorities to adopt, in their capacity as guarantors of public order, measures, even of a criminal-law nature, intended to react appropriately and without excess to such remarks (see *Incal* 1998, § 54). Finally, where such remarks incite to violence against an individual, a public official or a sector of the population, the State authorities enjoy a wider margin of appreciation when examining the need for an interference with freedom of expression.

35. The Court * * * takes note of the Turkish authorities' concern about the dissemination of views which they consider might exacerbate the serious disturbances which have been going on in Turkey for some fifteen years (see paragraph 28 above). In this regard, it should be noted that the article in issue was published shortly after the Gulf War, at a time when a large number of persons of Kurdish origin, fleeing repression in Iraq, were thronging at the Turkish border.

36. The Court observes, however, that the applicant was writing in his capacity as a trade-union leader, a player on the Turkish political scene, and that the article in question, despite its virulence, does not encourage the use of violence or armed resistance or insurrection. In the

Court's view, this is a factor which it is essential to take into consideration.

37. The Court also notes the severity of the penalty imposed on the applicant. * * * In this connection, the Court points out that the nature and severity of the penalty imposed are factors to be taken into account when assessing the proportionality of the interference.

38. In conclusion, Mr. Ceylan's conviction was disproportionate to the aims pursued and accordingly not "necessary in a democratic society." There has therefore been a violation of Article 10 of the Convention.

Mr. Judge Bonello, concurring * * *

* * * [T]he common test employed by the court seems to have been this: if the writings published by the applicants supported or instigated the use of violence, then their conviction by the national courts was justifiable in a democratic society. I discard this yardstick as insufficient.

I believe that punishment by the national authorities of those encouraging violence would be justifiable in a democratic society only if the incitement were such as to create "a clear and present danger." When the invitation to the use of force is intellectualized, abstract, and removed in time and space from the foci of actual or impending violence, then the fundamental right to freedom of expression should generally prevail.

I borrow what one of the mightiest constitutional jurists of all time had to say about words which tend to destabilize law and order: "We should be eternally vigilant against attempts to check the expression of opinions that we loathe and believe to be fraught with death, unless they so imminently threaten immediate interference with the lawful and pressing purposes of the law that an immediate check is required to save the country."[1]

The guarantee of freedom of expression does not permit a state to forbid or proscribe advocacy of the use of force except when such advocacy is directed to inciting or producing imminent lawlessness and is likely to incite or produce such action.[2] It is a question of proximity and degree. * * *[3] It is not manifest to me that any of the words with which the applicants were charged, however pregnant with mortality they may appear to some, had the potential of imminently threatening dire effects on the national order. Nor is it manifest to me that instant suppression of those expressions was indispensable for the salvation of Turkey.

Mr. Judge Gölcüklü dissenting.

* * * In my view, the quoted passages can in all good faith be construed as an incitement to hatred and extreme violence. Taking into account the margin of appreciation which must be left to the national authorities, I therefore conclude that the interference in issue cannot be

---

1. Justice Oliver Wendell Holmes in *Abrams v. United States*, 250 U.S. 616, 630 (1919).

2. *Brandenburg v. Ohio*, 395 U.S. 444, 447 (1969).

3. *Schenck v. United States*, 249 U.S. 47, 52 (1919).

described as disproportionate—with the result that it can be regarded as having been necessary in a democratic society.

Notes and Questions

1. Many contemporary courts are aware that speech restrictions dictated by fear of subversion might be abused. *Hector v. Attorney–General of Antigua and Barbuda*, [1990] 2 AC 312, 318:

> Finally, the same concern for preserving the security of the state is liable to have an injurious effect on the right to freedom of expression, equally by reason of the mistaken approach that it protects only the individual interest of the citizen, wherefore that interest ought, as it were, to be disregarded whenever it comes into conflict with the social interest embodied in the security of the state. In this way, the authorities are liable unwittingly to overlook the great social value which the principle of freedom of expression adds to the efficacy of the democratic process, and they are liable to do so where the expected damage that the publication is likely to cause to the state is not so great as to justify doing away with the right. In his important book, *Freedom of Speech in the U.S.A.*, Professor Chafee severely criticises the Federal Courts in the United States for being led away into such error when interpreting the Espionage Act during the First World War (*loc. cit.*, 1942 edition, p. 34).

2. Note that the Turkish law, as applied, was about advocacy of illegality, where the illegality was "incitement to hatred or hostility on the basis of a distinction between social classes, races, [and] religions." The European Court of Human Rights (ECHR) did not discuss the speech-restrictive nature of the laws (rather commonplace in countries where racial-, religious-, and ethnic-hate propaganda are criminalized). This is explained partly by the express provisions of the applicable Convention, which authorizes restrictions, and partly by the international nature of the Court: it must accommodate national (security) sensitivities. The ECHR simply reclassified the article from sedition to legitimate criticism of government and found the punishment disproportionate. Does this approach provide sufficient protection to speech during times of fear-generated government hysteria? Is this better for freedom of speech than the American approach?

A.3.   WHAT AMOUNTS TO PROTECTED EXPRESSION?

In most contemporary democracies, speech is understood to include many forms of expression. Traditionally, in France, regulation of the press was the subject of special regulation, and the constitutional provisions indicated that legislation is entitled to restrict speech. The 1881 Press Act (still in force with amendments) was a liberal regulation, but it did institutionalize, for example, the right to reply, which would be unconstitutional in the U.S. Only recently did the constitutional dimension of free expression emerge in France. "Today freedom of expression has constitutional status in France * * * but in France it provides only a limited guarantee." Roger Errera, *The Freedom of the Press: The United States, France, and Other European Countries*, in *Constitutionalism and*

Rights: The Influence of the United States Constitution Abroad 67 (Louis Henkin and Albert J. Rosenthal eds., 1990). The French Constitutional Council found (in the context of a broadcasting regulation) that objectives of constitutional character are to be considered in the regulation: the needs of public order, pluralism, and respect for the freedoms of others. Restrictions in the name of privacy protection (including preliminary permanent injunctions, as in the case of the memories by President Mitterand's physician on the late-President's illness) are not perceived as constitutionally problematic.

Some modern constitutions, like the German Basic Law, discuss not only speech and the press among protected forms of expression but also specify other forms and communicative institutions. Article 5 of the Basic Law provides for the protection of opinions (*Wahlkampf/"CSU: NPD Europas" Case*).[i]

> "Strictly speaking the communication of facts is not the expression of opinion. * * * [However,] the communication of facts is protected by the basic right of the freedom to express opinion because and to the extent it is a precondition of the formation of opinions. * * * What cannot contribute to * * * opinion formation is not protected, especially demonstrably or deliberately false statements of fact."

> 61 BVerfGE 1, 8 (1982) below.

> In the U.S., certain forms of low-value speech can be regulated, while others are simply not treated as speech. (For an alternative approach, see *R.A.V.* below.) On the other hand the offensive nature of expression, at least in certain circumstances, does not deprive speech and communicative conduct of First Amendment protection: "[W]e cannot indulge the facile assumption that one can forbid particular words without also running a substantial risk of suppressing ideas in the process. Indeed, governments might soon seize upon the censorship of particular words as a convenient guise for banning the expression of unpopular views." *Cohen v. California*, 403 U.S. 15, 26 (1971). Below we discuss commercial speech and symbolic communicative conduct as two areas that shed light on the underlying values of speech protection.

Notes on "Commercial" Speech

1. For constitutional systems that determine the value of speech with a balancing procedure, the nature of expression does not present specific theoretical problems. In *Irwin Toy* the Supreme Court of Canada applied a standard balancing test and found that prohibitions on toy advertisements were speech restrictions. The majority concluded that the protection of children was a legitimate goal and that a total ban on advertising was not an excessive means of protection (three judges dissented on this point). The U.S. categorical approach, however, raises difficult problems. In *Virginia State Board of Pharmacy v. Virginia Citizens Consumer Council, Inc.*, 425 U.S. 748 (1976),[j] the USSC was confronted with the question of whether speech that does "no more than propose a commercial transaction," and is so removed from any "exposition of ideas," and from "truth, science,

---

i. The German Basic Law also protects science and teaching (Art. 5 sec 3).

j. Virginia statute that made advertising the prices of prescription drugs "unprofessional conduct," held invalid.

morality, and arts in general, in its diffusion of liberal sentiments on the administration of government" (*Roth*), that it lacks all protection. It was found to be in the public interest that private actors be well informed in a market economy. However, government regulation of commercial speech is subject to lesser scrutiny than other forms of speech. "Special care" should attend the review of blanket bans, and the Court has pointedly remarked that "in recent years this Court has not approved a blanket ban on commercial speech unless the expression itself was flawed in some way, either because it was deceptive or related to unlawful activity." *Central Hudson Gas & Elec. Corp. v. Public Service Commission of New York*, 447 U.S., at 566 n.9.

2.   The European Union's Directive on Broadcasting (Council Directive 89/552) imposed a complete ban on the advertisement of tobacco products on television. Would this be unconstitutional in the U.S.? Directive 98/43/EC imposed a total ban on all advertising of tobacco. If a government is entitled to prohibit or restrict an unhealthy activity, is this to imply that the propaganda for such activity can be proscribed, too? The total ban was overturned, in 2000, by the European Court of Justice (ECJ), which annulled it on the grounds that EU lawmakers had no competence for introducing it on the basis of internal-market legislation. *Federal Republic of Germany v. European Parliament, et al.*, No. C–376/98, and *The Queen v. Secretary of State for Health and Others, ex parte Imperial Tobacco Ltd. and Others*, No. C–74/99, European Ct. of Justice.

3.   Consider Eric Barendt, *Freedom of Speech* 57 (1987):

Article 5 does specifically cover press freedom and the freedom of people to gain information from commonly available sources (*Informationsfreiheit*), so there is strong textual argument for holding at least some kinds of commercial speech to be constitutionally protected. However, in a later case the Karlsruhe Court without much discussion held that the advertisement by a chemist of non-professional goods, contrary to *Land* professional rules, was not covered by Article 5 because it did not assert an opinion [53 BVerfGE 96 (1980)]. It is possible that the Court was influenced by the chemist's economic motives for advertising; he was hardly seeking to contribute to the shaping of public opinion, which is generally regarded as the principal purpose of Article 5 [*Lüth*]. Elsewhere the Court made it plain that the Basic Law's protection of free speech is not removed merely because the publication of an opinion is designed to bring the publisher financial profits [30 BVerfGE 337, 352–53 (1971)], but as in the United States this factor may still influence the courts in controversial cases.

Do you agree with Barendt's statements, considering recent American developments in commercial speech, that is, in light of the increasing burdens imposed on the state to prove with a standard of less than strict scrutiny its interest in restricting nonmisleading advertising? The *Chemist Advertisement Case* can be viewed more as a freedom of occupation rather than a free speech case. Recent cases were decided in the context of fair competition and free choice of occupation.

4.   Speech protection is extended, either expressly or through interpretation, to forms of expression that were developed by modern technologies. However, the protection of expression in nontraditional media (other than print media) might be subject to special considerations; for example, because

of the direct, nonmediated impact of images on human behavior. See for India, *S. Rangarajan* below. Because totalitarian regimes exploited their monopoly over broadcasting for their own propaganda, posttotalitarian constitutions often contain specific rules regarding broadcasting freedoms and prohibiting political monopoly, and postcolonial constitutions emphasize the role of state broadcasting in education and development. Contemporary theories tend to extend free speech to a general communicative freedom.

A.3.1. PROTECTION OF SYMBOLS

An important issue concerns which forms of expressive conduct are protected as speech and which are purely conduct.

One of the best indicators of the nature of a liberal democracy is its attitude toward national symbols. In the U.S. flag burning cases the Supreme Court withstood prevailing national sentiment and allowed the symbolic (communicative) element of the conduct to prevail. In certain European countries, where state symbols are under criminal law protection against physical abuse, the laws involved are held constitutional not because flag burning lacks communicative value but simply because protection of national symbols is a constitutionally permissible, neutral-proportional restriction, given the goals of the protection and because of the low value level of the expression.

TEXAS v. JOHNSON

Supreme Court (United States).
491 U.S. 397 (1989).

Mr. Justice Brennan delivered the opinion of the Court.

After publicly burning an American flag as a means of political protest, Gregory Lee Johnson was convicted of desecrating a flag in violation of Texas law. This case presents the question whether his conviction is consistent with the First Amendment. We hold that it is not.

I

While the Republican National Convention was taking place in Dallas in 1984, respondent Johnson participated in a political * * * He set [the flag] on fire. While the flag burned, the protestors chanted: "America, the red, white, and blue, we spit on you. * * *" No one was physically injured or threatened with injury, though several witnesses testified that they had been seriously offended by the flag burning.

Of the approximately 100 demonstrators, Johnson alone was charged with a crime. The only criminal offense with which he was charged was the desecration of a venerated object in violation of Texas Penal Code Ann. § 42.09(a)(3) (1989).

II

We must first determine whether Johnson's burning of the flag constituted expressive conduct, permitting him to invoke the First

Amendment in challenging his conviction. If his conduct was expressive, we next decide whether the state's regulation is related to the suppression of free expression. *O'Brien*.[k] If the state's regulation is not related to expression, then the less stringent standard we announced in *O'Brien* for regulations of noncommunicative conduct controls. If it is, then we are outside of *O'Brien's* test, and we must ask whether this interest justifies Johnson's conviction under a more demanding standard. A third possibility is that the State's asserted interest is simply not implicated on these facts, and in that event the interest drops out of the picture.

In deciding whether particular conduct possesses sufficient communicative elements to bring the First Amendment into play, we have asked whether "[a]n intent to convey a particularized message was present, and [whether] the likelihood was great that the message would be understood by those who viewed it."

[I]n characterizing such action for First Amendment purposes, we have considered the context in which it occurred. * * *

III

In order to decide whether *O'Brien's* test applies here, we must decide whether Texas has asserted an interest in support of Johnson's conviction that is unrelated to the suppression of expression. The state offers two separate interests to justify this conviction: preventing breaches of the peace and preserving the flag as a symbol of nationhood and national unity. We hold that the first interest is not implicated on this record and that the second is related to the suppression of expression.

A

* * * [The Court found that the provocative idea expressed by the flag burning would not incite riot, nor did it represent "fighting words."]

B

The state also asserts an interest in preserving the flag as a symbol of nationhood and national unity. The state, apparently, is concerned that such conduct will lead people to believe either that the flag does not stand for nationhood and national unity, but instead reflects other, less positive concepts, or that the concepts reflected in the flag do not in fact exist, that is, that we do not enjoy unity as a nation. These concerns blossom only when a person's treatment of the flag communicates some message, and thus are related "to the suppression of free expression"

k. In *United States v. O'Brien*, 391 U.S. 367 (1968), the Court distinguished between pure expressive conduct and conduct that, on its face, does not necessarily convey any message and hence arguably could be regulated without effectively repressing one's ability to express oneself. In such cases "a government regulation is sufficiently justified if * * * it furthers an important or substantial government interest; if the government interest is unrelated to the suppression of free expression; and if the incidental restriction on alleged First Amendment freedom is not greater than is essential to the furtherance of that interest."

O'Brien was about draft-card burning, which violated a statute on the administration of military service. Compare the *O'Brien* test with the Canadian proportionality test in *Irwin Toy*.

within the meaning of *O'Brien*. We are thus outside of *O'Brien*'s test altogether.

IV

* * * Whether Johnson's treatment of the flag violated Texas law thus depended on the likely communicative impact of his expressive conduct. Our decision in *Boos v. Barry*, tells us that this restriction on Johnson's expression is content based. * * * According to the principles announced in *Boos*, Johnson's political expression was restricted because of the content of the message he conveyed. We must therefore subject the state's asserted interest in preserving the special symbolic character of the flag to "the most exacting scrutiny." *Boos v. Barry*.

According to Texas, if one physically treats the flag in a way that would tend to cast doubt on either the idea that nationhood and national unity are the flag's referents or that national unity actually exists, the message conveyed thereby is a harmful one and therefore may be prohibited.

If there is a bedrock principle underlying the First Amendment, it is that the government may not prohibit the expression of an idea simply because society finds the idea itself offensive or disagreeable.

We have not recognized an exception to this principle even where our flag has been involved.

The First Amendment does not guarantee that other concepts virtually sacred to our nation as a whole—such as the principle that discrimination on the basis of race is odious and destructive—will go unquestioned in the marketplace of ideas. See *Brandenburg*. We decline, therefore, to create for the flag an exception to the joust of principles protected by the First Amendment.

It is not the state's ends, but its means, to which we object. It cannot be gainsaid that there is a special place reserved for the flag in this nation, and thus we do not doubt that the government has a legitimate interest in making efforts to "preserv[e] the national flag as an unalloyed symbol of our country. * * * " [This] is not to say that it may criminally punish a person for burning a flag as a means of political protest.

We are tempted to say, in fact, that the flag's deservedly cherished place in our community will be strengthened, not weakened, by our holding today . . .

The way to preserve the flag's special role is not to punish those who feel differently about these matters. It is to persuade them that they are wrong.

Chief Justice Rehnquist, with whom Justice White and Justice O'Connor join, dissenting.

The American flag, then, throughout more than 200 years of our history, has come to be the visible symbol embodying our Nation. It does not represent the views of any particular political party, and it does not represent any particular political philosophy. The flag is not simply another "idea" or "point of view" competing for recognition in the marketplace of ideas.

* * *

But the Court insists that the Texas statute prohibiting the public burning of the American flag infringes on respondent Johnson's freedom of expression. Such freedom, of course, is not absolute. The public burning of the American flag by Johnson was no essential part of any exposition of ideas, and at the same time it had a tendency to incite a breach of the peace. * * *

Thus, in no way can it be said that Texas is punishing him because his hearers—or any other group of people—were profoundly opposed to the message that he sought to convey. Such opposition is no proper basis for restricting speech or expression under the First Amendment. It was Johnson's use of this particular symbol, and not the idea that he sought to convey by it or by his many other expressions, for which he was punished.

FLAG DESECRATION CASE

Federal Constitutional Court (Germany).
81 BVerfGE 278 (1990).[l]

[The German Criminal Code (Art. 90a) criminalizes, with a punishment of up to three years, the insult of Federal Germany and its constitutional order and the disparagement of its flag, coat of arms, and anthem. In various lower-court cases, the federal flag was used for caricatures and collages in highly disrespectful ways, including for a book jacket of a collection of antimilitary essays depicting people urinating on the flag during an army swearing-in ceremony.[m]]

Judgment of the First Senate:

* * *

B. II. 2. Although artistic freedom is guaranteed without reservation, this does not necessarily proscribe punishment of the complainants under § 90a (1) no.2 of the Criminal Code.

a) The guarantee of art. 5(3) first sentence GG is not limited solely by the basic rights of third parties. Rather, it can collide with all kinds of constitutional provisions; this is because a well-ordered human co-existence requires not only the mutual consideration of citizens, but also a functioning governmental order, which is a prerequisite for guaranteeing the effectiveness of any basic rights protection at all works of art

---

l. Decisions of the Bundesvervassungs-gericht–Federal Constitutional Court–Federal Republic of Germany, Volume 2/Part II: *Freedom of Speech*, published by the Members of the Court, Nomos Verlagsgesellschaft, Karlsruhe, 1998, p. 437.

m. § 90 a–Disparagement of the State and its symbols

(1) A person who publicly, in an assembly, or through the dissemination of writing

1. insults or maliciously disparages the Federal Republic of Germany, one of its regional states, or its constitutional order or

2. disparages the colors, the flag, the coat of arms of the anthem of the Federal Republic of Germany or one of its regional states shall be punished by a term of imprisonment up to 3 years or with a fine.

which damage the constitutionally guaranteed order are not, therefore, subject to limitation only if they directly endanger the continued existence of the state or the constitution. Rather, in all cases in which other constitutional principles conflict with the exercise of artistic freedom, a commensurate balance must be found among those opposing interests equally protected by the constitution, with the goal of their optimization (see BVerfGE 77, 240 [253]). The Bundesverfassungsgericht in an earlier decision, required a direct and present danger to the "highest-ranking basic values" of the constitution in order to overcome the guarantee of artistic freedom. This does not mean that art.5 (3) first sentence is absolutely pre-eminent in less extreme situations. In such cases, the conflict between artistic freedom and other constitutionally protected principles will be resolved through case-specific balancing. In the process, it will, however, be taken into consideration that limitations of these unconditionally guaranteed basic rights are not justified formalistically by general objectives like, for instance, "protection of the constitution" or the "functional ability of criminal justice;" rather, those constitutionally protected principles which, according to a realistic assessment of the circumstances, will collide with the safeguarding of rights under art.5 (3) first sentence GG, must be concretely carved out, guided by particular provisions of the Basic Law.

b) [The state has a constitutional duty to use the flag and other symbols to portray itself because the Basic Law itself describes the colors of the flag]. It is the purpose of these symbols to appeal to the citizens' sense of civic responsibility. * * * As a free state, the Federal Republic relies rather on the identification of its citizens with the basic values [i.e., the free democratic constitutional structure] represented by the flag. * * * The value of the criminal norm which conflicts with artistic freedom result from this meaning of the federal flag. The flag serves as an important integration device through the leading state goals it embodies; its disparagement can thus impair the necessary authority of the state.

c) In the light of art. 5 (3) first sentence GG, however, the protection of symbols must not lead to an immunization of the state against criticism and even against disapproval. Therefore, a balancing of the conflicting constitutional principles in the specific case is necessary.

Notes and Questions

1. A major political conflict erupted in the U.S., in 1989, when the USSC held in *Texas v. Johnson* that a statute prohibiting the "desecration" of the American flag for political purposes violated the First Amendment. Large segments of the country were outraged and sought a constitutional amendment to permit prosecution of flag burners. Norman Dorsen, *Flag Desecration in Courts, Congress and Country*, 17 Thomas M. Cooley L. Rev. 417, 440–42 (2000), comments:

> To many, flag desecration has become a metaphor for late 20th century permissiveness, self-indulgence and even anarchy, and it therefore must be opposed and stamped out. Professor Stephen Presser in 1998 congressional testimony supporting a flag amendment referred to the constitu-

tional goal of 'secur[ing] a certain baseline of civilized behavior' and said that 'the personal liberty element of our tradition has, in effect, spun out of constitutional control.'

These impulses are underscored in the proposed amendment by the word 'desecration,' which suggests a modern religious crusade rather than merely a conventional dispute over public policy. The despoilers of the flag, in this view, are not merely insulting one of the nation's great symbols, but indulging in blasphemy, leading to the charge from opponents [of a constitutional amendment] that such religious imagery 'veer[s] close to idolatry because the concept of 'desecration' applies only to religious objects and not to other things, no matter how justly admired.'

These attitudes, when added to the broad patriotic feeling about the flag, explain the zeal for an amendment. But this very zeal promotes a special danger to the rule of law. In the hands of some prosecutors, the elastic amendment, if ratified and implemented by a congressional statute, could be a license to proceed against the politically unpopular, the counter-culture and the despoilers of our body politic that Professor Presser, among others, deplores. * * *

[A] constitutional amendment restricting the substantive reach of the Bill of Rights for the first time in American history could compromise the First Amendment as protesters, for whatever reason, chose to burn or mutilate copies of the Constitution, Declaration of Independence, Great Seal of the United States, or other powerful national symbols. For this reason, among others, the 'bedrock principle' [announced in *Texas v. Johnson*] that 'the government may not prohibit expression of an idea simply because society finds the idea itself offensive or disagreeable' should remain the cornerstone of our freedom of speech.

2. Although in at least one case the German Federal Constitutional Court (GFCC) found that a direct and present danger to the highest-ranking values of the Basic Law is needed to overcome artistic freedom (33 BVerfGE 52 [71]), the criminalization of the disparagement of a state symbol per se has not raised a free speech issue in Germany. Neither the German courts nor scholarly articles ask what actual danger results from disparagement of the state and its symbols. Can this be explained in terms of the traditional stereotype about German culture, which allegedly maintains some state-respecting authoritarian traditions? An alternative explanation would emphasize that the unproblematic nature of the criminal protection of certain content is related to the constitutionally endorsed idea of militant democracy.

In the *Flag Desecration Case* the constitutionality per se of the provision in the Criminal Code was not raised in the complaints. Instead the Court found the sentences of the lower courts unconstitutional, arguing that the constitutional value of the flag was not properly balanced against artistic freedom. Although the Basic Law does not mention specific grounds for the restriction of artistic, scientific, and academic freedoms, artistic freedom can collide with several constitutional values. The protection of the constitutional order may prevail against artistic expression "because a well-ordered human co-existence requires * * * a functioning government order, which is a prerequisite for guaranteeing the effectiveness of any basic rights protection." (30 BVerfGE 173 [193].) In the *Flag Desecration Case* the GFCC took pains to show that the alleged attacks to the flag were not directed against the constitutional order but against the military. A few years later, in the *Tucholsky II Case*, 93 BVerfGE 266 (1995) (see below), institutional reputation became an issue. In Germany, respect for the state is considered a legitimate object of legal protection, including criminal law protection. However, the GFCC continues to diminish the impact of antidisparagement laws on speech by its balancing technique. The author of a leaflet that compared the Federal Republic and Bavaria with a fascist state obsessed by great-power politics was convicted for having maliciously reviled the state. On appeal, the Court emphasized that expressions must not be interpreted in case of ambiguity in a way that leads to conviction before other possibilities of interpretation have been excluded on convincing grounds. The Court argued that it is possible to interpret the statement as a criticism of indulgence over neofascist activities and not as an identification with fascist states. "Libelous criticism prevails only if in these statements, in their context, defamation of the State had pushed the dispute of facts completely into the background." (29.07.1998. 1 BvR 287/93. BCCL 1998, 233.)

3. In *Hong Kong Special Administrative Region v. Ng Kung Siu and Lee Kin Yun*, Court of Final Appeal of Hong Kong, Final Appeal No. 4 of 1999 (Criminal), the highest Hong Kong Court applied a proportionality test to a flag-desecration case where respondents, in a peaceful and orderly demonstration, were protesting against the system of government on the Mainland. The Chinese character "shame" had been written on the Chinese and Hong Kong flags. Desecration of the flag is a crime under national and regional (Hong Kong) law. The Court of Final Appeal of Hong Kong found that the ordinary meaning of "defiling" plainly includes the dishonoring of the flag. It also found a public interest in protecting the flag.

> The courts must give a generous interpretation to [the] constitutional guarantee [of free speech]. This freedom includes the freedom to express ideas which the majority may find disagreeable or offensive and the freedom to criticise governmental institutions and the conduct of public officials.

> It is common ground that the statutory provisions criminalising desecration of the national and regional flags restrict the freedom of expression. Before considering whether the restriction is justified, it is important to examine first the extent of the restriction. This is because when one comes to consider the issue of justification, one must have in mind what is that has to be justified, in particular, whether it is a wide or limited restriction that has to be justified. The wider the restriction, the more difficult it would be to justify. The appellant submits that the freedom of expression is implicated only in a minor way as only one mode of expression is prohibited. The respondent argues that the restriction is wide. The argument is that it prohibits not merely one mode of expression but by rendering unlawful one form of political protest also the substance of what may be expressed.

The Court of Final Appeal concluded that the restriction "is a limited one. It bans one mode of expressing whatever the message the person concerned may wish to express, that is the mode of desecrating the flags. It does not interfere with the person's freedom to express the same message by other modes." The Court found that the restriction serves public order as "the regional flag is the unique symbol of the Hong Kong Special Administrative

Region as an inalienable part of the People's Republic of China under the principle of 'one country, two systems'." Further, the Court stated that the restriction must be necessary: the "word 'necessary' in this test should be given its ordinary meaning and that no assistance is to be gained by substituting for 'necessary' a phrase such as 'pressing social need'." The requirement was met. The Court's understanding of necessity, admittedly, is dictated by the political situation that Hong Kong is within the People's Republic of China: "Hong Kong is at the early stage of the new order following resumption of the exercise of sovereignty by the People's Republic of China. The implementation of the principle of 'one country, two systems' is a matter of fundamental importance, as is the reinforcement of national unity and territorial integrity. Protection of the national flag and the regional flag from desecration, having regard to their unique symbolism, will play an important part in the attainment of these goals."

4. The protection of government institutions and symbols is quite common in Europe. In Hungary, one finds a strange mixture of the German and American reasonings. The Hungarian Constitutional Court (HCC) stated in Decision 30/1992 (V.26.) AB hat. (see below) that a criminal law which restricts speech should be given less weight in the balancing against the speech interest if the value protected by the act serves a constitutional right only indirectly, and even less weight is to be attributed to abstract interests, like "public order." Eight years later, in Decision 13/2000 (V.12.) AB hat., the Court found that the criminalization of disparagement of national symbols is constitutional because the flag is the means of expressing national sentiment and "pertinence to the national community," and, therefore, "in certain respects disparaging expressions are outside the constitutionally protected pluralism of opinions." Freedom of opinion is protected in order to allow criticism, but there is no criticism in disparagement. One possible reading of the HCC's view is that disparagement is conduct without expressive value. The Court found on the same day that national symbols are constitutionally protected by criminal law but that the use of symbols of despotic regimes (Nazi and communist) can be constitutionally criminalized (Decision 14/2000 (V.12.) AB hat.). It concluded that an opinion which is incompatible with constitutional values is not protected speech. Is this consistent with the approach in *Dennis*? Does the position of the HCC preclude the activities of political parties advocating communism or racial supremacy? Must murals in an avant-garde café depicting the communist red star be destroyed? What about the Nazi swastika in a bar frequented by extremists but not banned political party members? Is allowing the display of the symbols of antidemocratic totalitarian regimes necessary to protect the constitutional regime as the HCC suggests? Are there other possible reasons to criminalize such displays, such as the sensitivities of victims of past totalitarian regimes? Is the antidisplay law content-based discrimination? For arguments regarding content-based discrimination in regard to Nazism, see the *Holocaust Denial Case* below. Is the HCC's decision acceptable under a proportionality test?

Is the use of the flag strictly a matter of symbols and respect? In 1997, the mayor of the Albanian-populated municipality of Gostivar, in the Former Yugoslav Republic of Macedonia, organized a protest meeting to protect the "national" flag, that is, the Albanian flag. In his speech the mayor stated: "we give our life, but not our flag, [and] we will use the Albanian flag, there will be official use of Albanian language * * * within the framework of the project of regionalism." The Albanian flag was raised at the city hall, notwithstanding an interim stay by the Constitutional Court, which, at the time, was considering the Gostivar municipality's resolution on the flying of the Albanian flag. Two days later, a group of ethnic Macedonians desecrated the Albanian flag, and a fight erupted at the city hall. The police took action, two weeks later, to remove the flag from city hall. The action met with resistance, and three people were killed. The mayor was sentenced for inciting racial discord. The sentence was upheld by the Constitutional Court of the Former Yugoslav Republic of Macedonia, which argued that speech is protected but can be restricted for the security of society as a whole.

A.4. RESTRICTIONS IN THE PRIVATE AND PUBLIC INTERESTS: BALANCING

LÜTH CASE

Constitutional Court (Germany).
7 BVerfGE 198 (1958).

[During World War Two, Veit Harlan directed the notorious anti-Semitic film *The Jew Suess,* a piece of Nazi propaganda. In 1950, after being acquitted for Nazi crimes, Harlan directed his first postwar movie, *Immortal Beloved*. Incensed by the reemergence of a director of the Nazi period, Lüth, the Director of Information of the City of Hamburg, called for a boycott of Harlan's new film. Lüth believed that a boycott would demonstrate to the world that the new German cinema was not to be identified with an anti-Semitic director.

[The producer of *Immortal Beloved* obtained an injunction from the state court against Lüth, prohibiting him from issuing further calls for a boycott of the film. The plaintiffs used section 826 of the German Civil Code (BGB), which provides a remedy against a person who "intentionally causes injury to another person in a manner contrary to good morals." Finding that Lüth's statements injured the plaintiff's business in violation of section 826, the state court issued an injunction prohibiting Lüth from making further calls for a boycott of Harlan's firm. In response, Lüth filed a "constitutional complaint."]

Judgment of the First Senate:

B. II. The complainant claims that the superior court has violated his basic right to free speech as safeguarded by Article 5 (1) (I) of the Constitution.

1. The decision prohibits the complainant from making statements that could influence others to adhere to his opinion regarding Harlan's reappearance [as a film director]. * * * Seen objectively, this limits the complainant's freedom of expression * * * [But] such a ruling can violate the complainant's basic right under Article 5 (1) only if [a] provision of the Civil Code [Art. 826] would be so affected by a basic right as to render it an impossible basis for a decision. * * *

Whether and to what extent basic rights affect private law is controversial. The extreme positions in this dispute are, on the one hand, that basic rights are exclusively directed against the state and, on the other hand, that the basic rights as such, or at least some and in any case the more important of them, also apply in civil [i.e., private] law matters against everybody. Neither of these extremes finds support in the Constitutional Court's existing jurisprudence. * * * Nor is there any need here to resolve fully the dispute over the so-called effect of the basic rights on third persons [*Drittwirkung*]. The following discussion is sufficient to resolve this case.

* * * The primary purpose of the basic rights is to safeguard the liberties of the individual against interferences by public authority. They are defensive rights of the individual against the state. This [purpose] follows from the historical development of the concept of basic rights and from historical developments leading to the inclusion of basic rights in the constitutions of various countries. This also corresponds to the meaning of the basic rights contained in the Basic Law and is under-scored by the enumeration of basic rights in the first section of the Constitution, thereby stressing the primacy of the human being and his dignity over the power of the state. This is why the legislature allowed the extraordinary remedy * * * of the constitutional complaint to be brought only against acts of public authority.

An Objective Order of Values

It is equally true, however, that the Basic Law is not a value-neutral document [citations from numerous decisions]. Its section on basic rights establishes an objective order of values, and this order strongly rein-forces the effective power of basic rights. This value system, which centers upon dignity of the human personality developing freely within the social community, must be looked upon as a fundamental constitu-tional decision affecting all spheres of law [public and private], It serves as a yardstick for measuring and assessing all actions in the areas of legislation, public administration, and adjudication. Thus it is clear that basic rights also influence [the development of] private law. Every provision of private law must be compatible with this system of values, and every such provision must be interpreted in its spirit.

The legal content of basic rights as objective norms is developed within private law through the medium of the legal provisions directly applicable to this area of the law. Newly enacted statutes must conform to the system of values of the basic rights. The content of existing law also must be brought into harmony with this system of values. This system infuses specific constitutional content into private law, which from that point on determines its interpretation. A dispute between private individuals concerning rights and duties emanating from provi-sions of private law—provisions influenced by the basic rights—remains substantively and procedurally a private-law dispute. [Courts] apply and interpret private law, but the interpretation must conform to the Consti-tution.

The influence of the scale of values of the basic rights affects particularly those provisions of private law that contain mandatory rules of law and thus form part of the *ordre public*—in the broad sense of the term—that is, rules which for reasons of the general welfare also are binding on private legal relationships and are removed from the domination of private intent. Because of their purpose these provisions are closely related to the public law they supplement. Consequently, they are substantially exposed to the influence of constitutional law. In bringing this influence to bear, the courts may invoke the general clauses which, like Article 826 of the Civil Code, refer to standards outside private law. "Good morals" is one such standard. In order to determine what is required by social norms such as these, one has to consider first the ensemble of value concepts that a nation has developed at a certain point in its intellectual and cultural history and laid down in its constitution. That is why the general clauses have rightly been called the points where basic rights have breached the [domain of] private law.

Function of Lower Courts

The Constitution requires the judge to determine whether the basic rights have influenced the substantive rules of private law in the manner described. [If this influence is present] he must then, in interpreting and applying these provisions, heed the resulting modification of private law.

Freedom of Speech and General Laws

2. With regard to the basic right of free speech (Article 5), the problem of the relationship between basic rights and private law is somewhat different. As under the Weimar Constitution (Article 118), this basic right is guaranteed only within the framework of the "general laws" (Article 5 [2]). * * * One might take the view that the Constitution itself, by referring to limits imposed by the general laws, has restricted the legitimate scope of the basic right to that area left open to it by courts in their interpretation of these laws. Such an approach would mean that any general law restricting a basic right would never constitute a violation of that right.

However, this is not the meaning of the reference to "general laws" The basic right to freedom of opinion is the most immediate expression of the human personality [living] in society and, as such, one of the noblest of human rights. * * * It is absolutely basic to a liberal-democratic constitutional order because it alone makes possible the constant intellectual exchange and the contest among opinions that form the lifeblood of such an order; [indeed] it is "the matrix, the indispensable condition of nearly every other form of freedom" [Justice Cardozo, quoted in English].

Because of the fundamental importance of freedom of speech in the liberal-democratic state, it would be inconsistent to allow the substance of this basic right to be limited by an ordinary law (and thus necessarily by judicial decisions interpreting the law.) Rather, the same principle applies here that was discussed above in general terms with regard to the relationship between the basic rights and private law. [Courts] must evaluate the effect of general laws which would limit the basic right in the light of the importance of the basic right. * * * [They] must interpret these laws so as to preserve the significance of the basic right; in a free democracy this process [of interpretation] must assume the fundamentality of freedom of speech in all spheres, particularly in public life. * * * [Courts] may not construe the mutual relationship between basic rights and "general laws" as a unilateral restriction on the applicability of the basic rights by the "general laws;" rather, there is a mutual effect. According to the wording of Article 5, the "general laws": set bounds to the basic right but, in turn, those laws must be interpreted in light of the value-establishing significance of this basic right in a free democratic state, and so any limiting effect on the basic right must itself be restricted.

The Federal Constitutional Court is the court of last resort for constitutional complaints relating to the preservation of basic rights. Therefore it must have the legal right to control the decisions of the courts where, in applying a general law, they enter the sphere shaped by basic rights. * * * The Federal Constitutional Court must have the right to enforce a specific value found in the basic rights.

Meaning of General Laws as Applied to Speech

3.   The concept of "general laws" was controversial from the very beginning. * * * In any event * * * the phrase was interpreted as referring not only to laws that "do not prohibit an opinion or the expression of an opinion as such" but also to those that "are directed toward the protection of legal rights which need such protection regardless of any specific opinion;" in other words, laws that are directed toward the protection of a community value that takes precedence over the exercise of free speech [citations to legal literature]. * * *

If the term "general laws" is construed in this way, then we can say the following with regard to the purpose and scope of the protection of the basic right: [We] must reject the view that the basic right protects only the expression of an opinion but not the inherent or intended effect on other persons. * * * Article 5 (1) of the Basic Law protects value judgments, which are always aimed at having an intellectual impact, namely, at convincing others. Indeed, the protection of the basic right is aimed primarily at the personal opinion of the speaker as expressed in the value judgment. To protect the expression itself but not its effect would make no sense.

It understood in this way, the expression of an opinion in its purely intellectual effect is free. However, if someone else's legal rights are violated [and] the protection of these rights should take precedence over the protection of freedom of opinion, then this violation does not become permissible simply because it was committed through the expression of an opinion. [Courts] must weigh the values to be protected against each other. [They] must deny the right to express an opinion if the exercise of this right would violate a more important interest protected [by private law]. [Courts] must decide whether such interests are present on the basis of the facts of each individual case.

[In the light of this discussion, the Court noted: "there is no reason why norms of private law should not also be recognized as 'general laws' within the meaning of Article 5 (2)." The Court thus rejected the prevailing view, cited in the literature, that "general laws" embrace only public laws regulating the relations between individuals and the state."]

n. "In the years before *Lüth* a number of scholars had argued that the Basic Law, as an aspect of 'public law,' had no effect on rights of 'private law'—the body of rules

4. * * * The complainant fears that any restriction upon freedom of speech might excessively limit a citizen's chance to influence public opinion and thus no longer guarantee the indispensable freedom to discuss important issues publicly. * * * This danger is indeed present. * * * To counter the danger, however, it is unnecessary to exclude private law from the category of "general laws." Rather, we must strictly adhere to the character of the basic right as a personal freedom. This is especially important when the speaker is exercising his basic right not within the framework of a private dispute but for the purpose of influencing public opinion. Thus his opinion may possibly have an impact upon another's private rights even though this is not his intention. Here the relationship between ends and means is important. The protection of speech is entitled to less protection where exercised to defend a private interest—particularly when the individual pursues a selfish goal within the economic sector—than speech that contributes to the intellectual struggle of opinions. * * * Here the assumption is in favor of free speech.

[In section III of its opinion the Court closely examines the facts of the case and the judgment of the lower court. In noting that the advocacy of a boycott is not always contrary to "good morals" within the meaning of Art. 826 of the Civil Code, the Court said: " 'Good morals' are not unchangeable principles of pure morality; they are rather defined by the views of 'decent people' about what is 'proper' in social intercourse among legal partners." The Court then proceeds on its own to weigh Lüth's interests against those of Harlan and the film companies, holding that the district court had given insufficient attention to the motives of the complainant and the historical context of his remarks. The Court's concerns are captured in the following extracts.]

2. (b) * * * The complainant's statements must be seen within the context of his general political and cultural efforts. He was moved by the apprehension that Harlan's reappearance might—especially in foreign countries—be interpreted to mean that nothing had changed in German cultural life since the National Socialist period. * * * These apprehensions concerned a very important issue for the German people. * * * Nothing has damaged the German reputation as much as the cruel Nazi persecution of the Jews. A crucial interest exists, therefore, in assuring the world that the German people have abandoned this attitude and condemn it not for reasons of political opportunism but because through an inner conversion they have come to realize its evil. * * *

Because of his especially close personal relation to all that concerned the German–Jewish relationship, the complainant was within his rights to state his view in public: even at that time he was already known for his efforts toward reestablishing a true inner peace with the Jewish people. * * * It is understandable that he feared all these efforts might be 'disturbed and thwarted by Harlan's reappearance. * * *

which seeks to do justice between private individuals and which does not ordinarily   concern the state as a party." Quint, *op. cit.*

The demand that under these circumstances the complainant should nevertheless have refrained from expressing his opinion out of regard for Harlan's professional interests and the economic interests of the film companies employing him * * * is unjustified. * * * Where the formation of public opinion on a matter important to the general welfare is concerned, private and especially individual economic interests must, in principle, yield. This does not mean that these interests are without protection; after all, the basic right's value is underscored by the fact that it is enjoyed by everyone. Whoever feels injured by the public statements of someone else can make a public reply. Public opinion is formed, like the formation of a personal opinion, only through conflicts of opinion freely expressed. * * *

IV.   On the basis of these considerations, the Federal Constitutional Court holds that the superior court, in assessing the behavior of the complainant, has misjudged the special significance of the basic right to freedom of opinion. [Courts] must consider [the significance of this right] when it comes into conflict with the private interests of others. The decision below is thus based on an incorrect application of the standards applying to basic rights and violates the basic right of the complainant under Article 5 (1) of the Basic Law. It must therefore be quashed.

IRWIN TOY LTD. v. ATTORNEY GENERAL OF QUEBEC

Supreme Court (Canada).
[1989] 1 S.C.R. 927.

[Section 248 of Quebec's Consumer Protection Act, SQ 1978 (CPA) provides that, subject to the regulations, "no person may make use of commercial advertising directed at persons under 13 years of age." Irwin Toy broadcast messages that the *Office de la protection du consommateur* claimed were in contravention of ss. 248 and 249 of the Act.]

Dickson C.J.C., Lamer and Wilson JJ.:

* * *

VI.   Whether ss. 248 and 249 Limits Freedom of Expression as Guaranteed by the Canadian and Quebec Charters

* * *

B.   The First Step: Was the Plaintiff's Activity Within the Sphere of Conduct Protected by Freedom of Expression?

Does advertising aimed at children fall within the scope of freedom of expression? This question must be put even before deciding whether there has been a limitation of the guarantee. Clearly, not all activity is protected by freedom of expression * * *

We cannot * * * exclude human activity from the scope of guaranteed free expression on the basis of the content or meaning being conveyed. Indeed, if the activity conveys or attempts to convey a meaning, it has expressive content and *prima facie* falls within the scope of the guarantee. Of course, while most human activity combines expressive and physical elements, some human activity is purely physical and does not convey or attempt to convey meaning. It might be difficult to characterize certain day-to-day tasks, like parking a car, as having expressive content. To bring such activity within the protected sphere, the plaintiff would have to show that it was performed to convey a meaning. For example, an unmarried person might, as part of a public protest, park in a zone reserved for spouses of government employees in order to express dissatisfaction or outrage at the chosen method of allocating a limited resource. If that person could demonstrate that his activity did in fact have expressive content, he would, at this stage, be within the protected sphere and the s. 2(b) challenge would proceed.

* * *

46.   Thus, the first question remains: Does the advertising aimed at children fall within the scope of freedom of expression? Surely it aims to convey a meaning, and cannot be excluded as having no expressive content. * * *

Consequently, we must proceed to the second step of the inquiry and ask whether the purpose or effect of the government action in question was to restrict freedom of expression.

* * *

C.   The second step: was the purpose or effect of the government action to restrict freedom of expression?

a.   Purpose

* * *

50.   If the government's purpose is to restrict the content of expression by singling out particular meanings that are not to be conveyed, it necessarily limits the guarantee of free expression. If the government's purpose is to restrict a form of expression in order to control access by others to the meaning being conveyed or to control the ability of the one conveying the meaning to do so, it also limits the guarantee. On the other hand, where the government aims to control only the physical consequences of certain human activity, regardless of the meaning being conveyed, its purpose is not to control expression. * * *

Thus, for example, a rule against handing out pamphlets is a restriction on a manner of expression and is "tied to content," even if that restriction purports to control litter. * * *

52.   * * * In determining whether the government's purpose aims simply at harmful physical consequences, the question becomes: does the mischief consist in the meaning of the activity or the purported influence that meaning has on the behavior of others, or does it consist, rather, only in the direct physical result of the activity.

b.   Effects

53.   Even if the government's purpose was not to control or restrict attempts to convey a meaning, the Court must still decide whether the effect of the government action was to restrict the plaintiff's free expression. Here, the burden is on the plaintiff to demonstrate that such an effect occurred. In order so to demonstrate, a plaintiff must state her claim with reference to the principles and values underlying the freedom.

[The Act intended to prohibit particular content of expression in the name of protecting children; therefore, it constitutes limitations to freedom of expression.]

VII.   Whether the Limit on Freedom of Expression Imposed by ss. 248 and 249 Is Justified Under s. 9.1 of the Quebec Charter or s. 1 of the Canadian Charter

* * *

a.   Pressing and Substantial Objective

[The concern was for the protection of a group that is particularly vulnerable to the techniques of seduction and manipulation, abundant in advertising.]

[In establishing the factual basis for this generally identified concern, the Attorney General, relying heavily upon a U.S. Federal Trade Commission (FTC) report, argued that television advertising directed at young children is per se manipulative. The majority found that the Attorney General demonstrated that the concern which prompted the enactment of the impugned legislation is pressing and substantial and that the purpose of the legislation is one of great importance.]

75.   * * * The same can be said of evaluating competing credible scientific evidence and choosing thirteen, as opposed to ten or seven, as the upper age limit for the protected group here in issue. Where the legislature mediates between the competing claims of different groups in the community, it will inevitably be called upon to draw a line marking where one set of claims legitimately begins and the other fades away without access to complete knowledge as to its precise location. If the legislature has made a reasonable assessment as to where the line is most properly drawn, especially if that assessment involves weighing conflicting scientific evidence and allocating scarce resources on this basis, it is not for the court to second guess. * * *

b.   Means Proportional to the Ends

[The Court finds that the rational-connection test is satisfied. As to the issue of minimal impairment:]

* * *

80.   [I]n matching means to ends and asking whether rights or freedoms are impaired as little as possible, a legislature mediating between the claims of competing groups will be forced to strike a balance without the benefit of absolute certainty concerning how that balance is best struck. Vulnerable groups will claim the need for protection by the government whereas other groups and individuals will assert that the government should not intrude. * * *

When striking a balance between the claims of competing groups, the choice of means, like the choice of ends, frequently will require an assessment of conflicting scientific evidence and differing justified demands on scarce resources. Democratic institutions are meant to let us all share in the responsibility for these difficult choices. Thus, as courts review the results of the legislature's deliberations, particularly with respect to the protection of vulnerable groups, they must be mindful of the legislature's representative function. * * *

81. In other cases, however, rather than mediating between different groups, the government is best characterized as the singular antagonist of the individual whose right has been infringed. * * *

82. In the instant case, * * * [t]he question is whether the government had a reasonable basis, on the evidence tendered, for concluding that the ban on all advertising directed at children impaired freedom of expression as little as possible given the government's pressing and substantial objective.

　　　　* * *

88. Quebec's ban on advertising aimed at children is not out of proportion to measures taken in other jurisdictions. * * * Based on narrower objectives than those pursued by Quebec, some governments might reasonably conclude that self-regulation is an adequate mechanism for addressing the problem of children's advertising. But having identified advertising aimed at persons under thirteen as *per se* manipulative, the legislature of Quebec could conclude, just as reasonably, that the only effective statutory response was to ban such advertising.

89. * * * While evidence exists that other less intrusive options reflecting more modest objectives were available to the government, there is evidence establishing the necessity of a ban to meet the objectives the government had reasonably set. This Court will not, in the name of minimal impairment, take a restrictive approach to social science evidence and require legislatures to choose the least ambitious means to protect vulnerable groups. There must nevertheless be a sound evidentiary basis for the government's conclusions. * * *

iii. Deleterious effects

90. There is no suggestion here that the effects of the ban are so severe as to outweigh the government's pressing and substantial objective. Advertisers are always free to direct their message at parents and other adults. They are also free to participate in educational advertising. The real concern animating the challenge to the legislation is that revenues are in some degree affected. This only implies that advertisers will have to develop new marketing strategies for children's products.

[The impugned provisions are therefore upheld, under s. 1 of the Charter.]

Appeal dismissed.

Notes and Questions

1. *Lüth*, obviously, is *not* about the ultimate limits of speech exemplified by sedition. The case is about the damage caused to private economic interests by speech calling for a boycott, speech that was found acceptable under the circumstances. The case established the German constitutional standards of speech restriction based on "general laws," which Art. 5 sec. 2 explicitly allows. It rejected the possibility that *any* "general law," in other words any law that does not single out ideas, can restrict speech to the

extent a legislature thinks fit. It imposed a constitutional duty on ordinary courts to balance speech interests against other affected interests, in the specific circumstances. In rejecting the concept that a general law may restrict speech and in establishing the supervisory role of the Constitutional Court, freedom of opinion is protected not only as a private matter as the expression of the human personality but also under the American political understanding of speech as a condition of liberty. Many courts refer expressly to foreign courts in their formative years, as the *Lüth* court did to the Palko v. Connecticut, 302 U.S. 319 (1937) (Justice Cardozo). The French Constitutional Court, in the *Press Enterprises Case*, repeats the "indispensable-to-other-freedoms" argument, without a specific reference.[o]

2.   Peter E. Quint, *Free Speech and Private Law in German Constitutional Theory*, 48 Md. L. Rev. 247, 287 (1989) states:

> Even though the speech interest prevailed in *Lüth*, however, the opinion contained uncertain omens for the future. If in a subsequent case the constitutional interest in speech were to be balanced against 'general laws' protecting countervailing constitutional interests—or in the event that speech interests were to be balanced against interests that were for any reason stronger than Harlan's interests in *Lüth*—the interest in speech might not prevail. * * * Moreover, the delineation of a balancing technique as a basic technique relating to speech raises heightened problems of uncertainty. * * * If a new balance is to be struck on the manifold facts of each case, the result in any future speech decision (and consequently the future extent of protection of speech) will be particularly difficult to ascertain. * * * The resulting uncertainty may have the effect of discouraging the expression of opinions that are indeed constitutionally protected. * * * Instead, the [Supreme] Court has frequently adopted the technique of 'categorization,' through which it attempts to define with as much clarity as possible certain relatively narrow areas of unprotected speech and finds that most speech that does not fall into these categories is constitutionally protected.

To illustrate the difference between the two techniques, compare the opinion in *Lüth* with *N.A.A.C.P. v. Claiborne Hardware Co.*, 458 U.S. 886 (1982), where black residents of a Mississippi town organized a boycott against local merchants in an effort to achieve equal treatment. The boycott in *Claiborne* appeared to have been much more effective than the one sought by *Lüth*, but the speech and organizational activity engaged in by the defendants in *Claiborne* were held to be constitutionally protected. In a tort action brought by the merchants, the USSC found that the various forms of speech and association engaged in by the organizers of the boycott were covered by the First Amendment and did not fall into any unprotected category. Only those forms of speech that involved advocacy of imminent violent action—when such action actually was imminent—fell into a category of unprotected expression and could thus be subject to liability. For further discussion of balancing, see Melville B. Nimmer below.

o. "[Freedom of expression] is a fundamental liberty that is even more precious because its existence is one of the fundamental safeguards of the respect of other rights and liberties, and of the national sovereignty, and therefore the law may not regulate its exercise, but for making it more effective, or in order to reconcile it with other rules or principles of constitutional value." 84–181 DC of 10, 11 Oct. 1984. Roger Errera finds the statement to be an echo of Justice Cardozo's 1937 justification. Errera, *op. cit.* at 67.

A second leading German case, involving speech that affected private economic interests, is the *Blinkfüer Case*, 25 BVerfGE 256 (1969). A small-circulation procommunist weekly became the target of a proposed boycott by the Springer Press conglomerate. The High Court found that the call for a boycott was protected and that no damages should be paid. The GFCC reversed, arguing that the economic power of the Springer concern deprived the appellant of his possibility of expression. Contrary to *Lüth*, a speech interest—not an economic interest—was restrained by this call for a boycott.

3. The GFCC emphasizes that the actual balancing of constitutional values should be made in lower courts. For an apparently similar deference to trial courts' decisions, see *Edwards v. Aguillard* 482 U.S. 578, 608 (1987). Justice White, concurring, said:

> We usually defer to courts of appeals on the meaning of a state statute, especially when a district court has the same view. Of course, we have the power to disagree, and the lower courts in a particular case may be plainly wrong. But if the meaning ascribed to a state statute by a court of appeals is a rational construction of the statute, we normally accept it. *Brockett v. Spokane Arcades, Inc.*, 472 U.S. 491. We do so because we believe "that district courts and courts of appeals are better schooled in and more able to interpret the laws of their respective States." *Brockett v. Spokane Arcades, supra*, 472 U.S., at 500. *Brockett* also indicates that the usual rule applies in First Amendment cases.

4. The German position implies that the state has certain obligations to create conditions for the exercise of rights; for example, by protecting speech against private repression, including repression by more powerful speakers. At least in the context of electoral speech, most countries find such restriction on speech (electoral advertising and campaign financing) constitutional. See *Buckley v. Valeo,* 424 U.S. 1 (1976), in Chapter 11. As to the positive duties of the state to promote speech (and other negative) rights, see *Australian Capital Television v. The Commonwealth of Australia*, (1992) 177 C.L.R. 106, (see Chapter 2) where it was held that speech rights originate in the obligation of the state to promote representative democracy by allowing the public to be informed. What are the dangers of such governmental intervention? From an American perspective it may seem odd that a government is expected to promote a fundamental negative right (in other words, a right that consists of a protection against governmental interference). In *Platform "Ärzte für das Leben" v. Austria*, 139 ECHR (ser A) (1988), the ECHR held that the right to freedom of assembly includes the idea that demonstrators who annoy persons opposed to their ideas should be able to demonstrate without fear of violence from their opponents—those who are annoyed or even provoked. (Such fear, if reasonably held, would have a deterrent and, therefore, a speech-restricting impact. Thus in certain circumstances the right goes beyond the state's duty not to interfere and includes certain positive protective measures that affect the relations among private parties. (On third-party effect, see Chapter 10.) The ECHR left it to each member-state to determine the "appropriate measure" that would enable demonstrators to express themselves peacefully. For structural similarities in the U.S. free speech context, see *Feiner v. New York*, 340 U.S. 315 (1951) (street-corner speech attacking the establishment as anti-Negro attracts blacks and hostile whites; police arrest the agitator to prevent breach of peace). The USSC upheld the arrest: "[I]t is one thing to say that the police cannot be used as an instrument for the suppression of unpopular views, and

another to say that, when as here the speaker passes the bounds of argument or persuasion and undertakes incitement to riot, they are power-less to prevent a breach of peace." *Id.* at 321. Who should be arrested following the logic of the *Platform* decision? Justice Black dissented: "I reject the Court's opinion that the police had no obligation to protect petitioner's constitutional right to talk." *Id.* at 326. In *Edwards v. South Carolina*, 372 U.S. 229 (1963), the Court reversed a breach-of-peace conviction of civil rights demonstrators, saying that police protection should have been provid-ed so that the more than 200 onlookers did not threaten a violent disruption. Does this imply that the police must provide at least reasonable protection on every occasion that a violent conflict may arise because of speech? Are police entitled to ban a demonstration if they reasonably determine they lack sufficient resources to preserve order in the event of a speech at a demon-stration provoking violence or disorder? Is *Feiner* tacitly overruled?

GARDENER v. WHITAKER

Constitutional Court (South Africa).
1996 (4) SALR 337 (CC).

Kentridge A.J.:

[In 1993, the action committee of the City Council of East London (SA) had before it a report from officials of the Council, including the plaintiff. The defendant quoted a passage from the report and said: "I want to tell you emphatically that that is a lie." The judge found that the defamatory statement related to a matter of public interest and was made on an occasion where open and frank discussion of such matters was called for. In the circumstances he found a duty rested on the defendant to speak, and those present had a corresponding duty to receive his statement.

One of the constitutional issues for the judge was "whether the provisions of Chapter 3 of the Constitution dealing with fundamental rights apply to litigation between private individuals or entities. * * * [On this] issue, which for convenience he identified as being whether Chapter 3 had 'horizontal' as well as 'vertical' application, he identified the relevant sections of the Constitution as sections 7, 33(2), (3) and (4), and 35(3)."]

6. * * * Having analyzed these sections, and having considered the solutions offered to analogous questions in Canada, Sri Lanka, Germany, and the United States, [Justice Foreman] said this:

> From this brief comparative survey it is apparent that fundamental rights charters are primarily aimed at safeguarding the rights of individ-uals against the unjustified intrusion upon those rights by public organs of the State. This is apparent not only from the central position of importance of the respective charters within each system's broader constitutional structure, but also from the content of most of the protected rights and the explicit provisions in some charters restricting their application to instances involving State action. Despite this pri-mary aim, there is an apparent need to ensure that the values inherent in the charters should permeate throughout the entire legal system, albeit indirectly in most cases.

Later, with specific reference to the South African Constitution he said:

> Our constitution is also, obviously, primarily concerned with the protection of individual rights against state action. The content of most of the fundamental rights makes this apparent, as well as the thread of accountability of public institutions that runs throughout the Constitution. * * * But the Constitution is also concerned that the entire legal system, including the common law and customary law, should accord with the broader values of the Constitution. The courts are obliged to prevent the restriction of those rights if they are directly threatened (section 7[4]) and to adapt the common law to the broader objects of the Constitution even where they are not directly affected (sections 35[1] and 35[3]).

> * * * There is no uniform and single answer to the question whether an alleged breach of a fundamental right contained in Chapter 3 of the Constitution can found an action between private individuals and entitles [sic], or whether it only applies between individuals and State organs. It all depends on the nature and extent of the particular right, the values that underlie it, and the context in which the alleged breach of the right occurs.

[The Court found the decision a development of the common law, and for lack of jurisdiction it was upheld.]

Notes on "Third–Party Effect" and the "State–Action Doctrine"[p]

1. In many countries, the protection of speech applies only where it is imperiled by the state. This is a general position that applies to other rights as well. In Canada, the prevailing view is that

> the Charter, like most written constitutions, was set up to regulate the relationship between the individual and the government. * * * Private action is therefore excluded from the application of the Charter. Such actions as an employer restricting an employee's freedom of speech or assembly, a parent restricting the mobility of a child, or a landlord discriminating on the basis of race in his selection of tenants, cannot be breaches of the Charter, because in no case is there any action by the Parliament or government of Canada or by the Legislature or government of a province. * * * To hold otherwise would be to increase the scope of the Charter immeasurably.

> It is my view that s. 32 of the Charter specifies the actors to whom the Charter will apply. They are the legislative, executive and administrative branches of government. It will apply to those branches of government whether or not their action is invoked in public or private litigation. It would seem that legislation is the only way in which a legislature may infringe a guaranteed right or freedom. * * *

> * * * While in political science terms it is probably acceptable to treat the courts as one of the three fundamental branches of Government, that is, legislative, executive, and judicial, I cannot equate for the

p. See further in Chapter 10.

purposes of Charter application the order of a court with an element of governmental action.

Retail, Wholesale and Department Store Union, Local 580 v. Dolphin Delivery Ltd., [1986] 2 S.C.R. 573.

A more direct and close connection[q] to government action is needed for the application of the Charter to enforce the Charter rights of individuals.

The Canadian approach requires some kind of government involvement for the application of the Charter. This is the point of departure in the U.S., too. The USSC held in *New York Times v. Sullivan* (see below) that the libel law of Alabama was subject to the First Amendment. The Supreme Court extended considerably the sphere of *state action* by implicitly relying on the common law of Alabama as enforced by the Supreme Court of Alabama. Previously, the USSC required some sort of legislative or administrative action to underly the state action to invoke the Constitution. Similarly, in *Shelley v. Kraemer*, 334 U.S. 1 (1948) (see chapter 10.B), state action was found in the fact that certain restrictive terms of agreements (covenants) were enforced by state courts. The challenged deeds prohibited the sale of property to African Americans. In the view of the Supreme Court the racist discrimination could not have occurred without judicial enforcement of the deed.

This position was echoed in *Du Plessis and Others v. De Klerk and Ano*, 1996 (3) SALR 850 (CC), Constitutional Court of South Africa (below), by Justice Kriegler, who argued that "unless and until there is a resort to law, private individuals are at liberty to conduct their private affairs exactly as they please as far as the fundamental rights and freedoms are concerned. * * * A white bigot may refuse to sell property to a person of colour * * *." *Id.* at para. 135. Justice Mahomed refuted the approach as the freedom of unconstitutional bigotry would always occur in terms of law: "I am not persuaded that there is, in the modern State, any right which exists which is not ultimately sourced in some law. * * * Freedom is a fundamental ingredient of a defensible and durable civilization, but it is ultimately secured in modern conditions, only through the power, the sovereignty and the majesty of the law activated by the state's instruments of authority in the protection of those prejudiced through its invasion by others." *Id.* at para. 79.

2.   While the primary concern of free speech protection in the U.S. is to protect against governmental intervention, the *Lüth* decision indicates another dimension of the problem: the free speech rights of the speaker competing against the individual rights of other actors. One of the key issues in *Lüth* concerned the applicability of the Basic Law to civil litigation by ordinary courts. An unconditionally affirmative answer would have resulted in positioning the Constitutional Court above the other courts, opening a floodgate of litigation. Further, this would have made all private relations directly subject to, and reviewable under, the Basic Law. (A similar problem, although in relation to common law, emerged in South Africa after the fall of the apartheid regime, under the Interim Constitution. See *Gardener v. Whitaker*, 1996 (4) SALR 337 (CC). Both courts had to look into the "apparent need to ensure that the values inherent in the charters should

---

q. *Re Blainey and Ontario Hockey Association*, (1986) 26 DLR (4th) 728, was a lawsuit between private parties (a 12–year-old girl was restricted from playing hockey under the Association's rules). The Charter was applied because one of the parties acted on the authority of a statute, i.e., s. 19(2) of the Ontario Human Rights Code, which infringed the Charter rights of another.

permeate throughout the entire legal system, albeit indirectly in most cases." *Id.* at para. 6.) In the pre-*Lüth* period, the Federal Labor Court found the Basic Law directly applicable in labor relations. This was strongly criticized by conservative lawyers. The main argument in favor of direct application was that the Basic Law expresses "objective" values,[r] in other words, values present in the entire legal system. The policy dimension is also relevant. The Social Democrat President of the Federal Labor Court was dissatisfied with the rigid and unfair rules of the Labor Code inherited from an authoritarian regime. An even stronger concern was present in South Africa: "To leave those areas of the common law which are in conflict with the Constitution unaffected would in effect, if not by intent, perpetuate aspects of an undemocratic, discriminatory and unjust past." *Id.* at para. 6. The solution in *Lüth* was that the Basic Law has a third-party effect (*Drittwirkung Case*); Lüth's speech rights were taken into consideration in his private relations. The GFCC relied heavily on the all-encompassing impact of the objective values embedded in the Constitution:

> [I]f basic rights are seen as "objective" values essential for the public good, it is reasonable to suppose that rights may be impaired even under circumstances in which they have not been abridged by the state. If a citizen is guaranteed certain rights of speech, for example, and external pressure is applied that makes it impossible as a practical matter to exercise those rights, it may make little difference as far as the abstract rights are concerned whether that pressure comes from the state or from some other source—for example, from an authoritarian private employer. If the goal of the "objective" value is to encourage the optimal amount of speech for the good of society, that value can be significantly impaired by repression of speech whether the repression comes from the state or from private individuals or groups. Because the basic rights establish "objective" value, then, those rights must apply not only against the state exercising its authority under public law; according to the Constitutional Court, basic rights must also have an effect on the rules of private law which regulate legal relations among individuals.

Quint, *op. cit.* at 261.

3. The South African Constitutional Court (SACC) discussed the third-party effect in *Du Plessis and Others v. De Klerk and Ano*, 1996 (3) SALR 850 (CC). The defendant argued that his alleged defamation was protected by the freedom of expression clause of the Interim Constitution. The question referred to the Court was whether Chapter 3 on the fundamental rights of the Constitution applied to legal relationships between private parties. The majority found that the fundamental rights in the Constitution are generally not capable of horizontal application, and, more specifically, the provision relating to freedom of speech is not applicable to any relationship other than that between persons and legislative or executive organs of the state. However, Chapter 3 applied to all laws, including the common law. Where there is no direct constitutional issue, the courts must have due

---

r. "[I]n German legal theory, an 'objective' value is a value that is applicable in general and in the abstract, independently of any specified relationship—in contrast with a 'subjective' right, which is the right of a specified individual to some legal result against a specific party. * * * These values are not only specified rights of individuals but are also part of the general legal order, benefiting not only individuals who may be in a certain relationship with the state but possessing relevance for all legal relationships." Quint, *op. cit.*

regard to the "spirit, purport, and object" of Chapter 3. The dissenters in *Du Plessis* advocated direct horizontal effect, arguing that this is the only way to make good the institutional subjugation of apartheid and its common law. In an opinion concurring with the majority, Justice Sachs argued that discrimination in private employment is remedied more effectively through proper human rights legislation. Constitutional litigation is "clumsy." Perhaps as a reflection of these concerns[s] Art. 8(2) of the later-adopted South African Constitution provides: "A provision of the Bill of Rights binds a natural or a juristic person if, and to the extent that, it is applicable, taking into account the nature of the right and the nature of any duty imposed by the rights."

In *Du Plessis* the Court repeated its conclusion that "A comparative examination shows at once that there is no universal answer to [this] problem."

B. LIBEL

B.1. SPEECH INTERESTS AND DIGNITY: PRIMACY AND BALANCING

Expressive activities may hurt an audience and third parties, particularly by damaging reputations. Personal reputation, or honor, has long been the object of legal protection. Traditionally, the reputation interest was a governmental (and, to some extent, class) interest. The sedition acts of many constitutional states, in the nineteenth and twentieth centuries, criminalized speech that brought the government or its officials into contempt or hatred. Even without advocating violence or unlawful action against the government, such criticism was perceived as dangerous to the established authorities, which commanded unquestioned allegiance.[t] Some constitutions expressly recognize the need for the protection of public authority against speech. Article 40.6 of the Constitution of Ireland, for example, states: "The education of public opinion being, however, a matter of such grave import to the common good, the State shall endeavour to ensure that organs of public opinion, such as the radio, the press, the cinema, while preserving their rightful liberty of expression, including criticism of Government policy, shall not be used to undermine public order or morality or the authority of the State."

The French Press Act of 1881 proscribes the defamation of the President and important political functionaries. The provision was still used in the 1960s against disrespectful writers. The French legal atti-

---

s. The wording of the final Constitution was already known at the time *Du Plessis* was decided. The judicial reluctance to adopt an approach closer to the final wording indicates the strong judicial resistance to direct horizontal effect.

t. Authoritarianism may be found behind Lord Cockburn's still-influential nineteenth-century *dictum*: "It is said that it is for the interests of society that the public conduct of men should be criticised without any other limit than that the writer should

have an honest belief that what he writes is true. But it seems to me that the public have an equal interest in the maintenance of the public character of public men; and public affairs could not be conducted by men of honour with a view to the welfare of the country, if we were to sanction attacks upon them, destructive of their honour and character, and made without any foundation." *Campbell v. Spottiswode* (1863) 3 B. & S. 769, 777.

tude, which is expressed in one of the fundamental laws of the republic, is shared, among others, by German and Austrian statutes. For the ambiguous position of emerging democracies and the ECHR, see *Castells* and Decision 36/1994 (VI.24.) AB hat. (Hungarian Constitutional Court) below.

The Anglo–American legal tradition was more tolerant of strong criticism of the government. "For at least the past 200 years both Courts and legislatures in the common law world have recognised that 'the common convenience and welfare of society' may permit a person to make defamatory, untrue statements about another.'" This attitude is related to an increasingly antiauthoritarian understanding of government in democracy. Sir James Fitzjames Stephen, *A History of the Criminal Law of England* vol. II, 299–300 (1883) (on seditious libel, concluding somewhat too optimistically that "in this generation the time for prosecuting political libels has passed, and does not seem likely to return within any definable period"), stated that:

> Two different views may be taken of the relation between rulers and their subjects. If the ruler is regarded as the superior of the subject, as being by the nature of his position presumably wise and good, the rightful ruler and guide of the whole population, it must necessarily follow that it is wrong to censure him openly, that even if he is mistaken his mistakes should be pointed out with the utmost respect, and that whether mistaken or not no censure should be cast upon him likely or designed to diminish his authority.

> If on the other hand the ruler is regarded as the agent and servant, and the subject as the wise and good master who is obliged to delegate his power to the so-called ruler because being a multitude he cannot use it himself, it is obvious that this sentiment must be reversed. Every member of the public who censures the ruler for the time being exercises in his own person the right which belongs to the whole of which he forms a part. He is finding fault with his servant.

The change in elite political sentiment did not directly translate into law, although around the turn of the nineteenth century, the common

---

u. "Some see Lord Mansfield's judgment in 1786 in *Weatherston v. Hawkins* (1786) 1 Term Rep 110, about a servant's character reference as an early instance." *Lange v. Atkinson*, Court of Appeal [1998] 3 NZLR 424, 430. Ironically the "common convenience" was found not in a case regarding the press and public issues but in a case concerning a former master giving false information regarding the character of a discharged servant. The protection of press freedoms was recognized by the nineteenth century in common law without specific constitutional reference, among others, by Sir Alexander Cockburn, CJ (holding that a faithful report in a public newspaper of a parliamentary debate was protected by qualified privilege):

* * * The full liberty of public writers to comment on the conduct and motives of public men has only in very recent times been recognized. Comments on government, on ministers and officers of state, on members of both houses of parliament, on judges and other public functionaries, are now made every day, which half a century ago would have been the subject of actions or ex officio informations, and would have brought down fine and imprisonment on publishers and authors. Yet who can doubt that the public are gainers by the change, and that, though injustice may often be done, and though public men may often have to smart under the keen sense of wrong inflicted by hostile criticism, the nation profits by public opinion being thus freely brought to bear on the discharge of public duties? *Wason v. Walter* (1868) LR 4 QB 73 at pp 93–94.

Quoted in *Lange* at 440.

law of many states in the U.S. recognized qualified privilege to libel regarding government officials. As the Kansas Supreme Court found: " * * * it is of utmost consequence that the people should discuss the character and qualifications of candidates for their suffrages. The importance to the state and to society of such discussions is so vast and the advantage derived are so great that they more than counterbalance the inconvenience of private persons * * * and occasional injury to the reputation of individuals must yield to the public welfare." *Coleman v. MacLennan*, 98 Pac 281, at 286 (1908) (Justice Burch).

At the level of federal constitutional law, the criminalization of defamation (criminal libel) and the torts law protection of reputation were not seen as raising fundamental free speech concerns. In 1952, in a case upholding a conviction under a "group-defamation" law, the USSC held that libelous utterances are not constitutionally protected speech. *Beauharnais v. Illinois*, 343 U.S. 250. However, the tension between the protection of reputation and the protection of free speech persisted. Libel law has the potential, and was often used, to restrict criticism of government and discussion of public matters. The Sedition Act of 1798 (see above) not only prohibited antigovernmental agitation but also a fundamental element of both such agitation and the critical exchange of views on political matters, namely, disrespectful views regarding members of the government.[v]

The attitude of the Sedition Act was gradually disregarded, partly because of constitutional considerations. "[E]rroneous statement is inevitable in free debate, and * * * it must be protected if the freedoms of expression * * * are to have the 'breathing space' that they 'need * * * to survive.'" *N.A.A.C.P. v. Button*, 371 U.S. 415, 433 (1963). In libel law, opinions and, to a lesser extent, false statements were to some degree protected under the tort doctrine of fair comment. Nevertheless, only in 1964 did the USSC constitutionalize the law of defamation.

To understand the political implications of giving primacy to speech interests against political figures one should read the following case in its political context. Without the constitutional protection, defamation law could have been used to stifle the civil rights movement. Protecting the reputation of politicians always runs the risk of silencing political criticism of government.

NEW YORK TIMES CO. v. SULLIVAN

Supreme Court (United States).
376 U.S. 254 (1964).

[In the 1960s, civil rights activists sought the desegregation of public services. Southern politicians used force and intimidation to frustrate

---

v. In the Virginia Resolutions of 1798, the General Assembly of Virginia resolved that

it "doth particularly protest against the palpable and alarming infractions of the Constitution, in the two late cases of the 'Alien and Sedition Acts,' passed at the last session of Congress * * *. [The Sedition Act] exercises * * * a power not delegated by the Constitution, but, on the contrary, expressly and positively forbid-

den by one of the amendments thereto—a power which, more than any other, ought to produce universal alarm, because it is levelled against the right of freely examining public characters and measures, and of free communication among the people thereon, which has ever been justly deemed the only effectual guardian of every other right."

4 Elliot's Debates on the Federal Constitution. (1876), pp. 553–554.

the civil rights of blacks. State officials, among them, Sullivan, in Alabama, used state libel law to restrict criticism of police practices in the national media. Arguing for the defendant, Professor Wechsler emphasized the analogy between civil libel and criminal prosecution for sedition and their equal potential to silence government critics.]

Mr. Justice Brennan delivered the opinion of the Court.

We are required in this case to determine for the first time the extent to which the constitutional protections for speech and press limit a State's power to award damages in a libel action brought by a public official against critics of his official conduct. Respondent L. B. Sullivan is one of the three elected Commissioners of the City of Montgomery, Alabama. He brought this civil libel action against the four individual petitioners, who are Negroes and Alabama clergymen, and against petitioner the New York Times Company. * * * A jury in the Circuit Court of Montgomery County awarded [respondent] damages of $500,000. Respondent's complaint alleged that he had been libeled by statements in a full-page advertisement that was carried in the New York. * * *

[The advertisement described police abuses against black civil rights activists and students.]

* * *

On the premise that the charges * * * could be read as referring to him, respondent was allowed to prove that he had not participated in the events described. * * * And the police were not only not implicated in the bombings, but had made every effort to apprehend those who were. [There were many similar inaccuracies in the advertisement signed by prominent civil rights supporters.]

* * * [We] hold that the rule of law applied by the Alabama courts is constitutionally deficient for failure to provide the safeguards for freedom of speech and of the press.

* * *

I

* * * [The] publication here [communicated] information, expressed opinion, recited grievances, protested claimed abuses, and sought financial support on behalf of a movement whose existence and objectives are matters of the highest public interest and concern. That the Times was paid for publishing the advertisement is as immaterial in this connection as is the fact that newspapers and books are sold. Any other conclusion would discourage newspapers from carrying 'editorial advertisements' of this type, and so might shut off an important outlet for the promulgation of information and ideas by persons who do not themselves have access to publishing facilities.

II

Under Alabama law [once] "libel per se" has been established, the defendant has no defense as to stated facts unless he can persuade the jury that they were true in all their particulars. [His] privilege of "fair comment" for expressions of opinion depends on the truth of the facts upon which the comment is based. [Unless] he can discharge the burden of proving truth, general damages are presumed, and may be awarded without proof of pecuniary injury.

Respondent relies heavily, as did the Alabama courts, on statements of this Court to the effect that the Constitution does not protect libelous publications. Those statements do not foreclose our inquiry here. None of the cases sustained the use of libel laws to impose sanctions upon expression critical of the official conduct of public officials. [Libel] can claim no talismanic immunity from constitutional limitations. It must be measured by standards that satisfy the First Amendment.

* * * [Thus] we consider this case against the background of a profound national commitment to the principle that debate on public issues should be uninhibited, robust, and wide-open, and that it may well include vehement, caustic, and sometimes unpleasantly sharp attacks on government and public officials. The present advertisement, as an expression of grievance and protest on one of the major public issues of our time, would seem clearly to qualify for the constitutional protection. The question is whether it forfeits that protection by the falsity of some of its factual statements and by its alleged defamation of respondent.

* * * [Erroneous] statement is inevitable in free debate, and [it] must be protected if the freedoms of expression are to have the "breathing space" that they "need [to] survive."

* * * [Criticism] of government officials' conduct does not lose its constitutional protection merely because it is effective criticism and hence diminishes their official reputations.

[Brennan argues that the 1798 Sedition Act was unconstitutional[w] and that state criminal statutes criminalizing government criticism are likewise unconstitutional.] What a State may not constitutionally bring about by means of a criminal statute is likewise beyond the reach of its civil law of libel. The fear of damage awards under a rule such as that invoked by the Alabama courts here may be markedly more inhibiting than the fear of prosecution under a criminal statute.

A rule compelling the critic of official conduct to guarantee the truth of all his factual assertions—and to do so on pain of libel judgments virtually unlimited in amount—leads to a comparable "self-censorship." Allowance of the defense of truth, with the burden of proving it on the defendant, does not mean that only false speech will be deterred. * * * [Under] such a rule, would-be critics of official conduct may be deterred from voicing their criticism, even though it is believed to be true and

---

w. The position was advocated by Holmes, too: "I wholly disagree with the argument of the Government that the First Amendment left the common law as to seditious libel in force. History seems to me against the notion. I had conceived that the United States through many years had shown its repentance for the Sedition Act of 1798 (Act July 14, 1798, c.73, 1 Stat. 596), by repaying fines that it imposed. Only the emergency that makes it immediately dangerous to leave the correction of evil counsels to time warrants making any exception to the sweeping command, 'Congress shall make no law abridging the freedom of speech.'" *Abrams v. United States*, 250 U.S. 616, 630 (1919), Justice Holmes, dissenting.

even though it is in fact true, because of doubt whether it can be proved in court or fear of the expense of having to do so. They tend to make only statements which "steer far wider of the unlawful zone." The rule thus dampens the vigor and limits the variety of public [debate].

The constitutional guarantees require, we think, a federal rule that prohibits a public official from recovering damages for a defamatory falsehood relating to his official conduct unless he proves that the statement was made with "actual malice"—that is, with knowledge that it was false or with reckless disregard of whether it was false or [not].

Such a privilege for criticism of official conduct is appropriately analogous to the protection accorded a public official when he is sued for libel by a private citizen. In *Barr v. Matteo*, 360 U.S. 564, 575 (1959), this Court held the utterance of a federal official to be absolutely privileged if made 'within the outer perimeter' of his duties. * * * The reason for the official privilege is said to be that the threat of damage suits would otherwise "inhibit the fearless, vigorous, and effective administration of policies of government" and "dampen the ardor of all but the most resolute, or the most irresponsible, in the unflinching discharge of their duties." *Barr v. Matteo, supra*, at 571. Analogous considerations support the privilege for the citizen-critic of government. It is as much his duty to criticize as it is the official's duty to administer. As Madison said "the censorial power is in the people over the Government, and not in the Government over the people." It would give public servants an unjustified preference over the public they serve, if critics of official did not have a fair equivalent of the immunity granted to the officials themselves.

We conclude that such a privilege is required by the First and Fourteenth Amendments. * * *

III

* * * We also think the evidence was constitutionally defective in another respect: it was incapable of supporting the jury's finding that the allegedly libelous statements were made 'of and concerning' respondent. Respondent relies on the words of the advertisement and the testimony of six witnesses to establish a connection between it and himself.

* * *

This proposition[x] has disquieting implications for criticism of governmental conduct. For good reason, 'no court of last resort in this country has ever held, or even suggested, that prosecutions for libel on government have any place in the American system of jurisprudence.' *City of Chicago*. The present proposition would sidestep this obstacle by transmuting criticism of government, however impersonal it may seem

---

x. The Alabama Court position was this: "We think it common knowledge that the average person knows that municipal agents, such as police and firemen, and others, are under the control and direction of the city governing body, and more particularly under the direction and control of a single commissioner. In measuring the performance or deficiencies of such groups, praise or criticism is usually attached to the official in complete control of the body." *New York Times v. Sullivan*, 273 Ala. 656, at 674–675, 144 So.2d 25, at 39.

on its face, into personal criticism, and hence potential libel, of the officials of whom the government is composed. There is no legal alchemy by which a State may thus create the cause of action that would otherwise be denied for a publication which, as respondent himself said of the advertisement, 'reflects not only on me but on the other Commissioners and the community.' Raising as it does the possibility that a good-faith critic of government will be penalized for his criticism, the proposition relied on by the Alabama courts strikes at the very center of the constitutionally protected area of free expression.

Reversed and remanded.

Mr. Justice Black, with whom Mr. Justice Douglas joins (concurring).

* * * "Malice,"[y] even as defined by the Court, is an elusive, abstract concept, hard to prove and hard to disprove. The requirement that malice be proved provides at best an evanescent protection for the right critically to discuss public affairs and certainly does not measure up to the sturdy safeguard embodied in the First Amendment. Unlike the Court, therefore, I vote to reverse exclusively on the ground that the Times and the individual defendants had an absolute, unconditional constitutional right to publish in the Times advertisement their criticisms of the Montgomery agencies and [officials].

The half-million-dollar verdict [gives] dramatic proof [that] state libel laws threaten the very existence of an American press virile enough to publish unpopular views on public affairs. * * *

We would, I think, more faithfully interpret the First Amendment by holding that at the very least it leaves the people and the press free to criticize officials and discuss public affairs with impunity. * * * I doubt that a country can live in freedom where its people can be made to suffer physically or financially for criticizing their government, its actions, or its officials. * * * An unconditional right to say what one pleases about public affairs is what I consider to be the minimum guarantee of the First Amendment.[6]

Notes and Questions

1. What amounts to actual malice or recklessness? In the *New York Times* case, the USSC found that the failure of the editors of the *New York Times* to perform an accuracy check is sufficient for a finding of negligence. It was a sufficient defense that the editors relied on the reputation of those who made the claims regarding the Alabama police. A mere failure to investigate and even serious doubts regarding the truth of the communication are not enough for recklessness. *St. Amant v. Thompson* 390 U.S. 727 (1968).

y. Alabama law required that for recovering punitive damages, plaintiff should show "actual malice." This was satisfied in Alabama by showing that defendant was *negligent* in failing to ascertain the truth of factual allegations. Justice Brennan replaced the requirement with the showing intentional deceit or recklessness as to the truth. Justice Black believed that even that possibility would allow for abuse. Note the attitude of the all-white juries in the South in the libel cases.

6. Cf. Meiklejohn, Free Speech and Its Relation to Self–Government (1948).

2. The *New York Times* decision left open (in fn. 23) "how far down into the lower ranks of government employees" the rule would be applicable. In *Rosenblatt v. Baer*, 383 U.S. 75, 86 (1966), it was said that the rule applies to those who "appear to the public to [have] substantial responsibility for or control over the conduct of government affairs." Further, in *Garrison v. Louisiana*, 379 U.S. 64 (1964), anything that might touch on an official's "fitness for office" was held as a matter outside the traditional libel rules. The *New York Times* rule was further extended to public figures in *Curtis Publishing Co. v. Butts*, 388 U.S. 130 (1967). Chief Justice Warren based the extension, in part, on the increasing blurring of the "distinctions between governmental and private sectors." Many individuals "who do not hold public office at the moment are nevertheless intimately involved in the resolution of important public questions." He added that "as a class these 'public figures' have as ready access as 'public officials' to mass media of communication * * * to counter criticism."

3. For some time, the *New York Times* rule was applicable to defamatory statements involving matters of public or general interest, "without regard to whether the persons are famous or anonymous." *Rosenbloom v. Metromedia, Inc.*, 403 U.S. 29 (1971), (Justice Brennan). The trend came to an end in *Gertz v. Robert Welch, Inc.*, 418 U.S. 323 (1974).[z] In that decision, the Court found that the "extension of the *New York Times* test proposed by the *Rosenbloom* plurality [matters of public interest extend the test to anonymous persons] would abridge [the legitimate state interest to provide remedy against injurious defamation]. And it would occasion the additional difficulty of forcing state and federal judges to decide on an *ad hoc* basis which publications address issues of 'general or public interest' and which do not * * *." The Court left it to the states to define the appropriate standard of liability for a publisher of defamatory falsehood, so long as they do not impose liability without fault. In an effort to protect free speech, the Court, however, prohibited the use of punitive damages against the press with rare exceptions, which were subsequently developed, if the state law required a less demanding standard of liability than actual malice.

Ten years after *New York Times v. Sullivan*, in *Gertz v. Robert Welch, Inc.*, 418 U.S. 323 (1974), a new Supreme Court majority seemed uncomfortable determining what is a matter of public interest. In Germany, the characterization of speech being in the public interest (see *Lüth* above) is admittedly crucial. Is the Supreme Court's reluctance consistent with its readiness to determine who is a public figure? Before prematurely concluding that there is a difference, consider Justice Powell's plurality opinion in *Dun & Bradstreet v. Greenmoss Builders*, 472 U.S. 749, 757 (1985)[aa]:

> [We] have never considered whether the *Gertz* balance obtains when the defamatory statements involve no issues of public concern. To make this

z. Gertz served in a civil litigation as the attorney for the family of a man killed by a policeman. He was described in a right-wing monthly as a man of criminal record and long-time affiliate of the Communist party. These statements contained substantial inaccuracies. Respondent publisher asserted that the lawyer was a public figure, which might have entitled him to the reck-lessness privilege. Gertz was held to be a private individual.

aa. The petitioner, a private credit-reporting agency, provided a false report regarding the respondent. The respondent was awarded punitive damages without showing of actual malice. The Supreme Court upheld the decision.

determination, we must employ the approach approved in *Gertz* and balance the State's interest in compensating private individuals for injury to their reputation against the First Amendment interest in protecting this type of expression. [The] state interest [here] is identical to the one weighed in *Gertz*. We have long recognized that not all speech is of equal First Amendment importance. It is speech on 'matters of public concern' that is 'at the heart of the First Amendment's protection.' In contrast speech on matters of purely private concern is of less First Amendment concern.

Is there no public issue or public interest in protecting private credit-rating information? Is the threat to the robust debate of public issues less significant in the case of private communication than in the press cases? Why would there be a greater public issue at stake if the same credit information were published in a newspaper?

4. *Public Figures.* Individuals who have not assumed a role of special prominence in the affairs of society are not public figures, unless they have "thrust themselves to the forefront of particular controversies in order to influence the resolution of the issues involved." *Time, Inc. v. Firestone*, 424 U.S. 448 (1976). The Supreme Court found that a press conference regarding the divorce of an American magnate did not satisfy the test as it was not intended to influence the resolution of a public issue: it did not involve a "public controversy." Compare this with the way the Court has resolved questions about public issues and political issues. Which better promotes robust discussion and critical attitudes toward government? Which better protects private reputations? Consider the impact of the various approaches on the role of the judiciary. How much ad hockery is involved in the various approaches? The public-figure approach tends to extend some constitutional protection to all media's defamatory speech. Is this to say that the Court moved away from Meiklejohn's theory (quoted in *New York Times v. Sullivan*, Justice Black's concurring opinion), which was based on the need to protect speech regarding public issues? "It may be that the Court has refused to adopt the Meiklejohn 'public issues' test not because it believes that private speech (i.e., speech unrelated to public issues) is as important as public speech but rather because it doubts its ability to distinguish satisfactorily between the two. [B]y placing all defamatory media speech the Court may believe it has protected relatively little non-public speech." Steven H. Shiffrin, *Defamatory Non–Media Speech and First Amendment Methodology*, 25 U.C.L.A. L. Rev. 915, 929 (1978).

5. *Privacy concerns and free speech.* Free speech considerations might conflict with those of privacy. The USSC extended protection granted to speech in matters of public interest outside defamation to the tort of false light privacy when it found in *Time v. Hill*, 385 U.S. 374 (1967), that false publications which violate privacy are subject to the *New York Times* rule.[b]

b. Hill and his family involuntarily became the subjects of a front page news story, after being held hostage by three escaped convicts. The family was released unharmed. A play presented Hill as a heroic but suffering man, which was not the case. *Life Magazine* published an article describing the heroism of the family. Hill, who avoided the public spotlight, sued for damages on the basis of a New York privacy-protection statute.

[T]he constitutional protections for speech and press preclude the application of the New York statute to redress false reports of matters of public interest in the absence of proof that the defendant published the report with knowledge of its falsity or in reckless disregard of the truth [and that the instructions did not adequately advise the jury that a verdict for Hill required a finding of knowing or reckless falsity]. The guarantees for speech and press are not the preserve of political expression or comment upon public affairs, essential as those are to healthy government. One need only pick up any newspaper or magazine to comprehend the vast range of published matter which exposes persons to public view, both private citizens and public officials. Exposure of the self to others in varying degrees is a concomitant of life in a civilized community. The risk of this exposure is an essential incident of life in a society which places a primary value on freedom of speech and of press. [We] have no doubt that the subject of the *Life* article, the opening of a new play linked to an actual incident, is a matter of public interest. "The line between the informing and the entertaining is too elusive for the protection of [freedom of the press]." Erroneous statement is no less inevitable in such a case than in the case of comment upon public affairs.

The *New York Times* standard was held applicable to those who involuntarily became subjects of the public spotlight simply because of their newsworthiness. Note that in *Firestone* the privilege is extended to entertainment. The Court's broad vision of public exposure is justified on the ground that the line is elusive and judicial error would be detrimental to free speech.

6. *Worldwide reactions to* New York Times. *New York Times v. Sullivan* was enthusiastically received in the U.S.; Professor Harry Kalven called it a reason to dance in the streets. It is quoted in numerous jurisdictions worldwide, and since the 1960s, the defamatory criticism of politicians and governments is increasingly constitutionally protected. Nevertheless, its impact on press freedoms is mixed. Consider *Hill v. Church of Scientology of Toronto*, [1995] 2 S.C.R. 1130, in which the Supreme Court of Canada mentions, among others, the following shortcomings of the *New York Times* rule:

—It necessitates a detailed inquiry into matters of media procedure. This, in turn, increases the length of discoveries and of the trial which may actually increase, rather than decrease, the threat to speech interests. See D. A. Barrett, "Declaratory Judgments for Libel: A Better Alternative" (1986), 74 Cal. L. Rev. 847, at p. 855;

—It dramatically increases the cost of litigation;

—The fact that the dissemination of falsehoods is protected is said to exact a major social cost by deprecating truth in public discourse. See L. C. Bollinger, "The End of *New York Times v. Sullivan*: Reflections on *Masson v. New Yorker Magazine*," [1991] Sup. Ct. Rev. 1, at p. 6; J. A. Barron, "Access to the Press—A New First Amendment Right" (1966–67), 80 Harv. L. Rev. 1641, at pp. 1657–58.

The Supreme Court of Canada found *New York Times* inapplicable not only for policy reasons: "subjecting all private and public action to constitutional review would mean reopening whole areas of settled law and would be 'tantamount to setting up an alternative tort system'."

The New Zealand Court of Appeal (Wellington) remarked:

[T]he Canadian Court said at the end of its judgment [*Hill*], none of the factors prompting the United States Supreme Court were present. The appeal did not involve the media or political commentary about government policies, nor were the issues in *Theophanous v. Herald & Weekly Times Ltd.*, involving newspaper criticism of an Australian Federal Member of Parliament, raised. We have already seen that the more relevant Canadian cases present a divided picture. In the 1950s and 1960s, the Supreme Court of Canada gave qualified privilege a narrow role in cases involving political leaders while more recently provincial Courts of Appeal have given it a wider role in respect of actions brought by officials against Ministers.

Lange v. Atkinson, [1998] 3 NZLR 424, 450 (see below).

In *Reynolds*, below, Lord Cooke of Thorndon rejected the *New York Times* approach:

As to defamatory allegations of fact, even in the United States the opinions of jurists differ on the extent to which the collectively cherished right of free speech is to be preferred to the individually cherished right to personal reputation; and it is certain that neither in the United Kingdom nor anywhere else in the Commonwealth could it be maintained that the people have knowingly staked their all on unfettered freedom to publish falsehoods of fact about political matters, provided only that the writer or speaker is not actuated by malice. It would be a mistake to assume that commitment to the cause of human rights must lead to a major abandonment of established common law limitations on political allegations of fact. Sir Sydney Kentridge Q.C. argues against introducing a *New York Times Co. v. Sullivan* type defense for political discussion. 'It should not be beyond a court's ability * * * to distinguish in any particular case between hard-hitting political criticism and truly libellous allegations of fact.' I would follow that approach.

Reynolds at para. 115.

Lord Cooke had an additional concern: the peculiarity of the libel law in Alabama was that very high punitive damages could be awarded without proof of actual pecuniary loss. There is no comparable level of damages in Europe; hence the censorial effect of civil remedies that protect reputation is less severe (except for the right to reply).

MEPHISTO CASE

Constitutional Court (Germany).
30 BVerfGE 173 (1971).

[In the 1930s, while in exile from Nazi Germany, Klaus Mann published *Mephisto*, a satirical novel based on the career of his brother-in-law, Gustaf Gründgens, a successful and opportunistic actor of the Third Reich. Mann later admitted that, for him, Gründgens personified "the traitor par excellence, the macabre embodiment of corruption and cynicism * * * who prostitutes his talent for the sake of some tawdry fame and transitory wealth." Hendrik Höfgen was a caricature of the model on which Gründgens was based. When *Mephisto* was about to be reissued by a West German publisher, in 1964, the actor's adopted son secured an order from the Hamburg Court of Appeals, banning its distribution, a judgment affirmed by the High Court of Justice on the ground that the novel dishonored the good name and memory of the then-deceased actor. The publisher filed a constitutional complaint.]

Judgment of the First Senate:

The constitutional complaint is rejected.

* * *

C. III. First, Article 5 (3) [1] contains an objective norm that determines values and regulates the relationship between the realm of art and the state. At the same time this provision guarantees every person active in this sphere an individual right to freedom.

1. * * * The essential characteristic of artistic activity is the artist's free and creative shaping of impression, experiences, and events for direct display through a specific language of shapes. * * *

2. * * * Even if the artist describes actual occurrences, this reality is "poeticized" in a work of art. * * * The essence and purpose of the basic right contained in Article 5 (3) [1] are to keep free from state interference those processes, modes of behavior, and decisions based on the inherent laws of art and determined by aesthetic considerations. * * * For the narrative work of art, the constitutional guarantee includes free choice of subject and free presentation of that subject.

* * *

4. Article 5 guarantees autonomy of the arts without reservation. In view of the unambiguous text of Article 5 (3) [1], [one] may not restrict this guarantee by narrowing the concept of art on evaluative grounds, broadly interpreting other restrictive clauses in constitutional provisions, or analogizing restrictive clauses to the case of [artistic freedom]. * * *

* * * [We] must also reject the opinion that the constitutional order, the rights of others, and the moral code may restrict the freedom of the arts pursuant to Article 2 (1), second half of the sentence. This view is inconsistent with the subsidiary relationship of Article 2 (1) to the individual liberty rights specifically mentioned [in the Basic Law].

5. On the other hand, the right of artistic liberty is not unlimited. Like all basic rights, the guarantee of liberty in Article 5(3)[l] is based on the Basic Law's image of man as an autonomous person who develops freely within the social community. But the [fact that] this basic right contains no limiting proviso means that only the Constitution itself can determine limits on artistic freedom. Since freedom of the arts does not contain a provision entitling the legislature to limit [this basic right], it cannot be curtailed by [provisions of] the general legal system. [If] an indefinite clause, which applies when goods necessary for the continued

existence of the national community are endangered, has no anchor in the Constitution and does not sufficiently [conform] to the principle of the rule of law, it may not limit this right. Rather, [we] must resolve conflicts relating to the guarantee of artistic freedom by interpreting the Constitution according to the value order established in the Basic Law and the unity of its fundamental system of values. As a part of the Basic Law's value system, freedom of the arts is closely related to the dignity of man guaranteed in Article 1, which, as the supreme value, governs the entire value system of the Basic Law. But the guarantee of freedom of the arts can conflict with the constitutionally protected sphere of personality because a work of art can also produce social effects.

Because a work of art acts not only as an aesthetic reality but also exists in the social world, an artist's use of personal data about people in his environment can affect their rights to societal respect and esteem. * * *

6. * * * The obligation which Article 1 (1) imposes on all state authority to protect the individual against attacks on his dignity does not end with death. * * *

7. * * * The individual's right to societal respect and esteem does not have precedence over artistic freedom any more than the arts may disregard a person's general right to respect. * * *

[One] can only decide whether an artistic presentation's use of personal data threatens such a grave encroachment upon the protected private sphere of the person it describes that it could preclude publication of the work of art after carefully weighing all the facts of individual cases. * * * [One] must take into account whether and to what extent the "image" [of a particular person] appears so independent from the "original" because of the artistic shaping of the material and its incorporation into and subordination to the overall organism of the work of art that the individual, intimate aspects have become objective in the sense of a general, symbolic character of the "figure." If such a study * * * reveals that the artist has given or even wanted to give a "portrait" of the "original," then the [the resolution of this conflict] depends on the extent of artistic abstraction or the extent and importance of the "falsification" of the reputation or memory of the person concerned.

IV. 2. * * * [T]he last trial court has found that the case of Gründgens concerned a person of contemporary history and that his public memory is still alive. * * * The courts tried to solve [the] conflict [between reputation and art] by weighing the conflicting interests against each other.

* * *

3. * * * The Federal Constitutional Court is not empowered to set its own assessment of the individual case in the place of that of the competent judge. * * * Finally, [complainant] cannot challenge the conclusion of the courts * * * by arguing that the ban on publication is disproportional to the encroachment on the late Gustaf Gründgens's right to respect. It is true that the Federal Constitutional Court has repeatedly emphasized that the principle of proportionality has constitu-

tional rank and must therefore be considered whenever state authority encroaches on the citizen's sphere of liberty. But the instant case does not involve such an encroachment. The courts simply had to decide a claim based on private law made by one citizen against another; that is, to give concrete-definition to a relationship of private law in an individual case. * * * The primary function of private law is to settle conflicts of interests between persons of equal legal status in as appropriate a manner as possible.

* * *

Justice Stein, dissenting:

II. * * * The courts one-sidedly considered only tensions in the social sphere and, in so doing, ignored the novel's aesthetic aspect. This one-sided consideration affected the weighing of interests: * * * [T]hey compared the appearance and behavior of the fictitious Hendrik Höfgen with the personality of Gustaf Gründgens solely from the viewpoint of readers who see the novel as reality. * * *

This approach may be appropriate for a documentary or biography. * * * But a novel's artistic intent is not a realistic, truth-oriented description of historical events but rather a substantial, descriptive presentation of material based on the writer's imagination. An evaluation of a novel base solely on the effects that it produces outside its aesthetic existence neglects the specific relationship of art with reality and thus unlawfully restricts the right guaranteed by Article 5. * * *

Furthermore, the Federal High Court and the Appeals Court of Hamburg overemphasized the detrimental effects of the novel on the protected sphere of Gustaf Gründgens's personality when they undertook the required balancing of interests. * * *

Notes and Questions

1. *Dignity.* One way to explain the differences in the constitutional protection of reputation is to consider the role dignity plays in the constitutional systems of different countries. (See further, Chapter 5.) In *Lüth* the GFCC recognized the existence of an objective hierarchy of values. The hierarchy is structured around dignity. Strong criticism of the idea of a "closed" value system led the Court to abandon the concept in its more recent jurisprudence. However, dignity implies protection against state action that would violate human dignity (an individual right to "nonaction" or "noninterference") and, on the other hand, a right to state action to prevent violations of human dignity—in other words, a governmental duty of positive action. In German constitutional law every fundamental right has an objective component, which may lead to the state's duty to protect it. (See Professor Schlink's article in Chapter 2.) Generally, German and other European courts are much more concerned with human dignity in the speech context than U.S. courts.

Many post–1945 constitutions included provisions guaranteeing 'social dignity' or 'human dignity' that were clearly intended to mark the end of the Fascist era. * * * Human rights lawyers similarly explain and justify the campaign for human rights that is so vigorously prosecuted in the European Court of Human Rights in Strasbourg as the product of the horrific experience of Fascism. Even the new French law on bioethics has been presented to the world as a safeguard against Fascism. * * * Justice Lenoir, a top French jurist, ascribes the restrictiveness of French bioethics law to 'memories of Nazi racial and genetic practices.' FN 17, p. 1283 * * * [N]o such account of the rise of European dignitary law can be more than partially correct. First of all, the European law of honor is by no means exclusively about great issues of human rights. To the contrary, the European culture of honor and dignity reaches very deep into everyday social life, covering what to us seem astoundingly trivial matters of civility.

James Q. Whitman, *Enforcing Civility and Respect: Three Societies*, 109 Yale L. J. 1279, 1284 (2000).

According to a prevailing tenet in Germany, the founders of the Basic Law deliberately gave preference to dignity and personality rights, to the detriment of free speech.

In the Federal Republic of Germany * * * the Basic Law (Grundgesetz) guarantees freedom of opinion and speech but makes it expressly subject to limitations defined in "the general laws, the provision of law for the protection of youth, and by the right to inviolability of personal honour." The experience with the abuse of freedoms that contributed to the demise of the Weimar Republic and the suppression of these freedoms by the National Socialist regime left a deep imprint upon the Basic Law and subsequent legislation * * * [As a consequence of that experience,] free speech claims must be weighed against the values of human dignity and personal honor that are grounded in the Basic Law itself.

Eric Stein, *History Against Free Speech: German Law in European and American Perspective*, in *Verfassungsrecht und Völkerrecht: Gedächtnisschrift für Wilhelm Karl Geck* 831–32 (Wilfried Fiedler and Georg Ress eds., 1989).

Compare the similar position of the traditional common law in William Blackstone, *Commentaries on the laws of England*, vol. I, 129 (reprint, 1979), which treats reputation among security rights together with life.

The Basic Law did not randomly name explicitly the right to personal honour as the bound on freedom of opinion. Even without this special emphasis, the right to personal honour would, as an expression of the personality and a consequence of human dignity, protection and respect for which is an obligation on all State power (art. 1 (1) Basic Law), have importance in setting a limit, and especially so in the case of statements made in public. That was not sufficient for the constitutional legislature, whose concern was, through the limitation of the freedom of opinion embodied in the Basic Law, to act emphatically against the overflowing of the political clash of opinion into the personal sphere. Since protection of honour to date was, against the background particularly of experience in the time of the Weimar Republic on all sides seen as unsatisfactory, in 1949 the right to personal honour was taken into the Basic Law as an explicit limit on freedom of opinion, thereby creating a basis for protection of honour worthy of the name. This "protection of honour" remained undisputed from beginning to end in the debates in the Parliamentary Council. What was then a matter of course deserves respect today too. Refraining from personal defamation in the political opinion-forming process can only promote that process, by raising the culture of political conflict.

Justice Haas's dissent in the Tucholsky II Case. (For the dignity aspects of honor, see the *Life Imprisonment Case* in Chapter 5.)

The USSC has also recognized that "the constitutional right of free expression is * * * intended to remove governmental restraints from the arena of public discussion, putting the decision as to what views shall be voiced largely into the hands of each of us * * * in the belief that no other approach would comport with the premise of individual dignity upon which our political system rests." *Cohen v. California*, 403 U.S. 15, 24 (1971). This was not held to be decisive in speech matters:

> The Court has emphasized that the central meaning of the free expression guarantee is that the body politic of this Nation shall be entitled to the communications necessary for self-governance, and that to place restraints on the exercise of expression is to deny the instrumental means required in order that the citizenry exercise that ultimate sovereignty reposed in its collective judgment by the Constitution. Accordingly, we have held that laws governing harm incurred by individuals through defamation or invasion of privacy, although directed to the worthy objective of ensuring the 'essential dignity and worth of every human being'; necessary to a civilized society, *Rosenblatt v. Baer*, 383 U.S. 75, 92 (1966) (Stewart, J., concurring), must be measured and limited by constitutional constraints assuring the maintenance and well-being of the system of free expression.

Time Inc., v. Firestone, 424 U.S. 448, 471 (1976).

The supremacy of dignity stands in clear opposition to the USSC position in *Paul v. Davis*,[c] 424 U.S. 693 (1976), in which the Court refused to raise reputation alone to a protected liberty under the Fourteenth Amendment.

2. In *Mephisto* Justice Rupp-von Brünneck joined Justice Stein's dissent. She found the majority view a departure from previously established rules of balancing. Further, the lower courts failed to consider Klaus Mann's position as a member of the resistance to the Nazi regime.

c. Davis was charged with shoplifting, and his name was placed on a flyer distributed among local merchants describing him as an active shoplifter. The charge was dismissed, and he brought suit, claiming a deprivation of his constitutional right to reputation. He lost the case because he sought to recover for violation of his Fourteenth Amendment interest. (This is not to say that he might not have received damages under state privacy laws or under common law). In contrast, in *Lebach*, 35 BVerfGE 202 (1973), a convicted armed robber's story was presented on television before his release from prison. His name was released, and reference was made to his homosexual tendencies. The German Court found that the nondefamatory, or at least accurate, statements were an encroachment into the right to personality as these infringe the personal sphere. The Court, in the balancing process, recognized that.

weighty considerations suggest that the public should be fully informed of the commission of crimes, including the identity of the accused * * * In balancing these interests, * * * the public interest in receiving information must generally prevail when current crimes are being reported. * * * The right of personality does not, however, permit the media * * * to intrude indefinitely upon the * * * private sphere of the criminal. * * * Once [the defendant was convicted] and he has experienced the just reaction of the community, any further or repeated invasion of the criminal's personal sphere cannot normally be justified.

The Court found that the criminal's interest in rehabilitation might be decisive in determining limits on broadcasting.

According to Rupp-von Brünneck, the unlimited protection of GG art. 5, § 3, rests on the 'maturity of the citizen'—the citizen's ability to understand that a novel is something other than an expression of opinion and that it is, instead, a creation of the imagination. In this light, even if the countervailing rights of GG art. 1, § 1 should create a very narrow exception to the rights of artistic freedom, that exception should exist only when the novel is used solely as a pretext for personal attack without another motive.

Quint, *op. cit.* at 349.

"One of the most striking aspects of the *Mephisto* opinion is its apparent assumption, in sharp contrast with *Lüth*, that the interest in free expression is not significantly weightier than any other constitutional interest." Quint, *op. cit.* at 307. Do the dissenters propose departure from the role the Court envisioned in *Lüth*? Compare the Court's approach with that in *Tucholsky I*, 1 BvR 1423/92 (1994), below. Professor Quint discusses the pro-dignity position of the majority as deference dictated by considerations of efficient judicial administration:

The Federal Constitutional Court is the only federal court whose specific mission is to decide constitutional questions. Although the state courts and the Federal Supreme Court (BGH) also must pass on constitutional questions, the constitutional decisions of those courts are not nearly as authoritative as decisions handed down by the Constitutional Court. Moreover, the Constitutional Court is obliged to decide all constitutional issues appropriately presented to it—unless a committee of three justices decides that the result in the case is so clear that the complaint can be summarily rejected or sustained. In this light a deferential or adjustable scope of review might be seen as an acceptable method of controlling the Court's caseload. * * * Yet the use of an adjustable standard of review of this nature also raises its own problems. The use of an adjustable standard of review—in which the factors triggering a greater or lesser degree of scrutiny are themselves vague in nature—adds another layer of uncertainty to an already complex doctrine.

Quint, *op. cit.* at 326–329.

3. *Balancing.* Justice Black claimed that the protection of speech is absolute, but the majority of the USSC recognized that other values might deserve protection against speech interests. The choice requires some kind of balancing, as discussed in Melville B. Nimmer, *The Right to Speak from Times to Time: First Amendment Theory Applied to Libel and Misapplied to Privacy*, 56 Calif. L. Rev. 935, 941–47 (1968).

If such selection is to turn on rational rather than arbitrary considerations, it is obvious that the selection process requires a balancing of competing interests, and this returns us to the equally unacceptable alternative of ad hoc balancing.

Or does it? In *New York Times Company v. Sullivan* (376 U.S. 254 [1964]), the Supreme Court decision indicates a third approach which avoids the all or nothing implications of absolutism versus ad hoc balancing. *Times* points the way to the employment of the balancing process on the definitional rather than the litigation or ad hoc level. That is, the Court employs balancing not for the purpose of determining which litigant deserves to prevail in a particular case, but only define which forms of speech are to be regarded as "speech" within the meaning of the first amendment. This at first blush may appear to be only a verbal distinction, but a good deal more is involved.

There was balancing in the sense that not all defamatory speech was held to be protected by the first amendment. The Court could not determine which segment of defamatory speech lies outside the umbrella of the first amendment purely on logical grounds, and no pretense of logical inexorability was made. By in effect holding that knowingly and recklessly false speech was not speech within the meaning of the first amendment, the Court must have implicitly (since no explicit explanation was offered) referred to certain competing policy considerations. This is surely a kind of balancing, but it is just as surely not ad hoc balancing.

If the Court had followed the ad hoc approach, it would have inquired whether "under the particular circumstances presented," the interest of the defendants in publishing their particular advertisement outweighed the interest of the plaintiff in the protection of his reputation. This in turn would have led to such imponderable issues as: How important was it to the defendants (or possibly to the public at large) that this particular advertisement be published? How "serious" was the injury to the plaintiff's reputation caused by the advertisement?

The absence of a clear rule can also result in decisions unduly influenced by prevailing public emotions. Suppose in the next case, defamatory statements are made about a public official by reason of his conduct in connection with the Vietnam War. If the only reference available to the judges is the weight of the competing interests in speech and reputation, can anyone doubt that the speech is likely to have rough sledding, or at the very least, that a decision finding that speech outweighs reputation will require unusual judicial courage?

It is not necessarily true that the same considerations are weighed in both definitional and ad hoc balancing. In the latter, it is the interests presented in the particular circumstances of the case before the court which are weighed. For example, in a defamation case, the court would weigh not the interest in speech generally but rather the interest (and hence the importance) of the particular speech which is the subject of the litigation. On the other side, it would weigh not the interest in reputation generally, but the extent of the particular injury to reputation in the case before it. * * *

A more profound difference between the ad hoc and definitional lies in the fact that a rule emerges from definitional balancing which can be employed in future cases without the occasion for further weighing of interests.

I would make the concession that, *in vacuo*, ad hoc balancing is more likely to consider fine nuances and therefore produce a more just result. * * * But this likelihood may be offset by the fact that in ad hoc balancing weight is likely to be given only to the particular speech involved and not to 'speech' generally, so that the speech side of the balance may be underweighed when compared with the immediate impact of a particular injury to a particular reputation.

Is Nimmer's critique of balancing applicable to German balancing? Compare Quint's analysis with Nimmer's.

The Canadian Charter expressly recognizes that free speech can be restricted; restrictions are found acceptable if they satisfy a proportionality test. In *Hill v. Church of Scientology of Toronto*, [1995] 2 S.C.R. 1130,[d] the Canadian Supreme Court relies heavily on balancing, arguing the opposite of what the USSC claims. It recognizes the speech interest, but it finds little value for speech in false, defamatory statements and has no difficulty in finding that reputation and dignity will prevail. Is this the same kind of balancing that occurred in *Mephisto*?

In Germany, free speech is restricted when two fundamental rights clash. The conflict of fundamental rights, resulting in rights restrictions, is common in many jurisdictions. See proportionality in Chapter 2. In the U.S., however, the concern is about the impact of government regulation on speech. In a way, in Germany (or in countries following the German doctrine, see, for example, the Hungarian *Government Defamation Case* below), the courts are adjudicating conflicts among "subjective rights," while at the same time emphasizing, especially in broadcasting-regulation review, that fundamental rights have a certain institutional guarantee that the state should promote.

> Generally, in German legal theory, an 'objective' value is a value that is applicable in general and in the abstract, independently of any specified relationship—in contrast with a 'subjective' right, which is the right of a specified individual to some legal result against a specific party. In effect, by stating that the basic rights establish an 'objective' ordering of values, the Court was stating that those values are so important that they must exist apart from any specified legal relationship—that is, in this context, apart from any specific relationship between the individual and the state. These values are not only specified rights of individuals but are also part of the general legal order, benefiting not only individuals who may be in a certain relationship with the state but possessing relevance for all legal relationships.

> The Court's view that the basic rights form an 'objective' order appears to bear some relationship to the view that the Basic Law itself establishes certain fundamental principles that are permanent ends of the state and cannot be changed, even by constitutional amendment.

> Quint, *op. cit.* at 261.

4. Does the institutional protection of speech threaten First Amendment values? See Professor Schlink's views in Chapter 2. Professor Ingber states:

> [C]ourts that invoke the marketplace model of the first amendment justify free expression because of the aggregate benefits to society and not because an individual speaker receives a particular benefit. Courts

---

d. Hill, a Crown attorney, was publicly accused of misconduct. The statements were found to be untrue. Hill sued for damages and won. The major issues in this appeal were whether the common law of defamation is consistent with the Canadian Charter of Rights and Freedoms. The Canadian Supreme Court avoids the *New York Times* problem, among others, by demarcating the reputation of Hill, a prosecutor, into the public and the private. The defamatory criticism is classified as directed against his "private ego." Consequently, the Court balanced private honor against false statements.

that focus their concern on the audience rather than the speaker relegate free expression to an instrumental value, a means toward some other goal, rather than a value unto itself. Once free expression is viewed solely as an instrumental value, however, it is easier to allow government regulation of speech if society as a whole 'benefits' from a regulated system of expression.

Stanley Ingber, *The Marketplace of Ideas: A Legitimizing Myth*, 33 Duke L.J. 1, 4–5 (1984).

Protection of free speech, even to the detriment of personal reputation, as cultivated in the U.S., might be a function of the specific constitutional role of the state. In the U.S., government is not expected to provide specific positive protection to individual reputation.

B.2.   PUBLIC ISSUES, PUBLIC FIGURES

LEE KUAN YEW v. VINOCUR & ORS

High Court (Singapore).
1996–2 SLR 542 (1996).

JUDGMENT:

S. Rajendran

On 8 December 1994, the plaintiff, who is currently the Senior Minister in the Prime Minister's Office, commenced proceedings against the four defendants claiming damages for alleged libel contained in an article entitled "The Smoke Over Parts of Asia Obscures Some Profound Concerns" published in the *International Herald Tribune* (*IHT*) on 7 October 1994. * * * The second defendant was the author of the article containing the alleged defamation. * * *

The relevant part in the article published in the *IHT* that caused offence was as follows: "Intolerant regimes in the region reveal considerable ingenuity in their methods of suppressing dissent. * * * Others are more subtle: relying upon a compliant judiciary to bankrupt opposition politicians. * * * "

In the statement of claim filed on 9 January 1995 the plaintiff claimed that these words in the context of the said article were widely understood to refer to the plaintiff and that these words meant and were understood to mean, in their natural and ordinary meaning and/or by way of innuendo, that the plaintiff had cynically sought to suppress legitimate and democratic political activity in Singapore by the subtle means of:

(1) suing political opponents for defamation knowing that he did not have a meritorious claim or claims; and/or

(2) relying on a 'compliant judiciary' to grant judgment in his favour irrespective of the merits * * *

The first, third and fourth defendants had, in the 10–11 December 1994 issue of the IHT, apologised unreservedly to the plaintiff. * * *

The second defendant was at the relevant time living in Georgia, United States of America.

In the context in which the words were used it is clear that they referred to the plaintiff and to the judiciary of Singapore. An independent and impartial judiciary is a fundamental pillar of our society. Every judge of the Supreme Court is required by the Constitution to take an oath that he will discharge his duties 'without fear or favour, affection or ill-will' to the best of his abilities. To allege that the judiciary is compliant to the wishes of the plaintiff; to say or imply that the judiciary will find in favour of the plaintiff, whatever the merits of the plaintiff's case, is to undermine and degrade the judiciary. But it is not the undermining of the judiciary that is the issue in this case. It is the undermining of the plaintiff. The plaintiff has, throughout his political career, emphasized and advocated the need for honest government.

* * *

For the second defendant to suggest that court proceedings instituted by the plaintiff had no merits and that the plaintiff was able to obtain judgments in his favour because of a compliant judiciary is, in the absence of a reasonable defence, a scandalous and outrageous suggestion and a most severe slur on the honesty of the plaintiff.

When words defamatory of a person are published, the law presumes that the words are false and the burden of proving that they are true is placed on the defendant. If the second defendant wished to dispute the plaintiff's claims in these proceedings, the course open to the second defendant was to enter appearance and file his defence. * * * It appears to me that he chose not to defend the claim because he knew that he had made that statement recklessly and had no defence whatsoever.

LINGENS v. AUSTRIA

European Court of Human Rights.
8 E.H.R.R. 407 (1986).

[Referring to the acts and words of then-Chancellor of Austria Mr. Kreisky, Lingens, an Austrian journalist, wrote: "had they been made by someone else this would probably have been described as the basest opportunism." He then added that, in the circumstances, the position was more complex because Mr. Kreisky believed what he was saying. In a second article, published on October 21, 1975, titled "Reconciliation with the Nazis, but how?", he added: "In truth Mr. Kreisky's behaviour cannot be criticised on rational grounds but only on irrational grounds: it is immoral, undignified * * *." Lingens's comments were in regard to Kreisky's alleged attempts to form a coalition with the Freedom Party and its leader, Peters, who was a former Nazi.]

* * *

20.   * * * Article 111 of the Austrian Criminal Code * * * reads:

1.   Anyone who in such a way that it may be perceived by a third person accuses another of possessing a contemptible character or attitude or of behaviour contrary to honour or morality and of such a nature as to make him contemptible or otherwise lower him in public esteem shall be liable to imprisonment not exceeding six months or a fine.

* * *

3. The person making the statement shall not be punished if it is proved to be true. As regards the offence defined in paragraph 1, he shall also not be liable if circumstances are established which gave him sufficient reason to assume that the statement was true.

Under Article 112, "evidence of the truth and of good faith shall not be admissible unless the person making the statement pleads the correctness of the statement or his good faith." * * *

* * *

29. The Court of Appeal [found that Kreisky] was criticised in his capacity both as a party leader and as a private individual.

The expression "the basest opportunism" meant that the person referred to was acting for a specific purpose with complete disregard of moral considerations and this in itself constituted an attack on Mr. Kreisky's reputation.

[Lingens was sentenced.]

* * *

[THE COURT]

39. The adjective "necessary", within the meaning of Article 10 para. 2 (art. 10–2), implies the existence of a "pressing social need" (Barthold judgment, Series A no. 90, pp. 24–25, para. 55). The Contracting States have a certain margin of appreciation in assessing whether such a need exists (ibid.), but it goes hand in hand with a European supervision, embracing both the legislation and the decisions applying it, even those given by an independent court. * * *

40. * * * The Court must determine whether the interference at issue was "proportionate to the legitimate aim pursued" and whether the reasons adduced by the Austrian courts to justify it are "relevant and sufficient" (Barthold judgment).

41. In this connection, the Court has to recall that freedom of expression, as secured in paragraph 1 of Article 10 (art. 10–1), constitutes one of the essential foundations of a democratic society and one of the basic conditions for its progress and for each individual's self-fulfilment. Subject to paragraph 2 (art. 10–2), it is applicable not only to "information" or "ideas" that are favourably received or regarded as inoffensive or as a matter of indifference, but also to those that offend, shock or disturb. Such are the demands of that pluralism, tolerance and broadmindedness without which there is no "democratic society."

These principles are of particular importance as far as the press is concerned. Whilst the press must not overstep the bounds set, inter alia, for the "protection of the reputation of others", it is nevertheless incumbent on it to impart information and ideas on political issues just as on those in other areas of public interest. Not only does the press have the task of imparting such information and ideas: the public also has a right to receive (*Sunday Times* judgment, Series A no. 30, p. 40, para. 65). In this connection, the Court cannot accept the opinion, expressed in the judgment of the Vienna Court of Appeal, to the effect that the task of the press was to impart information, the interpretation of which had to be left primarily to the reader.

42.   Freedom of the press furthermore affords the public one of the best means of discovering and forming an opinion of the ideas and attitudes of political leaders. More generally, freedom of political debate is at the very core of the concept of a democratic society which prevails throughout the Convention.

The limits of acceptable criticism are accordingly wider as regards a politician as such than as regards a private individual. Unlike the latter, the former inevitably and knowingly lays himself open to close scrutiny of his every word and deed by both journalists and the public at large, and he must consequently display a greater degree of tolerance. No doubt Article 10 para. 2 (art. 10–2) enables the reputation of others— that is to say, of all individuals—to be protected, and this protection extends to politicians too, even when they are not acting in their private capacity; but in such cases the requirements of such protection have to be weighed in relation to the interests of open discussion of political issues.

43.   * * * The impugned expressions are therefore to be seen against the background of a post-election political controversy. * * *

[The Court found that the confiscation of the issues already printed was a violation of Art. 10.]

44.   * * * [T]he disputed articles had at the time already been widely disseminated, so that although the penalty imposed on the author did not strictly speaking prevent him from expressing himself, it nonetheless amounted to a kind of censure, which would be likely to discourage him from making criticisms of that kind again in future. * * *

46.   * * * In the Court's view, a careful distinction needs to be made between facts and value-judgments. The existence of facts can be demonstrated, whereas the truth of value-judgments is not susceptible of proof. The Court notes in this connection that the facts on which Mr. Lingens founded his value-judgment were undisputed, as was also his good faith.

Under paragraph 3 of Article 111 of the Criminal Code, read in conjunction with paragraph 2, journalists in a case such as this cannot escape conviction for the matters specified in paragraph 1 unless they can prove the truth of their statements (see paragraph 20 above).

As regards value-judgments this requirement is impossible of fulfilment and it infringes freedom of opinion itself, which is a fundamental part of the right secured by Article 10 of the Convention.

* * *

Peter Krug, CIVIL DEFAMATION LAW AND THE PRESS IN RUSSIA: PRIVATE AND PUBLIC INTERESTS, THE 1995 CIVIL CODE, AND THE CONSTITUTION,

PART ONE, 13 Cardozo Arts & Ent. L.J. 847, 849–850, 860–875 (1995);
PART TWO, 14 Cardozo Arts & Ent. L.J. 297, 303–306 (1996).

* * * [After the collapse of the Soviet system,] culminating in a new Civil Code effective January 1, 1995, the press has been made subject to a comprehensive system of post-publication civil responsibility for dissemination of statements injurious to personality interests. The scope of protection for individual rights of personality has been broadened incrementally to include new protected interests, such as a right to privacy, and a potent new remedy—recovery of monetary damages for non-material harm ("moral damages").

This expansion of personality rights protection has been accompanied by a significant increase in the number of civil lawsuits, many of them against press defendants.

In *Zhirinovskii v. Gaidar*, Deputy Vladimir Zhirinovskii sued former Prime Minister Egor Gaidar and the newspaper *Izvestiia*, seeking twenty-five million rubles (approximately $12,500) in moral damages for publication of a May 17, 1994, article in which Gaidar described Zhirinovskii as "a fascist populist" and "the most popular fascist in Russia." In September 1994, a Moscow district court determined that the statements were false and ordered the defendants to pay moral damages totalling one million rubles (approximately $500). In so ruling, the court rejected the defendants' argument that the article in question had been "a purely analytical one," investigating Zhirinovskii's "political essence," and therefore the term "fascist" was used as a "political characteristic only." The defense had also sought to refute Zhirinovskii's charge on a factual basis, introducing into evidence Adolf Hitler's *Mein Kampf*, Zhirinovskii's book *The Last Dash South*, and the *Encyclopedia of Philosophy*.

Two months later, that decision was upheld on appeal by the Moscow City Court. According to published accounts of the proceeding, the court's primary focus was upon the truth or falsity of the statement that the plaintiff was a "fascist." Zhirinovskii rejected this designation, stating instead that he considers himself a "national-socialist." * * *

In upholding the lower court's decision, the Moscow City Court ruled that the defendants had failed to meet their burden of proof. The court rejected the use of scholars' conclusions as evidence, stating that these conclusions represented "private opinion" and questioning the validity of claimed similarities between Zhirinovskii's writings and Hitler's *Mein Kampf*. * * *

[The Russian Supreme Court denied review initiated by the Deputy Procurator General, who argued on free speech grounds.]

* * *

Whether it is more accurate to say that the courts in the fascist cases treated the use of the term "fascist" as an assertion of fact or in reality viewed it as "abusive comment," it is clear that their approach was consistent with the statutory scheme governing protection of personality rights. * * *

The Constitutional Court's Decision in *Kozyrev* [Decision of Sept. 27, 1995].

In his complaint to the Constitutional Court, [the then-Foreign Minister] Andrei Kozyrev argued that article 29 of the Constitution should shield him from bearing the burden of proving the truthfulness of his statement, made over the air on television station NTV [Independent Television] in February 1994, that Vladimir Zhirinovskii holds "Fascist-like views." Specifically, his complaint called upon the Court to invalidate the civil code provisions supporting Zhirinovskii's civil defamation lawsuit because the absence in them of a fact/opinion distinction is inconsistent with paragraphs 1 and 3 of article 29.

In finding Kozyrev's complaint inadmissible, the Court paid close attention to the jurisdictional requirements of Russia's system of constitutional review. * * *

[T]he Court questioned Kozyrev's assertion that the civil code provision in question was constitutionally suspect, given that it represented statutory implementation of article 23(1) of the Constitution, which guarantees protection of one's honor and good name.

At the same time, however, the opinion states that Kozyrev's complaint posed "an important and topical question": how in a specific case to reconcile the protection of an individual's honor and good name with "the interest of free discussion of political issues in democratic society?" Having thereby articulated recognition of a public interest element in the defamation calculus, the Court declared to the ordinary courts that it would be necessary for them to determine whether the statement in question in a specific case "fits in the sphere of political discussion," how to distinguish generally between assertions of fact and political value judgments, and whether it is possible to make an objective evaluation of the truth or falsity of the latter. So that the ordinary courts will correctly carry out their duty to "insure the requisite equilibrium between the constitutional rights to protection of one's honor and dignity and the freedom of speech," the Court suggested strongly to the Russian Supreme Court that it issue "guiding explanations" for resolution of the difficult questions posed by Kozyrev's complaint.

Notes and Questions

1. Compare the position in *Lingens* with the efforts of the GFCC to create a sphere of political discussion where the balancing favors speech interests against reputation. A trial court must

> consider the vital importance of the status of the person [or entity] allegedly slandered and the degree to which he or she participated in the process of public opinion formation protected by Article 5 (1). A person who voluntarily exposes himself to public criticism forgoes part of his

protected private sphere. This principle, developed with natural persons in mind, is to be applied even more stringently to political parties, for their existence and activities—in contrast to those of private citizens or even individual politicians—are automatically and exclusively understood as being a part of political life. * * * Under the circumstances * * * a political party must endure even caustic remarks rightfully deemed as slanderous by any democratic party. [Such remarks] are not unusual in the heat of political battle, especially because the party had the opportunity to defend itself by political means.

Campaign Slur Case, 61 BVerfGE 1 (1982).[e]

2. *The Soviet State.* "[A] statement was injurious to reputation, and therefore defamatory, only if it accused the plaintiff of behavior violating a tenet of law or the Rules of Socialist Community Life or Communist Morality, as understood by one who adheres to those norms." Krug. *op. cit.* at 871 (Part One). Because defamation law was used for Communist Party initiated campaigns and, on the other hand, was very limited because of the above standards, the 1995 Civil Code and the courts took an individualistic and strict personality-rights-oriented turn.

[T]he role of the press was cut adrift from any 'public interest' foundation. As a result, information as a "public value" in the 1990s no longer functions as legal rationale and therefore has been rendered inapplicable to cases of personality rights protection.

The absence of a public ideology in civil defamation law is manifested in several significant ways. For one thing, the statutory and judicial criteria for measurement of moral damages do not include public interest factors.

* * *

In light of the current system's historical roots, however, it would be a mistake to assume blithely that these features are manifestations of authoritarianism or illustrative of a weakly-developed legal culture. Rather, Russia's current system is grounded in the civil law aspirations of nineteenth-century European liberalism, and the conviction that the strongest protection of individual autonomy rights is found in civil code codification. This ideology is marked by aversion to the infusion by outside forces, including the state, of public values outside those considered by the legislature.

Krug, *op. cit.* at 875 (Part One).

3. *The True–False Divide.* "[I]n post-Soviet Russian law it appears that * * * all defamatory statements [are treated] as susceptible to a determination as to their truth or falsity. As a result, because the burden of proof [regarding truth] in defamation lies on the defendant, the effect of such treatment is the imposition of liability even in cases where the statement in issue is arguably opinion and where an assertion of facts was not intended." Krug, *op. cit.* at 859 (Part One). This difficulty indicates the constitutional

e. The complainant was a candidate for election to the European Parliament on the SP federal list. At election meetings, he stated that the Christian Social Union (CSU) was the "NPD of Europe." The National Democratic Party, a legally operating right-wing party, was sometimes described as a "neo-Nazi" organization. The CSU, claiming that this was a derogatory statement of fact, obtained a temporary order enjoining the candidate from publicly repeating his charge.

importance of the legal characterization. In *Gertz* the unconditional constitutional protection of opinions was restated by the USSC as follows:

> Under the First Amendment there is no such thing as false idea. However pernicious an opinion may seem, we depend for its correction not on the conscience of judges and juries but on the competition of other ideas. But there is no constitutional value in false statements of facts * * * They belong to that category of utterances which "are no essential part of any exposition of ideas" [*Chaplinsky*].
>
> Although the erroneous statement of fact is not worthy of constitutional protection, it is nevertheless inevitable in free debate ... [The] First Amendment requires that we protect some falsehood in order to protect speech that matters.

Gertz v. Robert Welch, Inc., 418 U.S. 323, 339–40 (1974).

Are nonreckless false statements ideas? Are all opinions ideas? Until *Milkovich v. Lorain Journal Co.*, 497 U.S. 1 (1990), lower courts held opinions absolutely protected. In *Milkovich* the USSC denied any "wholesale defamation exception for anything that might be labelled opinion." In the context of the disclosure of factually correct private information, the USSC did not refuse "to hold broadly that truthful publication may never be punished." *Florida Star v. B.J.F.*, 491 U.S. 524 (1989). Information on private matters of public significance may be restricted only to further a state interest of the highest order.

4. In *Lingens* the ECHR rejected the position of an Austrian court that correct factual statements deserve more protection than opinions. It follows that opinions are as protected as factual statements. One may infer that opinion is fully protected (as long as the form of expression is not an offense in itself). The GFCC seems to see a certain fact–opinion continuity and may qualify a statement as opinion, depending on the context. In a public political context, lower courts are encouraged to qualify statements as opinions because this gives more protection to speech. "False information is not a protected good. The deliberate utterance of untruth is unprotected by Article 5 (1). The same holds true for incorrect quotations. * * * To the extent that incorrect allegations of fact are not automatically placed outside the protection of Article 5 (1) [l], they may be more easily restricted by general law than expressions of opinion." *Campaign Slur Case,* 61 BVerfGE 1 (1982). Compare *New York Times v. Sullivan*, where only reckless speech or actual malice was actionable. The New Zealand position is: "Where the matter complained of consists partly of statements of fact and partly of statements of opinion, the defence does not fail merely because the defendant does not prove the truth of every statement of fact if the opinion is shown to be a genuine opinion having regard to the facts proved to be true or not materially different from the truth or any other facts that were generally known at the time of the publication and are proved to be true." *Lange v. Atkinson*, Court of Appeal, Wellington, [1998] 3 NZLR 424, 436.

Contrary to *Lange* and in contrast to the constitutionalized American libel law, English common law provides that both statements of facts and opinions might amount to libel. See *Reynolds* below.

5. *Intensity.*

[T]he purpose of free speech is to form opinions, persuade, and exert an intellectual influence over other persons. This is why value judgments, always meant to convince others, are protected by Article 5 (1) [1] of the Basic Law. Designed primarily to protect a speaker's personal opinion, it is irrelevant whether an opinion is "valuable" or "worthless," "correct" or "false," or whether it is emotional or rational. If an opinion contributes to the intellectual struggle on an issue of public concern, it is presumed protected by the principle of free expression. Even caustic and exaggerated statements, particularly those uttered in the heat of an election campaign, are within the protection of Article 5 (1) [1].

Campaign Slur Case, 61 BVerfGE 1 (1982).

Nevertheless, a value judgment is expressed in an impermissible way, and when it causes damage to personality rights, defamation may occur. The issue is how intensely the opinion (and even fact) affects dignity.

In the *Political Satire Case*, 75 BVerfGE 369 (1987), Bavarian Minister–President Franz–Josef Strauss initiated criminal proceedings for insult to his honor. He was portrayed as a copulating pig in a sexual act with another pig wearing a judicial robe (representing justice). The GFCC upheld the lower courts injunction. In *Hustler Magazine v. Falwell*, 485 U.S. 46 (1988), the magazine, parodying a liquor advertisement, featured an "alleged interview" that contained a statement from the nationally famous fundamentalist minister Falwell regarding his "first time" with his mother in an outhouse. In both *Strauss* and *Hustler* the alleged offense to the defendant was caused by a work of art (satire–caricature and parody, respectively). In both cases the harm was caused by an extremely harsh expression of opinion regarding public figures, as part of an ongoing public debate regarding their character.[f] "A particularly intolerable (and socially unnecessary) mode of expressing" an idea excludes the expression from the protection of the First Amendment (see *R.A.V.* below). Nevertheless, Reverend Falwell lost. The USSC found that the statements were not factual allegations, and under the *New York Times* rule there was no libel. Only falsity can deprive someone of his reputation. As stated in *Gertz*, there are no false opinions. This is not to say that extremely harsh (indecent) expressions of opinions are fully protected. Under common law one is liable for the tort of emotional distress caused by expression, and in such cases the issue is not whether it is fact or opinion. The Court, however, extended the *New York Times v. Sullivan* rule regarding public figures, stating that only factual statements made with actual malice are considered in emotional distress cases. The public figure may have suffered injury, but the tort law interest to remedy injury was countered with speech considerations. Speaking out of hatred will not hamper the statement from contributing to the free exchange of ideas.

In the *Caricature Case*, the GFCC recognized the artistic nature of the Strauss caricature. Moreover, it took a position similar to the USSC regarding the incapacity of courts to determine artistic value. The German Court emphasized, however, that the artistic work had calumniatory content. In balancing artistic freedom against the general right to personality rights, the bestiality element in the caricature was decisive because it deprived the person of his dignity. The Court also emphasized that the politician's exposure did not divest him of dignity. What are the grounds for the

f. Reverend Falwell advocated the public's practice of traditional moral values and gave support to politicians who shared his views. He was publicly waging a moral war against Larry Flynt, the publisher of pornographic magazines. Flynt's attack on Falwell was a reaction to some of the actions taken by Falwell against Flynt.

difference? Are the positions of the two courts similar regarding the reasons for being deferential in matters of art? Would the result be the same if the Germans were more concerned with injury that is remedied by damages? The concept of personal honor, as expressed by the Civil Code, does not allow for monetary compensation in the event of nonpecuniary damage to honor. See the *Princess Soraya Case*, 34 BVerfGE 269 (1973) (finding such prohibition of damages unconstitutional), in Chapter 1.

6. In the *Stern-Strauss (Zwangsdemokrat* [constrained democrat]) *Case*, 82 BVerfGE 272, the German Court indicated that "belittlement" and "affront" were not protected speech. A journalist described Strauss as someone behaving like a democrat because of the constraints imposed on politics by the democratic nature of the Federal Republic. The Court extended constitutional protection to the *Stern* magazine article by construing a possibly nonbelittling, alternative meaning to the statement. In other cases the GFCC simply left to lower courts the attribution of meaning, although it reserved for itself the right to a more searching scrutiny of the civil courts' decisions, especially if the infringement of a constitutional right is extremely burdensome. The same technique was used by the Court in the *Tucholsky II Case* (see below). Judge Haas, dissenting, criticized the majority for disregarding the Court's allegedly prevailing position, which "always laid value on the position that it could not be its task to put its own assessment of the circumstances of the individual case in place of the competent judge." (Judge Haas was not on the Court during the *Stern-Strauss Case*.) In *Stern-Strauss* the Court followed its precedents regarding the protected nature of overstated and polemic criticism in public debate; insulting criticism is not protected. A belittling statement becomes insult if defamation becomes central to the detriment of debate on the issue. The GFCC is reluctant to give protection to strong and offensive formulations of opinions, especially where the defendant has other means to express itself. *Deutschland-Magazin Case*, 42 BVerfGE 143 (1976).

7. The uncertainty that results from the shifting evaluation of the intensity of the attack or size of harm is present in the ECHR's jurisprudence. In *Prager and Oberschlick v. Austria* (April 26, 1995) it held that exaggeration and even a degree of provocation by a journalist are protected, in view of the public-watchdog role of the press. In *De Haes and Gijsels v. Belgium* (1997) (para. 47), however, and contrary to *Lingens*, it said that opinions might be punished if they are "excessive, in particular, in the absence of any factual basis." Does this position echo the GFCC's position? Is an insulting act the same as an offending one? Is it the same as "excessive [without] factual basis"? Could one say that an insult is without ideas and all insults are directed primarily against dignity (personal honor), while in the case of protected offensive ideas the harm to, and degradation of, honor is secondary, that is, a kind of inevitable side effect?

8. In *Oberschlick v. Austria*, 19 E.H.R.R. 389 (No. 2) (1997), the ECHR revisited Austrian criminal libel law as applied. The journalist, Oberschlick, was found guilty of defamation (*üble Nachrede*) and insult (*Beleidigung*).[g] Commenting on a speech by Jörg Haider, the leader of the Austrian Freedom party, which glorified Nazis, Oberschlick wrote: "I will say of Jörg Haider, firstly, that he is not a Nazi and, secondly, that he is, however, an idiot."

---

g. Article 115 of the Criminal Code: "Anyone who, in public or in the presence of several others, insults, mocks, mistreats or threatens to mistreat a third person, shall be liable to imprisonment not exceeding three months or a fine."

The Austrian courts found that the word *Trottel* (a harsher expression than "idiot") was an insult and could only be used as a disparagement and not for any objective criticism.

The ECHR stated that a politician

is certainly entitled to have his reputation protected, even when he is not acting in his private capacity, but the requirements of that protection have to be weighed against the interests of open discussion of political issues, since exceptions to freedom of expression must be interpreted narrowly. * * * In the Court's view, the applicant's article, and in particular the word *Trottel*, may certainly be considered polemical, but they did not on that account constitute a gratuitous personal attack as the author provided an objectively understandable explanation for them derived from Mr. Haider's speech, which was itself provocative. As such they were part of the political discussion provoked by Mr. Haider's speech and amount to an opinion, whose truth is not susceptible of proof. Such an opinion may, however, be excessive, in particular in the absence of any factual basis, but in the light of the above considerations that was not so in this instance (see, *De Haes* and *Gijsels v. Belgium* [1997]).

The ECHR found that the offensive words were not disproportionate to the indignation knowingly aroused by Mr Haider. Are "insult" and "mockery" the equivalent of U.S. "fighting words"? Is there a difference between calling someone a "damned racketeer" or an "idiot"? In the Austrian and German cases the insulting words were made in an article, while in *Chaplinsky* the words were uttered face-to-face. Is this relevant?

BLADET TROMSØ AND STENSAAS v. NORWAY

European Court of Human Rights.
29 E.H.R.R. 125 (2000).

[*Bladet Tromsø* is a local newspaper in Norway and is used as a regular source by the Norwegian News Agency ("NTB").]

[Mr Lindberg was appointed seal hunting inspector for the 1988 season, on board the *Harmoni*.]

* * *

11.   The Ministry of Fisheries decided temporarily * * * to exempt Mr Lindberg's report from public disclosure relying on section 6, item 5, of a 1970 Act relating to Access of the Public to Documents in the Sphere of the Public. Under this provision, the Ministry was empowered to order that the report not be made accessible to the public, on the ground that it contained allegations of statutory offences.

* * *

13.   On 19 and 20 July 1988 *Bladet Tromsø* published the entire report in two parts[, reproducing the alleged breaches of the seal hunting regulations by members of crew of the *Harmoni*. Interviews with crew members, denying the facts of the report, were repeatedly published both before and after the publication of the report.]

* * *

30. [The allegations of the report, as well as its handling, became national and international news.] Seal hunting was debated in Parliament, the government announced that it would set up a Commission of Inquiry. Also banned with immediate effect the killing of baby seals.

31. * * * In its report the Commission of Inquiry found that the truth of most of Mr Lindberg's allegations relating to specifically named individuals had not been proved. * * *

On the other hand, the Commission identified several breaches of the hunting regulations (p. 69), which it deemed had been established by the footage presented by Mr Lindberg.

[The *Harmoni* crew initiated a number of successful criminal defamation cases against applicants.]

* * *

B.   The Court's assessment

1.   General principles

* * *

59. One factor of particular importance * * * is the essential function the press fulfils in a democratic society. Although the press must not overstep certain bounds, in particular in respect of the reputation and rights of others and the need to prevent the disclosure of confidential information, its duty is nevertheless to impart—in a manner consistent with its obligations and responsibilities—information and ideas on all matters of public interest (see *Jersild v. Denmark* 1994; *De Haes and Gijsels v. Belgium*). In addition, the Court is mindful of the fact that journalistic freedom also covers possible recourse to a degree of exaggeration, or even provocation (see *Prager and Oberschlick v. Austria* 1995). In cases such as the present one the national margin of appreciation is circumscribed by the interest of democratic society in enabling the press to exercise its vital role of "public watchdog" in imparting information of serious public concern (see *Goodwin v. the United Kingdom* 1996, § 39).

[The Court found that there was defamation by alleging untrue facts.]

* * *

62. * * * [However,] the contents of the impugned articles cannot be looked at in isolation of the controversy that seal hunting represented at the time in Norway and in Tromsø, the centre of the trade in Norway. Moreover, whilst the mass media must not overstep the bounds imposed in the interests of the protection of the reputation of private individuals, it is incumbent on them to impart information and ideas concerning matters of public interest. Not only does the press have the task of imparting such information and ideas: the public also has a right to receive them. Consequently, in order to determine whether the interference was based on sufficient reasons which rendered it "necessary," regard must be had to the public-interest aspect of the case.

63. * * * [According to the District Court, *Bladet Tromsø* was treating the issue in a sensationalist fashion.]

In the Court's view, however, the manner of reporting in question should not be considered solely by reference to the disputed articles. [The paper] published almost on a daily basis the different points of views, including the newspaper's own comments, [as well as those of the interested parties] * * * As the Court observed in a previous judgment, the methods of objective and balanced reporting may vary considerably, depending among other things on the medium in question; it is not for the Court, any more than it is for the national courts, to substitute its own views for those of the press as to what techniques of reporting should be adopted by journalists (see *Jersild*, § 31).

[T]he thrust of the impugned articles was not primarily to accuse certain individuals of committing. * * * The impugned articles were part of an ongoing debate of evident concern to the local, national and international public, in which the views of a wide selection of interested actors were reported.

      * * *

65. Article 10 of the Convention does not, however, guarantee a wholly unrestricted freedom of expression even with respect to press coverage of matters of serious public concern. Under the terms of paragraph 2 of the Article the exercise of this freedom carries with it "duties and responsibilities," which also apply to the press. * * * [T]he safeguard afforded by Article 10 to journalists in relation to reporting on issues of general interest is subject to the proviso that they are acting in good faith in order to provide accurate and reliable information in accordance with the ethics of journalism (see *Goodwin*, and *Fressoz and Roire*.)[h]

66. The Court notes that the expressions in question consisted of factual statements, not value-judgments. They did not emanate from the newspaper itself but were based on or were directly quoting from the Lindberg report, which the newspaper had not verified by independent research. It must therefore be examined whether there were any special grounds in the present case for dispensing the newspaper from its ordinary obligation to verify factual statements that were defamatory of private individuals. In the Court's view, this depends in particular on the nature and degree of the defamation at hand and the extent to which the newspaper could reasonably regard the Lindberg report as reliable with respect to the allegations in question. * * *

67. * * * More importantly, while *Bladet Tromsø* * * * named none of those accused of having committed the reprehensible acts. * * *

h. Article 10 "protects journalists' rights to divulge information on issues of general interest provided that they are acting in good faith and on an accurate factual basis and provide 'reliable and precise' information in accordance with the ethics of journalism" (*Fressoz*, § 54). *Fressoz and Roire v. France*, 31 E.H.R.R. 2 (2001), originated with the appellant journalists' publication of the tax forms of M. Calvet, the Chairman of the Peugeot Company, who refused salary increases to his employees but awarded himself, according to his tax return, a 46 percent raise. The journalists were convicted in relation to the breach of professional (fiscal) confidence. Although the Court agreed with the government that the punishment served the reputation of others, it found the publication a matter of general interest. In the present case the Court found that the public's interest in being informed outweighed the journalists' responsibilities.

Thus, while some of the accusations were relatively serious, the potential adverse effect of the impugned statements on each individual seal hunter's reputation or rights was significantly attenuated.

* * *

68. * * * In the view of the Court, the press should normally be entitled, when contributing to public debate on matters of legitimate concern, to rely on the contents of official reports without having to undertake independent research.

* * *

73. On the facts of the present case, the Court cannot find that the crew members' undoubted interest in protecting their reputation was sufficient to outweigh the vital public interest in ensuring an informed public debate over a matter of local and national as well as international interest. Accordingly, the Court holds that there has been a violation of Article 10 of the Convention.

Notes and Questions

1. In *Bladet Tromsø* the ECHR attempted to reconcile the role of newspapers covering stories in the public interest with the right to reputation of identifiable private individuals named in stories. Recognizing that the limits of acceptable criticism are wider for politicians and public figures than private persons, in *Janowski v. Poland*, 29 E.H.R.R. 705 (2000), the "applicant, a Polish journalist, was convicted and fined for 'insulting civil servants' with verbal insults ('oafs') during their action. The ECHR agreed and held that conviction was for relevant and sufficient reasons, and noted that Janowski's remarks were stated in his personal capacity, not as a journalist." Is the ECHR of the opinion that if a strong public interest is involved, newspapers should be exonerated from either the basic ethics of their trade or the laws of defamation?

2. The ECHR's reasoning implies that newspapers can dispense with verifying the facts of a story depending on (1) the nature and degree of the defamation and (2) whether it was reasonable in the circumstances to rely on external information. Compare the first position with the German one and the second one to the reasonableness requirement in *Lange* (Australia). Is this approach "recklessness" test? The *Bladet Tromsø* dissent argues:

> How could it have been 'reasonable' to rely on this report when the newspaper was fully aware that the Ministry had ordered that the report not be made public immediately because it had contained possibly libelous comments concerning private individuals? It was thus temporarily not in the public domain and rightly so." The dissenters would grant the privilege of reasonableness in cases of published official reports. How could this affect the watchdog function of the press? The dissenters are more concerned about press ethics: "Few stories can be so important in a democratic society or deserving of protection under Article 10 of the Convention, than the basic ethics of journalism—which require, *inter alia*, journalists to check their facts before going to press with a story in circumstances such as the present—can be sacrificed for the commercial gratification of an immediate scoop.

A similar distrust of the commercialization of the press is decisive in *Reynolds*.

3. The ECHR did not discuss the defamation itself, only the lack of verification of the statements of the person preparing the defamatory report. Although it found that the paper did not rely on independent sources, the press was not held responsible as it relied on official reports in contributing to the public debate.[i] The dissenters in *Bladet Tromsø* emphasized that plaintiffs (the seal hunters mentioned in the article) were private persons; thus the more relaxed rules regarding politicians did not apply. Were the seal hunters public figures simply because they were involved in a major public debate in a specific capacity that concerned the public?

4. *Group libel.* The contested statements in *Bladet Tromsø* did not refer to a specific person. Is there libel here? Whose reputation was at stake? The GFCC had no difficulty in finding reputation interest for members of an organization and no difficulty in criminalizing verbal attacks on public authorities. *Tucholsky II Case*, 93 BVerfGE 266 (1995). In a series of unrelated cases people used a quote ("Soldiers are Murderers") to express their dislike of the Army. (The well-known quote comes from the writer Tucholsky, an outspoken opponent of the Nazis, who killed him.) This time the convictions were based on Art. 185 of the German Criminal Code. The Court saw this as a general law serving a neutral interest: "Without a minimum of social acceptance, State institutions cannot carry out their functions. They may therefore in principle be protected against verbal attacks that threaten to undermine these requirements. Protection by the criminal law may not however have the effect of protecting State institutions against public criticism, possibly even in sharp forms." *Id.* at 678. General laws may restrict free speech. The GFCC found the convictions unconstitutional as the lower courts failed to recognize the "particularly high" importance of the expressed opinions as criticisms of government powers, an important speech value.

In *Beauharnais v. Illinois*, below, the USSC upheld a conviction for group libel concerning racial groups. In civil defamation the common law does not find numbers alone conclusive. Individuals can be defamed in the libeling of a group as long as they might be identified ("personally pointed" out). *Beauharnais* has not been formally overruled, but the dissenting views of Justice Black are now recognized as governing law:

> The Court condones this expansive state censorship by painstakingly analogizing it to the law of criminal libel. As a result of this refined analysis, the Illinois statute emerges labeled a "group libel law." This label may make the Court's holding more palatable for those who sustain it, but the sugar-coating does not make the censorship less deadly. However tagged, the Illinois law is not that criminal libel which has been "defined, limited and constitutionally recognized time out of mind." * * * [As] 'constitutionally recognized,' [criminal libel] has provided for punishment of false, malicious, scurrilous charges against individuals, not against huge groups. This limited scope of the law of criminal libel is of no small importance. It has confined state punishment of speech and expression to the narrowest of areas involving

i. In *Dalban v. Romania*, 31 E.H.R.R. 39 (2001), the press was held not to be liable for relying on an interim official report when it disregarded, at the same time, the final official reports or position when making defamatory accusations.

nothing more than purely private feuds. Every expansion of the law of criminal libel so as to punish discussions of matters of public concern means a corresponding invasion of the area dedicated to free expression by the First Amendment.

Id. at 271–72.

In *Tucholsky II* the GFCC recognized the special danger to speech in cases where a disparaging collective term is criminalized. The Court claimed that free speech is protected in such cases, by looking at the harm to the personal honor of individual members of a group. A feature that applies to all members within the very large group might be offensive to all (but the larger the group the lesser the likelihood of harm). Can institutions possess honor? Do they have identity? Is the symbolic protection of government institutions (see below) based on the protection of institutional reputation? Irrespective of free speech considerations, will the social esteem of an unidentified member of a defamed group be diminished if the group is described in offensive terms? Perhaps the suffering and loss of self-esteem of a group member is the concern that might trigger group protection. Does the application of the maxim "dirt in politics is inevitable" and hence the reduced protection against libel of political parties result from the GFCC's desire to mitigate the danger that group honor and the reputation of political parties in particular might extensively limit freedom of speech? Is the *Bladet Tromsø* article defaming the individual seal hunters of an identified ship (the *Harmoni*), or is it about seal hunting in general? The ECHR seems to endorse the second possibility: in the context of a hotly debated public issue the "thrust of the impugned articles was not primarily to accuse certain individuals."

5. In *Bladet Tromsø* the ECHR found that the presentation of the story was fair because it gave place to the crew members' views. Does this diminish defamation? Is the ECHR protecting editorial freedom as long as the editors offer a balanced presentation? The requirement of balanced presentation is required in the broadcasting laws of many European countries. Should newspapers follow the statutory requirements applicable to other media?

CASTELLS v. SPAIN

European Court of Human Rights.
4 E.H.R.R. 445 (1992).

[The applicant, Castells, at the material time, was a Senator elected on the Herri Batasuna list, a political grouping supporting independence for the Basque region, in Spain. In a weekly magazine, he published an article criticizing the government. In 1979, he was prosecuted for "insulting the government." The Senate withdrew the applicant's parliamentary immunity.[j] He was found guilty, and after many unsuccessful

j. The applicant's defense counsel challenged four of the five members of the relevant division of the Supreme Court. The Court took the view that, although the judges had indeed sat in the Criminal Division of the Supreme Court under the previous political regime, they had at that time merely applied the legislation in force. In 1983, the Constitutional Tribunal dismissed an appeal (*amparo*) that Castells had lodged, alleging a violation of Art. 24(2) of the Constitution (right to an impartial tribunal). It found that, while the judges in question might have political convictions differing from those of the applicant, it could not be regarded as being of direct or

appeals, the Supreme Court ruled, in 1986, that the term of imprisonment had been definitively served.]

* * *

B.   Relevant legislation

1.   Constitution of 1978

19.   * * * Article 18

1.   "The right to honour, to a private life and to a family life and the right to control use of one's likeness shall be protected."

* * *

Article 20

1.   The following rights shall be recognised and protected:

(a) the right freely to express and disseminate thoughts, ideas and opinions by word of mouth, in writing or by any other means of reproduction;

* * *

(d) the right to receive and communicate true information by any means of dissemination. The right to invoke the conscience clause and that of professional confidentiality shall be governed by statute.

* * *

2.   The Criminal Code

20.   The Institutional Act 8/1983 of 25 June 1983 reformed the Criminal Code. It provides that the offences of insulting the Government shall be punishable by the following penalties:

Article 161

The following shall be liable to long-term prison sentences:

Those who seriously insult, falsely accuse or threaten * * * the Government.

* * *

39.   * * * [I]n its decision of 10 April 1985—on which the Government relied—the Constitutional Court stressed that the security of the State could be threatened by attempts to discredit democratic institutions. In his article Mr. Castells did not merely describe a very serious situation, involving numerous attacks and murders in the Basque Country; he also complained of the inactivity on the part of the authorities, in particular the police, and even their collusion with the guilty parties and inferred therefrom that the Government was responsible.

It may therefore be said, and this conforms to the view held by the Government and the Commission, that in the circumstances obtaining in Spain in 1979 the proceedings instituted against the applicant were brought for the "prevention of disorder," within the meaning of Article 10(2), and not only for the "protection of the reputation * * * of others." * * *

* * *

indirect relevance to the solution of the dispute.

43. In the case under review Mr. Castells did not express his opinion from the senate floor, as he might have done without fear of sanctions, but chose to do so in a periodical. That does not mean, however, that he lost his right to criticise the Government.

In this respect, the pre-eminent role of the press in a State governed by the rule of law must not be forgotten. Although it must not overstep various bounds set, inter alia, for the prevention of disorder and the protection of the reputation of others, it is nevertheless incumbent on it to impart information and ideas on political questions and on other matters of public interest.

* * *

46. * * * The limits of permissible criticism are wider with regard to the Government than in relation to a private citizen, or even a politician. In the democratic system the actions or omissions of the Government must be subject to the close scrutiny not only of the legislative and judicial authorities but also of the press and public opinion. Furthermore, the dominant position which the Government occupies makes it necessary for it to display restraint in resorting to criminal proceedings, particularly where other means are available for replying to the unjustified attacks and criticisms of its adversaries or the media. Nevertheless it remains open to the competent State authorities to adopt, in their capacity as guarantors of public order, measures, even of a criminal law nature, intended to react appropriately and without excess to defamatory accusations devoid of foundation or formulated in bad faith.

47. In this instance, Mr. Castells offered on several occasions, before the Supreme Court and subsequently in the Constitutional Court, to establish that the facts recounted by him were true and well-known; in his view, this deprived his statements of any insulting effect. * * *

48. * * * In fact many of these assertions were susceptible to an attempt to establish their truth, just as Mr. Castells could reasonably have tried to demonstrate his good faith.

It is impossible to state what the outcome of the proceedings would have been had the Supreme Court admitted the evidence which the applicant sought to adduce; but the Court attaches decisive importance to the fact that it declared such evidence inadmissible for the offence in question. It considers that such an interference in the exercise of the applicant's freedom of expression was not necessary in a democratic society.

* * *

Notes and Questions

1. The ECHR did not discuss the acceptability of the criminalization of insulting the government. The House of Lords in *Derbyshire County Council v. Times Newspapers Ltd.*, [1993] AC 534, stated that, so far as public bodies (as opposed to their members and officials) are concerned, a local authority could not sue for libel at all:

The most important of these features [of a local authority] is that it is a governmental body. Further, it is a democratically elected body, the electoral process nowadays being conducted almost exclusively on party political lines. It is of the highest public importance that a democratically elected governmental body, or indeed any governmental body, should be open to uninhibited public criticism. The threat of a civil action for defamation must inevitably have an inhibiting effect on freedom of speech.

Lord Keith of Kinkel, *id.* at 547.

Does the denial of plaintiff standing in libel for government bodies also apply to what the Spaniards (or the Germans) call "insult"?

2. Some members of the European Commission of Human Rights, which at that time was responsible for referring complaints to the Court, considered the 1979 Spanish situation as one of "transition to democracy." The dissenting opinion calls Castells "a known * * * political representative of Basque extremism." The dissenters believed that the criminalization of the speech served the prevention of disorder in 1979, a couple of years after the end of the dictatorship. Castells was charged for serious accusations against the police and the state, which were not based on facts. The dissent disregarded that Castells wanted an internal investigation by the police, and he was not allowed to produce evidence. His speech might have served democracy.[k]

Contrary to the assumptions of the dissenters in *Castells*, the HCC stated, in 1994—five years after the collapse of communism—that

value judgments expressed in the conflict of opinions on public matters enjoy increased constitutional protection, even if they are exaggerated and intensified. * * * Even in the period of the establishment and consolidation of the institutional structure of democracy—when civilized debating of public matters has not yet taken root—there is no constitutional interest which would justify the restriction of communicating value judgments in the protection of authorities and official persons. The protection of the peace and democratic development of society does not require criminal law interference against criticism and negative judgment of the activity and operation of authorities and official persons even if it takes the form of defamatory and slanderous expressions and behavior.

Decision 36/1994 (VI.24.) AB hat.[l] (finding the special criminal protection of the reputation of a government official in violation of proportionality requirement as punishment is too restrictive of speech).

k. Nearly two decades after Castells made his claims, some members of the 1979 Spanish government were sentenced to very long imprisonment for covering up the actions of (and perhaps ordering) anti-Basque death squads working for and within the Spanish antiterrorist and secret services.

l. Article 232 of the Penal Code provided: "(1) The person who in the presence of another person states or spreads a rumour about a fact or uses an expression directly referring to such a fact which is capable of offending the honour of an official person or for offending the honour of an authority through an offence against an official person representing an authority, commits a misdemeanour, and shall be punishable with imprisonment of up to two years, public labour or fine." The defence of truth was restrictively admissible only. The provision was used against a journalist–political analyst, who stated at a nonacademic lecture that each member of the government had a price tag (when accepting bribes). The court of first instance found that the statement had a low level of social dangerousness and

While many jurisdictions are reluctant to apply criminal libel in the case of political speech, neither the ECHR nor other courts, operating in countries with established democratic traditions, are ready to go as far as the USSC in *New York Times* regarding civil wrongs. The various efforts and drawbacks are illustrated by libel cases in common law jurisdictions, where conflicting positions emerged regarding the protection of the press.

LANGE v. ATKINSON

Court of Appeal, Wellington (New Zealand).
3 NZLR 424 (1998).

Blanchard J:

2.   The alleged defamation

In this defamation proceeding the plaintiff, Mr David Lange, brings an appeal from an interlocutory judgment of Elias J in the High Court at Auckland [1997] 2 NZLR 22. Mr Lange claims that he was defamed in an article written by the first defendant, Mr Joe Atkinson. * * * Mr Lange was then a Member of Parliament and had formerly been Prime Minister of New Zealand. * * *

[T]he article is a generally critical review of Mr Lange's performance as a politician including his Prime Ministership and casts doubt on his recollection of certain events in which he was involved. Its flavour can perhaps be gauged from an accompanying cartoon, also said to defame, which depicts Mr Lange at breakfast being served a packet label led "Selective Memory Regression For Advanced Practitioners."

5.   High Court judgment

The Judge began her discussion by reviewing the balance which the law of defamation seeks to achieve between the important values of protection of reputation and freedom of speech. She said that the common law has recognised that political speech and the frank exchange of information and opinions bearing on the exercise of the franchise are necessary for the welfare of society. * * *

          * * *

Elias J concluded on the basis of the New Zealand Bill of Rights Act 1990 that it was for the "common convenience and welfare" of New Zealand society that the common law defence of qualified privilege should apply to claims for damages for defamation arising out of political discussion. She defined "Political discussion" as " * * * discussion which bears upon the function of electors in a representative democracy by developing and encouraging views upon government."

          * * *

applied no punishment. The second instance suspended the procedure and referred the case to the Constitutional Court. As the Court did not rule on the matter, the second-instance panel acquitted the journalist. The government, which initiated the criminal libel procedure, lost the elections.

Roughly six weeks later, the Constitutional Court declared the provision unconstitutional. It did not find unconstitutional that defamatory opinions are still subject to criminal law, partly because this was not the issue. Criminal libel is still the norm in many countries.

It was the Judge's view also that a requirement of reasonableness in the publication would introduce a wide factual inquiry as to fault which was not consistent with the Act's restatement of the defence of honest opinion.[m] * * * Once the circumstances of legitimate political discussion have been established, Elias J said, the only appropriate condition for raising qualified privilege should be honest belief.

14. Qualified privilege and political statements: conclusion

* * *

(1) The defence of qualified privilege may be available in respect of a statement which is published generally.

(2) The nature of New Zealand's democracy means that the wider public may have a proper interest in respect of generally-published statements which directly concern the functioning of representative and responsible government, including statements about the performance or possible future performance of specific individuals in elected public office.

(3) In particular, a proper interest does exist in respect of statements made about the actions and qualities of those currently or formerly elected to Parliament and those with immediate aspirations to such office, so far as those actions and qualities directly affect or affected their capacity (including their personal ability and willingness) to meet their public responsibilities.

(4) The determination of the matters which bear on that capacity will depend on a consideration of what is properly a matter of public concern rather than of private concern.

(5) The width of the identified public concern justifies the extent of the publication.

(b) The protection of private reputation: the role of § 19

The emphasis just placed on the requirement that the statements relate to matters of proper public concern provides some protection for private rights and reputation—to return to that critical balancing factor. It is clear from § 5 of the Bill of Rights read with arts 19(3) and 17 of the covenant that the law must have regard to that matter. Section 19(1) of the Act also provides such protection. To repeat, it provides that the defence of qualified privilege fails if the plaintiff proves that, in publishing the matter: " * * * the defendant was predominantly motivated by ill will towards the plaintiff or otherwise took improper advantage of the occasion of publication".

LANGE v. AUSTRALIAN BROADCASTING CORPORATION

High Court (Australia).
(1997) 189 C.L.R. 520.

[For the facts of this case, see *Lange*, New Zealand, above. The Lange story was reported by the Australian Broadcasting Corporation (ABC), in Australia.]

---

m. Prior to the new Act, the honest-opinion defence was known as fair com-   ment. The defendant must prove that the opinion was her genuine opinion.

Brennan CJ:

* * *

The defendant has relied on the decisions of this court in * * * *Theophanous*,[n] [where] this court by majority * * * declared that:

There is implied in the Commonwealth Constitution a freedom to publish material:

(a) discussing government and political matters;

(b) of and concerning members of the Parliament of the Commonwealth of Australia which relates to the performance by such members of their duties as members of the Parliament or parliamentary committees;

(c) in relation to the suitability of persons for office as members of the Parliament.

In the light of the freedom implied in the Commonwealth Constitution, the publication will not be actionable under the law relating to defamation if the defendant establishes that:

(a) it was unaware of the falsity of the material published;

(b) it did not publish the material recklessly, that is, not caring whether the material was true or false; and

(c) the publication was reasonable in the circumstances.

* * *

The principal reason why these general statements provide little guidance is that it is arguable that neither *Theophanous* nor *Stephens* contains a binding statement of constitutional principle.

* * *

* * * Without the statutory defence of qualified privilege, it is clear enough that the law of defamation, as it has traditionally been understood in New South Wales, would impose an undue burden on the required freedom of communication under the Constitution. * * *

* * * [T]his court should now declare that each member of the Australian community has an interest in disseminating and receiving information, opinions and arguments concerning government and political matters that affect the people of Australia. The duty to disseminate such information is simply the correlative of the interest in receiving it. The common convenience and welfare of Australian society are advanced by discussion—the giving and receiving of information—about government and political matters. The interest that each member of the Australian community has in such a discussion extends the categories of qualified privilege. Consequently, those categories now must be recognised as protecting a communication made to the public on a government or political matter.

n. *Theophanous v. Herald & Weekly Times, Ltd.*, (1994) 182 C.L.R. 104, 723. Chief Justice Mason, writing a plurality opinion, rejected *New York Times v. Sullivan*: "the efficacious working of representative democracy * * * [d]oes not warrant protecting statements made irresponsibly." Theophanous chaired the Australia House of Representatives Standing Committee on Migration Regulation, and the *Herald* newspaper published a letter accusing him of pro-Greek bias.

* * * Whether the making of a publication was reasonable must depend upon all the circumstances of the case. But, as a general rule, a defendant's conduct in publishing material giving rise to a defamatory imputation will not be reasonable unless the defendant had reasonable grounds for believing that the imputation was true, took proper steps, so far as they were reasonably open, to verify the accuracy of the material and did not believe the imputation to be untrue. Furthermore, the defendant's conduct will not be reasonable unless the defendant has sought a response from the person defamed and published the response made (if any) except in cases where the seeking or publication of a response was not practicable or it was unnecessary to give the plaintiff an opportunity to respond.

Notes and Questions

1. Although the Australian High Court has given sustained attention to what forms of communications are covered by that freedom, the question of how much protection such communication receives has not been clearly answered. If a particular communication falls within the coverage of the freedom of political communication, does this mean that no regulation of that communication can be justified? Or can reasonable regulation pursuing some legitimate interest be justified? Or, perhaps, does political communication or some type of it require special protection?

The High Court's answers to these kinds of questions has been rather unclear. Although at times the High Court appears to have settled on a proportionality test, at other times some members of the High Court have departed from this test and have held that a stricter standard of review, closely resembling the 'strict scrutiny' test seen in American constitutional law, should apply to certain categories of cases. These doctrinal swings, moreover, have been neither acknowledged by the Court nor the subject of sustained scholarly attention.

Adrienne Stone, *The Limits of Constitutional Text and Structure: Standards of Review and the Freedom of Political Communication*, 23 Melb. U. L. Rev. 668, 670 (1999).

2. *Lange v. Australian Broadcasting Corporation* seems to end an Australian revolution in free speech that was compared with *New York Times v. Sullivan*. In *Theophanus* and *Stephens*, referred to in the *Lange v. Australian Broadcasting Corporation* judgment, a plurality, concerned about the "chilling effects" of the existing common law, held that the disseminator of false information defaming a politician (in regard to his suitability to public office) is fully protected, except for recklessness to falsity, if "it was reasonable in the circumstances." Chief Justice Mason found that the meaning derived from the contemporary purpose of the Australian Constitution mandates that "it is incontrovertible that an implication of freedom of communication, the purpose of which is to ensure the efficacy of representative democracy, must extend to protect political discussion from exposure to onerous criminal and civil liability if the implication is to be effective in achieving its purpose." *Theophanus*, 68 AJLR 713, 721 (1994). Chief Justice Mason found that the rule applicable to political discussion "includes discussion of the political views and public conduct of persons who are engaged in activities that have become the subject of political debate, e.g., economic

commentators.'' *Id.* at 718. Is this broader than the American protection of "public figures''? Is (defamatory) speech regarding the nonpolitician media tycoon Rupert Murdoch not protected? Justice Brennan (as he then was advocating judicial deferentialism against judicial lawmaking) dissented in *Theophanus*, stating that the *Australian Capital Television* case (see Chapter 2) applies only negatively, i.e., regarding governmental speech restrictions, and not on the common law. In *Lange v. Australian Broadcasting Corporation* Brennan was already the Chief Justice, and he commanded a majority.

REYNOLDS v. TIMES NEWSPAPERS LIMITED

House of Lords (United Kingdom).
4 All E.R. 609 (1999).

Lord Nicholls of Birkenhead:

My Lords, this appeal concerns the interaction between two fundamental rights: freedom of expression and protection of reputation. The context is newspaper discussion of a matter of political importance. Stated in its simplest form, the newspaper's contention is that a libellous statement of fact made in the course of political discussion is free from liability if published in good faith. Liability arises only if the writer knew the statement was not true or he made the statement recklessly, not caring whether it was true or false, or if he was actuated by personal spite or some other improper motive. Mr. Reynolds' contention, on the other hand, is that liability may also arise if, having regard to the source of the information and all the circumstances, it was not in the public interest for the newspaper to have published the information as it did. Under the newspaper's contention the safeguard for those who are defamed is exclusively subjective: the state of mind of the journalist. Under Mr. Reynolds' formulation, there is also an objective element of protection.

The events giving rise to these proceedings took place during a political crisis in Dublin in November 1994. The crisis culminated in the resignation of Mr. Reynolds as Taoiseach (prime minister) of Ireland. * * * [T]he *Sunday Times* published in its British mainland edition an article entitled "Goodbye gombeen man.''

  * * *

In the libel proceedings which followed, Mr. Reynolds pleaded that the sting of the article was that he had deliberately and dishonestly misled the Dail. It was common ground before your Lordships that by instituting and prosecuting his libel action Mr. Reynolds had waived his immunity under the Irish constitution in respect of proceedings in the Dail. His ability to do so was not questioned in your Lordships' House.

The jury decided that the defamatory allegation of which Mr. Reynolds complained was not true. So the defence of justification failed. The jury decided that [the journalist] was not acting maliciously in writing and publishing the words complained of. So, if the occasion was privileged, and that was a question for the judge, the defence of qualified privilege would succeed. Despite their rejection of the defence of justification, the jury awarded Mr. Reynolds no damages.

  * * *

In the case of statements of opinion on matters of public interest, that is the limit of what is necessary for protection of reputation. Readers and viewers and listeners can make up their own minds on whether they agree or disagree with defamatory statements which are recognisable as comment and which, expressly or implicitly, indicate in general terms the facts on which they are based.

* * *

With defamatory imputations of fact the position is different and more difficult. Those who read or hear such allegations are unlikely to have any means of knowing whether they are true or not. In respect of such imputations, a plaintiff's ability to obtain a remedy if he can prove malice is not normally a sufficient safeguard. Malice is notoriously difficult to prove. If a newspaper is understandably unwilling to disclose its sources, a plaintiff can be deprived of the material necessary to prove, or even allege, that the newspaper acted recklessly in publishing as it did without further verification. Thus, in the absence of any additional safeguard for reputation, a newspaper, anxious to be first with a "scoop," would in practice be free to publish seriously defamatory misstatements of fact based on the slenderest of materials.

The appellant newspaper commends reliance upon the ethics of professional journalism. The decision should be left to the editor of the newspaper. Unfortunately, in the United Kingdom this would not generally be thought to provide a sufficient safeguard. The sad reality is that the overall handling of these matters by the national press, with its own commercial interests to serve, does not always command general confidence.

The investigative journalist has adequate protection [under the common law]. The contrary approach, which would involve no objective check on the media, drew a pertinent comment from Tipping J [dissenting] in *Lange v. Atkinson* [1998] 3 N.Z.L.R. 424 at 477:

> "It could be seen as rather ironical that whereas almost all sectors of society, and all other occupations and professions have duties to take reasonable care, and are accountable in one form or another if they are careless, the news media whose power and capacity to cause harm and distress are considerable if that power is not responsibly used, are not liable in negligence, and what is more, can claim qualified privilege even if they are negligent. It may be asked whether the public interest in freedom of expression is so great that the accountability which society requires of others, should not also to this extent be required of the news media."

* * *

My conclusion is that the established common law approach to misstatements of fact remains essentially sound. The common law should not develop "political information" as a new "subject-matter" category of qualified privilege, whereby the publication of all such information would attract qualified privilege, whatever the circumstances. That would not provide adequate protection for reputation.

Moreover, it would be unsound in principle to distinguish political discussion from discussion of other matters of serious public concern

* * *

A major expansion of the privilege, such as may have been achieved in Australia, shifts the focus of political defamation to the conduct of the defendant. In practice it may leave a politician plaintiff without redress. His or her private life may be immune from the extended privilege, but otherwise the opportunity of a public clearing of name may be virtually gone. If the Australian solution has disadvantages, they may lie in this change of focus and in the singling out of politicians as acceptable targets of falsehood.

Notes and Questions

1. In *Reynolds* the House of Lords rejected three attempts to enlarge the privileges of the press. First, they found the *New York Times* rule unacceptable, among other reasons, because Parliament recently (in the 1996 Defamation Act) considered that option and rejected it. In fact it was rejected at the drafting stage. Would one argue that the rejection of the actual malice rule was the view of Parliament? Is an express negative vote in Parliament material, after having turned the European HR Convention into the domestic law of the realm?

Second, the House of Lords rejected the circumstantial test ("were the nature, status and source of the material, and the circumstances of the publication should in the public interest be protected in the absence of proof of express malice") as one that does not offer clear guidance. The circumstantial test was developed by the Court of Appeal per Lord Bingham. Lord Bingham argued that "it is one thing to publish a statement taken from a government press release, or the report of a public company chairman, or the speech of a university vice-chancellor, and quite another to publish the statement of a political opponent, or a business competitor or a disgruntled ex-employee." [1998] 3All ER 961, 1004. Is this to say that if the information comes from a source that might be regarded as authoritative, the defamatory speech is protected? Does the respectability of a source establish a presumption in favor of the statement being in the public interest? Is an ex-employee likely to lie when she discloses corruption of her former employer? Compare Lord Bingham's position with Justice Elias's rejection of the authoritative-source rule. See *Lange* (New Zealand) below.

The third rejected possibility was that presented in the *Lange* (Australia) decision.

2. Notwithstanding his commitment to "informed choice," Lord Nicholls insisted that protection of reputation was also the legal and constitutional duty of the courts. One cannot expect that there will be due concern for reputation in the ethics of professional journalism. His concern was that the extension of the privilege would be counterproductive to personality rights because of the commercial nature of the British press. Can the public-watchdog function (the prevailing consideration in granting the press privileges) not operate in the environment of a commercialized press? Is there any effective press other than a commercial one? Lord Nicholls proposed an "elastic test": the political information could only be used for defense by the

press "if the public was entitled to know the information." In *Reynolds* the information provided was not what the public was entitled to know as the information was not balanced. [1999] 4 All ER 609, 627.

LANGE v. ATKINSON

Judicial Committee (New Zealand).
1 NZLR 257 (2000).

Lord Nicholls of Birkenhead:

As noted by Elias J, the issue raised by the application was whether, in the context of political speech, the common law currently strikes an appropriate balance between the two principles of reputation and free speech. * * * The Judge observed that the balance ultimately must be a value judgment informed by local circumstances and guided by principle.

The Court of Appeal gave its judgment on 25 May 1998. Six weeks later, on 8 July, the English Court of Appeal delivered its judgment in *Reynolds v. Times Newspapers Ltd.* * * *

In short, the English Court of Appeal declined to follow the approach of the New Zealand Court of Appeal in the present case * * * upheld the decision of the (English) Court of Appeal but not its formulation of three questions. The House decided that the common law should not develop "political information" as a new subject-matter category of qualified privilege, whereby the publication of all such information would attract qualified privilege, whatever its source and whatever the circumstances. * * *

Against this somewhat kaleidoscopic background, one feature of all the judgments, New Zealand, Australian and English, stands out with conspicuous clarity: the recognition that striking a balance between freedom of expression and protection of reputation calls for a value judgment which depends upon local political and social conditions. These conditions include matters such as the responsibility and vulnerability of the press' view, subject to one point mentioned later, this feature is determinative of the present appeal the Board does not substitute its own views, if different, for those of the New Zealand Court of Appeal.

     * * *

[The Court of Appeal had no opportunity to consider *Reynolds* and] an appraisal of the English case law is an important part of the background against which the Courts in New Zealand are assessing the best way forward on this important and difficult point of the common law. This is not surprising. Even on issues of local public policy, every jurisdiction can benefit from examinations of an issue undertaken by others. Interaction between the jurisdictions can help to clarify and refine the issues and the available options, without prejudicing national autonomy. * * * Their Lordships think it appropriate to give the New Zealand Court of Appeal the opportunity to reconsider the issue.[o] After all, the three countries are all parliamentary democracies with a common

---

o. It is not clear to what extent *Reynolds* will prevail after the Judicial Committee's decision. Consider the Chief Justice's pragmatism in regard to localism in matters of universal values.

origin. Whether the differences in details of their constitutional structure and relevant statute law have any truly significant bearing on the scope of qualified privilege for political discussion is among the aspects calling for consideration.

C. RACIST SPEECH

A great divide among constitutional democracies in the understanding of the limits to speech emerges in the context of racist speech (hate speech).[p] Speech is restricted for arousing hatred against others, primarily in relation to their belonging to a specific racial, ethnic, national, or religious community. On the other hand racist speech is often singled out irrespective of its possibly inciting effects; it is prohibited because its content is seen as humiliating to people belonging to the race. The assumptions regarding racially degrading and inciting speech often apply to nationalist and antiminority hate speech, too; it too may vary. Racism is condemned in most countries of the world. International conventions prohibit racial discrimination. It is argued that without the criminalization of racist propaganda, racist prejudice and even violence will increase, and discriminatory social practices will become the norm. It is also argued that without intervention at the level of communication, racist totalitarian political movements will endanger democracy. The prevailing American position, however, is that government interference with racist propaganda is likely to curtail free speech, while nonintervention by the state does not indicate any recognition of the "truth" of totalitarian racism:

> Some propositions seem true or false beyond rational debate. Some false and harmful, political and religious doctrine gain wide public acceptance. Adolf Hitler's brutal theory of a 'master race' is sufficient example. We tolerate such foolish and sometimes dangerous appeals not because they may prove true but because freedom of speech is indivisible. The liberty cannot be denied to some ideas and saved for others. The reason is plain enough: no man, no committee, and surely no government, has the infinite wisdom and disinterestedness accurately and unselfishly to separate what is true from what is debatable, and both from what is false. To license one to impose his truth upon dissenters is to give the same license to all others who have, but fear to lose, power. The judgment that the risks of suppression are greater than the harm done

p. The meaning of racist speech is unclear. Justice McLachlin noted in her dissent in *Keegstra*:

The *Shorter Oxford English Dictionary* defines "hatred" as: "The condition or state of relations in which one person hates another; the emotion of hate; active dislike, detestation; enmity, ill-will, malevolence." The wide range of diverse emotions which the word "hatred" is capable of denoting is evident from this definition. Those who defend its use in § 319(2) of the *Criminal Code* emphasize one end of this range—hatred, they say, indicates the most powerful of virulent emotions lying beyond the bounds of human decency and limiting § 319(2) to extreme materials. Those who object to its use point to the other end of the range, insisting that "active dislike" is not an emotion for the promotion of which a person should be convicted as a criminal. To state the arguments is to make the case; "hatred" is a broad term capable of catching a wide variety of emotion.

by bad ideas rests upon faith in the ultimate good sense and decency of free people.

Archibald Cox, *First Amendment*, 24 Society 8 (1986).

Democracies seem to handle racist speech partly in light of their historical experiences, but the differences are also related to the way democracy works in a given country and to the value attributed to free speech in the constitutional system. Moreover, most liberal democracies, with the notable exception of the U.S., have ratified antidiscrimination and antiracism conventions, which require states to take steps against racism and racist discrimination, including racist speech.

These international instruments embody quite a different conception of freedom of expression from the case law under the US First Amendment. The international decisions reflect the much more explicit priorities of the relevant documents regarding the relationship between freedom of expression and the objective of eradicating speech, which advocates racial and cultural hatred. The approach seems to be to read down freedom of expression to the extent necessary to accommodate the legislation prohibiting the speech in question.

R. v. Keegstra, below, at 822 (Justice McLachlin, dissenting).

In this section we first review how the U.S. moved away from "group libel," thus decriminalizing insulting racist speech. This is contrasted with incitement of hatred and the singling out of racist speech, in particular, Holocaust denial. For other aspects of inciting speech, see *Ceylan* above and *Hindutva* in Chapter 8.

BEAUHARNAIS v. PEOPLE OF THE STATE OF ILLINOIS

Supreme Court (United States).
343 U.S. 250 (1952).

[The Illinois law prohibited the exhibition in any public place on any publication portraying "depravity, criminality, unchastity, or lack of virtue of a class of citizens, of any race, color, creed or religion [which exposes such citizens] to contempt, derision or obloquy or which is productive of breach of the peace or riots." Beauharnais was convicted under the above provision for organizing the distribution of a leaflet that petitioned the Mayor of Chicago "to halt * * * the invasion of white people * * * by the Negro" and called white people to unite "to prevent the white race from becoming mongrelized by the Negro." A membership application form to the White Circle League was attached to the flyer. The statute and the convictions were upheld by the Supreme Court.]

Mr. Justice Frankfurter delivered the opinion of the Court.

* * *

Libel of an individual was a common-law crime, and thus criminal in the colonies. Indeed, at common law, truth or good motives was no defense. In the first decades after the adoption of the Constitution, this was changed by judicial decision, statute or constitution in most States, but nowhere was there any suggestion that the crime of libel be abolished. It has been well observed that such utterances are no essential part of any exposition of ideas, and are of such slight social value as a step to truth that any benefit that may be derived from them is clearly outweighed by the social interest in order and morality. [*Chaplinsky.*]

No one will gainsay that it is libelous falsely to charge another with being a rapist, robber, carrier of knives and guns, and user of marijuana. The precise question before us, then, is whether the protection of 'liberty' in the Due Process Clause of the Fourteenth Amendment prevents a State from punishing such libels—as criminal libel has been defined, limited and constitutionally recognized time out of mind—directed at designated collectivities and flagrantly disseminated.

If an utterance directed at an individual may be the object of criminal sanctions, we cannot deny to a State power to punish the same utterance directed at a defined group, unless we can say that this a willful and purposeless restriction unrelated to the peace and well-being of the State.

Illinois did not have to look beyond her own borders or await the tragic experience of the last three decades to conclude that willful purveyors of falsehood concerning racial and religious groups promote strife and tend powerfully to obstruct the manifold adjustments required for free, ordered life in a metropolitan, polyglot community. From the murder of the abolitionist Love-joy in 1837 to the Cicero riots of 1951, Illinois has been the scene of exacerbated tension between races, often flaring into violence and destruction. In many of these outbreaks, utterances of the character here in question, so the Illinois legislature could conclude, played a significant part.

In the face of this history and its frequent obligation of extreme racial and religious propaganda, we would deny experience to say that the Illinois legislature was without reason in seeking ways to curb false or malicious defamation of racial and religious groups, made in public places and by means calculated to have a powerful emotional impact on those to whom it was presented.

It may be argued, and weightily, that this legislation will not help matters; that tension and on occasion violence between racial and religious groups must be traced to causes more deeply embedded in our society than the rantings of modern Know–Nothings. Only those lacking responsible humility will have a confident solution for problems as intractable as the frictions attributable to differences of race, color or religion. This being so, it would be out of bounds for the judiciary to deny the legislature a choice of policy, provided it is not unrelated to the problem and not forbidden by some explicit limitation on the State's power. That the legislative remedy might not in practice mitigate the evil, or might itself raise new problems, would only manifest once more the paradox of reform. It is the price to be paid for the trial-and-error inherent in legislative efforts to deal with obstinate social issues.

It is not within our competence to confirm or deny claims of social scientists as to the dependence of the individual on the position of his racial or religious group in the community. It would be quite outside the scope of our authority for us to deny that the Illinois Legislature may warrantably believe that a man's job and his educational opportunities and the dignity accorded him may depend as much on the reputation of the racial and religious group to which he willy-nilly belongs, as on his own merits. This being so, we are precluded from saying that speech concededly punishable when immediately directed at individuals cannot be outlawed if directed at groups with whose position and esteem in society the affiliated individual may be inextricably involved.

We are warned that the choice open to the Illinois legislature here may be abused, that prohibiting libel of a creed or of a racial group, is but a step from prohibiting libel of a political party.

Every power may be abused, but the possibility of abuse is a poor reason for denying Illinois the power to adopt measures against criminal libels sanctioned by centuries of Anglo–American law.

* * *

Affirmed.

Mr. Justice Black, with whom Mr. Justice Douglas concurs, dissenting.

* * *

The Court's reliance on *Chaplinsky* is also misplaced. New Hampshire had a state law making it an offense to direct insulting words at an individual on a public street. *Chaplinsky* had violated that law by calling a man vile names 'face-to-face'. We pointed out in that context that the use of such 'fighting' words was not an essential part of exposition of ideas. Whether the words used in their context here are 'fighting' words in the same sense is doubtful, but whether so or not they are not addressed to or about individuals. Moreover, the leaflet used here was also the means adopted by an assembled group to enlist interest in their efforts to have legislation enacted. And the fighting words were but a part of arguments on questions of wide public interest and importance. Freedom of petition, assembly, speech and press could be greatly abridged by a practice of meticulously scrutinizing every editorial, speech, sermon or other printed matter to extract two or three naughty words on which to hang charges of 'group libel.' The *Chaplinsky* case makes no such broad inroads on First Amendment freedoms.

If there be minority groups who hail this holding as their victory, they might consider the possible relevancy of this ancient remark:

'Another such victory and I am undone.'

Mr. Justice Douglas dissenting.

My view is that if in any case other public interests are to override the plain command of the First Amendment, the peril of speech must be clear and present, leaving no room for argument, raising no doubts as to the necessity of curbing speech in order to prevent disaster.

COLLIN v. SMITH

["SKOKIE" CASES]
Court of Appeals (United States).
578 F.2d 1197 (7th Cir.1978).

[During the 1960s and 1970s, the civil rights movement relied heavily on aggressive speech and less on laws that promised protection against those who attacked minorities. The Supreme Court, in *Brandenburg* (above), in 1969, set broader limits on the advocacy of violence as a means of social action. The new standard—"inciting or producing imminent lawless action"—was generally about public order (disorderly conduct), but because racist speech was likely in many situations to result in or threaten breach of peace, the standard had an immediate impact on the handling of racist expression. It was in this context that *Skokie* arose. The National Socialist Party of America, a small neo-Nazi party, applied for a permit to hold a march displaying Nazi symbols. After a *writ of certiorari* granted by the Supreme Court, the Illinois Supreme Court found, "albeit reluctantly," that the Nazi demonstration could be enjoined, even in regard to the display of the Swastika, as it did not amount to "fighting words." The Village of Skokie, Illinois, with a sizable population of Holocaust survivors, enacted an ordinance making it a misdemeanor to disseminate (including display) any material that promoted or incited racial or religious hatred. The planned "peaceful demonstration" was not permitted. Collin, the party leader, appealed.]

Circuit Judge Pell

Any shock effect caused by such a uniform must be attributed to the content of the ideas expressed or to the onlookers' dislike of demonstrations by defendants. "But '(i)t is firmly settled that under our Constitution the public expression of ideas may not be prohibited merely because the ideas are themselves offensive to some of their hearers,' (citations) or simply because bystanders object to peaceful and orderly demonstrations." (*Bachellar v. Maryland*, 397 U.S. 564, 567 [1970]) The third issue on appeal is whether the plaintiff has overcome the presumptive invalidity of the prior restraint on defendants' "marching, walking or parading or otherwise displaying the swastika on or off their person," which is Part B of the injunction order. Since the display of the swastika is an expression of defendants' ideas, however odious and repulsive to most members of our society, it will generally be considered protected speech unless it falls within the exceptions discussed in connection with the wearing of the uniform. There is no showing that the display or wearing of the swastika will incite anyone to immediately commit mass murder in furtherance of the aims of the German Nazi Party, or to commit any unlawful act in furtherance of the goals of the defendant Party. *Brandenburg*.

R.A.V. v. CITY OF ST. PAUL, MINNESOTA

Supreme Court (United States).
505 U.S. 377 (1992).

Justice Scalia delivered the opinion of the Court.

In the predawn hours of June 21, 1990, petitioner and several other teenagers allegedly burned [a] cross inside the fenced yard of a black family.[q] * * * [The] St. Paul Bias–Motivated Crime Ordinance, St. Paul, Minn., Legis. Code § 292.02 (1990), provides:

"Whoever places on public or private property a symbol, object, appellation, characterization or graffiti, including, but not limited to, a burning cross or Nazi swastika, which one knows or has reasonable grounds to know arouses anger, alarm or resentment in others on the basis of race, color, creed, religion or gender commits disorderly conduct and shall be guilty of a misdemeanor."

* * *

In construing the St. Paul ordinance, we are bound by the construction given to it by the Minnesota court. Accordingly, we accept the Minnesota Supreme Court's authoritative statement that the ordinance reaches only those expressions that constitute "fighting words" within the meaning of *Chaplinsky*. * * * [From] 1791 to the present, however, our society, like other free but civilized societies, has permitted restrictions upon the content of speech in a few limited areas, which are "of such slight social value as a step to truth that any benefit that may be derived from them is clearly outweighed by the social interest in order and morality." (*Chaplinsky*.)

* * *

[We] have sometimes said that these categories of expression are "not within the area of constitutionally protected speech," *Roth; Beauharnais; Chaplinsky;* or that the "protection of the First Amendment does not extend" to them, *Bose Corp. v. Consumers Union of United States, Inc.; Sable Communications of Cal., Inc. v. FCC.* * * * [What] they mean is that these areas of speech can, consistently with the First Amendment, be regulated because of their constitutionally proscribable content (obscenity, defamation, etc.)—not that they are categories of speech entirely invisible to the Constitution, so that they may be made the vehicles for content discrimination unrelated to their distinctively proscribable content. Thus, the government may proscribe libel; but it may not make the further content discrimination of proscribing only libel critical of the government. * * *

[We] have not said that they constitute "*no* part of the expression of ideas, but only that they constitute "no *essential* part of any exposition of ideas." *Chaplinsky*. * * *

[Even] the prohibition against content discrimination that we assert the First Amendment requires is not absolute. It applies differently in

q. Cross burning is a traditional action   arson or the lynching of blacks.
of the Ku Klux Klan, often followed by

the context of proscribable speech than in the area of fully protected speech. The rationale of the general prohibition, after all, is that content discrimination "rais[es] the specter that the Government may effectively drive certain ideas or viewpoints from the marketplace," *Simon & Schuster*. But content discrimination among various instances of a class of proscribable speech often does not pose this threat.

When the basis for the content discrimination consists entirely of the very reason the entire class of speech at issue is proscribable, no significant danger of idea or viewpoint discrimination exists. Such a reason, having been adjudged neutral enough to support exclusion of the entire class of speech from First Amendment protection, is also neutral enough to form the basis of distinction within the class. To illustrate: A State might choose to prohibit only that obscenity which is the most patently offensive in its prurience—i.e., that which involves the most lascivious displays of sexual activity. But it may not prohibit, for example, only that obscenity which includes offensive *political* messages. * * *

II

Applying these principles to the St. Paul ordinance, we conclude that, even as narrowly construed by the Minnesota Supreme Court, the ordinance is facially unconstitutional. [T]he ordinance applies only to "fighting words" that insult, or provoke violence, "on the basis of race, color, creed, religion or [gender]." Those who wish to use "fighting words" in connection with other ideas to express hostility, for example, on the basis of political affiliation, union membership, or homosexuality—are not covered. The First Amendment does not permit St. Paul to impose special prohibitions on those speakers who express views on disfavored subjects.

In its practical operation, moreover, the ordinance goes even beyond mere content discrimination, to actual viewpoint discrimination. Displays containing some words—odious racial epithets, for example—would be prohibited to proponents of all views. But "fighting words" that do not themselves invoke race, color, creed, religion, or gender—aspersions upon a person's mother, for example—would seemingly be usable ad libitum in the placards of those arguing in *favor* of racial, color, etc., tolerance and equality, but could not be used by those speakers' opponents. [One] must wholeheartedly agree with the Minnesota Supreme Court that "[i]t is the responsibility, even the obligation, of diverse communities to confront such notions in whatever form they appear," but the manner of that confrontation cannot consist of selective limitations upon speech. St. Paul's brief asserts that a general "fighting words" law would not meet the city's needs because only a content-specific measure can communicate to minority groups that the "group hatred" aspect of such speech "is not condoned by the majority." The point of the First Amendment is that majority preferences must be expressed in some fashion other than silencing speech on the basis of its content. * * *

[The] reason why fighting words are categorically excluded from the protection of the First Amendment is not that their content communicates any particular idea, but that their content embodies a particularly intolerable (and socially unnecessary) *mode* of expressing whatever idea the speaker wishes to convey. St. Paul has not singled out an especially offensive mode of expression—it has not, for example, selected for prohibition only those fighting words that communicate ideas in a threatening (as opposed to a merely obnoxious) manner.

* * * According to St. Paul, the ordinance is intended, "not to impact on [*sic*] the right of free expression of the accused," but rather to "protect against the victimization of a person or persons who are particularly vulnerable because of their membership in a group that historically has been discriminated against." Even assuming that an ordinance that completely proscribes, rather than merely regulates, a specified category of speech can ever be considered to be directed only to the secondary effects of such speech, it is clear that the St. Paul ordinance is not directed to secondary effects within the meaning of *Renton*. As we said in *Boos v. Barry*, 485 U.S. 312 (1988), "[L]isteners' reactions to speech are not the type of 'secondary effects' we referred to in *Renton*."

* * *

Finally, St. Paul and its *amici* [assert] that the ordinance helps to ensure the basic human rights of members of groups that have historically been subjected to discrimination, including the right of such group members to live in peace where they wish. We do not doubt that these interests are compelling, and that the ordinance can be said to promote them. But the "danger of censorship" presented by a facially content-based statute, requires that that weapon be employed only where it is "*necessary* to serve the asserted [compelling] interest." The existence of adequate content-neutral alternatives thus "undercut[s] significantly" any defense of such a statute.

* * *

Justice White, with whom Justice Blackmun and Justice O'Connor join, and with whom Justice Stevens joins except as to Part I–A, concurring in the judgment.

* * *

I

A

* * * Today [the] Court announces that earlier Courts did not mean their repeated statements that certain categories of expression are "not within the area of constitutionally protected speech." *Roth.* * * * [It] is inconsistent to hold that the government may proscribe an entire category of speech because the content of that speech is evil, but that the government may not treat a subset of that category differently without violating the First Amendment; the content of the subset is by definition worthless and undeserving of constitutional protection.

The majority's observation that fighting words are "quite expressive indeed," is no answer. Fighting words are not a means of exchanging views, rallying supporters, or registering a protest; they are directed against individuals to provoke violence or to inflict injury.

* * * Indeed, by characterizing fighting words as a form of "debate" the majority legitimates hate speech as a form of public discussion. * * *

B

[Although] the First Amendment does not apply to categories of unprotected speech, such as fighting words, the Equal Protection Clause requires that the regulation of unprotected speech be rationally related to a legitimate government interest. A defamation statute that drew distinctions on the basis of political affiliation * * * would unquestionably fail rational basis review.

Turning to the St. Paul ordinance and assuming arguendo, as the majority does, that the ordinance is not constitutionally overbroad (but see Part II, *infra*), there is no question that it would pass equal protection review. The ordinance [reflects] the City's judgment that harms based in race, color, creed, religion, or gender are more pressing public concerns than the harms caused by other fighting words. In light of our Nation's long and painful experience with discrimination, this determination is plainly reasonable.

II

I would decide the case on overbreadth grounds. * * * Our fighting words cases have made clear, however, that such generalized reactions are not sufficient to strip expression of its constitutional protection. The mere fact that expressive activity causes hurt feelings, offense, or resentment does not render the expression unprotected. * * * Although the ordinance reaches conduct that is unprotected, it also makes criminal expressive conduct that causes only hurt feelings, offense, or resentment, and is protected by the First Amendment.

Justice Blackmun, concurring in the judgment.

I regret what the Court has done in this case. The majority opinion signals one of two possibilities: It will serve as precedent for future cases, or it will not. Either result is disheartening.

In the first instance, by deciding that a State cannot regulate speech that causes great harm unless it also regulates speech that does not (setting law and logic on their heads), the Court seems to abandon the categorical approach, and inevitably to relax the level of scrutiny applicable to content-based laws. As Justice White points out, this weakens the traditional protections of speech. If all expressive activity must be accorded the same protection, that protection will be scant. The simple reality is that the Court will never provide child pornography or cigarette advertising the level of protection customarily granted political speech. If we are forbidden to categorize, as the Court has done here, we shall reduce protection across the board. It is sad that in its effort to reach a satisfying result in this case, the Court is willing to weaken First Amendment protections.

In the second instance is the possibility that this case will not significantly alter First Amendment jurisprudence but, instead, will be regarded as an aberration—a case where the Court manipulated doctrine to strike down an ordinance whose premise it opposed, namely, that racial threats and verbal assaults are of greater harm than other fighting words. I fear that the Court has been distracted from its proper mission by the temptation to decide the issue over "politically correct speech" and "cultural diversity," neither of which is presented here. If this is the meaning of today's opinion, it is perhaps even more regrettable.

Mari J. Matsuda, PUBLIC RESPONSE TO RACIST SPEECH: CONSIDERING THE VICTIM'S STORY,

87 Mich. L. Rev. 2320, 2321–2322, 2326–2327, 2336, 2357–2358, 2360 (1989).*

* * *

In calling for legal sanctions for racist speech, this Article rejects an absolutist first amendment position. It calls for movement of the societal response to racist speech from the private to the public realm. The choice of public sanction, enforced by the state, is a significant one. The kinds of injuries and harms historically left to private individuals to absorb and resist through private means is no accident. The places where the law does not go to redress harm have tended to be the places where women, children, people of color, and poor people live. This absence of law is itself another story with a message, perhaps unintended, about the relative value of different human lives. A legal response to racist speech is a statement that victims of racism are valued members of our polity.

* * *

The identity of the person doing the analysis often seems to make the difference, however, in responding to racist speech. In advocating legal restriction of hate speech, I have found my most sympathetic audience in people who identify with target groups, while I have encountered incredulity, skepticism, and even hostility from others.

This split in reaction is also evident in case studies of hate speech. The typical reaction of target-group members to an incident of racist propaganda is alarm and immediate calls for redress. The typical reaction of non-target-group members is to consider the incidents isolated pranks, the product of sick-but-harmless minds. This is in part a defensive reaction: a refusal to believe that real people, people just like us, are racists. This disassociation leads logically to the claim that there is no institutional or state responsibility to respond to the incident. It is not the kind of real and pervasive threat that requires the state's power to quell.

* * *

* Appearing in final form in **Words that Wound: Critical Race Theory, Assaultive Speech, and the First Amendment** (M. J. Matsuda, C. R. Lawrence III, R. Delgado, and K. W. Crenshaw eds., 1993).

The negative effects of hate messages are real and immediate for the victims. Victims of vicious hate propaganda have experienced physiological symptoms and emotional distress ranging from fear in the gut, rapid pulse rate and difficulty in breathing, nightmares, post-traumatic stress disorder, hypertension, psychosis, and suicide. * * *

Victims are restricted in their personal freedom. In order to avoid receiving hate messages, victims have had to quit jobs, forgo education, leave their homes, avoid certain public places, curtail their own exercise of speech rights, and otherwise modify their behavior and demeanor. * * *

In order to respect first amendment values, a narrow definition of actionable racist speech is required. * * *

In order to distinguish the worst, paradigm example of racist hate messages from other forms of racist and nonracist speech, three identifying characteristics are suggested here:

    1.   The message is of racial inferiority;

    2.   The message is directed against a historically oppressed group; and

    3.   The message is persecutorial, hateful, and degrading.

Making each element a prerequisite to prosecution prevents opening of the dreaded floodgates of censorship.

The first element is the primary identifier of racist speech: racist speech proclaims racial inferiority and denies the personhood of target group members. All members of the target group are at once considered alike and inferior.

The second element attempts to further define racism by recognizing the connection of racism to power and subordination. Racism is more than race hatred or prejudice. It is the structural subordination of a group based on an idea of racial inferiority. Racist speech is particularly harmful because it is a mechanism of subordination, reinforcing a historical vertical relationship.

The final element is related to the "fighting words" idea. The language used in the worst form of racist speech is language that is, and is intended as, persecutorial, hateful, and degrading.

    * * *

What is argued here, then, is that we accept certain principles as the shared historical legacy of the world community. Racial supremacy is one of the ideas we have collectively and internationally considered and rejected. As an idea connected to continuing racism and degradation of minority groups, it causes real harm to its victims. We are not safe when these violent words are among us.

Treating racist speech as sui generis and universally condemned on the basis of its content and the harmful effect of its content is precisely the censorship that civil libertarians fear. I would argue, however, that explicit content-based rejection of narrowly defined racist speech is more protective of civil liberties than the competing-interests tests or the likely-to-incite-violence tests that can spill over to censor forms of political speech.

Notes and Questions

1. The actual holding of *Beauharnais* was that the prohibition of language that defames races or religions bore a rational relation to the state's goal of preventing violence and disorder. Professor Kalven was particularly concerned that *Beauharnais* moved dangerously close to declaring seditious libel laws constitutional. He wrote that seditious libel "is the doctrine that criticism of government officials and policy may be viewed as defamation of government and may be punished as a serious crime. [In] my view, the absence of seditious libel as a crime is the true pragmatic test of freedom of speech." Harry Kalven, *The Negro and the First Amendment* 15 (1965).

The Court has since abandoned the rational-relation-to-purpose approach to First Amendment cases and now requires that laws which restrict free speech and assembly be necessary to achieve compelling state purposes. See, e.g., *N.A.A.C.P. v. Button*, 371 U.S. 415, 438–44 (1963). Does *Beauharnais* survive *New York Times v. Sullivan*? In *Collin* the village introduced evidence in the district court tending to prove that some individuals, at least, might have had difficulty restraining their reactions to the Nazi demonstration. Would one rely on a fear of responsive violence to justify the ordinance? Look at *Brandenburg*. Would one use the argument in the context of the German *Holocaust Denial Case* (below) (prohibiting the public meeting where David Irving, the infamous revisionist historian, was scheduled to speak)?

2. *Collin* might be seen as a complete break with the *Beauharnais* position. The USSC has never overruled *Beauharnais*, but certiorari was not granted when review of the Seventh Circuit Skokie decision was asked for. See *Smith v. Collin*, 439 U.S. 916 (1978).

Justice Blackmun (joined by Justice White) dissented:

I feel the Seventh Circuit's decision is in some tension with *Beauharnais*. That case has not been overruled or formally limited in any way. I therefore would grant certiorari in order to resolve any possible conflict that may exist between the ruling of the Seventh Circuit here and *Beauharnais*. I also feel that the present case affords the Court an opportunity to consider whether, in the context of the facts that this record appears to present, there is no limit whatsoever to the exercise of free speech. There indeed may be no such limit, but when citizens assert, not casually but with deep conviction, that the proposed demonstration is scheduled at a place and in a manner that is taunting and overwhelmingly offensive to the citizens of that place, that assertion, uncomfortable though it may be for judges, deserves to be examined. It just might fall into the same category as one's "right" to cry "fire" in a crowded theater, for "the character of every act depends upon the circumstances in which it is done." *Schenck*.

3. The Circuit Court, in *Collin*, held that "because the ordinances turn on the content of the demonstration, they are necessarily not time, place, or manner regulations." *Police Dep't of City of Chicago v. Mosley* 408 U.S. 92, 99 (1972). Does the operation of a marketplace of ideas require the constitu-

tional protection of offensive speech? Is it not the case that the march of the Nazis would have brought nothing new to the market? Should that be decisive?

4. Justice Scalia, in *R.A.V.*, refers to the possibility of proscribing threatening words. What kind of threat is needed under the clear and present danger test? Compare the definitions of content based and viewpoint based discrimination offered by Justice Scalia and by the concurring opinions. Is "discrimination based on content" strictly a U.S.-based concern? What makes overbreadth[r] and vagueness a specific concern for free speech? It is a generally held canon in constitutional interpretation that wherever there is a possibility for a fair interpretation to be given to a statute that would be constitutional, the text should be read accordingly. Why is there a departure from that doctrine in the U.S.? "[P]unishment for an utterance already offends Art. 5 (1) when it does not possess the meaning that a court reads into it or when the court punishes one meaning [of the utterance] in the face of multiple meanings without [making an effort] convincingly to exclude [these] other possible meanings." Is the position of the *Tucholsky I* Court similar to the American concept of vagueness?[s]

5. The toleration of hate speech in *R.A.V.* was severely criticized, although not for the reasons hate speech is found impermissible in Europe. Judith Butler argues that cross burning is not speech but action.

> That the cross burns and thus constitutes an incendiary destruction is not considered as a sign of the intention to reproduce that incendiary destruction at the site of the house or the family; the historical correlation between cross-burning and marking a community, a family, or an individual for further violence is also ignored. How much of that burning is translatable into a declarative or constative proposition? And how would one know exactly what constative claim is being made by the burning cross? If the cross is the expression of a viewpoint, is it a declaration as in, 'I am of the opinion that black people ought not to live in this neighborhood' or even, 'I am of the opinion that violence ought to be perpetrated against black people,' or is it a perlocutionary performative, as in imperatives and commands which take the form of 'Burn!' or 'Die!'? Is it an injunction that works its power metonymically not only in the sense that the fire recalls prior burnings which have served to mark black people as targets for violence, but also in the sense that the fire is understood to be transferable from the cross to the target that is marked by the cross? The relation between cross-burning and torchings of both persons and properties is historically established. Hence, from this perspective, the burning cross assumes the status of a direct address and a threat and, as such, is construed either as the incipient moment of injurious action or as the statement of an intention to injure.

Judith Butler, *Excitable Speech: A Politics of the Performative* 57 (1997).

r. A law is void on its face if it "does not aim specifically at evils within the allowable area of [government] control, but sweeps within its ambit other activities that constitute an exercise" of free speech. *Thornhill v. Alabama*, 310 U.S. 88, 97 (1940).

s. A law is void on its face (violating due process) if it is so vague that persons "of common intelligence must necessarily guess at its meaning and differ as to its application." *Connally v. General Construction Co.*, 269 U.S. 385, 391 (1926). This doctrine is particularly important in the context of the First Amendment, for "where a vague statute '[abuts] upon sensitive areas of basic First Amendment freedoms,' it 'operates to inhibit the exercise of [those] freedoms.' Uncertain meanings inevitably lead citizens 'to steer far wider of the unlawful zone' [than] if the boundaries of the forbidden areas were clearly marked.'" *Grayned v. Rockford*, 408 U.S. 104, 109 (1972).

Owen Fiss suggests a political interpretation of the case: "The Supreme Court has been measured in its protection of subversive advocacy. Communists were allowed to engage in the general advocacy of revolution, but the Court drew the line when advocacy turned into incitement." Owen M. Fiss, *Liberalism Divided: Freedom of Speech and the Many Uses of State Power* 115 (1996).

6.   Friedrich Kübler, *How Much Freedom For Racist Speech? Transnational Aspects of a Conflict of Human Rights*, 27 Hofstra L. Rev. 335, 361–62 (1998):

> The European experience suggests a final observation. In *R.A.V. v. City of St. Paul*, the majority opinion framed the issue as one of protecting minorities 'who express views on disfavored subjects' against the majority's 'special hostility towards the particular biases thus singled out.' Even if this reflects an accurate understanding of the issue within the sophisticated web of the political process in a country like the United States, it is much less than an adequate description of what has happened and happens in other places. The construction of racial differences between people, and the propagandistic degradation and dehumanization of groups thus singled out and separated, is used as an efficient instrument to maximize power. In this game, the limits between 'private' and 'state' action become blurred and the rivaling factions grasp and usurp functions of government in order to enhance and stabilize their influence. The closer they get to public office, the more they become interested in gaining and retaining a certain amount of respectability in order to gain the support they need domestically and from abroad. Rules outlawing the language which denies individuals and groups the dignity of human beings can help to interfere with such a strategy; respectability will less easily be reconciled with permanent illegal action. Therefore, laws against racist speech can have symbolic importance; they show effects even before or without being enforced by courts. This impact will be strengthened if the law is supported by international agreements mandating such rules.

7.   The following opposing positions highlight the differences between Europe and the U.S.:

> The first inherent assumption is that once we concede to government the power to outlaw expression of an almost certainly false idea, we have opened the way for a general governmental power of suppressing unacceptable ideas. We cannot have a law prohibiting racist speech because it would allow government the power to suppress other speech on the basis of its content.[113]

> It appears to me that this is a typically American type of argument. Americans have two sensitivities which are not necessarily shared by civil libertarians in other democratic regimes.

> It is the assumption that restrictions on false ideas are placed solely because: (1) those ideas are false, and (2) we wish to prevent spread of false ideas in society. We have seen, however, that while limiting the spread of ideas is one ground for limiting racist speech, it is not the only

---

113.   T. Emerson, The System of Freedom of Expression 398 (1970): '[G]roup libel laws are premised on the proposition that the government is entitled to determine the social value of expression and to proscribe any expression it decides has insufficient value.'

ground. Just as important is the harm caused by the speech itself in undermining human dignity and the security people are entitled to enjoy as free, equal, autonomous individuals. It is difficult to see how anyone could demonstrate that the danger of overzealous suppression of speech by government outweighs the damage caused to Nazi victims forced to tolerate Nazis marching outside their houses, or to blacks bombarded with Ku Klux Klan propaganda.

David Kretzmer, *Freedom of Speech and Racism*, 8 Cardozo L. Rev. 445 (1987).

There is much respectable opinion that would ban public meetings of the National Front in the UK and the Nazi Party and the Ku Klux Klan in the U.S. While such appeals are superficially attractive, in my opinion it would be a serious mistake to adopt that position. Many sorts of ideas are repugnant to members of the community, and if government is allowed to ban some ideas it will surely ban others—including those that opponents of racist speech might find attractive. Democratic premises require protection of all points of view, even the most hateful. As Oliver Wendell Holmes once wrote, "If there is any principle of the Constitution that more imperatively calls for attachment than any other it is the principle of free thought—not free thought for those who agree with us, but freedom for the thought that we hate". Furthermore, from a practical standpoint, if the marketplace of ideas cannot be trusted to winnow out the hateful, there is no reason to believe that censorship will do it. The ideas will persist, and martyrs to an ugly cause will be created by operation of law.

In the UK, the law permits restriction of the right of protest if there is a threat of "serious public disorder", but even this standard could be mischievous. If there is such a threat, the proper remedy is to restrain those who would interfere with speech, not those who wish to express themselves. In the US the American Civil Liberties Union adhered to this position several years ago when a 'Nazi' group sought to demonstrate peaceably in the town of Skokie, Illinois, where many Jewish survivors of Hitler's death camps resided. ACLU lawyers represented the Nazis in extensive court proceedings, and eventually secured their right to march, which was short and nonviolent.

Norman Dorsen, *A Transatlantic View of Civil Liberties in the United Kingdom, in Civil Liberties* 358–59 (P. Wallington ed., 1984).

R. v. KEEGSTRA

Supreme Court (Canada).
[1990] 3 S.C.R. 697.

Dickson C.J.C. (Wilson, L' Heureux–Dubé, and Gonthier JJ., concurring)

2. * * * Keegstra was a high school teacher * * * from the early 1970s until his dismissal in 1982. In 1984, Mr. Keegstra was charged under s.319(2) (then 281.2[2]) of the Criminal Code with unlawfully promoting hatred against an identifiable group by communicating anti-Semitic statements to his students. He was convicted by a jury in a trial before McKenzie J of the Alberta Court of Queen's Bench.

3. * * * He taught his classes that * * * Jews "created the Holocaust to gain sympathy" * * * and expected his students to reproduce his teachings in class and on exams. If they failed to do so, their marks suffered.

[After conviction, Keegstra appealed, claiming that s. 319(2) of the Criminal Code unjustifiably infringed his freedom of expression as guaranteed by s. 2(b) of the Charter.ᵗ]

Criminal Code:

8. 319 * * *

(2) Every one who, by communicating statements, other than in private conversation, wilfully promotes hatred against any identifiable group is guilty of

(a) an indictable offence.

(3) No person shall be convicted of an offence under subsection (2)

(a) if he establishes that the statements communicated were true;

(b) if, in good faith, he expressed or attempted to establish by argument an opinion upon a religious subject;

(c) if the statements were relevant to any subject of public interest, the discussion of which was for the public benefit, and if on reasonable grounds he believed them to be true; or

(d) if, in good faith, he intended to point out, for the purpose of removal, matters producing or tending to produce feelings of hatred towards an identifiable group in Canada.

* * *

318(4) * * * "identifiable group" means any section of the public distinguished by colour, race, religion or ethnic origin.

* * *

V. The History of Hate Propaganda Crimes in Canada

* * *

23. * * * Following the Second World War and revelation of the Holocaust, in Canada and throughout the world a desire grew to protect human rights, and especially to guard against discrimination. Internationally, this desire led to the landmark Universal Declaration of Human

t. The Canadian Charter of Rights and Freedoms, 1982 provides as follows:

Section 1 [Limitation of Rights]

The Canadian Charter of Rights and Freedoms guarantees the rights and freedoms set out in it subject only to such reasonable limits prescribed by law as can be demonstrably justified in a free and democratic society.

Section 2 [Freedom of Religion, Speech, Association]

Everyone has the following fundamental freedoms:

(a) freedom of conscience and religion;

(b) freedom of thought, belief, opinion and expression, including freedom of the press and other means of communication;

(c) freedom of peaceful assembly; and

(d) freedom of association.

Rights in 1948, and, with reference to hate propaganda, was eventually manifested in two international human rights instruments.

* * *

VI.　Section 2(b) of the Charter–Freedom of Expression

* * *

35.　* * * Communications which wilfully promote hatred against an identifiable group without doubt convey a meaning, and are intended to do so by those who make them. [Hate speech is expression protected under 2(b). It is not a form of violence.]

VII.　Section I Analysis of s.319(2)

A.　General Approach to Section I

* * *

49.　Obviously, a practical application of s. I requires more than an incantation of the words "free and democratic society." These words require some definition, an elucidation as to the values that they invoke. To a large extent, a free and democratic society embraces the very values and principles which Canadians have sought to protect and further by entrenching specific rights and freedoms in the Constitution, although the balancing exercise in s. I is not restricted to values expressly set out in the Charter. * * *

C.　Objective of s. 319(2)

* * *

(i) Harm caused by expression promoting the hatred of identifiable groups

63.　Looking to the legislation challenged in this appeal, one must ask whether the amount of hate propaganda in Canada causes sufficient harm to justify legislative intervention of some type.

64.　* * * [T]he presence of hate propaganda in Canada is sufficiently substantial to warrant concern. Disquiet caused by the existence of such material is not simply the product of its offensiveness, however, but stems from the very real harm which it causes. Essentially, there are two sorts of injury caused by hate propaganda. First, there is harm done to members of the target group. It is indisputable that the emotional damage caused by words may be of grave psychological and social consequence. * * *

65.　In my opinion, a response of humiliation and degradation from an individual targeted by hate propaganda is to be expected. A person's sense of human dignity and belonging to the community at large is closely linked to the concern and respect accorded to the groups to which he or she belongs. * * * The derision, hostility and abuse encouraged by hate propaganda therefore have a severely negative impact on the individual's sense of self-worth and acceptance.

* * *

66.　A second harmful effect of hate propaganda which is of pressing and substantial concern is its influence upon society at large. * * * It is thus not inconceivable that the active dissemination of hate propaganda can attract individuals to its cause, and in the process create serious discord between various cultural groups in society. Moreover, the alteration of views held by the recipients of hate propaganda may occur subtly, and is not always attendant upon conscious acceptance of the communicated ideas. * * *

(ii) International human rights instruments

69.   * * * I would also refer to international human rights principles * * * for guidance with respect to assessing the legislative objective.

70.   Generally speaking, the international human rights obligations taken on by Canada reflect the values and principles of a free and democratic society, and thus those values and principles that underlie the Charter itself. * * * Moreover, international human rights law and Canada's commitments in that area are of particular significance in assessing the importance of Parliament's objective under s. 1. * * *

71.   No aspect of international human rights has been given attention greater than that focused upon discrimination. * * *

72.   In 1966, the United Nations adopted the *International Convention on the Elimination of All Forms of Racial Discrimination,* Can. TS 1970, No. 28 (hereinafter CERD). The Convention, in force since 1969 and including Canada among its signatory members, contains a resolution that States Parties agree to:

> * * * adopt all necessary measures for speedily eliminating racial discrimination in all its forms and manifestations, and to prevent and combat racist doctrines and practices in order to promote understanding between races and to build an international community free from all forms of racial segregation and racial discrimination.

Article 4 of the CERD is of special interest, providing that:

> States Parties condemn all propaganda and all organizations which are based on ideas or theories of superiority of one race or group of persons of one colour or ethnic origin, or which attempt to justify or promote racial hatred and discrimination in any form, and undertake to adopt immediate and positive measures designed to eradicate all incitement to, or acts of, such discrimination and, to this end, with due regard to the principles embodied in the *Universal Declaration of Human Rights* and the rights expressly set forth in article 5 of this Convention, *inter alia:*

> a.   Shall declare an offence punishable by law all dissemination of ideas based on racial superiority or hatred, incitement to racial discrimination, as well as all acts of violence or incitement to such acts against any race or group of persons of another colour or ethnic origin, and also the provision of any assistance to racist activities, including the financing thereof;

73.   Further, the *International Covenant on Civil and Political Rights,* 999 UNTS 171 (1966) (hereinafter ICCPR), adopted by the United Nations in 1966 and in force in Canada since 1976 * * *

guarantees the freedom of expression [in Art. 19] while simultaneously prohibiting the advocacy of hatred: * * * Article 20 [states]: "1. Any propaganda for war shall be prohibited by law. 2. Any advocacy of national, racial or religious hatred that constitutes incitement to discrimination, hostility or violence shall be prohibited by law."

* * *

(iii) Other provisions of the Charter

78. Significant indicia of the strength of the objective behind s. 319(2) are gleaned not only from the international arena, but are also expressly evident in various provisions of the Charter itself * * * Most importantly for the purposes of this appeal, ss. 15 and 27 represent a strong commitment to the values of equality and multiculturalism, and hence underline the great importance of Parliament's objective in prohibiting hate propaganda.

* * *

(iv) Conclusion respecting objective of s. 319(2)

85. In my opinion, it would be impossible to deny that Parliament's objective in enacting s. 319(2) is of the utmost importance. Parliament has recognized the substantial harm that can flow from hate propaganda, and in trying to prevent the pain suffered by target group members and to reduce racial, ethnic and religious tension in Canada has decided to suppress the wilful promotion of hatred against identifiable groups.

D. Proportionality

* * *

87. * * * [T]he interpretation of s. 2(b) under *Irwin Toy* gives protection to a very wide range of expression. Content is irrelevant to this interpretation, the result of a high value being placed upon freedom of expression in the abstract. This approach to s. 2(b) often operates to leave unexamined the extent to which the expression at stake in a particular case promotes freedom of expression principles. In my opinion, however, the s. I analysis of a limit upon s. 2(b) cannot ignore the nature of the expressive activity which the state seeks to restrict. While we must guard carefully against judging expression according to its popularity, it is equally destructive of free expression values, as well as the other values which underlie a free and democratic society, to treat all expression as equally crucial to those principles at the core of s. 2(b).

* * *

91. From the outset, I wish to make clear that in my opinion the expression prohibited by s. 319(2) is not closely linked to the rationale underlying s. 2(b). * * *

92. At the core of freedom of expression lies the need to ensure that truth and the common good are attained, whether in scientific and artistic endeavors or in the process of determining the best course to take in our political affairs. Since truth and the ideal form of political and social organization can rarely, if at all, be identified with absolute certainty, it is difficult to prohibit expression without impeding the free exchange of potentially valuable information. * * * Taken to its ex-

treme, this argument would require us to permit the communication of all expression, it being impossible to know with absolute certainty which factual statements are true, or which ideas obtain the greatest good. The problem with this extreme position, however, is that the greater the degree of certainty that a statement is erroneous or mendacious, the less its value in the quest for truth. Indeed, expression can be used to the detriment of our search for truth; the state should not be the sole arbiter of truth, but neither should we overplay the view that rationality will overcome all falsehoods in the unregulated marketplace of ideas. There is very little chance that statements intended to promote hatred against an identifiable group are true, or that their vision of society will lead to a better world. To portray such statements as crucial to truth and the betterment of the political and social milieu is therefore misguided.

[Chief Justice Dickson recognizes that self-fulfillment is also an important free speech objective. However, this self-fulfillment is realized in a community and it must "therefore be tempered insofar as it advocates with inordinate vitriol an intolerance and prejudice which views as execrable the process of individual self-development and human flourishing among all members of society."]

94. Moving on to a third strain of thought said to justify the protection of free expression, one's attention is brought specifically to the political realm. The connection between freedom of expression and the political process is perhaps the linchpin of the s. 2(b) guarantee, and the nature of this connection is largely derived from the Canadian commitment to democracy. Freedom of expression is a crucial aspect of the democratic commitment, not merely because it permits the best policies to be chosen from among a wide array of proffered options, but additionally because it helps to ensure that participation in the political process is open to all persons. * * *

* * *

95. * * * I am aware that the use of strong language in political and social debate—indeed, perhaps even language intended to promote hatred—is an unavoidable part of the democratic process. Moreover, I recognize that hate propaganda is expression of a type which would generally be categorized as "political," thus putatively placing it at the very heart of the principle extolling freedom of expression as vital to the democratic process. Nonetheless, expression can work to undermine our commitment to democracy where employed to propagate ideas anathemic to democratic values. Hate propaganda works in just such a way. * * *

96. Indeed, one may quite plausibly contend that it is through rejecting hate propaganda that the state can best encourage the protection of values central to freedom of expression, while simultaneously demonstrating dislike for the vision forwarded by hate-mongers. * * *

(ii) Rational connection

102. * * * [I]t would be difficult to deny that the suppression of hate propaganda reduces the harm such expression does to individuals who belong to identifiable groups and to relations between various cultural and religious groups in Canadian society.

103. Doubts have been raised, however, as to whether the actual effect of s. 319(2) is to undermine any rational connection between it and Parliament's objective. As stated in the reasons of MCLACHLIN J., there are three primary ways in which the effect of the impugned legislation might be seen as an irrational means of carrying out the Parliamentary purpose. First, it is argued that the provision may actually promote the cause of hate-mongers by earning them extensive media attention. In this vein, it is also suggested that persons accused of intentionally promoting hatred often see themselves as martyrs, and may actually generate sympathy from the community in the role of underdogs engaged in battle against the immense powers of the state. Second, the public may view the suppression of expression by the government with suspicion, making it possible that such expression— even if it be hate propaganda—is perceived as containing an element of truth. Finally, it is often noted * * * that Germany of the 1920s and 1930s possessed and used hate propaganda laws similar to those existing in Canada, and yet these laws did nothing to stop the triumph of a racist philosophy under the Nazis.

104. * * * I recognize that the effect of s. 319(2) is impossible to define with exact precision—the same can be said for many laws, criminal or otherwise. In my view, however, the position that there is no strong and evident connection between the criminalization of hate propaganda and its suppression is unconvincing. * * *

105. It is undeniable that media attention has been extensive on those occasions when s. 319(2) has been used. Yet from my perspective, s. 319(2) serves to illustrate to the public the severe reprobation with which society holds messages of hate directed towards racial and religious groups. The existence of a particular criminal law, and the process of holding a trial when that law is used, is thus itself a form of expression, and the message sent out is that hate propaganda is harmful to target group members and threatening to a harmonious society. * * *

106. In this context, it can also be said that government suppression of hate propaganda will not make the expression attractive and hence increase acceptance of its content.

     * * *

108. [I] therefore conclude that the first branch of the proportionality test has been met. * * *

(iii) Minimal impairment of the s. 2(b) freedom

     * * *

110. The main argument of those who would strike down s. 319(2) is that it creates a real possibility of punishing expression that is not hate propaganda. It is thus submitted that the legislation is overbroad, its terms so wide as to include expression which does not relate to Parliament's objective, and also unduly vague, in that a lack of clarity and precision in its words prevents individuals from discerning its meaning with any accuracy. In either instance, it is said that the effect of s. 319(2) is to limit the expression of merely unpopular or unconventional communications. Such communications may present no risk of causing

the harm which Parliament seeks to prevent, and will perhaps be closely associated with the core values of s. 2(b). This overbreadth and vagueness could consequently allow the state to employ s. 319(2) to infringe excessively the freedom of expression or, what is more likely, could have a chilling effect whereby persons potentially within s. 319(2) would exercise self-censorship. Accordingly, those attacking the validity of s. 319(2) contend that vigorous debate on important political and social issues, so highly valued in a society that prizes a diversity of ideas, is unacceptably suppressed by the provision.

* * *

111.   * * * In order to * * * determine whether s. 319(2) minimally impairs the freedom of expression, the nature and impact of specific features of the provision must be examined in some detail. * * *

118.   * * * The problem is said to lie in the failure of the offence to require proof of actual hatred resulting from a communication, the assumption being that only such proof can demonstrate a harm serious enough to justify limiting the freedom of expression under s. 1. It was largely because of this lack of need for proof of actual hatred that KERANS J.A. in the Court of Appeal held s. 319(2) to violate the Charter.

119.   * * * First, to predicate the limitation of free expression upon proof of actual hatred gives insufficient attention to the severe psychological trauma suffered by members of those identifiable groups targeted by hate propaganda. Second, it is clearly difficult to prove a causative link between a specific statement and hatred of an identifiable group. In fact, to require direct proof of hatred in listeners would severely debilitate the effectiveness of s. 319(2) in achieving Parliament's aim. * * *

124.   The factors mentioned above suggest that s. 319(2) does not unduly restrict the s. 2(b) guarantee. * * *

131.   * * * I should comment on a final argument marshalled in support of striking down s. 319(2) because of overbreadth or vagueness. It is said that the presence of the legislation has led authorities to interfere with a diverse range of political, educational and artistic expression, demonstrating only too well the way in which overbreadth and vagueness can result in undue intrusion and the threat of persecution. In this regard, a number of incidents are cited where authorities appear to have been overzealous in their interpretation of the law, including the arrest of individuals distributing pamphlets admonishing Americans to leave the country and the temporary holdup at the border of a film entitled *Nelson Mandela* and Salman Rushdie's novel *Satanic Verses* (1988)

132.   That s. 319(2) may in the past have led authorities to restrict expression offering valuable contributions to the arts, education or politics in Canada is surely worrying. I hope, however, that my comments as to the scope of the provision make it obvious that only the most intentionally extreme forms of expression will find a place within s. 319(2). In this light, one can safely say that the incidents mentioned above illustrate not over-expansive breadth and vagueness in the law,

but rather actions by the state which cannot be lawfully taken pursuant to s. 319(2). The possibility of illegal police harassment clearly has minimal bearing on the proportionality of hate propaganda legislation to legitimate Parliamentary objectives, and hence the argument based on such harassment can be rejected.

c.   Alternative modes of furthering Parliament's objective

133.   * * * [I]t is said that non-criminal responses can more effectively combat the harm caused by hate propaganda. * * *

134.   Given the stigma and punishment associated with a criminal conviction and the presence of other modes of government response in the fight against intolerance, it is proper to ask whether s. 319(2) can be said to impair minimally the freedom of expression. With respect to the efficacy of criminal legislation in advancing the goals of equality and multicultural tolerance in Canada, I agree that the role of s. 319(2) will be limited. * * *

135.   In assessing the proportionality of a legislative enactment to a valid governmental objective, however, s. 1 should not operate in every instance so as to force the government to rely upon only the mode of intervention least intrusive of a Charter right or freedom. It may be that a number of courses of action are available in the furtherance of a pressing and substantial objective, each imposing a varying degree of restriction upon a right or freedom. In such circumstances, the government may legitimately employ a more restrictive measure, either alone or as part of a larger programme of action, if that measure is not redundant, furthering the objective in ways that alternative responses could not, and is in all other respects proportionate to a valid s. 1 aim.

     * * *

138.   I thus conclude that s. 319(2) of the *Criminal Code* does not unduly impair the freedom of expression. * * *

[With respect to the third branch of the proportionality test, Chief Justice Dickson emphasizes the enormous importance of the objective of s. 319(2): "Few concerns can be as central to the concept of a free and democratic society as the dissipation of racism, and the especially strong value which Canadian society attaches to this goal must never be forgotten in assessing the effects of an impugned legislative measure." He then concludes that in light of that objective, the effects of s. 319(2), "involving as they do the restriction of expression largely removed from the heart of free expression values, are not of such a deleterious nature as to outweigh any advantage gleaned from the limitation of s. 2(b)." The infringement of freedom of expression is therefore upheld as a reasonable limit under s. 1. Chief Justice Dickson concludes that the presumption of innocence is infringed but that the limitation of the right can be upheld under s. 1.]

[Justice McLachlin (Justice Sopinka concurring), dissenting, finds lack of rational connection and refers to the chilling effects of the criminal provision.]

     [Appeal allowed.]

Notes and Questions

1. Chief Justice Dickson found the U.S. free speech doctrine, in the version that departed from *Beauharnais*, inapplicable, given the language of the Canadian Charter, which contains an express limitation. Is there any specific in Canadian society that makes the "clear and present danger" test irrelevant? Is it an acceptable argument that the protection of speech should be social-context bound? What could be the U.S. response to Chief Justice Dickson's harm concerns? Consider the following arguments of the HCC regarding the constitutionality of the criminal provision that makes "incitement of hatred" against any race or nation punishable:

> the whipped-up emotions against the group threaten the honor, dignity (and life, in the more extreme cases) of the individuals comprising the group, and by intimidation restricts them in the exercise of their other rights as well (including the right of freedom of expression). The behavior criminally sanctioned contains such a danger to individual rights as well, which gives such weight to public peace that the restriction on the freedom of expression may be regarded as necessary and proportionate.

Decision 30/1992 (V.26.) AB hat.[u] In the Court's view, "the intensity of the disruption of public peace justifies the restriction of the right to freedom of expression even above and beyond the threshold of 'clear and present danger'."

2. The Canadian justices disagree as to the practical advantages of antiracist regulations. The nature and effective use of antihate laws in the Weimar Republic are contested. Some scholars argue that there were no applicable antihatred laws to use against the Nazis in Germany before Hitler took power. To be sure, there was no group libel protection against defamation on racial grounds. See David Riesman, *Democracy and Defamation: Control of Group Libel*, 42 Colum. L. Rev. 727 (1942). Most contemporary European countries have specific antihate language in their criminal codes (for Germany, see above). In addition, a number of European countries (including France and Belgium) established as an offense the negation and minimization of the Holocaust. Multiethnic societies, like India, are keen to suppress race-based incitement because of the country's high level of ethnic violence.

3. The dissenters in *Keegstra* cite numerous examples where publication or distribution was delayed or hampered because of prosecutorial or administrative doubt regarding the appropriateness of circulating material. Do you agree with Chief Justice Dickson that this is only "minimal" police impairment? Or is it the functional equivalent of censorship? Consider in this regard the objections of Justice McLachlin: "The combination of overbreadth and criminalization may well lead people desirous of avoiding even the slightest brush with the criminal law to protect themselves in the best way they can—by confining their expression to non-controversial matters." *R. v. Keegstra*, above, at 860.

u. In this abstract review case the Court found that punishment for "incitement of hatred" against nations and national, ethnic, and religious groups, among others, is constitutional as it satisfies proportionality requirements. But use of offensive or denigrating expressions against such groups cannot be criminalized as there are less burdensome means (e.g., civil liability) to protect these interests.

Is it not the case that the possibilities of prosecution are of sufficiently chilling effect? Compare with the Greek Constitution (1975), which allows forfeiture by order of the state prosecutor in a number of circumstances (Art. 14). Prepublication forfeiture (seizure) is constitutionally permitted when the publication is offensive to recognized religions, the personality of the President, discloses military secrets, intends to overthrow the state with violence, or violates public morality. Are such measures necessary to protect democracy? Note that the Greek Constitution was written after the collapse of a military dictatorship.

4. Chief Justice Dickson argues that "in assessing the proportionality of a legislative enactment to a valid governmental objective, however, s. 1 should not operate in every instance so as to force the government to rely upon only the mode of intervention least intrusive of a Charter right or freedom." See *Keegstra* above. Is this position accepted by other courts? Cf. the Hungarian decision below.

ROBERT FAURISSON v. FRANCE

Human Rights Committee (United Nations).[v]
UN Doc CCPR/C/58/D/550/1993 (1996).

* * *

The facts as submitted by the author [i.e., Faurisson]

2.1 The author was a professor of literature at the Sorbonne University in Paris until 1973 and at the University of Lyon until 1991, when he was removed from his chair. Aware of the historical significance of the Holocaust, he has sought proof of the methods of killings, in particular by gas asphyxiation. While he does not contest the use of gas for purposes of disinfection, he doubts the existence of gas chambers for extermination purposes ("chambres à gaz homicides") at Auschwitz and in other Nazi concentration camps.

2.2 The author submits that his opinions have been rejected in numerous academic journals and ridiculed in the daily press, * * * nonetheless, he continues to question the existence of extermination gas chambers. * * *

2.3 On 13 July 1990, the French legislature passed the so-called "Gayssot Act," which amends the law on the Freedom of the Press of 1881 by adding an article 24 bis; the latter makes it an offence to contest the existence of the category of crimes against humanity as defined in the London Charter of 8 August 1945.

* * *

2.5 Shortly after the enactment of the "Gayssot Act", Mr. Faurisson was interviewed by the French monthly magazine *Le Choc du Mois*.

---

v. Under the Optional Protocol to the International Covenant on Civil and Political Rights (ICCPR), a state that becomes party to the Protocol recognizes the competence of the Human Rights Committee to receive and consider communications from individuals, subject to the jurisdiction of the participating state, who claim to be victims of a violation by that state of a right enumerated by the ICCPR. The Committee may publish a summary of its findings in its annual report. The Committee members consist of 18 nationals of the ICCPR's member-states, serving in their personal capacity.

* * * Following the publication of this interview, eleven associations of French resistance fighters and of deportees to German concentration camps filed a private criminal action against Mr. Faurisson and Patrice Boizeau, the editor of the magazine *Le Choc du Mois*.[w]

[Faurisson and Boizeau were fined an equivalent of approximately US$50,000 for having committed the crime of "*contestation de crimes contre l'humanité*".]

2.7. * * * The Court of Appeal did, *inter alia*, examine the facts in the light of articles 6 and 10 of the European Convention of Human Rights and Fundamental Freedoms and concluded that the court of first instance had evaluated them correctly.

2.8 The author observes that the "Gayssot Act" has come under attack even in the French National Assembly. Thus, in June 1991, Mr. Jacques Toubon, a member of Parliament for the *Rassemblement pour la République* (RPR) and currently the French Minister of Justice, called for the abrogation of the Act. Mr. Faurisson also refers to the criticism of the Gayssot Act by Mrs. Simone Veil, herself an Auschwitz survivor.

* * *

7.2. The State party * * * explains the legislative history of the "Gayssot Act." It notes, in this context, that anti-racism legislation adopted by France during the 1980s was considered insufficient to prosecute and punish, *inter alia*, the trivialization of Nazi crimes committed during the Second World War. The Law adopted on 13 July 1990 responded to the preoccupations of the French legislator vis-à-vis the development, for several years, of "revisionism," mostly through individuals who justified their writings by their (perceived) status as historians, and who challenged the existence of the Shoah. To the Government, these revisionist theses constitute "a subtle form of contemporary anti-semitism" which, prior to 13 July 1990, could not be prosecuted under any of the existing provisions of French criminal legislation.

* * *

7.4. The State party recalls that article 5, paragraph 1, of the Covenant allows a State party to deny any group or individual any right to engage in activities aimed at the destruction of any of the rights and freedoms recognized in the Covenant.

* * *

7.12. In support of its arguments, the State party refers to decisions of the European Commission of Human Rights addressing the interpretation of article 10 of the European Convention (the equivalent of para. 19 of the Covenant). In a case decided on 16 July 1982, / Case No. 9235/81 (*X. v. Federal Republic of Germany*), declared inadmissible 16 July 1982./ which concerned the prohibition, by judicial decision, of display and sale of brochures arguing that the assassination of millions of Jews during the Second World War was a Zionist fabrication, the

---

w. An amendment to the Press Act, 1881 granted standing to various human rights groups in hate-speech-publication cases, even if the association members were not directly injured.

Commission held that "it was neither arbitrary nor unreasonable to consider the pamphlets displayed by the applicant as a defamatory attack against the Jewish community and against each individual member of this community. By describing the historical fact of the assassination of millions of Jews, a fact which was even admitted by the applicant himself, as a lie and zionist swindle, the pamphlets in question not only gave a distorted picture of the relevant historical facts but also contained an attack on the reputation of all those * * * described as liars and swindlers." * * * The Commission further justified the restrictions on the applicant's freedom of expression, arguing that the "restriction was * * * not only covered by a legitimate purpose recognized by the Convention (namely the protection of the reputation of others), but could also be considered as necessary in a democratic society. Such a society rests on the principles of tolerance and broad-mindedness which the pamphlets in question clearly failed to observe. The protection of these principles may be especially indicated *vis-à-vis* groups which have historically suffered from discrimination."

     * * *

8.6. As to the violations of his right to freedom of expression and opinion, the author notes that this freedom remains severely limited: thus, he is denied the right of reply in the major media, and judicial procedures in his case are tending to become closed proceedings. * * * Precisely because of the applicability of the Law of 13 July 1990, it has become an offence to provide column space to the author or to report the nature of his defence arguments during his trials.

     * * *

Examination of the merits

     * * *

9.4. Any restriction on the right to freedom of expression must cumulatively meet the following conditions: it must be provided by law, it must address one of the aims set out in paragraph 3 (a) and (b) of article 19, and must be necessary to achieve a legitimate purpose.

     * * *

9.6. * * * [T]he rights for the protection of which restrictions on the freedom of expression are permitted by article 19, paragraph 3, may relate to the interests of other persons or to those of the community as a whole. Since the statements made by the author, read in their full context, were of a nature as to raise or strengthen anti-semitic feelings, the restriction served the respect of the Jewish community to live free from fear of an atmosphere of anti-semitism. The Committee therefore concludes that the restriction of the author's freedom of expression was permissible under article 19, paragraph 3 (a), of the Covenant.

9.7. Lastly the Committee needs to consider whether the restriction of the author's freedom of expression was necessary. The Committee noted the State party's argument contending that the introduction of the Gayssot Act was intended to serve the struggle against racism and anti-semitism. * * *

Friedrich Kübler, HOW MUCH FREEDOM FOR RACIST SPEECH?: TRANSNATIONAL ASPECTS OF A CONFLICT OF HUMAN RIGHTS

27 Hofstra L. Rev. 335, 336, 340, 344–345 (1998).

Specific laws against racist hate speech are largely a product of the second half of the twentieth century. In part, their origins are shaped by the specific national experience. This is particularly obvious in Germany, where its approach is primarily dictated by the trauma of the Holocaust. * * *

How has the German legal system reacted to racist speech?

* * *

The first approach has been based on the general provisions of criminal and civil law protecting individual integrity against insult, defamation, and similar forms of verbal aggression. * * * [T]here have been and still exist serious difficulties in coping with public statements of a general nature attacking and degrading anonymous collectives like 'the Jews' or 'the Turks.' In many cases, the courts have had to struggle with "the Auschwitz lie"—the denial of the fact that the Holocaust occurred.

A final problem has been explaining why a pure and simple denial of the fact of the Holocaust should constitute an insult or defamation of Jews living in Germany. Again, the most elaborate answer has been given by the Bundesgerichtshof in *Zivilsachen*. A defendant had publicly denounced the Holocaust as a 'Zionist lie.' The Federal Court confirmed an injunction issued by a lower court ordering defendant not to repeat this statement. The main issue was why the plaintiff, the grandson of a Jew killed in Auschwitz, should have standing to ask for such an injunction. The court reasoned that the Nazi prosecution provided the Jewish community in Germany with a new and specific identity which determines the relationship between individual German Jews and individual other Germans. For this reason, denying the Holocaust amounts to a refusal to respect the suffering of the victims and their relatives and to pay the esteem owed to the German Jews as a distinguishable group. For the Jewish part of the German population, this respect and esteem is an indispensable condition for living in Germany and a guarantee that anti-Semitic discrimination and prosecution will not happen again.

The difficulties of applying the general rules protecting individual integrity and reputation to the 'Auschwitz lie' have been a major reason to look for more specific remedies against racist hate speech. As a result, section 130 of the Penal Code ("StGB") was amended: [Notwithstanding these changes, the] simple lie cannot * * * be punished under section 130. The language used by the court is certainly not very appealing. But the basic idea that the mere denial of a historical event, even if made maliciously, does not by itself amount to a violation of human dignity has some merit. * * * As a result of this controversy, section 130 was included in a pending criminal law reform bill and thus amended again in [1994].

The new version of section 130 is more complicated. Its relevant parts read:

(1) Whosoever, in a manner liable to disturb the public peace,

  (a) incites hatred against parts of the population or invites violence or arbitrary acts against them, or

  (b) attacks the human dignity of others by insulting, maliciously degrading or defaming parts of the population shall be punished by imprisonment of no less than three months and not exceeding five years.

(2) Imprisonment, not exceeding five years, or fine will be the punishment for whoever

  (a) distributes,

  (b) makes available to the public,

  (c) makes available to persons of less than 18 years, or

  (d) produces, stores or offers for use as mentioned in letters (a) to (c) documents inciting hatred against part of the population or against groups determined by nationality, race, religion, or ethnic origin, or inviting to violent or arbitrary acts against these parts or groups, or attacking the human dignity of others by insulting, maliciously ridiculing or defaming parts of the population or such a group, or

  (e) distributes a message of the kind described in (1) by broadcast.

(3) Imprisonment, not exceeding five years or fine, will be the punishment for whoever, in public or in an assembly, approves, denies or minimizes an act described in section 220a paragraph 1 committed under the regime of National-socialism, in a manner which is liable to disturb the public peace.

This amendment has considerably enlarged the field of application of section 130 and thus intensified the conflict with the constitutional guarantee for freedom of expression. The basic rule of paragraph (1) provides for the punishment of racial speech without additionally requiring an attack on human dignity, but it retains the requirement of a threat to public peace.

HOLOCAUST DENIAL CASE

Federal Constitutional Court (Germany).
90 BVerfGE 241 (1994).

[In 1991, a regional association of the far-right National Democratic Party of Germany (NPD) issued invitations to a meeting intended to discuss "Germany's future in the shadow of political blackmail?" The featured speaker was David Irving, a revisionist historian, who has argued that the mass extermination of Jews during the Third Reich never occurred. The Bavarian state government, in Munich, placed the condition that the "Auschwitz Hoax" thesis not be promoted at the meeting. The government took this action on the authority of the Assembly Act, one provision of which allows the prohibition of meetings where the likelihood exists that things said will themselves constitute criminal violations. In this case the likely violations were denigration of the memory of the dead, criminal agitation, and, most importantly, criminal insult, all prohibited by the Criminal Code. The NPD argued that the condition constituted an unconstitutional intrusion on its right to free expression (although the meeting itself took place). The complaint was rejected by the lower courts, before being heard by the Federal Constitutional Court.]

Judgment of the First Senate:

* * *

B. II. The contested decisions do not constitute a violation of Art. 5 (1), first sentence of the Basic Law.

1. Art. 5 (1), first sentence, of the Basic Law guarantees everyone the right freely to express and disseminate his opinion.

a) These decisions have to be assessed primarily in terms of this basic right. It is true that the condition the complainant opposes relates to a meeting. Its subject, however, is certain utterances which the complainant, as organizer of the meeting, was neither allowed to make nor to tolerate. The constitutional assessment of the condition depends, above all, on whether such utterances are allowed or not. An utterance which cannot be prohibited on constitutional grounds, cannot give rise to a restrictive measure applying to a meeting pursuant to section 5 (4) of the Assemblies Act. The criteria for answering this question follow not from the basic right of freedom of assembly but from the right of freedom of expression.

b) The subject matter of the Basic Law's protection under Art. 5 (1) is opinions. Freedom of expression and dissemination relates to opinions. Opinions are shaped by the individual's subjective relationship towards the content of his utterance. The element of comment and appraisal is characteristic of opinions. To this extent, demonstration of their truth or untruth is not possible. They enjoy the protection of a basic right without it mattering whether their expression was well-founded or unfounded, or is deemed to be emotional or rational, valuable or worthless, dangerous or harmless. The protection of the basic right also extends to the form the utterance takes. An expression of opinion does not lose its protection as a basic right by being sharply or hurtfully worded. In this respect, the question can only be whether, and to what extent, limitations on freedom of expression ensue in accordance with Art. 5 (2) of the Basic Law.

Strictly speaking, representations of fact, on the other hand, are not expressions of opinion. By contrast with the latter, in their case it is the objective relationship between the utterance and reality that comes to the fore. Hence they are also amenable to an examination of their truth content. But this does not mean that representations of fact automatically lie outside the purview of Art. 5 (1) of the Basic Law. Since opinions are usually based on factual assumptions or they comment on factual circumstances, they are protected by the basic right at any rate to the extent that they are a condition for the formation of opinions, which Art. 5 guarantees as a whole [citing the *Campaign Slur Case*].

Consequently, the protection of a representation of fact only stops when it is unable to contribute anything to the constitutionally presupposed formation of opinion. From this angle incorrect information does not constitute an interest meriting protection. For this reason, the Federal Constitutional Court has constantly ruled that a deliberate or demonstrably untrue representation of fact is not covered by the protection enjoyed by freedom of expression [citing the *Böll Case*]. However, requirements affecting the duty of truth must not be assessed in such a way that the function of freedom of expression will suffer as a result or that permissible expressions of opinion are self-censored for fear of sanctions [citing the *Böll* and *Campaign Slur* cases].

Drawing the distinction between expressions of opinion and representations of fact can certainly be difficult because the two are often linked together and only jointly give sense to the utterance. In this case, severance of the factual from the evaluative elements is only permissible if this does not falsify the meaning of the utterance. If that is not possible the utterance must, in the interest of effective protection of the basic right, be viewed as an expression of opinion as a whole and be included within the ambit of the protection afforded freedom of expression because otherwise there would be the threat of substantial curtailment of basic right protection.

c) Freedom of expression is certainly not unconditionally guaranteed. Art. 5 (1) provides that it is limited by provisions of general law, statutory provisions for the protection of youth and of personal honor. Nevertheless, in the interpretation and application of laws that have a limiting effect on freedom of expression account must be taken of the significance of freedom of expression [citing the *Lüth Case*]. This usually requires balancing, in the light of the elements of the pertinent norms and on an individual basis, the limited basic right against the legal interest served by the law limiting this basic right.

In balancing, the Federal Constitutional Court has developed some rules according to which freedom of expression by no means always takes precedence over the protection of personality, as the complainant thinks. On the contrary, where expressions of opinion are regarded as a formal insult or vilification, protection of the personality normally comes before freedom of expression [citing the *Wallraff Case*]. Where expressions of opinion are linked to representations of fact, the protection merited can depend on the truth content of the factual assumptions on which they are based. If the latter are demonstrably untrue, freedom of expression will likewise usually come after the protection of personality [citing the *Campaign Slur Case*]. Otherwise it is a matter of which legal interest deserves to be given preference in an individual case. Here, however, it must be borne in mind that there is a presumption in favor of free speech as regards questions of importance to the public [citing the *Lüth Case*]. Hence, we must constantly take account of this presumption as well when balancing the legal positions of the persons involved.

2. Seen in these terms, a breach of Art. 5 (1) of the Basic Law has manifestly not been committed. The condition imposed on the complainant as the organizer of the meeting, namely to see to it that there would

be no denial or doubt cast on the persecution of the Jews during the Third Reich, is compatible with this basic right.

a) The complainant has not contested the prognosis of danger made by the authority dealing with the meeting and affirmed by the administrative courts, namely that utterances of this kind would be made during the course of the meeting. On the contrary, the complainant argues that it should be able to make such statements.

b) The prohibited utterance that there was no persecution of the Jews during the Third Reich is a representation of fact that is demonstrably untrue in the light of innumerable eye-witness accounts and documents, of the findings of courts in numerous criminal cases and of historical analysis. Taken on its own, a statement having this content therefore does not enjoy the protection of freedom of expression. Therein lies an important difference between denying the persecution of the Jews during the Third Reich and denying German guilt in respect of the outbreak of the Second World War—the subject of the decision handed down by the Federal Constitutional Court on 11 January 1994. [The *Historical Fabrication Case*.] Utterances concerning guilt and responsibility for historical events are always complex evaluations that cannot be reduced to representations of fact, whilst denial of an event itself will normally have the character of a representation of fact.

c) But even if we do not take the utterance to which the condition relates on its own but view it in connection with the subject of the meeting and thus as a precondition for forming opinion on the "susceptibility to blackmail" of German politics, the contested decisions will still withstand constitutional review. The prohibited utterance does, it is true to say, enjoy the protection of Art. 5 (1) of the Basic Law but there are no objections under constitutional law to its limitation.

aa) Such limitation has a lawful basis confirming to the constitution.

[The Court goes on to vindicate Section 5 (4) of the Assemblies Act, which authorizes the state government to prohibit meetings that support or provide the occasion for uttering views which "form the subject of a serious crime (*Verbrechen*) or a less-serious crime (*Vergehen*) prosecutable ex officio." The guarantee of freedom of assembly under Art. 8 (1), however, does require the legislature and government to observe the principle of proportionality. Similarly, the Act did not violate freedom of expression since the "Auschwitz Hoax" thesis had been held previously to constitute the offence of "insult" under the Criminal Code, the constitutionality of which the Court then affirmed in what follows.]

There are no doubts about the constitutionality of the criminal provisions on which the condition [i.e., that the "Auschwitz Hoax thesis not be promoted] was based here. The laws against defamation protect personal honor, which is expressly mentioned in Art. 5 (2) of the Basic Law as a legal interest justifying a limitation on freedom of expression. Section 130 of the Criminal Code is a general law within the meaning of Art. 5 (2) serving to protect humanity and ultimately having its foundation in Art. 1 (1) of the Basic Law [mandating the inviolability of the dignity of man]. * * *

(1) The administrative authorities and courts based their decisions on the criminal norm as interpreted by the ordinary courts. According to this [interpretation], the Jews living in Germany form an insultable (*beleidigungsfähige*) group in view of the fate of the Jewish population under national socialist rule; denial of the persecution of the Jews is regarded as an insult to this group. On this point, the Federal Court of Justice had the following to say:

> The historical fact itself that human beings were singled out according to the criteria of the so-called "Nuremberg Laws" and were robbed of their individuality for the purpose of extermination puts Jews living in the Federal Republic into a special personal relationship vis-à-vis their fellow citizens; what happened is also present in this relationship today. It is part of their personal self-perception to be comprehended as belonging to a group of people who stand out by virtue of their fate and in relation to whom there is a special moral responsibility on the part of all others and that this is a part of their dignity. Respect for this self-perception is virtually, for each individual, one of the guarantees against repetition of this kind of discrimination and forms a basic condition of their life in the Federal Republic. Whoever seeks to deny these events denies, vis-à-vis each individual, the personal worth due to each [Jewish person]. For the person concerned this means continuing discrimination against the group to which he belongs and, as part of that group, against himself.

(BGHZ 75, 160, 162 *et seq.*).

* * *

There is no cause for objection to the fact that, in the light of this court's jurisprudence, these contested decisions bear witness to a grave violation of the right of personality in so far as persecution of the Jews was denied. Constitutionally, no fault can be found with the explanatory connection established by the Federal Court of Justice between the racially motivated extermination of the Jewish population during the Third Reich and the attack on the right to respect and the human dignity of the Jews today. In this sense there is also a distinction between denying the persecution of the Jews and denying German war guilt [citing the *Historical Fabrication Case*]. At any rate, the last opinion referred to does not, irrespective of its being questionable from a historical point of view, injure the interests of third persons. * * *

(2) Balancing the defamation on the one hand against the limitation of freedom of expression on the other does not reveal any errors relevant to constitutional law. It is the gravity of the injury in each case that is decisive for this balancing. When insulting opinions are voiced, containing a representation of fact, it is crucial whether the representations of fact do not constitute an interest worth protecting. If they are inseparably connected with opinions, they will benefit from the protection of Art. 5 (1) of the Basic Law, but from the outset interference will be less serious than in the case of representations of fact that have not been shown to be untrue.

That is the case here. Even if one regards the utterance that the complainant was prohibited from permitting at its meeting as an expression of opinion in connection with the subject of the meeting, this does nothing to change the proven falsity of its factual content. Hence, interference relating to this is not particularly serious. In view of the weight attached to the insult, there can be no objection to the contested decisions' having given precedence to the protection of personality before freedom of expression.

Also, matters do not change if one considers that Germany's attitude to its national socialist past and the political consequences thereof, which were the subject of the meeting, is a question concerning the public in an important way. It is true that in this case there is a presumption in favor of free speech, but this does not apply if the utterance constitutes a formal insult or vilification [of the Jewish people], nor does it apply if the offensive utterance rests on demonstrably untrue representations of fact.

Overstretching the requirements of truth as regards the factual core of the utterance in a manner incompatible with Art. 5 (1) of the Basic Law is not then the result of this balancing. Limitation of the duty of care, from which the Federal Constitutional Court proceeds in the interest of free communication and of the critical and controlling function of the media, refers to representations of fact whose accuracy at the time of the utterance is still uncertain and which cannot be checked within a very short space of time. But it does not come into operation when the untruth of a statement is already established, as in this case.

Notes and Questions

1. As to the prohibition of antiracist ideas in Europe, "two basic, independent statutory models exist. One is an open statute which follows the dictates of the Convention for the Elimination of All Forms of Racial Discrimination, outlawing propagandizing racist ideas. The purest example of this model is the statute adopted by Italy upon ratification of the Convention that provides a prison sentence of one to four years for 'any person, who, in any way whatsoever, disseminates ideas based on racial superiority or racial hatred'." Kretzmer, *op. cit.* at 499. Statutes that follow this model have been adopted in other European countries, including The Netherlands, Norway, and Finland. The latter statutes refer, however, only to public statements, an element not explicitly mentioned in the Italian statute.

The second model is exemplified by the British statute.[194] [x] This statute applies to publication or distribution of written matter, or speech in public places, in which two conditions are satisfied: (1) the words or

---

194. Race Relations Act, 1976, ch. 74, § 70 (amending Public Order Act, 1936, 1 Edw. 8 & 1 Geo. 6, § 2).

x. Only a few cases were prosecuted under the Act. In an effort to strengthen incitement laws, Parliament enacted Part III of the Public Order Act, 1986. Under section 18, the use of "threatening, abusive, or

insulting words" is an offense if the speaker: (a) intends thereby to stir up racial hatred, or (b) having regard to all the circumstances, racial hatred is likely to be stirred up thereby. See Nathan Courtney, *British and United States Hate Speech Legislation: A Comparison*, 19 Brook. J. Int'l L. 727 (1993).

matter are threatening, abusive, or insulting, and (2) having regard to all the circumstances, hatred is likely to be stirred up against any racial group in Britain by the words or matter.

While the first of these two requirements obviously departs from the pure open approach adopted in the Italian statute, many of the other countries which adopt the open approach have an abusiveness requirement. What primarily distinguishes the second model from the first model, then, is not the abusiveness element, but the incitement to hatred element adopted in the British statute.

Id. at 445.

2. Explaining in the French National Assembly the draft of what became the Gayssot Act, the French government was of the opinion that racism did not constitute an opinion but an aggression and that every time racism was allowed to express itself publicly the public order was immediately and severely threatened. If this is true, then what about nonracist radical religious or political speech? Is there a difference?

UN Human Rights Committee member Rajsoomer Lallah, in a concurring opinion to the Committee position in *Faurisson*, states that the Gayssot Act is

> formulated in the widest terms and would seem to prohibit publication of bona fide research connected with principles and matters decided by the Nuremberg Tribunal. It creates an absolute liability in respect of which no defence appears to be possible. It does not link liability either to the intent of the author nor to the prejudice that it causes to respect for the rights or reputations of others as required under article 19, paragraph 3 (a), or to the protection of national security or of public order or of public health or morals as required under article 19, paragraph 3 (b).

Do you find the absolute-liability issue troubling? If none of the named grounds for restricting free speech is met, what makes the Committee believe that the Gayssot Act satisfies Art. 19 requirements? Would the Gayssot Act survive an overbreadth scrutiny?

3. It is certainly not out of the question for disparaging statements about large collectives to defame the persons belonging to them. This is particularly the case where the statements are associated with ethnic, racial, physical or mental characteristics from which the inferiority of a whole group of persons and therefore simultaneously each individual member of it is deduced. As a rule, however, only statements about particular persons or associations of persons can come into consideration as vilificatory criticism. The term has also to date been used only in this sense in the case law of the Federal Constitutional Court and the Federal Court of Justice. * * * Where instead groups of persons are concerned who are united by a particular social function, it is rather to be presumed that the statement is not marked by defamation of persons but associated with the activity done by them. The statement may then nonetheless be defamatory. It no longer falls, however, under the concept of vilificatory criticism, which makes a specific weighing against the interests of freedom of opinion, taking all circumstances of the case into account, superfluous.

Tucholsky II Case at 687–88.

4. The Belgian legislature made the negation, minimization, justification, or approval of the genocide committed by the German national socialist regime during the Second World War an offense (Act of 23 March 1995). A Holocaust revisionist challenged the Act, and the court accepted jurisdiction. But the challenge of a second person, who would have argued that the law did not go far enough, was held not to confer jurisdiction because disapproval of a law was held an insufficient interest to support standing. The Belgian Court of Arbitration held that opinions which are shocking to a fraction of the population are protected. Revisionism, however, intends to rehabilitate a criminal ideology hostile to democracy. The Court of Arbitration, following the standards of the ECHR, discussed the necessity of the restriction. The Act meets an imperative need because the expression of such opinions is offensive to the memory of the victims of genocide, its survivors, and in particular the Jewish people themselves. Cour d'Arbitration, 45/96, BCCL 184. Compare the Belgian position with the Hungarian one (below), which finds a group's disturbance insufficient to criminalize racist speech.

5. "While arguably consistent on a doctrinal level, American First Amendment jurisprudence has fairly consistently resulted in suppression of extremist speech coming from the left and in toleration of hate propaganda perpetrated by the extreme right." Michel Rosenfeld, *Pragmatism, Pluralism and Legal Interpretation: Posner's and Rorty's Justice Without Metaphysics Meets Hate Speech*, 18 Cardozo L. Rev. 97, 145 (1996). In view of the above cases, do you agree with Professor Rosenfeld's statement? Is the attitude in Europe the opposite one, at least since the mid–1980s? Some of the most spectacular German libel decisions—*Street Theater* (regarding Bavarian Prime Minister Strauss); *Tucholsky I*; and *Tucholsky II*—protected leftist (nonestablishment) activists against criminal libel. Note the impact of the European approach on the Web: in Germany, the prosecutorial initiative resulted in the change of access policy of a service provider regarding access to U.S.-and Canadian-based home pages devoted to hate; Yahoo France was ordered by a French Court to develop and apply a technology to hamper access to "Nazi sites." (See Section A. above.)

Does European antiracist legislation, and the criminalization of the Holocaust in particular, single out one political position? Might there be an element of action in these racist speech cases that would satisfy the test used by Judith Butler above?

6. *History and Speech Crimes.*

The potential harms resulting from incitement to hate, the subjecting of certain groups in a population to denigrating and humiliating treatment is amply documented in the annals of human experience.

* * * The tragic historical experiences of our century prove that views preaching racial, ethnic, national or religious inferiority or superiority, the dissemination of ideas of hatred, contempt and exclusion endanger the values of human civilization.

History, as well as current events, clearly demonstrates that any manifestation of inciting hatred against a certain group in the population is capable of intensifying social tensions, disturbing social harmony and peace and, in its most grievous forms, triggers violent clashes between certain groups in society.

In addition to those most extreme of the harmful consequences of incitement to hatred, demonstrated by current as well as historical experiences, those everyday dangers must also be borne in mind which accompany the unbridled expressions of ideas and thoughts capable of arousing hatred. These are the occurrences which prevent certain communities from living in harmony with other groups.

Hungarian Constitutional Court, Decision 30/1992 (V.26.) AB hat.

Compare the use of historical experience in evaluating the necessity to interfere into racial speech in the various countries. The experience of race riots in Illinois was an important element in the finding of constitutionality in *Beauharnais*.

7. The prohibition on racist speech affects political rights, too. In *Glimmerveen and Hagenbeek v. The Netherlands*, 4 E.H.R.R. 260 (1982), the applicants were earlier convicted for the distribution of racist leaflets and were leaders of small parties with racist programs. Their names appeared on a list of candidates for the municipal council elections of The Hague and Amsterdam. The Central Voting Board declared the list invalid, since the applicants were members of the governing board of a prohibited association and its discriminatory concepts conflicted with good morals and public order. The applicants considered that their rights to freedom of thought and freedom of expression, both in general and in the context of the elections, had been jeopardized. "The Commission recalls that it has held in the past that Article 3 of the First Protocol guarantees in principle the right to vote and the right to stand as a candidate at the election of the legislative body * * *." European Commission of Human Rights: Decisions and Reports, vol. 18, at 196. "The Commission therefore considers that, even assuming Article 3 of the First Protocol applies, the applicants cannot avail themselves of the right protected under that provision, having regard to Article 17 of the Convention. In conclusion the Commission finds that the applicants cannot, by reason of the provisions of Article 17 of the Convention, rely either on Article 10 of the Convention or Article 3 of the First Protocol." *Id*. at 197. (On militant democracy, see Chapter 11.)

Chapter 8

THE CONSTITUTION, FREEDOM OF RELIGION AND BELIEF

Article 9 of the European Convention for the Protection of Human Rights and Fundamental Freedoms (1950) provides one of the most comprehensive definitions of freedom of religion as an individual right:

1. Everyone has the right to freedom of thought, conscience and religion; this right includes freedom to change his religion or belief and freedom, either alone or in community with others and in public or private, to manifest his religion or belief, in worship, teaching, practice and observance.

2. Freedom to manifest one's religion or beliefs shall be subject only to such limitations as are prescribed by law and are necessary in a democratic society in the interests of public safety, for the protection of public order, health or morals, or for the protection of the rights and freedoms of others.

The Convention protects both religious and nonreligious beliefs. Historically, freedom of conscience in liberal constitutions was guaranteed as liberation from religious oppression. (Article 10 of the French Declaration of the Rights of Man and of the Citizen of 1789 reads: "no one should be disturbed on account of his opinions, even religious * * *." See also, e.g., Art. 20 of the Belgian Constitution.) Freedom *from* religion was one of the great liberating experiences of the Enlightenment; to this day those elements of religion that are repugnant to human rights and dignity are highly suspect and, in principle, not protected under the guise of free exercise. For this position, see Justice Chinnappa Reddy of the Indian Supreme Court (ISC) in *Bommai* below. One of the most spectacular conflicts of values today relate to religion-dictated practices that either harm members or are otherwise in conflict with secular or other concepts of dignity.

In countries where secularism dominates in the public sphere (like France), freedom of conscience and opinion is emphasized; free exercise of religion is merely a special form of manifesting one's conscience. Nevertheless, the focus in this chapter is on freedom of religion. This should not be understood as a value judgment. We make no claim that religion should deserve more protection than other dictates of conscience. Religious faith is only a distinct subcategory of conscience; the

French and, arguably, German approach is that religious beliefs are protected as a form of belief to the same extent that other beliefs are protected. Religion as a social phenomenon—as a more or less organized system of beliefs—may differ from other worldviews, but this results in no justified claim to special protection.

Further, we focus on religion partly because "freedom of religion" is the prevailing constitutional language in most constitutions and partly because most contemporary free exercise problems entail religion. Arguably, religion-based discrimination remains the most common form of human rights violation in the world, although freedom of religion is the oldest expressly recognized fundamental right. On the other hand, at least in some countries (e.g., The Netherlands: Union of Utrecht Treaty, 1579—freedom from the inquisition), freedom of religion is the oldest expressly recognized fundamental right.

The constitutional protection of religious freedom is determined to a great extent by the relations between the state and churches (discussed in Section B.). Free exercise and the legal status of churches are interrelated. The same problem—for example, accommodation, that is, legal exemptions from general rules of the state for the sake of religious practices—might often be discussed under both headings. Accommodation might be seen, on the one hand, as special endorsement of a religion or church that provides specific religious services or as a measure enabling an individual to practice religion.[a] Even where the constitutional issue concerns the permissible endorsement (support) of a church or religion, i.e., where the recipient addressee of government support is a collective entity or a belief, the endorsement is likely to affect individual free exercise. Government support of education may involve direct support to churches or denominational schools or support to parents whose children attend such schools. The latter undeniably serves free exercise of religion, although it might be impermissible as a governmental preference. While the latter approach enables individual free exercise, the former is about the permissible forms of state and church relations. The practical consequences are essentially identical: government funds are used for religious education.

The relation between free exercise and state endorsement of churches or religion is further complicated by the effect of endorsement of free exercise. Once Christendom was officially established, the features of an established church included prohibitions on the free exercise of dissenters, restrictions on access to public office for those who did not adhere to the established church (to be determined by church authori-

---

a. In *Sherbert v. Verner*, 374 U.S. 398, 409 (1963), cited in *Wisconsin v. Yoder*, 406 U.S. 205, 234 n. 22 (1972), the U.S. Supreme Court wrote:

Accommodating the religious beliefs of the Amish can hardly be characterized as sponsorship or active involvement. The purpose and effect of such an exemption are not to support, favor, advance, or assist the Amish, but to allow their centuries-old religious society, here long be-fore the advent of any compulsory education, to survive free from the heavy impediment compliance with the Wisconsin compulsory-education law would impose. Such an accommodation "reflects nothing more than the governmental obligation of neutrality in the face of religious differences, and does not represent that involvement of religious with secular institutions which it is the object of the Establishment Clause to forestall".

ties), and compelled contributions to the established church. State endorsement might be fatal to free exercise (both for those whose religion is, and is not, endorsed). Madison's original proposal to amend the U.S. Constitution would have required that "the civil rights of none shall be abridged on account of religious belief or worship, nor shall any national religion be established, nor shall the full and equal rights of conscience be in any manner, or on any pretext, infringed."

The involvement of the state in the free exercise right results in inevitable contradictions. In the U.S., for example, about 90 percent of the population believe in God. Many Americans expect government officials to be influenced by their faith; yet many of the same would not accept the state's involvement in religious matters. According to some traditions, the separation of church and state is important in order to protect minority religions and people of no faith, or simply as a convenient tool to avoid a topic so socially divisive. A different tradition suggests that separation is necessary to protect the purity of religion and the autonomy of the church. Thus the early Christian interpretation of the New Testament refused association of Christendom with state power.

In Section A. we approach these problems primarily from the perspective of individual practices, while in Section B. the collective aspects are emphasized.

A. FREE EXERCISE

Believers and nonbelievers would like to follow the dictates of their (not necessarily religious) conscience. But this may conflict with the tenets of other beliefs or the freedoms of other people. Or it might find conflict with the objectives and actions of the state or with public order.

In the first subsection we consider how religion is defined from a constitutional and judicial perspective. Religion's various definitions are not a matter of academic purity. They have important legal implications, including what is acceptable as religion. To be sure, specific definitions of religion may result in discrimination against other forms of belief.

The second subsection addresses violations of the right to free exercise of religion. Free exercise includes both freedom to practice religion and freedom from being forced to practice religion, especially in public life (government service, education, and the like). The simplest and most common problem of free exercise is that the government persecutes believers of a given religion or prohibits its public or even private practice. The most common reason for such persecution is that the state is deemed to be the protector of a "true faith." In the case of the communist states, official atheistic ideology dictated the persecution of religion and religious citizens. Other modern secular states are insensitive to the needs of free exercise. The dictates of one's religion may conflict with those of a state that follows purely secular considerations. Secular concerns are called "neutral" in the sense that they, allegedly, neither favor nor disfavor any religion. The requirements of neutrality, such as public order (or in the Italian Constitution, "good morals"), are the constitutionally recognized limits of free exercise. A neutral state is expected not to take sides in religious matters. It should be guided by nonsectarian perspectives based on the collective welfare and public good and not dictated by sectarian considerations. Owing to differences in cultural traditions, however, neutral rules may favor certain religious practices when they coincide with majority customs, for example, Sunday as a "day of rest." Such "secularization" may deny the religious relevance of certain events and practices. Moreover, the acceptance of majority religious practices as a common secular heritage disfavors minority religions. In *Employment Division v. Smith*, below, Justice O'Connor argues that the majority "suggests that the disfavoring of minority religions is an 'unavoidable consequence' under our system of government and that accommodation of such religions must be left to the political process. In my view, however, the First Amendment was enacted precisely to protect the rights of those whose religious practices are not shared by the majority and may be viewed with hostility." Religious freedoms are also protected because of considerations of equality, which set limits on the state's relation to religion and churches. Thus many constitutions expressly prohibit discrimination on grounds of religion, belief, and opinion. Article 11 of the Belgian Constitution, since 1994, prohibits discrimination and contains specific provisions to protect religious minorities: "the law and decree guarantee the rights and freedoms of the ideological and philosophical minorities."

A religious practice may violate the rights of other religious believers or other personal beliefs. Many religions require some form of proselytizing. Free exercise is often limited in the name of protecting other religions (generally the majority or mainstream religions). Specific practices (mostly minority) are held "destructive" or "nonrespectable."

Given the interest in free exercise, a state may allow some religious interests to prevail. We treat "accommodation" of religion in the third subsection, although it also bears on church–state relations. The exemptions granted to accommodate religious practices can be seen as endorsement, and special recognition may amount to a privilege granted to certain churches. Privileges always entail discrimination. If a state allows certain believers exemptions from general duties or prohibitions, others may feel discriminated against. In countries where there is a state church or where the state is multiconfessional (as in Germany), atheists and adherents to minority religions might feel discriminated against. In liberal democracies, it is expected that the state should be neutral.

A. 1. WHAT IS PROTECTED? WHAT IS RELIGION?

DECISION ON SCIENTOLOGY

Supreme Court (Italy).
Cass., sez. Sesta Penale, 8 Oct. 1997,
Registro Gen.n.116835/97.[b]

While some Italian courts (including Rome and Turin) have considered Scientology as a religion, a different conclusion was reached by the

b. Case summary by Cesnur at <www.cesnur.org>.

Court of Appeal of Milan. Reforming a first degree decision favorable to Scientology, on November 5, 1993 the Milan appeal judges found a number of Scientologists guilty of a variety of crimes, all allegedly committed before 1981, ignoring the question whether Scientology was a religion. The Italian Supreme Court, on February 9, 1995, annulled the Milan 1993 decision with remand, asking the Court of Appeal to reconsider whether Scientology was indeed a religion. On December 2, 1996 the Court of Appeal of Milan complied, but maintained that Scientology was not a religion. Not unlike their Turin homologues, the Milan appeal judges noted that "there is no legislative definition of religion" and "nowhere in the [Italian] law is there any useful element in order to distinguish a religious organization from other social groups". However, among a number of possible definitions, the Milan judges selected one defining religion as "a system of doctrines centered on the presupposition of the existence of a Supreme Being, who has a relation with humans, the latter having towards him a duty of obedience and reverence". The Milan judges, however, interpreted "Supreme Being" in a theistic sense. As a consequence, they could easily exclude the non-theistic worldview of Scientology from the sphere of religion.

On October 9, 1997, the Supreme Court annulled also the Milan 1996 decision, again with remand (meaning that another section of the Court of Appeal of Milan shall re-examine the facts of the case). The Supreme Court regarded the Milan theistic definition of religion as "unacceptable" and "a mistake", because it was "based only on the paradigm of Biblical religions." As such, the definition would exclude Buddhism, whose main Italian organization, the Italian Buddhist Union, has been recognized in Italy as a "religious denomination" since 1991. Buddhism, according to the Supreme Court, "certainly does not affirm the existence of a Supreme Being and, as a consequence, does not propose a direct relation of the human being with Him".

It is true, the Supreme Court observes, that "the self-definition of a group as religious is not enough in order to recognize it as a genuine religion". The Milan 1996 decision quoted the case law of the Italian Constitutional Court and its reference to the "common opinion" in order to decide whether a group is a religion. The relevant "common opinion", however, according to the Supreme Court is rather "the opinion of the scholars" than the "public opinion". The latter is normally hostile to religious minorities and, additionally, difficult to ascertain: one wonders, the Supreme Court notes, "from what source the Milan judges knew the public opinion of the whole national community". On other hand, most scholars—according to the Supreme Court—seem to prefer a definition of religion broad enough to include Scientology and, when asked, conclude that Scientology is in fact a religion, having as its aim "the liberation of the human spirit through the knowledge of the divine spirit residing within each human being". The Supreme Court also examined some of the arguments used by critics (and by the Milan 1996 judges) in order to deny to Scientology the status of religion.

1. First, critics object that Scientology is "syncretistic" and does not propose any really "original belief". This is, the Supreme Court argues, irrelevant, since syncretism "is not rare" among genuine religions, and

many recently established Christian denominations exhibit very few "original features" when compared to older denominations.

2. Second, it is argued that Scientology is presented to perspective converts as science, not as religion. The Supreme Court replies that, at least since Thomas Aquinas, Christian theology claims to be a science. On the other hand, science claiming to lead to non-empirical results such as "a knowledge of God" (or "of human beings as gods") may be both "bad science" and "inherently religious".

* * *

4. Fourth, texts by L. Ron Hubbard, the founder of Scientology, and by early Italian leaders seem to imply that Scientology's basic aim is to make money. Such texts' interest in money is, according to the Supreme Court, "excessive" but "perhaps appears much less excessive if we consider how money was raised in the past by the Roman Catholic Church". * * * The Supreme Court went on to observe that the more "disturbing" texts on money are but a minimal part of Hubbard's enormous literary production (including "about 8,000 works"); and that they were mostly circular letters or bulletins intended "for the officers in charge of finances and the economic structure, not for the average member". * * * What is, in fact, the ultimate aim of "selling Dianetics and Scientology"? There is no evidence, the Supreme Court suggests, that such "sales" are only organized in order to assure the personal welfare of the leaders. If they are intended as a proselytization tool, then making money is only an intermediate aim. The ultimate aim is "proselytization", and this aim "could hardly be more typical of a religion".
* * *

5. A fifth objection discussed by the Supreme Court is that Scientology is not a religion since there is evidence, in the Milan case itself, that a number of Scientologists were guilty of "fraudulent sales techniques" or abused of particularly weak customers, when "selling" Dianetics or Scientology. These illegal activities, the Supreme Court comments, should be prosecuted, but there is no evidence that they are more than "occasional deviant activities" of a certain number of leaders and members within the Milan branch, "with no general significance" concerning the nature of Scientology in general.

The Court * * * argues that the non-existence of a legal definition of religion in Italy (and elsewhere) "is not coincidental". Any definition would rapidly become obsolete and, in fact, limit religious liberty. It is much better, "not to limit with a definition, always by its very nature restrictive, the broader field of religious liberty". "Religion" is an ever-evolving concept, and courts may only interpret it within the frame of a specific historical and geographical context, taking into account the opinions of the scholars.

Notes and Questions

1. Some courts seek to avoid defining religion because a narrow definition would predetermine the outcomes of specific cases. Nevertheless, a court may implicitly compare questionable beliefs with practices and beliefs in a

given society that are held unquestionably religious. Thus, in Italy, religions were limited to those that were traditionally established. But as the courts avoided a definition of confession, increasingly more religions were recognized.[c] The question "What is religion?" is often replaced with the more specific one: "What is fundamental for a specific religion?" or "Is this position or behavior part of a specific religion?" Leaving the decisions of such matters to a secular court is problematic as the state assumes the right to decide matters of faith that affect church–state relations. Separation and church-autonomy theories claim that the church should exclusively determine matters of religious doctrine. The problem is further complicated where a state recognizes the jurisdiction of ecclesiastical or other church courts.

In other situations, especially when exceptions to general rules are claimed in the name of free exercise, courts may be more ready to claim the power of defining what is, and what is not, important for religion. The ISC in *Acharya Jagdishwaranand Avadhuta, etc. v. Commissioner of Police, Calcutta,* (1984) 1 S.C.R. 447, 448, said that:

> Courts have the power to determine whether a particular rite or observance is regarded as essential by the tenets of a particular religion. * * * The words 'religious denomination' in Article 26 of the Constitution must take their colour from the word 'religion' and if this be so, the expression 'religious denomination' must also satisfy three conditions:
>
> > (1) It must be a collection of individuals who have a system of beliefs or doctrines which they regard as conducive to their spiritual well-being, that is, a common faith; (2) common organisation, and (3) designation by a distinctive name.
>
> > Religion undoubtedly has its basis in a system of beliefs or doctrines which are regarded by those who profess that religion as conducive to their spiritual well being, but it would not be correct to say that religion is nothing else but a doctrine or belief. A religion may not only lay down a code of ethical rules for its followers to accept, it might prescribe rituals and observances, ceremonies and modes of worship which are regarded as integral parts of religion, and these forms and observances might extend even to matters of food and dress.

The ISC had no difficulty in finding that the Tandava Dance (carried out in public with a symbolic knife and prohibited by the police) was not essential for the Ananda Marga "religious denomination," notwithstanding the contrary statement of the group's founder. *Id.* at 449.

The willingness of courts to define religion is perhaps related to how they understand their role. The Indian courts are perceived as rather activist. Further, the Indian constitutional tradition is that the courts protect Indian secularism (see *Bommai* below). Note that the ISC relies on standard evidence (does dance occur in certain writings?); there is no discussion of theological necessities.

c. The Italian Constitutional Court found unconstitutional a regional law on subsidies that discriminated against confessions "without an Agreement with the state" (195/1993). It found that confessions without organization qualify as religions for purposes of state support.

In other countries, judges may take a relativistic and skeptical position in matters of religion, because either it follows from their agnostic worldview and judicial training or it follows from constitutional respect for religion and churches. In *A Letter Concerning Toleration*, John Locke's classic argument in favor of toleration was that no man can judge the merits of a religion. In the U.S., one could argue that "any definition of religion would seem to violate religious freedom in that it would dictate to religions, present and future, what they must [be]." Jonathan Weiss, *Privilege, Posture and Protection–"Religion" in the Law*, 73 Yale L.J. 593, 604 (1964). Respect for religion dictates that no secular authority should take a position in matters of faith. The reluctance to define religion might be related to the nature of the prevailing religion in a country and the state's relation to it. In 1944, the U.S. Supreme Court (USSC), per Justice Douglas, held that the First Amendment bars submitting to the jury a question of whether religious beliefs are true. "Men may believe what they cannot prove. * * * Religious experiences which are as real as life to some may be incomprehensible to others." *United States v. Ballard*, 322 U.S. 78, 86 (1944). In cases involving claims of conscientious objectors under the Universal Military Training and Service Act, which exempts persons from service by reason of their religious training and beliefs, the USSC was confronted with the question "What is religious belief?" and concluded:

> Within that phrase [belief] would come all sincere religious beliefs which are based upon a power or being, or upon a faith, to which all else is subordinate or upon which all else is ultimately dependent. The test might be stated in these words: A sincere and meaningful belief which occupies in the life of its possessor a place parallel to that filled by the God of those admittedly qualifying for the exemption comes within the statutory definition. This construction avoids imputing to Congress an intent to classify different religious beliefs, exempting some and excluding others, and is in accord with the well-established congressional policy of equal treatment for those whose opposition to service is grounded in their religious tenets.

United States v. Seeger, 380 U.S. 163, 176 (1965).

And the Constitution specifically prohibits making belief in God a condition to hold public office. See Torcaso v. Watkins, below.

The German Federal Constitutional Court (GFCC) extends free exercise rights to members of religious organizations that are not recognized churches. "The exercise of religious freedom depends neither upon an association's numerical size nor upon its social relevance. This follows from the command binding the state to ideological and religious neutrality and from the principle of parity of churches and creeds." *Blood Transfusion Case*, 32 BVerfGE 98 (1971). Religion may be exercised regardless of the legal status of the community. German authorities, on the other hand, have no difficulties determining what is and is not a religion, at least as far as Scientology is concerned. Should external factors (the number of believers, the "age-old form" of religion, or whether regular services are held) be given weight? Is it important that others share the religious belief? Is the centrality of God necessary? Should other forms of belief in transcendental forces be recognized? If constitutional protection is granted to religions, why not to secular rational beliefs, if these are sincerely held to be central? While the German position is nearly as reluctant to look at "external" criteria of religion as the USSC and some of the Italian courts, it is quite ready to use external criteria when it comes to recognizing churches. Article 137 (5) of the Weimar Constitution, which is in force in the Appendix to the Basic Law, states that public law status is granted to religious bodies "if their constitution, and the number of their members offer an assurance of their permanency." Should differentiation among religious bodies be separated from the equal treatment of religions?

2.   The U.S. Universal Military Training and Service Act granted exemption from military service on grounds of religious beliefs only. Justice Harlan (dissenting) found this distinction unconstitutional. For him, beliefs emanating from a purely ethical or philosophical source should be treated equally. "The common denominator must be the intensity of moral conviction with which a belief is [held]." *Welsh v. United States*, 398 U.S. 333, 358 (1970). Is it relevant that some constitutions, including the U.S., provide for freedom of religion but not of beliefs or conscience? In *Welsh* a plurality of four justices upheld an exemption where the applicant stated that his beliefs were "certainly religious in the ethical sense of that word." *Id.* at 341. Should there be a presumption in favor of sincerity of conviction with known religions that are shared as such, while with individual ethical beliefs the burden of proof should be on the individual? "Many activities that obviously are exercises of religion are not required by conscience or doctrine. * * * Any activity engaged in by a church as a body is an exercise of religion." Douglas Laycock, *Towards a General Theory of the Religion Clauses: The Case of Church Labor Relations and the Right to Church Autonomy*, 81 Colum. L. Rev. 1373, 1390 (1981). The European Commission found that pacifism is a protected "conviction." *Arrowsmith v. United Kingdom*, 3 E.H.R.R. 218 (1978). The applicant defined pacifism as "the commitment, in both theory and practice, to the philosophy of securing one's political or other objectives without resort to the threat or use of force against another human being under any circumstances, even in response to the threat or use of force" and was accepted by both the UK government and the Commission. *Id.* at para. 68. The Commission said that "pacifism as a philosophy and, in particular, as defined above, falls within the ambit of the right to freedom of thought and conscience." *Id.* at para. 69.

A number of constitutions protect nonreligious conscience and belief, including ideological and political convictions. In *Mitsubishi Resin, Inc. v. Takano* (1973), the Supreme Court of Japan considered the termination of a trial-term private-employment contract on grounds of nondisclosure of the employee's involvement in the student movement. The issue was whether the employee was discriminated against for his beliefs. Without ruling out some connection between past action and belief and stating that beliefs are protected, the Court found that the protection applies primarily in regard to government employment. (See Chapter 11, Section B.1.)

3.   The more a state is expected to be the defender of the true faith the more likely the authorities, including courts, will be inclined to enforce a prevailing theological understanding of religion. But this assumption is not always true. In 1952, the Chief Court of Sind (Pakistan) held that:

> [I]t is well-settled law, and one of the fundamental principle [*sic*] of the Muhammadan Law itself, that no Court can test or guage [*sic*] the sincerity of religious belief, and in order to hold that a person was Sunni Muslim, it was sufficient for a Court to be satisfied that he professed to

be a Sunni Muslim. It is not permissible to [*sic*] any Court to enquire further into the state of the mind and the beliefs of a person who professed to belong to a particular faith and inquire whether his actual beliefs conformed to the orthodox tenets of that particular faith * * *.

Moula Bux v. Charuk, 1952 P.L.D. (Sind) 54, 56 (Pak.).

Compare the judicial attitudes of Pakistan and the U.S. (*Seeger)* toward religion. Pakistani judges used to allow the individual to determine his or her religious identity (possibly against the evaluation of the church), while in the U.S., the question is whether belief amounts to religion.

4. State neutrality and the limits to the protection of beliefs are discussed in Germany in the *Tobacco Atheist Case*, 12 BVerfGE 1, 4 (1960).[d] A prisoner offered tobacco to fellow inmates in an attempt to persuade them to abandon the Christian church. For this activity he was denied parole. The prisoner complained, unsuccessfully, on grounds of freedom of belief.

[O]ne who violates limitations erected by the Basic Law' general order of values cannot claim freedom of belief. The Basic Law does not protect every manifestation of belief but only those historically developed among civilized people on the basis of certain fundamental moral opinions * * * The religiously neutral state cannot and should not define in detail the content of this freedom, because it is not allowed to evaluate its citizens' beliefs or nonbeliefs. Nevertheless, it must prevent misuse of this freedom. It follows from the Basic Law's order of values, especially from the dignity of the human being, that a misuse is especially apparent whenever the dignity of another person is violated. Recruiting for a belief and convincing someone turn from another belief, normally legal activities, become misuses of the basic right if a person tries, directly or indirectly, to use a base or immoral instrument to lure other persons from their beliefs. * * * A person who exploits the special circumstances of penal servitude and promises and rewards someone with luxury goods in order to make him renounce his beliefs does not enjoy the benefit of the protection of Article 4 (1) of the Basic Law.

The understanding of religion plays a crucial role in the persecution of religious minorities. The following two cases were decided at roughly the same time. In the first case the concern was about the majority's persecutorial animus directed against the minority religion; in the second the minority is understood to endanger the majority religion.

CHURCH OF THE LUKUMI BABALU AYE, INC. v. CITY OF HIALEAH

Supreme Court (United States).
508 U.S. 520 (1993).

Justice Kennedy delivered the opinion of the Court.

The principle that government may not enact laws that suppress religious belief or practice is so well understood that few violations are

d. Translated in Walter F. Murphy and   *tional Law* 467 (1977).
Joseph Tanenhaus, *Comparative Constitu-*

recorded in our opinions... Our review confirms that the laws in question were enacted by officials who did not understand, failed to perceive, or chose to ignore the fact that their official actions violated the Nation's essential commitment to religious freedom. The challenged laws had an impermissible object; and in all events the principle of general applicability was violated because the secular ends asserted in defense of the laws were pursued only with respect to conduct motivated by religious beliefs. We invalidate the challenged enactment and reverse the judgment of the Court of Appeals.

I

A

This case involves practices of the Santeria religion, which originated in the 19th century. When hundreds of thousands of members of the Yoruba people were brought as slaves from western Africa to Cuba, their traditional African religion absorbed significant elements of Roman Catholicism. The resulting syncretion, or fusion, is Santeria, "the way of the saints." * * * [O]ne of the principal forms of devotion is an animal sacrifice.

The animals are killed by the cutting of the carotid arteries in the neck.

* * * The District Court estimated that there are at least 50,000 practitioners in South Florida today.

B

Petitioner Church of the Lukumi Babalu Aye, Inc. (Church), is a not-for-profit corporation organized under Florida law in 1973. The Church and its congregants practice the Santeria religion. * * * In April 1987, the Church leased land in the City of Hialeah, Florida, and announced plans to establish a house of worship as well as a school, cultural center, and museum. * * * it appears that it received all needed approvals by early August 1987.

The prospect of a Santeria church in their midst was distressing to many members of the Hialeah community, * * *

[T]he city council adopted Resolution 87–66, which noted the "concern" expressed by residents of the city "that certain religions may propose to engage in practices which are inconsistent with public morals, peace or safety," and declared that "[t]he City reiterates its commitment to a prohibition against any and all acts of any and all religious groups which are inconsistent with public morals, peace or safety." Next, the council approved an emergency ordinance, Ordinance 87–40, which incorporated in full, except as to penalty, Florida's animal cruelty laws. Fla.Stat. ch. 828 (1987). Among other things, the incorporated state law subjected to criminal punishment "[w]hoever * * * unnecessarily or cruelly * * * kills any animal." § 828.12.

[Additionally] [o]rdinance 87–52 defined "sacrifice" as "to unnecessarily kill, torment, torture, or mutilate an animal in a public or private ritual or ceremony not for the primary purpose of food consumption," and prohibited owning or possessing an animal "intending to use such animal for food purposes."

II

The city does not argue that Santeria is not a "religion" within the meaning of the First Amendment. Nor could it. Although the practice of animal sacrifice may seem abhorrent to some, "religious beliefs need not be acceptable, logical, consistent, or comprehensible to others in order to merit First Amendment protection." *Thomas v. Review Bd. of Indiana Employment Security Div.*, 450 U.S. 707, 714 (1981).

In addressing the constitutional protection for free exercise of religion, our cases establish the general proposition that a law that is neutral and of general applicability need not be justified by a compelling governmental interest even if the law has the incidental effect of burdening a particular religious practice. See *Employment Div., Dept. of Human Resources of Ore. v. Smith*, supra. Neutrality and general applicability are interrelated, and, as becomes apparent in this case, failure to satisfy one requirement is a likely indication that the other has not been satisfied. A law failing to satisfy these requirements must be justified by a compelling governmental interest and must be narrowly tailored to advance that interest. These ordinances fail to satisfy the Smith requirements. We begin by discussing neutrality.

A

In our Establishment Clause cases we have often stated the principle that the First Amendment forbids an official purpose to disapprove of a particular religion or of religion in general. * * * These cases, however, for the most part have addressed governmental efforts to benefit religion or particular religions, and so have dealt with a question different, at least in its formulation and emphasis, from the issue here. Petitioners allege an attempt to disfavor their religion because of the religious ceremonies it commands, and the Free Exercise Clause is dispositive in our analysis.

* * *

At a minimum, the protections of the Free Exercise Clause pertain if the law at issue discriminates against some or all religious beliefs or regulates or prohibits conduct because it is undertaken for religious reasons. * * *

1

Although a law targeting religious beliefs as such is never permissible, * * * if the object of a law is to infringe upon or restrict practices because of their religious motivation, the law is not neutral, see *Employment Div., Dept. of Human Resources of Oregon v. Smith*; and it is invalid unless it is justified by a compelling interest and is narrowly tailored to advance that interest. * * * A law lacks facial neutrality if it refers to a religious practice without a secular meaning discernable from the language or context. * * * The ordinances, furthermore, define "sacrifice" in secular terms, without referring to religious practices.

* * *Facial neutrality is not determinative. * * * The Free Exercise Clause protects against governmental hostility which is masked, as well as overt.

* * * It becomes evident that these ordinances target Santeria sacrifice when the ordinances' operation is considered. * * * The subject at hand does implicate, of course, multiple concerns unrelated to religious animosity, for example, the suffering or mistreatment visited upon the sacrificed animals and health hazards from improper disposal. But the ordinances when considered together disclose an object remote from these legitimate concerns. * * * The definition excludes almost all killings of animals except for religious sacrifice, and the primary purpose requirement narrows the proscribed category even further, in particular by exempting kosher slaughter, * * * A pattern of exemptions parallels the pattern of narrow prohibitions. Each contributes to the gerrymander.

Ordinance 87–40 incorporates the Florida animal cruelty statute, Fla.Stat. § 828.12 (1987). Its prohibition is broad on its face, punishing "[w]hoever * * * unnecessarily * * * kills any animal." * * * Killings for religious reasons are deemed unnecessary, whereas most other killings fall outside the prohibition. * * * Thus, religious practice is being singled out for discriminatory treatment.

* * * In determining if the object of a law is a neutral one under the Free Exercise Clause, we can also find guidance in our equal protection cases. As Justice Harlan noted in the related context of the Establishment Clause, "[n]eutrality in its application requires an equal protection mode of analysis." *Walz v. Tax Comm'n of New York City*, 397 U.S. 664, 696 (1970).

B

* * *

The principle that government, in pursuit of legitimate interests, cannot in a selective manner impose burdens only on conduct motivated by religious belief is essential to the protection of the rights guaranteed by the Free Exercise Clause

* * *

Respondent claims that Ordinances 87–40, 87–52, and 87–71 advance two interests: protecting the public health and preventing cruelty to animals. The ordinances are underinclusive for those ends. [According to the other city ordinances,] * * * the eradication of insects and pests is "obviously justified"; and the euthanasia of excess animals "makes sense." *Id.*, at 22. These ipse dixits do not explain why religion alone must bear the burden of the ordinances, when many of these secular killings fall within the city's interest in preventing the cruel treatment of animals.

We conclude, in sum, that each of Hialeah's ordinances pursues the city's governmental interests only against conduct motivated by religious belief. The ordinances "ha[ve] every appearance of a prohibition that society is prepared to impose upon [Santeria worshippers] but not upon itself." *Florida Star v. B.J.F.*, 491 U.S. 524, 542 (1989).

III

* * *

A law burdening religious practice that is not neutral or not of general application must undergo the most rigorous of scrutiny. To satisfy the commands of the First Amendment, a law restrictive of religious practice must advance " 'interests of the highest order' " and must be narrowly tailored in pursuit of those interests.

First, even were the governmental interests compelling, the ordinances are not drawn in narrow terms to accomplish those interests.

Respondent has not demonstrated, moreover, that, in the context of these ordinances, its governmental interests are compelling. Where government restricts only conduct protected by the First Amendment and fails to enact feasible measures to restrict other conduct producing substantial harm or alleged harm of the same sort, the interest given in justification of the restriction is not compelling. It is established in our strict scrutiny jurisprudence that "a law cannot be regarded as protecting an interest 'of the highest order' * * * when it leaves appreciable damage to that supposedly vital interest unprohibited." *Florida Star*, 491 U.S., at 541–42,

IV

The Free Exercise Clause commits government itself to religious tolerance, and upon even slight suspicion that proposals for state intervention stem from animosity to religion or distrust of its practices, all officials must pause to remember their own high duty to the Constitution and to the rights it secures. Those in office must be resolute in resisting importunate demands and must ensure that the sole reasons for imposing the burdens of law and regulation are secular. Legislators may not devise mechanisms, overt or disguised, designed to persecute or oppress a religion or its practices. The laws here in question were enacted contrary to these constitutional principles, and they are void.

Reversed.

Justice Souter, concurring in part and concurring in the judgment.

While general applicability is, for the most part, self-explanatory, free-exercise neutrality is not self-revealing. Cf. *Lee v. Weisman*, 505 U.S. 577, 627 (1992) (Justice Souter, concurring) (considering Establishment Clause neutrality). A law that is religion neutral on its face or in its purpose may lack neutrality in its effect by forbidding something that religion requires or requiring something that religion forbids. * * * A secular law, applicable to all, that prohibits consumption of alcohol, for example, will affect members of religions that require the use of wine differently from members of other religions and nonbelievers, disproportionately burdening the practice of, say, Catholicism or Judaism. Without an exemption for sacramental wine, Prohibition may fail the test of religion neutrality.

THE AHMADIS CASES

Tayyab Mahmud, FREEDOM OF RELIGION & RELIGIOUS MINORITIES IN PAKISTAN: A STUDY OF JUDICIAL PRACTICE,

19 Fordham Int'l L.J. 40, 43, 47–50 (1995).

The record of Pakistan's superior judiciary in the area of protection of religious minorities * * * has gone through three distinct phases. The first phase is remarkable for its unequivocal protection of freedom of religion and religious minorities. The second phase represents a contraction of this protection through undue deference to the formal constitutional amendment process prescribed by the Constitution. The last, and current, phase is one in which the judiciary has capitulated before the ascendant forces of religious reaction and abdicated judicial protection of religious minorities. * * *

The Court reasoned that in prohibiting the use of distinguishing characteristics of Islam by the Ahmadis, Ordinance XX was in line with statutes that regulate commercial activity, target deceptive trade practices, and protect trademarks. The Court then noted that, "[f]or example, the Coca[-]Cola Company will not permit anyone to sell, even a few ounces of his own product in his own bottles or other receptacles, marked Coca[-]Cola, even though its price may be a few cents." [*Zaheeruddin*e at 1753–54.] The Court acknowledged that religious freedom is not confined to religious beliefs, but rather extends to "essential and integral" religious practices. It claimed, however, that the appellants had not explained how the prohibited epithets and public rituals were an essential part of their religion. The crux of the problem, according to the Court, was that the Ahmadis, whom the Court characterized as "an insignificant minority" and "hypersensitive," use epithets:

> [i]n a manner which to the Muslim mind looks like a deliberate and calculated act of defiling and desecration of their holy personages, [and which] is a threat to the integrity of 'Ummah' [Islamic community] and [the] tranquillity of the nation, and it is also bound to give rise to a serious law and order situation, like it happened many a time in the past.

In interpreting the phrase "subject to law" in Article 20 of the Constitution, the Court rejected the distinction made by the appellant between positive law and Islamic law. The Court took the position that due to the incorporation of the Objectives Resolution[f] as a substantive

---

e. 26 S.C.M.R. 1718 (1993) (Pak.). There were more than 2,300 cases pending, involving charges pursuant to Ordinance XX, at issue in *Zaheeruddin*.

f. In 1947, the leaders of the Pakistan Muslim League had no intention of conceding to demands for a theocratic state. Nevertheless, they compromised to diffuse the issue and deny the ulama a platform from

which to mobilize mass support. The mobilization must be understood in the context of the position of India; Muslims were in search of statehood. This compromise took form in the Objectives Resolution, adopted by the Constituent Assembly in 1949. The Objectives Resolution was a statement of intent regarding Pakistan's future constitution and contained a deliberately vague

part of the Constitution in 1985, injunctions of Islam as contained in the Qur'an and Sunnah are adopted as "the real and the effective law," and "are now the positive law." The Court claimed that due to this change "[t]he power of judicial review of the superior Courts also got enhanced," and "every man-made law must now conform to the Injunctions of Islam as contained in Qur'an and Sunnah * * * Therefore, even the Fundamental Rights as given in the Constitution must not violate the norms of Islam." The Court went on to say:

> Anything, in any fundamental right, which violates the Injunctions of Islam thus must be repugnant. It must be noted here that the Injunctions of Islam, as contained in Qur'an and the Sunnah, guarantee the rights of the minorities also in such a satisfactory way that no other legal order can offer anything equal. * * *

> [I]n this Ideological State, the appellants, who are non-Muslims want to pass off their faith as Islam[.] It must be appreciated that in this part of the world, faith is still the most precious thing to a Muslim believer, and he will not tolerate a Government which is not prepared to save him of such deceptions or forgeries.

NADEEM AHMAD SIDDIQ, ENFORCED APOSTASY: ZAHEERUDDIN v. STATE AND THE OFFICIAL PERSECUTION OF THE AHMADIYYA COMMUNITY IN PAKISTAN,

14 Law & Ineq. 275, 278–279, 282–285, 287–289,
291–292, 295–297, 299–307, 309–310 (1995).

* * * Ahmadis are a religious people who view themselves as members of a Muslim Community within the pale of Islam. * * *

The fundamental difference between Ahmadis and the Sunni Muslim majority in Pakistan concerns the identity of the Promised Messiah. * * *

The Islamic Republic of Pakistan was formed in 1947 * * * as a Muslim State but not as an Islamic theocracy per se. Pakistan was intended to function as a secular state accommodating other faiths but existing primarily to allow the free practice of Islam. * * * Pakistan has a population of about 130 million, of which approximately 3.5 to 4 million are Ahmadis.

Despite Pakistan's inception as a secular state, Muslim fundamentalist groups mounted increasing pressure to make it an Islamic theocracy. * * * Before 1953, Ahmadis were safe in Pakistan. Because there was no agreement amongst the ulama on fundamental questions of what a Muslim or an Islamic State was, "[the] government [in 1953] used this lack of unanimity to curb the activities of the fundamentalists."[38] [After the 1974 anti-Ahmadi disturbances, which spread throughout Pakistan, Prime Minister Zulfikar Ali Bhutto altered the Pakistan Constitution

pledge to incorporate Islamic principles. However, it also envisaged guaranteed fundamental rights, including religious freedom and rights of religious minorities, the rule of law, and an independent judiciary.

38. Rafiz Zakaria, *The Struggle within Islam: The Conflict Between Religion and Politics* 229 (1988).

and pronounced the Ahmadis a non-Muslim minority.[g] "Pakistan's Zia ul-Haqq regime, which fostered Islamic revivalism and the Islamization of Pakistani society, cracked down on Ahmadis through Martial Law Ordinance XX, issued on April 26, 1984, in an effort to regain Islamic 'purity'." After this ordinance took effect, Ahmadis no longer possessed the right to profess, practice, or propagate their beliefs either verbally or in writing for fear of being subject to fines or imprisonment. Ahmadi publications were banned and copies of Ahmadi translations of the Holy Quran were destroyed. * * * Ahmadis were accused of "masquerading as Muslims" and thus deceiving the general public. In order to safeguard the public from subversion, the government policy was to stop Ahmadis from identifying themselves as Muslims.

Under Ordinance XX, Ahmadis "pose as Muslims" and are punished. [They are prohibited from exercising religious activities required of Muslims.] * * * According to Ordinance XX, Ahmadis praying, using the call to prayer (Azan), calling their places of worship mosques (Masjid), or practicing any other tenet of Muslim faith is offensive to the religious sentiments of Pakistan's Sunni Muslims and is therefore a criminal offense.

Ahmadi mosques have been desecrated and destroyed * * * The Criminal Law (Amendment) Act of 1986, known as the "Blasphemy Law" of Section 295C of the Pakistan Penal Code makes blasphemy punishable by death alone. Ahmadis allegedly blaspheme by professing to be Muslims and have thus been repeatedly charged pursuant to Section 295C. * * *

III.   The Decision in Zaheeruddin v. State

Zaheeruddin was the first Pakistan Court case to consider the constitutionality of Ordinance XX. In Zaheeruddin, the Pakistan Court, on July 3, 1993, dismissed eight appeals brought by members of the Ahmadiyya Community. [See below.] The five Ahmadi criminal defendants, charged for wearing [badges bearing] the "Kalima"[h] on their persons and claiming to be Muslims, were returned to jail for the remainder of their sentences.

g. Even after the Ahmadis were declared non-Muslims by the Amendment, they were allowed to engage in Islamic religious practices. In 1976, when a group of ulama asked for an injunction prohibiting them from reciting the Koran, the Lahore High Court denied the petition and held that:

It is the policy of the State to protect all religions but to interfere with none. * * * [T]he right of conscience, i.e., the right of individual members of a community to hold certain religious beliefs and opinion is of course a religious one and one that cannot be called in question or adjudicated upon in the civil Court. The Lahore High Court recited "the fundamental principle of there being no compulsion in religious affairs. * * * It is not the province or duty of the Court to pronounce on the truth of religious tenets or to regulate religious rites or ceremonies." The Lahore High Court held that "every one has a right to follow the religion of his own liking and is at liberty to worship according to the dictates of his own conscience without being guided or governed in this respect by persons following a different religion.

Mobashir v. Bokhari, 1978 P.L.D. (Lahore High Ct.) 113 (Pak.), * * *.

h. The Kalima ("the word") is a covenant that is recited by a nonbeliever upon entering the fold of Islam. It is recited in the Arabic language and is exclusive to Muslims who recite it, not as proof of their faith but very often for spiritual well- being. The Kalima declares: "There is no God but Allah and Muhammad is His Prophet."

The Pakistan Court, in Zaheeruddin, held that laws restricting the religious practices of Ahmadis are constitutional. * * *

A.   The Pakistan Court Considers Ahmadis Non-Muslims

Article 260(3) of the Pakistan Constitution provides that Ahmadis are non-Muslims. Article 260(3)(a) of the Pakistan Constitution defines Muslim:

Muslim means a person who believes in the unity and oneness of Almighty Allah, in the absolute and unqualified Prophethood of Muhammad (peace be upon him), the last of the prophets and does not believe or recognize as a prophet or religious reformer, any person who claimed or claims to be a prophet, in any sense of the word or any description whatsoever, after Muhammad (peace be upon him). * * *

Support for the latter portion of the definition of Muslim [not shared by the Ahmadis] cannot be found in the Holy Quran or in the traditions of the Prophet Muhammad. * * *

B.   Company and Trademark Laws Do Not Prohibit Ahmadis from Muslim Practices

[The Court ruled that because Ahmadis are non-Muslims, any Ahmadi representation as a Muslim is fraud and deception upon the public.] Pakistani Courts frequently cite the laws of other common law jurisdictions, particularly the United States, Great Britain, Canada and Australia. Given Pakistan's "Anglo-Islamic" and post-colonial common law heritage, the Pakistan Supreme Court's respect for Anglo-American law is not surprising. The Pakistan Court relied on the company laws of Britain, India and Pakistan and trademark law from the United States, to justify prohibiting Ahmadis from using Islamic epithets or practices in the exercise of their faith. According to the Pakistan Court,

[i]ntentionally using trade names, trade marks, property marks or description of others in order to make [third parties believe] that they belong to the user thereof amounts to an offence. * * *

United States case law belies the fallacy of the Pakistan Court's reasoning. * * * In McDaniel v. Mirza Ahmad Sohrab, 27 N.Y.S.2d 525 (1941) * * * [t]he plaintiffs alleged that any representation or solicitation in the name of the Baha'i faith by defendants was a misrepresentation to the public that such use was officially authorized and sanctioned. The McDaniel court held that plaintiffs had no cause of action against defendants and stated, "[t]he plaintiffs have no right to a monopoly of the name of a religion. The defendants, who purport to be members of the same religion, have an equal right to use the name of the religion in connection with their own meetings, lectures, classes and other activities." *Id.* at 527. Defendants were thus permitted the "absolute right" to practice their faith and conduct their religious meetings. * * *

C.   The Pakistan Court Misused United States Freedom of Religion Precedent

The Pakistan Constitution does not contain a provision similar to the United States Constitution's Establishment Clause. The Pakistan Constitution, however, does include a Free Exercise component. Article

20 of the Pakistan Constitution guarantees the "[f]reedom to profess religion and to manage religious institutions" only "[s]ubject to law, public order and morality."[112] The Pakistan Court referred to the United States, where "fundamental rights are given top priority," as a country with "similar fundamental rights." * * * In Zaheeruddin, the Pakistan Court relied on United States case law to illustrate how religious practices may be restricted for public order and safety requirements. The Pakistan Court used Cantwell v. Connecticut, 310 U.S. 296 (1939), as authority for the proposition that the "freedom to act" on one's beliefs can be regulated for the protection of society. * * * The Pakistan Court quoted [among others] from Hamilton v. Regents, stating that, "Government owes a duty to the people within its jurisdiction to preserve itself in adequate strength to maintain peace and order and assure the enforcement of law. And every citizen owes the reciprocal duty, according to his capacity, to support and defend the Government against all enemies."

Finally, the Pakistan Court incorrectly quoted the United States Supreme Court as stating in Cox v. New Hampshire that

> [a] statute requiring persons using public streets for a parade or procession to procure a special license therefor[e] from the local authorities, does not constitute an unconstitutional interference with religious worship or the practice of religion, as applied to a group marching along a sidewalk in single file carrying signs and placards advertising their religious beliefs.[133]

The Pakistan Court * * * asserted that Ahmadi practices and centenary celebrations threaten Pakistani society by disturbing public peace, order and tranquility. The Court found such acts injure the feelings of the Muslim majority and therefore elicit violent reactions. Since violence results from Ahmadi practices, the Pakistan Court asserted that the Pakistan legislature has the authority to restrict these religious practices and that Ordinance XX was enacted pursuant to such authority. The Pakistan Court disingenuously applied United States case law that is over half a century old. The Court's reliance on old cases as precedent was hasty and self-serving. However, even if an analysis of Zaheeruddin is limited to these cases, Ordinance XX should still be found unconstitutional. The Pakistan Court took judicial statements out of context and misinterpreted United States law. * * * The United States decisions reveal that a constitutional statute must be neutral from its inception and thereafter applied equitably.

The Pakistan Court failed to recognize that in Cantwell the state could not completely ban certain religious practices and that a statute is

---

112. Pak. Const., art. 20. The full text of Article 20 is:

> Freedom to profess religion and to manage religious institutions.–Subject to law, public order and morality,–
>
> every citizen shall have the right to profess, practise and propagate his religion; and

every religious denomination and every sect thereof shall have the right to establish, maintain and manage its religious institutions.

133. *Zaheeruddin*, 1993 S.C.M.R. at 1764 (citing the above as an alleged direct quotation from *Cox*). The quotation does not, in fact, appear anywhere in the *Cox* opinion.

unconstitutional if it forbids religious, charitable or philanthropic solicitation. * * * In formulating its balancing test as to what conduct may be regulated, the Cantwell Court held that " 'breach of peace' embraces a great variety of conduct destroying or menacing public order and tranquillity." A "breach of peace" is limited to violent acts or words directed at and likely to produce violence in others and not by the mere communication of undesirable views. * * *

"When clear and present danger of riot, disorder, * * * or other immediate threat to public safety, peace or order, appears, the power of the State to prevent or punish is obvious. Equally obvious is it that a State may not unduly suppress free communication of views, religious or other, under the guise of conserving desirable conditions." 310 U.S. at 308.

The Pakistan Court did not mention that the law pertaining to the public practice of religion in Cox is only a time, place and manner regulation and not a prohibition.

* * * The Pakistan Government suppresses Ahmadi religious practice for the supposed protection of society because Ahmadi beliefs offend public sentiments and allegedly subvert law and order. Ahmadis, however, do not seek to create disorder. * * * Ahmadis do not commit violent acts in the practice of their faith nor do they direct their religious expression at others or intend to elicit violent reactions. * * * Furthermore, the practices of Ahmadis are similar to those of the majority Sunni population. * * *

Unlike polygamy in Reynolds, the practicing of Islam in Pakistan was never considered subversive of public order or "odious," nor was it ever criminal. In Pakistan, Islam is the religion of the majority and its practices are socially encouraged. Ahmadi practicing of Islam, however, is considered criminal. A perfectly moral act becomes criminal if an Ahmadi commits it. Ordinance XX therefore targets the religious practices of Ahmadis and prohibits them from performing otherwise socially encouraged acts. Ordinance XX, unlike other criminal laws, makes the actor, not the act, illegal. Ahmadis are therefore discriminated against for who they are and not what they do. Ordinance XX is a discriminatory law which names and targets a specific group and is not neutrally and generally applicable to all citizens.

The Pakistan Court * * * cited public safety to justify its prohibition, knowing, however, that Ahmadis would not engage in acts which would per se constitute a threat to society. Lights on buildings and Islamic inscriptions on walls, both of which were prohibited by the Jhang District Magistrate, are common sights and are not offensive in Pakistan. Further, the risk of disorder was minimal as the Ahmadi celebrations would have taken place in Rabwah, a predominantly Ahmadi village. * * *

Even older United States precedent demonstrates that intolerance and animosity against a religious community make that community worthy of governmental protection, not disdain. Instead, the Pakistan Government and Court participated in the intolerance and subversion of freedom of conscience and religion by deciding against the Ahmadiyya Community.

In order to thoroughly examine Free Exercise precedent and the protection of this fundamental right, the Pakistan Court should have applied more recent case law, * * * [which] demonstrate that the threat posed by religious beliefs must be substantial and not merely repugnant to the majority. They also emphasize that, for a law to be constitutional, it must be neutral in nature and application.

Notes and Questions

1. Compare *Church of Lukumi Babalu Aye v. Hialeah* with the facts in *Zaheeruddin*, which was argued at the same time. The minority nature of the religion was not an issue in either case. In the case of the Santeria, protection was granted against the majority (in the sense that the statute might have been motivated by the community's animus). In *Zaheeruddin* it was the majority religion and the community's animus that was protected. Is there any special reason for a court to side with the minority? Would the USSC have reached the same result if the Santeria religion had been more widespread and challenged mainstream religions?

2. Is it relevant that the ISC in *Acharya*, above, was addressing a religion in the context of reviewing a police order about possessing a knife at a public gathering, while the USSC was discussing a total ban on a religious practice?

3. From time to time there are campaigns or legal measures against so called sects and cults in Western democracies. The French government, for example, has established an "observatory" to follow sect activities; in Germany, state security authorities closely observed the Church of Scientology. These are considered disruptive systems of belief, which are often denied the protection of religion even if the teachings and most practices of the "cult" resemble the structure of recognized religions. The reasons given for disregarding the religious nature of the "cult" are its self-destructive nature (resulting, allegedly, in mass suicide) and the alleged techniques used in teaching ("brainwashing"), as well as the alleged "captivity" of the believers. A bill was tabled in the French Senate, in 2001, that would have imposed a sentence of up to five years detention and a fine of up to five million francs for causing a "state of subjection," either physical or psychological, through the "exercise of serious and repeated pressures or techniques aimed at altering the capacity of judgement." The bill did not define "sects," although the authorities prepared a list of more than 160 organizations that were viewed as "sects" and subject to official interest.

A.2.   RELIGIOUS PRACTICES AND FREEDOM OF CONSCIENCE

TORCASO v. WATKINS

Supreme Court (United States).
367 U.S. 488 (1961).

Mr. Justice Black delivered the opinion of the Court.

Article 37 of the Declaration of Rights of the Maryland Constitution provides:

'(N)o religious test ought ever to be required as a qualification for any office of profit or trust in this State, other than a declaration of belief in the existence of God * * *'

* * *

The appellant Torcaso was appointed to the office of Notary Public by the Governor of Maryland but was refused a commission to serve because he would not declare his belief in God. He then brought this action in a Maryland Circuit Court to compel issuance of his commission, charging that the State's requirement that he declare this belief violated 'the First and Fourteenth Amendments to the Constitution of the United States * * *'

* * * [T]here is much historical precedent for such laws. Indeed, it was largely to escape religious test oaths and declarations that a great many of the early colonists left Europe and came here hoping to worship in their own way. It soon developed, however, that many of those who had fled to escape religious test oaths turned out to be perfectly willing, when they had the power to do so, to force dissenters from their faith to take test oaths in conformity with that faith.

* * *

When our Constitution was adopted, the desire to put the people 'securely beyond the reach' of religious test oaths brought about the inclusion in Article VI of that document of a provision that 'no religious Test shall ever be required as a Qualification to any Office or public Trust under the United States.' * * * Not satisfied, however, with Article VI and other guarantees in the original Constitution, the First Congress proposed and the States very shortly thereafter adopted our Bill of Rights, including the First Amendment.

* * *

And a concurring opinion in *McCollum*,[i] written by Mr. Justice Frankfurter and joined by the other *Everson*[j] dissenters, said this:

'We are all agreed that the First and Fourteenth Amendments have a secular reach far more penetrating in the conduct of Government than merely to forbid an 'established church.' * * * We renew our conviction that 'we have staked the very existence of our country on the faith that complete separation between the state and religion is best for the state and best for religion.'[8]

Nothing decided or written in *Zorach*[k] lends support to the idea that the Court there intended to open up the way for government, state or federal, to restore the historically and constitutionally discredited policy of probing religious beliefs by test oaths or limiting public offices to

i. *Illinois ex rel. McCollum v. Board of Education*, 333 U.S. 203 (1948).

j. *Everson v. Board of Education*, 330 U.S. 1 (1947) (town reimburses parents for use of bus to parochial school—no violation of the Establishment Clause.)

8. 333 U.S. at 213, 232.

k. *Zorach v. Clauson* 343 U.S. 306 (1952) (program that allowed students to leave campus for off-campus religious instruction upheld).

persons who have, or perhaps more properly profess to have, a belief in some particular kind of religious concept.[9]

* * *

We repeat and again reaffirm that neither a State nor the Federal Government can constitutionally force a person 'to profess a belief or disbelief in any religion.' Neither can constitutionally pass laws or impose requirements which aid all religions as against non-believers, and neither can aid those religions based on a belief in the existence of God as against those religions founded on different beliefs.

In upholding the State's religious test for public office the highest court of Maryland said:

'The petitioner is not compelled to believe or disbelieve, under threat of punishment or other compulsion. True, unless he makes the declaration of belief he cannot hold public office in Maryland, but he is not compelled to hold office.'

The fact, however, that a person is not compelled to hold public office cannot possibly be an excuse for barring him from office by state-imposed criteria forbidden by the Constitution.

* * *

This Maryland religious test for public office unconstitutionally invades the appellant's freedom of belief and religion and therefore cannot be enforced against him.

Notes and Questions

1. Torcaso's claim is one of freedom of conscience and belief. He did not want to take the oath because that would have required him to falsely profess a belief. However, the USSC construed the issue in such a way that nonestablishment raised the difficult problems. The Maryland Court held that the issue was access to a public position and not of religious exercise (or lack of it). The USSC found that the religious-oath requirement barred the applicant, through use of criteria that violated the principle of separation of church and state. In countries where there are specific constitutional provisions against discrimination based on belief, to require an oath of belief might be discrimination on the basis of religion or worldview. (The GFCC finds no discrimination or imposition of religion in the prescribed oath. The oath, even a secular one, may be refused on grounds of one's faith as there is no constitutional value overriding it. This applies to witnesses but not to office holders. 33 BVerfGE 23, (1972).)

2. The European Court of Human Rights (ECHR) adopted the same position as *Torcaso*. The oath taken by members of San Marino's Parliament was "I, * * * swear on the Holy Gospels." This was held to represent religious indoctrination. *Buscarini and Others v. San Marino*, no. 24654/94,

---

9. In one of his famous letters of 'a Landholder,' published in December 1787, Oliver Ellsworth, a member of the Federal Constitutional Convention and later Chief Justice of this Court, included among his strong arguments against religious test oaths the following statement: 'In short, test-laws are utterly ineffectual: they are no security at all; because men of loose principles will, by an external compliance, evade them. If they exclude any persons, it will be honest men, men of principle, who will rather suffer an injury, than act contrary to the dictates of their consciences. * * * '

§ 8, 34–42, (ECHR) 1999–I. Secular-oath requirements may also raise issues of imposed belief. The Spanish Constitution specifies the conditions of membership in the Cortes. A House resolution created an additional requirement: elected members must take an oath to the Constitution before they are seated. Two duly elected Basque representatives, who belonged to a party fighting for the independence of the Basque region, refused to take the oath and were barred from exercising their mandate. In their complaint the representatives argued that, according to the Constitution, they became members by reason of their election; additional criteria could not be added. Moreover, they claimed discrimination on the basis of their constitutionally permissible beliefs; it is not unconstitutional to fight for the peaceful amendment of the Constitution. The Constitutional Tribunal found that the obligation to respect the constitutional order was not satisfied by mere nonviolation of the constitutional order. Respect required that those who exercise public power actively affirm the Constitution. This did not mean that public functionaries must identify themselves ideologically with the Constitution. To the Tribunal, the resolution requiring an oath was not an additional condition of membership; it simply manifests active respect for the Constitution (RTC 1983/101. 18 Nov. 1983).

3. In the *Rumpelkammer Case*, 24 BVerfGE 236 (1968), a charitable drive of a Catholic youth association to collect secondhand goods for the needy was supported from the pulpits of Catholic churches. A local court granted an injunction against the association upon request of a scrap dealer, who argued that 95 percent of the dealers would go out of business because of the drive. The GFCC found the complaint justified as the collection and the propaganda were religiously motivated and were "religious activities" protected by free exercise. The GFCC stated:

> The fundamental right to the free exercise of religion is included within the concept of freedom of belief. This concept— whether it concerns a religious creed or a belief unrelated to religion—not only embraces the personal freedom to believe or not to believe, i.e., to profess a faith, to keep it secret, to renounce a former belief and uphold another, but also includes the freedom to worship publicly, to proselytize, and to compete openly with other religions. * * * Because the "exercise of religion" has central significance for every belief and denomination, this concept must be expansively interpreted vis-à-vis its historical content. In support of this view, religious freedom can no longer be restricted by an express provision of the law, in contrast to Article 135 of the Constitution of the Weimar Republic, nor is it tied to other regulations concerning the relationship of church and state. The right is not subject to forfeiture under Article 18 of the Constitution. Moreover, several other constitutional provisions protect this right. * * * The right to free exercise extends not only to Christian churches but also to other religious creeds and ideological associations. This is a consequence of the ideological-religious neutrality to which the state is bound and the principle of equality with respect to churches and denominations. Thus there is no justification for interpreting the freedom to perform the rituals associated with religious beliefs more narrowly than freedom of belief or creed.

> Accordingly, the exercise of religion includes not only worship and practices such as the observance of religious customs like Sunday services, church collections, prayers, reception of the sacraments, processions, display of church flags, and the ringing of church bells, but also

religious education and ceremonies of nonestablished religions and atheists as well as other expressions of religious and ideological life.

Note that although the Basic Law does not permit statutory restrictions regarding the "undisturbed practice of religion," free exercise rights can be restricted for the sake of other people's rights and the constitutional order (community goods). The problem is similar to freedom of the arts. (See free speech in Chapter 7.)

4. Consider Tayyab Mahmud's description, op. cit. at 69:

In 1957 the Supreme Court of Pakistan had its first opportunity to rule directly on the nature and scope of religious freedom as enunciated in Article 18 of the Pakistan Constitution of 1956. The Court rejected the argument that because fundamental rights are made "subject to law,"[1] they may be taken away by legislation:

> The very conception of a fundamental right is that it being a right guaranteed by the Constitution cannot be taken away by the law, and it is not only technically inartistic but a fraud on the citizens for the makers of a Constitution to say that a right is fundamental but that it may be taken away by the law. I am unable to attribute any such intent to the makers of the Constitution who in their anxiety to regulate the lives of the Muslims of Pakistan in accordance with the Holy Quran and Sunnah could not possibly have intended to empower the legislature to take away from the Muslims the right to profess, practice and propagate their religion and to establish, maintain, and manage their religious institutions, and who in their conception of the ideal of a free, tolerant and democratic society could not have denied a similar right to the non-Muslim citizens of the State. * * * I refuse to be a party to any such pedantic, technical and narrow construction of the Article in question, for I consider it to be a fundamental canon of construction that a Constitution should receive a liberal interpretation in favour of the citizen, especially with respect to those provisions which were designed to safeguard the freedom of conscience and worship. *Jibendra Kishore Achharyya Chowdhury v. East Pakistan*, 1957 P.L.D. (S.Ct.) 9, 41-42 (Pak.).

While the Supreme Court recognized that law may regulate the manner in which religion may be professed, practiced, and propagated, and religious institutions may be established, maintained, and managed, it insisted that the term "subject to law" "cannot and do[es] not mean that such institutions may be abolished altogether by the Law."

JAPAN v. YASUKO NAKAYA
[GOKOKU (SHINTO) SHRINE CASE]
Supreme Court (Japan).
42 Minshū 5 at p. 277 (1988).

The Appellant has lodged a Jokoku Appeal against the judgment pronounced on June 1, 1982 by the Hiroshima High Court. The original judgment and the judgment of the first instance shall be quashed.

---

1. The ulema [Muslim clerics, religious scholars, and leaders] insisted that "law" here means the shari'a, hence a specifically interpreted religious law shall override the constitutionally guaranteed free exercise to all. The ulema's position prevailed with the victory of religious radicalism.

I.   The facts established by the original judgment are as below: 1. (1) The Appellee was baptized at the Yamaguchi Shin'ai Church of the United Church of Christians in Japan on April 4, 1958, and had believed in Christianity ever since. (2) The Appellee and Mr. Takafumi Nakaya (hereinafter called Takafumi), an officer of the Self–Defense Forces (hereinafter SDF), held a wedding ceremony involving no religious rituals on January 1, 1959,* * *; however, Takafumi was killed by a traffic accident * * * (3) Immediately after the death of Takafumi, the Appellee attended as a chief mourner at Takafumi's funeral with Buddhist rites arranged by the SDF Iwate Regional Liaison Office, * * * [but later] she deposited his ashes in the charnel vault [in a Christian] Church in 1969. Following the Christian faith, she attended, with her son, Takaharu, the memorial service for the deceased held by the Church in November of each year * * * (5) While living, Takafumi did not believe in any religion. 2. [In 1971 the Veterans Association initiated that Takafumi's ashes be enshrined at the Gokoku Shrine, a religious juridical entity. This was part of a joint enshrinement project for members of the SDF who had died while on duty. The idea was endorsed by the regional military commander. Appellee rejected the joint enshrinement because of her religious belief.]

II.   Upon above facts the original judgment ordered compensation for Appellee's damages * * *

III.   However, the ruling of the court below can not be accepted. The reason is as follows;

1.   The first issue is whether the application for the enshrinement should be regarded as a joint action of the Regional Office staff and the Veterans Association. It is obvious that to enshrine someone as Shinto deity relates to the enshrined Gods which are the fundamental of Shinto shrines and thus it is a matter to be conducted by independent decisions of the shrines. * * *

There were no facts showing that the Regional Office nor its staff directly approached Gokoku Shrine for the joint enshrinement. * * *

2.   To be examined next is the issue of whether the cooperation of the Regional Office staff with the Veterans Association for the application was a religious activity provided by paragraph 3, Article 20 of the Constitution.

The religious activity provided by the said article should not be construed to include any activities relating to religion but to mean only the activity whose purpose has a religious meaning and whose effect is to promote, to facilitate, to accelerate, to oppress or to intervene a religion. When we examine whether a certain action constitutes religious activity, we should decide objectively following common sense and considering various factors such as place of the action, the public's evaluation, intent, purpose and religious feelings of those who act, its effect and influence to the general public, etc.

It is as aforementioned that joint enshrinement is to be conducted by independent decisions of the shrines and therefore an application by someone for it does not constitute a prerequisite for it. * * *

The provision of separation of the State and religion in paragraph 3, Article 20 of the Constitution, which is known as a provision of the institutional guarantee, does not guarantee the religious freedom itself directly to individual persons, but rather it is an attempt to indirectly guarantee the freedom of religion by setting forth the parameters of actions which the State and its organs may not conduct. Therefore, the religious activity of the State or its organs which violates this provision should not necessarily be deemed unlawful in relation to individual persons unless the activity directly infringes upon their religious freedom as guaranteed by the Constitution, e.g., by imposing restriction on their exercise of religious freedom in violation of the first sentence of paragraph 1 of the said Article or by compelling individuals to attend religious activities in violation of paragraph 2 of the said Article.

3. [W]hen one's religious peacefulness is disturbed by religious activity of others, though it is natural for him to feel uncomfortable for that and to wish not to be disturbed any more, if we admit such a person to seek legal relief such as compensation or injunction on the ground of infringement of religious feelings, then, instead, it will obviously come to harm the religious freedom of others. The guarantee of freedom of religion requires tolerance for religious activities of others that are inconsistent with the religion that one believes in as long as such activity does not disturb his or her freedom of religion through compulsion or by giving rise to disadvantages. The same is true for cases of reminiscence or memorial of one's deceased spouse. * * * Appellee had never been compelled to attend the shrine's religious ceremonies, as found by the original judgment, and the Appellee does not assert any facts that any disadvantage was suffered because she did not attend the ceremonies nor any facts that she was prohibited, restricted, suppressed or intervened in any way to believe in Christianity or to mourn her late husband based on her religious faith.

The dissenting opinion of Justice Masami Ito is as follows:

I disagree with the opinion of the Court which quashed the original judgment and the judgment of the first instance and dismissed the case. The reasons are the following.

I. This is a tort case in which the Appellee seeks compensation for mental damages allegedly caused by an action of the State.

I am of the opinion that in modern society the interest of not being disturbed in one's mind by unwanted stimulus from others, i.e., the interest of mental peace, can be a legal interest under tort law. When this interest is acknowledged with respect to religion, we might call it the religious personal right or the religious privacy, though it is a matter of terminology. * * *

I think that it is necessary to take a view of protecting minorities when confronting issues relating to mental freedom and that such view is especially important in judicial review. That is the reason why, even in democracy ruled by the majority, protection is required for interests that cannot be deprived of by the majority's will as fundamental human rights. In the realm of thought or conscience, what the majority approve is unlikely to be infringed even without constitutional protection, but such protection works for minorities' thought or conscience that the majority would hate. In the realm of religion, since religious indifference prevails in our country because of the miscellaneousness of our religious consciousness, it is not rare to annoy religiously sensitive minorities. * * * This Court has ruled that the religious activity provided by paragraph 3, Article 20 of the Constitution does not mean to include all the activities relating to religion but means only the activity whose relation with religion exceeds appropriate limitation in light of social and cultural conditions of our country and whose purpose has a religious meaning and whose effect is to promote, to facilitate, to accelerate, to oppress or to intervene a religion (the judgment of July 13, 1977 by the Grand Bench, *supra*). The majority opinion follows this ruling. This is a three-pronged test for scrutiny of religious activity of the State prohibited by the separation clause, which test requires to examine the purpose, effect and extent of entanglement of the activity. This would be a correct standard in the abstract. The point is its application. Remembering that the ideal of paragraph 3, Article 20 of the Constitution, achieved by the lessons of past experiences in the country, is to serve the perfect separation of the State and religion, to apply this test to narrow the range of religious activity prohibited to the State would negate the purpose of the Constitution and should be inappropriate. It has often been pointed out that, while in European and American countries fundamental human rights have originated from the protection of the freedom of religion which is regarded as the core of the whole human rights, in Japan, together with the co-existence of various religious feelings in society, people in general do not have much concern about religion and lack sensitiveness for the freedom of religion. Under this situation, to loosen the separation principle should not be justified, and rather the principle should be applied strictly. * * *

BIJOE EMMANUEL & ORS. v. STATE OF KERALA & ORS.

Supreme Court (India).
(1986) 3 S. C. R. 518.

Chinappa Reddy, J.
 * * *

[In the Writ Petition petitioners say:] "The students who are Witnesses do not sing the Anthem though they stand up on such occasions to show their respect to the National Anthem. They desist from actual singing only because of their honest belief and conviction that their religion does not permit them to join any rituals except it be in their prayers to Jehovah their God." [The children were found by a commission to be "law abiding" and that they showed no disrespect to the National Anthem. However, under the instructions of the Deputy Inspector of Schools, the Head Mistress expelled the appellants from school.] It is evident that Jehovah's Witnesses, wherever they are, do hold religious beliefs which may appear strange or even bizarre to us, but the sincerity of their beliefs is beyond question. Are they entitled to be protected by the Constitution?

[The] National Honour Act was enacted in 1971. * * * [s]. 3 deals with the National Anthem and enacts, "Whoever, intentionally prevents the singing of the National Anthem or causes disturbance to any assembly engaged in such singing shall be punished with imprisonment for a term which extend to three years or with find, or with both." Standing up respectfully when the National Anthem is sung but not singing oneself clearly does not either prevent the singing of the National Anthem or cause disturbance to an assembly. * * *

The Kerala Education Act contains no provision of relevance. Section 36, however, enables the Government to make rules for the purpose of carrying into effect the provisions of the Act and in particular to provide for standards of education and courses of study. * * * Rule 8 of Chapter VIII provides for moral instruction and expressly says "Moral instruction should form a definite programme in every school but it should in no way wound the social or religious susceptibilities of the peoples generally." * * *

The Kerala Education Authorities rely upon two circulars of September 1961 and February 1970 issued by the Director of Public Instruction, Kerala. The first of these circulars is said to be a Code of Conduct for Teachers and pupils and stresses the importance of moral and spiritual values. * * *

The two circulars on which the department has placed reliance in the present case have no statutory basis and are mere departmental instructions. * * * [W]henever the Fundamental Right to freedom of conscience and to profess, practise and propagate religion is invoked, the act complained of as offending the Fundamental Right must be examined to discover whether such act is to protect public order, morality and health, whether it is to give effect to the other provisions of Part III of the Constitution or whether it is authorised by a law made to regulate or restrict any economic, financial, political or secular activity which may be associated with religious practice or to provide for social welfare and reform. It is the duty and function of the Court so to do. Here again as mentioned in connection with Art. 19(2) to (6), it must be a law having the force of a statute and not a mere executive or a departmental instruction. * * * [T]he question is not whether a particular religious belief or practice appeals to our reason or sentiment but whether the belief is genuinely and conscientiously held as part of the profession or practice of religion. Our personal views and reactions are irrelevant. If the belief is genuinely and conscientiously held it attracts the protection of Art. 25 but subject, of course, to the inhibitions contained therein.

In *Minersville School Dist. v. Gobitis*, 310 U.S. 586 (1940), the question arose whether the requirement of participation by pupils and public schools in the ceremony of saluting the national flag did not infringe the liberty guaranteed by the Fourteenth Amendment, in the case of a pupil who refused to participate upon sincere religious grounds. Justice Frankfurter, great exponent of the theory of judicial restraint that he was and speaking for the majority of the USSC, upheld the requirement regarding participation in the ceremony of the flag salutation primarily on the ground, "The wisdom of training children in patriotic impulses by those compulsions which necessarily prevade so much of the educational process is not for our independent judgment. * * * For ourselves, we might be tempted to say that the deepest patriotism is best engendered by giving unfettered scope to the most crochety beliefs. * * *'' In that very case Justice Stone dissented and said, "It (the Government) may suppress religious practices dangerous to morals, and presumably those also which are inimical to public safety, health and good order. But it is a long step, and one which I am unable to take, to the position that Government may, as a supposed, educational measure and as a means of disciplining young, compel affirmations which violate their religious conscience.'' * * *

Dealing with the argument that any interference with the authority of the school Board would in effect make the court the School Board for the country as suggested by Justice Frankfurter, Justice Jackson said,

> "There are village tyrants as well as village Hampdens, but none who acts under color of law is beyond reach of the Constitution. * * * We cannot, because of modest estimates of our competence in such specialities as public education, withhold the judgment that history authenticates as the function of this court when liberty is infringed."

* * *

Justice Jackson ended his opinion with the statement:

> "If there is any fixed star in our Constitutional constellation, it is that no official, high or petty, can prescribe what shall be orthodox in politics, nationalism, religion, or other matters of opinion or force citizens to confess by word or act their faith therein. If there are any circumstances which permit an exception, they do not now occur to us. We think the action of the local authorities in compelling the flag salute and pledge transcends constitutional limitations on their power and invades the sphere of intellect and spirit which it is the purpose of the First Amendment to our Constitution to reserve from all official control."

* * * We are satisfied, in the present case, that the expulsion of the three children from the school for the reason that * * * they do stand up respectfully when the anthem is sung, is a violation of their fundamental right to freedom of conscience and freely to profess, practice and propagate religion. * * * We only wish to add: our tradition teaches tolerance; our philosophy preaches tolerance; our constitution practices tolerance; let us not dilute it.

KOKKINAKIS v. GREECE

European Court of Human Rights.
17 E.H.R.R. 397 (1993).

Opinion of Judges Ryssdal, Bernhadt, and Rocha.

* * *

6. Mr. Minos Kokkinakis, of Greek nationality, * * * after becoming a Jehovah's Witness in 1936, * * * was arrested more than sixty times for proselytism. * * *

7. On 2 March 1986 he and his wife called at the home of Mrs. Kyriakaki in Sitia and engaged in a discussion with her. Mrs. Kyriakaki's husband, who was the cantor at a local Orthodox church, informed the police, who arrested Mr. and Mrs. Kokkinakis. * * *

A. Proceedings in the Lasithi Criminal Court

8. The applicant and his wife were prosecuted under section 4 of Law no. 1363/1938 making proselytism an offence [and sentenced].

9. [The Criminal Court found that the defendants told Mrs. Kyriakaki] "that they brought good news; by insisting in a pressing manner, they gained admittance to the house and began to read from a book on the Scriptures etc., encouraging her by means of their judicious, skilful explanations * * * to change her Orthodox Christian beliefs."

II. Relevant domestic law and practice

A. Statutory provisions

1. The Constitution

13. The relevant Articles of the 1975 Constitution read as follows:

Article 3

1. The dominant religion in Greece is that of the Christian Eastern Orthodox Church

* * *

3. The text of the Holy Scriptures is unalterable. No official translation into any other form of language may be made without the prior consent of the autocephalous Greek Church and the Great Christian Church at Constantinople.

Article 13

1. Freedom of conscience in religious matters is inviolable. The enjoyment of personal and political rights shall not depend on an individual's religious beliefs.

2. There shall be freedom to practice any known religion; individuals shall be free to perform their rites of worship without hindrance and under the protection of the law. The performance of rites of worship must not prejudice public order or public morals. Proselytism is prohibited.

3. The ministers of all known religions shall be subject to the same supervision by the State and to the same obligations to it as those of the dominant religion.

4. No one may be exempted from discharging his obligations to the State or refuse to comply with the law by reason of his religious convictions.

5. No oath may be required other than under a law which also determines the form of it.

* * *

14. The Christian Eastern Orthodox Church, which during nearly four centuries of foreign occupation symbolised the maintenance of Greek culture and the Greek language, took an active part in the Greek

people's struggle for emancipation, to such an extent that Hellenism is to some extent identified with the Orthodox faith.

* * *

2.   Law nos.1363/1938 and 1672/1939

16.   During the dictatorship of Metaxas (1936–40) proselytism was made a criminal offence. [Law no. 1672/1939 gave the following definition:]

2.   By 'proselytism' is meant, in particular, any direct or indirect attempt to intrude on the religious beliefs of a person of a different religious persuasion (eterodoxos), with the aim of undermining those beliefs, either by any kind of inducement or promise of an inducement or moral support or material assistance, or by fraudulent means or by taking advantage of his inexperience, trust, need, low intellect or naïvety.

* * *

23.   Since the revision of the Constitution in 1975 the Supreme Administrative Court has held on several occasions that the Jehovah's Witnesses come within the definition of a "known religion". * * *

24.   According to statistics provided by the applicant, 4,400 Jehovah's Witnesses were arrested between 1975 (when democracy was restored) and 1992, and 1,233 of these were committed for trial and 208 convicted. * * *

AS TO THE LAW

* * *

30.   In the Government's submission, there was freedom to practice all religions in Greece, * * * There was, however, a radical difference between bearing witness and "proselytism that is not respectable", the kind that consists in using deceitful, unworthy and immoral means, such as exploiting the destitution, low intellect and inexperience of one's fellow beings.

A.   General principles

31.   As enshrined in Article 9 (art. 9), freedom of thought, conscience and religion is one of the foundations of a "democratic society" within the meaning of the convention. It is, in its religious dimension, one of the most vital elements that go to make up the identity of believers and their conception of life, but it is also a precious asset for atheists, agnostics, sceptics and the unconcerned.

The pluralism indissociable from a democratic society, which has been dearly won over the centuries, depends on it.

32.   While religious freedom is primarily a matter of individual conscience, it also implies, inter alia, freedom to "manifest [one's] religion". Bearing witness in words and deeds is bound up with the existence of religious convictions.

According to Article 9 (art. 9), freedom to manifest one's religion is not only exercisable in community with others, "in public" and within the circle of those whose faith one shares, but can also be asserted "alone" and "in private"; furthermore, it includes in principle the right to try to convince one's neighbour, for example through "teaching", failing which, moreover, "freedom to change [one's] religion or belief", enshrined in Article 9 (art. 9), would be likely to remain a dead letter.

* * *

33.   [As to limitations, Art. 9] refers only to "freedom to manifest one's religion or belief". In so doing, it recognises that in democratic societies, in which several religions coexist within one and the same population, it may be necessary to place restrictions on this freedom in order to reconcile the interests of the various groups and ensure that everyone's beliefs are respected.

34.   According to the Government, such restrictions were to be found in the Greek legal system. * * *

B.   Application of the principles

* * *

36.   The sentence passed by the Lasithi Criminal Court and subsequently reduced by the Crete Court of Appeal (see paragraphs 9–10 above) amounts to an interference with the exercise of Mr. Kokkinakis's right to "freedom to manifest [his] religion or belief". Such an interference is contrary to Article 9 (art. 9) unless it is "prescribed by law", directed at one or more of the legitimate aims in paragraph 2 (art. 9–2) and "necessary in a democratic society" for achieving them.

1.   "Prescribed by law"

* * *

Mr. Kokkinakis * * * criticised the absence of any description of the "objective substance" of the offence of proselytism. He thought this deliberate, as it would tend to make it possible for any kind of religious conversation or communication to be caught by the provision. He referred to the risk of "extendibility" by the police and often by the courts too of the vague terms of the section. * * *

* * *

40.   The Court has already noted that the wording of many statutes is not absolutely precise. The need to avoid excessive rigidity and to keep pace with changing circumstances means that many laws are inevitably couched in terms which, to a greater or lesser extent, are vague (see, for example and mutatis mutandis, the *Müller and Others v. Switzerland* judgment of 24 May 1988, Series A no. 133, p. 20, para. 29). * * *

2.   Legitimate aim

* * *

42.   The Government contended that a democratic State had to ensure the peaceful enjoyment of the personal freedoms of all those living on its territory. If, in particular, it was not vigilant to protect a person's religious beliefs and dignity from attempts to influence them by immoral and deceitful means, Article 9 para. 2 (art. 9–2) would in practice be rendered wholly nugatory.

43. In the applicant's submission, religion was part of the "constantly renewable flow of human thought" and it was impossible to conceive of its being excluded from public debate. A fair balance of personal rights made it necessary to accept that others' thought should be subject to a minimum of influence, otherwise the result would be a "strange society of silent animals that [would] think but * * * not express themselves, that [would] talk but * * * not communicate, and that [would] exist but * * * not coexist".

44. Having regard to the circumstances of the case and the actual terms of the relevant courts' decisions, the Court considers that the impugned measure was in pursuit of a legitimate aim under Article 9 para. 2 (art. 9-2), namely the protection of the rights and freedoms of others, relied on by the Government.

3. "Necessary in a democratic society"

45. Mr. Kokkinakis did not consider it necessary in a democratic society to prohibit a fellow citizen's right to speak when he came to discuss religion with his neighbour. He was curious to know how a discourse delivered with conviction and based on holy books common to all Christians could infringe the rights of others. Mrs. Kyriakaki was an experienced adult woman with intellectual abilities * * *

* * *

47. * * * The Court's task is to determine whether the measures taken at national level were justified in principle and proportionate. * * *

48. First of all, a distinction has to be made between bearing Christian witness and improper proselytism. The former corresponds to true evangelism, which a report drawn up in 1956 under the auspices of the World Council of Churches describes as an essential mission and a responsibility of every Christian and every Church. The latter represents a corruption or deformation of it. It may, according to the same report, take the form of activities offering material or social advantages with a view to gaining new members for a Church or exerting improper pressure on people in distress or in need; it may even entail the use of violence or brainwashing; more generally, it is not compatible with respect for the freedom of thought, conscience and religion of others.

Scrutiny of section 4 of Law no. 1363/1938 shows that the relevant criteria adopted by the Greek legislature are reconcilable with the foregoing if and in so far as they are designed only to punish improper proselytism, which the Court does not have to define in the abstract in the present case.

49. The * * * Greek courts established the applicant's liability by merely reproducing the wording of section 4 and did not sufficiently specify in what way the accused had attempted to convince his neighbour by improper means. None of the facts they set out warrants that finding.

That being so, it has not been shown that the applicant's conviction was justified in the circumstances of the case by a pressing social need. * * *

Partly Concurring Opinion of Judge Pettiti

* * * I take the view that what contravenes Article 9 (art. 9) is the Law. I agree with acknowledging its foreseeability. But the definition is such as to make it possible at any moment to punish the slightest attempt by anyone to convince a person he is addressing. * * *

Proselytism is linked to freedom of religion; a believer must be able to communicate his faith and his beliefs in the religious sphere as in the philosophical sphere. Freedom of religion and conscience is a fundamental right and this freedom must be able to be exercised for the benefit of all religions and not for the benefit of a single Church, even if this has traditionally been the established Church or "dominant religion".

Freedom of religion and conscience certainly entails accepting proselytism, even where it is "not respectable" * * *

The only limits on the exercise of this right are those dictated by respect for the rights of others where there is an attempt to coerce the person into consenting or to use manipulative techniques.

Notes and Questions

1. *Gobitis* was overruled in *West Virginia State Bd. of Education v. Barnette*, 319 U.S. 624 (1943). In *Barnette* the Court found that "to sustain the compulsory flag salute we are required to say that a Bill of Rights which guards the individual's right to speak his own mind, left it open to public authorities to compel him to utter what is not in his mind.* * * The very purpose of the Bill of Rights was to withdraw certain subjects from the vicissitudes of political controversy, to place them beyond the reach of majorities and officials and to establish them as legal principles to be applied by the courts." *Id.* at 634, 638. Is there any reason for the Indian Court to rely on the *Gobitis* dissents instead of *Barnette*?

2. The *Barnette* majority rejected the justification accepted in *Gobitis*, namely, that the flag salute promoted national unity:

Those who begin coercive elimination of dissent soon find themselves exterminating dissenters. Compulsory unification of opinion achieves only the unanimity of the graveyard. It seems trite but necessary to say that the First Amendment to our Constitution was designed to avoid these ends by avoiding these beginnings. * * * If there is any fixed star in our constitutional constellation, it is that no official, high or petty, can prescribe what shall be orthodox in politics, nationalism, religion, or other matters of opinion or force citizens to confess by word or act their faith therein.

Id. at 642.

3. If the practices in a Shinto shrine are merely a community custom, as the Japanese Supreme Court held, is this decisive from the perspective of the Catholic widow? Is belief not to be protected against state-endorsed customs? To the extent the custom endorses religion, the Court seems to be more concerned about the violation of other people's beliefs. Why would a state-inflicted violation of a faith be more damaging than the endorsement of a custom? Does the "neutral" nature of the custom diminish the injury to religious or secular sensitivity? Note that the Japanese custom may disguise

religion. In *Kakunaga v. Sekiguchi* (Supreme Court of Japan, Grand Bench, 1977), when public authorities participated at a Shinto groundbreaking ceremony paid for by the authorities, it was argued that "it is general practice today in the construction industry for the contractor [here, the municipality] to sponsor and attend a ceremony like the one in this case; those involved in the building, moreover, regard the ritual as indispensable for safety. * * * [T]he motive of the contractor in holding this ceremony is merely an extremely secular response to the demands for a customary groundbreaking ceremony from those involved in the building process." Lawrence W. Beer and Hiroshi Itoh, *The Constitutional Case Law of Japan, 1970 through 1990*, at 482 (1996).

4. Are differences in the U.S., Japanese, and Indian outcomes related to the intensity of the violation? Note that the Japanese Court and the USSC majority, in *Employment Division*, argue that some level of injury to beliefs is simply inevitable. Is this the position in *Gobitis*?

5. Compare the contested religious practices in the different cases. In the flag salute and oath cases a state practice required an action that conflicted with religious beliefs, and the rules made it more difficult for people of certain convictions to participate in the political community. In the Greek case, while the applicable rules—and perhaps the Constitution itself— might be seen as discriminatory, the faith-motivated activity (proselytizing) affected private parties. Is this difference sufficient to justify more-restrictive standards?

6. Consider John Witte, Jr., *A Dickensian Era of Religious Rights: An Update on Religious Human Rights in Global Perspective*, 42 Wm. & Mary L. Rev. 707, 764 (2001):

> To my mind, the preferred solution to the modern problem of proselytism is not so much further state restriction as further self-restraint on the part of both local and foreign religious groups. Again, the 1966 International Covenant on Civil and Political Rights provides some useful cues. International Covenant on Civil and Political Rights, 99 U.N.T.S. 171, 6 I.L.M. 368 (entered into force March 23, 1976). Article 27 of the Covenant reminds us of the special right of local religious groups, particularly minorities, 'to enjoy their own culture, to profess and practice their own religion.' *Id*. Such language might well empower and encourage vulnerable minority traditions to seek protection from aggressive and insensitive proselytism by missionary mavericks and 'drive-by' crusaders who have emerged with alacrity in the past two decades. It might even have supported a moratorium on proselytism for a few years in places like Russia so that local religions, even the majority Russian Orthodox Church, had some time to recover from nearly a century of harsh oppression that destroyed most of its clergy, seminaries, monasteries, literature, and icons. But Article 27 cannot permanently insulate local religious groups from interaction with other religions.

Do proselytism and other religious practices require self-restriction on the practicing party? Is proselytizing a special problem if it is conducted by foreigners? Is protection of a national or religious identity sufficient ground for restriction?

A.3. ACCOMMODATION AND OTHER EXCEPTIONS TO GENERAL RULES

To what extent should government make exceptions to its general rules to allow the free exercise of specific religious practices and forms of behavior in everyday life if such activities are dictated by a religion? Does a sincere respect of religion mandate a legal environment that will not force a person to act against fundamental religious or other convictions?

Assuming that the state strictly follows secular goals, exceptions favoring dictates of free exercise of religion present difficult problems, even if the state intends only to promote free exercise. First, the goals and means of the secular state may simply contradict the dictates of religion; for example, in matters of population policy the government may advocate practices that are impermissible to a religion. Further, government endorsement of the dictates of one or another religion in general rules, and even as an exception from the general rules, would discriminate against other citizens who are not so privileged. By recognizing an exception from generally applicable rules in favor of one or another denomination, even if this exception applies to members of a religious community, other believers may feel discriminated against, insofar as their concerns are not granted special treatment. In addition, the recognition of exceptions in the name of promoting free exercise may increase social factionalism and conflict. (Similar arguments were made in government decisions denying conscientious-objector status.) Where religion is ethnically divisive, the dimension of religious accommodation of the religious practices of a given ethnic group may be seen as siding with that community, and thus it may prove socially divisive.[m]

GOLDMAN v. WEINBERGER

Supreme Court (United States).
475 U.S. 503 (1986).

Justice Rehnquist delivered the opinion of the Court.

Petitioner Goldman is an Orthodox Jew and ordained rabbi. [He] entered active service in the United States Air Force as a commissioned officer, * * * and served as a clinical psychologist at the mental health clinic on the base.

Until 1981, petitioner was not prevented from wearing his yarmulke on the base. * * * [I]n April 1981, after he testified as a defense witness at a court-martial wearing his yarmulke but not his service cap, opposing counsel lodged a complaint with the Hospital Commander, arguing that petitioner's practice of wearing his yarmulke was a violation of Air Force Regulation (AFR) 35–10. This regulation states in pertinent part that

---

m. This tension is illustrated in the case of a person of Finnish nationality, who refused to pay a tax that was imposed to support the Swedish state church. The ECHR found the tax to be in violation of freedom of religion. *Darby v. Sweden*, 176 ECHR (ser. A) at paras. 28–36 (1990).

"[h]eadgear will not be worn * * * [w]hile indoors except by armed security police in the performance of their duties."

Petitioner argues that AFR 35–10, as applied to him, prohibits religiously motivated conduct and should therefore be analyzed under the standard enunciated in *Sherbert v. Verner*, 374 U.S. 398, 406 (1963)* * * But we have repeatedly held that "the military is, by necessity, a specialized society separate from civilian society." *Parker v. Levy*, 417 U.S. 733, 743 (1974) "[T]he military must insist upon a respect for duty and a discipline without counterpart in civilian life," *Schlesinger v. Councilman*, 420 U.S. 738, 757 (1975).

Our review of military regulations challenged on First Amendment grounds is far more deferential than constitutional review of similar laws or regulations designed for civilian society. The military need not encourage debate or tolerate protest to the extent that such tolerance is required of the civilian state by the First Amendment; to accomplish its mission the military must foster instinctive obedience, unity, commitment, and esprit de corps.

In the context of the present case, when evaluating whether military needs justify a particular restriction on religiously motivated conduct, courts must give great deference to the professional judgment of military authorities concerning the relative importance of a particular military interest. * * *

The considered professional judgment of the Air Force is that the traditional outfitting of personnel in standardized uniforms encourages the subordination of personal preferences and identities in favor of the overall group mission. Uniforms encourage a sense of hierarchical unity by tending to eliminate outward individual distinctions except for those of rank. The Air Force considers them as vital during peacetime as during war because its personnel must be ready to provide an effective defense on a moment's notice. * * *

Petitioner Goldman contends that the Free Exercise Clause of the First Amendment requires the Air Force to make an exception to its uniform dress requirements for religious apparel unless the accouterments create a "clear danger" of undermining discipline and esprit de corps. He asserts that in general, visible but "unobtrusive" apparel will not create such a danger and must therefore be accommodated. He argues that the Air Force failed to prove that * * *

[W]hether or not expert witnesses may feel that religious exceptions to AFR 35–10 are desirable is quite beside the point. The desirability of dress regulations in the military is decided by the appropriate military officials, and they are under no constitutional mandate to abandon their considered professional judgment. Quite obviously, to the extent the regulations do not permit the wearing of religious apparel such as a yarmulke, a practice described by petitioner as silent devotion akin to prayer, military life may be more objectionable for petitioner and probably others. But the First Amendment does not require the military to accommodate such practices in the face of its view that they would detract from the uniformity sought by the dress regulations.

Justice Stevens, with whom Justice White and Justice Powell join, concurring.

Justice Brennan [in dissent] is unmoved by the Government's concern that "while a yarmulke might not seem obtrusive to a Jew, neither does a turban to a Sikh, a saffron robe to a Satchidananda Ashram–Integral Yogi, nor do dreadlocks to a Rastafarian." He correctly points out that "turbans, saffron robes, and dreadlocks are not before us in this case," and then suggests that other cases may be fairly decided by reference to a reasonable standard based on "functional utility, health and safety considerations, and the goal of a polished, professional appearance." As the Court has explained, this approach attaches no weight to the separate interest in uniformity itself.

The interest in uniformity, however, has a dimension that is of still greater importance for me. It is the interest in uniform treatment for the members of all religious faiths. If exceptions from dress code regulations are to be granted on the basis of a multifactored test such as that proposed by Justice Brennan, inevitably the decisionmaker's evaluation of the character and the sincerity of the requester's faith—as well as the probable reaction of the majority to the favored treatment of a member of that faith—will play a critical part in the decision. For the difference between a turban or a dreadlock on the one hand, and a yarmulke on the other, is not merely a difference in "appearance"—it is also the difference between a Sikh or a Rastafarian, on the one hand, and an Orthodox Jew on the other. The Air Force has no business drawing distinctions between such persons when it is enforcing commands of universal application.

EMPLOYMENT DIVISION, DEPARTMENT OF HUMAN RESOURCES OF OREGON v. SMITH

Supreme Court (United States).
494 U.S. 872 (1990).

Justice Scalia delivered the opinion of the Court.

This case requires us to decide whether the Free Exercise Clause of the First Amendment permits the State of Oregon to include religiously inspired peyote use within the reach of its general criminal prohibition on use of that drug, and thus permits the State to deny unemployment benefits to persons. [Smith, who used peyote as member of the Native American Church, was fired from his job and was denied unemployment compensation.]

II

Respondents' claim for relief rests on our decisions in [*Sherbert v. Verner*, 374 U.S. 398 (1963), *Thomas v. Review Board*, 450 U.S. 707 (1981), and *Hobbie v. Unemployment Appeals Commission*, 480 U.S. 136 (1987)] in which we held that a State could not condition the availability of unemployment insurance on an individual's willingness to forgo conduct required by his religion. [However,] the conduct at issue in those cases was not prohibited by law. * * *

A

The "exercise of religion" often involves not only belief and profession but the performance of (or abstention from) physical acts: assembling with others for a worship service, participating in sacramental use of bread and wine, proselytizing, abstaining from certain foods or certain modes of transportation.

* * *

Respondents * * * contend that their religious motivation for using peyote places them beyond the reach of a criminal law that is not specifically directed at their religious practice, and that is concededly constitutional as applied to those who use the drug for other reasons. They assert, in other words, that "prohibiting the free exercise [of religion]" includes requiring any individual to observe a generally applicable law that requires (or forbids) the performance of an act that his religious belief forbids (or requires). As a textual matter, we do not think the words must be given that meaning.

We have never held that an individual's religious beliefs excuse him from compliance with an otherwise valid law prohibiting conduct that the State is free to regulate. On the contrary, the record of more than a century of our free exercise jurisprudence contradicts that proposition. [We] first had occasion to assert that principle in *Reynolds* [*v. United States* 98 U.S. 145, 166 (1878)] where we rejected the claim that criminal laws against polygamy could not be constitutionally applied to those whose religion [i.e. the Mormons] commanded the practice. * * *

The only decisions in which we have held that the First Amendment bars application of a neutral, generally applicable law to religiously motivated action have involved not the Free Exercise Clause alone, but the Free Exercise Clause in conjunction with other constitutional protections, such as freedom of speech and of the press, see [*Cantwell*], or the right of parents, acknowledged in *Pierce v. Society of Sisters*, 268 U.S. 510 (1925), to direct the education of their children, see *Wisconsin v. Yoder*, 406 U.S. 205 (1972)[below].

The present case does not present such a hybrid situation, but a free exercise claim unconnected with any communicative activity or parental right. Respondents urge us to hold, quite simply, that when otherwise prohibitable conduct is accompanied by religious convictions, not only the convictions but the conduct itself must be free from governmental regulation. We have never held that, and decline to do so now.

B

Respondents argue that even though exemption from generally applicable criminal laws need not automatically be extended to religiously motivated actors, at least the claim for a religious exemption must be evaluated under the balancing test set forth in *Sherbert v. Verner*. Under the *Sherbert* test, governmental actions that substantially burden a religious practice must be justified by a compelling governmental interest. [We] have never invalidated any governmental action on the basis of the *Sherbert* test except the denial of unemployment compensation.[n] Although we have sometimes purported to apply the *Sherbert* test in contexts other than that, we have always found the test satisfied. In recent years we have abstained from applying the *Sherbert* test (outside the unemployment compensation field) at all.

Even if we were inclined to breathe into *Sherbert* some life beyond the unemployment compensation field, we would not apply it to require exemptions from a generally applicable criminal law. The *Sherbert* test, it must be recalled, was developed in a context that lent itself to individualized governmental assessment of the reasons for the relevant conduct.

[The] government's ability to enforce generally applicable prohibitions of socially harmful conduct, like its ability to carry out other aspects of public policy, "cannot depend on measuring the effects of a governmental action on a religious objector's spiritual development." [*Lyng v. Northwest Indian Cemetery Protective Association*, 485 U.S. 439, 451 (1988).] To make an individual's obligation to obey such a law contingent upon the law's coincidence with his religious beliefs, except where the State's interest is "compelling"—permitting him, by virtue of his beliefs, "to become a law unto himself," [*Reynolds*]—contradicts both constitutional tradition and common sense.

* * *

Nor is it possible to limit the impact of respondents' proposal by requiring a "compelling state interest" only when the conduct prohibited is "central" to the individual's religion. It is no more appropriate for judges to determine the "centrality" of religious beliefs before applying a "compelling interest" test in the free exercise field, than it would be for them to determine the "importance" of ideas before applying the "compelling interest" test in the free speech field.[4]

Precisely because "we are a cosmopolitan nation made up of people of almost every conceivable religious preference," *Braunfeld v. Brown*, 366 U.S. 599 (1961) and precisely because we value and protect that religious divergence, we cannot afford the luxury of deeming presumptively invalid, as applied to the religious objector, every regulation of conduct that does not protect an interest of the highest order.

Values that are protected against government interference through enshrinement in the Bill of Rights are not thereby banished from the political process. * * * It is therefore not surprising that a number of States have made an exception to their drug laws for sacramental peyote

n. South Carolina denied unemployment-compensation benefits to a Sabbatarian who refused to work on Saturdays and therefore refused to accept available employment. This was seen as an unconstitutional forced choice between religion and benefits. "Governmental imposition of such a choice puts the same kind of burden upon the free exercise of religion as would a fine imposed against [her] for Saturday worship." *Sherbert v. Verner*, 374 U.S. 404 (1963).

4. [Dispensing] with a "centrality" inquiry is utterly unworkable. It would require, for example, the same degree of "compelling state interest" to impede the practice of throwing rice at church weddings as to impede the practice of getting married in church. There is no way out of the difficulty that, if general laws are to be subjected to a "religious practice" exception, both the importance of the law at issue and the centrality of the practice at issue must reasonably be considered.

use. But to say that a nondiscriminatory religious-practice exemption is permitted, or even that it is desirable, is not to say that it is constitutionally required, and that the appropriate occasions for its creation can be discerned by the courts. It may fairly be said that leaving accommodation to the political process will place at a relative disadvantage those religious practices that are not widely engaged in; but that unavoidable consequence of democratic government must be preferred to a system in which each conscience is a law unto itself or in which judges weigh the social importance of all laws against the centrality of all religious beliefs. * * *

Justice O'Connor concurring in the judgment. [Today's] holding dramatically departs from well-settled First Amendment jurisprudence, appears unnecessary to resolve the question presented, and is incompatible with our Nation's fundamental commitment to individual religious liberty.

II

* * *

A

* * *

Because the First Amendment does not distinguish between religious belief and religious conduct, conduct motivated by sincere religious belief, like the belief itself, must be at least presumptively protected by the Free Exercise Clause.

The Court today, however, interprets the Clause to permit the government to prohibit, without justification, conduct mandated by an individual's religious beliefs, so long as that prohibition is generally applicable. But a law that prohibits certain conduct—conduct that happens to be an act of worship for someone—manifestly does prohibit that person's free exercise of his religion. * * *

To say that a person's right to free exercise has been burdened, of course, does not mean that he has an absolute right to engage in the conduct. The compelling interest test effectuates the First Amendment's command that religious liberty is an independent liberty, that it occupies a preferred position, and that the Court will not permit encroachments upon this liberty, whether direct or indirect, unless required by clear and compelling governmental interests "of the highest order," [*Yoder*] ...

[A] State that makes criminal an individual's religiously motivated conduct burdens that individual's free exercise of religion in the severest manner possible, for it "results in the choice to the individual of either abandoning his religious principle or facing criminal prosecution." I would have thought it beyond argument that such laws implicate free exercise concerns....

Legislatures, of course, have always been "left free to reach actions which were in violation of social duties or subversive of good order." Reynolds, 98 U.S., at 164; Yet [O]nce it has been shown that a government regulation or criminal prohibition burdens the free exercise of religion, we have consistently asked the government to demonstrate that unbending application of its regulation to the religious objector "is essential to accomplish an overriding governmental interest," [*Lee*] or represents "the least restrictive means of achieving some compelling state interest," [*Thomas*]. [The] approach more consistent with our role as judges to decide each case on its individual merits.

There is nothing talismanic about neutral laws of general applicability or general criminal prohibitions, for laws neutral toward religion can coerce a person to violate his religious conscience or intrude upon his religious duties just as effectively as laws aimed at religion. As the language of the Clause itself makes clear, an individual's free exercise of religion is a preferred constitutional activity. Finally, the Court today suggests that the disfavoring of minority religions is an "unavoidable consequence" under our system of government and that accommodation of such religions must be left to the political process. In my view, however, the First Amendment was enacted precisely to protect the rights of those whose religious practices are not shared by the majority and may be viewed with hostility. [Justice O'Connor found that the Oregon statute satisfies the compelling state- interest test, given the interest in the uniform application of the criminal prohibition at issue.]

Justice Blackmun, with whom Justice Brennan and Justice Marshall join, dissenting.

I

In weighing the clear interest of respondents Smith and Black (hereinafter respondents) in the free exercise of their religion against Oregon's asserted interest in enforcing its drug laws, it is important to articulate in precise terms the state interest involved. It is not the State's broad interest in fighting the critical "war on drugs" that must be weighed against respondents' claim, but the State's narrow interest in refusing to make an exception for the religious, ceremonial use of peyote. [Failure] to reduce the competing interests to the same plane of generality tends to distort the weighing process in the State's favor.

The State's interest in enforcing its prohibition, in order to be sufficiently compelling to outweigh a free exercise claim, cannot be merely abstract or symbolic. The State's asserted interest thus amounts only to the symbolic preservation of an unenforced prohibition. But a government interest in "symbolism, even symbolism for so worthy a cause as the abolition of unlawful drugs," *Treasury Employees v. Von Raab*, 489 U.S. 656, (1989) (SCALIA, J., dissenting), cannot suffice to abrogate the constitutional rights of individuals ...

The State * * * offers, however, no evidence that the religious use of peyote has ever harmed anyone.

The carefully circumscribed ritual context in which respondents used peyote is far removed from the irresponsible and unrestricted recreational use of unlawful drugs.[6]

6. In this respect, respondents' use of peyote seems closely analogous to the sacra- mental use of wine by the Roman Catholic Church. During Prohibition, the Federal

III

* * *

[Respondents] believe, and their sincerity has never been at issue, that the peyote plant embodies their deity, and eating it is an act of worship and communion. Without peyote, they could not enact the essential ritual of their religion.

If Oregon can constitutionally prosecute them for this act of worship, they, like the Amish, may be "forced to migrate to some other and more tolerant region." *Yoder.* This potentially devastating impact must be viewed in light of the federal policy—reached in reaction to many years of religious persecution and intolerance—of protecting the religious freedom of Native Americans. See American Indian Religious Freedom Act, 42 U.S.C. § 1996 ("it shall be the policy of the United States to protect and preserve for American Indians their inherent right of freedom to believe, express, and exercise the traditional religions * * * including but not limited to access to sites, use and possession of sacred objects, and the freedom to worship through ceremonials and traditional rites").

Notes and Questions

1. "[C]onstitutionally compelled exemptions [from generally applicable laws regulating conduct] were within the contemplation of the framers and ratifiers as a possible interpretation of the free exercise clause." Michael W. McConnell, *The Origins and Historical Understanding of Free Exercise of Religion,* 103 Harv. L. Rev. 1409, 1415 (1990).

> The wide berth granted to the value of free exercise seems greater in Germany than in the United States. The negative and positive character of this freedom, like that of free speech, means that both governments and private enterprises must accommodate the religious practices of citizens and employees. My sense is that German constitutional doctrine requires a higher measure of accommodation than does American doctrine. For example, Goldman v. Weinberger, 475 U.S. 503 (1986), and Estate of Thornton v. Caldor, Inc., 472 U.S. 703 (1985) would probably have been decided the other way, favoring religious exercise, in Germany.

> Donald P. Kommers, *The Constitutional Jurisprudence of the Federal Republic of Germany* 573 n. 7 (1989).

2. Should specific military interests result in diminished protection of fundamental rights? Is there a compelling state interest that necessitates respect for uniforms? Consider that Goldman was a professional soldier: Does this matter? See, e.g., Kenneth Lasson, *Religious Liberty in the Military: The First Amendment Under "Friendly Fire",* 9 J.L. & Religion 471 (1992).

3. *The Aftermath of the* Smith *Case.* Congress enacted the Religious Freedom Restoration Act of 1993 (RFRA) in direct response to *Smith.* RFRA

Government exempted such use of wine from its general ban on possession and use of alcohol. However compelling the Government's then general interest in prohibiting the use of alcohol may have been, it could not plausibly have asserted an interest sufficiently compelling to outweigh Catholics' right to take communion.

prohibited "[g]overnment" from "substantially burden[ing]" a person's exercise of religion even if the burden results from a rule of general applicability, unless the government can demonstrate the burden "(1) is in furtherance of a compelling governmental interest; and (2) is the least restrictive means of furthering that interest." RFRA mandated the application of the *Sherbert* test, which was disregarded by the majority in *Smith*. Congress relied on the Fourteenth Amendment, which, inter alia, guarantees that no state shall make or enforce any law depriving any person of "life, liberty, or property, without due process of law," or denying any person the "equal protection of the laws" (§ 1) and empowers Congress "to enforce" those guarantees by "appropriate legislation" (§ 5). In *City of Boerne v. Flores*, 521 U.S. 507 (1997), the USSC found that Congress's attempt to overrule the Court's constitutional interpretation was unconstitutional, arguing in terms of a lack of legislative powers.[o] The Court found no "widespread pattern of religious discrimination in this country" that would have justified "direct" congressional enforcement of this "liberty." "RFRA's most serious shortcoming, however, lies in the fact that it is so out of proportion to a supposed remedial or preventive object that it cannot be understood as responsive to, or designed to prevent, unconstitutional behavior. It appears, instead, to attempt a substantive change in constitutional protections, proscribing state conduct that the Fourteenth Amendment itself does not prohibit." *Id.* at 509. RFRA gave Congress a power to intrude into traditional areas of state responsibility, a power inconsistent with the design of the Constitution.

> It is a reality of the modern regulatory state that numerous state laws, such as the zoning regulations at issue here, impose a substantial burden on a large class of individuals. When the exercise of religion has been burdened in an incidental way by a law of general application, it does not follow that the persons affected have been burdened any more than other citizens, let alone burdened because of their religious beliefs. In addition, the Act imposes in every case a least restrictive means requirement—a requirement that was not used in the pre-Smith jurisprudence RFRA purported to codify—which also indicates that the legislation is broader than is appropriate if the goal is to prevent and remedy constitutional violations.

Id. at 535.

Is the USSC more reluctant to find an "incidental burden" on speech than in the case of religion? This is perhaps related to the object of the regulation: in free speech cases there is no action, but the *Smith* approach is related to acts. "Laws are made for the government of actions and while they cannot interfere with mere religious belief and opinions, they may with practices." *Reynolds v. United States*, 98 U.S. 145, 166 (1878). However, as Professor Tribe states, "[t]his belief-action dichotomy, much like the speech-conduct dichotomy, is at best an oversimplification. * * * [T]he state does not directly attack citizens' religious beliefs. Rather, the state rewards or punishes beliefs indirectly, by encouraging or discouraging actions that are

o. The Catholic Archbishop of San Antonio had applied for a building permit, which was denied under an ordinance governing historic preservation in a district that included the church. Justice Stevens, concurring, stated that "If the historic landmark on the hill in Boerne happened to be a museum or an art gallery owned by an atheist, it would not be eligible for an exemption from the city ordinances that forbid an enlargement of the structure. Because the landmark is owned by the Catholic Church, it is claimed that RFRA gives its owner a federal statutory entitlement to an exemption from a generally applicable, neutral civil law."

based on beliefs." Laurence H. Tribe, *American Constitutional Law* 1184 (2d ed. 1988).

Respondent in *City of Boerne* contended that RFRA was a proper exercise of Congress's remedial or preventive power and a reasonable means of protecting the free exercise of religion as defined by *Smith*. It prevents and remedies laws that are enacted with the unconstitutional object of targeting religious beliefs and practices. In view of such antireligious regulations as the Hialeah city ordinance (*Lukumi Babalu Aye*), had Congress practical reasons to enforce accommodation as a means of antidiscrimination? Is the enforcement of the First Amendment to be left exclusively to the courts?

Citing pre-First Amendment American practices, Justices Breyer, O'Connor, and Souter (on different grounds) dissented in *City of Boerne*, claiming that the Free Exercise Clause "is best understood as an affirmative guarantee of the right to participate in religious practices and conduct without impermissible governmental interference, even when such conduct conflicts with a neutral, generally applicable law"; thus even neutral laws of general application may be invalid if they burden religiously motivated conduct. 521 U.S. at 546. "The Religion Clauses of the Constitution represent a profound commitment to religious liberty. Our Nation's Founders conceived of a Republic receptive to voluntary religious expression, not of a secular society in which religious expression is tolerated only when it does not conflict with a generally applicable law." *Id.* at 564.

4. *Accommodation as a constitutional obligation?* The prohibition of kosher butchering, i.e., slaughtering of animals according to Jewish and Islamic rituals, was a misdemeanor in the province (*Land*) of Vorarlberg, Austria. The local chapter of the Prevention of Cruelty to Animals required anesthesia in all butchering. The Basic Law of 1867 and the Peace Treaty of St. Germain-en-Laye guarantee the free exercise of faith in Austria. According to the Peace Treaty, the exercise is free unless it is inconsistent with public order. The Austrian Constitutional Court ruled that the intervention into free exercise is justified if the religious practice severely disturbs the living together of the people, as this would amount to disturbance of public order. The prevention of cruelty is a recognized public interest, but in this case, it did not justify intervention because it did not exceed in importance the public interest at stake. VfGH Beschluss B3028/97.

5. In the *Blood Transfusion Case*, 32 BVerfGE 98 (1971), the defendant and his wife were members of the Association of Evangelical Brotherhood. The defendant's wife, who was of sound mind, refused a blood transfusion and hospitalization during complications related to childbirth. She died and the defendant was convicted for failing to provide assistance. The GFCC said: "In this type of case criminal law cannot require two people with the same beliefs to influence one another so as to convince themselves of the danger of their religious decision." It mandated privileged treatment of religiously motivated action:

Freedom of religion, as part of that value system, is also a part of the mandate of tolerance, especially in reference to the guarantee of human dignity in Article 1 (1) of the Basic Law, which governs the entire value system of fundamental rights as its paramount value * * *

With respect to criminal law, one who acts or fails to act on the basis of a religious conviction may find himself in conflict with the governing morality and the legal obligations flowing from this morality. When someone commits a punishable act on the basis of his religion, then a conflict arises between Article 4 (1) of the Basic Law and the goals of criminal law. This offender is not resisting the legal order out of any lack of respect for that order; he too wishes to preserve the legal value embodied in that penal law. He sees himself, however, as being in a borderline situation where the general legal order is competing with the dictates of faith. Even if this personal decision objectively conflicts with the values governing society, it is not so reprehensible as to justify the use of society's harshest weapon, the criminal justice system, to punish the offender. Criminal punishment, no matter what the sentence, is an inappropriate sanction for this constellation of facts under any goal of the criminal justice system (retribution, prevention, rehabilitation of the offender). The duty of all public authority to respect serious religious convictions, [as] contained in Article 4 (1) of the Basic Law, must lead to a relaxation of criminal laws when an actual conflict between a generally accepted legal duty and a dictate of faith results in a spiritual crisis for the offender that, in view of the punishment labeling him a criminal, would represent an excessive social reaction violative of his human dignity.

6.   The Children's Aid Society of Ontario, Canada, received a court order for wardship authority over the daughter of a Jehovah's Witnesses couple to enable it to give permission for a blood transfusion, which the parents refused to permit on religious grounds. In *B. v. Children's Aid Society of Metropolitan Toronto*, [1995] 1 S.C.R. 315, in a 5–4 decision, the majority, per Justice La Forest, held:

> [I]it is the freedom of religion of the appellants—Sheena's parents—that is at stake in this appeal, not that of the child herself. * * * [The purpose of the] *Children's Protection Act* is nothing more or less than the protection of children. But if the purpose of the Act does not infringe on the freedom of religion of the appellants, the same cannot be said of its effects. * * * While it is difficult to conceive of any limitations on religious beliefs, the same cannot be said of religious practices, notably when they impact on the fundamental rights and freedoms of others * * *. In my view, it appears sounder to leave to the state the burden of justifying the restrictions it has chosen. Any ambiguity or hesitation should be resolved in favour of individual rights. Not only is this consistent with the broad and liberal interpretation of rights favoured by this Court, but s.1 is a much more flexible tool with which to balance competing rights than s. 2(a). * * * As I am of the view that the Act seriously infringed on the appellants' freedom to choose medical treatment for their child in accordance with the tenets of their faith; it remains to be determined whether this infringement was justified under s. 1 of the *Charter*.

Id. at 381–85.

The other four justices structured the conflict between the right to life of the child and the religious freedoms of the parents, where the right to life had precedence. Which position is closer to the German decision discussed above?

7.   *Conscientious objectors.* One of the most spectacular conflicts between beliefs and obligations to the state is related to military service. In the U.S., Quakers were granted an exemption during the War of Independence as the revolutionary government did not want to antagonize important

supporters. American legislation traditionally recognized an exemption to religious objectors; the constitutional issue (especially during the Vietnam War) was what amounted to religion. Many European constitutions, enacted after the collapse of one or another dictatorship, expressly recognize conscientious-objector status and allow for alternative service (Germany, as amended in 1968, Spain, Hungary, Russia, and Poland). This can be seen as recognition of the freedom of conscience, allowing departure from generally applicable laws. In the first German conscientious-objector case, 12 BVerfGE 45 (1960), the GFCC stated that "conscience is to be understood as an experimental and spiritual phenomenon that absolutely compels a person, in demonstrating his concern for fellow human beings, to commit himself unreservedly to an ideal." The test applied regarding conscientious objectors was "an inner moral command against the use of arms of any kind and in all circumstances, an interior force that touches the very depths of his personality." The GFCC does not require this moral command to be rooted in religion. What matters is the internal commitment. The GFCC is demanding in determining the personal commitment: selective objection to a particular war is unacceptable. The GFCC found unconstitutional a system where the potential conscripts simply notify the authorities about their beliefs and apply for alternative service (48 BVerfGE 127 (1975)). The conscience is actually examined by the authorities. In view of the GFCC, this is mandated by equality considerations. In 1983, the then-conservative government introduced a new "postcard" notification system, requiring objectors to serve in the compulsory civilian service for a period that was one-third longer than armed conscripts' required service. Article 12 (a) of the Basic Law states that the duration of civilian service shall not exceed that of military service. Nevertheless, the GFCC found the longer period constitutional, 69 BVerfGE 1 (1985), on the ground that acceptance of a longer, less intensive service indicates sincere belief. Does the new system satisfy equality requirements, especially equality of beliefs?

Compare the German position with the "less permissive" one of the Italian Constitutional Court (ICC):

> The Italian Constitution * * * contains a set of normative elements which, taken together, uniformly establish the principle that so-called rights of conscience must be safeguarded.

> However, this protection cannot be considered to be free of limitations and conditions. It is primarily the responsibility of the legislator to balance individual conscience and the right it claims for itself on the one hand, and the overall, indefeasible duty to practice political, economic and social solidarity under article 2 of the Italian Constitution on the other, in order to safeguard the orderly running of society and guarantee that the obligations and burdens they create are fairly shared between all the citizens, without creating privileges.

> The state can require service of a sentence—in the absence of more valid alternatives—as the *quid pro quo* for evading constitutionally imposed duties (in this case, under article 52 of the Italian Constitution, regarding the obligation to defend the country in every possible manner). But once the element of conscience has been given a value which characterizes the positive law in this respect, it cannot subsequently be ignored by introducing measures to bring pressure to bear on an individual to

persuade him to change his convictions and act other than in accordance with his conscience.

Conscientious Objector Case, Judgement n. 43/1997.[p]

The Spanish and German courts found constitutional the replacement of military service with alternative community service. In addition, they found that the criminalization of refusal of alternative community service did not violate freedom of conscience. But if the rule establishing the period and conditions for the performance of the alternative community service exceeded reasonable limits, this could infringe the right to object to military service. 55/1996, TC 1996; 19 BVerfGE 135 (1965); 24 BVerfGE 178 (1968).

8. *Sabbath.* The governmental choice of a day of rest and related prohibitions on commerce have resulted in constitutional litigation that indicates the potential for religious discrimination via accommodating a national, all-encompassing norm that has religious roots or establishes a state religion. Most courts that try to respect equality of religions and state neutrality seek to explain away the survival of the Sunday (or other Sabbath) observance. However, the Supreme Court of Canada found the Lord Day's Act of 1970, which prohibits gainful employment or work in one's calling on Sunday, to be a violation of freedom of religion. In *R. v. Big M Drug Mart, Ltd.*, [1985] 1 S.C.R. 295, the Calgary police charged Big M Drug Mart with selling groceries. Big M argued that the Lord's Day Act *establishes* Christian religious practice. The Court said:

> There are obviously two possible ways to characterize the purpose of Lord's Day legislation, the one religious, namely securing public observance of the Christian institution of the Sabbath and the other secular, namely providing a uniform day of rest from labour. * * * Historically, there seems little doubt that it was religious purpose, which underlay the enactment of English Lord's Day legislation.

> * * * [T]he American Supreme Court, in its quartet on Sunday observance legislation, suggest that the purpose of legislation may shift, or be transformed over time by changing social conditions. [The Supreme Court found the US approach unacceptable:] To the extent that it binds all to a sectarian Christian ideal, the *Lord's Day Act* works a form of coercion inimical to the spirit of the *Charter* and the dignity of all non-Christians. In proclaiming the standards of the Christian faith, the Act creates a climate hostile to, and gives the appearance of discrimination against, non-Christian Canadians. * * * [U]niversal observance of the day of rest preferred by one religion] is contrary to the expressed provisions of s. 27, which as earlier noted reads:

>> 'This Charter shall be interpreted in a manner consistent with the preservation and enhancement of the multicultural heritage of Canadians.'

p. An Italian law of 1972 granted conscientious-objector status. However, if the person refused to accept some alternative obligation he was subject to punishment. After such conviction, the individual was exonerated from the performance of compulsory military service. However, when the sentence has been conditionally suspended by the courts, the military authorities may have considered that the term must be served once again, using the standard procedures for calling up recruits to military service and following the servicing of the new call-up papers as a repeat refusal to perform.

* * * For the present case it is sufficient in my opinion to say that whatever else freedom of conscience and religion may mean, it must at the very least mean this: government may not coerce individuals to affirm a specific religious belief or to manifest a specific religious practice for a sectarian purpose. * * * The legislative preservation of a Sunday day of rest should be secular, the diversity of belief and non-belief, the diverse socio-cultural backgrounds of Canadians make it constitutionally incompetent for the federal Parliament to provide legislative preference for any one religion at the expense of those of another religious persuasion. * * * It seems disingenuous to say that the legislation is valid criminal law and offends s. 2(a) because it compels the observance of a Christian religious duty, yet is still a reasonable limit demonstrably justifiable because it achieves the secular objective the legislators did not primarily intend.

In *State v. Lawrence*, 1997 (4) SALR 1176 (CC), the South African Constitutional Court (SACC) upheld restrictions on the sale of wine on "closed days" (Sundays, Good Friday, and Christmas Day). President Chaskalson found that:

the selection of a Sunday for purposes which are not purely religious and which do not constrain the practice of other religions would be unlawful simply because Sunday is the Christian sabbath. * * * In South Africa, Sundays have acquired a secular as well as a religious character. * * * The section does not compel licensees or any other persons, directly or indirectly, to observe the Christian sabbath. It does not in any way constrain their right to entertain such religious beliefs as they might choose, or to declare their religious beliefs openly, or to manifest their religious beliefs. It does not compel them to open or close their businesses on a Sunday.

Id. at paras. 89–97.

Are there factual differences between the Canadian and South African cases that would explain the differences? Note that both decisions strongly emphasized the impact of the selection of a religious holiday on religious minorities.

The Hungarian Constitutional Court (HCC) found no difficulty in the government's choice of Sunday and major Christian religious holidays to be days of rest as "these days are held festive days by the overwhelming majority, are part of the folk-lore, and based on tradition which is observed in most countries of the world; the day of rest is not a Sunday observance prohibition" (Decision 8/1993 (II.27.) AB hat.). To some extent the Hungarian case was an easier one because it was decided in an abstract review where there were no prohibitions on the exercise of a particular trade in the case. In the U.S., the legislative choice of Sunday as a universal day of rest was found not to violate the Establishment Clause of the Constitution, and the secular goal of providing a day of rest was found sufficiently compelling. *McGowan v. Maryland,* 366 U.S. 420 (1961). A Connecticut law provided "that those who observe a Sabbath any day of the week as a matter of religious conviction must be relieved of the duty to work on that day, no matter what burden or inconvenience this imposes on the employer or fellow workers." The USSC found in *Thornton v. Caldor, Inc.,* 472 U.S. 703 (1985), that the Connecticut law was in violation of the Establishment Clause as it advanced religion. Does the Sabbath observance law prefer one religion?

Note that the Sabbath could be observed on "any day" of the week. Title VII of the Civil Rights Act requires employers to reasonably accommodate the religious practices of employees.

> In my view, a statute outlawing employment discrimination based on race, color, religion, sex or national origin has the valid secular purpose of assuring employment opportunity to all groups in our pluralistic society. Since Title VII calls for reasonable rather than absolute accommodation and extends that requirement to all religious beliefs and practices rather than protecting only the Sabbath observance, I believe an objective observer would perceive it as an antidiscrimination law rather than an endorsement of religion or a particular religious practice.

> Justice O'Connor, concurring in *Thornton* at 711.

In *Braunfeld* the Sunday-closing laws of 21 states, exempting Sabbatarians, were held unconstitutionally discriminative as these laws did not provide exemptions to others who claimed a day of rest on nonreligious grounds.

> Challenges to "sabbatarian laws" that restrict ordinary, everyday activities, like shopping or driving, on days that for some are reserved for reflection and prayer, provide a clear example of the normative superiority of the pragmatic approach. Laws of this kind have been tested all over the world; in Canada, Ireland, Israel, Hungary, and South Africa as well as in the United States. To varying degrees, the Supreme Courts in the first three countries concentrated on the impact such laws had on different individuals and groups who were affected by their provisions and, as a result, were able to provide greater protection for religious liberty than the courts in the United States and South Africa which did not. Indeed, by using a principle of proportionality which (like the German's principle of "practical concordance") tries to maximize all of the interests at stake in a case, they were able to protect religious liberty in their communities without restricting the sovereignty of the people to express its collective identity in the laws it enacts to any significant degree. * * * Israel's Supreme Court * * * in *Lior Horev v. Minister of Communication/ Transportation*, [1997] provides a dramatic example of the capacity of pragmatic reasoning to resolve highly charged political issues of church/state relations in a way that is equally sensitive to the interests of both. At issue was a Government regulation that would have closed a major artery running through the heart of Jerusalem—Bar Ilan Street—during the hours of prayer on the Jewish sabbath. The street ran through a number of orthodox neighborhoods. * * * The dispute was "deep and bitter" one that divided the country and even spilled over into violence on the street.

> [Chief Justice] Barak was very aware of the political dimension of the dispute but he insisted the Court could not concern itself with the general state of relations between the orthodox and secular communities. The issue in law was the authority of the relevant state official to enforce a partial closing on Bar Ilan Street. * * * He disagreed with three of his colleagues who voted to strike down the regulation because they thought it would act as a precedent for other closings. He thought "slippery slope" arguments of this kind were "dangerous" because they were based on fears and speculation that had no basis in fact. As a

pragmatist, he took the view that each road closing had to be judged on its own set of facts.

* * *

Barak * * * read [the Basic Law's] declaration that Israel was a "democratic state" to mean that Governments could pass laws for the purpose of protecting the religious sentiments of their people so long as they did not entail any religious coercion and they respected a basic principle of proportionality or "toleration". "Toleration", he wrote, "is a basic value in every democratic conception. * * * It is crucial to a democracy based on pluralism. It was this principle, rather than anything actually written in the Basic Law, that Barak used to evaluate the closing of Bar Ilan Street. First, he endorsed the idea of a partial closing. Stopping traffic during the hours of prayer was much more in keeping with the principle of toleration than either of the all or nothing (open or closed for the entire day) positions of the parties. * * * By comparison, the inconvenience most Israelis would suffer from being denied access to the street during such times would be trivial. Commuters who used the street as a thoroughfare would be obliged to take an alternative route which, Barak calculated, would add an additional two minutes to their trip. At least during the times when prayers were being said, the proportionalities—in the significance of the closing for the two communities—were clear.

David M. Beatty, *The Forms and Limits of Constitutional Interpretation*, 49 Am. J. Comp. Law 79, 101–103 (2001).

In Israel, a government measure was challenged as violating the Sabbath. Is this important for the outcome of the case? It seems there was no attempt to define the state as neutral and deprive the day of rest of its religious nature in Israel. The Sabbath was protected for the sake of religion. Does the pragmatism of the Israeli Supreme Court "accommodate" secular considerations in the prevailingly religious constitutional setting? In view of Justice O'Connor's willingness to uphold Title VII as an antidiscrimination measure, while finding the mandated accommodation of Connecticut unconstitutional, do you agree that the USSC is directed by principles whereas other courts are pragmatic? What is the meaning of judicial pragmatism? As to Israel, see further *Shavit* below.

B. CHURCH AND STATE

In this section we deal with contemporary problems in church–state relations. The American literature often refers to these as (non)establishment issues, in view of the First Amendment's prohibition of any law "respecting an establishing of religion."[q] This provision was intended to

q. In *Everson v. Board of Education*, 330 U.S. 1, 16 (1947), the USSC wrote: The 'establishment of religion' clause of the First Amendment means at least this: Neither a state nor the Federal Government can set up a church. Neither can pass laws which aid one religion, aid all religions, or prefer one religion over another. Neither can force nor influence a person to go to or to remain away from church against his will or force him to profess a belief or disbelief in any religion. No person can be punished for entertaining or professing religious beliefs or disbeliefs, for church attendance or non-attendance. No tax in any amount, large or small, can be levied to support any religious activities or institutions, whatever they may be called, or whatever from they may adopt to teach or practice limit only the federal Congress. The majority of the founding states had state-church systems, in 1791, when the Bill of Rights was ratified. "Relations between church and state at the end of the 1780s fell into two quite different categories. In several European countries, one national religion, such as the Church of England in Great Britain, was established. The established church typically was supported by tax revenues, by laws conferring privileges only upon members, and sometimes by violent persecution of nonadherents. In contrast, although several American colonies had assessed taxes to support one chosen faith, none of the newly United States subsidized a single religion." *County of Allegheny v. A.C.L.U.*, 492 U.S. 573 646 (1989) (Justice Stevens, concurring). This system survived for many years in state constitutions; for example, in Massachusetts until 1833.

The institutional relations between church and state should serve free exercise values. However, the language of contemporary constitutions reflects other concerns, too, often recognizing that one or more churches have special status in society. Moreover, many religions are based on the assumption that religion is not a matter of individual rights; religion is not only an individual right. It cannot be exercised outside a specific community. In this approach the rights holder should be the community that is organized according to religious tenets. (Article 16 of the Spanish Constitution treats freedom of religion as an individual and collective right—it pertains to communities, too.) A constitutional argument for the privileged status of churches is that there can be no protection of religion outside the church, which is the only depository of religious rights; or at least freedom of religion cannot be fully protected without giving adequate protection (power of self-determination and autonomy) to the church.

The protection of free exercise of religion does not entail the recognition of specific organizations that provide the structure and framework for religious practices (e.g., in France, the Republic is "lay"; the Dutch[r] and Armenian constitutions contain no reference to any "church"). But many constitutions have provisions, regarding the relationship between the church and state, that reflect the social power of the church at the time of constitution making. (For the historical meaning of establishment, see *Allegheny* below.) Liberal democracies have moved away from the idea of a state church, in order to satisfy the constitutional requirement of equality among citizens; but they may still single out the majority church as the national church. This was the solution in Italy, in 1947; followed by Spain, in 1977; and Poland, in 1997.

religion. Neither a state nor the Federal Government can, openly or secretly, participate in the affairs of any religious organizations or groups and vice versa. In the words of Jefferson, the clause against establishment of religion by law was intended to erect 'a wall of separation between Church and State.' *Reynolds v. United States*, 98 U.S. 145, at 164.
See Wilber G. Katz, *Religion and American Constitutions* 8–10 (1964). The author ar-

gues that the religion clauses were adopted to protect the states' rights from congressional interference with existing establishments in the states.

r. The Dutch Civil Code recognizes churches and independent units of churches as sui generis legal entities. The general principles on legal entities do not apply to churches.

The first subsection of this section is dedicated to the various models, in particular to the problem of the state's identification with a specific church or with religious worldviews. The second subsection deals with a special area of the relationship: To what extent can religion play a role in education? Of course, church–state relations entail important problems outside the school context, like special access to government agencies and services (e.g., military or prison chaplains), access to public funding of churches or special church services, tax exemption to churches, and other forms of preferential treatment provided to churches or to individuals exercising religious practices. The interrelations are extremely complex. For example, Germany is multiconfessional, that is, a number of churches have special state recognition; for instance, through the collection of church taxes by the state revenue service. At the same time, the state is expected to remain neutral, which means that religion cannot be a governmental consideration in public life. For example, if two equally qualified candidates seek a position in a school, the state cannot give preference to the Catholic one, even if the overwhelming majority of students are Catholics. As the cases below indicate, the teacher, as the representative of the state, must follow the neutrality requirements and cannot use his or her position to indoctrinate children. State neutrality, however, remains a contested, ambiguous ideal. One interpretation is that, to protect freedom of religion, state neutrality cannot be hostile, nor even indifferent, to religion; but this "implies the state guarantee of religious freedom in a regime of confessional and cultural pluralism" (Italian Constitutional Court, 12 April 1989, No. 203).

B.1. MODELS OF CHURCH–STATE RELATIONS: SECULARISM, SEPARATION, COEXISTENCE, BENEVOLENCE AND STATE RELIGION

Most religions require communal action; hence the importance of the organization for religious practices. The forms of religious organizations differ considerably. Churches typically are nationwide, though not necessarily centralized. Historically, the prevailing church dominated society. As soon as religious minority groups emerged, the dominant church often took to persecuting them (branding them heretics, cults, sects, and the like). Although there were various religions that managed to peacefully co-exist, Europe and other parts of the world suffered long periods of religious persecution. The European experience, together with the experience of the American descendants of the persecuted, contributed to the basic ideas of religious freedom and church–state relations in liberal constitutions. The U.S. Constitution adopted solutions developed in the state constitutions. It attempted to enable the co-existence of religious communities that seek to live according to their own religious tenets. These tenets are often in conflict with one another. This was the fundamental problem in Europe, which led to the Reformation. Only after desperate wars did a degree of tolerance emerge. Tolerance meant, for John Locke and others, that the state would not interfere in religious practices. Tolerance implies that the practice of all religions is permitted, and citizens are not discriminated against on the basis of religion. Historically, such tolerance was often limited to the private sphere, and in public affairs (office-holding) certain churches were afforded religious preferences and prerogatives. One meaning of tolerance is that the state should be neutral, that is, the state should not interfere in matters of faith or proclaim any religion as the "truth." It is perhaps in the domain of church–state relations that the greatest differences exist today among constitutional governments. While many constitutions preserved specific historical arrangements between a dominant church and the state, others were written with the intent to keep churches out of politics or even out of the public sphere. In some cases such depoliticization was facilitated by the predominantly private and customary nature of the predominant religion, as in Japan after World War Two. Certain countries are particularly keen to disregard churches and religions in public life; e.g., in Singapore it is assumed that this is required by the extreme sensitivities in a religiously diverse society. Were the state to allow a religious approach in governmental practices, it would antagonize other religious groups, endangering public order. Hence the state must keep equal distance from all churches. If a church is believed to promote political activities (even through the legitimate political process, as in parliamentary activities), those in political power might feel this is an impermissible interference in state affairs. This, in principle, is the Indian attitude, dictated by concerns of interethnic and interdenominational conflict. For such reasons, Bismarck, the statesman responsible for the unification of Germany in the nineteenth century, pushed legislation through Parliament that resulted in a sort of state neutrality that was hostile to the Roman Catholic Church and to parliamentary representatives who followed its political platform. A somewhat similar model of hostile neutrality (*laïcité*) emerged in France, resulting from the political struggle between republicans and the political supporters of the Roman Catholic Church. As a result, the 1905 Law on the *Separation* expressly barred churches from having a public function. Today private denominational education is entitled to public subsidies, although the curriculum must meet general secular standards.[s] The history of separation indicates that "at some point, aggressive separationism becomes hostility towards religion,"[t] although the state's identification with one religion, or perhaps with religions, might also be oppressive and discriminatory, endangering freedom of religion.

s. Consider John Finnis, *On the Practical Meaning of Secularism*, 73 Notre Dame L. Rev. 491 (1998):

'Secular' is a word minted by Latin Christians * * * signifying the affairs of this world. * * * Aquinas uses it regularly, and often quite without negative connotations: he will say, for example, that in matters which concern the good of the political community (*bonum civile*), Christians should generally obey the directives of the secular rather than the ecclesiastical authorities.

Aquinas is pointing out a distinction of competences which exemplifies a social process of differentiation that goes much wider. Modern historians and sociologists have often called this wider social process 'secularization.'

t. W. Cole Durham, *Perspectives on Religious Liberty: A Comparative Framework*, in *Religious Human Rights in Global Perspective: Legal Perspectives* (Johan D. van der Vyver and John Witte, Jr. eds., 1996).

In the U.S., church–state relations are understood in the light of the constitutional precept of the nonestablishment of religion and churches. (Endorsement, in Europe and in Islamic states, means the constitutional recognition of a state church and, perhaps, of a state religion.) Government cannot function in a way that would recognize or rely upon anything religious. The few known exceptions, like prayer at the opening of a legislative session, are justified as historical customs. Religious considerations cannot be made part of governmental activities. The permissible impact of government on churches and religious practices is more complicated; it is contested and controversial. Discriminatory endorsement is prohibited. Tax-exempt status to churches is permissible but only within the class of charities. Other government support of activities that might benefit churches or religious believers remains highly suspect and, in principle, impermissible. Related issues are decided on an ad hoc basis, turning on the assumed neutrality of the given measure.

A more benevolent secularism is advocated by many Indian thinkers and politicians. The Indian Constitution expressly guarantees the autonomy of churches in their own affairs. However, the benevolence has its dangers in the Indian context, given the socially divisive nature of religion. The Supreme Court used to vigorously defend the laws that prohibit the use of religion in politics (religious parties or symbols in elections are prohibited). However, religious implications of political parties were recently understood as expressions of national identity.

The German Basic Law (especially in its Appendix, which incorporates the religious-entities articles of the 1919 Weimar Constitution) and the social and legal practices developed around the inherited constitutional arrangements provide public law status to churches that were recognized by the state in the pre-Weimar period. After the religious wars of the sixteenth and seventeenth centuries, the German states agreed that the religion of the ruler of each state should be decisive for its subjects. Much later, after the repeal of the Bismarckian system of "state neutrality," the previous arrangements were consolidated. The current privileges of churches include tax collection by the state, publicly financed denominational and interdenominational schools, religion classes as part of the educational curricula, and others.

The German approach to church–state relations is often considered as "cooperationist." Regardless of the relevant constitutional provisions, Spain, Italy, Poland, Hungary, as well as some Latin American countries cooperate with an increasing number of (major) churches, through agreements and concordats with the Vatican.

State recognition of the dictates of a religion and the authority it grants to a church (or churches) to determine matters regulated by the tenets of religion may empower church authorities to decide the fate of church members. Such arrangements challenge ordinary concepts of state neutrality and point to theocracy. (Article 3 of the Greek Constitution may serve as an example. See *Kokkinakis* above.) Apostasy (leaving one's religion) is a crime punishable by death in certain Islamic republics, in accordance with the Koran. Given the protected and endorsed status of churches, special state authorities (Ministry of Religious Affairs, in Israel; Ministry of Cults, often together with the Ministry of Education, in Greece) handle matters related to church support and exercise control over the tolerated churches.

Churches insist that in personal matters of believers, church law and church courts should have jurisdiction. This is the case in Israel and the rule in Islamic republics. Even secular India had to grant such personal powers. As the *Burial Society* case (burial of nonreligious Jews in rabbinically administered cemeteries) indicates, the liberal need to protect the personal beliefs of citizens inevitably challenges such endorsement.

Krystyna Daniel and W. Cole Durham, Jr., RELIGIOUS IDENTITY AS A COMPONENT OF NATIONAL IDENTITY: IMPLICATIONS FOR EMERGING CHURCH–STATE RELATIONS IN THE FORMER SOCIALIST BLOC, in THE LAW OF RELIGIOUS IDENTITY: MODELS FOR POST–COMMUNISM

117, 120–126 (András Sajó and Shlomo Avineri eds., 1999).

* * *

Modalities of Relationship Between Religion and Politics. The possible modes of relation are finite, though the basic relationships are subject to infinite variations. A first possibility is that religious and political institutions may simply be fused in a particular society. In certain types of primitive societies, for example, it is virtually impossible to distinguish political and religious notions. Historical societies, however, virtually always display differentiation of religious and political institutions. Where differentiation is present, there are essentially three possibilities: either political institutions are subordinate to religious institutions, religious institutions are subject to political institutions, or the two are in some type of equipoise.

These relationships are, of course, dynamic. Much about the interrelationship depends on the beliefs and objectives of the individuals and institutions involved in any particular setting. Thus, the attitude of the church toward state institutions can make a major difference with respect to the likelihood of church-state tensions. For example, if the fundamental attitude of a religious belief system and its institutions is to withdraw from the world to a monastic retreat, and to leave the world to the powers that be, tensions are likely to be minimal. Similarly, if the church traditionally accepts political authority, either as part of a relationship such as the Orthodox ideal of 'symphony' or as a reflection of something like the medieval 'two swords' doctrine, with its recognition of the legitimacy in appropriate contexts of secular power, conflict is likely to be restrained. But if the religious organization believes that its role is to transform the state and society, tension is likely to be much more acute. More generally, different religious traditions adopt different postures toward their surrounding cultures, and this can have significant ramifications for church-state interactions. The impact of the second Vatican Council on Roman Catholic attitudes toward liberal democracy and human rights and the resulting liberalization of attitudes toward religious freedom in predominantly Catholic countries is one of the most striking examples of this in our century.

Similarly, the state may adopt various postures toward religious groups within its jurisdiction. The state almost always encounters religion in some regulatory context or another, and in sufficiently extreme cases, the state feels compelled to proscribe or limit extreme religious practices.[21] (It may also regulate in innocuous ways necessary for general coordination in society and not objectionable to the church. For example, churches seldom have deeply principled objections to reasonable parking regulations applicable to the street in front of a church building.)[22] What is important from a religious freedom standpoint in this context is how deferential the state is to matters about which the religious organization genuinely cares, and how extreme the circumstances must be to justify the state in overriding religious freedom claims.[23] These issues have to do fundamentally with the outer limits of religious freedom.

Leaving these matters aside, the state may seek to identify with religion to varying degrees. This is in a sense the obverse of concerns

---

21. See, *e.g.*, *Sherbert v. Verner*, 374 U.S. 398 (1963); *Wisconsin v. Yoder*, 406 U.S. 205 (1972). The compelling state interest' test was substantially weakened by the U.S. Supreme Court's decision in *Employment Division v. Smith*, 494 U.S. 872 (1990), but was substantially restored by Congress in the Religious Freedom Restoration Act, 42 U.S.C. § 2000bb to 2000bb–4 (Supp V. 1993) and then eliminated again when the Supreme Court declared RFRA unconstitutional in *City of Boerne v. Flores*, 521 U.S. 507 (1997) (on grounds of lack of Congressional power under Section 5 of the 14th Amendment to promulgate religious freedom requirements effective as against the states).

22. However, they may have objections to zoning or historical preservation rules. For examples, see *Keeler v. Mayor & City Council of Cumberland*, 940 F.Supp 879 (D.Md.1996); *St. John's Roman Catholic Church Corp. v. Town of Darien*, 184 A.2d 42 (Conn.1962); *Messiah Baptist Church v. County of Jefferson*, 859 F.2d 820 (10th Cir.1988); and *Bethel Evangelical Lutheran Church v. Village of Morton*, 559 N.E.2d 533 (Ill. App.Ct.1990).

23. Germany, for example, gives church autonomy great deference. The German Basic Law, by incorporating Article 137(3) of the Weimar Constitution, provides that 'every religious community independently regulates and administers its own affairs within the boundaries of the laws that are valid for all.' The Federal Constitutional Court has recognized that not any law can override religious autonomy, but rather that a barrier to religious activity is raised only by general laws when the law represents a provision of particular importance to the common weal. BVerfGE 42, 312 (334); 66, 1 (20). See G. Robbers, *State and Church in Germany*, in *State and Church in the European Union*, 57, 62–63 (1996).

The right of religious associations to autonomy is not limited to a narrow class of specifically religious, worship-type activities. Rather, it extends to other areas of religiously motivated conduct, such as 'the running of hospitals, kindergartens, retirement homes, private schools and universities.' *Id.* at 63. It includes matters of dogma, liturgy, structuring of the religious organization, its hierarchy, and subordinate organizations, administration of church affairs, determination of the organization of the religious body and of the rights and duties of members, relationships with ministers and other religious officials, financial structure and arrangements of the religious association (but not state tax matters), the independence of religious jurisdiction (in its own affairs), territorial organization of religious affairs, and so forth. K. Hesse, 'Selbstbestimmungsrecht der Kirchen und Religionsgemeinschaften' in *Handbuch des Staatskirchenrechts der Bundesrepublik Deutschland* 521, 537–43 (J. Llistl & Pirson, eds. 2d. ed. 1994). Even state supervision of a religious body's administration of its own affairs is held to be impermissible. *Id.* The dominant view today gives substantial deference to a religious association's own self-understanding of what constitutes its own affairs. See, *e.g.* BVerfGE 24, 236 (247–48); BVerfGE 53, 366 (401); BVerfGE 66, 1 (22); BVerfGE 70, 138 (167–68).

with religious identity in society. At one extreme, the state may identify strongly with a particular religious tradition. In the extreme case, this may lead to a virtual theocracy such as that in Iran, or it may lead to official establishment of religion (with varying degrees of toleration or non-toleration for other religions). A milder version of state identification involves endorsement of a particular religious tradition and the special role it has played in a country's history and culture, without necessarily making it the official established church in a country. At the other extreme, a state may adopt an official stance that opposes religion. Communist Albania was probably the extreme version of this position, but most Marxists regimes shared at least to some degree this hostility toward religion. In a sense, Marxist regimes with their pronounced negative identification with religion tended to pose the flip-side of regimes with strong positive identification of religion. Marxism was in effect a secular world view that played the same role in society as an established church: it wanted to assert a monopoly position with respect to the belief systems that would be permissible in society. Dissident views were anathema. Of course, hostility to religion can emanate from other sources besides militant Marxism. Anticlericalism has been a familiar phenomenon in many cultures since the Enlightenment, and has led to a number of regimes that have been extremely hostile to religion. Still another position falls short of intentional hostility to religion, but may have the same effect. This is the situation where a state adopts a general law that is neutral on its face and addresses some legitimate state objective, but works a hardship on a particular religious group. If the state insists on imposing this burden, even where there is no compelling state objective for doing so, or where the state objective could be substantially achieved in a way that would avoid the burden on religion, it is in fact negatively identified with religion (at least with the burdened religion).[27]

Between the extremes of positive and negative identification of state with religion, there are a range of intermediate positions, virtually all of which have representatives among contemporary western nations. Despite their diversity, virtually all such systems lay claim to the legitimacy-conferring notion of neutrality, but each conceives of neutrality in rather different ways. One model of neutrality is state inaction. This was the original theory of the religion clause of the first amendment of the United States Constitution: 'Congress shall make no law respecting an establishment of religion or prohibiting the free exercise thereof.' The provision was drafted with the idea that liberty is best protected not by defining individual rights, but by restricting the assertion of governmental power. The problem with this model in the contemporary setting is that government has grown so large and exerts such intense gravitational influence on all of social life that one can no longer be assured that inaction is an automatic guarantor of neutrality. Critics who view deprivatization of religion in the United States as a departure from original separationist axioms often overlook this reality.

27. See, *e.g.*, *Munn v. Algee*, 924 F.2d 568, 574 (5th Cir.1991) (holding that a Jehovah Witness's refusal to accept a blood transfusion was unreasonable, and therefore precluded wrongful death recovery).

A second model of neutrality is the impartiality of the unbiased umpire. As applied to religion, neutrality in this sense contends that the state should be neutral in the sense that it should always act in religion-blind ways. It should never act on the basis of exclusively religious premises. Generally, advocates of this position assume that there is some way of demarcating the realms of reason and religion, and from their perspective, politics is an enterprise that should be carried out within the limits of reason alone. Deliberation in the public square, under this view, must be carried out exclusively on the basis of rational premises that are not predicated on claims of privileged access to truth and that can be understood without resort to religious beliefs. Even the institutions that prepare citizens for participation in public deliberation (*i.e.*, the schools) must be preserved as a temple of (secular) reason, and woe to the poor Muslim girl who dares to wear religious clothing while attending school, thereby tainting the rationalist antechambers of the public square!

A third model conceives of the state as the monitor of an open forum. The state can impose time, place, and manner restrictions on the marketplace of ideas and can take certain precautions to avoid violence and fraud in the operations of the market, but essentially the state is a night watchman minimalist exerting no control on the content of ideas that flow into the market and raising no barriers to access. It sets the stage for the members of society to engage in discourse, recognizing that in doing so, it provides a venue in which various ideas can be represented and can attempt to establish some pecking order of the quality of truth claims. That is, efforts at persuasion will go on in the market place, and in addition, symbolic positioning can be expected as well. But with respect to all of this, the state simply attempts to remain neutral, and to assure that its agents are not captured or subjected to any illicit manipulation as they monitor the boundaries and operations of the market.

A fourth model of neutrality calls for substantive equal treatment. In general, all citizens and groups should be treated alike, but the state in making laws and engaging in other actions may take significant differences into account in making decisions and in serving its citizenry. Among other things, the fact that a person or group holds religious beliefs that would be burdened by a decision or allocation of resources or by a governmental regulation or prohibition is a relevant fact that the state can permissibly take into account. Indeed, since religious beliefs go to the core of human dignity, it is a consideration of preeminent rank that should be taken into account and that overrides most other considerations, and indeed warrants differential treatment (*i.e.*, an exemption) in the absence of compelling state interests that can be furthered in no other way. This view of neutrality yields an accommodationist church-state theory.

The fifth model of neutrality is in effect the 'second generation rights' version of the fourth. That is, it views the actualization of substantive rights as an affirmative obligation of the state (or in weaker versions, it sees no constitutional constraints on providing economic or other means to facilitate (even) religious groups in the actualization of their religious freedom rights). That is, the state is willing to affirmatively cooperate with religious groups in helping them to carry out their mission as they perceive it. There are difficulties in carrying out this vision of neutrality, since there are no clear principles that govern allocation of resources among groups with very different sizes and needs, but the state concern to assure that groups receive the help they need tends to outweigh concerns about making the distribution precisely equal.

These models of neutrality correspond to a range of possible ways that a neutral state can seek to structure church-state relations. It can take a cooperationist approach along the lines of the German model. It can follow an accommodationist model that is leery of the complexities of equality once one moves into heavy funding of religious organizations but willing to make the accommodations necessary to carve out room for religion in an increasingly cluttered public realm. This is the approach that tends to be favored by those in the U.S. that are sympathetic to some measure of deprivatized religion. Or one can take a more formalist approach and contend that all public discourse must be assimilated into rational secularism, and that even the minimal accommodations necessary to respect religious difference in the public square may impermissibly compromise state neutrality.

Most credible church-state regimes in the modern world inhabit a range somewhere in the neutralist zone. A few cluster on the positive identification periphery of this zone, maintaining endorsement regimes (with considerable but varying levels of toleration for other groups). Still others cluster at the negative periphery where separationism slips over into inadvertent or knowing (but not purposeful) hostility toward religion in terms of the burdens it is willing to impose on religion. Very often, such hostility is a reflection of bureaucratic intransigence. (The area of life administered is perceived as being rife with compelling state interests, and requests for religious exemptions are given no quarter.) Obviously, the various types of neutrality overlap in significant and not always predictable ways. The question for the remainder of this paper is which of these models best describes the types of regimes toward which former socialist bloc countries are evolving, and how religious identity and nationalism interact with transitional state-building to complicate this picture.

CHAN HIANG LENG COLIN & ORS
v. PUBLIC PROSECUTOR

High Court (Singapore).
[1994] 3 S.L.R. 662.

HEADNOTES: The appellants were tried and convicted under s 4(2) of the Undesirable Publications Act (Cap 358) (the UPA) of charges of being in possession of publications published by the Watch Tower Bible & Tract Society (WTBTS), which were prohibited by gazette notification No 123 dated 14 January 1972 (Order 123), made pursuant to s 3 of the UPA. The contents of the prohibited publications were related to the doctrine of the sect known as the Jehovah's Witnesses. Part of the doctrine of the Jehovah's Witnesses advocated that its adherents should refuse to do any form of military duty. As a result, a number of Jehovah's Witnesses refused to do national service. It was on this basis that the Jehovah's Witnesses were de-registered as a society by the Minister for Home Affairs.[u]

At the same time, Order 123 was passed by the Minister for Culture banning all publications by WTBTS, the parent body of the Jehovah's Witnesses.

Judges: Yong Pung How CJ

The relevant provisions of art 15 of the Constitution are as follows:

"Every person has [Art. 15] the right to profess and practise his religion and to propagate it.

No person shall be compelled to pay any tax the proceeds of which are specially allocated in whole or in part for the purposes of a religion other than his own.

Every religious group has the right—to manage its own religious affairs; to establish and maintain institutions for religious or charitable purposes; and to acquire and own property and hold and administer it in accordance with law.

This Article does not authorise any act contrary to any general law relating to public order, public health or morality."

In the course of the hearing of this appeal, Mr. How referred me to various judicial pronouncements in the United States on the right to freedom of religion. There is a fundamental difference between the right to freedom of religion under the First Amendment to the United States Constitution and art 15. Significantly, the Singapore Constitution does not prohibit the 'establishment' of any religion. The social conditions in Singapore are, of course, markedly different from those in the United States. On this basis alone, I am not influenced by the various views as enunciated in the American cases cited to me but instead must restrict my analysis of the issues here with reference to the local context.

The basic proposition in judicial review is that the court will not question the merits of the exercise of the ministerial discretion. There can be no enquiry as to whether it was a correct or proper exercise or whether it should or ought to have been taken. The court cannot substitute its own view as to how the discretion should be exercised with that actually taken

In addition, there is a presumption that the orders were valid and the burden of proving that they were ultra vires or unconstitutional therefore lay on the appellants who challenged them on such grounds (*Chng Suan Tze v. Minister for Home Affairs*).

Mr. How's first contention was that a purposive construction ought to be adopted in considering art 15. He claimed that the right of freedom of religion was required for the protection of the religious liberties of

u. The Deregistration Order was issued in 1972, on the basis that the sect's doctrines were inimical to public order. At that time there were 175 members of the church, and no charges of wrongdoing had been brought against them prior to the order.

minority groups. Article 152(1) It shall be the responsibility of the Government constantly to care for the interests of the racial and religious minorities in Singapore.

Mr. How's submissions centred upon the concept of broad unreasonableness, and little legal argument was presented in support of this allegation. * * * [if] I understood him correctly, one of the challenges he was making was with respect to whether the minister had exercised his discretion based upon the correct criteria as stipulated under the relevant empowering sections. He * * * referred to art 15(4), which provides that the right of freedom of religion can only be constrained if public order, public health or morality is affected, and s 24(1)(a) of the Societies Act, which states that registered organizations can be dissolved on the ground that they are a threat to public peace, welfare or good order. * * * The test to be adopted in determining whether an act affects law and order or public order is this: Does it lead to disturbance of the current of life of the community so as to amount to disturbance of the public order or does it affect merely an individual leaving the tranquillity of the society undisturbed?

* * * In my view, Mr. How's submission that it must be shown that there was a clear and immediate danger was misplaced for one simple reason. It cannot be said that beliefs, especially those propagated in the name of 'religion', should not be put to a stop until such a scenario exists. If not, it would in all probability be too late as the damage sought to be prevented would have transpired.

The appellants contended that there was no evidence produced or even alleged to show that the Jehovah's Witnesses were a threat to public order. Article 15(4) clearly envisages that the right of freedom of religion is subject to inherent limitations and is therefore not an absolute and unqualified right.

I am of the view that religious beliefs ought to have proper protection, but actions undertaken or flowing from such beliefs must conform with the general law relating to public order and social protection. * * * The sovereignty, integrity and unity of Singapore are undoubtedly the paramount mandate of the Constitution and anything, including religious beliefs and practices, which tend to run counter to these objectives must be restrained.

But we have no alternative, as I learned, because they are violating the law. In many Western European countries, they would count as conscientious objectors. But the idea of conscientious objection does not apply in Singapore. There is no such tradition in Singapore. If we try to introduce the practice here, the whole system of universal National Service will come unstuck. Many other people will ask: why should I also not decide to have conscientious objections and therefore exempt myself from National Service?

[In] my view, it was not for this court to substitute its view for the minister's as to whether the Jehovah's Witnesses constituted a threat to national security. As I have outlined earlier, the appellants had the burden of showing that the minister had exercised his powers wrongly.

I now come to Order 123. Section 3 of the UPA reads:

If the Minister is of opinion that the importation, sale or circulation of any publication or series of publications published or printed outside Singapore or within Singapore by any person would be contrary to the public interest, he may in his discretion, by order published in the Gazette, prohibit the importation * * * it was not unreasonable, in my view, for the minister to prohibit all publications by WTBTS. The minister's actions were clearly to stop the dissemination and propagation of beliefs of the Jehovah's Witnesses and this would of necessity include every publication by WTBTS. Any order other than a total blanket order would have been impossible to monitor administratively.

The final submission made by the appellants was that the orders were disproportionate to the interests of the State and operated unfairly. The Court of Appeal has already held in *Chng Suan Tze* that the principle of proportionality was not a separate ground for judicial review but was subsumed under the ground of 'irrationality' in the sense that no reasonable authority could have come to such a decision.

As I understood it, the respective ministers were clearly of the view that the continued existence of the Jehovah's Witnesses was prejudicial to the national interest. The basis for the de-registration clearly flowed from the danger of allowing absolute freedom of religion which might create a complete denial of a government's authority and ability to govern individuals or groups asserting a religious affiliation.

S.R. BOMMAI v. UNION OF INDIA

Supreme Court (India).
(1994) 2 S.C.R. 644.

[In *Bommai* the Court upheld the presidential dissolution of certain Indian state governments and legislatures that were considered to favor Hindu religious fundamentalism, resulting in the destruction of the "Babur's mosque" and related massacres in Ayodhya and elsewhere. For the exercise of dissolution power in emergency, see the excerpt in Chapter 3, Section E.]

P.B. Sawant, J. (on behalf of himself and Kuldip Singh, J.)

* * *

147. * * * [T]he ideal of a secular State in the sense of a State which treats all religions alike and displays benevolence towards them is in a way more suited to the Indian environment and climate than that of a truly secular State by which (is) meant a state which creates complete separation between religion and the State

147. * * * Chinnappa Reddy, delivering his Ambedkar Memorial Lecture on 'Indian Constitution and Secularism' has observed that

"Indian constitutional secularism is not supportive of religion at all but has adopted what may be termed as permissive attitude towards religion out of respect for individual conscience and dignity. There, even while recognising the right to profess and practise religion, etc., it has excluded all secular activities from the purview of religion and also of practices which are repugnant to public order, morality and health and are abhorrent to human rights and dignity, as embodied in the other fundamental rights guaranteed by the Constitution."

148.   One thing which prominently emerges from the above discussion on secularism under our Constitution is that whatever the attitude of the State towards the religions, religious sects and denominations, religion cannot be mixed with any secular activity of the State. In fact, the encroachment of religion into secular activities is strictly prohibited. This is evident from the provisions of the Constitution to which we have made reference above. The State's tolerance of religion or religions does not make it either a religious or a theocratic State. When the State allows citizens to practise and profess their religions, it does not either explicitly or implicitly allow them to introduce religion into non-religious and secular activities of the State. The freedom and tolerance of religion is only to the extent of permitting pursuit of spiritual life which is different from the secular life. The latter falls in the exclusive domain of the affairs of the State. This is also clear from sub-section (3) of Section 123 of the Representation of the People Act, 1951 which prohibits an appeal by a candidate or his agent or by any other person with the consent of the candidate or his election agent to vote or refrain from voting for any person on the ground of his religion, race, caste, community or language or the use of or appeal to religious symbols.

K. Ramaswamy, J:

177.   Secularism became the means and consciously pursued for full practical necessities of human life to liberate the human spirit from bondage, ignorance, superstition which have held back humanity.

178.   Freedom of faith and religion is an integral part of social structure. Such freedom is not a bounty of the State but constitutes the very foundation on which the State is erected. Human liberty sometimes means to satisfy the human needs in one's own way. Freedom of religion is imparted in every free society because it is a part of the general structure of the liberty in such a society and secondly because restrictions imposed by one religion would be an obstacle for others. In the past religious beliefs have become battlegrounds for power and root cause for suppression of liberty. Religion has often provided a pretext to have control over vast majority of the members of the society. Democratic society realises folly of the vigour of religious practices in society. Strong religious consciousness not only narrows the vision but hampers rule of law. The Founding Fathers of the Constitution, therefore, gave unto themselves "we people of India", the Fundamental Rights and Directive Principles of State Policy to establish an egalitarian social order for all sections of the society in the supreme law of the land itself. Though the concept of "secularism" was not expressly engrafted while making the Constitution, its sweep, operation and visibility are apparent from fundamental rights and directive principles and their related provisions. It was made explicit by amending the preamble of the Constitution 42nd Amendment Act. The concept of secularism of which religious freedom is the foremost appears to visualise not only of the subject of God but also an understanding between man and man. Secularism in the Constitution

is not anti-God and it is sometimes believed to be a stay in a free society. Matters which are purely religious are left personal to the individual and the secular part is taken charge by the State on grounds of public interest, order and general welfare. The State guarantee individual and corporate religious freedom and dealt with an individual as citizen irrespective of his faith and religious belief and does not promote any particular religion nor prefers one against another. The concept of the secular State is, therefore, essential for successful working of the democratic form of Government. There can be no democracy if anti-secular forces are allowed to work dividing followers of different religious faith flying at each other's throats. The secular Government should negate the attempt and bring order in the society. Religion in the positive sense, is an active instrument to allow the citizen full development of his person, not merely in the physical and material but in the non-material and non-secular life.

* * *

180. In Ziyauddin Burhanuddin Bukhari v. Brijmohan Ramdass Mehra 33 this Court held that: (SCR p. 297: SCC p. 32, para 44)

"The Secular State rising above all differences of religion, attempts to secure the good of all its citizens irrespective of their religious beliefs and practices. It is neutral or impartial in extending its benefits to citizens of all castes and creeds. Maitland had pointed out that such a state has to ensure, through its laws, that the existence or exercise of a political or civil right or the right or capacity to occupy any office or position under it or to perform any public duty connected with it does not depend upon the profession or practice of any particular religion.

* * *

"Thereby this Court did not accept the wall of separation between law and the religion with a wider camouflage to impress control of what may be described exploitative parading under the garb of religion. Throughout ages endless stream of humans of diverse creeds, cultures and races have come to India from outside regions and climes and contributed to the rich cultural diversity. Hindu religion developed resilience to accommodate and imbibe with tolerance the cultural richness with religious assimilation and became a land of religious tolerance."

COUNTY OF ALLEGHENY v. A.C.L.U.

Supreme Court (United States).
492 U.S. 573 (1989).

Justice Blackmun [other Justices joining in certain parts]
* * *

I

* * *

Since 1981, the county has permitted the Holy Name Society, a Roman Catholic group, to display a creche[v] in the county courthouse

---

v. In the Nativity scene there was an angel bearing a banner that proclaimed "Gloria in Excelsis Deo! (Luke)." The county also placed a small evergreen tree, deco-

during the Christmas holiday season. * * * As observed in this Nation, Christmas has a secular, as well as a religious, dimension.[3]

* * *

B

* * *

At least since 1982, the city has expanded its Grant Street holiday display to include a symbolic representation of Chanukah, an 8–day Jewish holiday. * * *

* * *

[T]he District Court denied respondents' [a civil liberties organization and individuals] request for a permanent injunction.

* * *

III

A

This Nation is heir to a history and tradition of religious diversity that dates from the settlement of the North American Continent. Sectarian differences among various Christian denominations were central to the origins of our Republic. Since then, adherents of religions too numerous to name have made the United States their home, as have those whose beliefs expressly exclude religion.

Precisely because of the religious diversity that is our national heritage, the Founders added to the Constitution a Bill of Rights, the very first words of which declare: "Congress shall make no law respecting an establishment of religion, or prohibiting the free exercise thereof. * * *" Perhaps in the early days of the Republic these words were understood to protect only the diversity within Christianity, but today they are recognized as guaranteeing religious liberty and equality to "the infidel, the atheist, or the adherent of a non-Christian faith." * * *

In the course of adjudicating specific cases, this Court has come to understand the Establishment Clause to mean that government may not promote or affiliate itself with any religious doctrine or organization, may not discriminate among persons on the basis of their religious beliefs and practices, may not delegate a governmental power to a religious institution, and may not involve itself too deeply in such an institution's affairs....

* * *

Our subsequent decisions [after *Lemon*] further have refined the definition of governmental action that unconstitutionally advances religion. In recent years, we have paid particularly close attention to whether the challenged governmental practice either has the purpose or

---

rated with a red bow, behind each of the two endposts of the fence.

3. "[T]he Christmas holiday in our national culture contains both secular and sec-

tarian elements." *Lynch v. Donnelly*, 465 U.S. 668, 709, (1984) (Justice Brennan, dissenting).

effect of "endorsing" religion, a concern that has long had a place in our Establishment Clause jurisprudence. See *Engel v. Vitale*, 370 U.S. 421, 436, (1962). Thus, in *Wallace v. Jaffree*, 472 U.S. at 60, the Court held unconstitutional Alabama's moment-of-silence statute because it was "enacted * * * for the sole purpose of expressing the State's endorsement of prayer activities." * * *

Of course, the word "endorsement" is not self-defining. Rather, it derives its meaning from other words that this Court has found useful over the years in interpreting the Establishment Clause. Thus, it has been noted that the prohibition against governmental endorsement of religion "preclude[s] government from conveying or attempting to convey a message that religion or a particular religious belief is favored or preferred." *Wallace v. Jaffree*, 472 U.S., at 70 (O'Connor, J., concurring in judgment) * * *

Whether the key word is "endorsement," "favoritism," or "promotion," the essential principle remains the same. The Establishment Clause, at the very least, prohibits government from appearing to take a position on questions of religious belief or from "making adherence to a religion relevant in any way to a person's standing in the political community." *Lynch v. Donnelly*, 465 U.S. 668, 687 (1984) (O'Connor, J., concurring).

B

[In] *Lynch v. Donnelly*, *supra*, in which we considered whether the city of Pawtucket, R.I., had violated the Establishment Clause by including a crèche in its annual Christmas display, located in a private park within the downtown shopping district. By a 5–to–4 decision in that difficult case, the Court upheld inclusion of the crèche in the Pawtucket display, holding, inter alia, that the inclusion of the creche did not have the impermissible effect of advancing or promoting religion.

* * *

[D]espite divergence at the bottom line, the five Justices in concurrence and dissent in *Lynch* agreed upon the relevant constitutional principles: the government's use of religious symbolism is unconstitutional if it has the effect of endorsing religious beliefs, and the effect of the government's use of religious symbolism depends upon its context. * * * Accordingly, our present task is to determine whether the display of the crèche and the menorah, in their respective "particular physical settings," has the effect of endorsing or disapproving religious beliefs.

* * *

IV

We turn first to the county's crèche display. There is no doubt, of course, that the crèche itself is capable of communicating a religious message. * * * Here, unlike in *Lynch*, nothing in the context of the display detracts from the crèche's religious message. * * *

[H]ere, in contrast [to *Lynch*], the crèche stands alone: it is the single element of the display on the Grand Staircase.

* * *

The fact that the creche bears a sign disclosing its ownership by a Roman Catholic organization * * * demonstrates that the government is endorsing the religious message of that organization, rather than communicating a message of its own. But the Establishment Clause does not limit only the religious content of the government's own communications. It also prohibits the government's support and promotion of religious communications by religious organizations.

* * *

V

C

* * *

Justice Kennedy's accusations are shot from a weapon triggered by the following proposition: if government may celebrate the secular aspects of Christmas, then it must be allowed to celebrate the religious aspects as well because, otherwise, the government would be discriminating against citizens who celebrate Christmas as a religious, and not just a secular, holiday. This proposition, however, is flawed at its foundation. The government does not discriminate against any citizen on the basis of the citizen's religious faith if the government is secular in its functions and operations. On the contrary, the Constitution mandates that the government remain secular, rather than affiliate itself with religious beliefs or institutions, precisely in order to avoid discriminating among citizens on the basis of their religious faiths.

A secular state, it must be remembered, is not the same as an atheistic or antireligious state. A secular state establishes neither atheism nor religion as its official creed. Justice Kennedy thus has it exactly backwards when he says that enforcing the Constitution's requirement that government remain secular is a prescription of orthodoxy. It follows directly from the Constitution's proscription against government affiliation with religious beliefs or institutions that there is no orthodoxy on religious matters in the secular state * * *

To be sure, in a pluralistic society there may be some would-be theocrats, who wish that their religion were an established creed, and some of them perhaps may be even audacious enough to claim that the lack of established religion discriminates against their preferences. But this claim gets no relief, for it contradicts the fundamental premise of the Establishment Clause itself. The antidiscrimination principle inherent in the Establishment Clause necessarily means that would-be discriminators on the basis of religion cannot prevail.

For this reason, the claim that prohibiting government from celebrating Christmas as a religious holiday discriminates against Christians in favor of nonadherents must fail. Celebrating Christmas * * * necessarily entails professing * * * that Jesus is * * * the Messiah, a specifically Christian belief.

* * *

VI

The display of the Chanukah menorah in front of the City–County Building may well present a closer constitutional question. The menorah, one must recognize, is a religious symbol * * *.

* * *[t]he menorah here stands next to a Christmas tree and a sign saluting liberty. * * * The necessary result of placing a menorah next to a Christmas tree is to create an "overall holiday setting". * * *

[T]he simultaneous endorsement of Judaism and Christianity is no less constitutionally infirm than the endorsement of Christianity alone.

* * *

[T]he combination of the tree and the menorah communicates, not a simultaneous endorsement of both the Christian and Jewish faiths, but instead, a secular celebration of Christmas coupled with an acknowledgment of Chanukah as a contemporaneous alternative tradition.

Although the city has used a symbol with religious meaning as its representation of Chanukah, this is not a case in which the city has reasonable alternatives that are less religious in nature. * * *

* * * [T]he sign states that during the holiday season the city salutes liberty.

* * *

Justice Kennedy, with whom The Chief Justice, Justice White, and Justice Scalia join, concurring in the judgment in part and dissenting in part.

I

* * *

Rather than requiring government to avoid any action that acknowledges or aids religion, the Establishment Clause permits government some latitude in recognizing and accommodating the central role religion plays in our society. Any approach less sensitive to our heritage would border on latent hostility toward religion, as it would require government in all its multifaceted roles to acknowledge only the secular, to the exclusion and so to the detriment of the religious. A categorical approach would install federal courts as jealous guardians of an absolute "wall of separation," sending a clear message of disapproval. In this century, as the modern administrative state expands to touch the lives of its citizens in such diverse ways and redirects their financial choices through programs of its own, it is difficult to maintain the fiction that requiring government to avoid all assistance to religion can in fairness be viewed as serving the goal of neutrality.

* * * [I]n *Zorach v. Clauson*, 343 U.S. 306 (1952), for example, we permitted New York City's public school system to accommodate the religious preferences of its students by giving them the option of staying

in school or leaving to attend religious classes for part of the day. Justice Douglas wrote for the Court:

"When the state encourages religious instruction * * * it follows the best of our traditions. For it then respects the religious nature of our people and accommodates the public service to their spiritual needs. To hold that it may not would be to find in the Constitution a requirement that the government show a callous indifference to religious groups. That would be preferring those who believe in no religion over those who do believe." *Id.* at 313–314.

Nothing in the First Amendment compelled New York City to establish the release-time policy in *Zorach*, but the fact that the policy served to aid religion, and in particular those sects that offer religious education to the young, did not invalidate the accommodation. Likewise, we have upheld government programs supplying textbooks to students in parochial schools, * * * and exempting churches from the obligation to pay taxes, *Walz v. Tax Comm'n of New York City*, 397 U.S. 664 (1970).

* * *

"The general principle deducible from the First Amendment and all that has been said by the Court is this: that we will not tolerate either governmentally established religion or governmental interference with religion. Short of those expressly proscribed governmental acts there is room for play in the joints productive of a benevolent neutrality which will permit religious exercise to exist without sponsorship and without interference." 397 U.S. at 669.

This is most evident where the government's act of recognition or accommodation is passive and symbolic, for in that instance any intangible benefit to religion is unlikely to present a realistic risk of establishment. Absent coercion, the risk of infringement of religious liberty by passive or symbolic accommodation is minimal. * * *

* * * [N]oncoercive government action within the realm of flexible accommodation or passive acknowledgment of existing symbols does not violate the Establishment Clause unless it benefits religion in a way more direct and more substantial than practices that are accepted in our national heritage.

II

* * * [I]n permitting the displays on government property of the menorah and the creche, the city and county sought to do no more than "celebrate the season," and to acknowledge, along with many of their citizens, the historical background and the religious, as well as secular, nature of the Chanukah and Christmas holidays. This interest falls well within the tradition of government accommodation and acknowledgment of religion that has marked our history from the beginning. * * *

Notes and Questions

1. Consider Thio Li–Ann, *The Secular Trumps the Sacred: Constitutional Issues Arising from* Colin Chan v. Public Prosecutor, 16 Sing L. Rev. 26, 59–60 (1995):

In Singapore, where religious loyalties are potentially a source of desta-bilising conflict, the government has insisted on the strict separation of religion from politics, to the extent these two areas can be satisfactorily identified. This is best exemplified in the *raison d'être* motivating the enactment of the Maintenance of Religious Harmony Act (MRHA). Since Singapore is multi-religious, religious harmony is crucial to her survival and there is a fear that 'the social fabric of Singapore will be threatened if religious groups venture into politics or if political parties use religious sentiments to garner popular support . . . if one religious group does this, others must inevitably follow . . . the end result will again be conflict between religions . . . added to political instability and factional strife.' The crux of the issue is the fear of religion being used as a guise for communal politics.

The MRHA gives the executive control over the religious groups' propa-gation activities through the issuance of restraining orders under one of four grounds enumerated in s 8. Broad non-justiciable discretionary power is conferred upon the relevant Minister to police the nebulous religion-politics divide and to issue an order 'gagging' religious free speech and expression when the divide is breached.

On the other hand the state of Singapore takes restrictive measures *because* it intends to be "neutral" in religious matters.

[I]n Singapore society the word 'cult' has a sinister connotation. * * * What is it in such group called a 'cult' that raises such grave concern? Given that Singaporean society is multi-racial, multi-cultural and multi-religious with very high degree of religious tolerance, why deviant religious beliefs or doctrines alone would, in our opinion, probably not cause such grave concern and anxiety * * * to the ordinary man the word 'cult' means a religious group with teachings and practices that are abhorrent or harmful to society.

Chen Cheng & Anor v. Central Christian Church and other appeals, Court of Appeal of Singapore [1999] 1 SLR 94 para. 27 (1998).

The Singapore decisions against Jehovah's Witnesses illustrate the close relationship between free individual exercise and collective representation of the religious community. In principle, worship by Jehovah's Witnesses remained constitutionally protected. The Witnesses were prosecuted on grounds other than their religious affiliation. However, the possession of religious publications (not on the specific grounds of possible statements in specific issues) was held to be a crime as such possession was part of the activity of the banned religious organization. Note that the ban is based on the supposed impact on public order, i.e., on neutral and secular concerns. Is the emphasis on state neutrality needed because of the religious pluralism in Singapore society? Is this concern similar to the nonestablishment concern of the American founding fathers? Why are the solutions different? Compare the concern for neutrality of the law with the position of the majority in *Smith.* Would the ban on publications be constitutional under *Smith*? Is a particular religion singled out in the Singapore decision? (See *Lukumi Babalu Aye.*) Chief Justice Yong finds American precedents irrelevant. What makes American precedents respectable in secular India and irrelevant in secular Singapore? Is the rule of law observed in the Singapore High Court reasoning? Note that Chief Justice Yong accepted the position of the Minis-ter regarding the dangerousness of a belief without questioning it, and he put the burden on appellants to show that the Minister exercised his powers wrongly. Thio Li–Ann argues that the position of Chief Justice Yong, who claimed that "national service . . . is a fundamental tenet in Singapore[,] [and then] * * * singles out a government policy, national service, confers a sacrosanct quality to it and exalts it above the Constitution—hardly a conventional mode of constitutional interpretation." Li–Ann, *op. cit.* at 82. In *Bommai*, Justices Sawant and Kuldip Singh argued that secularism is part of the basic structure of the Indian Constitution. Consequently, the President has the power to dissolve such governments that promote political actions going against secularism (which occurred where certain state governments supported political groups that were violent toward other religions). Are the positions of India and Singapore similar in their militant defense of secularism? Are the two courts defending the same kind of secularism?

2.   The Court of Appeal of Singapore, in *Chan Hiang Leng Colin & Ors v. Minister for Information and the Arts* [1996] 1 S.L.R. 609, was confronted with an attempt to review the Minister's order to ban importing publications of the International Bible Students Association. The appeal was dismissed because dissemination of the beliefs of an unlawful society was a matter of national security, which was found nonjusticiable. The court's role was to see that there was evidence that the disputed decision was based on national-security considerations (the refusal of military service by the Witnesses was found to be a "self-evident" factual basis for a national-security concern). The court ruled there was no violation of freedom of religion: "The only effect of Order 179/72 is that the society known as the SCJW had been deregistered and it is, therefore, an offence to be a member of it. It does not, however, follow that it is illegal to profess * * * the beliefs of Jehovah's Witnesses. It may be that group participation in [their activities] may invoke a presumption * * * of being a member of an unlawful society." *Id.* at 614.

3.   Writing strict separation into a constitution does not necessarily create a wall between church and state, as the Hungarian and Japanese examples indicate. Interestingly, the erosion of the wall of separation occurred in countries where most people were not particularly religious. In Japan, beginning in the Meiji period (after the end of isolation), state support for Shintoism increased, and from the beginning of 1928 to the end of World War Two, Shinto became the state religion. General MacArthur believed that Shintoism and militarism were related, and in his plans to reorganize and demilitarize Japan he mandated the strict separation of state and politics from all religions. The Japanese Constitution is, therefore, one of the strongest examples of written secularism and separationism.

Article 20

1.   Freedom of religion is guaranteed to all. No religious organization shall receive any privileges from the State, nor exercise any political authority.

2.   No person shall be compelled to take part in any religious act, celebration, rite or practice.

3.   The State and its organs shall refrain from religious education or any other religious activity.

Nevertheless, in *Kakunaga* a divided Grand Bench of the Supreme Court found that a government-paid Shinto groundbreaking ceremony at a public construction site was not in violation of the constitutionally mandated separation because the ritual was standard practice in the construction industry. Moreover, since those involved in the construction regarded the ceremony as an essential safety measure, it was held not to violate the separation principle. The dissenters argued that "the definition of prohibited religious activity in Article 20, paragraph 3 should not be limited to the propagation of religious doctrine * * * as the majority contends. * * * A public entity undertaking to sponsor such activities is fundamentally at odds with the religious neutrality of the State." Beer and Itoh, *op. cit.* at 485. The majority concluded that strict separation between church and state was impossible and that the state was required only to be neutral; thus the Court should be concerned only if the state interferes with religious affairs or vice versa.

4. *Neutral (Lay) State.*

In Western Europe there is a common model of relationship between the state and religious faiths. It is frequently summarized in the French phrase *"la laïcité de l'Etat"* but this model is also applicable to countries where a national church or state church exists.

This common European model appears to be defined by the following coordinates:

> The state is neutral (impartial) toward the various individual religious subjects.

> A religious subsector is singled out within the public sector. This may be understood as a "playing field" or "protected area." Inside it the various collective religious subjects (churches, denominations, and religious communities) are free to act in conditions of substantial advantage compared to those collective subjects that are not religious.

> The state has the right to intervene in this area only to see that the players respect the rules of the game and the boundaries of the playing field.[9]

Silvio Ferrari, *The New Wine and the Old Cask: Tolerance, Religion, and the Law in Contemporary Europe*, in *The Law of Religious Identity: Models for Post–Communism* 1, 3–4 (András Sajó and Shlomo Avineri eds., 1999).

Professor Ferrari finds that impartiality of the public powers, internal autonomy of the religious communities with greater protection than that afforded to other associations (including support for some of their external religious activities), and limits to public manifestations of religion for reasons of public order, health, morals, or for the protection of the rights and freedoms of others, are the main characteristics of Western European church–state relations.

---

9. Understanding of this common model is obscured by persistent recourse to an outmoded classification of the relations between the state and religious faiths. This classification divides states into three categories, namely: separatist states (such as France and the Netherlands), states with concordats (Germany, Italy, Spain), and states with national (or state) churches (England and the Scandinavian states). The classification grants excessive importance to the formal element of the relationship between church and state, in other words to the type of association that exists between the two institutions, and overlooks its legal substance. Consequently, this classification is unable to grasp the process of rapprochement that is going on between the national laws of the various countries of Western Europe.

Professor Troper, a French legal scholar, offers a different perspective on French *laïcité*:

As traditionally understood in the 19th century, the object of the principle of *laïcité* was to govern the relationship between religion and the state. It comprised two basic policies that were based upon a clear division between public and private spheres:

The state was to be neutral in the performance of all its activities. This included all activities in the public sphere. Thus, religion was not to be a part of public celebrations, no religion was to be subsidized, and no religion was to be taught in the schools.

Religion was to belong only to the private sphere. It was a matter to be governed only by the conscience of the individual. The state was to respect complete freedom of belief. From this point of view, *laïcité* implied freedom of religion and tolerance.

During the third and fourth republics, the first (strict) interpretation of *laïcité* prevailed. In 1959, under Gaullist and conservative governments, the second interpretation prevailed, and new laws authorized the state and local authorities to subsidize private (primarily religious) schools. But, at the same time, there was a broad consensus in favor of the neutrality of the state established under the law of separation of 1905. Even when there were pressures to give more public funding to private schools, it was generally agreed that government should remain neutral. This had a symbolic dimension—no public ceremony was to have a religious element. But there was also a policy dimension. The organizing and the running of public services was to be perfectly neutral. As regards education, this principle had both a negative and a positive aspect. The negative aspect was that schools were not to discriminate against any individual because of religion and were not to teach any religious values. It followed that teachers were prohibited from expressing their personal beliefs, because pupils could be influenced by such expressions. This is the reason why it was decided that a Catholic priest could not become a teacher in a public school and that a woman teacher who was wearing a small cross in her *décolleté* could be disciplined. The positive aspect was that schools were to teach common values imbedded in the republic, especially *laïcité* and tolerance. This was meant to facilitate social and political integration, a function which was to be performed as well by the military draft. Sometimes, the principle of *laïcité* was understood in an anti-religious, especially anti-Catholic, fashion, but, more generally, it was agreed that schools were to be a part of the integrating machinery of the state.

Michel Troper, *The Problem of the Islamic Veil and the Principle of School Neutrality in France*, in *The Law of Religious Identity: Models for Post Communism* 89, 90–92 (András Sajó and Shlomo Avineri eds., 1999.)

5. *Church autonomy.* Free exercise and separation considerations require the noninterference of state authorities into the internal affairs of religious organizations. Noninterference dictates that government authorities should not take positions in matters of religious teachings and organization. How far autonomy goes otherwise is not determined by principles. The Indian Constitution (2. Art. 26) guarantees to all denominations management "of [their] own affairs in matters of religion."

The question is, where is the line to be drawn between what are matters of religion and what are not. It will be seen that besides the right to manage its own affairs in matters of religion, which is given by clause (b), the next two clauses of article 26 guarantee to a religious denomination the right to acquire and own property and to administer such property in accordance with law. The administration of its property by a religious denomination has thus been placed on a different footing from the right to manage its own affairs in matters of religion. The latter is a fundamental right which no legislature can take away, whereas the former can be regulated by laws which the legislature can validly impose. * * * As we have already indicated, freedom of religion in our Constitution is not confined to religious beliefs only; it extends to religious practices as well subject to the restrictions which the Constitution itself has laid down. Under article 26(b), therefore, a religious denomination or organization enjoys complete autonomy in the matter of deciding as to what rites and ceremonies are essential according to the tenets of the religion they hold and no outside authority has any jurisdiction to interfere with their decision in such matters. Of course, the scale of expenses to be incurred in connection with these religious observances would be a matter of administration of property belonging to the religious denomination and can be controlled by secular authorities. * * * [However,] a law which takes away the right of administration from the hands of a religious denomination altogether and vests it in any other authority would amount to a violation of the right guaranteed under clause (d) of article 26.

The Commissioner, Hindu Religious Endowments, Madras (Petitioner) v. Sri Lakshmindra Thirtha Swamiar of Sri Shirur Mutt (Respondent), A.I.R. 1954 S.C. 282.

6. In many countries, if an organization is granted specific religious status it may have structures of governance that may otherwise be impermissible under the general rules on associations, especially where the law on association, in conformity with the constitution, requires a democratic structure and transparency of democratic decisionmaking. *Non*-interference has its own problems. It may contribute to the prevalence of existing hierarchical structures. For example, Italian law leaves it to the Catholic hierarchy to determine which religious organizations qualify for not-for-profit status. Noninterference may leave individuals abandoned vis-à-vis church authorities and majorities within their own religious communities. Such noninterference may amount to the denial of legal protection to individuals that is otherwise required and provided in public and most private spheres. In a number of situations the principle of noninterference requires exceptions to generally applicable rules, including accommodation of church practices, which are essentially nonreligious and which would not be accommodated if they were activities outside the church. Title VII of the U.S. Civil Rights Act allows religious organizations to discriminate on religious grounds in employment. When the janitor of a Mormon Church which operated an athletic facility that was open to the public was discharged for not being a Church member, the action was found not to violate the First Amendment. The exception was held constitutional because it was not the government itself that advanced religion; the law simply allowed churches to do so. *Corporation of the Presiding Bishop of the Church of Jesus Christ of Latter–Day Saints v. Amos,* 483 U.S. 327 (1987).

7. Greek authorities convicted a Mufti (a local Muslim religious leader) for having usurped the functions of a "known religion." He had won election to his position in conformity with Muslim religious law, but Greece had failed for many years to create legislation permitting such elections. After the Mufti was elected by the believers, Greek authorities appointed a different person. The ECHR found this discriminatory and in violation of international treaty obligations requiring respect for the Muslim religious minority.

> [The] Court does not consider that, in democratic societies, the State needs to take measures to ensure that religious communities remain or are brought under a unified leadership. * * * It is true that the Government argued that, in the particular circumstances of the case, the authorities had to intervene in order to avoid the creation of tension among the Moslems in Rodopi and between the Moslems and the Christians of the area as well as Greece and Turkey. Although the Court recognises that it is possible that tension is created in situations where a religious or any other community becomes divided, it considers that this is one of the unavoidable consequences of pluralism. The role of the authorities in such circumstances is not to remove the cause of tension by eliminating pluralism, but to ensure that the competing groups tolerate each. [The] Court considers that nothing was adduced that could warrant qualifying the risk of tension between the Moslems and Christians or between Greece and Turkey as anything more than a very remote possibility.

Serif v. Greece, (2001) 31 E.H.R.R. 20 (1999).

8. In *Allegheny* Justice Kennedy and the three justices who joined him would find the display of the crèche consistent with the establishment clause. Justice Kennedy argues that this conclusion necessarily follows from the Court's decision in *Marsh v. Chambers*, 463 U.S. 783 (1983), which sustained the constitutionality of legislative prayer. In *Marsh* it was decisive that the prayer represented a long-established historical tradition. Justice Kennedy also asserts that the crèche, even in this setting, poses "no realistic risk" of "represent[ing] an effort to proselytize," having repudiated the Court's endorsement inquiry in favor of a "proselytization" approach. The Court's analysis of the crèche, he contends, "reflects an unjustified hostility toward religion." *Id*. What are the grounds of government neutrality in the U.S.? Is it "equality of citizens" (the prohibition of discrimination among religions amounting to discrimination among the various believers as well as nonbelievers)? Compare this with the understanding of neutrality in Germany—noninvolvement in religious matters but support to churches. In most European countries, religion plays a much less intense social role than in the U.S., where the number of practicing believers is far greater. Nevertheless, over the decades a narrow majority of the USSC's justices more or less consistently rejected the argument that the government should, or at least may, express its respect to the fundamental beliefs of the vast majority of the population in a nondiscriminatory manner. Is Justice Kennedy advocating the same benevolent neutrality that prevails in Germany? Would Justice Kennedy find impermissibly nonneutral the German or Greek constitutional approach to governmental recognition of certain churches in general and the direct funding of denominational schools in particular?

9. The Establishment Clause forbids the enactment of any law "respecting an establishment of religion." The USSC has applied a three-

pronged test to determine whether legislation satisfies the Establishment Clause: "First, the statute must have a secular purpose; second, its principal or primary effect must be one that neither advances nor inhibits religion; finally, the statute must not foster an excessive entanglement of government with religion." *Lemon v. Kurtzman*, 403 U.S. 602, 612–613, (1971).

In *Edwards v. Aguillard*, 482 U.S. 578 636 (1987), Justice Scalia, dissenting, criticized the *Lemon* test: "I think the pessimistic evaluation that The Chief Justice made of the totality of Lemon is particularly applicable to the 'purpose' prong: it is a 'constitutional theory [that] has no basis in the history of the amendment it seeks to interpret, is difficult to apply and yields unprincipled results. * * * ' " cited in *Wallace v. Jaffree*, 472 U.S. 38, 112 (1985) (Justice Rehnquist, dissenting). Note the ad hoc approach of the USSC. A similar approach prevails in the school-funding context.

> Judicial review of government action under the Establishment Clause is a delicate task. The Court has avoided drawing lines which entirely sweep away all government recognition and acknowledgment of the role of religion in the lives of our citizens for to do so would exhibit not neutrality but hostility to religion. Instead the courts have made case-specific examinations of the challenged government action * * * Unfortunately, even the development of articulable standards and guidelines has not always resulted in agreement among the Members of this Court on the results in individual cases. And so it is again today.

County of Allegheny v. A.C.L.U., 492 U.S. 573, 624 (1989) (Justice O'Connor, concurring).

10.   Consider John Finnis's criticism of state neutrality:

> The thought that basic value judgments have no truth scarcely coheres with, say, the Constitution's proclamation and defence of fundamental human rights. So the polite form taken in this context by secularism's unreadiness to acknowledge basic human goods as true is the demand for a kind of constitutional neutrality about them. * * * To support this value-neutral autonomy right, the Court points to a line of cases beginning in 1923 with *Meyer v. Nebraska* [to] *Eisenstadt v. Baird* in 1972. But if one reads these cases in sequence, it is instantly obvious that the decisions before 1972 utterly reject the conception that politics, government, and law must preserve neutrality about such basic human goods as education in good and useful knowledge (goods celebrated in the cases from the 1920s), or marriage (honoured in its procreativity in *Skinner* and in its domesticity and friendship in Harlan's dissent in *Poe* and even in *Griswold*). The break comes with the judgment of the radically secularised Justice Brennan in *Eisenstadt v. Baird*, which assumes a double neutrality of values and corresponding symmetry of normative judgments. * * * There is just the single neutral category: 'the decision [of the individual, whether married or single,] * * * whether to bear or beget a child.' The key word is 'whether.'

John Finnis, *On the Practical Meaning of Secularism*, 73 Notre Dame L. Rev. 491, 505–506 (1998).

Is Finnis's criticism of state neutrality an argument in favor of Justice Kennedy's position?

"A secular state, it must be remembered, is not the same as an atheistic or antireligious state. A secular state establishes neither atheism nor religion as its official creed." *County of Allegheny v. A.C.L.U.*, 492 U.S. 573, 610 (1989) (Justice Blackmun). Is "religion-friendly secularism" an oxymoron? Is U.S. "government neutrality" based on the same principles as the concept by the same name in India?

11. The German position regarding the special protection of former state churches was consolidated in the Weimar Constitution of 1919; the church-related provisions of the Weimar Constitution were declared to remain in force by the Basic Law. The Weimar system accepted that a special category of religious associations would continue to exist as corporations of public law that grant special rights and responsibilities to these entities, including the right to impose church taxes to be collected by the state. Other religious associations may be granted the status of a public law body if the "constitution" and the membership of the association guarantee long-lasting existence to it. As the case of Jehovah's Witnesses long-lasting difficulties indicate, the recognition of a church is subject to special scrutiny. In 1997, the German Federal Administrative Court rejected the registration claim of the Witnesses. (They could continue the collective exercise of religion as an association.) The GFCC reversed the decision in 2000 (2 BvR 1500/97), asserting that the belief of the Witnesses in an impeding end of the world was not contrary to the requirement of durability. The Court, in conformity with preexisting understanding, emphasized that the public law bodies are related to the neutral state as they take over certain functions of the public power. In granting special status, the state must guarantee the protection of human dignity. It follows that a religious association must satisfy the requirements of faithfulness to the law (*Rechtstreu*) in order to qualify as a public law body. Many religions require their believers to give priority to religious prescriptions in any conflict with the law of the state. However, a religious community that is basically ready to follow law and order and participates in the constitutional order may satisfy the qualification requirements. The basis of the evaluation in the neutral state is not based on articles of faith but on actual behavior. Any attempt to realize a theocratic domination would violate the constitutional order, but loyalty to the state cannot be required. The position of the Witnesses, that the state is part of Satan's world, cannot be seen as a lack of loyalty. Likewise, the religious position that prohibits participation in elections is not a danger to democracy; it is merely an indication of being apolitical.

As the German Basic Law recognizes the status of conscientious objectors, the rejection of military service by the Witnesses was not an issue of loyalty, although this is a crucial test in countries with a concept of loyalty that does not know of exceptions to the constitutional duties on the basis of otherwise recognized constitutional rights. This is the case in Singapore (see above), where the problem, however, is that of free exercise. Do you find that states which have strong pretensions to define culture and national identity are more concerned about church loyalty? Is recognition as a church a matter of the self-perception of the state? (In the U.S., qualifying as a church requires a low level of symbolic identification.) Or is the loyalty requirement an expression of the actual perception of perils to the public order? In a multiculturally precarious society like Singapore, with special, recent experience of disorder in neighboring countries, perhaps a higher level of protection of public order prevails and hence the stricter concern for loyalty. Is this public-order-related concern satisfactory from the perspective of fundamental rights protection?

12. *Postcommunist constitutions.* The postcommunist constitutions, like that of Hungary, use expressions indicating that the state is separate from churches. The 1993 Russian Constitution requires the state to remain neutral in matters of worldviews and expressly separates church and state. ("Separation" was the term used in all the communist constitutions.) The references to separation were intended to discontinue governmental control over churches. In communism, after a period of open persecution, strict commands and secret service methods were used to turn the remaining church organizations into loyal servants of communist goals. Soon after the collapse of communism, conservative political groups and "more-established" churches felt that they were menaced by new "cults." These groups insisted that separation was not a "wall" and the state should promote the right to free exercise by granting certain public means to churches, primarily to those churches that were established in the various countries before communism. Poland signed a Concordat with the Holy See, followed by Hungary; notwithstanding the separation clause in the Hungarian Constitution, budgetary powers were transferred to churches. Of course, in Poland the Catholic Church was a foremost opponent of communism, and the overwhelming majority are practicing Catholics. The 1997 Polish Constitution, instead of separation, refers to mutual autonomy. This was not the case in Hungary. Should majority religious practices matter in the interpretation of the constitution? Is it possible that state neutrality has a special importance where there is a strong religious culture? (Compare with secularism in India.) The HCC found no religious discrimination in the privileges (greater internal autonomy, educational facilities, access to prisons, etc.) granted to "bigger" churches but not to "smaller" ones and other religious organizations.

> The separation of the Church and the State does not mean that the State could not consider the characteristics of the Churches and that the legal status of the 'Church' should be regulated in the same way as other social organizations. The State has neither such a unified regulating obligation in connection with social organizations * * *. The State— while the freedom of the religion and within the right of the common exercise of religion are not violated by it—can also determine, at its discretion, the conditions of the foundation of the 'Church' and its legal status.

Decision 8/ 1993 (II.27.) AB hat.

The 1997 Polish Constitution reflects a compromise between socialists and Catholic forces. It provides (in Art. 25) that the relationship between the state and churches and other religious organizations should be based on the principle of respect for their autonomy, the mutual independence of each in its own sphere, and the principle of cooperation. The same article establishes that relations between Poland and the Catholic Church are to be determined by international treaty. (The Italian Constitution recognizes the Lateran Treaty, but its meaning was reinterpreted. See below.) The Polish Concordat, among others, allows cemeteries to be administered by the Catholic Church even where there is no other cemetery. Compare with the Israeli *Burial Society* case below. Public broadcasters are statutorily required to observe Christian values. In light of these developments and the manner, for example, that denominational schools are administered in some countries (see below), do you agree with Ferrari's position that there is a convergence toward a neutral lay state in Europe?

13.   Professor Ann Elizabeth Mayer, in *Universal Versus Islamic Human Rights: A Clash of Cultures or a Clash with a Construct?*, 15 Mich. J. Int'l L. 307, 351–58 (1994), writes:

> Partly because of their commitment to the traditional notion that all laws are to be founded in Islamic sources and that there is no place for human legislation in an Islamic system, Saudi leaders were reluctant to adopt a constitution. * * * [In Saudi Arabia] change was officially inaugurated on March 1, 1992, when a Basic Law of Government, a Shura Council Decree, and a Decree on Provinces were issued * * * Article 6 tells the citizens that they 'are to pay allegiance to the king in accordance with the Holy Koran and the Prophet's tradition, in submission and obedience and in times of ease and difficulty, fortune and adversity.'

> Article 23 * * * affirms that the State protects Islam and implements Islamic law and calls on the State to order people to do right and to shun evil. In context, the principle set forth in article 23 is tantamount to an endorsement of the traditional functions of Saudi Arabia's notorious religious police. * * * It has been under the auspices of a committee that is assigned to propagate virtue and to prohibit vice that the Kingdom's mutawwa'in, or religious police, have operated. * * * Moreover, it appears that they have undertaken to monitor worship by nonMuslims, even though all nonMuslim worship must be conducted in private in Saudi Arabia, so that policing religious services entails invading private quarters. Article 23 also calls on the State to fulfill the obligation to propagate the faith, thereby engaging the government in the task of proselytizing on behalf of Islam, which in context can only mean the officially-approved Sunni Wahhabism.

> As in the Cairo Declaration, there is no provision for freedom of religion, an omission that seems especially ominous given the upswing in religiously-based persecutions of nonMuslims that has occurred since the Gulf War. However, it is ultimately Muslims who have the most to fear from the absence of any protection for religious freedom. Members of Saudi Arabia's large Shi'i minority are often condemned as infidels or apostates by defenders of the State-sponsored Wahhabi orthodoxy. In part due to intercommunal tensions, which have been exacerbated by the antagonism between the Saudis and the Islamic Republic of Iran, the Saudis treat members of their Shi'i minority as if they are likely to be disloyal, subjecting Shi'is to discrimination and religious persecution * * *

> The most critical principle in the Basic Law that specifically relates to human rights is article 26, which, as in other Islamic human rights schemes, borrows the concept of human rights but subordinates such rights to Islamic law. It provides that 'the state protects human rights in accordance with the Islamic shari'a.' The shari'a limits on rights cannot be definitely fixed, since Saudi law is uncodified and the legal sources remain open to a variety of interpretations.

14.   Many Muslim governments and Western commentators present Islam as a single religious position with one approach to religion's role in public and private life, in line with "schemes like the Cairo Declaration and the Saudi Basic Law, [which] are designed to shore up the political interests of those promoting them and have only a tenuous connection to Islamic

culture. [These positions] mine the Islamic heritage only very selectively—shutting out the enlightened, modern perspectives of Muslims who are supportive of human rights." Mayer, *op. cit.* at 376.

The Supreme Court of Pakistan restated in the *Zaheeruddin v. State,* above, certain assumptions that might be characteristic of Islamic theocracy. These features include:

> (i) Islamic law or Shari'ah is the supreme law of the land, and all legislation, including the Constitution, must yield to it; (ii) Islamic law is a self-evident and fixed normative code, one that can be deployed without any revision or development to seek answers to all problems confronting a state in modern times, including issues of constitutional governance and fundamental individual rights; ... (iv) the historical record of the independence movement and pronouncements of the Founding Fathers of Pakistan about religious freedom and the rights of religious minorities are not relevant to a judicial resolution of the issue at hand; (v) in a Muslim-majority state, no protection needs to be provided to religious beliefs and practices which are out of step with, and offend, the majority; and (vi) the dictates of international human rights law must yield to the pronouncements of Islamic law and are thus irrelevant with respect to questions regarding the freedom of religion in a Muslim state.

Mahmud, *op. cit.* at 51.

Theocracy should not be seen as the inevitable constitutional position in a country with a prevailing Muslim population. Turkey's leaders chose secularism after World War One. Pakistan's post–1947 constitutional system, although intended to create a Muslim state, did not subordinate the secular to the religious. Dr. Muhammad Iqbal, who is credited with originating the concept of a separate homeland for the Muslims of India, in his first clearly articulated call for separate Muslim states in the Muslim-majority areas of India, offered assurances to non-Muslims in his Presidential Address at the December 1930 session of the All–India Muslim League.

> After stating that "[a] community which is inspired by feelings of ill-will towards other communities is low and ignoble," he affirmed that "I entertain the highest respect for the customs, laws, religious and social institutions of other communities." Iqbal then assured that "[n]or should the Hindus fear that the creation of autonomous Muslim states will mean the introduction of a kind of religious rule in such states." Iqbal argued that:

>> The claim of the present generation of Muslim Liberals to reinterpret the foundational legal principles, in the light of their own experience and the altered conditions of modern life, is, in my opinion, perfectly justified. The teaching of the Qur'an that life is a process of progressive creation necessitates that each generation, guided but unhampered by the work of its predecessors, should be permitted to solve its own problems.

> In Iqbal's view, the revitalized institutionalization of ijtiha'd[w] would be the best vehicle for accomplishing this legislative agenda. The first step

w. Ijtiha'd is the exertion of mental faculties in the search for legal principles in areas where the Koran and Sunnah may be silent, to accommodate changes in the context of the application of settled principles. However, after the formative phase of Is-in this process was the rejection of an "intellectual attitude which has reduced the Law of Islam practically to a state of immobility." The second step was to recognize that the representative elected legislature in a republic was the appropriate forum for ijtiha'd. Thus, Iqbal's vision understood ijtiha'd as a 'complete authority in legislation,' which had traditionally been reserved for the founders of religious schools.

For Iqbal: The essence of Tauhid [unity of God], as a working idea, is equality, solidarity, and freedom. The state, from the Islamic standpoint, is an endeavor to transform these ideal principles into space-time forces, an aspiration to realize them in a definite human organization. It is in this sense alone that the state in Islam is a theocracy, not in the sense that it is headed by a representative of God on Earth who can always screen his despotic will behind his supposed infallibility.

Iqbal approved of the Turkish position of vesting the Caliphate or Imamate in the elected Assembly. Iqbal also believed that the republican form of government had become a necessity in the Islamic World.

Mahmud, *op. cit.* at 59–61.

SHAVIT v. THE CHEVRA KADISHA (HEREAFTER, "BURIAL SOCIETY") OF RISHON LE ZION

Supreme Court (Sitting as a Court of Civil Appeals) (Israel).
C.A. 6024/97 (1999).

Justice M. Cheshin [majority opinion, together with Chief Justice Barak].

[The local rabbi in charge of the cemetery refused a family request to have the deceased's name inscribed on the tombstone in both Hebrew and Latin characters.]

2. * * * Speaking for the Court, District Court Judge Yehuda Zaft dismissed Dr. Shavit's petition, leading to the appeal before this Court today.

Legal Background—The Gideon *and* Kestenbaum *Affairs*

3. [In] the *Gideon*[x] case * * * Justice Etzioni [stated]:

"I am thoroughly convinced, unequivocally that it is everyman's right to pay proper respect to loved-ones who have passed on, in accordance with their way of life and tradition, provided doing so does not harm the feelings or legitimate interests of their fellow. * * *

6. [Eighteen years later, this was confirmed in the *Kestenbaum* affair.] * * * It appears that the District Court mainly relies on the legislation passed after the *Gideon* and *Kestenbaum* cases were decided,

---

lamic jurisprudence, by roughly 900 A.D., ijtiha'd was confined to the explanation, application, and, at the most, interpretation of the doctrine as it had been laid down once and for all.

x. Civil Appeal, 280/71 *Gideon v. Chevra Kadisha*, PD 27(1) 10. In that case, the Burial Society was following the halakhic opinion of Rabbi Ovadia Yosef, a leading Halakhic authority who held as follows:

"Foreign (general) calendar dates on tombstones must be absolutely forbidden, as there is a Biblical (Torah) prohibition to this effect." Rabbi Ovadia is the spiritual leader of the Shas party, which has participated in a number of government coalitions, depending on the cabinet's willingness to sponsor Shas's Orthodox school system.

that is the Right to Alternative Civil Burial Law, 5756–1996 (hereon, The Alternative Burial Law), which, in the District Court's view, justifies the overruling of those decisions.

Clearly, we are all aware that a later statute may overturn an earlier law or decision, the question in each case being simply whether the later law contradicts its predecessors irreconcilably * * *

The Alternative Burial Law For Our Purposes

7. The [Alternative Burial] law provides that the Minister of Religious Affairs determines the places which may serve as alternative civil places of burial in accordance with the law, and that the cemeteries are to be located across the country at reasonable distances between them (article 4 of the law). Alternative civil cemeteries are intended to be administered by corporations dealing with burial related matter (article 5 of the law). Moreover, the Minister of Religious Affairs is authorized to enact regulations, among them regulations authorizing corporations dealing with burial related matters and burial directives (article 6 of the law). * * *

8. * * * the Minister of Religious Affairs procrastinated in enacting the regulations necessary for applying the Alternative Burial Law. * * *

11. * * * the Alternative Burial Law's purpose was essentially to *add an alternative* to the repertoire of available modes of burial—for those who seek to be buried in accordance with their worldview, rather than according to the traditional worldview. * * *

15. The significance of the District Court's decision is that the Alternative Burial Law struck down the rule set out in *Gideon-Kestenbaum* by implication. We cannot agree with that conclusion. The rule set out by the Supreme Court is founded on the basic principles of the Israeli legal system—Human Dignity, public policy, public law principles—and it is so entrenched and mighty that it is difficult to accept that it was supposedly struck down by implication, by the mere enactment of the Alternative Burial Law; * * *

16. * * * And these were the words of Justice Barak in the *Kestenbaum* decision (ibid. 524):

"Human Dignity in Israel is not a metaphor. This is a normative reality which begs an operative conclusion. For our purposes, the required conclusion is that a state authority's general authorization to carry out particular activities—such as the administration of a cemetery—cannot be interpreted as granting that authority permission to effect a concrete and serious infringement on Human Dignity of those affected by the matter. A state authority which seeks to infringe on Human Dignity must obtain explicit and clear authorization from the Legislator to this end."

* * *

The Burial Society's Rabbi's Ruling; Human Dignity; The Private and Public Sphere

18.   In addition, the Burial Society submits that it is subject to the ruling of its Chief Rabbi and to the instructions of Rishon le Zion's local rabbi. Furthermore, it argues that the halakhic ruling of these rabbis forbids it from inscribing non-Hebrew (foreign) letters, and marking the birth and death dates according to the Gregorian calendar. We do not accept this argument either.

[I]t appears that there is no sweeping, all encompassing [halakhic] ruling prohibiting the inscription of non-Hebrew characters or dates of birth and death as per the Gregorian calendar on tombstones. In fact, many cemeteries in Israel do not follow such a rule. * * *

The principle that grants the local Rabbi superior authority in history jurisdiction, the principle of the Mara DeAtra (Local Rabbinical Authority) can only subject those who are observant, or by virtue of an explicit statutory provision to this effect. In bygone days, when the communities of Israel were scattered among the nations, in all the nations, this was the absolute rule. This is equally the ruling, as it turns out, in Jewish communities around the world even today. See also, Menachem Elon, *Jewish Law* (Jerusalem: 5752–1992, 3rd edition, updated and expanded) Volume 1 at 547 and following. This is not the case in Israel, where we assembled in our land, and I do not see any reason from a legal point of view to impose the Halakha of the Mara DeAtra (Local Rabbinical Authority) on all—including practicing Jews and those who are not—is though it were the law of the land ...

20.   The argument [that the impugned inscriptions] disrespect the dead and infringe upon their families' feelings is not new to us. It was explicitly raised in the *Kestenbaum* case, where the Court answered it explicitly. Thus, for instance, President Shamgar stated as follows:

"The dignity of the deceased before the Court—his dignity and that of his family—are determining. The prohibition imposed by the Burial Society on the Appellant considerably exceeds the allowable proportionality."

* * *

26.   [In regard to Justice Englard's dissent,] [t]he differences of opinion that arose between the parties are, in truth, debates between the will and dignity of the individual—the Appellant before us—and the Halakha of the Mara DeAtra (Local Rabbinical Authority) as instructed by the Burial Society. However, the opinion of the Mara DeAtra (Local Rabbinical Authority) only obligates only practicing Jews or when it is accompanied by a legal statute which cloaks it with legal authority. We must remember that the State of Israel is not a State of Halakha. It is a state of Law. Israel is a democracy, ruled by the law—the Rule of Law, that is. Our consideration is preserving the individual's rights, a person's will, his good, his welfare—and all in accordance to the country's laws.

Justice I. Englard:

3. * * * [T]he judges are being dragged in this controversy, which is essentially an ideological one. As it is well known, adjudication cannot resolve ideological battles fought inside the Jewish people on the essence of Judaism and the relationship between State and religion in Israel, the

Jewish and Democratic State. The form of inscribing dates on a tombstone is but one aspect of this conflict. * * *

4. * * * I will state from the onset that an objective test, probing reasonableness is, to my mind, incapable of measuring or evaluating human emotions, in the realm of beliefs and opinions. Before us lies the realm of ideology, centering around symbols, whose degree of centrality to human lives cannot be measured by an external standard of reasonableness. Any determination regarding the reasonableness of a given symbol will necessarily be the expression of a subjective scale of values. Moreover, the status of a given symbol in a particular society is not necessarily fixed for a prolonged period of time.

* * *

13. All agree that there is a threshold of sensitivity of the observant community that must not be crossed. * * * I asked myself if it is really the Court's role to determine the "legitimate" limits of the sensitivities of the observant public in general, and of those who live by the Commandments of the Torah, in particular. Moreover, delimiting the realm of "reasonable" sensitivities in general, is to a decisive degree predicated upon a subjective perspective, as attested to by the differences of opinion between the judges themselves.

* * *

18. The great question before us at present refers to the relationship between the principle of the Burial Society's freedom of religion, and that of the observant Jews found among the deceased's relatives—on one side, and the principle of the deceased's relatives' freedom to act in accordance with their world view—on the other. * * * To my mind, we have no right to rank conflicting values, ascribing to them a particular status, according to a hierarchy of values which is necessarily idiosyncratic. * * * As noted, the real struggle takes place outside the bounds of the cemetery itself; Behind the debate lies the battle for the very shape of Judaism and the State of Israel. This is the reality with which this Court is faced—one which cannot be ignored.

* * *

20. * * * This situation constitutes the true problem of justice: namely, where, to our chagrin, it is impossible to achieve the preservation of all the legitimate interests involved, but rather compels us to prefer one interest over the other. In this context, many speak of a process of balancing between conflicting interests. I am not convinced that this image correctly describes the judicial process which, at the end of the day, compels us to reject one right for another. Be that as it may, I am of the opinion that concerning the present issue, the deceased's family's right to design the grave according to their viewpoint must withdraw in the face of the Burial Society's right to act in accordance with the Halakhic injunction of the Local Rabbinical Authority. Why is this so? The Burial Society is, as its name suggests, Holy this is to say an institution charged with a religious function, defined by Jewish tradition as the doing of true loving kindness. It incumbs upon the Burial Society to act in accordance with the Jewish Halakha, as it is determined by the

Local rabbinical Authority. Such has been the situation since the days of old, so it is written in the conditions of the franchise, so it is written in the documents, so were the expectations of many among the city's dead, and so demand many among the deceased persons' relatives.

21. In my opinion, this Court is not, in principle, authorized, to coerce a religious body—be it public or private—to conduct itself in a manner contrary to the religious law to which it ascribes. For coercion of this nature, constitutes a severe infringement to the principle of freedom of religion. This infringement is only permissible by clear decree of the Legislator.

Chief Justice A. Barak:

6. Thus it appears, that in the *Kestenbaum* case, the value of preserving the Hebrew language was placed on one side of the scales of justice, while on the second lies the value (and liberty) of Human Dignity. At present, we must add on one hand, alongside preserving the Hebrew language, the value (and liberty) of freedom of religion, which is, in my view, simply an aspect of Human Dignity. In a parallel manner, we similarly add, to the other side, an additional aspect of a Human Dignity infringement, namely the harm that occurs when an individual's dignity is injured, for religious reasons. Indeed, to my mind, freedom from religion equally constitutes an aspect of Human Dignity. This being the case, freedom of religion on one hand, is to be measured against the freedom to act in accordance to one's individual autonomous will, on the other. This refers to the individual's freedom not to find himself bound by a religious prohibition, to which he does not adhere. This is the individual's freedom to make out his own path—in life and in death—according to his worldview.

The answer provided to this question, since the time of Israel's independence, has been that the Court must place the conflicting considerations on the scales of justice. It must balance between the clashing values and principles.

* * *

7. * * * At the basis of this approach, lies the pronouncement that the values and principles—and the liberties which flow from them—are not absolute in character. No "absolute" value is attached to values, principles and liberties. Their weight is always relative. Their status is determined in relation to the values, principles and liberties with which they are likely to collide.

9. * * * It is not possible to conclude that in a clash between freedom of religion and freedom from religion, one or the other always has the upper hand. Had we reached that conclusion, we would in fact be negating the constitutional status of one of the two freedoms in question. Rather, the proper approach is one that balances between values and principles that collide within the confines of one freedom. This balancing framework requires us to aspire to a result in which the "nucleus" of each of the freedoms in question will be preserved, and the infringement limited to its "peripheries" (Compare: article 19(2) of the German Constitution which establishes that "In no case may the essence of a

basic right be infringed"). Hence, we must consider both the magnitudes of the infringement and its essence. The decision itself must flow from considerations of reasonableness, fairness and tolerance.

10.   This having been said, we shall now turn to the case at bar. On *one* side of the balancing scale lies the Human Dignity of the Deceased and his relatives, who request to inscribe a non-Hebrew inscription on the tombstone. This freedom protects their feelings from harm. It protects them from religious coercion. Failing to allow them to inscribe the name of the deceased and relevant dates on the tombstone, in the language of their choosing, severely, substantially and substantively infringes on this freedom * * *

11. On the second side of the balance lies the freedom of religion of the Burial Society's personnel that abide by the ruling of the Local Rabbinical Authority. On the same side of the balancing scale lie the dignity of the Dead and the sentiments of their relatives who are harmed by the use of a foreign language on the monuments in the cemetery— even if these are not the monuments of their dears. This harm too has to be taken into consideration. It constitutes part of the deceased's dignity and that of his or her relatives.

12. How shall we strike a balance between these conflicting considerations?

It seems to me that in the circumstances of the case at bar, the deceased and his relatives, requesting that non-Hebrew characters be inscribed on the tombstone, prevail. The reasoning underlying my approach is twofold: *First*, the harm to the deceased and his relatives—in instances where they are denied the inscription of their choice—is direct and severe. By contrast, a scenario where others are permitted to display non-Hebrew inscriptions only constitutes an indirect and benign injury to a deceased and his relatives. * * *

13. Secondly, prohibiting non-Hebrew inscriptions on religious grounds—as distinguished from considerations pertaining to the Hebrew language—constitutes religious coercion. * * * By contrast, the harm to the Observant Jew—an injury that I recognize and take into account— resulting from their inability to fulfill the Halakhic injunction of the Mara DeAtra (Local Rabbinical Authority), is not as severe and poignant. Let us not forget that at issue here is a "local" religious ruling, since every Mara DeAtra (Local Rabbinical Authority) has his own rulings.

15. The following argument could be raised: the view that gave preference to those values and principles supporting non-Hebrew inscriptions on tombstones, is a secular one. Had the balancing been conducted from a religious perspective, the results would have been different. I cannot accept this argument. The viewpoint animating the balancing in question is neither secular nor religious. The perspective underlying the balancing reflects the clash between values and principles from the proper angle, that of the totality of values of a Jewish and Democratic state. This is an integrative perspective, based on a synthesis of Jewish and democratic values. The Court is neither secular nor religious; The Court considers everyone's feelings; The Court takes into account all freedoms; The Court expresses all these values—Jewish values and

democratic values alike. To the best of its abilities, it balances between conflicting feelings, freedoms and values.

16. * * * According to Justice England's approach, the religious precept is to be followed in every case where a religious body—even one exercising public authority—acts upon Halakhic norms—based on its freedom of religion. According to my colleague's approach, the balancing doctrine is not applicable in instances where the liberty in question is freedom of religion.

19. Negating the Court's power to decide the proper boundaries respecting the protection of religious sensitivities—in a non-theocratic Israel—shall inevitably lead to these sensitivities not being taken into account. Indeed, a democratic society, seeking to recognize and protect the human rights of all its residents, must recognize human sentiments and balance between them, taking into account the degree of harm inflicted upon them. Only harm beyond the proper "tolerable limit" shall merit protection.

Notes and Questions

1. Are religious tenets decisive in structuring church–state relations, or is this a matter of ordinary secular politics? Dr. Gidon Sapir, *Religion and State in Israel: The Case for Reevaluation and Constitutional Entrenchment*, 22 Hastings Int'l & Comp. L. Rev. 617, 619–26 (1999), discusses the problem in the Israeli context:

> At the time of its establishment and during the first years of statehood, Israel incorporated and crystallized arrangements that originated from two sources. First, it incorporated legal arrangements that prevailed in Palestine prior to the establishment of the state, first during the period of the Ottoman rule and then under the British mandate.[2]
>
> Second, Israel incorporated resolutions that were passed and implemented prior to the establishment of the state by some Zionist institutions. The status quo doctrine is the outcome of this incorporation and crystallization. * * *
>
> * * * [T]he status quo doctrine does not contain a set of principles, but rather a collection of arrangements concerning various issues having to do with the relationship between religion and state. First, the status quo incorporates an understanding of the legal status of religious courts and their exclusive jurisdiction over matters of personal status. Israel allows all religious communities, including Muslim, Christian, and Druze, to maintain autonomous, judicial institutions and follow their own laws in matters of personal status, which are then binding on all members of the community. With respect to the Jewish denomination, the religious courts, known as the Rabbinical Courts, are an integral part of the state's judicial system, supported by state funds, and retain exclusive

2. The Ottoman Empire's 'Millet' system allowed recognized religious communities to maintain an autonomous judicial system and follow their religious laws in matters of religious status. The British empire left this arrangement intact (see The Palestine Order in Council (1922–47), Paragraph 83, III Laws of Palestine 2569 (1934)), and the State of Israel made very minor modifications to this arrangement, mainly related to the fact that after the establishment of the state Jews were no longer a minority religious community.

jurisdiction over matters of marriages and divorces [in accordance with Jewish religious law].

Second, the State of Israel established several other religious institutions, in addition to the rabbinical courts. The State established religious councils, which are administrative bodies in each locality that provide religious services and distribute public funding for their maintenance. [The state- established] Chief Rabbinate does enjoy partial jurisdiction over several issues, including licensing of marriages and divorces, kashrut (conformity with dietary law) and authorization of judges of the religious courts. The Ministry of Religious Affairs, which is the major governmental department that provides funds and services for all religious communities, retains authority over the religious councils. One of the religious parties traditionally controls this ministry.

The third element of the status quo is the educational system. State educational law divides the state educational system between state schools and state religious schools. The law allows a parent to choose between state (secular) education and state religious education when he registers his child in the state education system. State funding of religious education in Israel is not confined to state schools, but includes private schools, both elementary and secondary. These "recognized private schools" receive state financial support that is substantially equivalent to that received by official state schools.

The fourth component of the status quo involves observance of the Sabbath and religious holidays. On these days all governmental offices close, interurban and urban public transportation in most areas of the State come to a halt, and military casual activities are restricted to a minimum. Moreover, the Law of Working Hours and Rest obliges all Jewish employers to rest on the Jewish Holidays and permits work only in factories essential to the economy or the security of the state with a work permit. In 1969, the law was amended to include the self-employed.

Fifth, the status quo includes observance of Jewish dietary laws: production of pork is restricted by state law;[20] dietary laws are observed by government kitchens, at official state events and all military facilities. * * *

The sixth element is the de facto exemption from army service granted to Orthodox yeshiva students. * * *

[There are a number of arguments in favor of the status quo.] * * * [T]he subject of the relationship between religion and state is extremely complicated and potentially explosive. A dispute over this issue threatens, therefore, the stability of Israeli society. * * * proponents argue that Israeli Jewish society is divided into two, diametrically opposed, subgroups: religious (or Orthodox) and secular. These two groups allegedly maintain contradictory and irreconcilable positions respecting the desirable relationship between religion and state. Orthodox Jews feel they cannot compromise their halakhic [Jewish legal code] vision of the state and therefore cannot accept less than a full halakhic resolution.

---

20. Pig Raising Prohibition Law, 16 L.S.I. 93 (1962). The law applies to Jews and Muslims, who are forbidden by their religion to raise pigs, but exempts Christian communities and specifies "permitted areas"—localities in which Christians form a majority.

The secularists, on the other side, can hardly compromise their secular, democratic, vision of the state and therefore cannot accept anything less than a fully democratic system. * * * Proponents claim that Israel faces life-threatening dangers that are much more urgent than issues of religion and state.

Dr. Sapir considers the possibility that "the status quo might be a product of 'politics of omission.'" *Id.* at 626. According to Stephen Holmes, *Gag Rules or the Politics of Omission*, in *Constitutionalism and Democracy* 19 (Jon Elster and Rune Slagstad eds. 1988), such omission can be a prudent strategy: "to avoid destructive conflicts, we suppress controversial themes. By tying our tongues about a sensitive question, we can secure forms of cooperation and fellowship otherwise beyond reach." Is removing certain items from the democratic agenda acceptable in a democracy? Imagine what would happen if matters of religion were left to the ordinary democratic process, especially where there is a clear (and salvation-offering) religious majority? Is such removal, as Holmes suggests, "a necessary condition for the emergence and stability of democracies"? Is the Israeli system unique, or is it simply a system that makes unprincipled concessions to theocracy? In 1919, the Weimar Constitution affirmed the existing status quo by confirming that churches which had the recognized status of "public law corporation[s]" could continue in that capacity with special privileges. These were former state churches in the various German kingdoms, duchies, and the like that constituted the German empire. In 1949, the "church–state-relations" rules of the Weimar Constitution were incorporated into the Basic Law. Is the Weimar arrangement, as accepted by the German Basic Law, another case of unprincipled recognition of the status quo?

2. In *Abd-Allah Lucien Meyers v. Hausen a. A* (2P.361/1997) Tribunal Federal, 1999, the Swiss Federal Court denied Meyers's right to decent burial in his municipality of origin. The right to decent burial itself is guaranteed by the federal Constitution (Art. 53.2), but it is provided by local authorities. The Constitution forbids religious discrimination, but it does not grant a right to special burial in nonconformance with local customs. Specially designated cemeteries for members of religions that are not accommodated by local customs are a constitutional possibility, and religious communities must provide their own cemeteries. Abd–Allah Lucien Meyers asked to be buried in Hausen, where he was born. The municipality could not guarantee that his body would remain there indefinitely, as required by the precepts of Islam ("eternal rest"). It was held immaterial that there was no cemetery in the canton of Zurich where the religious precepts of Islam could be satisfied.

THE HINDUTVA CASES

Brenda Cossman and Ratna Kapur, SECULARISM'S LAST SIGH?: THE HINDU RIGHT, THE COURTS, AND INDIA'S STRUGGLE FOR DEMOCRACY,
38 Harv. Int'l L.J. 113, 113–114, 120–123 (1997).

"India forces us to think, sometimes in tragic moments, of the function of religious thought within secularism. This is again a challenge for the times. If you look around the world today this is a very important issue;

this particular kind of sometimes fundamentalist, of other times religious orthodoxy erupting within secularism, not simply in opposition to it."

Homi Bhabha[1]

The struggle to secure the constitutional and political protection of secularism in India has been long and difficult, and secularism's enemies remain numerous. Recently, as Homi Bhabha suggests, these enemies are waging their war not in opposition to secularism, but in and through it. Increasingly, secularism has become the subject of intense political contestation in which right wing religious and fundamentalist forces endeavor to claim the secularist terrain as their own. In India, the Hindu Right—a nationalist and right wing political movement devoted to creating a Hindu State—increasingly has staked out its own claim, arguing that it alone is committed to upholding secularism. Indeed, secularism has become a central and powerful weapon in the Hindu Right's quest for discursive and political power. * * * A series of recent and highly controversial cases involved the prosecution of elected representatives of the Hindu nationalist Shiv–Sena/Bhartiya Janta Party alliance Government in the western state of Maharashtra for corrupt practices under the Representation of the People Act, 1951. In *Manohar Joshi v. Nitin Bhaurao Patil*[3] and eleven other cases (collectively known as the "Hindutva" cases), the Supreme Court of India delivered a mixed message to the cause of secularism.

* * *

The main opinion on the interpretation of the Representation of the People Act, 1951, and whether an appeal to Hindutva constituted a violation of the Act, was set forth in *Prabhoo v. Prabhakar Kasinath Kunte et al.*[23] This case involved charges of corrupt practices against Dr. Prabhoo, the mayor of Bombay, and his agent Bal Thackeray. The Bombay High Court found Prabhoo and Thackeray guilty of corrupt practices on grounds that they had appealed for votes on the basis of religion and promoted feelings of enmity and hatred between different classes of citizens of India. On appeal, Prabhoo argued that the High Court had erred in finding that an appeal to Hindutva constituted a violation of the Act. It was argued that Hindutva means Indian culture, not Hindu culture, and moreover that the public speeches of the candidate "criticized the anti-secular stance of the Congress Party in practicing discrimination against Hindus and giving undue favor to the minorities which is not an appeal for votes on the ground of Hindu religion. * * *"

The Court first turned to the meaning of section 123(3) [of RPA] and its prohibition of appeals to religion to gain votes. In the Court's view, the prohibition did not mean that religion could never be mentioned in election speeches. A speech with a secular stance that raised questions about discrimination against a particular religion would not be

---

1. Secularism as an Idea Will Change, HINDU, Dec. 17, 1995, at XIX.

3. *Manohar Joshi v. Nitin Bhaurao Patil*, 1995 S.C.A.L.E. 30.

23. *Dr. Romesh Yeshaunt Prabhoo v. Prabhakar Kashinath Knute*, 1995 S.C.A.L.E. 1.

caught by section 123(3). Rather, section 123(3) was intended to prohibit a candidate from either seeking votes on the basis of his religion or trying to alienate votes from another candidate on the basis of that candidate's religion. The Court then considered the meaning of the prohibition on the promotion of feelings of enmity or hatred between different religious communities contained in section 123(3A). In its view, the clear objective of the section was to curb "the tendency to promote or attempt to promote communal, linguistic or any other factional enmity or hatred to prevent the divisive tendencies."

* * * On the meaning of Hindutva, the Court concluded:

> that the term "Hindutva" is related more to the way of life of the people in the subcontinent. It is difficult to appreciate how in the face of these decisions the term "Hindutva" or "Hinduism" per se, in the abstract, can be assumed to mean and be equated with narrow fundamentalist Hindu religious bigotry, or be construed to fall within the prohibition in (section 123(3) or (3A)).

* * * Accordingly, the Court concluded that simply referring to Hindutva or Hinduism in a speech does not automatically make the speech one based on the Hindu religion and thus an appeal to religion. Nor, in the Court's view, does such a reference necessarily "depict an attitude hostile to all persons practicing any religion other than the Hindu religion" but rather, it is the particular "use made of these words and the meaning sought to be conveyed in the speech which has to be seen." Such words may be used in a speech "to promote secularism or to emphasize the way of life of the Indian people and the Indian culture or ethos or to criticize the policy of any political party as discriminatory or intolerant." * * *

In the case against Prabhoo and his agent, Thackeray, the Court found that all three of Thackeray's speeches at issue constituted a clear appeal to the Hindu voters to vote for Prabhoo because he was a Hindu, and thus violated section 123(3). * * * By way of contrast, in the case against Manohar Joshi, for a speech in which he stated that "the first Hindu State will be established in Maharashtra," the Court held that Joshi was not guilty of violating section 123(3) or (3A). Such a statement was not an appeal to voters on the basis of religion, but simply "the expression, at best, of such a hope."

Notes and Questions

1. In some respects the "secularism" in *Bommai* reminds one of the contempt for religion voiced by Enlightenment philosophers and some Indian administrators, who often perceive religious practices as detrimental to the individual and the common good. Some Indian justices were ready to accept freedom of religion as a private matter, but Justice Ramaswamy referred to the Hindu tradition of cultural tolerance. This tolerance was increasingly challenged in India by Hindu politicians, culminating in the *Hindutva* cases. Does the justification of tolerance by a stylized version of the majority religion make the secularism argument more convincing? Note the position of Justices Reddy and Agrawal in *Bommai*, A.I.R. 1994 S.C. 2068, para. 243, who held that "any party or organization which seeks to fight the elections

on the basis of a plank which has the proximate effect of eroding the secular philosophy of the Constitution would certainly be guilty of following an unconstitutional course of action." The unconstitutionality apparently rests in the politicizing of religion and the danger of a de facto establishment of state religion: "if a political party espousing a particular religion comes to power, that religion tends to become, in practice, the official religion. All other religions come to acquire a secondary status, at any rate, a less favourable position." *Id.*

2. Brenda Cossman and Ratna Kapur (*op. cit.* at 115) find that the Court failed

> to take account of the Hindu Right's discursive strategies and to pay sufficient attention to manipulations of secularism by the Hindu Right. * * * Hindu Right has hijacked the dominant understanding of secularism as the equal respect of all religions in order to promote its vision of Hindutva and its agenda of establishing a Hindu State. In its hands, the equal respect of all religions becomes a tool for attacking the rights of minority religious communities. Its emphasis on the formal equal treatment of all religions operates as an unmodified majoritarianism whereby the dominant Hindu community becomes the norm against which all others are to be judged.

Compare Daniel Gold: "[t]he Hinduism of ritual and law displays an extreme preoccupation with the play of cosmic order on earth, a concern for following codes of behavior deemed divinely ordained and morally proper. Building the Hindu Nation, by contrast, demands staunch identification with the group, an evocation of group loyalty and assertiveness that need not inherently respect traditional codes—thus belying the professed broad aims of the Hindu demonstrators at Ayodhya." Daniel Gold, *Organized Hinduisms: From Vedic Truth to Hindu Nation*, in *Fundamentalisms Observed* 582 (Martin E. Marty and R. Scott Appleby eds., 1991).

3. To be sure, the constitutional problem of the secularization of religion is not limited to India. After the collapse of Yugoslavia, Catholic values were identified with Croatia, Bosnian identity was Muslim, and Serbs were Orthodox Christians. Currently, in many countries, mainstream Christian traditions are imposed on the nonreligious as "part of the national identity," for example, in finding constitutional Catholic religious holidays as part of a national tradition. (See Note on the Sabbath above.)

B.2. SECULAR EDUCATION AND DENOMINATIONAL SCHOOLS

It is one of the "missions" of the modern state to provide education, both by operating a school system (national and/or local) and supervising what is taught. Freedom of religion, on the other hand, challenges the effort of the state to govern school matters.[y] Here we look into a few of the potential conflicts, particularly to what extent members of a faith-or

---

y. In many liberal democracies, public support of denominational schools is full of inconsistencies. See France, above. As to the U.S., the commitment to the separation of church and state could not stop the Supreme Court from allowing ad hoc exceptions to satisfy public needs and sentiments.

belief-based community or individuals with special convictions may choose their own system of education. See *Interdenominational School Case*; and *Kjeldsen, Busk Madsen and Pedersen v. Denmark* below. The mirror view of that problem is this: To what extent ought the state finance such religion-driven (or other beliefs-driven) school systems? If religious communities are allowed to own and operate educational systems apart from the secular-education system, how far may this go? Are these communities entitled to become separate societies within the state? (This problem is discussed in the Note following *Yoder* below.) A second problem is the permissibility of religion in state schools (as a curricular subject; as a symbol, e.g., crucifix, robe, and the like; and as a practice, like prayer). The answers partly depend on the effect on students; otherwise, church–state relations and the understanding of free exercise and cultural identities will matter. In this context we deal only summarily with the use of state funds to support religion or a religious institution, although some of the cases address the issue. Several dimensions of this problem were touched on in the context of state neutrality.

WISCONSIN v. YODER

Supreme Court (United States).
406 U.S. 205 (1972).

Mr. Chief Justice Burger delivered the opinion of the Court.

Respondents Yoder and Miller are members of the Old Order Amish religion. Wisconsin's compulsory school-attendance law required them to cause their children to attend public or private school until reaching age 16 but the respondents declined to send their children, ages 14 and 15, to public school after they complete the eighth grade.

On complaint of the school district administrator for the public schools, [Respondents were charged, tried, and convicted of violating the compulsory-attendance law.]

I

There is no doubt as to the power of a State, having a high responsibility for education of its citizens, to impose reasonable regulations for the control and duration of basic education. See, e.g., *Pierce v. Society of Sisters*, 268 U.S. 510, 534, (1925). Providing public schools ranks at the very apex of the function of a State. Yet even this paramount responsibility was, in *Pierce*, made to yield to the right of parents to provide an equivalent education in a privately operated system.

II

* * * A way of life, however virtuous and admirable, may not be interposed as a barrier to reasonable state regulation of education if it is based on purely secular considerations; to have the protection of the Religion Clauses, the claims must be rooted in religious belief.

* * *

[W]e see that the record in this case abundantly supports the claim that the traditional way of life of the Amish is not merely a matter of personal preference, but one of deep religious conviction, shared by an organized group, and intimately related to daily living.

III

* * * It is true that activities of individuals, even when religiously based, are often subject to regulation by the States in the exercise of their undoubted power to promote the health, safety, and general welfare, or the Federal Government in the exercise of its delegated powers. But to agree that religiously grounded conduct must often be subject to the broad police power of the State is not to deny that there are areas of conduct protected by the Free Exercise Clause of the First Amendment and thus beyond the power of the State to control, even under regulations of general applicability.

Nor can this case be disposed of on the grounds that Wisconsin's requirement for school attendance to age 16 applies uniformly to all citizens of the State and does not, on its face, discriminate against religions or a particular religion, or that it is motivated by legitimate secular concerns. A regulation neutral on its face may, in its application, nonetheless offend the constitutional requirement for governmental neutrality if it unduly burdens the free exercise of religion. *Sherbert v. Verner, supra*; cf. *Walz v. Tax Commission*, 397 U.S. 664 (1970).

Where fundamental claims of religious freedom are at stake, * * * we must searchingly examine the interests that the State seeks to promote by its requirement for compulsory education to age 16, and the impediment to those objectives that would flow from recognizing the claimed Amish exemption.

The State advances two primary arguments in support of its system of compulsory education. It notes, as Thomas Jefferson pointed out early in our history, that some degree of education is necessary to prepare citizens to participate effectively and intelligently in our open political system if we are to preserve freedom and independence. Further, education prepares individuals to be self-reliant and self-sufficient participants in society. We accept these propositions.

It is neither fair nor correct to suggests that the Amish are opposed to education beyond the eighth grade level. What this record shows is that they are opposed to conventional formal education of the type provided by a certified high school because it comes at the child's crucial adolescent period of religious development.

* * * There can be no assumption that today's majority is 'right' and the Amish and others like them are 'wrong.' A way of life that is odd or even erratic but interferes with no rights or interests of others is not to be condemned because it is different.

Indeed, the Amish communities singularly parallel and reflect many of the virtues of Jefferson's ideal of the 'sturdy yeoman' who would form the basis of what he considered as the ideal of a democratic society. Even their idiosyncratic separateness exemplifies the diversity we profess to admire and encourage.

IV

[I]t seems clear that if the State is empowered, as parens patriae, to 'save' a child from himself or his Amish parents by requiring an additional two years of compulsory formal high school education, the State will in large measure influence, if not determine, the religious future of the child. Even more markedly than in Prince, therefore, this case involves the fundamental interest of parents, as contrasted with that of the State, to guide the religious future and education of their children. The history and culture of Western civilization reflect a strong tradition of parental concern for the nurture and upbringing of their children. This primary role of the parents in the upbringing of their children is now established beyond debate as an enduring American tradition.

* * * To be sure, the power of the parent, even when linked to a free exercise claim, may be subject to limitation under *Prince v. Massachusetts* if it appears that parental decisions will jeopardize the health or safety of the child, or have a potential for significant social burdens. * * * The record strongly indicates that accommodating the religious objections of the Amish by forgoing one, or at most two, additional years of compulsory education will not impair the physical or mental health of the child, or result in an inability to be self-supporting or to discharge the duties and responsibilities of citizenship, or in any other way materially detract from the welfare of society.

V

For the reasons stated we hold, with the Supreme Court of Wisconsin, that the First and Fourteenth Amendments prevent the State from compelling respondents to cause their children to attend formal high school to age 16.[22] Our disposition of this case, however, in no way alters our recognition of the obvious fact that courts are not school boards or legislatures, and are ill-equipped to determine the 'necessity' of discrete aspects of a State's program of compulsory education. This should suggest that courts must move with great circumspection in performing the sensitive and delicate task of weighing a State's legitimate social concern when faced with religious claims for exemption from generally applicable education requirements. * * *

Mr. Justice Douglas, dissenting in part.

* * *

22. * * * Accommodating the religious beliefs of the Amish can hardly be characterized as sponsorship or active involvement. The purpose and effect of such an exemption are not to support, favor, advance, or assist the Amish, but to allow their centuries-old religious society, here long before the advent of any compulsory education, to survive free from the heavy impediment compliance with the Wisconsin compulsory-education law would impose. Such an accommodation 'reflects nothing more than the governmental obligation of neutrality in the face of religious differences, and does not represent that involvement of religious with secular institutions which it is the object of the Establishment Clause to forestall.' *Sherbert v. Verner*, 374 U.S. 398, 409, (1963).

It is the future of the student, not the future of the parents, that is imperiled by today's decision. If a parent keeps his child out of school beyond the grade school, then the child will be forever barred from entry into the new and amazing world of diversity that we have today. The child may decide that that is the preferred course, or he may rebel. It is the student's judgment, not his parents', that is essential if we are to give full meaning to what we have said about the Bill of Rights and of the right of students to be masters of their own destiny. If he is harnessed to the Amish way of life by those in authority over him and if his education is truncated, his entire life may be stunted and deformed. The child, therefore, should be given an opportunity to be heard before the State gives the exemption which we honor today. * * *

Note on Religious Self-government and Secession

The problem of allowing self-government on religious grounds is described by Justice Douglas (dissenting): "When racial or religious lines are drawn by the State, the multiracial, multireligious communities that our Constitution seeks to weld together as one become separatist; antagonisms that relate to race or to religion rather than to political issues are generated; communities seek not the best representative but the best racial or religious partisan. Since that system is at war with the democratic ideal, it should find no footing here." *Wright v. Rockefeller*, 376 U.S. 52, 67 (1964).

Justice Kennedy said in *Kiryas Joel* below: "Religion flourishes in community, and the Establishment Clause must not be construed as some sort of homogenizing solvent that forces unconventional religious groups to choose between assimilating to mainstream American culture or losing their political rights." The issue is how far the state should go in allowing religious communities to live as they see fit. Such permissiveness may undermine social homogeneity, increase factionalism, and allow for the denial of social values and individual rights that are cherished in a liberal constitution.

In *Wisconsin v. Yoder* the USSC allowed members of the Old Order Amish religion not to send their children to public schools after they completed the eighth grade. The state, having a high responsibility for education of its citizens, can impose reasonable regulations for basic education. However, "the traditional way of life of the Amish is not merely a matter of personal preference, but one of deep religious conviction, shared by an organized group, and intimately related to daily living," and, therefore, a free exercise exemption is applicable. The Court found that the protection of the traditional way of life is "beyond the power of the State to control, even under regulations of general applicability."

Yoder may be celebrated as a model of accommodating multiculturalism. Yet it is more an exception than a model, both in comparative terms and in U.S. law. The Amish showing was one that few other religious groups or sects could make, and the USSC became reluctant to grant exceptions to a way of life understood as religious conduct. See *Smith* above. As indicated in *Board of Education of Kiryas Joel Village School District v. Grumet*, 512 U.S. 687 (1994), the USSC is aware of the political implications of religious secessionism. The village of Kiryas Joel is a religious enclave of Satmar

Hasidim, practitioners of a strict form of Judaism. A special New York statute carved out a separate school district along village lines, "giving the sect exclusive control of the political subdivision." The USSC found this arrangement invalid because the benefit was not applicable to other religious and nonreligious groups. Justice Stevens, with whom Justices Blackmun and Ginsburg joined concurring, found that the New York law

> affirmatively supports a religious sect's interest in segregating itself and preventing its children from associating with their neighbors. The isolation of these children, while it may protect them from 'panic, fear and trauma,' also unquestionably increased the likelihood that they would remain within the fold, faithful adherents of their parents' religious faith. By creating a school district that is specifically intended to shield children from contact with others who have 'different ways,' the state provided official support to cement the attachment of young adherents to a particular faith."

Id. at 711.

Justice O'Connor perceived here an abuse of people's right of self-government, leading to the establishment of their religion:

> People who share a common religious belief or lifestyle may live together without sacrificing the basic rights of self-governance that all American citizens enjoy, so long as they do not use those rights to establish their religious faith. * * * There is more than a fine line, however, between the voluntary association that leads to a political community comprised of people who share a common religious faith, and the forced separation that occurs when the government draws explicit political boundaries on the basis of peoples' faith. In creating the Kiryas Joel Village School District, New York crossed that line, and so we must hold the district invalid.

Id.at 730.

In *Kiryas Joel* the community sought to use government funds for its secular educational purposes (a special school for the mentally retarded), while the Old Amish wanted merely to be left out of compulsory education.

Compare *Kiryas Joel* with the use of the democratic process in Rijssen (a municipality in The Netherlands). The majority of the community in Rijssen are orthodox Protestants with very negative views on theater and performing arts. The municipality refused to rent a hall under its management to a hypnosis show. The Supreme Court of The Netherlands found that the municipality restricted the free speech rights of the performer on the basis of the show's content. The Court said that the public had an obligation to protect the public interest, which includes observing principles of good governance and respect for fundamental rights of the public when entering into agreements. But the principle of freedom of contract, relied upon by the municipality, cannot prevail against the speech interest. The Netherlands Supreme Court, First Division, 26.04.1996. 15.951. BCCL 1996. 243. (See further, state action in Chapter 10.)

TEACHING OF THE CATHOLIC RELIGION CASE

Constitutional Court (Italy).
Judgment n. 203/1989.

* * *

1. The Magistrate of Florence referred the question of constitutionality, with respect to articles 2, 3 and 19 of the Constitution, of article 9, number 2, of the 1985 Law on Ratifying the Amendment (Ratification and Execution of the agreement and amendment to the Lateran Pacts of February 11, 1929 between the Republic of Italy and The Holy See), asserting that such provisions might discriminate against the students who do not opt for the teaching of the Catholic religion, unless said norms can be interpreted in a way according to which the religious teaching qualifies merely as an optional additional subject.

2. * * * The "judge *a quo*" [the Magistrate], by describing also the discriminatory effects upon the students opting for the teaching of the Catholic religion, underscores the reciprocity of the potential discrimination and sets forth in a proper and adequate manner the constitutional issue. Such question is whether the teaching of the Catholic religion, located in the educational plan among the other subjects with equal cultural dignity, as mandated by the legislation implementing the above mentioned agreements, is a cause of discrimination or not.

* * *

3. This Court has ruled and followed it constantly in various occasions that the supreme principles of the constitutional order "override the other norms or laws having constitutional standing". The provisions in the Lateran Pacts, which enjoy the special constitutional protection granted by article 7.2 of the Constitution, must be subject to a conformity review [conformity to the supreme principles of the constitutional order.

[C]onsidering the underlying facts of the present case, articles 3 [non-discrimination on grounds of religion] and 19 [free exercise of religion] are relevant because they affirm the freedom of religion in two senses of prohibition:

a) that there shall be no discrimination among citizens on the basis of religion;

b) that there shall be no constraint imposed, in the name of religious pluralism, on the negative liberty not to profess any religion;

4. The mentioned values, together with other constitutional values (articles 7, 8 and 20 of the Court), concur in the formation of the supreme principle of the secularity of the State, which is an essential institutional feature of the State, as designed in the constitutional charter of the Republic.

The principle of the secular State does not entail that the State has an indifferent attitude towards religions, but that the State ensures the protection of freedom of religion, in a regime of confessional and cultural pluralism. The additional Protocol to the law n.121 of 1985, which ratifies, implements and executes the Agreement between the Republic of Italy and The Holy See, with reference to article 1 provides that: "the principle according to which the Catholic religion is the sole religion of the Italian state, originally affirmed in the Lateran Pacts, is not considered valid anymore". Article 1 of the 1929 Treaty [the Lateran Pacts], in fact, stated that: "Italy recognizes and reaffirms the principle, established by article 1 of the Statute of the Realm of March 4, 1848, pursuant to which the Catholic, apostolic, roman religion is the sole religion of the State".

The confessional choice of the *Statuto albertino* [the Constitution of 1848], confirmed in the Lateran Treaty of 1929, has therefore been relinquished in the additional Protocol to the 1985 Agreement and the secular nature of the Republic of Italy has consequently been reaffirmed in the bilateral relationship.

5. We will know turn to the analysis of the text of article 9, number 2, law n.121 of 1985, in order to fully understand how and why the teaching of the Catholic religion in the public schools (with the exception of Universities) has been kept within a legislative framework that now recognizes the secularity of the State.

Four important points arise out of the first sentence ("The Republic of Italy, recognizing the value of the religious culture and having regard to the fact that the principles of Catholicism are part of the historical heritage of the Italian People, will continue to ensure the teaching of the Catholic religion, in the context of the goals of school, in every level and grade of the public schools, except for Universities"):

1) the recognition of the value of the religious culture;

2) the recognition of the fact that the principles of Catholicism are part of the historical heritage of the Italian People;

3) the continuing commitment of the Italian State to ensure, as before, the teaching of the Catholic religion in every level and grade of the public schools, except for Universities;

4) the administration of such teaching in the context of the goals of education.

The points sub 1), 2) and 4) represent new concepts, which are perfectly compatible with the secular nature of the Republic of Italy.
* * *

7. In the historical development of Italy, religion has first been used as a tool to improve and sustain common morality, this was followed by the positivistic opposition between science and religion, followed by the use of religion as the ethical foundation of the totalitarian State. Finally, religion played a crucial role in the long-lasting dispute between the Monarchy and the Pope, which began during the *Risorgimento*. Having completed the above historical cycle, today the Republic exactly, in its capacity as a secular State, is able to justify the teaching of the Catholic religion on the following bases:

a) the educational value of the religious culture, meaning not just a single religion, but the religious pluralism of the civil society;

b) the acquisition of the principles of Catholicism in "The historical heritage of the Italian People".

The *genus* ("value of the religious culture") and the *species* ("the principles of Catholicism in the historical heritage of the Italian People") together define the secular attitude of the State-community, which does not entail the ideological and abstract hostility or, conversely, benevolence of the State-person or of the governing parties with respect to the religion in general or to a particular faith. It means, instead, that the State must pay attention to the actual needs of the civil and religious conscience of its citizens.

The teaching of the Catholic religion shall be administered, pursuant to article 9, "in the context of the goals of education", that is to say: in a manner compatible with the other scholastic disciplines.

8. The second sentence of article 9, number 2, law n.121 of 1985 ("in order to safeguard the freedom of conscience and the educational responsibilities of the parents, everyone has the right to decide whether to take the above mentioned course or not") is the most relevant from a constitutional perspective.

With respect to the teaching of the Catholic religion, a special mention is dedicated to the safeguard of the freedom of conscience and of the educational responsibilities of the parents, which are protected by articles 19 and 30, respectively, of the Constitution of the Republic.

As far as the teaching of a positive religion—administered "in conformity to the doctrine of the Church" according to section 5, letter a) of the additional Protocol—is concerned, however, the secular State has the duty to ensure that the freedom recognized in article 19 and the educational responsibilities of the parents affirmed in art. 30 of the Constitution shall not be impaired or limited.

This is the instrumental logic of the State-community, which recognizes and protects the right of self-determination of its citizens by granting them the subjective right to decide whether to avail themselves of the teaching of the Catholic religion or not.

Such right is entrusted to the parents and, with regard to high schools, directly to the students, pursuant to article 1, point 1, law of June 18, 1986 n.281 (Educational choices and Enrollment in the High School). Such subjective right has no precedents in the field.

The shift from the arguments of the liberal age (religion is a private affair and religious education a matter exclusively managed by the parents) to those of the ethical State (religion is a feature of the national identity that deserves to be cultivated in the public schools) is apparent.

A peculiar character of the teaching of a positive religion emerges in connection with the Agreement of February 18, 1984. The proposal to substantially endorse a specific doctrine might conflict with issues of personal conscience and with the educational preferences of the family. In order to avoid such potential conflicts, the secular State grants the right to make a free choice.

The third sentence of article 9, number 2 of the Agreement ("At the time of enrollment, the students or their parents shall exercise such right to choose, upon demand of the scholastic authority, and the choice will not give rise to any form of discrimination") fully complies with the principle of secularity and with its various corollaries, because of the agreed guarantee that the choice will not give rise to any form of discrimination.

Section 5, number 2 of the additional Protocol does not comprise any provision directly related to the present controversy and, therefore, the alleged constitutional violation cannot concern the mentioned norm.

9.   The mandatory enrollment in an alternative course or subject of those who decided not to avail themselves of the teaching of the Catholic religion would amount to a patent discrimination to their detriment. The right to choose with respect to the teaching of the Catholic religion is a constitutional right of free determination of a very serious and conscientious character. Therefore, it cannot be degraded to a mere option between two alternative obligations as if the decision concerned two equivalent school subjects.

The State is obliged, pursuant to the Agreement with the Holy See, to ensure the teaching of the Catholic religion. For the students and their families, however, it is merely optional: only the decision to opt for it creates the scholastic duty to attend the classes.

Those who decide not to avail themselves of the teaching of the Catholic religion, instead, face no further obligations. The mandatory enrollment in an alternative course or subject would unduly influence the moral decision, which involves—and must involve only—the conscious exercise of the constitutional freedom of religion.

For these reasons the Constitutional Court *declares* that the question of constitutionality is groundless. * * *

INTERDENOMINATIONAL SCHOOL CASE

Federal Constitutional Court (Germany).
41 BVerfGE 29 (1975).

[Education is within the exclusive authority of the *Land* (state) in Germany. In 1967, Baden–Württemberg amended Art. 15 (1) of its Constitution to establish Christian interdenominational schools as the uniform type of public grade school within the state. Because their children attended school in this state, the complainants asserted a violation of their right to religious freedom under Art. 4 (1) of the Basic Law. They objected to their children being educated according to any religious or ideological precepts. Complainants also alleged a violation of their parental right to determine the care and upbringing of their children, pursuant to Art. 6 of the Basic Law.]

Judgment of the First Senate:
* * *

C.1.i.(a) As did the Federal Constitutional Court in the Concordat decision, the Basic Law presupposes the organizational freedom of the states in educational matters. Article 7 * * * establishes the principles for the denominational organization of schools. Accordingly, persons charged with child-rearing have the right to determine if the child may participate in a religion class (Article 7 (2) of the Basic Law) that is offered as a regular subject in state schools (Article 7 (3) [I]). If no state elementary school of this type exists in the local community, a private elementary school is to be licensed as an interdenominational, or ideological school (Article 7 (5) of the Basic Law). Article 7 does not provide for more far-reaching parental influence on the denominational organization of the state school. To this extent this constitutional norm differs substantially from the so-called school compromise of the Weimar Constitution. [In that document] Article 146 (2) determined that, upon parental petition, [the state was to establish] elementary schools of the parents' denomination or ideology within the community as long as the orderly operation of the school was not affected. It also provided that the wishes of the parents be respected as much as possible.

(b) The history of Article 7 of the Basic Law illustrates that the states were intended to be largely independent with respect to the ideological and denominational character of state schools. * * * [t]he state legislature was granted extensive freedom to make democratic decisions concerning the actual organization of school systems.

Article 7 (5) of the Basic Law assumes that state elementary schools can be established as interdenominational, denominational, or ideological schools.

[T]he Basic Law refers the parents to private schools. Basically, it allows the states to decide whether they want to grant parents an affirmative right to control and participate in the denominational organization of public schools beyond the scope set forth in Article 7 of the Basic Law. * * *

2.(a) Insofar as the denominational nature of the state elementary school encroaches upon religious freedom, it is primarily the constitutional position of the child who must attend such a school which is affected. But parents' constitutional rights can also be affected when they are compelled to expose their school-age children to an education which does not correspond to their own ideas of religion and ideology.

[The parents' fundamental right to religious freedom] also includes the rights of parents to pass on to their children the kind of religious and ideological convictions they consider right. It is true that parents cannot derive from this right a claim against the state to have their children educated in the desired ideological way. However, parents' obligation to allow their children to be exposed to ideological and religious influences which contradict their own convictions may adversely affect this right. Those charged with the child's upbringing may, by virtue of their right to freedom under Article 4 of the Basic Law, protect themselves from governmental actions which adversely affect their personal, constitutionally protected sphere. * * *

(b) * * * In the instant case the complainants' request to keep the education of their children free from all religious influences, base on Articles 4 (1) and 4 (2) of the Basic Law, must inevitably conflict with the desire of other citizens to afford their children a religious education, also based on Article 4 of the Basic Law. There is a tension here between "negative" and "positive" religious freedom. The elimination of all ideological and religious references would not neutralize the existing ideological tensions and conflicts, but would disadvantage parents who desire a Christian education for their children and would result in compelling them to send their children to a lay school that would roughly correspond with the complainants' wishes. * * *

(c) Because life in a pluralistic society makes it practically impossible to take into consideration the wishes of all parents in the ideological organization of compulsory state schools, [we] must assume that the individual cannot assert his right to freedom pursuant to Article 4 of the Basic Law free of any limitation at all. [In] school matters the task of resolving the inevitable tension between negative and positive religious freedom falls to the democratic state legislature. In the process of making public policy, the legislature must seek a compromise which is reasonable for all while considering the varying views. * * * One can only resolve this [problem] by assessing the conflicting interests through a balancing [process] and categorizing the constitutional aspects previously discussed. At the same time one must take into consideration the constitutional commandment of tolerance (compare Article 3 (3), Article 33 (3) of the Basic Law) as well as the safeguarding of state independence in matters of school organization. Further, one must keep in mind that individual states may pass differing regulations due to differences in school traditions, the denominational composition of the population, and its religious roots.

3. As a result, the state legislature is not absolutely prohibited from incorporating Christian references when it establishes a state elementary school, even though a minority of parents have no choice but to send their children to this school and may not desire any religious education for their children. However, the [legislature] must choose a type of school which, insofar as it can influence children's decisions concerning faith and conscience, contains only a minimum of coercive elements. Thus the school may not be a missionary school and may not demand commitment to Christian articles of faith. Also, it must remain open to other ideological and religious ideas and values. The [legislature] may not limit a school's educational goals to those belonging to a Christian denomination, except in religion classes, which no one can be forced to attend. Affirming Christianity within the context of secular disciplines refers primarily to the recognition of Christianity as a formative cultural and educational factor which has developed in Western civilization. It does not refer to the truth of the belief. With respect to non-Christians, this affirmation obtains legitimacy as a progression of historical fact. * * * Confronting non-Christians with a view of the world in which the formative power of Christian thought is affirmed does not cause discrimination either against minorities not affiliated with Christianity or against their ideology—at least, not if the issue focuses on striving to develop the autonomous personality in the ideological and religious realm according to the basic decision of Article 4 rather than focusing on an absolute claim to the truth of a belief.

CLASSROOM CRUCIFIX II CASE

Federal Constitutional Court (Germany).
93 BVerfGE 1(1995).

[A Bavarian school ordinance required the display of the crucifix in every elementary school classroom.]

Judgment of the First Senate:

* * *

C. The constitutional complaint [of parents of schoolchildren] is well founded. The rejection of the plaintiff's claim is incompatible with Article 4 (1) and Article 6 (2). * * *

1. Article 4 (1) of the Basic Law protects freedom of belief. [Including] guarantees to refrain from participating in such activities. To be sure, in a society that tolerates a wide variety of faith commitments, the individual clearly has no right to be spared exposure to quaint religious manifestations, cultish activities, or religious symbols. However, a different situation arises when the state itself exposes an individual to the influence of a given faith, without giving the child a chance to avoid such influence.

* * * The state is thus committed to protect the individual from attacks or obstructions by adherents of different beliefs or competing religious groups. Article 4 (1), however, grants neither to the individual nor to religious communities the right to have their faith commitments supported by the state. On the contrary, freedom of faith as guaranteed by Article 4(1) of the Basic Law requires the state to remain neutral in matters of faith and religion. A state in which members of various or even conflicting religious and ideological convictions must live together can guarantee peaceful coexistence only if it remains neutral in matters of religious belief. And when the state supports or works together with [these religious communities], it must take care not to identify itself with a particular community.

2.(a) * * * Given the context of compulsory education, the presence of crosses in classrooms amounts to state-enforced ''learning under the cross'', with no possibility to avoid seeing it. This constitutes the crucial difference between the display of the cross in a classroom and the religious symbols people frequently encounter in their daily lives.

(b) The cross is the symbol of a particular religious conviction, and not merely an expression of cultural values that have been influenced by Christianity.

Any support of [Christian] faith tenets by the state would undermine freedom of religion, a matter already determined by the Federal Constitutional Court in its ruling on the constitutionality of so-called [*Simultanschulen*] (citing 41 BVerfGE 29, 52). In affirming the Christian character of the biconfessional public elementary schools', the court ruled that the state may legitimately recognize Christianity's imprint on culture and education over the course of Western history, but not the particular tenets of the Christian religion.

The cross now as before represents a specific tenet of Christianity; it constitutes its most significant faith symbol. It symbolizes man's redemption from original sin through Christ's sacrifice just as it represents Christ's victory over Satan and death and his power over the world. Accordingly, the cross symbolizes both suffering and triumph. [N]on-Christians and atheists perceive [the cross] to be the symbolic expression of certain faith convictions and a symbol of missionary zeal. To see the cross as nothing more than a cultural artifact of the Western tradition without any particular religious meaning would amount to a profanation contrary to the self-understanding of Christians and the Christian church.

(c) One cannot deny, as do the challenged decisions of the administrative courts, that the cross also has an effect on students.

Education is more than just transmitting fundamental cultural values and developing cognitive facilities. It also involves the development of pupils' emotional and affective abilities. [The] presence [of the cross] constitutes a deeply moving appeal; it underscores the faith commitment it symbolizes, thus making that faith exemplary and worthy of being followed. This is particularly true with young and impressionable people who are still learning to develop their critical capacities and principles of right conduct.

3.(a) * * * No state, even one that universally guarantees freedom of religion and is committed to religious and ideological neutrality, is in a position completely to divest itself of the cultural and historical values on which social cohesion and the attainment of public goals depend. The Christian religion and the Christian churches have always exerted a tremendous influence in our society, regardless of how this influence is evaluated today. * * * Furthermore, any state that requires children to attend state schools must respect the religious freedom of those parents who want their children to receive a religiously based education.

In a pluralistic society, needless to say, the state, in setting up a system of compulsory public school instruction, cannot possibly satisfy all educational goals or needs. Problems will always arise, and it will be particularly difficult to implement the negative as well as the positive aspects of religious freedom in one and the same public institution. So far as education is concerned, no one can claim an absolute right under Article 4 (1) of the Basic Law.

In resolving the inevitable tension between the negative and positive aspects of religious freedom, and in seeking to promote the tolerance that the Basic Law mandates, the state, in forming the public will, must strive to bring about an acceptable compromise.

The Federal Constitutional Court has concluded [in its previous case law] that the state legislature is not forbidden to introduce Christian values into the organization of public elementary schools. * * * Christianity's influence on culture and education may be affirmed and recognized, but not particular articles of faith. Christianity as a cultural force incorporates in particular the idea of tolerance toward people of different persuasions. Confrontation with a Christian worldview will not lead to discrimination or devaluation of a non-Christian ideology so long as the state does not impose the values of the Christian faith on non-Christians; indeed, the state must foster the autonomous thinking that Article 4 of the Basic Law secures within the religious and ideological realms.

The display of crosses in classrooms, however, exceeds [these guidelines and constitutional limits]. As noted earlier, the cross cannot be separated from its reference to a particular tenet of Christianity;

(b) Parents and pupils who adhere to the Christian faith cannot justify the display of the cross by invoking their positive freedom of religious liberty. All parents and pupils are equally entitled to the positive freedom of faith, not just Christian parents and pupils. The resulting conflict cannot be resolved on the basis of majority rule. * * * Inasmuch as schools heed the Constitution, leaving room for religious instruction, school prayer, and other religious events, all of these activities must be conducted on a voluntary basis and the school must ensure that students who do not wish to participate in these activities are excused from them and suffer no discrimination because of their decision not to participate. The situation is different with respect to the display of the cross. Students who do not share the same faith are unable to remove themselves from its presence and message.

Justices Otto Seidl, Alfred Söllner, and Evelyn Haas, dissenting.

* * * According to Article 135 (2) of the amended Bavarian Constitution, Christianity is not to be understood in a confessional sense. * * * In affirming Christianity, the state is merely acknowledging the West's cultural and educational indebtedness to Christianity.

3. Under Article 7 (1) and (5) of the Basic Law, individual states enjoy a large measure of discretion in determining the [nature] and organization of elementary schools. . . . The rule that mandates the display of a cross in every classroom does not exceed that discretion. Since the state legislature is permitted to establish a Christian community school, it cannot be prevented from expressing, through the symbol of the cross, the values and ideals which characterize this type of school.

(a) Section 13 (1.3) of the Bavarian Elementary School Ordinance implements the organization of the Christian community school. For teachers and students alike, the display of the cross in classrooms symbolizes Western values and ethical norms that transcend confessional considerations and are to be taught in this type of school. In enacting this law, the state legislature was permitted to consider the fact that the majority of citizens residing in Bavaria belong to one or another form of the Christian church.

        * * *

4. The state has a constitutional mandate to remain neutral in religious and ideological matters. But the principle of neutrality must not be construed as indifference toward such matters. The church-state articles of the Weimar Constitution, which have been incorporated into Article 140 of the Basic Law, envision neutrality in the sense of cooperation between the state, churches, and religious communities. These articles [may even require the state] to support churches and religious communities.

The mere presence of the cross demands no particular mode of conduct and does not convert the school into a missionary enterprise.

KJELDSEN, BUSK MADSEN AND PEDERSEN v. DENMARK

European Court of Human Rights.
1 E.H.R.R. 711 (1976).

[A 1970 amendment to the State Schools Act introduced, among other items, mandatory sex education into the curriculum of Danish state primary schools to address sexual insecurities and promote responsibility among students. Applicant Kjeldsen's daughter was a student in a state school; the School Board refused to grant her free private education. The closest private school was 19 kilometers from the family's home. The daughter had diabetes and could not be away from home for long periods of time. The ministry refused to exempt her from attending sex-education classes. The applicants consider themselves wronged in relation to their "Christian convictions" as a result of the obligation on their children to take part in "detailed" and vulgar teachings on sexual matters.]

* * *

I.   ON THE ALLEGED VIOLATION OF ARTICLE 2 OF PROTOCOL No. 1 (P1–2)

49.   The applicants invoke Article 2 of Protocol No. 1 (P1–2) which provides: "No person shall be denied the right to education. In the exercise of any functions which it assumes in relation to education and to teaching, the State shall respect the right of parents to ensure such education and teaching in conformity with their own religious and philosophical convictions."

50.   * * * The Government * * * emphasised that Denmark does not force parents to entrust their children to the State schools; it allows parents to educate their children, or to have them educated, at home and, above all, to send them to private institutions to which the State pays very substantial subsidies, thereby assuming a "function in relation to education and to teaching", within the meaning of Article 2 (P1–2). Denmark, it was submitted, thereby discharged the obligations resulting from the second sentence of this provision.

The Court notes that in Denmark private schools co-exist with a system of public education. The second sentence of Article 2 (P1–2) is binding upon the Contracting States in the exercise of each and every function—it speaks of "any functions"—that they undertake in the sphere of education and teaching, including that consisting of the organisation and financing of public education. Furthermore, the second sentence of Article 2 (P1–2) must be read together with the first which enshrines the right of everyone to education. It is on to this fundamental right that is grafted the right of parents to respect for their religious and philosophical convictions, and the first sentence does not distinguish, any more than the second, between State and private teaching. * * * The second sentence of Article 2 (P1–2) aims in short at safeguarding the possibility of pluralism in education which possibility is essential for the preservation of the "democratic society" as conceived by the Convention. In view of the power of the modern State, it is above all through State teaching that this aim must be realised.

The Court thus concludes, as the Commission did unanimously, that the Danish State schools do not fall outside the province of Protocol No. 1 (P1). In its investigation as to whether Article 2 (P1–2) has been violated, the Court cannot forget, however, that the functions assumed by Denmark in relation to education and to teaching include the grant of substantial assistance to private schools. Although recourse to these schools involves parents in sacrifices which were justifiably mentioned by the applicants, the alternative solution it provides constitutes a factor that should not be disregarded in this case * * *

51. The Government pleaded in the alternative that the second sentence of Article 2 (P1–2), assuming that it governed even the State schools where attendance is not obligatory, implies solely the right for parents to have their children exempted from classes offering "religious instruction of a denominational character".

The Court does not share this view. Article 2 (P1–2), which applies to each of the State's functions in relation to education and to teaching, does not permit a distinction to be drawn between religious instruction and other subjects. It enjoins the State to respect parents' convictions, be they religious or philosophical, throughout the entire State education programme.

52. As is shown by its very structure, Article 2 (P1–2) constitutes a whole that is dominated by its first sentence. By binding themselves not to "deny the right to education", the Contracting States guarantee to anyone within their jurisdiction "a right of access to educational institutions existing at a given time" and "the possibility of drawing", by "official recognition of the studies which he has completed", "profit from the education received" (judgment of 23 July 1968 on the merits of the "Belgian Linguistic" case, Series A no. 6, pp. 30–32, paras. 3–5).

The right set out in the second sentence of Article 2 (P1–2) is an adjunct of this fundamental right to education (paragraph 50 above). It is in the discharge of a natural duty towards their children—parents being primarily responsible for the "education and teaching" of their children—that parents may require the State to respect their religious and philosophical convictions. Their right thus corresponds to a responsibility closely linked to the enjoyment and the exercise of the right to education. * * *

53. * * * [T]he setting and planning of the curriculum fall in principle within the competence of the Contracting States. * * * In particular, the second sentence of Article 2 of the Protocol (P1–2) does not prevent States from imparting through teaching or education information or knowledge of a directly or indirectly religious or philosophical kind. It does not even permit parents to object to the integration of such teaching or education in the school curriculum, for otherwise all institutionalised teaching would run the risk of proving impracticable. In fact, it seems very difficult for many subjects taught at school not to have, to

a greater or lesser extent, some philosophical complexion or implications. The same is true of religious affinities if one remembers the existence of religions forming a very broad dogmatic and moral entity which has or may have answers to every question of a philosophical, cosmological or moral nature.

The second sentence of Article 2 (P1–2) implies on the other hand that the State, in fulfilling the functions assumed by it in regard to education and teaching, must take care that information or knowledge included in the curriculum is conveyed in an objective, critical and pluralistic manner. The State is forbidden to pursue an aim of indoctrination that might be considered as not respecting parents' religious and philosophical convictions. That is the limit that must not be exceeded. * * *

54. * * * The [sex] instruction, as provided for and organized by the contested legislation, is principally intended to give pupils better information; this emerges from, inter alia, the preface to the "Guide" of April 1971.

Even when circumscribed in this way, such instruction clearly cannot exclude on the part of teachers certain assessments capable of encroaching on the religious or philosophical sphere; for what are involved are matters where appraisals of fact easily lead on to value-judgments. * * * [T]he Danish State, by providing children in good time with explanations it considers useful, is attempting to warn them against phenomena it views as disturbing, for example, the excessive frequency of births out of wedlock, induced abortions and venereal diseases. * * *

These considerations are indeed of a moral order, but they are very general in character and do not entail overstepping the bounds of what a democratic State may regard as the public interest. Examination of the legislation in dispute establishes in fact that it in no way amounts to an attempt at indoctrination aimed at advocating a specific kind of sexual behaviour. It does not make a point of exalting sex or inciting pupils to indulge precociously in practices that are dangerous for their stability, health or future or that many parents consider reprehensible. Further, it does not affect the right of parents to enlighten and advise their children, to exercise with regard to their children natural parental functions as educators, or to guide their children on a path in line with the parents' own religious or philosophical convictions.

Certainly, abuses can occur as to the manner in which the provisions in force are applied by a given school or teacher and the competent authorities have a duty to take the utmost care to see to it that parents' religious and philosophical convictions are not disregarded at this level by carelessness, lack of judgment or misplaced proselytism. However, it follows from the Commission's decisions on the admissibility of the applications that the Court is not at present seised of a problem of this kind (paragraph 48 above). * * * The Court consequently reaches the conclusion that the disputed legislation in itself in no way offends the applicants' religious and philosophical convictions to the extent forbidden by the second sentence of Article 2 of the Protocol (P1–2), interpreted in the light of its first sentence and of the whole of the Convention.

Besides, the Danish State preserves an important expedient for parents who, in the name of their creed or opinions, wish to dissociate their children from integrated sex education; it allows parents either to entrust their children to private schools, which are bound by less strict obligations and moreover heavily subsidized by the State or to educate them or have them educated at home, subject to suffering the undeniable sacrifices and inconveniences caused by recourse to one of those alternative solutions.

* * *

Separate Opinion of Judge Verdross

* * *

Article 2 (P1–2) * * * requires the States, in an unqualified manner, to respect parents' religious and philosophical convictions; it makes no distinction at all between the different purposes for which the education is provided. Since the applicants consider themselves wronged in relation to their "Christian convictions" as a result of the obligation on their children to take part in "detailed" teaching on sexual matters, the Court ought to have restricted itself to ascertaining whether, should there have been any doubt, this complaint tallied or not with the beliefs professed by the applicants. * * * The distinction between information on the knowledge of man's sexuality in general and that concerning sexual practices is recognised under the Danish legislation itself. While private schools are required under the legislation to include in their curricula a biology course on the reproduction of man, they are left the choice whether or not to comply with the other rules compulsory for State schools in sexual matters. The legislature itself is thereby conceding that information on sexual activity may be separated from other information on the subject and that, consequently, an exemption granted to children in respect of a specific course of the first category does not prevent the integration in the school system of scientific knowledge on the subject.

The Danish Act on State schools does not in any way exempt the children of parents having religious convictions at variance with those of the legislature from attending the whole range of classes on sex education. The conclusion must therefore be that the Danish Act, within the limits indicated above, is not in harmony with the second sentence of Article 2 of Protocol No. 1 (P1–2).

Notes and Questions

1. The USSC's position on religious education (and state support to students in denominational schools) in a system of separation is extremely complex:

> [A] provision for therapeutic and diagnostic health services to parochial school pupils by public employees is invalid if provided in the parochial school, but not if offered at a neutral site, even if in a mobile unit adjacent to the parochial school. Reimbursement to parochial schools for the expense of administering teacher-prepared tests required by state law is invalid, but the state may reimburse parochial schools for the expense of administering state-prepared tests. The state may lend school

textbooks to parochial school pupils because, the Court has explained, the books can be checked in advance for religious content and are 'self-policing'; but the state may not lend other seemingly self-policing instructional items such as tape recorders and maps. The state may pay the cost of bus transportation to parochial schools, which the Court has ruled are 'permeated' with religion; but the state is forbidden to pay for field trip transportation visits 'to governmental, industrial, cultural, and scientific centers designed to enrich the secular studies of students.'

Jesse H. Choper, *The Religion Clauses of the First Amendment: Reconciling the Conflict*, 41 U. Pitt. L. Rev. 673, 680–681 (1980) (footnotes omitted).

2.   The ICC finds the Protocol to the Lateran Treaty to be constitutional. The Court envisions a regime where all students have to make an express declaration regarding enrollment in Catholic instruction. If there is no declaration, there is no religious instruction. Does this interpretation conform with the Protocol Treaty? Does a default rule that requires positive action to be enrolled for religious instruction impose a burden on free exercise? Is this burden greater or lesser than the burden on the nonreligious student who must opt out? Is the position of the majority in the classroom relevant in this context? Is it relevant that the instruction takes place in state-sponsored public (secular) schools? The ICC describes a certain historical trend in church–state relations. Where would you put the current German arrangement on that continuum? While an increasing number of liberal constitutions expressly reject the idea of a state church, there is a continued trend to single out a national church allegedly because it represents the majority religion or it played a particular role in the nation's history. Such a privileged position creates serious tensions with the equality provisions of constitutions. This was the case with the Italian Constitution, in particular, because the Lateran Agreement (including the Concordat) implied that the Catholic religion be accepted as the state religion, which further implied the prohibition of abortion and divorce. Only in 1984, with the Additional Protocol to the Concordat, was the state-religion status expressly abolished. See the liberal interpretation of the Additional Protocol above. Italian governments continued with the practice of individual agreements with churches. It is argued that the individual agreements better serve the interests of churches and religions than neutral general laws; such individualized treatment acknowledges the individual identity of the religions. Would a general, uniform treatment simply impose the dictates and concerns of a majority religion?

The ICC found that the respect for religious freedom is a matter of individual conscience that is related to personal intimacy. This might be called the "privatization of religion." The Court concluded that the choice of having, or not having, religious education in school should not be conditioned upon the choice of another school subject. (In practical terms there is no need to provide alternative classes to the religion class.) Does this personal choice in education reflect the new understanding of church–state relations? Is it related to a personal (private) concept of religion?

The dissenters in the *Crucifix Case* argue that the negative freedom of religion of the complaining parents must not be allowed to negate the positive right to manifest one's religious freedom. Can the official placement of the cross in the classroom be characterized as the exercise of the positive right of religious parents? What if the crucifix is brought to class upon the initiative of the majority of parents? What are the rights to be balanced against such parental rights?

3. Consider Bernhard Schlink, *Between Secularization and Multiculturalism*, in *The Law of Religious Identity: Models for Post–Communism* 77–80 (András Sajó and Shlomo Avineri eds., 1999):

> [O]ne reason the reaction in Germany was so strong to the [*Crucifix*] decision was that previous Constitutional Court decisions had intimated the possibility of a different decision, one that would accept the hanging of crucifixes in courtrooms to be unconstitutional only under very specific conditions: the plaintiff had been Jewish and unwilling, because of Jewish history, to participate in a trial "under the cross." The Court had then assumed that a crucifix or cross in the courtroom would not, as a rule, be an imposition, as it required neither identification with the content it symbolized, nor any other behavior.[2] * * * Here and there the foreign press, reporting on the crucifix decision, called it a delayed German extension of secularization, even an overdue one in comparison with other countries. In fact, the German Constitutional Court's crucifix decision fits smoothly, if not into its line of precedent, then into the line of social development. The crucifix in the courtroom, though rescued by the Court, is hardly ever seen anymore, and school prayer, despite its justification by the Court, is rarely heard. Like the crucifix in the courtroom and school prayer, the crucifix in the classroom has no real function. In the past it existed because it, and its acceptance, were taken for granted. But the legal battle—which was covered by the media, catalyzed parallel trials, and led to negotiations, and eventually to debates in Parliament—ended the taking for granted of the crucifix in the classroom. That is secularization: when the worldly unity of the spiritual and the secular ceases to be taken for granted. * * * But religious feelings and customs are not brought to class by students alone. The state itself introduces them: in Germany, the state of North Rhine–Westphalia was the first to introduce Muslim religious instruction into the schools, and other states followed its lead. At the same time, North Rhine–Westphalia is attempting to gain better, stricter control over, and under some circumstances to prohibit, Koran schools sponsored by Islamic associations in which children between 7 and 16 are given religious training, sometimes in a boarding school situation.[11]

This simultaneity of two opposing trends calls forth the fear expressed on the occasion of the crucifix decision. Retreat and expulsion of Christian and European values from the public and educational spheres to make way for Muslims or sects? Loss of an Occidental orientation in favor of what? What cultural identity can be passed on to our children under these conditions?

In the case of Muslim students in a predominantly Christian society, whose interests should prevail in matters of religious education? Should the educational and religious rights of the Muslim parents be respected against the interest of social homogenization? Is it not the case that by protecting religious freedoms it is the minority group coherence that is protected? Why do France, Germany, and the UK differ so markedly? Is this related to

---

2. 35 BVerfGE 366, 375.

11. OVG Münster, RdJB (1989) 346 ff.

secular differences? Is it because of the differences in social tensions related to the size and difference of the immigrant minorities?

4.   The German and Italian constitutions do not provide for the separation of church and state; state support for denominational schools, in principle, is permissible. In Ireland, the Constitution expressly provides for state aid to denominational schools. In *Campaign to Separate Church and State*[z] Justice Barrington found that "Article 42.2 [of the Irish Constitution] establishes that * * * children may receive 'religious education in schools recognised or established by the State but in accordance with the wishes of the parents' (p 25). Those children are entitled to 'religious education' and not merely 'religious instruction.' Barrington J. explains that the former term is a much wider one than the latter, though he does not explain what precisely either means." Rory O'Connell, *Theories of Religious Education in Ireland* 14 J.L. & Religion 433, 510–11 (1999–2000). Contrary to the constitutions mentioned above, the Hungarian Constitution states that the church is separate from the state. Nevertheless, the HCC found it constitutional that denominational schools be supported by the state and that nonreligious parents should send their children to denominational schools if there is no other state-operated public school available:

> The State's neutrality in connection with the right to freedom of religion does not mean inactivity. The State's obligation is to ensure a field, where the declaration of religious convictions, its teaching and following in life, the work of churches as well as the denial of religion—and to ensure situations under which different ideas can occur and develop and enable the free formation of personal convictions. On the one hand the State should ensure this process of expression which actually comes from the right to freedom of thought and public speech. On the other hand it should concern itself with the defence of other fundamental rights against the freedom of religion. Finally there could be a need for the positive regulation of the right to freedom of religion. The State should make a regulated compromise where the State structure creates such a situation in which the religious and non-religious limits are mutually exclusive. Such a "situation" for example would be ideological education under compulsory school education. * * * The State cannot refuse the legal possibility of establishing denominational or atheist schools, it should enact a law to satisfy these needs. The State is not

z. *Campaign to Separate Church and State v. Minister of Education* [1998] 3 IR 321. "The Campaign to Separate Church and State, a secularist lobby group, initiated legal action challenging the constitutionality of the State paying chaplains in community schools * * * The group argued that the (£) 1.2 million in payments made annually to chaplains in such schools represented a breach of Article 44 (2.2) of the Constitution, which gives a guarantee that the State would not endow any religion." Andy Pollack, *Challenge on Chaplains Pay Initiated in 1988*, The Irish Times, March 26, 1998.

Rory O'Connell, *Theories of Religious Education in Ireland* 14 J.L. & Religion 433, 519 (1999–2000):

In Campaign to Separate Church and State Barrington J. sought to decide not just the issue of chaplains' salaries, which was before the Court, but also the integrated curriculum controversy which was not before the Court. He decides, even though it is not an issue, that: "A religious denomination is not obliged to change the general atmosphere of its school merely to accommodate a child of a different religious persuasion who wishes to attend the school."

Barrington J. took advantage of this opportunity to give a narrow interpretation to the conscience clause in Article 44.2.4, an interpretation which is strikingly indifferent to the powerfully expressed concerns of the German Constitutional Court in the Classroom Crucifix case.

obliged to establish non-neutral schools. If the church or parents establish or run committed schools, the State should support them in proportion to their undertaking the State's programmes at these institutions and also cannot withhold support if it supports another institution very similar in ideas to the non-supported one and so there is no constitutional reason for making such a difference.

Decision 4/ 1993 (II.12.) AB hat.

The HCC followed almost literally the GFCC's reasoning in the *Interdenominational School Case*, notwithstanding the clear differences in the constitutional text and in the role of religion in the two societies. (Only 10 percent of the Hungarians are active Churchgoers, primarily Catholic.) In this case, are cultural convictions more important than the constitutional text? Is the Hungarian approach related to the specific needs of postcommunism? Postcommunist societies were in search of "normalcy" that implied, at least for the conservative majority in political power, similarity to Germany, a country perceived as the model of "normalcy."

5. The funding of denominational schools also came up in Canada:

[F]ailure to act in order to facilitate the practice of religion cannot be considered state interference with freedom of religion. The fact that no funding is provided for private religious education cannot be considered to infringe the appellants' freedom to educate their children in accordance with their religious beliefs where there is no restriction on religious schooling. As submitted by the intervener, the Canadian Civil Liberties Association, there are many spheres of government action which hold religious significance for religious believers. It does not follow that the government must pay for the religious dimensions of spheres in which it takes a role. If this flowed from s. 2(a), then religious marriages, religious corporations, and other religious community institutions such as churches and hospitals would all have a Charter claim to public funding.

Adler et al. v. The Queen in Right of Ontario et al., [1996] 3 S.C.R. 609, 702–03 (Justice Sopinka).[aa]

Does the requirement of compulsory education in Canada infringe upon the freedom of religion of parents who must pay to send their children to denominational schools by imposing a burden on them not borne by persons of other religions or without religion? In Hungary, the government decided that both public and denominational schools are state funded. Is the Hun-

---

aa. In *Adler et al. v. The Queen in Right of Ontario et al.*, [1996] 3 S.C.R. 609, 702–03, Justice Sopinka wrote:

The appellants are parents who, by reason of religious or conscientious beliefs, send their children to private religious schools. As I see the issues before us, this case is to be resolved with reference to S. 93 of the *Constitution Act, 1867*. Section 93 grants to the provinces the power to legislate with regard to education. This grant is subject to certain restrictive conditions, among them s. 93(*l*) which provides that no law may prejudicially affect any right or privilege with respect to denominational schools which any class of

persons had at the time of Union. The effect of this subsection is to entrench constitutionally a special status for such classes of persons, granting them rights which are denied to others.

The appellants [argue that] s. 2(a)'s guarantee of freedom of religion requires the Province of Ontario to provide public funding for independent religious schools. * * * [It] is my opinion that the s. 2(a) claim fails because any claim to public support for religious education must be grounded in s. 93(i), which is a "comprehensive code" of denominational school rights.

garian approach more equitable from the perspective of freedom of religion? In the Hungarian case the issue was whether the restitution of school buildings to churches (which triggers public funding) was constitutional. The schools were confiscated by the Communists. In the Canadian case the issue for the majority was whether the right to free exercise combined with equality obliges the state to fund private-school (primarily denominational-school) attendance. In Hungary, the result of the Court's holding was that certain churches that were established before communism and owned buildings were entitled to school buildings, which triggered funding for teaching activities. Certain religions, e.g., Jehovah's Witnesses, which were not "recognized" by the state before World War Two and could not, therefore, own property, did not qualify for such treatment. The same applies to newer religions that could not own schools because they could not acquire property during the communist era. The return of buildings re-created a precommunist disparity.

6. *Poland.*

Religious classes in the public school system were taught under communism until 1961. However, since 15 September 1945 religious classes were not obligatory as they were before World War II. In 1961 religious classes were removed from public schools on the legal basis of the Statute of 15 July 1961, which dealt with the educational system.

Religious education was provisionally re-introduced in public schools in 1990 on the basis of instruction promulgated by the Minister of Education on 3 August (for the Catholic Church) and on 24 August (for other denominations). However, this action was subsequently challenged by the Ombudsman. The Constitutional Tribunal decided that this regulation was valid and did not recognize that this low level regulation was in conflict with statutory regulations.[37] * * *

According to the binding legal regulations, religious classes may be organized in public schools (elementary and secondary level) at the request of parents of students. For secondary level students who do not participate in religious classes, ethics classes are substituted. Schools have the obligation to organize religious classes if there are at least seven pupils of the same denomination. Further, schools can provide gratuitously the school building for religious teachings organized outside of the public educational system by other, smaller churches and denominations. Religious classes are organized within the curriculum of studies.

Schools employ teachers of religion appointed by the diocesan bishop or another superior of the church. The authorities of particular churches evaluate the professional qualifications of teachers of religious classes and make decisions on dismissal of the teachers. School authorities supervise the educational qualifications of teachers and inform them of their conclusion about the effectiveness of the teacher, whether average or superior.

Teachers of religious classes are included in the pedagogical board of teachers, but cannot perform duties of a form master (class patrol). There are two religious classes per week under ordinary approval, or one hour of religious teaching with another superior's approval. In practice there is usually only one hour. A student's grade in religion classes is

37. The decision of the Constitutional Tribunal of 30 January 1991, No. K. 11/90.

placed on the school's certificate, but the grade of religious teaching doesn't affect promotion to the next class. Pupils attending religious classes have three consecutive days off for Lent retreat.

It is permissible to place a cross in the classroom. Pupils can also say prayers before and after classes.

* * * It is worth noting that the preamble to the Statute on Education of 1991 indicates that Christian values should be respected in the process of education.

Krystyna Daniel and W. Cole Durham, Jr., *Religious Identity as a Component of National Identity: Implications for Emerging Church–State Relations in the Former Socialist Bloc*, in *The Law of Religious Identity: Models for Post–Communism* 117, 132–33 (András Sajó and Shlomo Avineri eds., 1999).

7. In France, the 1959 *loi* Debré grants the possibility of state support to denominational schools that enter into contractual agreements with local municipalities. Given the principle of *laïcité*, the support is not to denominational but to private educational facilities. The Act states that:

> The State proclaims and respects the freedom of education, and guarantees its exercise to all private establishments operating lawfully. * * * In the private establishments that have made a contract as provided above, the teaching taking place under the regime of the contract is subject to control by the State. The establishment, while retaining its own specific character, has to provide this teaching in total respect for freedom of conscience. All children shall have access to it, without discrimination as to origins, opinions, or beliefs.

The issue was never considered fully settled. In 1977, the Right introduced an amendment (the *loi* Guermeur) to the 1959 Act, to make the contracts of association easier, turning the system into a direct-grant system and requiring educators within private institutions, who are appointed and paid by the state, to respect the character of the private educational establishment (primarily religion). The requirement of respect for the religious character of the establishment, an expression not used in the "neutral" approach to private education, was challenged on grounds of freedom of conscience. The Constitutional Council found that freedom of conscience is a fundamental principle recognized by the laws of the Republic (77–87 DC of 23 Nov. 1977). (It was not discussed as a right, although this was a possibility under the French Declaration of 1789.) The Council found that the law, by imposing the obligation of respect, did not violate the principle. In other words the "duty to respect" is permissible per se, as long as it does not violate the freedom of conscience in practice.

In 1984, the Left introduced changes to the 1959 arrangement, requiring private schools to operate according to requirements applicable to state schools. It repealed the provision of the 1977 amendment that required teachers to respect the specific character of the establishment where they taught. During the debates, mass demonstrations were held, and the Catholic Church condemned the draft. In 84–185 DC of 18 Jan. 1985, the Constitutional Council considered the matter again as a problem of the principle of freedom of education and not one of religion, and the repealing amendment was interpreted to mean that it would not violate freedom of education. It reasoned that even if the 1977 amendment were repealed, respect for the specific character of an establishment applied, and, therefore, the repeal did not violate the Constitution. Did the Council agree to the repeal of the affirmative formulation only because it found it immaterial (repetitive)? Do the French jurists play word games when they claim *laïcité* while the state provides money and respect to religious schools? Whose rights are recognized in the French scheme? Is the French system acceptable under a strict separationist model? (See Chapter 6 for the equality aspects.)

8. *The veil in class.* The observance of Islamic dress codes in secular Western schools resulted in a number of high-profile cases. If teachers wear scarves etc., the issue is whether the free exercise right of the teacher should be accommodated. The right is generally recognized, but it is not held inviolable, as the following Swiss decision indicates: "It follows that in the same way as other constitutional liberties the freedom of religion of the appellant can be limited as long as the restriction is based on a sufficient legal basis, responds to a preponderant public interest and respects the principle of proportionality." Swiss Federal Tribunal, Second Court of Public Law of 12 Nov. 1997.[bb] The court found prevailing public interest in the neutrality of education in a state where the church is separate from the state and ruled that, in such circumstances, coercion of children had to be prevented.

In the U.S., the Supreme Court of Oregon upheld a teacher's dismissal. *Cooper v. Eugene School District No. 4J*, 723 P.2d 298 (1986), concerned a Sikh teacher, whose teaching certificate was revoked for violating the dress code—wearing a white turban. The Court said that: "If such a law is to be valid, it must be justified by a determination that religious dress necessarily contravenes the wearer's role or function at the time and place beyond any realistic means of accommodation." *Id.* at 307. The "revocation of teaching certificate was * * * based upon one's doing so in manner incompatible with that function, rather than 'sanction' by reason of hostility to religious and political belief." *Id.* at 313. In *United States v. Board of Education for the School District of Philadelphia*, 911 F.2d 882 (1990), in a Title VII action against the school board challenging its refusal to allow a public school teacher to wear religious attire in the course of her duties, the U.S. Court of Appeals, Third Circuit, held that it would have imposed undue hardship to require the school board to accommodate a Muslim public school teacher by allowing her to teach in religious garb. Is a dress code a "general rule" (like in *Smith*), or is it directed against religion? Both the Swiss and American approaches are based on the assumption that the dress code is the least burdensome solution to the requirements of school neutrality. Do you think that state neutrality means that free exercise claims are or might be disregarded for government employees? Is this consistent with the accommo-

---

bb. Other foreign decisions were quoted in this respect by the Swiss Court:

In Germany, on September 9, 1985 the Superior Administrative Tribunal of Munich confirmed the prohibition directed to a public school teacher to wear within the confines of the school clothes of a color dictated by the prescriptions of the Bhagwan religious movement (red tones, ranging from pink to dark purple). The Administrative Tribunal held that a teacher who constantly and routinely conveys, by his dress, that he adheres to certain religious convictions, necessarily brings his students to be preoccupied with his ideas. * * * In France, in an opinion dated October 20, 1994, the Administrative Tribunal of Bordeaux accepted an appeal made by a nursing student who was dismissed from her school because she refused to give up wearing her veil or a surgical cap, even though the veil or cap could deeply trouble certain patients in the psychiatric unit where she was to perform her rotation.

dation of school children's beliefs? Note that in most contested cases the teachers are religious minorities.

The problem of Muslim children wearing scarfs was discussed, in France, in the context of school neutrality. Michel Troper, *The Problem of the Islamic Veil and the Principle of School Neutrality in France, op.cit.*, at 90, 96-97, said:

> On 7 October 1989, three female students at a public secondary school in the Paris area repeatedly refused to remove their Islamic veils in class and were expelled from school. Thereafter, several other schools took similar action. The incidents raised a storm of controversy in France. * * * [The North–African immigrants seemed foreign to French traditions and were subject to strong prejudice. In its advisory opinion, the *Conseil d'État*[cc] considered the implications of *laïcité* and emphasized (a) neutrality of the schools and (b) freedom of conscience of the students. It found applicable 'limits on the freedom of students to wear symbols where such symbols are used as instruments of religious propaganda within the school (this would be incompatible with the principle of neutrality) or where they begin to hinder normal school activities or jeopardize public order within the schools.' The determination whether a specific use is permissible was left to the school principal.] In the *Aoukili* case,[9] the *Conseil d'État* upheld the punishment of two girls who had refused to take off their veil during a physical education class. The punishment was considered justified in that case:

> a) because it is dangerous to take part in sports with a veil and

> b) because the girls' parents stood outside the school demonstrating for a strict observance of Islam and handing out brochures, which the court interpreted as evidence that the veil was not a mere symbol but an instrument of religious propaganda.

In Germany, a ruling of the German Federal Administrative Court[dd] excused Muslim schoolgirls from coeducational swimming lessons.

> The administrative court with jurisdiction over the matter first decided that a Muslim girl could, and was required to, participate in gym classes in loose clothing that "on the one hand concealed her body contours, and on the other permitted the necessary freedom of movement for sports activities," as well as in a head covering.[7] The schoolgirl argued on appeal before the Federal Administrative Court not only that she "feared that even in such clothing, her body's contours would be visible, and she might lose her head covering," but that she was "forced to look at the boys exercising in their short or tight sports clothing, which she was also not permitted to do." The Federal Administrative Court found in her favor, saying her freedom of religion could be honored only if she were excused from gym classes.[8]

cc. Opinion of 27 November 1989 concerning *laïcité*, RFSP (1991) 45.

9. 10 March 1995, AJDA (1995) 322, concl. Aguila. On 27 November 1996 the *Conseil d'Etat* decided a large number of appeals in cases involving the veil. In 23 cases, it upheld decisions by school principals to exclude girls wearing the veil, based on some interference with public order. On the other hand, seven decisions were struck down because the girls had been punished for no other reason than the wearing of the veil.

dd. 94 BVerwGE 82.

7. OVG Münster, RdJB 409, 411 (1992).

8. 94 BVerfGE 82, 89ff.

Schlink, *op. cit.* at 79.

The European Commission found in *Karaduman v. Turkey* (Application no. 16278/90, 74 DR 93 (1993)) that the wearing of a Muslim headscarf by a student was not a manifestation of a religious belief.

9.   There is a certain constitutional permissiveness as to general public funding of religious education, not necessarily to promote the free exercise right but simply because courts, with the exception of the U.S., find this basically to be a legitimate legislative choice. In some Continental countries, religious education (including instruction) is permissible in public schools, as long as it is not coercive. What amounts to "coercive" differs among countries. In addition, as the German cases indicate, there is an ongoing change in the sensitivity within the country. The USSC found coercion at a graduation ceremony where a nondenominational prayer was delivered. *Lee v. Weisman* 505 U.S. 577, 580 (1992). But in *Good News Club et al. v. Milford Central School,* 533 U.S. 98 (2001), it found permissible a school's decision that authorized district residents to use its building after school for, among other things (arguably religiously motivated), educational and social uses. In the Court's view the children would not perceive that the school was endorsing the club and would not feel coerced to participate because the club's activities occurred on school grounds. "[E]ven if we were to inquire into the minds of schoolchildren in this case, we cannot say the danger that children would misperceive the endorsement of religion is any greater than the danger that they would perceive a hostility toward the religious viewpoint if the Club were excluded from the public forum." 533 U.S. at 100. Cf. *Capitol Square Review and Advisory Bd. v. Pinette*, 515 U.S. 753, 779–80 (1995) (Justice O'Connor, concurring in part and concurring in judgment) ("[B]ecause our concern is with the political community writ large, the endorsement inquiry is *not about the perceptions of particular individuals* or saving isolated nonadherents from * * * discomfort") (emphasis added).

When it comes to the school curricula, certain countries are reluctant to grant exceptions on grounds of religious freedoms (*Kjeldsen* in Europe, and *Edwards*[ee] in the U.S.; see further, the reluctance to allow concessions to Muslims in the classroom). Is such reluctance understandable in light of the possibilities that exist to opt entirely out of the state school system? Note once again the homogenizing public function of state education!

ee. Louisiana statute that forbade "the teaching of the theory of evolution in public schools unless accompanied by instruction in 'creation science' " held unconstitutional.

Chapter 9

CRIMINAL PROCEDURE (DUE PROCESS)

Due process of law is the primary and indispensable foundation of individual freedom. It is the basic and essential term in the social compact which defines the rights of the individual and delimits the powers which the state may exercise....

In re Gault, 387 U.S. 1, 20 (1967)

Criminal procedure—which covers a range of issues that arise in pretrial, trial, and posttrial proceedings—is a large and often technical body of law. It is frequently treated as a separate topic and taught as a separate course. Much of it is nonconstitutional in nature. This chapter introduces some important criminal procedure issues that have constitutional dimensions.

A state's power to investigate, arrest, interrogate, try, and sentence an individual directly implicates the constitutional values of liberty, dignity, equality, fairness, and due process of law. (Constitutional issues concerning punishment are discussed in Chapter 5.) Procedural rules are designed to protect individual rights and constrain abusive and arbitrary behavior by state agents, such as the police, prosecutors, and judges. In this sense the constitutional nature of criminal procedure can be seen as an attempt to mediate the imbalance in power between the individual and the state.

While a detainee's or defendant's rights to fair treatment and a fair trial are guaranteed in most countries today, the specific rights that flow from these guarantees vary: as will be seen in this chapter, rights to silence, confrontation of witnesses, and speedy trial, among others, are often interpreted differently from country to country. Variations in interpretation may reflect genuine disagreement about the normative content of these rights, or they may result from the fact that they are being interpreted under very different systems of criminal procedure. In addition, an issue that is considered constitutional in one country can be nonconstitutional in another, complicating any comparative analysis.

The sources of criminal procedure rights vary greatly. In some cases such rights are explicit in a constitutional document; in others they have been recognized via national legislation (statute), ratification of international legal instruments, or judicial action. For example, in countries that fairly recently have experienced authoritarian or totalitarian government, such as Germany, Spain, and many in Eastern Europe and Latin America, constitutions and subsequent enabling legislation contain detailed and comprehensive lists of procedural rights designed to protect individuals from the arbitrary exercise of state power. In France, such rights are derived from the 1789 Declaration of the Rights of Man and of the Citizen, the principles listed in the Preamble of the 1946 Constitution, and the "unenumerated fundamental principles of the Republic." The French Constitutional Council has "discovered" that these principles contain rights such as the right to personal liberty and to a legal defense, thus elevating these rights to constitutional status. See Alec Stone Sweet, *Governing With Judges: Constitutional Politics In Europe* 99 (2000). Similarly, India initially had a limited approach to due process: Art. 21 of the Constitution provides that "[n]o person shall be deprived of his life or personal liberty except according to *procedure established by law*" (emphasis added). This approach was altered in 1978, when the Supreme Court of India construed the expression "procedure established by law" as meaning a procedure that is reasonable, fair, and just. *Maneka Gandhi v. Union of India,* A.I.R. 1978 S.C. 597, para. 56. Since this decision, India's Court has interpreted Art. 21 expansively, finding that it requires, among other things, that detainees have a speedy trial and a right to counsel and that conditions of detention must satisfy reasonableness, justice, and fairness (e.g., prisoners must be allowed to see their family members).

In the United States, the development of what is now called constitutional criminal procedure was a long, slow process, complicated by the federal structure of government. In the words of one commentator:

> [The U.S.] Constitution contained some restraints on the prosecution and punishment of individuals. No conviction for treason, for example, was permitted unless there were two corroborating witnesses, and the writ of habeas corpus could not be suspended. To promote individual autonomy, [the Bill of Rights] guaranteed rights to freedom of expression and against unreasonable searches and seizures. It assured criminal defendants the rights not to testify against themselves, to have assistance of counsel, and to be tried by an impartial jury. * * *

> Little enforcement occurred in the early history of the United States, however, largely because the U.S. Supreme Court held that the Bill of Rights constrained only the federal and not the state governments. The Court adhered to a doctrine of dual sovereignty, which accorded states maximal freedom to operate in areas not ceded in the Constitution itself. Among those areas was the administration of criminal justice.

> The dual sovereignty doctrine eroded as a result of decisions interpreting the Fourteenth Amendment, which provides in part that "[n]o State shall * * * deprive any person of life, liberty, or property, without due process of law." Litigation, sometimes supported by civil liberties and other organizations, drew national attention to states' abuses of defendants. Members of the U.S. Supreme Court further expressed concern that greater cooperation between federal and state officers, prompted by increasing cross-border crime, threatened the rights of the accused. In a

series of decisions spanning the twentieth century, the Court held that the Due Process Clause required the states to obey provisions in the Bill of Rights that served "fundamental fairness," a concept variously amplified as entailing principles of liberty and justice that are "at the base of all our civil and political institutions; "implicit in the concept of ordered liberty * * * enshrined in the history and the basic constitutional documents of English-speaking people" part of the Anglo–American legal heritage; "and essential to a fair trial." * * * Defendants, whether in state or federal court, were entitled to appointment of counsel, to a privilege against self-incrimination, to be free from illegal searches, and to a public trial before a jury of their peers. A government that denied those rights faced stiff sanctions, ranging from exclusion of evidence to reversal of conviction.

Out of this case law, decided by a Court that took seriously its constitutional role as a "bulwark" of liberty, a new model of criminal procedure emerged. It was derived not from any precise text, but from the Court's interpretation of the broad principles on which the United States was founded. Through this model the Court endeavored to serve both individual autonomy and public order, in a manner that is just and equal; that is, to use the Court's term, "fundamentally fair." The model has come to be called constitutional criminal procedure. It is constitutional" not because its rules appear in a constitution, though they may. Rather, it is "constitutional" in that it assumes that certain rights are part of the constitutive nature of civil society.

Diane Marie Amman, *Harmonic Convergence? Constitutional Criminal Procedure in an International Context*, 75 Ind. L.J. 809, 811–14, 833–35 (2000).

Whether due process rights are explicitly listed in a constitution, added to the constitutional fabric by subsequent action, or derived from higher principles via judicial interpretation, the reader should focus on the value accorded such rights and their practical effects. In order for rights to be genuine rather than paper guarantees, they must be embedded in cultures committed to the rule of law.

A state needs more than political will to ensure that these guarantees are enforced. Due process rights impose costly and burdensome obligations upon the state. A state needs sufficient financial and human resources and the administrative capacity to put them to use. "The constitutional right to due process—like the private right to bring an action in contract or tort—presupposes that * * * the state maintains and makes accessible complex and relatively transparent legal institutions within which the cumbersome formalities of fair, public, and understandable adjudication occur." Stephen Holmes and Cass Sunstein, *The Cost of Rights: Why Liberty Depends on Taxes* 53 (1999).

For example, a state must have the budget and the means to provide adequate and sufficient courtrooms; to recruit, train, monitor, and retain qualified personnel; to locate and compel witnesses to appear and testify; to appoint and pay for counsel if the defendant cannot afford a lawyer; to allow and process appeals; and to maintain and operate a bail system that allows a defendant the right to remain free pending trial. The logistical, financial, and technical burden of operating such a complex system helps explain why, in many countries, the gap between the promises of procedural protections and its realities remains vast.

Some nations that do provide a complex panoply of rights have developed short cuts to render the workload and cost manageable. It is not uncommon for a country to offer an abbreviated trial for very minor crimes. In addition, a trial can sometimes be replaced by either plea bargaining (as in the United States or England) or a penal order (as in Germany and many other Western European countries). In a plea bargain, the accused makes a deal with the prosecution to plead guilty, waiving the right to a trial in exchange for a more lenient sentence or some other benefit. The "deal" is then brought before a judge for approval. In the United States, where full-blown trials can be costly and can take a long time (in part because of the jury system), incentives to bargain are high. In some U.S. jurisdictions, up to 90 percent of cases are plea-bargained. The process has been criticized for denying the accused the full reach of their procedural and substantive rights, undermining the integrity of the criminal justice system, and being coercive. The United States Supreme Court, in *Santobello v. New York*, 404 U.S. 257, 260 (1971), found plea-bargaining to be "an essential component of the administration of justice. Properly administered, it is to be encouraged." Many European systems do not have the equivalent of the guilty plea. Bargaining can sometimes occur, however, although it differs from the U.S. practice. Bargaining developed incrementally in Germany, where it is used far less often than in the United States, is rare in cases involving violent or serious crimes, and shortens rather than replaces a trial. In Italy a form of bargaining was written into the 1988 Criminal Procedure Code. The penal order, used in much of Western Europe for routine and minor offenses, is a written summary procedure. See Craig Bradley, *Reforming the Criminal Trial*, 68 Ind. L.J. 659 (1991), and Joachim Herrmann, *Models for the Reform of the Criminal Trial in Eastern Europe: A Comparative Perspective*, 1996 St. Louis–Warsaw Transatlantic L.J. 27, 147.

A. ADVERSARIAL VS. INQUISITORIAL SYSTEMS

Because the protection and provision of procedural rights depend so heavily on state institutions, the structure and organization of institutions—and perceptions of their purpose and functions—color the quality and nature of these rights. A sophisticated analysis of procedural systems has classified them according to two sets of models. A system is "hierarchical or co-ordinate," depending on how procedural authority is structured within a system, and is either "conflict-solving or policy-implementing," depending on whether the system perceives the purpose of adjudication primarily as a means to settle a conflict that has arisen in society or as a means to impose state policy choices. Mirjan Damaska, *The Faces of Justice and State Authority: A Comparative Approach to the Legal Process* (1986). See also Oscar G. Chase, *American "Exceptionalism" and Comparative Procedure*, 50 Am. J. Comp. L. 277 (2002) (primarily from a civil case perspective).

More commonly, systems of criminal procedure are classified as either adversarial or inquisitorial. Adversarial systems are associated with the English and U.S. common law tradition, and inquisitorial systems are associated with the European civil law tradition. Adversarial systems are typically described as being dominated by the parties, who collect and present evidence before a judge with limited supervisory authority and a jury. The underlying rationale of such systems is that truth is more likely to be uncovered where parties advocate zealously on their own behalf. Inquisitorial systems, on the other hand, typically allow the police and prosecution to develop the initial case file, with the judge playing a central role at trial in the calling and questioning of witnesses. The rationale for this system is that it is better to have the state leading an investigation into the truth, rather than allowing the parties perhaps to obscure the truth by manipulating the evidence to suit their respective objectives.

In adversarial systems the police work with the prosecution, developing a case against the accused and sharing their findings only with the prosecution. The defendant may gain access to this information only through discovery rules, designed to counteract the inequality in resources between the two parties. In inquisitorial systems police are supposed to play an impartial role in working alongside other state employees (e.g., forensic psychiatrists and scientists) to develop a single case file out of which everyone at trial (prosecution, defense, and judge) will work. Lay juries, which decide questions of fact, are characteristic of adversarial systems, while in inquisitorial systems questions of law and fact are decided together by judges or by mixed bodies of judges and laypersons.

Scholars have increasingly recognized that adversarial and inquisitorial traditions represent opposite ends of a spectrum describing the type and degree of the state's role in prosecuting citizens. Most systems of criminal procedure do not conform to a purely adversarial or inquisitorial model: they combine elements from each.

Even where distinctions between adversarial and inquisitorial systems may once have been fairly clear, there appears to be a gradual convergence between the two types of systems. Nico Jörg, Stewart Field, and Chrisje Brants comment: "[I]nquisitorial procedure is increasingly influenced by the necessity of fairness in truth-finding at the trial stage, while there are some (less developed) indications that adversarial procedure is beginning to take on more direct truth-finding characteristics. * * * All of this suggests gradual convergence. [But] we must not lose sight of the risk involved in adopting strategies and safeguards from each other's procedural styles. Each depends on its own historically developed institutions and the faith that different societies place in them." *Are Inquisitorial and Adversarial Systems Converging?*, in *Criminal Justice in Europe* 41 (Christopher Harding, Phil Fennell, Nico Jörg, and Bert Stewart eds., 1995).

Examples of these trends may be seen in Italy and Latin America.

Italy. In 1988, Italy promulgated a new Code of Criminal Procedure, which established an adversarial system of procedure in place of the previous inquisitorial one. The move responded, among other things, to complaints that the inquisitorial system, by allowing the judge both to investigate and determine guilt, created the potential for prejudice against defendants. The new system puts the prosecution and defense on equal ground. The judge's function is to try both law and fact.

The new system has been criticized for retaining elements of the previous inquisitorial system and thus undermining the goal of fairness between the parties. See Elisabetta Grande, *Italian Criminal Justice: Borrowing and Resistance*, 48 Am. J. Comp. L. 227 (2000). In particular, it appears that truth-seeking is still a central goal of the system, to the detriment of parity. For example, in 1992 the Italian Constitutional Court (ICC) held partially unconstitutional a section of the new Code that would have excluded out-of-court statements by witnesses, on the ground that in order to discover the truth, trial judges, as the triers of fact, need to be able to take such information into account. See Judgment n. 255/1992.

Latin America. Efforts are underway in several Latin American countries (including Bolivia, Chile, and Ecuador) to move from an inquisitorial system to a more adversarial one. The transition requires substantial modification in the functions performed by governmental institutions like the Public Ministry, which under the inquisitorial system had a relatively passive role and will now supervise the investigation phase of the criminal process. In Chile, where there was formerly no such ministry, one has been created. As a result of the change, penal judges are no longer in charge of conducting investigations; their function is now exclusively adjudicatory. The transitions were motivated, in part, by problems resulting from the lack of resources of judges, who faced great difficulties and delays in conducting investigations. Nonetheless, concerns remain about the ability of the different institutions, without substantial training and new funding, to perform their new roles adequately.

Adversarial systems emphasize parity, and inquisitorial systems emphasize the search for truth. Will a combination of elements from the two models simply result in a watering down of both goals without any benefits?

Should the relative wealth or poverty of a country affect an assessment of whether criminal procedure should be more adversarial or inquisitorial? In an inquisitorial system the judiciary requires substantial funding, while in an adversarial system prosecutors and defense attorneys will probably require even more resources. Is judicial or governmental corruption a greater concern under one system than another? Or is the locus of corruption merely different?

A.1. THE EXPANDING ROLE OF INTERNATIONAL LAW AND SUPRANATIONAL JUDICIAL BODIES

One of the reasons for the growing convergence or agreement around issues of criminal procedure is the harmonizing effect of international law. Most countries have come to recognize that some criminal procedure rights are fundamental human rights and have ratified international agreements to that effect.[a] Some of these international agreements have established regional or multinational judicial bodies as official interpreters, for example, the Inter–American Court of Human Rights and the European Court of Human Rights (ECHR).[b] The decisions of these courts, in the course of reviewing the performance of national judicial systems, lend persuasive or even binding authority to the protection of human rights within and across borders. Although the highest national court of a country may resist "interference" from without, the influence of supranational judicial bodies is on the rise, and some domestic courts are adopting the reasoning of extraterritorial cases into their decisions. An example of such a decision occurred after the ECHR, in reviewing a claim brought by a Spaniard that the Spanish judicial system had denied him a fair trial, found that the plaintiff had been denied the opportunity to confront adverse witnesses (a right guaranteed by the European Convention for the Protection of Human Rights and Fundamental Freedoms, hereafter, European HR Convention) and thus had been denied a fair trial (a right also protected in the European HR Convention). The ECHR returned the case to the Spanish judicial system, whereupon the Spanish Constitutional Tribunal declared the decision of the European Court to be merely advisory, not binding. The Tribunal went on to note, however, that under the Spanish Constitution, all treaties, once ratified, are akin to domestic law. Accordingly, the Tribunal held that a violation of the European HR Convention constituted a violation of the Spanish Constitution. In particular, the Tribunal found that violations of the European HR Convention's right to fair trial amounted to a violation of the due process and fair trial clauses of the Spanish Constitution. See Spanish Constitution, Art. 17.1 (due process) and Art. 24.2 (public hearing–fair trial). The national judiciary, while not allowing itself to be bound by the decision of a supranational judiciary, reached findings in accord with it, even though the Spanish Constitution's fair trial clause, unlike its counterpart in the European HR Convention, does not explicitly include the right to confront adverse witnesses. *Barberà, Messegué and Jabardo v. Spain*, 11 E.H.R.R. 360

a. E.g., the International Covenant on Civil and Political Rights, Dec. 16, 1966, 999 U.N.T.S. 171 (entered into force Mar. 23, 1976) (Art. 14 provides that "everyone shall be entitled to a fair and public hearing by a competent, independent and impartial tribunal established by law"); the African Charter on Human and People's Rights, June 27, 1981 (Arts. 3–7), reprinted in 21 I.L.M. 59 (reprinted as "Banjul Charter on Human and People's Rights"); the American Convention on Human Rights, O.A.S. Treaty Series No. 36, 1144 U.N.T.S. 123 entered into force July 18, 1978 (see Arts. 7, 8, and 9); and the Convention for the Protection of Human Rights and Fundamental Freedoms, Nov. 4, 1950, 213 U.N.T.S. 221 ("European Convention"). Article 6(1) of the European Convention provides the de-

fendant the right to "a fair and public hearing * * * by an independent and impartial tribunal." Article 6(3)(e) provides the defendant the right "to examine or have examined witnesses against him."

b. Established, respectively, under the American Convention on Human Rights, and the Convention for the Protection of Human Rights and Fundamental Freedoms ("European Convention"). In addition, an optional protocol to the International Covenant on Civil and Political Rights allows individuals to complain of violations to the U.N. Human Rights Committee. See Optional Protocol to the International Covenant on Civil and Political Rights, art. 1, 999 U.N.T.S. 302 (1976) (entered into force Mar. 23, 1976).

(1988); Dennis P. Riordan, *The Rights to a Fair Trial and to Examine Witnesses Under the Spanish Constitution and the European Convention on Human Rights*, 26 Hastings Const. L.Q. 373 (1999).

B. GENERAL PRINCIPLES OF FAIRNESS AND DUE PROCESS

B.1. FAIR TRIAL

The right to a fair trial is the broad principle from which most other procedural rights of an accused flow. Whereas the fair trial right is often mentioned by courts in support of decisions, it is rarely defined independently from the specific rights that flow from it. In general, the right to a fair trial serves the goal of protecting individuals from arbitrary deprivation of fundamental rights. One commentator has argued that the right to a fair trial should be understood as protecting the search for truth: "[C]haracteristics [such as] an impartial decision maker, an atmosphere conducive to consideration, with relevant evidence considered and irrelevant evidence excluded[,] are aimed primarily at improving the chances of arriving at a verdict that accords with some notion of preexisting, objective truth." Danny J. Boggs, *The Right to a Fair Trial*, U. Chi. Legal F. 1, 4 (1998).

Many constitutions, especially recent ones, contain sections that explicitly provide for a fair trial. In a 1993 survey, M. Cherif Bassiouni found that no fewer than 38 national constitutions contained provisions that protected the right to a fair trial or hearing in criminal cases. In addition, Bassiouni found that many other constitutions contained language that could be interpreted as guaranteeing the right to a fair trial:

> For example, seven national constitutions guarantee the right to a procedure with all safeguards necessary for a defense. The right to a defense is related to the right to a fair trial and is dealt with in conjunction with this right. The "right to defense," without more, is guaranteed in twenty-one national constitutions, but the specific interpretation attached to this rubric is not evident from the constitutional text alone. It could imply the right to a fair trial, but also the right to counsel, or even simply the right to defend oneself. In ten additional constitutions the right to defense is guaranteed in terms such as "at every level of the proceedings," which seems to designate a right to counsel or self-representation. The elusiveness of this term is exemplified by the constitution of Sao Tome and Principe which guarantees the "right of defense" * * * to accuser and accused.

M. Cherif Bassiouni, *Human Rights in the Context of Criminal Justice: Identifying International Procedural Protections and Equivalent Protections in National Constitutions*, 3 Duke J. Comp. & Int'l. L. 235, 267–68 (1993).

The right to a fair trial is closely associated with other rights, such as the right to be heard, the right to a public trial, and the right to a reasoned decision. The right to be heard includes subsidiary rights, e.g., to receive notice of the initiation of proceedings, to present favorable and rebut unfavorable evidence, and to be present at all stages of the proceedings, many of which are explored below.

The right to a public trial can be viewed both as a right of the defendant and as a public right to open or transparent government. According to one commentator, Judith Resnik, five rationales are typically cited in the U.S. for providing public access to a trial. First, because criminal trials historically have been open, they should remain so. Second, public trials have therapeutic value for the community. Third, trials educate the public about the judicial system. Fourth, the presence of an audience serves to check judicial power. Fifth, the publicity of a trial may enhance fact-finding, by causing new evidence to turn up and by persuading those who testify to speak more truthfully than if permitted to testify in private. Resnik maintains that these rationales are not all solid; for example, the argument that trials have therapeutic value is flawed because trials usually occur long after the events at issue occurred. Resnik proposes a further rationale based on the values of interaction and the generation of norms:

> We the public sit not only to learn about the norms and to prevent application of the 'wrong' norm, but also to be part of the process of changing norms. We create our social rules out of individual sagas of claims of right. By understanding that a role for the public in process is based in part on this need for interaction, we stress the expressive qualities of procedure, the use of process as one way to give meaning to cultural values such as dignity of individuals. Further, by having public participation, we gain the possibility of generating shared narratives of powerful significance. Process may provide a vehicle for—briefly—creating a shared community and, of course, process may also be the occasion by which the war of our many communities is plainly revealed. * * * [B]ecause I believe that adjudication is one aspect of political life * * * I believe that our polity needs to play some role in the process.

Judith Resnik, *Due Process: A Public Dimension*, 39 U. Fla. L. Rev. 405, 419 (1987).

With the rise of powerful and sometimes sensational news media, trial publicity is sometimes considered detrimental to due process because it can erode the impartiality of decision-makers. Nevertheless, the right to a public trial is often important in countries where the media are weak and where, due to social unrest, terrorism, or the declaration of a state of emergency, there is danger of prosecutorial excess. In the Zimbabwe case of *Hayes v. Baldachin*, 1980 ZLR 442 AD, the Court found the holding of a secret trial under emergency powers constituted a serious irregularity calculated to prejudice the defendant because witnesses whose evidence is open to public scrutiny are likely to be more meticulous and truthful than if what they say is examined by only one or two people in a closed courtroom.''

The right to a reasoned decision is considered an essential element of a fair trial because it allows the losing party to ascertain whether full attention has been paid to its arguments and it serves as a basis for an appeal. While this element of fairness is usually left unstated in constitutions, the constitutions of Spain (Art. 120(3)), Italy (Arts. 13(3), 111(6)), and Belgium (Art. 149), among others, expressly require reasoned judicial decisions.

Notes and Questions

1. In drafting a constitution, how would you ensure that all defendants received a fair trial? Would you include a blanket right to a fair trial in the constitution, or would you, instead, enumerate specific rights that ensure the trial's fairness? If you opt for the latter, how would you decide which rights to include? Or should both approaches be used? Consider these questions throughout the chapter as you study particular procedural rights.

2. Which rationales discussed in Judith Resnik's article strike you as persuasive justifications for a public trial? Are there any additional justifications? Note that some of the rationales, such as the therapeutic value of the trial for the community, might in some instances conflict with a defendant's right to a fair trial.

B.2. THE PRESUMPTION OF INNOCENCE AND REVERSE-ONUS PROVISIONS

The presumption of an accused's innocence is considered a core principle in many human rights instruments (e.g., the African Charter on Human and People's Rights, Art. 7(2); American Convention on Human Rights, Art. 8(2); the European HR Convention, Art. 6(2); and the International Covenant on Civil and Political Rights, Art. 14(2)). One commentator has found that the presumption of innocence is guaranteed in at least 67 constitutions, but several constitutions provide only for a narrower right not to be presumed guilty. See Bassiouni, *op. cit.* at 266–67. In the U.S., this principle has been found to be implicit in the Fourteenth Amendment's due process clause. *In re Winship,* 397 U.S. 358 (1970). The presumption of innocence places the burden of proving a case against the accused on the prosecution. But in some countries that guarantee the presumption of innocence there are reverse-onus provisions, which place the burden of proof on the defendant on specific issues.

The South African Constitutional Court (SACC) and the Irish Supreme Court have dealt with reverse-onus provisions differently.

Note that the presumption of innocence is also at issue in other contexts, such as the right to bail (Subsection C.2.), in cases of preventive detention (Subsection C.3.), and with the right to silence, particularly at trial (Subsection D.2.).

S. v. MBATHA

Constitutional Court (South Africa).
1996 (2) SALR 464 (CC).

Langa J:

2. * * * [T]he applicant appealed against his conviction on two counts under the provisions of the Arms and Ammunition Act 75 of 1969

(the Act). The charge concerned the unlawful possession of two AK47 rifles and twelve rounds of ammunition. * * *

4.   The issue * * * is the validity of the presumption contained in section 40(1) of the Act in the light of the provisions of section 25(3)(c) and (d) of the Constitution. * * * Section 40(1) of the Act provides:

> Whenever in any prosecution for being in possession of any article contrary to the provisions of this Act, it is proved that such article has at any time been on or in any premises, including any building, dwelling, flat, room, office, shop, structure, vessel, aircraft or vehicle or any part thereof, any person who at that time was on or in or in charge of or present at or occupying such premises, shall be presumed to have been in possession of that article at that time, until the contrary is proved.

6.   * * * [The relevant parts of section 25(3) of the Constitution read:]

> Every accused person shall have the right to a fair trial, which shall include the right. . . . (c) to be presumed innocent

9.   * * * It was common cause that the provision amounts to a legal presumption; it is a reverse onus provision. * * * The effect of the provision is to relieve the prosecution of the burden of proof with regard to an essential element of the offence. It requires that the presumed fact must be disproved by the accused on a balance of probabilities. * * * As pointed out by O'Regan J in *Bhulwana*'s case, a presumption of this nature is in breach of the presumption of innocence since it could result in the conviction of an accused person despite the existence of a reasonable doubt as to his or her guilt.

10.   No legal system can guarantee that no innocent person can ever be convicted. Indeed, the provision of corrective action by way of appeal and review procedures is an acknowledgement of the ever-present possibility of judicial fallibility. Yet it is one thing for the law to acknowledge the possibility of wrongly but honestly convicting the innocent and then provide appropriate measures to reduce the possibility of this happening as far as is practicable; it is another for the law itself to heighten the possibility of a miscarriage of justice by compelling the trial court to convict where it entertains real doubts as to culpability and then to prevent the reviewing court from altering the conviction even if it shares in the doubts.

12.   * * * The conclusion I come to, therefore, is that section 40(1) of the Act offends against the right of an accused person to be presumed innocent, in terms of section 25(3)(c) of the Constitution. The provision can accordingly only be permissible if it is saved by the provisions of section 33(1) of the Constitution.

13.   [This section] provides as follows:

The rights entrenched in this Chapter may be limited by law of general application, provided that such limitation—

(a) shall be permissible only to the extent that it is—

  (i) reasonable; and

(ii) justifiable in an open and democratic society based on freedom and equality; and

(b) shall not negate the essential content of the right in question, and . . . shall . . . also be necessary.

[The decision then goes on to describe and apply a proportionality test that weighs the competing values at stake. The government argued that the provision was necessary to combat an escalation in crime. Although the Court expressed sympathy with the government's position, it concluded:]

24.   If the purpose of the provision is to promote the legitimate law enforcement objective of separating innocent bystanders from genuine suspects, then it should be cast in terms limited to serving that function only. A legislative limitation motivated by strong societal need should not be disproportionate in its impact to the purpose for which that right is limited. If restrictions are warranted by such societal need, they should be properly focused and appropriately balanced. The foundations of effective law enforcement procedures should always be the thorough collection of evidence and the careful presentation of a prosecution case. The sweeping terms of the presumption, however, encourage dragnet searches followed by dragnet prosecutions in which innocent bystanders, occupants and travelers can be required to prove their innocence and the normal checks and balances operating at the pre-trial stage cease to operate. Immense discretionary power is given to the police, in the first instance and to the prosecuting authorities thereafter, as to whether or not to proceed with arrest and indictment. From a practical point of view, the focus of crucial decision-making on guilt or innocence thus shifts from the constitutionally controlled context of a trial to the unrestrained discretion of police and prosecutor. The possibility cannot be excluded that overworked police and prosecuting authorities would understandably be tempted to focus on merely getting sufficient evidence to raise the presumption of possession; they can then rely on a poor showing by the accused in the witness box to secure a conviction. Yet the law gives no guidance to investigators and prosecutors as to when it is appropriate to rely on the presumption to proceed with a case and when not. Innocent persons may be put to the inconvenience, indignity and expense of a trial simply because they were in a bus, on a ship, or in a taxi, restaurant or house where weapons happened to be discovered. At the same time, the objectivity and professionalism of the police and prosecution are undermined by the lack of principled criteria governing their actions. In my view, in order to catch offenders and secure their convictions, it is not reasonable and justifiable either to expose honest citizens to such open-ended jeopardy or to impose such ill-defined responsibility upon those charged with law enforcement.

25.   The presumption is not only too wide in its application with regard to persons, it also casts a heavy burden on those who are caught by it to disprove guilt. * * *

27.   I accordingly find that although the provision in question is a law of general application, it has not been shown to be reasonable as required by section 33(1) of the Constitution. It is furthermore so

inconsistent with the values which underlie an open and democratic society based on freedom and equality that it cannot be said to be justifiable. * * * Section 40(1) of the Act is unconstitutional inasmuch as it is an unreasonable and unjustifiable violation of the presumption of innocence.

O'LEARY v. THE ATTORNEY GENERAL

Supreme Court (Ireland).
1990 No. 363 (1990).

[The defendant was found in possession of posters, showing the picture of a man in a paramilitary uniform brandishing a rifle and with the words "IRA calls the shots" displayed on it. Under Art. 24 of the Offences Against the State Act of 1939, proof of the possession of incriminating documents, by itself, would constitute evidence of membership in an unlawful organization. At trial, the defendant accepted that the posters were in his possession but said he had them as a member of Sinn Fein, a political party, and denied membership in the IRA. Nonetheless, in reliance on the presumption established in Art. 24, the court convicted him of both membership in an unlawful organization and possession of incriminating documents, in violation of sections 21 and 12 of the Act. The defendant challenged the conviction, arguing that Art. 24 of the Act violated the constitutionally protected right to the presumption of innocence.]

The learned High Court judge, in regard to the presumption of innocence, said the following: * * *

The first task that must engage the Court is to declare afresh that the presumption of innocence in a criminal trial is implicit in the requirement of Article 38(1) of the Constitution that no person shall be tried on any criminal charge save in due course of law. The Court does not need to go any further than to assert that such a principle is required by this Article of the Constitution.

The Court's next task is to analyse section 24 of the Act of 1939 to find out whether there is a breach of that principle. In turn, the Court must test the validity of the section in question by reference to the formula laid down in the case: *East Donegal Co-operative v. Attorney General* [1970] IR 317. At p. 340 of the report, Walsh J, delivering the judgment of the Court, said the following:

In testing the validity of Acts of the Oireachtas which were passed since the coming into force of the Constitution, the approach is that laid down by this Court in *McDonald v. Bord na gCon* [1965] IR 317. It was pointed out in that case that there was a presumption of constitutionality operating in favour of all such statutes and it was stated at p 239 of the report that "one practical effect of this presumption is that if in respect of any provision or provisions of the Act two or more constructions are reasonably open, one of which is constitutional and the other or others are unconstitutional, it must be presumed that the Oireachtas intended only the constitutional construction and a Court called upon to adjudicate upon the constitutionality of the statutory provision should uphold the constitutional construction. It is only when there is no construction reasonably open which is not repugnant to the Constitution that the provision should be held to be repugnant." * * *

For the appellant, Miss Finlay's essential submission was that the words "until the contrary is proved" imposed the burden on the accused of proving that he was not a member of an unlawful organisation, which in effect means that the burden is thrown on him to prove that he is not guilty of the offence.

The Court does not accept this submission.

In the opinion of the Court the section permits no more than the following: if an incriminating document is proved to be in the possession of a person (and that is all that the Court has to consider in this case because actual possession of the documents was proved and, indeed, admitted by the accused) that shall, without more, be evidence until the contrary is proved that such person was a member of an unlawful organisation. It is clear that such possession is to amount to evidence only; it is not to be taken as proof and so the probative value of the possession of such a document might be shaken in many ways: by cross-examination; by pointing to the mental capacity of the accused or the circumstances by which he came to be in possession of the document, to give some examples. The important thing to note about the section is that there is no mention of the burden of proof changing, much less that the presumption of innocence is to be set to one side at any stage.

So, if a charge of membership of an unlawful organisation were being tried on indictment by a judge with a jury, the judge's charge might go along the following lines—this in a case where the accused did not give evidence and, indeed, assuming that there had been no cross-examination of the prosecution witnesses:

> Members of the jury, the accused has been found in possession of a document and it will be for you to find beyond reasonable doubt whether it is an "incriminating document" within the definition that I have given to you as set forth in the legislation. If you are satisfied beyond reasonable doubt on that you must also be satisfied beyond reasonable doubt that it was in the possession of the accused. Now if you are satisfied on both of these elements you are entitled to convict the accused because the section provides that the possession of an incriminating document shall, without more, be evidence until the contrary is proved that the accused was a member of an unlawful organisation. Here nothing to the contrary has been proved, and therefore you are entitled to convict the accused of the offence etc.

There is no doubt that in the example quoted the evidentiary burden of proof would have shifted to the accused. This, as the learned High Court judge pointed out, is applicable in many statutes and he gave instances of them. The Hardy case, already referred to, is an example of one such. Further, if someone is caught red-handed in any particular situation the presumption of innocence is not dispensed with if the trial judge points to the apparent strength of the case against the accused.

Courts, whether comprising a judge sitting with a jury or a judge or judges only, will not act as automatons in the assessment of evidence.

With a statutory provision setting out what is to be regarded as evidence–and whether it is called a presumption or not is of no moment—the Court must always approach its task in a responsible manner and have proper regard to the paramount place that the presumption of innocence occupies in any criminal trial. * * *

In the circumstances, the Court is satisfied that none of the grounds of appeal has been made out. The Court holds that it has not been established that section 24 of the Offences Against the State Act, 1939 is invalid having regard to the provisions of the Constitution.

Accordingly, the appeal is dismissed.

Notes and Questions

1. In *Mbatha* the Court struck down the statute at issue, while in *O'Leary* the statute was upheld. In *Mbatha* the Court left open the possibility that a statute violating the presumption of innocence could be upheld if it met the Court's test. In *O'Leary* the presumption of innocence was deemed absolute, but the Court interpreted the statute to comply with it. Which decision provides stronger protections for the presumption of innocence? Which approach is preferable?

2. Are there situations where reverse-onus provisions are justifiable and necessary? Does your analysis depend on other aspects of the system? Should the nature of the offense influence interpretation of a reverse-onus prohibition? Is it relevant that the defendant in *O'Leary* was charged with a crime against the state?

B.3. RIGHT TO A TRIAL BEFORE AN IMPARTIAL TRIBUNAL

B.3.1. IMPARTIALITY

The impartiality of a tribunal is essential to the proper functioning of the judiciary. When a judge or magistrate, presiding over the conviction and sentencing of an accused, has already participated in another aspect of the proceedings (such as conducting initial investigations, as might occur in a civil law system) or has a personal stake in the proceedings, a relationship with a party, or some other indication of bias, the trial may be tainted. An impartial tribunal has ramifications beyond an individual case because impartiality and the appearance of impartiality preserve the integrity of the judicial system as a whole and instill public respect for the administration of justice.

As noted earlier, the right to a public hearing may affect the impartiality of a tribunal. In a Spanish case, Judgment of the Spanish Constitutional Tribunal 136/99 (July 20, 1999), leading members of the Basque Nationalist Party were found guilty of collaboration with a terrorist organization and sentenced to imprisonment. The defendants challenged the decision before the Constitutional Tribunal, arguing that political institutions had influenced the sentencing court through public speeches and that social pressure had made the court lose its impartiality. The Tribunal dismissed the appeal, holding that, while the Constitution protects defendants from being tried by the media, this protection must be balanced against the right to freedom of expression and to a public trial. To reverse a decision of the lower court, there must be an objective reason to suspect a lack of impartiality. In this case the Tribunal found that the sentencing court was fully independent and that political messages in the media were harmless.

The African Committee on Human and People's Rights, in interpreting the African [Banjul] Charter on Human and People's Rights 7(1)(d)ᶜ commented on the creation of a tribunal consisting of one judge plus four senior military officials that would judge and sentence cases of civil disturbance: "Regardless of the character of the individual members of such tribunals, its composition alone creates the appearance, if not the actual lack of impartiality." *The Constitutional Rights Project (in respect of Zamani Lakwot and six others) v. Nigeria, (87/93)*, 8th Annual Activity Report of the African Committee on Human and People's Rights, 1994–1995, AVHPR/RPT/8th/Rev.1 at 14, para. 10).

The ECHR has decided several cases on this issue. It found no lack of impartiality where a juvenile judge had participated in pretrial procedures and had decided that the accused should be held in pretrial custody. The Court stated that "[t]he mere fact that [the judge] also made pre-trial decisions, including decisions relating to detention on remand, cannot be taken in itself as justifying fears as to his impartiality; what matters is the scope and nature of these decisions." *Nortier v. The Netherlands*, 17 E.H.R.R. 273 (1994), 24 August 1993, at 12. Similarly, the Court found that the judge's detailed knowledge of a case, based on his role in the preliminary phases, did not in itself mean that he was prejudiced in a way that prevented him from being impartial when the case came to trial; what mattered were the scope and nature of the pretrial measures he had taken. *Saraiva de Carvalho v. Portugal*, 18 E.H.R.R. 534 (1994), 22 April 1994, at 11. On the other hand the European Court found a lack of impartiality where the presiding judge of the appeal court, who had extensive powers, had previously been in an influential position in the public prosecutor's department. The Court found that the impartiality of the tribunal was "capable of appearing open to doubt"; although the mere fact that a judge was once a member of the public prosecutor's office was not determinative of itself. *Piersack Case*, 5 E.H.R.R. 169 (1983), 1 October 1982, para. 31.

B.3.2. COMPOSITION AND ALLOCATION OF RESPONSIBILITIES

Before what sort of a tribunal does an accused have the right to be tried? Some constitutions, such as those of the U.S. and the Russian Federation, provide for a right to a trial by jury in certain types of cases (in Russia, in cases "determined by law"). In countries where French or German approaches to procedure prevail, many criminal trials are con-

---

c. "(1) Every individual shall have the right to have his cause heard. This comprises * * * (d) the right to be tried within a reasonable time by an impartial court or tribunal."

ducted by a single judge or by a panel of judges without a jury. Where there is a panel of judges, the panel often comprises a mixture of professional and lay judges, who work together at all stages of the case. In France, nine laypersons sit with three professional judges; in Germany, two laypersons interact with one or more professional judges. The panels hear evidence and decide issues of fact and law. Probably because of the intermingling of professional and lay participants and the parallel assumption that the professionals (by virtue of their knowledge and experience) will be able to discern what is truly probative, the German system contains relatively loose laws of evidence. This process differs greatly from the Anglo–American system, where lay juries are solely responsible for interpreting the meaning and weight of evidence. In such countries, far more attention is paid to defining the evidence that reaches the jury.

In France, before judges and juries retire together to deliberate, the judge reads aloud the following from the Code of Criminal Procedure (Art. 353):

> The law does not demand of Judges and Jurors that you take account of the means by which you were convinced; the law does not prescribe rules according to which the completeness or sufficiency of evidence can be determined, it only requires that you reflect in silence and with careful thought in order to determine, in the sincerity of your consciences, what impression has been made upon your reasoning by the evidence adduced against the defendant and the way he/she has defended him/herself. The law asks only one question which sums up your entire duty. Do you have an 'inner belief' (*intime conviction*)?

One text, noting that this article is read aloud and posted on the walls of jury rooms, comments that "[e]valuation of evidence is free and unconstrained by formal exclusionary rules as the courts are concerned more with the 'weight' or 'value' of evidence than its admissibility." Richard Vogler, *Criminal Procedure in France*, in *Comparative Criminal Procedure* 29 (John Hatchard, Barbara Huber, and Richard Vogler eds., 1996).

The issue of what sort of tribunal is required raises not only the question of judges versus juries, but also questions regarding the nature of the tribunal itself. May administrative bodies adjudicate some cases? What about military tribunals? The underlying question is which decisions must be made by a court and which decisions may be made by other branches of government. For more detailed discussion, see the material on separation of powers in Chapter 3.

C. PRETRIAL DUE PROCESS

Liberty-related issues dominate the pretrial stage, a stage at which an individual is peculiarly vulnerable to arbitrary power and abuse by executive agents of the state. Arrest, search and seizure, police interrogation, and detention all occur outside a courtroom and beyond the sight of a trial judge. The dangers inherent in this arrangement, and their implications, are raised by Bostjan Zupancic:

If * * * the immediate use of power becomes decisive in the resolution of a particular controversy between * * * an individual subject and the state, as for example in [the] criminal process * * * then the legal process and the rule of law with it have been subverted. * * *

The causes of this subversion lie in the constitutional imbalance of power between the judicial branch and the State's executive branch, i.e. its police. The latter uses torture, physical coercion, and other forms of pressure during custodial interrogation and without the presence of a lawyer–while the criminal justice system later, during criminal trial, is pressured to pretend that the evidence was obtained legally, i.e. that the controversy between the individual and the State is now being resolved without resort to power. The judicial branch, while pretending to know nothing of the abuses in the police station, ratifies the abuses and becomes an accomplice of the executive branch. If the separation of powers, here the separation of [the] judicial branch from the abuses of the executive branch, is not consistently carried out, if the judges become the accomplices of police abuses, then we have a collapse of the judicial power into the executive power. The consequence is, of course, the collapse of constitutional legitimacy and the rule of law.

Bostjan M. Zupancic, *The Privilege Against Self–Incrimination as a Human Right*, 13, 17–18 (1999) (unpublished manuscript).

These matters are addressed in this section. Two other important issues, the right to silence and the right to counsel, which come into play at both pretrial and trial stages, are discussed in Sections D. and E. below.

C.1. ARREST, SEARCH AND SEIZURE

Standards for stops, searches, and arrests vary greatly. As the following cases make clear, both liberty and privacy issues may be at stake. Privacy is discussed in greater depth in Chapter 5.

What standard of evidence or suspicion do police need to stop a person or to search a person, vehicle, or home? In many countries, police are authorized to stop people simply to check their papers. In France, for example, police can conduct ID checks, without individualized suspicion, that can last up to four hours and can frisk for weapons without suspicion of danger.

The U.S. and French cases, immediately below, discuss limitations on searches and seizures and the role of judicial supervision at this stage of the process. The next section addresses the difficult question of remedies. If a defendant's rights have been violated during the investigative process, should the court be allowed to consider the evidence thus obtained?

KATZ v. UNITED STATES

Supreme Court (United States).
389 U.S. 347 (1967).

[Katz was convicted of transmitting betting information over the telephone, in violation of a federal statute. At trial the government introduced evidence of Katz's conversations, which had been obtained by a recording device attached to the telephone booth where he made his calls.]

Mr. Justice Stewart delivered the opinion of the Court.

* * * We granted certiorari in order to consider the constitutional questions thus presented.

The petitioner has phrased those questions as follows:

A. "Whether a public telephone booth is a constitutionally protected area so that evidence obtained by attaching an electronic listening recording device to the top of such a booth is obtained in violation of the right to privacy of the user of the booth."

B. "Whether physical penetration of a constitutionally protected area is necessary before a search and seizure can be said to be violative of the Fourth Amendment to the United States Constitution."

* * * Because of the misleading way the issues have been formulated, the parties have attached great significance to the characterization of the telephone booth from which the petitioner placed his calls. The petitioner has strenuously argued that the booth was a "constitutionally protected area." The Government has maintained with equal vigor that it was not. But this effort to decide whether or not a given "area," viewed in the abstract, is "constitutionally protected" deflects attention from the problem presented by this case. For the Fourth Amendment protects people, not places. What a person knowingly exposes to the public, even in his own home or office, is not a subject of Fourth Amendment protection. * * * But what he seeks to preserve as private, even in an area accessible to the public, may be constitutionally protected. * * *

The Government stresses the fact that the telephone booth from which the petitioner made his calls was constructed partly of glass, so that he was as visible after he entered it as he would have been if he had remained outside. But what he sought to exclude when he entered the booth was not the intruding eye—it was the uninvited ear. He did not shed his right to do so simply because he made his calls from a place where he might be seen. No less than an individual in a business office, in a friend's apartment, or in a taxicab, a person in a telephone booth may rely upon the protection of the Fourth Amendment. One who occupies it, shuts the door behind him, and pays the toll that permits him to place a call is surely entitled to assume that the words he utters into the mouthpiece will not be broadcast to the world. To read the Constitution more narrowly is to ignore the vital role that the public telephone has come to play in private communication.

* * * The Government's activities in electronically listening to and recording the petitioner's words violated the privacy upon which he justifiably relied while using the telephone booth and thus constituted a "search and seizure" within the meaning of the Fourth Amendment. The fact that the electronic device employed to achieve that end did not happen to penetrate the wall of the booth can have no constitutional significance.

The question remaining for decision, then, is whether the search and seizure conducted in this case complied with constitutional standards.

* * * It is apparent that the agents in this case acted with restraint. Yet the inescapable fact is that this restraint was imposed by the agents themselves, not by a judicial officer. They were not required, before commencing the search, to present their estimate of probable cause for detached scrutiny by a neutral magistrate. They were not compelled, during the conduct of the search itself, to observe precise limits established in advance by a specific court order. Nor were they directed, after the search had been completed, to notify the authorizing magistrate in detail of all that had been seized. In the absence of such safeguards, this Court has never sustained a search upon the sole ground that officers reasonably expected to find evidence of a particular crime and voluntarily confined their activities to the least intrusive means consistent with that end. Searches conducted without warrants have been held unlawful "notwithstanding facts unquestionably showing probable cause," *Agnello v. United States*, 269 U.S. 20, 33, for the Constitution requires "that the deliberate, impartial judgment of a judicial officer . . . be interposed between the citizen and the police. . . ." *Wong Sun v. United States*, 371 U.S. 471, 481–82. "Over and again this Court has emphasized that the mandate of the [Fourth] Amendment requires adherence to judicial processes," *United States v. Jeffers*, 342 U.S. 48, 51, and that searches conducted outside the judicial process, without prior approval by judge or magistrate, are per se unreasonable under the Fourth Amendment— subject only to a few specifically established and well-delineated exceptions.

It is difficult to imagine how any of those exceptions could ever apply to the sort of search and seizure involved in this case. Even electronic surveillance substantially contemporaneous with an individual's arrest could hardly be deemed an "incident" of that arrest. Nor could the use of electronic surveillance without prior authorization be justified on grounds of "hot pursuit." And, of course, the very nature of electronic surveillance precludes its use pursuant to the suspect's consent.

* * * [T]he judgment must be reversed.

Mr. Justice Harlan, concurring:

As the Court's opinion states, "the Fourth Amendment protects people, not places." The question, however, is what protection it affords to those people. Generally, as here, the answer to that question requires reference to a "place." My understanding of the rule that has emerged from prior decisions is that there is a twofold requirement, first that a person have exhibited an actual (subjective) expectation of privacy and, second, that the expectation be one that society is prepared to recognize as "reasonable." Thus, a man's home is, for most purposes, a place where he expects privacy, but objects, activities, or statements that he exposes to the "plain view" of outsiders are not "protected," because no intention to keep them to himself has been exhibited. On the other hand, conversations in the open would not be protected against being overheard, for the expectation of privacy under the circumstances would be unreasonable.

INCREASED POLICE POWERS
TO COMBAT TERRORISM

Constitutional Council (France).
96–377 DC of 16 July 1996.

[This decision considered the constitutionality of the "Act to strengthen enforcement measures to combat terrorism and violence against holders of public office or public service functions and to enact measures relating to the criminal investigation police."]

* * * Section 10 of the Act referred amends section 706–24 of the Code of Criminal Procedure by adding four paragraphs; under the first three, with regard to offences within the definition of acts of terrorism, visits, searches and seizures may henceforth be made at night if the needs of the investigation so require. * * *

15. The Senators making the first reference submit that the rule laid down by section 59 of the Code of Criminal Procedure, which prohibit visits and searches between 9 p.m. and 6 a.m., is a fundamental principle recognized by the laws of the Republic; the Senators and Deputies making the references submit that there can be no departures from the principle of personal freedom guaranteeing the inviolability of the residence unless they are necessary to safeguard law and order, and that this requirement for a perceived undeniable need does not exist at the preliminary investigation stage; they submit, finally, that a warrant issued by the judicial authority does not on its own guarantee respect for personal freedom;

16. The search for offenders is necessary for safeguarding constitutional principles and rights; it is for the legislature to reconcile this constitutional objective with the exercise of the public liberties secured by the Constitution, among them individual liberty and the inviolability of the home;

17. Given the demands of public policy, it is legitimate for the legislature to provide for the possibility of visits, searches and seizures by night where an offence potentially classifiable as an act of terrorism is being or has just been committed, provided the warrant is given by the judicial authorities as guardians of individual liberties and provided the measures are surrounded by appropriate procedural guarantees; the law in this case empowers senior judges in the persons of the President of the *Tribunal de grande instance* or a person appointed by him to issue the warrants by written decision giving reasons and specifying the offence for which evidence is sought, the address of execution, and the facts of the case justifying the search etc.; moreover, operations are subject to control by the judge authorizing them to ensure compliance with the Act's requirements; and the operations would be void as a matter of public policy unless directed solely to detecting and establishing offences of the relevant categories; the concept of the 'needs of the investigation' is to be interpreted as allowing a visit, search or seizure to

be made only if it cannot otherwise be done within the time scales allowed by section 59 of the Code of Criminal Procedure; and once the warrant has been given the visit, search or seizure must be made with all due dispatch; the legislature has accordingly not excessively violated the principle of inviolability of the home, given the needs of the investigation in the event of *flagrante delicto.*

18. In contrast, the possibility of visits, searches and seizures by night, at unspecified times, in all places, including those used exclusively for residential purposes, in the event of a preliminary investigation and in the course of a preparatory inquiry, on the understanding that they are within the discretion of the Prosecutor or carried out under his control by officers of the criminal investigation police and that the authority responsible for the inquiry is now empowered to authorize, direct and control the relevant operations, constitutes an excessive violation of individual liberty;

19. It follows that section 706–24 of the Code of Criminal Procedure, as it applies to the preliminary investigation, is unconstitutional; it follows in turn that the words 'or of the investigation' and 'unless they are authorized by the examining magistrate', which refer to the case of a judicial inquiry, must be considered unconstitutional and that the remainder of section 10 of the Act can be considered constitutional only insofar as it refers solely to investigations in cases of *flagrante delicto.*

Notes and Questions

1. In *Klass v. Germany*, 2 E.H.R.R. 214 (1979–80), the ECHR considered a challenge to German legislation that permitted state authorities to open and inspect mail and listen to telephone conversations in order to protect against "imminent dangers" threatening the "free democratic constitutional order" and "the existence or the security of the State." The challengers claimed that the legislation infringed Arts. 6 (right to a fair hearing), 8 (right to respect for correspondence), and 13 (effective remedy before a national authority in respect of breaches of the Convention) of the European HR Convention. Although the challengers accepted the state's right to have recourse to such measures, they objected to the legislation on the grounds that it contained no requirement to notify the persons after surveillance had ceased and that it excluded any remedy before the courts against the ordering and implementation of the measures. The German government responded that the law fell within an exception in Art. 8(2) as being "necessary in a democratic society in the interests of national security" or "for the prevention of disorder or crime."

The Court found that the legislation infringed the rights protected by Art. 8 and that the exception in paragraph 2 should be narrowly construed. Nonetheless, the Court held that the legislation did fall within the exception, since the purposes of surveillance were limited by the legislation itself and because the implementation of the legislation was subject to strict conditions. "Democratic societies nowadays find themselves threatened by highly sophisticated forms of espionage and by terrorism, with the result that the State must be able, in order effectively to counter such threats, to undertake the secret surveillance of subversive elements operating within its jurisdiction." Moreover, the Court held that the secrecy of the surveillance measures was permissible under both Arts. 8 and 13 because the secrecy was necessary to ensure the efficacy of the measures, individuals would be notified of the surveillance as soon as possible after the surveillance had concluded, and individuals who believed themselves to be under surveillance could complain to the Constitutional Court. Finally, the Court held that Art. 6 was not violated by the legislation. The decision to place someone under surveillance did not amount to an interference with a "civil right" or to the laying of a "criminal charge" within the meaning of Art. 6(1) because such surveillance was validly secret under Art. 8. Also, after termination of the surveillance, the individual had "at his disposal several legal remedies against the possible infringements of his rights" that would satisfy Art. 6. See Chapter 1, Subsection E.2. for the resolution in the same case of issues arising under the German Basic Law by the German Federal Constitutional Court.

2. Is the protection of "people not places" described in *Katz* a workable rule? Does Justice Harlan's concurrence offer a better approach? Should some places, such as homes at night, be off-limits even to searches pursuant to warrant except in the most exigent circumstances? Are there other locations that may also merit special protection?

3. Law enforcement officials have become increasingly reliant on high-tech devices, including aerial surveillance, infrared devices and heat sensors, systems to monitor e-mail communications, and even satellite imagery. Should use of these techniques constitute searches requiring warrants? How do technological advances affect expectations of privacy? In *Kyllo v. United States*, 533 U.S. 27, 34 (2001), the U.S. Supreme Court (USSC) considered the use of heat sensors to detect marijuana-growing lights: "The question we confront is what limits there are upon the power of technology to shrink the realm of guaranteed privacy." In a 5–4 decision, the Court held that where the government uses a device that is not in general public use in order to explore details of a private home that would previously have been unknowable without physical intrusion, the surveillance constitutes a Fourth Amendment search and requires a warrant.

C.1.1. EXCLUSIONARY RULE

What remedies are available when the police have acted illegally to obtain evidence? In some countries, illegally seized evidence may not be introduced into evidence against the defendant. Those who advocate such exclusion argue that the use of illegally obtained evidence in court taints the administration of justice, or, as in the U.S., that without exclusion the police will not be deterred from lawless invasion of property or persons. Those who reject an exclusionary rule often claim that there are other remedies available for police lawlessness, such as civil actions or disciplinary proceedings against the police.

In 1961, the U.S. held that evidence obtained in violation of the defendant's Fourth, Fifth, or Sixth Amendment rights was to be excluded. *Mapp v. Ohio*, 367 U.S. 643 (1961). It broadened the doctrine in *Wong Sun v. United States*, 371 U.S. 471 (1963), holding that all evidence obtained or derived from the exploitation of illegally obtained evidence was to be excluded. The issue has remained controversial, and the Court has reacted by narrowing the doctrine over the years. Generally, the Court will not apply the exclusionary rule when it will not likely deter government misconduct. For example, if the prosecution can show "inevitable discovery," that is, that the police would have discovered the evidence even if they had acted constitutionally, then the evidence will be admissible. *Nix v. Williams*, 467 U.S. 431 (1984). Similarly, an intervening act of free will by the defendant will break the causal chain between the evidence and the original illegality so that the evidence is admissible. *Wong Sun v. United States*, above (defendant's voluntary return to the police station after an illegal arrest rendered his confession admissible). Also, the exclusionary rule does not apply to parole-revocation proceedings (*Pennsylvania v. Scott*, 524 U.S. 357 (1998)) or when the police act in good faith based on a defective search warrant (*United States v. Leon*, 468 U.S. 897 (1984)).

In Canada, § 24(2) of the Charter of Rights and Freedoms says that evidence obtained in violation of rights contained in the Charter must be excluded if its admission would bring the administration of justice into disrepute. There are two tests for exclusion. Under *R. v. Burlingham* (excerpted below in Section E., "Right to Counsel") the evidence will be excluded if its admission would render the trial unfair. Under *R. v. Grant,* [1993] 3 S.C.R. 223, it is necessary to look at the motivations of the state actor: if the rights violation was a knowing, gross violation, then the evidence is excluded; if the violation occurred despite the good intentions of the actor, it is not excluded.

JAPAN v. HASHIMOTO

Supreme Court (Japan).
32 Keishū 6 at p. 1672 (1978).[d]

[A man was stopped on the street by a police officer who suspected he was carrying drugs. The officer put a hand in the man's pocket and seized a bag of illegal drugs. The man was acquitted by lower courts because of inadmissibility of the evidence. The Supreme Court found:]

Upon considering the purpose, the nature and the activities of both the official interrogation and examination of personal effects, it would be an improper interpretation to say the police could examine the personal effects only after receiving the owner's consent. Instead, considering the necessity of examining the personal effects and the urgency, and comparing impartially the infringement of the legal right of an individual with the public interest which should be protected, an officer could examine personal effects without the owner's consent, within a reasonable limit suitable to the situation, so long as it was not a search. * * * [In this case the officer] seriously violated the privacy of the individual. The officer's action was an unreasonable search. [Thus] the evidence must be said to have been seized unlawfully.

[Interpreting the Code of Criminal Procedure, the Court decided:] Since it is an important task of a criminal trial to apply the Criminal Code fairly and to maintain order in society, it is imperative to clarify

d. Reproduced from Lawrence W. Beer and Hiroshi Itoh, *The Constitutional Case* *Law of Japan, 1970 through 1990*, at 427, 432–33 (1996).

the facts of a case as much as possible. Even if the material for evidence were obtained through an illegal procedure, the substance itself would not change its shape or quality, nor would its value as evidence per se or its shape change. It would be inappropriate for the Court to reject immediately material as evidence simply because it was seized illegally. On the other hand, the fact finding should be carried out under adequate procedures that secure the individuals human rights from unlawful intrusion. [Here] the officer exceeded only a little the limits of the law [and] had no intention to neglect any law.

EDWARDS v. POLICE

High Court, Christchurch (New Zealand).
2 NZLR 164 (1994).

[The defendant had been stopped while riding a motorcycle and had then been followed onto private property by a policeman, who forcibly seized him and ordered him to go to a station for a breath test for suspicion of intoxication. When the man refused, the police officer arrested him. A subsequent blood test was positive for alcohol.]

Tipping, J.

* * * [Mr.] Edwards was subjected to unlawful restraint and detention amounting to assault and false imprisonment. What is more, the evidence in relation to alcohol and the failure to accompany was obtained as a direct result of the constable's unlawful conduct. It is obvious that Mr. Edwards was seeking the sanctity of his home. He would probably have achieved his objective if the constable had not unlawfully detained him. There is a considerable element of unfairness in the prosecution being able to produce evidence which would probably not have been available if the constable had not acted unlawfully. * * *

[A] balance must be struck between the interests of society in having offences prosecuted and the interests of citizens in having the police observe the law. [While] at one level it may be thought wrong for Mr. Edwards to escape the consequences of drinking and driving and refusing to accompany a traffic officer, at another level there has been a substantial breach of his civil rights. While I have some general sympathy for the position in which the constable found himself, it is of fundamental importance that citizens are not unlawfully detained by law enforcement officers; the more so when substantial force is used in doing so.

[It] is important in a case such as this that the Court vindicate and give tangible recognition to the substantial breach of rights which has occurred. The only way in which that can be done is by excluding the evidence which resulted in a direct and material way from the breach.

Notes and Questions

1. The assumption underlying the exclusionary rule is that even if police powers are precisely defined, the police will sometimes exceed their authority to obtain evidence against the accused. What set of police incen-

tives create this danger? Would the exclusionary rule still be constitutionally required if these incentives were altered? Do technological advances in evidence-gathering techniques complicate the picture?

2. What values underlie the exclusionary rule? If we take truth-seeking to be the most important value of criminal procedure, would we still want an exclusionary rule?

3. In *Hashimoto*, above, the Court mentions that the police officer exceeded the limits of the law "only a little." In *Edwards* the Court mentions that a "substantial breach of rights" occurred. Should the magnitude of the illegal police act be a determining factor in exclusion? Can a constitutional violation be large or small? Should the police officer's intention make a difference? What if the officer made an "honest mistake"?

4. In *Schenk v. Switzerland*, 13 E.H.R.R. 242 (1991), Pierre Schenk claimed that the introduction at trial of an illegally made tape recording rendered his trial unfair within the meaning of Art. 6, para. 1 of the European HR Convention, which provides: "everyone is entitled to a fair and public trial * * *." The Swiss Federal Court, which had upheld Schenk's conviction for trying to arrange the murder of his ex-wife, acknowledged the unauthorized nature of the recording but held (para. 30b): "the public interest in having the truth established in the matter of an offence relating to murder [overrode] Schenk's interest in maintaining the confidentiality of a telephone conversation which in no way bore upon his privacy." The ECHR agreed. After noting that rules on admissibility of evidence are primarily a matter for national law, it stated (para. 46): "The Court therefore cannot exclude as a matter of principle and in the abstract that unlawfully obtained evidence of the present kind may be admissible. It has only to ascertain whether Mr. Schenk's trial as a whole was fair." After finding that Schenk had been allowed to conduct a full defense and noting that the tape recording was not the only piece of evidence used to reach a determination of guilt, the Court concluded that Schenk's trial had been fair.

C.2. PRETRIAL DETENTION, BAIL, AND PROMPT JUDICIAL REVIEW

Generally speaking, the presumption of innocence militates against detaining or holding in custody persons who are awaiting trial. Some states allow for release of the accused on bail unless just cause exists for detention, such as the likelihood that the accused will flee the jurisdiction, tamper with evidence (including potential witnesses), or commit further crimes.

To assure that law enforcement authorities detain only those for whom just cause for detention exists, states may provide that the accused be brought before a judicial official without unreasonable delay. Under British law the maximum period of ordinary detention, without charge, is 24 hours; this period may be extended for up to 96 total hours, with authorizations from magistrate courts. However, a separate scheme of pretrial detention was established for persons arrested under the Prevention of Terrorism Act of 1989 (PTA). The PTA provides that detainees may be held for up to 48 hours after arrest and, with authorization of the Secretary of State, for an additional five days. These procedures have had their most important impact on the criminal justice system in Northern Ireland. The United Kingdom has retained this detention policy, despite a ruling by the ECHR that a detention under the PTA that exceeded four days and six hours violated Art. 5(3) of the European HR Convention. See *Brogan v. United Kingdom,* 11 E.H.R.R. 117 (1989). Rather than modify its procedure, the United Kingdom has derogated from Art. 5(3).

Sometimes the availability of a legal challenge to the denial of release from detention is only a formality. In Mexico, once an accused has been indicted, judicial review of the detention must occur within 72 hours, but in practice virtually all detentions are validated. The Mexican Supreme Court has stated that a detention that was illegal when carried out becomes legal once the judge, and not the police, is keeping the defendant in jail. Miguel Sarre and Fernando Figueroa, *Perspectives on a Right to Fair Trial (Mexico),* in *Right to a Fair Trial* 90 (David Weissbrodt and Rudiger Wolfrum eds., 1997).

In countries that lack bail provisions or where bail provisions are ineffective or underused, people may be held in pretrial detention for long periods. The 2001 Amnesty International Report on Rwanda found that some 125,000 people were still being held in squalid detention camps, awaiting trial on charges stemming from the 1994 genocide. Detainees, because they are under investigation, are vulnerable to coercion and even torture to extract evidence or confessions. In addition, poor living conditions—for example, conditions in pretrial detention centers in Eastern Europe are often considerably worse than in prison, with detainees facing severe overcrowding, inadequate food and medical care, and widespread disease—may push people to talk or confess simply to speed up the investigative process.

Even in countries that have and use bail, an accused can be detained by a magistrate who knowingly sets a prohibitively high bail, thereby effectively denying the detainee the option of being released on his or her own recognizance. In some circumstances such judicial discretion can yield discriminatory results; for example, studies in Canada revealed that indigenous peoples and blacks were more likely than whites to be held in pretrial detention. See *Manitoba Aboriginal Justice Inquiry Report* 102 (1991); *Report of the Commission on Systemic Racism in the Ontario Criminal Justice System* 113 (Dec. 1995). Similar problems occur in the U.S. and Australia.

C.3. PREVENTIVE DETENTION

Preventive detention refers to the detention of a person in advance of commission of a crime because of the belief that the person will, or is likely to, commit a crime. Preventive detention is usually considered to be contrary to due process rights, but it exists in different forms in some systems.

In the U.S., before passage of the 1984 Bail Reform Act, 18 USC 3141 *et seq.* (BRA), pretrial detention was usually available only when a judicial officer found a defendant presented a risk of flight. The BRA, however, provided for preventive detention if the federal government demonstrated by clear and convincing evidence, after an adversary hearing, that no release conditions would reasonably assure the safety of another person and the community. In the following case the USSC upheld the facial constitutionality of the statute under the due process and excessive bail clauses of the U.S. Constitution. While recognizing the individual's interest in liberty, the majority held that Congress could provide for detention as an exercise of its regulatory powers and that pretrial detention under the BRA did not amount to punishment without trial.

UNITED STATES v. SALERNO

Supreme Court (United States).
481 U.S. 739 (1987).

Chief Justice Rehnquist delivered the opinion of the Court.

* * * [A]s our cases hold, this right [the interest in liberty—Eds.] may, in circumstances where the government's interest is sufficiently weighty, be subordinated to the greater needs of society. We think that Congress' careful delineation of the circumstances under which detention will be permitted satisfies this standard. When the Government proves by clear and convincing evidence that an arrestee presents an identified and articulable threat to an individual or the community, we believe that, consistent with the Due Process Clause, a court may disable the arrestee from executing that threat. Under these circumstances, we cannot categorically state that pretrial detention 'offends some principle of justice so rooted in the traditions and conscience of our people as to be ranked as fundamental.'

[Justice Marshall, joined by Justice Brennan, dissented, expressing the view that the pretrial detention provisions were unconstitutional since they violated the presumption of innocence:]

The essence of this case may be found, ironically enough, in a provision of the Act to which the majority does not refer. Title 18 USC § 3142(j) (1982 ed., Supp. III) provides that 'nothing in this section shall be construed as modifying or limiting the presumption of innocence.' But the very pith and purpose of this statute is an abhorrent limitation of the presumption of innocence. The majority's untenable conclusion that the present Act is constitutional arises from a specious denial of the role of the Bail Clause and the Due Process Clause in protecting the invaluable guarantee afforded by the presumption of innocence.

'The principle that there is a presumption of innocence in favor of the accused is the undoubted law, axiomatic and elementary, and its enforcement lies at the foundation of the administration of our criminal law.' *Coffin v. United States*, 156 U.S. 432, 453 (1895). Our society's belief, reinforced over the centuries, that all are innocent until the state has proved them to be guilty, like the companion principle that guilt must be proved beyond a reasonable doubt, is "implicit in the concept of ordered liberty," *Palko v. Connecticut*, 302 U.S. 319, 325 (1937). * * *

But let us suppose that a defendant is indicted and the Government shows by clear and convincing evidence that he is dangerous and should be detained pending a trial, at which trial the defendant is acquitted. May the Government continue to hold the defendant in detention based upon its showing that he is dangerous? The answer cannot be yes, for that would allow the Government to imprison someone for uncommitted crimes based upon "proof" not beyond a reasonable doubt. * * * [O]ur fundamental principles of justice declare that the defendant is as innocent on the day before his trial as he is on the morning after his acquittal. Under this statute an untried indictment somehow acts to permit a detention, based on other charges, which after an acquittal would be unconstitutional. * * *

To be sure, an indictment is not without legal consequences. It establishes that there is probable cause to believe that an offense was committed, and that the defendant committed it. Upon probable cause a warrant for the defendant's arrest may issue; a period of administrative detention may occur before the evidence of probable cause is presented to a neutral magistrate. See *Gerstein v. Pugh*, 420 U.S. 103 (1975). * * *

In India, the Constitution permits preventive detention, and it is recognized that individual liberty may be subordinated to larger social interests. Article 21 of the Indian Constitution provides that "[n]o person shall be deprived of his life or personal liberty except according to procedure established by law." In addition, Art. 22(1)-(2) protects a person's rights to notice of the grounds of arrest, to counsel, and to be produced before a magistrate within 24 hours of arrest. However, Art. 22(3) recognizes the possibility of preventive detention under laws so providing. In such cases, the Constitution continues:

(4) No law providing for preventive detention shall authorize the detention of any person for a period longer than three months unless—

an advisory Board consisting of persons who are qualified to be appointed as, Judges of High Court has reported before the expiration of the said period that there is, in its opinion sufficient cause for such detention:

Provided that nothing in this clause shall authorize such detention beyond the period specified by any law made by Parliament.

(5) When any person is detained in pursuance of an order made under any law providing for preventive detention, the authority making the order shall, as soon as may be, communicate to such person the grounds on which the order has been made and shall afford him the earliest opportunity of making a representation against the order.

(6) Nothing in clause (5) shall require the authority making such order to disclose the facts which such authority considers to be against the public interest to disclose.

The following decision by a Constitutional Bench of the Supreme Court of India (a special panel comprising five or more judges to hear and rule on a constitutional issue) upheld the constitutional validity of the Maintenance of Internal Security Act of 1971 as regards preventive detention.

A.D.M., JABALPUR v. S. SHUKLA
Supreme Court (India).
A.I.R. 1976 S.C. 1207 (1976).

Beg, J.

213.   * * * Article 22 merely makes it clear that deprivations of liberty by means of laws regulating preventive detention would be included in 'procedure established by law' and indicates what that procedure should be. In that sense, it could be viewed as, substantially, an elaboration of what is found in Article 21, although it also goes beyond it inasmuch as it imposes limits on ordinary legislative power.

328.   * * * [A] prima facie valid detention order, that is to say, one duly authenticated and passed by an officer authorized to make it recording a purported satisfaction to detain the petitioner under the Maintenance of Internal Security Act, which is operative either before or after its confirmation by the Government, is a complete answer to a petition for a writ of Habeas Corpus. Once such an order is shown to exist in response to a notice for a writ of Habeas Corpus, the High Court cannot inquire into its validity or vires on the ground of either mala fides of any kind or of non-compliance with any provision of the Maintenance of Internal Security Act in Habeas Corpus proceedings.

In *A.K. Roy v. Union of India*, A.I.R. 1982 S.C. 710, the Constitutional Bench of the Supreme Court of India, while upholding the constitutionality of the National Security Act, 1980 observed:

Chandrachud C.J. (for himself and on behalf of Bhagwati & Desai J.J.)

35.   * * * [I]t is evident that the power of preventive detention was conferred by the Constitution in order to ensure that the security and safety of the country and the welfare of the people are not put in peril. So long as a law of preventive detention operates within the general scope of the affirmative words used in the respective entries of the Union and concurrent lists which give that power and so long as it does not violate any condition or restriction placed upon that power by the Constitution, the Court cannot invalidate that law on the specious ground that it is calculated to interfere with the liberties of the people.

Notes and Questions

1.   Should preventive detention be contrary to due process per se? One may argue, with the majority in *Salerno*, that the requirement that the prosecution present "clear and convincing evidence" justifying detention without bail, is sufficient to satisfy due process. On the other hand, one may argue that the requirement that a person be proven guilty beyond a reasonable doubt is an essential component of due process. What is the strongest justification for each approach?

2. If you conclude that preventive detention is justifiable in some circumstances, should it be limited to the denial of bail prior to trial or allowed, as it is by the Constitution of India, whenever it is authorized by law? Does Justice Marshall's hypothetical defendant, who is acquitted but then still detained upon a showing of dangerousness, change the analysis?

3. Closely related to the issue of preventive detention is a right that is commonly found in modern constitutions—a detainee's right to be charged promptly or released and to be informed in detail of the nature of the charges. In the New Zealand case of *R. v. Gibbons*, [1997] 2 NZLR 585, a defendant claimed that he was not promptly charged after his arrest, and he was not informed in detail of the charges against him. The Court held that "[w]hat is prompt will depend on what is reasonably practical in the circumstances of the case. It will also depend on the nature of the right in issue and the interests in need of protection." Thus by the time the detainee is charged, he should already have been informed of his right to consult a lawyer. But the charging itself need not be immediate upon arrest. In this case, where the detainee was charged at the police station after he had consulted a lawyer, the delay in charging was reasonable. Similarly, "the level of detail required will vary with the circumstances of the case and the stage of the prosecutorial process. * * * In this case he was told in some detail of the nature of the charges he was facing at the time he was charged. * * * By that time he was already aware of the reasons for his arrest and had consulted and instructed a lawyer. Therefore, there has been no breach of his rights under s 24(a) of the Bill of Rights Act either."

C.4. INTERROGATION AND DETENTION: THE PROBLEM OF TORTURE

One of the dangers of pretrial detention—and interrogation in general—is that persons held in custody can be coerced or abused in an attempt to extract evidence or confessions. The problems of abuse and torture can thus be seen as related to the right to silence, discussed in the next section. In some jurisdictions, torture can also be a violation of the right to dignity. The following cases discuss how torture should be defined, whether it can ever be justifiable in situations of national security or emergency, and what remedies are appropriate.

PUBLIC COMMITTEE AGAINST TORTURE IN ISRAEL, ET AL. v. THE STATE OF ISRAEL, THE GENERAL SECURITY SERVICE, ET AL.

Supreme Court (Israel).
H.C. 5100/94.

Sitting as the High Court of Justice, 9/6/1999.

Chief Justice Barak:

The State of Israel has been engaged in an unceasing struggle for both its very existence and security, from the day of its founding. Terrorist organizations have established as their goal Israel's annihilation. Terrorist acts and the general disruption of order are their means of choice * * * The main body responsible for fighting terrorism is the [General Security Service] GSS.

In order to fulfill this function, the GSS also investigates those suspected of hostile terrorist activities. The purpose of these interrogations is, among others, to gather information regarding terrorists and their organizing methods for the purpose of thwarting and preventing them from carrying out these terrorist attacks. In the context of these interrogations, GSS investigators also make use of physical means. The legality of these practices is being examined before this Court in these applications * * *

The Means Employed for Interrogation Purposes

* * * [I]t was argued before this Court that some of the physical means employed by the GSS investigators are permitted by the "law of interrogation" itself. For instance, this is the case with respect to some of the physical means applied in the context of waiting in the "Shabach" position: the placing of the head covering (for preventing communication between the suspects); the playing of powerfully loud music (to prevent the passing of information between suspects); the tying of the suspect's hands to a chair (for the investigators' protection) and the deprivation of sleep, as deriving from the needs of the interrogation. Does the "law of interrogation" sanction the use of physical means, the like used in GSS interrogations?

An interrogation, by its very nature, places the suspect in a difficult position. . . .

Indeed, the authority to conduct interrogations, like any administrative power, is designed for a specific purpose, which constitutes its foundation, and must be in conformity with the basic principles of the [democratic] regime. In crystallizing the interrogation rules, two values or interests clash. Our concern lies in the clash of values and the balancing of conflicting values. The balancing process results in the rules for a 'reasonable interrogation' * * * These rules are based, *on the one hand*, on preserving the "human image" of the suspect * * * and on preserving the "purity of arms" used during the interrogation * * * *On the other hand*, these rules take into consideration the need to fight the phenomenon of criminality in an effective manner generally, and terrorist attacks specifically. These rules reflect "a degree of reasonableness, straight thinking (right mindedness) and fairness" * * *

* * * The "law of interrogation" by its very nature, is intrinsically linked to the circumstances of each case. This having been said, a number of general principles are nonetheless worth noting:

First, a reasonable investigation is necessarily one free of torture, free of cruel, inhuman treatment of the subject and free of any degrading handling whatsoever. There is a prohibition on the use of "brutal or inhuman means" in the course of an investigation * * * Human dignity also includes the dignity of the suspect being interrogated * * * This conclusion is in perfect accord with (various) International Law treaties—to which Israel is a signatory—which prohibit the use of torture, "cruel, inhuman treatment" and "degrading treatment" * * * These prohibitions are "absolute". There are no exceptions to them and there is no room for balancing. Indeed, violence directed at a suspect's body or spirit does not constitute a reasonable investigation practice. The use of violence during investigations can potentially lead to the investigator being held criminally liable * * * *Second,* a reasonable investigation is likely to cause discomfort * * * The conditions under which it is conducted risk being unpleasant. Indeed, it is possible to conduct an effective investigation without resorting to violence * * * In the end result, the legality of an investigation is deduced from the propriety of its purpose and from its methods. Thus, for instance, sleep deprivation for a prolonged period, or sleep deprivation at night when this is not necessary to the investigation time wise may be deemed a use of an investigation method which surpasses the least restrictive means ...

Physical Means and the "Necessity" Defence

We have arrived at the conclusion that the GSS personnel who have received permission to conduct interrogations (as per the Criminal Procedure Statute [Testimony]) are authorized to do so. This authority— like that of the police investigator—does not include most of the physical means of interrogation which are the subject of the application before us. Can the authority to employ these interrogation methods be anchored in a legal source beyond the authority to conduct an interrogation? This question was answered by the State's attorneys in the affirmative. As noted, an explicit authorization permitting GSS to employ physical means is not to be found in our law. An authorization of this nature can, in the State's opinion, be obtained in specific cases by virtue of the criminal law defense of "necessity", prescribed in the Penal Law. The language of the statute is as follows: (Article 34 (1):

> "A person will not bear criminal liability for committing any act immediately necessary for the purpose of saving the life, liberty, body or property, of either himself or his fellow person, from substantial danger of serious harm, imminent from the particular state of things [circumstances], at the requisite timing, and absent alternative means for avoiding the harm."

The State's position is that by virtue of this "defence" to criminal liability, GSS investigators are also authorized to apply physical means, such as shaking, in the appropriate circumstances, in order to prevent serious harm to human life or body, in the absence of other alternatives. The State maintains that an act committed under conditions of "necessity" does not constitute a crime. Instead, it is deemed an act worth committing in such circumstances in order to prevent serious harm to a human life or body. We are therefore speaking of a deed that society has an interest in encouraging, as it is deemed proper in the circumstances. It is choosing the lesser evil. Not only is it legitimately permitted to engage in the fighting of terrorism, it is our moral duty to employ the necessary means for this purpose. * * * As this is the case, there is no obstacle preventing the investigators' superiors from instructing and guiding them with regard to when the conditions of the "necessity" defence are fulfilled and the proper boundaries in those circumstances. From this flows the legality of the directives with respect to the use of physical means in GSS interrogations. In the course of their argument, the State's attorneys submitted the "ticking time bomb" argument. A given suspect is arrested by the GSS. He holds information respecting the location of a bomb that was set and will imminently explode. There is no way to diffuse the bomb without this information. If the information is obtained, however, the bomb may be diffused. If the bomb is not diffused, scores will be killed and maimed. Is a GSS investigator authorized to employ physical means in order to elicit information regarding the location of the bomb in such instances? * * *

[W]e are prepared to presume * * * that if a GSS investigator—who applied physical interrogation methods for the purpose of saving human life—is criminally indicted, the "necessity" defence is likely to be open to him in the appropriate circumstances * * *

This however, is not the issue before this Court * * * The question before us is whether it is possible to infer the authority to, in advance, establish permanent directives setting out the physical interrogation means that may be used under conditions of "necessity". Moreover, we are asking whether the "necessity" defence constitutes a basis for the GSS investigator's authority to investigate, in the performance of his duty. According to the State, it is possible to imply from the "necessity" defence, available (*post factum*) to an investigator indicted of a criminal offence, an advance legal authorization endowing the investigator with the capacity to use physical interrogation methods. Is this position correct?

In the Court's opinion, a general authority to establish directives respecting the use of physical means during the course of a GSS interrogation cannot be implied from the "necessity" defence. The "necessity" defence does not constitute a source of authority, allowing GSS investigators to make use of physical means during the course of interrogations. The reasoning underlying our position is anchored in the nature of the "necessity" defence. This defence deals with deciding those cases involving an individual reacting to a given set of facts; It is an ad hoc endeavour, in reaction to a event. * * * Thus, the very nature of the defence does not allow it to serve as the source of a general administrative power * * *

Similarly, the individual GSS investigator—like any police officer—does not possess the authority to employ physical means which infringe upon a suspect's liberty during the interrogation, unless these means are inherently accessory to the very essence of an interrogation and are both fair and reasonable.

A Final Word

This decision opens with a description of the difficult reality in which Israel finds herself security wise. We shall conclude this judgment by re-addressing that harsh reality. We are aware that this decision does not ease dealing with that reality. This is the destiny of democracy, as not all means are acceptable to it, and not all practices employed by its enemies are open before it. Although a democracy must often fight with one hand tied behind its back, it nonetheless has the upper hand. Preserving the Rule of Law and recognition of an individual's liberty constitutes an important component in its understanding of security. At the end of the day, they strengthen its spirit and its strength and allow it to overcome its difficulties. This having been said, there are those who argue that Israel's security problems are too numerous, thereby requiring the authorization to use physical means. If it will nonetheless be decided that it is appropriate for Israel, in light of its security difficulties to sanction physical means in interrogations (and the scope of these means which deviate from the ordinary investigation rules), this is an issue that must be decided by the legislative branch which represents the people. We do not take any stand on this matter at this time. It is there that various considerations must be weighed. The pointed debate must occur there. It is there that the required legislation may be passed, provided, of course, that a law infringing upon a suspect's liberty "befitting the values of the State of Israel," is enacted for a proper purpose, and to an extent no greater than is required. (Article 8 to the Basic Law: Human Dignity and Liberty) * * *

Given the possibility that a state may be unable or unwilling to police itself in cases where national security is thought to be at stake or in cases of official wrongdoing, the role of supranational instruments and tribunals may be particularly important. In the following case excerpt, the ECHR considers Art.3 of the European HR Convention, which forbids subjecting an individual to torture or inhuman and degrading treatment, and Art. 13, which requires states to provide effective remedies for violations of the Convention.

AYDIN v. TURKEY

European Court of Human Rights.
25 E.H.R.R. 251 (1997).

[The Court addressed the claim of a 17–year-old Kurdish woman who, along with her family, was arrested by Turkish security forces. The Turkish government has been engaged in an armed struggle with its Kurdish minority for many years. The woman alleged that her treatment during detention amounted to torture and that the government failed to conduct an adequate investigation of her allegations.]

74. The applicant contended that the rape and ill-treatment to which she had been subjected gave rise to separate violations of Article 3 of the [European HR] Convention, both of which should be characterised as torture. Article 3 provides:

"No one shall be subjected to torture or to inhuman or degrading treatment or punishment."

75. She was 17 years old at the time of her detention. She was kept blindfolded and isolated from her father and sister-in-law throughout the period of detention. During that time she was debased by being raped and has suffered long-term psychological damage as a result of that particular act of torture.

Furthermore, she was stripped naked, questioned by strangers, beaten, slapped, threatened and abused. She was forced into a tyre, spun around and hosed with ice-cold water from high-pressure jets. Having regard to her sex, age and vulnerability she requested the Court to find that the deliberately inflicted and calculated physical suffering and sexual humiliation of which she was the victim was of such severity as to amount to an additional act of torture. * * *

81. * * * Article 3 of the Convention enshrines one of the fundamental values of democratic societies and as such it prohibits in absolute terms torture or inhuman or degrading treatment or punishment. Article 3 admits of no exceptions to this fundamental value and no derogation from it is permissible under Article 15 even having regard to the imperatives of a public emergency threatening the life of the nation or to any suspicion, however well-founded, that a person may be involved in terrorist or other criminal activities (see, for example, the *Aksoy* judgment * * *)

82. In order to determine whether any particular form of ill-treatment should be qualified as torture, regard must be had to the distinction drawn in Article 3 between this notion and that of inhuman treatment or degrading treatment. This distinction would appear to have been embodied in the Convention to allow the special stigma of "torture" to attach only to deliberate inhuman treatment causing very serious and cruel suffering (see *Ireland v. the United Kingdom* * * * p. 66, § 167).

83. While being held in detention the applicant was raped by a person whose identity has still to be determined. Rape of a detainee by an official of the State must be considered to be an especially grave and abhorrent form of ill-treatment given the ease with which the offender can exploit the vulnerability and weakened resistance of his victim. Furthermore, rape leaves deep psychological scars on the victim which do not respond to the passage of time as quickly as other forms of physical and mental violence. The applicant also experienced the acute physical pain of forced penetration, which must have left her feeling debased and violated both physically and emotionally.

84. The applicant was also subjected to a series of particularly terrifying and humiliating experiences while in custody at the hands of the security forces at Derik gendarmerie headquarters having regard to her sex and youth and the circumstances under which she was held. She was detained over a period of three days during which she must have been bewildered and disoriented by being kept blindfolded, and in a constant state of physical pain and mental anguish brought on by the beatings administered to her during questioning and by the apprehension of what would happen to her next. She was also paraded naked in humiliating circumstances thus adding to her overall sense of vulnerability and on one occasion she was pummelled with high-pressure water while being spun around in a tyre.

85. The applicant and her family must have been taken from their village and brought to Derik gendarmerie headquarters for a purpose, which can only be explained on account of the security situation in the region * * * and the need of the security forces to elicit information. The suffering inflicted on the applicant during the period of her detention must also be seen as calculated to serve the same or related purposes.

86. Against this background the Court is satisfied that the accumulation of acts of physical and mental violence inflicted on the applicant and the especially cruel act of rape to which she was subjected amounted to torture in breach of Article 3 of the Convention. * * *

103. * * * Article 13 guarantees the availability at the national level of a remedy to enforce the substance of the Convention rights and freedoms in whatever form they might happen to be secured in the domestic legal order. The effect of this Article is thus to require the provision of a domestic remedy allowing the competent national authority both to deal with the substance of the relevant Convention complaint and to grant appropriate relief, although Contracting States are afforded some discretion as to the manner in which they conform to their obligations under this provision. The scope of the obligation under Article 13 varies depending on the nature of the applicant's complaint under the Convention. Nevertheless, the remedy required by Article 13 must be "effective" in practice as well as in law, in particular in the sense that its exercise must not be unjustifiably hindered by the acts or omissions of the authorities of the respondent State. * * *

Furthermore, the nature of the right safeguarded under Article 3 of the Convention has implications for Article 13. Given the fundamental importance of the prohibition of torture and the especially vulnerable position of torture victims * * * Article 13 imposes, without prejudice to any other remedy available under the domestic system, an obligation on States to carry out a thorough and effective investigation of incidents of torture.

Accordingly, where an individual has an arguable claim that he or she has been tortured by agents of the State, the notion of an "effective remedy" entails, in addition to the payment of compensation where appropriate, a thorough and effective investigation capable of leading to the identification and punishment of those responsible and including effective access for the complainant to the investigatory procedure. It is true that no express provision exists in the Convention such as can be found in Article 12 of the 1984 United Nations Convention against Torture and Other Cruel, Inhuman or Degrading Treatment or Punishment, which imposes a duty to proceed to a "prompt and impartial" investigation whenever there is a reasonable ground to believe that an act of torture has been committed. * * * However, such a requirement is implicit in the notion of an "effective remedy" under Article 13. * * *

104. Having regard to these principles, the Court notes that the applicant was entirely reliant on the public prosecutor and the police acting on his instructions to assemble the evidence necessary for corroborating her complaint. The public prosecutor had the legal powers to interview members of the security forces at Derik gendarmerie headquarters, summon witnesses, visit the scene of the incident, collect forensic evidence and take all other crucial steps for establishing the truth of her account. His role was critical not only to the pursuit of criminal proceedings against the perpetrators of the offences but also to the pursuit by the applicant of other remedies to redress the harm she

suffered. The ultimate effectiveness of those remedies depended on the proper discharge by the public prosecutor of his functions.

[The Court, after discussion of the official investigation, found:]

109. * * * [I]t must be concluded that no thorough and effective investigation was conducted into the applicant's allegations and that this failure undermined the effectiveness of any other remedies which may have existed given the centrality of the public prosecutor's role to the system of remedies as a whole, including the pursuit of compensation.

In conclusion, there has been a violation of Article 13 of the Convention.

Notes and Questions

1. The Israeli and Turkish cases define judicial limits on interrogation procedures that include torture. Is this a proper judicial role when a country regards itself at war? Are decisions forbidding the use of physical force laudatory because they underline the importance of the rule of law and set out enduring principles that transcend particular contexts? What is the role for a court if the legislature has explicitly allowed physical force in interrogations? Should the answer depend on whether the judgments of the courts can be enforced against executive branch wrongdoers?

2. What remedies are appropriate for torture cases? And what should be their purpose—e.g., deter future misconduct, restore public faith in the integrity of the system, make the victim whole?

3. The well-known U.S. case of *Miranda v. Arizona*, excerpted in the next section, discusses, among other issues, police violence during custodial interrogation. As you read the following sections on right to silence and right to counsel, consider how these rights may afford some protection from police abuse.

D. RIGHT TO SILENCE AND PRIVILEGE AGAINST SELF–INCRIMINATION

An accused's right to silence and privilege against self-incrimination can be found in at least 48 national constitutions. See Bassiouni, *op. cit.* at 265. There is significant variation in the interpretation of the privilege, especially as to whether it applies immediately upon arrest or only at trial and whether adverse inferences may be drawn from the silence of the accused. The following cases explore these variations, but first we present a discussion of rationales for the privilege.

David Dolinko, IS THERE A RATIONALE FOR THE PRIVILEGE AGAINST SELF–INCRIMINATION?,
33 UCLA L. Rev. 1063, 1065–66 (1986).

The rationales for the privilege against self-incrimination fall, very roughly, into two categories. Systemic rationales are policies their proponents believe to be crucial to our particular kind of criminal justice system. Individual rationales are principles claimed to be entailed by a proper understanding of human rights or by a proper respect for human dignity and individuality. Among systemic rationales are the suggestions that the privilege "encourages third-party witnesses to appear and testify by removing the fear that they might be compelled to incriminate themselves" and "remov[es] the temptation to employ short cuts to conviction that demean official integrity." Individual rationales include the arguments that compelled self-incrimination works an unacceptable cruelty or invasion of privacy, as well as the notion of "respect for the inviolability of the human personality," and the belief that punishing an individual for silence or perjury when he has been "place[d] ... in a position in which his natural instincts and personal interests dictate that he should lie ... is an intolerable invasion of his personal dignity."

D.1. THE PRIVILEGE BEFORE TRIAL

Not all countries extend the privilege against self-incrimination to the pretrial stage of the criminal process. In countries where the privilege does apply pretrial, there is usually an additional constitutional requirement that detainees be informed of their right to silence before being interrogated. In the well-known *Miranda* case, excerpted below, the USSC held that the interrogation of an individual in custody implicates the privilege against self-incrimination.

MIRANDA v. ARIZONA

Supreme Court (United States).
384 U.S. 436 (1966).

Mr. Chief Justice Warren delivered the opinion of the Court.

The cases before us raise questions which go to the roots of our concepts of American criminal jurisprudence: the restraints society must observe consistent with the Federal Constitution in prosecuting individuals for crime. More specifically, we deal with the admissibility of statements obtained from an individual who is subjected to custodial police interrogation and the necessity for procedures which assure that the individual is accorded his privilege under the Fifth Amendment to the Constitution not to be compelled to incriminate himself. * * *

We start * * * with the premise that our holding is not an innovation in our jurisprudence, but is an application of principles long recognized and applied in other settings. We have undertaken a thorough re-examination of the *Escobedo* decision and the principles it announced, and we reaffirm it. That case was but an explication of basic rights that are enshrined in our Constitution—that "No person ... shall be compelled in any criminal case to be a witness against himself," and that "the accused shall * * * have the Assistance of Counsel"—rights which were put in jeopardy in that case through official overbearing. These precious rights were fixed in our Constitution only after centuries of persecution and struggle. And in the words of Chief Justice Marshall, they were secured "for ages to come, and ... designed to approach immortality as nearly as human institutions can approach it," *Cohens v. Virginia*, 6 Wheat. 264, 387 (1821).

In stating the obligation of the judiciary to apply these constitutional rights, this Court declared in *Weems v. United States*, 217 U.S. 349, 373 (1910):

> "* * * our contemplation cannot be only of what has been but of what may be. Under any other rule a constitution would indeed be as easy of application as it would be deficient in efficacy and power. Its general principles would have little value and be converted by precedent into impotent and lifeless formulas. Rights declared in words might be lost in reality. And this has been recognized. The meaning and vitality of the Constitution have developed against narrow and restrictive construction."

This was the spirit in which we delineated, in meaningful language, the manner in which the constitutional rights of the individual could be enforced against overzealous police practices. It was necessary in *Escobedo*, as here, to insure that what was proclaimed in the Constitution had not become but a "form of words," *Silverthorne Lumber Co. v. United States*, 251 U.S. 385, 392 (1920), in the hands of government officials. And it is in this spirit, consistent with our role as judges, that we adhere to the principles of *Escobedo* today. * * *

I

* * * An understanding of the nature and setting of this in-custody interrogation is essential to our decisions today. The difficulty in depicting what transpires at such interrogations stems from the fact that in this country they have largely taken place incommunicado. From extensive factual studies undertaken in the early 1930's, * * * it is clear that police violence and the "third degree" flourished at that time. * * * In a series of cases decided by this Court long after these studies, the police resorted to physical brutality—beating, hanging, whipping—and to sustained and protracted questioning incommunicado in order to extort confessions. * * * Unless a proper limitation upon custodial interrogation is achieved—such as these decisions will advance—there can be no assurance that practices of this nature will be eradicated in the foreseeable future. * * *

[T]he modern practice of in-custody interrogation is psychologically rather than physically oriented. As we have stated before, "Since *Chambers v. Florida*, 309 U.S. 227, this Court has recognized that coercion can be mental as well as physical, and that the blood of the accused is not the only hallmark of an unconstitutional inquisition." *Blackburn v. Alabama*, 361 U.S. 199, 206 (1960). Interrogation still takes place in privacy. Privacy results in secrecy and this in turn results in a gap in our knowledge as to what in fact goes on in the interrogation rooms. * * *

[T]he very fact of custodial interrogation exacts a heavy toll on individual liberty and trades on the weakness of individuals. * * * In the cases before us today, given this background, we concern ourselves primarily with this interrogation atmosphere and the evils it can bring. In No. 759, *Miranda v. Arizona*, the police arrested the defendant and took him to a special interrogation room where they secured a confession. * * *

In these cases, we might not find the defendants' statements to have been involuntary in traditional terms. Our concern for adequate safeguards to protect precious Fifth Amendment rights is, of course, not lessened in the slightest. In each of the cases, the defendant was thrust into an unfamiliar atmosphere and run through menacing police interrogation procedures. The potentiality for compulsion is forcefully apparent, for example, in *Miranda*, where the indigent Mexican defendant was a seriously disturbed individual with pronounced sexual fantasies. * * * To be sure, the records do not evince overt physical coercion or patent psychological ploys. The fact remains that in none of these cases did the officers undertake to afford appropriate safeguards at the outset of the interrogation to insure that the statements were truly the product of free choice.

It is obvious that such an interrogation environment is created for no purpose other than to subjugate the individual to the will of his examiner. This atmosphere carries its own badge of intimidation. To be sure, this is not physical intimidation, but it is equally destructive of human dignity. The current practice of incommunicado interrogation is at odds with one of our Nation's most cherished principles—that the individual may not be compelled to incriminate himself. Unless adequate protective devices are employed to dispel the compulsion inherent in custodial surroundings, no statement obtained from the defendant can truly be the product of his free choice. * * *

II

* * * [W]e may view the historical development of the privilege as one which groped for the proper scope of governmental power over the citizen. As a "noble principle often transcends its origins," the privilege has come rightfully to be recognized in part as an individual's substantive right, a "right to a private enclave where he may lead a private life. That right is the hallmark of our democracy." *United States v. Grunewald*, 233 F.2d 556, 579, 581–582 (Frank, J., dissenting), rev'd, 353 U.S. 391 (1957). . . . [T]he constitutional foundation underlying the privilege is the respect a government—state or federal—must accord to the dignity and integrity of its citizens. To maintain a "fair state-individual balance" * * * our accusatory system of criminal justice demands that the government seeking to punish an individual produce the evidence against him by its own independent labors, rather than by the cruel, simple expedient of compelling it from his own mouth. *Chambers v. Florida*, 309 U.S. 227, 235–238 (1940). In sum, the privilege is fulfilled only when the person is guaranteed the right "to remain silent unless he chooses to speak in the unfettered exercise of his own will." *Malloy v. Hogan*, 378 U.S. 1, 8 (1964).

* * * We are satisfied that all the principles embodied in the privilege apply to informal compulsion exerted by law-enforcement officers during in-custody questioning. An individual swept from familiar surroundings into police custody, surrounded by antagonistic forces, and

subjected to the techniques of persuasion described above cannot be otherwise than under compulsion to speak. As a practical matter, the compulsion to speak in the isolated setting of the police station may well be greater than in courts or other official investigations, where there are often impartial observers to guard against intimidation or trickery. * * *

III

Today, then, there can be no doubt that the Fifth Amendment privilege is available outside of criminal court proceedings and serves to protect persons in all settings in which their freedom of action is curtailed in any significant way from being compelled to incriminate themselves. We have concluded that without proper safeguards the process of in-custody interrogation of persons suspected or accused of crime contains inherently compelling pressures which work to under-mine the individual's will to resist and to compel him to speak where he would not otherwise do so freely. In order to combat these pressures and to permit a full opportunity to exercise the privilege against self-incrimination, the accused must be adequately and effectively apprised of his rights and the exercise of those rights must be fully honored.

It is impossible for us to foresee the potential alternatives for protecting the privilege which might be devised by Congress or the States in the exercise of their creative rule-making capacities. Therefore we cannot say that the Constitution necessarily requires adherence to any particular solution for the inherent compulsions of the interrogation process as it is presently conducted. Our decision in no way creates a constitutional straitjacket which will handicap sound efforts at reform, nor is it intended to have this effect. We encourage Congress and the States to continue their laudable search for increasingly effective ways of protecting the rights of the individual while promoting efficient enforce-ment of our criminal laws. However, unless we are shown other proce-dures which are at least as effective in apprising accused persons of their right of silence and in assuring a continuous opportunity to exercise it, the following safeguards must be observed.

At the outset, if a person in custody is to be subjected to interroga-tion, he must first be informed in clear and unequivocal terms that he has the right to remain silent. For those unaware of the privilege, the warning is needed simply to make them aware of it—the threshold requirement for an intelligent decision as to its exercise. More impor-tant, such a warning is an absolute prerequisite in overcoming the inherent pressures of the interrogation atmosphere. It is not just the subnormal or woefully ignorant who succumb to an interrogator's impre-cations, whether implied or expressly stated, that the interrogation will continue until a confession is obtained or that silence in the face of accusation is itself damning and will bode ill when presented to a jury. Further, the warning will show the individual that his interrogators are prepared to recognize his privilege should he choose to exercise it.

The Fifth Amendment privilege is so fundamental to our system of constitutional rule and the expedient of giving an adequate warning as to the availability of the privilege so simple, we will not pause to inquire in individual cases whether the defendant was aware of his rights without a warning being given. Assessments of the knowledge the defendant possessed, based on information as to his age, education, intelligence, or prior contact with authorities, can never be more than speculation; a warning is a clearcut fact. More important, whatever the background of the person interrogated, a warning at the time of the interrogation is indispensable to overcome its pressures and to insure that the individual knows he is free to exercise the privilege at that point in time.

The warning of the right to remain silent must be accompanied by the explanation that anything said can and will be used against the individual in court. This warning is needed in order to make him aware not only of the privilege, but also of the consequences of forgoing it. * * *

The circumstances surrounding in-custody interrogation can operate very quickly to overbear the will of one merely made aware of his privilege by his interrogators. Therefore, the right to have counsel present at the interrogation is indispensable to the protection of the Fifth Amendment privilege under the system we delineate today. Our aim is to assure that the individual's right to choose between silence and speech remains unfettered throughout the interrogation process. * * *

The presence of counsel at the interrogation may serve several significant subsidiary functions as well. If the accused decides to talk to his interrogators, the assistance of counsel can mitigate the dangers of untrustworthiness. With a lawyer present the likelihood that the police will practice coercion is reduced, and if coercion is nevertheless exercised the lawyer can testify to it in court. The presence of a lawyer can also help to guarantee that the accused gives a fully accurate statement to the police and that the statement is rightly reported by the prosecution at trial. * * *

An individual need not make a pre-interrogation request for a lawyer. While such request affirmatively secures his right to have one, his failure to ask for a lawyer does not constitute a waiver. No effective waiver of the right to counsel during interrogation can be recognized unless specifically made after the warnings we here delineate have been given. The accused who does not know his rights and therefore does not make a request may be the person who most needs counsel. * * *

Accordingly we hold that an individual held for interrogation must be clearly informed that he has the right to consult with a lawyer and to have the lawyer with him during interrogation under the system for protecting the privilege we delineate today. As with the warnings of the right to remain silent and that anything stated can be used in evidence against him, this warning is an absolute prerequisite to interrogation. No amount of circumstantial evidence that the person may have been aware of this right will suffice to stand in its stead. Only through such a warning is there ascertainable assurance that the accused was aware of this right. * * *

In order fully to apprise a person interrogated of the extent of his rights under this system then, it is necessary to warn him not only that he has the right to consult with an attorney, but also that if he is indigent a lawyer will be appointed to represent him. Without this additional warning, the admonition of the right to consult with counsel would often be understood as meaning only that he can consult with a lawyer if he has one or has the funds to obtain one. The warning of a right to counsel would be hollow if not couched in terms that would convey to the indigent—the person most often subjected to interrogation—the knowledge that he too has a right to have counsel present. As with the warnings of the right to remain silent and of the general right to counsel, only by effective and express explanation to the indigent of this right can there be assurance that he was truly in a position to exercise it.

Once warnings have been given, the subsequent procedure is clear. If the individual indicates in any manner, at any time prior to or during questioning, that he wishes to remain silent, the interrogation must cease. At this point he has shown that he intends to exercise his Fifth Amendment privilege; any statement taken after the person invokes his privilege cannot be other than the product of compulsion, subtle or otherwise. Without the right to cut off questioning, the setting of in-custody interrogation operates on the individual to overcome free choice in producing a statement after the privilege has been once invoked. If the individual states that he wants an attorney, the interrogation must cease until an attorney is present. At that time, the individual must have an opportunity to confer with the attorney and to have him present during any subsequent questioning. If the individual cannot obtain an attorney and he indicates that he wants one before speaking to police, they must respect his decision to remain silent.

If the interrogation continues without the presence of an attorney and a statement is taken, a heavy burden rests on the government to demonstrate that the defendant knowingly and intelligently waived his privilege against self-incrimination and his right to retained or appointed counsel. *Escobedo v. Illinois,* 378 U.S. 478, 490, n. 14 * * *.

IV

A recurrent argument made in these cases is that society's need for interrogation outweighs the privilege. This argument is not unfamiliar to this Court. * * * The whole thrust of our foregoing discussion demonstrates that the Constitution has prescribed the rights of the individual when confronted with the power of government when it provided in the Fifth Amendment that an individual cannot be compelled to be a witness against himself. That right cannot be abridged. * * *

In announcing these principles, we are not unmindful of the burdens which law enforcement officials must bear, often under trying circumstances. We also fully recognize the obligation of all citizens to aid in enforcing the criminal laws. * * * As we have noted, our decision does not in any way preclude police from carrying out their traditional investigatory functions. Although confessions may play an important role in some convictions, the cases before us present graphic examples of the overstatement of the "need" for confessions. In each case authorities conducted interrogations ranging up to five days in duration despite the presence, through standard investigating practices, of considerable evidence against each defendant. * * *

The experience in some other countries also suggests that the danger to law enforcement in curbs on interrogation is overplayed. [The Court here discusses the experiences of England and Scotland, India, and Sri Lanka.] * * * Conditions of law enforcement in our country are sufficiently similar to permit reference to this experience as assurance that lawlessness will not result from warning an individual of his rights or allowing him to exercise them. Moreover, it is consistent with our legal system that we give at least as much protection to these rights as is given in the jurisdictions described. We deal in our country with rights grounded in a specific requirement of the Fifth Amendment of the Constitution, whereas other jurisdictions arrived at their conclusions on the basis of principles of justice not so specifically defined. * * *[64]

Note on Miranda

While *Miranda* occupies a central position in U.S. criminal procedure, its effect has been limited through subsequent decisions. *Harris v. New York,* 401 U.S. 222 (1971), held that statements by a defendant preceded by defective warnings, while inadmissible in the prosecution's case in chief, were admissible to impeach the defendant's credibility. In *Oregon v. Hass,* 420, U.S. 714 (1975), the Court made clear that a defendant's statements were available for impeachment even if they resulted from interrogations conducted after the defendant had received *Miranda* warnings and had asserted his rights. Under *New York v. Quarles,* 467 U.S. 649 (1984), if police interrogation is reasonably prompted by concern for public safety, responses to the questions may be used in court, even if *Miranda* warnings are not given.

Miranda has been criticized on the grounds that its costs (possibly allowing a large number of guilty persons to go free) outweigh its benefits and that its rule is not constitutionally required but is merely prophylactic. See, e.g., Paul G. Cassell, Miranda*'s Social Costs: An Empirical Reassessment,* 90 Nw. U. L. Rev. 387 (1996). Cassell proposes that *Miranda* be replaced with alternative methods of protecting suspects from police coercion, such as videotaping of interrogations. *Miranda*'s defenders contest the factual basis for this view, arguing that *"Miranda*'s detectable social costs are vanishingly small and its benefits are substantial—for anyone who may someday be arrested and for police departments themselves. Yet we cannot afford to treat compliance with *Miranda*'s safeguards as an optional matter." Stephen J. Schulhofer, Miranda's *Practical Effect: Substantial Benefits and Vanishingly Small Social Costs,* 90 Nw. U. L. Rev. 500, 562 (1996).

The Supreme Court recently revisited the *Miranda* decision in *Dickerson v. United States,* 530 U.S. 428 (2000). In *Dickerson* the Court addressed a challenge to *Miranda* based on a federal statute that would have eliminated the *Miranda* requirements. Thus the case raised the question of whether

---

64. Although no constitution existed at the time confessions were excluded by rule of evidence in 1872, India now has a written constitution which includes the provision that "No person accused of any offence shall be compelled to be a witness against himself." Constitution of India, Article 20 (3). See Tope, The Constitution of India 63–67 (1960).

the *Miranda* warnings were constitutionally required or were simply prophylactic measures to prevent police abuse that could be annulled through
legislative action. The Court found that the holding of *Miranda* was based on
the requirements of the Fifth Amendment, and, therefore, Congress cannot
eliminate the *Miranda* requirements by statute.

The *Miranda* decision is a still quite rare example of the use of foreign
authorities in U.S. constitutional decisionmaking as it discussed the laws
and experience of Scotland, England, and India.

While other countries provide for a privilege against self-incrimination,
they have implemented it variously. In several cases foreign systems go
beyond the requirements of *Miranda* in their imposition of limits on police
questioning. Australia and England require videotaping of interrogations.
Also,

> suspects in England and France must be allowed to contact family or
> friends, and must be told of that right; police detention of longer than a
> fixed number of hours requires approval of designated higher-level
> police officers, prosecutors, or judges; and a detailed record, signed by
> the suspect, must be kept of all in-custody proceedings (including, inter
> alia, not only the suspect's statements, but also all warnings, waivers,
> and approvals of extensions of detention). In Germany, suspects must be
> warned, before questioning, of their right to remain silent, even when
> the suspect is not arrested or otherwise in custody, and the use of police
> deceit and questioning by informants or undercover officers is more
> restricted than in the U.S. Of course, in each of these systems suspects
> lack some protections which American suspects have during interroga-
> tion (particularly with respect to the right to counsel and waiver rules).

Richard S. Frase, *The Search for the Whole Truth About American and
European Criminal Justice,* 3 Buff. Crim. L. Rev. 785, 801 (2000).

The following cases and the notes following illustrate the variations
among countries in protecting a detainee's right to silence before trial.

R. v. HEBERT

Supreme Court (Canada).
[1990] 2 S.C.R. 151.

The accused was arrested on a charge of robbery and informed upon
arrest of his right to counsel. At the police station, after consulting
counsel, he advised the police that he did not wish to make a statement.
The accused was then placed in a cell with an undercover police officer
posing as a suspect under arrest. The officer engaged the accused in
conversation, during which the accused made incriminating statements
implicating him in the robbery. Prior to trial, there was a voir dire to
determine the admissibility of these statements. The judge held that the
accused's right to counsel under s. 10(b) of the Canadian Charter of
Rights and Freedoms and his right to remain silent asserted under s. 7
of the Charter had been violated and excluded the statements pursuant
to s. 24(2) of the Charter. The Crown offered no evidence, and the
accused was later acquitted. The Court of Appeal set aside the accused's
acquittal and ordered a new trial. The Court found that the police
conduct did not violate the accused's right to counsel or his right to
remain silent.

The judgment of Dickson C.J. and Lamer, La Forest, L'Heureux–Dubé, Gonthier, Cory and McLachlin JJ. was delivered by McLachlin J.

This case raises the issue of whether a statement made by a detained person to an undercover police officer violates the rights of the accused under the *Canadian Charter of Rights and Freedoms*. * * *

Canadian Charter of Rights and Freedoms

7. Everyone has the right to life, liberty and security of the person and the right not to be deprived thereof except in accordance with the principles of fundamental justice.

10. Everyone has the right on arrest or detention * * * (*b*) to retain and instruct counsel without delay and to be informed of that right;

24. * * * (2) Where, in proceedings under subsection (1), a court concludes that evidence was obtained in a manner that infringed or denied any rights or freedoms guaranteed by this Charter, the evidence shall be excluded if it is established that, having regard to all the circumstances, the admission of it in the proceedings would bring the administration of justice into disrepute.

* * * The scheme under the *Charter* to protect the accused's pre-trial right to silence may be described as follows. Section 7 confers on the detained person the right to choose whether to speak to the authorities or to remain silent. Section 10(*b*) requires that he be advised of his right to consult counsel and permitted to do so without delay.

The most important function of legal advice upon detention is to ensure that the accused understands his rights, chief among which is his right to silence. The detained suspect, potentially at a disadvantage in relation to the informed and sophisticated powers at the disposal of the state, is entitled to rectify the disadvantage by speaking to legal counsel at the outset, so that he is aware of his right not to speak to the police and obtains appropriate advice with respect to the choice he faces. Read together, ss. 7 and 10(*b*) confirm the right to silence in s. 7 and shed light on its nature.

The guarantee of the right to consult counsel confirms that the essence of the right is the accused's freedom to choose whether to make a statement or not. The state is not obliged to protect the suspect against making a statement; indeed it is open to the state to use legitimate means of persuasion to encourage the suspect to do so. The state is, however, obliged to allow the suspect to make an informed choice about whether or not he will speak to the authorities. To assist in that choice, the suspect is given the right to counsel. * * *

I should not be taken as suggesting that the right to make an informed choice whether to speak to the authorities or to remain silent necessitates a particular state of knowledge on the suspect's part over and above the basic requirement that he possess an operating mind. The *Charter* does not place on the authorities and the courts the impossible task of subjectively gauging whether the suspect appreciates the situation and the alternatives. Rather, it seeks to ensure that the suspect is in a position to make an informed choice by giving him the right to counsel. The guarantee of the right to counsel in the *Charter* suggests that the suspect must have the right to choose whether to speak to the police or not, but it equally suggests that the test for whether that choice has been violated is essentially objective. Was the suspect accorded his or her right to consult counsel? By extension, was there other police conduct which effectively deprived the suspect of the right to choose to remain silent, thus negating the purpose of the right to counsel?

The second *Charter* right relevant to the ambit of the right to silence conferred by s. 7 is the privilege against self-incrimination. This right has been enshrined in s. 11(*c*) of the *Charter*, which provides that no one can be required to give evidence against himself, and echoed in s. 13 of the *Charter*, which prevents evidence given by a witness being used against the witness in a subsequent proceeding. * * * [T]he *Charter* guarantees against self-incrimination at trial are to be given their full effect, an effective right of choice as to whether to make a statement must exist at the pre-trial stage.

* * *

The scope of the right to silence must be defined broadly enough to preserve for the detained person the right to choose whether to speak to the authorities or to remain silent, notwithstanding the fact that he or she is in the superior power of the state. On this view, the scope of the right must extend to exclude tricks which would effectively deprive the suspect of this choice. To permit the authorities to trick the suspect into making a confession to them after he or she has exercised the right of conferring with counsel and declined to make a statement, is to permit the authorities to do indirectly what the *Charter* does not permit them to do directly. This cannot be in accordance with the purpose of the *Charter*.

* * *

I am of the view that the evidence sought to be adduced in this case would render the trial unfair. I should not be taken as suggesting that violation of an accused's right to silence under s. 7 automatically means that the evidence must be excluded under s. 24(2). I would not wish to rule out the possibility that there may be circumstances in which a statement might be received where the suspect has not been accorded a full choice in the sense of having decided, after full observance of all rights, to make a statement voluntarily. But where, as here, an accused is conscripted to give evidence against himself after clearly electing not to do so by use of an unfair trick practised by the authorities, and where the resultant statement is the only evidence against him, one must surely conclude that reception of the evidence would render the trial unfair. The accused would be deprived of his presumption of innocence and would be placed in the position of having to take the stand if he wished to counter the damaging effect of the confession. The accused's conviction if obtained would rest almost entirely on his own evidence against himself, obtained by a trick in violation of the *Charter*.

I am also satisfied that the *Charter* violation was a serious one. The conduct of the police was wilful and deliberate. They intentionally set out on a course to undermine the appellant's right to silence notwithstanding his express assertion of that right, by having the undercover police officer engage the appellant in conversation. * * *

The effect of the exclusion in this case is serious. It would result in an acquittal, since virtually the only evidence against the accused was his statement to the undercover policeman.

Balancing these factors, I arrive at the conclusion that the test in s. 24(2) is met. As the authorities to which I earlier referred amply demonstrate, it has long been felt inappropriate that an accused should be required to betray himself. Where virtually the only evidence against him is such a betrayal, the effect is that the accused is required to secure his own conviction. That is contrary to the notions of justice fundamental to our system of law and calculated, in my opinion, to bring the administration of justice into disrepute.

I would allow the appeal and restore the acquittal.

NANDINI SATPATHY v. P. L. DANI

Supreme Court (India).
A.I.R. 1978 S.C. 1025 (1978).

[Nandini Satpathy, former Chief Minister of Orissa and one-time national minister, was directed to appear at a police station for questioning in connection with cases filed against her under the Prevention of Corruption Act and the Indian Penal Code. On the strength of this first information, an investigation was opened, and Satpathy was interrogated with reference to a long string of questions given to her in writing. The questioning soon broadened into other areas.]

V.R. Krishna Iyer, J.

6. * * * The gravamen of the accusation was one of acquisition of assets disproportionate to the known, licit sources of income and probable resources over the years. The dimensions of the offences naturally broadened the area of investigation, and to do justice to such investigation, the net of interrogation had to be cast wide. Inevitably, a police officer who is not too precise, too sensitive and too constitutionally conscientious is apt to trample under foot the guaranteed right of testimonial tacitness. This is precisely the grievance of the appellant, and the defense of the respondent is the absence of the 'right of silence' * * *.

19. * * * There are only two primary queries involved in this clause [Article 20(3) of the Constitution of India reads "No person accused of any offence shall be compelled to be a witness against himself."—Eds.] that seals the lips into permissible silence: (i) Is the person called upon to testify 'accused of any offence'? (ii) Is he being compelled to be witness against himself? A constitutional provision receives its full semantic range and so it follows that wider connotation must be imparted to the expressions 'accused of any offence' and 'to be witness against himself.'

53. * * * We hold that Section 161 of the Criminal Procedure Code, 1973 enables the police to examine the accused during investiga-

tion. The prohibitive sweep of art. 20(3) goes back to the stage of police interrogation—not, as contended, commencing in Court only. In our judgement the provisions of art. 20(3) and s. 161(1) substantially cover the same area, so far as police investigations are concerned. The ban on self-accusation and the right to silence, while an investigation or trial is under way, goes beyond that case and protects the accused in regard to other offences pending or imminent, which may deter him from voluntary disclosure of criminatory matter. We are disposed to read 'compelled testimony' as evidence procured not merely by physical threats or violence but by psychic torture, atmospheric pressure, environmental coercion, tiring interrogative prolixity, overbearing and intimidatory methods and the like * * *. [T]he legal perils following upon refusal to answer, or answer truthfully, cannot be regarded as compulsion within the meaning of art. 20(3). The prospect of prosecution may lead to legal tension in the exercise of a constitutional right, but then, a stance of silence is running a calculated risk. On the other hand, if there is any mode of pressure, subtle or crude, mental or physical, direct or indirect, but sufficiently substantial, applied by the policeman for obtaining information from an accused strongly suggestive of guilt, it becomes 'compelled testimony', violative of art. 20(3).

54. * * * A police officer is clearly a person in authority. Insistence on answering is a form of pressure especially in the atmosphere of the police station unless certain safeguards erasing duress are adhered to. Frequent threats of prosecution if there is failure to answer may take on the complexion of undue pressure violating art. 20(3). Legal penalty may by itself not amount to duress but the manner of mentioning it to the victim of interrogation may introduce an element of tension and tone of command perilously hovering near compulsion.

55. * * * The accused person cannot be forced to answer questions merely because the answers thereto are not implicative when viewed in isolation and confined to that particular case. He is entitled to keep his mouth shut if the answer sought has a reasonable prospect of exposing him to guilt in some other accusation actual or imminent, even though the investigation under way is not with reference to that. In determining the incriminatory character of an answer the accused is entitled to consider—and the Court while adjudging will take note of—the setting, the totality of circumstances, the equation, personal and social, which have a bearing on making an answer substantially innocent but in effect guilty in import. However, fanciful claims, unreasonable apprehensions and vague possibilities cannot be the hiding ground for an accused person. He is bound to answer where there is no clear tendency to criminate.

29. * * * We have said sufficient to drive home the anxious point that this cherished principle which prescribes compulsory self-accusation, should not be dangerously over-broad not illusorily whittled down. And it must openly work in practice and not be a talismanic symbol. The *Miranda* ruling clothed the Fifth Amendment with flesh and blood and so must we, if Article 20(3) is not to prove a promise of unreality. Aware that the questions raised go to the root of criminal jurisprudence we seek light from *Miranda* for interpretation, not innovation, for principles in

their settings, not borrowings for our conditions. The spiritual thrust of the two provisions is the same. * * *

Notes and Questions

1. Are the rationales for the right to silence suggested by Dolinko or those given in the cases persuasive?

2. Does your answer to the first question support extending the right to silence to pretrial interrogation? Consider the conflicting values, discussed in the introductory sections of this chapter, of truth-seeking and equality between the parties. Should a willingness to extend the right to pretrial interrogation depend on the role played by the police in the criminal justice system (i.e., on whether the police are aligned with the prosecution or are formally neutral)?

3. Assuming that the right to silence does extend to pretrial interrogation, are *Miranda*-style warnings necessary to protect that right? If warnings are necessary, are the specific warnings required by the *Miranda* decision sufficient? In a recent decision the International Court of Justice held that the U.S. violated its obligations under the Vienna Convention on Consular Relations, Art. 36, para. 1(b), by failing to inform the LaGrand brothers (German nationals), shortly after their arrest, of their right to contact their consulate. See *LaGrand Case* (*Germany v. United States of America*), 2001 I.C.J. (June 27). Should a warning about this right be required? What about other rights of the accused?

D.2. THE RIGHT TO SILENCE AT TRIAL: ADVERSE INFERENCES

In some common law countries, including the U.S., defendants rarely speak at trial. In Continental Europe, the opposite is true. This difference is partly due to legal rules and partly to the difference in trial environments and cultures. In reading the following cases, consider whether the drawing of adverse inferences from silence at trial is a serious limitation on a defendant's right to silence or on the presumption of innocence.

In the following case the USSC held that the Fifth Amendment prohibits both comment by the prosecution on a defendant's silence (either before or during trial) and instructions by the court that such silence is evidence of guilt. Compare the case to the decision of the European Court of Human Rights which follows.

GRIFFIN v. CALIFORNIA
Supreme Court (United States).
380 U.S. 609 (1965).

Mr. Justice Douglas delivered the opinion of the Court.

Petitioner was convicted of murder in the first degree after a jury trial in a California court. He did not testify at the trial on the issue of guilt, though he did testify at the separate trial on the issue of penalty. The trial court instructed the jury on the issue of guilt, stating that a defendant has a constitutional right not to testify. But it told the jury:

As to any evidence or facts against him which the defendant can reasonably be expected to deny or explain because of facts within his knowledge, if he does not testify or if, though he does testify, he fails to deny or explain such evidence, the jury may take that failure into consideration as tending to indicate the truth of such evidence and as indicating that among the inferences that may be reasonably drawn therefrom those unfavorable to the defendant are the more probable.

It added, however, that no such inference could be drawn as to evidence respecting which he had no knowledge. It stated that failure of a defendant to deny or explain the evidence of which he had knowledge does not create a presumption of guilt nor by itself warrant an inference of guilt nor relieve the prosecution of any of its burden of proof.

Petitioner had been seen with the deceased the evening of her death, the evidence placing him with her in the alley where her body was found. The prosecutor made much of the failure of petitioner to testify:

'The defendant certainly knows whether Essie Mae had this beat up appearance at the time he left her apartment and went down the alley with her. * * *

'He would know that. He would know how she got down the alley. He would know how the blood got on the bottom of the concrete steps. He would know how long he was with her in that box. He would know how her wig got off. He would know whether he beat her or mistreated her. He would know whether he walked away from that place cool as a cucumber when he saw Mr. Villasenor because he was conscious of his own guilt and wanted to get away from that damaged or injured woman.

'These things he has not seen fit to take the stand and deny or explain.

'And in the whole world, if anybody would know, this defendant would know.

'Essie Mae is dead, she can't tell you her side of the story. The defendant won't.'

The death penalty was imposed and the California Supreme Court affirmed. * * *

The question remains whether * * * the comment rule, approved by California, violates the Fifth Amendment. * * *

We think it does. [The California rule allowing comment] is in substance a rule of evidence that allows the State the privilege of tendering to the jury for its consideration the failure of the accused to testify. No formal offer of proof is made as in other situations; but the prosecutor's comment and the court's acquiescence are the equivalent of an offer of evidence and its acceptance. The Court in the *Wilson* case [149 U.S. 60, 66 (1893)] stated: * * *

It is not every one who can safely venture on the witness stand, though entirely innocent of the charge against him. Excessive timidity, nervousness when facing others and attempting to explain transactions of a suspicious character, and offenses charged against him, will often confuse and embarrass him to such a degree as to increase rather than remove prejudices against him. It is not every one, however honest, who would therefore willingly be placed on the witness stand.

* * * [C]omment on the refusal to testify is * * * a penalty imposed by courts for exercising a constitutional privilege. It cuts down on the privilege by making its assertion costly. It is said, however, that the inference of guilt for failure to testify as to facts peculiarly within the accused's knowledge is in any event natural and irresistible, and that comment on the failure does not magnify that inference into a penalty for asserting a constitutional privilege. What the jury may infer, given no help from the court, is one thing. What it may infer when the court solemnizes the silence of the accused into evidence against him is quite another.

We * * * hold that the Fifth Amendment * * * forbids either comment by the prosecution on the accused's silence or instructions by the court that such silence is evidence of guilt.

MURRAY v. UNITED KINGDOM

European Court of Human Rights.
22 E.H.R.R. 29 (1996).

On 8 May 1991, the applicant was found guilty of aiding and abetting unlawful imprisonment and sentenced to eight years in prison. He had been arrested on 7 January 1990 under the Prevention of Terrorism (Temporary Provisions) Act 1989. Following arrest, he was cautioned under the Criminal Evidence (Northern Ireland) Order 1988 ("the Order") and informed that adverse inferences could be drawn at his trial if he elected to remain silent and not answer police questions. * * * On finding the applicant guilty, the judge informed him that he had drawn adverse inferences from the fact that he had not answered police questions and that he had not given evidence at his trial.

I.   Alleged violation of Article 6 of the Convention

40.   The applicant alleged that there had been a violation of the right to silence and the right not to incriminate oneself contrary to Article 6(1) and (2) of the Convention. * * * The relevant provisions provide as follows:

1.   In the determination of * * * any criminal charge against him, everyone is entitled to a fair and public hearing within a reasonable time by an independent and impartial tribunal established by law * * *

2.   Everyone charged with a criminal offence shall be presumed innocent until proved guilty according to law. * * *

41.   In the submission of the applicant, the drawing of incriminating inferences against him under the Criminal Justice (Northern Ireland) Order 1988 ("the Order") violated Article 6(1) and (2) of the Convention. * * *

He contended that a first, and most obvious element of the right to silence is the right to remain silent in the face of police questioning and not to have to testify against oneself at trial. In his submission, these have always been essential and fundamental elements of the British criminal justice system. Moreover the Commission in *Saunders v. United Kingdom* and the Court in *Funke v. France* have accepted that they are an inherent part of the right to a fair hearing under Article 6. In his view these are absolute rights which an accused is entitled to enjoy without restriction.

A second, equally essential element of the right to silence was that the exercise of the right by an accused would not be used as evidence against him in his trial. However, the trial judge drew very strong inferences, under Articles 4 and 6 of the Order, from his decision to remain silent under police questioning and during the trial. Indeed, it was clear from the trial judge's remarks and from the judgment of the Court of Appeal in his case that the inferences were an integral part of his decision to find him guilty.

Accordingly, he was severely and doubly penalised for choosing to remain silent: once for his silence under police interrogation and once for his failure to testify during the trial. To use against him silence under police questioning and his refusal to testify during trial amounted to subverting the presumption of innocence and the onus of proof resulting from that presumption: it is for the prosecution to prove the accused's guilt without any assistance from the latter being required. * * *

44. The Court must, confining its attention to the facts of the case, consider whether the drawing of inferences against the applicant under Articles 4 and 6 of the Order rendered the criminal proceedings against him—and especially his conviction—unfair within the meaning of Article 6 of the Convention. * * * It is not the Court's role to examine whether, in general, the drawing of inferences under the scheme contained in the Order is compatible with the notion of a fair hearing under Article 6.

45. Although not specifically mentioned in Article 6 of the Convention, there can be no doubt that the right to remain silent under police questioning and the privilege against self-incrimination are generally recognised international standards which lie at the heart of the notion of a fair procedure under Article 6. * * *

47. On the one hand, it is self-evident that it is incompatible with the immunities under consideration to base a conviction solely or mainly on the accused's silence or on a refusal to answer questions or to give evidence himself. On the other hand, the Court deems it equally obvious that these immunities cannot and should not prevent that the accused's silence, in situations which clearly call for an explanation from him, be taken into account in assessing the persuasiveness of the evidence adduced by the prosecution.

Wherever the line between these two extremes is to be drawn, it follows from this understanding of "the right to silence" that the question whether the right is absolute must be answered in the negative. * * *

Whether the drawing of adverse inferences from an accused's silence infringes Article 6 is a matter to be determined in the light of all the circumstances of the case * * *

48. As regards the degree of compulsion involved in the present case, it is recalled that the applicant was in fact able to remain silent. Notwithstanding the repeated warnings as to the possibility that inferences might be drawn from his silence, he did not make any statements

to the police and did not give evidence during his trial. Moreover under Article 4(5) of the Order he remained a non-compellable witness. * * * Thus his insistence in maintaining silence throughout the proceedings did not amount to a criminal offence or contempt of court. Furthermore, as has been stressed in national court decisions, silence, in itself, cannot be regarded as an indication of guilt.

49. The facts of the present case accordingly fall to be distinguished from those in *Funke v. France* where criminal proceedings were brought against the applicant by the customs authorities in an attempt to compel him to provide evidence of offences he had allegedly committed. Such a degree of compulsion in that case was found by the Court to be incompatible with Article 6 since, in effect, it destroyed the very essence of the privilege against self-incrimination.

50. Admittedly a system which warns the accused—who is possibly without legal assistance (as in the applicant's case)—that adverse inferences may be drawn from a refusal to provide an explanation to the police for his presence at the scene of a crime or to testify during his trial, when taken in conjunction with the weight of the case against him, involves a certain level of indirect compulsion. However, since the applicant could not be compelled to speak or to testify, as indicated above, this factor on its own cannot be decisive. The Court must rather concentrate its attention on the role played by the inferences in the proceedings against the applicant and especially in his conviction.

51. In this context, it is recalled that these were proceedings without a jury, the trier of fact being an experienced judge. Furthermore, the drawing of inferences under the Order is subject to an important series of safeguards designed to respect the rights of the defence and to limit the extent to which reliance can be placed on inferences.

In the first place, before inferences can be drawn under Article 4 and 6 of the Order appropriate warnings must have been given to the accused as to the legal effects of maintaining silence. Moreover, as indicated by the judgment of the House of Lords in *R. v. Kevin Sean Murray* the prosecutor must first establish a prima facie case against the accused, i.e. a case consisting of direct evidence which, if believed and combined with legitimate inferences based upon it, could lead a properly directed jury to be satisfied beyond reasonable doubt that each of the essential elements of the offence is proved.

The question in each particular case is whether the evidence adduced by the prosecution is sufficiently strong to require an answer. The national court cannot conclude that the accused is guilty merely because he chooses to remain silent. It is only if the evidence against the accused "calls" for an explanation which the accused ought to be in a position to give that a failure to give an explanation "may as a matter of common sense allow the drawing of an inference that there is no explanation and that the accused is guilty". Conversely if the case presented by the prosecution had so little evidential value that it called for no answer, a failure to provide one could not justify an inference of guilt. In sum, it is only common sense inferences which the judge considers proper, in the light of the evidence against the accused, that can be drawn under the Order.

In addition, the trial judge has discretion whether, on the facts of the particular case, an inference should be drawn. As indicated by the Court of Appeal in the present case, if a judge accepted that an accused did not understand the warning given or if he had doubts about it, "we are confident that he would not activate Article 6 against him". Furthermore in Northern Ireland, where trial judges sit without a jury, the judge must explain the reasons for the decision to draw inferences and the weight attached to them. The exercise of discretion in this regard is subject to review by the appellate courts.

52.   In the present case, the evidence presented against the applicant by the prosecution was considered by the Court of Appeal to constitute a "formidable" case against him * * *

53.   The trial judge drew strong inferences against the applicant under Article 6 of the Order by reason of his failure to give an account of his presence in the house when arrested and interrogated by the police. He also drew strong inferences under Article 4 of the Order by reason of the applicant's refusal to give evidence in his own defence when asked by the court to do so.

54.   In the Court's view, having regard to the weight of the evidence against the applicant, as outlined above, the drawing of inferences from his refusal, at arrest, during police questioning and at trial, to provide an explanation for his presence in the house was a matter of common sense and cannot be regarded as unfair or unreasonable in the circumstances. As pointed out by the Delegate of the Commission, the courts in a considerable number of countries where evidence is freely assessed may have regard to all relevant circumstances, including the manner in which the accused has behaved or has conducted his defence, when evaluating the evidence in the case. It considers that, what distinguishes the drawing of inferences under the Order is that, in addition to the existence of the specific safeguards mentioned above, it constitutes, as described by the Commission, "a formalised system which aims at allowing common sense implications to play an open role in the assessment of evidence".

Nor can it be said, against this background, that the drawing of reasonable inferences from the applicant's behaviour had the effect of shifting the burden of proof from the prosecution to the defence so as to infringe the principle of the presumption of innocence.

55.   The applicant submitted that it was unfair to draw inferences under Article 6 of the Order from his silence at a time when he had not had the benefit of legal advice. In his view the question of access to a solicitor was inextricably entwined with that of the drawing of adverse inferences from pre-trial silence under police questioning. In this context he emphasised that under the Order once an accused has remained silent a trap is set from which he cannot escape: if an accused chooses to give evidence or to call witnesses, he is, by reason of his prior silence, exposed to the risk of an Article 3 inference sufficient to bring about a conviction;

on the other hand, if he maintains his silence inferences may be drawn against him under other provisions of the Order.

56. The Court recalls that it must confine its attention to the facts of the present case. The reality of this case is that the applicant maintained silence right from the first questioning by the police to the end of his trial. It is not for the Court therefore to speculate on the question whether inferences would have been drawn under the Order had the applicant, at any moment after his first interrogation, chosen to speak to the police or to give evidence at his trial or call witnesses. Nor should it speculate on the question whether it was the possibility of such inferences being drawn that explains why the applicant was advised by his solicitor to remain silent.

Immediately after arrest the applicant was warned in accordance with the provisions of the Order but chose to remain silent. The Court, like the Commission, observed that there is no indication that the applicant failed to understand the significance of the warning given to him by the police prior to seeing his solicitor. Under these circumstances the fact that during the first 48 hours of his detention the applicant had been refused access to a lawyer does not detract from the above conclusion that the drawing of inferences was not unfair or unreasonable.

57. Against the above background, and taking into account the role played by inferences under the Order during the trial and their impact on the rights of the defence, the Court does not consider that the criminal proceedings were unfair or that there had been an infringement of the presumption of innocence.

58. Accordingly, there has been no violation of Article 6(1) and (2) of the Convention.

Gordon Van Kessel, EUROPEAN PERSPECTIVES ON THE ACCUSED AS A SOURCE OF TESTIMONIAL EVIDENCE,

100 W. Va. L. Rev. 799, 833–35 (1998).

For a number of reasons, very few Continental defendants remain silent at trial. First, Continental rules of procedure and evidence place fewer impediments in the way of defendants actively participating at trial than do American rules. For example, use of prior convictions does not turn on whether the accused decides to testify. Also, the presiding judge already has seen defendant's record in the dossier, though technically the dossier is not considered evidence in some countries. Finally, because the Continental defendant is not sworn as a witness, he is not subject to prosecution for perjury.

Second, the Continental trial process offers more inducements and strongly encourages the defendant to respond to questions by exacting a heavy price for remaining silent. Judges and other participants expect the accused to speak. For example, in France, although the accused technically has the right to remain silent at trial without the risk of negative inferences, he is strongly encouraged to speak, and as a practical matter, defendant's complete silence will lead to adverse inferences by the judges such that the silence right is rarely invoked. The unitary trial (in which guilt and punishment issues are decided in one proceeding) also induces defendants to speak. At trial, the accused may contest guilt and present factors mitigating punishment, but if he refuses to speak at all, he forfeits the opportunity to give mitigating evidence respecting punishment. The unitary trial not only induces defendant to speak, but to confess if he wishes to mitigate his guilt, as when he desires to point out that although he participated in the robbery, he did not have a gun and told his accomplice not to kill the victim.

The environment and choreography of Continental trials also strongly focuses on the accused and encourages him to be an active participant and assist in the presentation of his defense. In Continental courtrooms, defense lawyers usually sit behind the defendant, in contrast to American lawyers who sit protectively at defendant's side. Also, Continental defendants usually are called upon to speak first, before either prosecution or defense witnesses, and are always given the opportunity to speak last. This is the case even under Spain's new jury trial procedure in which the taking of testimony begins with questioning of the defendant by the public and private prosecutors and then by the defense attorney. Although Spanish defendants have a Constitutional right to remain silent, are not under oath, and have no duty to tell the truth, they have always testified at the outset in response to prosecutorial questioning in the first year in which the new Spanish jury trials were conducted.

Throughout the trial, the Presiding Judge continuously focuses the inquiry on the accused, seeking to involve him in the case, for example, asking him if he wishes to respond to the testimony of witnesses. The informality of the proceedings and the discussion format of trial, in contrast to our formal direct and cross-examination procedure, emphasizes participation by all, including questioning of the accused by both professional and lay judges. Even in countries still using the English-style jury, lay jurors are active. For example, in a Belgian jury trial which I witnessed, following the presiding judge's questioning of the accused, the jurors were asked whether they had any questions. Some posed questions which initially were rephrased by the presiding judge, but eventually defendant answered jurors directly, resulting in an unfiltered discussion between the accused and some of the jurors. Consequently, with the trial focused on the defendant and the defendant expected to participate, the practical effect of defendant's unmasked refusal is so damaging that, despite the general rule against drawing adverse inferences from defendant's silence, it is a rare event in Continental trials for a defendant to remain completely silent. Contrast trials in the United States where defendants are sidelined and fact-finders are silenced. The American judge generally deals with defense only through defendant's lawyer, and the defendant cannot directly address the fact-finder unless he agrees to take the stand and testify under oath subject to cross-examination. Fact-finders also are discouraged from participating. Members of the jury panel may speak during the selection process, but once chosen as fact-finders, usually jurors are silenced. During jury selection in the Oklahoma City bombing case, prosecutors often would ask prospective jurors if they would be bothered by the fact that they might have some unanswered questions about the case. One prospective juror answered, "Like if something isn't clear, we can ask the judge?" Judge Matsch replied, "The answer to that is: No. You can't ask questions."

Notes and Questions

1. As noted in the *Murray* case, it may seem reasonable in certain instances to expect a defendant to explain himself to the jury or judge. If the defendant refuses to do so, why shouldn't the prosecutor be able to note that fact? Consider that in some jurisdictions a defendant who decides to testify may be subject to cross-examination and impeachment, which may be damaging to the defendant's case.

2. Is it futile to forbid the drawing of adverse inferences because the trier of fact will probably draw them regardless of the prohibition? Does it matter whether the trier of fact is a judge or a jury?

3. Are there stronger reasons for forbidding the drawing of adverse inferences in the U.S. than in Continental Europe?

E.   RIGHT TO COUNSEL

The right to the assistance of counsel is guaranteed in many constitutions. It provides, at a minimum, that the accused may select and retain counsel for assistance at trial. Several constitutions also explicitly protect the right to counsel upon detention, and some provide that the state will furnish (and pay for) counsel on behalf of any accused person who cannot afford to retain counsel. In addition, some constitutional systems consider that the right to counsel includes the right to effective assistance of counsel.

E.1.   RIGHT TO COUNSEL PRETRIAL

Some constitutions provide for the right to counsel at all stages of the criminal proceedings. See, e.g., Bulgaria Const. ch. 2, art. 30(4); Guatemala Const. tit. II, ch. I, art. 19(c); Italy Const. pt. I, tit. I, art. 24; Japan Const. ch. III, art. 37. Others specifically provide for the right to counsel at trial and in the pretrial stages but do not state that the right is protected at all stages. See, e.g., Bolivia Const. pt. 1, tit. 2, art. 16; The Netherlands Const. ch. I, art. 18(1). And several constitutions simply provide for the right to counsel or the right to a defense, without specifying when this right applies. See, e.g., U.S. Const., VI Am.

Also important is the right of the accused to *notice* of his right to counsel. In some countries, such as the United Kingdom, the accused has a right to be informed of the right to counsel. In other countries, such as The Netherlands and France, the accused does not have the right to counsel prior to trial and, accordingly, has no right to be informed of a right to counsel at that initial stage.

As noted in the section on the right to silence, the *Miranda* decision has two elements: the defendant has a right to be notified upon arrest not only of his right to silence but also of the right to counsel. This pretrial right to counsel is rooted not in the Sixth Amendment right to counsel (which is triggered only after formal proceedings begin) but rather in the due process clause of the U.S. Constitution. Under the due process clause, the defendant has a right to an attorney during custodial interrogation. Unless a defendant waives this right, interrogation must cease until an attorney is provided. Similar protections are provided in other constitutions. In *S. v. Woods & Ors,* 1993 (2) ZLR 258 (S), the Constitutional Court of Zimbabwe held that a refusal of access to counsel of prisoners held in police custody violated the right to a fair trial and warranted the exclusion of statements or indications made by the defendant prior to his access to a lawyer.

In the Canadian case of *R. v. Burlingham* the Supreme Court considered the effect of a denial of the right to counsel during pretrial stages on the admissibility of the fruits of the police interrogation of a defendant.

R. v. BURLINGHAM

Supreme Court (Canada).
[1995] 2 S.C.R. 206.

The appellant, who had been charged with one murder and was suspected in a second, was subjected to an intensive and often manipulative interrogation by the police. He was systematically questioned, although he stated repeatedly that he would not speak unless he could consult with his lawyer. The police interrogators constantly denigrated the integrity of defence counsel.

The police offered the appellant a "deal": he would be charged with second degree murder if he provided the police with the location of the gun and other ancillary information related to that murder. When the appellant refused to accept the "deal" without consulting his lawyer, the officers continued to badger him about the reliability of his lawyer and informed him this "one-time" chance would be kept open only for the weekend—the period when appellant's counsel was unavailable. The appellant eventually agreed, despite his being advised by another lawyer not to talk to the police, and fulfilled his part of the deal by giving police a full confession, bringing them to the murder site and telling them where the murder weapon had been thrown. The appellant recounted the events of the day and the information he had given to the police to his girlfriend.

A misunderstanding arose as to the deal. The appellant understood that he would be allowed to plead not guilty to a charge of second degree murder, whereas the Crown insisted that he would have to plead guilty to that charge. The trial judge found as a fact that the police officers had made an honest mistake.

The appellant was charged with first degree murder. At trial, the Crown sought to introduce all of the evidence obtained while the appellant had been under the misunderstanding that he was participating in a valid agreement. The trial judge found that appellant's right to counsel (s. 10(b) of the Canadian Charter of Rights and Freedoms) had been breached and held that appellant's confession, his disclosure of the location of the weapon, and his directions and gestures to the police were inadmissible. [The judge] admitted the fact of finding the gun, the actual gun, testimony of a witness, testimony identifying the gun, and the testimony of his girlfriend regarding the statements appellant made to her. The appellant was convicted of the first degree murder and the Court of Appeal affirmed that decision. At issue here is whether or not appellant was denied his right to counsel guaranteed by s. 10(b) of the Charter, and if so, what was the just and appropriate remedy under s. 24(2) of the Charter?

Per Iacobucci J. (La Forest, Sopinka, Cory and Major JJ., concurring):

B.   * * * (i) Was there a denial of the accused's right to counsel?

[The accused's right to counsel had been violated in several ways.] First, the police continually questioned him despite his repeated statements that he would say nothing absent consultation with his lawyer. * * * Second, s. 10(b) specifically prohibits the police * * * from belittling an accused's lawyer with the express goal or effect of undermining the accused's confidence in and relationship with defence counsel. * * * Third, * * * s. 10(b) was violated when the officers pressured the accused into accepting the "deal" without first having the opportunity to consult with his lawyer. * * * The end result of this badgering was that the accused did not understand the full content of his right to counsel. * * * [P]olice have the duty to advise a suspect of the right to counsel where there is a fundamental and discrete change in the purpose of an investigation which involves a different and unrelated offence or a significantly more serious offence than that contemplated at the time of the original instruction of the right to counsel. Such a situation arose in the case at bar. The deal offered by the police involved a different offence * * *. [A] genuine effort should have been made to contact the accused's own lawyer.

[S]ection 10(b) mandates the Crown or police, whenever offering a plea bargain, to tender that offer either to accused's counsel or to the accused, while in the presence of his or her counsel, unless the accused has expressly waived the right to counsel. It is a constitutional infringement to place such an offer directly to an accused, especially * * * when the police coercively leave it open only for the short period of time during which they know defence counsel to be unavailable. * * * Mere expediency or efficiency is not sufficient to create enough "urgency" to permit a s. 10(b) breach. * * * [T]o the extent that the plea bargain is an integral element of the Canadian criminal process, the Crown and its officers engaged in the plea bargaining process must act honourably and forthrightly.

(ii) What is the just and appropriate remedy?

[The Court found that this was not a case for a stay of proceedings. A judicial stay is the most dramatic of remedies and should be limited to the clearest of cases.]

Section 24(2) provides that when evidence is obtained in a manner that infringes an accused's Charter rights, this evidence shall be excluded from the trial process if it is established that, having regard to all the circumstances, [admission] would bring the administration of justice into disrepute. * * * [Under the *Collins* test, the factors to be considered are] (1) those affecting the fairness of the trial, (2) those relating to the seriousness of the violation, and (3) those relating to the effect on the reputation of the administration of justice of excluding the evidence. * * * [S]elf-incriminatory evidence obtained as a result of a Charter breach * * * will generally go to the fairness of the trial and should generally be excluded. This Court has consistently shied away from the differential treatment of real evidence. * * * [The classification of evidence] as real or conscriptive should not in and of itself be determinative. [Although] theoretically the onus rests on the accused to show that the impugned evidence would not have been found but for the unconstitutional conduct, in practice the burden will often fall on the Crown as it possesses superior knowledge. [T]he "but-for" test will be met by the Crown when it satisfies the court on a balance of probabilities that the law enforcement authorities would have discovered the impugned derivative evidence regardless of the information arising from the unconstitutional conduct. [C]onsideration of what evidence should or should not be excluded [should commence] with the evidence obtained most proximate to the Charter breach and then work towards [more remote evidence. M]ore remote evidence might not be admitted if its admission would have the same effect as admitting the proximate evidence.

[Here,] the derivative real evidence, the gun, *would not* have been found but for the information [obtained in breach of s. 10(b)]. The gun was at the bottom of the frozen Kootenay River and the only person who knew of its location was the appellant.

[The Court then found that the evidence of the accused's statement to his girlfriend that he had directed the police to the location of the gun was also derivative evidence made as a result of the breach. There was no satisfactory indication on a balance of probabilities that this evidence would have been found regardless of the unconstitutionally obtained information. Admission of the girlfriend's statement "would directly affect the fairness of the trial."] [E]xcluding the gun while including the statements effectively eviscerates the Charter of most of its protective value to the accused in this case; including both would totally eliminate any such value. * * *

Moreover, the serious nature of the Charter breach in this case also supports the conclusion that the administration of justice would be brought into disrepute by the admission of the evidence. * * * [T]he violation was willful and flagrant. It is also * * * clear that there was no element of urgency.

As to the third branch of the *Collins* test, I am satisfied that the effect of excluding evidence on the reputation of the administration of justice will be incidental and far outweighed by the negative consequences that would follow were this unconstitutional evidence to be included. * * * The accused was charged with a serious offence but there would be a new trial on lawful evidence adduced against him.

Given the seriousness of the Charter violations, this was not a case for applying [the no substantial wrong or miscarriage of justice proviso in s. 686(1)(b)(iii) of the Criminal Code]. * * * [T]he improperly obtained evidence formed a critical component of the Crown's case and it could not be said that there as no reasonable possibility that the verdict would have been different had the evidence been properly excluded at trial. * * * Consideration should be given to [deciding that the proviso should be applied only in] cases in which it can be shown beyond a reasonable doubt that the impugned evidence excluded under s. 24(2) * * * did not contribute at all to the original verdict.

[Held: The appeal was allowed; the conviction was set aside, and a new trial was ordered.]

Per Iacobucci J. (La Forest, Sopinka, Cory and Major JJ. concurring):

Notes and Questions

1. The right to counsel at the pretrial stage is not expressly set out in the International Covenant on Civil and Political Rights, the American Convention on Human Rights, the African Charter on Human and People's Rights, or the European HR Convention. But the corresponding supranational courts (Inter–American Court of Human Rights and the European Court of Human Rights) have found that the right to access to a lawyer, during detention, interrogation, and preliminary investigation, is an implicit aspect of the right to a fair trial. Amnesty International, *Fair Trials Manual* (1998). For example, in *Murray v. United Kingdom*, above, the accused was denied access to counsel during the first 48 hours of detention. During this time, the accused needed to decide whether to exercise his right of silence, a decision that in turn might affect whether he was charged. The ECHR found that denial of access to counsel during the first 48 hours after arrest violated the fair trial right of the European HR Convention, Art. 6.

2. Should the right to counsel attach before formal proceedings begin? Why? Even if the right to counsel does attach before trial, should evidence obtained from an accused who was denied access to counsel be excluded? Are there alternative methods to discourage the denial of access to counsel?

E.2. RIGHT TO COUNSEL APPOINTED AND PAID FOR BY THE STATE

Given the large number of criminal defendants who are unable to afford counsel, the right to appointment of counsel paid for by the state is frequently considered a requirement of constitutional rights to counsel, a fair trial, and equal protection under law. There are, however, variations in the scope of this right, for example, as to whether the defendant may waive or forfeit the right to counsel paid for by the state. Also, there is often a substantial distance between the constitutional promise of free legal representation and the fulfillment of that promise.

The South African and Japanese cases that follow illustrate some of the difficulties in implementing the right to counsel.

THE STATE v. WESSEL ALBERTUS VERMAAS

Constitutional Court (South Africa).
1995 (3) SALR 292 (CC).

Didcott J:

1. A question that came to the fore in recent years, sparking a lively controversy in our law, was whether persons standing trial on criminal charges who could not afford to pay for their legal representation were entitled to be provided with it at public expense once its lack amounted to a handicap so great that to try them on their own lay beyond the pale of justice. The controversy . . . has been settled decisively by our new Constitution (Act 200 of 1993), section 25(3)(e) of which declares that:

> "Every accused person shall have the right to a fair trial, which shall include the right * * * to be represented by a legal practitioner of his or her choice or, where substantial injustice would otherwise result, to be provided with legal representation at state expense, and to be informed of these rights".

2. We now have before us for simultaneous adjudication the cases of Vermaas and Du Plessis, where the right thus proclaimed has been invoked in circumstances rather different from those that were generally envisaged while the controversy lasted and we might have expected to encounter when such a matter first appeared on our agenda. For a trial of huge dimensions is a feature of each case, exacerbating the difficulties of both providing legal representation and proceeding with none * * *

4. A series of advocates [appeared for Vermaas] at earlier phases of the trial, but they had either withdrawn or been dismissed from it, in turn, because of problems that had arisen, mainly financial. * * * Vermaas [himself] started addressing the court on a record of the oral evidence presented and the documentary exhibits produced, which amounted in bulk to about 40,000 pages. Changing tack, however, he applied, during June 1994, for an order directing that throughout the remainder of the trial he be furnished with legal representation at the cost of the state.

5. * * * The services of successive advocates were obtained by Du Plessis, too, and, through a shortage of funds, likewise lost. So * * * he sought the same order as the one that Vermaas requested soon afterwards, claiming in addition the right to choose the lawyer whom he wanted the state to procure for him * * *

15. * * * Hartzenberg J held that no such right was derived from section 25(3)(e) when the state supplied the lawyer's services. That is certainly so. The effect of the disjunctive "or", appearing in the section immediately before the reference to the prospect of "substantial injustice", is to differentiate clearly between two situations, the first where the accused person makes his or her own arrangements for the representation that must be allowed, the second in which the assistance of the

state becomes imperative, and to cater for the personal choice of a lawyer in the first one alone.

16. A word or two had better be added, as I draw to a close, on a subject of public importance which prompted some discussion when the present cases were argued. No counsel on either side could then tell us of any steps taken yet to establish the financial and administrative structures that were necessary to give effect to the part of section 25(3)(e) providing for legal representation at the expense of the state. We gained the impression that nothing of much significance had been done in that direction since the Constitution came into force a year ago. The impression, if true, is most disturbing. We are mindful of the multifarious demands on the public purse and the machinery of government that flow from the urgent need for economic and social reform. But the Constitution does not envisage, and it will surely not brook, an undue delay in the fulfillment of any promise made by it about a fundamental right. One can safely assume that, in spite of section 25(3)(e), the situation still prevails where during every month countless thousands of South Africans are criminally tried without legal representation because they are too poor to pay for it. They are presumably informed in the beginning, as the section requires them peremptorily to be, of their right to obtain that free of charge in the circumstances which it defines. Imparting such information becomes an empty gesture and makes a mockery of the Constitution, however, if it is not backed by mechanisms that are adequate for the enforcement of the right.

OGAWA ET AL. v. JAPAN

[THE DEFENSE REJECTION CASE]
Supreme Court (Japan).
33 Keishū 5 at p. 416 (1979).[e]

This case arose as part of an incident in connection with the '4–28 Okinawa Day Struggle' of April 28, 1970, and approximately 240 persons were indicted in the Tokyo District Court in relation to this conflict. * * * [N]inety of these engaged ten defense attorneys of their own choice, [arguing] for the "combination formula," [whereby] a combined group of attorneys takes charge of the entire case while holding oral proceedings and arguments jointly or separately. * * * [A] conference of judges at the Tokyo District Court, determining that there was no other reasonable and concrete resolution, decided to divide the indicted into [two groups (A and B), assigning each to a separate division of the court].

[Before the first public hearing date for Groups A and B, all of the defense attorneys resigned,] and on the very day of the first public hearing, the accused requested the assignment of state-appointed counsel. [The court appointed new counsel for both groups, but these counsel also resigned shortly thereafter. The defendants claimed, among other things, a violation of Art. 37, para 3 of the Japanese Constitution, which provides: "At all times the accused shall have the assistance of compe-

e. Reproduced from Lawrence W. Beer and Hiroshi Itoh, *The Constitutional Case*   *Law of Japan, 1970 through 1990*, at 443 (1996).

tent counsel who shall, if the accused is unable to secure the same by his own efforts, be assigned to his use by the State." Eds.]

[W]hen the court made inquiries into the circumstances which led to the submission of the resignations, it found the facts as follows:

The accused from the outset demanded the holding of so-called integrated public hearings and did not cooperate at all with the concrete requests deemed necessary by state appointed counsel for their defense. On May 18, 1971, during a meeting of the parties * * * they used such abusive language as: "To speak bluntly, we do not trust counsel. Therefore, expect nothing [of value] from the opening statement by counsel." Furthermore, on May 25 * * * the accused bitterly condemned and criticized the activities of their attorneys in language such as the following: "You're not prepared to be the defense counsel of this case" * * * They then heaped outrageous insults upon the lawyers, continuing their abuse and denunciations. As a result, the six state-appointed attorneys reached the conclusion that the accused no longer had any serious intention to accept the services of counsel * * *

[T]he accused asked for reappointment of counsel; the court * * * asked for an explanation of the above facts from each of the accused, and asked whether each would vow not to engage in similar activities in the future. Thereafter, when the court attempted to continue its inquiry on the above two points by calling the accused one by one into the judge's chamber, all the accused refused * * * [T]he court rejected the request for reappointment of state-appointed attorneys.

Thereafter, the accused made three more requests for the reappointment of the state-appointed attorneys. When the first instance court * * * attempted to secure from the accused an assurance that they would not repeat the acts described above, the accused refused to respond, saying: "It is the duty of the court to assign attorneys with no conditions attached." * * * The first instance court rejected all their requests for the reappointment of state-appointed attorneys * * *

Based on the above facts, the accused should be deemed to have expressed through their own acts that they had no intention to carry into effect, through the offices of state-appointed counsel, a proper defense for the protection of their rights, and that the court was for this reason forced to release the state-appointed attorneys from the case. Furthermore, since it should be recognized that the accused attempted in unison to maintain and continue the above situation thereafter, every request by the accused for the reappointment of state-appointed counsel should be judged to be far from a sincere exercise of their rights. In such an instance, a proper interpretation is that even where a formal request for the appointment of state-appointed counsel has been made, the court has no obligation to accede to it.

As clearly stated in * * * the Rules of Criminal Procedure, procedural rights must be exercised with sincerity and not be abused. The precedents of this Court purport that when these rights are abused by the accused, their [binding power] need not be recognized, even if they assume a form of compliance with the exercise of rights prescribed in the constitution * * * Under this interpretation, if the accused should request anew with sincerity the appointment of state-appointed counsel, then the court could proceed with the task of appointment and this would not substantially limit the proper exercise by the accused of their right to make such a request. It is clear in light of the purport of the above precedents that the above-mentioned measures taken by the first instance court do not violate Article 37, paragraph 3 of the Constitution.

Notes and Questions

1.   Consider Richard S. Frase and Thomas Weigend, *German Criminal Justice as a Guide to American Law Reform* * * * 18 Bost. Coll. Int'l. & Comp. L. Rev. 317, 323–25 (1995):

> In some countries, such as Germany, the assistance of counsel is sometimes not a right but, rather, an obligation. That is, in German district courts, counsel is mandatory and will be appointed for the defendant if the defendant has not retained private counsel. This state-appointment of counsel will occur even over the defendant's objection. In county courts, the accused does not have a right to counsel, but one will be appointed if the case involves a felony or is complicated, in which case counsel is mandatory and cannot be waived by the accused.

> German civil law approach to fair trial requires that the right to counsel be viewed as the right not of the defendant but of society: there is a public interest in the rational and fair conduct of the criminal process that is independent of the preferences or financial means of the accused.

2.   How should budgetary concerns affect an analysis of what process is due? Consider the *Vermaas* case, which held that the accused has a right to counsel but not a right to counsel of his choice. If the state were wealthy, would due process require providing counsel of the defendant's choice? Or is there some minimum quality of counsel that must be provided to satisfy due process regardless of the state's ability to pay?

3.   Is it appropriate to require defendants to treat their counsel respectfully? Assuming that the defendants in the Japanese case were right in their claim that defense counsel were untrustworthy, does the requirement that they accept them as counsel effectively deny the defendants the right to counsel? The *Ogawa* facts suggest that there is a tension between the *Vermaas* rule that the defendant does not have the right to counsel of his choice and the interest in providing counsel that effectively represents the defendant. Consider this problem in light of the materials that follow on the effective assistance of counsel.

E.3.   RIGHT TO THE EFFECTIVE ASSISTANCE OF COUNSEL

The USSC has recognized a right to "effective assistance of counsel" under the Sixth Amendment to the Constitution. Other countries do not recognize this right in the same terms but do scrutinize the performance of counsel in varying degrees. As the following material suggests, the extent to which a defendant's right to effective assistance of counsel is protected may depend heavily on a court's ability and willingness to supervise counsel's behavior.

In the U.S., there is significant controversy over what "effective assistance of counsel" means in a concrete case. In *Strickland v. Washington*, 466 U.S. 668 (1984), the Court held that a convicted defendant's claim that counsel's assistance was so defective as to require reversal of a conviction or death sentence requires the defendant to show, first, that counsel's performance was deficient and, second, that the deficient performance prejudiced the defense so as to deprive the defendant of a fair trial. The first prong of the test requires that the defendant prove that counsel's representation fell below an "objective standard of reasonableness." The Court said that judicial scrutiny of counsel's performance must be highly deferential: courts must indulge a strong presumption that counsel's conduct falls within the wide range of reasonable professional assistance. Under the second prong of the test, in *United States v. Cronic*, 466 U.S. 648, 658 (1984), decided the same day as *Strickland*, the Court noted that "there are circumstances * * * so likely to prejudice the accused that the cost of litigating their effect in a particular case is unjustified." In other words, the Court recognized that in some cases prejudice would be presumed. The "[s]uch circumstances include: (1) 'the complete denial of counsel' * * * (2) situations in which 'counsel entirely fails to subject the prosecution's case to meaningful adversarial testing'; (3)'when counsel was either totally absent, or prevented from assisting the accused during a *critical stage* of the proceeding'; and (4) 'when counsel labors under an actual conflict of interest.' "

DAUD v. PORTUGAL

European Court of Human Rights.
30 E.H.R.R. 400 (1998).

The applicant, an Argentinean citizen, was sentenced to nine years' imprisonment for drug trafficking and using a false passport. Relying on Articles 6(1) and (3)(c) and (e) of the Convention, he complained that he had not received a fair hearing. In particular, he complained of inadequate legal assistance, the shortcomings of his officially assigned lawyer, the refusal of his application for a judicial investigation and the poor quality of the interpreting at his trial * * *

I.   Alleged violation of Article 6(1) and (3)(c) and (e) of the Convention

32.   * * * In support of his complaints he relied on paragraphs 1 and 3(c) and (e) of Article 6 of the Convention, which provide:

1.   In the determination of * * * any criminal charge against him, everyone is entitled to a fair and public hearing within a reasonable time by an independent and impartial tribunal established by law * * *

3.   Everyone charged with a criminal offence has the following minimum rights: * * *

(c) to defend himself in person or through legal assistance of his own choosing or, if he has not sufficient means to pay for legal assistance, to be given it free when the interests of justice so require; * * *

(e) to have the free assistance of an interpreter if he cannot understand or speak the language used in court.

A. Legal assistance

34. In the applicant's submission, the lawyers assigned to him by the Portuguese authorities by way of legal assistance, particularly the first one, did not provide him with effective legal assistance in preparing and conducting his defence, so that he was obliged to apply in person, but unsuccessfully, to the investigating judge and subsequently to the Criminal Court. The refusal to initiate judicial investigation proceedings had seriously infringed his rights. Seeing that he was a foreigner, he should have been given appropriate assistance. * * *

36. The Government, on the other hand, maintained that the obligation to provide legal assistance had been discharged by appointing and replacing the officially assigned lawyers and paying their fees. A replacement had been appointed as soon as the circumstances had required. The applicant had never informed the judge of any shortcomings on the part of his representative or asked for a different one. The second lawyer, appointed on 18 January 1993, had not sought any extra time to study the file. The authorities could not go beyond appointing Counsel and replacing him if the defence was manifestly inadequate. They could never aim to rectify any technical or procedural errors. Lastly, the domestic court's refusal of the applicant's requests and, more particularly, the lack of any judicial investigation had in no way impaired the fairness of the trial, as the defendant had been able to adduce the same evidence at the trial as he would have been able to do during a judicial investigation.

38. The Court reiterates that the Convention is designed to "guarantee not rights that are theoretical or illusory but rights that are practical and effective, and that assigning Counsel does not in itself ensure the effectiveness of the assistance he may afford an accused." (*Imbrioscia v. Switzerland* * * *.)

"Nevertheless, a State cannot be held responsible for every shortcoming on the part of a lawyer appointed for legal aid purposes ... It follows from the independence of the legal profession from the State that the conduct of the defence is essentially a matter between the defendant and his Counsel, whether Counsel be appointed under a legal aid scheme or be privately financed ... [T]he competent national authorities are required under Article 6(3)(c) to intervene only if a failure by legal aid Counsel to provide effective representation is manifest or sufficiently brought to their attention in some other way." (*Kamasinski v. Austria*.)

39. In the instant case the starting-point must be that, regard being had to the preparation and conduct of the case by the officially assigned lawyers, the intended outcome of Article 6(3) was not achieved. The Court notes that the first officially assigned lawyer, before reporting sick, had not taken any steps as Counsel for Mr. Daud, who tried unsuccessfully to conduct his own defence. As to the second lawyer, whose appointment the applicant learned of only three days before the beginning of the trial at the Criminal Court, the Court considers that she did not have the time she needed to study the file, visit her client in

prison if necessary and prepare his defence. The time between notification of the replacement of the lawyer and the hearing was too short for a serious, complex case in which there had been no judicial investigation and which led to a heavy sentence. The Supreme Court did not remedy the situation, since in its judgment of 30 June 1993 it declared the appeal inadmissible on account of an inadequate presentation of the grounds.

Mr. Daud consequently did not have the benefit of a practical and effective defence as required by Article 6(3)(c).

40.   The Court must therefore ascertain whether it was for the relevant authorities, while respecting the fundamental principle of the independence of the Bar, to act so as to ensure that the applicant received the effective benefit of his right, which they had acknowledged.

42.   In his letter of 15 December 1992, after more than eight months had elapsed, the applicant also asked the court for an interview with his lawyer, who had still not contacted him. Because the letter was written in a foreign language, the judge disregarded the request. Yet the request should have alerted the relevant authorities to a manifest shortcoming on the part of the first officially assigned lawyer, especially as the latter had not taken any step since being appointed in March 1992. For that reason, and having regard to the refusal of the two applications made during the same period by the defendant himself, the court should have inquired into the manner in which the lawyer was fulfilling his duty and possibly replaced him sooner, without waiting for him to state that he was unable to act for Mr. Daud. Furthermore, after appointing a replacement, the Lisbon Criminal Court, which must have known that the applicant had not had any proper legal assistance until then, could have adjourned the trial on its own initiative. The fact that the second officially assigned lawyer did not make such an application is of no consequence. The circumstances of the case required that the court should not remain passive.

43.   Taken as a whole, these considerations lead the Court to find a failure to comply with the requirements of paragraph 1 in conjunction with paragraph 3(c) of Article 6 from the stage of the preliminary inquiries until the beginning of the hearings before the Lisbon Criminal Court. There has therefore been a violation of those provisions.

Notes and Questions

1.   The *Strickland* test is deferential to defense counsel, creating the possibility that a range of behavior by counsel that may appear inappropriate will be accepted. On the other hand, if the standard to prove ineffective assistance of counsel were lowered this might encourage frivolous claims by defendants. How should the balance be struck between protecting a defendant from poor counsel and preventing frivolous claims? Might it depend on the nature of the case?

2.   Is closer court scrutiny of defense counsel's actions during the trial desirable? The *Daud* decision suggests one problem with court supervision might be an excessive interference with counsel's work. The ECHR's solu-

tion is to require the defendant himself to complain about counsel to the court. How likely is it that a defendant, who is usually dependent on defense counsel, will approach the court directly with complaints?

3. The U.N. Human Rights Committee held that a Jamaican's right to counsel was violated (ICCPR Art 14(3)) when his pro bono counsel refused to raise grounds for an appeal, did not inform defendant, and told the court that "my client's appeal is without merit." *Grant v. Jamaica*, UNHRC Communication No. 353/1988, adopted March 1994 (p. 236).

F. RIGHT TO PREPARE AND CONDUCT A DEFENSE

Several constitutions and international instruments include provisions that protect the defense's role in the trial process. Such protections include the right of access to the prosecution's case, adequate time and facilities to prepare a defense, and the right to call and cross-examine witnesses. In the U.S., many of these rights are understood to stem from the due process clauses of the U.S. and state constitutions, while in Europe and other countries they are often encompassed by the principle of "equality of arms." (See Chapter 6, Subsection C.4. for further discussion from the standpoint of equality rights.) In addition, protections have developed against prosecutorial excesses. For example, the prosecution's ability to present certain types of evidence, such as evidence that was illegally obtained, is often limited through exclusionary rules, as discussed earlier.

> [H]uman rights instruments * * * evince a definite move towards adversarial criminal procedures and away from the inquisitorial mode. The right to equality of arms is guaranteed in * * * the ICCPR [International Covenant for Civil and Political Rights], the AMCHR [American Convention on Human Rights], and the Fundamental Freedoms. * * * The right to equality of arms, as expressed in the ICCPR and the Fundamental Freedoms, is also noted in more than twenty-seven national constitutions. In these constitutions, the specific language of the right incorporates the guarantee in a cluster of rights, which also include the right to adequate time and facilities for preparation of the defense. In large part it can be said that this right is the European counterpart to the common law right of due process.

Bassiouni, *op. cit.* at 277–78.

F.1. PREPARATION OF A DEFENSE

F.1.1. ADEQUATE TIME AND FACILITIES

An evidentiary principle found in several constitutions is the requirement of adequate time and facilities to prepare a defense. This issue was raised in *Vacher v. France*, 24 E.H.R.R. 482 (1997), 17 December 1996, where the ECHR found that the French Court of Cassation's dismissal of Vacher's appeal for failure to lodge grounds of appeal violated his right to adequate time and facilities for the preparation of his defense (encompassed in para. 6(3)(b) of the Convention). There was no fixed date for filing a pleading, and the Court of Cassation heard the appeal promptly. Vacher, who was not warned of the hearing date by the registry nor able to foresee it, was thus deprived of the opportunity to present his case in the Court of Cassation in an effective manner.

Other cases have rejected similar claims. In *Koigi Wa Wamwere v. Attorney General* (1990 unreported) (available in Kivuthu Kibwana and Kathurima M'Inoti, *Human Rights Issues in the Criminal Justice System of Kenya and the African Charter of Human and People's Rights*, in *The Protection of Human Rights in African Criminal Proceedings* 126 (M. Cherif Bassiouni and Ziyad Motala eds., 1995)) the High Court of Kenya interpreted Kenya's Constitution, Section 77(2)(c)'s requirement of adequate time and facilities to prepare a defense. The applicant, who had been detained in prison prior to trial, alleged that his prison guards frequently raided his cell, confiscating notes he had prepared for consultation with defense counsel. Subsequently, the applicant was denied all access to pen and paper and thus was unable to prepare a defense. The court held that the claim was without merit as there were many other prisoners awaiting trial under similar circumstances and yet none had complained that their ability to prepare a defense was hampered.

In the *Tadic* judgment by the International Criminal Tribunal for the Former Yugoslavia (Appeals Chamber, July 15, 1999), the Court considered Tadic's claim that lack of cooperation by the authorities in the Republika Srpska had the effect of denying the appellant adequate time and facilities to prepare for trial, resulting in denial of a fair trial. The Appeals Chamber held that while domestic courts had the capacity to control matters that could materially affect the fairness of a trial, the International Tribunal faced the dilemma of having to rely upon the cooperation of states without having the power to compel them to cooperate through enforcement measures. It then established that the principle of equality of arms under the International Tribunal needs a more liberal interpretation, meaning that the trial chamber must provide every practicable facility it is capable of granting under its rules and statute when faced with a request by a party for assistance in presenting a case. The Appeals Chamber ruled that there was no evidence that the trial chamber had failed to provide assistance or was negligent in responding to a request for assistance and that, therefore, the fact that the defense could not present such evidence did not detract from the fairness of the trial.

F.1.2. ACCESS TO THE PROSECUTION'S CASE/DISCOVERY RULES

There are marked differences between the U.S. system and Continental European systems with regard to the defense's access to the prosecution's file. Such access is limited in the U.S., while Continental European countries generally have open-file policies. As noted by one author, "[e]ven the recent Italian Criminal Code revision adopting many accusatorial characteristics retained mandatory full pretrial discovery for the defense. The rationale for retaining open discovery while moving toward an adversary style was explained by an Italian professor and a judge: 'Such an expansive defense discovery reflects the purpose of rejecting the sporting theory of justice. To Italian lawyers, a trial by surprise would be an unbearable violation of the constitutional provision on due process of law.' Gordon Van Kessel, *Adversary Excesses in the American Criminal Trial*, 67 Notre Dame L. Rev. 403, 454 (1992).

The leading U.S. case is *Brady v. Maryland*, 373 U.S. 83 (1963). In that case, after petitioner was convicted of murder and sentenced to death, he learned the state had withheld a statement in which another individual involved in the crime admitted the homicide. Daniel J. Capra, *Access to Exculpatory Evidence: Avoiding the Agurs Problems of Prosecutorial Discretion and Retrospective Review*, 53 Fordham L. Rev. 391, 392–97 (1984), discusses *Brady* and a subsequent decision, *United States v. Agurs*, 427 U.S. 97 (1976):

> [T]he Supreme Court stated that 'the suppression by the prosecution of evidence favorable to an accused upon request violates due process where the evidence is material either to guilt or to punishment, irrespective of the good faith or bad faith of the prosecution.' * * * The two major problems of implementing the *Brady* right are that: the prosecutor—an understandably biased party—is left to decide which information is in fact favorable to the defendant; and when a defendant is denied access to exculpatory evidence, he must rely on a speculative post-trial review to determine the effect such evidence would have had on his case. * * * In the years since Brady, the problems * * * have been exacerbated. In *United States v. Agurs*, the Court tacitly recognized the difficult position of the prosecutor after *Brady*: Because of his role as an advocate, the prosecutor cannot determine the favorability of evidence in the way that an independent factfinder (not to speak of defense counsel) would. However, the Court chose a strange solution for the prosecutor's dilemma: It shifted to defense counsel the burden of determining which evidence is exculpatory. In other words, under *Agurs* it is defense counsel's obligation to put the prosecutor on notice that certain evidence is or could be exculpatory. Thus, directed by defense counsel, the prosecutor supposedly can act more objectively. The problem with this solution is that in many if not most cases, defense counsel is given the virtually impossible task of specifically identifying evidence that by definition he does not know exists. Defense counsel must in effect rummage through the prosecutor's file without having access to the file.

The *Agurs* decision drew a distinction between situations where the defense made a general request for exculpatory evidence and those in which it made a specific request for evidence, putting a heavier burden on the prosecution to disclose evidence that was specifically requested. The Court later eliminated this distinction in *United States v. Bagley*, 473 U.S. 667 (1985), prescribing a single standard of materiality for both types of evidence. Under *Bagley* the prosecution is obligated to disclose evidence that is material to guilt or innocence; evidence is material if there is a reasonable probability that disclosure of the evidence would have changed the outcome of the proceeding. In *Kyles v. Whitley*, 514 U.S. 419 (1995), the Court explained that the issue is whether "the favorable evidence could reasonably be taken to put the whole case in such a different light as to undermine confidence in the verdict." *Id.* at 435.

In *Shabalala v. Attorney General of Transvaal*, 1996 (1) SALR 64 (CC), the Supreme Court of South Africa considered the impact of the new Constitution's fair trial guarantee on the preconstitutional "blanket docket privilege" for documents in possession of the state. The Court (in paragraphs 43 and 50) noted that:

> If an accused requires the documents protected by the rule * * * in order to have a fair trial, it is argued that both justice and the public interest require that these documents should not be denied to the defence. * * * This is obviously a formidable argument. The interests of the accused must, however, be balanced against other legitimate considerations. * * * If the conflicting considerations are weighed, there appears to be an overwhelming balance in favour of an accused person's right to disclosure in those circumstances where there is no reasonable risk that such disclosure might lead to the disclosure of the identity of informers or State secrets or to intimidation or obstruction of the proper ends of justice. The 'blanket docket privilege' which effectively protects even such statements from disclosure therefore appears to be unreasonable, unjustifiable in an open and democratic society and is certainly not necessary.

The Court held that a different rule applied where there is a reasonable risk that disclosure might interfere with protection of state secrets, methods of police investigation, identity of informers, and communications between a legal advisor and his clients, or where there is reasonable risk that disclosure might lead to intimidation of witnesses or otherwise impede the proper ends of justice. In such cases, found the Court in paragraphs 52 and 72 (a) (6): "it might be proper to protect the disclosure of witnesses' statements. * * * Even in such cases, however, it does not follow that the disclosure of the statements concerned must always be withheld if there is a risk that the accused would not enjoy a fair trial. [The Court] should balance the degree of risk involved in attracting the potential prejudicial consequences (if such access is permitted) against the degree of the risk that a fair trial may not insure for the accused (if such access is denied)."

F.2. RIGHT TO CALL AND TO CROSS– EXAMINE WITNESSES

The right to call and cross-examine witnesses is primarily a feature of adversarial systems of criminal procedure. In the U.S., this right is established in the Sixth Amendment to the Constitution, which provides that "the accused shall enjoy the right * * * to be confronted with the witnesses against him; to have compulsory process for obtaining witnesses in his favor * * *." In contrast, countries with inquisitorial systems tend not to include these rights in their constitutions or to provide for a somewhat softer right to introduce witnesses and respond to evidence. For example, Colombia's Constitution, Art. 29, provides for the accused's right to "present proof and controvert that which is brought against him."

The cases that follow adopt different approaches to the issue.

VAN MECHELEN AND OTHERS
v. THE NETHERLANDS

European Court of Human Rights.
25 E.H.R.R. 647 (1997).

[The applicants were convicted of attempted manslaughter and robbery. They were identified through statements made before the trial by anonymous police officers, none of whom gave evidence before either the Regional Court or the investigating judge. On appeal, the Court of Appeal referred the case to the investigating judge, who arranged hearings in which he, a registrar, and the anonymous witnesses were in one room and the applicants, their lawyers, and the Advocate General were in another room. The two rooms were connected by a sound link. Reasons given by the police witnesses for retaining anonymity included fear for the safety of their families and the need to remain anonymous in the interests of police service. In addition, a number of named witnesses were heard. The Court of Appeal upheld the convictions. Relying on Arts. 6(1) and (3)(d), the applicants complained to the ECHR that their convictions were based to a decisive extent upon the evidence of anonymous witnesses.]

1. *Applicable principles*

49. As the requirements of Article 6 § 3 are to be seen as particular aspects of the right to a fair trial guaranteed by Article 6 § 1, the Court will examine the complaints under Article 6 §§ 1 and 3 (d) taken together (see, among many other authorities, the above-mentioned Doorson judgment, pp. 469–70, § 66).

50. The Court reiterates that the admissibility of evidence is primarily a matter for regulation by national law and as a general rule it is for the national courts to assess the evidence before them. The Court's task under the Convention is not to give a ruling as to whether statements of witnesses were properly admitted as evidence, but rather to ascertain whether the proceedings as a whole, including the way in which evidence was taken, were fair * * *

51. In addition, all the evidence must normally be produced at a public hearing, in the presence of the accused, with a view to adversarial argument. There are exceptions to this principle, but they must not infringe the rights of the defence; as a general rule, paragraphs 1 and 3 (d) of Article 6 require that the defendant be given an adequate and proper opportunity to challenge and question a witness against him, either when he makes his statements or at a later stage. * * *

52. As the Court had occasion to state in its Doorson judgment * * * the use of statements made by anonymous witnesses to found a conviction is not under all circumstances incompatible with the Convention.

53. In that same judgment the Court noted the following:

"It is true that Article 6 does not explicitly require the interests of witnesses to be taken into consideration. However, their life, liberty or security of person may be at stake, as may interests coming generally within the ambit of Article 8 of the Convention. Such interests of witnesses and victims are in principle protected by other, substantive provisions of the Convention, which imply that Contracting States should organise their criminal proceedings in such a way that those interests are not unjustifiably imperilled. Against this background, principles of fair trial also require that in appropriate cases the interests of the defence are balanced against those of witnesses or victims called upon to testify." (see the above-mentioned Doorson judgment, p. 470, § 70)

54.   However, if the anonymity of prosecution witnesses is maintained, the defence will be faced with difficulties which criminal proceedings should not normally involve. Accordingly, the Court has recognised that in such cases Article 6 § 1 taken together with Article 6 § 3 (d) of the Convention requires that the handicaps under which the defence labours be sufficiently counterbalanced by the procedures followed by the judicial authorities (ibid., p. 471, § 72).

55.   Finally, it should be recalled that a conviction should not be based either solely or to a decisive extent on anonymous statements (ibid., p. 472, § 76).

2.   *Application of the above principles*

56.   In the Court's opinion, the balancing of the interests of the defence against arguments in favour of maintaining the anonymity of witnesses raises special problems if the witnesses in question are members of the police force of the State. Although their interests—and indeed those of their families—also deserve protection under the Convention, it must be recognised that their position is to some extent different from that of a disinterested witness or a victim. They owe a general duty of obedience to the State's executive authorities and usually have links with the prosecution; for these reasons alone their use as anonymous witnesses should be resorted to only in exceptional circumstances. In addition, it is in the nature of things that their duties, particularly in the case of arresting officers, may involve giving evidence in open court.

57.   On the other hand, the Court has recognised in principle that, provided that the rights of the defence are respected, it may be legitimate for the police authorities to wish to preserve the anonymity of an agent deployed in undercover activities, for his own or his family's protection and so as not to impair his usefulness for future operations.
* * *

58.   Having regard to the place that the right to a fair administration of justice holds in a democratic society, any measures restricting the rights of the defence should be strictly necessary. If a less restrictive measure can suffice then that measure should be applied.

59.   In the present case, the police officers in question were in a separate room with the investigating judge, from which the accused and even their counsel were excluded. All communication was via a sound link. The defence was thus not only unaware of the identity of the police

witnesses but were also prevented from observing their demeanour under direct questioning, and thus from testing their reliability * * *

60.   It has not been explained to the Court's satisfaction why it was necessary to resort to such extreme limitations on the right of the accused to have the evidence against them given in their presence, or why less far-reaching measures were not considered.

In the absence of any further information, the Court cannot find that the operational needs of the police provide sufficient justification. It should be noted that the Explanatory Memorandum of the Bill which became the Act of 11 November 1993 (see paragraph 42 above) refers in this connection to the possibilities of using make-up or disguise and the prevention of eye contact.

61.   Nor is the Court persuaded that the Court of Appeal made sufficient effort to assess the threat of reprisals against the police officers or their families. It does not appear from that court's judgment that it sought to address the question whether the applicants would have been in a position to carry out any such threats or to incite others to do so on their behalf. Its decision was based exclusively on the seriousness of the crimes committed (see paragraph 26 above). * * *

62.   It is true—as noted by the Government and the Commission (see paragraph 48 above)—that the anonymous police officers were interrogated before an investigating judge, who had himself ascertained their identity and had, in a very detailed official report of his findings, stated his opinion on their reliability and credibility as well as their reasons for remaining anonymous.

However these measures cannot be considered a proper substitute for the possibility of the defence to question the witnesses in their presence and make their own judgment as to their demeanour and reliability. It thus cannot be said that the handicaps under which the defence laboured were counterbalanced by the above procedures.

63.   Moreover, the only evidence relied on by the Court of Appeal which provided positive identification of the applicants as the perpetrators of the crimes were the statements of the anonymous police officers. That being so the conviction of the applicants was based "to a decisive extent" on these anonymous statements. * * *

65.   Against this background the Court cannot find that the proceedings taken as a whole were fair.

R. v. TAYLOR AND CRABB

Court of Appeal (Criminal Division) (United Kingdom).
Crim. L.R. 253 (1995).

Evans LJ (reading the judgment of the court): This appeal by Gary Taylor arises out of a trial which took place at the Central Criminal Court in June–July 1993 before His Honour Judge Denison QC and a jury.

* * * The question raised by this appeal is whether the learned judge's ruling, which was that Miss A was entitled to give her evidence

anonymously and with a certain amount of physical protection by means of a screen, was correct or not. We are told that in fact arrangements were made whereby counsel and the jury could see her direct and she could see them. The defendants, however, could not see her, nor could she see them, but there was a video camera which enabled the defendants to see her by that means whilst she was giving evidence. That was a device which meant that she was not conscious as she gave evidence of the defendants looking at her. Equally, it meant that the defendants were able to see for themselves whether or not Miss A was a person whom they knew or could recognise. * * *

The fact that the defence were not made aware of Miss A's identity meant, of course, that they were unable to make any enquiries with regard to her or her background or to obtain a statement from her. Had they done so, it is submitted, they might have been able to unearth further information which would be of value to them in cross-examination. But it must also be stated that the prosecution had themselves made enquiries into Miss A and her background. The way in which it was put by counsel for the prosecution in the hearing before the learned judge was this: "The Crown have complied with their duty to provide the defence with all relevant material in this case. I am having her background treble checked this morning before she gives evidence to make absolutely sure that there is nothing that we know of which ought to be disclosed."

The defence, therefore, had the assurance that those enquiries had been made and that there was no unused material which was being withheld from them. * * *

We would express our conclusions on the law in the following terms. [The defense] asserts a fundamental right of a defendant to see and to know the identity of his accusers, including witnesses for the prosecution brought against him. By that, [the defense] does not mean that there are no exceptions, because, as already indicated, he concedes that cases of national security might be one. However, in so far as he submits that it is a fundamental right, in the sense that it is one which should only be denied to a defendant in rare and exceptional circumstances, then that is a submission with which we can and do agree. Whether or not in a particular case the exception should be made is preeminently a matter for the exercise of discretion by the trial judge. Apart from all other considerations it is a question which has to be decided in the course of the trial when, or possibly before, the witness comes to the witness-box, and it may be at a stage when relatively little evidence has been given.

Since we must regard this as an exercise of discretion, the next consideration is, what factors are or may be relevant to that exercise of discretion by the trial judge? * * * First and foremost, there must be real grounds for being fearful of the consequences if the evidence is given and the identity of the witness is revealed. In practical terms and in most cases it may well be sufficient to draw a parallel with the statutory provisions of s 23(3)(b) of the Criminal Justice Act 1988. That provides for statements to be admissible in evidence when the person who made it does not give oral evidence through fear. However, we think it worth noting that in principle it may not be necessary for the witness himself or herself to be fearful, or it may not be the case that they are fearful alone. There can be cases where concern is expressed by other persons; in fact the present is such a case, having regard to the statement from the witness' mother, Mrs. A, already read. A second comment should be added, which is this. The consequences need not necessarily be limited to those for the witness herself. There could be cases of concern for the consequences for the family of the witness rather than the individual, for example.

Secondly, the evidence must be sufficiently relevant and important to make it unfair to the prosecution to compel them to proceed without it. But the greater its importance, the greater the potential unfairness to the defendant in allowing the witness to remain anonymous. In this context, it seems to us, that a distinction can properly be drawn, as the learned judge drew it here, between cases where the creditworthiness of the witness is or is likely to be in issue and others where the issue for the jury is the reliability and accuracy of the witness rather than credit.

Thirdly, the prosecution must satisfy the court that the creditworthiness of the witness has been fully investigated and the results of that enquiry disclosed to the defence so far as is consistent with the anonymity sought.

Fourthly, the court must be satisfied that no undue prejudice is caused to the defendant. "Undue" is a necessary qualification because some prejudice is inevitable if the order in question is made, even if that prejudice is only the qualification placed on the right to confront the witness as one of the defendant's accusers.

But there may be factors pointing the other way. Here, for example, the defendants could see the witness on the television video screen as she gave evidence. They could be sure, therefore, that she was no one whom they recognised or who, so far as they were aware, had any motive for giving evidence against them. That factor eliminates part of even the so-called "theoretical possibility" * * * that any actual prejudice was caused.

Finally, the court can balance the need for protection, including the extent of any necessary protection, against the unfairness or appearance of unfairness in the particular case. By referring to the extent of protection, we have in mind other courses which can be taken short of allowing anonymity to the witness. These include, for example, screening, a voice camera, a hearing in camera or whatever it may be.

By way of comment, it seems to us that there is no reason in principle why the same considerations should not apply when it is the defence who seek to call a witness whose identity is not to be revealed; but that is not a factor which arises in the present case.

The question we have to consider is whether that exercise of the learned judge's direction discloses any error of law or otherwise can be said to be clearly wrong, as [defense counsel] submits that it is. It seems to us that it was in fact close to being a model exercise of the discretion which the learned judge was called upon to exercise in the present case.

* * * Not only was the balancing exercise fully and carefully carried out, but it has also to be said that this is not a case where there are any grounds for supposing that the witness was not impartial or that she did have an axe to grind. One can think of many examples of cases where that situation would not arise. But it did arise here, and therefore the learned judge, in our view, was entitled to come to the conclusion which he did, that this witness should be allowed to give her evidence anonymously and in the way in which she did.

Notes and Questions

1. On what grounds is the right to confrontation an element of due process? Does the argument depend on an assumption that the criminal justice system is adversarial?

2. Can the decisions in *Van Mechelen* and *Taylor* be reconciled, or do they reflect different understandings of the basis for the right to confrontation?

3. What is the proper scope of the right to confrontation? Is it sufficient to allow the defendant to cross-examine the witness? Must the defendant be able to see the witness and know the witness's identity? What is gained by these rights?

4. Should there be limits to confrontation? Many systems establish rules to protect witnesses from discriminatory or painful questions from counsel. Consider the situation in rape trials where the victim testifies or when children are on the stand.

G. RIGHT TO A SPEEDY TRIAL

The right to a speedy trial protects detainees from indefinite confinement, permits all accused to clear themselves of charges within a reasonable period of time, and ensures that trials occur while the evidence and memories of witnesses are still fresh. Nevertheless, according to Bassiouni, "the right to a speedy trial * * * is qualified by the threat of expedited proceedings which jeopardize a fair trial. The counterbalance to this right, then, is the accused's right to adequate time and facilities for the preparation of his or her defense." Bassiouni, *op. cit.* at 286.

The right to a speedy trial is guaranteed in many constitutions, but there are many variations as to who may claim the right, what time limits apply, and what the remedies are for its violation.

In the U.S., the right to a speedy trial is explicitly protected by the Sixth Amendment to the U.S. Constitution. *Barker v. Wingo*, 407 U.S. 514 (1972), established that to determine whether the speedy trial right had been violated, courts must balance four factors: length of delay, reason for the delay, the point at which the defendant asserted the right, and the prejudice suffered by the defendant as a result of the delay. This analysis was later sharpened in the case reproduced, in part, below.

DOGGETT v. UNITED STATES

Supreme Court (United States).
505 U.S. 647 (1992).

[In February 1980, petitioner Doggett was indicted on federal drug charges, but he left the country before the Drug Enforcement Agency could secure his arrest. The DEA knew that he was later imprisoned in Panama, but after requesting that he be sent back to the U.S., it never followed up on his status. After the DEA discovered that Doggett had left Panama for Colombia, it made no further attempt to locate him. Thus it was unaware that he reentered the U.S. in 1982 and subsequently married, earned a college degree, found steady employment, lived openly under his own name, and stayed within the law. The Marshall's Service eventually located Doggett, during a simple credit check on individuals with outstanding warrants. He was arrested in September 1988, eight and a half years after his indictment. He moved to dismiss the indictment on the ground that the government's failure to prosecute him earlier violated his Sixth Amendment right to a speedy trial. The District Court denied the motion, and Doggett entered a conditional guilty plea. The Court of Appeals affirmed.]

Justice Souter delivered the opinion of the Court.

In this case we consider whether the delay of 8–1/2 years between petitioner's indictment and arrest violated his Sixth Amendment right to a speedy trial. We hold that it did. * * *

II

The Sixth Amendment guarantees that, "[i]n all criminal prosecutions, the accused shall enjoy the right to a speedy * * * trial * * *." On its face, the Speedy Trial Clause is written with such breadth that, taken literally, it would forbid the government to delay the trial of an "accused" for any reason at all. Our cases, however, have qualified the literal sweep of the provision by specifically recognizing the relevance of four separate enquiries: whether delay before trial was uncommonly long, whether the government or the criminal defendant is more to blame for that delay, whether, in due course, the defendant asserted his right to a speedy trial, and whether he suffered prejudice as the delay's result. See *Barker*, 407 U.S. 514, at 530.

The first of these is actually a double enquiry. Simply to trigger a speedy trial analysis, an accused must allege that the interval between accusation and trial has crossed the threshold dividing ordinary from "presumptively prejudicial" delay * * * since, by definition, he cannot complain that the government has denied him a "speedy" trial if it has, in fact, prosecuted his case with customary promptness. If the accused makes this showing, the court must then consider, as one factor among several, the extent to which the delay stretches beyond the bare minimum needed to trigger judicial examination of the claim. * * * This latter enquiry is significant to the speedy trial analysis because, as we discuss below, the presumption that pretrial delay has prejudiced the accused intensifies over time. In this case, the extraordinary 8–1/2 year lag between Doggett's indictment and arrest clearly suffices to trigger the speedy trial enquiry; its further significance within that enquiry will be dealt with later.

As for *Barker*'s second criterion, the Government claims to have sought Doggett with diligence. The findings of the courts below are to the contrary, however, and we review trial court determinations of negligence with considerable deference. * * *

The Government goes against the record again in suggesting that Doggett knew of his indictment years before he was arrested. Were this true, *Barker*'s third factor, concerning invocation of the right to a speedy trial, would be weighed heavily against him. But here again, the Government is trying to revisit the facts. * * *

III

The Government is left, then, with its principal contention: that Doggett fails to make out a successful speedy trial claim because he has not shown precisely how he was prejudiced by the delay between his indictment and trial.

A

We have observed in prior cases that unreasonable delay between formal accusation and trial threatens to produce more than one sort of harm, including "oppressive pretrial incarceration," "anxiety and concern of the accused," and "the possibility that the [accused's] defense will be impaired" by dimming memories and loss of exculpatory evidence. * * * Of these forms of prejudice, "the most serious is the last, because the inability of a defendant adequately to prepare his case skews the fairness of the entire system." * * * Doggett claims this kind of prejudice, and there is probably no other kind that he can claim, since he was subjected neither to pretrial detention nor, he has successfully contended, to awareness of unresolved charges against him. * * *

B

This brings us to an enquiry into the role that presumptive prejudice should play in the disposition of Doggett's speedy trial claim. We begin with hypothetical and somewhat easier cases and work our way to this one.

Our speedy trial standards recognize that pretrial delay is often both inevitable and wholly justifiable. The government may need time to collect witnesses against the accused, oppose his pretrial motions, or, if he goes into hiding, track him down. * * * Thus, in this case, if the Government had pursued Doggett with reasonable diligence from his indictment to his arrest, his speedy trial claim would fail. * * *

The Government concedes, on the other hand, that Doggett would prevail if he could show that the Government had intentionally held back in its prosecution of him to gain some impermissible advantage at trial. * * * That we cannot doubt. *Barker* stressed that official bad faith in causing delay will be weighed heavily against the government, 407 U.S., at 531, and a bad-faith delay the length of this negligent one would present an overwhelming case for dismissal.

Between diligent prosecution and bad-faith delay, official negligence in bringing an accused to trial occupies the middle ground. While not compelling relief in every case where bad-faith delay would make relief virtually automatic, neither is negligence automatically tolerable simply because the accused cannot demonstrate exactly how it has prejudiced him. It was on this point that the Court of Appeals erred, and on the facts before us, it was reversible error.

Barker made it clear that "different weights [are to be] assigned to different reasons" for delay. * * * Although negligence is obviously to be weighed more lightly than a deliberate intent to harm the accused's defense, it still falls on the wrong side of the divide between acceptable and unacceptable reasons for delaying a criminal prosecution once it has begun. And such is the nature of the prejudice presumed that the weight we assign to official negligence compounds over time as the presumption of evidentiary prejudice grows. Thus, our toleration of such negligence varies inversely with its protractedness, cf. *Arizona v. Youngblood*, 488 U.S. 51 (1988), and its consequent threat to the fairness of the accused's trial. * * *

To be sure, to warrant granting relief, negligence unaccompanied by particularized trial prejudice must have lasted longer than negligence demonstrably causing such prejudice. But even so, the Government's egregious persistence in failing to prosecute Doggett is clearly sufficient. The lag between Doggett's indictment and arrest was 8–1/2 years, and he would have faced trial 6 years earlier than he did but for the Government's inexcusable oversights. The portion of the delay attributable to the Government's negligence far exceeds the threshold needed to state a speedy trial claim; indeed, we have called shorter delays "extraordinary." * * * When the Government's negligence thus causes delay six times as long as that generally sufficient to trigger judicial review * * * and when the presumption of prejudice, albeit unspecified, is neither extenuated, as by the defendant's acquiescence * * * nor persuasively rebutted. The defendant is entitled to relief.

In many countries, overburdened systems are unable to process cases expeditiously. With cases sometimes taking up to 15 years to try, the Supreme Court of India has laid down guidelines for lower courts. The Court has recognized speedy trial as a fundamental right implicit in Art. 21 of the Constitution of India, which provides that no person be deprived of life or personal liberty except according to procedure established by law. The following decision is by a Constitutional Bench of the Indian Supreme Court.

ABDUL REHMAN ANTULAY & OTHERS v. R.S. NAYAK

Supreme Court (India).
A.I.R. 1992 S.C. 1701 (1992).

Jeevan Reddy, J.

86.   * * * (2) Right to speedy trial flowing from Article 21 encompasses all the stages, namely the stages of investigation, inquiry, trial, appeal, revision and re-trial * * *

(3) The concerns underlying the right to speedy trial from the point of view of the accused are:

(a) the period of remand and pre-conviction detention should be as short as possible. In other words, the accused should not be subjected to unnecessary or unduly long incarceration prior to his conviction;

(b) the worry, anxiety, expense and disturbance to his vocation and peace, resulting from an unduly prolonged investigation, inquiry or trial should be minimal; and

(c) undue delay may well result in impairment of the ability of the accused to defend himself, whether on account of death, disappearance or non-availability of witnesses or otherwise.

(4) At the same time, one cannot ignore the fact that it is usually the accused who is interested in delaying the proceedings. As is often pointed out, "delay is a known defence tactic". Since the burden of proving the guilt of the accused lies upon the prosecution, delay ordinarily prejudices the prosecution. Non-availability of witnesses, disappearance of evidence by lapse of time really works against the interest of the prosecution. Of course, there may be cases where the prosecution, for whatever reason, also delays the proceedings. Therefore, in every case, where the right to speedy trial is alleged to have been infringed, the first question to be put and answered is—who is responsible for the delay? Proceedings taken by either party in good faith, to vindicate their rights and interest, as perceived by them, cannot be treated as delaying tactics nor can the time taken in pursuing such proceedings be counted towards delay. It goes without saying that frivolous proceedings or proceedings taken merely for delaying the day of reckoning cannot be treated as proceedings taken in good faith. The mere fact that an application/petition is admitted and an order of stay granted by a superior court is by itself no proof that the proceeding is not frivolous. Very often these stays are obtained on *ex parte* representation.

(5) While determining whether undue delay has occurred (resulting in violation of Speedy Trial) one must have regard to all the attendant circumstances, including nature of offence, conditions and so on—what is called, the systemic delays. It is true that it is the obligation of the State to ensure a speedy trial and State includes judiciary as well, but a realistic and practical approach should be adopted in such matters instead of a pedantic one.

(6) Each and every delay does not necessarily prejudice the accused. Some delays may indeed work to his advantage. As has been observed by

Powell, J. in *Barker* (33 L Ed 2d 101) "it cannot be said how long a delay is too long in a system where justice is supposed to be swift but deliberate...."

However, inordinately long delay may be taken as presumptive proof of prejudice. In this context, the fact of incarceration of accused will also be a relevant fact. The prosecution should not be allowed to become a persecution. * * *

(7) We cannot recognise or give effect to, what is called the 'demand' rule. An accused cannot try himself; he is tried by the court at the behest of the prosecution. Hence, an accused's plea of denial of speedy trial cannot be defeated by saying that the accused did at no time demand a speedy trial. * * *

(8) Ultimately, the court has to balance and weigh the several relevant factors—'balancing test' or 'balancing process'—and determine in each case whether the right to speedy trial has been denied in a given case.

(9) Ordinarily speaking, where the court comes to the conclusion that right to speedy trial of an accused has been infringed the charges or the conviction, as the case may be, shall be quashed. But this is not the only course open. The nature of the offence and other circumstances in a given case may be such that quashing of proceedings may not be in the interest of justice. In such a case, it is open to the court to make such other appropriate order—including an order to conclude the trial within a fixed time where the trial is not concluded or reducing the sentence where the trial has concluded—as may be deemed just and equitable in the circumstances of the case.

(10) It is neither advisable nor practicable to fix any time-limit for trial of offences. Any such rule is bound to be [a] qualified one. Such rule cannot also be evolved merely to shift the burden of proving justification on to the shoulders of the prosecution. In every case of complaint of denial of right to speedy trial, it is primarily for the prosecution to justify and explain the delay. At the same time, it is the duty of the court to weigh all the circumstances of a given case before pronouncing upon the complaint.

Notes and Questions

1. The tests in *Barker,* as applied in *Doggett* and *Antulay,* have common elements, such as the degree to which the defendant was prejudiced by the delay and the causes of the delay. Both elements inject flexibility into the test. Is such flexibility desirable, or would it be better to have strict rules regarding time frames?

2. Should it matter whether the defendant asserted the right to a speedy trial or whether the prosecution or defense caused the delay? Should the reasons for the delay or its length be linked to the possible remedies?

3. In *Park et al. v. Japan,* 26 Keishū 10 at 631 (1972), available in Beer and Itoh, *op. cit.* at 434, the Japanese Supreme Court addressed a claim under the speedy trial right guaranteed by Art. 37, paragraph 1 of the

Japanese Constitution. The case arose out of incidents in 1952, in which demonstrators attacked the Takada Police Box and stoned the vehicles of U.S. servicemen. Thirty-one people were indicted for various crimes of violence and arson; 20 of these were also among the accused in a different case (*Osu*), stemming from related incidents. At defense counsel's request, the trial was suspended so that the court could try the *Osu* case first. The suspension lasted 15 years.

The Japanese Supreme Court held that the delay violated the "fundamental human right" of the accused to receive a speedy trial. The Court noted that "a 'speedy trial' is a relative notion to be determined in relation to various conditions in each concrete case." Whether the postponement of a criminal trial violates the right to a speedy trial should take into account elements "such as: the causes and reasons for the delay; whether the delay was unavoidable; to what degree the constitutionally protected interest was damaged." Although the defense had asked for the suspension, the Court found this did not constitute a waiver of the speedy trial right because nobody had foreseen the length of the *Osu* trial. The Court also found that the defendants' interest in a speedy trial was seriously damaged because, among other reasons, no evidence had been taken on a variety of important issues, and the memories of witnesses and the defendants "might have become vague and uncertain." The Court held "the instant case has come within such a category that the court can apply emergency measures to terminate the proceedings against the defendants."

H. RIGHT TO APPEAL

The right to appeal is explicitly protected by the constitutions of many countries, see, e.g., the constitutions of Colombia (Art. 31), Peru (Art. 139(6)), and Venezuela (Art. 49), and it is protected by the European HR Convention. The U.S. Constitution does not explicitly provide for a right to appeal a conviction, and the Supreme Court has not recognized the right. However, the right to a direct appeal is statutorily protected and almost universally available. The materials below include excerpts from an article regarding the justifications for an appeal as a right in the U.S. and a decision by the ECHR that interprets the right of access to a court as including the right to an appeal.

Harlon Leigh Dalton, TAKING THE RIGHT TO APPEAL (MORE OR LESS) SERIOUSLY,
95 Yale L.J. 62, 62–63, 66–73 (1985).

The right to appeal at least once without obtaining prior court approval is nearly universal—within the universe bounded by the Atlantic and Pacific Oceans, Mexico and Canada. Although its origins are neither constitutional nor ancient, the right has become, in a word, sacrosanct. During the past decade of high anxiety over the burdens placed on our judicial system by what has fairly been termed a litigation explosion, the basic right to take an appeal has remained virtually untouched and, indeed, uncommented upon.

At the same time, the right to appeal has in practice begun to shrink to a mere formality in many jurisdictions as appellate judges severely restrict oral argument, deliberate alone, write skeletal opinions, write unpublished opinions, affirm without opinion, and in some cases rule from the bench. It takes little prescience to predict that someday, erelong, the same forces that have led to the "reforms" listed above will drive judicial managers to consider whether the right to appeal should itself be abandoned. * * *

[Some statements suggest that] appeal of right furthers the substantive goal of a correct decision in every case. Simply bringing a dispute to an end and diffusing hostilities is not enough. No matter how much we value resolution per se, we also want to achieve the "right results." After all, had Solomon actually split the baby in half, he would have successfully terminated the dispute over its parentage. Instead, he merely threatened to bisect the child, not because he thought splitting the difference had a ring of fairness, but rather as a means of determining who the real mother was—of achieving the right result.

[Another suggestion is] that appeal of right is also rooted in process values; that is to say that (quite apart from arriving at correct decisions) we are committed to arriving at decisions correctly, in a manner that assures that litigants are, and feel they are, treated fairly. At a minimum, we insist that the process be fair in form: that the parties be afforded an adequate opportunity to present their cases and to respond to their adversaries; that tribunals be competent and unbiased; and that appropriate rules of decision be followed. Related to this concern with formal fairness is a desire that the legal process provide appropriate satisfactions to the parties caught up in it. The underlying assumption is that the way in which parties experience a process may be as important as its outcome. For the injured party, the opportunity to participate meaningfully in the vindication of her rights (or, less loftily, the chance to see the other side squirm) may be a far greater and even more socially useful reward than is money damages. For the injuring party, the realization that she has been treated fairly and has had a full opportunity to put matters in the best possible light arguably promotes an acceptance of outcome and a belief in the legitimacy of the system that is essential to the success of both private ordering and official compulsion.

This appreciation of the value of participation is manifested in the appeals process as we hold ourselves ready to honor the litigant's classic boast: "If need be, I'll take this case all the way to the Supreme Court." * * *

The litigants are not the only players whom we might have the system satisfy. The attention we pay to the job satisfaction of trial judges doubtless determines in part who will perform the judging function and with what degree of avidity and creativity. * * *

And then there is the jury, those "twelve [sic] men [sic] good and true" whose sense of efficacy and importance we would do well to cater to, in part because they can spread the word should it appear that the game is rigged or that the professionals are playing it solely for their own amusement, but more importantly because they are a stand-in for "the people," in whose name and for whose account public norms are elaborated and enforced. Moreover, to the extent that trials are intended to lead to public catharses, it is the jurors who most directly experience release; to the extent that trials are morality plays in which issues of public moment are explored, it is the jurors who observe the drama and divine lessons appropriate to us all. But unless a case is sufficiently important or notorious for its appellate meanderings to be reported in the press, the jury by which it was tried is not likely to have a clue about whether its verdict was challenged and, if so, how well the verdict stood up. Thus, the taking of an appeal and its outcome are usually non-events from the standpoint of juror satisfaction with the judicial process. However, even in the midst of trial the right to appeal may compromise jury satisfaction if one of the litigants is focused more on an anticipated appeal than on the immediate drama. * * *

Although little has been written on why the right to appeal has attained the status of a right, a fair amount has been said about the larger question: Why do we have appeals in the first place? Among the more compelling answers to that question are that appellate courts exist to correct errors; to develop legal principles; and to tie geographically dispersed lower courts into a unified, authoritative legal system. As we have seen, the first-listed justification for having appellate courts—to correct errors—is also an argument for permitting recourse to those courts in every case. It remains to be seen whether the other justifications for maintaining an appellate structure likewise support access to it at will.

It is by now a commonplace that courts do and should engage in judicial lawmaking, in interpreting, shaping, and articulating the law, when statutory and constitutional pronouncements fall short or land wide. Although in matters of first impression or initial application it falls to the trial court to perform this function, in general we look to appellate courts to abandon, reaffirm, or reformulate old principles and to enunciate or select from among new ones. Given a mechanism for alerting appellate courts to the existence of issues on which legal clarification is desirable, the law-making function of an intermediate appellate court is not inconsistent with its having discretion to decide which cases it will hear.

Unless we insist that every judgment be appealed, we necessarily rely on some mechanism to sort out what gets reviewed and what does not. Traditionally, we leave it to the parties, a choice that is far from value-neutral inasmuch as party initiative and control is one of the pillars of the ideational structure underlying adjudication in this country. Party initiative not only resonates with radical individualism and distrust of the state, major strains in the American ethos; it also is an attempt to power the judicial engine with the fuel of individual self-interest. Party initiative is, furthermore, commonly viewed as a means of allocating scarce judicial resources on the basis of intensity of felt need as expressed by willingness to pay to play. However, the ends served by party initiative could be served nearly as well by letting courts select from among those cases presented for appeal by the parties. Self-interest would still propel would-be appellants to the court's door, and relative desire would still determine the universe from which the appellate docket would be drawn. * * *

The appellate court arguably is in the best position to determine whether, where, when and how the law is in need of clarification or revision. Quite obviously there are occasions in which trial judges are acutely aware that the state of the law they are asked to apply is sorry; and litigants, too, are sometimes more concerned with the mess the law is in than with winning and losing. But even where appellate courts have control over their own dockets, these other actors are free to play a major role in guiding law reform.

More troubling is the possibility that appellate courts, left to their own devices, will on occasion knowingly duck issues in need of resolution. There is no question that supreme courts in the exercise of their discretion sometimes decline to hear cases that are undeniably certworthy. When that occurs in three-tier systems, the immediate dispute already has been reviewed by at least one court. Thus, the high court's "no thank you," whether based on considerations jurisprudential or political, does not leave the litigants at the mercy of a single decision-maker. This would not be the case, however, were intermediate appellate courts permitted to exercise discretionary review. In view of the fact that individual case oversight is a principal function of intermediate courts, we would do well to ensure that such courts not have the discretion to forego review in a case they believe to have been wrongly decided simply because the case is too hot to handle, because the issues it raises might be more (or less) sympathetically framed in a subsequent case, or for any other like prudential reason.

Setting limits on the exercise of discretion would not be easy. One means would be to invert the standard for review so that the exercise of discretion will be seen as an exception to the rule. The statute might read: "The court of appeals shall entertain all cases properly presented to it, except that the court may in its discretion decline to review cases in any of the categories hereinafter enumerated. [etc.]." * * *

The concern that intermediate appellate courts might duck politically tough issues if given control over their own dockets could be addressed in other ways as well. For example, trial courts could be allowed to certify cases which appellate courts would then be bound to hear. Alternatively, the effect of trial court certification could be to place upon the appellate court the burden of justifying in writing any decision to decline review. I float these various possibilities not because I think any of them is unproblematic, but rather because they suggest that the case for or against discretionary appeal at the intermediate level need not turn on whether that discretion might be abused.

Less need be said about the remaining justification for maintaining the current appellate structure—to bind scattered local courts into a unified and authoritive judicial system. It is having the appellate system in place, rather than resorting to it in any given case, that accomplishes these purposes. Thus, an appellate court's supervisory power over the trial courts within its geographic domain, together with an inclination to step in whenever the latter are in disarray, is itself a sufficient unifier. Similarly, the fact that the power trial courts exercise ultimately emanates from somewhere on high is sufficient to lend authority to their pronouncements, and to promote acceptance of their word as final in most cases, without regard for whether an appeal could have been taken as of right.

OMAR v. FRANCE

European Court of Human Rights.
29 E.H.R.R. 210 (1998).

[The applicants were convicted of laundering the proceeds of drug trafficking. They complained that their right to a fair trial had been infringed by the Court of Cassation's decision to rule their appeals on points of law inadmissible on the ground that they had not complied with warrants for their arrest.]

* * *

I. Alleged violation of Article 6(1) of the Convention

31. The applicants submitted that the decision to declare their appeal on points of law inadmissible on the ground that they had not complied with the warrants for their arrest had infringed their right of access to a court, one of the elements of the right to a fair trial. They relied on Article 6(1) of the [European HR] Convention, the relevant part of which provides:

In the determination ' * * * of any criminal charge against him, everyone is entitled to a fair * * * hearing * * * by [a] * * * tribunal.
* * *

Such inadmissibility, they submitted, was not prescribed by law but had been introduced by case law and was contrary to the "presumption of innocence", since it was based on the idea that the accused had deliberately sought to evade justice. In the present case, however, they had never failed to appear in court and had complied whenever summoned by judges or experts. Before the Court of Cassation they had instructed a lawyer (Mr. Monod) to represent them and they had not left the address given as their place of residence in the case file. There was accordingly no proportionality between their failure to comply with the arrest warrants and the sanction that had been imposed for that reason. The Code of Criminal Procedure did not lay down any positive obligation to surrender to custody and it had not been asserted that they had resisted any attempts to enforce the warrants.

32. The Government submitted that the Court of Cassation's ruling that the applicants' appeal was inadmissible satisfied the criteria laid down by the Court's case law, in so far as the limitation concerned did not "restrict or reduce the access left to the individual in such a way or to such an extent that the very essence of the right [was] impaired". Access to the Court of Cassation was not denied to an absconding defendant but only made subject to certain conditions intended to ensure a fair balance between the protection of public interests and respect for the rights of the defence. In the present case the applicants had deliberately failed to comply with the warrants for their arrest, since they had not attended the hearing for the delivery of the Court of Appeal's judgment, the date of which had been duly notified to them. They had

lodged their appeal on points of law three days later, and could therefore not maintain that, not having been served in person with a copy of the arrest warrant, they were not obliged to comply with it. The ruling that the appeal was inadmissible had thus been proportionate to the aim pursued, which was to make it possible to enforce the court's order against the applicants, regard being had in addition to the level of the court which had ruled it inadmissible.

* * *

34. The Court reiterates that the right to a court, of which the right of access is one aspect, is not absolute; it may be subject to limitations permitted by implication, particularly regarding the conditions of admissibility of an appeal. However, these limitations must not restrict exercise of the right in such a way or to such an extent that the very essence of the right is impaired. They must pursue a legitimate aim and there must be a reasonable proportionality between the means employed and the aim sought to be achieved.

35. In the present case the Court of Cassation declared the applicants' appeal on points of law inadmissible on the grounds that:

> It follows from the general principles of criminal procedure that a convicted person who has not complied with a warrant for his arrest is not entitled to act through a representative in order to lodge an appeal on points of law. It could not be otherwise unless he supplied evidence of circumstances making it absolutely impossible for him to surrender to custody at the appropriate time. As no such evidence has been supplied by the three appellants, against whom arrest warrants were issued after they had appeared in court for the hearing, their appeal, which has been lodged by an attorney practising in the Court of Appeal, must be declared inadmissible.

36. The Court must therefore determine whether, in the circumstances of the present case, the fact that the applicants' appeal on points of law was automatically declared inadmissible because they had not complied with the warrants for their arrest infringed their right of access to a court.

37. The Court notes in the first place that the obligation for a defendant sentenced to a non-suspended term of imprisonment accompanied by a warrant for his arrest to surrender to custody at the time when he gives notice of his intention to appeal on points of law, that is within five days of delivery of the Court of Appeal's judgment, is derived from the very long-established and consistent case law of the Criminal Division of the Court of Cassation.

38. At the hearing the Agent of the Government emphasised that this rule had an essentially moral basis and was underpinned by the idea "that it would be shocking to allow a person who has deliberately failed to comply with a court order to appeal on points of law". It was not absolute and was no longer applied where the appellant's good faith could be presumed, as, for example, when he came in person to sign his notice of appeal.

39.   However, some French legal writers have criticised the rule, arguing that the decision, when considering an appeal on points of law, to declare it inadmissible ipso jure when the defendant has not surrendered to custody within the five-day time limit is based on a presumption that he is at fault, whereas his fault is not necessarily intentional.

40.   The Court can only note that, where an appeal on points of law is declared inadmissible solely because, as in the present case, the appellant has not surrendered to custody pursuant to the judicial decision challenged in the appeal, this ruling compels the appellant to subject himself in advance to the deprivation of liberty resulting from the impugned decision, although that decision cannot be considered final until the appeal has been decided or the time limit for lodging an appeal has expired.

This impairs the very essence of the right of appeal, by imposing a disproportionate burden on the appellant, thus upsetting the fair balance that must be struck between the legitimate concern to ensure that judicial decisions are enforced, on the one hand, and the right of access to the Court of Cassation and exercise of the rights of the defence on the other.

41.   In that connection, the Court emphasises the crucial role of proceedings in cassation, which form a special stage of the criminal proceedings whose consequences may prove decisive for the accused.

Article 6(1) of the Convention does not, it is true, compel the Contracting States to set up courts of appeal or of cassation. Nevertheless, a State which does institute such courts is required to ensure that persons amenable to the law shall enjoy before these courts the fundamental guarantees contained in Article 6.

42.   In its *Poitrimol* judgment the Court held:

The inadmissibility of the appeal on points of law, on grounds connected with the applicant's having absconded * * * amounted to a disproportionate sanction, having regard to the signal importance of the rights of the defence and of the principle of the rule of law in a democratic society.

43.   That finding is even more valid in the present case. Whereas Mr. Poitrimol had left French territory and was on the run abroad with his two children, none of the applicants attempted to evade enforcement of the arrest warrants. They did not leave their work or the address given as their place of residence in the case file. They attended the hearings in the Court of Appeal. They were not in court for the delivery of the judgment, but no statutory provision obliged them to attend, since in French law such attendance is a right, not an obligation.

The police could have apprehended them at any time, and indeed did apprehend Mr. Cheniti Omar, who was arrested at his place of work on 27 May 1993.

44.   Having regard to all the circumstances of the case, the Court considers that the applicants suffered an excessive restriction of their right of access to a court, and therefore of their right to a fair trial.

There has accordingly been a breach of Article 6(1).

Questions

Omar v. France and the excerpts from the Dalton article address the question of whether an appeal is required for a fair trial. Is an appeal as a right necessary for fairness? If so, why?

I. PROHIBITION AGAINST DOUBLE JEOPARDY

In broad terms, the prohibition against double jeopardy prevents a state from prosecuting a person more than once for the same offense or for offenses arising out of the same transaction. The equivalent of this prohibition in civil law countries is the principle of *non bis in idem* (that is, one should not be tried twice for the same crime). While most countries abide by this principle in some form, there are significant variations.

One important variation in constitutional protections for double jeopardy has to do with the definition of "same offense." The U.S. test for what constitutes the "same offense" for double jeopardy purposes has changed a few times. The main question is whether "same offense" should be defined in terms of "same conduct" or "same elements." The "same conduct" test is a broad rule that bars prosecutions if, to establish an essential element of an offense charged in that prosecution, the government will prove conduct that constitutes an offense for which the defendant has already been prosecuted. The "same elements" test is a less protective rule, which provides that two offenses are not the same if each offense contains an element not contained in the other offense. The same elements test was established by the Supreme Court in *Blockburger v. United States*, 284 U.S. 299 (1932), and was replaced with a "same conduct" test in *Grady v. Corbin*, 495 U.S. 508 (1990). But in *United States v. Dixon*, 509 U.S. 688 (1993), the Supreme Court returned to a "same elements" test.

The ECHR has followed a similar approach. In *Oliveira v. Switzerland*, 28 E.H.R.R. 289 (1999), the Court considered whether prosecution of a person for multiple offenses arising out of a single act results in a violation of the *non bis in idem* principle. In *Oliveira* a driver hit two other cars, causing serious injuries to one of the other drivers, was convicted by a Police Magistrate for failing to control her vehicle, and fined 200 Swiss francs (Sfr). More than a year later, the District Attorney's Office issued a penal order, fining her 2,000 Sfr for negligently causing physical injury contrary to the Criminal Code. Oliveira challenged the District Attorney's order in Zurich District Court, which held that a person may be prosecuted for a more serious offense after having been convicted on a summary basis of a minor offense. However, it reduced the 2,000 Sfr fine to 1,500 Sfr and deducted the 200 Sfr. from that. After this decision was affirmed within the Swiss court system, Oliveira challenged it before the ECHR, claiming a violation of Art. 4 of Protocol No. 7 to the Convention, which provides that "no one shall be liable to be tried or punished again in criminal proceedings under the jurisdiction of the same State for an offence for which he has already been finally acquitted or convicted in accordance with the law and penal procedure of that State." The Court found that there had been no violation of the Article, stating that this case was:

> a typical example of a single act constituting various offences. The characteristic feature of this notion is that a single criminal act is split up into two separate offences, in this case the failure to control the vehicle and the negligent causing of physical injury. In such cases, the greater penalty will usually absorb the lesser one. There is nothing in that situation which infringes Article 4 of Protocol No. 7 since that provision prohibits people being tried twice for the same offence whereas in cases concerning a single act constituting various offences one criminal act constitutes two separate offences.

An additional distinction among constitutional protections against successive prosecutions is that the prohibition on double jeopardy applies only within a single sovereign, barring multiple prosecutions for a single offense by the same sovereign but allowing prosecutions for the same offense by different sovereigns. For example, after prosecution by a state government in the U.S., the federal government may prosecute the individual for the same offense under federal law. *Bartkus v. Illinois,* 359 U.S. 121 (1959). In contrast, *non bis in idem* forbids prosecutions for a single offense by separate sovereigns. In *R. v. Van Rassel,* reproduced below, the Supreme Court of Canada confronted the question of whether a conviction after an acquittal by a court of a foreign government for offenses arising out of related conduct violated the principle of double jeopardy.

R. v. VAN RASSEL

Supreme Court (Canada).
[1990] 1 S.C.R. 225.

The appellant, an R.C.M.P. [Royal Canadian Mounted Police] officer and a member of an international drug enforcement team, was arrested in Florida and charged in the U.S. with soliciting and accepting bribes in exchange for information given to him by the American authorities. The appellant was acquitted at trial. He was subsequently charged in Canada with breach of trust under s. 111 of the Criminal Code. The trial judge held that the appellant had already been acquitted of the same offences in the U.S. and ordered a stay of proceedings. The Court of Appeal allowed the Crown's appeal, rejected the plea of autrefois acquit, and ordered that the trial proceed.

MCLACHLIN J.

* * * Discussion

1. Do the Principles Relating to the Concept of Double Jeopardy Apply Between Two Nations?

The common law authorities have accepted the proposition that the concept of double jeopardy may apply between two nations: Halsbury's Laws of England (4th ed. 1976), vol. 2, para. 88; *R. v. Thomas,* [1985] Q.B. 604 (C.A.) In this regard, MARTIN J.A. of the Ontario Court of

Appeal wrote in *R. v. Stratton* (1978), 3 C.R. (3d) 289, at p. 298 (obiter), that the plea of autrefois acquit applies to foreign convictions. In his view, s. 535(5)(a) of the Criminal Code refers to an acquittal or to a conviction, including a conviction or acquittal in another country. * * *

Additionally, the American courts have held that the double jeopardy rule does not preclude two prosecutions for the same offence, one for a breach of federal law and the other for a breach of State law, noting that applying the double jeopardy principle in such circumstances could adversely affect the sovereignty of each government: *Abbate v. United States*, 359 U.S. 187 (1959); *Bartkus v. Illinois*, 359 U.S. 121 (1959). The problem does not arise in this form in Canada, in view of the federal Parliament's supreme powers. Still, it can be argued by analogy that a rule which prohibits the Canadian government from prosecuting someone because of an earlier conviction or acquittal in another country adversely affects Canadian sovereignty.

In view of the conclusion I have arrived at on the second question, it is not necessary to decide in this case which of these two positions should prevail.

2.   If the Answer to the First Question is Yes, Does Applying the Principles of Double Jeopardy Lead to the Conclusion That the Trial Judge Was Right in Ordering a Stay of Proceedings Against the Accused?

Before answering this question, an answer must first be given to the following question: did the Court of Appeal err in considering only the defence of autrefois acquit, without dealing with the other principles relied on by the accused, namely res judicata, the rule in *Kienapple*, the Latin maxim *nemo debet bis vexari pro una et eadem causa* and s. 11(h) of the Charter?

I would answer this question in the affirmative. The double jeopardy concept expressed in the Latin maxim cited is a principle of general application which is expressed in the form of more specific rules, such as the plea of autrefois acquit, issue estoppel and the rule stated in *Kienapple*. The term res judicata, likewise, has sometimes been used in a broad sense to comprise all of these various principles, though since LASKIN J. (as he then was) expressed his preference for the term in *Kienapple*, at p. 748, to describe the principle in that case it has often been used as a term of art. The case law shows that these principles differ in the way they are applied, despite their common origin. The application of s. 11(h) of the Charter must be determined by considering the wording of this provision. For these reasons, each of the defences put forward by the accused must be considered separately.

(a) Autrefois acquit

The defence of autrefois acquit is codified in the Criminal Code. * * * To make out the defence of autrefois acquit, the accused must show that the two charges laid against him are the same. In particular, he must prove that the following two conditions have been met:

> (1) the matter is the same, in whole or in part; and

> (2) the new count must be the same as at the first trial, or be implicitly included in that of the first trial, either in law or on

account of the evidence presented if it had been legally possible at that time to make the necessary amendments.

It is sometimes difficult to apply the principle of autrefois acquit to charges arising in criminal law systems completely different from our own. While the laws of different countries are rarely the same, it must be recognized that the plea of autrefois acquit is based on the principle of justice and fairness and that the Criminal Code does not require that the charges be absolutely identical. Despite the technical form of the relevant sections of the Criminal Code, the substantive point is a simple one: could the accused have been convicted at the first trial of the offence with which he is now charged? If the differences between the charges at the first and second trials are such that it must be concluded that the charges are different in nature, the plea of autrefois acquit is not appropriate. On the other hand, the plea will apply if, despite the differences between the earlier and the present charges, the offences are the same. For example, the presence under foreign law of a defence which does not exist under domestic law will not prevent the principle of autrefois acquit from applying: *R. v. Aughet* (1918), 118 L.T. 658 (C.A.)

* * *

Applying the principle of autrefois acquit, the question which arises in this case is the following: could the accused have been convicted on the American charges of the offences with which he is charged in Canada if the necessary amendments (not altering the nature of the offence) had been made?

In my opinion the answer to this question must be no. First, the Canadian charges are limited to events which occurred in Canada. None of the American charges would have been laid if, for example, the accused had copied the telex in Canada without taking the copies to the United States. Only the first American charge mentions Montreal, and it does so only with reference to the question of "interstate travel", which does not arise in the Canadian charges.

Second, the conduct referred to in the American and Canadian charges is different. American counts 1 and 3 require that the accused be an American official (according to a very broad definition) and that there should have been a transaction, that is an exchange of money for information or to exert illegal influence. The Canadian charges, for their part, require that the accused be a *Canadian* official and make no reference to any exchange of money. * * *

I am of the view, however, that the identity test in s. 537(1)(b) has not been met. Even as amended, the second American charge would not include one essential element of the Canadian charge, that of being a Canadian official, because this latter element is not part of the offence defined in 18 U.S.C. 641. (The American provision in question does not require that the accused be an official.)

This analysis leads me to conclude that the accused could not have been convicted in the United States for offences of the same nature as those in the Canadian charges. Since the Canadian charges deal with Canadian events, require no proof of payment in exchange for information or illegal influence and are based on a breach of trust by a Canadian official in relation to the people of Canada, they are clearly different from the American charges.

For these reasons, I conclude that the plea of autrefois acquit does not apply in the circumstances.

* * *

(c) Issue Estoppel

The rule that a court should not rule on an issue that has already been decided by another court is a fundamental principle of our system of justice. The fact that a matter has already been the subject of a judicial decision may raise an estoppel against the party seeking to relitigate the matter. This is the principle of issue estoppel, and it too is related to the principle of res judicata. Issue estoppel is recognized in Canadian criminal law: *Gushue v. The Queen*, [1980] 1 S.C.R. 798.

The respondent suggests that issue estoppel could not apply with respect to a foreign criminal judgment since the parties involved are not the same. It will not be necessary to decide this point since it is well established that the principle applies only in circumstances where it is clear from the facts that the question has already been decided. * * *

In the present case there is nothing to indicate that the American jury found in the accused's favour on the particular issues raised in the Canadian charges. The jury might have acquitted the accused for reasons entirely distinct from those underlying the Canadian jury's decision. This becomes apparent when we consider the differences between the American and Canadian charges. The result might perhaps have been different if the appellant had adduced in evidence the opinion of an expert in American law establishing that an issue in the Canadian proceedings had been decided in his favour in the United States, but he did nothing in this regard. This defence thus does not assist the accused's case.

(d) Section 11(h) of the Charter

Section 11(h) reads as follows:

11. Any person charged with an offence has the right . . .

(h) if finally acquitted of the offence, not to be tried for it again and, if finally found guilty and punished for the offence, not to be tried or punished for it again;

Section 11(h) of the Charter applies only in circumstances where the two offences with which the accused is charged are the same. In *R. v. Wigglesworth*, [1987] 2 S.C.R. 541, this Court held that the same act can give rise to different offences, each offence being based on a separate duty. Wilson J. said, at p. 566:

I would hold that the appellant in this case is not being tried and punished for the same offence. The "offences" are quite different. One is an internal disciplinary matter. The accused has been found guilty of a major service offence and has, therefore, accounted to his profession. The other offence is the criminal offence of assault. The accused must now account to society at large for his conduct. He cannot complain, as a member of a special group of individuals subject to private internal discipline, that he ought not to account to society for his wrongdoing. His conduct has a double aspect as a member of the R.C.M.P. and as a member of the public at large. To borrow from the words of the Chief Justice quoted above, I am of the view that the two offences were "two different 'matters', totally separate one from the other and not alternative one to the other". While there was only one act of assault there were two distinct delicts, causes or matters which would sustain separate convictions.

In the present case the American and Canadian offences are different because they are based on duties of a different nature. Even though the American and Canadian offences are purely criminal in nature, the alleged conduct of the accused has a double aspect: first, wrongdoing as a Canadian official with a special duty to the Canadian public under s. 111 of the Criminal Code, and second, wrongdoing as an American official or member of the American public, temporarily subject to American law. The accused must now account for his conduct to the Canadian public as well as to the American public, as the offences relate to different duties. For this reason, I am of the opinion that s. 11(h) of the Charter is of no assistance to the accused.

Conclusion

For all these reasons, I would dismiss the appeal and refer the matter back to the trial judge for the trial to proceed.

Notes and Questions

1. What is the justification or justifications for the prohibition on double jeopardy? Is the exception for prosecutions by different sovereigns consistent with the most persuasive justification?

2. What test should determine whether the prohibition on double jeopardy has been violated? Does the "same elements" or "same conduct" test provide an individual with more security and fairer treatment? From the court's perspective, is one more efficient than the other?

J. PROHIBITION AGAINST RETROACTIVITY OF THE PENAL LAW

The prohibition against ex post facto laws has ancient roots, extending at least as far back as the Roman principle *nullum crimen sine lege, nulla poena sine lege* (no crime without law, no penalty without law), which generally forbids the retroactive application of criminal law. The principle is found in one form or another in all legal systems, be they civil, common law, or Islamic. Nonetheless, as specific questions arise there may be variations in the application of the principle. For example, there are differences in terms of whether the application of a vague law would violate the principle and whether laws that are beneficial to the accused may, or must, be applied retroactively. Frequently, an important element in determining whether the prohibition on retroactivity has been violated is the foreseeability of a particular interpretation of the law. In the cases below the ECHR and the U.S. Court of Appeals for the Eighth Circuit address the matter of foreseeability. A third case examines the issue of foreseeability in the context of a transition from an authoritarian to a democratic regime. A second set of materials deals with the principle, common in many countries, that the most beneficial law to the accused should be applied. See also the material in Chapter 1, Section C.

CANTONI v. FRANCE

European Court of Human Rights.
1996–V E.H.R.R. 1641 (1996).

* * * 7. Mr. Michel Cantoni, a French national who was born in 1947, is the manager of a supermarket owned by the Euromarché chain at Sens (Yonne). * * *

8. In 1988 criminal proceedings were brought, at the instigation of the Yonne Pharmacists' Association and several individual pharmacists, against the applicant and other managers of supermarkets in the region for unlawfully selling pharmaceutical products. He had sold in his shop aqueous eosin at 1% strength, 70% modified alcohol, 10–volume hydrogen peroxide, vitamin C (tablets of 500 mg and sachets of powder of 1000 mg), inhalations made out of plant essences, pocket inhalers, antiseptic sprays and mineral supplements.

In their defence the applicant and his fellow accused maintained that the products in question were not medicinal products within the meaning of Article L. 511 of the Public Health Code (see paragraph 18 below) and were accordingly not covered by the pharmacists' monopoly.

9. On 30 September 1988 the Sens Criminal Court found the applicant guilty as charged, fined him 10,000 francs and ordered him to pay damages of 1 franc to each of the civil parties. After considering the products in question individually, it took the view that they were medicinal products, in some cases on account of their function and in others on account of their presentation. * * *

26. The applicant complained of a violation of Article 7 of the Convention, which is worded as follows:

"1. No one shall be held guilty of any criminal offence on account of any act or omission which did not constitute a criminal offence under national or international law at the time when it was committed. Nor shall a heavier penalty be imposed than the one that was applicable at the time the criminal offence was committed.

2. This Article shall not prejudice the trial and punishment of any person for any act or omission which, at the time when it was committed, was criminal according to the general principles of law recognised by civilised nations."

He maintained that the definition of medicinal product contained in Article L. 511 of the Public Health Code was very imprecise and left a wide discretion to the courts. The Court of Cassation's case-law in this field was marked by arbitrariness and a lack of certainty which were themselves directly responsible for the conflicting classifications given to parapharmaceutical products by the lower courts. This state of affairs still persisted and concerned all the substances in question, whether hydrogen peroxide, 70% strength alcohol or vitamin C. * * *

In short, the definition found in the legislation and the case-law failed to afford the requisite foreseeability and accessibility. It followed that Mr. Cantoni could not reasonably have been expected to appreciate, before putting the products in question up for sale, what constituted the material element of the offence in respect of which he was prosecuted. * * *

28.   Referring to the case-law of the Court, the Government argued that a law could be formulated in relatively general terms making it possible for its provisions to be adapted, through the process of interpretation, to changing situations. Even the most perfectly drafted law required a judge to clarify its limits and Article L. 511 of the Public Health Code was no exception.

The definition given in Article L. 511 was based in particular on extensive case-law concerning the notion of medicinal product and was no more open to criticism than any other statutory definition. Indeed it was actually far more precise than many of the definitions to be found in the Criminal Code. Above all the legislature had no alternative but to have recourse to such a definition because to date no more satisfactory definition of medicinal product had been established. The only other solution—the drawing up of exhaustive lists—was not practicable because in this field there were thousands of different products and their number varied on an almost daily basis. A list would therefore never correspond to the reality. * * *

In addition, the definition of medicinal product had given rise to hardly any problems in the criminal courts until the end of the nineteen eighties. The disputes that occurred at that time had been created artificially and deliberately by supermarket chains. They had succeeded in disorientating some of the lower courts, but not the Court of Cassation, which had applied the same principles for more than a century.

29.   As the Court has already held, Article 7 embodies, *inter alia*, the principle that only the law can define a crime and prescribe a penalty (*nullum crimen, nulla poena sine lege*) and the principle that the criminal law must not be extensively construed to an accused's detriment, for instance by analogy. From these principles it follows that an offence must be clearly defined in the law. This requirement is satisfied where the individual can know from the wording of the relevant provision and, if need be, with the assistance of the courts' interpretation of it, what acts and omissions will make him criminally liable.

When speaking of "law" Article 7 alludes to the very same concept as that to which the Convention refers elsewhere when using that term, a concept which comprises statutory law as well as case-law and implies qualitative requirements, notably those of accessibility and foreseeability. * * * In the present case only that last aspect is in issue. * * *

31.   As the Court has already had occasion to note, it is a logical consequence of the principle that laws must be of general application

that the wording of statutes is not always precise. One of the standard techniques of regulation by rules is to use general categorisations as opposed to exhaustive lists. The need to avoid excessive rigidity and to keep pace with changing circumstances means that many laws are inevitably couched in terms which, to a greater or lesser extent, are vague. The interpretation and application of such enactments depend on practice. * * *

32. Like many statutory definitions, that of "medicinal product" contained in Article L. 511 of the Public Health Code is rather general. * * * When the legislative technique of categorisation is used, there will often be grey areas at the fringes of the definition. This penumbra of doubt in relation to borderline facts does not in itself make a provision incompatible with Article 7, provided that it proves to be sufficiently clear in the large majority of cases. The role of adjudication vested in the courts is precisely to dissipate such interpretational doubts as remain, taking into account the changes in everyday practice.

The Court must accordingly ascertain whether in the present case the text of the statutory rule read in the light of the accompanying interpretive case-law satisfied this test at the relevant time. * * *

34. Nor is the Court persuaded by the argument based on the decisions of the lower courts cited by the applicant and concerning the type of "borderline" product for the sale of which he was convicted. There were indeed divergencies in the decisions of the lower courts * * *. According to the Government, these may be explained essentially by the fact that the comparisons of decisions did not take account of prosecutions brought in respect of different concentrations of the products in question.

The Court notes in the first place that the applicant did not indicate whether the decisions cited classified these products as medicinal products by virtue of their function or by virtue of their presentation, and, in the latter case, whether the presentation was the same on each occasion.

Even assuming that the decisions dealt with identical cases, the questions before the lower courts were principally questions of fact. For the first category of decisions, concerning products regarded as medicinal by virtue of their function, it was essentially a matter of establishing the current state of scientific knowledge. For the second category, that is decisions relating to products regarded as medicinal by virtue of their presentation, the courts aimed to gauge the impression gained by the averagely well-informed consumer.

Moreover, there is, in the Court's view, one decisive consideration. From, at the latest, 1957 onwards the Court of Cassation has always either confirmed the decisions of the courts below classifying a parapharmaceutical-type product as medicinal or quashed decisions which denied that classification. It has never upheld a decision by a lower court finding that such a product fell outside the notion of medicinal product (see paragraph 21 above). Thus, well before the events in the present case, the Court of Cassation had adopted a clear position on this matter, which with the passing of time became even more firmly established.

35. The Court recalls that the scope of the notion of foreseeability depends to a considerable degree on the content of the text in issue, the field it is designed to cover and the number and status of those to whom it is addressed. * * * A law may still satisfy the requirement of foreseeability even if the person concerned has to take appropriate legal advice to assess, to a degree that is reasonable in the circumstances, the consequences which a given action may entail. * * * This is particularly true in relation to persons carrying on a professional activity, who are used to having to proceed with a high degree of caution when pursuing their occupation. They can on this account be expected to take special care in assessing the risks that such activity entails.

With the benefit of appropriate legal advice, Mr. Cantoni, who was, moreover, the manager of a supermarket, should have appreciated at the material time that, in view of the line of case-law stemming from the Court of Cassation and from some of the lower courts, he ran a real risk of prosecution for unlawful sale of medicinal products.

36. There has accordingly been no breach of Article 7.

HAGAN v. CASPARI

Court of Appeals, Eighth Circuit (United States).
50 F.3d 542 (1995).

Circuit Judge Bowman.

Donald Hagan, a Missouri prisoner, filed a petition for a writ of habeas corpus pursuant to 28 U.S.C. 2254 (1988). The District Court, adopting the report and recommendation of a magistrate judge finding merit in Hagan's due process claim, granted the petition. The State of Missouri, through Paul D. Caspari, superintendent of the Missouri Eastern Correctional Center, timely appeals. We reverse. * * *

I

* * * The trial court sentenced Hagan to concurrent prison terms of fifteen years for the first-degree robbery conviction, fifteen years for the second-degree robbery conviction, and seven years for the stealing conviction. Thus his aggregate sentence for the three crimes is fifteen years.

Hagan filed a timely motion for post-conviction relief, see Mo. S. Ct. R. 24.035 (1989), arguing, inter alia, that to convict him of stealing the van on top of second-degree robbery for forcibly taking the keys to the van violates the Double Jeopardy Clause. See U.S. Const., amend. V. The trial court denied the motion, but the Missouri Court of Appeals (Eastern District) reversed, finding merit in Hagan's double jeopardy argument and throwing out his conviction for stealing the van. * * * The Supreme Court of Missouri reversed the court of appeals and affirmed the trial court's denial of Hagan's Rule 24.035 motion. * * * In the course of its decision, the supreme court overruled State v. Lewis, 633 S.W.2d 110 (Mo. Ct. App. 1982), a Missouri Court of Appeals (Western District) decision that Hagan had relied on for his double jeopardy argument. * * *

Hagan subsequently filed the present petition for federal habeas corpus relief. In his petition, Hagan claims that the decision of the Missouri Supreme Court in his case * * * retroactively applied an unforeseeable change in state law in violation of his rights under the Due Process Clause. See U.S. Const., amends. V, XIV. * * *

II

* * * The retroactive application of an unforeseeable interpretation of a criminal statute, if detrimental to a defendant, generally violates the Due Process Clause. * * * As the Supreme Court held in *Bouie v. City of Columbia*, 378 U.S. 347 (1964), such action deprives a defendant of "due process of law in the sense of fair warning that his contemplated conduct constitutes a crime." * * * Not every retroactive application of a judicial construction of the law, however, violates the Due Process Clause; it does so only if it "punishes as a crime an act previously committed, which was innocent when done; * * * makes more burdensome the punishment for a crime, after its commission; or * * * deprives one charged with a crime of any defense available according to the law at the time when the act was committed * * *." *Davis*, 958 F.2d at 833 (quoting *Collins v. Youngblood*, 497 U.S. 37, 42 (1990) (quoting *Beazell v. Ohio*, 269 U.S. 167, 169 (1925))); see also *Calder v. Bull*, 3 U.S. (3 Dall.) 386, 390 (1798) (ex post facto clause).

The state contends that the decision in Hagan was entirely foreseeable, and therefore its application to Hagan did not violate the Due Process Clause. Missouri law, according to the state, was unsettled at the time of Hagan's conviction and the state supreme court, having never addressed the precise question at issue, is not obligated to apply an erroneous decision of a lower state court in order to avoid violating the Due Process Clause.

Hagan argues that while the state supreme court "could" have overruled Lewis it is not clear that the court "would" have overruled the decision. As evidence for this proposition, Hagan notes that (1) the state supreme court refused to review Lewis in 1982 "which implies that it agreed or at least did not disagree" with the rule in that case; (2) prosecutors, defense attorneys, and judges relied on the Lewis rule for more than a decade; and (3) the Lewis decision cites Supreme Court and state supreme court opinions. All of these arguments are irrelevant. A court's refusal to exercise discretionary review of a lower court's decision implies nothing about the merits of the lower court's decision. * * * The reliance of prosecutors, et al., and the citation of authorities does not make the overruling of Lewis more or less foreseeable. To resolve the foreseeability issue, we must examine Lewis and its legal underpinnings. * * *

Factually, *Lewis* and this case are indistinguishable. The Missouri Court of Appeals (Western District) reversed Lewis's stealing conviction and held that convictions for both second-degree robbery and stealing would contravene Mo. Rev. Stat. 556.041, which prohibits convictions for two offenses when one is a lesser included offense of the other, and Missouri's single-larceny rule, codified as Mo. Rev. Stat. 570.050, which defines the stealing of several articles of property during the same scheme or course of conduct as a single offense of stealing. *Lewis*, 633 S.W.2d at 113–16.

Stealing, in certain cases, can be a lesser included offense of second-degree robbery but, as a review of the applicable Missouri statutes shows, it can also be a separate offense. The Missouri code defines stealing as the appropriation of property or services of another "with the purpose to deprive him thereof, either without his consent or by means of deceit or coercion." Mo. Rev. Stat. 570.030 (1986). Second-degree robbery is defined as forcibly stealing property. Mo. Rev. Stat. 569.030. The code defines forcible stealing as the use or threat of immediate use of physical force during the course of stealing that prevents or overcomes resistance or that compels another to deliver the property or to engage in other conduct aiding the commission of the theft. Mo. Rev. Stat. 569.010(1).

An included offense under Missouri law is one "established by proof of the same or less than all of the facts required to establish the commission of the offense charged * * *." Mo. Rev. Stat. 556.046.1(1). The *Lewis* court noted that Missouri's definition of an included offense is based on *Blockburger v. United States*, 284 U.S. 299 (1932). In *Blockburger* the Supreme Court held that when "the same act or transaction constitutes a violation of two distinct statutory provisions, the test to be applied to determine whether there are two offenses or only one, is whether each provision requires proof of a fact which the other does not." *Id.* at 304. In *Blockburger,* the defendant had engaged in one drug transaction that violated two provisions of the Narcotics Act, and the Court affirmed his two convictions because the two provisions required proof of different facts.

Based on its reading of the applicable Missouri statutes, the Missouri Supreme Court concluded in *Hagan* that *Lewis* was wrongly decided. Its core holding was at odds with the plain meaning of section 556.046.1 and *Blockburger*. To prove the offense of second-degree robbery of the keys, the state had to show that the keys were taken forcibly from the victim without her consent. The state did not have to prove that a vehicle was also taken without the victim's consent. To prove the offense of stealing a motor vehicle in this case, the state had to prove that the vehicle was taken without the victim's consent. The state did not have to prove that the vehicle's keys were taken forcibly without consent. Each statutory offense requires proof of at least one fact that the other does not.

The Missouri single-larceny rule, Mo. Rev. Stat. 570.050, provides as follows:

> "Amounts stolen pursuant to one scheme or course of conduct, whether from the same or several owners and whether at the same or different times, constitute a single criminal episode and may be aggregated in determining the grade of the offense."

The state supreme court, in the course of overruling *Lewis*, stated that "by its own terms, the statute applies solely to charges of stealing." *Hagan*, 836 S.W.2d at 462. The limited purpose of the statute is to combine the value of all property stolen to determine the grade of the stealing offense charged. Thus the single-larceny rule provided no impediment to Hagan's convictions on both robbery and stealing charges. * * * Again, it follows that the Lewis court was wrong, and plainly so, for the decision was contrary to the clear language of the statute the court was interpreting.

Given this background, we conclude that the state supreme court's decision to overrule Lewis was eminently foreseeable. We have some doubt whether a state supreme court's overruling of an intermediate appellate court decision ever can constitute a change in state law for due process purposes. In fact, we are strongly inclined to agree with the state that until the state's highest court has spoken on a particular point of state law, the law of the state necessarily must be regarded as unsettled. Here, however, we need not decide whether the overruling of Lewis "changed" state law, because in this case it is perfectly clear that anyone reading the pertinent Missouri statutes could easily have concluded that Lewis was contrary to their plain meaning. It therefore was readily foreseeable that Lewis was likely to be overruled once a case calling it into question reached the Missouri Supreme Court. Hagan's due process rights were not violated when the Missouri Supreme Court used his case as the occasion to overrule the intermediate appellate court decision in Lewis. This result was readily foreseeable, and Hagan was not denied fair notice of the extent of his liability for his crimes.

The interpretation and exposition of state law is the prerogative of the state's highest court. The Supreme Court of Missouri is entitled to correct a lower court's mistaken reading of a state statute without running afoul of the Due Process Clause. The extent of the criminal liability for the acts Hagan committed was clear on the face of the applicable Missouri statutes. See *Bouie*, 378 U.S. at 354–55 (holding that due process is implicated when defendant is deprived of fair warning of criminal nature of conduct or of potential consequences). We hold that Hagan's due process rights were not violated when the Missouri Supreme Court overruled the lower state court's decision in Lewis and affirmed all of Hagan's convictions. * * *

Notes and Questions: Retroactivity of Statutes and Judicial Decisions in the U.S.

1. As noted in *Hagan*, Art. I §§ 9 and 10 of the U.S. Constitution prohibits state and federal governments from enacting any "ex post facto law." This prohibition has been interpreted as providing that "any statute which punishes as a crime an act previously committed, which was innocent when done; which makes more burdensome the punishment for a crime, after its commission, or which deprives one charged with a crime of any defense available according to law at the time when the act was committed, is prohibited as *ex post facto*." *Beazell v. Ohio*, 269 U.S. 167, 169–70 (1925). The Supreme Court recently held that the ex post facto clause's prohibition on retroactivity applies only to criminal statutes and not to common law decisionmaking, see *Rogers v. Tennessee*, 532 U.S. 451 (2001), and the only limits on retroactivity of judicial decisionmaking are rooted in due process.

In *Rogers* the USSC upheld the Tennessee Supreme Court's abolition of the common law "year-and-a-day" rule, under which a defendant could not be convicted of murder unless the victim died by the defendant's act within a year and a day of the act. The Court found that the abolition of the rule was not "unexpected and indefensible" as advances in medicine had rendered the rule obsolete, the rule had been abolished in the majority of jurisdictions to address the issue, and the rule existed only as common law and had not served as a ground of decision in murder prosecutions in the state. Earlier, the Court held that a statute providing for the deportation of aliens who had ever been a member of the Communist Party was sustained against an ex post facto claim by an alien who had been a Communist from 1925 to 1939. *Harisiades v. Shaughnessy*, 342 U.S. 580 (1952).

2. A further retroactivity issue that has been raised in U.S. courts has to do with the effect of judicial decisions on statutes. If a judicial decision holds that a statute is unconstitutional, is the statute in effect repealed? Or, if a later judicial decision overrules the first, does this revitalize the statute? *Jawish v. Morlet*, 86 A.2d 96 (D.C. Mun. Ct. App. 1952), said that "[t]here are comparatively few cases dealing with the question * * * but they are unanimous in holding that a law once declared unconstitutional and later held to be constitutional does not require reenactment by the legislature in order to restore its operative force. They proceed on the principle that a statute declared unconstitutional is void in the sense that it is inoperative or unenforceable, but not void in the sense that it is repealed or abolished * * * if the decision is reversed the statute is valid *from its first effective date*." (emphasis added). The *Jawish* principle would seem inapplicable if it permitted, after the second decision, a person to be prosecuted for behavior undertaken during the time the statute was "inoperative." See also Chapter 2, Subsection B.3.2.

The issues of retroactivity and foreseeability often arise after a regime change. The following case examines the difficult problem of punishing acts permitted or encouraged under an authoritarian government but not under a democratic successor state. Cf. the Hungarian *Retroactive Criminal Legislation Case* involving crimes under communist law not prosecuted by the postcommunist regime for political reason in Chapter 1, Subsection C.1.

STRELETZ, KESSLER AND KRENZ v. GERMANY

European Court of Human Rights.
33 E.H.R.R. 31 (2001).

[This case addressed the claims of three former nationals of the German Democratic Republic (GDR), who, after German reunification, were convicted of the indirect homicides of people attempting to cross the border into the Federal Republic of Germany. The applicants occupied senior positions in the GDR's state apparatus and were found by the German courts to be responsible for decisions authorizing the use of deadly force (including mines and firearms) to protect the border. On appeal to the Federal Constitutional Court, they submitted that their actions had been justified under the law applicable in the GDR at the material time and should not have made them liable to criminal prosecution. Thus the lower court's decision, they argued, had infringed Art. 103

§ 2 of the Basic Law, which provides that "[a]n act shall not be punishable unless it has been so defined by law before it was committed." The Constitutional Court dismissed the appeals, noting that:

> this legal situation, in which the Federal Republic has to exercise its authority in criminal matters on the basis of the law of a State that neither practiced democracy and the separation of powers nor respected fundamental rights, may lead to a conflict between the mandatory rule-of-law precepts of the Basic Law and the absolute prohibition of retroactiveness in Article 103 § 2 thereof, which, as has been noted, derives its justification in terms of the rule of law * * * in the special trust reposed in criminal statutes when these have been enacted by a democratic legislature required to respect fundamental rights. This special basis of trust no longer obtains where the other State statutorily defines certain acts as serious criminal offences while excluding the possibility of punishment by allowing grounds of justification covering some of those acts and even by requiring and encouraging them notwithstanding the provisions of written law, thus gravely breaching the human rights generally recognised by the international community.

The Constitutional Court applied "Radbruch's Formula," which holds that "positive law must be considered contrary to justice where the contradiction between statute law and justice is so intolerable that the former must give way to the latter." Accordingly, in this case "a ground of justification derived from State practice and purporting to allow 'border violators' to be killed must be disregarded as an instance of extreme State injustice. * * *"

[In their appeal to the ECHR, the applicants claimed, among other things, that the Federal Constitutional Court's decision violated Art. 7(1) of the European HR Convention, which provides that "[n]o one shall be held guilty of any criminal offence on account of any act or omission which did not constitute a criminal offence under national or international law at the time when it was committed * * *."]

67. Since the term "law" in Article 7 § 1 of the Convention includes unwritten law, the Court must also, before going further into the merits of the case, analyse the nature of the GDR's State practice, which was superimposed on the rules of written law at the material time.

68. In that context, it should be pointed out that at the time of the offences in issue none of the applicants was prosecuted for them in the GDR. This was because of the contradiction between the principles laid down in the GDR's Constitution and its legislation, on the one hand, which were very similar to those of a State governed by the rule of law, and the repressive practice of the border-policing regime in the GDR and the orders issued to protect the border, on the other.

69. To staunch the endless flow of fugitives, the GDR built the Berlin Wall on 13 August 1961 and reinforced all the security measures along the border between the two German States with anti-personnel mines and automatic-fire systems. In addition to these measures, border guards were ordered "not to permit border crossings, to arrest border

violators (*Grenzverletzer*) or to annihilate them (*vernichten*) and to protect the State border at all costs". * * *

71. Thus the aim of the above State practice, implemented by the applicants, had been to protect the border between the two German States "at all costs" in order to preserve the GDR's existence, which was threatened by the massive exodus of its own population.

72. However, the Court points out that the reason of State thus invoked must be limited by the principles enunciated in the Constitution and legislation of the GDR itself; it must above all respect the need to preserve human life, enshrined in the GDR's Constitution, People's Police Act and State Borders Act * * *.

73. The Court considers that recourse to anti-personnel mines and automatic-fire systems, in view of their automatic and indiscriminate effect, and the categorical nature of the border guards' orders to "annihilate border violators (*Grenzverletzer*) and protect the border at all costs", flagrantly infringed the fundamental rights enshrined in Articles 19 and 30 of the GDR's Constitution, which were essentially confirmed by the GDR's Criminal Code (Article 213) and successive statutes on the GDR's borders (section 17(2) of the People's Police Act 1968 and section 27(2) of the State Borders Act 1982). This State practice was also in breach of the obligation to respect human rights and the other international obligations of the GDR, which, on 8 November 1974, had ratified the International Covenant on Civil and Political Rights, expressly recognising the right to life and to the freedom of movement * * * regard being had to the fact that it was almost impossible for ordinary citizens to leave the GDR legally. * * *

75. Moreover, irrespective of the GDR's responsibility as a State, the applicants' acts as individuals were defined as criminal by Article 95 of the GDR's Criminal Code, which already provided in its 1968 version, in terms repeated in 1977: "Any person whose conduct violates human or fundamental rights ... may not plead statute law, an order or written instructions in justification; he shall be held criminally responsible". * * *

iv. Foreseeability of the convictions

77. However, the applicants argued that in view of the reality of the situation in the GDR their conviction by the German courts had not been foreseeable * * *

78. The Court is not convinced by that argument. The broad divide between the GDR's legislation and its practice was to a great extent the work of the applicants themselves. Because of the very senior positions they occupied in the State apparatus, they evidently could not have been ignorant of the GDR's Constitution and legislation, or of its international obligations and the criticisms of its border-policing regime that had been made internationally. * * *

79. Moreover, the fact that the applicants had not been prosecuted in the GDR, and were not prosecuted and convicted by the German courts until after the reunification, on the basis of the legal provisions

applicable in the GDR at the material time, does not in any way mean that their acts were not offences according to the law of the GDR.

80. In that connection, the Court notes that the problem Germany had to deal with after reunification as regards the attitude to adopt *vis-à-vis* persons who had committed crimes under a former regime has also arisen for a number of other States which have gone through a transition to a democratic regime.

81. The Court considers that it is legitimate for a State governed by the rule of law to bring criminal proceedings against persons who have committed crimes under a former regime; similarly, the courts of such a State, having taken the place of those which existed previously, cannot be criticised for applying and interpreting the legal provisions in force at the material time in the light of the principles governing a State subject to the rule of law.

82. Indeed, the Court reiterates that for the purposes of Article 7 § 1, however clearly drafted a provision of criminal law may be, in any legal system, there is an inevitable element of judicial interpretation. There will always be a need for elucidation of doubtful points and for adaptation to changing circumstances. * * * Admittedly, that concept applies in principle to the gradual development of case-law in a given State subject to the rule of law and under a democratic regime, factors which constitute the cornerstones of the Convention, as its preamble states (see paragraph 83 below), but it remains wholly valid where, as in the present case, one State has succeeded another.

83. Contrary reasoning would run counter to the very principles on which the system of protection put in place by the Convention is built. The framers of the Convention referred to those principles in the preamble to the Convention when they reaffirmed "their profound belief in those fundamental freedoms which are the foundation of justice and peace in the world and are best maintained on the one hand by an effective political democracy and on the other by a common understanding and observance of the human rights upon which they depend" and declared that they were "like-minded" and had "a common heritage of political traditions, ideals, freedom and the rule of law". * * *

87. The Court considers that a State practice such as the GDR's border-policing policy, which flagrantly infringes human rights and above all the right to life, the supreme value in the international hierarchy of human rights, cannot be covered by the protection of Article 7 § 1 of the Convention. That practice, which emptied of its substance the legislation on which it was supposed to be based, and which was imposed on all organs of the GDR, including its judicial bodies, cannot be described as "law" within the meaning of Article 7 of the Convention. * * *

89. Having regard to all of the above considerations, the Court holds that at the time when they were committed the applicants' acts constituted offences defined with sufficient accessibility and foreseeability in GDR law. * * *

107. Accordingly, the applicants' conviction by the German courts after the reunification was not in breach of Article 7 § 1.

Note on Applying the Most Favorable Law to the Accused

Some countries couple the prohibition on ex post facto laws with a requirement that the most beneficial law to the accused always be applied. Thus, if different laws or penalties would cover a defendant's action at different points in time after his arrest and before judgment, the law that would be most favorable to the defendant is the one that must be applied. This principle is common in the constitutions of Latin American countries. See, e.g., the constitutions of Bolivia (Art. 16), Colombia (Art. 29), Chile (Art. 19), Ecuador (Art. 24), and Peru (Arts. 103 and 139). The Canadian Charter of Rights and Freedoms, Art. 11(i), also recognizes the right of the defendant "if found guilty of the offense and if the punishment for the offense has been varied between the time of commission and the time of sentencing, to the benefit of the lesser punishment."

In the U.S., the Constitution neither prohibits nor requires retrospective effect, and there is no express constitutional requirement that the most beneficial law be applied to the accused. A respected California Supreme Court justice, Roger Traynor, discussed the issue in *Quo Vadis, Prospective Overruling: A Question of Judicial Responsibility*, 28 Hastings L.J. 533, 553–54 (1977):

> Sometimes there are legislative changes in punishment. They are usually subject to a rule precluding retroactive application to defendants whose convictions have become final. Such a rule is of course inevitable as to increases in punishment, where retroactive application would not be constitutionally permissible under the usual ex post facto clause. As to statutes mitigating punishment, however, there is no constitutional barrier to retroactive application, and there are compelling arguments in its favor. Once the legislature adopts a lesser penalty as adequate, the retention of the harsher penalty no longer serves any legitimate penological goal. Hence we declared in California that when a criminal statute is amended to mitigate punishment after the prohibited act was committed, but before a final judgment of conviction is entered, the amended statute governs. *See In re Estrada*, 408 P.2d 948 (Cal.1965).

Issues concerning the "most favorable law" and retroactivity were raised when the USSC, starting in the early 1960s, revised earlier doctrine and applied Bill of Rights protections—including, among many others, the right to counsel, the right to be free of unreasonable searches and seizure, and the privilege against self-incrimination—to state trials, whereas previously they had applied only to federal trials. The question arose whether an incarcerated person convicted under the earlier process, which did not include the relevant provision of the Bill of Rights, should now receive a new trial with the new constitutional protection in force. The Court was sharply divided, granting retroactivity in some cases, e.g., *Robinson v. Neil*, 409 U.S. 505, 509 (1973) (protection against double jeopardy), and not in others, e.g., *Linkletter v. Walker*, 381 U.S. 618 (1965) (exclusion of evidence seized in violation of the Fourth Amendment). For discussion, see Francis Beytagh, *Ten Years of Non–Retroactivity: A Critique and a Proposal*, 61 Va. L. Rev. 1557 (1975). The issue arose more recently in a series of collateral attacks on convictions in state court, when the USSC, in *Teague v. Lane*, 489 U.S. 288

(1989), held that the "new" constitutional rules would be applied to all cases on direct review that were not yet final but would not be applied to final judgments challenged on collateral review except in extraordinary situations. For a comprehensive analysis, see Richard Fallon and Daniel Meltzer, *New Law, Non–Retroactivity, and Constitutional Remedies,* 104 Harv. L. Rev. 1731 (1991).

In Argentina, the principle of application of the most beneficial law to the accused, along with the rule against retroactivity of penal laws, came into play in an interesting manner in the trials of members of the military and of the military junta, in the mid–1980s. Before leaving office, General Bignone signed a self-amnesty law that would apply to all countersubversive activities. This law, along with the fact that the military appeared to have jurisdiction over the cases and that the Penal Code provided a defense of due obedience to members of the military, created significant legal obstacles for prosecutors. The following excerpt from Carlos Nino's *Radical Evil on Trial* 70 (1996) describes these obstacles and how they were surmounted:

> The first obstacle arose from article 2 of the Penal Code, which, in turn, could not retroactively be abrogated without violating article 18 of the constitution. Article 2 gave the defendant the benefit of the least harsh law in effect. [If this principle were applied to the junta, the self-amnesty law would have to be given effect.] This obstacle was surmounted by formulating a new theory * * * that permitted nullification [of laws passed by de facto regimes. This theory of de facto laws allowed nullification] * * * of the amnesty law, refuting its binding force from its inception.

> The second obstacle involved the impossibility of retroactively modifying the military jurisdiction in the face of article 18 of the constitution, which proscribes ex post facto laws. This obstacle was overcome by invoking article 95 of the constitution, which prohibits the president, and the courts dependent on him, such as the military one, from trying people and imposing punishment. To satisfy these two conflicting constitutional provisions, we compromised, recognizing military jurisdiction in the first instance and establishing a broad appellate review in the civilian courts. * * *

> The third obstacle was the retroactive modification, without violating article 18 of the constitution, of the provisions of the Penal Code and Military Code that provided for a broad defense of due obedience that could cover practically all human rights abuses. This difficulty was resolved by reinterpreting, rather than modifying, the existing due obedience laws for the period March 24, 1976 to December 10, 1983. As already recognized by most scholars, even those attached to the military, the due-obedience defense was triggered only when there was a mistake about the legitimacy of the orders. The proposed reinterpretation created a rebuttable presumption that, unless the agent held decision-making authority, all those invoking the defense of due obedience either mistakenly believed that the orders were legitimate due to intense propaganda or, alternatively, were subject to an overall climate of compulsion.

Notes and Questions

1.   If foreseeability is the only basis for the prohibition against retroactivity, judicial decisions or statutes might be applied retroactively whenever a rule is objectively foreseeable, regardless of whether the defendant was in fact aware of the possibility. The *Hagan* decision illustrates this view. Can you think of arguments, based on foreseeability, that would forbid retroactivity in these cases?

2.   Are there additional justifications for the prohibition against retroactivity? If the prohibition is justified on the basis of fairness, in what sense of the concept is this so? Is there a relationship between the prohibition on retroactivity and the transparency of a legal system?

3.   Are the techniques described by Carlos Nino to overcome the "obstacles" raised by the principle of applying the most beneficial law to the accused persuasive? Or do they stretch the principle to the point of distortion? If there is distortion, can it be justified by the necessity of prosecuting the egregious human rights violations of the military junta in Argentina?

Chapter 10

RIGHTS IN ECONOMIC
AND SOCIAL LIFE

Since time immemorial, rulers were expected to provide for the welfare of their subjects. The liberal revolutions intended to liberate the individual and were unconcerned about constitutionalizing the promotion of public welfare, although the 1791 French Constitution prescribes certain governmental welfare obligations (e.g., the state should "provide work for the able-bodied poor who may not have been able to obtain it for themselves"). The liberal constitutions were concerned about the safeguard of those rights that enable citizens to care for themselves—entrepreneurial freedoms (including freedom of contract) and the right to own property. Beginning in the 1880s, specific rights in the workplace and to social security were considered by legislation, primarily in an effort to solve the "social question." Conservatives, like the German Chancellor Bismarck, wrote labor laws to neutralize their political adversaries, accommodating the demands of various socialist workers' movements, Christian social thought (see Pope Leo XIII, *Rerum Novarum* of 1939), and progressive ideas. These were influential in shaping new constitutions—Mex. Const. of 1917; German (Weimar Rep.) Const. of 1919; Soviet Const. of 1918—and, as "new" rights, they won international recognition as "second-generation rights" in the Universal Declaration of Human Rights of 1948 and the International Covenant on Economic and Social Rights of 1966.

This chapter discusses both traditional rights, regarding economic activities, and some "second-generation" rights. The first two sections concern the traditional economic liberties (property, contract, and entrepreneurship). Often these fundamental liberties were, and are, only partially or indirectly guaranteed (as general liberties) in constitutions; thus they may be easily restricted by legislation. Although these rights are deemed to be crucial for liberal market economies, the cases presented here indicate that the primary legislative and judicial concern has been whether to recognize new grounds to restrict them.

The third section is devoted to social and welfare rights. Here the cases and problems, in a way, are the inverse of those presented in the context of liberal economic rights. Most of these rights (with the exception of those that refer to the workplace and employment relations) presuppose government action or consist in state-provided services. The socioeconomic and welfare rights confer obligations but generally do not create individual entitlements, at least not directly. The cases deal with how courts may push the government to enforce and materialize these rights. These rights, however, are generally not judicially enforceable. Nevertheless, the right to shelter, free and accessible healthcare, and education (to refer to issues we discuss in more detail) are of immense social importance in a world where millions live in extreme poverty and not only in the developing world. Understandably, constitutional law cannot simply neglect these basic needs.

A. PROPERTY

Most cases relating to property discuss the extent to which it can be restricted, and the grounds for restrictions are to be found in the constitutional nature of private property. Classic (though not all) human rights theories and political theories, including Locke's, advocated private property rights, to the extent that eighteenth-century revolutionary declarations placed property in the same class of sacrosanct rights as life and liberty. As Blackstone put it in the eighteenth century: "So great moreover is the regard of the law for private property, that it will not authorize the least violation of it; no, not even for the general good of the whole community." William Blackstone, *Commentaries on the laws of England*, vol. I, 139 (reprint, 1979). It was this shared belief, perhaps, that made it unnecessary for the constitutions of possessive individualism to grant special protection to property beyond the takings clause. The constitutional protection of property in liberal market systems seems to be limited to compensation against takings, at least as far as the property of an individual or corporation is concerned. While such ownership underwent all sorts of restrictions, the institution of private property proved a different matter: it is unlikely that any nationalization scheme making the dominant role of private property impractical would be held constitutional in a Western democracy. Contrary to natural law, which influenced the formulations of the Declaration of Independence and the 1789 French Declaration, one possible reason for such limited protection of private property is that it is viewed, for practical reasons, as an artificial creation of law and not a human right pertaining to human liberty. To the extent that property is an obstacle to other people's dignity, it may be restricted (see the Indian Supreme Court (ISC) position in *Kesavananda* below). German judicial theory looks at property as a value to be protected in its individual autonomy-enhancing capacity. And in a 1993 concurring opinion the Hungarian Chief Justice (Decision 15/1993 (III.12.) AB hat.) closely following the German doctrine, argued that the communists took away private property, which is an important guarantee of personal autonomy. To assure the autonomy-granting function of property, the functional equivalent of property, namely, welfare entitlement, should also receive property-like protection. In other words, the autonomous citizen of postcommunism is made independent of government so long as government does not deprive him of government-provided services and benefits.

Is this the basis of individual autonomy in a market society? What are the material conditions of such "autonomy"? It certainly presupposes that the social welfare status quo is financially affordable. How will such welfare-enabled autonomy influence political decisionmaking? Will people vote for more welfare services that will result in heavier direct taxes on others?

The cases below deal with fundamental questions of expropriation and legitimate restrictions of ownership: What are the legitimate public interests that justify the use of eminent domain? What is fair compensation? What are the inherent social and permissible regulatory limits to property? How far may regulation go in defining what property is? And, what regulation amounts to regulatory taking, restricting the activities of the possessor to the extent that it amounts to expropriation?

PENNSYLVANIA COAL CO. v. MAHON

Supreme Court (United States).
260 U.S. 393 (1922).

Mr. Justice Holmes delivered the opinion of the Court.

This is a bill in equity brought by the defendants in error to prevent the Pennsylvania Coal Company from mining under their property in such way as to remove the supports and cause a subsidence of the surface and of their house. The bill sets out a deed executed by the Coal Company in 1878, under which the plaintiffs claim. The deed conveys the surface but in express terms reserves the right to remove all the coal under the same and the grantee takes the premises with the risk and waives all claim for damages that may arise from mining out the coal. But the plaintiffs say that whatever may have been the Coal Company's rights, they were taken away by an Act of Pennsylvania, approved May 27, 1921 P. L. 1198, commonly known there as the Kohler Act. * * *

The statute forbids the mining of anthracite coal in such way as to cause the subsidence of, among other things, any structure used as a human habitation ... As applied to this case the statute is admitted to destroy previously existing rights of property and contract. The question is whether the police power can be stretched so far.

Government hardly could go on if to some extent values incident to property could not be diminished without paying for every such change in the general law. As long recognized, some values are enjoyed under an implied limitation and must yield to the police power. But obviously the implied limitation must have its limits, or the contract and due process clauses are gone. One fact for consideration in determining such limits is the extent of the diminution. When it reaches a certain magnitude, in most if not in all cases there must be an exercise of eminent domain and compensation to sustain the act. So the question depends upon the particular facts. The greatest weight is given to the judgment of the legislature, but it always is open to interested parties to contend that the legislature has gone beyond its constitutional power.

* * *

It is our opinion that the act cannot be sustained as an exercise of the police power, so far as it affects the mining of coal under streets or cities in places where the right to mine such coal has been reserved. * * * What makes the right to mine coal valuable is that it can be exercised with profit. To make it commercially impracticable to mine certain coal has very nearly the same effect for constitutional purposes as appropriating or destroying it. This we think that we are warranted in assuming that the statute does.

* * *

* * * The protection of private property in the Fifth Amendment presupposes that it is wanted for public use, but provides that it shall not be taken for such use without compensation. When this seemingly absolute protection is found to be qualified by the police power, the natural tendency of human nature is to extend the qualification more and more until at last private property disappears. But that cannot be accomplished in this way under the Constitution of the United States.

The general rule at least is that while property may be regulated to a certain extent, if regulation goes too far, it will be recognized as a taking. * * * In general it is not plain that a man's misfortunes or necessities will justify his shifting the damages to his neighbor's shoulders. * * *

* * * So far as private persons or communities have seen fit to take the risk of acquiring only surface rights, we cannot see that the fact that their risk has become a danger warrants the giving to them greater rights than they bought.

Mr. Justice Brandeis dissenting.

* * *

Every restriction upon the use of property imposed in the exercise of the police power deprives the owner of some right theretofore enjoyed, and is, in that sense, an abridgment by the state of rights in property without making compensation. But restriction imposed to protect the public health, safety or morals from dangers threatened is not a taking. The restriction here in question is merely the prohibition of a noxious use.

HAWAII HOUSING AUTHORITY v. MIDKIFF

Supreme Court (United States).
467 U.S. 229 (1984).

Justice O'Connor delivered the opinion of the Court.

* * *

The Hawaiian Islands were originally settled by Polynesian immigrants from the western Pacific. These settlers developed an economy around a feudal land tenure system in which one island high chief, the *ali'i nui*, controlled the land and assigned it for development to certain subchiefs. * * *

* * * The legislature concluded that concentrated land ownership was responsible for skewing the State's residential fee simple market, inflating land prices, and injuring the public tranquility and welfare.

To redress these problems, * * * [and] to accommodate the needs of both lessors and lessees, the Hawaii Legislature enacted the Land Reform Act of 1967 (Act), which created a mechanism for condemning residential tracts and for transferring ownership of the condemned fees simple to existing lessees. By condemning the land in question, the Hawaii Legislature intended to make the land sales involuntary, thereby making the federal tax consequences less severe while still facilitating the redistribution of fees simple.

Under the Act's condemnation scheme, tenants * * * are entitled to ask the Hawaii Housing Authority (HHA) to condemn the property on which they live. When 25 eligible tenants,[1] or tenants on half the lots in the tract, whichever is less, file appropriate applications, the Act authorizes HHA to hold a public hearing to determine whether acquisition by the State of all or part of the tract will "effectuate the public purposes" of the Act (§ 516–22). If HHA finds that these public purposes will be served, it is authorized to designate some or all of the lots in the tract for acquisition. It then acquires, at prices set either by condemnation trial or by negotiation between lessors and lessees, the former fee owners' full "right, title, and interest" in the land.

After compensation has been set, HHA may sell the land titles to tenants who have applied for fee simple ownership. HHA is authorized to lend these tenants up to 90% of the purchase price. * * *

     * * *

III

A

The starting point for our analysis of the Act's constitutionality is the Court's decision in *Berman v. Parker*, 348 U.S. 26, (1954). In *Berman*, the Court held constitutional the District of Columbia Redevelopment Act of 1945. That Act provided both for the comprehensive use of the eminent domain power to redevelop slum areas and for the possible sale or lease of the condemned lands to private interests. In discussing whether the takings authorized by that Act were for a "public use," *id.*, at 31, the Court stated:

> "We deal, in other words, with what traditionally has been known as the police power. * * * The definition is essentially the product of legislative determinations addressed to the purposes of government, purposes neither abstractly nor historically capable of complete definition. Subject to specific constitutional limitations, when the legislature has spoken, the public interest has been declared in terms well-nigh conclusive. In such cases the legislature, not the judiciary, is the main guardian of the public needs to be served by social legislation * * * *Id.*, at 32.
>
>   * * *
>
> * * * Here one of the means chosen is the use of private enterprise for redevelopment of the area. Appellants argue that this makes the project a taking from one businessman for the benefit of another businessman. But the means of executing the project are for Congress and Congress

---

1. The eligible tenant is one who [owns] a house on the lot.

alone to determine, once the public purpose has been established." *Id.*, at 33.

* * *

To be sure, the Court's cases have repeatedly stated that "one person's property may not be taken for the benefit of another private person without a justifying public purpose, even though compensation be paid." *Thompson v. Consolidated Gas Corp.*, 300 U.S. 55, 80 (1937). * * * But where the exercise of the eminent domain power is rationally related to a conceivable public purpose, the Court has never held a compensated taking to be proscribed by the Public Use Clause.

On this basis, we have no trouble concluding that the Hawaii Act is constitutional. The people of Hawaii have attempted, much as the settlers of the original 13 Colonies did,[5] to reduce the perceived social and economic evils of a land oligopoly traceable to their monarchs. * * *

* * *

Of course, this Act, like any other, may not be successful in achieving its intended goals. But "whether in fact the provision will accomplish its objectives is not the question: the [constitutional requirement] is satisfied if . . . the . . . [state] Legislature rationally could have believed that the [Act] would promote its objective." *Western & Southern Life Ins. Co. v. State Bd. of Equalization*, 451 U.S. 648, 671–672, * * *

B

* * *

The mere fact that property taken outright by eminent domain is transferred in the first instance to private beneficiaries does not condemn that taking as having only a private purpose. The Court long ago rejected any literal requirement that condemned property be put into use for the general public. "It is not essential that the entire community, nor even any considerable portion, . . . directly enjoy or participate in any improvement in order [for it] to constitute a public use." *Rindge Co. v. Los Angeles*, 262 U.S., at 707. "[W]hat in its immediate aspect [is] only a private transaction may . . . be raised by its class or character to a public affair." *Block v. Hirsh*, 256 U.S., at 155. As the unique way titles were held in Hawaii skewed the land market, exercise of the power of eminent domain was justified.

HAMBURG FLOOD CONTROL CASE

Federal Constitutional Court (Germany).
24 BVerfGE 367 (1986).

[The city-state of Hamburg adopted the Dikes and Embankments Act of 1964, after considerable damages caused by extensive flooding in 1962. The Act provided for the conversion of all grassland classified as "dikeland" in the land register into public property. The Act terminated

---

5. After the American Revolution, the colonists in several States took steps to eradicate the feudal incidents with which large proprietors had encumbered land in the Colonies.

all private rights over the property and provided compensation to the land owners. Several owners filed constitutional complaints, alleging a violation of their fundamental right under Art. 14.]

Judgement of the First Senate:

* * *

D.I.1. Article 14 (1) [1] of the Basic Law guarantees property both as a legal institution and as a concrete right held by the individual owner. To hold property is an elementary constitutional right which must be seen in close context with the protection of personal liberty. Within the general system of constitutional rights, its function is to secure its holder a sphere of liberty in the economic field and thereby enable him to lead a self-governing life. The protection of property as a legal institution serves to secure this basic right. [And] this constitutional right of the individual is conditioned upon legal institution of "property". Property could not be effectively secured if lawmakers were empowered to replace private property with something no longer deserving the label of owner-ship. * * * The regulation of property may be adjusted to social and economic conditions. The legislature's task is to regulate property in the light of fundamental constitutional values. The institutional guarantee, however, prohibits any revision of the private legal order which would remove the fundamental catalog of constitutionally protected activities relating to the area of property and which would substantially curtail or suspend the protected sphere of liberty protected by this fundamental right. * * *

[Despite these broad principles protecting the property right, the Court went on to hold that the state could legitimately place the dikeland properties under public control as the property was to be used for a particular public purpose, the construction of flood-prevention dikes.]

* * *

E.III. 1.a) * * * Article 14 (3) permits the expropriation of real property if the common good requires it. [But] the overriding standard of the common good limits the legal power to take property ordinarily within the protection of Article 14. This standard—and only this stan-dard—permits an expropriation of property under Article 14 (3) * * * The object of a valid taking under Article 14 (3) must be clearly specified in the law. The Basic Law establishes that in the recurring tension between the property interest of the individual and the needs of the public, the public interest may, in case of conflict, take precedence over the legally guaranteed position of the individual. * * * The Constitution does not leave the resolution of this conflict to the legislature but settles the issue itself.

b) The terms of Article 14 (3) [1]—[the common good requirement] limit the taking of property under the terms of Article 14 (3) [2]—[the "by law" and "compensation" requirements] * * * If these require-ments are not met, the basic right to property is violated. The owner's duty to tolerate an intrusion against his right to property is limited to the terms established by the Constitution itself. * * *

Beyond all this, the right to property as specified in Article 14 (3) is secured by the fact that property may not be taken in the absence of just compensation. The core guarantee under a permissible expropriation is the value of the property in question. * * *

The function of Article 14 is not primarily to prevent the taking of property without compensation—although in this respect it offers greater protection than Article 153 of the Weimar Constitution—but rather to secure existing property in the hands of its owners. The view propounded under the Weimar Constitution, and to some extent also under Article 14, is that the property guarantee is essentially a guarantee of the value of property and that its expropriation is acceptable so long as the parties are adequately compensated. Yet this view does not reflect the [full] purpose and spirit of Article 14. Because the Weimar Constitution had no provisions for testing the constitutionality of expropriation laws, and because judicial review was [severely] restricted, the judiciary had to be concerned primarily with protecting property owners through compensation. Thus the basic right [of property] emerged more and more into a demand for adequate compensation. By contrast, the property guarantee under Article 14 (1) [2] must be seen in relationship to the personhood of the owner—i.e., to the realm of freedom within which persons engage in self defining, responsible activity. The property right is not primarily a material but rather a personal guarantee. The basic right protects the individual against every unjustified infringement of the entire range of protected goods.

MELLACHER v. AUSTRIA

European Court of Human Rights.
12 E.H.R.R. 391 (1989).

[A new Rent Act was adopted in Austria, in 1981.]

35. * * * It has * * * been suggested in many quarters that there is no justification for applying the system of square metre rents to existing leases and for leaving it to the tenants concerned to apply for a reduction.

* * * According to the relevant provisions of the [Austrian] Federal Constitution, the individuals concerned have no right to apply directly to this court if the civil courts are competent. The civil appellate courts can request a review by the Constitutional Court if they have doubts as to the constitutionality of a legal provision which they are required to apply in a particular case. However, as the present cases show, the competent civil courts had no such doubts concerning section 44 of the 1981 Rent Act.

36. This is confirmed by a decision of the Supreme Court of 3 July 1984, in which it held that there was no doubt as to the constitutional validity of this provision. The Supreme Court stated as follows:

"In passing the Rent Act, the legislature has, for reasons which are understandable from a historical point of view, limited freedom of contract with regard to the amount of rent payable for properties covered by the Act. Over a number of decades, always with reference to current needs, further properties were removed from the sphere of freely negotiated rents, determined by supply and demand. * * *

The legislature * * * regarded the fundamental aim of the transitional provisions as being to achieve the gradual and smoothest possible adjustment of existing leases to the new rules. * * *

Undeniably this constitutes an interference with existing leases. Indeed this was the legislature's declared intention.

In this connection it must not be overlooked that the obligation to pay rent for an apartment constitutes a continuing obligation and that in general such obligations are not entirely immune to certain adjustments and changes....

* * * ([Constitutional Court Case 7423/1974]: 'There is no provision in the Federal Constitution which in principle prevents ordinary legislation from interfering with lawfully acquired rights'). * * * [T]he legislature has neither acted arbitrarily nor exceeded its powers. It has remained within the bounds of the freedom to form legislative policy which, in case of doubt, it must be assumed to have. To place too many limits on this freedom would lead to inflexibility with regard to legal situations and hamper innovations even where necessary.

The possibility available to tenants of applying for a reduction in rent under section 44(2) and (3) of the Rent Act is clearly disadvantageous to landlords who have concluded an agreement on the amount of rent to be paid by the tenant under existing legislation and now find that their confidence in the law has been misplaced. It should however be recognised that this is counterbalanced by a series of provisions as a result of which rent is no longer frozen at the 1914 level. * * *

Of course the new system may bring more disadvantages for some landlords and more advantages for others. However, at all events, it is merely a restriction on the right of property (*Eigentumsbeschränkung*) since the rent for a sitting tenant may still exceed the amount chargeable under the new legislation by 50%. The legislature may authorise an expropriation only if such a measure serves the public good and the general interest. Article 5 of the Basic Law provides that an expropriation may be effected only if it is justified in the general interest. Although the first sentence of Article 5 of the Basic Law does indeed apply to restrictions on the right of property, the legislature can lay down such restrictions without fear of acting in breach of the constitution, provided that they do not threaten the very substance of the fundamental right to the inviolability of property or otherwise violate a constitutional principle binding on the legislature. * * * * "

* * *

AS TO THE LAW

I. ALLEGED VIOLATION OF ARTICLE 1 OF PROTOCOL No. 1

40. According to the applicants, the reduction of rent granted to various tenants pursuant to section 44(2) of the 1981 Rent Act (see paragraphs 13, 18, 25 and 32 above) constituted a violation of Article 1 of Protocol No. 1, which is worded as follows:

"Every natural or legal person is entitled to the peaceful enjoyment of his possessions. No one shall be deprived of his possessions except in the public interest and subject to the conditions provided for by law and by the general principles of international law.

The preceding provisions shall not, however, in any way impair the right of a State to enforce such laws as it deems necessary to control the use of property in accordance with the general interest or to secure the payment of taxes or other contributions or penalties.''

The applicants complained that the Austrian authorities had interfered with their freedom of contract and deprived them of a substantial proportion of their future rental income. * * *

A.   The Article 1 rule applicable in this case

42.   Article 1 guarantees in substance the right of property (see the *Marckx* judgment of 13 June 1979, Series A no. 31, pp. 27–28, § 63). * * *

43.   * * * In the applicants' view, the 1981 Rent Act had had the result of turning them into mere administrators of their property, receiving remuneration controlled by the public authorities. They claimed that the effect of the reductions was such that they could be regarded as equivalent to a deprivation of possessions. * * * They also alleged that they had been deprived of a contractual right to receive payment of the agreed rent.

44.   The Court finds that the measures taken did not amount either to a formal or to a *de facto* expropriation. There was no transfer of the applicants' property nor were they deprived of their right to use, let or sell it. The contested measures which, admittedly, deprived them of part of their income from the property amounted in the circumstances merely to a control of the use of property. Accordingly, the second paragraph of Article 1 applies in this instance.

B.   Compliance with the conditions laid down in the second paragraph

45.   The second paragraph reserves to States the right to enact such laws as they deem necessary to control the use of property in accordance with the general interest.

Such laws are especially called for and usual in the field of housing, which in our modern societies is a central concern of social and economic policies.

In order to implement such policies, the legislature must have a wide margin of appreciation both with regard to the existence of a problem of public concern warranting measures of control and as to the choice of the detailed rules for the implementation of such measures. The Court will respect the legislature's judgment as to what is in the general interest unless that judgment be manifestly without reasonable foundation (see the James and Others judgment of 21 February 1986, Series A no. 98, p. 32, § 46).

1.   Aim of the interference

46.   The applicants disputed the legitimacy of the aim of the 1981 Rent Act. They claimed that it was not intended to redress a social injustice but to bring about a redistribution of property * * * They

maintained, and produced statistics to support this view, that in 1981 there had been no shortage of accommodation, either in quantitative or in qualitative terms. * * * [The Act] was intended to satisfy a section of the electors of the socialist government, which was in power at the time.

* * *

47. * * * The easing of rent controls, in 1967, had increased the disparities between rents for equivalent apartments. * * * [T]he 1981 Rent Act was intended to reduce excessive and unjustified disparities between rents for equivalent apartments and to combat property speculation.

Through these means, the Act also had the aims of making accommodation more easily available at reasonable prices to less affluent members of the population, while at the same time providing incentives for the improvement of substandard properties.

In the Court's view, the explanations given for the legislation in question are not such as could be characterised as being manifestly unreasonable. The Court therefore accepts that the 1981 Rent Act had a legitimate aim in the general interest.

2. Proportionality of the interference

48. [An interference into property rights] must achieve a "fair balance" between the demands of the general interest of the community and the requirements of the protection of the individual's fundamental rights. The search for this balance is reflected in the structure of Article 1 as a whole and therefore also in the second paragraph thereof. There must be a reasonable relationship of proportionality between the means employed and the aim pursued.

* * *

51. The Court observes that, in remedial social legislation and in particular in the field of rent control, which is the subject of the present case, it must be open to the legislature to take measures affecting the further execution of previously concluded contracts in order to attain the aim of the policy adopted.

52. The applicants also complained * * * [that] the right conferred by section 44(2) of the Act was available without distinction to all tenants and not only to the most disadvantaged of them. A genuinely social measure would have been to accord rent subsidies to the most needy * * *

53. [The system] may place some landlords at a greater disadvantage than others. [However,] * * * [i]t would hardly be consistent with these aims nor would it be practicable to make the reductions of rent dependent on the specific situation of each tenant. * * *

The possible existence of alternative solutions does not in itself render the contested legislation unjustified. Provided that the legislature remains within the bounds of its margin of appreciation, it is not for the Court to say whether the legislation represented the best solution for dealing with the problem or whether the legislative discretion should have been exercised in another way.

* * *

56. * * * It is undoubtedly true that the rent reductions are striking in their amount, in particular in the cases of the applicants * * *. But it does not follow that these reductions constitute a disproportionate burden. The fact that the original rents were agreed upon and corresponded to the then prevailing market conditions does not mean that the legislature could not reasonably decide as a matter of policy that they were unacceptable from the point of view of social justice.

* * *

JOINT DISSENTING OPINION OF JUDGES Cremona, Bindschedler–Robert, Gölcüklü, Bernhardt AND Spielmann

* * *

Contrary to the majority opinion, we are of the view, however, that in these two cases the interferences in question do not satisfy the proportionality requirement in that, with regard to them, there was a failure to respect the requisite fair balance (which, , as has been said before by the Court, is inherent in the whole structure of the Convention) between the demands of the general interest and the interest of the individual or individuals concerned.

* * *

As regards application [of Mellacher], the monthly rent * * * was reduced * * * to 17.6 per cent of the original amount which was freely and at the time lawfully negotiated and which, as accepted by the majority (paragraph 56), corresponded to the prevailing market conditions. The applicants do not seem to be far wrong when they say that the reduced rent now corresponds to the price of a simple meal for two persons in a cheap restaurant.

* * *

Taking due account of the State's margin of appreciation, we do not consider that the proportionality requirement is satisfied in these cases. The applicants bore an individual and excessive burden which was not legitimate in the circumstances, with an upsetting of the requisite fair balance which is to be struck between the demands of the general interest of the community and the requirements of the protection of the individual applicants' fundamental rights.

Like the unanimous Commission, we therefore find a violation in both these cases.

PENNELL v. CITY OF SAN JOSE

Supreme Court (United States).
485 U.S. 1 (1988).

[Under a San Jose, Cal., rent-control ordinance (Ordinance), a landlord may automatically raise the annual rent of a tenant in possession by as much as 8 percent, but if a tenant objects to the increase, a hearing is required to determine whether the landlord's proposed increase is "reasonable under the circumstances," and the hearing officer is directed to consider specified factors, including "the hardship to a tenant." Any tenant whose household income and monthly housing expense meet [certain income requirements] shall be deemed to be suffering under financial and economic hardship, which must be weighed.]

Chief Justice Rehnquist delivered the opinion of the Court.

* * *

[T]here is nothing in the Ordinance requiring that a hearing officer in fact reduce a proposed rent increase on grounds of tenant hardship. * * * Given the "essentially ad hoc, factual inquir[y]" involved in the takings analysis, *Kaiser Aetna v. United States*, we have found it particularly important in takings cases to adhere to our admonition that "the constitutionality of statutes ought not be decided except in an actual factual setting that makes such a decision necessary." * * *

* * * [Petitioners] argue, however, that * * * "The objective of alleviating individual tenant hardship is ... not a 'policy the legislature is free to adopt' in a rent control ordinance."

* * * [But] the Ordinance establishes a scheme in which a hearing officer considers a number of factors in determining the reasonableness of a proposed rent increase which exceeds eight percent *and* which exceeds the amount deemed reasonable * * * [T]he Hearing Officer examines the history of the premises, the landlord's costs, and the market for comparable housing. Section 5703.28(c)(5) also allows the landlord to bring forth any other financial evidence—including presumably evidence regarding his own financial status—to be taken into account by the Hearing Officer. It is in only this context that the Ordinance allows tenant hardship to be considered and * * * "balance[d]" with the other factors * * *. Within this scheme, [the Ordinance] represents a rational attempt to accommodate the conflicting interests of protecting tenants from burdensome rent increases while at the same time ensuring that landlords are guaranteed a fair return on their investment. * * * We accordingly find that the Ordinance, which so carefully considers both the individual circumstances of the landlord and the tenant before determining whether to allow an *additional* increase in rent over and above certain amounts that are deemed reasonable, does not on its face violate the Fourteenth Amendment's Due Process Clause. * * *

Justice Scalia, with whom Justice O'Connor joins, concurring in part and dissenting in part.

* * *

* * * [T]he "hardship" provision is invoked to meet a [distinct] social problem: the existence of some renters who are too poor to afford even reasonably priced housing. But *that* problem is no more caused or exploited by landlords than it is by the grocers who sell needy renters their food * * *. And even if the neediness of renters could be regarded as a problem distinctively attributable to landlords in general, it is not remotely attributable to the *particular* landlords that the Ordinance singles out * * *.

The traditional manner in which American government has met the problem of those who cannot pay reasonable prices for privately sold necessities—a problem caused by the society at large—has been the distribution to such persons of funds raised from the public at large through taxes, * * *

The politically attractive feature of regulation is not that it permits wealth transfers to be achieved that could not be achieved otherwise; but rather that it permits them to be achieved "off budget," with relative invisibility and thus relative immunity from normal democratic processes. * * * Once the door is opened it is not unreasonable to expect price regulations requiring private businesses to give special discounts to senior citizens (no matter how affluent), or to students, the handicapped, or war veterans. Subsidies for these groups may well be a good idea, but because of the operation of the Takings Clause our governmental system has required them to be applied, in general, through the process of taxing and spending, where both economic effects and competing priorities are more evident.

That fostering of an intelligent democratic process is one of the happy effects of the constitutional prescription—perhaps accidental, perhaps not. Its essence, however, is simply the unfairness of making one citizen pay in some fashion other than taxes, to remedy a social problem that is none of his creation. * * *

I would hold that the seventh factor in § 5703.28(c) of the San Jose Ordinance effects a taking of property without just compensation.

RUSTOM CAVASJEE COOPER v. UNION OF INDIA

Supreme Court (India).
(1970) 3 S.C.R. 530.

[In 1969, an Ordinance of the acting president of India transferred the undertakings of 14 named commercial banks to corresponding new banks that were created by the Ordinance. Parliament enacted the Banking Companies (Acquisition and Transfer of Undertakings) Act, 1969. The object of the Act was to provide for the acquisition and transfer of the undertakings of certain banking companies in order to better serve the development of the economy in conformity with national policy and objectives. A compensation scheme was contained in a schedule to the Act. Shareholders of the named banks challenged the Act, arguing that the measures were not within Parliament's legislative competence because (a) to the extent to which the Act vested in the corresponding new banks the assets of businesses other than in the Banking Act, namely, their buildings and land, it trenched upon the authority of the state legislature and the statutorily required acquisition did not satisfy conditions of reasonableness; and (b) the provisions of the Act, which transferred the undertakings of the named banks and prohibited them from carrying on banking business and practically prohibited them from carrying on nonbanking business, impaired property rights and were discriminatory.]

[pp. 570, 575–76 of the decision.]

The Judgment of J.C. Shah, S.M. Sikri, J.M. Shelat, V. Bhargava, G.K. Mitter, C.A. Vaidalingam, K.S. Hedge, A.N. Grover, P. Jaganmohan Reddy and I.D. Dua, JJ. was delivered by Shah, J. A.N. Ray, J. gave a dissenting opinion.

* * *

Under the Constitution, protection against impairment of the guarantee of fundamental rights is determined by the nature of the right, the interest of the aggrieved party and the degree of harm resulting from the State action. Impairment of the right of the individual and not the object of the State in taking the impugned action, is the measure of protection * * * In this Court, there is, however, a body of authority that the nature and extent of the protection of the fundamental rights is measured not by the operation of the State action upon the rights of the individual, but by its object. Thereby the constitutional scheme which makes the guaranteed rights subject to the permissible restrictions within their allotted fields, fundamental, got blurred * * *.

* * * Again to hold that the extent of, and the circumstances in which, the guarantee of protection is available depends upon the object of the State action, is to seriously erode its effectiveness. * * *

But this Court has held in some cases to be presently noticed that Art. 19 (1) (f) and Art. 31 (2) are mutually exclusive. * * *

* * * In [a number of authorities under *Gopalan*] it was held that the substantive provisions of a law relating to acquisition of property were not liable to be challenged on the ground that they imposed unreasonable restrictions on the right to hold property. [However, beginning in 1960, a second line of precedents emerged.]

* * *

[According to the new trend,] Art. 31 (1) is liable to be tested on the ground that it violates other fundamental rights and freedoms including the right to hold property guaranteed . . .

[I]t follows that the extent of protection against impairment of a fundamental right is determined not by the object of the Legislature nor by the form of the action, but by its direct operation upon the individual's rights. * * *

* * * Each freedom has different dimensions. Article 19 (1) (f) enunciates the right to acquire, hold and dispose of property: cl. (5) of Art. 19 authorizes imposition of restrictions upon the right. Article 31 assures the right to property and grants protection against the exercise of the authority of the State. Clause (5) of Art. 19 and cis. (1) & (2) of Art. 31 prescribe restrictions upon State action, subject to which the right to property may be exercised. Article 19 (5) is a broad generalization dealing with the nature of limitations, which may be placed by law on the right to property. The guarantees under Arts. 31 (1) & (2) arise out of the limitations imposed on the authority of the State by law to take over the individual's property. The true character of the limitations under the two provisions is not different.

* * *

* * * Imposition of restrictions which are incidental or subsidiary to the carrying on of trade by the State whether to the exclusion of the citizens or not must, however, satisfy the test of the main limb.

The law which prohibits after July 19, 1969, the named banks from carrying on banking business, being a necessary incident of the right assumed by the Union, is not liable to be challenged because of Art. 19 (6) (ii) in so far as it affects the right to carry on business.

There is no satisfactory proof in support of the plea that the enactment of Act 22 of 1969 was not in the larger interest of the nation, but to serve political ends, i.e. not with the object to ensure better banking facilities, or to make them available to a wider public, but only to take control over the deposits of the public with the major banks, and to use them as a political lever against industrialists who had built up industries by decades of industrial planning and careful management.

* * *

Protection of Art. 14.

By Art. 14 of the Constitution the State is enjoined not to deny any person equality before the law or the equal protection of the laws within the territory of India. The Article forbids class legislation, but not reasonable classification in making laws. The test of permissible classification under an Act lies in two cumulative conditions: (i) classification under the Act must be founded on an intelligible differentia distinguishing persons, transactions or things grouped together from others left out of the group; and (ii) the differentia has a rational relation to the object sought to be achieved by the Act: there must be a nexus between the basis of classification and the object of the Act. * * *

The Courts recognize in the Legislature some degree of elasticity in the matter of making a classification between persons, objects and transactions. Provided the classification is based on some intelligible ground, the Courts will not strike down that classification, 'because in the view of the Court it should have proceeded on some other ground or should have included in the class selected for special treatment some other persons, objects or transactions which are not included by the Legislature. The Legislature is free to recognize the degree of harm and to restrict the operation of a law only to those cases where the need is the clearest. The Legislature need not extend the regulation of a law to all cases it may possibly reach, and may make a classification founded on practical grounds of convenience. Classification to be valid must, however, disclose a rational nexus with the object sought to be achieved by the law, which makes the classification. * * *

[However, b]y reason of the transfer of the undertaking of the named banks, the interests of the banks and the shareholders are vitally affected. * * *

* * *

The object of Act 22 of 1969 is according to the long title to provide for the acquisition and transfer of the undertakings of certain banking companies in order to serve better the needs of development of the economy in conformity with the national policy and objectives and for matters connected therewith or incidental thereto. The national policy may reasonably be taken to be the policy contained in the directive principles of State policy, especially Arts. 38 & 39 of the Constitution. For achieving the need's of a developing economy in conformity with the national policy and objectives, the resources of all banks foreign as well as Indian-are inadequate. * * *

* * * [I]n the absence of any reliable data, we do not think it necessary to express an opinion on the question whether selection of the undertaking of some out of many banking institutions, for compulsory acquisition, is liable to be struck down as hostile discrimination, on the ground that there is no reasonable relation between the differentia and the object of the Act which cannot be substantially served even by the acquisition of the undertakings of all the banks out of which the selection is made. * * *

* * *

The fourteen named banks are prohibited from carrying on banking business—a disability for which there is no rational explanation * * *

For reasons set out by us for holding that the restriction is unreasonable, it must also be held that the guarantee of equality is impaired by preventing the named banks carrying on the non-banking business.

Protection of the guarantee under Art. 31(2)—

* * *

The law providing for acquisition must again either fix the amount of compensation or specify the principles on which, and the manner in which, the compensation is to be determined and given.

* * * In all States where the rule of law prevails, the right to compensation is guaranteed by the Constitution or regarded as inextricably involved in the right to property.

By the 5th Amendment in the Constitution of the U.S.A. the right of eminent domain is expressly circumscribed by providing "Nor shall private property be taken for public use, without just, compensation". Such a provision is to be found also in every State Constitution in the United States. The Japanese Constitution, 1946, by Art. 25 provides a similar guarantee. Under the Commonwealth of Australia Constitution, 1900, the Commonwealth Parliament is invested with the power of acquisition of property on "just terms": s. 57 (XXXI).

Under the Common Law of England, principles for payment of compensation for acquisition of property by the State are stated by Blackstone in his "Commentaries on the Laws of England", 4th Ed., Vol. I, at p. 109:

"So great moreover is the regard of the law for private property, that it will not authorize the least violation of it; no, not even for the general good of the whole community ... Besides, the public good is in nothing more essentially interested, than in the protection of every individual's private rights, as modeled by the municipal law. In this and similar cases the legislature alone can, and indeed frequently does, interpose, and compel the individual to, acquiesce. But how does it interpose and compel? Not by absolutely stripping the subject of his property in an arbitrary manner; but giving him a full indemnification and equivalent for the injury thereby sustained. The public is now considered as an individual, treating with an individual for an exchange. All that the legislature does, is to oblige the owner to alienate his possession for a reasonable price ..."

The British Parliament is supreme and its powers are not subject to any constitutional limitations. But the British Parliament has rarely, if at all, exercised power to take property without payment of the cash value of the property taken. In *Attorney General v. De Keyser's Royal Hotel* L.R. [1920] A.C. 508 the House of Lords held that the Crown is not entitled as of right either by virtue of its prerogative or under any statute, to take possession of the land or building of a subject for administrative purposes in connection with the defense of the realm, without compensation for their use and occupation.

[T]he expression "just equivalent" meant "full indemnification" and the expropriated owner was on that account entitled to the market value of the property on the date of deprivation of the property.

P.P. Rao, BASIC FEATURES OF THE CONSTITUTION

(2000) 2 S.C.C. (j) 1–6.

* * *

[T]he Supreme Court declared in *Kesavananda Bharati v. State of Kerala*, (1973) Supp. S.C.R. 1, below] that Article 368 did not enable Parliament to alter the basic structure or framework of the Constitution. This decision is not just a landmark in the evolution of constitutional law, but a turning point in constitutional history. No other court in the world had taken this position. Subsequently, the Supreme Court of Bangladesh adopted the doctrine of basic structure relying on *Kesavananda Bharati*. In Pakistan the Lahore High Court and the Baluchistan High Court took the same view but not the Supreme Court. The new Constitution of Nepal (1990) contains some provisions which cannot be amended at all. * * *

The theory of basic structure has a background rooted in the right to property. The Congress Party was committed to land reforms long before independence. * * * After the dawn of independence, the State Legislatures lost no time in enacting land reforms. The Patna High Court struck the first blow when it declared the Bihar Land Reforms Act, 1950 arbitrary and violative of Article 14. * * * It came as a rude shock to the framers of the Constitution whose mindset was different. Speaking on the Draft Constitution, Jawaharlal Nehru had said in the Constituent Assembly on 10–9–1949:

"The policy of the abolition of big estates is not a new policy but one that was laid down by the National Congress years ago. So far as we are concerned, we, who are connected with the Congress, shall, naturally, give effect to that pledge completely—one hundred per cent—and no legal subtlety, no change, is going to come in our way. That is quite clear. We will honour our pledges. Within limits, no Judge and no Supreme Court will be allowed to constitute themselves into a third chamber. No Supreme Court and no judiciary will sit in judgment over the sovereign will of Parliament which represents the will of the entire community. If we go wrong here and there, they can point it out; but in the ultimate analysis, where the future of the community is concerned, no judiciary must come in the way. Ultimately, the whole Constitution is a creature of Parliament."[8]

Parliament could not remain complacent after the judgment of the Patna High Court. The Constitution (First Amendment) Act, 1951 was the legislative response to the legalistic interpretation of fundamental rights by the judiciary. Moving the amendment, Jawaharlal Nehru said:

"Even in the last three years or so, some very important measures passed by the State Assemblies have been held up. No doubt, as I said, the interpretation of the courts must be accepted as right but in the meantime you, I and the country have to face social and economic upheavals. How are we to meet this challenge of the times? ... Therefore, we have to think of big changes and that is why we thought of amending Article 31."[9]

* * * Successive amendments not only made changes in the provisions relating to the right to property, but also enlarged the Ninth Schedule by including a large number of Acts. The Seventeenth Amendment was challenged in *I.C. Golaknath v. State of Punjab*, [(1967) 2 S.C.R. 762: A.I.R. 1967 S.C. 1643] on the ground that the impugned amendment was "law" within the meaning of Article 13 and it violated the right to property conferred by Article 31. * * * In effect, *Golaknath*, amounted to a warning to Parliament not to amend the Constitution in future so as to abridge or take away any of the fundamental rights enshrined in Part III as interpreted by the Court. The ruling placed a serious fetter on the amending power of Parliament which Parliament was however not prepared to accept. By the 24th Amendment, Article 368 was amended to get over *Golaknath case*. The amended Article 368 enabled Parliament, in exercise of its constituent power, to amend by way of addition, variation or repeal any provision of the Constitution in accordance with the procedure laid down therein. Further, it declared that nothing in Article 13 shall apply to any amendment made under Article 368. Parliament asserted itself once again by enacting the Constitution (Twenty-fifth) Amendment Act, 1971 substituting the word "amount" for the word "compensation" * * * The 29th Amendment included in Schedule IX the Kerala Land Reforms (Amendment) Acts, 1969 and 1971 making them immune from attack on the ground of violation of fundamental rights.

The validity of the Twenty-fifth Amendment was challenged in *Kesavananda Bharati v. State of Kerala* along with the Twenty-fourth

8. *Jawaharlal Nehru's Speeches* (1949–1953), the Publications Division, Government of India, Second Impression, p. 485.

9. *Ibid*, p. 503.

and Twenty-ninth Amendments. * * * While upholding the validity of
the 24th and the 29th Amendment Acts and Section 2(*a*) and (*b*) and the
first part of Section 3 of the 25th Amendment Act, 1971, the Court by a
majority of 7:6 struck down the second part of Section 3 which made the
declaration that the law was immune from judicial review as it was made
for giving effect to the directive principles of the State policy final. The
Court overruled *Golaknath* and declared that Article 368 did not enable
Parliament to alter the basic structure or framework of the Constitution.

* * * This single decision has deflected the balance of power decisively in favour of the judiciary at the cost of Parliament and cast a cloud
of uncertainty over the amending power. Previously Parliament had the
last word in law-making and amending the Constitution. Now the
Supreme Court has the final say. Amendments to the Constitution are
made amenable to judicial review. This far-reaching decision pronounced
on 24–4–1973 had its immediate repercussions. Within two days, the
Union Government retaliated by superseding the three seniormost
puisne Judges * * *

* * *

A common feature of the decisions in *Golaknath* and *Kesavananda
Bharati* is the wafer-thin majority. It shows that two views are possible
on the issues involved. It also shows that the dividing line between
constitutional law and constitutional politics is very thin indeed. Even in
Golaknath, the Judges who were in a minority strongly felt that an
unamendable Constitution would not be conducive to progress. For
instance, R.S. Bachawat, J. expressed the unhappy situation thus:

> "A static system of laws is the worst tyranny that any Constitution can
> impose upon a country. An unamendable Constitution means that all
> reform and progress are at a standstill. If Parliament cannot amend
> Part III of the Constitution even by recourse to Article 368, no other
> power can do so."[19]

The constitutional limitation in the form of basic structure came to
be appreciated better when Parliament enacted the 39th Amendment
which inserted Article 329–A placing a dispute regarding the election of
a person holding the office of Prime Minister or Speaker beyond the
purview of judicial review. The sole object of the exercise was to save
Indira Gandhi's election, after it was set aside by J.M.L. Sinha, J. of the
Allahabad High Court. In *Indira Nehru Gandhi v. Raj Narain* [(1975)
Supp. S.C.C. 1], a Constitution Bench of the Supreme Court analysed the
various judgments delivered in *Kesavananda Bharati* in order to ascertain the content of the basic structure for judging the validity of the
impugned amendment. * * * Following the ratio of *Kesavananda Bharati*, the Court declared that the 39th Amendment violated the basic
structure of the Constitution, but the Judges differed in their perception
of the basic structure and its application to the case on hand.

19. *I.C. Golaknath v. State of Punjab*
[(1967) 2 S.C.R. 762: A.I.R. 1967 S.C. 1643],
at p. 918.

HIS HOLINESS KESAVANANDA BHARATI SRIPADAGLAVARU v. STATE OF KERALA

Supreme Court (India).
(1973) SUPP. S.C.R.

[The question whether the fundamental rights set out in Part III of the Constitution could be taken away or abridged by amendment of the Constitution was first considered by this Court in *Sankari Prasad v. Union of India*, (1952) S.C.R. 89, in which the validity of the Constitution (First Amendment) Act, 1951 was challenged. The First Amendment made changes in Arts. 15 and 19 of the Constitution and inserted Arts. 31A and 31B. The principal contention was that the First Amendment, insofar as it purported to take away or abridge the rights conferred by Part III of the Constitution, fell within the prohibition of Art. 13(2) of the Constitution. The Court unanimously held that the limits in 13(2) do not invalidate constitutional amendments. Later amendment cases, however, resulted in different positions. In *Rustom Cavasjee Cooper v. Union of India*, (1970) 3 S.C.R. 530, the Court, by a majority of ten against one, held that even after the Fourth Amendment, "Compensation" meant "the equivalent in terms of money of the property compulsory acquired * * * according to relevant principles which * * * must be appropriate to the determination of compensation for the particular class of property sought to be acquired."

[Arguments were addressed mainly in Writ Petition No. 135 of 1970. In it the petitioner challenged the validity of the Kerala Land Reforms Amendment Act, 1969 and the Kerala Land Reforms Amendment Act, 1971, for the reason that some of their provisions violated Arts. 14, 19(1)(f), 25, 26, and 31 of the Constitution. During the pendency of the Writ Petition, Parliament passed three constitutional amendments, the Twenty–Fourth, Twenty–Fifth and Twenty–Ninth Amendment Acts.

[The Constitution Twenty–Fourth Amendment Act amended Art. 368. It provided that Parliament may, in exercise of its constituent power, amend by way of addition, variation, or repeal, any provision of the Constitution in accordance with the procedure laid down in that article. The other part of the amendment provides that nothing in Art. 13 shall apply to any amendment under Art. 368.

[The Constitution Twenty–Fifth Amendment Act enabled state legislatures to expropriate in order to secure "directive principles" (see below) without the possibility of judicial review of such legislation; instead of compensation, only an "amount" was to be paid, exempt again from judicial review. The Amendments were intended to seal the Kerala Land Reforms, which were based on these techniques.

[The Constitution Twenty–Ninth Amendment Act included the Kerala and Reforms Acts in the Ninth Schedule to the Constitution, making them immune from attack on the ground of violation of fundamental rights. The petitioner challenged the validity of the three acts.]

[pp. 4, 120, 164–66, 193, 196–97, 203, 455, 457, 571, 611–13 of the decision.]

HELD—(By Full Court): The Constitution (Twenty Fourth) Amendment Act, Section 2(a) and 2(b) of the Constitution (Twenty Fifth) Amendment Act and the Constitution (Twenty Ninth) Amendment Act are valid.

By majority: Per Hegde, Ray, Jaganmohan Reddy, Palekar, Khanna, Mathew, Beg, Dwivedi, Mukherjea and Chandrachud, JJ: The decision of the majority in Golaknath that the word "law" in article 13(2) included amendments to the Constitution and the article operated as a limitation upon the power to amend the Constitution in article 368 is erroneous and is overruled.

By majority: Per Ray, Palekar, Khanna, Mathew, Beg, Dwivedi and Chandrachud, JJ: The power of amendment is plenary. It includes within itself the power to add, alter or repeal the various articles of the Constitution including those relating to fundamental rights.

By majority: Per Sikri, C.J. and Shelat, Hegde, Grover, Khanna, Jaganmohan Ikeddy and Mukherjea, JJ. (Ray, Palekar, Mathew, Beg, Dwivedi and Chandrachud, JJ. dissenting): The power to amend does not include the power to alter the basic structure, or framework of the Constitution so as to change its identity.

* * *

By majority: The first part of article 31C is valid. The second part of the article, viz., "and no law containing a declaration that it is for giving effect to such policy shall be called in question in any court on the ground that it does not give effect to such policy" is invalid.

Sikri C.J.

* * *

Part IV of the Constitution contains directive principles of State policy. Article 37 specifically provides that "the provisions contained in this Part shall not be enforceable by any court, but the principles therein laid down are nevertheless fundamental in the governance of the country and it shall be the duty of the State to apply these principles in making laws." This clearly shows, and it has also been laid down by this Court, that these provisions are not justiciable and cannot be enforced by any Court. The Courts could not, for instance, issue a mandamus directing the State to provide adequate means of livelihood to every citizen, or that the ownership and control of the material resources of the community be so distributed as best to subserve the common good, or that there should be equal pay for equal work for both men and women.

Some of the directive principles are of great fundamental importance in the governance of the country. But the question is whether they override the important fundamental rights. In other words, can Parliament abrogate the fundamental rights in order to give effect to some of the directive principles?

* * *

It was the common understanding that fundamental rights would remain in substance as they are and they would, not be amended out of existence. It seems also, to have been a common understanding that the fundamental features of the Constitution, namely, secularism, democracy and the freedom of the individual would always subsist in the welfare state.

In view of the above reasons, a necessary implication arises that there are implied limitations on the power of Parliament that the expression "amendment of this Constitution" has consequently a limited meaning in our Constitution and not the meaning suggested by the respondents.

* * * [T]he appeal by the respondents to democratic principles and the necessity of having absolute amending power to prevent a revolution to buttress their contention is rather fruitless, because if their contention is accepted the very democratic principles, which they appeal to, would disappear and a revolution would also become a possibility.

However, if the meaning I have suggested is accepted a social and economic revolution can gradually take place while preserving the freedom and dignity of every citizen.

For the aforesaid reasons, I am driven to the conclusion that the expression "amendment of this Constitution" in art. 368 means any addition or change in any of the provisions of the Constitution within the broad contours of the Preamble and the Constitution to carry out the objectives in the Preamble and the Directive Principles. Applied to fundamental rights, it would mean that while fundamental rights cannot be abrogated reasonable abridgements of fundamental rights can be effected in the public interest.

It is of course for Parliament to decide whether an amendment is necessary. The Courts will not be concerned with wisdom of the amendment.

* * *

The true position is that every provision of the Constitution can be amended provided in the result the basic foundation and structure of the constitution remains the same. The basic structure may be said to consist of the following features:

(1) Supremacy of the Constitution;

(2) Republican and Democratic form of Government;

(3) Secular Character of the Constitution;

(4) Separation of Powers between the Legislature, the Executive and the Judiciary;

(5) Federal Character of the Constitution.[a]

The above structure is built on the basic foundation, i.e., the dignity and freedom of the individual. This is of supreme importance. This cannot by any form of amendment be destroyed.

* * *

The meaning of the expression "Amendment of the Constitution" does not change when one reads the proviso. If the meaning is the same,

a. Other judges came down with a different list on the basic structure. By some counts the elements of the basic structure exceed 13. See also *Bommai* in Chapter 8.

Art. 368 can only be amended so as not to change its identity completely. Parliament, for instance, could not make the Constitution uncontrolled by changing the prescribed two third majority to simple majority. Similarly it cannot get rid of the true meaning of the expression "Amendment of the Constitution" so as to derive power to abrogate fundamental rights.

* * *

Let us then see if the other part of the article throws any light on the word "amount". The article postulates that in some cases principles may be laid down for determining the amount and these principles may lead to an adequate amount or an inadequate amount. So this shows that the word "amount" here means something to be given in lieu of the property to be acquired but this amount has to and can be worked out by laying down certain principles. These principles must then have a reasonable relationship to the property which is sought to be acquired, if this is so, the amount ultimately arrived at by applying the principles must have some reasonable relationship with the property to be acquired; otherwise the principles of the Act could hardly be principles within the meaning of art. 31(2).

* * * The amount has to be fixed by law but the amount so fixed by law must also be fixed in accordance, with some principles because it could not have been intended that if the amount is fixed by law, the legislature would fix the amount arbitrarily.

* * *

In this connection it must be borne in mind that art. 31(2) is still a fundamental right. Then, what is the change that has been brought about by the amendment? It is no doubt that a change was intended, it seems to me that the change effected is that a person whose property is acquired can no longer claim full compensation or just compensation but he can still claim that the law should lay down principles to determine the amount which he is to get and these principles must have a rational relation to the property sought to be acquired.

* * *

It seems to me that in effect, art. 31C [the provision created by the Constitution Twenty Fifth Amendment] enables States to adopt any policy they like and abrogate arts. 14, 19 and 31 of the Constitution at will. * * * In short, it enables a State Legislature to set up complete totalitarianism in the State. * * *

Parliament equally cannot enable the legislatures to abrogate [fundamental rights].

* * *

Ray, J.

* * * [I]f compensation means market price then the concept of property right in Part III is an absolute right to own and possess property or to receive full price while the concept of property right in Part IV is conditioned by social interest and social justice. There would be an inherent conflict in working out the Directive Principles of Part IV with the guarantee in Part III.

* * *

Social justice will require modification or restriction of rights under Part III. The scheme of the Constitution generally discloses that the principles of social justice are placed above individual rights and whenever or wherever it is considered necessary individual, rights have been subordinated or cut down to give effect to the principles of social justice. Social justice means various concepts, which are evolved in the Directive Principles of the State.

Palekar, J.

* * *

The absolute concepts of Liberty and Equality are very difficult to achieve as goals in the present day organized society. * * * England developed these rules in its day to day Government under the rule of law and does not make a song and dance about them. British rules of India tried to introduce these rules in the governance of this country, * * *. Nobody can deny that when Imperial interests were in jeopardy, these rules of good government were applied with an unequal hand, and when the agitation for self rule grew in strength these rules were thrown aside by the rulers by resorting to repressive laws. It was then that people in this country clamoured for these elementary human rights. * * * Indeed the framers of the constitution took good care not to confer the fundamental rights in absolute terms because that was impractical. Knowing human capacity for distorting and misusing all liberties and freedoms, the framers of the constitution put restrictions on them in the interest of the people and the State thus emphasizing that fundamental rights i.e. rules of civilized government are liable to be altered, if necessary, for the common good and in the public interest.

And yet, as we have seen above, even in U.K. individual liberty as it was understood a generation or two ago is no longer so sacrosanct, especially, in relation to ownership of property. * * * If U.K. had stood staunchly by its Victorian concept of laissez faire and individual liberty, the progress in social and economic justice which it has achieved during the last half a century would have been difficult. Even so, though very much more I advanced than our country, U.K. cannot claim that it has fully achieved social and economic justice for all its citizens. * * * In a country like ours where we have, on the one hand, abject poverty on a very large scale and great concentration of wealth on the other, the advance towards social and economic justice is bound to be retarded if the old concept of individual liberty is to dog our footsteps. In the ultimate analysis, liberty or freedom which are so much praised by the wealthier sections of the community arc the freedom to amass wealth and own property and means of production, which, as we have already seen, our constitution does not sympathize with. If the normal rule is that all rules of civilized government are subject to public interest and the common weal, those rules will have to undergo new adjustments in the implementation of the Directive Principles. A blind adherence to the concept of freedom to own disproportionate wealth will not take us to the important goals of the Preamble, while a just and sympathetic implementation of the Directive Principles has at least the potentiality to take us to those goals, although on the way, a few may suffer some diminution of the unequal freedom they now enjoy. That being the philosophy underlying the Preamble the fundamental rights and the Directive Principles taken together, it will be incorrect to elevate the fundamental rights as essentially an elaboration of the objectives of the Preamble. As a matter of fact a law made for implementing the Directive Principles of Article 39(b) and (c), instead of being contrary to the Preamble, would be in conformity with it because while it may cut down individual liberty of a few, it widens its horizon for the many.

* * * The Preamble read as a whole, therefore, does not contain the implication that in any genuine implementation of the Directive Principles, a fundamental right will not suffer any diminution. Concentration and control of community resources, wealth and means of production in the hands of a few individuals, are, in the eyes of the constitution, an evil which must be eradicated from the social organization, and hence, any fundamental right, to the extent that it fosters this evil, is liable to be abridged or taken away in the interest of the social structure envisaged by the constitution. The scheme of the fundamental rights in Part III itself shows that restrictions on them have been placed to guard against their exercise in an evil way.

FRENCH NATIONALIZATIONS CASE

Constitutional Council (France).
81–132 DC of 16 January 1982.[b]

[*Background*: The Socialist Government elected in May–June 1981 sought to nationalize a number of strategic companies as well as the major banks. In its 1979 *programme commun* with the Communists it was envisaged that these nationalizations would require a constitutional amendment. Since the Socialists were in a minority in the Senate, a *loi* to amend the Constitution could not be passed. In any case, this would have taken some time, and thus impeded progress on implementing the policy. The Government adopted the course of having an ordinary *loi* passed by Parliament, with the National Assembly imposing its will over the Senate. The *loi* was referred to the Conseil constitutionnel by opposition deputies and senators. Among other questions, the issue was raised of whether such a reform could be undertaken within the existing Constitution, or whether an amendment was necessary. The Conseil d'État had advised that an amendment was necessary. The Conseil constitutionnel found that it was not, but it did impose strict limits on the power to nationalize by giving priority to the Declaration of 1789 over the Preamble to the 1946 Constitution.]

DECISION

On the principle of nationalizations

13. Considering that article 2 of the Declaration of the Rights of Man and of the Citizen of 1789 proclaims that 'The ultimate purpose of

b. Reproduced from John Bell, *French Constitutional Law* 273–75, 338–41 (1992).

every political institution is the preservation of the natural and impre-scriptible rights of man. These rights are to liberty, property, security, and resistance to oppression', and that article 17 of the same Declaration also proclaims that 'Property, being an inviolable and sacred right, none can be deprived of it, except when public necessity, legally ascertained, evidently requires it and on condition of a just and prior indemnity';

14. Considering that the French people, by the referendum of 5 May 1946, rejected a draft Constitution that would have preceded the provisions on the institutions of the Republic with a new Declaration of the Rights of Man, including, notably, a statement of principles differing from those proclaimed in 1789 by the above-mentioned articles 2 and 17;

15. Considering that, by contrast, by the referendums of 13 October 1946 and 28 September 1958, the French people have approved texts conferring constitutional value on the principles and rights proclaimed in 1789; that, in fact, the Preamble to the 1946 Constitution 'solemnly reaffirms the rights and liberties of man and of the citizen consecrated by the Declaration of Rights of 1789', and aims simply to complete them by the formulation of 'political, economic, and social principles as partic-ularly necessary for our times'; that, in the terms of the Preamble to the Constitution of 1958, 'the French people solemnly proclaims its attach-ment to the rights of man and to the principles of national sovereignty such as are defined by the Declaration of 1789, confirmed and completed by the Preamble to the 1946 Constitution';

16. Considering that, if, since 1789 until today, the objectives and the conditions for the exercise of the right of property have undergone an evolution characterized both by a significant extension of its sphere of application to particular new areas and by limitations required in the name of the public interest, the same principles proclaimed by the Declaration of the Rights of Man retain full constitutional value both in so far as they concern the fundamental character of the right of proper-ty, whose preservation constitutes one of the purposes of political soci-ety, and which is placed on the same level as liberty, security, and resistance to oppression, and in so far as they concern the safeguards given to the holders of this right and the prerogatives of public authori-ties; that the freedom which, in the terms of article 4 of the Declaration, consists in the power to do anything that does not cause harm to another itself cannot be preserved if arbitrary or abusive restrictions are imposed on the freedom of enterprise;

17. Considering that article 9 of the Preamble to the 1946 Consti-tution provides that: 'Any property or business whose exploitation has or acquires the character of a national public service or a *de facto* monopoly should become the property of the community'; that this provision has neither the purpose nor the effect of rendering inapplicable the princi-ples of the Declaration of 1789 recalled above to the operations of nationalizations;

18. Considering that, if article 34 of the Constitution places within the province of *loi* 'the nationalization of undertakings, and the transfer of undertakings from the public to the private sector', this provision, just like the one confiding to *loi* the determination of the fundamental

principles of the regime for property, does not dispense the legislature, in the exercise of its powers, from respecting the principles and rules of constitutional value that bind all organs of the State;

19. Considering that it appears from the preparatory materials for the *loi* submitted for scrutiny by the Conseil constitutionnel that the legislature intended to justify the nationalizations effected by the said *loi* by claiming that they are necessary to give public authorities the means to deal with the economic crisis, to promote growth, and to combat unemployment, and that they therefore arise from a public necessity within the meaning of article 17;

20. Considering that the legislature's judgment of the necessity of the nationalizations decided upon by the *loi* submitted for scrutiny by the Conseil constitutionnel should not be called into question by the latter, in the absence of any manifest error of evaluation, so long as it is not established that the transfers of property and businesses currently effected would restrict the area of private property and the freedom of enterprise to such an extent as to violate the said provisions of the Declaration of 1789. * * *

      * * *

Unequal treatment

21. Considering that, as far as the nationalization of banks is concerned, article 13 of the *loi* declares first, in paragraph I the general rule according to which the companies covered by the nationalization are identified, as well as the exceptions made to this rule, then, in paragraph II, it draws up a list of the companies nationalized. * * * [The grounds of the complaint were the exclusion of (i) banks with credit of less than 1 milliard francs; (ii) mutualist and co-operative banks; and (iii) banks whose majority capital was held by foreigners, since they infringed equality.]

      * * *

28. Considering that the principle of equality is no less applicable between legal persons as between physical persons, because, legal persons being groupings of physical persons, because, legal persons being groupings of physical persons, breach of the principle of equality between the former would be equivalent to breach of equality between the latter;

29. Considering that the principle of equality does not prevent a *loi* from establishing non-identical rules with respect to categories of persons who are in different situations, but this can only be the case where the non-identity is justified by a difference in situation and is not incompatible with the purpose of the *loi*;

30. Considering that the exclusion of banks with the status of commercial or industrial property companies or the status of discount houses is not contrary to the principle of equality, as certain of the features of the status of these establishments are specific to them;

31. Considering that even if banks whose majority capital belongs directly or indirectly to physical persons not resident in France, or to legal persons not having their registered office in France, have the same

legal status as other banks, the legislature may exclude them from nationalization without breaching the principle of equality, because of the difficulties that nationalizing these banks might cause at an international level, which eventuality would in its view, harm the public interest that the objectives pursued by the *loi* on nationalization would serve;

32. Considering that, by contrast, the exception made for banks whose majority share capital belongs directly or indirectly to companies of a mutualist or co-operative character does breach the principle of equality; that, in fact, it is justified neither by the specific character of their status, nor by the nature of their activity, nor by potential difficulties in applying the *loi* that would work against the public interest goals that the legislature intends to pursue;

33. Considering that, thus, the following provisions of article 13–I of the *loi* submitted for scrutiny by the Conseil constitutionnel must be declared incompatible with the Constitution: 'Banks the majority of whose share capital belongs directly or indirectly to companies of a mutualist or co-operative character' * * *

Compensation

[The method of compensation was to give former shareholders in the nationalized companies some interest-bearing bonds, which could be redeemed after a period of seven and a half years.]

  * * *

43. Considering that, by virtue of the provisions of article 17 of the Declaration of the Rights of Man and of the Citizen, the deprival of a property right for public necessity requires a just and prior indemnity * * *

53. Considering that it is true that, according to the [provisions of the *loi*], the reference to the average stock-market price for the years 1978, 1979, and 1980 only forms 50 per cent of the calculation of the exchange value of the shares, and is complemented as to 25 per cent by reference to the net accounting position, and 25 per cent by reference to ten times the net average profit;

54. Considering that, according to the intentions of the legislature, the appeal to criteria other than the average stock-market price was precisely to correct the imperfections in the reference to the average stock-market value * * *

55. But considering that this goal is unequally achieved by the provisions currently examined; that, in particular, the reference to the net accounting position, excluding the assets of subsidiaries, as well as the reference to the net average profit, excluding the profits of subsidiaries, lead to very different results for the companies in question, determined not by a difference in objective economic and financial facts, but by the diversity of the management techniques and methods of presenting accounts followed by the companies, which, in itself, should have no bearing on the assessment of compensation;

56. Considering that, furthermore, as a necessary consequence, the provisions of the articles currently examined deprive the former share-

holders of the dividends that they would have received for the 1981 financial year, and which are not made up for by the interest that the bonds given in exchange will produce in 1982;

57.   Considering that, overall, as far as the shares of the companies quoted on the stock exchange are concerned, the method of calculating the value of exchange leads to inequalities in treatment, the extent of which is not justified alone by practical considerations of speed and simplicity; that the inequalities of treatment are compounded, in a number of cases, by a substantial underestimate of the said exchange value; that, finally, the refusal to give former shareholders the benefit of dividends relating to the financial year 1981, or to provide them with an equivalent advantage in an appropriate form, removes without justification the compensation to which the former shareholders are entitled;

    * * *

60.   Considering that it follows from what has been said that articles 6, 18, and 32 of the *loi* submitted for scrutiny by the Conseil constitutionnel are incompatible with the requirements of article 17 of the Declaration of the Rights of Man and of the Citizen as far as the just character of the compensation is concerned * * *

Notes and Questions

1.   Liberal constitutions hardly ever prescribed a specific economic order. "[A] constitution is not intended to embody a particular economic theory," said Justice Holmes in *Lochner v. New York*, 198 U.S. 45, 75 (1905). Likewise the German Federal Constitutional Court (GFCC) stated that "[t]he Basic Law guarantees neither the neutrality of the executive or legislative power in economic matters nor a 'social market economy.' * * * The Basic Law's neutrality in economic matters consists merely in the fact that the 'constituent power' has not adopted a specific economic system. This omission enables the legislature to pursue economic policies deemed proper for the circumstances, provided the Basic Law is observed." *Investment Aid I Case*, 4 BVerfGE 7 (1954). Economic policy affecting ownership rights is within the legislative powers of the federation. Do liberal constitutions fail to protect private property as a fundamental value except, perhaps, to the extent of a limited compensation interest? Is private property secondary to other social interests determined in the democratic process? Communist constitutions were very clear about the economic system and property relations they found acceptable. Note that market imperfections and economic and political crises may imperatively require structural intervention of the state (subsidies, nationalization, antitrust) in the operation of the economy. The nature of the economic order presents considerable problems in developing countries, where, as *Kesavananda* indicates, this is a central issue of constitutional contest, given that many governments hold to the belief that only various socialist measures can improve the conditions of their populations and, further, that the social justice provisions enable or even mandate such an economic order.

2.   As Professor Bruce Ackerman has shown in his *Private Property and the Constitution* (1977), "taking" is a concept based on commonly held assumptions regarding fundamental changes in the use and protection of

land. Restrictions on the future use of property, where the value-diminishing change originates in amended laws and other regulations, are not seen as expropriatory takings. Such changes may affect even the content of land ownership. In *Goldblatt v. Hempstead*, 369 U.S. 590 (1962), the U.S. Supreme Court (USSC) found no indication of any diminution of value as a result of changes in a zoning law "to prohibit any excavating below the water table." The GFCC found in the *Groundwater Case*, 58 BVerfGE 300 (1981), that "[b]oth public and private law contribute equally to the determination of the constitutional legal position of the property owner." A new Water Resources Act, which resulted in the restriction of the use of ground water for a gravel pit, was found to be applicable, although the Civil Code provided that the right of the land owner extends to the terrestrial body under the surface. The revocation of the owner's land use rights, which the previous law and the Civil Code considered property, was held constitutional as the owner was granted a generous lead time.

One argument for the low level of protection of property is that it is an artificial creature of law. On the other hand property is important for the free development of the individual. This is the position of the GFCC, as quoted above. Locke wedded property with life and liberty. Human beings could not be autonomous without a guaranteed personal economic basis of their independence and initiative. *Co-determination Case*, 50 BVerfGE 290 (1979).[c] In Germany, "[t]he individual has to accept those limits of his freedom of action which the legislature imposes to cultivate and maintain society." *Investment Aid I Case*, 4 BVerfGE 7 (1954).

Property-related constitutional review is concerned primarily with (a) the constitutionally acceptable grounds of expropriation; (b) the constitutionality of statutorily imposed restrictions on property, resulting in specific obligations of owners and reductions in the value of property; and (c) the extent of statutory restrictions of property rights that amount to regulatory takings, requiring compensation. In specific historical circumstances denationalization or restoration of property results in extensive litigation. This was the case in most countries in transition from communism and in Germany in 1961. *Volkswagen Denationalization Case*, 12 BVerfGE 354 (1961). Sometimes it is also discussed in the constitutional context whether a specific right amounts to property, triggering the level of the property protection.[d] Professor Konrad Hesse, a leading German commentator, argues

c. The German Co-determination Act of 1976 requires employee representation on the supervisory board of any firm with more than 2,000 employees. The Act was unsuccessfully challenged on grounds that it violated ownership rights and the right of occupational freedom, as well as the freedom of economic activity, based on the general freedom of personality rights (Art. 2.)

d. In the German *Civil Servant Case* the issue was whether certain rights (entitlements) created by public law constitute property. (In the event of a financial benefit, expropriation is difficult to imagine as the entitlement to a pension or other recurrent presentations have to be compensated for by a similar monetary service.) Although the Weimar Constitution protected the benefits of civil servants, the 1951 legis-

lation on dislocated civil servants excluded ex-Nazis from certain benefits. The Constitutional Court found that this was not an expropriation, 3 BVerfGE 58 (1953). See Hans W. Baade, *Social Science Evidence and the Federal Constitutional Court of West Germany*, 23 Journal of Politics 421 (1961). In the *Equalization of Maintenance Case*, 53 BVerfGE 257 (1980), property-rights protection was extended to insurance-based rents (annuities), where the rent amounted to an expectation based on statute. Social insurance replaced private insurance. The precondition of the rent expectation is the satisfaction of the individual duty to contribute to the insurance fund. Social and child (youth) support are not part of property-like protected rents, 63 BVerfGE 152 (1983).

that the ownership of specific objects has lost its importance as a guarantee of private existence and the individual shaping of one's life and as a factor in the shaping of the social order. Private ownership, for example, of farmland or a family business, is no longer the foundation of private existence, particularly after two world wars and bouts of wild inflation. Private ownership, in the civil law sense, no longer serves as the foundation of the individual's guarantee of existence and self-government. Now the foundation is grounded in one's work and participation in state-provided social services and welfare services.[e] Should social welfare entitlements receive property-like protection? On what grounds? See welfare rights below.

3. *Public use (public purpose); private beneficiaries.* What amounts to public purpose in the use of eminent domain (expropriation)? Is it the breadth of the class of beneficiaries? In *Pennsylvania Coal* the concern was private transfers of property interests by legislation. The willingness of the public to promise fair compensation was seen to indicate that no such private transfer occurred. In *Midkiff* the public nature of the purpose seems to be abandoned as the beneficiaries of the condemnation are identifiable individuals. What might be wrong with the transfer of property to another person (who might be a much more efficient user)?[f] In Germany, the restriction that serves the common interests of a class of owners, where the affected owner is a member of that class, can satisfy public purpose requirements. Restrictions on specific winegrowers (in regard to new cultivations) were upheld as serving the common interests of the growers. *Vineyard Case,* 21 BVerfGE 150 (1967). The cultivation restrictions were based, in part, on European Community law and were intended to ban all new cultivations for three years, in an attempt to address the Community's vine surplus. The European Court of Justice (ECJ), having reaffirmed that fundamental rights form an "integral" part of Community law, reviewed the constitutional protection to property in the member-states and concluded that:

> some constitutions refer to the obligations arising out of the ownership of property, to its social function, to the subordination of its use to the requirements of the common good, or of social justice. * * * Even if it is not possible to dispute in principle the Community's ability to restrict the exercise of the right to property * * * it is still necessary to examine whether the restrictions * * * in fact correspond to objectives of general interest pursued by the Community or whether, with regard to the aim pursued, they constitute a disproportionate and intolerable interference with the rights of the owner, impinging upon the very substance of the right to property. * * * It is therefore necessary to identify the aim pursued by the disputed regulation and to determine whether there exists a reasonable relationship between the measures provided for in the regulation and the aim pursued by the Community in this case.

> *Hauer v. Land Rheinland–Pfalz,* [1979] E.C.R. 3727, 3746–47. (See Chapter 2.)

The Court found its own test satisfied, particularly because the ban was applied in a nondiscriminatory manner and only temporarily.

---

e. Konrad Hesse, *Verfassungsrecht,* 19. Aufl. 1993. S. 181 Rdnr. 443.

f. This action is sometimes described as a "naked" wealth transfer. See Cass R.

Sunstein, *Naked Preferences and the Constitution,* 84 Colum. L. Rev. 1689 (1984).

4. *Legitimate use restrictions.* In 1922, in *Pennsylvania Coal Co. v. Mahon*, the USSC found the statutory restriction on preestablished use rights unconstitutional. Justice Brandeis, dissenting, found the new law an application of the police power. In *Miller v. Schoene*, 276 U.S. 272 (1928), the Court upheld the Cedar Rust Act of Virginia, which authorized the state entomologist to cut down red cedar trees on citizens' private property to prevent the communication of plant disease to neighboring apple orchards. No compensation was paid. "When forced to such a choice a state does not exceed its constitutional powers by deciding upon the destruction of one class of property in order to save another which, in the judgment of the legislature, is of greater value to the public." *Id.* at 279.

The USSC moved further in the direction of enabling government to impose restrictive burdens on property in *Penn Central Transportation Co. v. New York City*, 438 U.S. 104 (1978). The Court upheld landmark protection, which resulted in restricting development rights and serving aesthetic concerns and was applicable to single owners, saying that "government may execute laws or programs that adversely affect recognized economic values." *Id.* at 124. Will any legislative finding of public interest satisfy the requirements of eminent domain in the U.S.? Will any finding of public interest (including prevention from harming other owners) justify property restrictions so long as they do not amount to taking (or in the German terminology, "the restrictive regulation is not too dense")? Is the Pennsylvania Act discussed in *Pennsylvania Coal* a regulatory taking? In *Keystone Bituminous Coal Association v. DeBenedictis*, 480 U.S. 470 (1987), a 1966 Pennsylvania statute, which was analogous to the Kohler Act, was held constitutional. The Act as applied prohibited mining that caused subsidence damage to human habitation. Fifty percent of the coal beneath such structures was required to be kept in place. The USSC distinguished *Pennsylvania Coal* by finding that the government action in *Keystone* was directed against a "significant threat to the common welfare." *Id.* at 485. The Court found that, contrary to *Pennsylvania Coal*, there was no showing that the mine operators were unable to operate profitably or that their investment expectations were unduly diminished.

What makes a regulation a taking? Is it the extent of the intrusion? See Justice Holmes in *Pennsylvania Coal* above: if the regulation "goes too far" there is a taking—but which intrusions go too far? Is the extent of the intrusion determined in terms of the loss of value (the income not generated)? Is it physical invasion that matters? Is the legitimacy of the state–public interest protected by the regulation decisive? Should the state interest be taken into consideration in qualifying a regulatory restriction as a taking? Is a statutory restriction directly affecting a specific economic activity functionally different from a general restriction serving regulatory interests (a mine-operation rule favoring affected homeowners versus an environmental regulation applicable to all operations affecting the environment)?

5. The French Constitutional Council discussed the regulatory restriction of property rights in the *Eiffel Tower Amendment Case* (on the *Loi modifiant la loi n° 82–652 du 29 juillet 1982 et portant diverses dispositions relatives à la communication audiovisuelle*) (85–198 DC of 13 Dec. 1985). An amendment to a law permitted a national public company to install and use equipment on the superstructures of private buildings. The law aimed in particular at the Eiffel Tower, although it was not singled out by name or size in the Act. The Council ruled that an administrative easement of this

kind are constitutional "insofar as it only imposes a tolerable inconvenience, is not a deprivation of property * * * but a public-interest easement affecting buildings by reason of their height and elevation * * *." The easement amounts to a taking only if property is emptied of all its content or if it affects those occupying the building. Compare *Loretto v. Teleprompter Manhattan CATV Corp.*, 458 U.S. 419 (1982) (roof-top space ordered by city to be made available for installation of television cables found a compensable taking).

6. Article 14(2) of the German Basic Law imposes limits on property by acknowledging that it entails obligations and that it can be used only for the public good. That ownership entails social obligations is an idea dating back to the 1794 Prussian General Law. The GFCC stated in the *Co-determination Case*, 50 BVerfGE 290 (1979),[g] that there are restrictions inherent in the nature of ownership as property owners have "commitments * * * to society in general; and these commitments increase in scope as the relationship between the property in question and its social environment as well as its social function narrows." Further, the use of property should take into consideration the interests of nonowners. Even the USSC has upheld property restrictions in the exercise of nonowners' constitutional rights.[h]

7. In Germany, the interests of the tenant must be considered if an owner wishes to terminate a lease to make his property available for personal use. "The majority of the population not being in the situation to provide a home relying on their own resources * * * [, therefore] the acceptance of an unlimited termination of the lease would disregard the social importance of the home for the affected tenants." *Termination for Personal Use I Case*, 68 BVerfGE 361 (1985). The GFCC had no difficulty in upholding federal laws that limited the increase of rent and the right of owners to terminate rent contracts that would have enabled owners to evict tenants and offer their apartments at market prices. In principle, of course, even if ownership might be subject to far-reaching restrictions, the core of ownership is respected. But beyond this core protection (against takings), owners have social obligations, and their property rights are subject to constitutional limitations, such as the public interest in social housing. Public interest restrictions are subject only to proportionality considerations in Germany. See the *Tenancy and Rent Control Case*, 37 BVerfGE 132 (1974). According to proportionality considerations, termination of a rent contract cannot be constitutionally prohibited where it serves the owner's personal needs; but even here the tenants' interests must be considered, namely, these interests should be balanced against the landlord's housing—not property—interests). For example, to the extent that an owner's personal-and family-use claims reflect "excessive" or disproportionate use, not even his personal-use claims are acceptable grounds for a contract's termination.

g. Compare with the *Democratization of the Public Sector Case* where the French Constitutional Council held constitutional the requirement that workers-directors sit on the board in partly (50 percent or more) state-owned companies, but the appointment by the Minister for Commerce of a director to represent the private shareholders was held unconstitutional as it had the potential to deprive shareholders of their ownership rights (83–162 DC of 19, 20 July 1983) (employee representation in supervising boards found constitutional).

h. *PruneYard Shopping Center v. Robins*, 447 U.S. 74 (1980) (picketers' free speech right allows them to exercise that right on shopping center property; no unreasonable impairment of value or use of property). For additional developments on picketing, see Chapter 2, Subsection C.2.3.c., Note 2.

Termination for Personal Use I Case, 68 BVerfGE 361 (1985); *Termination for Personal Use II Case*, 79 BVerfGE 292 (1989). Note that the GFCC often discusses the owner's interests as simply the interests of one of the parties to a contract where the tenants have quasi-ownership interests that are legitimately protected by legislation, given the importance (in a social state) to provide housing to those in need where there is a shortage. The European Court of Human Rights (ECHR) applies principles of proportionality to ownership control in its "necessary-in-a-democratic-society" analysis. In light of *Mellacher*, might proportionality concerns result in some kind of heightened scrutiny? Should property-restricting public interests be such that only the selected remedies are capable of serving the public interest? Is the *Mellacher* approach offering more protection to private property than the rationality review in the U.S. cases? Note that the ECHR did not find it relevant that no housing shortage existed at the time the additional restrictions in rent controls (reducing rents) were introduced in Austria.

8. *Economic hardship.* Compare the radically different levels of intervention in Austria (*Mellacher*) and in the City of San Jose (*Pennell*). The USSC found the ordinance was acceptable because it required a case-by-case consideration of each request for rent control. The Austrian legislation uses a generally applicable scheme, while San Jose relies on individual determination, following a hearing. The impact on property is very different, too. Is this due to varying perceptions of social justice? Austria is certainly a social welfare state. Do the City of San Jose and the USSC have a different understanding of the public interest than Austrian courts and legislators? What kind of interest is protected in the case of protecting tenants? Why are these cases discussed in terms of ownership rights? Is the legislation protecting the needy, a special interest group, or is it intended to mitigate a specific socioeconomic hardship? Do you agree with the dissenters in *Pennell* that the tenants' hardship was not caused by the landlords and thus they should not be forced to bear the costs of the "solution" to the hardship? Is the San Jose solution justified by *Midkiff*, where a specific group of owners is also singled out to bear the costs of solving a social problem? Are the Hawaiian landowners and the large estate owners different from building owners? Is the radical interference in the contractual relations limiting ownership in Germany and Austria justified by the theory of "social obligations of ownership"?

9. Given the liberal constitutions' lack of clear commitment to any specific economic order, nationalization (i.e., the expropriation of whole industrial sectors where the enterprises become state property) and land reform (where large estates were distributed among peasants without land) may go very far in a market economy. In *Rustom Cavasjee Cooper* it was not the far-reaching Indian nationalization scheme itself but only the lack of adequate compensation and the arbitrary singling out of the named banks that was found unconstitutional. In the French *Nationalizations Case*, the Constitutional Council raised only minor objections about the scheme. Both the Preamble of the 1946 French Constitution and the German Basic Law expressly authorize nationalizations, with the latter allowing for the nationalization of entire economic sectors. The Indian Constitution holds similar provisions.

The most commonly litigated issue in nationalization cases concerns the appropriate level of compensation. Far-reaching nationalization was held to conform to Protocol No. 1 of the European Convention for the Protection of

Human Rights and Fundamental Freedoms (hereafter, European HR Convention), even when the compensation paid was below market prices. See *Lithgow v. United Kingdom*, 8 E.H.R.R. 329 (Judgment of 8 July 1986). In 1997 the British Labor government enacted legislation that nationalized named companies. The value of (unlisted) shares was determined on the basis of "a hypothetical Stock Exchange quotation over a six-month 'Reference Period' in 1973–74." Following negotiations, the actual compensation paid was below the average of the reference period. The ECHR found that a measure depriving a person of his property had to strike a fair balance between the general interests of the community and individual rights. The amount of compensation must be considered in striking such a balance. In the case of a nationalization the compensation might differ from the just compensation applied in other expropriation contexts, given the public interest. (Further, in ECHR cases the member-states have broad discretion.) The Court found the compensation scheme reasonable, concluding that the difference in the various market prices was an ordinary business risk, especially since the compensation formula was established at the outset.

The French Constitutional Council considered that the express authorization of nationalizations must be read in conjunction with the Declaration of 1789, which guarantees that expropriations may occur only in cases of public necessity and when full compensation is paid. In determining when such public necessity exists, the Council has the power to control the legislative branch in matters of nationalization. The constitutional provisions that govern nationalization and privatization do relieve "the legislature, in the exercise of its powers, from respecting the principles and rules of constitutional value that bind all organs of the State." The Council did not agree with the socialist position that nationalization decisions are simply at the discretion of the democratic process under the authorization of the 1946 Preamble. As the *Nationalizations Case* indicates, the Council did not impose strict scrutiny on public necessity as it limited its intervention to cases of manifest error. Interestingly, the Council hinted that in order to turn the Fifth Republic from a "social" state to a "socialist" one, an amendment to the Constitution was needed, because Art. 17 of the 1789 Declaration prevails over the nationalization clause of the Preamble of 1946.

The Indian cases represent a more dramatic conflict, partly because the social problem was more pressing. In India, in order to remedy pressing social injustice, the Congress Party government was ready to go beyond the text of the Constitution as understood by the ISC, especially in regard to compensation. To bypass the Court's objections, the Constitution was amended to free nationalization decisions from judicial review. But the Court, relying on a doctrine of "unconstitutional amendments," limited that effort. At the same time, the Court became an independent force of social change (see below), pushing states to carry out socialistic constitutional policies foreseen in the state policy sections of the Constitution, which were otherwise unenforceable in court. In the Indian case specific constitutional goals of economic and social justice were interpreted as justifying massive nationalizations and other ownership restrictions. "In the early fifties when Parliament was keen to push through radical socio-economic reforms, the judiciary put speed breakers on the way. In the late seventies and early eighties when the court was in a mood to give a fillip to the directive principles, Parliament and the State Legislatures did not take full advantage of the situation. The result is obvious. The directive principles of State policy still remain a distant dream for 'We, the people of India'." Rao, *op. cit.* at 8.

10. Would the European and American considerations regarding the protection of private property make sense in the Indian context, where some nationalizations serve state-development policies in an underdeveloped country while others intend to create social justice?

B. FREEDOM OF ECONOMIC INITIATIVE AND THE POWER TO REGULATE THE ECONOMY

Liberal constitutions were created to protect individual liberty and, at the same time, to create a stable framework for free-market transactions. Increasingly, for reasons related to social and economic stability, the state felt compelled to interfere more with the economy, abandoning its night-watchman role. Such intervention soon came in conflict with entrepreneurship and interfered with the content of contracts, which had been seen as the quintessential domain of liberty in the economy. In the first subsection we discuss the constitutional changes affecting freedom of contract, while the next subsection addresses the regulation of economic activities. Somewhat surprisingly, new possibilities for the protection of individual initiative emerged in constitutional law, notwithstanding the general increase in economic regulation.

B.1. FREEDOM OF CONTRACT

The principle of freedom of contract is not found in constitutions. Constitutions refer to contracts in terms of undertaking budgetary obligations or in regard to regulatory powers of one or another state body. Agreements are mentioned in the context of the binding force of collective contracts in labor law. The "contract clause" of the U.S. Constitution is about the impairment of existing contracts and was inserted because of a special crisis due to debt relief, one of the factors leading to the Philadelphia Convention. " 'The sober people of America' were convinced that some 'thorough reform' was needed which would 'inspire a general prudence and industry, and give a regular course to the business of society.' The Federalist, No. 44." See *Blaisdell* at 236 (below). Nevertheless, in the liberal economies of the nineteenth century, contractual freedom was uncontested, though there were some statutory limits dictated by the needs of public order. Such regulations were generally held to be unproblematic uses of the police power. Increased legislative intervention in the name of social protection, especially in labor contracts, led the USSC to intervene. In the name of the due process clause, which protects liberty (contractual freedom being a liberty), the USSC engaged in a substantive review of economic legislation affecting contractual freedom. The approach, exemplified by *Lochner*, was seen as extreme judicial activism. The position became politically untenable at the time of the Great Depression, when people expected the government to act quickly and aggressively to remedy the ailing economy. The result was an extreme judicial deference to economic legislation that, with some recent exceptions, lasts to this day, as *Williamson* exemplifies.

LOCHNER v. NEW YORK

Supreme Court (United States).
198 U.S. 45 (1905).

Mr. Justice Peckham delivered the opinion of the Court.

The indictment * * * charged that the plaintiff in error violated * * * the labor law of the state of New York, [1897] in that he wrongfully and unlawfully required and permitted an employé working for him to work more than sixty hours in one week. * * * The employee may desire to earn the extra money, which would arise from his working more than the prescribed time, but this statute forbids the employer from permitting the employé to earn it.

The statute necessarily interferes with the right of contract between the employer and employees, concerning the number of hours in which the latter may labor in the bakery of the employer. The general right to make a contract in relation to his business is part of the liberty of the individual protected by the 14th Amendment of the Federal Constitution. Under that provision no state can deprive any person of life, liberty, or property without due process of law. The right to purchase or to sell labor is part of the liberty protected by this amendment, unless there are circumstances, which exclude the right. There are, however, certain powers, existing in the sovereignty of each state in the Union, somewhat vaguely termed police powers, the exact description and limitation of which have not been attempted by the courts. Those powers, broadly stated, and without, at present, any attempt at a more specific limitation, relate to the safety, health, morals, and general welfare of the public. Both property and liberty are held on such reasonable conditions as may be imposed by the governing power of the state in the exercise of those powers, and with such conditions the 14th Amendment was not designed to interfere.

* * *

[A] state law has been upheld by this court [in] *Holden v. Hardy*, 169 U.S. 366. A provision in the act of the legislature of Utah was there under consideration, the act limiting the employment of workmen in all underground mines or workings, to eight hours per day, 'except in cases of emergency, where life or property is in imminent danger.' * * * It was held that the kind of employment, mining, smelting, etc., and the character of the employees in such kinds of labor, were such as to make it reasonable and proper for the state to interfere. "* * * This law applies only to the classes subjected by their employment to the peculiar conditions and effects attending underground mining * * *."

* * * There is nothing in *Holden v. Hardy* which covers the case now before us.

* * *

It must, of course, be conceded that there is a limit to the valid exercise of the police power by the state. * * * In every case that comes before this court, therefore, where legislation of this character is concerned, and where the protection of the Federal Constitution is sought, the question necessarily arises: Is this a fair, reasonable, and appropriate exercise of the police power of the state, or is it an unreasonable, unnecessary, and arbitrary interference with the right of the individual to his personal liberty * * *.

This is not a question of substituting the judgment of the court for that of the legislature. If the act be within the power of the state it is valid, although the judgment of the court might be totally opposed to the enactment of such a law. But the question would still remain: Is it within the police power of the state? And that question must be answered by the court.

The question whether this act is valid as a labor law, pure and simple, may be dismissed in a few words. There is no reasonable ground for interfering with the liberty of person or the right of free contract, by determining the hours of labor, in the occupation of a baker. There is no contention that bakers as a class are not equal in intelligence and capacity to men in other trades or manual occupations, or that they are not able to assert their rights and care for themselves without the protecting arm of the state, interfering with their independence of judgment and of action. They are in no sense wards of the state. * * * Clean and wholesome bread does not depend upon whether the baker works but ten hours per day or only sixty hours a week. The limitation of the hours of labor does not come within the police power on that ground.

* * * The mere assertion that the subject relates, though but in a remote degree, to the public health, does not necessarily render the enactment valid. The act must have a more direct relation, as a means to an end, and the end itself must be appropriate and legitimate, before an act can be held to be valid which interferes with the general right of an individual to be free in his person and in his power to contract in relation to his own labor.

* * * Some occupations are more healthy than others, but we think there are none which might not come under the power of the legislature to supervise and control the hours of working therein, if the mere fact that the occupation is not absolutely and perfectly healthy is to confer that right upon the legislative department of the government.

     * * *

Mr. Justice Harlan (with whom Mr. Justice White and Mr. Justice Day concurred) dissenting.

[L]iberty of contract is subject to such regulations as the state may reasonably prescribe for the common good and the well-being of society, what are the conditions under which the judiciary may declare such regulations to be in excess of legislative authority and void? * * * In *Jacobson v. Massachusetts*, 197 U.S. 11, 25, we said that the power of the courts to review legislative action in respect of a matter affecting the general welfare exists *only* 'when that which the legislature has done comes within the rule that, if a statute purporting to have been enacted to protect the public health, the public morals, or the public safety has no real or substantial relation to those objects, or is, beyond all question, a plain, palpable invasion of rights secured by the fundamental law,'—citing *Mugler v. Kansas*, 123 U.S. 623, 661. * * *

* * * the state is not amenable to the judiciary, in respect of its legislative enactments, unless such enactments are plainly, palpably, beyond all question, inconsistent with the Constitution * * *. We cannot say that the state has acted without reason, nor ought we to proceed upon the theory that its action is a mere sham. * * *

Mr. Justice Holmes dissenting.

* * *

This case is decided upon an economic theory, which a large part of the country does not entertain. * * * It is settled by various decisions of this court that state constitutions and state laws may regulate life in many ways which we as legislators might think as injudicious, or if you like as tyrannical, as this, and which, equally with this, interfere with the liberty to contract. * * * But a constitution is not intended to embody a particular economic theory, whether of paternalism and the organic relation of the citizen to the state or of *laissez faire*. It is made for people of fundamentally differing views, and the accident of our finding certain opinions natural and familiar, or novel, and even shocking, ought not to conclude our judgment upon the question whether statutes embodying them conflict with the Constitution of the United States.

General propositions do not decide concrete cases. The decision will depend on a judgment or intuition more subtle than any articulate major premise. But I think that the proposition just stated, if it is accepted, will carry us far toward the end. Every opinion tends to become a law. I think that the word 'liberty,' in the 14th Amendment, is perverted when it is held to prevent the natural outcome of a dominant opinion, unless it can be said that a rational and fair man necessarily would admit that the statute proposed would infringe fundamental principles as they have been understood by the traditions of our people and our law. It does not need research to show that no such sweeping condemnation can be passed upon the statute before us. A reasonable man might think it a proper measure on the score of health. * * *

NEBBIA v. NEW YORK

Supreme Court (United States).
291 U.S. 502 (1934).

Mr. Justice Roberts delivered the opinion of the Court.

The Legislature of New York established by chapter 158 of the Laws of 1933, a Milk Control Board with power, among other things to 'fix minimum and maximum * * * retail prices to be charged by * * * stores to consumers for consumption off the premises where sold.' [Consol.

Laws, c. 69 s 312]. * * * [Nebbia, the proprietor of a grocery store in Rochester, sold milk for less than the fixed price and was convicted].

The question for decision is whether the Federal Constitution prohibits a state from so fixing the selling price of milk. We first inquire as to the occasion for the legislation and its history.

During 1932 the prices received by farmers for milk were much below the cost of production. The decline in prices during 1931 and 1932 was much greater than that of prices generally. The situation of the families of dairy producers had become desperate and called for state aid similar to that afforded the unemployed, if conditions should not improve [291 U.S. 502, 516].

* * *

Milk is an essential item of diet. * * *

* * *

Curtailment or destruction of the dairy industry would cause a serious economic loss to the people of the state.

* * *

A satisfactory stabilization of prices for fluid milk requires that the burden of surplus milk be shared equally by all producers and all distributors in the milk shed. * * *

* * *

Under our form of government the use of property and the making of contracts are normally matters of private and not of public concern. The general rule is that both shall be free of governmental interference. But neither property rights nor contract rights are absolute; for government cannot exist if the citizen may at will use his property to the detriment of his fellows, or exercise his freedom of contract to work them harm. Equally fundamental with the private right is that of the public to regulate it in the common interest. As Chief Justice Marshall said, speaking specifically of inspection laws, such laws form 'a portion of that immense mass of legislation which embraces everything within the territory of a state, * * * all which can be most advantageously exercised by the states themselves. Inspection laws, quarantine laws, health laws of every description, as well as laws for regulating the internal commerce of a state, * * * are component parts of this mass.'

* * *

The court has repeatedly sustained curtailment of enjoyment of private property, in the public interest. The owner's rights may be subordinated to the needs of other private owners whose pursuits are vital to the paramount interests of the community. * * *

* * * The Constitution does not secure to any one liberty to conduct his business in such fashion as to inflict injury upon the public at large, or upon any substantial group of the people. Price control, like any other form of regulation, is unconstitutional only if arbitrary, discriminatory, or demonstrably irrelevant to the policy the Legislature is free to adopt, and hence an unnecessary and unwarranted interference with individual liberty.

* * *

Separate opinion of Mr. Justice McReynolds.

* * * There was an oversupply of an excellent article [milk]. The affirmation is 'that milk has been selling too cheaply * * * and has thus created a temporary emergency; this emergency is remedied by making the sale of milk at a low price a crime.'

The XIV Amendment wholly disempowered the several states to 'deprive any person of life, liberty, or property, without due process of law.' The assurance of each of these things is the same. If now liberty or property may be struck down because of difficult circumstances, we must expect that hereafter every right must yield to the voice of an impatient majority when stirred by distressful exigency. * * *

Regulation to prevent recognized evils in business has long been upheld as permissible legislative action. But fixation of the price at which "A," engaged in an ordinary business, may sell, in order to enable "B," a producer, to improve his condition, has not been regarded as within legislative power. This is not regulation, but management, control, dictation—it amounts to the deprivation of the fundamental right which one has to conduct his own affairs honestly and along customary lines. * * * And if it be now ruled that one dedicates his property to public use whenever he embarks on an enterprise which the Legislature may think it desirable to bring under control, this is but to declare that rights guaranteed by the Constitution exist only so long as supposed public interest does not require their extinction. To adopt such a view, of course, would put an end to liberty under the Constitution.

* * *

Here, we find direct interference with guaranteed rights defended upon the ground that the purpose was to promote the public welfare by increasing milk prices at the farm. Unless we can affirm that the end proposed is proper and the means adopted have reasonable relation to it, this action is unjustifiable.

* * *

Not only does the statute interfere arbitrarily with the rights of the little grocer to conduct his business according to standards long accepted—complete destruction may follow; but it takes away the liberty of 12,000,000 consumers to buy a necessity of life in an open market. It imposes direct and arbitrary burdens upon those already seriously impoverished with the alleged immediate design of affording special benefits to others. * * *

HOME BUILDING & LOAN ASS'N v. BLAISDELL

Supreme Court (United States).
290 U.S. 398 (1934).

[In 1933, Minnesota, reacting to the economic hardship of the Great Depression, passed a mortgage-moratorium law to provide relief for homeowners threatened with foreclosure. The law declared an emergency and said that, during the emergency period, courts could postpone mortgage sales and redemption periods. Its provisions were to apply "only during the continuance of the emergency and in no event beyond May 1, 1935."]

Mr. Chief Justice Hughes delivered the opinion of the Court.

* * *

In determining whether the provision for this temporary and conditional relief exceeds the power of the state by reason of the clause in the Federal Constitution prohibiting impairment of the obligations of contracts, we must consider the relation of emergency to constitutional power, the historical setting of the contract clause, the development of the jurisprudence of this Court in the construction of that clause, and the principles of construction which we may consider to be established.

Emergency does not create power. Emergency does not increase granted power or remove or diminish the restrictions imposed upon power granted or reserved. The Constitution was adopted in a period of grave emergency. Its grants of power to the Federal Government and its limitations of the power of the States were determined in the light of emergency, and they are not altered by emergency. * * *

The widespread distress following the revolutionary period, and the plight of debtors, had called forth in the States an ignoble array of legislative schemes for the defeat of creditors and the invasion of contractual obligations. * * * The occasion and general purpose of the contract clause are summed up in the terse statement of Chief Justice Marshall in [Ogden]:

"* * * [T]his mischief had become so great, so alarming, as not only to impair commercial intercourse, and threaten the existence of credit, but to sap the morals of the people, and destroy the sanctity of private faith. To guard against the continuance of the evil, was an object of deep interest with all the truly wise, as well as the virtuous, of this great community, and was one of the important benefits expected from a reform of the government." * * *

* * *

[The] constitutional provision [is] qualified by the measure of control which the state [retains] to safeguard the vital interests of its people. * * * Not only are existing laws read into contracts in order to fix obligations as between the parties, but the reservation of essential attributes of sovereign power is also read into contracts as a postulate of the legal order. The policy of protecting contracts against impairment presupposes the maintenance of a government by virtue of which contractual relations are worth while—a government which retains adequate authority to secure the peace and good order of society. This principle of harmonizing the constitutional prohibition with the necessary residuum of state power has had progressive recognition in the decisions of this Court.

* * *

[There] has been a growing appreciation of public needs and of the necessity of finding ground for a rational compromise between individual rights and public welfare. The settlement and consequent contraction of the public domain, the pressure of a constantly increasing density of population, the interrelation of the activities of our people and the complexity of our economic interests, have inevitably led to an increased use of the organization of society in order to protect the very bases of individual opportunity. Where, in earlier days, it was thought that only the concerns of individuals or of classes were involved, and that those of the state itself were touched only remotely, it has later been found that the fundamental interests of the state are directly affected; and that the question is no longer merely that of one party to a contract as against another, but of the use of reasonable means to safeguard the economic structure upon which the good of all depends.

It is no answer to say that this public need was not apprehended a century ago, or to insist that what the provision of the Constitution meant to the vision of that day it must mean to the vision of our time. If by the statement that what the Constitution meant at the time of its adoption it means today, it is intended to say that the great clauses of the Constitution must be confined to the interpretation which the framers, with the conditions and outlook of their time, would have placed upon them, the statement carries its own refutation. It was to guard against such a narrow conception that Chief Justice Marshall uttered the memorable warning: 'We must never forget, that it is a constitution we are expounding' [*McCulloch v. Maryland*] 'a constitution intended to endure for ages to come, and, consequently, to be adapted to the various crises of human affairs.' When we are dealing with the words of the Constitution * * * , 'we must realize that they have called into life a being the development of which could not have been foreseen completely by the most gifted of its begetters. * * * The case before us must be considered in the light of our whole experience and not merely in that of what was said a hundred years ago.'

* * * The vast body of law, which has been developed, was unknown to the fathers, but it is believed to have preserved the essential content and the spirit of the Constitution. With a growing recognition of public needs and the relation of individual right to public security, the court has sought to prevent the perversion of the clause through its use as an instrument to throttle the capacity of the states to protect their fundamental interests. This development is a growth from the seeds, which the fathers planted. * * *

Applying the criteria established by our decisions, we conclude:

1. An emergency existed in Minnesota, which furnished a proper occasion for the exercise of the reserved power of the state to protect the vital interests of the community. [The] finding of the Legislature and state court has support in the facts of which we take judicial notice. * * *

2. The legislation was addressed to a legitimate end; that is, the legislation was not for the mere advantage of particular individuals but for the protection of a basic interest of society.

3. In view of the nature of the contracts in question—mortgages of unquestionable validity—the relief afforded and justified by the emergency, in order not to contravene the constitutional provision, could only be of a character appropriate to that emergency, and could be granted only upon reasonable conditions.

4. The conditions upon which the period of redemption is extended do not appear to be unreasonable. * * *

5. The legislation is temporary in operation. It is limited to the exigency, which called it forth. * * *

We are of the opinion that the Minnesota statute as here applied does not violate the contract clause of the Federal Constitution. Whether the legislation is wise or unwise as a matter of policy is a question with which we are not concerned. * * *

* * *

The judgment of the Supreme Court of Minnesota [upholding the law] is affirmed.

Mr. Justice Sutherland, dissenting.

* * *

A provision of the Constitution, it is hardly necessary to say, does not admit of two distinctly opposite interpretations. It does not mean one thing at one time and an entirely different thing at another time. If the contract impairment clause, when framed and adopted, meant that the terms of a contract for the payment of money could not be altered [by] a state statute enacted for the relief of hardly pressed debtors to the end and with the effect of postponing payment or enforcement during and because of an economic or financial emergency, it is but to state the obvious to say that it means the same now * * *

* * *

The defense of the Minnesota law is made upon grounds, which were discountenanced by the makers of the Constitution. * * *

* * * [The Minnesota] statute, therefore, is not merely a modification of the remedy; it effects a material and injurious change in the obligation. * * *

* * * If the provisions of the Constitution be not upheld when they pinch as well as when they comfort, they may as well be abandoned. Being unable to reach any other conclusion than that the Minnesota statute infringes the constitutional restriction under review, I have no choice but to say so.

[Justices Van Devanter, McReynolds, and Butler joined in this dissent.]

SHELLEY v. KRAEMER

Supreme Court (United States).
334 U.S. 1 (1948).

Mr. Chief Justice Vinson delivered the opinion of the Court.

These cases present for our consideration questions relating to the validity of court enforcement of private agreements, generally described as restrictive covenants, which have as their purpose the exclusion of persons of designated race or color from the Basic constitutional issues of obvious importance have been raised. [One of the sets of the covenants signed in 1911 by the majority of owners of property in a given neighborhood restricted the sale of property to non-Caucasians for a period of 50 years. Shelley, who was Negro, bought a house from among those who were subject to the covenant. Respondents, as owners of other property subject to the terms of the restrictive covenant, brought suit for reinvestment of title in the immediate grantor. The Missouri Supreme Court granted the relief.]

* * *

Petitioners * * * urge that they have been denied the equal protection of the laws, deprived of property without due process of law, and have been denied privileges and immunities of citizens of the United States. We pass to a consideration of those issues.

* * *

* * * The restrictions of these agreements, rather, are directed toward a designated class of persons and seek to determine who may and who may not own or make use of the properties for residential purposes. The excluded class is defined wholly in terms of race or color.; "simply that and nothing more."

It cannot be doubted that among the civil rights intended to be protected from discriminatory state action by the Fourteenth Amendment are the rights to acquire, enjoy, own and dispose of property. * * *

It is likewise clear that restrictions on the right of occupancy of the sort sought to be created by the private agreements in these cases could not be squared with the requirements of the Fourteenth Amendment if imposed by state statute or local ordinance.

* * *

But the present cases * * * do not involve action by state legislatures or city councils. Here the particular patterns of discrimination and the areas in which the restrictions are to operate, are determined, in the first instance, by the terms of agreements among private individuals. Participation of the State consists in the enforcement of the restrictions so defined.

* * *

* * * These are cases in which the purposes of the agreements were secured only by judicial enforcement by state courts of the restrictive terms of the agreements.

II

That the action of state courts and of judicial officers in their official capacities is to be regarded as action of the State within the meaning of the Fourteenth Amendment, is a proposition which has long been established by decisions of this Court. * * *

III

* * *

We have no doubt that there has been state action in these cases in the full and complete sense of the phrase. * * * It is clear that but for the active intervention of the state courts, supported by the full panoply of state power, petitioners would have been free to occupy the properties in question without restraint.

These are not cases, as has been suggested, in which the States have merely abstained from action, leaving private individuals free to impose such discriminations as they see fit. Rather, these are cases in which the States have made available to such individuals the full coercive power of government to deny to petitioners, on the grounds of race or color, the enjoyment of property rights in premises which petitioners are willing and financially able to acquire and which the grantors are willing to sell.

* * *

We hold that in granting judicial enforcement of the restrictive agreements in these cases, the States have denied petitioners the equal protection of the laws and that, therefore, the action of the state courts cannot stand. We have noted that freedom from discrimination by the States in the enjoyment of property rights was among the basic objectives sought to be effectuated by the framers of the Fourteenth Amendment. That such discrimination has occurred in these cases is clear.

* * * The rights created by the first section of the Fourteenth Amendment are, by its terms, guaranteed to the individual. The rights established are personal rights.

* * *

Mr. Justice Reed, Mr. Justice Jackson, and Mr. Justice Rutledge took no part in the consideration or decision of these cases.

Notes and Questions

1. In the U.S., substantive due process analysis was used to protect individual economic liberties, primarily freedom of contract. Such review, as applied in *Lochner*, allows a court to closely scrutinize both the legislative ends and means employed in legislation. The relationship had to be "real and substantial." Many laws designating specific working hours and wages of special groups satisfied this requirement. The measures, however, had to protect the general welfare, except where the protected group was unable to protect itself (women, children). As to the means, the *Lochner* majority was skeptical about the findings of experts who advocated workplace reform measures. The Court sometimes required that a measure affecting liberty (contract) or property should be the only option available for that purpose.

As noted above, the departure from substantive due process analysis occurred during the Great Depression. Congress sought to correct some of the imbalances of the market, including remedies for improving employment conditions. The first case where the majority upheld legislation that curtailed freedom of contract was *West Coast Hotel Co. v. Parrish,* 300 U.S. 379 (1937), which upheld a general minimum wage law in the District of Columbia. Justice O'Connor recently discussed the process:

> * * * [*West Coast Hotel*] signaled the demise of *Lochner* by overruling *Adkins.*[i] In the meantime, the Depression had come and, with it, the lesson that seemed unmistakable to most people by 1937, that the interpretation of contractual freedom protected in *Adkins* rested on fundamentally false factual assumptions about the capacity of a relatively unregulated market to satisfy minimal levels of human welfare. * * * The facts upon which the earlier case had premised a constitutional resolution of social controversy had proved to be untrue, and history's demonstration of their untruth not only justified, but required the new choice of constitutional principle that *West Coast Hotel* announced. Of course, it was true that the Court lost something by its misperception, or its lack of prescience, and the Court-packing crisis only magnified the loss; but the clear demonstration that the facts of economic life were different from those previously assumed warranted the repudiation of the old law.
>
> * * *
>
> *West Coast Hotel* and *Brown* [*v. Board of Education*] each rested on facts, or an understanding of facts, changed from those which furnished the claimed justifications for the earlier constitutional resolutions. * * * In constitutional adjudication as elsewhere in life, changed circumstances may impose new obligations, and the thoughtful part of the Nation could accept each decision to overrule a prior case as a response to the Court's constitutional duty.
>
> * * * To overrule prior law for no other reason than that would run counter to the view repeated in our cases, that a decision to overrule should rest on some special reason over and above the belief that a prior case was wrongly decided.

Planned Parenthood of Southeastern Pa. v. Casey, 505 U.S. 833, 861–64 (1992).

2. *The impact of the constitution on private relations.* Economic relations cannot be fully immune to the prevailing value system of the political order. But there are considerable differences in the extent to which constitutions may directly (or even indirectly) affect private economic and social relations. After all, certain constitutions were specifically intended to determine the way government works, leaving the nonpublic sphere, in principle, to private arrangements. Intrusion into the private sphere would have been a violation of private liberty.

The problem of defining the scope of the restrictions which the Federal Constitution imposes upon exertions of power by the States has given rise to many of the most persistent and fundamental issues which this

---

i. *Adkins v. Children's Hosp.*, 261 U.S. 525 (1923) (striking down minimal-wage laws for women).

Court has been called upon to consider. That problem was foremost in the minds of the framers of the Constitution, and since that early day, has arisen in a multitude of forms. The task of determining whether the action of a State offends constitutional provisions is one, which may not be undertaken lightly. Where, however, it is clear that the action of the State violates the terms of the fundamental charter, it is the obligation of this Court so to declare.

Shelley v. Kraemer, 334 U.S. at 22–23 (1948).

3. Non–Americans find it somewhat artificial that the USSC, in the absence of a governing statute, must find state action in order to apply the Constitution to private relations. The differences between the U.S. and other modern welfare states are considerable. In Germany, for example, constitutional doctrine requires the state to take positive action to ensure that citizens enjoy their constitutional rights. (On the "intermediate" impact of the German Basic Law on private relations, see *Lüth*, 7 BVerfGE 198 (1958), in Chapter 7). The practical differences might be less than the differences in principle as the U.S. federal government and the states through legislation, at least to some extent, provide for the enjoyment of certain fundamental and other (primarily welfare) rights without a constitutionally mandated obligation.

4. Outside the U.S., economic legislation in general and labor legislation in particular are more frequently reviewed under the constitution. In 1998, in an effort to reduce unemployment, the Socialist government in France enacted the "Law of orientation and initiative to reduce working hours of employees" of 19 May 1998. The law offered a framework for industry to carry out the overall reduction primarily through negotiated settlements. A plaintiff complained, among other things, that the freedom of entrepreneurship and the liberty of employers and employees were violated. Such rights follow from Art. 4 of the 1789 Declaration, which is a constituent part of the 1958 Constitution. The Constitutional Council found in its decision, 98–401 DC of 10 June 1998, that the liberty of Art. 4, which "consists in the power of doing whatever does not injure another," is subject to limits justified by the general interest and constitutional exigencies, as long as such limitations do not deprive the right of its very nature. The legislature possessed the competence to legislate on the fundamental principles of labor law, which permit the imposition of rules that, in line with recital Five of the Preamble of the 1946 Constitution, provide for the right of all to have employment. The law satisfied these requirements, and it did not constitute an attack on the existing contracts that was of such gravity as to manifestly disregard the liberty of Art. 4. The Council did not explain what would amount to such manifest disregard under the circumstances.

For additional review of legislation affecting existing contracts, see the German and Austrian rent control cases. *Termination for Personal Use I Case*, 68 BVerfGE 361 (1985); *Mellacher v. Austria* above. As there is no special provision on contracts, the German courts approach the constitutional problem from the perspective of property rights, where expectations and material interests are considered as property or quasi property. The Austrian Supreme Court, on the other hand, refused to discuss contractual interests in terms of constitutionally protected values: "There is no provision in the [Austrian] Federal Constitution which in principle prevents ordinary legislation from interfering with lawfully acquired rights."

B.2. CHOICE AND PRACTICE OF OCCUPATION

The complexities of modern economies resulted in an increasingly dense web of bureaucratic regulations, formally justified by the modern state's role as the promoter of the general welfare. In practice, however, economic regulation is often dictated by special interest groups. The results may be unfair, discriminatory, or simply limiting of economic initiative and liberty because of, for instance, barriers to entry. Paralyzed by the *Lochner* experience, the U.S. acquiesces in all nondiscriminatory economic legislation through a "rational basis" test (see *Williamson v. Lee Optical*, 348 U.S. 483, below), but most other jurisdictions developed a constitutional right of choice of occupation that is broadly interpreted.

Depending on the nature of the occupational choice or practice, courts offer various levels of protection. The judicial tests include deferential rationality tests, proportionality analysis, and compelling state interest standards.

PHARMACY CASE

Federal Constitutional Court (Germany).
7 BVerfGE 377 (1958).

[Bavaria's Apothecary Act provided for the issuance of additional licenses to new pharmacies but only if they were commercially viable and would cause no economic harm to nearby competitors. In 1955, Bavaria invoked this statute to deny a license to a person who had recently migrated from East Germany, where he had been a licensed pharmacist.]

Judgement of the First Senate: * * *

Section 3 (1) of the Bavarian Apothecary Act of 16 June 1952, as amended on 10 December, 1955, is void. * * *

B. IV. Whether Article 3 (1) of the Apothecary Act is consistent with Article 12 (1) requires a discussion of the fundamental propositions concerning the importance of the right to choose a trade.

1. Article 12 (1) protects the citizen's freedom in an area of particular importance to a modern society based on the division of labor. Every individual has the right to take up any activity which he believes himself prepared to undertake as a "profession"—that is, to make [the activity] the very basis of his life * * *

[Article 12 (1)] guarantees the individual more than just the freedom to engage independently in a trade. To be sure, the basic right aims at the protection of economically meaningful work but it views work as a "vocation" (*Beruf*). Work in this sense is seen in terms of its relationship to the human personality as a whole: It is a relationship that shapes and completes the individual over a lifetime of devoted activity; it is the foundation of a person's existence, through which that person simultaneously contributes to the total social product. * * *

2. * * * The idea of a "profession" within the meaning of the Basic Law embraces not only those occupations identified by custom or by law, but also freely chosen activities that do not correspond to the legal or traditional conception of a trade or profession.

b) The text of Article 12 (1), when viewed against the backdrop of the real significance of the basic right, suggests that the legislature may regulate the practice but not the choice of an occupation. But this cannot be the [true] meaning of the provision, for the concepts of "choice" and "practice" are not mutually exclusive. * * * Both concepts represent a complex unity and, although viewed from different angles, are incorporated into the notion of "vocational activity". * * *

* * * [A] legal regulation purporting primarily to limit the practice of an occupation would survive constitutional analysis even if it has an indirect effect on the choice of an occupation. This situation occurs primarily where the choice of an occupation is largely dependent upon admission standards. * * *

In any case, Article 12 (1) is a unified basic right in the sense that the reservation clause of sentence 2 ["The practice of trades, occupations, and professions may be regulated by or pursuant to a law."] grants the legislature the power to make regulations affecting either the choice or the exercise of an occupation. But this does not mean that the legislature is empowered to regulate each of these aspects of vocational activity to the same degree. For it is clear from the text of Article 12 (1) that occupational choice is to remain "free" while the practice of an occupation may be regulated. This language does not permit an interpretation that assumes an equal degree of legislative control over each of these "aspects". The more legislation affects the choice a profession, the more limited is the regulatory power. This interpretation accords with the basic concepts of Constitution and the image of man founded on those concepts. The choice of an occupation is an act of self-determination, of the free will of the individual; it must be protected as much as possible from state encroachment. In practicing an occupation, however, the individual immediately affects the life of society; this aspect of [vocational activity] is subject to regulation in the interest of others and of society.

The legislature is thus empowered to make regulations affecting either the choice or the practice of a profession. The more a regulatory power is directed to the choice of a profession, the narrower are its limits; the more it is directed to the practice of a profession, the broader are its limits. * * *

c) * * * The general principles governing the regulation of vocational activity may be summarized as follows: The practice of an occupation may be restricted by reasonable regulations predicted on considerations of the common good. The freedom to choose an occupation, however, may be restricted only for the sake of a compelling public interest; that is, if, after careful deliberation, the legislature determines that a common interest must be protected, then it may impose restrictions in order to protect that interest—but only to the extent that the protection cannot be accomplished by a lesser restriction on freedom of choice. In the event that an encroachment on freedom of occupational choice is unavoidable, lawmakers must always employ the regulative means least restrictive of the basic right.

A graduated scale of possible restrictions governs the legislature's authority to regulate vocational activity:

Lawmakers are freest when they regulate the practice of an occupation. In regulating such practice, they may broadly consider calculations of utility. Lawmakers may impose limitations on the right to practice a profession so as to prevent detriment and danger to the general public; they may also do so to promote an occupation for the purpose of achieving greater total performance within society. Here the Constitution protects the individual only against excessively onerous and unreasonable encroachments. Apart from these exceptions, such restrictions on the freedom of occupation do not greatly affect the citizen since he already has an occupation inviolate.

On the other hand, if [the legislature] conditions the right to take up an occupational activity on the fulfillment of certain requirements, thus impinging on the choice of an occupation, then regulations for the public good are legitimate only when such action is absolutely necessary to protect particularly important community interests; in all such cases the restrictive measures selected must entail the least possible interference. But the nature of a regulation prescribing conditions for admission to a profession depends on whether the legislation deals with individual conditions, such as those of educational background and training, or with objective conditions irrelevant to one's personal qualifications and over which one exercises no control.

The regulation of individual (subjective) conditions [for admission to an occupation] is a legitimate exercise of legislative authority. Only those applicants possessing the proper qualifications, determined in accordance with preestablished formal criteria, will be admitted to a trade or profession. * * * Such limits are reasonable because applicants for various professions know well in advance of their choice whether or not they have the proper qualifications. The principle of proportionality governs here; any requirements laid down must bare a reasonable relationship to the end pursued [i.e., the safe and orderly practice of a profession].

The situation is different, however, when the state proceeds to control the objective conditions of admission. Here the matter is simply out of the individual's hands. Such restrictions contradict the spirit and purpose of the basic right because even one whom the state has permitted to make his choice by meeting the requirements of admission may nevertheless be barred from an occupation. This encroachment on a person's freedom cuts all the more deeply the longer he has had to attend school and the more specialized his training. * * * In this case it appears that [the legislature] intends to impose the restriction on admission in order to protect practicing pharmacists from further competition, a motive that, by general consensus, can never justify a restriction on the freedom to choose an occupation. This crude and most radical means of barring professionally and presumably morally qualified applicants from their chosen profession thus violates the individual's right to choose an occupation, quite apart from any possible conflict with the principle of equality. Limits upon the objective conditions of admission are permissible on very narrowly defined terms. Generally speaking, [the legislature] may impose them only when they are needed for the prevention of demonstrable or highly probable dangers to community interests of overriding importance. * * *

V.   * * * Public health is doubtless an important community interest [whose] protection may justify encroachments on the freedom of the individual. Additionally, there is no doubt that an orderly supply of drugs is crucial for the protection of public health. "Orderly" in this context means that needed drugs will be available to the general public and that their distribution will also be controlled. * * * The Bavarian legislature presumably had these objectives in mind, but between the lines of the legislation we can also discern the political aims of a pharmacy profession at work to protect its [narrow] interests and the traditional concept of the "apothecary".

The decisive question before us is whether the absence of this restriction on the establishment of new pharmacies would * * * in all probability disrupt the orderly supply of drugs in such a way as to endanger public health.

We are not convinced that this danger is impending.

VII.   * * * Section 3 (1) of the Bavarian Apothecary Act is unconstitutional because it violates the basic right of the complainant under Article 12 (1). * * *

KABUSHIKI KAISHA SUMIYOSHI v. GOVERNOR OF HIROSHIMA PREFECTURE [JAPAN DRUG STORE CASE]

Supreme Court (Japan).
29 Minshū 4 at p. 572 (1975).

[The plaintiff company applied for a license to establish a general drug sales store. The law empowers the governor to refuse the issuance of licenses in cases where the location of the pharmacy or the store to be established is near those already established. The request was denied and the governor's decision was upheld by the Hiroshima High Court.]

1.   Freedom of Choice of Occupation under the Constitution article 22, paragraph 1 and Licensing Systems.

(1) Article 22, paragraph 1 of the Constitution provides that every person shall have freedom to choose his occupation to the extent that it does not interfere with the public welfare. An occupation is a continuous activity in which an individual engages in order to maintain his own livelihood. Furthermore, in a society in which there is a division of labor, an occupation is by nature an activity apportioned by social function through which one contributes to the continuity and development of society, and as the locus where each person fulfills his personally endowed individuality, it also has an inseparable relationship to the personal worth of the individual. * * * [T]herefore, the said provision

should be interpreted to include not only freedom to choose an occupation in the narrow sense, but also a guarantee of freedom of occupational activity.

(2) Indeed, because occupation, as previously stated, is in essence a social and, moreover, principally an economic activity, and by its nature something in which mutual social relations are great; in comparison to other constitutionally guaranteed freedoms, especially the so-called "mental" freedoms, the demand for regulation by public authority is stronger. * * *

Occupation is consequently a social activity within which the necessity for some sort of restrictions is inherent * * *

(3) * * * [L]icensing systems go beyond simple regulation of the content and form of occupational activities and impose restrictions upon the freedom to choose an occupation itself in the narrow sense. Thus, because they are powerful limitations upon freedom of occupation, in principle in order to be able to affirm their constitutionality, they are required to be necessary and reasonable measures for an important public interest. Also in cases where they are not measures for a positive purpose with respect to social or economic policy, but rather negative, police measures for the purpose of preventing harm to the public brought about by free occupational activities, it is necessary to find that the above purpose could not be fully achieved through regulation of simply the form and content of the occupational activities, which is, in comparison with a licensing system, a looser restriction upon freedom of occupation. * * *

2. Concerning the Licensing System under the Pharmaceutical Affairs Low Licensing System.

(1) * * *

Because drugs and other medical supplies, in addition to being necessities with respect to the maintenance of the life and health of the people, * * * not only regulation of the content of the business, but also adoption of a licensing system limiting dealers to persons having fixed qualifications and forbidding the establishment of businesses by persons other than these, may in itself be affirmed as a measure both necessary and reasonable for a purpose that accords with the public welfare.* * *

(2) * * * Under paragraph 2 instances are recognized in which a license may not be issued from the standpoint of the suitability of the location of the facilities, and under paragraph 4 the specifics of these provisions are left to prefectural ordinance. Among the standards related to these licensing conditions, in contrast to those set under each item of paragraph 1 of the same article, which in every case are matters directly related to the purpose of preventing the dispensing of substandard drugs and other medical supplies, and whose necessity and reasonableness may be affirmed relatively easily * * *

3. Concerning the Legislative Purpose and Reasons Underlying the Regulations for the Suitable Location of Pharmacies and General Drug and Medical Supplies Sales Store (hereafter referred to as "Pharmacies").

(1) * * *

[T]he regulations on the suitable location of pharmacies are regulatory measures for the negative, police purpose of preventing hazards to the life and health of the people. Prevention of excessive competition among pharmacies and of instability of business operations contemplated therein, are not themselves the aims, but are recognized clearly to be nothing more than means for preventing substandard drugs from being dispensed. That is, the social and economic policy objective of protecting the business operations of pharmacies, among which small and medium enterprises are numerous, is not the intent of the regulations on the suitable location of pharmacies * * *

(2) * * * [Defendant argued that in some areas there were no pharmacies, while in large cities there was excessive competition, resulting in unstable business and therefore negligent handling of drugs. The restrictions intended to promote the proper location of drug stores to prevent the above anomalies. The Court refers to evidence in the legislative history of excessive competition.]

4. Concerning the Constitutionality of Regulations on the Proper Location of Pharmacies.

(2) b. (a) * * * [A]s an ultimate measure for the complete prevention of the dangers to the health of the people resulting from the dispensing of substandard drugs, it is not without merit to proceed further and devise preventative measures for eliminating to the greatest possible extent all potential causes for violations. We cannot say that this is absolutely unnecessary. However, in order to uphold the constitutionality of geographical restrictions on the establishment of pharmacies, which involve substantial limitations on freedom of occupation, as such acceptable preventative measures, it does not suffice merely that we cannot say that there is no necessity for such restrictions in relation to the health of the people in the above sense; we must find it reasonable to say that if such restrictions were not enforced, there would be a danger of hazards arising to the health of the people to the extent of outweighing the restriction on freedom of occupation imposed by the above measures.

(b) * * *[I]t would be unusual in the extreme for proprietors of pharmacies in general, especially pharmacists who are restrained from behind by penalties for any violation of laws and regulations and are under constant administrative supervision, to dare to resort to violation of laws and regulations merely for economic reasons.* * *

(c) * * *[I]t is unreasonable to conclude that there exists to a considerable degree the danger of dispensing substandard drugs which originates principally in the instability of business operations of pharmacies, and which cannot be prevented by strict enforcement of supervision and regulation of dispensing businesses. * * *

STATE v. LAWRENCE

Constitutional Court (South Africa).
1997 (4) SALR 1176 (CC).

[For the facts of this case, see Notes and Questions, Chapter 8, Subsection A.3.]

Chaskalson P:

* * *

[7] The appellants contended that the prohibition imposed by [Liquor Act] section 90(1)(a) on the selling of wine "after hours" on week days and on closed days, and by section 88(1) on the sale of liquor other than wine, which made the sale of cider and beer unlawful, is inconsistent with the right to economic activity guaranteed by s 26 of the interim Constitution and that the prohibition against selling wine on Sundays was inconsistent with the right to freedom of religion, belief and opinion guaranteed by s 14.

* * *

[26] Section 26 of the interim Constitution, on which the appellants rely for their challenge to the provisions under which they were convicted, provides:

"26. Economic activity

(1) Every person shall have the right freely to engage in economic activity and to pursue a livelihood anywhere in the national territory.

(2) Subsection (1) shall not preclude measures designed to promote the protection or the improvement of the quality of life, economic growth, human development, social justice, basic conditions of employment, fair labour practices or equal opportunity for all, provided such measures are justifiable in an open and democratic society based on freedom and equality."

* * *

[52] The purpose of particular legislative provisions has ordinarily to be established from their context, which would include the language of the statute and its background. Where the purpose is one sanctioned by s 26(2) the question whether that purpose is justifiable in an open and democratic society based on freedom and equality is essentially a question of law; so too is the question whether there is a rational basis for the means used to achieve the legislative purpose. * * *

* * *

[56]   * * * Measures designed to curtail some of the harmful effects of trade in liquor are clearly measures designed to protect or improve the quality of life. * * * [The] challenges [of the appellants] were confined to the particular constraints imposed on them by the licensing system. It is necessary, therefore, to consider the particular constraints to which objection was taken in each of the appeals.

After hours sales—the Lawrence appeal

* * *

[61] The appellant's objection is that the restrictions imposed by the Liquor Act on the hours during which the holder of a grocer's wine license may sell table wine during week days interferes with the freedom of such license holders to trade lawfully and with the freedom of consumers to purchase wine at times most convenient to them.

* * *

[63] Freedom to engage in economic activity in an open and democratic society does not imply a totally unconstrained freedom. Economic activity is subject to regulation and a shop keeper cannot claim to have "an unconstrained right to transact business whenever one wishes".

* * *

[65] The scheme of the legislation is to effect controls through licenses. The licenses control who may sell liquor, what liquor may be sold, and when and where sales may take place. It is not necessary to deal with the different types of licenses that may be given or the conditions attaching to them. Restriction on the hours of selling apply to all licenses though different selling times are fixed for different types of licenses. The distinctions drawn between the different types of licenses are rationally related to the differences in the nature of the businesses and no point was made of this in argument. The basis of the appellant's argument was that restrictions on the hours of sale do not reduce alcohol related problems, and that an increase in the hours of sale would not lead to an increase in alcohol consumption or alcohol related problems. The restrictions on hours of selling were therefore irrational.

* * *

[68] * * * The question to be decided is not whether the policy underlying the Liquor Act is an effective policy; it is whether there is a rational basis for such policy related to the purpose of the legislation.

[69] What is clear from the affidavit of Mr. Makan—one of the appellants' own experts—is that the control of the availability of alcohol is a recognised means of combatting the adverse effects of alcohol consumption. * * *

[70] I am satisfied that even if the burden of proof is on the Attorney General to establish the rational basis, and not on the appellants to negative it, it has been established that there is a rational basis for measures restricting the hours of sale as part of a legislative scheme designed to curtail the consumption of liquor. In the circumstances the restrictions do not in my view constitute a breach of section 26 of the interim Constitution.

WILLIAMSON v. LEE OPTICAL OF OKLAHOMA

Supreme Court (United States).
348 U.S. 483 (1955).

Mr. Justice Douglas delivered the opinion of the Court.

The District Court held unconstitutional portions of three sections of [an Oklahoma] Act. First, it held invalid under the Due Process

Clause of the Fourteenth Amendment the portions of s 2 which make it unlawful for any person not a licensed optometrist or ophthalmologist to fit lenses to a face or to duplicate or replace into frames lenses or other optical appliances, except upon written prescriptive authority of an Oklahoma licensed ophthalmologist or optometrist.

An ophthalmologist is a duly licensed physician who specializes in the care of the eyes. An optometrist examines eyes for refractive error, recognizes (but does not treat) diseases of the eye, and fills prescriptions for eyeglasses. The optician is an artisan qualified to grind lenses, fill prescriptions, and fit frames.

The effect of s 2 is to forbid the optician from fitting or duplicating lenses without a prescription from an ophthalmologist or optometrist. In practical effect, it means that no optician can fit old glasses into new frames or supply a lens, whether it be a new lens or one to duplicate a lost or broken lens, without a prescription. * * *

* * *

The Oklahoma law may exact a needless, wasteful requirement in many cases. But it is for the legislature, not the courts, to balance the advantages and disadvantages of the new requirement. It appears that in many cases the optician can easily supply the new frames or new lenses without reference to the old written prescription. * * * [Th]e legislature may have concluded that eye examinations were so critical, not only for correction of vision but also for detection of latent ailments or diseases, that every change in frames and every duplication of a lens should be accompanied by a prescription from a medical expert. To be sure, the present law does not require a new examination of the eyes every time the frames are changed or the lenses duplicated. For if the old prescription is on file with the optician, he can go ahead and make the new fitting or duplicate the lenses. But the law need not be in every respect logically consistent with its aims to be constitutional. It is enough that there is an evil at hand for correction, and that it might be thought that the particular legislative measure was a rational way to correct it.

The day is gone when this Court uses the Due Process Clause of the Fourteenth Amendment to strike down state laws, regulatory of business and industrial conditions, because they may be unwise, improvident, or out of harmony with a particular school of thought. We emphasize again what Chief Justice Waite said in *Munn v. State of Illinois,* 94 U.S. 113, 134, 'For protection against abuses by legislatures the people must resort to the polls, not to the courts.'

Secondly, the District Court held that it violated the Equal Protection Clause of the Fourteenth Amendment to subject opticians to this regulatory system and to exempt, as s 3 of the Act does, all sellers of ready-to-wear glasses. The problem of legislative classification is a perennial one, admitting of no doctrinaire definition. Evils in the same field may be of different dimensions and proportions, requiring different remedies. Or so the legislature may think. Or the reform may take one step at a time, addressing itself to the phase of the problem, which seems most acute to the legislative mind. The legislature may select one phase of one field and apply a remedy there, neglecting the others. The prohibition of the Equal Protection Clause goes no further than the invidious discrimination. We cannot say that that point has been reached here. For all this record shows, the ready-to-wear branch of this business may not loom large in Oklahoma or may present problems of regulation distinct from the other branch.

* * *

Fourth, the District Court held unconstitutional, as violative of the Due Process Clause of the Fourteenth Amendment, the provision of s 4 of the Oklahoma Act, which reads as follows:

'No person, firm, or corporation engaged in the business of retailing merchandise to the general public shall rent space, sublease departments, or otherwise permit any person purporting to do eye examination or visual care to occupy space in such retail store.'

It seems to us that this regulation is on the same constitutional footing as the denial to corporations of the right to practice dentistry. *Semler v. Dental Examiners*, 294 U.S. 608, 611 (1935). It is an attempt to free the profession, to as great an extent as possible, from all taints of commercialism. It certainly might be easy for an optometrist with space in a retail store to be merely a front for the retail establishment. In any case, the opportunity for that nexus may be too great for safety, if the eye doctor is allowed inside the retail store. Moreover, it may be deemed important to effective regulation that the eye doctor be restricted to geographical locations that reduce the temptations of commercialism. Geographical location may be an important consideration in a legislative program, which aims to raise the treatment of the human eye to a strictly professional level. We cannot say that the regulation has no rational relation to that objective and therefore is beyond constitutional bounds.

* * *

Notes and Questions

1. The interpretation of the German Basic Law that "democratized" the old rule of free access to the professions (once a major victory of freedom against the self-protective measures of the professions and professional estates) extended general liberty to entrepreneurial freedom, or, conversely, entrepreneurial freedom is a part of general liberty. Once the GFCC found a fundamental right in pursuing an economic activity, the regulatory freedom of the state came under substantive judicial scrutiny, necessitating some kind of balancing and proportionality.

2. The German approach was widely followed. This is exemplified by the Japanese case where the Supreme Court of Japan extended the liberty to choose a profession to the way in which it is exercised, at least in cases where an individual's personal development is involved. Is there any attempt to follow the German balancing approach in the Japanese decision?

Some jurisdictions, even those with the same judicial standards and constitutional provisions, may allow for more economic protectionism (acceptance of entry barriers) than others. The Austrian Constitutional Court (2/3/1998 (G 37/97)) upheld a law requiring any new pharmacy to be at least

500 meters distance from the nearest existing pharmacy. It annulled the requirement that at least 5,500 persons had to be supplied with pharmaceutical products by the new pharmacy on the ground that it restricted the right to work for remuneration in a way that did not support any public interest. As to additional restrictions, however, the Court found that a high public interest exists to provide efficient service to consumers. Such service presupposes a certain inventory of pharmaceuticals, which is safeguarded by the requirement that the number of persons already served by the existing pharmacy not be reduced to less than 5,500 by the opening of any new pharmacy. (BCCL, 1998. 15).

In Spain, the postdictatorship Constitution of 1977 follows the German Basic Law in guaranteeing the right to work and the free choice of occupation (profession) and office.[j] Nevertheless, the fundamental right to choose one's occupation was not applied to restrictions on opening a pharmacy, which the Court characterized as a simple liberty interest subject to regulation. The Spanish Constitution provides that "the exercise of such rights and liberties be regulated only by law, which in every case must respect the essential content [of fundamental rights]." A law of 1944 limited the opening of new pharmacies, taking into consideration the number of inhabitants, just as the Austrian legislation did. The Constitutional Tribunal upheld the law, denying entry to new pharmacists in certain areas. It found that the regulation of a profession or entrepreneurial activities is not a restriction of the free exercise of the fundamental right. The restricted right in the case of opening pharmacies is only a restriction of general liberty, which can be subject to any (nondiscriminatory) legal restriction. Decision 83/1984. Does the Austrian–Spanish position satisfy requirements of equality and nondiscrimination? In view of the decision in the German *Pharmacy Case*, are the Austrian and Spanish decisions convincing? The Swiss Federal Court (2d Public Law Chamber, (2P.68/1998) 125 I 474), in *MediService SA v. State Council of the Canton of Vaud*, applied a proportionality test in analyzing a canton's health-protection measure against a claim that it restricted freedom of trade and industry guaranteed by the federal Constitution. The Vaud canton law permitted postal delivery of medicine into the canton only for special reasons. The federal Court recognized the danger of postal delivery of medicine but found MediService's preventive measures satisfactory. Thus the special requirements of the Canton of Vaud violated the appellant's right of access to the market.

In a later case the German Court went further in protecting occupational freedom, holding that the right entails a corresponding duty of the state to provide access to free higher education, including admission to medical school. See *Numerus Clausus I* below. On the other hand the free development of the individual protected in the German *Pharmacy Case* had to be reconciled with a strong social perception of entrepreneurial freedom:

j. Article 35 [Work]

(1) All Spaniards have the duty to work and the right to work, to the free election of profession or office career, to advancement through work, and to a sufficient remuneration to satisfy their needs and those of their family, while in no case can there be discrimination for reasons of sex.

(2) The law shall regulate a statute for workers.

Article 38 [Free Enterprise]

Free enterprise within the framework of a market economy is recognized. The public authorities guarantee and protect its exercise and the defense of productivity in accordance with the demands of the general economy, and as the case may be, in keeping with planning.

The individual has to accept those limits on his freedom of action which the legislature imposes to cultivate and maintain society. In turn, such acceptance depends upon the limits of what can reasonably be demanded in a particular case, provided the autonomy of the person is preserved. * * * The Basic Law guarantees neither the neutrality of the executive or the legislative power in economic matters nor does it guarantee a 'social market economy' * * * The Constitutional Court is not authorized to judge the wisdom of legislation. * * * The principle of equality does not extend the authority of review granted to the Constitutional Court. * * * In principle, the constitutional authority even includes power to pass laws in the interest of particular groups. Such laws must, however, be aimed at the public welfare.

Investment Aid I Case, 4 BVerfGE 7 (1954).

3. It is remarkable that entrepreneurial liberty is practically left unprotected in the U.S. Judicial history explains this reluctance. See *Lochner*, 198 U.S. 45; *Williamson*, 348 U.S. 483.

A corporate applicant for a pharmacy permit appealed the application's denial by the North Dakota State Board of Pharmacy. The state statute required that an applicant for such a permit be "a registered pharmacist in good standing" or "a corporation or association, the majority stock in which is owned by registered pharmacists in good standing, actively and regularly employed in and responsible for the management, supervision, and operation of such pharmacy." The Supreme Court, by Justice Douglas, held that North Dakota's statutory requirements did not violate the due process clause of the Fourteenth Amendment. The state was well within its authority

'to legislate against what (it) found to be injurious practices in (its) internal commercial and business affairs,' * * * We refuse to sit as a 'superlegislature to weigh the wisdom of legislation,' and we emphatically refuse to go back to the time when courts used the Due Process Clause 'to strike down state laws, regulatory of business and industrial conditions, because they may be unwise, improvident, or out of harmony with a particular school of thought.' Nor are we able or willing to draw lines by calling a law 'prohibitory' or 'regulatory.' Whether the legislature takes for its textbook Adam Smith, Herbert Spencer, Lord Keynes, or some other is no concern of ours. The Kansas debt adjusting statute may be wise or unwise. But relief, if any be needed, lies not with us but with the body constituted to pass laws for the State of Kansas.

North Dakota State Board of Pharmacy, v. Snyder's Drug Stores, Inc., 414 U.S. 156, 165–66 (1973) (citations omitted).

4. Freedom of occupation is typically a right that is used against protectionist or other regulatory interferences. At times it may conflict with other rights, too:

[A] year after the enactment of [the Israeli] Basic Law: Freedom of Occupation, the Supreme Court nullified administrative regulations, which restricted the importation of non-kosher meat on the ground that the restrictions violated freedom of occupation. The nullification of these regulations generated angry reactions from the religious parties that correctly considered the outcomes of these decisions to be a violation of the status quo. The religious parties struggled to find ways to restore the previous arrangement. They did not bother to reestablish the status quo doctrine in primary legislation because they were concerned that the Supreme Court would use judicial review to nullify that primary legislation as well. Instead, employing a different strategy, they succeeded in amending Basic Law: Freedom of Occupation to include an overriding clause similar to the Canadian 'notwithstanding' clause. As a result, section 8 of Basic Law: Freedom of Occupation now states that 'a statutory provision which infringes freedom of occupation will be valid * * * if it is included in a statute enacted by a majority of the Knesset members and expressly declares that it is valid despite the Basic Law.' Following this amendment, the Knesset enacted legislation that enables the government to restrict the importation of non-Kosher meat. Non-Kosher meat importers appealed again to the Supreme Court to nullify this new law. In December 1996, the Supreme Court found the legislation contradicted freedom of occupation. However, the court did not nullify the law because it found that it satisfied the overriding clause.[80]

Dr. Gidon Sapir, *Religion and State in Israel: The Case for Reevaluation and Constitutional Entrenchment*, 22 Hastings Int'l & Comp. L. Rev. 617, 638–39 (1999).

5. *Rustom Cavasjee Cooper v. Union of India*, (1970) 3 S.C.R. 530, 585–86, states:

In *Mohammad Yasin v. The Town Area Committee, Jalalabad and Another* (1952) S.C.R. 572 [the Supreme Court of India] observed that under Art. 19(1)(g) of the Constitution a citizen has the right to carry on any occupation, trade or business and the only restriction on 'this right is the authority of the State to make a law relating to the carrying on of such occupation, trade or business as mentioned in cl. (6) of that Article as amended by the Constitution (First Amendment) Act, 1951.' In Mohammad Yasin's case, by-laws of the Municipal Committee, provided that no person shall sell or purchase any vegetables or fruit within the limits of the municipal area of Jalalabad, wholesale or by auction, without paying the prescribed fee. It was urged on behalf of a wholesale dealer in vegetables that although there was no prohibition against carrying on business in vegetables by anybody, in effect the by-laws brought about a total stoppage of the wholesaler's business in a commercial sense, for he had to pay prescribed fee to the contractor, and under the bye-laws the wholesale dealer could not charge a higher rate of commission than the contractor. The wholesale dealer, therefore, could charge the growers of vegetables and fruit only the commission permissible under the by-laws, and he had to make over the entire commission to the contractor without retaining any part thereof. The wholesale dealer was thereby converted into a mere tax-collector for the contractor or the Town Area Committee without any remuneration. The by-laws in this situation were struck down as impairing the freedom to carry on business.

6. The right to practice a profession is protected under the Fourteenth Amendment of the U.S. Constitution as a liberty, but subject to appropriate regulation. In *Conn v. Gabbert*, 526 U.S. 286 (1999), a lawyer, who accompanied his client, was subject to a search while his client was questioned by a grand jury. The Supreme Court found that it is a protected liberty to practice one's profession without undue and unreasonable government interference. While complete prohibition on the practice of one's employment is

80. *See Meatrael v. Knesset*, 50(5) P.D. 15 (1996).

generally unconstitutional, the temporary interruptions exercised as part of a legitimate government function, as in the actual case, is not a violation of the due process requirement. Is the distinction here between choice and practice of occupation similar to the German one? In the German approach access to a profession is a core value, given its importance for the development of the individual. In the U.S., notwithstanding the liberty of profession, issues are not structured as freedom to choose a profession. Professional liberty does not trigger as demanding a scrutiny as in Germany. In *Regents of the Univ. of California v. Bakke*, 438 U.S. 265 (1978), (see Chapter 6) the alleged injury was impermissible racial discrimination in the allocation of places in a medical school, a program receiving federal funds. The issue was framed around the constitutionality of discrimination and not Bakke's right to occupational choice.

7. The USSC appears ready to go a great distance to uphold restrictions on professions and economic activities in general. It might be surprising in this context that, notwithstanding the exceptional deferentialism of the post-*Lochner* era, once a constitutional value—especially equal protection—is at stake, even what might seem to be a convincing measure to protect the public interest will not suffice. An Oklahoma statutory scheme prohibited the sale of "nonintoxicating" 3.2 percent beer to males under the age of 21 and to females under the age of 18. Statistical evidence regarding young males' drunk-driving arrests and traffic injuries demonstrated for the lower court that the gender-based discrimination was substantially related to the achievement of traffic safety on Oklahoma roads. In the 18–to–20–year-old age group, .18 percent of females and 2 percent of males were arrested for driving while under the influence of alcohol. In *Craig v. Boren*, 429 U.S. 190 (1976), the Supreme Court found the statute unconstitutional. (See Chapter 6.)

8. Like in the U.S. Constitution, there is no specific provision on entrepreneurial freedoms in the French Constitution, only a general freedom of action—the "freedom to do anything that does not cause harm to another" of Art. 4 of the 1789 Declaration. On the other hand it was recognized as early as 1791 that "any person is free to conduct such business or to exercise such profession, art, or trade as suits him." *Loi* Chapelier, Art. 7. The Constitutional Council recognized, in 1976, that the freedom to exercise a profession is a civil liberty (76–88 L of 3 March 1976). The constitutional basis for such a position is unclear. Arbitrary or abusive restrictions to the freedom of enterprise were held to endanger the general freedom in the *Nationalizations Case* (above, para. 16.). The Council finds that the freedom of enterprise is neither general nor absolute as it exists within the framework of regulation (84–176 DC of 25 July 1984). Although freedom of enterprise receives limited protection, it is considered important enough to justify the restriction of other rights. Its constitutional status requires that it be restricted only by *loi* and, therefore, subject to constitutional review. The Council considered that in the case of restricting press ownership for the sake of freedom of communication and pluralism, freedom of enterprise sets a certain limit on such a restriction. In reviewing the legislation intended to limit the share of the press market, the Council found that the ceiling could not be such that it inhibited the growth of existing titles (84–181 DC of 10, 11 Oct. 1984).

C. SOCIAL AND WELFARE RIGHTS

"Social rights" and "welfare rights" might refer to the same rights, or welfare might be part of social rights, or it might be a separate set of rights with a different basis than social rights. The International Covenant of Economic, Social and Cultural Rights refers to "social, economic, and cultural" rights. American lawyers and many economists generally refer to welfare rights, which may refer to all social services and monetary support provided by the government to individuals, according to their social status. Welfare may include pensions for the retired and the handicapped, illness or injury benefits (including a universal and free healthcare system), child, maternity, and family support (both monetary supplements and special care), unemployment benefits, and free or subsidized housing, including low-interest loans. Sometimes welfare service is provided without a prior contribution from the beneficiary. Many social rights are entitlements provided through a social security scheme based on the principle of social solidarity. Free education, subsidized cultural activities, and even telecommunications are, or were, provided as free or heavily subsidized ("social") government services. All of this is generally referred to as the "social insurance scheme." The fundamental preconditions of existence (health, food, water, shelter) are often provided as part of welfare services. Other welfare services (like pensions) are termed as social rights in some contexts, although the term may express an institutional claim and not an individual one. Economic rights may refer to entrepreneurial liberty as well as special guarantees regarding labor, including conditions of employment and the right to create professional associations. The relevance of socioeconomic rights to more traditional rights and to the core value of dignity is stressed in the following position of the ISC:

> The structure of the Constitution has been erected on the concept of an egalitarian society. But the Constitution makers did not desire that it should be a society where the citizen will not enjoy the various freedoms and such rights as are the basic elements of those freedoms, e.g., the right to equality, freedom of religion etc., so that his dignity as an individual may be maintained. It has been strongly urged on behalf of the respondents that a citizen cannot have any dignity if he is economically or socially backward. No one can dispute such a statement but the whole scheme underlying the Constitution is, to bring about economic and social changes without taking away the dignity of the individual. Indeed, the same has been placed on such a high pedestal that to ensure the freedoms etc. their infringement has been made justiciable by the highest court in that land.
>
> *Kesavananda v. Kerala*, (1973) Supp. S.C.R. 1, 280 (Justices Shelat and Grover).

Some constitutions discuss socioeconomic rights as state tasks (Spain) or nonenforceable rights (Weimar Constitution); others, like Italy, use a language that is sometimes different from that of first generation rights. The Italian Constitution mentions what the Republic provides and not what one is entitled to, but it does accord certain employment-related rights to employees. The Slovak Constitution uses standard rights language, but it adds that the content of these rights is to be determined by legislation. The German Basic Law is silent on welfare rights, except that it puts the family under the protection of the state; however, the self-definition of the state as being social was sufficient for the legislature to create welfare rights. The former British colonies were to some extent influenced by the solution of the 1937 Irish Constitution. The Directive Principles of Social Policy of the Irish Constitution were addressed to the Oireachtas (Parliament), and the same provisions expressly prohibited the Principles to be "cognizable by any Court." As we will see, the ISC has extensively used the Indian Directive Principles in reinterpreting fundamental values to order the government to implement enforceable rights so that the Directive Principles are carried out. Recently the High Court of Ireland has also created rights using similar reasoning, notwithstanding the prohibition against judicial action.

Most cases in this section deal with housing, health, and education rights. First we look at the notion of human dignity as the source of a claim to receive minimum livelihood from the state. Such a minimum is intended to allow the integration of the individual into society; thus it varies. The International Covenant of Economic, Social and Cultural Rights and the official comments on the Covenant specify how states should progressively satisfy these rights claims. The matter is of particular importance in developing countries, where a number of courts have sought to direct their governments to satisfy international and constitutional obligations in regard to social and economic rights. Given the limited resources in these economies, it is unclear how successful this "judicial steering" will prove. The attempt also deserves consideration from the perspective of judicial activism. Their understanding of the welfare state leads some West European courts to protect and extend welfare rights, partly on grounds of equality considerations. The U.S. presents a different trend: federal and state authorities provide substantial welfare services, but the courts are not ready to award constitutional protection to welfare-entitlement claims. Although welfare concerns at one time were high on the American political agenda (President Roosevelt's Four Freedoms included "freedom from want"), the marked contrast between Europe and the U.S. suggests that what matters is not the function of the state but the judicial understanding of its proper role. In many European countries, India, and, with some caveat, South Africa, the constitution is understood to have a direct impact on private relations, and the state has a constitutional obligation to provide services to individuals. In the U.S., government is not seen to be affirmatively responsible for the welfare of its citizens. This problem is discussed at the conclusion of this section.

FAMILY BURDEN COMPENSATION CASE

Federal Constitutional Court (Germany).
99 BVerfGE 216 (1998).

Principles of the Resolution

1. Article 6 Paragraph 1 of the Basic Law contains a special principle of equality prohibiting discrimination against marriage and

traditional families as compared to other forms of cohabitation and child-rearing communities. This prohibition of discrimination is an impediment to the imposition of any burden upon the existence of marriage (Article 6 paragraph 1 of the Basic Law) or the exercise of parental rights within a marital family community (Article 6 paragraphs 1 and 2 of the Constitution).

2. The economic resources of parents are generally reduced by their children's need of care, beyond children's essential material needs and their need for care due to their parents' employment. It is necessary for the minimal livelihood of families that care-giving for children be unburdened by income taxes without differentiation as to how this care-giving function is satisfied.

3. a) When equalizing children's maintenance requirements, the legislature also must take into account the need to care for children. This is true for all parents who receive a child allowance or a child benefit, regardless of the parents' family status.

b) In accordance with the constitutional principle of foreseeability, as far as a family's minimal needs are determined by personal data such as family status, number of children, and age, the law must be formulated so that it can be applied solely by reference to that data.

* * *

Judgment of the Second Senate

A. The constitutional complaints concern the question of whether or not it is consistent with the Basic Law that parents living in a matrimonial community can be denied, on the one hand, the right to deduct from their income tax base the cost of taking care of their children resulting from their employment, and, on the other hand, be denied the grant of a household allowance.

I. 1. The notion of, and the requirements for, possible tax deductions regarding costs of taking care of children are regulated in § 33c of the Income Taxation Act (hereafter ITA). The relevant wording is as follows:

Cost of Taking Care of Children in the Case of Single Persons

Expenditures for child-minding services concerning a child living in a single household (§ 32 Paragraph 4, 1st sentence) are treated as extraordinary charges within the meaning of § 33 if the child is fully subject to income taxation and is not sixteen years old as of the beginning of the calendar year, and insofar as the expenditures arise out of the parents' employment. Expenditures can only be considered as far as they are necessary according to the circumstances and do not exceed a reasonable amount. Expenditures for school education, teaching special abilities, sports, and other leisure activities will not be considered.

The notion of single persons covers unmarried persons and married persons who are permanently separated from their spouses. Married individuals are regarded as single persons if their spouses are not fully subject to income taxation.

* * *

In connection with later changes [of the Income Taxation Act], the Federal Government reconsidered extending tax relief for costs of child-minding arising out of parents' employment to married parents in general. However, in the view of the Federal Government, the Basic Law did not impose such a rule. The need to make expenditures for child-minding seemed to be more evident to the Government in the case of single parents than in the case of married parents looking after their children. Furthermore, by dividing the income, spouses are usually treated in such a way that additional child-minding costs typically do not arise or can be borne more easily by spouses than by single parents. * * *

B. * * *

I. 1. a) Taking care of and bringing up children are the natural rights of parents and their primary duties (Article 6 Paragraph 1 Sentence 1 of the Basic Law). Parents fulfill these duties within the family. * * *

b) The duty to bring up children (Article 6 Paragraph 2 Sentence 1 of the Basic Law) is parents' strictly personal responsibility, though it is not theirs alone. Article 6 Paragraph 1 of the Basic Law provides—in the sense of a protective right—the freedom to decide how to structure living together as a married couple or family. Hence, the state must respect the family both in terms of immaterial or personal and material or economic values, according to the individual organization of each family. * * *

2. a) Article 6 Paragraph 1 of the Basic Law also contains a special principle of equality prohibiting discrimination against marriage and traditional families compared to other forms of cohabitation and child-rearing communities (prohibition of discrimination). Article 6 Paragraph 1 prohibits discrimination between spouses and singles, parents and childless couples and married couples and other types of family arrangements. This prohibition of discrimination is an impediment to imposing any burden upon the existence of marriage (Article 6 paragraph 1 of the Basic Law) or the exercise of parental rights in a traditional marital family (Article 6 paragraphs 1 and 2 of the Basic Law).

b) It is also discriminatory when spouses or parents are excluded from tax relief because of their marriage or their family organization. The principle of tax equality, at least for direct taxes, requires taxation to be applied according to people's financial capacities.

The Federal Constitutional Court clarifies the constitutional principle of means-based income taxation by obligating the tax legislature to exempt non-disposable income that is necessary for a family's livelihood.

3. a) From Article 1 Paragraph 1 of the Basic Law and the "social state" principle in Article 20 Paragraph 1 of the Constitution, a constitutional principle results whereby the state must exempt income that is minimally necessary for a humane existence—a "subsistence minimum"—from taxation. Taking further into consideration Article 6 Paragraph 1 of the Basic Law, this principle applies to the minimal needs of all members of the family. Hence, in considering someone's financial capacity to be taxed, the state must exempt expenditures for the up-

bringing of the child to the extent necessary to guarantee children's minimum care needs. These minimum requirements are computed on the basis of demand and not on actual expenditures. Furthermore, the court emphasizes that children's maintenance requirements cannot be legally analogized with the private satisfaction of needs. Hence, the tax legislature may not reach resources that are necessary for the care and the upbringing of children in the same way that it reaches resources used for the satisfaction of other needs.

* * *

b) * * * The Income Tax Act always must exempt the cost of bringing up a child, no matter if the parents take care of the child personally, if they prefer for some pedagogical reasons to have someone else temporarily take care of the child (e.g., in a Kindergarten), or if they decide to work and therefore to have someone else take care of the child.

4.* * * Raising children is an activity that is also in the interest of society and requires its support. Accordingly, the state must ensure that parents are equally able to temporarily forego employment to look after their children personally or to combine raising children and employment. The state also must create conditions under which the assumption of child-care obligations does not lead to professional disadvantages, under which returning to employment and raising children while working is possible for both parents, and under which the availability of institutional child-care is improved.

II. 1. a) * * * The distinction drawn in § 33c paragraph 2 ITA between "singles" entitled to a deduction and married persons not entitled to a deduction is therefore not based on their different financial capacity to be taxed. * * *

C. In addition to discrimination against the traditional marital family as compared to other child-rearing communities in violation of Article 6 Paragraphs 1 and 2 of the Basic Law, the tax treatment of the reduced financial capacity of parents does not meet the constitutional requirements of Article 6 Paragraphs 1 and 2, and discriminates against them—as they are unable to benefit from the taxable relief provided for by § 33c and § 32 paragraph 7—compared to childless taxpayers.

I. Child allowances and child benefits only cover children's minimum material requirements. Until now, in contradiction to the principle of equality (see B.II.1. above), the requirements of raising a child have only been considered if they arise in connection with a single person's employment, illness, or disability, or if one spouse is ill or disabled and the other spouse is either employed, ill, or disabled (§ 33c paragraphs 1 to 3 and 5 ITA). These regulations do not sufficiently take into account the fact that the obligation to care for children exists independent of illness, disability, or employment, and that it does not depend on the manner in which the obligation is fulfilled. Hence, when providing a new rule for exempting child care from taxation, the legislature will have to consider an equal tax reduction for all parents—independent of the way children are cared for and of actual expenditures—and therefore will have to increase the child allowance or the child benefits.

II. The Income Tax Act not only does not take into consideration the cost of providing child-care (§ 33c ITA), but also does not take into consideration the expenses necessary for children's individual development toward self-sufficiency. * * * Therefore, the legislature, when designing a new child allowance regulation * * *, must take into account the child-care requirements of all parents who are entitled to a child allowance or child benefits, regardless of their family status.

The cost of raising a child is not sufficiently satisfied by a child allowance and child benefits. The minimum standard of living that is relevant for granting social aid, and therefore for determining the minimum maintenance needs to be exempt from taxation, includes food, housing, clothing, body care, household goods, heating, and personal needs of daily life * * *. Within a reasonable scope, maintaining relations with one's environment and participation in cultural life are also included * * *. For children and adolescents, it also includes meeting special needs related to their development and growth. * * *

When this need is quantified, however, parents' general costs of affording children the opportunity to develop toward a responsible life in this society are not sufficiently taken into consideration. Contrary to § 33c paragraph 1 sentence 5 ITA, the following examples are also to be included in these costs: membership in associations and other ways of meeting children or adolescents outside the family home, learning and experimenting with modern techniques of communication, acquiring cultural and linguistic skills, using spare time responsibly, and arranging vacations. * * *

CESCR GENERAL COMMENT NO. 3

U.N. ESCOR, Comm. On Econ., Soc., & Cultural Rights,
5th Sess., Supp. No. 2A at 83.
U.N. Doc. E/1991/22–E/CN.4/1991/1 Annex III (1990).[k]

The nature of States parties obligations

(Art. 2, para. 1 of the Covenant)

(Fifth session, 1990) * * *

1. * * * Those obligations include both what may be termed (following the work of the International Law Commission) obligations of conduct and obligations of result. * * *

2. * * * [T]he undertaking in article 2 (1) "to take steps", which in itself, is not qualified or limited by other considerations. * * * Thus while the full realization of the relevant rights may be achieved progressively, steps towards that goal must be taken within a reasonably short time after the Covenant's entry into force for the States concerned. Such steps should be deliberate, concrete and targeted as clearly as possible towards meeting the obligations recognized in the Covenant.

* * *

---

k. The U.S. is not party to the Covenant. The General Comment is not binding, but it is authoritative.

5. Among the measures, which might be considered appropriate, in addition to legislation, is the provision of judicial remedies with respect to rights, which may, in accordance with the national legal system, be considered justiciable. The Committee notes, for example, that the enjoyment of the rights recognized, without discrimination, will often be appropriately promoted, in part, through the provision of judicial or other effective remedies. * * * [T]here are a number of other provisions in the International Covenant on Economic, Social and Cultural Rights, including articles 3, 7 (a) (i), 8, 10 (3), 13 (2) (a), (3) and (4) and 15 (3) which would seem to be capable of immediate application by judicial and other organs in many national legal systems. Any suggestion that the provisions indicated are inherently non-self-executing would seem to be difficult to sustain.

* * *

7. Other measures may also be considered "appropriate" for the purposes of article 2 (1) include, but are not limited to, administrative, financial, educational and social measures.

8. The Committee notes that the undertaking "to take steps * * * by all appropriate means including particularly the adoption of legislative measures" neither requires nor precludes any particular form of government or economic system being used as the vehicle for the steps in question, provided only that it is democratic and that all human rights are thereby respected. Thus, in terms of political and economic systems the Covenant is neutral and its principles cannot accurately be described as being predicated exclusively upon the need for, or the desirability of a socialist or a capitalist system, or a mixed, centrally planned, or *laisser-faire* economy, or upon any other particular approach. Covenant are susceptible of realization within the context of a wide variety of economic and political systems, provided only that the interdependence and indivisibility of the two sets of human rights, as affirmed *inter alia* in the preamble to the Covenant, is recognized and reflected in the system in question. The Committee also notes the relevance in this regard of other human rights and in particular the right to development.

9. The principal obligation of result reflected in article 2 (1) is to take steps "with a view to achieving progressively the full realization of the rights recognized" in the Covenant. The term "progressive realization" is often used to describe the intent of this phrase * * * the phrase must be read in the light of the overall objective, indeed the raison d'être, of the Covenant which is to establish clear obligations for States parties in respect of the full realization of the rights in question. It thus imposes an obligation to move as expeditiously and effectively as possible towards that goal. Moreover, any deliberately retrogressive measures in that regard would require the most careful consideration and would need to be fully justified by reference to the totality of the rights provided for in the Covenant and in the context of the full use of the maximum available resources.

10. * * * [A] minimum core obligation to ensure the satisfaction of, at the very least, minimum essential levels of each of the rights is incumbent upon every State party. Thus, for example, a State party in

which any significant number of individuals is deprived of essential foodstuffs, of essential primary health care, of basic shelter and housing, or of the most basic forms of education is, *prima facie*, failing to discharge its obligations under the Covenant. * * *

12. Similarly, the Committee underlines the fact that even in times of severe resources constraints whether caused by a process of adjustment, of economic recession, or by other factors the vulnerable members of society can and indeed must be protected by the adoption of relatively low-cost targeted programmes. * * *

AHMEDABAD MUNICIPAL CORPORATION v. NAWAB KHAN GULAB KHAN & ORS

Supreme Court (India).
(1996) SUPP. 7 S.C.R. 548.

[In *Olga Tellis* case [see note below], the Constitution Bench had considered the right to dwell on pavements or in slums by the indigent and the same was accepted as a part of right to life enshrined under Article 21; their ejectment from the place nearer to their work would be deprivation of their right to livelihood. They will be deprived of their livelihood if they are evicted from their slum and pavement dwellings. Their eviction tantamount to deprivation of their life. The right to livelihood is a traditional right to live, the easiest way of depriving a person of his right to life would be to deprive him of his means of livelihood to the point of abrogation. * * * The deprivation of right to life, therefore, must be consistent with the procedure established by law.]

K. Ramaswamy J.

[pp. 557, 558–65, 567, 571, 573, 574–77 of the decision.]

Leave granted.

* * * 29 persons had filed the writ petition in the High Court. They are pavement-dwellers in unauthorised occupation of footpaths of the Rakhial Road in Ahmedabad which is a main road. They have constructed huts thereon. * * * [T]he Corporation sought to remove their encroachments on December 10, 1982. * * * The High Court granted interim stay of removal of the encroachment. By the impugned judgment, the High Court directed the Municipal Corporation not to remove their huts until suitable accommodation was provided to them. The High Court also further held that before removing the unauthorised encroachments the procedure of hearing, consistent with the principles of natural justice should be followed. * * * [On] September 11, 1995, this Court directed the appellant thus: "We think that the Municipal Corporation should frame a Scheme to accommodate them at the alternative places * * *" Pursuant thereto, a Scheme has been framed and placed before this Court.

* * *

A Constitution Bench of this Court in *Sadan Singh etc. v. New Delhi Municipal Committee & Anr. etc.* [(1989) 2 S.C.R. 1038] was confronted with and had considered the question "can there be at all a fundamental right of a citizen to occupy a particular place on the pavement where he can squat and engage in trading business? We have no hesitation in answering the issue against the petitioners. The petitioners do have the fundamental right to carry on a trade or business of their choice, but not to do so on a particular place * * *."

It is for the Court to decide in exercise of its constitutional power of judicial review whether the deprivation of life or personal liberty in a give case is by procedure which is reasonable, fair and just or it is otherwise. Footpath, street or pavement are public property which are intended to serve the convenience of general public. They are not laid for private use indeed, their use for a private purpose frustrates the very object for which they carved out from portions of public roads. * * *

The Constitution does not put an absolute embargo on the deprivation of life or personal liberty but such a deprivation must be according to the procedure, in the given circumstances, fair and reasonable. To become fair, just and reasonable, it would not be enough that the procedure prescribed in law is a formality. It must be pragmatic and realistic one to meet the given fact-situation.

* * *

But the question is; whether the respondents are entitled to alternative settlement before ejectment of them?

Article 19(1) (e) accords right to residence and settlement in any part of India as a fundamental right. Right to life has been assured as a basic human right under Article 21 of the Constitution of India. Article 25(1) of the Universal Declaration of Human Rights declares that everyone has the right to standard of living adequate for the health and well-being of himself and his family; it includes food, clothing, housing, medical care and necessary social service. * * * Article 11(1) of the International Covenant on Economic, Social and Cultural Rights lays down that State parties to the Covenant recognise that everyone has the right to standard of living for himself and his family including food, clothing, housing and to the continuous improvement of living conditions. In *Chameli Singh & Ors. v. State of U.P. & Anr.* [(1996) 2 S.C.C. 549], a Bench of three Judges of this Court had considered and held that the right to shelter is a fundamental right available to every citizen and it was read into Article 21 of the Constitution of India as encompassing within its ambit, the right to shelter to make the right to life more meaningful. In paragraph 8 it has been held thus:

"In any organised society, right to live as a human being is not ensured by meeting only the animal needs of man. It is secured only when he assured of all facilities to develop himself and is freed from restrictions which inhibit his growth. All human rights are designed to achieve this object. Right to live guaranteed in any civilised society implies the right to food, water, decent environment, education, medical care and shelter. These are basic human rights known to any civilised society. All civil, political, social and cultural rights enshrined in the Universal Declaration of Human Rights and Convention or under the Constitution of India cannot be exercised without these basic human rights. Shelter for a human being, therefore, is not a mere protection of his life and limb. It is home where he has opportunities to grow physically, mentally, intellectually and spiritually. Right to shelter, therefore, includes adequate living space, safe and decent structure, clean and decent surroundings, sufficient light, pure air and water, electricity, sanitation and other civic amenities like roads etc. so as to have easy right to shelter, therefore, does not mean a mere right to a roof over one's head but right to all the infrastructure necessary to enable them to live and develop as human being. Right to shelter when used as an essential requisite to the right to live should be deemed to have been guaranteed as a fundamental right. As is enjoined in the Directive Principles, the State should be deemed to be under an obligation to secure it for its citizens, of course subject to its economic budgeting. * * *"

Socio-economic justice, equality of status and of opportunity and dignity of person to foster the fraternity among all the sections of the society in an integrated Bharat is the arch of the Constitution set down in its Preamble. Articles 39 and 38 enjoins the State to provide facilities and opportunities. Article 38 and 46 of the Constitution enjoin the State to promote welfare of the people by securing social an economic justice to the weaker sections of the society to minimise inequalities in income and endeavor to eliminate inequalities in status. In that case, it was held that to bring the Dalits and Tribes into the mainstream of national life, the State was to provide facilities and opportunities as it is the duty of the State to fulfil the basic human and constitutional rights to residents so as to make the right to life meaningful. * * * In *P.G. Gupta v. State of Gujarat* [(1995)] Supp. 2 S.C.C. 182], another Bench of three Judges had considered the mandate of human right to shelter and read it into Article 19(1)(e) and Article 21 of the Constitution and the Universal Declaration of Human Rights and the Convention of Civic, Economic and Cultural Rights and had held that it is the duty of the State to construct houses at reasonable cost and make them easily accessible to the poor. The aforesaid principles have been expressly embodied and in built in our Constitution to secure socio-economic democracy so that everyone has a right to life, liberty and security of the person. Article 22 of the Declaration of Human Rights envisages that everyone has a right t social security and is entitled to its realisation as the economic, social and cultural rights and indispensable for his dignity and free development of his personality. It would, therefore, be clear that though no person has a right to encroach and erect structures or otherwise on footpath, pavement or public streets or any other place reserved or earmarked for a public purpose, the State has the Constitutional duty to provide adequate facilities and opportunities by distributing its wealth and resources for settlement of life and erection of shelter over their heads to make the right to life meaningful, effective and fruitful. Right to livelihood is meaningful because no one can live without means of his living, that is the means of livelihood. The deprivation of the right to life in that context would not only denude right of the effective content and meaningfulness but it would make life miserable and impossible to life. It would, therefore, be the duty of the State to provide right to shelter to the poor and indigent weaker sections of the society in fulfillment of the Constitutional objectives.

[The Corporation provided evidence that a complex scheme for housing with amenities and land was developed and offered to the hutment dwellers. The hutment dwellers argued that the proposed] units are situated at a far away place and direction to vacate the pavements and occupation of the premises would deprive the respondents of their livelihood. * * *

It is rather unfortunate that even after half the century from date of independence, no constructive planning has been implemented to ameliorate the conditions of the rural people by providing regular source of livelihood or infrastructural facilities like health, education, sanitation etc. * * * Article 38,39 and 46 mandate the State, as its minimise inequalities in income and in opportunities and status. It positively charges the State to distribute its largess to the weaker sections of the society envisaged in Article 46 to make socio-economic justice a reality, meaningful and fruitful so as to make the life worth living with dignity of person and equality of status and to constantly improve excellence. [Under the Constitution] municipalities [are] constitutional instrumentalities to elongate the socio-economic and political democracy under the rule of law. * * *

* * * The appellant-Corporation, therefore, has Constitutional duty and authority to implement the directives contained in Articles 38, 39 and 46 and all cognate all the citizens as meaningful. It would, therefore, be the duty of the appellant to enforce the schemes in a planned manner by annual budgets to provide right to residence to the poor.

As regards the question of budgeting, it is true that Courts cannot give direction to implement the scheme with a particular budget as it being the executive function of the local bodies and the State to evolve their annual budget. As an integral passing annual budget, they should also earmark implementation of socio-economic justice to the poor. * * * It is common knowledge that when Government allows largess to the poor, by pressures or surreptitious means or in the language of the appellant-Corporation "the slum lords" exert pressures on the vulnerable sections of the society to vacate their place of occupation and shift for settlement to other vacant lands belonging to the State or municipalities or private properties by encroachment. * * * The facts in this case do disclose that out of 29 encroachers who have constructed the houses on pavements, 19 of them have left the places, obviously due to such pressures and interests of rest have come into existence by way of purchase. When such persons part with possession in any manner known to law, the alienation or transfer is opposed to the Constitutional objectives and public policy. Therefore, such transfers are void ab initio conferring no right, title or interest therein.

* * *

As regards the direction given by the High Court to provide accommodation as a condition to remove the encroachment * * * the financial condition of the Corporation may also be kept in view but that would not be a constraint on the Corporation to avoid its duty of providing residence/plot to the urban weaker sections. It would, therefore, be the duty of the Corporation to evolve the schemes. In the light of the schemes now in operation, we are of view that opportunity should be given to the 10 named petitioner encroachers to opt for any one of the three schemes. * * *

Notes and Questions

1. The German Court finds that the right to a minimum standard of living applies to expenses related to childcare maintenance, given the special protection to family and children in the Basic Law. In determining the needs of life, self-development requirements must be considered. This is in conformity with the GFCC's understanding of the human personality as a development process. The Austrian Constitutional Court came to similar conclusions in a series of cases regarding that portion of the personal income tax that is levied to cover childcare costs. The case could have been decided on grounds of the rights of children. Instead, the Court considered how childcare maintenance affected the statutory obligation of a minimum standard of living (whether after-tax income was sufficient to maintain the minimum standard). The Court found that social welfare prestations (subsidies, transfers) and communal services must be taken into consideration when calculating childcare costs. The provided childcare is not a matter of choice in one's private life. One has to take into consideration, for tax purposes, what remains after the deduction of maintenance obligations. (G 168, 285/96 (17.11.1997) (VfSlg. 14.992)).

2. *Dignity and social-existence minimums.* The GFCC confronted the problem of minimum living standards in a series of decisions. (*Kinderfreibeträge* (Children's allowance), 43 BVerfGE 108,121; *Steuerfreies Existenzminimum* (Tax-free minimum standard of living (*Minimum Livelihood Case*)), 82 BVerfGE 60, etc.) The Basic Law has provisions to protect the family, but these do not require the state to equalize family burdens. The state provides other services to families, such as education. The state must give proper consideration to the burdens of childcare, through tax relief or child-support subsidies (prestations). The state must leave such an amount of income tax free that would allow the safeguard "of the minimum conditions of an existence that is worthy of human dignity." The USSC seems to implicitly deny the right to a social minimum. (See *Dandridge v. Williams*, 397 U.S. 471 (1970), in Chapter 6, Subsection A.1.)

3. Like in Germany, most constitutional courts tend to leave the determination of child-support services to the legislature. The Korean Supreme Court, in the *Standards for Protection of Livelihood Case*, found that:

> In a judicial review of whether the state performed its constitutional duty to guarantee people to have living condition worthy of human beings, the state action can be adjudged unconstitutional only where the state did not legislate for livelihood protection at all or where legislation is so irrational that the state abused its discretion.

> Whether the standards for livelihood protection are reasonable has to be determined by considering all relevant payments for livelihood protection and all reduced or exempted burdens. Taking into account all these elements, i.e., livelihood protection payment, winter subsidy, elderly

allowance, free transportation, exemption of charge for TV, reduction of utility fare, etc., the standards in question did not transgress the petitioners' right to pursue happiness and to enjoy life worthy of human beings.

9–1 KCCR 543, 94 HunMa 33, May 29, 1997.[1]

4. In *Asahi v. Japan* (see *The Constitutional Case Law of Japan: Selected Supreme Court Decisions, 1961–70*, at 131–47 (Hiroshi Itoh and Lawrence W. Beer eds., 1978)), a tuberculosis patient was receiving 600 yen a month from the government, in addition to free meals and medical treatment. The payment was stopped once Asahi's brother began to provide him financial support. Asahi's claim for reinstatement was based on the Livelihood Protection Act and Art. 25 of the Constitution. The Supreme Court held that Art. 25 "merely proclaims that it is the duty of the state to administer national policy in such a manner as to enable all the people to enjoy at least the minimum standards of wholesome and cultivated living; and it does not grant the people as individuals any concrete rights." The rights are protected through the specific enactment. A "concrete right consists of a right to receive such assistance as is stipulated in the schedule that the minister of Health and Welfare establishes on the belief that the schedule is sufficient to maintain minimum standards of living." How does this compare with the position of the GFCC in the *Minimum Livelihood Case*? Is the German Court more active because of a different understanding of separation of powers? Or does the tax context versus the welfare context make the difference? Note, once again, how little guidance the constitutional text provides regarding the individual enforceability of social welfare rights.

Does human dignity, "in conjunction with the social state principle," require the state to provide special support to enable the citizen to live a meaningful life? If the state is constitutionally required not to take away what is needed to live a socially acceptable life, called in German the "existential minimum," is it also required to provide this for people who have inadequate incomes? If there are such obligations, do free social services satisfy them? Note that all these decisions came up in the context of child support, although the care and upbringing of children are the "natural right of, and a duty primarily incumbent on, the parents." Basic Law, Art. 6. (2). (On dignity, see Chapter 5.)

5. The German concept of the social state is the basis of the state's legal obligations. The legislature has a constitutional mandate to realize the social state. Assumptions about the social nature of the state may result in welfare-enhancing interpretations. The Preamble of the 1946 French Constitution, which is part of the current 1958 Constitution, contains openly socialistic aspirations. It is on this basis that the French Constitutional Council considers certain social rights (health, decent housing) as objectives

---

1. A translation of the summary of the Court's rationale can be found at the Court's web page. The petitioners, a couple whose livelihood was protected under the Protection of Minimum Living Standards Act, filed a constitutional complaint, alleging that the payment level, suggested by the "Livelihood protection standards of 1994" in the "Directions for Livelihood Protection Project of 1994" notified by the

Minister of Health and Welfare, was far short of the minimum cost of living. The issue was whether the challenged "Livelihood protection standards of 1994" transgressed the petitioners' right to pursue happiness and to enjoy life worthy of human beings, i.e., a guaranteed minimal quality of life. See <http://www.ccourt.go.kr/english/case50.html>. The Court dismissed the petition.

with constitutional value.[m] The Council interprets such objectives as a result of the state's obligation to provide services. The legislature has to provide for adequate realization of the Preamble (89–269 DC of 22 Jan. 1990). The *Conseil d'État* held that the public healthcare expenditure should be fixed at a level that is compatible with the healthcare needs of the population.

The social-state requirement also has an impact on the interpretation of other provisions in the Basic Law, including social justice, which, as the *Minimum Livelihood Case* indicates, has a strong equality component. In view of the CESCR, are the social rights in a rich, developed welfare state, like Germany, the same as those in a developing country? Recall that housing problems in Germany are discussed in terms of the quasi-property rights of tenants, entrenched by legislation, while the issue in India is that of access to housing that is not implemented by legislation. The Indian courts argue that the state has a constitutional duty to provide housing to the needy. Can you infer such a duty from the German concept of the social state? Compare also the affirmative state duties stemming from human dignity in India, Germany, and France.[n] Dignity is used much less aggressively by Western courts in regard to the state's economic duties. Can this difference be attributed to the fact that in Germany the state provides for what is needed, and thus the level of poverty, as affecting dignity, is not comparable in the two countries?

6. Compare the ISC's position with the following two comments on the relation between dignity and social rights. Is the dignity concern the same?

[T]he United Nations estimates that there are over 100 million persons homeless worldwide and over 1 billion inadequately housed. * * * In the Committee's view, the right to housing should not be interpreted in a narrow or restrictive sense which equates it with, for example, the shelter provided by merely having a roof over one's head or views shelter exclusively as a commodity. Rather it should be seen as the right to live somewhere in security, peace and dignity. This is appropriate for at least two reasons. In the first place, the right to housing is integrally

---

m. A constitutional objective may serve to limit a fundamental right or liberty. Moreover, the Council may find unconstitutional a provision of law or regulation that does not serve the pursuit of, or hampers, a constitutional objective. Cf. Bernard Mathieu, *La protection du droit à la santé par le juge constitutionnel. A propos et a partir de la decision de la Cour constitutionnelle italienne no 185 du 20 mai 1998* (protection of the right to health by the constitutional judge, by the way of and starting from the decision of the Italian Constitutional Court No 185 of May 20, 1998), *Cahiers du Conseil constitutionnel*, No. 6. 1998.

n. Once the French Constitutional Council recognized the principle of respect for the dignity of the human person, the principle was applied to decent housing. In 94–359 DC of 19 Jan. 1995, *Loi relative à la diversité de l'habitat* (Law relating to the diversity of the habitat) and 98–403 of 29 July 1998, *Loi d'orientation relative à la lutte contre les exclusions* (law of orientation relating to the fight against exclusions)

the possibility for all to have decent housing was found to be an objective of constitutional value, which enables the Council to review legislation. The source of this objective was found in the rights and freedoms of the human person of para. 1 of the Preamble of 1946, in conjunction with paras. 10–11 (on conditions necessary for development and the guarantee of material security and means of decent existence for those unable to work). The objective was found not to be violated in regard to certain contraventions, which punished irregularities of stay of foreigners. See 96–377 DC of 16 July 1996, *Loi tendant à renforcer la répression du terrorisme et des atteintes aux personnes dépositaires de l'autorité publique ou chargées d'une mission de service public et comportant des dispositions relatives à la police judiciaire* (law tending to reinforce the repression of terrorism and the attacks to the agents of the public authority or in charge of a mission of public utility and comprising provisions relating to the Criminal Investigation Department).

linked to other human rights and to the fundamental principles upon which the Covenant is premised. This "the inherent dignity of the human person" from which the rights in the Covenant are said to derive requires that the term "housing" be interpreted so as to take account of a variety of other considerations, most importantly that the right to housing should be ensured to all persons irrespective of income or access to economic resources. Secondly, the reference in article 11 (1) must be read as referring not just to housing but to adequate housing. As both the Commission on Human Settlements and the Global Strategy for Shelter to the Year 2000 have stated: "Adequate shelter means * * * adequate privacy, adequate space, adequate security, adequate lighting and ventilation, adequate basic infrastructure and adequate location with regard to work and basic facilities—all at a reasonable cost.

CESCR General Comment No. 4, "The right to adequate housing." (art. 11(1) of the Covenant), U.N. ESCOR, Comm. On Econ., Soc., & Cultural Rights, 6th Sess., Supp. No. 3, at 114, U.N. Doc. E/1992/23–E/C.12/1991/4 Annex III (1991), paras. 5, 7.

Lawrence Tribe, *American Constitutional Law* 778–79 (2d ed. 1988), writes:

People who cannot buy bread cannot follow the suggestion that they eat cake; people bowed under the weight of poverty are unlikely to stand up for their constitutional rights. Yet the Constitution cannot readily be construed to make income support an affirmative duty of the state.

The effort to identify the "indispensable conditions of an open society" thus proves inseparable from the much larger enterprise of identifying the elements of being human—and deciding, which of those elements are entirely to politics to protect, and which are entrusted to protection by judicial decree. * * * [T]he supposed dichotomy between economic and personal rights must fail, * * *. The day may indeed come when a general doctrine under the fifth and fourteenth amendments recognizes for each individual a constitutional right to a decent level of affirmative governmental protection in meeting the basic human needs of physical survival and security, health and housing, work and schooling. * * * But * * * that time has not yet come.[15]

7. *Justiciabilty*. In Germany, it is taken for granted that social obligations that serve as the guarantee of a minimum that cannot be taken away from the individual do not amount to individual rights that could be claimed in a court. The enforceability of constitutional provisions on welfare rights and the proper role of judicial review are often subject to debate in other jurisdictions. In its first judgment on the certification of the Constitution, the South African Constitutional Court (SACC) said that socioeconomic rights are justiciable to a certain extent. "At the very minimum, socioeconomic rights can be negatively protected from improper invasion." *Ex parte Chairperson of the Constitutional Assembly: In re Certification of the Constitution of the Republic of S. Afr.*, 1996 (4) SALR 744, 801 (CC) (para. 78). Is "protection from governmental invasion" a realistic judicial strategy in the field of welfare rights?

The SACC said:

15. See, e.g., *Maher v. Roe*, 432 U.S. 464, 469 (1977) (upholding state refusal to fund nontherapeutic abortions): "The Constitution imposes no obligation on the States to pay the pregnancy-related medical expenses of indigent women, or indeed to pay any of the medical expenses of indigents."

it is true that the inclusion of socio-economic rights may result in courts making orders which have direct implications for budgetary matters. However, even when a court enforces civil and political rights such as equality, freedom of speech and the right to a fair trial, the order it makes will often have such implications. * * *

[W]e are of the view that these rights are, at least to some extent justiciable. * * * [M]any of the civil and political rights entrenched in the NT will give rise to similar budgetary implications without compromising their justiciability. The fact that socio-economic rights will almost inevitably give rise to such implications does not seem to is a bar to their justiciability.

Id. at 800, para. 77.

Do you agree with the Court that there is no fundamental difference between various rights as all rights have budgetary implications? Confronted with actual spending limits, the SACC took a more cautious position on state-financed dialysis in the *Soobramoney Case* below.

8. *Courts writing the state budget?* The constitutional recognition of welfare rights and entitlements has multiple meanings and consequences, ranging from establishing legitimate budget expenditures to individual-rights claims enforceable in a court of justice. The various options are not exclusive. The Indian *Ahmedabad* case, above, indicates that welfare rights may trigger special governmental programs that may (as is the case in India), or may not, be subject to substantive review. Compare the judicial position regarding budgetary allocations required by the making good of a social right. In the South African dialysis case the court was satisfied with the amount allocated by the government. In Germany, the GFCC did not go into the analysis of the adequacy of the funding provided by the state for universities in *Numerus Clausus I* (below), where the funding serves the satisfaction of the right of free choice of occupation; it required only that the most efficient regulatory scheme be applied in using the resources. The ISC, on the other hand, ordered an unspecified budgetary allocation for housing; in this case, however, the budget appropriation was completely absent. Can you envision a situation where the courts will probe the adequacy of a fundamental social right enabling spending? Where there is a social right in the constitution, a "Directive Policy" (in India) or a "State Task" (in Spain), would the failure to enact rights-protecting legislation amount prima facie to a violation of state duties? The Russian Constitution, in addition to state obligations regarding public housing, requires that municipalities take proper measures to promote the right to housing for the needy. Does this impose an obligation on the central budget to allocate resources to municipalities to help them satisfy their obligations?

9. *Are there economic limits to the state's obligations to satisfy welfare rights?* The minimum common expectation generated by a social right is that the state should provide regulations that enable access to rights-enhancing services. The standard position of the Italian Constitutional Court (ICC) is that the protection of the right to health is subject to the constraints that are present in the redistribution of the available resources. But the Court found that the demands of public finance cannot destroy the hard core of the right to health, which is protected as an inviolable part of human dignity. The free healthcare of poorer citizens is therefore protected. This applies even if the poor citizen travels abroad as such travel might be part of

personal development (309/1999, ICC). (The Act under review on the national health service granted free healthcare abroad only to certain categories of the poor, depending on the reason for the foreign stay—e.g., employment or study reasons but not family visits or leisure.) If extra expenses in the healthcare system are triggered by the self-development rights of the citizen, are extra benefits dictated by core elements of that self-development? For example, are additional medical costs to be covered as part of the equal right to health if the additional spending is dictated by religious considerations? When a Spanish Jehovah's Witness was refused treatment for objecting to a blood transfusion in a public healthcare hospital, he had the surgery at a private clinic, without the blood transfusion. He petitioned the public insurance scheme for reimbursement, which was denied. The Spanish Constitutional Tribunal held that the duty of the state to ensure effective and genuine operation of the right to freedom of religion did not entail any obligation to provide alternative medical services for adherents of a given faith so that they might fulfil a requirement of their religion (166/1996, BCCL 1996, 421).

10. *Directive Principles of State Policy (India).* Consider Mahendra P. Singh, *V.N. Shukla's Constitution of India* A45–46 (9th ed. 1996):

Part IV of the [Indian] Constitution enumerates certain Directive Principles of State Policy, which are declared as fundamental in the governance of the country. These principles are intended to be the imperative basis of State policy.

* * *

The Directive Principles of State Policy differ in one vital respect from the fundamental rights. Whereas the former are non-justiciable rights, the latter are justiciable rights. They have expressly been excluded from the purview of the courts.

* * *

In the nature of things the rights enumerated in this part can only be directives and cannot be justiciable rights. This is so because the directive principles require positive action on the part of the State, and, therefore, can be guaranteed only so far as practicable. * * * However, the significant thing to note about the Directive Principles of State Policy is, as Matthew, J. pointed out in the Kesavananda Bharati case, that, although they are expressly made unenforceable, that does not affect their fundamental character. They still very much form part of the constitutional law of the land. They are as important as the fundamental rights of individuals. They are fundamental in the governance of the country.

* * *

Mathew, J. went a step further and explained that whether at a particular moment in the history of the nation, a particular fundamental right should have priority over the moral claims embodied in Part IV or must yield to them is a matter which must be left to be decided by each generation in the light of its experience and values.

* * * It is * * * not correct to say that under the constitutional scheme, Fundamental Rights are superior to Directive Principles or Directive Principles must yield to Fundamental Rights. Both are in fact equally fundamental and an effort should be made to harmonise them by

importing the Directive Principles in the construction of Fundamental Rights. This harmony must be maintained even by constitutional amendments. The Constitution is founded on the bed-rock of the balance between Parts III and IV.

11.   The right to adequate housing first came up in India in *Olga Tellis v. Bombay Municipal Corporation*, (1985) 3 S.C.C. 545. The Bombay Municipality, without prior notice, forcefully evicted pavement dwellers from their shacks on one of the main streets of Bombay. The court found a right to shelter in the right to life. Though the state was not held responsible for providing shelter, a just and fair procedure established by law was found to be necessary for deprivation of the right to livelihood, similar to U.S. due process protection or German social justice. At this time, however, the recognition of a right to livelihood in the right to life did not trigger positive state action, nor did the ISC invalidate the eviction law. But it did set stringent conditions for removal in requiring alternative sites for resettlements. The Court gradually moved toward finding that the right to shelter results in a corresponding duty of the state to develop adequate, judicially supervised programs to realize the right. The movement toward more active government involvement results from a reading of the Directive Principles, first as a negative duty: "This right to live with human dignity enshrined in Article 21 derives its life breath from the Directive Principles of State Policy ... No state * * * has the right to take any action which will deprive a person of the enjoyment of * * * basic essentials [from health protection to protection of children against abuse, education, and humane work conditions]." *Id.* at 183, para. 10.

12.   When reviewing the law on housing lease and housing benefits (Act of July 2, 1994), the Polish Constitutional Tribunal found that the provisions of the Act that allowed the eviction of pregnant women, minors, handicapped persons and their caretakers, or persons entitled to social housing was unconstitutional. (Judgement of April 4, 2001, K. 11/00.)

> The case was initiated by Ombudsman Andrzej Zoll, who asked the Tribunal to review a section of the Law on Rent dealing with evictions. Overall, the law has made it more difficult to evict people by forbidding the evictions of pregnant women, families with children, or disabled persons and their cohabitants. It also established that the court must review the economic situation of any person threatened by eviction and decide about his or her right to receive public housing. But another amendment also permitted carrying out evictions that had already been ordered before these new provisions were adopted. The ombudsman argued that this was unconstitutional. On April 4, the Tribunal agreed, ruling the measures unconstitutional. The Tribunal found them a violation of Art. 30 ("The inherent and inalienable dignity of the person shall constitute a source of freedoms and rights of persons and citizens. It shall be inviolable. The respect and protection thereof shall be the obligation of public authorities") and Art. 71.1 ("The State, in its social and economic policy, shall take into account the good of the family. Families, finding themselves in difficult material and social circumstances—particularly those with many children or a single parent—shall

have the right to special assistance from public authorities"). The ruling did not overturn the previous eviction orders but opened the possibility for appeal. During 2000, the number of removals quadrupled, with 90 percent of the cases due to unpaid rent.

Poland Update, E. Eur. Const. Rev., vol. 10, nos. 2–3, at 35 (2001).

13. The Hungarian Constitutional Court (HCC) held that the right to social security (Art. 70/E, Hungarian Constitution) does not include a right to housing. Nonetheless, the Court said that the right to social security requires the state to provide for minimum sustenance, by establishing and maintaining a welfare system within the government's fiscal capacities. The state's obligation stems from its duty to protect human life and dignity (Art. 54(1), Hungarian Constitution). Although the Court refused to identify the specific rights that might be contained in the right to social security, the justices said that it follows from the duty of the state to provide housing in cases where the lack of shelter endangers one's life. Decision 42/2000 (XI.8.) AB hat. on the abstract interpretation of Art. 70/E of the Constitution.

In light of the above cases, is the scope of protection offered against "eviction to the street" the same in both Hungary and Poland? Compare the approach of the Indian, Polish, and Hungarian courts to the right to life and dignity. Was human dignity used to impose an obligation on the state to provide shelter (protection against eviction) on a novel ground, or was it used to specify an existing constitutional right? Considering the Hungarian case on the right to housing, why would a constitutional court refuse to specify the components of the right to social security? Why might it specify such rights?

14. In *Government of South Africa v. Grootboom*, 2001 (1) SALR 46 (CC), the SACC defined the scope of the right of access to adequate housing in Section 26(1) and the extent of the government's obligation to "take reasonable legislative and other measures to achieve the progressive realization of the right within available resources" in Section 26(2). The legislature enacted a program in furtherance of the obligation to construct low cost housing. After having been on the waiting list of the housing program for years, applicants in the case moved from their "informal settlement" and occupied the land designated for low-cost housing, from which they were evicted by a court order with all their belongings demolished. After constructing shacks from sheets of plastic, the applicants claimed a violation of their right of access to adequate housing (Section 26).

When interpreting Section 26(2), the Constitutional Court said:

> "[The] State is obliged to take positive action to meet the needs of those living in extreme conditions of poverty, homelessness or intolerable housing. * * * The right of access to adequate housing is entrenched because we value human beings and want to ensure that they are afforded their basic human needs. A society must seek to ensure that the basic necessities of life are provided to all if it is to be a society based on human dignity, freedom and equality."

Id. at 62, 69, paras. 24, 44.

The Court found that while the government's program was capable of fulfilling midterm and long-term objectives of housing development, it failed to respond to the needs of those in desperate situations. The Court emphasized that Section 26(2) does not create direct individual claims for access to adequate housing, but the constitutional right of access to adequate housing means that the government has a duty to establish and maintain a system that provides adequate access to housing.

The scope of the *Grootboom* decision is not easy to define. In a subsequent decision, *Minister of Public Works v. Kyalami Ridge Environmental Association*, (3) SALR 1151 (CC), the Court faced a fact scenario resembling *Grootboom*. The government had offered temporary shelter to flood victims on a prison farm, without prior consultation with the residents of the nearby township. The residents of the township challenged the establishment of the camp for the flood victims with reference to environmental protection legislation and argued, also, that the actions of the government were ultra vires. The Court held that the government's power to offer temporary shelter to the flood victims was valid because the government owned the land on which the transit camp was established.

The SACC decided *Kyalami* on the basis of property rights and not with reference to Section 26 of the Constitution. Is the government wholly free to use its property as it sees fit, or are there constraints on the government when it acts as an owner? In a broader context, is not *Kyalami* about the very situation described in *Grootboom*? If so, why did the Court not apply the same doctrine? In light of *Kyalami*, may the Court's willingness to apply Section 26 and the right to access to housing in *Grootboom* be regarded as an exception? Does the decision in *Kyalami* suggest that the Court prefers to settle issues on formal or nonconstitutional grounds?

15.   *Access to housing under the European HR Convention.* The European HR Convention does not expressly protect the right to housing. Article 8 (1) of the Convention provides that everyone has the right to respect for his private and family life, his home, and his correspondence. While Art. 8 of the Convention is generally considered as a "privacy clause," the decision of the ECHR in *Chapman v. United Kingdom*, 33 E.H.R.R. (2001), indicates that the Court is willing to afford some protection to a right to housing under Art. 8.

The applicant was a gypsy (Roma), living with her family in a caravan (mobile home), shuttling constantly between unofficial sites. The family was on the waiting list for an official site, without ever being offered one. In 1985, the applicant bought a piece of land with the intention of living on it in a mobile home. Over the years, her numerous applications for permission to live in a mobile home or to erect a bungalow on the land were refused on environmental considerations. An alternative site for a home was never offered, and the applicant's family refused to leave their land. The applicant challenged the actions of the UK authorities, claiming inter alia that her right to a home was infringed under Art. 8 of the European HR Convention. The ECHR found that

"the applicant's occupation of her caravan is an integral part of her ethnic identity as a gypsy, reflecting the long tradition of that minority of following a travelling lifestyle. * * * Measures which affect the applicant's stationing of her caravans have therefore a wider impact than on the right to respect for home. They also affect her ability to maintain her identity as a gypsy and to lead her private and family life in accordance with that tradition."

Id. at 421, para. 73.

An issue in the case was whether the limitation imposed by the government on the applicant's right to a home was necessary in a democratic society. The Court emphasized the government's "wide margin of appreciation," but, acknowledging that the gypsies constitute a vulnerable minority, the Court held they were entitled to special consideration and to accommodation of their lifestyle: "To this extent there is thus a positive obligation imposed on the Contracting States by virtue of Article 8 to facilitate the gypsy way of life." *Id.* at 427, para. 96. Nonetheless, the Court said that it could not impose an obligation on the government to provide housing to the gypsies in fulfillment of its positive obligation under Art. 8 of the European HR Convention, not even in light of a clear housing shortage.

The Court held that:

Article 8 does not in terms give a right to be provided with a home. Nor does any of the jurisprudence of the Court acknowledge such a right. While it is clearly desirable that every human being has a place where he or she can live in dignity and which he or she can call home, there are unfortunately in the Contracting States many persons who have no home. Whether the State provides funds to enable everyone to have a home is a matter for political not judicial decision. In sum, the issue for determination before the Court in the present case is not the acceptability or not of a general situation, however deplorable, in the United Kingdom in the light of the United Kingdom's undertakings in international law, but the narrower one whether the particular circumstances of the case disclose a violation of the applicant's, Mrs. Chapman's, right to respect for her home under Article 8 of the Convention.

* * *

The humanitarian considerations which might have supported another outcome at national level cannot be used as the basis of a finding by the Court which would be tantamount to exempting the applicant from the implementation of the national planning laws and obliging governments to ensure that every gypsy family has available for its use accommodation appropriate to its needs.

Id. at 427–29, paras. 99, 100, 105.

The Court did not attribute special significance to the fact that the applicant's family was limited in using the land it owned. The applicant's claim was based on the environmental restrictions on land use. The Court tied the protection of the home to the protection of dignity. Was this a strong argument? If the state cannot be required under Art. 8 of the Convention to provide housing even when there is an apparent shortage, what does a positive obligation under Art. 8 mean? Can the Court's deference be attributed to the fact that it is not a domestic forum of rights protection? If so, how do we explain cases where the Court recognizes rights?

SOOBRAMONEY v. MINISTER OF HEALTH (KWAZULU–NATAL)

Constitutional Court (South Africa).
1998 (1) SALR 765 (CC).

Chaskalson P:

[1] The appellant, a 41 year old unemployed man, is a diabetic * * * In 1996 his kidneys also failed. Sadly his condition is irreversible

and he is now in the final stages of chronic renal failure. His life could be prolonged by means of regular renal dialysis. He has sought such treatment from the renal unit of the Addington state hospital in Durban. The hospital can, however, only provide dialysis treatment to a limited number of patients.

* * *

[3]   * * * Only patients who suffer from acute renal failure, which can be treated and remedied[1] by renal dialysis are given automatic access to renal dialysis at the hospital. Those patients who, like the appellant, suffer from chronic renal failure which is irreversible are not admitted automatically to the renal programme. * * *

[4]   * * * The appellant suffers from ischaemic heart disease and [according to the guidelines,] he is therefore not eligible for a kidney transplant.

* * *

[7]   The appellant based his claim on section 27(3) of the 1996 Constitution which provides: "No one may be refused emergency medical treatment" and section 11 which stipulates "Everyone has the right to life."[o]

* * *

[11]   What is apparent from these provisions is that the obligations imposed on the state by sections 26 and 27 in regard to access to housing, health care, food, water and social security are dependent upon the resources available for such purposes, and that the corresponding rights themselves are limited by reason of the lack of resources. Given this lack of resources and the significant demands on them that have already been referred to, an unqualified obligation to meet these needs would not presently be capable of being fulfilled. This is the context within which section 27(3) must be construed.

* * *

1. Where the renal failure can be cured by dialysis, it is usually achieved within a period of four to six weeks from the commencement of the treatment.

o. Section 26 Housing

(1) Everyone has the right to have access to adequate housing.

(2) The state must take reasonable legislative and other measures, within its available resources, to achieve the progressive realisation of this right.

(3) No one may be evicted from their home, or have their home demolished, without an order of court made after considering all the relevant circumstances. No legislation may permit arbitrary evictions.

Section 27 Health care, food, water and social security

(1) Everyone has the right to have access to–

  (a) health care services, including reproductive health care;

  (b) sufficient food and water; and

  (c) social security, including, if they are unable to support themselves and their dependants, appropriate social assistance.

(2) The state must take reasonable legislative and other measures, within its available resources, to achieve the progressive realisation of each of these rights.

(3) No one may be refused emergency medical treatment.

[14] Counsel for the appellant argued that section 27(3) should be construed consistently with the right to life entrenched in section 11 of the Constitution and that everyone requiring life-saving treatment who is unable to pay for such treatment herself or himself is entitled to have the treatment provided at a state hospital without charge.

* * *

[19] * * * If section 27(3) were to be construed in accordance with the appellant's contention it would make it substantially more difficult for the state to fulfill its primary obligations under sections 27(1) and (2) to provide health care services to "everyone" within its available resources. It would also have the consequence of prioritising the treatment of terminal illnesses over other forms of medical care and would reduce the resources available to the state for purposes such as preventative health care and medical treatment for persons suffering from illnesses or bodily infirmities which are not life threatening. In my view much clearer language than that used in section 27(3) would be required to justify such a conclusion.

[20] Section 27(3) itself is couched in negative terms—it is a right not to be refused emergency treatment. The purpose of the right seems to be to ensure that treatment be given in an emergency, and is not frustrated by reason of bureaucratic requirements or other formalities. A person who suffers a sudden catastrophe which calls for immediate medical attention * * * should not be refused ambulance or other emergency services which are available and should not be turned away from a hospital which is able to provide the necessary treatment.[10] What the section requires is that remedial treatment that is necessary and available be given immediately to avert that harm.

[21] The applicant suffers from chronic renal failure. To be kept alive by dialysis he would require such treatment two to three times a week. This is not an emergency which calls for immediate remedial treatment. It is an ongoing state of affairs resulting from a deterioration of the applicant's renal function which is incurable. In my view section 27(3) does not apply to these facts.

[22] The appellant's demand to receive dialysis treatment at a state hospital must be determined in accordance with the provisions of sections 27(1) and (2) and not section 27(3). These sections entitle everyone to have access to health care services provided by the state "within its available resources".

* * *

[29] The provincial administration which is responsible for health services in KwaZulu–Natal has to make decisions about the funding that should be made available for health care and how such funds should be spent. These choices involve difficult decisions to be taken at the political level in fixing the health budget, and at the functional level in deciding

10. We have only recently emerged from a system of government in which the provision of health services depended on race. On occasions seriously injured persons were refused access to ambulance services or admission to the nearest or best equipped hospital on racial grounds.

upon the priorities to be met. A court will be slow to interfere with rational decisions taken in good faith by the political organs and medical authorities whose responsibility it is to deal with such matters.

* * *

[31]   * * * There are also those who need access to housing, food and water, employment opportunities, and social security. These too are aspects of the right to "... human life: the right to live as a human being, to be part of a broader community, to share in the experience of humanity."ᵖ

The State has to manage its limited resources in order to address all these claims. There will be times when this requires it to adopt a holistic approach to the larger needs of society rather than to focus on the specific needs of particular individuals within society.

* * *

[37]   (dismissed.)

Madala J:

* * *

[42]   The Constitution is forward-looking and guarantees to every citizen fundamental rights in such a manner that the ordinary person-in-the-street, who is aware of these guarantees, immediately claims them without further ado—and assumes that every right so guaranteed is available to him or her on demand. Some rights in the Constitution are the ideal and something to be strived for. They amount to a promise, in some cases, and an indication of what a democratic society aiming to salvage lost dignity, freedom and equality should embark upon. They are values which the Constitution seeks to provide, nurture and protect for a future South Africa.

[43]   However, the guarantees of the Constitution are not absolute but may be limited in one way or another. In some instances, the Constitution states in so many words that the state must take reasonable legislative and other measures, within its available resources "to achieve the progressive realisation of each of these rights." In its language, the Constitution accepts that it cannot solve all of our society's woes overnight, but must go on trying to resolve these problems. One of the limiting factors to the attainment of the Constitution's guarantees is that of limited or scarce resources.

* * *

Sachs J:

* * *

[54]   * * * Traditional rights analyses * * * have to be adapted so as to take account of the special problems created by the need to provide a broad framework of constitutional principles governing the right of access to scarce resources and to adjudicate between competing rights

p.   Per Justice O'Regan in *S. v. Makwanyane*, [see Chapter 2, note 5 at para. 326.]

bearers. When rights by their very nature are shared and inter-dependent, striking appropriate balances between the equally valid entitlements or expectations of a multitude of claimants should not be seen as imposing limits on those rights (which would then have to be justified in terms of section 36), but as defining the circumstances in which the rights may most fairly and effectively be enjoyed.

SMOKING IN CLOSED AREAS CASE

Constitutional Court (Italy).
Judgment n. 399 of Dec. 11, 1996.

* * * The constant jurisprudence of this Court holding that health is a primary benefit which rises to a fundamental right of the person and requires full and exhaustive protection, so as to operate in the public and private spheres of the law, must be recognized.

It has also been repeatedly affirmed that the protection of health regards to the general and common expectation an individual has to conditions of life, environment and work that do not put this essential benefit at risk. Such protection implicates not only active situations of the expectation, but includes, other than preventive measures, the duty not to harm or put the health of others at risk. Therefore, where an incompatibility exists between the constitutionally protected right to the protection of health and freedom of action without [specific] constitutional protection, the former shall prevail.

The Tribunal now refers a case not in regard to the prohibition on smoking in the areas considered in Decision n. 202 of 1991, but with regard to the harm deriving from second-hand smoke in closed areas of the workplace, for specific consideration of these premises. The referring magistrate advises that "this is not a request for damages, rather a preventive action for the adoption of measures to avoid the actualization of a harm." The referral points out that subsequent to [ICC] Decision n. 202 of 1991, the legislator, in effectuating European Community directives, has regulated (in legislative decree n. 626 of 1994) the subject of the protection of workers' health and security, without, nevertheless introducing a general and absolute prohibition on smoking at the workplace.

The referral indicates that the law, while expressly demanding the "protection of non-smokers against the inconveniences of smoke" with regard to certain premises (hospital wards, schools, means of public transportation), and other places "for public gatherings," as well as in a number of "premises for entertainment" [and all premises open to the public belonging to the public administration and to private entities offering public services], it does not provide for analogous prohibitions in workplace premises which numerous employees must occupy for long periods of time.

* * *

It is * * * unreasonable to maintain that these prohibitions should pertain only to businesses in their recreational premises—as accepted by the banking institute in the present case—or common areas (coffee shops, cafeterias, etc.) used by employees rather than to premises they need to occupy in order to fully and energetically perform their [primary activities].

* * *

* * * [Although] an absolute and general prohibition on smoking in all closed areas of the workplace is not recognizable in the positive laws, it is also true that provisions intended to protect the health of workers from all that may harm it, including passive smoke, already exist in the ordinance.

The fact that certain norms legislatively prescribe an absolute prohibition on smoking in special circumstances, does not exclude the legitimacy of an analogous prohibition with regard to different locations. * * *

In * * * the fulfillment of these provisions of a pragmatic but also preceptive nature, employers must engage themselves to concretely verify that the health of workers is adequately protected [without specific command of the law].

It is not for this Court to specify the various possible measures and procedures of such interventions (change of locations, schedules, facilities, and possible prohibitions), since these originate, other than from compliance with the legislative proscriptions, from diligent evaluations by employers taking the particular circumstances in which specific jobs must be performed into consideration, as well as through supervision by workers, inspectors and labor judges.

It is for the Court to note, instead, that, the duty to supervise and to provide for adequately, [which is] present in the rights of workers (Art. 9 of the Statute, and Art. 19 of law n. 626 of 1994) is already deductible from positive norms, interpreted as actualization of the constitutional principles of the protection of health. Within this framework, the employer will find the organizational measures necessary to effectuate the goal of protection from second-hand smoke in conformity with the constitutional principle of Article 32.[q] The respect for this principle in the present issue must be understood in the following manner: the preventive protection of non-smokers in the workplace can be considered satisfied when, through a series of measures adopted in light of particular circumstances, the risk deriving from second-hand smoke is reduced, if not eliminated, to a level so low as to reasonably exclude that the health of workers is in danger.

Once it is ascertained that the enacted law provides for an appropriate framework to adequately protect the health of workers even from the danger of second-hand smoke, the request for consideration of a final intervention extending an absolute and general prohibition on smoking in all closed areas of the workplace is exhausted. The remitting judge, on

---

q. Article 32 [Health]

(1) The Republic shall protect the health as a basic right of the individual and as an interest of the community, and shall grant free medical care to the poor.

(2) No one shall be forced to undergo any medical treatment, except as provided for by law. In no case shall the law violate the limits set by respect for the human being.

the other hand, believed that such an intervention would be the only efficient way to protect health according to Article 32 of the Constitution.

NUMERUS CLAUSUS I CASE

Federal Constitutional Court (Germany).
33 BVerfGE 303 (1972).

[Until the mid–1960s, all applicants to university with a specially demanding high school degree (Abitur) were admitted to their school of choice. University education is provided by the state (within the competence of the *Länder*), free of charge. The number of applicants increased dramatically and an admission quota (a numerical limit, or *numerus clausus*, in Latin) was introduced in the most popular areas of study. Admissions were based on admission-exam criteria. Applicants to the Hamburg and Munich medical schools were rejected.]

Judgement of the First Senate: * * *

A.III.1. [The university repeatedly] refused plaintiff's application [to medical school] because of insufficient places for students [studying medicine]. [On appeal,] [p]laintiff asserts that it is unconstitutional to restrict admission to study medicine for so many years despite the fact that doctors are urgently needed in various branches of the medical profession. [Plaintiff further claims that the university] admitted considerably more applicants in previous years and sufficient time has been available to expand training and educational capacity. * * *

2. The Administrative Court suspended the procedures under Article 100 (1).

C. The Hamburg and Bavarian university admission policies are not fully consistent with the Basic Law.

I. The primary standard used in assessing the constitutionality of admission restrictions, as established by [our] precedents and in the legal literature, is the guaranteed right of all Germans under Article 12 (1) to choose where they are to be educated.

The inclusion of this right in the Basic Law, and its initial interpretation, clearly indicate the Article 12 (1) was designed as a right of the individual to defend himself from official encroachments on educational freedom. * * *

Overcrowded educational facilities highlight another important aspect of the right to choose freely the place of one's training; that is, the closely related right, also guaranteed by Article 12 (1), to choose freely an occupation. As a rule, education is the first step in taking up a profession; both are integral parts of a coordinated life process. * * * [In light of the Pharmacy Law, we shall] judge any restrictions on the admission to a course of study as stringently as restrictions on the choice of the occupation when the choice of an occupation—e.g., the medical profession—involves a prescribed program of study.

In the field of education the constitutional protection of basic rights is not limited to the function of protection from governmental intervention traditionally ascribed to the basic liberty rights. The Federal Constitutional Court has repeatedly declared that basic rights in their capacity as objective norms also establish a value order that represents a fundamental constitutional decision in all areas of the law. Therefore, [the Court has said] that basic rights are not merely defensive rights of the citizen against the state. The more involved a modern state becomes in assuring the social security and cultural advancement of its citizens, the more the complementary demand that participation in governmental services assume the character of a basic right will augment the initial postulate of safeguarding liberty from state intervention. This development is particularly important in the field of education. * * * The freedom to choose an occupation—apart from the special provisions of Article 33 relating to civil service employment—is at present predominantly put into practice in the private sector and is largely directed toward protecting the individual's chosen lifestyle; that is, its purpose is to insure freedom from any coercion or prohibition with respect to one's choice or practice of a profession. By contrast, freedom of choice with respect to one's place of education is geared, by its very nature, toward free access to institutions; this right would be worthless without the actual ability to exercise it. Accordingly, the proposed federal guidelines for higher education proceed from the initial assumption that every German is entitled to carry out his chosen program of study if he demonstrates the requisite qualifications.

It is not within the discretion of the legislature to recognize this right * * * [W]hen the state has created certain educational institutions, claims of access to these institutions may arise from the principle of equality in tandem with Article 12 (1) and with the principle of the state based on social justice. This is especially true when the state has laid claim to a factual monopoly that cannot easily be abandoned, as in the sphere of education, and when participation in governmental services is also an indispensable precondition for the exercise of basic rights as in the field of training for academic professions. In a free social welfare state based on the rule of law, [one] cannot leave it to the limited discretion of governmental agencies to determine the circle of beneficiaries and to exclude some citizens from these privileges, especially since this would result in the [government] steering the choice of a profession. On the contrary, every citizen qualified for university studies has the right to share equally in the opportunity being offered. [This] conclusion flows from the fact that the state offers these services. Therefore, Article 12 (1) together with Article 3 (1) [the principle of equality] and the mandate of a social welfare state guarantee any citizen meeting the individual admission requirements the right to be admitted to the [institution of] higher education of his choice.

2. * * * [T]he Hamburg Administrative Court, in its reference to this court, maintains that the state must expand educational facilities * * *

Normally, with regard to social services—that is, financial benefits— [the legislature] can to some extent redistribute [funds] to deal with the disadvantageous consequences of confining services to existing means. An absolute restriction on admission to the university, however, leads to the glaring inequality that one class of applicants receives everything and the other receives nothing—at least for a more or less long and possibly decisive period. * * * Because of these effects, absolute admissions restrictions are undisputedly on the edge of constitutional acceptability. In the long run, expanding capacity is the only way to deal with these effects. [As a consequence] the following question arises: Whether the value decisions manifested in basic rights together with the state's educational monopoly vest a social state with an objective constitutional mandate to provide sufficient educational capacities for all courses of study. [We] need not decide whether this question should be answered in the affirmative or whether, under certain circumstances, an individual citizen can use this constitutional mandate as the basis for an enforceable claim [against the state] to create opportunities for higher study. For constitutional consequences would arise only if that constitutional mandate were manifestly violated. * * * [We] can ascertain no such violation with respect to the field of medical studies today.

Even to the extent that participatory rights are not entirely restricted to existing benefits, they are still subject to the limitation of what is possible, meaning that which the individual may reasonably claim from society. The legislature has the primary responsibility for determining [what may be reasonably claimed]. According to the explicit provision of Article 109 (2) the legislature must consider other public welfare concerns as well as the demands of overall economic balance when setting its spending policy. It is also incumbent on the legislature to decide whether to enlarge [existing] facilities as well as which construction [projects] have priority, considering too that the enlargement and new construction of universities are to be regarded as joint tasks of the federation and the states within the meaning of Article 91.

a) * * * Any constitutional obligation [of the legislature] that may exist does not include the duty to supply a desired place of education at any time to any applicant. This would make costly investments in the realm of higher education exclusively dependent upon individual demands, which often fluctuate and are influenced by manifold circumstances. It would [also] lead to a misunderstanding of [the concept of] freedom, to a failure to recognize that personal liberty, in the long run, cannot be effectuated in isolation either from its equilibrium or from the ability of the whole to function effectively. The idea that the individual has an unlimited claim [which is enforceable] at the expense of the community as a whole is incompatible with the principle of a social welfare state. * * * It would be contrary to the [state's] mandate [to achieve] social justice as articulated by the principle of equality [if the state] gave only a privileged portion of the population the benefit of limited public financial resources while neglecting other important concerns of the public welfare. * * *

[The Court concluded that the states had made adequate efforts to expand the number of openings in medical schools but found that regulations governing admission to existing facilities fell short of constitutional requirements. After noting under the terms of Article 12 (1) the right to choose an occupation, the Court set forth the conditions under which admission might be restricted. The state may limit admissions to the university but only on the basis of criteria clearly defined by law. Every applicant must be given a fair chance to be admitted under specified selection procedures. Additionally, the *numerus clausus* would survive constitutional analysis only if the state could demonstrate that all places in a given academic department were filled to capacity.]

c) In light of these considerations, any absolute limit on admissions must meet strict requirements. According to the Federal Constitutional Court's gradation theory [citing the *Pharmacy Case*], the more the freedom of occupation is affected the more the regulatory power of the state is limited.

* * *

[A]n absolute restriction on the admission of beginning students is constitutional only if (1) [the legislature] imposes [the restriction only] when absolutely necessary, after having exhausted currently available publicly funded facilities, and (2) [the statute] bases the choice and distribution [of openings] on equitable criteria and provides each applicant with the opportunity to compete [for an opening], devoting the greatest possible attention to where the individual's wishes to study.

* * *

[T]hose responsible for admitting [students] are obliged to make a selection which is reasonably acceptable to the rejected applicants, always using the principle of fairness as a guideline. * * *

If the legislature authorizes a delegation of its authority [regarding admissions], it must at least determine the selection criteria and their order of importance.

Section 17 of the "Hamburg University Law" of April 25, 1969, is incompatible with the federal Constitution because the [state] legislature failed to determine the type and priority of selection criteria for absolute admissions restrictions. * * *

Section 3 (2) of the "Bavarian Admission Law" of July 8, 1970 is incompatible with the Constitution insofar as [it allows] the general admission of applicants with their legal residence in Bavaria or neighboring states, even when the capacity of [Bavarian] educational institutions are completely exhausted. [The statute is also unconstitutional] insofar as [it] give these applicants preferential ranking. * * *

FREE TEXTBOOKS CASE

Constitutional Court (Czech Republic).
Pl. US 25/94 (1995).[r]

The petition is rejected on the merits.

I. On 4 November 1994, the Constitutional Court of the Czech Republic received from a group of Deputies of the Assembly of Deputies of the Parliament of the Czech Republic a petition instituting a proceeding on the annulment of Government Regulation No. 15/1994 Sb., on the Provision Free of Charge of Textbooks, Teaching Texts, and Basic School Materials.

r. This case is available at <www.conc­ourt.cz/angl_verze/doc/p–25–94.html>.

The Government of the Czech Republic * * * Regulation No. 15/1994 Sb. was based upon authority given it under § 4 para. 2 of Act No. 29/1984 Sb., on the Basic and Secondary School System (the Education Act), pursuant to which the Government is to designate the extent to which textbooks, teaching texts, and basic school materials will be provided to students free of charge. It added that education free of charge as called for in Article 33 para. 2 of the Charter of Fundamental Rights and Basic Freedoms ["Citizens have the right to free education in elementary and secondary schools"] is to be understood (in connection with the mentioned § 4 of the Education Act) as referring to the right of students to be provided with instruction in suitable buildings, the wages of qualified instructors and further personnel, the costs of the operation and maintenance of the buildings, free use of educational aids, that is, those which are owned by the school and which it uses for its own instruction (models, chemicals, chalk, wall maps and pictures, etc.). Students, or their parents, are to pay for educational materials which are owned and used by the students, with the exception of materials which the state provides to students in the first year of elementary school, worth 200 Czech Crowns per student. The above-mentioned Government Regulation provides that textbooks for elementary school are also lent to the students free of charge, but they do not become their property. In secondary school, the students purchase textbooks, and they become their property. * * *

The Convention on the Rights of the Child, Article 28 para. 1, letters a) and b) provides that

> States Parties recognize the right of the child to education, and with the view to achieving this right progressively and on the basis of equal opportunity, they shall, in particular:
>
> (a) Make primary education compulsory and available free to all;
>
> (b) Encourage the development of different forms of secondary education, including general and vocational education, make them available and accessible to every child, and take appropriate measures such as the introduction of free education and offering financial assistance in case of need;

Article 5 para. 2 of the International Covenant on Economic, Social, and Cultural Rights, promulgated under No. 120/1976 Sb., provides that

> no restriction upon or derogation from any of the fundamental human rights recognized or existing in any country in virtue of law, conventions, regulations or custom will be admitted on the pretext that the present Covenant does not recognize such rights or that it recognizes them to a lesser extent. * * *

The mentioned Government Regulation, No. 15/1994 Sb., does not restrict the right to education free of charge nor does it affect it substantially. Education free of charge unquestionably means that the state shall bear the costs of establishing schools and school facilities, of their operation and maintenance, but above-all it means that the state may not demand tuition, that is, the provision of primary-and secondary-level education for payment. An exception is allowed for private and religious schools, which exist apart from the network of "state" schools, which to the necessary degree secure the right to education free of charge. The provision on the degree to which the government provides free textbooks, teaching texts, and basic school materials can not be placed under the heading of the right to education free of charge. According to the interpretation of this concept proposed by the petitioners, the state should see to the provision of everything directly related to attendance at elementary and secondary schools, for example, galoshes, briefcases, pencil cases, writing equipment, physical education gear, etc. It is clear that education free of charge cannot consist in the fact that the state bears all costs incurred by citizens when pursuing their right to education and the Government undoubtedly has authority to proceed in this way. In no way does this cast into doubt the principle of elementary and secondary education free of charge.

Art. 13. Para. 1 of the International Covenant on Economic, Social, and Cultural Rights provides that, "States Parties to the present Covenant recognize the right of everyone to education", and Art. 13 para. 2 of the same Covenant provides that

> States Parties to the present Covenant recognize that, with a view to achieving the full realization of this right:

> (a) Primary education shall be compulsory and available free to all;

> (b) Secondary education * * * shall be made generally available and accessible to all by every appropriate means, and in particular by the progressive introduction of free education.

The costs connected with putting the right to education into effect can be divided between the state and the citizen, or his legal representative. It is appropriate to keep in mind that it is in the citizen's own interest to obtain education (and by this way also higher qualifications and better opportunities to make one's way in the labor market) and to make effort himself to achieve it. The expenses connected with putting the right to education into effect are a long-term investment into the life of the citizen. The state bears the essential part of these costs, however, it is not obliged to bear all of them.

GOLDBERG v. KELLY

Supreme Court (United States).
397 U.S. 254 (1970).

Mr. Justice Brennan delivered the opinion of the Court.

The question for decision is whether a State that terminates public assistance payments to a particular recipient without affording him the opportunity for an evidentiary hearing prior to termination denies the recipient procedural due process in violation of the Due Process Clause of the Fourteenth Amendment.

      * * *

The State Commissioner of Social Services amended the State Department of Social Services' Official Regulations to require that local social services officials proposing to discontinue or suspend a recipient's financial aid do so according to a procedure that conforms to either subdivision (a) or subdivision (b) of s 351.26 of the regulations as amended. The City of New York elected to promulgate a local procedure according to subdivision (b). That subdivision, so far as here pertinent, provides that the local procedure must include the giving of notice to the recipient of the reasons for a proposed discontinuance or suspension at least seven days prior to its effective date, with notice also that upon request the recipient may have the proposal reviewed by a local welfare official holding a position superior to that of the supervisor who approved the proposed discontinuance or suspension, and, further, that the recipient may submit, for purposes of the review, a written statement to demonstrate why his grant should not be discontinued or suspended. The decision by the reviewing official whether to discontinue or suspend aid must be made expeditiously, with written notice of the decision to the recipient. The section further expressly provides that '(a)ssistance shall not be discontinued or suspended prior to the date such notice of decision is sent to the recipient and his representative, if any, or prior to the proposed effective date of discontinuance or suspension, whichever occurs later.'

* * * Appellees' challenge to this procedure emphasizes the absence of any provisions for the personal appearance of the recipient before the reviewing official, for oral presentation of evidence, and for confrontation and cross-examination of adverse witnesses. However, the letter does inform the recipient that he may request a post-termination 'fair hearing.' This is a proceeding before an independent state hearing officer at which the recipient may appear personally, offer oral evidence, confront and cross-examine the witnesses against him, and have a record made of the hearing. If the recipient prevails at the 'fair hearing' he is paid all funds erroneously withheld. * * *

* * *

Appellant does not contend that procedural due process is not applicable to the termination of welfare benefits. Such benefits are a matter of statutory entitlement for persons qualified to receive them. Their termination involves state action that adjudicates important rights. The constitutional challenge cannot be answered by an argument that public assistance benefits are "a 'privilege' and not a 'right'." *Shapiro v. Thompson*, 394 U.S. 618, 627 n. 6 (1969). Relevant constitutional restraints apply as much to the withdrawal of public assistance benefits as to disqualification for unemployment compensation * * *

* * * [W]hen welfare is discontinued, only a pre-termination evidentiary hearing provides the recipient with procedural due process. For qualified recipients, welfare provides the means to obtain essential food, clothing, housing, and medical care. * * *

Moreover, important governmental interests are promoted by affording recipients a pre-termination evidentiary hearing. From its founding the Nation's basic commitment has been to foster the dignity and well-being of all persons within its borders. We have come to recognize that forces not within the control of the poor contribute to their poverty. This perception, against the background of our traditions, has significantly influenced the development of the contemporary public assistance system. Welfare, by meeting the basic demands of subsistence, can help bring within the reach of the poor the same opportunities that are available to others to participate meaningfully in the life of the community. At the same time, welfare guards against the societal malaise that may flow from a widespread sense of unjustified frustration and insecurity. Public assistance, then, is not mere charity, but a means to 'promote the general Welfare, and secure the Blessings of Liberty to ourselves and our Posterity.' The same governmental interests that counsel the provision of welfare, counsel as well its uninterrupted provision to those eligible to receive it; pre-termination evidentiary hearings are indispensable to that end.

* * *

The city's procedures presently do not permit recipients to appear personally with or without counsel before the official who finally determines continued eligibility. Thus a recipient is not permitted to present evidence to that official orally, or to confront or cross-examine adverse witnesses. These omissions are fatal to the constitutional adequacy of the procedures.

* * *

Mr. Justice Black, dissenting.

In the last half century the United States, along with many, perhaps most, other nations of the world, has moved far toward becoming a welfare state, that is, a nation that for one reason or another taxes its most affluent people to help support, feed, clothe, and shelter its less fortunate citizens. The result is that today more than nine million men, women, and children in the United States receive some kind of state or federally financed public assistance in the form of allowances or gratuities, generally paid them periodically, usually by the week, month, or quarter. Since these gratuities are paid on the basis of need, the list of recipients is not static, and some people go off the lists and others are added from time to time. These ever-changing lists put a constant administrative burden on government and it certainly could not have reasonably anticipated that this burden would include the additional procedural expense imposed by the Court today.

* * *

* * * In my judgment there is not one word, phrase, or sentence from the beginning to the end of the Constitution from which it can be inferred that judges were granted any such legislative power. * * * Hence my dissent.

* * *

* * * [T]his Court today adopts the views of the District Court 'that to cut off a welfare recipient in the face of . . . 'brutal need' without a prior hearing of some sort is unconscionable,' and therefore, says the Court, unconstitutional. The majority reaches this result by a process of weighing 'the recipient's interest in avoiding' the termination of welfare benefits against 'the governmental interest in summary adjudication.' Today's balancing act requires a 'pre-termination evidentiary hearing,' yet there is nothing that indicates what tomorrow's balance will be.

Although the majority attempts to bolster its decision with limited quotations from prior cases, it is obvious that today's result doesn't depend on the language of the Constitution itself or the principles of other decisions, but solely on the collective judgment of the majority as to what would be a fair and humane procedure in this case.

* * *

Notes and Questions

1. It is unclear whether a right to education triggers a positive obligation of the state at all. In the context of education, the Czech Constitutional Court took the typical position that even if there is an express constitutional right to free services, it is left to the legislature to determine the extent of the right as it is materialized by government. The Czech Court takes a deferential position regarding the level of service provided by government. The GFCC found in *Numerus Clausus I* and its progeny, without a specific right to education mentioned in the Basic Law, that it has the power to set the conditions of state services in higher education that serve the constitutional right to free choice of occupation. Likewise, the Interim Constitution in South Africa was silent regarding the role of the state in education.[s] In *Ex Parte Gauteng Provincial Legislature: In re Dispute Concerning the Constitutionality of Certain Provisions of the Gauteng School Education Bill of 1995*, 1996 (3) SALR 165 (CC), but the SACC per Justice Mahomed stated that the right to basic education protected in the Interim Constitution creates a positive obligation of the state so that citizens can effectively enjoy certain individual rights.

According to the welfare-state theory[t] of *Numerus Clausus I*, the state has affirmative duties to promote social rights through the active provision of state-sponsored and state-operated services, including higher education. The Court avoided the recognition that an individual may have enforceable claims against the state to create an opportunity for higher education and left it to the legislature to determine the proper level of government-provided services in light of other welfare considerations and overall economic conditions. But it took a firm position in reviewing the fairness of the regulatory handling of the fundamental right to education. The position of the GFCC resulted in a series of additional cases, reviewing the entire regulatory system of admissions and forcing the legislature to rewrite, in nondiscriminatory terms, an area that traditionally fell within the university's autonomy and state-spending discretion. The GFCC forced the creation of a national admissions system and required universities to make maximum use of their capacities. (Compare with the somewhat similar equality concerns resulting in the review of state university admissions criteria in *Regents of the Univ. of California v. Bakke*, 438 U.S. 265 (1978). See Chapter

---

s. Art. 29(1) of the Constitution of South Africa (1996) states that "the state must take reasonable measures to make progressively available and accessible" further education.

t. Compare the German concept of the welfare state, which is a service provider to all citizens equal in dignity, with the American concept, which is concerned with the poor: "In the last half century the United States, along with many, perhaps most, other nations of the world, has moved far toward becoming a welfare state, that is, a nation that for one reason or another taxes its most affluent people to help support, feed, clothe, and shelter its less fortunate citizens." *Goldberg v. Kelly*, 397 U.S. 254, 271 (1970) (Justice Black, dissenting).

6.) The GFCC does not take a stand as to how the state will satisfy its constitutional social obligations to promote a social right; it may choose both direct provision of a service as a state service or simply provide social planning for private institutions that will permit the enjoyment of the right.[u] If the state undertakes such activity itself, through public institutions, constitutional requirements apply, and citizens have equal rights of participation.

Compare the application of the equality clause of the Fourteenth Amendment in the case of state action in the U.S. Compare further with *Ahmedabad*: Is the Indian Court more activist? Note there was state action in *Ahmedabad*, but no specific action was taken regarding housing. Of course, by German standards the welfare state, one way or another, should have done something about housing.

2. The impact of social rights, beyond the material provision of state services, includes government spending (discussed above), proper regulation, influences and restrictions on other constitutional rights, and formalities regarding the manner of regulations.[v] In the *Smoking in Closed Areas Case* the ICC refrained from specifying the proper legislative solutions expected from the state; in a few other cases courts may single out the proper legislative measure to implement the social right.

Courts are reluctant to review the adequacy of welfare services, although they may indicate the factors that need consideration. As the Indian and South African housing cases show, guidance might be given as to the formal measures that authorities must take (though not by legislation). Like the Korean and German courts, the French Constitutional Council avoids scrutinizing the sufficiency of state-provided services. The issue was not what happens to all recipients but, instead, the validity of giving benefits to contributors to the fund. The Act established an upper-wealth limit for the award of a noncontributory benefit. When the Council examined the Act establishing universal-illness insurance, its approach was limited to equality issues, and it was unwilling to examine the possible unconstitutionality of the Act on other grounds. The Council found itself not competent in the matter, as long as the details of the Act were not manifestly inappropriate, to examine whether the goals set out could have been achieved by other means. Decision on the *"Loi portant création d'une couverture maladie universelle"* (Act on creating universal-illness protection), 99–416 DC of 23 July 1999.

3. In some cases the ICC came close to granting individual access to government welfare service provisions, at least in the context of equality; at the same time, it recognizes certain welfare rights as grounds for restricting other constitutional interests. The Court stated that the right to healthcare entails the right to preventative medical treatment and is "guaranteed to every person as a right that is constitutionally dependent on its implementation by law, through the balancing of the interests protected by this right with the other interests protected by the Constitution." ICC 267/1998, BCCL

---

u. Only in regard to public broadcasting did the GFCC recognize a duty of the state to provide a specific service to promote the right to communicate. This was understood as an exception related to the specificity of broadcasting freedoms. *Broadcasting Case*, 87 BVerfGE 181, 198. (1992).

v. The Czech Constitutional Court ruled in Pl. US 35/95 (1996) that the right to health can be regulated and restricted only by statute because it is a constitutional right.

1998, 260. The requirement of prior authorization for urgent treatment in secondary healthcare is unconstitutional as it impairs effective health protection. The clause prohibiting nonreimbursement for such services from the mandatory insurance scheme is therefore void. Does this approach yield results different from those that legislation might achieve under the police power in the U.S.? Is the Italian approach closer to substantive due process in economic-social matters as exemplified in *Lochner*? Note that the right to private life, protected by Art. 8 (1) of the European HR Convention, includes a person's physical and psychological integrity (*Botta v. Italy*, 26 E.H.R.R. 241 (1998)). Such a right to integrity does not merely compel the state to refrain from interference with people's private lives. It also implies a positive obligation on the state to effectively respect private life. The European Commission of Human Rights found in the case of an Italian applicant that in a public healthcare system based on compulsory contributions, "the State has an obligation to provide medical care" and "an excessive delay of the public health service in providing a medical service to which the patient is entitled" could raise an issue under Art. 8. (1). *Passannante v. Italy*, 94–A Eur. Comm'n H.R. Dec. & Rep. 91 (1998) (declaring application inadmissible).

A Greek Council of State decision offers a different technique for restricting property rights in the service of social rights. The Council of State recognized that social rights might justify exceptions to general rules, favoring certain protected groups. Family, marriage, mothers, and children enjoy the protection of the state under the Greek Constitution, and the homeless and poorly housed are subject to special attention by the government (not a constitutional right). For example, lawmakers may allow exemptions to building regulations with a view to meeting the housing needs of lower income families. 550/99 BCCL 1999, 385.

4.   Fundamental welfare rights can burden other interests, as illustrated by the *Nowinski Case*. A Buenos Aires Province law required pensioners to register and pay contributions to the Medical and Social Insurance Institute. They could not derive any advantage from contributing. The Supreme Court of the Nation (Argentina) held that the law was constitutional as the measure intends to satisfy the right to social security, which is based on social solidarity. The Court did not consider the case as one of distributive justice, which governs individual benefits on a strict equality basis, but, instead, it came under the heading of social justice (23.02.1999. N.36.XXXIII BCCL 1999. 13).

The ICC found it self-evident that the constitutional right to health imposed an active duty on employers to protect the health interests of nonsmoking employees.

5.   In 1998 (Judgment n. 185 of May 20, 1998), the ICC confronted a service-rationing issue, somewhat similar to the South African *Soobramoney* (dialysis) *Case*. Amidst a major public debate and strong criticism of government carelessness, Act 94/1998 authorized access to a multidrug treatment (the "Di Bella therapy") for terminally ill cancer patients, which was in a clinical-experimental stage. The law-decree provided that for some terminally ill cancer patients, the Di Bella therapy would be made available free of charge for purposes of experiment. Other terminally ill cancer patients, who were not eligible for the experiment, could obtain the treatment upon medical prescription but only if they paid for it. The Council of State, which

made the referral to the Constitutional Court, considered that the law discriminated among drugs, and hence it created an unjustified distinction among the terminally ill patients. The Court found (Judgment n. 185 of May 20, 1998, first *Di Bella Treatment Case*) that the law violated Art. 3 of the Constitution, which provides that all citizens have equal social dignity and are equal before the laws, irrespective of personal and social conditions. Section 2 of Art. 3 provides: "It is the duty of the Republic to eliminate the social and economic obstacles, which impede * * * the full development of the human personality." Further, the Court ruled that by allowing the prescription of the drug, an expectation was created among cancer patients. The enjoyment of this fundamental right cannot depend on the financial means of patients. The Court found insufficient that the Ministry of Health negotiated a price reduction with the drug companies and that a fixed sum of support to buy the drug was allocated to the municipalities. The Court admitted, however, as in the *Smoking in Closed Areas Case*, that it would not substitute its judgment for that of the legislation regarding the efficiency of drugs. In consequence of the ruling, the Italian government amended the law (law-decree 186/1998) and had to increase the budgetary contribution to the Health Fund, in an effort to provide the drug to the poor.

Compare the Italian position with that of the GFCC. On March 5, 1997, the GFCC[w] found that there was no constitutional right to have a medical prescription of a pharmaceutical reimbursed where the drug is not subject to pharmaceutical approval. The Court said that the decision was based on "the expertise of competent authorities," and patients had no right to a specific treatment. The only constitutionally prescribed obligation in regard to health protection is that the public authorities should take measures that "are not completely inappropriate or totally inadequate." The German Basic Law has no specific provisions regarding the right to health; such rights derive from the social-state clause and Art. 2 (2) on the right to bodily integrity. Other courts also extend care without specific social rights, relying on general expectations of respect for human beings. In this view, the French Constitutional Council and the ECHR hold that noncitizens are entitled to emergency services.

6. *Maintaining the level of social services.* The postcommunist constitutions, like those of postapartheid South Africa, expressly recognize the right to health or to free healthcare. Both the Hungarian and the Polish constitutional courts interpreted these rights as nonindividual rights that are satisfied by state-provided services. The HCC held that the state was duty bound, even during economic hardship, to maintain the level of services provided during the communist era.

In 1995, the social-liberal coalition government in Hungary introduced an austerity package to avoid a major fiscal crisis, partly due to previous welfare overspending. State spending on, among others, maternity leave, government-provided child support, etc., was cut back,[x] and paid sick leave was reduced. Many elements of the welfare package were held unconstitutional, including the introduction of a means test for child support, intended

---

w. *Medicine Case*, 1 BvR 1071/95.

x. The law would have reduced or denied, among others, the pregnancy allowance, maternity benefit, childcare benefit, childcare fee, and childcare allowance (a three-year monthly supplement to mothers who remain at home with their children). The Court found that the level of benefits was to be maintained even for children that were born within 300 days as of the promulgation of the law (Decision 43/1995 (VI.30.) AB hat.).

to replace the system by which all parents received benefits irrespective of their financial situation.

One of the main reasons the HCC rejected welfare reductions was that it contradicts legal certainty (only to a lesser extent did the Court argue that reductions violate the right to social security). This was a guiding principle at certain points in the Hungarian and Polish cases. Neither court denied the need both to preserve the state budget balance and to affect the conditions of preexisting agreements (or statutory promises). These changes might prove unfavorable to certain groups. The changes are limited, however, by requirements of legal certainty. Legal certainty follows from the constitutional provision of the rule-of-law state. (Polish Constitutional Tribunal, 17.12.1997, 22/96, BCCL, 1998. 99.) The HCC considered legal certainty the "most important conceptual element of a rule-of-law system." The Preamble to the Hungarian Constitution states that it was created as a means of transition to a social market economy, and Art. 2.2 states that Hungary is a rule-of-law state. Article 1 of Poland's Little Constitution, in force between 1992 and 1997, stated that Poland is a democratic state ruled by law. While the Polish Tribunal applied "legal certainty" against pension reductions from the early 1990s (see the *Pension Case* in Chapter 2), in Hungary, at the beginning of the economic transition, legal certainty in the early pension cases meant only the "relative stability of the legal system" (Decision 32/1991 (VI.6.) AB hat.). The drastic reduction in pensions, resulting from a lack of adjustment to inflation, was held constitutional. In the 1995 context, the Court added that legal certainty was "of particular importance for the stability of the social [welfare] system as [it serves as] the theoretical foundation of the protection of acquired rights" (Decision 43/1995 (VI.30.) AB hat.).

The French Constitutional Council, in direct contrast to the ECJ, continues to reject the idea that legal certainty is a constitutional value. The Council found that there is no written constitutional norm in this regard. Of course, it must be respected by legislation. However, in its decision on the law on social security funding (Decision on the *Loi de financement de la sécurité sociale pour 1999*) (Law on financing of social security for 1999), 98–404 DC of 18 Dec. 1998), a stricter scrutiny seems to emerge that is not necessarily related to welfare. The decision recognizes that Parliament is entitled to adopt fiscal measures with retrospective effect, if it serves a "sufficient general interest." The "sufficiency" analysis allows a certain proportionality analysis between the scope of the retrospective measure and the importance of the aim pursued.

The Hungarian Constitution clearly states that Hungary is not a welfare state. Nevertheless, in the 1989 revision the language of the Universal Declaration was transcribed into the text, promising "social security." An earlier dissenting opinion argued that it is part of the right to social security "that the state should refrain from those legal interferences into citizens' material [financial] relations that would impose on large masses of the population disproportionate burdens which exceed their capacity to comply (in the domain of taxation, increased interest rates, housing rent, etc.) without compelling necessity" (Decision 24/1991 (V.18.) AB hat., 356). At that time, the majority found pension and other welfare reductions acceptable. In each case the HCC reaffirmed that there were constitutional limits, albeit not specified, to cutbacks in social rights. The 1995 "austerity-package" decisions of the Court were based on the assumption that the legislature did not observe the "constitutional limits." In this conclusion the Court developed a material (substantive) concept of legal certainty. The way the notion has now been extended amounts to material social certainty, as desired earlier by the dissenters. The HCC has now gone beyond the position of the Constitutional Court of the rich German welfare state, which limits its own control over guaranteed welfare to securing a minimum level of subsistence.

The stability of the level of social services might be based on the UN Covenant. This was the position of the Supreme Court of Argentina. The Court ruled that family allowances are social rights; such allowances are subject to regulation but can never be withdrawn, even in unforeseen circumstances. The right was based on Art. 14 (b) of the Constitution, which secures full protection for the family, and on Art. 10.1 of the International Covenant on Economic, Social and Cultural Rights of 1966, which has constitutional force in Argentina[y] (19.08.1999., V.916.XXXII, BCCL 1999, 344; see also Chapter 3, Section E.). The UN Committee on Economic, Social and Cultural Rights in its General Comment No. 4 on the right to adequate housing, stated that "a general decline in living and housing conditions, directly attributable to policy and legislative decisions by state parties, and in the absence of accompanying compensatory measures, would be inconsistent with the obligations under the Covenant." U.N. ESCOR, Comm. On Econ., Soc., & Cultural Rights, 6th Sess., Supp. No. 3, at 114, U.N. Doc. E/1992/23–E/C.12/1991/4 Annex III (1991), at para. 11. Is this to say that retrogressive measures are a prima facie infringement of a right? Is retrogression regarding a special welfare right justified if the measure achieves an overall protection of welfare rights through other services?

Contrast the Hungarian and Argentine position with the French one. The French doctrine of constitutional objectives does not apply the doctrine that social welfare payments, once granted, cannot be withdrawn. This so-called ratchet effect is reserved in France to fundamental rights and principles. Consider also the position of the Norwegian Supreme Court, which has never found an act of Parliament unconstitutional. The 1990 amendments to the 1966 National Insurance Act resulted in the termination of the "spouse-supplement for old-age pensioners" whose incomes exceeded a certain level. The applicant had lost all of her spouse-supplement, which amounted, earlier, to half of the annual basic pension. The Supreme Court of Norway found that pension entitlements are protected against unreasonable retroactivity, and the Court should take into consideration pensioners' future-benefit expectations (or, in the specific case, the expectations regarding benefits to the spouse). These expectations were considered against the needs served by the restriction, and the Court held that the services could be terminated. One judge held that, although there should be considerable protection against retroactivity, there was no violation because the spouse did not contribute toward the benefit. *Insurance Act Case*, Supreme Court of Norway, Plenary, Inr 76B/1996, BCCL 1996, 384. Should it make any difference if the benefit reduction would affect a person who personally contributed toward an insurance scheme? The European Commission of

---

y. Art. 10.1 of the Covenant states that "the widest possible protection and assistance should be accorded to the family * * * particularly for its establishment and while it is responsible for the care and education of dependent children." The Argentine Court obviously interprets "protec-tion and assistance" as meaning material support. Article 2 of the Covenant expressly sets the level of rights protection "to the maximum of [the state's] available resources, with a view to achieving progressively the full realization of the rights recognized."

Human Rights has found that there is no entitlement to specific predetermined fixed benefits in social insurance schemes.

7. The affordability of maintaining welfare services at levels provided under state socialism and the efficiency of the structures and institutions that provided these services were hotly debated after the transition to market economies in postcommunist Europe. American scholar Cass Sunstein, in particular, was concerned about the wisdom of writing into the new constitutions these welfare entitlements as enforceable or vested rights, state goals, state promises or, for that matter, in any other form.

András Sajó, *How the Rule of Law Killed Hungarian Welfare Reform*, E. Eur. Const. Rev., vol. 5, no. 1, at 31, 32–33 (1996), gave the following description of the debate:

> [Sunstein argued that] constitutionalizing social rights at this state of economic and social development may undermine private property rights and economic development itself. Other authors emphasize the importance of local East European political realities and pragmatically invoke the political impossibility of omitting such rights. * * * Others assert that social and economic rights are indeed fundamental human rights, heralded in the United Nations Universal Declaration of Human Rights. Socialists claim that such social rights were indeed provided under state socialism: they belong to the people, and therefore the people cannot be deprived of these services or of social security in general.

> The counterargument is that, by constitutionalizing welfare rights and thus obliging the state to provide welfare services, the relatively poor countries of East Europe are destined either to stagnation and eventual economic collapse, or to a cavalier disregard of constitutional provisions. * * *

> * * * [B]oth the inherited bureaucracy and the clients or recipients of the welfare system insist on welfare spending that is excessive given deficit-riddled budgets and scant public resources. In 1993, for example, welfare spending in Hungary was 27.7 percent of GDP, compared to 23.3 percent in France (which the Juppé government in 1995 believed to be inhibiting growth even in France.) Welfare spending in Hungary is much higher than in most other countries with a comparable level of economic development (*Hungary: Structure reforms for sustainable growth. A World Bank Country Study*, EBRD: Washington, 1995).

Losers in the market transition, in any case, may find that constitutional courts are ready to spring to their support. This help is somewhat unexpected, as constitutional courts are not designed to respond to special group interests. Nevertheless, some of these courts, notably the Hungarian and the Polish ones, seem prepared to give more protection to welfare entitlements than is any political party in power.

8. *Equality and Welfare*. In the first *Di Bella Treatment Case* (Judgment n. 185 of May 20, 1998) the deference to science would have resulted in accepting differentiation among patients dictated by professional considerations of drug development. The ICC finds that the legislative authorization for the use of a drug is a legislative fact of objective nature, which generates an expectation on behalf of the concerned patients. The expectation is part of the inherent minimum in the right to health, and nondiscrimination criteria apply. As there is no alternative therapy for the terminally ill, those who are

not selected to participate in the pharmaceutical experiment have the right to free access. In other words, contrary to the South African decision, at least in this context, a subjective, individual right to healthcare (within the social insurance scheme) is guaranteed because of equality concerns. Is this to say that once a healthcare service is provided it must be accessible to all? Remember the concern of the South African Court regarding available resources. Is the Italian Court's position in the multidrug treatment context different from that in the *Smoking* decision, where the protective regulatory measures of the state satisfied the right to health?

The individual right to (free) treatment with experimentally available means in the Italian case is at least limited as it applies in a situation where there is no alternative treatment. Where there are various treatment alternatives, is the government or the social service operator entitled to choose the cheapest one? What if the cheaper alternative is less effective? The World Health Organization's Charter of 1946 is based on the assumption that there is a fundamental right to the "highest level of health." It is unclear whether this imposes a service-provision obligation on the state (or society). Is the Italian decision simply a special situation where there was an actual attempt to treat the terminally ill and there was clear legislative discrimination that directly affected dignity? Consider the terminal nature of the illness of the South African diabetic patient, on the one hand, and the lack of alternative treatments in Italy, where the experimental multitreatment seemed to provide healing. In Italy, the multitreatment provided by the state was the only medically recognized hope for the patients. There was no hope for Mr. Soobramoney. When someone is under the total control of state authorities, as in a prison or a mental institution, even the U.S. courts recognize an obligation of the state to provide welfare services and security. See *DeShaney v. Winnebago County Dept. of Social Services* below.

The problem underlying the right of free access to social services (including healthcare) is one of social equality. While the poor and the less well to do depend on social services, and their access is often restricted on professional and resource grounds, healthcare and other services are more a matter of liberty for the better off. In South Africa, the access restrictions did not apply to private clinics and their patients. An alternative (egalitarian) approach would be to maintain public control on all dialysis machines and allow access to public and private clients on medical grounds only. Is this feasible? Desirable?

9. *New Property.* The idea of a property-like protection of welfare expectations was developed by Professor Charles Reich in *The New Property*, 73 Yale L.J. 733 (1964). The USSC granted property-like protection to welfare recipients in *Goldberg v. Kelly*, 397 U.S. 254 (1970). Interestingly, the HCC found that certain social security services (including sick leave and pensions in cases where the contribution to the mandatory, state-operated social security fund is minimal) are to receive property-like protection. Given the textual differences between the U.S. and the Hungarian constitutions, "property likeness" means opposite things in the two countries. In the U.S., property-like protection means procedural due process protection, that is, an individual cannot be deprived of a welfare service without some kind of hearing. In Hungary, property-like protection of statutory entitlements means a flat prohibition on takings.

The Supreme Court of Argentina considers pensions as property, which, however, is not infringed as long as its reduction is justified by considerations of public policy, provided the reduction is not confiscatory or arbitrarily disproportionate (25.08.1998. M.653.XXVIII. BCCL 1998. 373)

In *Bowen v. Gilliard*, 483 U.S. 587, 604–5 (1987), in the context of a governmental child-support program, Justice Stevens wrote: "Congress is not, by virtue of having instituted a social welfare program, bound to continue it at all, much less at the same benefit level. * * * It would be quite strange indeed if, by virtue of an offer to provide benefits to needy families through the entirely voluntary AFDC program, Congress or the States were deemed to have taken some of those very family members' property."

In countries where the constitution expressly provides for the protection of children and families, is there a violation if a welfare program is terminated? Should states create an obligation to provide for the needy where they cannot provide for their welfare?

The GFCC jurisprudence, which the HCC has followed, leads to a different conclusion. As a leading commentator summarized the German position: "one cannot deduce from the concept of a social welfare state the general prohibition of irrevocability [*Rückschrittsverbot*]." The HCC refused to accept (or even consider) the government's position as to the compelling nature of the new circumstances that would allow a restriction of rights.

As to the concept of benefits as property, this otherwise established approach presupposes actual contributions. This is the position of the GFCC. See, for example, 1 BvR 609/90 (1996). Given the elements of uncertainty in insurance, the individual contribution to a welfare fund does not establish a right to a specific return. The ECHR found in *Gaygusuz v. Austria*, 23 E.H.R.R. 364 (1996), that even the right to emergency assistance is a property-like protected possession under Art. 1. Protocol No. 1 of the European HR Convention because it is sponsored by the unemployment insurance fund, which operates from contributions; it is not a state-provided emergency service that is granted on the basis of need.

DeSHANEY v. WINNEBAGO COUNTY DEPARTMENT OF SOCIAL SERVICES

Supreme Court (United States).
489 U.S. 189 (1989).

Chief Justice Rehnquist delivered the opinion of the Court.

Petitioner is a boy who was beaten and permanently injured by his father, with whom he lived. Respondents are social workers and other local officials who received complaints that petitioner was being abused by his father and had reason to believe that this was the case, but nonetheless did not act to remove petitioner from his father's custody. Petitioner sued respondents claiming that their failure to act deprived him of his liberty in violation of the Due Process Clause of the Fourteenth Amendment to the United States Constitution. We hold that it did not.

II

* * * The claim is one invoking the substantive rather than the procedural component of the Due Process Clause; petitioners do not

claim that the State denied Joshua protection without according him appropriate procedural safeguards, but that it was categorically obligated to protect him in these circumstances.[2]

But nothing in the language of the Due Process Clause itself requires the State to protect the life, liberty, and property of its citizens against invasion by private actors. The Clause is phrased as a limitation on the State's power to act, not as a guarantee of certain minimal levels of safety and security. It forbids the State itself to deprive individuals of life, liberty, or property without "due process of law," but its language cannot fairly be extended to impose an affirmative obligation on the State to ensure that those interests do not come to harm through other means. Nor does history support such an expansive reading of the constitutional text. Like its counterpart in the Fifth Amendment, the Due Process Clause of the Fourteenth Amendment was intended to prevent government "from abusing [its] power, or employing it as an instrument of oppression," *Davidson v. Canon,* 474 U.S. at 348. * * *

Consistent with these principles, our cases have recognized that the Due Process Clauses generally confer no affirmative right to governmental aid, even where such aid may be necessary to secure life, liberty, or property interests of which the government itself may not deprive the individual. * * * As we said in *Harris v. McRae:* "Although the liberty protected by the Due Process Clause affords protection against unwarranted *government* interference * * *, it does not confer an entitlement to such [governmental aid] as may be necessary to realize all the advantages of that freedom." 448 U.S., at 317–318. If the Due Process Clause does not require the State to provide its citizens with particular protective services, it follows that the State cannot be held liable under the Clause for injuries that could have been averted had it chosen to provide them. As a general matter, then, we conclude that a State's failure to protect an individual against private violence simply does not constitute a violation of the Due Process Clause.

Petitioners contend, however, that even if the Due Process Clause imposes no affirmative obligation on the State to provide the general public with adequate protective services, such a duty may arise out of certain "special relationships" created or assumed by the State with respect to particular individuals. Brief for Petitioners 13–18. Petitioners argue that such a "special relationship" existed here because the State knew that Joshua faced a special danger of abuse at his father's hands, and specifically proclaimed, by word and by deed, its intention to protect him against that danger. Id., at 18–20. Having actually undertaken to protect Joshua from this danger—which petitioners concede the State played no part in creating—State acquired an affirmative "duty," enforceable through the Due Process Clause, to do so in a reasonably competent fashion. * * *

---

2. Petitioners also argue that the Wisconsin child protection statutes gave Joshua an "entitlement" to receive protective services in accordance with the terms of the statute, an entitlement which would enjoy due process protection against state depri- vation under our decision in *Bd. of Regents of State Colleges v. Roth,* 408 U.S. 564 (1972). But this argument is made for the first time in petitioners' brief to this Court. * * * We therefore decline to consider it here.

We reject this argument. It is true that in certain limited circumstances the Constitution imposes upon the State affirmative duties of care and protection with respect to particular individuals. * * * We reasoned that because the prisoner is unable " 'by reason of the deprivation of his liberty [to] care for himself,' " it is only " 'just' " that the State be required to care for him. *Ibid.*, quoting *Spicer v. Williamson*, 191 N.C. 487, 490, 132 S. E. 291, 293 (1926).

In *Youngberg v. Romeo*, 457 U.S. 307 (1982), we extended this analysis beyond the Eighth Amendment setting, holding that the substantive component of the Fourteenth Amendment's Due Process Clause requires the State to provide involuntarily committed mental patients with such services as are necessary to ensure their "reasonable safety" from themselves and others. * * *

But these cases afford petitioners no help. Taken together, they stand only for the proposition that when the State takes a person into its custody and holds him there against his will, the Constitution imposes upon it a corresponding duty to assume some responsibility for his safety and general well being. * * * In the substantive due process analysis, it is the State's affirmative act of restraining the individual's freedom to act on his own behalf—through incarceration, institutionalization, or other similar restraint of personal liberty—which is the "deprivation of liberty" triggering the protections of the Due Process Clause, not its failure to act to protect his liberty interests against harms inflicted by other means.

The *Estelle-Youngberg* analysis simply has no applicability in the present case. * * * While the State may have been aware of the dangers that Joshua faced in the free world, it played no part in their creation, nor did it do anything to render him any more vulnerable to them. * * *

* * * A State may, through its courts and legislatures, impose such affirmative duties of care and protection upon its agents as it wishes. But not "all common-law duties owed by government actors were * * * constitutionalized by the Fourteenth Amendment." *Daniels v. Williams*, 474 U.S. at 335–36. Because, as explained above, the State had no constitutional duty to protect Joshua against his father's violence, its failure to do so—though calamitous in hindsight—simply does not constitute a violation of the Due Process Clause.

Justice Brennan, with whom Justice Marshall and Justice Blackmun join, dissenting.

      * * *

It may well be, as the Court decides, ante, at 194–97, that the Due Process Clause as construed by our prior cases creates no general right to basic governmental services. * * *

* * * In a constitutional setting that distinguishes sharply between action and inaction, one's characterization of the misconduct alleged under § 1983 might effectively decide the case. * * *

* * * Cases from the lower courts also recognize that a State's actions can be decisive in assessing the constitutional significance of subsequent inaction. For these purposes, moreover, actual physical re-

straint is not the only state action that has been considered relevant. * * *

* * * The cases that I have cited tell us that (recognizing entitlement to welfare under state law), can stand side by side with *Dandridge v. Williams*, 397 U.S. 471, 484 (1970) (implicitly rejecting idea that welfare is a fundamental right), [Chapter 6, Subsection A.2.] and that *Goss v. Lopez*, 419 U.S. 565, 573 (1975) (entitlement to public education under state law), is perfectly consistent with *San Antonio Independent School Dist. v. Rodriguez*, 411 U.S. 1, 29–39 (1973) (no fundamental right to education). To put the point more directly, these cases signal that a State's prior actions may be decisive in analyzing the constitutional significance of its inaction. * * *

Wisconsin has established a child-welfare system specifically designed to help children like Joshua. * * * Wisconsin law invites—indeed, directs—citizens and other governmental entities to depend on local departments of social services such as respondent to protect children from abuse.

* * * As the Court today reminds us, "the Due Process Clause of the Fourteenth Amendment was intended to prevent government from abusing [its] power, or employing it as an instrument of oppression." *Ante*, at 196, quoting *Davidson, supra*, at 348. My disagreement with the Court arises from its failure to see that inaction can be every bit as abusive of power as action, that oppression can result when a State undertakes a vital duty and then ignores it. Today's opinion construes the Due Process Clause to permit a State to displace private sources of protection and then, at the critical moment, to shrug its shoulders and turn away from the harm that it has promised to try to prevent. Because I cannot agree that our Constitution is indifferent to such indifference, I respectfully dissent.

CARMICHELE v. MINISTERS OF SAFETY AND SECURITY AND OF JUSTICE AND CONSTITUTIONAL DEVELOPMENT

Constitutional Court (South Africa).
2001 (4) SALR 938 (CC).

[A woman was viciously attacked and injured by a man. The attack occurred at the home of another woman, at a small secluded village on the sea. Before this, the man had been charged with rape and attempted murder of a girl he knew but had been released. The police and the prosecutor did not inform the judge of all the facts known to them about the man. When the other woman spoke to officials in an attempt to have the man detained because of her fear of sexual violence, she was told that there was no law to protect her until he acted again. After that, the man was in psychiatric treatment, appeared again in court, and was eventually released. He then went to the woman's house, and again, fearing violence, she had her friend contact the police. The police again responded that they could do nothing.]

[34] * * * [U]nder the Constitution there can be no question that the obligation to develop the common law with due regard to the spirit,

purport and objects of the Bill of Rights is an obligation which falls on all of our courts including this Court.

* * *

[36] In exercising their powers to develop the common law, judges should be mindful of the fact that the major engine for law reform should be the legislature and not the judiciary. In this regard it is worth repeating the dictum of Iacobucci J in *R. v. Salituro* [a Canadian case].
* * *

In South Africa, the IC [Interim Constitution] brought into operation, in one fell swoop, a completely new and different set of legal norms, according to which the courts must remain vigilant and not hesitate to bring the common law into line with the Bill of Rights. * * *

[45] * * * We would adopt the following statement [of the ECHR] in *Osman v. United Kingdo*m:

"It is common ground that the State's obligation in this respect extends beyond its primary duty to secure the right to life by putting in place effective criminal law provisions to deter the commission of offences against the person backed up by law-enforcement machinery for the prevention, suppression and sanctioning of breaches of such provisions. It is thus accepted by those appearing before the Court that Article 2 of the Convention may also imply in certain well-defined circumstances a positive obligation on the authorities to take preventive operational measures to protect an individual whose life is at risk from the criminal acts of another individual."

* * *

[49] * * * A public interest immunity excusing [public officials] from liability that they might otherwise have in the circumstances of the present case, would be inconsistent with our Constitution and its values.
* * *

[54] Our Constitution is not merely a formal document regulating public power. It also embodies, like the German Constitution, an objective, normative value system. As was stated by the German Federal Constitutional Court:

"The jurisprudence of the Federal Constitutional Court is consistently to the effect that the basic right norms contain not only defensive subjective rights for the individual but embody at the same time an objective value system which, as a fundamental constitutional value for all areas of the law, acts as a guiding principle and stimulus for the legislature, executive and judiciary." [39 BVerfGE 1, 41.]

* * *

[57] Following this route it might be easier to cast the net of unlawfulness wider because constitutional obligations are now placed on the state to respect, protect, promote and fulfil the rights in the Bill of Rights and, in particular, the right of women to have their safety and security protected. * * *

[62] Thus one finds positive obligations on members of the police force both in the IC and the Police Act. In addressing these obligations

in relation to dignity and the freedom and security of the person, few things can be more important to women than freedom from the threat of sexual violence. * * * The police is one of the primary agencies of the state responsible for the protection of the public in general and women and children in particular against the invasion of their fundamental rights by perpetrators of violent crime.

Notes and Questions

1. The state's obligation to protect the fundamental interests of those under its control has the potential to become a source of welfare services. That possibility was rejected in *DeShaney*. It may also be the source of a duty to protect fundamental nonwelfare rights. This is the alternative reading of *DeShaney*: the authorities were supposed to protect life ("reasonable safety") not welfare (*Romeo*). Does a state have a duty to remove poverty-based obstacles to the exercise of rights, given that there are good reasons to believe that poverty threatens freedom and equality? Is this to say that subsidies should be paid to remove obstacles to the exercise of fundamental rights? In *Harris v. McRae*, 448 U.S. 297 (1980), federal funding limits barred payments from Medicaid for most medically necessary abortions. The Court said:

> [I]t simply does not follow [from *Roe v. Wade*] that a woman's freedom of choice carries with it a constitutional entitlement to the financial resources to avail herself of the full range of protected choices * * * [A]lthough government may not place obstacles in the path of a woman's exercise of her freedom of choice, it need not remove those not of its own creation. Indigency falls in the latter category. The financial constraints that restrict an indigent woman's ability to enjoy the full range of constitutionally protected freedom of choice are the product not of governmental restrictions on access to abortions, but rather of her indigency. * * *
>
> Although the liberty protected by the Due Process Clause affords protection against unwarranted governmental interference with freedom of choice in the context of certain governmental decisions, it does not confer an entitlement to such funds as may be necessary to realize all the advantages of that freedom.

> *Id.* at 316–18.

Justice Brennan, dissenting, said: "The proposition for which [*Roe* and its progeny stand] is not that the State is under an affirmative obligation to ensure access to abortions for all who may desire them; it is that the State must refrain from wielding its enormous power and influence in a manner that might burden the pregnant woman's freedom to choose * * *." *Id.* at 330.

2. *DeShaney* recognized as a matter of principle that the state must protect the rights of those who are under its direct supervision, within reasonable limits. This has had little impact on the condition of prison inmates in the last decades. Contrast the performance of the ISC, which revolutionized detention conditions and mental hospitals. *Lakshmi Kant Pandey v. Union of India*, (1984) 2 S.C.C. 244, and *Laxmikant Pandey v. Union of India*, (1991) 4 S.C.C. 33, imposed principles and norms on the state in the matter of adoption of Indian children by foreigners. The Child Aid Society (CAP) was created by existing legislation to oversee such

adoptions. CAP allegedly failed to prevent the continued practice of selling babies abroad. It was found that CAP had special duties being a government-established agency; and in that capacity it violated (by omission) the constitutional right to life (understood broadly as livelihood, in light of the Directive Principles). The Indian Court's decisions contained detailed regulations on how to conduct the adoption of children.

The state's positive obligation to promote individual rights is increasingly recognized by the ECHR. In *Guerra v. Italy*, 266 E.H.R.R. 357 (1998), the issue was whether the Italian government should provide the local population with information about environmental risks. The ECHR found that there is no obligation of the state to collect and disseminate environmental information on its own initiative under Art. 10, which safeguards the freedom to receive and impart information. However, to the extent a noxious industrial emission of a private party violated an applicant's private or family life, the privacy right of Art. 8 is applicable as privacy is not limited to protection against state action; there are positive obligations of the state to respect the right to family life. As pollution might have affected private life adversely, as in the actual case, where applicants were not informed in a way that would have enabled them to assess their risks, the Court held that the state failed to satisfy its obligation.

3. In *Carmichele* the SACC blurs the traditional line between the public and the private, by granting that private persons have a right to public protection from the actions of other private persons rather than just a right not to have their rights violated by public actors. However, such rights to protection are ambivalent in nature and can be applied in complex ways. Note that the South African Court relies on the German *Abortion I Case* (see Chapter 5), in which the right to protection was designed as a right directed against a woman's choice to terminate a pregnancy. Can a constitutional argument be made that women have a right to protection against violence *as well as* to freedom of choice regarding a pregnancy based on, say, equality? For a discussion of positive rights, see Heléne Combrinck, *Positive State Duties to Protect Women from Violence: Recent South African Developments*, 20 Human Rights Quarterly 666–90 (1998).

4. Compare the South African position with the English one in *Hill v. Chief Constable of West Yorkshire*, [1989] 1 AC 53 (HL). The House of Lords found it necessary to protect the police from delictual claims with the view that the interests of the community as a whole were best served by a police force that is not distracted from its primary duties by the fear of liability: "The result would be a significant diversion of police manpower and attention from their most important function, that of the suppression of crime." Per Lord Keith of Kinkel, *id*. at 63G.

Chapter 11

CONSTITUTIONAL GUARANTEES
OF DEMOCRACY

Constitutionalism derives from a modern understanding of democracy as much as democracy flows from a constitutional form of government. In this chapter we consider the political rights and constitutional institutions that are essential to civic participation in government and the legitimization of state power by those subject to its will.

"Demos" means "people" in Greek; democracy means "government by the people." To Aristotle, democracy was one of three forms of rule, as opposed to monarchy or tyranny as government by only one person or aristocracy or oligarchy as government by just a few. Such a quantitative definition, however, allowed for versions of democracy that excluded, for example, women, noncitizens, servants, and slaves, from any right to participate. Much later, Montesquieu still referred to democracy but meant government of the privileged. In the Middle Ages, some religious forces denounced democracy as a denial of the God-given differences among people, while others—Calvinists, levellers, and diggers—sought democratic reform in pursuit of a Christian ideal of equality. Later, French Enlightenment theorist Jean Jacques Rousseau conceived of democracy as the "general will" of all people—based on the natural equality of all humankind—and inspired the drafting of a French bill of rights following the 1789 Revolution. But "Liberty, Equality, and Fraternity" remained mere declarations rather than reality in France—as well as in the United States, following its Bill of Rights in 1791—until liberalism and the growth of social forces favoring equality combined individuality with socially shared power; thus the modern form of democracy. The U.S. Declaration of Independence of 1776 asserted a rather radical proposition: that governments, instituted to secure the "unalienable rights" of their citizens, derive "their just powers from the consent of the governed." For many years, however, racial minorities and women remained excluded from the enjoyment of such rights, and the democratic rights of these and other groups are subject to debate around the world.

A. DEMOCRACY AND LAW

Most nation-states today call themselves democracies. Yet constitutions do not explain what is meant by this term. Thus democracy's meaning must be deduced from a variety of rights and principles. The question regarding constitutional guarantees of democracy is *where* exactly *which aspect* of *what kind* of democracy is a reality for *whom*?

A.1. THE NATURE AND EXTENT OF CONSTITUTIONAL PROTECTION OF DEMOCRACY

McGINTY v. WESTERN AUSTRALIA

High Court (Australia).
(1996) 186 C.L.R. 140.

[Members of the Legislative Assembly of Western Australia complained of the definition of election areas in a law based on outdated population numbers, resulting in disparities between metropolitan and nonmetropolitan districts.]

The plaintiffs submit that disparities in voting power are inconsistent with the principle of representative democracy as that principle is understood at the present time. Representative democracy, so the argument runs, requires that

(a) every legally capable adult has the vote; and

(b) each person's vote be equal to the vote of every other person.

Of course, the term "legally capable adult" assumes without defining the scope of the franchise. In this century, the age of legal adulthood has been reduced from 21 to 18 and the legal incapacity of women to vote has been removed. Aborigines, who were once constitutionally disqualified from the franchise, are no longer so disqualified. But age, sex and race are not the only qualifications that have governed an adult's right to vote. Other qualifications have related to ownership of property and education or a period of residence within the electoral district. Disqualifications still include the status of convicted criminal and mental infirmity or absence from registered address. In view of the fact that the franchise has historically expanded in scope, it is at least arguable that the qualifications of age, sex, race and property which limited the franchise in earlier times could not now be reimposed so as to deprive a citizen of the right to vote. * * * The term "representative democracy" implies that the franchise be so general in its scope and voting power be so distributed among those who have the franchise that those who are elected to govern can fairly be seen to be representatives of the people who are governed. * * *

However, it is unnecessary and, for reasons presently to be stated, impermissible to determine the validity of the [law] by reference to its consistency with the requirements of a general principle of representative democracy. "Representative democracy" has been used as a shorthand description of the form of government prescribed by the Commonwealth Constitution in order to explain how the freedom to discuss governments and political matters is implied in the Constitution. As "the people" are to choose their elected representatives, it has been held that the people must be left free to discuss political and economic matters in order to perform their constitutional functions.

* * * Although the term "representative democracy" is useful to explain the text on which the implied freedom depends, the term is not to be found in either the Constitution of the Commonwealth or the Constitution of Western Australia. It is logically impermissible to treat "representative democracy" as though it were contained in the Constitution, to attribute to the term a meaning or content derived from sources extrinsic to the Constitution and then to invalidate a law for inconsistency with the meaning or content so attributed. The text of the Constitution can be illuminated by reference to representative democracy but the concept neither alters nor adds to the text. * * *

AUSTRALIAN CAPITAL TELEVISION v. THE COMMONWEALTH OF AUSTRALIA

High Court (Australia).
(1992) 177 CLR 106.

[This case is presented in Chapter 2.]

REFERENCE RE SECESSION OF QUEBEC

Supreme Court (Canada).
[1998] 2 S.C.R. 217.

[This case is presented in Chapter 2.]

Notes and Questions

1. *Criteria of democracy.* How does one assess a state's claim to democracy? Can a state be democratic if it does not protect human rights? What about a government that is dominated by a small minority, for example, of one ethnicity, class, sex, or religion? Can a government be democratic if it is based on the limited exercise of franchise, or does democracy require legitimization by the widest possible participation of voters?

2. *Human Rights.* Constitutions are not the sole guarantors of democracy. In international law the Universal Declaration of Human Rights mentions popular sovereignty, the universal and equal right to vote in elections, the right to participate in government, and equal access to public service. Also, Art. 25 of the International Covenant on Civil and Political Rights (ICCPR) states that "every citizen shall have the right and the opportunity," without discrimination "and without unreasonable restrictions," "to take part in the conduct of public affairs, directly or through freely chosen representatives," "to vote and to be elected," and "to have access, on general terms of equality, to public service in his country."

3. *Theories.* Courts display particular understandings of democracy, just as theorists do. Consider what political theorist John Stuart Mill wrote in his 1861 treatise *Considerations on Representative Government*:

There is no difficulty in showing that the ideally best form of government is that in which the sovereignty, or supreme controlling power in the last resort, is vested in the entire aggregate of the community; every citizen not only having a voice in the exercise of that ultimate sovereignty, but being, at least occasionally, called on to take an actual part in the government, by the personal discharge of some public function, local or general.

* * *

But while it is essential to representative government that the practical supremacy in the state should reside in the representatives of the people, it is an open question what actual functions, what precise part in the machinery of government, shall be directly and personally discharged by the representative body. Great varieties in this respect are compatible with the essence of representative government, provided the functions are such as secure to the representative body the control of everything in the last resort.

John Stuart Mill, *Utilitarianism, Liberty, and Representative Government* 207, 229 (Ernest Rhys ed., 1910).

4. *Right or principle?* National constitutions often invoke democracy in their opening provisions. The constitutions of Bulgaria, Estonia, Greece, Italy, Luxembourg, and Austria, among others, do so in their first article. Others make no mention of the term, but they protect rights to political activities. Democracy may be guaranteed as rights, like the right to vote, or as principles, like the principle of representation. Some aspects of democracy, like the idea of self-government, may exist only on paper but not in practice, owing to social exclusion. Other aspects of democracy, like an active citizenry, may exist in social practice but not in the constitutional text. Which aspects form democracy, according to the *McGinty* decision? Does this differ from the arguments in *Australian Capital Television* or the decision on Quebec? How do the concepts differ when compared with Mill's theory?

A.2.   LIMITS TO DEMOCRACY AND UNMAKING AUTHORITARIANISM

Democracy rests on equal voting powers, but more fundamentally it is rooted in the idea of individual self-determination and thus on liberty and freedom. But if the people are free to decide, then they may also select a nondemocratic form of government. Can democracy survive if it tolerates its enemies? The following cases discuss governing systems in transition. While the Czechoslovak case describes the practices of anti-democratic (totalitarian, authoritarian) regimes, we will consider anti-democratic political parties at the end of this chapter.

LUSTRATION CASE

Constitutional Court (Czech and Slovak Federal Republic).
Pl. US 1/92 (Sb.).[a]

[Deputies of the Federal Assembly of the Czech and Slovak Federal Republic petitioned the Court to declare unconstitutional an Act that set

a. Available, in translation, at the web page of the Constitutional Court of the Czech Republic, at <www.concourt.cz/angl_verze/doc/p–1–92.html>.

down some additional preconditions to holding certain offices in governmental bodies and organizations. The Act said that certain people, based on information and a commission's decision, were barred from holding public offices and acquiring a business license.]

Justice Valko, Chairman of the Court:

* * * In the period from 1948 until 1989, which [the] Act defines as "the era of non-freedom", the totalitarian regime violated not only human rights, but also its own laws, which it had adopted for the purpose of establishing and maintaining its hold on power. * * * [State] bodies and organizations also took part in the suppression of rights and freedoms without having any foundation at all in law for their activities. * * * In keeping with the theory of a permanent class struggle and of the leading role of the Communist Party of Czechoslovakia, the totalitarian regime deprived hundreds of thousands of persons not only of their freedom or their lives, but also even of their employment. Thus, this arbitrariness became subsequently legalized * * *

[After] the [1968] occupation of Czechoslovakia by the Warsaw Pact * * *, procedures and decision-making were regulated by [a rule] which provided: "Anyone who, by his actions, disrupts the socialist societal order and, as a consequence, loses the trust needed to hold the office or work position he is currently holding, may be removed from that office, or his employment relations may be immediately severed * * *

Until the end of 1989, every crucial position at all levels of administration (as well as those in bodies and organizations of state and economic teams) was filled in accordance with these cadre orders, so that the influence of the Communist Party of Czechoslovakia on events in all areas of public and economic life was decisively guaranteed * * *. To maintain its position of power, the totalitarian regime relied above all on the tools of repression, the decisive component of which consisted of State Security and the network of clandestine collaborators. * * *

In conformity with these principles, those holding totalitarian power in the preceding regime tried to preserve, to the greatest possible extent, a mutually connected and conspiratorial team which would enable it, even under a changed internal political situation, to influence even the ensuing democratic developments, or to reverse these developments at a propitious time. * * *

Considering all of these facts both individually and in their entirety, the Court has come to the conclusion that this calculated and malicious conduct created a real and potentially very perilous source of destabilization and danger, which could easily threaten the developing constitutional order. * * *

A democratic state has not only the right but also the duty to assert and protect the principles upon which it is founded, thus, it may not be inactive in respect to a situation in which the top positions at all levels of state administration, economic management, and so on, were filled in accordance with the now unacceptable criteria of a totalitarian system. Of course, a democratic state is, at the same time, entitled to make all efforts to eliminate an unjustified preference enjoyed in the past by a favored group of citizens in relation to the vast majority of all other citizens where such preference was accorded exclusively on the basis of membership in a totalitarian political party and where, as was already inferred earlier, it represented a form of oppression and discrimination in regard to these other citizens.

In a democratic society, it is necessary for employees of state and public bodies (but also of workplaces which have some relation to the security of the state) to meet certain criteria of a civic nature, which we can characterize as loyalty to the democratic principles upon which the state is built. * * *

In comparison with the situation that existed during the communist regime, * * * the statute under consideration affects only a very limited group of employees, exclusively in the power, administrative, and economic apparatus, and it affects licensed trades which are or could be the source of certain risks, be it merely from the perspective of protecting the establishment of democracy and its principles, the security of the state, or the protection of state secrets or of those positions from which it is possible, either overtly or covertly, to influence the development of society and the desirable performances of jobs in individual bodies or organizations.

In addition, * * * the statute * * * shall apply only during a relatively short time period by the end of which it is foreseen that the process of democratization will have been accomplished * * *.

As a result of the considerations mentioned above, the Court is convinced that it cannot deny the state's right * * * to lay down in its domestic law conditions or prerequisites crucial for the performance of leadership or other decisive positions if * * * its own safety, the safety of its citizens and, most of all, further democratic developments are taken into consideration * * *. If compared with the preceding legal order, these conditions might appear to be, from a formal perspective, a restriction on civil rights; however, in the current legal order the basic criteria which will serve as the guide for our actions in the future are those found in [the Constitution]. [This is in] contrast to the totalitarian system, which was founded on the basis of the goals of the moment and was never bound by legal principles, much less principles of constitutional law * * *

Each state or rather those which were compelled over a period of forty years to endure the violation of fundamental rights and basic freedoms by a totalitarian regime has the right to enthrone democratic leadership and to apply such legal measures as are apt to avert the risk of subversion or of a possible relapse into totalitarianism, or at least to limit those risks.

The law-based state which, after the collapse of totalitarianism, is tied to the democratic values enthroned after the collapse of totalitarianism, cannot in the final analysis be understood as amorphous with regard to values. * * * Thus, the concept of the law-based state does not have to do merely with the observance of any sort of values and any sort of rights, even if they are adopted in the procedurally proper manner, rather it is concerned first and foremost with respect for those norms that are not incompatible with the fundamental values of human society as they are expressed in the * * *Charter of Fundamental Rights and Basic Freedoms.

Therefore, * * * the Court [does not grant the petition].

* * * [However, the] Court has determined that the petition is well-founded to the extent it raises objections to the inclusion of the group of persons * * * in so far as files may have been kept on persons designated in the statute as collaborators without some written commitment and without their knowledge. * * *

OMAR JALLOW CASE

Inter–Parliamentary Council (Gambia).
CASE No. GMB/03 (27 September 2002).[b]

[In 1996, Gambia issued the Political Activities Decree 89, which bans all persons who held the offices of President, Vice–President, and Ministers in the Government of Gambia, before the transition, from participating in any political activity. The Decree thus bans indefinitely Mr. Omar Jallow, a former Minister, from participating in any political activity.]

* * * Considering that, according to one of the sources, [two Ministers] were admitted to membership of the ruling party [in] breach of Decree 89,

Considering that legislative elections are due later this year in the Gambia,

Bearing in mind that the Gambia is a party to the International Covenant on Civil and Political Rights and the African Charter on Human and People's Rights, both of which guarantee freedom of expression, assembly and association; that these rights are also embodied in the Constitution of the Gambia, Section 4 of which stipulates that "... *any other law found to be inconsistent with any provision of this Constitution shall, to the extent of its inconsistency, be void"*,

1. *Deeply regrets* that the parliamentary authorities have failed to respond, particularly since the core problem raised by this case calls for parliamentary action;

2. Insists forcefully that Decree 89, which deprives parties and specific persons, including Mr. Jallow, of their civil and political rights, violates the Constitution and the international obligations which the Gambia pledged to observe when it ratified the ICCPR and the African Charter on Human and People's Rights, as the Decree has the effect of annulling the human rights and fundamental freedoms guaranteed to them under the Constitution and the aforesaid two instruments;

3. Notes, moreover, that the authorities appear to apply Decree 89 selectively;

b. Available at <www.ipu.org/hr-e/168/ Gmb03.htm>.

4. Urges therefore the National Assembly, as guardian of the human rights of all Gambian citizens, to take legislative action to bring Decree 89 into conformity with the Constitution as required under its Section 4, and with the international human rights law subscribed to by the Gambia, so as to ensure that Mr. Jallow and the other persons concerned may fully exercise their fundamental rights to freedom of association, assembly and participation in the political affairs of their country and may stand in the next parliamentary elections;

5. Recalls that international law has precedence over national law, as has the Constitution over national statutory law, including any decrees;

6. Remains confident that the Supreme Court will rule on the question of the constitutionality of Decree 89 in conformity with the Constitution, as well as with the international human rights norms to which the Gambia has subscribed * * *.

Notes and Questions

1. *The relevance of history.* Do specific historical situations change your assessment of constitutional rights? Compare the Czechoslovak *Lustration Case* with the Gambian decision, which also reacts to the transition of a political system: Does history matter? In the *Stasi Collaboration Case*, 1 BvR 2111/94 (1997), the German Federal Constitutional Court (GFCC) stated that constitutional rights to the free choice of employment protect against any request to provide information even on activities in an oppressive political system, if such information would lead to self-incrimination. Therefore, according to the Court, obligations to provide such information touch upon the general rights of the individual, and false responses cannot be grounds for dismissal. Is this a sound reaction to the transformation from dictatorship to democracy? And does it hold for all information and for all positions in any government? The dissent in *Glasenapp* (see below) argues that forcing teachers to actively teach Christianity is as unconstitutional as forcing them to actively distance themselves from communism. Such questions emerged in the context of the rise of Nazism in Europe, in the 1930s, and the Cold War, in the 1970s. Do such circumstances make a difference from the standpoint of constitutional law? If constitutions endorse political pluralism, as well as protect freedoms of speech and religion, how much can a state ask of its civil servants? Consider that in times of transition such issues might be vitally important. As the above cases on background checks demonstrate, a state may have an interest in terminating the employment of those who served a nondemocratic government. Is this constitutionally justifiable?

2. *Courts and coups d'etat.* On four occasions Pakistan's highest court has justified military takeovers of the country. In a February 2, 2001 judgment by the Supreme Court of Pakistan,[c] lawyers argued that "[The] provisions relating to fundamental rights in our constitution are meant for highly sophisticated societies and not for a politically primitive country like Pakistan." They convinced the Court to allow military rulers three years to implement their programs. One lawyer commented that "courts have no

---

c. Available at <www.law-firm.org.pk/Military–Review.htm>.

business [giving] ideological and political leadership to society." Do you agree? The Pakistan Court used the "doctrine of state necessity." (On emergency powers, see Chapter 3, Section E.) The Human Rights Commission of Pakistan responded that "[t]he government has jeopardized the independence of the judiciary by forcing the judges to take a fresh oath [of allegiance to the military rulers]." Five justices subsequently resigned.[d] In consequence, the decision about who becomes a justice on a constitutional court becomes an issue of democracy as well.

3. *Democracy and authoritarianism.* American scholar Richard Pildes has argued that "Authoritarianism is an inherent structural tendency of democratic regimes." For example, he says, there is a "tendency of the partisan forces that gain temporary democratic control to attempt to leverage that control into more enduring and effective political domination." Richard Pildes, *The Inherent Authoritarianism in Democratic Regimes,* in *Out of and Into Authoritarian Law* (András Sajó ed., 2002.) Applying this argument to systems in transition, Leszek Lech Garlicki, former Justice of the Polish Constitutional Tribunal, comments:

> It is not necessary, therefore—as during the period of communism—to resort to underground activities in order to overthrow by force those in power. The same goal can be achieved equally well by utilizing the democratic procedures, but the end result might consist in bringing to power—legally and democratically—parties and politicians whose views of democracy and pluralism might be rather far from the standards of the beginning of the 21st century. The experience of Central Europe provides a lesson, however, that the democratic procedures and the functioning of a 'free market of ideas' may also lead to different results. After all, there have been known cases of democratic elections elevating criminal figures to power, and also, much more frequently, situations in which the disillusionment with the effects of applying democratic procedures has produced the social acceptance of a coup d'etat and the rule of 'enlightened' dictators.

The Democratic Limits to Authoritarianism in Democracy (When the State Knows Better What is Good for the People), in *id.*

4. *Individuals.* The Czechoslovak and Gambian courts restricted the right to hold public office, basing their decisions on historical arguments. The Hungarian Constitutional Court (HCC) decided (Decision 60/1994 (XII.24.) AB hat.), however, that lustration laws should be judged by normal standards rather than by the exceptional conditions of a transition. It stated that "it may be necessary to disclose the personal records of public officials that bear upon their present office or political role. The right of individuals—especially voters—to access information of public interest enjoys precedence over protecting the personal records of persons in key political roles or other public offices, given that the term 'public interest' presumes the information could be a key factor in evaluating the suitability for further office of those in the latter category."

The HCC further held that "in the interest of the democratic functioning of the State and likewise in the democratic formulation of public opinion, the constitutionally protected 'personal space' of public officials and key

d. See Inter–Press Service at <www.atimes.com/ind-pak/ BE16Df01.html>.

political players is smaller than that of other individuals; for they must especially allow themselves to be subjected to the criticism of others." Decision 36/1994 (VI.24.) AB hat. Some disclosure may thus be needed, though some may also go too far. How does one draw the line? Which rights are at issue here: democracy, voting, privacy, informational self-determination, occupation?

5. *Means of change.* Constitutions can be used to justify problematic practices. After 1945, the Allied Forces established a system of "de-Nazification," which included firing former German Nazis from their state positions. Civil servants were required to answer questionnaires describing their duties under the Hitler regime. If doubts were raised, they were tried in special "courts," to which "judges" had been selected based on their political persuasions. The post-War German state and federal Constitution excluded any claim to fundamental rights against such practices. Should there be constitutional limits to constitutional change? Would such limits endanger or enhance democracy? More recent lustration laws have been criticized for their overly zealous generalizations and, like the "de-Nazification" rules, for their inability to solve the problem they are meant to address. What would be the constitutional means to ensure democracy in the circumstances of a transition?

A.3. MILITANT DEMOCRACY

Democracies are based on the guarantee of individual freedom and equality. But freedom can be exploited to destroy democracy as well. While lustration is an issue in periods of transition, the protection of democracy against its enemies is a matter that states confront at all times.

SOCIALIST REICH PARTY CASE

Federal Constitutional Court (Germany).
2 BVerfGE 1 (1952).[e]

[The Socialist Reich Party (SRP) was founded in 1949 as a successor to the rightist German Imperial Party. Its publications, campaign appeals, and leadership displayed a strong neo-Nazi orientation. Finding that the SRP "seeks to impair the liberal democratic order," the federal government petitioned the Court to declare the new party unconstitutional, based on a specific provision in the Constitution, Art. 21 sec. 2, which allows for such.]

E. * * * German constitutions following World War I hardly mentioned political parties, although even at that time * * * political parties to a large extend determined democratic constitutional life. The reasons for this omission are manifold, but in the final analysis the cause lies in a democratic ideology that refused to recognize groups mediating between the free individual and the will of the entire people composed of the sum of individual wills and represented in parliament by parliamen-

e. Editor's note: translation from Donald P. Kommers, *The Constitutional Jurisprudence of the Federal Republic of Germa-* ny 218–222 (2d ed. 1997), in slightly altered form.

tarians "as representatives of the entire people." * * * The Constitution abandoned this viewpoint and, more realistically, expressly recognizes parties as agents—even if not the sole ones—forming the political will of the people.

The Constitution's attempt to regulate political parties encounters [a] problem [that] relates to the principle of democracy, which permits any political orientation to manifest itself in political parties, including—to be consistent—antidemocratic orientations. * * *

In a free democratic state * * * freedom of political opinion and freedom of association—including political association—are guaranteed to individual citizens as basic rights. On the other hand, part of the nature of every democracy consists in the people exercising their supreme power in elections and voting. In the reality of the large modern democratic state, however, this popular will can emerge only through parties as operating political units. Both fundamental ideas lead to the basic conclusion that the establishment and activity of political parties must not be restrained.

The framers of the German Constitution had to decide whether they could fully implement this conclusion or whether, enlightened by recent experiences, they should * * * draw certain limits * * *. They had to consider whether principles governing every democracy should limit the absolute freedom to establish parties on the basis of any political idea, and whether parties seeking to abolish democracy by using formal democratic means should be excluded from political life. [They] also had to take into account the danger that the government might be tempted to eliminate troublesome opposition parties.

[The] Constitution has tried to resolve these problems. On the one hand, it establishes the principle that formation of political parties shall be free. On the other hand, it offers a means of preventing activity by "unconstitutional" parties. To avert the danger of an abuse of this power, [it] authorizes the Federal Constitutional Court to decide the question of unconstitutionality and attempts to determine as far as possible the factual requirements for this declaration. * * * Because of the special importance of parties in a democratic state [the Court] is justified in eliminating them form the political scene if, but only if, they seek to topple supreme fundamental values of the free democratic order which are embodied in the Constitution. * * *

Conceptually, parties are also "associations" * * *. Hence, [the Constitution] would prohibit them under the conditions mentioned there and would subject them to the authority of the executive in general. * * * [But] if an association is a political party, it is [also] entitled to the privileges * * * because of the special status granted only to parties. * * *

[A] party may be eliminated from the political process only if it rejects the supreme principles of a free democracy. If a party's internal organization does not correspond to democratic principles, [one] may generally conclude that the party seeks to impose upon the state the structural principles that it has implemented within its own organization. * * * Whether or not this conclusion is justified must be determined in each individual case. * * *

[The Court then analyzes the history of German political parties, especially the NSDAP, the party of Adolf Hitler, and examines, in detail, letters between Socialist Reich party leaders and with potential recruits. The documents reveal that most SRP leaders have been Nazis with positions in their organizations and that they were actively seeking out former Nazis.] * * *

G. II. 3. (e) The SRP claims in its defense that other parties have also tried to enlist former National Socialists. * * * This objection shows that the SRP misunderstands the situation. [We] do not reproach the SRP for having tried to enlist former National Socialists, but rather for collecting the particularly hard-core individuals who have "remained true to themselves." [The SRP recruited these persons] not in order to gain positive forces for democracy, but to preserve and propagate National Socialist ideas. * * *

(f) Former Nazis hold key positions in the party to such an extent as to determine its political and intellectual image. [N]o decision can be made against their will.

III. (a) [The SRP's] organization is also similar to that of the Nazi party. * * * Its internal structure is not in keeping with democratic principles * * *. In brief, a party must be structured from the bottom up; that is, members must not be excluded from decision-making processes, and the basic equality of members as well as the freedom to join or to leave [the party] must be guaranteed. It would also contravene democratic principles * * * either to promise absolute obedience to party leaders or to demand such a promise. * * *

[The SRP] does not accept members of trial tribunals, political persecutees. * * *

(d) (3) [Expulsion] practice corresponds exactly with the procedure in the Nazi party. * * * These facts demonstrate that the SRP was governed in a dictatorial manner. * * *

H. 1. The SRP is thus unconstitutional within the meaning of * * * the Basic Law. * * * Therefore, the party must be dissolved.

UNITED COMMUNIST PARTY OF TURKEY v. TURKEY

European Court of Human Rights.
26 E.H.R.R. 121 (1998).

[The United Communist Party of Turkey (TBKP) was dissolved by the Constitutional Court for having sought to establish the domination of one social class over the others, which is prohibited under Turkish general and constitutional law, for using the word "communist" in its name, contrary to a law, and for having carried on activities likely to undermine the territorial integrity of the state and the unity of the nation, contrary to laws and the Constitution, particularly related to the independence of the Kurdish people. A Grand Chamber decided that the

Turkish Court's decision violated the European Convention for the Protection of Human Rights and Fundamental Freedoms.]

45. Democracy is without doubt a fundamental feature of the "European public order" * * *. That is apparent, firstly, from the Preamble to the Convention, which establishes a very clear connection between the Convention and democracy by stating that the maintenance and further realization of human rights and fundamental freedoms are best ensured on the one hand by an effective political democracy and on the other by a common understanding and observance of human rights * * *. The Preamble goes on to affirm that European countries have a common heritage of political tradition, ideals, freedom and the rule of law. The Court has observed that in that common heritage are to be found the underlying values of the Convention * * *; it has pointed out several times that the Convention was designed to maintain and promote the ideals and values of a democratic society * * *.

In addition, Articles 8, 9, 10 and 11 of the Convention require that interference with the exercise of the rights they enshrine must be assessed by the yardstick of what is "necessary in a democratic society". The only type of necessity capable of justifying an interference with any of those rights is, therefore, one which may claim to spring from "democratic society". Democracy thus appears to be the only political model contemplated by the Convention and, accordingly, the only one compatible with it. * * *

57. [One] of the principal characteristics of democracy [is] the possibility it offers of resolving a country's problems through dialogue, without recourse to violence, even when they are irksome. Democracy thrives on freedom of expression. From that point of view, there can be no justification for hindering a political group solely because it seeks to debate in public the situation of the State's population and to take part in the nation's political life in order to find, according to democratic rules, solutions capable of satisfying everyone concerned.

CHRISTIAN DEMOCRACY PARTY CASE

Constitutional Tribunal (Poland).
Decision dated 13 March 2000 (K. 1/99).

[The Christian Democracy of the Republic of Poland (ChDRP) party introduced amendments to its articles of association, providing that the chairmen of the regional party councils were to be appointed by the Chairman of the National Committee. The court that was to register the ChDRP's amendments was concerned that they violated the Constitution and referred the matter to the Constitutional Tribunal. The question of principle was whether the Constitution implied that the internal structure of a party meet certain democratic standards.]

[O]ne could neither overestimate nor treat too lightly the factor of internal organization. In the light of the Constitution, a political party, defined as a voluntary association * * * should constitute a dynamic unity of its internal and external structures and methods of activity. That unity should assure the citizens organized in political parties the possibility of organized and effective impact or participation in democratically exercised governance. This implies the existence of a link between the internal structures and methods of activity of political parties, and the fulfillment by those parties of their constitutional role and the democratic nature of their methods of influencing the policy of the state. Those links, however, are of a relative nature, and the subjection of the internal methods and structures of * * * political parties to their role and methods of shaping state policy [is] not * * * a necessary requirement. Undemocratic elements of internal organization need not always directly and substantially bear upon the fulfillment by a party of its role in the political system or upon the external methods of activity which it applies. Therefore, the liberty of shaping the internal structures and principles of the functioning of a party cannot be restricted, as long as it does not exclude the democratic nature of the methods by which a party intends to influence or actually influences the shaping of the policy of the state. * * * That implies the necessity to judge in relation always to a specific case * * *. Such assessments should, above all, take into account: first, whether, and if so, to what extent the structures and methods of internal organization prevent or restrict the influence of the party members upon the shaping of significant elements of its program, its statutes and policies; secondly, whether, and if so, to what extent, the structures and internal organizational methods prevent or inhibit the party members from influencing the composition of the highest bodies of the party * * *; and thirdly, whether and if so, to what extent, the structures and methods of internal organization prevent or inhibit the party members from exerting influence upon the possible activities of their representatives * * *.

The only limitations of the freedom to organize the internal structures and methods of conducting party activities that are specified in absolute terms consist of the prohibitions contained in [the Constitution itself]. [The] Constitution is in favor of observing far-going restraint with regards to the possibility and scope of interference by the public authorities, including the legislature, with the internal structures and principles of activity of the political parties.

[Based on these premises, the Constitutional Tribunal said that "the method of formation of the internal structures of that party diverges to a considerable extent from the principle of the election of all the organs of a party in favor of special creative prerogatives of the chairman of that party. That may give rise to doubts." This does not mean, however, that the Constitution has been violated in that way.]

It should be taken into account that the autonomy of the formation of the internal structures is derived from the liberty to form parties. External interference may be [constitutional] only when such a structure unequivocally and obviously diverges from the standards of a democratic state governed by the law and its corresponding value system. In this case the Constitutional Tribunal has not found any such obvious and unequivocal incompatibility.

REFAH PARTISI (THE WELFARE PARTY) v. TURKEY

European Court of Human Rights.
Application nos. 41340/98, 41342/98, 41343/98, 41344/98 (2001).

[Refah, a political party founded in 1983, became the largest party in the Turkish Parliament in 1995 and a member of the coalition government in 1996. In 1998, the Turkish Constitutional Court dissolved Refah on grounds that it was a "center" of activities contrary to the principles of secularism. Refah had nothing undemocratic in its platform. But prominent members advocated women wearing Islamic headscarves in public places, which violates the Turkish Constitution, discussed whether social change that the party sought would be "peaceful or violent" and would be achieved "harmoniously or by bloodshed," stated it sought to establish the supremacy of the Koran through a holy war (jihad), and had called for a theocratic regime.]

34. The applicants alleged that Refah's dissolution and the prohibition barring its leaders * * * from holding similar office in any other political party had infringed their right to freedom of association * * *. Such an interference [is justified if it was] "prescribed by law", pursued one or more legitimate aims * * * and was "necessary in a democratic society" for the achievement of those aims. * * *

43. * * * Democracy requires that the people should be given a role. Only institutions created by and for the people may be vested with the powers and authority of the State; statute law must be interpreted and applied by an independent judicial power. There can be no democracy where the people of a State, even by a majority decision, waive their legislative and judicial powers in favour of an entity which is not responsible to the people it governs, whether it is secular or religious.

The rule of law means that all human beings are equal before the law, in their rights as in their duties. However, legislation must take account of differences, provided that distinctions between people and situations have an objective and reasonable justification, pursue a legitimate aim and are proportionate and consistent with the principles normally upheld by democratic societies. But the rule of law cannot be said to govern a secular society when groups of persons are discriminated against solely on the ground that they are of a different sex or have different political or religious beliefs. Nor is the rule of law upheld where entirely different legal systems are created for such groups.

There is a very close link between the rule of law and democracy. As it is the function of written law to establish distinctions on the basis of relevant differences, the rule of law cannot be sustained over a long period if persons governed by the same laws do not have the last word on the subject of their content and implementation.

44. * * * There can be no democracy without pluralism. It is for that reason that freedom of expression * * * is applicable * * * not only to "information" or "ideas" that are favourably received or regarded as inoffensive or as a matter of indifference, but also to those that offend,

shock or disturb. The fact that their activities form part of a collective exercise of the freedom of expression in itself entitles political parties to seek the protection of * * * the Convention. * * *

47. The Court takes the view that a political party may campaign for a change in the law or the legal and constitutional basis of the State on two conditions: (1) the means used to that end must in every respect be legal and democratic; (2) the change proposed must itself be compatible with fundamental democratic principles. It necessarily follows that a political party whose leaders incite recourse to violence, or propose a policy which does not comply with one or more of the rules of democracy or is aimed at the destruction of democracy and infringement of the rights and freedoms afforded under democracy cannot lay claim to the protection of the Convention against penalties imposed for those reasons. * * *

49. Moreover, the Court reiterates that * * * freedom of thought, conscience and religion is one of the foundations of a "democratic society" within the meaning of the Convention. It is, in its religious dimension, one of the most vital elements that go to make up the identity of believers and their conception of life, but it is also a precious asset for atheists, agnostics, sceptics and the unconcerned. The pluralism indissociable from a democratic society, which has been dearly won over the centuries, depends on it. That freedom entails, *inter alia*, freedom to hold or not to hold religious beliefs and to practise or not to practise a religion. * * *

51. The State's role as the neutral and impartial organiser of the practising of the various religions, denominations and beliefs is conducive to religious harmony and tolerance in a democratic society. * * *

65. * * * The parties agreed before the Court that preserving secularism is necessary for protection of the democratic system in Turkey. However, they did not agree about the content, interpretation and application of the principle of secularism. But interpretation of that principle, which underlies all of the grounds for dissolution, was based, according to the Constitutional Court, on the context of the history of Turkish law. It pointed out that Turkish society had undergone the experience of a theocratic political regime during the Ottoman Empire and that it had founded the secular republican regime in Turkey by putting an end to theocracy. The Court accordingly finds, at this stage of its examination, that the establishment of a theocratic regime, with rules valid in the sphere of public law as well as that of private law, is not completely inconceivable in Turkey, account being taken, firstly, of its relatively recent history and, secondly, of the fact that the great majority of its population are Muslims.

70. Like the Government, the Court considers that Refah's proposal that there should be a plurality of legal systems would introduce into all legal relationships a distinction between individuals grounded on religion, would categorise everyone according to his religious beliefs and would allow him rights and freedoms not as an individual but according to his allegiance to a religious movement. The Court takes the view that such a societal model cannot be considered compatible with the Conven-

tion system, for two reasons. Firstly, it would do away with the State's role as the guarantor of individual rights and freedoms and the impartial organiser of the practice of the various beliefs and religions in a democratic society, since it would oblige individuals to obey, not rules laid down by the State in the exercise of its above-mentioned functions, but static rules of law imposed by the religion concerned. But the State has a positive obligation to ensure that everyone within its jurisdiction enjoys in full, and without being able to waive them, the rights and freedoms guaranteed by the Convention. Secondly, such a system would undeniably infringe the principle of non-discrimination between individuals as regards their enjoyment of public freedoms, which is one of the fundamental principles of democracy. * * *

72. [In addition, it] is difficult to declare one's respect for democracy and human rights while at the same time supporting a regime based on sharia, which clearly diverges from Convention values, particularly with regard to its criminal law and criminal procedure, its rules on the legal status of women and the way it intervenes in all spheres of private and public life in accordance with religious precepts. * * * In the Court's view, a political party whose actions seem to be aimed at introducing sharia in a State party to the Convention can hardly be regarded as an association complying with the democratic ideal * * *.

74. * * * While it is true that Refah's leaders did not, in government documents, call for the use of force and violence as a political weapon, they did not take prompt practical steps to distance themselves from those members of Refah who had publicly referred with approval to the possibility of using force against politicians who opposed them. * * *

77. The Court further considers that Refah's political aims were neither theoretical nor illusory, but achievable. * * *

81. Consequently, the Court * * * takes the view that, even though the margin of appreciation left to States must be a narrow one where the dissolution of political parties is concerned, since the pluralism of ideas and parties is itself an inherent part of democracy, a State may reasonably forestall the execution of such a policy, which is incompatible with the Convention's provisions, before an attempt is made to implement it through concrete steps that might prejudice civil peace and the country's democratic regime.

Justices Fuhrmann, Loucaides and Bratza, dissenting:

We regret that we are unable to share the view of the majority of the Court * * *. [We] can readily accept the Government's argument as to the vital importance of secularism in Turkish society. * * * [But] not only was Refah democratically elected in 1995 * * * but * * * it is common ground that the party was organised on democratic lines and that there was nothing in its statute or programme to demonstrate or even suggest any departure from the principle of secularism or any encouragement to the use of violent or undemocratic means to replace the existing constitutional structure of the Turkish society. [Although parties may conceal their aims, courts must seek good evidence to prove as much.] * * * [The] use of the blunt instrument of dissolving a party is to be seen as a genuine alternative to the taking of steps against the individual person responsible. * * *

The question * * * is * * * whether the extreme measure of dissolution * * * could be considered as responding to a pressing social need and as a measure which was proportionate to the legitimate aims served. * * * What is in our view lacking is any compelling or convincing evidence to suggest that the party, whether before or after entering Government, took any steps to realise political aims which were incompatible with Convention norms, to destroy or undermine the secular society, to engage in or to encourage acts of violence or religious hatred, or otherwise to pose a threat to the legal and democratic order in Turkey.

Notes and Questions

1. *Limitations?* The Supreme Court of Israel has argued that freedom "is no axe to strike at democracy"; thus freedom of speech may be limited for reasons of state security. H.C. 88/680 *Shnitzer v. Military Censor*, P.D. (1988), 21. The jurisprudence of the U.S. Supreme Court (USSC) takes a different approach. Although *Gitlow v. New York*, 268 U.S. 652 (1925), held that even a tendency of speech to lead to crime would justify restricting speech, the case is no longer followed. Today advocacy of (as opposed to incitement to) violence is protected speech in the U.S. What are the constitutional arguments to support such divergent holdings? Do democracies need legal protection? This is the idea of "militant democracy," an expression coined by Karl Loewenstein in *Militant Democracy and Fundamental Rights*, 31 Am. Pol. Sci. Rev. 417, 417–32, 638–58 (1937). Are the Cold War, the threat of terrorist attacks, or the danger of the establishment of the Sharia as a legal system (rejected by the European Court of Human Rights (ECHR) in *Refah*) sufficient justifications to limit political activity? Should it depend on the imminence or the likelihood of the danger? Is there a difference between political speech and a call to hatred? Many European countries prohibit the public display of emblems or symbols or the wearing of clothes connected with extreme-right ideologies or racial hatred; the U.S. does not. Is this a question of speech, violence, democracy, or the protection of minorities and thus equality? In comparison, consider *Refah*. We also discuss these issues in chapters 6 and 7.

2. *Substance and Procedure.* How can a democracy be intolerant toward antidemocratic actors without relinquishing its claim to democratic legitimacy? By depriving some antidemocratic actors of their civil rights, does militant democracy destroy rather than protect the democratic state? Gregory Fox and Georg Nolte characterize the problem of tolerance as the central paradox of democratic regimes in *Intolerant Democracies*, 36 Harv. Int'l. L.J. 1, 14 (1995). A fundamental principle of liberal democratic theory is the requirement of diversity of public opinion as a minimum condition of political life, with society being best served by fair competition between factions. The presence of antidemocratic ideologies thus creates a dilemma for the democratic state. Suppression of these ideologies offends the foremost democratic principle, yet their presence threatens the survival of a system in which the principle of tolerance is institutionalized. Fox and Nolte describe

two approaches democracies take to resolving this dilemma: one they call the procedural model, the other substantive.

> Procedural democrats view democracy as a set of institutional arrangements, a framework for decision-making which does not prescribe the content of the decisions. Rooted in Enlightenment opposition to traditional authority, procedural democracy rests on faith that rational discourse ensures liberty. The social contract is not a priori; democracy means actual majority rule of the people. A procedural democracy thus exists only so long as there is a political will to be democratic. Proceduralists rely on free speech to counter antidemocratic speech.

> The substantive democrat rejects the proceduralist claim that a democracy must allow itself to become undemocratic if the majority so desires. Substantive democrats find it contradictory to say tolerance is the fundamental organizing principle of government and to preserve the possibility of intolerant government. Thus, substantive democrats prioritize the long-term survival of the democratic form over the political rights of antidemocratic actors.

> *Id.*

In Fox and Nolte's terms militant democracy is a substantive democracy. By contrast, the Weimar Republic, Germany's first constitutional state based on the principle of popular sovereignty, reflected the influence of procedural, or liberal, democratic theory. In his 1932 essay on legality and legitimacy (*Legalität und Legitimität*, in *Verfassungsrechtliche Aufsätze aus den Jahren 1924–1954*, at 263 (reprint 1993)), a prominent constitutional scholar, Carl Schmitt, attacked liberal constitutional democracy as vulnerable, recommending in its place a constitution with an unalterable core. On the eve of Nazi rule, he, with many others, challenged the procedural positivism and relativism that prevailed in the Weimar Republic. He argued that elected representatives should not sweep away fundamental interests of the people, even by constitutional amendment procedures. He found implied limitations in procedural rules because they could not be meant to destroy the "essence" of what they were designed to effect. Schmitt's theory also legitimized the existence of legal institutions designed to prevent a democratic constitution from being turned against itself. Note that Schmitt became famous as the legal defender of the Nazi regime once Hitler was in power, which suggests that his is not a theory of democracy but rather a theory of state preservation. Fox and Nolte, *op. cit.* at 19–20.

Regarding German history, the Allied democratic impulse in Germany did not derive from pure democratic good will. It also served as ideological legitimization for the otherwise problematic provision of massive aid to a recent enemy, a policy that reflected underlying military, economic, and anticommunist Allied interests. After an initially vigorous de-Nazification effort, Western Allies accepted that Nazism was prevalent among highly skilled and administratively capable members of society and that removing them from key government and civic positions would have had an overall adverse effect. Can democracy live with representatives who were actively involved in a dehumanizing, totalitarian system? What kind of qualities (and qualifications) are needed for such positions? Compare this to the decision on lustration, above, in Subsection A.2.

From the perspective of the Allies immediately after World War Two, allowing West Germany to construct a liberal regime slowly was unacceptable. Since the Weimar constitution had opened the door to the electoral assumption of power by the National Socialists, or Nazis, despite the party's clearly antidemocratic means and aims, the postwar Basic Law intended to prevent this history from repeating itself. According to American commentator Donald P. Kommers, Germany "crafted [a] negative revolution opposing all utopian schemes for rebuilding the political order." *German Constitutionalism: A Prolegomenon*, 40 Emory L.J. 837, 852–53 (1991). The postwar German state was established as a conservative regime, one meant to be insulated at once from radical or extreme political movements of any kind and from excesses of state power. In 1949, the Basic Law was adopted, which formally states in Art. 20 that the Federal Republic of Germany is a "democratic and social federal state." It protects fundamental rights, which are interpreted to affirmatively require the state to respect them and to provide the conditions for their enjoyment. No individual right is seen to be absolute, but all may be limited by each other, and some allow for proportional limitations by statute as well. However, no right may be absolutely eclipsed or restricted. In this sense individual rights represent the unalterable core of a substantive democracy. But in other provisions the Basic Law also provides for its own defense. It allows the GFCC to suspend the individual rights of those who "abuse" their freedom of expression, it guarantees a rather theoretical yet symbolically important right of resistance in defense of democracy if there is no alternative, it restricts amendments of the Basic Law itself, and it allows the GFCC, if called upon by Parliament, to ban antidemocratic political parties and associations. These provisions form the constitutional basis of what the GFCC defined, in 1956, as "militant democracy." "[T]he Basic Law represents a conscious effort to achieve a synthesis between the principle of tolerance with respect to all political ideas and certain inalienable values of the political system. Article 21(2) ... expresses the conviction of the [drafters], based on their concrete historical experience, that the state could no longer afford to maintain an attitude of neutrality toward political parties. [The Basic Law] has in this sense created a "militant democracy," a constitutional [value] decision that is binding on the Federal Constitutional Court." *Communist Party Case*, 5 BVerfGE 85, 141–142 (1956), translated in Donald P. Kommers, *The Constitutional Jurisprudence of the Federal Republic of Germany* 228 (1989). Are constitutional courts a reliable safeguard against abuses of power?

Where are the limits for restricting democratic parties? According to Art. 13 of the Polish Constitution, "The existence of political parties and other organizations referring in their programs to totalitarian methods and practices of nazism, fascism and communism is prohibited, and concerns also those, the programs or activities of which assume or allow for racial and nationalistic hatred, the use of violent force in order to win power or influence the policy of the state, or foresee the secrecy of their structures or membership." Article 21 section 2 of the German Basic Law states: "Parties which, by reason of their aims or the behavior of their adherents, seek to impair or abolish the free democratic basic order or to endanger the existence of the Federal Republic of Germany are unconstitutional." The GFCC decides the question of unconstitutionality. In *Sidiropoulos and Others v. Greece*, 27 E.H.R.R. 633, the ECHR decided, in 1998, that the Greek court's refusal to register an applicants' association deprived the applicants of any possibility to jointly or individually pursue their stated aims, thus depriving them of their right to associate. Are there some aims that are not legitimate?

3. *Theory as Law?* The German *Socialist Reich Party Case* was followed by a decision in 1956, in the midst of the Cold War, that declared the Communist Party unconstitutional. The decision presents an exhaustive analysis of Marxism–Leninism and thus also purports to be a strong statement of political philosophy. Is this proper constitutional reasoning? Are such matters for the courts to decide, or should they be left to the political process? The USSC has held that mere membership in a communist party is insufficient to deprive someone, e.g., of the right to travel. *Aptheker v. Secretary of State*, 378 U.S. 500 (1964). What kind of constitutional argument could prevent a government from targeting opposition parties? In the spring of 2002, the GFCC stopped a procedure to prohibit the neofascist NPD because most party members who were referred to as witnesses of the antidemocratic activity were undercover agents or informers for the German secret service (the official name of which is "Agency for the Protection of the Constitution"). What results from this in constitutional law?

B. DEMOCRATIC ACTIVITY: RIGHTS OF A CIVIL SOCIETY

Political participation in democracies is not limited merely to voting in elections (discussed below); it covers a whole range of activities. In recent political theory active citizenship and associational democracy are sometimes considered even more important than traditional institutions and forms of organizing. Citizens may lobby parties or representatives, join parties or associations, make campaign contributions, or pressure organizations that work for causes they favor. They may also take more direct action, like staging demonstrations and protests, writing letters, or uniting with others to shape public opinion. Constitutions thus offer guarantees for democracy in addition to those that protect the general franchise, plurality of political parties, or rights of minorities within or outside of Parliament.

B.1. ACTIVE CITIZENS

MITSUBISHI RESIN, INC. v. TAKANO

Supreme Court (Japan).
27 Minshū 11 at p. 1536 (1973).[f]

* * * The appellee passed the company entrance test that the appellant company conducted for university graduates while he was a student * * *. [The following year] he graduated and at the same time entered the appellant company on a three-month trial basis. [He was then notified] that at the end of the trial period he would be dismissed. This case is in dispute of the validity of such action. According to the allegations of the [company, the appellee] made a number of deceptively false remarks in the personal history he was asked to file[,] concealed a

f. Reproduced from Lawrence W. Beer and Hiroshi Itoh, *The Constitutional Case*   *Law of Japan, 1970 through 1990*, at 170–179 (1996).

number of facts that should have been noted on the requested documents and made false statements in response to questions at his interview. [The matters of interest were, among others, that he joined the Student Council, which conducted extremely radical activities, and he was involved in unregistered demonstrations.]

[Relating] to the appellee's concealment of certain matters as the reason for refusal to take the appellee in as a permanent employee, we shall consider whether this is related to the thoughts and beliefs of the appellee. * * * There is a close relationship between peoples thoughts and their behavior. * * * This is particularly so in this type of case where the problem involves activities related to student movements. Even if it is not always possible to say that participation in student movements is related to specific thoughts and beliefs, in many cases there is undeniably some kind of connection. An investigation by an enterprise about whether or not a worker was involved in the past in any student movements will be used as data upon which to determine his qualifications for employment from the standpoint of the enterprise's operations. * * *

[Certain] provisions of the Constitution were created to guarantee the basic equality and liberty of individuals in relation to the activities of the government or other public entities. They are wholly for the regulation of relations between individuals and the government and public entities, and were not intended to regulate directly the relations between private parties. * * *

In relations between private parties, these rights of each person to equality and liberty in actuality [encounter] the possibility of conflict. The regulation of this conflict in a modern free society is entrusted to private self-regulation. However, where one party exceeds what is socially permissible in manner and degree in injuring another party, the law in principle intervenes and regulates the relationship between the parties. * * *

There are differences in societal power relationships between private parties, and there are situations where one party's position is superior to that of another party. * * * [Where] actual damage or a fear of damage to an individual's basic equality or freedom exceeds socially permissible limits in mode or extent, this can be corrected through legislative action.

* * * While guaranteeing freedom of belief and equality under the law, the Constitution also guarantees as basic human rights * * * the right to use and manage private property and other wider freedoms of economic activity. Entrepreneurs enjoy freedom of contract as one type of that kind of economic activity. For the benefit of his own enterprise, an entrepreneur can, in principle, freely decide, unless there are some other legal restrictions to the contrary, what kind of conditions should be set in hiring people, and what kind of people should be hired. Even if an enterprise should refuse to hire someone based on his particular beliefs or ideas, we cannot say that this is per se illegal. * * * [Consequently,] there is no reason to regard as an illegal act prohibited by law an investigation of a worker's beliefs and ideas. * * *

* * * [Unless] otherwise proscribed by law, the above activities by the enterprise should be construed to be legally permissible.

LEVY v. VICTORIA

High Court (Australia).
(1997) 189 C.L.R. 579.

[Levy was charged with offences pursuant to the Wildlife (Game) (Hunting Season) Regulations * * * of "enter[ing] into or upon a permitted hunting area during prohibited times without holding an authority to do so." He was not the holder of a valid game license, but entered a hunting area where he was intercepted by authority, interviewed, and removed against his will from that area. He pleaded that he entered the area for the purpose of protesting against the laws of the Victorian Parliament, which authorized the holders of game licenses to shoot game birds.]

Justice Brennan:

* * * Speech is the chief vehicle by which ideas about government and politics are communicated. Hence it is natural to regard the freedom of communication about government and politics implied in the Constitution as a freedom of speech. But actions as well as words can communicate ideas. In the United States where "freedom of speech" is protected by the First Amendment of the Constitution, non-verbal activity which expresses ideas may be protected as a form of speech. Thus a "protest by silent and reproachful presence" or by a burning of the flag of the United States have been held to be protected by the First Amendment. However, American decisions on the protection of "expressive activity" under the First Amendment must be viewed with caution in the context of our Constitution. The freedom of discussion implied in the Constitution of the Commonwealth, unlike the subject of protection under the First Amendment of the United States Constitution, does not require consideration of the connotation of "speech" or of the conduct which might be thought to constitute a form of "speech". The implication denies legislative or executive power to restrict the freedom of communication about the government or politics of the Commonwealth, whatever be the form of communication, unless the restriction is imposed to fulfil a legitimate purpose and the restriction is appropriate and adapted to the fulfilment of that purpose. In principle, therefore, non-verbal conduct which is capable of communicating an idea about the government or politics of the Commonwealth and which is intended to do so may be immune from legislative or executive restriction so far as that immunity is needed to preserve the system of representative and responsible government that the Constitution prescribes.

Televised protests by non-verbal conduct are today a commonplace of political expression. A law which simply denied an opportunity to make such a protest * * * would be as offensive to the constitutionally implied freedom as a law which banned political speech-making * * *. However, while the speaking of words is not inherently dangerous or productive of a tangible effect that might warrant prohibition or control in the public interest, non-verbal conduct may, according to its nature and effect, demand legislative or executive prohibition or control even though it conveys a political message. Bonfires may have to be banned to prevent the outbreak of bushfires, and the lighting of a bonfire does not escape such a ban by the hoisting of a political effigy as its centrepiece. A law which prohibits non-verbal conduct for a legitimate purpose other than the suppressing of its political message is unaffected by the implied freedom if the prohibition is appropriate and adapted to the fulfilment of that purpose. * * *

In the present case, the plaintiff entered upon the proclaimed area and, had he not been removed, he would have stayed there to make a dramatic and televised protest against duck shooting and the laws and policies which permitted or encouraged the practice. He was prohibited from being able lawfully to make that protest and he was removed from the proclaimed area in exercise of an authority arising from the * * * Hunting Season Regulations. The conduct in which the plaintiff desired to engage and which was proscribed * * * was calculated to express and was capable of expressing a political message. It was therefore conduct of the kind which, if the criteria presently to be mentioned existed, would be immune from legislative prohibition.

* * * If the prohibition or regulation is reasonably appropriate and adapted to the protection of life or limb there can be no doubt as to its validity. [Such law] is not invalidated * * * merely because an opportunity to discuss matters of government or politics is thereby precluded.

The permitted hunting areas * * * were the areas on which duck shooters would be engaged in shooting ducks at the opening of the season. * * * Some analogy is seen in the decision of the Supreme Court of the United States in *Schenck v. Pro Choice Network of Western New York* in which that Court determined the extent of a buffer zone that ought to be maintained between persons entering an abortion clinic and those who picket the clinic in protest. The analogy is attractive unless the different criterion of validity under our Constitution is steadily kept in mind. Under our Constitution, the courts do not assume the power to determine that some more limited restriction than that imposed by an impugned law could suffice to achieve a legitimate purpose. The courts acknowledge the law-maker's power to determine the sufficiency of the means of achieving the legitimate purpose, reserving only a jurisdiction to determine whether the means adopted could reasonably be considered to be appropriate and adapted to the fulfilment of the purpose. * * *

Notes and Questions

1. *Civil disobedience.* An active citizenry is often considered an essential ingredient of a well-functioning democracy, and its absence a sign of crisis, social disintegration, or destabilization. Yet an active citizenry may not only strengthen democracy, it may also endanger it. Civil disobedience is a case in point, where citizens break the law in protesting injustice. Is such behavior constitutionally protected? (See also the discussion on free speech in Chapter 7.) If broken laws are interpreted in light of political rights, can a court balance the rule of law against the rights to democratic activity? In Great Britain, the Queen's Bench Division, in *Hirst and Agu v. Chief*

Constable of West Yorkshire, 85 Cr. App. R. 330 (1987), addressed whether animal-rights supporters who demonstrated on a highway outside a fur shop could be arrested and convicted for willfully obstructing, without lawful authority or excuse, free passage along the highway. The Court stated:

> The question * * * is whether we correctly interpreted the meaning of the words 'willfully obstruct', and whether the facts of the case are capable as a matter of law of justifying a conviction. "[Willful Obstruction] is when obstruction is caused purposely or deliberately". However, precedents have indicated two further elements must be satisfied before any one can be convicted of these offenses. First, the defendant must have no lawful authority or excuse to engage in the act in question. Second, the court must determine whether the acts engaged in are reasonable.

The Court then said it depends on all the circumstances, including the length of time the obstruction continues, the place where it occurs, the purpose for which it is done, and, of course, whether it does in fact cause an actual obstruction as opposed to a potential obstruction. The GFCC argued similarly in the *Coercion Case*, 73 BVerfGE 206 (1986), in which protesters blocked traffic and were charged with coercion of motorists. The Court held that criminal law on coercion should be interpreted in light of the Basic Law and that violence which consists of blocking traffic is thus not automatically objectionable. Do you agree?

2. *Shocking speech.* If democracy rests on speech, when should constitutions limit what can be said? The ECHR in *Handyside v. United Kingdom*, 1 E.H.R.R. 737 (1976), decided:

[49.] * * * The Court's supervisory functions oblige it to pay the utmost attention to the principles characterising a 'democratic society.' Freedom of expression constitutes one of the essential foundations of such a society, one of the basic conditions for its progress and for the development of every man ... it is applicable not only to information or ideas that are favourably received or regarded as inoffensive or as a matter of indifference, but also to those which offend, shock, or disturb the state or any other sector of the population. Such are the demands of pluralism, tolerance and broad-mindedness without which there is no 'democratic society.'

In 1990, the Indian Supreme Court (ISC), in *Rangarajan v. Jagjivran Ram*, (1989) 2 S.C.R. 204, held that: "In a democracy it is not necessary that everyone should sing the same song * * *. Democracy is a government by the people via open discussion * * *. The public discussion with people's participation is a basic feature * * * of democracy * * * democracy can neither work nor prosper unless people go out to share their views. The truth is that public discussion on issues relating to administration has positive value." Compare this to the influential opinion of Justice Louis Brandeis in *Whitney v. California*, 274 U.S. 357, 372 (1926), in Chapter 7, Section A.

3. *Which rights?* In *Levy* Justice Kirby argued that the "sovereignty of the people [implies] the capacity of the people to enjoy their democratic rights or to express and agitate their views in a manner appropriate to a society where the people are the ultimate sovereign." What rights are infringed when individual political activity is prohibited?

4. *More than rational motives.* Democracy, as some courts argue, relies on informed decisions by the people. Can activities based on emotions, like love or hate, also be protected political activity? Are provocative acts protected as art or individual self-determination but not as politics? Justices Toohey and Gummow stated in *Levy*:

> It may be conceded that television coverage of actual events * * * would attract public attention * * * even if it would portray or stimulate appeals to emotion rather than to reason. The appeal to reason cannot be said to be, or ever to have been, an essential ingredient of political communication or discussion.

> [Justice Gaudron added:] A rudimentary knowledge of human behaviour teaches that people communicate ideas and opinions by means other than words spoken or written. Lifting a flag in battle, raising a hand against advancing tanks, wearing symbols of dissent, participating in a silent vigil, public prayer and meditation, turning away from a speaker, or even boycotting a big public event clearly constitutes political communication although not a single word is uttered. The constitutionally protected freedom of communication in Australia must therefore go beyond words. But where may the boundary be set to put limits so that the constitutional protection is not debased by extending it to every activity of ordinary life?

5. *More than speech.* The above decisions focus on freedom of expression as fundamental to democracy, but they offer strikingly different interpretations of the sphere such rights protect. Is free speech the only right active citizens require? What protects citizens from a government collecting individual data on their political activities, as occurred in the wake of *Glasenapp* below? Is such government screening compatible with democratic constitutions? In 1988, in *Noriega v. Hernandez Colon* the Puerto Rican Supreme Court (126 P.R. Dec. 42, (1990)) held that the government practice of opening records and making lists of citizens and organizations, based exclusively on their political ideologies and affiliations, violated the right to privacy. Do you agree? We also discuss this in Chapter 5.

6. *Publicity?* In *McIntyre v. Ohio Elections Commission*, 514 U.S. 334 (1995), the USSC upheld a ban on anonymous political leafleting. Does public disclosure further democracy? Does it make a difference knowing who is responsible for any published content? Is a law that requires transparency, not only regarding the responsibility for content but also regarding the financing of the publication, constitutional? Is there a difference between a law that requires notification of a paid publication and one that requires publication of the name of who paid?

B.2. CITIZENS IN THE CIVIL SERVICE

Democracy means government by the people, and people's participation in public affairs may take different forms. A form we consider now is work in the civil service, originally a privilege of the few and today an employment sector encompassing various different kinds of positions. States tend to require loyalty from their civil service personnel to ensure that the state survives even in times of crises. At the same time, such requirements may violate the very rights the state is meant to protect. We will see that history, as well as the kind of job in question, tends to influence how courts deal with such issues.

GLASENAPP v. GERMANY

European Court of Human Rights.
9 E.H.R.R. 25 (1986).

14. * * * Julia Glasenapp * * * [applied] to the appropriate authority * * * for appointment as a secondary-school teacher with the status of probationary civil servant * * *. When making her application she had signed [a declaration stating that she upheld "the principles of the free democratic constitutional system"]. The information preceding the declaration * * * explained * * * the meaning of the expression "free democratic constitutional system" as defined by the Federal Constitutional Court * * *:

"The fundamental principles of this system include: respect for human rights as defined in the Basic Law, in particular the right to life and free development of the personality; the sovereignty of the people, the separation of powers, the Government's responsibility to Parliament; the principle that administrative acts are governed by the rule of law, the independence of the courts, the plurality of political parties; equal opportunity for all political parties; the right to found an opposition and to contend with those in power, in accordance with the Constitution." * * * "Candidates for civil-service posts may not be appointed if they support activities inimical to the Constitution. Disciplinary proceedings for dismissal will be brought against civil servants guilty of such a breach of duty."

15. The legal basis of the declaration * * * was the [state's] Civil Servants Act * * * [which] provides that in order to be appointed * * * a candidate must give the guarantee that at all times he will uphold the free democratic constitutional system within the meaning of the Basic Law [and] must undertake to bear witness to and to uphold this system by his every word and deed.

The * * * declaration * * * corresponded to the decree on the employment of extremists in the civil service * * * [which was meant to] ensure uniformity of administrative practice in the matter [and which] provides:

" * * * If a candidate belongs to an organisation engaging in activities inimical to the Constitution, this fact shall cast doubt on whether he is prepared at all times to uphold the free democratic constitutional system. As a rule this doubt shall be sufficient reason for not appointing him. * * * "

16. In accordance with the directives * * *, the * * * authority * * * asked the [state] for information about possible extremist activities of Mrs. Glasenapp. [The] Ministry replied as follows:

"From 1970 to 1972, G lived in Berlin in a commune to which members of Maoist Communist organisations belonged. * * * Mrs. Glasenapp did not attract attention by activities of her own."

17. * * * [Glasenapp was very anxious to point out that she had not lived in a commune but as a subtenant.]

19. [The] authority [soon after appointed] her as a secondary-school teacher with the status of probationary civil servant. * * *

20. [She then] distributed in the school copies of a "personal statement" and of the Minister of the Interior's letter * * * [and during break] discussed with pupils outside the school the decree on the employment of extremists. [She also held another press conference, after which] one of the daily newspapers * * * published an article on her case. She [wrote] to the paper. This newspaper did not publish her letter but the journal of the communist party did so. The letter, referring to the appointment interview stated that "I pointed out in the discussion that I support the KPD's policy, e.g. in the north of the city. I am a member of a committee to set up an international people's kindergarten." [Based on these activities the authority considered whether she should be dismissed for "wilful deceit".]

23. [The authority] wrote to her * * * as follows:

"So long as you do not certify in writing that you do not support the KPD's policies we must assume that you do not agree to abide by your declarations * * *." The authority pointed out that the KPD, according to its own statements * * *, was trying to overthrow the political system in the Federal Republic of Germany by force and that to support its policies was contrary to the duties of a civil servant. * * * [It decided] that Mrs. Glasenapp should be dismissed for "wilful deceit". * * *

29. [Mrs. Glasenapp went to court, which stated that it] was undisputed and a matter of common knowledge that the former * * * KPD banned by the Federal Constitutional Court, together with the present party of the same name—still tolerated in the Federal Republic, apparently for reasons of foreign policy—and the other communist groups * * * sought to set up the "dictatorship of the proletariat" or the "dictatorship of the working class". * * * But it did not exist where Communists were in control. A Communist form of government was incompatible with the Basic Law. A candidate for a civil-service post was clearly not upholding the free democratic system within the meaning of the Basic Law if he belonged to a Communist group. If he was not a member of such an organisation or if his membership could not be proved but he worked for it or for similar ends, he did not afford a guarantee that he would uphold the system.

[Glasenapp claimed a violation of her rights to freedom of speech and against discrimination, based on Arts. 10 and 14 of the European Convention for the Protection of Human Rights and Fundamental Freedoms.]

39. The Government pleaded * * * incompatibility of the application with the [European] Convention * * * [because] Glasenapp was claiming a right that was not secured in the Convention. In their view, the [case] concerned issues of access to the civil service * * * and not the right to freedom of expression * * *.

41. [We hold that such complaints] do not fall "clearly outside the provisions of the Convention". They relate to the interpretation and application of the Convention: in order to decide the case, the Court

must inquire whether the disputed revocation of appointment amounted to an "interference" with the exercise of the applicant's freedom of expression * * *.

47. Glasenapp contended that the revocation of her appointment contravened [the right to freedom of expression, the exercise of which, according to the Convention, is subject to restrictions]. * * *

48. The Universal Declaration of Human Rights * * * and the International Covenant on Civil and Political Rights * * * provide, respectively, that "everyone has the right of equal access to public service in his country" * * * and that "every citizen shall have the right and the opportunity ... to have access, on general terms of equality, to public service in his country" * * *. In contrast, neither the European Convention nor any of its Protocols sets forth any such right. Moreover, as the Government rightly pointed out, the signatory States deliberately did not include such a right. * * *

49. [But] it does not follow that in other respects civil servants fall outside the scope of the Convention. * * * [The] Convention stipulates that "everyone within the jurisdiction" of the Contracting States must enjoy the rights and freedoms * * * "without discrimination on any ground". And [it] allows States to impose special restrictions on the exercise of the freedoms of assembly and association by "members of the armed forces, of the police or of the administration of the State" [and thus] confirms that as a general rule the guarantees in the Convention extend to civil servants. * * *

50. [In] order to determine whether it was infringed it must first be ascertained whether the disputed measure amounted to an interference with the exercise of freedom of expression * * *.

51. The annulment of Mrs. Glasenapp's appointment was * * * prompted by * * * the expression of a particular opinion in her letter and the refusal to express another opinion during the interview proceedings.

52. [The requirement that] she gave the guarantee that she would consistently uphold the free democratic constitutional system within the meaning of the Basic Law. This is one of the personal qualifications required of anyone seeking a post as a civil servant * * * in Germany. This requirement applies to recruitment to the civil service, a matter that was deliberately omitted from the Convention, and it cannot in itself be considered incompatible with the Convention. * * *

53. It follows from the foregoing that access to the civil service lies at the heart of the issue submitted to the Court. In refusing Glasenapp such access, the State authority took account of her opinions and attitude merely in order to satisfy itself as to whether she possessed one of the necessary personal qualifications for the post in question.

That being so, there has been no interference with the exercise of the right [of freedom of speech.]

Justice Cremona, concurring:

While agreeing with the finding of no violation in the judgment, I am unable to agree with the essential reasoning behind it.

* * * Essentially everything revolves around the applicant's letter published in the Rote Fahne. The net result was that she lost her job because of her political opinions, thus suffering a serious prejudice. This in my view discloses an interference with freedom of expression. * * * In this case, therefore, as in a picture, civil service status provides no more than the general background, whereas the dominant feature in the foreground is a prejudice suffered because of the holding and expression of opinions. * * * Having said that, I would add briefly that in my view the interference in question was justified under paragraph 2 of that Article * * *.

Justice Spielmann, partly dissenting:

* * * The present judgment could, however, have brought out more clearly the principle that even in the case of access to the civil service, * * * the Convention obviously may apply. * * * This would have served as a reminder that, in the Court's view, pluralism, tolerance and broad-mindedness are the best guarantees of survival for a true democratic State, which can only be strong when it is democratic.

* * * The Glasenapp case brings to mind a case which arose in Luxembourg in 1934. * * * The decision taken by the Government of Luxembourg in 1934—at a time, then, when the Star of David had already been introduced in Germany and when the first concentration camp, at Dachau, was already operating full time to silence those who exercised the rights which are today enshrined in * * * the Convention—deserves to be mentioned. It is all the more worthy of mention as there are points of curious similarity between it and the Glasenapp case, as if History was refusing not to repeat itself.

[The Judge referred to a 1934 Luxembourg case, in which teachers were dismissed for being members of the legal Communist Party, on grounds that they would not teach Christian virtues as required by the Education Act.] [The Luxembourg] case and the Glasenapp case have features in common. * * * In both cases the main criteria which the relevant authorities took as a basis was that of an obligation to perform something, which was difficult for those affected to discharge—or, at least, difficult to prove. How, in fact, is a primary-school teacher, who is responsible for teaching children to read and write, to prove that he or she has always "presented the Christian and civic order as an ideal"? (It should be noted that by this time, religious instruction was already the responsibility of the clergy.) How can a drawing teacher, such as Glasenapp, whose main task is to teach the art of drawing to young pupils, prove that she has "constantly upheld the free democratic system"?

* * * I consider the point raised by Glasenapp to be of primary importance in a democratic society. I thus entirely share the Commission's opinion on the admissibility of the application, which reads as follows:

"The Commission considers that the fact that the applicant was required to express her opinions about the KPD * * * brings her present application within * * * the Convention. The mere fact that the applicant was * * * a civil servant on probation does not preclude the Commission from examining her complaint * * *. Nor can the fact that the right of access to or employment in the public service is not one of those rights and freedoms restrict the scope of the operation and protection of the Convention in respect of rights which it does guarantee * * *."

[A]t the heart of the issue were the freedoms of expression and opinion * * *. [Then,] the crucial point * * * seems to me to be whether such interference was necessary in a democratic society * * *. In this connection, it is of interest to bear in mind the position taken up by the Government * * *:

"The fall of the Weimar Republic was due among other things to the fact that the State took too little interest in the political views of its civil servants, judges and soldiers as a result of a misunderstanding of liberal principles. The officials of the Weimar Republic thus included those whose sympathies lay more with the former monarchy or with movements of the far right or far left and who, in the economic recession of the 1920s and the many political conflicts of that period, did not uphold the democratic Constitution, or the State based on the rule of law. That was a crucial contributing factor in the repeal of the democratic Weimar Constitution, which had established a State based on the rule of law, and in the emergence of the National Socialist dictatorship. The lessons from this historical experience were learned, and special provisions were included in the Basic Law of the Federal Republic of Germany, covering among other things the organisation of the civil service, which was thus constitutionally safeguarded. That is why, in the Federal Republic of Germany, no one can become a civil servant who does not afford a guarantee of constant loyalty to the order established in the Basic Law."

I cannot share this excessively generalised view. History has shown beyond any doubt that the Weimar Republic did not collapse on account of a few civil servants "whose sympathies lay more with the former monarchy or with movements of the far right or far left", but for infinitely more complex and more deep-seated reasons. In this respect * * * Germany is not comparable with the Weimar Republic.

U.S. CIVIL SERVICE COMMISSION v. NATIONAL ASSOCIATION OF LETTER CARRIERS

Supreme Court (United States).
413 U.S. 548 (1973).

[Employees organized in the National Association of Letter Carriers filed complaints against the Civil Service Commission, which enforced the Hatch Act, which prohibited political activity of public employees.]

Justice White delivered the opinion of the Court.

[We ask] the single question whether the prohibition * * * against federal employees taking "an active part in political management or in political campaigns," is unconstitutional on its face. * * *

[Such a question] has been here before. This very prohibition was attacked in the Mitchell case by a labor union and various federal employees as * * * being vague and indefinite, arbitrarily discriminatory, and a deprivation of liberty. * * * The Court held that "the practice of excluding classified employees from party offices and personal political activity at the polls ha[d] been in effect for several decades," and the Court had previously upheld the longstanding prohibition forbidding federal employees "from giving or receiving money for political purposes from or to other employees of the government". "The conviction that an actively partisan governmental personnel threatens good administration has deepened * * *," Congress having recognized the "danger to the service in that political rather than official effort may earn advancement and to the public in that governmental favor may be channeled through political connections." The Government, the Court thought, was empowered to prevent federal employees from contributing energy as well as from collecting money for partisan political ends * * *

We unhesitatingly reaffirm the Mitchell holding that Congress had, and has, the power to prevent [federal employees] from holding a party office, working at the polls, and acting as party paymaster for other party workers. An Act of Congress going no farther would in our view unquestionably be valid. So would it be if, in plain and understandable language, the statute forbade activities such as organizing a political party or club; actively participating in fund-raising activities for a partisan candidate or political party; becoming a partisan candidate for, or campaigning for, an elective public office; actively managing the campaign of a partisan candidate for public office; initiating or circulating a partisan nominating petition or soliciting votes for a partisan candidate for public office; or serving as a delegate, alternate or proxy to a political party convention. Our judgment is that neither [freedom of speech] nor any other provision of the Constitution invalidates a law barring this kind of partisan political conduct by federal employees.

Such decision on our part would no more than confirm the judgment of history, a judgment made by this country over the last century that it is in the best interest of the country, indeed essential, that federal service should depend upon meritorious performance rather than political service, and that the political influence of federal employees on others and on the electoral process should be limited. * * *

The restrictions so far imposed on federal employees are not aimed at particular parties, groups, or points of view, but apply equally to all partisan activities of the type described. They discriminate against no racial, ethnic, or religious minorities. Nor do they seek to control political opinions or beliefs, or to interfere with or influence anyone's vote at the polls.

But, as the Court held in *Pickering v. Board of Education*, 391 U.S. 563, 568 (1968), the government has an interest in regulating the conduct and "the speech of its employees that differ[s] significantly from those it possesses in connection with regulation of the speech of the citizenry in general. The problem * * * is to arrive at a balance between the interests of the [employee], as a citizen, in commenting upon matters of public concern and the interest of the [government], as an employer, in promoting the efficiency of the public services it performs through its employees." Although Congress is free to strike a different balance than it has, if it so chooses, we think the balance it has so far struck is sustainable by the obviously important interests sought to be served by the limitations on partisan political activities * * *.

* * * A major thesis of the [law in question] is that to serve this great end of Government—the impartial execution of the laws—it is essential that federal employees, for example, not take formal positions in political parties, not undertake to play substantial roles in partisan political campaigns, and not run for office on partisan political tickets. * * * [In addition,] it is not only important that the Government and its employees in fact avoid practicing political justice, but it is also critical that they appear to the public to be avoiding it, if confidence in the system of representative Government is not to be eroded to a disastrous extent.

* * * A related concern * * * was to further serve the goal that employment and advancement in the Government service not depend on political performance, and at the same time to make sure that Government employees would be free from pressure and from express or tacit invitation to vote in a certain way or perform political chores in order to curry favor with their superiors rather than to act out their own beliefs. It may be urged that prohibitions against coercion are sufficient protection; but for many years the joint judgment of the Executive and Congress has been that to protect the rights of federal employees with respect to their jobs and their political acts and beliefs it is not enough merely to forbid one employee to attempt to influence or coerce another. * * * Neither the right to associate nor the right to participate in political activities is absolute in any event. Nor are the management, financing, and conduct of political campaigns wholly free from governmental regulation. * * *

But however constitutional the proscription of identifiable partisan conduct in understandable language may be, the [argument] was that [it] was both unconstitutionally vague and fatally overbroad. [We cannot agree.] * * * As we see it, our task is not to destroy the Act if we can, but to construe it, if consistent with the will of Congress, so as to comport with constitutional limitations. * * * It is also important in this respect that the Commission has established a procedure by which an employee in doubt about the validity of a proposed course of conduct may seek and obtain advice from the Commission and thereby remove any doubt there may be as to the meaning of the law, at least insofar as the Commission itself is concerned.

Justices Douglas, Brennan and Marshall, dissenting:

The [law in question] prohibits federal employees from taking "an active part in political management or in political campaigns." Some of the employees, whose union is speaking for them, want "to run in state and local elections for the school board, for city council, for mayor"; "to write letters on political subjects to newspapers"; "to be a delegate in political convention"; "to run for an office and hold office in a political party or political club"; "to campaign for candidates for political office"; "to work at polling places in behalf of a political party."

There is no definition of what "an active part . . . in political campaigns" means. * * *

The chilling effect of these vague and generalized prohibitions is so obvious as not to need elaboration. * * * We deal here with a * * * right to speak, to propose, to publish, to petition Government, to assemble. Time and place are obvious limitations. Thus no one could object if employees were barred from using office time to engage in outside activities whether political or otherwise. But it is of no concern of Government what an employee does in his spare time, whether religion, recreation, social work, or politics is his hobby—unless what he does impairs efficiency or other facets of the merits of his job. * * * [I]t is now settled that Government employment may not be denied or penalized "on a basis that infringes [the employee's] constitutionally protected interests—especially, his interest in freedom of speech." If Government, as the majority stated in Mitchell, may not condition public employment on the basis that the employee will not "take any active part in missionary work," it is difficult to see why it may condition employment on the basis that the employee not take "an active part . . . in political campaigns." * * *

AHMED v. UNITED KINGDOM

European Court of Human Rights.
29 E.H.R.R. 1 (1998).

[In Great Britain, legislative measures were designed to limit the involvement of local government officials in political activities; the applicants, who were employees of the local authorities, were unable to stand for elected office.]

42. The Court observes that the above-mentioned interferences give rise to a breach of Article 10 unless it can be shown that they were "prescribed by law", pursued one or more legitimate aim or aims * * * and were "necessary in a democratic society" to attain them. * * *

52. The Court does not accept the applicants' argument that the protection of effective democracy can only be invoked as a justification for limitations on the rights guaranteed under Article 10 in circumstances where there is a threat to the stability of the constitutional or political order. To limit this notion to that context would be to overlook both the interests served by democratic institutions such as local authorities and the need to make provision to secure their proper functioning where this is considered necessary to safeguard those interests. The Court recalls in this respect that democracy is a fundamental feature of the European public order. * * *

53. The Court observes that the local government system of the respondent State has long rested on a bond of trust between elected members and a permanent corps of local government officers who both advise them on policy and assume responsibility for the implementation of the policies adopted. That relationship of trust stems from the right of council members to expect that they are being assisted in their functions by officers who are politically neutral and whose loyalty is to the council

as a whole. Members of the public also have a right to expect that the members whom they voted into office will discharge their mandate in accordance with the commitments they made during an electoral campaign and that the pursuit of that mandate will not founder on the political opposition of their members' own advisers; it is also to be noted that members of the public are equally entitled to expect that in their own dealings with local government departments they will be advised by politically neutral officers who are detached from the political fray.

The aim pursued by the Regulations was to underpin that tradition and to ensure that the effectiveness of the system of local political democracy was not diminished through the corrosion of the political neutrality of certain categories of officers. * * * [The Regulations were also based on a "pressing social need" and] pursued a legitimate aim * * * namely to protect the rights of others, council members and the electorate alike, to effective political democracy at the local level. * * *

65. Having regard to * * * the margin of appreciation which the respondent State enjoys in this area, the restrictions imposed on the applicants cannot be said to be a disproportionate interference with their rights * * *.

Justices Spielmann, Pekkanen, and Van Dijk, dissenting:

1. To our regret we are not able to join the majority in their conclusion that Article 10 has not been violated in the present case. * * * We cannot persuade ourselves, however, that the interference was "necessary in a democratic society", given, on the one hand, the scope of its effects and, on the other hand, the aims pursued. * * *

3. * * * There is no reason, and indeed no room, for an inherent limitation in respect of the civil service. Article 10 does, of course, refer in its second paragraph to "duties and responsibilities", but that does not mean that this provision contains an implied limitation for certain individuals or groups; it is primarily up to those exercising their right to freedom of expression to fulfil those duties and responsibilities. Only if they fail to do so in one or more concrete cases, or if there is the imminent danger of such a failure, would there be grounds for introducing legislative or administrative measures to ensure the proper fulfilment of these duties and responsibilities; but even then only to the extent "necessary in a democratic society". * * *

5. Was there a pressing social need for the Regulations in issue and for their application to the applicants? * * * The mere fact that [a reporting] Committee noticed a change of atmosphere in recent years in the direction of stronger party affiliation of civil servants, especially at the local government level, does not in itself mean that the same standard of political neutrality in public service could not be maintained without recourse to such restrictive regulations as those in issue. In particular, it has not convincingly been argued by the Government why civil servants would not, as a rule, be responsible enough to decide for themselves the sort of political action their position permits and does not permit, subject to *ex post facto* disciplinary supervision. * * *

6. Even if there is a pressing social need for the interference concerned, the latter must be proportionate to the legitimate aim pursued. * * * The Regulations are said to affect only 2% of civil servants. However, that still is a considerable number. * * * [The] civil servants concerned may feel under what could be called permanent self-censorship in order not to endanger their positions. * * *

7. For all the above-stated reasons we are of the opinion that the interference complained of was not necessary in a democratic society and, consequently, was not justified. * * *

REKVÉNYI v. HUNGARY

European Court of Human Rights.
30 E.H.R.R. 519 (1999).

[A police officer and Secretary General of the Police Independent Trade Union challenged, on freedom of expression and association grounds, an amendment to the Constitution that prohibited members of the armed forces, police, and security services from joining a political party and from engaging in political activity.]

26. The Court takes it for granted that the pursuit of activities of a political nature comes within the ambit of Article 10 in so far as freedom of political debate constitutes a particular aspect of freedom of expression. Indeed, freedom of political debate is at the very core of the concept of a democratic society. Furthermore, [it does] extend to military personnel and civil servants. The Court sees no reason to come to a different conclusion in respect of police officers. * * *

34. According to the Court's well-established case-law, one of the requirements flowing from the expression "prescribed by law" is foreseeability. Thus, a norm cannot be regarded as a "law" unless it is formulated with sufficient precision to enable the citizen to regulate his conduct: he must be able, if need be with appropriate advice, to foresee, to a degree that is reasonable in the circumstances, the consequences which a given action may entail. Those consequences need not be foreseeable with absolute certainty: experience shows this to be unattainable. Again, whilst certainty is highly desirable, it may bring in its train excessive rigidity and the law must be able to keep pace with changing circumstances. Accordingly, many laws are inevitably couched in terms which, to a greater or lesser extent, are vague and whose interpretation and application are questions of practice. The role of adjudication vested in the courts is precisely to dissipate such interpretational doubts as remain. The level of precision required of domestic legislation which cannot in any case provide for every eventuality depends to a considerable degree on the content of the instrument in question, the field it is designed to cover and the number and status of those to whom it is addressed. Because of the general nature of constitutional provisions, the level of precision required of them may be lower than for other legislation.

35. The Court notes the * * * term "political activities" is subject to interpretation and is to be read in conjunction with complementary

provisions * * *. As to the wording of these provisions, it is inevitable, in the Court's opinion, that conduct which may entail involvement in political activities cannot be defined with absolute precision.

41. * * * [The] Court concludes that the restriction in question pursued legitimate aims * * *, namely the protection of national security and public safety and the prevention of disorder. * * *

46. * * * In view of the particular history of some Contracting States, the national authorities of these States may, so as to ensure the consolidation and maintenance of democracy, consider it necessary to have constitutional safeguards to achieve this aim by restricting the freedom of police officers to engage in political activities and, in particular, political debate.

What remains to be determined is whether the particular restrictions imposed in the present case can be regarded as "necessary in a democratic society".

47. The Court observes that between 1949 and 1989 Hungary was ruled by one political party. Membership of that party was, in many social spheres, expected as a manifestation of the individual's commitment to the regime. This expectation was even more pronounced within the military and the police, where party membership on the part of the vast majority of serving staff guaranteed that the ruling party's political will was directly implemented. This is precisely the vice that rules on the political neutrality of the police are designed to prevent. It was not until 1989 that Hungarian society succeeded in building up the institutions of a pluralistic democracy * * *. Regard being had to the margin of appreciation left to the national authorities in this area, the Court finds that, especially against this historical background, the relevant measures taken in Hungary in order to protect the police force from the direct influence of party politics can be seen as answering a "pressing social need" in a democratic society. [The means were also not disproportionate, and thus there was no violation of the European Convention for the Protection of Human Rights and Fundamental Freedoms.]

Justice Fisach, partly dissenting:

While I agree with the majority that there has been no violation of [freedom of expression], I regret that I am unable to share its view that there has been no breach of [freedom of association]. [Restrictions] on freedom of association must not only be lawful * * *, they must also be necessary in a democratic society. I can see no convincing argument which, in a pluralist, democratic society, could justify a ban on joining a political party.

On the contrary, I consider that the unhappy experiences suffered under the communist regime ought to encourage political leaders to advocate a fresh approach so that the democratic process can be consolidated and the future prepared for in a spirit of open-mindedness and tolerance.

As the police are now no longer at the service of the communist party, but of democracy, it is essential that change be accompanied by an approach fostering awareness of democratic pluralism through divergent political views that fuel debate over ideas.

Banning the police from joining a political party amounts to depriving them of a right, if not the democratic duty, which all citizens have to hold opinions and political convictions, to take a close interest in public affairs and to participate in the fashioning of the will of the people and of the State.

Notes and Questions

1. *The Aftermath of* Glasenapp. Ms. Vogt, an active member of the German Communist Party (KPD) in her student years, was appointed to a teaching position and became a civil servant. She remained an active member of the party, which was legally active in Germany. There was no evidence that her membership affected her performance as a teacher. In 1982, the authorities began disciplinary proceedings against Vogt, on the ground that her membership in the KPD violated the duty of political loyalty required by civil servants. German courts upheld her dismissal, but the ECHR disagreed.

In *Vogt v. Germany*, 21 E.H.R.R. 205 (1996), the ECHR, in a ten-to-nine decision, held: "[61.] that, although the reasons put forward by the Government in order to justify their interference with Ms. Vogt's right[s] * * * are certainly relevant, they are not sufficient to establish convincingly that it was necessary * * * to dismiss her. Even allowing for a certain margin of appreciation, the conclusion must be that to dismiss Ms. Vogt by way of disciplinary sanction from her post as a secondary-school teacher was disproportionate to the legitimate aim pursued."

The Court distinguished *Vogt* from *Glasenapp,* arguing that the case did not concern a "right to a civil service position." Ms. Vogt was already employed. The Court conceded that:

> [59.] [A] democratic state is entitled to require civil servants to be loyal to the constitutional principles on which it is founded. In this connection [the Court] takes into account Germany's experience under the Weimar Republic and during the bitter period that followed the collapse of that regime up to the adoption of the Basic Law in 1949. Germany wished to avoid a repetition of those experiences by founding its new State on the idea that it should be a 'democracy capably of defending itself'. Nor should Germany's position in the political context of the time be forgotten. These circumstances understandably lent extra weight to this underlying notion and to the corresponding duty of political loyalty imposed on civil servants.

Nevertheless, the Court found that there was an insufficiently pressing social need to justify such severe action against Ms. Vogt. The Court found that her dismissal interfered with her freedom of association rights (Art. 11 of the European HR Convention) because she "was dismissed from her post * * * for having persistently refused to dissociate herself from the KPD on the ground that in her personal opinion membership of that party was not incompatible with her duty of loyalty." The second clause of Art. 11 allows the state to impose "lawful restrictions on the exercise of these rights by members of the armed forces, of the police or of the administration of the state." The Court found that her dismissal was out of proportion to the goal pursued, for the reasons given in its discussion of Art. 10.

Does the *Vogt* Court's position contradict Justice Holmes, who pointed out that "[t]he petitioner may have a constitutional right to talk politics. But he has no constitutional right to be a policeman." *McAuliffe v. New Bedford*, 155 Mass. 216, 220 (1892). (For a more recent position of the USSC, see *Pickering v. Board of Education*, 391 U.S. 563 (1968) (speech rights granted to public employees).) Should it be a decisive difference that Ms. Vogt held a position while Ms. Glasenapp was not yet fully employed? Is the new approach in *Vogt* the result of historical changes, i.e., that communism had collapsed several years before 1995?

2. *History*. Some justices rely on historical arguments. In *Letter Carriers* the USSC stated, in 1939, that a rapidly expanding government workforce could not be employed to build a powerful, invincible, and perhaps corrupt political machine. Compare this with the decisions on lustration, above at Subsection A.2., as well as with the *Rekvényi* decision on the Hungarian police. There, the dissenting opinion argues that history necessitates a "fresh approach." Is history an argument only in periods of transition or significant change? Does it also apply to situations in which one political party has governed for a long period of time? Consider, for example, that the conservative government in Germany lasted for 16 years. Is there a danger of filling civil service posts with political allies? How can constitutional law prevent such practices?

3. *Incompatibilities*. Decisions on the civil service address a variety of professions: letter carriers, police personnel, teachers, and the like. Are there differences to the limits of political activity with regard to the type of employee, between teaching and carrying letters, for example, or, if you consider the British case, between local and national civil service? If so, why?

In South Korea, national electoral law prohibited local officeholders from seeking national office while holding a local position, and it limited publication by candidates of informative literature during the 180 days preceding election day. Compare this with *Ahmed*. Do you agree with the majority or with the dissent? The Korean Constitutional Court, in *Ban on Local Government Heads' Mid-term Candidacy*, 11–1 KCCR 675, 98Hun–Ma214 (1999), decided that:

> State entities and local self-governing entities should not use their public functions to support or oppose a particular party or candidate. They especially should not influence voters' decisions through campaign activities. If they do so, it violates the state's duty of neutrality and the principle of equal opportunity. Biased intervention of a state entity in public officials' elections is not allowed even in form of informative publishing activities. * * * The closer to the election, the greater influence the publicity will have * * *. In those periods, local self-governing entities have a more important duty to permit formation of the political opinion of the local residents free of intervention of public authority than to publicize its accomplishments. The instant provision's ban on any 'self-glorifying' publication of informative literature is not an excessive limitation on freedom of expression where it allows informative publishing activities incidental to the regular operation of the local self-governing entity.

B.3. ASSOCIATION AND ASSEMBLY

Democratic activity rests on sharing political opinions with others. The right to associate and freedom of assembly are thus fundamental aspects of democracy as well.

CITIZENS AGAINST RENT CONTROL v. BERKELEY

Supreme Court (United States).
454 U.S. 290 (1981).

[A Berkeley ordinance limited contributions to certain political groups. The citizens' association against rent control received an amount exceeding that limit and was forced to turn the funds over to the city. The association challenged the ordinance.]

Chief Justice Burger delivered the opinion of the Court.

The issue on appeal is whether a limitation of $250 on contributions to committees formed to support or oppose ballot measures violates the First Amendment. * * *

We begin by recalling that the practice of persons sharing common views banding together to achieve a common end is deeply embedded in the American political process. The 18th-century Committees of Correspondence and the pamphleteers were early examples of this phenomena and the *Federalist Papers* were perhaps the most significant and lasting example. The tradition of volunteer committees for collective action has manifested itself in myriad community and public activities; in the political process it can focus on a candidate or on a ballot measure. Its value is that by collective effort individuals can make their views known, when, individually, their voices would be faint or lost.

The Court has long viewed the First Amendment as protecting a marketplace for the clash of different views and conflicting ideas. That concept has been stated and restated almost since the Constitution was drafted. The voters of the city of Berkeley adopted the challenged ordinance which places restrictions on that marketplace. It is irrelevant that the voters rather than a legislative body enacted 602, because the voters may no more violate the Constitution by enacting a ballot measure than a legislative body may do so by enacting legislation.

The Court has acknowledged the importance of freedom of association in guaranteeing the right of people to make their voices heard on public issues:

> "Effective advocacy of both public and private points of view, particularly controversial ones, is undeniably enhanced by group association, as this Court has more than once recognized by remarking upon the close nexus between the freedoms of speech and assembly." *NAACP v. Alabama*, 357 U.S. 449, 460 (1958). * * *

Under the Berkeley ordinance an affluent person can, acting alone, spend without limit to advocate individual views on a ballot measure. It is only when contributions are made in concert with one or more others in the exercise of the right of association that they are restricted by 602.

There are, of course, some activities, legal if engaged in by one, yet illegal if performed in concert with others, but political expression is not one of them. To place a Spartan limit—or indeed any limit—on individuals wishing to band together to advance their views on a ballot measure, while placing none on individuals acting alone, is clearly a restraint on the right of association. Section 602 does not seek to mute the voice of one individual, and it cannot be allowed to hobble the collective expressions of a group.

(Justice WHITE dissented.)

DIRECTOR OF PUBLIC PROSECUTIONS v. JONES (MARGARET)

House of Lords (United Kingdom).
2 A. C. 240 (H.L. 1999).

Lord Irvine of Lairg L.C.:

My Lords, this appeal raises an issue of fundamental constitutional importance: what are the limits of the public's rights of access to the public highway? Are these rights so restricted that they preclude in all circumstances any right of peaceful assembly on the public highway?

[Twenty-one people assembled on the roadside adjacent to the perimeter fence of the monument at Stonehenge wearing banners of the Stonehenge Campaign. They were arrested; Jones was charged with "trespassory assembly" because the assembly was held by entering land to which they had no right of access. The demonstration was peaceful and nonobstructive of the highway. The Divisional Court of the Queen's Bench Division upheld the conviction.]

The central issue in the case thus turns on two interrelated questions: (i) what are the "limits" of the public's right of access to the public highway at common law? and (ii) what is the "particular purpose" for which the public has a right to use the public highway?

[In] the lead case, *Harrison v. Duke of Rutland* [1893] 1 Q.B. 142 the plaintiff had used the public highway, which crossed the defendant's land, for the sole and deliberate purpose of disrupting grouse-shooting upon the defendant's land, and was forcibly restrained by the defendant's servants from doing so. The plaintiff sued the defendant for assault; and the defendant pleaded justification on the basis that the plaintiff had been trespassing upon the highway. Lord Esher M.R. held, at page 146:

"... on the ground that the plaintiff was on the highway, the soil of which belonged to the Duke of Rutland, not for the purpose of using it in order to pass and repass, or for any reasonable or usual mode of using the highway as a highway, I think he was a trespasser".

Plainly Lord Esher M.R. contemplated that there may be "reasonable or usual" uses of the highway beyond passing and repassing. He continued, at pages 146–147:

"Highways are, no doubt, dedicated prima facie for the purpose of passage; but things are done upon them by everybody which are recognised as being rightly done, and as constituting a reasonable and usual mode of using a highway as such. If a person on a highway does not transgress such reasonable and usual mode of using it, I do not think that he will be a trespasser." * * *

The question to which this appeal gives rise is whether the law today should recognise that the public highway is a public place, on which all manner of reasonable activities may go on. * * *

[Based on the concept that the original purpose of dedication is untenable,] I conclude therefore the law to be that the public highway is a public place which the public may enjoy for any reasonable purpose, provided the activity in question does not amount to a public or private nuisance and does not obstruct the highway by unreasonably impeding the primary right of the public to pass and repass: within these qualifications there is a public right of peaceful assembly on the highway. Since the law confers this public right, I deprecate any attempt artificially to restrict its scope. It must be for the magistrates in every case to decide whether the user of the highway under consideration is both reasonable in the sense defined and not inconsistent with the primary right of the public to pass and repass. In particular, there can be no principled basis for limiting the scope of the right by reference to the subjective intentions of the persons assembling. Once the right to assemble within the limitations I have defined is accepted, it is self-evident that it cannot be excluded by an intention to exercise it. Provided an assembly is reasonable and non-obstructive, taking into account its size, duration and the nature of the highway on which it takes place, it is irrelevant whether it is premeditated or spontaneous: what matters is its objective nature. To draw a distinction on the basis of anterior intention is in substance to reintroduce an incidentality requirement. For the reasons I have given, that requirement, properly applied, would make unlawful commonplace activities which are well accepted. Equally, to stipulate in the abstract any maximum size or duration for a lawful assembly would be an unwarranted restriction on the right defined. These judgments are ever ones of fact and degree for the court of trial. * * *

Article 11 of the European Convention on Human Rights

If, contrary to my judgment, the common law of trespass is not as clear as I have held it to be, then at least it is uncertain and developing, so that regard should be had to the Convention in resolving the uncertainty and in determining how it should develop (*ref. omitted*). The effect of the Divisional Court's decision in this case would be that any peaceful assembly on the public highway, no matter how minor or harmless, would involve the commission of the tort of trespass. Its conclusion is that all peaceful assemblies on the highway are tortious, whilst seeking to justify that state of affairs by observing that peaceful assemblies are in practice usually tolerated. In my judgment it is none to the point that restrictions on the exercise of the right of freedom of assembly may under Article 11 be justified where necessary for the protection of the rights and freedoms of others. If the Divisional Court were correct, and an assembly on the public highway was always trespassory, then there is not even a prima facie right to assembly on the public highway in our law. Unless the common law recognises that assembly on the public highway may be lawful, the right contained in Article 11(1) of the Convention is denied. Of course the right may be subject to restrictions (for example, the requirements that user of the highway for purposes of assembly must be reasonable and non-obstructive, and must not contravene the criminal law of wilful obstruction of the highway). But in my judgment our law will not comply with the Convention unless its starting-point is that assembly on the highway will not necessarily be unlawful. I reject an approach which entails that such an assembly will always be tortious and therefore unlawful.

[Allowing the appeal, Lord Slynn and Lord Hope, dissenting.]

CHRISTINE MULUNDIKA v. THE PEOPLE

Supreme Court (Zambia).
1995/SCZ/25 (unreported) SCZ Judgment No. 25.g

The appellants challenged the constitutionality of * * * the Public Order Act [which, after the country's transition from authoritarian to democratic government,] requires any person wishing to hold a peaceful assembly to obtain a permit and contravention of which is criminalized. * * *

[The] broader question * * * is whether in this day and age * * * it is justifiable in a democracy that the citizens of this country can only assemble and speak in public with prior permission * * * and whether the law under attack is consistent with the guaranteed freedoms of assembly and speech.

[It] was common cause between the parties that there is absolutely nothing wrong with provisions which are purely regulatory in the interests of public order as envisaged by the constitution itself. * * * [But a] major argument [was] that although the freedoms under the constitution are not absolute, they should only be regulated but not abridged, diminished or denied. It was submitted that the [law] could not reasonably be justifiable in a democratic society when it reduced the fundamental freedoms to the level of a mere license to be granted or denied on the subjective satisfaction of a regulating officer.

* * * The fact or possibility that permission to assemble and to speak may be refused—so that the constitutional freedoms are denied altogether—on improper or arbitrary grounds or even on unknown grounds, renders the subsection objectionable for a variety of reasons. [Quite] apart from the possibility of unconstitutionally denying the fundamental rights, the absence of adequate and objective guidelines * * * leaves it seriously flawed. * * *

[The Court accepted a proportionality test that was developed by the Court of Appeal of Tanzania in *Pumbun v. Attorney General and Another*, (1993) 2 L.R.C. 317.] * * *

[The] framers of the constitution could not have contemplated criminalization of gatherings in this wholesale fashion by some surviving colonial statute. In [addition,] the subsection is highly subjective and expressed in negative terms when it speaks of the regulating officer issuing a permit only if "satisfied that such assembly, public meeting or procession is unlikely to cause or lead to a breach of the peace." The

g. Available at <http://zamlii.zam-net.zm/courts/supreme/full/95scz25.htm>.

implication is that the permit must be refused unless the regulating officer is able to satisfy himself or herself to the contrary. It is difficult to imagine a clearer recipe for possible arbitrariness and abuse. The constitutional arrangements for democracy can hardly survive if the free flow of ideas and information can be torpedoed by a misguided regulating officer.

The other aspect is whether there are any effective controls on the exercise of the power to grant or refuse a permit * * *. There are in fact none so that the regulating officer is not required to give reasons for refusal and there is no procedure provided to act as a safeguard for an aggrieved unsuccessful applicant which is reasonable, fair and just. Fundamental constitutional rights should not be denied to a citizen by any law which permits arbitrariness and is couched in wide and broad terms. In the *State of Bihar v. K.K. Misra and Others* AIR 1971 1667 at 1675, the Supreme Court of India [said that] "... in order to be a reasonable restriction, the same must not be arbitrary or excessive and the procedure and the manner of imposition of the restriction must also be fair and just. Any restriction which is opposed to the fundamental principles of liberty and justice cannot be considered reasonable. One of the important tests to find out whether a restriction is reasonable is to see whether the aggrieved party has a right of representation against the restriction imposed or proposed to be imposed." * * *

This brings us to consider if [the rule] is reasonably justifiable in a democratic society, especially one that is re-establishing the essential elements of democracy based on plural politics and the genuine exercise by the people of their free will and choice and their freedoms. Even in the best of the democratic traditions, some regulation of public gatherings is required. For example, the Public Order Act 1986 of England which both sides referred to is instructive. Provision is made for notifications to be given by organisers of processions of gatherings so that the regulating authorities have the opportunity to perform the very necessary function of giving directions and imposing conditions, if any, for the sake of upholding public order and preserving the peace. The giving of notice to a regulating authority for the latter to give regulatory directions is one thing; the giving or refusal of permission to meet and speak is quite another matter.

For an attempt at the definition of what is "democratic society", [we] begin from the premise that there are certain minimum attributes in any democracy, including the availability of a Government which reflects the will of the majority of the people expressed at periodic and genuine elections; the power of the state should reside in the people and where this is exercised on their behalf, the mandatory is accountable. Apart from the free and informed consent and maximum participation of the governed, it is also common to expect that the people have and actually enjoy basic rights and freedoms and available to the majority as well as to any minority. Although there are many shades of democracy and an adequate definition elusive—and certainly not necessary for our present purposes—the courts have long recognised the importance of freedom of speech and assembly in a democratic society. * * *

[The] requirement of prior permission to gather and to speak, which permission can be denied sometimes for good and at other times for bad cause not contemplated by the constitutional derogation, directly affects the guaranteed freedoms of speech and assembly. It is little wonder that these are the freedoms most discussed by the courts whenever a democratic society is being considered. The weight of judicial authority in Commonwealth countries argues against the constitutionality of a provision like [the one at issue here].

Unfortunately, experience teaches and it is sadly not hypothetical that in this country, the requirement for a permit to gather and speak has been used since 1953 to muzzle critics and opponents as well as alleged troublemakers. * * *

Of course, we do not share [the] view that the politicians in this country are immature and irresponsible and that those in Zimbabwe are more responsible and mature. On the contrary, the people of this country have come a long way and would not like ever again to be oppressed or caged by any other individual or group of individuals. It is therefore not true that there would be chaos and anarchy if the requirement of obtaining permission with the chance of being denied such permission is pronounced against. For one thing, there are other laws [that may be applicable]. For another, the holding * * * will simply mean that the police and other authorities can no longer deny the citizens of this country their freedom to assemble and speak. The requirement of a prior permit is a left over from the days of Her Majesty's Governors and the British themselves do not require permission to assemble and speak. Why should we require it?

Although not guided by concern for the administrative consequences, we readily accept and acknowledge that there are many regulatory features * * * which are perfectly constitutional and very necessary for the sake of public peace and order. * * * Though therefore the police can no longer deny a permit because the requirement for one is about to be pronounced against, they will be entitled—indeed they are under a duty in terms of the remainder of the Public Order Act—to regulate public meetings, assemblies and processions strictly for the purpose of preserving public peace and order. The police and any other regulating authority can only perform this other very necessary function of giving directions and imposing conditions if they are notified, in advance, of any gathering proposed to be held. Such notification would necessarily differ in form and content from an application for permission under the subsection challenged in these proceedings. While, therefore, we would urge that the whole Public Order Act should be reviewed and modernize in its entirety to enable the police to carry out their duties effectively without contravening any provision in our constitution, we are satisfied that, meanwhile, it would not be unlawful for the Inspector–General of Police, as the appropriate authority under the Act, to devise some simple and practical method of receiving notifications. * * *

In sum and for the reasons which we have given, we hold that [the law in question is] null and void, and therefore invalid for unconstitutionality. It follows also that the invalidity and the constitutional guarantee of the rights of assembly and expression preclude the prosecution of persons and the criminalization of gatherings in contravention of the subsection pronounced against.

Justice Chaila, dissenting:

[I] have with greatest respect disagreed with the conclusion on and interpretation of [the] Public Order Act and its annullment. I have observed that the majority decision has mainly been based on the persuasion by various authorities from the United States, Tanzania, Ghana, and Zimbabwe. I would like to point out that these authorities are based on their countries' constitutions and their environments.

[I] totally agree with the position [on] the authorities cited to us. They have a big force but they are not binding on this court. What matters to this court is to look at the wording of our constitution itself and to interpret it and apply it. * * * In this case it is common cause that there is need to have some regulating law. [All rights guaranteed by the Constitution] depend for their very existence and implementation upon civil society—that is the ordered society—established by the Constitution. The continuance of that society itself depends upon national security, for without security any society is in danger of collapse or overthrow. National security is thus paramount not only in the interests of the State but also in the interests of each individual member of the State; and measures designed to achieve and maintain that security must come first; and, subject to the provisions of the Constitution, must override, if need be, the interests of individuals and of minorities with which they conflict. * * *

The appellants must prove that Parliament did not act constitutionally in passing [the law and that it] is not necessary and is not reasonably justifiable in a democratic society. * * * The big question is if [the rule] is declared inconsistent with the constitution how will the regulating authority legally and effectively regulate the meetings, processions and demonstrations? If three persons or political parties or groups of people decide to hold a meeting on a particular day, at a particular venue and the meetings happen to be at the same time, same date, and same place, how will the regulating officer handle the situation if there is no element of the regulating officer having to give some form of permit? If the holders of the meeting may decide not to inform the police, what happen? The * * * Constitution is worded in such a way that the police in considering the applications should not prevent or reject an application any how. The police should not prevent people to enjoy their rights; if anything they should assist people to enjoy their rights, but the police must be fully involved. The police should further give reasons why they refuse to give a permit. If [the law] is completely struck out, the regulating officer will not be in a position to perform properly his regulating duties * * *. In my opinion [such law] is necessary. It allows the regulating officer some say in maintaining law and order.

THOMAS v. CHICAGO PARK DISTRICT

Supreme Court (United States).
534 U.S. 316 (2002).

Justice Scalia delivered the opinion of the Court.

This case presents the question whether a municipal park ordinance requiring individuals to obtain a permit before conducting large-scale events must, consistent with the First Amendment, contain the procedural safeguards described in [a case on prior licensing of motion pictures].

I

[The Chicago] Park District adopted an ordinance that requires a person to obtain a permit in order to "conduct a public assembly, parade, picnic, or other event involving more than fifty individuals," or engage in an activity such as "creat[ing] or emit[ting] any Amplified Sound." The ordinance provides that "[a]pplications for permits shall be processed in order of receipt," and the Park District must decide whether to grant or deny an application within 14 days unless, by written notice to the applicant, it extends the period an additional 14 days. Applications can be denied on any of 13 specified grounds.

If the Park District denies an application, it must clearly set forth in writing the grounds for denial and, where feasible, must propose measures to cure defects in the application. When the basis for denial is prior receipt of a competing application for the same time and place, the Park District must suggest alternative times or places. An unsuccessful applicant has seven days to file a written appeal to the General Superintendent of the Park District, who must act on the appeal within seven days. If the General Superintendent affirms a permit denial, the applicant may seek judicial review in state court by common-law certiorari.

Petitioners have applied to the Park District on several occasions for permits to hold rallies advocating the legalization of marijuana. The Park District has granted some permits and denied others. Not satisfied, petitioners filed an action * * * alleging, inter alia, that the Park District's ordinance is unconstitutional on its face. * * *

II

[But the] licensing scheme at issue here is not subject-matter censorship but content-neutral time, place, and manner regulation of the use of a public forum. The Park District's ordinance does not authorize a licensor to pass judgment on the content of speech: None of the grounds for denying a permit has anything to do with what a speaker might say. Indeed, the ordinance (unlike the classic censorship scheme) is not even directed to communicative activity as such, but rather to all activity conducted in a public park. The picnicker and soccer-player, no less than the political activist or parade marshal, must apply for a permit if the 50–person limit is to be exceeded. And the object of the permit system (as plainly indicated by the permissible grounds for permit denial) is not to exclude communication of a particular content, but to coordinate multiple uses of limited space, to assure preservation of the park facilities, to prevent uses that are dangerous, unlawful, or impermissible under the Park District's rules, and to assure financial accountability for damage caused by the event. * * *

Regulations of the use of a public forum that ensure the safety and convenience of the people are not "inconsistent with civil liberties but ... [are] one of the means of safeguarding the good order upon which [civil liberties] ultimately depend." *Cox v. New Hampshire.* Such a traditional exercise of authority does not raise the censorship concerns that prompted us to impose the extraordinary procedural safeguards on the film licensing process.

III

Of course, even content-neutral time, place, and manner restrictions can be applied in such a manner as to stifle free expression. Where the licensing official enjoys unduly broad discretion in determining whether to grant or deny a permit, there is a risk that he will favor or disfavor speech based on its content. We have thus required that a time, place, and manner regulation contain adequate standards to guide the official's decision and render it subject to effective judicial review.

* * * As we have described, the Park District may deny a permit only for one or more of the reasons set forth in the ordinance. It may deny, for example, when the application is incomplete or contains a material falsehood or misrepresentation; when the applicant has damaged Park District property on prior occasions and has not paid for the damage; when a permit has been granted to an earlier applicant for the same time and place; when the intended use would present an unreasonable danger to the health or safety of park users or Park District employees; or when the applicant has violated the terms of a prior permit. Moreover, the Park District must process applications within 28 days, and must clearly explain its reasons for any denial. These grounds are reasonably specific and objective, and do not leave the decision "to the whim of the administrator." They provide "narrowly drawn, reasonable and definite standards" to guide the licensor's determination.

ASSOCIATIONS LAW DECISION

Constitutional Council (France).
71–41 DC of 16 July 1971.

[An excerpt of this case is presented in Chapter 2, Subsection B.1., Notes and Questions.]

Notes and Questions

1. *The kind of government. Citizens against Rent Control* accepts the right of association as a fundamental ingredient of democratic constitutionalism. The following cases reveal a number of resulting problems. In the Zambia decision the issue is not only prior licensing of political activity but, in addition, procedural safeguards of the opportunity to use political rights.

In *Park District* the USSC argues that content-neutral regulation and old-fashioned authority do not endanger the active involvement of citizens. What kind of government do you imagine to use authority in favor of active citizens? What kind would not? What additional constitutional safeguards ensure that democracy blossoms rather than withers? What kind of practice, rather than the text of a law, will lead to unconstitutionality? In the Indian case of *Thappar v. State of Madagascar*, (1950) S.C.R. 594, 603, the ISC argued: "Where a law purports to authorise the imposition of restrictions on a fundamental right in a language wide enough to cover restrictions both within and without the limits of constitutionally permissible legislative action affecting such a right, it is not possible to uphold it even so far as it may be applied within the constitutional limits, as it is not severable. So long as the possibility of its being applied for purposes not sanctioned by the constitution cannot be ruled out, it must be held to be wholly unconstitutional and void."

2. *Civic Obligations?* Do the organizers of meetings and marches have a corresponding obligation to enable the police to carry out their regulatory function by giving notice of their activities? The GFCC requires cooperation between protesting citizens and the police to lift the threshold of police action against rallies. *Brokdorf Case*, 69 BVerfGE 315 (1985). The Supreme Court of Zimbabwe, *In re Munhemeso*, 1994 (1) Zimb. L. Rep. 49, considered the constitutionality of the Law and Order (Maintenance) Act, under which members of the Congress of Trade Unions had been charged after they had unsuccessfully applied to a regulating officer for a permit for a procession that was denied without explanation. The Court held:

> [T]he Law in question is unconstitutional because, when certain features are taken cumulatively, the provision is not reasonably justifiable in a democratic society. The features are firstly the uncontrolled nature of the discretionary power vested in the regulating authority; secondly the fact that the regulating authority was not obliged, when imposing a ban, to take into account whether disorder or breach of the peace could be averted by attaching conditions upon the conduct of the procession such as relating to time, duration and route; thirdly, the fact that although the rights to freedom of expression and assembly are primary and the limitations thereon secondary, section 6(2) reversed the order, in effect denying such rights unless the public procession was unlikely to cause or lead to a breach of the peace or public disorder; and fourthly the criminalisation of a procession held without a permit irrespective of the likelihood or occurrence of any threat to public safety or public order.

3. *Order in democracy.* How much order does democracy require? A vibrant community, with active citizens' associations concerned with public issues and a diverse set of political activities, is important to democracy. But recall the concept of militant democracy in Subsection A.3. above. In *Mulundika* the dissent argues that chaos will ensue if laws do not uphold a prior licensing system. However, the dissent also implies that police should enable citizens to enjoy their rights. The Polish Constitutional Tribunal held constitutional, in U. 10/92, 26 Jan. 1993, restraints on the bylaws of the lower house of Parliament (the Sejm) to establish parliamentary caucuses, to safeguard the effectiveness of Parliament. In Germany, the GFCC frequently accepts arguments referring to the effectiveness of Parliament and balances

it, for example, against the individual rights of its members. (On parliamentary autonomy, see Chapter 3, Section A.) Do you agree with such reasoning?

4. *Neutrality?* In *Chicago Park District* the USSC argues that the licensing of public gatherings is constitutional if it is neutral, while laws that regulate content are incompatible with fundamental rights. What defines neutrality? Take the example of three groups, each of whose activities would cause damage to the local environment: one wants to play soccer, a second seeks to protest government policy, and a third wishes to display their minority culture. Is banning all three groups a neutral decision? Should the lack of an alternative public space make a difference? In German constitutional law even neutral regulation requires a "constitutional interpretation" to take into account that political activity has priority over, in our example, soccer. But does this satisfy the requirements of legal certainty?

5. *Endurance.* In Poland, a law prohibited citizens from forming cooperatives and organizations consisting of legal persons. In 1991, the Constitutional Tribunal, in _____, K. 6/90, held:

> The freedom of association is aimed at the joint development of citizens' political, social, business and cultural activities. The kinds of activity enumerated are defined only very generally, which means that joint active participation of citizens in social life may take various forms in specific situations, and that the specific aims of joint activity of citizens may be diverse, too. [Not] all kinds of group activity [fall within the scope of the Constitution], but only those kinds that are organized and exhibit a certain permanence. [The] Constitution does not include spontaneous actions taken by large groups of citizens (e.g., fighting a fire in common, or even joint organized activities but not permanent as for instance a demonstration or fundraising).

This means that the state may define what association is recognized by law, based on its endurance. But what about spontaneous single-issue associations fighting for civil rights or minority associations with insufficient resources to operate for extended periods of time?

C. THE RIGHT TO VOTE AND ELECTIONS

In representative democracies the right to vote is the most fundamental political right. As a dissent in the Canadian Supreme Court decision in *Reference re Provincial Electoral Boundaries (Sask.)*, [1991] 2 S.C.R. 158, stated: "[t]he right to vote is synonymous with democracy." The USSC, in *Reynolds v. Sims*, 377 U.S. 533 (1964), maintained:

> [The] right of suffrage is a fundamental matter in a free and democratic society. Especially since the right to exercise the franchise in a free and unimpaired manner is preservative of other basic civil and political rights, any alleged infringement of the right of citizens to vote must be carefully and meticulously scrutinized. * * * A citizen, a qualified voter, is no more nor no less so because he lives in the city or on the farm. This is the clear and strong command of our Constitution's Equal Protection Clause. This is an essential part of the concept of a government of laws and not men. This is at the heart of Lincoln's vision of 'government of the people, by the people, [and] for the people.' The Equal Protection Clause demands no less than substantially equal state

legislative representation for all citizens, of all places as well as of all races. * * *

A number of questions arise. Who is allowed to vote? Do voters only elect representatives, or do they also have a direct voice in public affairs? How should elections be organized? And what is the function of a vote once it is cast?

NEW NATIONAL PARTY v. SOUTH AFRICA

Constitutional Court (South Africa).
1999 (3) SALR 191 (CC).

[The National Party challenged the legal requirement of specific IDs for voters.]

Justice Yacoob:

[10]   [The] Electoral Act * * * regulate[s] the way in which citizens must register and vote. The question which must be answered is whether these requirements constitute an infringement of the right to vote. * * *

[11]   The Constitution effectively confers the right to vote for legislative bodies at all levels of government only on those South African citizens who are 18 years or older. * * * The importance of the right to vote is self-evident and can never be overstated. * * * [The] right is fundamental to a democracy for without it there can be no democracy. But the mere existence of the right to vote without proper arrangements for its effective exercise does nothing for a democracy; it is both empty and useless.

[12]   The Constitution takes an important step in the recognition of the importance of the right * * * by providing that all South African citizens have the right to free, fair and regular elections. * * * The right to vote is of course indispensable to, and empty without, the right to free and fair elections; the latter gives content and meaning to the former. * * * [This implies that] each citizen entitled to do so must not vote more than once in any election; any person not entitled to vote must not be permitted to do so. The extent to which these deviations occur will have an impact on the fairness of the election. This means that the regulation of the exercise of the right to vote is necessary so that these deviations can be eliminated or restricted in order to ensure the proper implementation of the right to vote. * * *

[13]   The existence of, and the proper functioning of a voters roll, is therefore a constitutional requirement * * *.

[14]   The details of the system are left to Parliament. * * *

[15]   The requirement that only those persons whose names appear on the national voters roll may vote, renders the requirement that * * * citizens must register before they can exercise their vote, a constitutional imperative. It is a constitutional requirement of the right to vote, and not a limitation of the right.

[17]   * * * Some form of easy and reliable identification is necessary to facilitate [the voter identification] process. * * *

[18] The appellant did not dispute that proof of identity [is a] necessary component of the electoral system contemplated by the Constitution. What was disputed was whether the Electoral Act could prescribe that the only means for such proof was a bar-coded ID * * *. [The] argument was that [many people] * * * would not be able to vote for a variety of inter-related reasons. The submissions were that the Department of Home Affairs, charged with the responsibility of issuing these documents, did not have the capacity to produce them in a timely way, that the cost of acquiring the documents constituted a real impediment and that potential voters were not aware, or had not been made sufficiently aware, of the documentary requirements to enable them to apply * * * in time. * * *

[19] It is to be emphasised that it is for Parliament to determine the means by which voters must identify themselves. This is not the function of a court. But this does not mean that Parliament is at large in determining the way in which the electoral scheme is to be structured. There are important safeguards aimed at ensuring appropriate protection for citizens who desire to exercise this foundational right.

The first of the constitutional constraints placed upon Parliament is that there must be a rational relationship between the scheme which it adopts and the achievement of a legitimate governmental purpose. Parliament cannot act capriciously or arbitrarily. * * *

[20] A second constraint is that the electoral scheme must not infringe any of the fundamental rights enshrined in * * * the Constitution. * * * The decisive question * * * is, * * * when can it legitimately be said that a legislative measure designed to enable people to vote in fact results in a denial of that right? * * *

[21] The exercise to be carried out by a court entails an evaluation of the consequences of a statutory provision in the process of its implementation. * * * Parliament must ensure that people who would otherwise be eligible to vote are able to do so * * * if they take reasonable steps in pursuit of the right to vote. More cannot be expected of Parliament. * * *

[23] [It] might well happen that the right may be infringed or threatened because a governmental agency does not perform efficiently in the implementation of the statute. This will not mean that the statute is invalid. The remedy for this lies elsewhere. The appellant must fail if it does not establish that the right is infringed by the impugned provisions * * *.

[24] * * * The first question to be decided, therefore, is whether the * * * Electoral Act is rational. * * *

[26] An examination of the 1986 Act shows that the requirement of the bar-coded ID as the principal method of identification is, on the face of it, rationally connected to the legitimate governmental purpose of enabling the effective exercise of the vote. * * * The bar-code on the document facilitates quick, easy and reliable verification of the fact that the name of the person has been entered on the population register. * * *

[28] [The next question is whether it is] arbitrary or capricious * * *.

[30] [Surveys] indicate * * * that about 5 million people who were eligible to vote did not have bar-coded IDs. * * *

[32]   Once it is accepted, however, that the bar-coded ID is appropriate as the main identification document for the purpose of registration and voting and that some reliable form of identification is indispensable, it follows, that it is futile to require people in this category to acquire some other form of identity document instead of the bar-coded ID. Those who have no identification documents have been obliged to apply for them and have not done so. * * * It follows that it is also rational that the bar-coded ID should be the main identification document for this category as well.

[33]   The next question to be answered is whether it is arbitrary not to provide that the two and a half million people who have other identity documents be allowed to use them as alternative methods of identification for purposes of registration and voting. * * *

[35]   [But there] are * * * essential differences between the bar-coded ID and other forms of identity documents. * * * [Other] forms of identification contended for have a common feature: they constitute a powerful symbol and reminder of a shameful past characterised by racial discrimination, oppression and exploitation, untold misery and suffering and the denial to the majority of South African citizens not merely of their right to vote but also of their essential humanity. This is a factor of considerable significance. These documents were issued on a racial basis, and reflect the race of the person to whom they were issued. They constituted a pillar on which racialism could be effectively structured. For many in our country the use of these documents for electoral purposes would be highly embarrassing if not positively offensive.

[36]   On the other hand, the documentary requirements pose no real disadvantage to most people * * *. Furthermore, there is no evidence that the cost and inconvenience mentioned in argument is a real factor [and that] the impugned provisions discriminate against people on the ground of their poverty. * * *

[37]   The facial analysis reveals nothing that suggests any denial of the right to vote. * * *

[41]   It must be borne in mind that the responsibility of ensuring that people know of the requirements for voting is not only that of the government. Indispensable to any democratic process is that political parties will ensure that their potential supporters are aware of the prerequisites of voting and comply with them. * * *

[44]   The mere possibility of people not being able to register does not begin to carry the day.

[46] [This] does not mean however, that the only remaining alternative to declaring the legislation unconstitutional, is that the freeness and fairness of the election must be determined after the election is held. If the Commission did not allow sufficient time for registration, had too few registration points, or acted in any other way that was tantamount

to a denial of the vote, any aggrieved party could apply for an appropriate mandamus against the Commission.

[49] [But the] attack on the constitutionality of these provisions fails.

Justice O'Regan, dissenting.

[118] * * * The right to vote and the right to free and fair elections based on a national common voters-roll cannot be observed unless the government, both the legislature and the executive, and, of course, the Electoral Commission, take the necessary positive steps to ensure that a voters-roll is compiled and the election is held. [The] primary obligation [imposed] upon government is not a negative one, requiring government to refrain from conduct which could cause an infringement of the right, but a positive one, requiring government to take positive steps to ensure that the right is fulfilled. * * *

[119] South African democracy is still in its infancy and requires nurturing and care to ensure it becomes firmly established.

[120] [The] obligation to afford citizens the right to vote in regular, free and fair elections is important not only because of the relative youth of our constitutional democracy but also because of the emphatic denial of democracy in the past. * * *

[127] In my view, the proper approach is to require legislative regulation of the right to vote to be reasonable. * * * It will enable appropriate scrutiny of legislative measures regulating elections * * *.

[128] [It] will depend upon the circumstances of each case. * * *

[160] [Here] a large number of voters who had lawful and valid forms of identification have been compelled to obtain other forms of identification in a short period of time in order to be able to register and vote. Failure to obtain the prescribed forms of identification will result in disenfranchisement. In my view, this result betrays a disregard for the importance of the right to vote in free and fair elections in a country where such a right is only in its infancy. The provisions cannot, in my view, be considered reasonable or justifiable in the circumstances.

HARPER v. VIRGINIA STATE BOARD OF ELECTIONS

Supreme Court (United States).
383 U.S. 663 (1966).

[The state of Virginia imposed a small annual poll tax on all persons over age 21. Those who did not pay were disenfranchised.]

Mr. Justice Douglas delivered the opinion of the Court.

[Once] the franchise is granted to the electorate, lines may not be drawn which are inconsistent with the Equal Protection Clause * * *. That is to say, the right of suffrage "is subject to the imposition of state standards which are not discriminatory and which do not contravene any restriction that Congress, acting pursuant to its constitutional powers, has imposed." * * * We conclude that a State violates the Equal Protection Clause * * * whenever it makes the affluence of the voter or payment of any fee an electoral standard. Voter qualifications have no relation to wealth nor to paying or not paying this or any other tax. Our cases demonstrate that the Equal Protection Clause * * * restrains the States from fixing voter qualifications which invidiously discriminate. Thus without questioning the power of a State to impose reasonable residence restrictions on the availability of the ballot, we held * * * that a State may not deny the opportunity to vote to a bona fide resident merely because he is a member of the armed services [and thus travels abroad]. * * * The principle that denies the State the right to dilute a citizen's vote on account of his economic status or other such factors by analogy bars a system which excludes those unable to pay a fee to vote or who fail to pay.

It is argued that a State may exact fees from citizens for many different kinds of licenses; that if it can demand from all an equal fee for a driver's license, it can demand from all an equal poll tax for voting. But we must remember that the interest of the State, when it comes to voting, is limited to the power to fix qualifications. Wealth, like race, creed, or color, is not germane to one's ability to participate intelligently in the electoral process. Lines drawn on the basis of wealth or property, like those of race are traditionally disfavored. * * * The degree of the discrimination is irrelevant.

[The] Equal Protection Clause is not shackled to the political theory of a particular era. In determining what lines are unconstitutionally discriminatory, we have never been confined to historic notions of equality, any more than we have restricted due process to a fixed catalogue of what was at a given time deemed to be the limits of fundamental rights. Notions of what constitutes equal treatment for purposes of the Equal Protection Clause do change. This Court in 1896 held that laws providing for separate public facilities for white and Negro citizens did not deprive the latter of the equal protection and treatment that the Fourteenth Amendment commands. * * * [But] in 1954—more than a half-century later—we repudiated the "separate-but-equal" doctrine * * * as respects public education. * * *

Our conclusion * * * is founded not on what we think governmental policy should be, but on what the Equal Protection Clause requires.

Justices Black, Harlan, and Stewart dissented.

FOREIGN VOTERS CASE

Federal Constitutional Court (Germany).
83 BVerfGE 37 (1990).

[A German state (*Land*) granted its foreign resident aliens the right to vote in municipal elections. Some seven thousand Danes, Irish, Dutch, Norwegians, Swedes, and Swiss, who had resided for at least five years in the *Land*, would have been eligible to vote. Christian Democratic representatives in the federal Parliament brought an abstract judicial proceeding, claiming that the state law "undermined the democratic right of the German people to self-determination."]

C. * * * The [state] government's amendment to the * * * Election Act violates [the Constitution, which] permits the people to elect representatives at communal and district levels; the concept of "the people" is employed in the same way as in [the Constitution's provision on democracy], which defines "the people" as the German people. The concept of "the people" within a community and district includes only the German people. Foreigners cannot be given the right to vote at the municipal level.

I. 1. The constitutional assertion that "all state authority shall emanate from the people" * * * contains not just the principle of popular sovereignty (evidenced by its location and connection with other norms); it also defines the people who exercise state authority through elections, voting, specific legislative organs, executive power, and the judiciary; it is the body politic of the Federal Republic of Germany, [the Constitution] identifies [the republic] as a democratic, social federal state, based on the rule of law and the division of powers; there can be no democratic state without a body politic that is both subject to and object of the state authority vested in it and exercised through its organs. This body politic is the people, from whom all state authority emanates. This does not mean that all state decisions must be approved by the people; rather, it means that the subject of state authority must be a cohesive, unified group.

2. According to the [Constitution], the people, from whom state authority emanates in the Federal Republic of Germany, comprises German citizens and all persons of similar status. Membership in this body politic is determined by citizenship. Citizenship is both the legal precondition for the equal status of individuals and the foundation for equal rights and duties; exercise of legal rights and duties legitimates democratic state authority.

Other provisions of the [Constitution] that relate to "the people" are unequivocal in [identifying] the body politic as the German people. The Preamble declares that it is the German people who adopted the [Constitution] by virtue of their constituent power, [Art. 28 does] guarantee every German in every Land the same political rights and duties; [others] require the federal president and members of the cabinet to swear that they will dedicate their efforts to the well-being of the German people; [one article] grants the German people the right to adopt a [new] constitution * * *. Notably, the Preamble and article 28 article both declare the German people to be subject and object to the state of the FRG. And Article 116, which attributes the characteristic of being German to so called status Germans only, derives its meaning from its own definition of the subject of German state authority as all German citizens. The drafters of the [Constitution] expressly addressed this issue, even while modifying the principle somewhat in consideration of the circumstances of the post-war era.

3. If the [Constitution] conceives being German as necessary to being part of "the people" as the subject of state authority, then it must follow that [being German] is a precondition of the right to vote, which is a direct exercise of the state authority possessed by the people. This

does not mean that the legislator is unable to influence the composition of "the people". [It] empowers the legislator to set conditions for gaining or losing citizenship status * * * and thereby to establish the criteria for membership in the body politic. Through the Citizenship Act, the legislator can also change residence requirements to influence political rights.

It is incorrect to state that an increase in the population of foreigners within the FRG changes the constitutional concept of "the people". Underlying this misperception is the concept that democracy and the inherent concept of freedom demand [complete] congruence between those who hold democratic rights and those who are subject to state domination. This is the correct starting point, but it cannot eliminate the relationship between being German and being a member of the body politic, and thus vested with state authority. * * *

KRAMER v. UNION FREE SCHOOL DISTRICT

Supreme Court (United States).
395 U.S. 621 (1969).

Mr. Chief Justice Warren delivered the opinion of the Court.

[We] are called on to determine whether * * * the New York Education Law is constitutional. [It] provides that in certain * * * school districts residents who are otherwise eligible to vote in state and federal elections may vote in the school district election only if they (1) own (or lease) taxable real property within the district, or (2) are parents (or have custody of) children enrolled in the local public schools. Appellant, a bachelor who neither owns nor leases taxable real property, filed suit in federal court claiming that [it] denied him equal protection of the laws. * * *

* * * "In determining whether or not a state law violates the Equal Protection Clause, we must consider the facts and circumstances behind the law, the interests which the State claims to be protecting, and the interests of those who are disadvantaged by the classification." And, in this case, we must give the statute a close and exacting examination. "[S]ince the right to exercise the franchise in a free and unimpaired manner is preservative of other basic civil and political rights, any alleged infringement of the right of citizens to vote must be carefully and meticulously scrutinized." This careful examination is necessary because statutes distributing the franchise constitute the foundation of our representative society. Any unjustified discrimination in determining who may participate in political affairs or in the selection of public officials undermines the legitimacy of representative government.

[Therefore, a] rigid examination is applicable to statutes denying the franchise to citizens who are otherwise qualified by residence and age. Statutes granting the franchise to residents on a selective basis always pose the danger of denying some citizens any effective voice in the governmental affairs which substantially affect their lives. Therefore, if a challenged state statute grants the right to vote to some bona fide residents of requisite age and citizenship and denies the franchise to others, the Court must determine whether the exclusions are necessary to promote a compelling state interest. And, for these reasons, the deference usually given to the judgment of legislators does not extend to decisions concerning which resident citizens may participate in the election * * * [The] general presumption of constitutionality afforded state statutes and the traditional approval given state classifications if the Court can conceive of a "rational basis" for the distinctions made are not applicable. * * *

The need for exacting judicial scrutiny of statutes distributing the franchise is undiminished simply because, under a different statutory scheme, the offices subject to election might have been filled through appointment. States do have latitude in determining whether certain public officials shall be selected by election or chosen by appointment and whether various questions shall be submitted to the voters. In fact, we have held that where a county school board is an administrative, not legislative, body, its members need not be elected. However, "once the franchise is granted to the electorate, lines may not be drawn which are inconsistent with the Equal Protection Clause of the Fourteenth Amendment."

Nor is the need for close judicial examination affected because the district meetings and the school board do not have "general" legislative powers. Our exacting examination is not necessitated by the subject of the election; rather, it is required because some resident citizens are permitted to participate and some are not. * * *

Besides appellant and others who similarly live in their parents' homes, the statute also disenfranchises the following persons (unless they are parents or guardians of children enrolled in the district public school): senior citizens and others living with children or relatives; clergy, military personnel, and others who live on tax-exempt property; boarders and lodgers; parents who neither own nor lease qualifying property and whose children are too young to attend school; parents who neither own nor lease qualifying property and whose children attend private schools. [Appellant argues that all] members of the community have an interest in the quality and structure of public education, appellant says, and he urges that "the decisions taken by local boards ... may have grave consequences to the entire population." * * *

The State apparently reasons that since the schools are financed in part by local property taxes, persons whose out-of-pocket expenses are "directly" affected by property tax changes should be allowed to vote. Similarly, parents of children in school are thought to have a "direct" stake in school affairs and are given a vote. * * *

We need express no opinion as to whether the State in some circumstances might limit the exercise of the franchise to those "primarily interested" or "primarily affected." Of course, we therefore do not reach the issue of whether these particular elections are of the type in which the franchise may be so limited. For, assuming, arguendo, that New York legitimately might limit the franchise in these school district elections to those "primarily interested in school affairs," close scrutiny of the [law] demonstrates that they do not accomplish this purpose with sufficient precision to justify denying appellant the franchise. * * *

[The] classifications must be tailored so that the exclusion of appellant and members of his class is necessary to achieve the articulated state goal. [The law] does not meet the exacting standard of precision we require of statutes which selectively distribute the franchise. The classifications * * * permit inclusion of many persons who have, at best, a remote and indirect interest in school affairs and, on the other hand, exclude others who have a distinct and direct interest in the school meeting decisions. * * *

Justices Stewart, Black, and Harlan, dissenting:

* * * Clearly a State may reasonably assume that its residents have a greater stake in the outcome of elections held within its boundaries than do other persons. Likewise, it is entirely rational for a state legislature to suppose that residents, being generally better informed regarding state affairs than are nonresidents, will be more likely than nonresidents to vote responsibly. And the same may be said of legislative assumptions regarding the electoral competence of adults and literate persons on the one hand, and of minors and illiterates on the other. It is clear, of course, that lines thus drawn cannot infallibly perform their intended legislative function. Just as "[i]lliterate people may be intelligent voters," nonresidents or minors might also in some instances be interested, informed, and intelligent participants in the electoral process. Persons who commute across a state line to work may well have a great stake in the affairs of the State in which they are employed; some college students under 21 may be both better informed and more passionately interested in political affairs than many adults. But such discrepancies are the inevitable concomitant of the line drawing that is essential to law making. So long as the classification is rationally related to a permissible legislative end, therefore—as are residence, literacy, and age requirements imposed with respect to voting—there is no denial of equal protection. Thus judged, the statutory classification involved here seems to me clearly to be valid.

* * * [The] asserted justification for applying such a standard cannot withstand analysis. * * * The voting qualifications at issue have been promulgated, not by Union Free School District * * *, but by the New York State Legislature, and the appellant is of course fully able to participate in the election of representatives in that body. * * * [Therefore, a strict standard need not be applied.] Nor is there any other justification for imposing the Court's "exacting" equal protection test. This case does not involve racial classifications, which in light of the genesis of the Fourteenth Amendment have traditionally been viewed as inherently "suspect." And this statute is not one that impinges upon a constitutionally protected right, and that consequently can be justified only by a "compelling" state interest. For "the Constitution of the United States does not confer the right of suffrage upon any one".

Notes and Questions

1. *Governed, but no vote.* Who should have a voice in the public affairs of a nation? Puerto Ricans became U.S. citizens in 1917, but the courts continue to uphold a position developed in the "Insular Cases" (around

1901) that Puerto Rico is not a state and thus cannot have electors in the Presidential Electoral College. The same applies to representation in the Congress, although there is a Puerto Rican "delegate" to the House of Representatives. In *Balzac v. People of Puerto Rico*, 258 U.S. 298 (1922), it was held that the right to trial by jury does not apply to Puerto Rican citizens. Citizenship was not a sufficient ground to extend rights (resulting from the constitutional obligation of the states) to "those distant ocean communities of a different origin and language from those of our continental people." Is it for constitutional courts to decide such issues? A strong concurrence in *Igartua De La Rosa v. United States*, 229 F.3d 80 (2000), Court of Appeals for the First Circuit, United States 2000, stated that:

> [The] civil rights of United States citizens residing in Puerto Rico, particularly their national political rights, have remained dormant at best, subject to the vagaries of Congress, and the conspicuous inattention of the judiciary. The granting of so-called "Commonwealth" status in 1952, itself an enigmatic condition which merely allowed the residents of Puerto Rico limited self-government, did nothing to correct Puerto Rico's fundamental condition of national unempowerment, embodied most notably in the lack of voting representation in the Congress and the ineligibility to vote for President and Vice–President. The United States citizens residing in Puerto Rico to this day continue to have no real say in the choice of those who, from afar, really govern them, nor as to the enactment, application, and administration of the myriad of federal laws and regulations that control almost every aspect of their daily affairs. * * * The present conundrum cannot be justified or perpetuated further under the subterfuge of labeling it a "political question." Undoubtedly, this situation is "political" in the sense that it involves the political rights of a substantial number of United States citizens. It is also "political" because it is one that should, in the normal course of things, be resolved by the political process and the political branches of government. But * * * this problem is no more "political" than that presented to and resolved by the Supreme Court in *Brown v. Board of Education*, [which ordered the integration of schools and thus put an end to legal segregation as a form of racism in the U.S.].

Consider that in the *Foreign Voters Case* the GFCC, like the USSC, defers to the legislature in defining who belongs and who has a voice. Do you agree? Or are there standards of democracy, like the protection of minority rights, that require a different approach?

2. *Efforts of Government.* In South Korea, the Electoral Act denied Korean citizens living overseas the right to vote. Citizens who were living in Japan complained when they could not participate in the December 18, 1997 presidential election. In 1999, the Constitutional Court, in *Overseas Citizens Voting Rights Ban*, 11–1 KCCR 54, 97Hun–Ma253,[h] unanimously held:

> It is needed to impose residential requirements on voting rights in order to protect the essential content of the voting right, the fairness in voting, and other public interests. Such requirements may effectively deny overseas citizens the right to vote. However, it is unrealistic to recognize the voting rights of North Korean citizens or other Japanese

h. Quoted summary available at <www.ccourt.go.kr/english/Decision- Eng.html#2–3>.

residents participating in the pro-North Chosun Federation ('jo-chong-ryeon') when the nation remains divided. It is difficult to assure the fairness in voting once it is open to overseas citizens. Also, it is practically impossible to deliver the election and candidate information, campaign, and send ballots to all overseas residents, and retrieve them within the statutory election period. Furthermore, the right to vote is correlated to the duty to pay tax and serve in the military, and overseas residents have not performed these duties. Therefore, the restriction on overseas residents' voting rights is not only aimed at legitimate legislative purposes but also balances well the public interest served and the basic rights infringed by it. It is also an appropriate means to accomplish the end.

It will be ideal to grant all overseas residents voting rights and thereby promote their national pride as Korean citizens, elevate their love of the country, and generate in their daily lives keener interest in the fate of the country. This issue of an ideal is different from the question of whether a restriction on voting rights necessarily violates the Constitution. Even if it is undesirable to deny overseas residents the voting rights, as long as there is a reasonable basis, such denial is not excessive restriction on basic rights. Therefore, the above provision does not depart from the Article 37 (2) limit on restriction on basic rights.

To make overseas residents' voting rights contingent on their national values or level of national awareness may be like putting the cart before the horse. Fairness in voting can be achieved with government efforts, and many technical problems can be overcome through advanced means of communication. In light of such possibilities, is the decision still sound? The Court later reviewed a law that denied the absentee voting of study-abroad students and overseas representatives of Korean companies and upheld it on the grounds that overseas absentee ballots are costly and difficult to administer fairly. The Court also reasoned that, unlike domestic absentee voters, these groups are responsible for their absence. The Court finally argued that absentee voting was merely an administrative amenity made available to voters and that its lack does not deny the voting right itself.

The South African Constitutional Court (SACC) has said that certain realities are not decisive ("whether the department has been performing efficiently * * * and whether it presently has the capacity to issue these documents to all those who require them is, strictly speaking, irrelevant to the determination of the constitutionality * * * "). Is it not the duty of the court, however, to prevent any abuse of, or any lack of effort and investment of resources in, administrative systems? Consider the constitutional arguments of the USSC regarding vagueness in free speech regulations (discussed in Chapter 7) as well as the argument by the Supreme Court of Zambia in *Mulundika* above.

3. *Local or national?* In *Kim v. Osaka Electoral Commission,* 49 Minshū 639, (Sup. Ct., Feb. 28, 1995), the Japanese Supreme Court decided that the Constitution does not secure local suffrage for settled aliens (*Teiju gaikokujin*). At the same time, it also held that the constitutional principle of local autonomy does not prohibit the Diet from granting this right to foreigners, such as permanent residents, who have an especially close relationship with a local public entity. As in Germany, the Court held that local

elections for denizens is a matter of legislative adjustment. Are voting rights local or national matters or, perhaps, even international human rights matters?

4. *Citizens' obligations?* In looking at the South African decision, do "formal" requirements for a specific ID further or limit democracy? Is it justifiable to establish "material" requirements, like law-abiding behavior? In *Sauvé v. Canada,* [1999] 180 D.L.R. (4th ser.) 385, the Canadian Federal Court of Appeal considered a law that denied the right to vote to prisoners serving a sentence of two years or more. The Court stated:

> Whether [the] Act is good penal policy or good public policy is not at issue * * * This case is about what, if anything, Parliament may or may not do to interfere with prisoner voting rights * * *. Having found that the objectives of enhancement of civic responsibility and respect for rule of law and enhancement of the penal sanction were those which motivated Parliament, I [think] that those objectives are sufficiently pressing and substantial as to warrant an infringement of a Charter right. * * * In * * * this case, the Parliament has chosen to deny the rights of a group of relatively powerless people—those serving prison sentences of two years or more—and must therefore be subject to a certain degree of scrutiny regarding its choice to do so. On the other hand, this statute represents an example of the state setting the ground-rules for its electoral process. While the notion of ensuring a "decent" or "moral" electorate may have little place in today's society, it is Parliament's role to maintain and enhance the integrity of the electoral process. Such considerations are by definition political and therefore warrant deference. This statute also represents an exercise of the criminal law power which is necessarily linked to the criminal sanction. It is my view that Parliament is entitled to a great deal of deference when it makes choices regarding penal policy. * * * I would, therefore, hold that [the law] is a reasonable limit demonstrably justified in a free and democratic society * * *.

The dissent maintained that the law was invalid, since it would be less intrusive to decide on a case-by-case basis:

> Refusing to grant the right to vote to inmates must be seen as a remnant of the exclusion practices of the past. On the one hand, these practices involved excluding criminals from society through banishment, deportation, loss of citizenship or civil death.* * * On the other hand, universal suffrage has progressed very gradually, even in the most democratic countries. * * * The poor, the illiterate, Blacks, Aboriginal people and women were all excluded from the democratic process. People who were convicted or incarcerated were excluded both from society and from the right to vote. The modern trend is toward equality of rights and participation in political life by everyone, even the members of unpopular or marginal groups. Canada may be seen as one of the front runners among democratic countries when it comes to legal and political equality. * * * Exclusions are becoming less and less acceptable, and we believe that there ought to be no exceptions to the right to vote and that the Canada Elections Act should be revised to grant the right to vote to all prison inmates.

Note that the SACC, in *August v. Electoral Commission,* 1999 (3) SALR 1 (CC), held that an electoral law that prevents prisoners incarcerated for severe crimes from exercising their voting rights is unconstitutional and emphasized that governments carry a positive obligation to ensure that all citizens are able to vote regardless of their status.

In 1999, the French Constitutional Council, reviewing the *Institutional Act Concerning New Caledonia*, Decision 99–410 DC, assessed the constitutionality of an act that disqualifies from public elective office, for at least five years, any natural person against whom a personal bankruptcy order, a specific prohibition, or a judicial winding-up order has been made, without the court expressly ordering the disqualification. The Council declared:

> [Part of the Act] * * * relates to the conditions of ineligibility and to incompatibilities. * * * [We note that by] the Declaration of Human and Civic Rights: "Only punishments that are strictly and evidently necessary shall be prescribed; and no one shall be punished except by virtue of a law passed and promulgated before the offence is committed, and legally applied". The principle that punishments must be necessary implies that disqualification from public elective office may be applied only if the court has expressly ordered it, having regard to the circumstances of the specific case; the possibility for the court to release the offender from his disqualification, at his request, if he has made a sufficient contribution to paying off his liability, does not in itself suffice to secure respect for the requirements imposed by the principle of necessity laid down by article 8 of the Declaration of Human and Civic Rights. * * * [This part of the] Act violates the principle that penalties must be necessary.

On what grounds can access to voting be limited? For example, is it constitutional to exclude voters who cannot read? What if information on public matters is solely available in print? Can a vote be cast only in writing? In *Lassiter v. Northampton Election Bd.*, 360 U.S. 45 (1959), the USSC found that literacy requirements are not in and of themselves contrary to the Fifteenth Amendment. But in *South Carolina v. Katzenbach*, 383 U.S. 301 (1966), the Court upheld the Voting Rights Act of 1965, which prohibited such state qualifications, arguing that literacy requirements tended "to perpetuate that discrimination which the Fifteenth Amendment was designed to uproot."

5. *Levels of scrutiny.* Should the constitutional test of the equality of political rights require mere rationality or a stricter scrutiny? In *Kramer* the USSC majority applies a more rigid test than the dissent. With whom do you agree? Does it make a difference, as the dissent argues, whether the Constitution explicitly guarantees universal franchise? If a constitution constitutes a democratic state, what follows for the interpretation of rights to political activity, like the vote?

6. The scope of minority democracy is often a source of conflict in multicultural societies. In *Tse Kwan Sang v. Pat Heung Rural Committee*, the Hong Kong Court of First Instance, [1999] 3 HKLRD 267, 3 HKC 457 (Justice Cheung), upheld on final appeal Nos. 11 and 13 of 2000 (Civil),[i] considered the constitutionality of election rules that restricted the right to stand for election of "indigenous villagers" and female voters. Mr. Tse, who was born in a village, challenged the validity of the election, in light of the Hong Kong Constitution and the International Covenant on Civil and Political Rights (ICCPR). The Court stated:

---

i. Available   at   /cfa/judmt/facv
<www.info.gov.hk/jud/guide2cs/html   _11_13_00.htm>.

To vote and stand as a candidate in the village representative election is to take part in the conduct of public affairs. * * * On the face of it, the exclusionary rule is contrary to [higher law]. [But the opponents argue that the law] expressly protects the lawful traditional rights and interest of the indigenous inhabitants of the New Territories. The Kuk is an advisory body which historically and, as a matter of fact, represents predominantly the interest of indigenous villagers. It does not represent the interest of the rural population as a whole. There are other avenues open to the rural population to take part in public affairs, namely, through the District Board elections. * * * [But] whatever may be the rules governing the village representative election, they are arbitrary and inconsistent in nature. * * * [It also] had never been explained why according to Election Rules married female indigenous villagers must have remained living in the village for seven years or over before she could register as a voter. * * *

The principles embodied in the ICCPR are not some hollow, high-sounding principles. Its preamble refers to the 'inherent dignity, equal and inalienable rights of human beings' and that 'the ideal of free human beings enjoying civil and political freedom and freedom from fear and want can only be achieved if conditions are created, whereby everyone may enjoy his civil and political rights'. Let us not be cynical and construe or apply the ICCPR in such a way as to render it totally meaningless.

In the above decision, counsel referred to a Canadian case, *Issac v. Davey*, [1974] 51 D.L.R. (3rd ser.) 170, in which the Ontario Court of Appeal, following the Supreme Court of Canada in *Attorney General of Canada v. Lavell*, [1974] 38 D.L.R. (3rd ser.) 481, held that provisions in the Indian Act for the election of aboriginal councilors in reserve land, and for the government of the Band by the elected council, were not rendered inoperative by the antidiscrimination provision of the Canadian Bill of Rights. The judge replied: "In my view, the rights of the aborigines in Canada should be considered in the context of Canada. Their rights are governed by treaties and the decision of *Issac* is not helpful as a general proposition that election of village representatives in the New Territories cannot be challenged." Do you agree? Is democracy a universal principle, and if so, is the right to stand in elections (free from discrimination) a universal right? (On minority rights protection in a federal system, see Chapter 4, Section E.)

Conflicts between the autonomy of institutions or groups within society and the right of individuals to participate led to a decision by the USSC in *Santa Clara Pueblo v. Martinez*, 436 U.S. 49 (1978). (See also Chapter 6.) In *Martinez* a female member of the Santa Clara Pueblo tribe and her daughter brought an action for relief against the tribe, alleging that an ordinance denying tribal membership to the children of female members who marry outside the tribe—but not to similarly situated children of men—violated the right to equality. The Court held that:

Indian tribes are "distinct, independent political communities, retaining their original natural rights" in matters of local self-government. Although no longer "possessed of the full attributes of sovereignty," they remain a "separate people, with the power of regulating their internal and social relations." They have power to make their own substantive law in internal matters, and to enforce that law in their own forums. As separate sovereigns pre-existing the Constitution, tribes have historically been regarded as unconstrained by those constitutional provisions framed specifically as limitations on federal or state authority. Thus, * * * this Court held that the Fifth Amendment did not "operat[e] upon" "the powers of local self-government enjoyed" by the tribes. * * * As the Court * * * recognized, however, Congress has plenary authority to limit, modify or eliminate the powers of local self-government which the tribes otherwise possess. [In the Indian Civil Rights Act] Congress acted * * * by imposing certain restrictions upon tribal governments similar, but not identical, to those contained in the Bill of Rights and the [constitutional right to equality]. * * * [But providing] a federal forum for [more] issues * * * constitutes an interference with tribal autonomy and self-government beyond that created by the change in substantive law itself. * * *

We note * * * that a central purpose of the [Indian Civil Rights Act] was to "secur[e] for the American Indian the broad constitutional rights afforded to other Americans," and thereby to "protect individual Indians from arbitrary and unjust actions of tribal governments." * * * [But two] distinct and competing purposes are manifest in the provisions of the ICRA: In addition to its objective of strengthening the position of individual tribal members vis-à-vis the tribe, Congress also intended to promote the well-established federal "policy of furthering Indian self-government." [The law] in some instances modified the safeguards of the Bill of Rights to fit the unique political, cultural, and economic needs of tribal governments. * * * [Unless] and until Congress makes clear its intention to permit the additional intrusion on tribal sovereignty that adjudication of such actions in a federal forum would represent, we are constrained to find that 1302 does not impliedly authorize actions for declaratory or injunctive relief against either the tribe or its officers. * * *

Dissenting, Justice White argued that, since the purpose of the Indian Civil Rights Act is to insure fundamental rights to all Indians, "not only is a private cause of action consistent with that purpose, it is necessary for its achievement. The legislative history indicates that Congress was concerned, not only about the Indian's lack of substantive rights, but also about the lack of remedies to enforce whatever rights the Indian might have." Since the Pueblos' powers lie in one body, and since Martinez has no recourse beyond that, restriction from constitutional jurisprudence in the case deprives her of legal protection. The majority defines the issue as the autonomy of the collective, while the dissent argues that even collectives are bound to respect individuals. One might also argue that the case is about gender discrimination. Can a collective be democratic if it denies the right to belong to some but not to others? How does the Hong Kong case differ?

7. *Individual or collective?* Are political rights (within the electoral context and outside it) individual rights, or do these rights serve group interests, which are often directly recognized? Vikram David Amar and Alan Brownstein, in *The Hybrid Nature of Political Rights*, 50 Stan. L. Rev. 915, 972–73 (1998), argue that political rights are of hybrid nature:

Judicial decisions commonly recognize or emphasize either the individual or group aspect of political rights. Less frequently, a court directly addresses both dimensions of voting rights in a single case. Rarer still are opinions that coherently explain how the individual and group nature of political rights fit together in deciding constitutional questions. The uncertainty reflected in the case law does not undermine our contention that political rights have a hybrid composition. In fact, the hybrid nature of political rights causes much of the ambiguity in the case law. The hybrid nature of political rights presents complex constitutional issues for courts that cannot be resolved by reference to any simple hierarchy of values.

Even cases ostensibly resting on the individual dimension of political rights cannot avoid the importance of group issues or the tension between these conflicting aspects of political rights. The seminal reapportionment cases of *Baker v. Carr* [369 U.S. 186 (1962) (holding that equal protection challenges to legislative apportionment are justiciable)] and *Reynolds v. Sims* [above], for example, illustrate the essential duality of voting rights. On the one hand, Carr and Sims—with their ringing endorsement of the "one person, one vote" principle and concern for the unequal weight assigned to the votes of single voters—seem to endorse a uniquely individualistic understanding of the right to vote.

As Richard Briffault[j] and others have suggested, however, the Court also recognizes a significant group dimension to the right to vote in these cases. As *Sims* illustrates, gerrymandering the demographic size of voting districts is unconstitutional because it provides unequal representation to large political groups, as well as to individual voters—so much so that the very essence of majority rule is jeopardized as a minority of voters threatens to take control of political decisionmaking in a state. This concern about proportionality in representation necessarily radiates from the group nature of the right to vote.

Also, consider that in critical legal and feminist theory, group rights are challenged based on the experience that individuals have diverse and shifting attachments and that groups change and shift as well, just as groups may form the basis of identity and belonging as well as threaten individual freedom. What does this mean for a concept of group rights? Can you imagine individual rights that protect collective aspects of identity? (On group rights, see also Chapter 6.)

C.1. THE IMPACT OF VOTING

Possessing the right to vote does not define what a vote actually does, nor does it guarantee the substance of its use. In some situations force may compel citizens to vote a certain way, or their votes may be taken only to legitimate an inherently nondemocratic government. A vote may also ensure the legitimacy of a body that is itself governed by other institutions or laws, on which it has no, or only limited, influence, as in the European integration cases, in which nation-states are members of a supranational entity—the European Union. Many European constitutional courts required that their constitutions be changed to allow for integration. But the issue may be more complex.

j. *Race and Representation After* Miller v. Johnson, U. Chi. Legal F. 23, 27–30, 60–63 (1995).

MAASTRICHT II DECISION

Constitutional Council (France).
92–312 DC of 2 Sept. 1992.k

[This case is presented in Chapter 1.]

* * * The authors of the referral proceed from the concept that the French constitutional order is constructed around the central notion of national sovereignty to ask the Constitutional Council how far it is possible to go with revisions of the Constitution to effect successive inroads into "the essential conditions for the exercise of sovereignty".

[But this Council only decides] whether a given international agreement referred to does or does contain clauses contrary to the Constitution; the question put by the authors of the referral is not Whether the Treaty on European Union contains clauses contrary to the Constitution; the argument must accordingly be disregarded.

MAASTRICHT TREATY CASE

Federal Constitutional Court (Germany).
89 BVerfGE 155 (1994).

[This case is presented in Chapter 1.]

[The constitutional right to vote] forbids the weakening * * * of the legitimation of State power gained through an election, and of the influence on the exercise of such power, by means of a transfer of duties and responsibilities of the Federal Parliament, to the extent that the principle of democracy [is] violated.

HAIG v. CANADA

Supreme Court (Canada).
[1993] 2 S.C.R. 995.

Justices La Forest, L'Heureux–Dubé, Sopinka, Gonthier, and Major:

[Two] referenda were held in Canada, each concerning proposed amendments to the Canadian Constitution. Haig was not able to cast a ballot in either. This was unfortunate. The only issue in the present appeal is this: Was [he] entitled to cast a ballot in the federal referendum?

At that specific moment in Canadian history, there was a confluence of political pressures, concerns and events. Among these was the ongoing and often politically heated constitutional dialogue. * * * It was in this context that the federal government undertook to hold a referendum in those provinces where a provincial referendum would not otherwise be held. This choice was in accord with the desire and the authority of the provinces to consult their own electors as they saw fit.

In the end, only two referenda were held: one in Quebec pursuant to Quebec's provincial referendum legislation, the other in the rest of

---

k. Available, in French, at <www.con-   sion/1992/92312dc.htm>.
seil-constitutionnel.fr/deci-

Canada pursuant to the federal referendum legislation. [The] mechanics of the two referenda were governed by the elections legislation of each government. [The] residency provisions of the Quebec elections legislation, in particular, diverge from those in the federal legislation by requiring six months residency in order to be eligible to vote. It was this residency requirement which resulted in some Quebec residents, Mr. Haig in particular, not being able to cast their vote, and which is at the heart of this case.

* * * The appellants submit that, to the extent that they were unable to participate in the federal referendum, they were deprived of their constitutional right to vote, of their freedom of expression, and of their right to equal benefit of the law. * * *

[There] is nothing in the Canadian Constitution which relates to referenda, let alone anything that mandates or prevents this type of consultation by either the federal or provincial governments. [The] decision to hold a federal referendum in nine provinces and two territories was a constitutionally permissible one. It was a political choice, a choice open under the legislation, and a choice consistent with principles of federalism. What is left to consider, then, is whether this choice was also consistent with the obligations of the federal government under the Charter. It is to that issue that I now turn.

Does * * * the Charter guarantee to every citizen of Canada the right to participate in a federal referendum, independently of the terms of the federal referendum legislation? Section 3 of the Charter reads as follows:

> "Every citizen of Canada has the right to vote in an election of members of the House of Commons or of a legislative assembly and to be qualified for membership therein."

The wording of the section, as is immediately apparent, is quite narrow, guaranteeing only the right to vote in elections of representatives of the federal and the provincial legislative assemblies. The purpose * * * is, then, to grant every citizen of this country the right to play a meaningful role in the selection of elected representatives who, in turn, will be responsible for making decisions embodied in legislation for which they will be accountable to their electorate.

[The] democratic rights guaranteed in the Charter are also positive ones. Federal and provincial governments have a mandate to hold regular elections to allow citizens to select their representatives. The failure to hold such regular elections would violate the Charter, would open the government to account for such constitutional infringements, and would undoubtedly provoke a constitutional crisis. Since the results of an election are clearly binding upon citizens in a democratic society, failure to act upon such results would entail a serious constitutional breach.

A referendum, on the other hand, is basically a consultative process, a device for the gathering of opinions. Voting in a referendum differs significantly from voting in an election. First, unless it legislatively binds itself to do so, a government is under no obligation to consult its citizens through the mechanism of a referendum. It may, as did Quebec under Bill 150, bind itself to conduct a specific referendum but, in the absence of such legislation, there is no obligation to hold this type of consultation. Second, though a referendum may carry great political weight and a government may choose to act on the basis of the results obtained, such results are non-binding in the absence of legislation requiring a government to act on the basis of the results obtained. In the absence of binding legislation, the citizens of this country would not be entitled to a legal remedy in the event of non-compliance with the results. Were a government to hold a referendum and then ignore the results, the remedy would be in the political and not the legal arena. These differences provide further evidence that the constitutionally guaranteed right to vote does not contemplate the right to vote in a referendum.

Section 3 of the Charter is clear and unambiguous as is its purpose: it is limited to the elections of provincial and federal representatives. Consequently, since a referendum is in no way such a selection, the citizens of this country cannot claim a constitutional right to vote in a referendum under * * * the Charter. Accordingly, Mr. Haig's s. 3 Charter rights were not infringed because he could not cast his ballot in the federal referendum.

Notes and Questions

1. *Dimensions of a Right.* The French decision emphasizes national sovereignty as a limit to integration, while the German case addresses whether a national vote can allow a national government to give power to an international body. There, European integration becomes a question of violating individual rights to representation. What is sovereignty from the perspective of individual political rights?

2. *Do votes matter?* The impact of votes differs between direct and indirect (be they representative, or group-based, or elitist, or other) forms of participation. If democracy means government by the *demos*, popular referenda may be the highest form of democracy. The Canadian Supreme Court, above, was of a different opinion. Throughout the world, referenda have sometimes been exploited for opposite ends, such as bypassing an elected parliament or discriminating against minorities who have little power in such a (purely) majoritarian process. The GFCC held that the constitutional principle of democracy does not necessarily entail a right to direct democracy; it is satisfied if a political system provides only for representative democracy (8 BVerfGE 104 (1958)). See further on referendum in Chapter 3, Subsection B.3.

3. *Democracy within democratic bodies.* The reach of the vote is also an issue when parliaments decide who works on which issue. In Germany, in the 1980s, though the Green party won seats in Parliament, it was considered ''radical'' by the majority, which decided to exclude Green party

representatives from certain parliamentary committees. In 1986, the GFCC upheld the exclusion in 70 BVerfGE 324. A dissenting judge, Böckenförde, stated:

> I am unable to agree with the decision of the court. The exclusion of the Green party from participation in the budgetary deliberations concerning the secret service violates [constitutional law regarding elections and democracy] * * *. As the direct representatives of the German people, all the delegates [elected to Parliament] have the right to participate in its deliberations. * * *. Each individual delegate is a representative of all the people; jointly they make up the "representation of the people" and they are empowered by the people, in their capacity as an active citizenry, to represent the people as a whole.
>
> * * * Each [representative] has a specific and equal right to * * * participation. Only in this way can a representative responsibly carry out the official function for which he has been elected. Representatives are not to be divided into classes * * *.
>
> It is precisely this general participation in the formation of the political will of parliament—a process emanating from general intellectual and political discussion and argumentation—which legitimates the inherent right of a parliamentary majority to decide [issues of public policy.] One [process] cannot be separated from the other.
>
> * * * Parliament may not [surrender] its right to deliberate by transferring certain aspects of budgetary planning to a small committee operating in secret. * * *
>
> A parliamentary majority thus cannot do away with this principle, not even within the framework of its admitted authority over matters of procedure. * * *
>
> The [situation here] clearly illustrates [the arbitrariness of Parliament's action]. Parliament has never charged the representative or the parliamentary party requesting participation [in its committee deliberations] with failing to maintain secrecy in similar cases; nor did Parliament declare with certainty that [the representatives from the Green party] would not maintain secrecy * * *. Without any further explanation and without any procedural measures, a path was chosen for deliberating on these economic plans which was * * * calculated to effectively exclude the parliamentary party from participating in the deliberations. * * *

C.2. APPORTIONMENT

Numbers can define the effect of a vote. Population and seats are thus put into meaningful relationships when legislatures decide how to design electoral districts. This is called apportionment.

McGINTY v. WESTERN AUSTRALIA

High Court (Australia).
(1996) 186 C.L.R. 140.

Chief Justice Brennan:

* * * Unaffected by context, the phrase "chosen by the people" admits of different meanings. It might connote that candidates are chosen by popular direct election as distinct from election by an electoral college; or it might connote some requirement of equality or near equality of voting power among those who hold the franchise; or it might go further and import some requirement of a franchise that is held generally by all adults or all adult citizens unless there be substantial reasons for excluding them. Equally, these meanings might be attributed to the notion of "representative democracy". * * *

There are hundreds of electoral systems in existence today by which a form of representative government might be achieved. Their merits must be judged by a number of different criteria which are likely to be incompatible with one another. As one commentator has put it (Bogdanor, *The People and the Party System*, (1981) at 209):

"High priority amongst conflicting criteria would generally be given to such considerations as the extent to which a particular system promoted stable and effective government, fairness of representation, a wide choice of representatives, and contact between the electorate and its chosen representatives. But there will be disagreement on the relative priorities to be attached to each of these aims. Frequently a balance will have to be struck between them. Fair representation is a valuable aspiration, but not perhaps at the expense of encouraging the growth of too many splinter groups which could weaken the effectiveness of government. On the other hand, it would be foolish to pursue the aim of strong government so single-mindedly as to prevent the natural diversity of opinion amongst the electorate from being reflected in the composition of the legislature."

There can be no implication that a particular electoral system, of the many available, is required by the Constitution. There is, of course, the express requirement that whatever system is employed it must result in a direct choice by the people. That must mean direct choice by the people through those eligible to vote at elections, but beyond that the matter of electoral systems, including the size of electoral divisions, and indeed whether to have divisional representation at all, is left to the parliament.

Whatever those responsible for framing the Constitution may have regarded as the most appropriate electoral system for federal elections, their views are not contained in that instrument. They remain at best "unexpressed assumptions upon which the framers of the instrument supposedly proceeded" and are not to be confused with those intentions which are expressed. Whilst implications can be and have been drawn from the Constitution, it is clear beyond question that implications may only properly be drawn where they are necessary or obvious. [They] must appear from the terms of the instrument itself and not from extrinsic circumstances. * * *

Once it is recognised, as in my view it must be, that electorates of equal numerical size are not a necessary characteristic of representative government, the plaintiffs are driven in their argument to find in the system of representative government laid down by the Constitution a requirement that there be, as nearly as practicable, electorates of equal size. But that requirement is nowhere to be found in any express provision of the Constitution and this Court has denied * * * that there is any basis for its implication. It is not to be found in the expression "directly chosen by the people" contained [in the Constitution, which indeed contains] requirements which are to the contrary. * * *

Clearly there is force in the contrary view which holds that the effect of unequal electoral divisions—malapportionment—is to weight the value of votes in the numerically smaller divisions. But the extra weight is only in the consequence that an elector in a smaller electorate is required to share his or her representative with a lesser number of electors than in the larger electorate. There are other ways, perhaps more significant, in which the value of a vote may be affected as, for example, where electoral divisions are defined in such a way as to allow one party in a two party system to return a majority of representatives with less than a majority of the total votes, which may occur whether or not malapportionment also exists. Disproportion of this kind may be intentionally caused by a gerrymander.

Of course, the problems arising from malapportionment and disproportion would largely disappear if there were no electoral divisions within a State and a system of proportional representation were adopted * * *. But such a system may be to the detriment of a two party system by encouraging the growth of splinter groups. [It] would be unwise to freeze into a constitutional requirement a particular aspect of an electoral system the attraction of which might vary at different times, in different conditions and to different eyes. The wisdom of those who were responsible for framing our Constitution in recognising the political nature of such matters, and in leaving them to parliament, ought not to be overborne by drawing an implication which is neither apparent nor necessary. * * *

Justice Toohey:

The view I take of representative democracy as found in the Constitution of Western Australia is that it is not a fixed concept but rather is responsive to the time and circumstances in which it falls for consideration. Therefore, rather than answer the questions as asked, it is appropriate to say no more than that if an election were now held for the Legislative Assembly or Legislative Council in accordance with the impugned statutory provisions, the members would not be chosen by the people in accordance with the constitutional dictates of representative democracy.

REFERENCE RE PROVINCIAL ELECTORAL
BOUNDARIES (SASK.)

Supreme Court (Canada).
[1991] 2 S.C.R. 158.

[Proposed changes to the electoral-boundaries law were claimed to infringe the Canadian Charter. The law imposed a strict quota of urban and rural ridings and required that urban ridings coincide with existing municipal boundaries. The resulting distribution map revealed a number of ridings with variations in excess of 15 percent from the provincial quotient and indicated a problem of underrepresentation in urban areas.]

Justices La Forest, Gonthier, McLachlin, Stevenson, and Iacobucci:

At issue here was whether the variances and distribution reflected in the constituencies themselves violated the Charter guarantee of the right to vote. The validity of The Representation Act, 1989 in so far as it defined the constituencies, was indirectly called into question.

The definition of provincial voting constituencies is subject to the Charter and is not a matter of constitutional convention relating to the provincial constitution which is impervious to judicial review. Although legislative jurisdiction to amend the provincial constitution cannot be removed from the province without a constitutional amendment and is in this sense above Charter scrutiny, the provincial exercise of its legislative authority is subject to the Charter. The province is empowered by convention to establish its electoral boundaries but that convention is subject to s. 3 of the Charter.

The content of the Charter right to vote is to be determined in a broad and purposive way, having regard to historical and social context. The broader philosophy underlying the historical development of the right to vote must be sought and practical considerations, such as social and physical geography, must be borne in mind. The Court, most importantly, must be guided by the ideal of a "free and democratic society" upon which the Charter is founded. The purpose of the right to vote enshrined in s. 3 of the Charter is not equality of voting power per se but the right to "effective representation". The right to vote therefore comprises many factors, of which equity is but one. The section does not guarantee equality of voting power.

Relative parity of voting power is a prime condition of effective representation. Deviations from absolute voter parity, however, may be justified on the grounds of practical impossibility or the provision of more effective representation. Factors like geography, community history, community interests and minority representation may need to be taken into account to ensure that our legislative assemblies effectively represent the diversity of our social mosaic. Beyond this, dilution of one citizen's vote as compared with another's should not be countenanced.

The history or philosophy of Canadian democracy does not suggest that the framers of the Charter in enacting s. 3 had the attainment of voter parity as their ultimate goal. Their goal, rather, was to recognize the right long affirmed in this country to effective representation in a system which gives due weight to voter equity but admits other considerations where necessary. Effective representation and good government in this country compel that factors other than voter parity, such as geography and community interests, be taken into account in setting electoral boundaries. Departures from the Canadian ideal of effective representation, where they exist, will be found to violate s. 3 of the Charter.

The actual allocation of seats between urban and rural areas closely followed the population distribution between those areas and effectively increased the number of urban seats to reflect population increases in urban areas. In general the variations between boundaries in the southern part of the province appeared to be justifiable on the basis of factors such as geography, community interests and population growth patterns. The northern boundaries were appropriate, given the sparse population and the difficulty of communication in the area. A violation of s. 3 of the Charter was not established.

Justice Sopinka, concurring:

* * * The framers of the Charter did not intend to create a new right and accordingly the primary inquiry was to determine on what principles the right to vote was based. Historically, the drawing of electoral boundaries has been governed by the attempt to achieve voter equality with liberal allowances for deviations based on the kinds of considerations enumerated in s. 20 of The Electoral Boundaries Commission Act. Deviations were avoided which deprived voters of fair and effective representation. Under the Charter, deviations are subjected to judicial scrutiny and must not be such as to deprive voters of fair and effective representation.

The Charter guarantee in s. 3 does not extend to the process. * * *

Chief Justice Lamer, Justices L'Heureux–Dubé, and Cory, dissenting:

In Canada, each citizen as a minimum must have the right to vote, to cast that vote in private and to have that vote honestly counted and recorded. Equally important, each vote must be relatively equal to every other vote; there cannot be wide variations in population size among the 64 southern constituencies. Deviations from equality will be permitted where they can be justified as contributing to the better government of the people as a whole, giving due weight to regional issues involving demographics and geography. * * *

The fundamental importance of the right to vote demands a reasonably strict surveillance of legislative provisions pertaining to elections. Scrutiny under s. 3 attaches not only to the actual distribution in question but also to the underlying process from which the electoral map was derived. While the actual distribution map may appear to have achieved a result that is not too unreasonable, the effect of the statutory conditions interfered with the rights of urban voters. Once an independent boundaries commission is established, it is incumbent on the legislature to ensure that the Commission was able to fulfill its mandate freely and without unnecessary interference. The right to vote is so fundamental that this interference is sufficient to constitute a breach of s. 3 of the Charter.

[Regarding the northern ridings, geography] and demography demonstrated a pressing and substantial need and the creation of these constituencies was rationally connected to the concept that they have effective representation.

The southern ridings were in a different position legally and geographically. While the differing representational concerns of urban and rural areas may properly be considered in drawing constituency boundaries, the voter population of each constituency should be approximately equal and the type of mandatory conditions imposed here are therefore precluded. * * * Earlier and more equitable distributions indicated that the rights of urban voters could be interfered with to a lesser extent.

KUROKAWA v. CHIBA PREFECTURE ELECTION COMMISSION

Supreme Court (Japan).
30 Minshū 3 at p. 223 (1976).[1]

[In the 1962 elections in Japan, legislative seats were apportioned based on the 1946 census and a 1964 law. This resulted in the need to gain up to four votes in metropolitan Tokyo to equal one vote in rural areas. A resident of Tokyo complained to the Court, alleging that the Electoral Law violated his rights to equality and universal suffrage. A court rejected the claim and left apportionment to the discretionary power of the legislature. In the case presented here elections were held in 1972 based on the 1964 census and faced a discrepancy of five votes in the city to one in the countryside. Kurokawa complained again that the right to equality was violated by the electoral law. The Court held:]

The 1972 general election for the House of Representatives in the Chiba First District is unconstitutional. * * *

* * * The election of December 10, 1972, in the First Election District of Chiba Prefecture for the House of Representatives is illegal. * * *

Our Constitution * * * in noting that the number of members of members of each House and other matters pertaining to the election of members shall be fixed by law * * *, leaves the decision concerning the actual mechanics of the election to the discretion of the Diet. Therefore, the Constitution does not deem equality in the value of each vote to be the sole aspect of an electoral system to be taken into account by the Diet. The Diet may also consider other factors as long as they create an appropriate electoral system that can effectuate impartial and effective representation. The equality of each vote should be harmonized with other political purposes and elements * * *.

[It] is not unusual when a nation is divided into election districts and a single ballot system is adopted, that the number of voters in each

1. Reproduced from Lawrence W. Beer and Hiroshi Itoh, *The Constitutional Case* *Law of Japan, 1970 through 1990*, at 355–63 (1996).

election district is not always perfectly proportional to the number of delegates from that district. However, when the variation form the ideal becomes too great to be overlooked, it may raise the constitutional question of whether the electoral system entails an unreasonable unequal weighing of each vote on the basis of the voter's residence. This case is one of those instances.

* * *

The apportionment provision in this case is an offshoot of the partial amendment of the Election Law * * * of 1964. * * * [The variance today] seems to have been purely a result of the change of population since the amendment * * *.

[I]f the defect is a result of gradual change in circumstances, it is necessary to carefully examine exactly when the law became unconstitutional. It is neither practical nor appropriate to frequently reform the election districts * * *. [I]t should be held unconstitutional only when no rectification, which the Constitution requires to be made within a reasonable period of time, has been made within such a time period.

Arts. 43 and 47 of the Constitution state that the Diet shall establish the electoral system and determine the method of voting, the number of legislators, the boundaries of districts, and the apportionment of seats among those districts. In principle, then, decisions regarding the electoral system should be left to the discretion of the Diet. * * * [The] Diet can establish the system most appropriate to provide fair and effective representation. But its decisions on particular electoral arrangements for both houses have to be continually checked to determine if they infringe on the Constitution's command of electoral equality.

* * * Decisions regarding districting and apportioning seats involve complex political and technical considerations. There are no objective standards specifying how these factors should be reflected in actual decisions. Thus wide discretion must be left to the Diet. If, however * * * any inequality of votes still seems unreasonable, judges must assume that the Diet has exceeded its discretion. Unless some reasons to justify inequality are given, judges have no alternative but to hold the arrangements unconstitutional.

* * * At the time of the 1972 election for the House of Representatives, however, the actual discrepancy in voters represented by individual Diet members had grown to a maximum of 5 to 1. Such a deviation violates the constitutional requirement for equality in the right to vote. The cause of deviations can be attributed mainly to shifts in population. * * * Reapportionments based on changes in population should be carried out within a reasonable period of time; and when the Diet does not do so, it violates the Constitution.

In Chiba, there had been no revision for more than eight years, after the 1964 apportionment in spite of the fact that the Public Office Election Law requires reapportionment of the Diet every five years, based on the most recent national census. Thus the actual apportionment of seats at the time of the election violated the constitutional requirement of equality of voting rights.

SHAW v. RENO

Supreme Court (United States).
509 U.S. 630 (1993).

[The state of North Carolina submitted to a reapportionment plan with one majority black district. The U.S. Attorney General objected to the plan on the ground that a second district could have been created to give effect to minority voting strength. The state's revised plan contained a second majority black district, which stretches approximately 160 miles and, for much of its length, is no wider than the I–85 corridor. Citizens filed an action against the state and federal officials, claiming that the state had created an unconstitutional racial gerrymander in violation of the equality clause.]

Justice O'Connor delivered the opinion of the Court.

This case involves two of the most complex and sensitive issues this Court has faced in recent years: the meaning of the constitutional "right" to vote, and the propriety of race-based state legislation designed to benefit members of historically disadvantaged racial minority groups. [The North Carolina legislature adopted] legislation creating a second majority-black district. [Appellants argue that the law,] which contains district boundary lines of dramatically irregular shape, constitutes an unconstitutional racial gerrymander. * * *

The voting age population of North Carolina is approximately 78% white, 20% black, and 1% Native American; the remaining 1% is predominantly Asian. The black population is relatively dispersed; blacks constitute a majority of the general population in only 5 of the State's 100 counties. * * *

"The right to vote freely for the candidate of one's choice is of the essence of a democratic society...." For much of our Nation's history, that right sadly has been denied to many because of race. The Fifteenth Amendment, ratified in 1870 after a bloody Civil War, promised unequivocally that "[t]he right of citizens of the United States to vote" no longer would be "denied or abridged ... by any State on account of race, color, or previous condition of servitude."

But "[a] number of states ... refused to take no for an answer and continued to circumvent the * * * prohibition through the use of both subtle and blunt instruments, perpetuating ugly patterns of pervasive racial discrimination." Blumstein, *Defining and Proving Race Discrimination: Perspectives on the Purpose vs. Results Approach from the Voting Rights Act*, 69 Va. L. Rev. 633, 637 (1983). Ostensibly race-neutral devices such as literacy tests with "grandfather" clauses and "good character" provisos were devised to deprive black voters of the franchise. Another of the weapons in the States' arsenal was the racial gerrymander—"the deliberate and arbitrary distortion of district boundaries ... for [racial] purposes." * * *

* * * Congress enacted the Voting Rights Act of 1965 as a dramatic and severe response to the situation. * * *

But it soon became apparent that guaranteeing equal access to the polls would not suffice to root out other racially discriminatory voting practices. Drawing on the "one person, one vote" principle, this Court recognized that "[t]he right to vote can be affected by a dilution of voting power as well as by an absolute prohibition on casting a ballot." Where members of a racial minority group vote as a cohesive unit, practices such as multimember or at-large electoral systems can reduce or nullify minority voters' ability, as a group, "to elect the candidate of their choice." Accordingly, the Court held that such schemes violate the Fourteenth Amendment when they are adopted with a discriminatory purpose and have the effect of diluting minority voting strength. Congress * * * amended the Voting Rights Act to prohibit legislation that results in the dilution of a minority group's voting strength, regardless of the legislature's intent. * * *

It is against this background that we confront the questions presented here. * * * Our focus is on appellants' claim that the State engaged in unconstitutional racial gerrymandering. That argument strikes a powerful historical chord: it is unsettling how closely the North Carolina plan resembles the most egregious racial gerrymanders of the past.

* * * In their complaint, appellants did not claim that the * * * reapportionment plan unconstitutionally "diluted" white voting strength. They did not even claim to be white. Rather, appellants' complaint alleged that the deliberate segregation of voters into separate districts on the basis of race violated their constitutional right to participate in a "color-blind" electoral process. Despite their invocation of the ideal of a "color-blind" Constitution, appellants appear to concede that race-conscious redistricting is not always unconstitutional. That concession is wise: this Court never has held that race-conscious state decisionmaking is impermissible in all circumstances. What appellants object to is redistricting legislation that is so extremely irregular on its face that it rationally can be viewed only as an effort to segregate the races for purposes of voting, without regard for traditional districting principles and without sufficiently compelling justification. For the reasons that follow, we conclude that appellants have stated a claim upon which relief can be granted under the Equal Protection Clause.

The Equal Protection Clause provides that "[n]o State shall . . . deny to any person within its jurisdiction the equal protection of the laws." Its central purpose is to prevent the States from purposefully discriminating between individuals on the basis of race. Laws that explicitly distinguish between individuals on racial grounds fall within the core of that prohibition.

No inquiry into legislative purpose is necessary when the racial classification appears on the face of the statute. Express racial classifications are immediately suspect * * *. Classifications of citizens solely on the basis of race "are by their very nature odious to a free people whose institutions are founded upon the doctrine of equality." * * * Accordingly, we have held that the Fourteenth Amendment requires state legislation that expressly distinguishes among citizens because of their race to be narrowly tailored to further a compelling governmental interest.

These principles apply not only to legislation that contains explicit racial distinctions, but also to those "rare" statutes that, although race neutral, are, on their face, "unexplainable on grounds other than race." * * * [This is the case here, too.]

[We] believe that reapportionment is one area in which appearances do matter. A reapportionment plan that includes in one district individuals who belong to the same race, but who are otherwise widely separated by geographical and political boundaries, and who may have little in common with one another but the color of their skin, bears an uncomfortable resemblance to political apartheid. * * *

Racial classifications of any sort pose the risk of lasting harm to our society. They reinforce the belief, held by too many for too much of our history, that individuals should be judged by the color of their skin. Racial classifications with respect to voting carry particular dangers. Racial gerrymandering, even for remedial purposes, may balkanize us into competing racial factions; it threatens to carry us further from the goal of a political system in which race no longer matters—a goal that the [Constitution embodies], and to which the Nation continues to aspire. It is for these reasons that race-based districting by our state legislatures demands close judicial scrutiny. * * * Today we hold only that appellants have stated a claim under the Equal Protection Clause * * *, and that the separation lacks sufficient justification.

Justice White, dissenting:

The grounds for my disagreement * * * are simply stated: appellants have not presented a cognizable claim, because they have not alleged a cognizable injury. [We] have insisted that members of the political or racial group demonstrate that the challenged action have the intent and effect of unduly diminishing their influence on the political process. * * * Because extirpating such considerations from the redistricting process is unrealistic, the Court has not invalidated all plans that consciously use race, but rather has looked at their impact.

Redistricting plans also reflect group interests, and inevitably are conceived with partisan aims in mind. To allow judicial interference whenever this occurs would be to invite constant and unmanageable intrusion. Moreover, a group's power to affect the political process does not automatically dissipate by virtue of an electoral loss. Accordingly, we have asked that an identifiable group demonstrate more than mere lack of success at the polls to make out a successful gerrymandering claim. * * * [We] have limited such claims by insisting upon a showing that "the political processes ... were not equally open to participation by the group in question—that its members had less opportunity than did other residents in the district to participate in the political processes and to elect legislators of their choice." *White v. Regester*, 412 U.S. 755, at 766 (1973). * * *

[It] strains credulity to suggest that North Carolina's purpose in creating a second majority-minority district was to discriminate against members of the majority group by "impair[ing] or burden[ing their] opportunity ... to participate in the political process." The State has made no mystery of its intent, * * * by improving the minority group's prospects of electing a candidate of its choice. I doubt that this constitutes a discriminatory purpose as defined in the Court's equal protection cases—i.e., an intent to aggravate "the unequal distribution of electoral power."

Justice Stevens, dissenting:

* * * Finally, we must ask whether otherwise permissible redistricting to benefit an underrepresented minority group becomes impermissible when the minority group is defined by its race. The Court today answers this question in the affirmative, and its answer is wrong. If it is permissible to draw boundaries to provide adequate representation for rural voters, for union members, for Hasidic Jews, for Polish Americans, or for Republicans, it necessarily follows that it is permissible to do the same thing for members of the very minority group whose history in the United States gave birth to the Equal Protection Clause. A contrary conclusion could only be described as perverse.

APPORTIONMENT II CASE

Federal Constitutional Court (Germany).
16 BVerfGE 130 (1963).

[Petitioner challenged the validity of the 1961 federal election, in which one state (*Land*) had been allegedly divided into too many election districts relative to its population, and the result left one political party with three additional seats.]

B. I. 3. (a) * * * The principle of equal suffrage means that everyone should be able to exercise his right to vote in as formally an equal way as possible. * * * In a pure majority [voting] system consisting of electoral districts of equal size, the weight of each individual vote is equal when all ballots have the same value; electoral equality in a system of proportional requires a similar [weighting of votes].

The requirement of fundamental equality in [casting ballots] * * * can also be satisfied when proportional representation is wedded to elements of a [single-district, winner-take-all system] as provided in the Federal Election Act (FEA). * * * [W]hen all district seats have been assigned * * * within the framework of the proportional seat distribution based on second-ballot votes, the size of a district and thus the weight attached to individual votes for the purpose of determining which party-slated candidate will get the nod in a [particular] district has little to do with the principle of electoral equality.

(c) The weight of ballots does differ to a degree in those situations in which, pursuant to * * * the FEA [a party retains all the district seats it has gained, even if the seats exceed the total number arrived at under proportional representation]. In the light of the formal principle of equality that governs in a system based on proportional representation, it is not unconditionally permissible to give more weight to these ballots than to those cast for parties which fail to gain district seats in excess of [what they are allowed under proportional representation]. * * *

Rather, such a result is consistent with the principle of electoral equality only to the extent that it represents a necessary consequence of a personalized election system. The Federal Election Act modifies proportional representation [by combining] it with the election of particular individuals in single member constituencies on the basis of a relative majority. [Indeed the district ballot precedes the list ballot.] The [primacy] of the single-member-district system is rooted in [this] closer personal relationship between district candidates and their constituencies. This special concern of the personalized proportional election system justifies the [slight inequality] that results from the admission of excessive mandates [under the FEA]. Thus excessive mandates are constitutionally unobjectionable only to the extent that their allocation represents the necessary consequence of the specific purpose of personalized proportional elections. In view of the formal nature of the equality of the right to vote a differentiation in the weight of ballots that would go beyond this peculiarity of the personalized election system cannot be justified.

For this reason districts with approximately equal population figures must be created when it is technically possible so that no state will end up with more districts than its * * * share of the total population in the federal territory would warrant. If all districts are of approximately the same size, then their appropriate distribution among the states will be guaranteed, thus keeping the number of excessive mandates at a constitutionally permissible minimum.

* * * On the other hand, every district must be a balanced and coherent entity under the terms of the Federal Election Act. But historically rooted administrative boundaries ought also to coincide as much as possible with district boundaries. Demographic figures, of course, do not remain constant. * * * Consequently, the constitutional requirement that district boundaries be adjusted to demographic change in the interest of equality cannot be met completely. Federal legislation has taken these inherent difficulties into account; [for example,] the FEA limits the extremes of permissible deviation from the average population of the constituencies to 33 1/3 percent. * * *

4. However, the fact that during the last parliamentary election the districts no longer completely satisfied the required equality of the right to vote does not mean that the division of districts was unconstitutional at that time.

(a) * * * 37 districts * * * exceeded the limits set forth in * * * the FEA. * * * At the same time [another state] had three districts too many while [others] had a surplus of four; [still others] on the other hand, were short seven, one, and three seats, respectively. Because these inequalities spilled over to influence the differential weight of votes in [this state], the current apportionment statute may not [constitutionally] be applied to the next [federal] parliamentary election. [The existing legislative] districting has become unconstitutional because it * * * no longer corresponds to up-to-date demographic figures and because we can no longer expect an automatic readjustment of the current discrepancies. The federal legislature is therefore obliged, during the current legislative period, to reorganize the districts by reducing to a permissible level the deviations in their population from the national average and by adjusting constituency lines to each state's share in the total population.

(b) The unconstitutionality of the apportionment of districts was, however, not so clearly evident [at the time of election], as to invalidate the apportionment from that date. * * *

5. Because the apportionment did not violate the principle of equal elections * * *, to a degree that would have appeared to jeopardize its constitutionality, one cannot speak of a flaw in the election which would have influenced the 1961 elections in a constitutionally objectionable fashion. Consequently, the federal parliament rightfully rejected the challenge to the validity of the fourth parliamentary election on the ground that the districting system was unconstitutional. * * *

Notes and Questions

1. *Universality?* Many national courts have confronted the question of the weight or value of a vote. Should constitutional interpretation differ according to a country's history, geography, or party system? The Canadian Supreme Court of British Columbia, in *Dixon v. British Columbia*, [1989] 59 D.L.R. (4th ser.) 247, comments on the U.S. jurisprudence:

> The American emphasis on a pure population standard for electoral apportionment may be seen as a product of that country's unique history and conception of democracy. The decisions upholding this standard are heavily influenced by the courts' understanding of the intentions of the framers of the US Constitution * * *

> Democracy in Canada is rooted in a different history. Its origins lie not in the debates of the founding fathers, but in the less absolute recesses of the British tradition. Our forefathers did not rebel against the English tradition of democratic government as did the Americans; on the contrary, they embraced it and changed it to suit their own perceptions and needs.

> What is that tradition? It was a tradition of evolutionary democracy, of increasing widening of representation through the centuries. But it was also a tradition which, even in its more modern phases, accommodates significant deviation from the ideals of equal representation. Pragmatism, rather than conformity to a philosophical ideal, has been its watchword.

Consider also the comment from a separate opinion by Justice McHugh in *McGinty* above:

> [Plaintiffs] argue that the decisions of the United States Supreme Court on equality of electoral districts are directly relevant to Australia because the Constitution, like the United States Constitution, has adopted a structure of representative government. * * *

> [The] United States Supreme Court, said: "We hold that, construed in its historical context, the command * * * that Representatives be chosen 'by the People of the several States' means that as nearly as is practicable one man's vote in a congressional election is to be worth as much as another's. * * * To say that a vote is worth more in one district than in another would not only run counter to our fundamental ideas of democratic government, it would cast aside the principle of a House of Representatives elected 'by the People' * * * While it may not be possible to draw congressional districts with mathematical precision,

that is no excuse for ignoring our Constitution's plain objective of making equal representation for equal numbers of people the fundamental goal for the House of Representatives.

The equal representation for equal numbers principle has been rigorously applied by the Supreme Court. [The] Court invalidated a plan which allowed a difference of 4.2 per cent between the most populous and least populous congressional district in Texas. [In another case] the Court was even more rigorous. It invalidated a plan in which the difference between the largest district and the smallest district in New Jersey was only 0.7 per cent.

The plaintiffs contend that the statement [in another U.S. decision] is equally applicable to our Constitution. His Honour said: "The right to vote freely for the candidate of one's choice is of the essence of a democratic society, and any restrictions on that right strike at the heart of representative government. And the right of suffrage can be denied by a debasement or dilution of the weight of a citizen's vote just as effectively as by wholly prohibiting the free exercise of the franchise.

Legislators represent people, not trees or acres. Legislators are elected by voters, not farms or cities or economic interests. As long as ours is a representative form of government, and our legislatures are those instruments of government elected directly by and directly representative of the people, the right to elect legislators in a free and unimpaired fashion is a bedrock of our political system. It could hardly be gainsaid that a constitutional claim had been asserted by an allegation that certain otherwise qualified voters had been entirely prohibited from voting for members of their state legislature. And, if a State should provide that the votes of citizens in one part of the State should be given two times, or five times, or 10 times the weight of votes of citizens in another part of the State, it could hardly be contended that the right to vote of those residing in the disfavoured areas had not been effectively diluted.

The plaintiffs also rely on decisions of the United States Supreme Court that hold that the equal protection clause in * * * the United States Constitution requires that, whenever the members of a legislature are elected from districts within a State or city or local government area, each district, so far as practicable, should have an equal number of voters who elect a proportionately equal number of members. * * *

In my opinion, the United States decisions do not govern the construction of the Constitution. The decisions * * * were heavily influenced by United States history * * *. The Australian history is different. * * *

2. *Latitude?* Many courts have given some degree of latitude to the legislature in designing which votes count, where, and how much. Is this compatible with the doctrine of formal equality in the area of voting rights, which most courts endorse? The GFCC, for example, held that "the constitutional requirement that district boundaries be adjusted to demographic change in the interest of equality cannot be met completely." Do constitutions thus require state procedures that ensure the constant modification of voting districts according to shifts in population? After considering the Japanese holding on the issue in the Kurokawa case, do you agree? In 1985, in *Kanao et al. v. Hiroshima Election Commission*, the Supreme Court of Japan held that: "[The Constitution includes] not only a ban on discrimina-

tion with respect to voters' qualifications * * * but also equality in the substance of the voting right, or the equal value of votes; in other words, equality in the influence which each elector has on the election of representatives. The election system in a parliamentary democracy should be established to reflect fairly and effectively people's opinions and interests in national politics, and to meet the requirement of stability in politics and the actual circumstances in each country. There is no universal formula." 39 Minshū 5, at p. 1100 (1985). Quoted from Beer and Itoh, *op. cit.* at 394–95. What position might one take from a perspective of comparative constitutional law and human rights?

D. POLITICAL PARTIES

To ensure democracy, constitutions often focus on the rights that govern political parties. In some countries, like Germany, political parties are explicitly recognized in the constitution as the prime sites for forming political opinions and making decisions. Political theorists thus sometimes speak of the "party state" rather than the citizens' state. In mass democracies open meetings, in which everyone participates, are unmanageable on a national scale. Parties are therefore the substructure that provides the basis for elections and thus the legitimating procedure to form parliaments and governments. Constitutional law thus confronts the question of which organizations have a right to be recognized as parties—an issue we touched upon in the discussion of militant democracy—as well as who has access to political power under what conditions, whether internal party structures are subject to control, and how presence in public debates and financing can be regulated.

D.1. POLITICAL PARTIES AND ELECTIONS: ACCESS TO POWER

Recognition of an association as a political party does not ensure access to power. The following cases discuss when parties may be obstructed in their attempts to represent small constituencies in parliaments.

WILLIAMS v. RHODES

Supreme Court (United States).
393 U.S. 23 (1968).

Mr. Justice Black delivered the opinion of the Court.

The State of Ohio in a series of election laws has made it virtually impossible for a new political party, even though it has hundreds of thousands of members, or an old party, which has a very small number of members, to be placed on the state ballot to choose electors pledged to particular [presidential] candidates * * *. [The election law] requires a new party to obtain petitions signed by qualified electors totaling 15% of the number of ballots cast in the last preceding gubernatorial election, [and there are] substantial additional · burdens * * * Together these various restrictive provisions make it virtually impossible for any party to qualify on the ballot except the Republican and Democratic Parties. These two Parties face substantially smaller burdens because they are allowed to retain their positions on the ballot simply by obtaining 10% of the votes in the last gubernatorial election and need not obtain any signature petitions. Moreover, Ohio laws make no provision for ballot position for independent candidates * * *.

The Ohio American Independent Party * * * and the Socialist Labor Party * * * both brought suit to challenge the validity of these Ohio laws * * * on the ground that they deny these Parties and the voters who might wish to vote for them the equal protection of the laws. * * *

* * * It is true that this Court has firmly established the principle that the Equal Protection Clause does not make every minor difference in the application of laws to different groups a violation of our Constitution. But we have also held many times that "invidious" distinctions cannot be enacted without a violation of the Equal Protection Clause. In determining whether or not a state law violates the Equal Protection Clause, we must consider the facts and circumstances behind the law, the interests which the State claims to be protecting, and the interests of those who are disadvantaged by the classification. In the present situation the state laws place burdens on two different, although overlapping, kinds of rights—the right of individuals to associate for the advancement of political beliefs, and the right of qualified voters, regardless of their political persuasion, to cast their votes effectively. Both of these rights, of course, rank among our most precious freedoms. [We] have said with reference to the right to vote: "No right is more precious in a free country than that of having a voice in the election of those who make the laws under which, as good citizens, we must live. Other rights, even the most basic, are illusory if the right to vote is undermined."

No extended discussion is required to establish that the Ohio laws before us give the two old, established parties a decided advantage over any new parties struggling for existence and thus place substantially unequal burdens on both the right to vote and the right to associate. The right to form a party for the advancement of political goals means little if a party can be kept off the election ballot and thus denied an equal opportunity to win votes. So also, the right to vote is heavily burdened if that vote may be cast only for one of two parties at a time when other parties are clamoring for a place on the ballot. * * * The State has here failed to show any "compelling interest" which justifies imposing such heavy burdens on the right to vote and to associate.

The State * * * claims that [it] may validly promote a two-party system in order to encourage compromise and political stability. The fact is, however, that the Ohio system does not merely favor a "two-party system"; it favors two particular parties—the Republicans and the Democrats—and in effect tends to give them a complete monopoly. There is, of course, no reason why two parties should retain a permanent monopoly on the right to have people vote for or against them. Competition in ideas and governmental policies is at the core of our electoral process * * *. New parties struggling for their place must have the time and opportunity to organize in order to meet reasonable requirements for ballot position, just as the old parties have had in the past.

* * * Finally Ohio claims that its highly restrictive provisions are justified because without them a large number of parties might qualify for the ballot, and the voters would then be confronted with a choice so confusing that the popular will could be frustrated. But the experience of many States, including that of Ohio prior to 1948, demonstrates that no more than a handful of parties attempts to qualify for ballot positions even when a very low number of signatures, such as 1% of the electorate, is required. It is true that the existence of multitudinous fragmentary groups might justify some regulatory control but in Ohio at the present time this danger seems to us no more than "theoretically imaginable." No such remote danger can justify the immediate and crippling impact on the basic constitutional rights involved in this case.

Justice Douglas, concurring:

* * * Cumbersome election machinery can effectively suffocate the right of association, the promotion of political ideas and programs of political action, and the right to vote. The totality of Ohio's requirements has those effects. It is unnecessary to decide whether Ohio has an interest, "compelling" or not, in abridging those rights, because "the men who drafted our Bill of Rights did all the 'balancing' that was to be done in this field." Appellees would imply that "no kind of speech is to be protected if the Government can assert an interest of sufficient weight to induce this Court to uphold its abridgment." I reject that suggestion. * * *

FIVE PERCENT HURDLE CASE

Constitutional Court (Czech Republic).
N. 88/1997 Sb.[m]

* * * [In] 1996, the political party DU filed a constitutional complaint against the [decisions of the Central Electoral Commission and the Constitutional Court of the Czech Republic, on the validity of elections]. The petitioning party holds the view that the contested norms of the Electoral Act contravene [the] Czech Constitution and likewise infringe the constitutionally guaranteed fundamental rights enshrined in [the] Charter of Fundamental Rights and Basic Freedoms [among which is] the principle of a universal, equal, and direct right to vote by secret ballot and on the basis of proportional representation, * * * the equal right to stand for election to all citizens of the Czech Republic who have attained 21 years of age and have the right to vote, [the right of] access to any elective or other public office and [the] right to participate in the administration of public affairs either directly or through the free election of their representatives. * * *

[The Court held:]

m. Available in translation at html>. <www.concourt.cz/angl_verze/doc/p–25–96.-

The fact that DU did not receive any seat in the Assembly of Deputies in the most recent election despite receiving 170,000 votes can undoubtedly be ascribed to the direct effect of the Electoral Act provision concerning the five-percent closing clause * * *

[The first democratic Constitution of Czechoslovakia required proportional representation, and the electoral system was purely proportional.] As for the 1920 Constitution, one can scarcely deduce from it any binding consequences for the conception of the Electoral Act, issued on the basis of the Constitution of 1993. The period after World War I was that of a victorious crusade for proportional representation across Europe. Only later did the European states gain experience with the character and function of proportional representation. At that time a limitation clause was neither conceived of in theory nor implemented in practice. Therefore the 1920 Constitution's formulation on proportional representation is * * * neutral and does not per definicionem contain a priori either a limitation clause or a prohibition thereof. It was only the experience of European parliaments before World War II, and after it as well, that led to the search for a system that would limit an excessive splintering of the political spectrum in Parliament. It was the experience not only of the Imperial Assembly of the Weimar Republic or of the Czechoslovak First Republic, but also of France, quite decidedly in the Fourth Republic (1946–1958), which confirmed that excessive diversification in the Assembly's composition and unrestricted proportional representation may become a tool of political de-stabilization and an element destructive of a constitutional state.

The theoretical re-evaluation of the proportional representation principle and a change in the political practice of contemporary representative democracies confirm the overwhelming opinion that, provided there are serious reasons therefore, the introduction of certain measures limiting the scope of the proportional representation principle is not in contradiction with the character of the electoral system * * * as one of proportional representation, if and to the extent that such provisions do not fundamentally limit proportional representation. Over time democratic states have introduced the proportional representation system, furnished with a five-percent or a three-percent clause, without considering that they thereby devalued the principle of proportional representation. In this respect, the Constitution of the Czech Republic does not draw upon the 1920 Constitution; rather upon the theoretical foundation and institutional solution of contemporary democratic states which make use of proportional representation in a more or less limited form. * * *

According to DU, the requirement of direct election was violated by the allocation of seats to candidates of parties which did not gain the number of votes necessary for them to be elected. To determine this issue, it is necessary to elucidate the concept, "direct election". The principle that elections should be direct is meant to ensure a direct relation between the votes of the electorate and the resulting filling of seats, a relation excluding a further decision-maker that would select a Deputy at its discretion. An example of just such a decision-maker would, for example, be electors chosen by voters with the intention that an electoral college decide who should fill the elective function.

* * * Therefore, the electoral procedure must be adjusted so that every vote cast may be ascribed to specific persons. The principle of direct election * * * does not prohibit election on the basis of mass candidate lists * * * because, although the candidates for the upcoming elections are selected by another decision-making body (political party), this selection occurs prior to the elections themselves * * * and can be understood as—sui generis—a choice offered to the voters. As far then as actual voting by the voters is concerned, for an election to be considered direct, it is sufficient if the stipulated order of candidates is known to the voters in advance and if each vote cast can be ascribed to specific, clearly identifiable persons, who are standing as candidates to the elected office. This condition is met even if, on the basis of the five-percent clause, a particular party acquires the right to an additional seat or seats in excess of what strictly proportional representation would allow. Even in this case, however, seats must be filled by those candidates whom their political party duly inscribed on the list and who the voters could expect when voting might possibly gain a seat if the party, for which the candidates stood, acquires the right to an additional seat as a result of other parties' failure to meet the five-percent requirement. * * *

A common denominator of DU's objections, and at the same time its most serious objection, is the reference to the violation [of the right of] access, under equal conditions, to any elective or other public office, and the reference to the violation of * * * the principle of equality of the voting right.

The principle of equality of the voting right can be considered from two basic perspectives: the first consists in the comparison of the numerical weight of individual votes * * *. The equality of the voting right requires that in the count all the votes are of equal value, that is, of the same numerical weight (quantitative equality) and consequence, so that the count would enable an exact numerical differentiation of the electorate, that is, an exact numerical "identification" of support given to individual candidate lists. The second perspective on equality of the voting right conceives of the equality of votes in light of the democratic principle, that is * * * a claim to a proportionate number of seats, that is one corresponding to the proportion of votes cast. * * *

[A] certain limitation upon the differentiation during seat allocation is inevitable and, therefore, permissible. [It results] from the practical impossibility of appropriately expressing an exact proportion * * *. Nevertheless, there may exist other significant grounds for placing restrictions upon equality * * *. While the purpose of voting is, undoubtedly, to differentiate the electorate, the objective of elections is not, however, to obtain a mere expression of political preference by individual voters and a mere differentiated mirror image of opinion streams and the voters' political positions. Since it is the people who exercise state power * * * and since [this] presupposes the capacity to adopt decisions, elections * * * must have * * * the capacity to adopt such decisions on the basis of the majority's will. To base the composition of the Assembly of Deputies on a strict proportional image of voting results might give rise to a political representation fragmented into a large number of small groups promoting diverse interests, which would make the formation of a majority much more difficult if not entirely impossible.

The principle of differentiation and the principle of integration must come into conflict at the stage of the electoral process where seats are allocated * * *. Therefore, * * * it is acceptable to incorporate into the electoral mechanism itself certain integrative stimuli * * *. After the bad experiences with the excessive fragmentation of parliamentary composition, the European states * * * adopted as well integrative stimuli, in particular, the limitation clause, which in most cases is five percent. It is generally recognized that the legislature has the right to * * * treat political parties in a disparate manner, if such is absolutely necessary to ensure integration character of elections * * *. The existence of the limitation clause must * * * be made conditional on there being serious grounds * * *. It must be noted that any increase in * * * the limitation clause cannot be unlimited, so that, for example, a ten-percent clause could already be considered such an intrusion upon the proportional system as to threaten its democratic substance. [T]he principle of minimal intervention * * * in proportion to the prescribed objective applies to the limitation clause too. For this reason, even the need for electoral limitation must be construed strictly.

From this perspective, no fixed value may be assigned to the * * * limitation clause, rather it is relative and always must depend on the specific proportion of forces in the country * * *. In Germany, for instance, some * * * asserted that, due to stability which the country has reached over time, the right of smaller, especially new, parties to obtain seats in the Assembly is threatened by the clause, to the degree that it has already lost its indispensable character. In contrast * * * the * * * majority object[s] that the danger of fragmentation is still very real because the current stabilized system is * * * also a result of the clause * * *.

A comparison of the limitation clause with the majority system speaks in favor of the limitation clause. Constitutional courts unconditionally conceive of the majority electoral system as democratic, despite the fact that the political views of a large percent of the voters are not represented * * *. [Solely] the votes cast for the winning candidate represent success whereas the other votes "fall out of the picture". * * *

[Thus] the five-percent limitation clause may not a limine be rejected as an unconstitutional limitation of the equal right to vote. [What] remains to be considered is whether in the case of the Czech Republic the five-percent clause is the minimal measure * * *. As is well known, the political spectrum of the Czech Republic is the result of a relatively short development and is not as yet quite clearly structured or visibly stabilized. A characteristic feature of all Czech parliamentary elections so far * * * has been the marked splintering of political forces into a large number of political parties * * *. Even though the number * * * fell to 20, the election results demonstrate that, were proportional representation to be respected in full, at least three other political parties would have had to join the three presently-governing coalition parties in order to form a governing coalition representing even a frail majority. * * * Experience with similar coalitions, in particular, in the fourth French Republic justify fears and skepticism. Therefore, if a certain distortion of proportionality in political representation, resulting from the five-percent clause, does not in its overall effect constitute a disproportion which would justify doubts about the democratic nature of the political representation, the Constitutional Court has no choice but to reject DU's objections. * * *

ALL GERMANY ELECTION CASE

Federal Constitutional Court (Germany).
82 BVerfGE 322 (1990).

[Three small political parties, one of which was the newly formed socialist party in East Germany, wanted to participate in the first postunification nationwide election and complained that various election-law hurdles violated the Basic Law. In addition, candidates complained that such election laws violated their constitutional rights. The Court held that the applications and constitutional complaints were well founded.]

The principle of election equality * * * is * * * to be understood in the sense of a strict and formal equality because of the connection with the egalitarian democratic principle. The democratic order set up by the [constitution] thus, in the realm of elections, weighs votes of all citizens of the State equally without regard to the differences existing between them. Therefore, differences in the computed value as well as, in principle and for an election of proportional representation, differences in the effective value of the electors' votes is unconstitutional.

As there are primarily parties which unite the citizens organisationally for the elections into political operational units, it follows from the formalised equality requirement in the realm of elections that the principle of equal opportunities of competition for the political parties and electoral alliances is also to be understood in the same formal sense. The right of the parties to equality of opportunities in the elections follows from their constitutional status * * * and from the importance attributed by the constitution to the freedom of party formation and from the multi-party principle in a free democracy. It controls the election procedure in the same way as preparation for the election. Democracy cannot function if the parties do not enter the election contest in principle under the same legal conditions. When the legislator regulates the area of formation of political will in elections in a manner which can change the equality of opportunities of political parties and electoral alliances, especially narrow boundaries are set for its creative latitude; in principle, any different treatment of parties or electoral groupings is, by virtue of the Constitution, denied.

It therefore follows from the principles of formal electoral equality and equality of opportunities of parties that only a narrow margin of appreciation remains for the legislator in the regulation of elections * * *. Any differentiations always need a pressing reason * * *. To secure the functional capability of the representatives * * * has repeatedly been regarded * * * as a reason of sufficiently pressing character * * *. The principle peculiar to the system of proportional representation, to portray the political will of the electorate as closely as possible to reality * * *, can result in the splitting up of the elected representatives of the people into many small groups, which would impede or prevent the formation of a stable majority. Insofar as it is required to secure the capability of parliament to operate and decide, the legislator may for that reason weigh the effective value of the votes differently in a proportional representation election.

For the sake of this objective, the legislator is permitted, in principle, to secure the functional capability of the representatives * * * by a barrier clause. In this regard, a quorum of 5% is as a rule not objectionable under constitutional law. However, the Court emphasised early on that the reconcilability of a barrier clause with the principle of equality in elections cannot be abstractly assessed once and for all. A provision of electoral law could be justified in one state at a certain point in time and not in another state at another point in time * * *. [An] assessment of the barrier clause which diverges from the traditional one can afterwards prove to be necessary—even if only temporarily—if circumstances within a state change substantially * * *.

If the legislator finds such special circumstances, he must take them into account. [He] is free in principle to forego a barrier clause, to reduce its limit or to take other appropriate measures. If he regards it as advisable to adhere to a barrier clause of 5% but to mitigate its effects, the means * * * must * * * be reconcilable with the constitution and especially satisfy the principles of electoral law equality and equality of opportunities of parties. * * * Rather, a requirement can only survive constitutional scrutiny if it operates neutrally with regard to the election contest of the parties. This neutrality can also require that the legislator may not, in connection with barrier clauses, ignore distortions of the election contest which are caused by law and which present themselves as special circumstances in the sense mentioned.

* * * The first election for the whole of Germany takes place only a year after the peaceful revolution in the German Democratic Republic. Between the restoration of an electoral area of the whole of Germany, which unites two territories separated for 40 years and the day of the first election for the whole of Germany there will be just three months. This development leaves a number of parties no sufficient possibility to * * * present themselves * * * with the prospect of success and to solicit the votes of electors. * * * [Therefore,] a 5% barrier clause applied to the whole electoral area burdens parties which were until now active only on the territory of the German Democratic Republic much more heavily than the parties which were only active in the Federal Republic of Germany. * * *

A further special circumstance * * * arises from the fact that parties and political alliances * * * could only organise themselves and become active since the revolutionary change in the German Democratic Republic. In comparison to the parties which had been active over a long period, their organisational, personnel and financial fundamentals of operation are therefore not so fully developed; and only a short time is available to them for the development of their programme and their collaboration with other political groups. * * * .

Accordingly, the regime under discussion is to be examined to see whether it removes, in a way that cannot be faulted in constitutional law, the special difficulty * * * for political parties * * * of the widening of the electoral area and, connected with that, the increased exclusionary effect of a barrier clause of 5% * * *.

This question is to be answered in the negative. * * * Only some of the smaller parties receive, from the start, a chance to participate * * * in spite of non-attainment of the quorum. In the abstract, the possibility of combination of lists is available to all parties * * *. But electoral law must orientate itself not to abstractly invented cases, but to political reality. If one takes this into account, the number of possible combinations of lists is reduced drastically. * * *. Therefore * * * only a very small part of the parties * * * has any real chance of finding a partner which could help to overcome the 5% clause. That violates the equality of opportunities of the parties. * * *

It does not follow * * * that the legislator is constrained by virtue of the Constitution to abandon a barrier clause regime altogether in the first election * * *. Certainly a general lowering * * * does not come into consideration.

* * * A strict and formal equality corresponding with the democratic principle can only be restored in the face of the unequal starting point existing here by attaching formal equality to the actual reference area. The fact that * * * in the one reference area more votes must be cast to attain this share of the votes than in the other does not lead to an infringement of equality if—as here—the reference areas are for their part formed according to the standpoint of equality.

The simple regionalisation of a barrier clause * * * certainly does not yet satisfy the requirements of equality of opportunities. On its own it cannot sufficiently make up for the different starting conditions for this first election * * *. They exist [because] some of them are * * * in a position in the election campaign to rely on resources which could build them up in the time of the party dictatorship * * * whilst others, which were suppressed and persecuted by this dictatorship, were only able to begin to get organised for the first time after its overthrow. * * * It needs to be compensated for.

Notes and Questions

1. *Whose rights?* In *Williams v. Rhodes* the USSC addressed whether the access of parties to the ballot is governed by the constitutional right to vote or by the right to equality, that is, the equal opportunity of parties. Does this make a difference? What if a voter wants his or her voice to count in the process and thus wants access to be eased by law?

2. *Who decides?* A dissenting opinion in *Williams v. Rhodes* argues that legislatures, and not courts, should ultimately determine who has access to the ballot and under what conditions. Does it make a difference whether elections are held for an electoral college, as in the U.S., or to form a

parliament, as in Germany? If the constitution should protect minorities, what are the implications with regard to access rights?

3. *Affirmative measures.* If there is no barrier to ballot access or if the barrier is low, are equal opportunities automatic? The Constitution of Uganda states that: "The state shall ensure gender balance and fair representation of marginalised groups on all constitutional and other bodies." Is this compatible with the idea of general representation? In France, the law guarantees a certain percentage of positions on the ballot in local elections to women, and the Constitutional Council upheld a modified version of the law. (See the discussion in Chapter 6 Sections D and E.) Though a strict quota of male and female candidates was found unconstitutional (98–407 DC of 14 Jan. 1999), gender quotas in local elections remain part of French law, after Parliament amended the Constitution to provide for equality in the candidacy requirement. Also consider the *Declaration and Platform for Action from the United Nations 4th World Conference on Women at Beijing,* at U.N. Doc. A/CONF.177/20, (1995):

> Despite the widespread movement towards democratization in most countries, women are largely underrepresented at most levels of government * * * and have made little progress in attaining political power * * *. Globally, only 10 per cent of the members of legislative bodies and a lower percentage of ministerial positions are now held by women. Indeed, some countries, including those that are undergoing fundamental political, economic and social changes, have seen a significant decrease in the number of women represented * * *. Although women make up at least half of the electorate in almost all countries and have attained the right to vote and hold office in almost all States Members of the United Nations, women continue to be seriously underrepresented as candidates for public office. The traditional working patterns of many political parties and government structures continue to be barriers to women's participation in public life. Women may be discouraged from seeking political office by discriminatory attitudes and practices, family and child-care responsibilities, and the high cost of seeking and holding public office. Women in politics and decision-making positions in Governments and legislative bodies contribute to redefining political priorities, placing new items on the political agenda that reflect and address women's gender-specific concerns, values and experiences, and providing new perspectives on mainstream political issues. * * *

> Actions to be taken by Governments: (a) Commit themselves to establishing the goal of gender balance in governmental bodies and committees, as well as in public administrative entities, and in the judiciary, including, inter alia, setting specific targets and implementing measures to substantially increase the number of women with a view to achieving equal representation of women and men, if necessary through positive action, in all governmental and public administration positions; (b) Take measures, including, where appropriate, in electoral systems that encourage political parties to integrate women in elective and non-elective public positions in the same proportion and at the same levels as men; * * * (g) Encourage greater involvement of indigenous women in decision-making at all levels; (h) Encourage and, where appropriate, ensure that government-funded organizations adopt non-discriminatory policies and practices in order to increase the number and raise the position of women in their organizations; * * *.

Can nation-states implement the U.N. recommendations from Beijing without violating their constitutions? Or would they enhance the quality of constitutional culture by doing so? How can equality and pluralism, as well as freedoms of speech and association, be respected to ensure the participation of minorities?

D.2. RIGHTS TO PRESENCE IN PUBLIC

Democratic activity, be it by citizens or by parties, relies on the opportunity to present one's views to a larger public. Therefore, constitutional protection of democracy may extend to rights of access to such opportunities, including the media.

RADICAL GROUPS CASE

Federal Constitutional Court (Germany).
47 BVerfGE 198 (1978).

[In various election campaigns, radio and television stations in three German states (*Länder*) denied campaign broadcasting time to three radical left-wing parties. The stations declined to carry the parties' campaign ads because of their revolutionary rhetoric calling for the destruction of the existing political order. Administrative courts sustained the actions of the broadcasters. The affected parties, all with communist political persuasions, challenged these judicial decisions.]

The constitutional complaints are valid.

1. The contested decisions are predicated on the fact that the complainants constitute political parties * * * within the meaning of * * * [c]onstitutional and party law. According to the law, political parties represent associations of citizens who permanently or for an extended period influence the formation of the political will * * * and who wish to take part in representing the people in * * * parliament if the totality of their [activity] particularly [as measured by] the size of the party, the stability of its organization, its membership, and public prominence is sufficient to underscore the seriousness of these goals. This definition harmonizes with * * * the Constitution * * *.

The complainants [display all the characteristics to meet that definition]. The fact that [they] were possibly engaged in pursuing unconstitutional goals, especially the abolition of the parliamentary system, does not strip them of their character as political parties. [The Constitution] states that [political] parties which, by reason of their aims or the behaviour of their adherents, seek to impair or to abolish the free democratic basic order or to endanger the existence of the Federal Republic are unconstitutional. This phraseology reveals that a political organization's status as a political party is to be judged independently of its constitutional or unconstitutional nature. If constitutionality were an essential characteristic of political parties, there would be no need for [a section of the Constitution] authorizing proceedings against unconstitutional parties. * * *

I. While the right of all parties to equal opportunity is not expressly mentioned in the Constitution, [it] may be inferred form the significance associated with the multiparty principle * * * and the freedom to establish political parties. * * * This basic right [to equality] extends not only to the election itself but also, since [elections] are influenced by measures of public authority, to campaign propaganda [the dissemination of which] is so necessary for electioneering in modern mass democracy. * * *

Thus the principle of equal opportunity bars radio and television stations from denying broadcasting time to political parties admitted to participation in the electoral process on the ground that [these] parties are too insignificant or even harmful. On the other hand, the equal opportunity principle does not bar [these stations] form differentiating between parties in allotting broadcasting time so long as they grant small and new parties adequate airtime.

[Another] question raised by the constitutional complaints is whether the principle of equal opportunity is violated where broadcasting stations, after screening ads submitted by political parties, refuse to run them on the ground that the messages [conveyed] have nothing to do with the election or are either anticonstitutional or just plain criminal.

2. The principle of equal opportunity demands that every political party receive fundamentally the same opportunity * * * maintaining an equal chance in the competition for electoral votes. * * *

3. Radio and television stations have no right to refuse broadcasting [time to a party] merely because its election ad contains anticonstitutional ideas. This [view] stands opposed to the provisions of [party prohibition procedure] as well as to the [spirit] of the Constitution's principle of equal opportunity.

(a) The principle of equal opportunity bars public authority from any differentiation of treatment among parties * * * unless justified by a special, that is, cogent, reason. * * * Even in the case of political parties whose goal is to destroy the democratic state and to abolish at least in part the constitutional order * * *, and which, if they were to win seats in parliament, would constitute a political danger, even then radio and television stations are not authorized to meet this danger by refusing to broadcast election campaign ads * * *. The unwritten political party privilege found in [the Constitution] will not permit such far-reaching station control over the contents of election campaign messages. * * *

The jurisdictional monopoly of the Federal Constitutional Court categorically precludes administrative action against the existence of a political party, regardless of how anticonstitutional the party's program may be. To be sure, the possibility of political opposition against such a party exists; however, [the party] must be free to act politically without in any way being impeded. The Constitution tolerates the dangers inherent in the activities of such a political party until it is declared unconstitutional. * * * This [principle] must also be respected by radio and television stations.

(b) * * * [Thus even] a violation of a general criminal law must be evident if a [broadcasting station] is to refuse an * * * ad. * * * This will always be the case whenever political parties encourage, also indirectly, the commission of criminal acts. * * *

[This] Court has repeatedly ruled that the participation of political parties in elections represents the core of their activity. * * * A denial of airtime to political parties without sufficient reason is a rather severe violation [of the Constitution]. Such a denial would curtail the process of freely forming the political will [on which] political elections [depend]; citizens would find it difficult or even impossible to exercise their entrusted right to decide on the merits of political party programs. * * *

Notes and Questions

1. *Public and Private Media.* In Canada, a complaint regarding the participation of small political parties in televised election debates was rejected because the television station was not considered to be bound by basic rights. *Trieger v. Canadian Broadcasting Corp.*, [1988] 54 D.L.R. (4th ser.) 143. Should there be a right to such participation if the state operates the station? Should constitutional protection extend to private stations? Does the government have a duty to regulate time and appearance on television? The Canadian Supreme Court, in *Thomson Newspapers Co. v. Canada,* [1998] 1 S.C.R. 877, upheld a rule that prohibited newspapers from publishing poll results three days before an election:

> There were other measures which would have achieved the government's purpose equally well or even better than the publication ban, and which would have been far less intrusive to the freedom of expression. * * * This is a complete ban on political information at a crucial time in the electoral process. [It] interferes with the rights of voters who want access to the most timely polling information available, and with the rights of the media and pollsters who want to provide it. It is an interference with the flow of information pertaining to the most important democratic duty which most Canadians will undertake in their lives: their choice as to who will govern them. Such a polling ban also sends the message that the media in their role as a reporter of information, and not as an advertiser, can be muzzled by the government. Rather than approaching the problem of inaccurate polls as a question of too little information, or added incentives for preventing the publication of inaccurate polls, the government constrains the range of evaluations that a voter is permitted to make in fulfilling their sacred democratic function as a citizen. It justifies such a measure on the basis that some indeterminate number of voters might be unable to spot an inaccurate poll result and might rely to a significant degree on the error, thus perverting their electoral choice.

The dissent by Justice Gonthier referred to political theory to justify the ban on polls: "Conversation, as theorists from Tarde to Habermas have argued, is fundamental to the construction of a democratic public sphere, and polls do not seem to generate interpersonal communication. In a way, polls make many political discussions superfluous, since they give the illusion that the public has already spoken in a definitive manner." Do you agree?

2. *Single issues.* The European Commission of Human Rights, in *Bowman v. United Kingdom*, 22 E.H.R.R. C.D. 13 (1996), considered legislation that restricted "single-issue" campaigning by individuals other than electoral candidates. A woman had been charged for distributing leaflets outlining the abortion views of three electoral candidates. The Commission held that this was an unjustified violation of freedom of expression. With regard to the right to vote, it wrote:

> The Commission has had regard to whether the expression of opinion or information on "single issues" addressed by individuals or groups with strongly-held views may operate in particular constituencies so as to "distort" election results. It has previously considered * * * that one of the legitimate objectives of national electoral systems is to channel currents of thought so as to promote the emergence of a sufficiently clear and coherent political will. * * * The Government has not, however, produced any argument to the effect that "single issue" campaigning [as in this] case would distract voters from the political platforms which are the basis of national party campaigns to such a degree as would hinder the electoral process.

D.3.   FINANCING OF POLITICAL ACTIVITIES

The dissemination of political opinions in public depends largely on financial resources, particularly needed by parties and candidates to capture votes. Constitutional challenges to financing schemes thus raise issues of equality as well as the nature of the democratic process in free-market societies in general and in the media in particular.

BUCKLEY v. VALEO

Supreme Court (United States).
424 U.S. 1 (1976).

[The Federal Election Campaign Act limited political contributions to candidates and spending by candidates and requires committees to keep detailed financial records and to file quarterly reports with the Federal Election Commission, which was created by that law.]

Per Curiam:

* * * The intricate statutory scheme adopted * * * to regulate federal election campaigns includes restrictions on political contributions and expenditures that apply broadly to all phases of and all participants in the election process. The major contribution and expenditure limitations in the Act prohibit individuals from contributing more than $25,000 in a single year or more than $1,000 to any single candidate for an election campaign and from spending more than $1,000 a year "relative to a clearly identified candidate." Other provisions restrict a candidate's use of personal and family resources in his campaign and limit the over-all amount that can be spent by a candidate in campaigning for federal office. The constitutional power of Congress to regulate federal elections is well established and is not questioned by any of the parties in this case. Thus, the critical constitutional questions presented here go * * * to whether the * * * legislation * * * interferes with

[constitutional] freedoms or invidiously discriminates against nonincumbent candidates and minor parties * * *.

The Act's contribution and expenditure limitations operate in an area of the most fundamental restore * * * activities. Discussion of public issues and debate on the qualifications of candidates are integral to the operation of the system of government established by our Constitution. [It] affords the broadest protection to such political expression in order "to assure [the] unfettered interchange of ideas for the bringing about of political and social changes desired by the people." Although [constitutional] protections are not confined to "the exposition of ideas," there is practically universal agreement that a major purpose of [the Constitution] was to protect the "free discussion of governmental affairs, . . . of course includ[ing] discussions of candidates. . . ." This no more than reflects our "profound national commitment to the principle that debate on public issues should be uninhibited, robust, and wide-open". In a republic where the people are sovereign, the ability of the citizenry to make informed choices among candidates for office is essential, for the identities of those who are elected will inevitably shape the course that we follow as a nation. * * *

We cannot share the view that the present Act's contribution and expenditure limitations are comparable to the restrictions on conduct upheld in [other cases]. The expenditure of money simply cannot be equated with such conduct as destruction of a draft card. Some forms of communication made possible by the giving and spending of money involve speech alone, some involve conduct primarily, and some involve a combination of the two. Yet this Court has never suggested that the dependence of a communication on the expenditure of money operates itself to introduce a nonspeech element or to reduce the exacting scrutiny required by the [Constitution]. * * *

The interests served by the Act include restricting the voices of people and interest groups who have money to spend and reducing the over-all scope of federal election campaigns. Although the Act does not focus on the ideas * * *, it is aimed in part at equalizing the relative ability of all voters to affect electoral outcomes by placing a ceiling on expenditures for political expression. * * * [It] is beyond dispute that the interest in regulating the alleged "conduct" of giving or spending money "arises in some measure because the communication allegedly integral to the conduct is itself thought to be harmful."

The Act's contribution and expenditure limitations also impinge on protected associational freedoms. Making a contribution, like joining a political party, serves to affiliate a person with a candidate. In addition, it enables like-minded persons to pool their resources in furtherance of common political goals. The Act's contribution ceilings thus limit one important means of associating with a candidate or committee, but leave the contributor free to become a member of any political association and to assist personally * * * on behalf of candidates, [and] permit associations and candidates to aggregate large sums of money * * *. By contrast, the Act * * * precludes most associations from effectively amplifying the voice of their adherents, the original basis for the recognition * * * freedom of association. [This] "is simultaneously an interference with the freedom of [their] adherents."

In sum, * * * the Act's * * * expenditure ceilings impose significantly more severe restrictions on protected freedoms of political expression and association than do its limitations on financial contributions.

* * * It is unnecessary to look beyond the Act's primary purpose—to limit the actuality and appearance of corruption resulting from large individual financial contributions—in order to find a constitutionally sufficient justification for the $1,000 contribution limitation. Under a system of private financing of elections, a candidate lacking immense personal or family wealth must depend on financial contributions from others * * *. The increasing importance of the communications media and sophisticated mass-mailing and polling operations to effective campaigning make the raising of large sums of money an ever more essential ingredient of an effective candidacy. To the extent that large contributions are given to secure a political quid pro quo from current and potential office holders, the integrity of our system of representative democracy is undermined. Although the scope of such pernicious practices can never be reliably ascertained, * * * deeply disturbing examples * * * demonstrate that the problem is not an illusory one.

Of almost equal concern * * * is the impact of the appearance of corruption stemming from public awareness of the opportunities for abuse inherent in a regime of large individual financial contributions. [This] Court found that the danger to "fair and effective government" posed by partisan political conduct on the part of federal employees charged with administering the law was a sufficiently important concern to justify broad restrictions on the employees' right of partisan political association. Here, as there, Congress could legitimately conclude that the avoidance of the appearance of improper influence "is also critical . . . if confidence in the system of representative Government is not to be eroded to a disastrous extent."

* * * The Act's $1,000 contribution limitation focuses precisely on the problem of large campaign contributions * * * while leaving persons free to engage in independent political expression, to associate actively through volunteering their services, and to assist to a limited but nonetheless substantial extent * * * with financial resources. Significantly, the Act's contribution limitations in themselves do not undermine to any material degree the potential for robust and effective discussion of candidates and campaign issues by individual citizens, associations, the institutional press, candidates, and political parties. We find that, under the rigorous standard of review * * *, the weighty interests served by restricting the size of financial contributions to political candidates are sufficient to justify the limited effect upon * * * freedoms * * *.

[But the] Act's expenditure ceilings impose direct and substantial restraints on the quantity of political speech. The most drastic * * * restricts individuals and groups, including political parties that fail to place a candidate on the ballot, to an expenditure of $1,000 "relative to a clearly identified candidate during a calendar year." * * *. Other expenditure ceilings limit spending by candidates, * * *, their campaigns, * * *, and political parties in connection with election campaigns * * *. It is clear that a primary effect of these expenditure limitations is to restrict the quantity of campaign speech by individuals, groups, and candidates. The restrictions, while neutral as to the ideas expressed, limit political expression "at the core of our electoral process and of [constitutional] freedoms." * * * We find that the governmental interest in preventing corruption and the appearance of corruption is inadequate to justify [this].

First, assuming, arguendo, that large independent expenditures pose the same dangers of * * * quid pro quo arrangements as do large contributions, [the law] does not provide an answer that sufficiently relates to the elimination of those dangers. Unlike the contribution limitations' total ban, [it] prevents only some large expenditures. So long as persons and groups eschew expenditures that in express terms advocate the election or defeat of a clearly identified candidate, they are free to spend as much as they want * * *. It would naively underestimate the ingenuity and resourcefulness of persons and groups desiring to buy influence to believe that they would have much difficulty devising expenditures that skirted the restriction on express advocacy of election or defeat, but nevertheless benefited the candidate's campaign. [No] substantial societal interest would be served by [this].

Second, * * * the independent advocacy restricted * * * does not presently appear to pose dangers of real or apparent corruption comparable to those identified with large campaign contributions. * * * The ceiling on personal expenditures by candidates on their own behalf * * * imposes a substantial restraint on the ability of persons to engage in protected * * * expression. The candidate, no less than any other person, has a * * * right to engage in the discussion of public issues and vigorously and tirelessly to advocate his own election and the election of other candidates. Indeed, it is of particular importance that candidates have the unfettered opportunity to make their views known so that the electorate may intelligently evaluate the candidates' personal qualities and their positions on vital public issues before choosing among them on election day. Mr. Justice Brandeis' observation that, in our country "public discussion is a political duty," applies with special force to candidates for public office. [The] ceiling on personal expenditures by a candidate in furtherance of his own candidacy thus clearly and directly interferes with constitutionally protected freedoms.

* * * The ancillary interest in equalizing the relative financial resources of candidates competing for elective office, therefore, provides the sole relevant rationale for [the] expenditure ceiling. That interest is clearly not sufficient to justify the provision's infringement of fundamental * * * rights. First, the limitation may fail to promote financial equality among candidates. A candidate who spends less of his personal resources on his campaign may nonetheless outspend his rival as a result of more successful fundraising efforts. Indeed, a candidate's personal wealth may impede his efforts to persuade others that he needs their financial contributions or volunteer efforts to conduct an effective campaign. Second, and more fundamentally, the [Constitution] simply can-

not tolerate [this] restriction upon the freedom of a candidate to speak without legislative limit on behalf of his own candidacy. We therefore hold [it to be] unconstitutional. * * *

[Furthermore,] no governmental interest that has been suggested is sufficient to justify the restriction.* * * The campaign expenditure ceilings appear to be designed primarily to serve the governmental interests in reducing the allegedly skyrocketing costs of political campaigns. * * * [But] the mere growth in the cost of federal election campaigns * * * provides no basis for governmental restrictions * * *. [The Constitution] denies government the power to determine that spending to promote one's political views is wasteful, excessive, or unwise. In the free society ordained by our Constitution, it is not the government, but the people * * * who must retain control over the quantity and range of debate on public issues in a political campaign. For these reasons, we hold that [this rule] is constitutionally invalid.

* * * [The] disclosure requirements impose no ceiling on campaign-related activities. But we have repeatedly found that compelled disclosure * * * can seriously infringe on privacy of association and belief. * * * [A] strict test is necessary because compelled disclosure has the potential for substantially infringing the exercise of [constitutional] rights. [Yet] there are governmental interests sufficiently important to outweigh the possibility of infringement, particularly when the "free functioning of our national institutions" is involved. [They fall into three categories.] First, disclosure provides the electorate with information "as to where political campaign money comes from and how it is spent by the candidate" in order to aid the voters in evaluating those who seek federal office. It allows voters to place each candidate in the political spectrum more precisely * * *. The sources of a candidate's financial support also alert the voter to the interests to which a candidate is most likely to be responsive * * *. Second, disclosure requirements deter actual corruption and avoid the appearance of corruption by exposing large contributions and expenditures to the light of publicity. * * * A public armed with information about a candidate's most generous supporters is better able to detect any post-election special favors that may be given in return. And * * * Congress could reasonably conclude that full disclosure during an election campaign tends "to prevent the corrupt use of money to affect elections." [As Brandeis said,] "Publicity is justly commended as a remedy for social and industrial diseases. Sunlight is said to be the best of disinfectants; electric light the most efficient policeman." Third, and not least significant, recordkeeping, reporting, and disclosure requirements are an essential means of gathering the data necessary to detect violations of the contribution limitations described above.

* * * We are not unmindful that the damage done by disclosure to the associational interests of the minor parties and their members and to supporters of independents could be significant. These movements are less likely to have a sound financial base, and thus are more vulnerable to fall-offs in contributions. * * * [Yet in the case before us, and on] this record, the substantial public interest in disclosure identified by the legislative history of this Act outweighs the harm generally alleged.

TRADE UNIONS' POLITICAL
CONTRIBUTIONS CASE

Constitutional Court (South Korea).
11–2 KCCR 555, 95 Hun–Ma 154 (1999).[n]

[A labor union filed constitutional complaints against a statute's ban on labor unions' political contributions.]

Today, individuals can realize their political identities through groups that synthesize, prioritize, and reconcile their various interests and desires. Interest groups and political parties are indispensable elements of democratic opinion-making. Social organizations are second to political parties in acting as bridges between the state and the people. The statute is based on the premise that a labor organization must perform only its regular task of 'improvement of working conditions' through collective bargaining and agreement and cannot engage in any political activity. Such legislative intent make the meaning and substantive availability of political freedom vacuous. The statute allows political contributions by other social organizations, especially management, but bans political contributions by labor unions. It is intended to restrain labor unions' influence on political parties and labor unions' participation in political discourse. Such scheme can undermine the reconciliation of social interests between labor and management, and bias the political discourse against labor.

The legislative purposes of preventing the draining of labor union budgets or excessive financial burdens on union members do not justify the ban, either. Weak finance of a labor union merely means that the 'balance of power' and the 'equality in weapons' are broken against labor union while labor and management, two private organizations, are determining working conditions under the principle of private autonomy. Therefore, the fear of weak finance cannot justify the statute. The statute is further unjust because the state, through the statute, even further worsens the relative position of labor by regulating political contributions adversely to labor. 'Independence' required of labor unions does not mean political neutrality, or neutrality in religion or other values. It only means independence of the organization in fact and independence of the decision-making structure in law. Therefore, the workers, who are in the same social and economic positions, may find themselves a common political objective and, through union activities, not only improve working conditions but also participate in the formation of the people's political judgment without compromising their independence as long as they are acting out of their free wills and according to the union's organizing principles. In the end, given the meaning of political freedom guaranteed by the Constitution, 'prevention of politicization of labor union' and 'protecting labor union's finance' are not legitimate legislative purposes. [They] are not compelling interests [and

n. Quoted summary available at Eng.html#2–12>.
<www.ccourt.go.kr/english/Decision-

the statute] violates the complainant's freedom of expression and association and is unconstitutional.

The provision is also violative of the principle of equality. The role of social organizations in the people's political decision-making is equally applicable to labor unions. The statute * * * allows political contributions to interest groups such as corporations * * * or the association of management entities * * *. We cannot help but finding that the statute discriminates against labor unions in the area of political activities.

PARTY FINANCE II CASE
Federal Constitutional Court (Germany).
8 BVerfGE 51 (1958).

[Laws permitted citizens to deduct from their net taxable income a portion of their donations to political parties. A state (*Land*) government challenged the constitutionality of these deductions, claiming they favored political parties backed by wealthy individuals and large corporations.]

II.   * * * By declaring donations to political parties deductible, the federal legislature renounces that part of income or corporate tax which would otherwise accrue. * * * This renunciation benefits political parties. Recognizing donations to political parties as deductible expenses means, therefore, that the government indirectly participates, by the amount of revenue it loses, in financing parties. When the legislature exercises its authority it is bound by higher constitutional principles. The challenged provision would be unconstitutional if the Constitution prohibited any direct or indirect governmental financial support of political parties as petitioner claims. But this is not the case. * * *

[The challenged provisions of the tax laws,] however, violate the basic right of political parties to equal opportunity. * * *

2.   The challenged provisions permit every taxpayer * * * to donate money to any political party and to enjoy * * * deductibility * * *. According to its wording, the regulation gives every political party the same chance to obtain donations. But even if a law avoids unequal treatment on its face * * *, it may be contrary to the principle of equality if its practical application results in an obvious inequality and if this unequal effect is directly due to the legal formulation [of the statute]. It is not the outward form that is decisive, but the substantive legal content. * * *

3.   If the legislature interferes with the formation of the political will by enacting a statute which could possibly have even an indirect effect on the equal opportunity of political parties, then it must bear in mind that its discretion in this area is very limited. As a matter of principle, all parties must be treated formally in an equal manner. This principle prohibits [the legislature] from treating parties differently unless [this] is justified by an especially "compelling reason." * * *

Today, all political parties are dependent on donations, due to the huge financial expenditures required by modern electoral campaigns, no party can cover its entire financial needs * * * from member contributions. In a democratic, multiparty state, all political parties are equally called upon to take part in forming the people's political will. * * * It is true that the state need not pass laws to ensure * * * that parties' financial needs are satisfied. [But] if the legislature passes any regulation to promote party financing, the provision must be constitutional and, in particular, must not violate parties' basic right of equal opportunity. * * * Since the income tax rate increases with the size of taxable income, * * * the possibility of deducting donations to a political party from taxable income creates an incentive primarily for corporate taxpayers and those with high incomes to make donations. Pursuant to the new law, these taxpayers can even double their donations without paying more than before, under certain circumstances. [The statute] does not * * * produce greater incentive for taxpayers with low incomes, because the donations that they can afford are usually so small as not to exceed the standard deductions for deductible expenses.

General experience shows that, in contrast to donations made for charitable, religious, or scientific purposes, [taxpayers] make donations to a political party with a special interest in mind. * * * Thus a donor will tend to contribute to the party which he believes will foster his special interests * * *. [But] this fact can be of importance only if political parties differ so clearly from each other * * * that the donor must choose one party * * * over another if he wants to safeguard his interests. Such differences do in fact exist between certain parties in the Federal Republic. * * * The challenged provisions, therefore favor those parties whose programs and activities appeal to wealthy circles. * * * [They are thus unconstitutional.]

Notes and Questions

1. *Money.* Canadian, U.S., and European courts cherish democracy as well as freedom of expression, yet each arrives at different conclusions on how to preserve both. British experts have uniformly criticized the sums of money involved in American elections, describing the system as an "administrative nightmare" or "almost openly corrupt." See Lisa E. Klein, *On the Brink of Reform: Political Party Funding in Britain,* 31 Case W. Res. J. Int'l L. 1 (1999). Europe and Canada also tend to emphasize equality more than the U.S. For example, the German system provides public funding for parties relative to their success in elections. What are the consequences for democracy of the different approaches? Compare Sanford Levinson, Book Review, *Regulating Campaign Activity: The New Road to Contradiction,* 83 Mich. L. Rev. 939, 945 (1985): "Overtly, justifying restriction of campaign spending by reference to the idea of fair access to the public forum may seem content neutral. However, it is worth considering to what extent we in fact support such restrictions because of tacit assumptions about the content of the views held by the rich, who would obviously feel most of the burden of the restrictions."

The Canadian Supreme Court, in *Native Women's Association v. The Queen,* [1994] 3 S.C.R. 627, discussed the participatory rights of the Native Women's Association, which claimed it had no political voice in, and compared to, male-dominated institutions and that it had inadequate access to political speech, including money and a forum. What is the difference between this problem and the cases above? The Court held that: "It cannot be claimed that NWAC has a constitutional right to receive government funding aimed at promoting participation, 'since the Government already funded Native groups.' It cannot be said that every time the Government of Canada chooses to fund or consult a certain group, thereby providing a platform upon which to convey certain views, that the Government is also required to fund a group purporting to represent the opposite point of view."

2. *Limits.* Is the fight against corruption a valid argument for limiting the freedom to finance politics? Can constitutional law limit donations to restrict the costs of campaigning? How would such a law affect the equality of candidates? If a cap on spending limits the options of candidates to present themselves to the public, will it violate the rights of equality for new or unknown parties, the rights of individual voters who may not be well informed about who runs for office, or the rights of candidates? The USSC stated that caps may not hinder "effective advocacy," i.e., the ability to wage an effective campaign. Who determines what is effective? Turkish law requires independent candidates to pay for the printing of their ballots, while political parties, mentioned as essential in the Constitution, receive funding for that purpose. Is this satisfactory from an equality perspective? In most countries, the budgets of candidates are not subject to control, while in Moldova, parties are controlled by the Constitutional Court, including their finances.

3. *Canvassing.* The solicitation of votes can take many forms. In *Taniguchi v. Japan,* 21 Keishū 9 at p. 1245 (Sup. Ct. Nov. 21, 1967*),* the Japanese Court decided that a law that prohibits door-to-door election canvassing was constitutional because "canvassing may encourage various evils and impair fair elections." Do you agree? What if canvassing takes place in front of an election site?

4. *"Campaigning tactics"?* In *Zimbabwe African National Union v. United African National Council*, 1980 Zimb. L. Rep. 69, a court decided that while a party could provide food, drink, and entertainment at a rally, it could not conduct a drawing for six cars as prizes, as this would constitute bribery. In Turkey, the law prohibits candidates and political parties from distributing gifts to voters. In 2001, the Macedonian Constitutional Court invalidated sections of the party law that allowed parties to own businesses that would generate income for their activities. In Japan, the Supreme Court held in *Arita v. Kojima,* 24 Minshū 6, at p. 625 (Sup. Ct. June 24, 1970), that corporations could make large political contributions to political parties in the name of their companies. A stockholder lost his suit against the company managers because the Court said that "a company, like a natural person, has a social position as a constituent entity in the nation * * * and as such must undertake certain social functions. The company can therefore properly engage in acts, which at first glance may appear to have no relation to its charter purposes, so long as the acts are demanded or expected of the company by common conception, and so long as the company is responding to such expectations." Beer and Itoh, *op. cit.* at 406–07. Is this argument convincing?

5. *Criteria for democracy.* Should the success of democracy be evaluated? Most states are members of the United Nations, with roughly 110 of them legally dedicated to democracy in that they promise to hold free and general elections. Democracy on paper, however, does not always translate to

democracy in fact. For example, though Senegal is a multiparty state with universal franchise and a secret ballot, the results of the 1988 national elections were rejected as fraudulent, both by opposition parties and by other social institutions. Local elections were boycotted, and the legitimacy of the government was rejected. Is acceptance by political opposition forces required for democratic legitimization? Is acceptance by the international legal regime becoming the defining factor? Which is the paramount right: freedom of speech, association, assembly, or equality? What kind of constitutional system furthers all of these rights for as many people as possible?

6. Regulation of the financing of political campaigns remains sharply contested in the U.S. Soon after *Buckley v. Valeo* was decided the USSC invalidated a Massachusetts criminal statute that prohibited banks and business corporations from making contributions or expenditures to influence a referendum. *First Nat'l. Bank v. Bellotti,* 435 U.S. 765 (1978). The majority relied on the importance of maximizing speech from any source and rejected any special risk of corruption. Three Justices argued in dissent that the statute was justifiable to prevent institutions of great wealth "from using that wealth to acquire an unfair advantage in the political process." 435 U.S. at 809. On the other hand, in *Austin v. Michigan Chamber of Commerce,* 494 U.S. 652 (1990), the Court upheld a law barring the Chamber of Commerce, a nonprofit corporation composed mainly of profit-making members, from making contributions to candidates. Lawsuits are pending that are designed to overrule or modify the holdings of *Buckley v. Valeo.*

INDEX

References are to pages

Speech, freedom of expression and racist speech, 885-921

†